VISUAL C++® .NET

HOW TO PROGRAM

Deitel® Books, Cyber Classrooms, Complete Tra
published by

How To Program Series

Advanced Java™ 2 Platform How to Program
C How to Program, 4/E
C++ How to Program, 4/E
C#® How to Program
e-Business and e-Commerce How to Program
Internet and World Wide Web How to Program, 3/E
Java™ How to Program, 5/E
Perl How to Program
Python How to Program
Visual Basic® 6 How to Program
Visual Basic® .NET How to Program, 2/E
Visual C++® .NET How to Program
Wireless Internet & Mobile Business How to Program
XML How to Program

.NET How to Program Series

C# How to Program
Visual Basic® .NET How to Program, 2/E
Visual C++® .NET How to Program

Visual Studio® Series

C# How to Program
Getting Started with Microsoft® Visual C++® 6 with an Introduction to MFC
Simply C#: An Application-Driven Tutorial Approach
Simply Visual Basic® .NET: An Application-Driven Tutorial Approach (Visual Studio .NET 2002 Edition)
Simply Visual Basic® .NET: An Application-Driven Tutorial Approach (Visual Studio .NET 2003 Edition)
Visual Basic® 6 How to Program
Visual Basic® .NET How to Program, 2/E
Visual C++® .NET How to Program

CS1 Programming Series

Java™ Software Design

Simply Series

Simply C#: An Application-Driven Tutorial Approach
Simply Java™ Programming: An Application-Driven Tutorial Approach
Simply Visual Basic® .NET: An Application Driven Tutorial Approach (Visual Studio .NET 2002 Edition)
Simply Visual Basic® .NET: An Application Driven Tutorial Approach (Visual Studio .NET 2003 Edition)

Deitel® Developer Series

Java™ Web Services for Experienced Programmers
Web Services A Technical Introduction

Computer Science Series

Operating Systems, 3/E

For Managers Series

e-Business and e-Commerce for Manager

ining Courses and Web-Based Training Courses Prentice Hall

The Complete Training Course Series

The Complete C++ Training Course, 4/E
The Complete C# Training Course
The Complete e-Business and e-Commerce Programming Training Course
The Complete Java™ 2 Training Course, 5/E
The Complete Perl Training Course
The Complete Python Training Course
The Complete Visual Basic® 6 Training Course
The Complete Visual Basic® .NET Training Course, 2/E
The Complete Wireless Internet & Mobile Business Programming Training Course
The Complete XML Programming Training Course

Interactive _Multimedia Cyber Classroom_ Series

C++ Multimedia Cyber Classroom, 4/E
C# Multimedia Cyber Classroom
e-Business and e-Commerce Multimedia Cyber Classroom
Java™ 2 Multimedia Cyber Classroom, 5/E
Perl Multimedia Cyber Classroom
Python Multimedia Cyber Classroom
Visual Basic® 6 Multimedia Cyber Classroom
Visual Basic® .NET Multimedia Cyber Classroom, 2/E
Wireless Internet & Mobile Business Programming Multimedia Cyber Classroom
XML Multimedia Cyber Classroom

Interactive _Web-Based Training_ Series

Premium CourseCompass Version of Visual Basic® .NET Multimedia Cyber Classroom, 2/E
Premium CourseCompass Version of Java 2 Multimedia Cyber Classroom, 5/E
Premium CourseCompass Version of C++ Multimedia Cyber Classroom, 4/E

To follow the Deitel publishing program, please register at:

`www.deitel.com/newsletter/subscribe.html`

for the *Deitel™ Buzz Online* e-mail newsletter.

To communicate with the authors, send e-mail to:

`deitel@deitel.com`

For information on corporate on-site seminars offered by Deitel & Associates, Inc. worldwide, visit:

`www.deitel.com`

For continuing updates on Prentice Hall and Deitel publications visit:

```
www.deitel.com,
www.prenhall.com/deitel
www.InformIT.com/deitel
```

Library of Congress Cataloging-in-Publication Data

On file

Vice President and Editorial Director, ECS: *Marcia J. Horton*
Senior Acquisitions Editor: *Kate Hargett*
Assistant Editor: *Sarah Parker*
Project Manager: *Jennifer Cappello*
Vice President and Director of Production and Manufacturing, ESM: *David W. Riccardi*
Executive Managing Editor: *Vince O'Brien*
Managing Editor: *Tom Manshreck*
Production Editors: *John F. Lovell, Chirag G. Thakkar*
Production Editor, Media: *Bob Engelhardt*
Director of Creative Services: *Paul Belfanti*
Creative Director: *Carole Anson*
Art Director: *Geoffrey Cassar*
Cover Art and Chapter Opener Art: *David Merrell*
Cover Designer: *Geoffrey Cassar, Dr. Harvey Deitel*
Manufacturing Manager: *Trudy Pisciotti*
Manufacturing Buyer: *Lisa McDowell*
Marketing Manager: *Pamela Shaffer*
Marketing Assistant: *Barrie Reinhold*

PEARSON
Prentice Hall

Printed in the United States of America

10 9 8 7 6 5 4 3 2

ISBN 0-13-437377-4

Pearson Education Ltd., *London*
Pearson Education Australia Pty. Ltd., *Sydney*
Pearson Education Singapore, Pte. Ltd.
Pearson Education North Asia Ltd., *Hong Kong*
Pearson Education Canada, Inc., *Toronto*
Pearson Educacion de Mexico, S.A. de C.V.
Pearson Education–Japan, *Tokyo*
Pearson Education Malaysia, Pte. Ltd.
Pearson Education, Inc., *Upper Saddle River, New Jersey*

VISUAL C++® .NET
HOW TO PROGRAM

H. M. Deitel
Deitel & Associates, Inc.

P. J. Deitel
Deitel & Associates, Inc.

J. P. Liperi
Microsoft Corporation

C. H. Yaeger
Deitel & Associates, Inc.

PEARSON
Prentice
Hall

PEARSON EDUCATION, INC., Upper Saddle River, New Jersey 07458

Trademarks

In memory of Edsger W. Dijkstra:

It is a privilege to keep learning from your work in the fields of programming languages, software engineering and operating systems.

Harvey and Paul Deitel

To my friends back home in NJ (Luke, Craig, Kutch, Mark, Tara, Pio, Phil, Greg, Pete, Redder, Hoffman, and Nikki), my friends from BU (Wass, Chet, Jake, Chay, Hoss, Meenan, Bill, Katie, and my dearest Avital), my loving sister, Veronica, and my brother-in-law, Scott:

For constantly encouraging me to push myself, for having endless faith in me, and for making it all worth it. "We did it, man."

Jon

To Judith Broadwin:

Thank you for always believing in me.

Cheryl

Contents

Preface

Live in fragments no longer. Only connect.
Edward Morgan Forster

We wove a web in childhood,
A web of sunny air.
Charlotte Brontë

Welcome to Visual C++ .NET and the world of Windows, Internet and World-Wide-Web programming with Visual Studio® .NET and the .NET platform! At Deitel & Associates, we write college-level programming-language textbooks and professional books. Writing *Visual C++ .NET How to Program* was a joy. This book and its support materials have everything instructors and students need for an informative, interesting, challenging and entertaining educational experience. Also, we have included a tour of the book in this preface to help instructors, students and professionals get a sense of the rich coverage this book provides of Visual C++ .NET programming.

In this preface, we overview the conventions we use in *Visual C++ .NET How to Program*, such as syntax coloring the code examples, "code washing" and highlighting important code segments to help focus students' attention on key concepts introduced in each chapter. We also overview the features of *Visual C++ .NET How to Program.*

This textbook is up-to-date with Microsoft's latest release of Visual Studio—Visual Studio .NET 2003, which includes an updated version of Visual C++ .NET. Every example and exercise solution was built and tested using the Visual C++ .NET Standard Edition version 2003 software. For the educational market only, this textbook is available in a "value pack" with the Microsoft® Visual C++® .NET Standard Edition version 2003 integrated development environment as a free supplement. The standard edition is fully functional and is shipped on 5 CDs. There is no time limit for using the software. [*Note:* Professionals using this publication will have to purchase the necessary software to build and run the applications in this textbook.]

We discuss *Visual C++ .NET How to Program*'s comprehensive suite of educational materials that help instructors maximize their students' learning experience. These include an Instructor's Resource CD with solutions to the book's chapter exercises and a Test-Item File with hundreds of multiple-choice examination questions and answers. Additional instructor resources are available at the book's Companion Web Site (`www.prenhall.com/deitel`), which includes a Syllabus Manager and customizable PowerPoint® Lecture Notes. PowerPoint slides and additional support materials are available for students at the Companion Web Site, as well.

Visual C++ .NET How to Program was reviewed by a team of distinguished academics and industry professionals. We list their names and affiliations so you can get a sense of how carefully this book was scrutinized. The preface concludes with information about the authors and about Deitel & Associates, Inc. As you read this book, if you have any questions, please send an e-mail to `deitel@deitel.com`; we will respond promptly. Please visit our Web site, `www.deitel.com`, regularly and be sure to sign up for the *DEITEL® Buzz Online* e-mail newsletter at `www.deitel.com/newsletter/subscribe.html`, which provides information about our publications, company announcements, links to informative technical articles, programming tips, teaching tips, challenges and anecdotes.

Features of Visual C++ .NET How to Program

This book contains many features, including:

Syntax Highlighting

We syntax highlight all the Visual C++ .NET code in a manner similar to that of Visual Studio .NET. This greatly improves code readability—an especially important goal, given that this book contains over 22,000 lines of code. Our syntax-highlighting conventions are as follows:

```
comments appear like this
keywords appear like this
constants and literal values appear like this
errors and ASP .NET directives appear like this
all other code appears in black
```

Code Highlighting and User-Input Highlighting

We have added extensive code highlighting to make it easier for readers to spot the featured segments of each program. This feature also helps students review the material rapidly when preparing for exams or labs. We have also highlighted in our screen dialogs all user inputs to distinguish them from program outputs.

"Code Washing"

This is our term for applying comments, using meaningful identifiers, applying indentation and using vertical spacing to separate meaningful program units. This process results in programs that are much more readable and self-documenting. We have added descriptive comments to all of the code to help the student clearly understand the flow of the program. We have done extensive code washing of all the source code programs in the text and the ancillaries.

Web Services

Microsoft's .NET strategy embraces the Internet and Web as integral to software development and deployment. Web-services technology enables information sharing, e-commerce and other interactions using standard Internet protocols and technologies, such as Hypertext Transfer Protocol (HTTP), Extensible Markup Language (XML) and Simple Object Access Protocol (SOAP). Web services enable programmers to package application functionality in a manner that turns the Web into a library of reusable software components. Chapter 20, *Web Services*, presents a Web service that allows users to manipulate "huge integers"—integers too large to be stored in .NET's built-in data types. In this example, a user enters two huge integers and presses buttons to invoke a Web service that adds, subtracts or compares the two huge integers.

Object-Oriented Programming

Object-oriented programming is the most widely employed technique for developing robust, reusable software. This text offers a rich treatment of Visual C++ .NET's object-oriented programming features. Chapter 8, Object-Based Programming, introduces how to create classes and objects. These concepts are extended in Chapter 9, Object-Oriented Programming: Inheritance, which discusses how programmers can create powerful new classes quickly by "absorbing" the capabilities of existing classes. Chapter 10, Object-Oriented Programming: Polymorphism, focuses on the relationships between classes in a hierarchy.

XML

Extensible Markup Language (XML) use is exploding in the software-development industry, in the e-business and e-commerce communities, and is pervasive throughout the .NET platform. Because XML is a platform-independent technology for describing data and for creating markup languages, XML's data portability integrates well with Visual C++ .NET based applications and services. Chapter 18, Extensible Markup Language (XML), introduces XML. In this chapter, we present XML markup and discuss the Document Object Model (DOM™), which is used to manipulate XML documents programmatically.

Multithreading

Computers enable programmers to perform many tasks in parallel (i.e., concurrently), such as printing documents, downloading files from a network and surfing the Web. Multithreading is the technology through which programmers can develop applications that perform concurrent tasks. Historically, a computer has contained a single, expensive processor, which its operating system would share among all applications. Today, processors are becoming increasingly inexpensive, making it possible to build affordable computers with many processors working in parallel—such computers are called multiprocessors. Multithreading is effective on both single-processor and multiprocessor systems. .NET's multithreading capabilities make the platform and its related technologies better prepared to handle today's sophisticated multimedia-intensive, database-intensive, network-based, multiprocessor-based, distributed applications. Chapter 14, Multithreading, introduces this powerful capability.

ADO .NET

Databases store vast amounts of information that individuals and organizations must access to conduct business. As an evolution of Microsoft's ActiveX Data Objects (ADO) technology, ADO .NET represents a new approach to building applications that interact with databases. ADO .NET uses XML and an enhanced object model to provide developers with the tools they need to access and manipulate databases for large-scale, extensible, mission-critical, multi-tier applications. Chapter 19, Database, SQL and ADO .NET, introduces ADO .NET and the Structured Query Language (SQL) for manipulating databases.

Graphical User Interfaces

Visual Studio .NET 2003 and Visual C++ .NET Standard Edition version 2003 include a *Windows Form designer*. This form designer simplifies the creation of graphical user interfaces (GUIs) for the programmer by generating the GUI code. GUI applications are programs that display graphical elements, such as buttons and labels, with which the user interacts. This book presents many GUI applications to demonstrate different topics in Visual C++ .NET. Visual Studio .NET contains built-in GUI development tools for C#, Visual Basic® .NET and Visual C++ .NET.

XHTML™

The World Wide Web Consortium (W3C) has declared HTML to be a legacy technology that will undergo no further development. HTML is being replaced by the Extensible Hypertext Markup Language (XHTML)—an XML-based technology that is rapidly becoming the standard for describing Web content. We use XHTML in Chapter 18, Extensible Markup Language (XML), and offer an introduction to the technology in Appendix E, Introduction to XHTML: Part 1 and Appendix F, Introduction to XHTML: Part 2. These appendices overview headers, images, lists, image maps and other XHTML features.

Unicode®

As computer systems evolved worldwide, computer vendors developed numeric representations of character sets and special symbols for the local languages spoken in different countries. In some cases, different representations were developed for the same languages. Such disparate character sets hindered communication among computer systems. Visual C++ .NET supports the *Unicode Standard* (maintained by a non-profit organization called the *Unicode Consortium*), which maintains a single character set that specifies unique numeric values for characters and special symbols in most of the world's languages. Appendix D, Unicode, discusses the standard, overviews the Unicode Consortium Web site, `www.unicode.org` and presents an Visual C++ .NET application that displays "Welcome to Unicode!" in several languages.

Bit Manipulation

Computers work with data in the form of binary digits, or bits, which can assume the values 1 or 0. Computer circuitry performs various simple bit manipulations, such as examining the value of a bit, setting the value of a bit and reversing a bit (from 1 to 0 or from 0 to 1). Operating systems, test-equipment, networking software and many other kinds of software require that programs communicate "directly with the hardware" by using bit manipulation. Appendix I, Bit Manipulation, overviews the bit manipulation capabilities that the .NET Framework provides.

Teaching Approach

Visual C++ .NET How to Program contains a rich collection of examples, exercises and projects drawn from many fields and designed to provide students with a chance to solve interesting, real-world problems. The book concentrates on the principles of software engineering and stresses program clarity. We avoid arcane terminology and syntax specifications in favor of teaching by example. Our code examples have been fully tested using Microsoft's Visual C++ .NET Standard Edition version 2003 software.

We are educators who teach edge-of-the-practice topics in industry classrooms worldwide. This text emphasizes good pedagogy.

Font Conventions

We use fonts to distinguish between IDE features (such as menu names and menu items) and other elements that appear in the IDE. Our convention is to emphasize IDE features in a sans-serif bold **Helvetica** font (for example, **Properties** window) and to emphasize program text in a serif `Lucida` font (`int x = 5`).

Learning Visual C++ .NET with the Live-Code Approach

Visual C++ .NET How to Program is loaded with live-code examples (provided on the accompanying CD)— each new concept is presented in the context of a complete, working program that is immediately followed by one or more sample executions showing the program's input/output dialog. This style exemplifies the way we teach and write about programming. We call this method of teaching and writing the LIVE-CODE approach. *We use programming languages to teach programming languages.* Reading the examples in the text is much like typing and running them on a computer.

World Wide Web Access

All of the source-code examples for *Visual C++ .NET How to Program* (and our other publications) are available on the Internet as downloads from the following Web sites:

```
www.deitel.com
www.prenhall.com/deitel
```

Registration is quick and easy and the downloads are free. We suggest downloading all the examples, then running each program as you read the corresponding text. Making changes to the examples and immediately seeing the effects of those changes is a great way to enhance your learning experience. Any instructions we provide for running this book's examples assume that the user is running Windows 2000 or Windows XP and is using Microsoft's Internet Information Services (IIS). Additional setup instructions for IIS and other software can be found at our Web sites—`www.deitel.com` and `www.prenhall.com/deitel`—along with the examples. [*Note*: This is copyrighted material. Feel free to use it as you study, but you may not republish any portion of it in any form without explicit permission from Prentice Hall and the authors.]

Objectives

Each chapter begins with a statement of objectives. This tells the student what to expect and gives the student an opportunity, after reading the chapter, to determine if he or she has met these objectives. It is a confidence builder and a source of positive reinforcement.

Quotations

The learning objectives are followed by a series of quotations. Some are humorous, some are philosophical and some offer interesting insights. Our students enjoy relating the quotations to the chapter material. You may appreciate some of the quotations more *after* reading the chapters.

Outline

The chapter outline enables students to approach the material in top-down fashion. This, too, helps students anticipate future topics and set a comfortable and effective learning pace.

22,000+ Lines of Code in 187 Example Programs (with Program Outputs)

We present Visual C++ .NET features in the context of complete, working programs. The programs range in size from just a few lines of code to substantial examples containing hundreds of lines of code. All examples are available on the accompanying CD and as downloads from our Web site, `www.deitel.com`.

884 Illustrations/Figures

An abundance of charts, line drawings and program outputs is included.

417 Programming Tips

We have included programming tips to help readers focus on important aspects of program development. We highlight hundreds of these tips in the form of *Good Programming Practices*, *Common Programming Errors*, *Error-Prevention Tips*, *Performance Tips*, *Portability Tips*, *Software Engineering Observations* and *Look-and-Feel Observations*. These tips and practices represent the best the authors have gleaned from many decades of programming and teaching experience. One of our customers—a mathematics major—told us that she feels this approach is like the highlighting of axioms, theorems and corollaries in mathematics books; it provides a foundation on which to build good software.

72 Good Programming Practices

Good Programming Practices *are tips for writing clear programs. These techniques help students produce programs that are more readable, self-documenting and easier to maintain.*

135 Common Programming Errors

Students learning a language—especially in their first programming course—tend to make certain kinds of errors frequently. Focusing on these Common Programming Errors *helps students avoid making the same errors. It also helps reduce long lines outside instructors' offices during office hours!*

31 Error-Prevention Tips

When we first designed this "tip type," we thought we would use it strictly to tell people how to test and debug programs. In fact, many of the tips describe aspects of Visual C++ .NET that reduce the likelihood of "bugs" and thus simplify the testing and debugging processes.

49 Performance Tips

In our experience, teaching students to write clear and understandable programs is by far the most important goal for a first programming course. But students want to write the programs that run the fastest, use the least memory, require the smallest number of keystrokes, or dazzle in other nifty ways. Students really care about performance. They want to know what they can do to "turbo charge" their programs. So we highlight opportunities for improving program performance—making programs run faster or minimizing the amount of memory that they occupy.

10 Portability Tips

Software development is a complex and expensive activity. Organizations that develop software must often produce versions customized to a variety of computers and operating systems. So there is a strong emphasis today on portability, i.e., on producing software that will run on a variety of computer systems with few, if any, changes.

104 Software Engineering Observations

The object-oriented programming paradigm necessitates a complete rethinking of the way we build software systems. Visual C++ .NET is effective for achieving good software engineering. The Software Engineering Observations *highlight architectural and design issues that affect the construction of software systems, especially large-scale systems.*

16 Look-and-Feel Observations

We provide Look-and-Feel Observations *to highlight graphical-user-interface conventions. These observations help developers design attractive, user-friendly graphical user interfaces that conform to industry norms.*

Summary (759 Summary bullets)

Each chapter ends with additional pedagogical devices. We present an extensive, bullet-list-style *Summary* in every chapter. This helps the student review and reinforce key concepts. There is an average of 35 summary bullets per chapter.

Terminology (2225 Terms)

We include a *Terminology* section with an alphabetized list of the important terms defined in the chapter—again, further reinforcement. There is an average of 101 terms per chapter. Each term also appears in the index, so the student can locate terms and definitions quickly.

507 Self-Review Exercises and Answers (Count Includes Separate Parts)

Extensive *Self-Review Exercises* and *Answers to Self-Review Exercises* are included for self study. This gives the student a chance to build confidence with the material and prepare to attempt the regular exercises.

174 Exercises (Solutions in Instructor's Manual; Count Includes Separate Parts)

Each chapter concludes with a substantial set of exercises including simple recall of important terminology and concepts; writing individual program statements; writing small portions of functions and Visual C++ .NET classes; writing complete functions, Visual C++ .NET classes and programs; and writing major term projects. The large number of exercises enables instructors to tailor their courses to the unique needs of their audiences and to vary course assignments each semester. Instructors can use these exercises to form homework assignments, short quizzes and major examinations. [***NOTE:* Please do not write to us requesting the instructor's manual. Distribution of this publication is strictly limited to college professors teaching from the book. Instructors may obtain the solutions manual from their regular Prentice Hall representatives. We regret that we cannot provide the solutions to professionals.**]

Approximately 5,838 Index Entries (with approximately 7,261 Page References)

We have included an extensive *Index* at the back of the book. This helps the student find any term or concept by keyword. The *Index* is useful to people reading the book for the first time and is especially useful to practicing programmers who use the book as a reference. Most of the terms in the *Terminology* sections appear in the *Index* (along with many more index entries from each chapter). Thus, the student can use the *Index* in conjunction with the *Terminology* sections to be sure he or she has covered the key material of each chapter.

Software Included with Visual C++ .NET How to Program

For the educational market only, this textbook is available in a "value pack" with the Microsoft Visual C++ .NET Standard Edition version 2003 integrated development environment as a free supplement. The standard edition is fully functional and is shipped on 5 CDs. There is no time limit for using the software. [*Note:* Professionals using this publication will have to purchase the necessary software to build and run the applications in this textbook.]

DIVE-INTO™ Series Tutorial for Visual C++ .NET

Our *DIVE-INTO™ SERIES* of tutorials helps readers get started with many popular program-development environments. These are available free for download at `www.deitel.com/books/downloads.html`. *DIVE-INTO Microsoft® Visual C++® .NET 2003* shows how to compile, execute and debug Visual C++ .NET applications in Visual Studio .NET Standard Edition version 2003. The document also provide step-by-step instructions with screen shots to help readers install the software, and overviews the compiler and its online documentation.

Ancillary Package for Visual C++ .NET How to Program

Visual C++ .NET How to Program has extensive ancillary materials for instructors. The *Instructor's Resource CD (IRCD)* contains solutions to most of the end-of-chapter exercises. This CD is available only to instructors through their Prentice Hall representatives. [***NOTE:* Please do not write to us requesting the instructor's CD. Distribution of this CD is limited strictly to college professors teaching from the book. Instructors may obtain the solutions manual only from their Prentice Hall representatives.**] The ancillaries for this book also include a *Test Item File* of multiple-choice questions. In addition, we provide PowerPoint slides containing all the code and figures in the text and bulleted items that summarize the key points in the text. Instructors can customize the slides. The PowerPoint slides are downloadable from `www.deitel.com` and are available as part of Prentice Hall's Companion Web Site (`www.prenhall.com/deitel`) for *Visual C++ .NET How to Program*, which offers resources for both instructors and students. For instructors, the Companion Web Site provides a Syllabus Manager, which helps instructors plan courses interactively and create online syllabi.

Students also benefit from the functionality of the *Companion Web Site*. Book-specific resources for students include:

- Customizable PowerPoint slides
- Source code for all example programs
- Reference materials from the book appendices (such as operator-precedence chart, character set and Web resources)

Chapter-specific resources available for students include:

- Chapter objectives
- Highlights (e.g., chapter summary)

- Outline
- Tips (e.g., *Common Programming Errors*, *Good Programming Practices*, *Portability Tips*, *Performance Tips*, *Look-and-Feel Observations*, *Software Engineering Observations* and *Error-Prevention Tips*)
- Online Study Guide—contains additional short-answer self-review exercises (e.g., true/false and matching questions) with answers and provides immediate feedback to the student

Students can track their results and course performance on quizzes using the *Student Profile* feature, which records and manages all feedback and results from tests taken on the *Companion Web Site*. To access the DEITEL® *Companion Web Sites*, visit `www.prenhall.com/deitel`.

DEITEL® e-Learning Initiatives

e-Books and Support for Wireless Devices

Wireless devices will have an enormous role in the future of the Internet. Given recent bandwidth enhancements and the emergence of 2.5 and 3G technologies, it is projected that, within a few years, more people will access the Internet through wireless devices than through desktop computers. Deitel & Associates is committed to wireless accessibility and has published *Wireless Internet & Mobile Business How to Program*. We are investigating new electronic formats, such as wireless e-books so that students and professors can access content virtually anytime, anywhere. For periodic updates on these initiatives subscribe to the *DEITEL® Buzz Online* e-mail newsletter, `www.deitel.com/newsletter/subscribe.html` or visit `www.deitel.com`.

DEITEL® Buzz Online E-mail Newsletter

Our free e-mail newsletter, the *DEITEL® Buzz Online*, includes commentary on industry trends and developments, links to free articles and resources from our published books and upcoming publications, product-release schedules, errata, challenges, anecdotes, information on our corporate instructor-led training courses and more. To subscribe, visit

```
www.deitel.com/newsletter/subscribe.html
```

Tour of the Book

In this section, we tour the chapters and appendices of *Visual C++ .NET How to Program*. In addition to the topics presented in each chapter, several of the chapters contain an Internet and Web Resources section that lists additional sources from which readers can enhance their knowledge of Visual C++ programming.

Chapter 1—Introduction to .NET and Visual C++® .NET

The first chapter presents the history of the Internet, World Wide Web and various technologies (such as XML and SOAP) that have led to advances in computing. We introduce the Microsoft .NET initiative and Visual C++ .NET, including Web services. We explore the impact of .NET on software development and software reusability.

Chapter 2—Introduction to the Visual Studio® .NET IDE

Chapter 2 introduces Visual Studio .NET, an integrated development environment (IDE) that allows programmers to create applications using standard C++ and Managed Extensions for C++ (Visual C++ .NET). Visual Studio .NET contains tools for debugging and writing code. The chapter presents features of Visual Studio .NET, including its key windows, and shows how to compile and run programs. The chapter also introduces readers to console-application and Windows-application programming in Visual C++ .NET. Every concept is presented in the context of a complete working Visual C++ .NET program and is followed by one or more screen shots showing actual inputs and outputs as the program executes.

Chapter 3—Introduction to Visual C++ .NET Programming

This chapter introduces readers to our LIVE-CODE approach. Every concept is presented in the context of a complete working Visual C++ .NET program and is followed by one or more sample outputs depicting the program's execution. In our first example, we print a line of text and carefully discuss each line of code. We then discuss fundamental tasks, such as how a program inputs data from its users and how to write programs that perform arithmetic.

Chapter 4—Control Statements: Part 1

This chapter formally introduces the principles of structured programming, a set of techniques that will help the reader develop clear, understandable, maintainable programs throughout the text. The first part of this chapter presents program-development and problem-solving techniques. The chapter demonstrates how to transform a written specification to a program by using such techniques as *pseudocode* and *top-down, stepwise refinement*. We then progress through the entire process, from developing a problem statement into a working Visual C++ .NET program. The notion of algorithms is also discussed. We build on information presented in the previous chapter to create programs that are interactive (i.e., they change their behavior to suit user-supplied inputs). The chapter then introduces the use of control statements that affect the sequence in which statements are executed. Control statements produce programs that are easily understood, debugged and maintained. We discuss the three forms of program control—sequence, selection and repetition—focusing on the `if...else` and `while` control statements. Flowcharts (i.e., graphical representations of algorithms) appear throughout the chapter, reinforcing and augmenting the explanations.

Chapter 5—Control Statements: Part 2

Chapter 5 introduces more complex control statements and the logical operators. It uses flowcharts to illustrate the flow of control through each control structure, including the `for`, `do...while` and `switch` statements. We explain the `break` and `continue` statements and the logical operators. Examples include calculating compound interest and printing the distribution of grades on an exam (with some simple error checking). The chapter concludes with a structured programming summary, including each of Visual C++ .NET's control statements. The techniques discussed in Chapters 4 and 5 constitute a large part of what has been taught traditionally under the topic of structured programming.

Chapter 6—Functions

A *function* allows the programmer to create a block of code that can be called upon from various points in a program. Groups of related functions can be separated into functional blocks (classes), using the "divide and conquer" strategy. Programs are divided into simple components that interact in straightforward ways. We discuss how to create our own functions that can take input, perform calculations and return output. We examine the FCL's `Math` class, which contains methods for performing complex calculations (e.g., trigonometric and logarithmic calculations). The FCL (Framework Class Library) is .NET's code library, or collection of classes that provides numerous capabilities to the programmer. *Recursive* functions (functions that call themselves) and function overloading, which allows multiple functions to have the same name, are introduced. We demonstrate overloading by creating two `Square` functions that take an integer (i.e., whole number) and a floating-point number (i.e., a number with a decimal point), respectively.

Chapter 7—Arrays

Chapter 7 discusses arrays, our first data structures. (Chapter 22 discusses the topic of data structures in depth.) Data structures are crucial to storing, sorting, searching and manipulating large amounts of information. *Arrays* are groups of related data items that allow the programmer to access any element directly. Rather than creating 100 separate variables that are all related in some way, the programmer instead can create an array of 100 elements and access these elements by their location in the array. We discuss how to declare and allocate managed arrays, and we build on the techniques of the previous chapter by passing arrays to functions. In addition, we discuss how to pass a variable number of arguments to methods. Chapters 4 and 5 are essential for array processing, because repetition statements are used to iterate through elements in an array. The combination of these concepts helps the reader create highly-structured and well-organized programs. We then demonstrate how to sort and search arrays. We discuss multidimensional arrays, which can be used to store tables of data.

Chapter 8—Object-Based Programming

Chapter 8 begins our deeper discussion of classes. The chapter represents a wonderful opportunity for teaching data abstraction the "right way"—through a language (MC++) expressly devoted to implementing new types. The chapter focuses on the essence and terminology of classes (programmer-defined types) and objects. The chapter discusses implementing MC++ classes, accessing class members, enforcing information hiding with access modifiers, separating interface from implementation, using properties and utility methods and initializing objects with constructors. The chapter discusses declaring and using constants, *composition*, the `this` reference, `static` class members and examples of popular abstract data types such as stacks and queues. We overview how to create reusable software components with assemblies, namespaces and Dynamic Link Library (DLL) files.

Chapter 9—Object-Oriented Programming: Inheritance

Chapter 9 introduces one of the most fundamental capabilities of object-oriented programming languages, inheritance, which is a form of software reusability in which new classes are developed quickly and easily by absorbing the capabilities of existing classes and adding appropriate new capabilities. The chapter discusses the notions of base classes and derived classes, access modifier `protected`, direct base classes, indirect base classes, use of constructors in base classes and derived classes, and software engineering with inheritance. The chapter compares inheritance ("is a" relationships) with composition ("has a" relationships).

Chapter 10—Object-Oriented Programming: Polymorphism

Chapter 10 deals with another fundamental capability of object-oriented programming, namely polymorphic behavior. *Polymorphism* permits classes to be treated in a general manner, allowing the same method call to act differently depending on context (e.g., "move" messages sent to a bird and a fish result in dramatically different types of action—a bird flies and a fish swims). In addition to treating existing classes in a general manner, polymorphism allows new classes to be added to a system easily. This chapter distinguishes between abstract classes and concrete classes. A feature of this chapter is its three polymorphism case studies—a payroll system, a shape hierarchy headed up by an abstract class and a shape hierarchy headed up by an interface. These programming techniques and those of the previous chapter allow the programmer to create extensible and reusable software components.

Chapter 11—Exception Handling

Exception handling is one of the most important topics in Visual C++ .NET from the standpoint of building mission-critical and business-critical applications. People can enter incorrect data, data can be corrupted and clients can try to access records that do not exist or are restricted. A simple division-by-zero error may cause a calculator program to crash, but what if such an error occurs in the navigation system of a flying airplane? Programmers must deal with these situations, because in some cases, the results of program failure could be disastrous. Programmers need to know how to recognize the errors (*exceptions*) that might occur in software components and handle those exceptions effectively, allowing programs to deal with problems and continue executing instead of "crashing." This chapter overviews exception-handling techniques. We cover the details of Visual C++ .NET exception handling, the termination model of exception handling, throwing and catching exceptions, and the FCL class `Exception`. Programmers who construct software systems from reusable components built by other programmers often deal with the exceptions that those components throw when a problem occurs.

Chapter 12—Graphical User Interface Concepts: Part 1

Chapter 12 explains how to add graphical user interfaces (GUIs) to our programs, providing a professional look and feel. By using the techniques of rapid application development (RAD), we can create a GUI from reusable controls, rather than explicitly programming every detail. The Visual Studio .NET IDE makes developing GUIs even easier by allowing the programmer to position components in a window through so-called visual programming. We discuss how to construct user interfaces with *Windows Forms* GUI controls such as labels, buttons, text boxes, scroll bars and picture boxes. We also introduce *events*, which are messages sent by a program to signal to an object or a set of objects that an action has occurred. Events are most commonly used to signal user interactions with GUI controls, but also can signal internal actions in a program. We overview event handling and discuss how to handle events specific to controls, the keyboard and the mouse. Tips are included throughout the chapter to help the programmer create visually appealing, well-organized and consistent GUIs.

Chapter 13—Graphical User Interface Concepts: Part 2

Chapter 13 introduces more complex GUI controls, including menus, link labels, panels, list boxes, combo boxes and tab controls. In a challenging exercise, readers create an application that displays a disk drive's directory structure in a tree—similar to that created by

Windows Explorer. The *Multiple Document Interface* (*MDI*) is presented, which allows multiple windows to be open simultaneously in a single GUI. We conclude with a discussion of how to create custom controls by combining existing controls. The techniques presented in this chapter allow readers to create sophisticated and well-organized GUIs, adding style and usability to their applications.

Chapter 14—Multithreading

We have come to expect much from our applications. We want to download files from the Internet, listen to music, print documents and browse the Web—all at the same time! To do this, we need a technique called multithreading, which allows applications to perform multiple activities concurrently. Visual C++ .NET gives programmers access to the multithreading classes provided by the FCL, while shielding programmers from complex details. Visual C++ .NET is better equipped to deal with more sophisticated multimedia, network-based and multiprocessor-based applications than other languages that do not have multithreading features. This chapter overviews the threading classes in the FCL and covers threads, thread life-cycles, time-slicing, scheduling and priorities. We analyze the producer-consumer relationship, thread synchronization and circular buffers. This chapter lays the foundation for creating the impressive multithreaded programs that clients demand.

Chapter 15—Strings, Characters and Regular Expressions

In this chapter, we discuss the processing of words, sentences, characters and groups of characters. In Visual C++ .NET, *strings* (groups of characters) are objects. This is yet another benefit of Visual C++ .NET's emphasis on object-oriented programming. `String` objects contain methods that can copy, search, extract substrings and concatenate strings with one another. We introduce class *`StringBuilder`*, which defines string-like objects that can be modified after initialization. As an interesting example of strings, we create a card shuffling-and-dealing simulation. We discuss regular expressions, a powerful tool for searching and manipulating text.

Chapter 16—Graphics and Multimedia

In this chapter, we discuss *GDI+* (an extension of the *Graphics Device Interface—GDI*), the Windows service that provides the graphical features used by .NET applications. The extensive graphical capabilities of GDI+ can make programs more visual and fun to create and use. We discuss Visual C++ .NET's treatment of graphics objects and color control. We also discuss how to draw arcs, polygons and other shapes. The chapter demonstrates how to use various pens and brushes to create color effects and includes an example that demonstrates gradient fills and textures. We also introduce techniques for turning text-only applications into aesthetically pleasing programs that even novice programmers can write with ease. The second half of the chapter focuses on audio, video and speech technology. We discuss adding sound, video and animated characters to programs (primarily via existing audio and video clips). You will see how easy it is to incorporate multimedia into Visual C++ .NET applications. This chapter introduces a technology called *Microsoft Agent* for adding *interactive animated characters* to a program. Each character allows users to interact with the application, using more natural human communication techniques, such as speech. The agent characters respond to mouse and keyboard events, speak and hear (i.e., they support speech synthesis and speech recognition). With these capabilities, your applications can speak to users and actually respond to their voice commands!

Chapter 17—Files and Streams

Imagine a program that could not save data to a file. Once the program is closed, all the work performed by the program is lost forever. For this reason, this chapter is one of the most important for programmers who will be developing commercial applications. We introduce FCL classes for inputting and outputting data. A detailed example demonstrates these concepts by allowing users to read and write bank account information to and from files. We introduce the FCL classes and methods that help perform input and output conveniently—they demonstrate the power of object-oriented programming and reusable classes. We discuss benefits of sequential files, random-access files and buffering. This chapter lays the groundwork for the material presented in Chapter 21, Networking: Streams-Based Sockets and Datagrams.

Chapter 18—Extensible Markup Language (XML)

The Extensible Markup Language (XML) derives from SGML (Standard Generalized Markup Language), which became an industry standard in 1986. Although SGML is employed in publishing applications worldwide, it has not been incorporated into the mainstream programming community because of its sheer size and complexity. XML is an effort to make SGML-like technology available to a much broader community. XML, created by the World Wide Web Consortium (W3C), describes data in a portable format. XML differs in concept from markup languages such as HTML, which only describes how information is rendered in a browser. XML is a technology for creating markup languages for virtually any type of information. Document authors use XML to create entirely new markup languages to describe specific types of data, including mathematical formulas, chemical molecular structures, music, recipes and much more. Markup languages created with XML include XHTML (Extensible HyperText Markup Language, for Web content), MathML (for mathematics), VoiceXML™ (for speech), SMIL™ (Synchronized Multimedia Integration Language, for multimedia presentations), CML (Chemical Markup Language, for chemistry) and XBRL (Extensible Business Reporting Language, for financial data exchange). The extensibility of XML has made it one of the most important technologies in industry today and is being integrated into almost every field. Companies and individuals constantly are finding new and innovative uses for XML. In this chapter, we present examples that illustrate the basics of marking up data with XML. We demonstrate several XML-derived markup languages, such as *XML Schema* (for checking an XML document's grammar), and *XSLT (Extensible Stylesheet Language Transformations*, for transforming an XML document's data into another text-based format such as XHTML). (For readers who are unfamiliar with XHTML, we provide Appendices E and F, which present a detailed introduction to XHTML.)

Chapter 19—Database, SQL and ADO .NET

Data storage and access are integral to creating powerful software applications. This chapter discusses .NET support for database manipulation. Today's most popular database systems are relational databases. In this chapter, we introduce the *Structured Query Language* (*SQL*) for performing queries on relational databases. We also introduce *ActiveX Data Objects* (*ADO .NET*)—an extension of ADO that enables .NET applications to access and manipulate databases. ADO .NET allows data to be exported as XML, which enables ADO .NET applications to communicate with programs that understand XML. The reader will learn how to create database connections, using tools provided in Visual Studio .NET, and how to use ADO .NET classes to query a database.

Chapter 20—Web Services

Previous chapters demonstrated how to create applications that execute locally on the user's computer. In this chapter, we introduce Web services, which are programs that "expose" services (i.e., methods) to clients over the Internet, intranets and extranets. Web services offer increased software reusability by allowing services on disparate platforms to interact with each other seamlessly. We discuss .NET Web services basics and related technologies, including *Simple Object Access Protocol* (*SOAP*) and *Active Server Pages* (*ASP*) .NET. This chapter presents an interesting example of a Web service that manipulates huge integers (up to 100 digits). We present a Blackjack application that demonstrates session tracking, a form of personalization that enables the application to "recognize" a user. We conclude with a discussion of Microsoft's Global XML Web Services Architecture (GXA), a series of specifications that provide additional capabilities to Web services developers.

Chapter 21—Networking: Streams-Based Sockets and Datagrams

Chapter 21 introduces the fundamental techniques of streams-based networking. We demonstrate how streams-based *sockets* allow programmers to hide many networking details. With sockets, networking is as simple as if the programmer were reading from and writing to a file. We also introduce *datagrams,* in which packets of information are sent between programs. Each packet is addressed to its recipient and sent out to the network, which routes the packet to its destination. The examples in this chapter focus on communication between applications. One example demonstrates using streams-based sockets to communicate between two Visual C++ .NET programs. Another, similar example sends datagrams between applications. We also show how to create a multithreaded-server application that can communicate with multiple clients in parallel. In this client/server tic-tac-toe game, the server maintains the status of the game, and two clients communicate with the server to play the game.

Chapter 22—Data Structures and Collections

This chapter discusses arranging data into aggregations such as linked lists, stacks, queues and trees. Each data structure has properties that are useful in many applications, from sorting elements to keeping track of method calls. We discuss how to build each of these data structures. This is also a valuable experience in crafting useful classes. In addition, we cover prebuilt collection classes in the FCL. These classes store sets, or collections, of data and provide functionality that allow the developer to sort, insert, delete and retrieve data items. Different collection classes store data in different ways. This chapter focuses on classes `Array`, `ArrayList`, `Stack` and `Hashtable`, discussing the details of each. When possible, Visual C++ .NET programmers should use appropriate FCL collections, rather than implementing similar data structures themselves. This chapter reinforces much of the object technology discussed in Chapters 5–7, including classes, inheritance and composition.

Appendix A—Operator Precedence Chart

This appendix lists Visual C++ .NET operators and their precedence.

Appendix B—Number Systems

This appendix explains the binary, octal, decimal and hexadecimal number systems. It also reviews the conversion of numbers among these bases and illustrates mathematical operations in each base.

Appendix C—ASCII Character Set
This appendix contains a table of the 128 ASCII (American Standard Code for Information Interchange) alphanumeric symbols and their corresponding integer values.

Appendix D—Unicode®
This appendix introduces the Unicode Standard, an encoding scheme that assigns unique numeric values to the characters of most of the world's languages. We include a Windows application that uses Unicode encoding to print welcome messages in several languages.

Appendices E and F—Introduction to XHTML: Parts 1 & 2
In these appendices, we introduce the Extensible HyperText Markup Language (XHTML), a W3C technology designed to replace HTML as the primary means of describing Web content. As an XML-based language, XHTML is more robust and extensible than HTML. XHTML incorporates most of HTML's elements and attributes—the focus of these appendices. Appendices E and F are included for our readers who do not know XHTML or who would like a review of XHTML before studying Chapter 18, Extensible Markup Language (XML).

Appendix G—XHTML Special Characters
This appendix provides many commonly used XHTML special characters, called *character entity references*.

Appendix H—XHTML Colors
This appendix lists commonly used XHTML color names and their corresponding hexadecimal values.

Appendix I—Bit Manipulation
This appendix discusses Visual C++ .NET's powerful bit-manipulation capabilities. This helps programs process bit strings, set individual bits on or off and store information more compactly. Such capabilities are characteristic of low-level assembly languages and are valued by programmers writing systems software, such as operating system and networking software.

Acknowledgments

One of the great pleasures of writing a textbook is acknowledging the efforts of many people whose names may not appear on the cover, but whose hard work, cooperation, friendship and understanding were crucial to the production of the book. Many people at Deitel & Associates, Inc. devoted long hours to this project:

Abbey Deitel
Barbara Deitel
Christi Kelsey
Tem Nieto
Christina Courtemarche
Rashmi Jayaprakash
Laura Treibick
Betsy DuWaldt

We would also like to thank the participants in the Deitel & Associates, Inc., College Internship Program who contributed to this publication.[1] We would like to extend a special thank you to Jim Bai of Carnegie Mellon University, who helped us with the completion of the text and instructor's manual under tight deadlines.

Jim Bai (Carnegie Mellon)
Bei Zhao (Northeastern)
Jimmy Nguyen (Northeastern)
Nicholas Cassie (Northeastern)
Thiago da Silva (Northeastern)
Mike Dos'Santos (Northeastern)
Emanuel Achildiev (Northeastern)

We are fortunate to have worked on this project with the talented and dedicated team of publishing professionals at Prentice Hall. We especially appreciate the extraordinary efforts of our Computer Science Editor, Kate Hargett and her boss and our mentor in publishing—Marcia Horton, Editorial Director of Prentice-Hall's Engineering and Computer Science Division. Vince O'Brien and Tom Manshreck did a marvelous job managing the production of the book. Sarah Parker managed the publication of the book's extensive ancillary package.

We wish to acknowledge the efforts of our reviewers and to thank Carole Snyder and Jennifer Cappello of Prentice Hall, who managed the review process. Adhering to a tight time schedule, these reviewers scrutinized the text and the programs, providing countless suggestions for improving the accuracy and completeness of the presentation. We sincerely appreciate the time these people took from their busy professional schedules to help us ensure the quality, accuracy and timeliness of this book.

Visual C++ .NET How to Program Reviewers:
Shishir Abhyanker (Accenture)
Rekha Bhowmik (Winona State University)
Chadi Boudiab (Georgia Perimeter College)
Steve Chattargoon (Northern Alberta Institute of Technology)
Kunal Cheda (Syntel India, Ltd.)
Dean Goodmanson (Renaissance Learning, Inc.
Keith Harrow (Brooklyn College)
Doug Harrison (Eluent Software)
James Huddleston (Independent Consultant)
Terrell Hull (Sun Certified Java Architect, Rational Qualified Practitioner)
Shrawan Kumar (Accenture)
Andrew Mooney (American Continental University)

1. The *Deitel & Associates, Inc. College Internship Program* offers a limited number of salaried positions to Boston-area college students majoring in Computer Science, Information Technology, Marketing, Management and English. Students work at our corporate headquarters in Maynard, Massachusetts full-time in the summers and (for those attending college in the Boston area) part-time during the academic year. We also offer full-time internship positions for students interested in taking a semester off from school to gain industry experience. Regular full-time positions are available from time to time to college graduates. For more information, please contact our president—`abbey.deitel@deitel.com`—and visit our Web site, `www.deitel.com`.

Neal Patel (Microsoft Corporation)
Paul Randal (Microsoft Corporation)
Christopher Whitehead (Columbus State University)
Warren Wiltsie (Fairleigh Dickinson University)

***Visual C++ .NET: A Managed Code Approach for Experienced Programmers* Reviewers:**
Neal Patel (Microsoft)
Paul Randal (Microsoft)
Scott Woodgate (Microsoft)
David Weller (Microsoft)
Dr. Rekha Bhowmik (St. Cloud State University)
Carl Burnham (Hosting Resolve)
Kyle Gabhart (StarMaker Technologies)
Doug Harrison (Eluent Software)
Christian Hessler (Sun Microsystems)
Michael Hudson (Blue Print Tech)
John Paul Mueller (DataCon Services)
Nicholas Paldino (Exis Consulting)
Chris Platt (RealAge Inc./ UC San Diego Extension)
Teri Radichel (Radical Software)
Ivan Rancati
Tomas Restrepo (Intergrupo S.A)

Contacting Deitel & Associates

We would sincerely appreciate your comments, criticisms, corrections and suggestions for improving the text. Please address all correspondence to:

`deitel@deitel.com`

We will respond promptly.

Errata

We will post all errata for this publication at `www.deitel.com`.

Customer Support

Please direct all software and installation questions to Pearson Education Technical Support:

- By phone: 1-800-677-6337
- By email: `media.support@pearsoned.com`
- On the Web: `247.prenhall.com`

Please direct all Visual C++ .NET language questions to `deitel@deitel.com`. We will respond promptly.

Welcome to the exciting world of programming in Visual C++ .NET. We sincerely hope you enjoy learning with this book.

Dr. Harvey M. Deitel
Paul J. Deitel
Jonathan P. Liperi
Cheryl H. Yaeger

About the Authors

Dr. Harvey M. Deitel, Chairman of Deitel & Associates, Inc., has 42 years experience in the computing field, including extensive industry and academic experience. Dr. Deitel earned B.S. and M.S. degrees from the Massachusetts Institute of Technology and a Ph.D. from Boston University. He worked on the pioneering virtual memory operating-systems projects at IBM and MIT that developed techniques now widely implemented in systems such as UNIX, Linux and Windows XP. He has 20 years of college teaching experience and served as the Chairman of the Computer Science Department at Boston College before founding Deitel & Associates, Inc., with his son, Paul J. Deitel. He is the author or co-author of several dozen books and multimedia packages. With translations published in numerous foreign languages, Dr. Deitel's texts have earned international recognition. Dr. Deitel has delivered professional seminars to major corporations, government organizations and various branches of the military.

Paul J. Deitel, CEO and Chief Technical Officer of Deitel & Associates, Inc., is a graduate of the Massachusetts Institute of Technology's Sloan School of Management, where he studied information technology. Through Deitel & Associates, Inc., he has delivered professional seminars to numerous industry and government clients and has lectured on C++ and Java for the Boston Chapter of the Association for Computing Machinery. He and his father, Dr. Harvey M. Deitel, are the world's best-selling Computer Science textbook authors.

Jonathan P. Liperi is a graduate of Boston University with a Master's degree in Computer Science. His research at BU focused on dimensionality reduction techniques and matching functions for temporal databases. Jon also co-authored Deitel & Associates, Inc. publications, *Visual C++ .NET: A Managed Code Approach for Experienced Programmers* and *Python How to Program*. Jon currently works as a Software Development Engineer in Test on the Enterprise Frameworks and Tools team at Microsoft.

Cheryl H. Yaeger, Director of Microsoft Software Publications with Deitel & Associates, Inc., is a graduate of Boston University with a degree in Computer Science. Cheryl has co-authored various Deitel & Associates, Inc. publications, including *Visual C++ .NET: A Managed Code Approach for Experienced Programmers*, *C# How to Program*, *C#: A Programmer's Introduction*, *C# for Experienced Programmers*, *Simply C#*, *Visual Basic .NET for Experienced Programmers*, *Simply Visual Basic .NET*, *Simply Visual Basic .NET 2003* and *Simply Java™ Programming* and has contributed to several others.

About Deitel & Associates, Inc.

Deitel & Associates, Inc., is an internationally recognized corporate training and content-creation organization specializing in Internet/World Wide Web software technology, e-business/e-commerce software technology, object technology and computer programming languages education. The company provides instructor-led courses on Internet and World Wide Web programming, wireless Internet programming, object technology, and major programming languages and platforms, such as C, C++, Visual C++ .NET, Visual Basic .NET, C#, Java, Advanced Java, XML, Perl, Python and more. The founders of Deitel & Associates, Inc., are Dr. Harvey M. Deitel and Paul J. Deitel. The company's clients include many of the world's largest computer companies, government agencies, branches of the military and business organizations. Through its 28-year publishing partnership with

Prentice Hall, Deitel & Associates, Inc., publishes leading-edge programming textbooks, professional books, interactive CD-based multimedia *Cyber Classrooms*, *Complete Training Courses*, Web-based training courses and course management systems e-content for popular CMSs such as WebCT™, Blackboard™ and CourseCompass℠. Deitel & Associates, Inc., and the authors can be reached via e-mail at:

```
deitel@deitel.com
```

To learn more about Deitel & Associates, Inc., its publications and its worldwide corporate on-site training curriculum, see the last few pages of this book or visit:

```
www.deitel.com
```

Individuals wishing to purchase Deitel books, *Cyber Classrooms*, *Complete Training Courses* and Web-based training courses can do so through bookstores, online booksellers and:

```
www.deitel.com
www.prenhall.com/deitel
www.InformIT.com/deitel
www.InformIT.com/cyberclassrooms
```

Bulk orders by corporations and academic institutions should be placed directly with Prentice Hall. See the last few pages of this book for worldwide ordering instructions.

1

Introduction to .NET and Visual C++® .NET

Objectives

- To learn the history of the Internet and the World Wide Web.
- To become familiar with the World Wide Web Consortium (W3C).
- To learn what the Extensible Markup Language (XML) is and why it is an important technology.
- To understand the impact of object technology on software development.
- To understand the Microsoft® .NET initiative.
- To introduce Managed Extensions for C++.

Things are always at their best in their beginning.
Blaise Pascal

High thoughts must have high language.
Aristophanes

Our life is frittered away by detail…Simplify, simplify.
Henry David Thoreau

Before beginning, plan carefully….
Marcus Tullius Cicero

Look with favor upon a bold beginning.
Virgil

I think I'm beginning to learn something about it.
Auguste Renoir

Outline

1.1 Introduction

Welcome to Visual C++ .NET! We have worked hard to provide programmers with the most accurate and complete information regarding Visual C++ .NET and the .NET platform. We hope that this book will provide an informative, entertaining and challenging learning experience for you. In this chapter, we present the history of the Internet and World Wide Web and introduce Microsoft's .NET initiative.

1.2 History of the Internet and World Wide Web

In the late 1960s, at a conference at the University of Illinois Urbana-Champaign, *ARPA*—the *Advanced Research Projects Agency* of the Department of Defense—rolled out the blueprints for networking the main computer systems of approximately a dozen ARPA-funded universities and research institutions. The computers were to be connected with communications lines operating at a then-stunning 56 Kbps (1 Kbps is equal to 1,024 bits per second), at a time when most people (of the few who had access to networking technologies) were connecting over telephone lines to computers at a rate of 110 bits per second. Researchers at Harvard talked about communicating with the Univac 1108 "supercomputer," which was located across the country at the University of Utah, to handle calculations related to their computer graphics research. Many other intriguing possibilities were discussed. Academic research was about to take a giant leap forward. Shortly after this conference, ARPA proceeded to implement what quickly became known as the *ARPAnet*, the grandparent of today's *Internet*.

Things worked out differently from the original plan. Although the ARPAnet did enable researchers to network their computers, its chief benefit proved to be its capability for quick and easy communication via what came to be known as *electronic mail* (*e-mail*). This is true even on today's Internet, with e-mail, instant messaging and file transfer facilitating communications among hundreds of millions of people worldwide.

The network was designed to operate without centralized control. This meant that if a portion of the network should fail, the remaining working portions would still be able to route data packets from senders to receivers over alternative paths.

- Math::Pow(x, y)

  $\Rightarrow x^y$

- String::Concat(s"____", s"____")
- Use decimal type for $ calcs.
- do {

  ____

  ____

  } while (condition);

- for (; ;) {

  ____

  ____

  }

- switch ( ) {

  case '_':

  case '_':

  ⋮

  break;

  → default:

  break;

  }

The protocol (i.e., set of rules) for communicating over the ARPAnet became known as the *Transmission Control Protocol (TCP)*. TCP ensured that messages were routed properly from sender to receiver and that those messages arrived intact.

In parallel with the early evolution of the Internet, organizations worldwide were implementing their own networks to facilitate both intra-organization (i.e., within the organization) and inter-organization (i.e., between organizations) communication. A huge variety of networking hardware and software appeared. One challenge was to enable these diverse products to communicate with each other. ARPA accomplished this by developing the *Internet Protocol* (*IP*), which created a true "network of networks," the current architecture of the Internet. The combined set of protocols is now commonly called *TCP/IP*.

Initially, the use of the Internet was limited to universities and research institutions; later, the military adopted the technology. Eventually, the government decided to allow access to the Internet for commercial purposes. When this decision was made, there was resentment among the research and military communities—it was felt that response times would become poor as "the Net" became saturated with so many users.

In fact, the opposite has occurred. Businesses rapidly realized that, by making effective use of the Internet, they could refine their operations and offer new and better services to their clients. Companies started spending vast amounts of money to develop and enhance their Internet presence. This generated fierce competition among communications carriers and hardware and software suppliers to meet the increased infrastructure demand. The result is that *bandwidth* (i.e., the information-carrying capacity of communications lines) on the Internet has increased tremendously, while hardware costs have plummeted. The Internet has played a significant role in the economic growth that many industrialized nations experienced over the last decade.

The *World Wide Web* allows computer users to locate and view multimedia-based documents (i.e., documents with text, graphics, animations, audios or videos) on almost any subject. Even though the Internet was developed more than three decades ago, the introduction of the World Wide Web (WWW) was a relatively recent event. In 1989, Tim Berners-Lee of CERN (the European Organization for Nuclear Research) began to develop a technology for sharing information via hyperlinked text documents. Basing the new language on the well-established *Standard Generalized Markup Language* (*SGML*)—a standard for business data interchange—Berners-Lee called his invention the *HyperText Markup Language* (*HTML*). He also wrote communication protocols, such as the *Hypertext Transfer Protocol* (*HTTP*), to form the backbone of his new hypertext information system, which he referred to as the World Wide Web.

Surely, historians will list the Internet and the World Wide Web among the most important and profound creations of humankind. In the past, most computer applications ran on "stand-alone" computers (computers that were not connected to one another). Today's applications can be written to communicate among the world's hundreds of millions of computers. The Internet and World Wide Web merge computing and communications technologies, expediting and simplifying our work. They make information instantly and conveniently accessible to large numbers of people. They enable individuals and small businesses to achieve worldwide exposure. They are changing the way we do business and conduct our personal lives.

1.3 World Wide Web Consortium (W3C)

In October 1994, Tim Berners-Lee founded an organization, called the *World Wide Web Consortium* (*W3C*), that is devoted to developing nonproprietary, interoperable technologies for the World Wide Web. One of the W3C's primary goals is to make the Web universally accessible—regardless of its users' disabilities, languages or cultures.

The W3C is also a standardization organization and is composed of three *hosts*—the Massachusetts Institute of Technology (MIT), ERCIM (European Research Consortium in Informatics and Mathematics) and Keio University of Japan—and approximately 450 members. Members provide the primary financing for the W3C and help set the strategic direction of the Consortium. To learn more about the W3C, visit `www.w3.org`.

Web technologies standardized by the W3C are called *Recommendations*. Current W3C Recommendations include Extensible HyperText Markup Language (XHTML™) for marking up content for the Web (discussed in Section 1.4), *Cascading Style Sheets (CSS™)* for describing how content is formatted and the *Extensible Markup Language (XML)* for creating markup languages. Recommendations are not actual software products, but documents that specify the role, syntax and rules of a technology. Before becoming a W3C Recommendation—a document passes through three major phases: *Working Draft*, which, as its name implies, specifies an evolving draft; *Candidate Recommendation*, a stable version of the document that industry can begin to implement; and *Proposed Recommendation*, a Candidate Recommendation that is considered mature (i.e., has been implemented and tested over a period of time) and is ready to be considered for W3C Recommendation status. For detailed information about the W3C Recommendation track, see the World Wide Web Consortium Process Document at

`www.w3.org/Consortium/Process`

1.4 Extensible Markup Language (XML)

As the popularity of the Web exploded in the 1990s, HTML's limitations became apparent. Although HTML was created as a common format for the Web, HTML's lack of *extensibility* (the ability to change or add features) frustrated developers, and the lack of correctly structured documents allowed erroneous HTML to proliferate. Browser vendors attempting to gain market share created platform-specific tags. This forced Web developers to support multiple browsers, which significantly complicated Web development. To address these and other problems, the W3C developed XML.

XML combines the power and extensibility of its parent language, SGML, with simplicity. XML is a *meta-language*—a language used as a basis for other languages—that offers a high level of extensibility. Using XML, the W3C created the *Extensible HyperText Markup Language (XHTML)*, an XML *vocabulary* (i.e., an XML-based markup language that is developed for a specific industry or purpose) that provides a common, extensible format for the Web. XHTML is expected to replace HTML. The W3C also developed the *Extensible Stylesheet Language (XSL)*, which is composed of several technologies, to manipulate data in XML documents for presentation purposes. XSL provides developers the flexibility to transform data from an XML document into other types of documents—for example, Web pages or reports. In addition to serving as the basis for other markup languages, developers use XML for data interchange and e-commerce systems. At the time of this writing, there were more than 450 XML vocabularies.

Unlike many technologies, which begin as proprietary solutions and become standards, XML was defined as an open, standard technology. XML's development has been supervised by the W3C's *XML Working Group*, which prepared the XML specification and approved it for publication. In 1998, the XML version 1.0 specification (`www.w3.org/TR/REC-xml`) was accepted as a *W3C Recommendation.* This means that the technology is stable for wide deployment in industry.

The W3C continues to oversee the development of XML, as well as Simple Object Access Protocol (SOAP), a technology for the distribution of data (marked up as XML) over the Internet. Developed initially by Microsoft and DevelopMentor, SOAP is a W3C Working Draft that provides a framework for expressing application semantics and encoding and packaging data. Microsoft .NET (discussed in Section 1.6 and Section 1.8) uses XML and SOAP to mark up and transfer data over the Internet. XML and SOAP are at the core of .NET—they allow software components to interoperate (i.e., communicate easily with one another). SOAP is supported by many platforms, because of its foundations in XML and HTTP. We discuss XML in Chapter 18, Extensible Markup Language (XML), and SOAP in Chapter 20, Web Services.

1.5 Key Software Trend: Object Technology

What are objects, and why are they special? Object technology is a packaging scheme that facilitates the creation of meaningful software units. These units are large and focused on particular application areas. There are date objects, time objects, paycheck objects, invoice objects, audio objects, video objects, file objects, record objects and so on. In fact, almost any noun can be represented as a software object. Objects have *properties* (i.e., *attributes*, such as color, size and weight) and perform *actions* (i.e., *behaviors*, such as moving, sleeping and drawing). Objects can also have events that they can respond to, like a mouse-click. Classes are a blueprint for an object. This class blueprint can be used to create many occurrences of that object. Classes represent groups of related objects. For example, all cars belong to the "car" class, even though individual cars vary in make, model, color and options packages. A class specifies the general format of its objects; the properties and actions available to an object depend on its class.

We live in a world of objects. Just look around you—there are cars, planes, people, animals, buildings, traffic lights, elevators and so on. Before object-oriented languages appeared, *procedural programming languages* (such as Fortran, Pascal, BASIC and C) focused on actions (verbs) rather than things or objects (nouns). We live in a world of objects, but earlier programming languages forced individuals to program primarily with verbs. The paradigm shift to object-oriented programming made writing programs a bit awkward. However, with the advent of popular object-oriented languages, such as C++, Java™ and C#, programmers can program in an object-oriented manner that reflects the way in which they perceive the world. This process, which seems more natural than procedural programming, has resulted in significant productivity gains.

One of the key problems with procedural programming is that the program units created do not mirror real-world entities effectively and therefore are difficult to reuse. Programmers often write and rewrite similar software for various projects. This wastes precious time and money as programmers repeatedly "reinvent the wheel." With object technology, properly designed software entities (called objects) can be reused on future projects. Using libraries of reusable components can reduce the amount of effort required to implement certain kinds of systems (compared with the effort that would be required to reinvent these capabilities in new projects). Visual C++ .NET programmers use the .NET Framework Class Library (known commonly as the FCL), which is introduced in Section 1.8.

Some organizations report that software reusability is not, in fact, the key benefit of object-oriented programming. Rather, they indicate that *object-oriented programming* (*OOP*) tends to produce software that is more understandable because it is better organized and has fewer maintenance requirements. As much as 80 percent of software costs are not associated with the original efforts to develop the software, but instead are related to the continued evolution and maintenance of that software throughout its lifetime. Object orientation allows programmers to abstract the details of software and focus on the "big picture." Rather than worrying about minute details, the programmer can focus on the behaviors and interactions of objects. A roadmap that showed every tree, house and driveway would be difficult, if not impossible, to read. When such details are removed and only the essential information (the roads) remains, the map becomes easier to understand. In the same way, a program that is divided into objects is easy to understand, modify and update because it hides much of the detail. It is clear that object-oriented programming will be the key programming methodology for at least the next decade.

Software Engineering Observation 1.1

Use a building-block approach to create programs. By using existing pieces in new projects, programmers avoid reinventing the wheel. This is called software reuse, *and it is central to object-oriented programming.*

[*Note*: We will include many of these *Software Engineering Observations* throughout the book to explain concepts that affect and improve the overall architecture and quality of a software system and, particularly, of large software systems. We also will highlight *Good Programming Practices* (practices that can help programmers write programs that are clearer, more understandable, more maintainable and easier to test and debug), *Common Programming Errors* (problems we highlight to ensure that programmers avoid the most common errors), *Performance Tips* (techniques that will help programmers write programs that run faster and use less memory), *Portability Tips* (techniques that will help programmers write programs that can run, with little or no modification, on a variety of computers), *Testing and Debugging Tips* (techniques that will help programmers remove bugs from their programs and, more importantly, write bug-free programs in the first place) and *Look-and-Feel Observations* (techniques that will help programmers design the "look and feel" of their graphical user interfaces for appearance and ease of use). Many of these techniques and practices are only guidelines; you will, no doubt, develop your own preferred programming style.]

The advantage of writing your own code is that you will know exactly how it works. The code will be yours to examine, modify and improve. The disadvantage is the time and effort that goes into designing, developing and testing new code.

Performance Tip 1.1

Reusing proven code components instead of writing your own versions can improve program performance, because these components normally are written to perform efficiently.

Software Engineering Observation 1.2

Extensive class libraries of reusable software components are available over the Internet and the World Wide Web; many are offered free of charge.

1.6 Introduction to Microsoft .NET

In June 2000, Microsoft announced its *.NET* (pronounced "dot-net") *initiative*. The *.NET platform* is one that provides significant enhancements to earlier developer platforms. .NET offers a new software-development model that allows applications created in disparate programming languages to communicate with each other. The platform also allows developers to create Web-based applications that can be distributed to a great variety of devices (even wireless phones) and to desktop computers.

Microsoft's .NET initiative is a broad new vision for embracing the Internet and the Web in the development, engineering and use of software. One key aspect of the .NET strategy is its independence from a specific language or platform. Rather than requiring programmers to use a single programming language, developers can create a .NET application by using any combination of .NET-compatible languages (Fig. 1.1). Programmers can contribute to the same software project, writing code in the .NET languages (such as Visual C++ .NET, C#, Visual Basic® .NET and many others) in which they are most proficient.

Programming Languages	
APL	Mondrian
C#	Oberon
COBOL	Oz
Component Pascal	Pascal
Curriculum	Perl
Eiffel	Python
Forth	RPG
Fortran	Scheme
Haskell	Smalltalk
J#	Standard ML
JScript .NET	Visual Basic .NET
Mercury	Visual C++ .NET

Fig. 1.1 .NET Languages (tabular information from Microsoft Web site, `msdn.microsoft.com/netframework/technologyinfo/Overview/default.aspx`).

A key component of the .NET architecture is *Web services*, which are applications that expose (i.e., make available) functionality to applications (also called clients) via the Internet. Clients and other applications can use these Web services as reusable building blocks. One example of a Web service is Dollar Rent A Car's reservation system, known as Quick Keys.[1] Dollar wanted to expose the functionality of its mainframe-based system so that other companies could provide customers with the ability to make car-rental reservations. Dollar could

1. Microsoft Corporation, "Dollar Rent A Car Breathes New Life Into Legacy Systems Using .NET Connected Software," 15 March 2002 `<www.microsoft.com/business/casestudies/b2c/dollarrentacar.asp>`.

have created individual, proprietary solutions for its business partners. To expose its functionality in a reusable way, Dollar implemented its solution using Web services. Through the newly created Web service, airlines and hotels can use Dollar's reservation system to reserve cars for their clients. Dollar's business partners do not need to use the same platform as Dollar uses, nor do they need to understand how the reservation system is implemented. Reimplementing its application as a Web service has provided Dollar with millions of dollars of additional revenue, as well as thousands of new customers.

Web services extend the concept of software reuse by allowing programmers to concentrate on their specialties without having to implement every component of every application. Instead, companies can buy Web services and devote their time and energy to developing their products. Object-oriented programming has become popular, because it enables programmers to create applications easily, using prepackaged components. Similarly, programmers may create an application using Web services for databases, security, authentication, data storage and language translation without having to know the internal details of those components.

When companies link their products via Web services, a new user experience emerges. For example, a single application could manage bill payments, tax refunds, loans and investments, using Web services from various companies. An online merchant could buy Web services for online credit-card payments, user authentication, network security and inventory databases to create an e-commerce Web site.

The key technologies in such interactions are XML and SOAP, which enable Web services to communicate. XML gives meaning to data, and SOAP is the protocol that allows Web services to communicate easily with one another. XML and SOAP act as the "glue" that combines various Web services to form applications.

Universal data access is another essential .NET concept. If two copies of a file exist (e.g., on a personal and a company computer), the oldest version must be updated constantly—this is called file *synchronization*. If the files are different, they are *unsynchronized*, a situation that could lead to errors. With .NET, data can reside in one central location rather than on separate systems. Any Internet-connected device can access the data (under tight control, of course), which would then be formatted appropriately for use or display on the accessing device. Thus, the same document could be seen and edited on a desktop PC, a PDA, a wireless phone or some other device. Users would not need to synchronize the information, because it would be fully up-to-date in a central location.

.NET is an immense undertaking. We discuss various aspects of .NET throughout this book. Additional information is available at `www.microsoft.com/net`.

1.7 Visual C++ .NET

Standard C++ evolved from C, which was developed from two previous programming languages, BCPL and B. BCPL was developed in 1967 by Martin Richards as a language for writing operating systems software and compilers. Ken Thompson modeled many features in his B language after their counterparts in BCPL and used B in 1970 to create early versions of the UNIX operating system at Bell Laboratories on a DEC PDP-7 computer. Both BCPL and B were "typeless" languages—every data item occupied one "word" in memory and the burden of typing variables fell on the shoulders of the programmer.

The C language was evolved from B by Dennis Ritchie at Bell Laboratories and was originally implemented on a DEC PDP-11 computer in 1972. C uses many important concepts of BCPL and B while adding data typing and other powerful features. C initially became widely known as the development language of the UNIX operating system. Today, virtually all new major operating systems are written in C and/or C++. C is available for most computers. C is also hardware independent. With careful design, it is possible to write C programs that are *portable* to most computers.

By the late 1970s, C had evolved into what now is referred to as "traditional C." The publication in 1978 of Kernighan and Ritchie's book, *The C Programming Language,* brought attention to the language. This publication became one of the most successful computer science books of all time.

The rapid expansion of C over various types of computers (sometimes called *hardware platforms*) led to many variations that were similar but often incompatible. This was a serious problem for program developers who needed to develop code that would run on several platforms. It became clear that a standard version of C was needed. In 1983, the X3J11 technical committee was created under the American National Standards Committee on Computers and Information Processing (X3) to "provide an unambiguous and machine-independent definition of the language." In 1989, the standard was approved; this standard was updated in 1999. The standards document is referred to as *INCITS/ISO/IEC 9899-1999*. Copies of this document may be ordered from the American National Standards Institute (`www.ansi.org`) at `webstore.ansi.org/ansidocstore`.

Portability Tip 1.1

C is a standardized, hardware-independent, widely available language; therefore, applications written in C often can be run with little or no modifications on a wide range of different computer systems.

C++ is a superset C developed by Bjarne Stroustrup in the early 1980s at Bell Laboratories. C++ provides a number of features that "spruce up" the C language, but more importantly, it provides capabilities for object-oriented programming.

Building software quickly, correctly and economically remains an elusive goal, and this is true at a time when the demand for new and more powerful software is soaring. Objects, as discussed earlier, are essentially reusable software *components* that model items in the real world. Software developers are discovering that using a modular, object-oriented design and implementation approach can make software development groups much more productive than is possible with previous popular programming techniques, such as structured programming. Object-oriented programs are easier to understand, correct and modify.

Developed in the early 1990s, Visual C++ is a Microsoft implementation of C++ that includes Microsoft's proprietary extensions to the language. Over the past decade, Microsoft has released several versions of Visual C++—most recently, Visual C++ .NET. Visual C++ .NET is known as a *visual programming language*—the developer uses graphical tools, such as Visual Studio .NET, to create applications. We discuss Visual Studio .NET later in this section.

Early graphics and *graphical user interface* (*GUI*) programming (i.e., the programming of an application's visual interface) with Visual C++ was implemented using the *Microsoft Foundation Classes* (*MFC*). The *MFC library* is a collection of classes that help Visual C++ programmers create powerful Windows-based applications. Now, with the introduction of .NET, Microsoft provides an additional library (.NET's FCL, discussed in

Section 1.8) for implementing GUI, graphics, networking, multithreading and other capabilities. This library is available to .NET-compliant languages such as Visual C++ .NET, Visual Basic .NET and Microsoft's new language, C#. However, developers still can use MFC—Microsoft has, in fact, upgraded MFC to MFC 7, which includes new classes and documentation that can be accessed using Visual Studio .NET. MFC often is used to develop *unmanaged code*, or code that does not make use of the .NET Framework.

The .NET platform enables Web-based applications to be distributed to a variety of devices, including desktop computers and cell phones. The platform offers a new software-development model that allows applications created in disparate programming languages to communicate with each other. Visual C++ .NET was designed specifically for the .NET platform so Visual C++ programmers could migrate easily to .NET. However, Microsoft also designed Visual C++ .NET to be backward compatible with its previous version of Visual C++, 6.0, and has continued to emphasize compliance with the ANSI/ISO standard for C++.

Visual C++ .NET introduces *Managed Extensions for C++* (*MC++*) that enable a programmer to access the .NET Framework. Programmers can use the .NET Framework to create objects that provide automatic memory management and language interoperability (with other .NET languages). Such objects are known as *managed objects*; the code that defines these objects is known as *managed code*. [*Note*: The different implementations of C++ and Visual C++ have yielded several industry terms. For the remainder of this book, we use the term "C++" when referring to standard C++. We use the term "Managed Extensions for C++ (MC++)" when referring to features of managed C++ or code that uses these features. Finally, we use the term "Visual C++ .NET" when referring to the Microsoft product/compiler, which can be used to write both managed and unmanaged code.]

MC++ provides the programmer access to new data types provided by the .NET Framework. These new data types aid in standardization across different platforms and .NET programming languages. In MC++, standard C++ data types are mapped to these new types. [*Note*: We discuss .NET data types in more detail in Chapter 3, Introduction to Visual C++ .NET Programming.]

In Visual C++ .NET, programs are created using Visual Studio .NET, an *Integrated Development Environment* (*IDE*). With the IDE, a programmer can create, run, test and debug programs conveniently, thereby reducing the time it takes to produce a working program to a fraction of the time it would have taken without using the IDE. The process of rapidly creating an application using an IDE typically is referred to as *Rapid Application Development (RAD)*. For fast Windows application programming, Visual Studio .NET provides a *Windows Form designer*, a visual programming tool that simplifies GUI and database programming. With the Windows Form Designer, Visual Studio .NET generates program code from various programmer *actions* (such as using the mouse for pointing, clicking, dragging and dropping).

Visual C++ .NET enables a new degree of language interoperability: Software components from different languages can interact as never before. Developers can package even old software to work with new Visual C++ .NET programs. In addition, Visual C++ .NET applications can interact via the Internet, using industry standards such as the Simple Object Access Protocol (SOAP) and XML, which we discuss in Chapter 18, Extensible Markup Language (XML) and Chapter 20, Web Services. The programming advances embodied in .NET and Visual C++ .NET will lead to a new style of programming, in which applications are created from building blocks available over the Internet.

1.8 .NET Framework and the Common Language Runtime

The *.NET Framework* is at the heart of .NET. This framework manages and executes applications, contains a class library (called the *Framework Class Library*, or *FCL*) that all .NET languages can share, enforces security and provides many other programming capabilities. Details of the .NET Framework are found in the *Common Language Infrastructure* (*CLI*). The CLI is now an ECMA International (the European Computer Manufacturers Association) standard.[2] This allows independent software vendors to create the .NET Framework for other platforms. The .NET Framework exists only for the Windows platform, but is being developed for other platforms, as well. Microsoft's *Shared Source CLI* (*Common Language Infrastructure*) is an archive of source code that provides a subset of the Microsoft .NET Framework for Windows XP, FreeBSD[3] operating system and Mac OS X 10.2. The source code in the Shared Source CLI is written to the ECMA International CLI standard. There are also other projects underway to provide the .NET Framework to other platforms. The Mono project (`www.go-mono.com`) provides a subset of the .NET Framework for the UNIX and Linux systems, and also runs on Windows systems. The DotGNU Portable .NET project (`www.southern-storm.com.au/portable_net.html`) provides software tools that enable programmers to write .NET applications on several operating systems (although it is targeted mainly at the Linux operating system).

The *Common Language Runtime (CLR)*, which executes managed code, is another central part of the .NET Framework. Programs are compiled into machine-specific instructions in two steps. First, the program is compiled into *Microsoft Intermediate Language (MSIL)*, which defines instructions for the CLR. Code converted into MSIL from other .NET languages and sources is woven together by the CLR. Then, another compiler in the CLR compiles the MSIL into machine code (for a particular platform), creating a single application.

Why bother having the extra step of converting from Visual C++ .NET to MSIL, instead of compiling directly into machine language? The key reasons are portability between operating systems, interoperability between languages and execution-management features such as memory management and security.

If the .NET Framework is installed on a platform, that platform can run any .NET program. The ability of a program to run (without modification) across multiple platforms is known as *platform independence*. Code written once can be used on another machine without modification, saving both time and money. In addition, software can target a wider audience—previously, companies had to decide whether converting (sometimes called *porting*) their programs to different platforms was worth the cost. With .NET, porting is simplified.

The .NET Framework also provides *language interoperability*. Programs written in different languages are all compiled into MSIL—the different parts can be combined to create a single, unified program. MSIL allows the .NET Framework to be *language independent*, because MSIL is not tied to a particular programming language. Any language that can be compiled into MSIL is called a *.NET-compliant language*.

Language interoperability offers many benefits to software companies. Visual C++ .NET, Visual Basic .NET and C# developers, for example, can work side-by-side on

---

2. More information for the CLI standard can be found at `www.ecma-international.org/publications/standards/Ecma-335.htm`.
3. The FreeBSD project provides a freely available and open-source UNIX-like operating system that is based on UC Berkeley's *Berkeley System Distribution* (*BSD*). For more information on BSD, visit `www.freebsd.org`.

the same project without having to learn another programming language—all their code is compiled into MSIL and linked together to form one program. In addition, the .NET Framework can package preexisting components (i.e., components created using tools that predate .NET) and .NET components to work together. This allows companies to reuse the code that they have spent years developing and integrate it with the .NET code that they write. Integration is crucial, because companies cannot migrate easily to .NET unless they can stay productive, using their existing developers and software.

Another benefit of the .NET Framework is the CLR's execution-management features. The CLR manages memory, security and other features, relieving the programmer of these responsibilities. With languages like C++, programmers must manage their own memory. This leads to problems if programmers request memory and never release it—programs could consume all available memory, which would prevent applications from running. By managing the program's memory, the .NET Framework allows programmers to concentrate on program logic.

This book explains how to develop .NET software with Visual C++ .NET and the FCL. Steve Ballmer, Microsoft's CEO, stated in May 2001 that Microsoft was "betting the company" on .NET. Such a dramatic commitment surely indicates a bright future for Visual C++ .NET and its community of developers.

1.9 Web Resources

`www.deitel.com`
This is the official Deitel & Associates, Inc. Web site. Here you will find updates, corrections, downloads and additional resources for all Deitel publications. In addition, this site provides information about Deitel & Associates, Inc., information on international translations and much more.

`www.deitel.com/newsletter/subscribe.html`
You can register here to receive the *DEITEL® BUZZ ONLINE* e-mail newsletter. This free newsletter updates readers on our publishing program, instructor-led corporate training courses, hottest industry trends and topics and much more. The newsletter is available in full-color HTML and plain-text formats.

`www.prenhall.com/deitel`
This is Prentice Hall's Web site for Deitel publications, which contains information about our products and publications, downloads, Deitel curriculum and author information.

`www.InformIT.com/deitel`
This is the Deitel & Associates, Inc. page on Pearson's InformIT Web site. (Pearson owns our publisher Prentice Hall.) InformIT is a comprehensive resource for IT professionals providing articles, electronic publications and other resources for today's hottest information technologies.

`www.w3.org`
The World Wide Web Consortium (W3C) is an organization that develops and recommends technologies for the Internet and World Wide Web. This site includes links to W3C technologies, news, mission statements and frequently asked questions (FAQs).

`www.microsoft.com`
The Microsoft Corporation Web site provides information and technical resources for all Microsoft products, including .NET, enterprise software and the Windows operating system.

`www.microsoft.com/net`
The .NET home page provides downloads, news and events, certification information and subscription information.

SUMMARY

- In the late 1960s, at a conference at the University of Illinois Urbana-Champaign, ARPA—the Advanced Research Projects Agency of the Department of Defense—rolled out the blueprints for networking the main computer systems of approximately a dozen ARPA-funded universities and research institutions. Shortly after this conference, ARPA proceeded to implement the ARPAnet, the grandparent of today's Internet.
- Although the ARPAnet did enable researchers to network their computers, its chief benefit proved to be its capability for quick and easy communication via what came to be known as electronic mail (e-mail). This is true even on today's Internet, with e-mail, instant messaging and file transfer facilitating communications among hundreds of millions of people worldwide.
- The protocol (i.e., set of rules) for communicating over the ARPAnet became known as the Transmission Control Protocol (TCP). TCP ensured that messages were routed properly from sender to receiver and that those messages arrived intact.
- ARPA developed the Internet Protocol (IP), which created a true "network of networks," the current architecture of the Internet. The combined set of protocols is now commonly called TCP/IP.
- In 1989, Tim Berners-Lee of CERN (the European Organization for Nuclear Research) began to develop a technology for sharing information via hyperlinked text documents. Berners-Lee called his invention the HyperText Markup Language (HTML). He also wrote communication protocols to form the backbone of his new hypertext information system, which he referred to as the World Wide Web.
- The World Wide Web allows computer users to locate and view multimedia-based documents (i.e., documents with text, graphics, animations, audios or videos) on almost any subject.
- In October 1994, Berners-Lee founded the World Wide Web Consortium (W3C), an organization that is devoted to developing nonproprietary, interoperable technologies for the World Wide Web. One of the W3C's primary goals is to make the Web universally accessible—regardless of an individual's disabilities, language or culture.
- XML combines the power and extensibility of its parent language, SGML, with simplicity.
- XML is a meta-language that offers a high level of extensibility.
- Using XML, the W3C created the Extensible HyperText Markup Language (XHTML), an XML vocabulary that provides a common, extensible format for the Web.
- In addition to serving as the basis for other markup languages, developers use XML for data interchange and e-commerce systems. At the time of this writing, there were more than 450 XML vocabularies.
- Unlike many technologies, which begin as proprietary solutions and become standards, XML was defined as an open, standard technology. XML's development has been supervised by the W3C's XML Working Group, which prepared the XML specification and approved it for publication.
- In 1998, the XML version 1.0 specification was accepted as a W3C Recommendation.
- Object technology is a packaging scheme that facilitates the creation of meaningful software units.
- Objects have properties (i.e., attributes, such as color, size and weight) and perform actions (i.e., behaviors, such as moving, sleeping or drawing).
- Classes represent groups of related objects.
- With the advent of popular object-oriented languages, such as C++, Java and C#, programmers can program in an object-oriented manner that reflects the way in which they perceive the world. This process, which seems more natural than procedural programming, has resulted in significant productivity gains.

- With object technology, properly designed software entities (called objects) can be reused on future projects.
- Using libraries of reusable componentry can reduce the amount of effort required to implement certain kinds of systems (as compared to the effort that would be required to reinvent these capabilities in new projects).
- Visual C++ .NET programmers use the .NET Framework Class Library (FCL).
- In June 2000, Microsoft announced its .NET initiative. The .NET platform is one that provides significant enhancements to earlier developer platforms.
- .NET offers a new software development model that allows applications created in disparate programming languages to communicate with each other. The platform also allows developers to create Web-based applications that can be distributed to a great variety of devices (even wireless phones) and to desktop computers.
- One key aspect of the .NET strategy is its independence from a specific language or platform. Rather than requiring programmers to use a single programming language, developers can create a .NET application by using any combination of .NET-compatible languages. Programmers can contribute to the same software project, writing code in the .NET languages in which they are most proficient.
- A key component of the .NET architecture is Web services, which are applications that expose functionality to clients via the Internet. Clients and other applications can use these Web services as reusable building blocks.
- Universal data access is another essential .NET concept. With .NET, data can reside in one central location rather than on separate systems. Any Internet-connected device can access the data (under tight control, of course), which would then be formatted appropriately for use or display on the accessing device.
- Developed in the early 1990s, Visual C++ is a Microsoft implementation of C++ that includes Microsoft's proprietary extensions to the language. Over the past decade, Microsoft has released several versions of Visual C++—most recently, Visual C++ .NET.
- Visual C++ .NET is known as a visual programming language—the developer uses graphical tools provided in Visual Studio .NET to create applications.
- Early graphics and graphical user interface (GUI) programming (i.e., the programming of an application's visual interface) with Visual C++ was implemented using the Microsoft Foundation Classes (MFC). The MFC library is a collection of classes that help Visual C++ programmers create powerful Windows-based applications.
- Now, with the introduction of .NET, Microsoft provides an additional library (.NET's FCL) for implementing GUI, graphics, networking, multithreading and other capabilities.
- The FCL is available to .NET-compliant languages such as Visual C++ .NET, Visual Basic .NET and Microsoft's new language, C#.
- Developers still can use MFC—Microsoft has upgraded MFC to MFC 7, which includes new classes and documentation that can be accessed using Visual Studio .NET. MFC often is used to develop unmanaged code, or code that does not make use of the .NET Framework.
- Visual C++ .NET introduces Managed Extensions for C++ (MC++) that enable a programmer to access the .NET Framework.
- Programmers can use the .NET Framework to create objects that provide automatic memory management and language interoperability (with other .NET languages). Such objects are known as managed objects; the code that defines these objects is known as managed code.
- In Visual C++ .NET, programs are created using Visual Studio .NET, an Integrated Development Environment (IDE). With the IDE, a programmer can create, run, test and debug programs conve-

niently, thereby reducing the time it takes to produce a working program to a fraction of the time it would have taken without using the IDE.

- The process of rapidly creating an application using an IDE typically is referred to as Rapid Application Development (RAD).
- The .NET Framework is at the heart of .NET. This framework manages and executes applications, contains the FCL, enforces security and provides many other programming capabilities.
- The details of the .NET Framework are found in the Common Language Infrastructure (CLI).
- The Common Language Runtime (CLR) executes Visual C++ .NET managed-code programs. Programs are compiled into machine-specific instructions in two steps. First, the program is compiled into Microsoft Intermediate Language (MSIL), which defines instructions for the CLR. Code converted into MSIL from other languages and sources is woven together by the CLR. Then, another compiler in the CLR compiles the MSIL into machine code (for a particular platform), creating a single application.

TERMINOLOGY

action
Advanced Research Projects Agency (ARPA)
ARPAnet
attribute
bandwidth
behavior
C programming language
C++ programming language
Cascading Style Sheets (CSS™)
Common Language Infrastructure (CLI)
Common Language Runtime (CLR)
component
DotGNU Portable .NET project
extensibility
Extensible HyperText Markup Language (XHTML)
Extensible Markup Language (XML)
Extensible Stylesheet Language (XSL)
Framework Class Library (FCL)
graphical user interface (GUI)
hardware platform
HyperText Markup Language (HTML)
Hypertext Transfer Protocol (HTTP)
Integrated Development Environment (IDE)
Internet
Internet Protocol (IP)
language independent
language interoperability
managed code
Managed Extensions for C++ (MC++)
managed object
meta-language
Microsoft Foundation Classes (MFC)
Microsoft Intermediate Language (MSIL)
Mono project
.NET Framework
.NET initiative
.NET platform
.NET-compliant language
object
object-oriented programming (OOP)
platform independence
porting
procedural programming language
property
Rapid Application Development (RAD)
Shared Source CLI (Common Language Infrastructure)
Standard Generalized Markup Language (SGML)
synchronization
TCP/IP
Transmission Control Protocol (TCP)
universal data access
unmanaged code
unsynchronized
Visual Basic .NET
Visual C++
Visual C++ .NET
visual programming language
Visual Studio .NET
vocabulary (XML)
W3C Recommendation
Web service
Windows Form designer
World Wide Web (WWW)
World Wide Web Consortium (W3C)
XML Working Group

SELF-REVIEW EXERCISES

1.1 Fill in the blanks in each of the following statements:

a) C is widely known as the development language of the __________ operating system.
b) The __________ provides a large programming library for .NET languages.
c) __________ are applications that expose (i.e., make available) functionality to clients via the Internet.
d) Visual Studio .NET is a(n) __________ in which Visual C++ .NET programs are developed.
e) Objects have __________ (i.e., attributes, such as color, size and weight) and perform __________ (i.e., behaviors, such as moving, sleeping and drawing).
f) __________ represent groups of similar objects.
g) If two copies of a file exist (e.g., on a personal and a company computer), the oldest version must be updated constantly—this is called file __________.
h) __________ tends to produce software that is more understandable because it is better organized and has fewer maintenance requirements.
i) MFC often is used to develop __________, or code that does not make use of the .NET Framework
j) The process of rapidly creating an application using an IDE typically is referred to as __________.
k) The ability of a program to run (without modification) across multiple platforms is known as __________.

1.2 State whether each of the following is *true* or *false*. If *false*, explain why.

a) Universal data access is an essential part of .NET.
b) W3C standards are called recommendations.
c) C++ is an object-oriented language.
d) The Common Language Runtime (CLR) requires that programmers manage their own memory.
e) Visual C++ is the only language available for programming .NET applications.
f) Procedural programming models the world more naturally than object-oriented programming.
g) MSIL is the common intermediate format to which all .NET programs compile, regardless of their original .NET language.
h) The .NET Framework can package preexisting components (i.e., components created using tools that predate .NET) and .NET components to work together.
i) With the introduction of the FCL, programmers can no longer use MFC.
j) If the .NET Framework is installed on a platform, that platform can run any .NET program.

ANSWERS TO SELF-REVIEW EXERCISES

1.1 a) UNIX. b) Framework Class Library (FCL). c) Web Services. d) integrated development environment (IDE). e) properties, actions. f) classes. g) synchronization. h) object-oriented programming (OOP). i) unmanaged code. j) rapid application development (RAD). k) platform independence.

1.2 a) True. b) True. c) True. d) False. The CLR handles memory management. e) False. Visual C++ is one of many .NET languages (others include Visual Basic and C#). f) False. Object-oriented programming is a more natural way to model the world than is procedural programming. g) True. h) True. i) False. Microsoft has, in fact, upgraded MFC to MFC 7, which includes new classes and documentation that can be accessed using Visual Studio .NET. j) True.

EXERCISES

1.3 Distinguish between the following terms:
a) C.
b) C++.
c) Visual C++.
d) Visual C++ .NET.
e) Managed Extensions for C++ (MC++).

1.4 What are HTML, XML and XHTML?

1.5 What two steps are used to compile a .NET program? Why are two steps used?

1.6 What is needed to run a .NET program on a new type of computer (machine)?

1.7 Expand each of the following acronyms:
a) W3C
b) XML
c) SOAP
d) TCP/IP
e) GUI
f) CLR
g) CLI
h) FCL
i) MSIL

1.8 What are the key benefits of the .NET Framework and the CLR?

2

Introduction to the Visual Studio® .NET IDE

Objectives

- To become familiar with the Visual Studio .NET integrated development environment (IDE).
- To become familiar with the types of commands contained in the IDE's menus and toolbox.
- To identify and understa
  nd the use of various kinds of windows in Visual Studio .NET.
- To understand the features provided by the **Toolbox**.
- To understand Visual Studio .NET's help features.
- To create, compile and execute a simple Visual C++ .NET program.

Seeing is believing.
Proverb

Form ever follows function.
Louis Henri Sullivan

Intelligence … is the faculty of making artificial objects, especially tools to make tools.
Henri-Louis Bergson

Outline

2.1 Introduction

Visual Studio .NET is Microsoft's integrated development environment (IDE) for creating, running and debugging programs written in a variety of .NET programming languages. Visual Studio .NET also offers editing tools for manipulating several types of files. Visual Studio .NET is a powerful and sophisticated tool for creating business-critical and mission-critical applications. This chapter provides an overview of the Visual Studio .NET features needed to create a simple Visual C++ .NET program. You will learn additional IDE features throughout the book.

2.2 Visual Studio .NET Integrated Development Environment (IDE) Overview

When you execute Visual Studio .NET for the first time, the ***Start Page*** in Fig. 2.1 appears in the Visual Studio .NET window. This page contains three tabs. Users can click the name of a tab to browse its contents. Select the ***Projects*** tab. We refer to single-clicking with the left mouse button as *selecting* or *clicking*. We refer to single-clicking with the right mouse button as *right-clicking*. We refer to clicking twice with the left mouse button as *double-clicking*. [*Note*: Please be aware that there are slight differences in the way Visual Studio .NET appears based on the version you are using. This book assumes you are using Visual C++ .NET Standard Edition version 2003; the examples in this book will not run in older versions of Visual Studio.]

Figure 2.1 shows the **Projects tab on** the **Start Page**. The **Projects** section will contain links to recently opened projects and the modification dates of the projects. A *project* is a group of files and objects that make up an application. You can also view recently opened projects by selecting **Recent Projects** from the **File** menu. If you do not have any recent projects to load, the **Projects** list will be empty. Notice the two *buttons* on the page: ***New Project*** and ***Open Project***. A button is a rectangular area that performs an action when clicked.

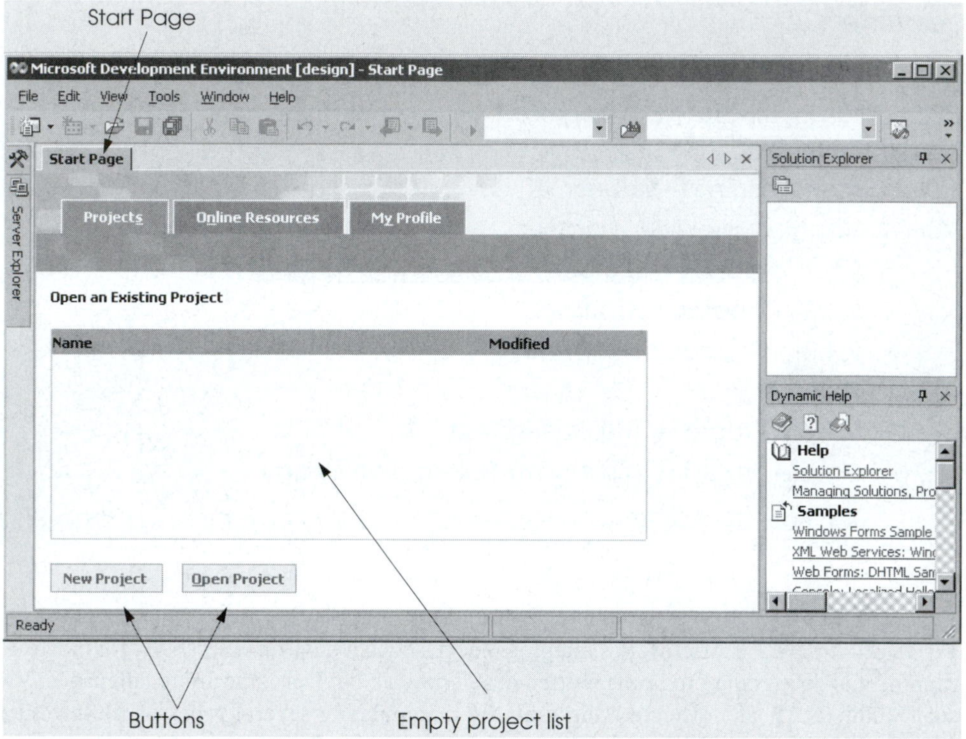

Fig. 2.1 **Start Page** in Visual Studio .NET, with an empty project list.

We now provide a brief overview of the ***Online Resources*** tab, shown in Fig. 2.2. The left side of the page contains some helpful links, such as ***Get Started***, ***What's New*** and ***Online Community***.[1] The **Get Started** link enables the user to search for sample code based on a topic. The **What's New** link displays new features and updates for Visual Studio .NET, including downloads for code samples and new programming tools. The **Online Community** provides ways to contact other software developers, using newsgroups, Web pages and other online resources. The ***Headlines*** link enables you to browse news articles and how-to guides. The ***Search Online*** link allows you to browse through the *MSDN* (*Microsoft Developer Network*) online library (`msdn.microsoft.com/library`). The MSDN site includes numerous articles, downloads and tutorials for many technologies. The ***Downloads*** link allows you to obtain updates and code samples. The ***XML Web Services*** page provides programmers with information about *Web services*, which are reusable pieces of software accessible via the Internet. ***Web Hosting*** provides information for developers who wish to post their software (such as Web services) online for public use.

1. Note that, for many of the links provided by the **Online Resources** tab, an Internet connection is required.

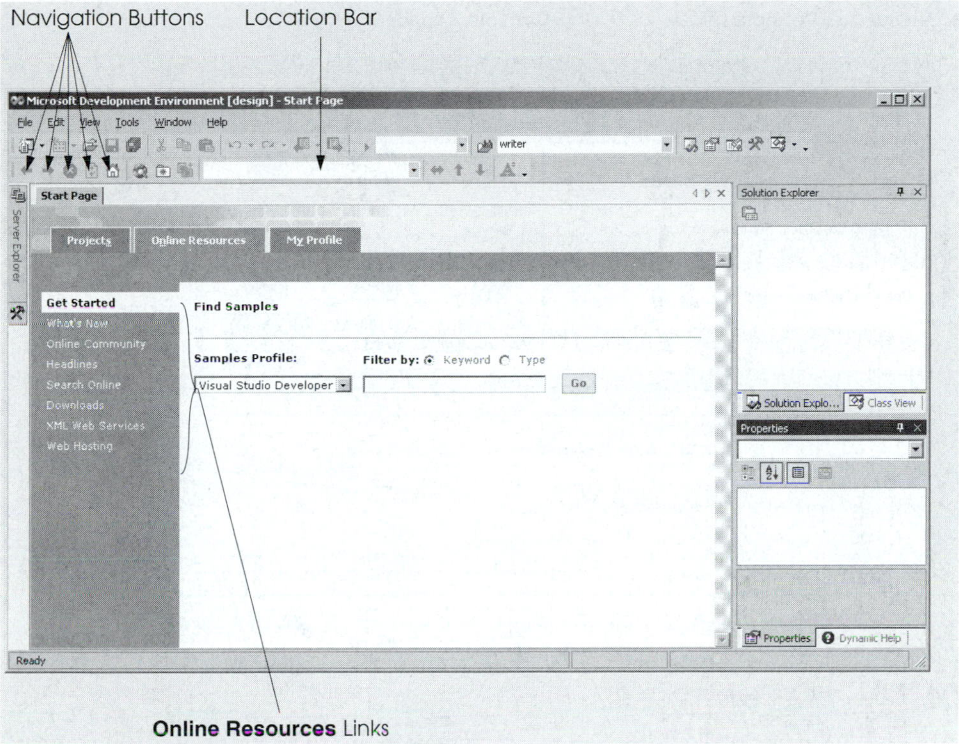

Fig. 2.2 **Start Page** in Visual Studio .NET, with the **Online Resources** tab selected.

The ***My Profile*** tab allows users to customize Visual Studio .NET, such as by setting keyboard and window layout preferences. Users also can customize Visual Studio .NET by selecting **Options…** or **Customize…** from the **Tools** menu. [*Note*: We use the **>** character to indicate the selection of a menu command. For example, we use the notation **Tools > Options…** and **Tools > Customize…** to indicate the selection of the **Options…** and **Customize…** items, respectively, from the **Tools** menu.]

Users can browse the Web through Visual Studio .NET—the Internet Explorer Web browser is accessible from within the IDE. To access a Web page, select **View > Toolbars > Web**, then type the Web page's address into the location bar (Fig. 2.2). Several other windows appear in the IDE in addition to the **Start Page**. We discuss these windows in the upcoming sections.

To create a new Visual C++ .NET program, click the **New Project** button on the **Projects** tab of the **Start Page**. This action displays the ***New Project*** *dialog* shown in Fig. 2.3 (alternatively, the **New Project** dialog can be opened via **File > New > Project**…. Visual Studio .NET organizes programs into projects and solutions. A project, as mentioned earlier, is a group of related files, such as C++ code, images and documentation. A *solution* is a group of projects that represents a complete application or a set of related applications. Each project in the solution may perform a different task. In this chapter, we create two single-project solutions.

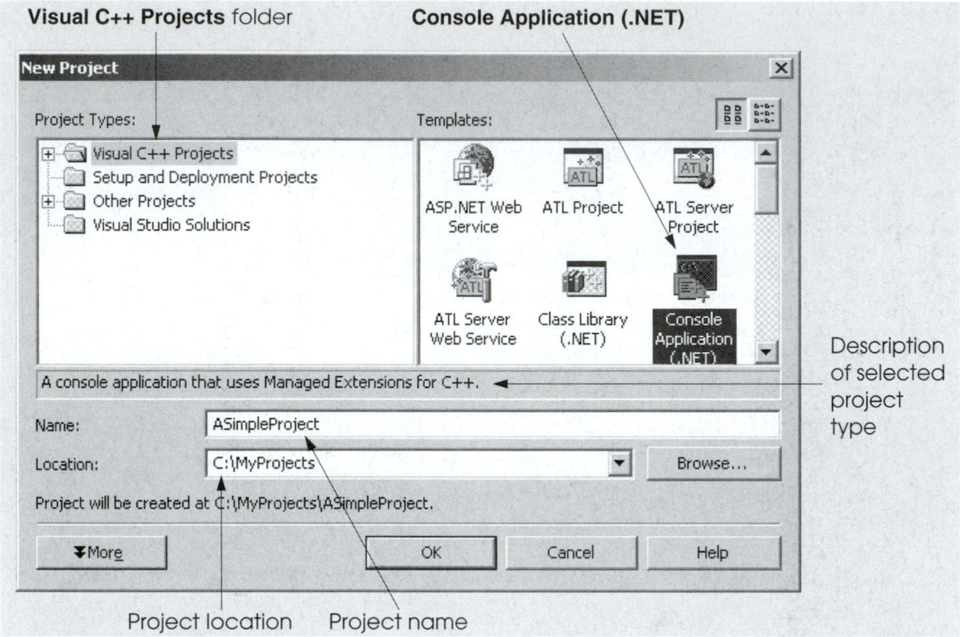

Fig. 2.3 **New Project** dialog.

Visual Studio .NET allows you to create projects in a variety of programming languages. This book focuses on Managed Extensions for C++ (MC++), so select the **Visual C++ Projects** folder (Fig. 2.3). There are many project types from which to choose, several of which are used throughout this book. Select ***Console Application (.NET)***. [*Note*: You might not have all the project types shown in Fig. 2.3 (or you might have more types) based on the version of Visual Studio .NET installed.]

Console applications are applications that execute in a *console window* (also called the ***Command Prompt***). Throughout this book, we create console and Windows applications. *Windows applications* are applications that execute inside the Windows operating system (OS) and appear in their own windows, like Microsoft Word, Internet Explorer and Visual Studio .NET. Typically, Windows applications contain *controls*—graphical elements, such as buttons and labels—with which the user interacts. These controls are placed on a window, or *form*. In Chapters 12–13, we will introduce how to create applications with graphical elements. In these early chapters, we create primarily console applications for simplicity. In this chapter, we create one console application and one Windows application to introduce you to creating applications using Visual Studio .NET.

The default location for new projects or files is the folder where the last project or file was created. You can change both the name and the location of the folder in which to save the project. To name the project, type `ASimpleProject` in the **Name:** field of Fig. 2.3. To save the project (Fig. 2.3), click the **Browse…** button, which opens a **Project Location** dialog (Fig. 2.4). Navigate through the directories to the location where you want to store the project and select **Open**. This selection returns the user to the **New Project** dialog; the selected folder appears in the **Location** text field. When you are satisfied with the project's name, location and type, click **OK**. Visual Studio .NET will create and load the new project. When you create a new project or open an existing project, the IDE appears, as shown in Fig. 2.5.

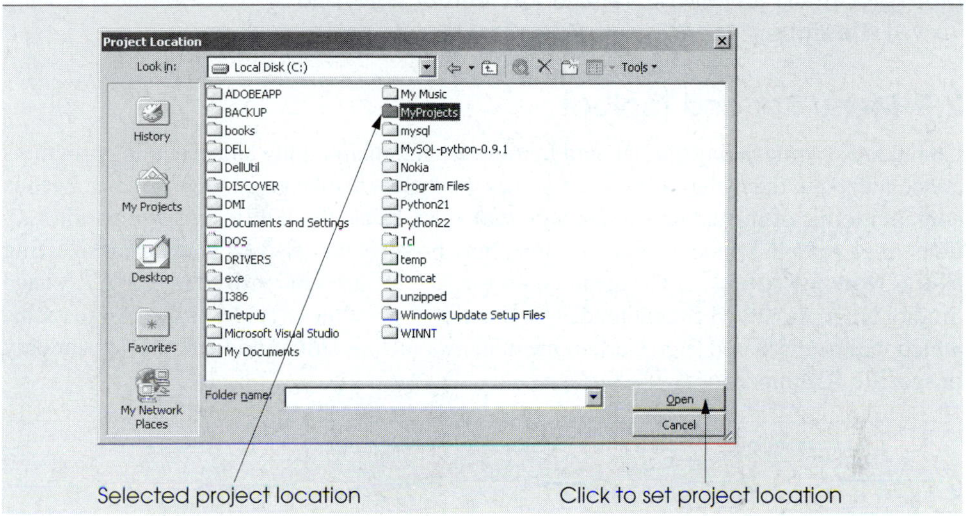

Fig. 2.4 Setting the project location.

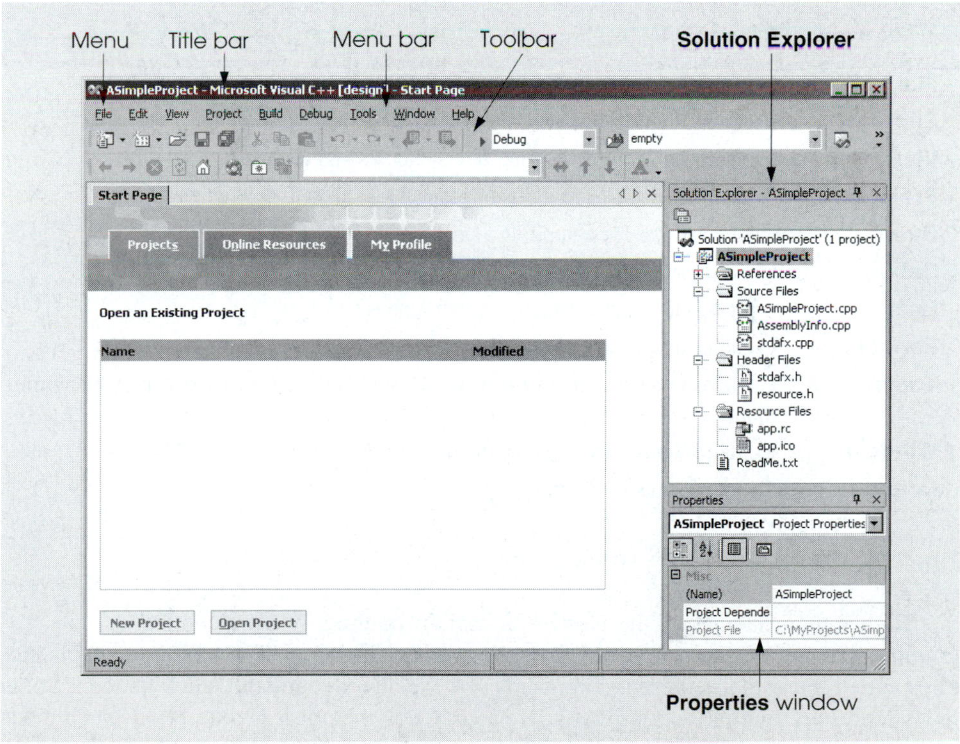

Fig. 2.5 Visual Studio .NET environment after a new project has been created.

The top of the IDE window (the *title bar* in Fig. 2.5) displays **ASimpleProject - Microsoft Visual C++ [design]**. This title provides the name of the project (**ASimpleProject**), the project type (**Microsoft Visual C++**) and the mode of the file being viewed (**Design** mode). We discuss the various modes in Section 2.6.

2.3 Menu Bar and Toolbar

Commands for managing the IDE and for developing, maintaining and executing programs are contained in the menus. Figure 2.6 shows the menus displayed on the menu bar. Menus contain groups of related items that, when selected, cause the IDE to perform various actions (e.g., open a window). For example, new projects can also be created by selecting **File > New > Project...**. The menus shown in Fig. 2.6 are summarized in Fig. 2.7. Visual Studio .NET provides different modes for the user. One of these modes is the design mode, which will be discussed later. Certain menu items (such as **Data** and **Format**) appear only in specific IDE modes.

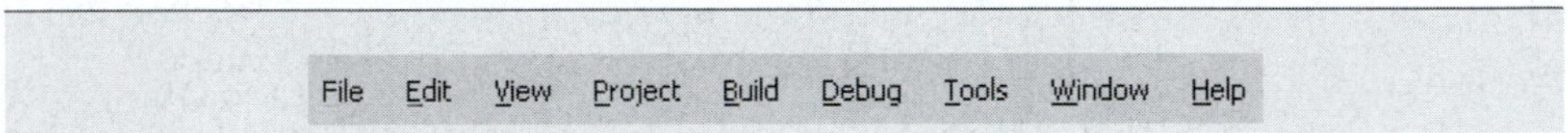

Fig. 2.6 Visual Studio .NET menu bar.

Menu	Description
File	Contains items for opening projects, closing projects, printing files, etc.
Edit	Contains items such as cut, paste, find, undo, etc.
View	Contains items for displaying IDE windows and toolbars.
Project	Contains items for adding features, such as image files, to the project.
Build	Contains items for compiling a program.
Debug	Contains items for debugging and executing a program.
Data	Contains items for interacting with databases.
Format	Contains items for arranging a form's controls.
Tools	Contains items for additional IDE tools and options for customizing the environment.
Window	Contains items for arranging and displaying windows.
Help	Contains items for getting help.

Fig. 2.7 Visual Studio .NET menus summary.

Rather than navigating the menus for certain commonly used commands, the programmer can access the commands from the *toolbar* (Fig. 2.8). The toolbar contains pictures called *icons* that represent commands. To execute a command, click its icon. Some icons represent multiple actions that are related. Click the *down arrows* beside such icons to display a list of commands. Figure 2.8 shows the standard (default) toolbar and an icon that provides access to two items.

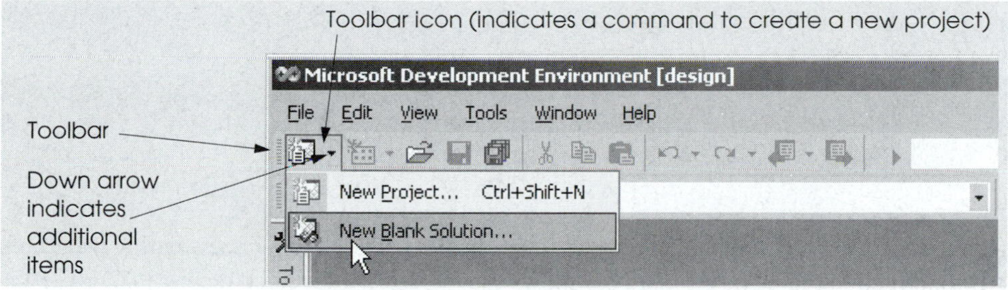

Fig. 2.8 Visual Studio .NET toolbar.

Placing the mouse pointer over an icon on the toolbar highlights that icon and displays a description called a *tool tip* (Fig. 2.9). Tool tips help users understand the purposes of unfamiliar icons.

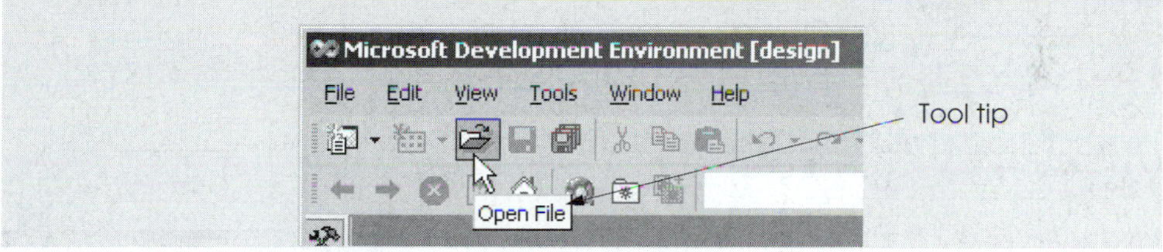

Fig. 2.9 Tool tip demonstration.

Toolbars can be further customized via the **Toolbars** tab on the **Customize** dialog that is displayed when you select **Tools > Customize**.... Here you can delete icons, rename icons and change icon images (among other options).

Notice that Visual Studio .NET provides keyboard shortcuts (also called *mnemonics*) for some menu items, such as *Ctrl+Shift+N* for the **File > New > Project**... menu item (Fig. 2.8). These keyboard shortcuts provide another way to access commonly used commands. More information about keyboard shortcuts in Visual Studio .NET can be found by entering the following URL into the location bar:

```
ms-help://MS.VSCC.2003/MS.MSDNQTR.2003FEB.1033/vsintro7/html/
vxorikeyboardshortcuts.htm
```

2.4 Visual Studio .NET Windows

Visual Studio .NET provides you with windows for exploring files and customizing controls. In this section, we discuss the windows that are essential for developing MC++ applications. These windows can be accessed using the toolbar icons below the menu bar and on the right edge of the toolbar (Fig. 2.10), or by selecting the name of the desired window from the **View** menu. We will discuss in detail three of the windows (**Properties**, **Toolbox** and **Solution Explorer**) in the following sections. **Class View** will be discussed in Chapter 8. The **Object Browser** is not used in this text.

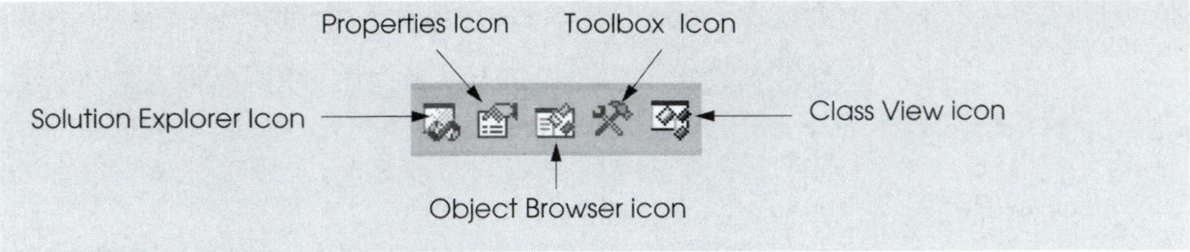

Fig. 2.10 Toolbar icons for two Visual Studio .NET windows.

2.4.1 Solution Explorer

The ***Solution Explorer*** window (Fig. 2.11) lists all the files in the solution. When Visual Studio .NET is first loaded, the **Solution Explorer** is empty—there are no files to display. After a new project has been created or an existing project has been loaded, the **Solution Explorer** displays that project's contents.

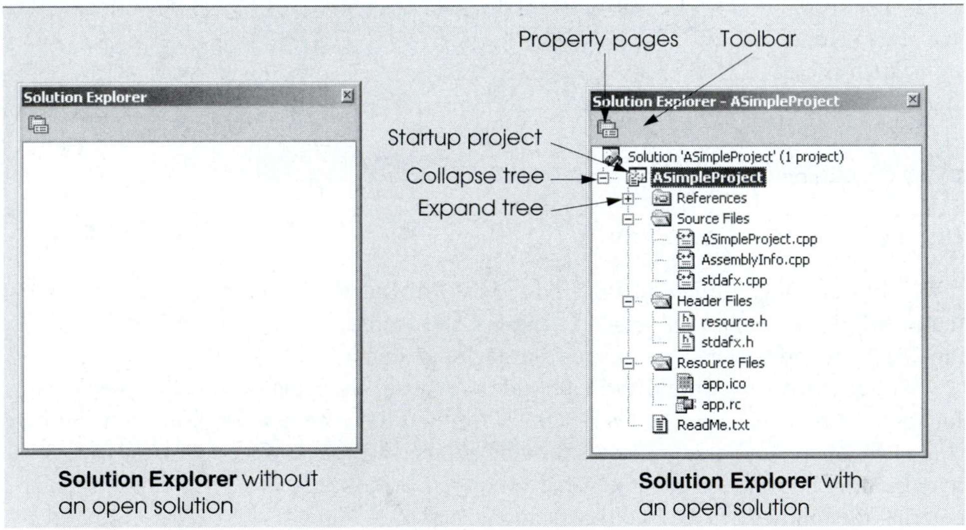

Fig. 2.11 **Solution Explorer** window.

The *startup project* of the solution is the project that runs when you execute the solution. The startup project appears in bold text in the **Solution Explorer**. For our single-project solution, the startup project (`ASimpleProject`) is the only project. When creating a project of type **Console Application (.NET)**, Visual Studio .NET generates various files, including a program file named *ProjectName*`.cpp`, where *ProjectName* is the name of the new project. In this case, the generated file is called `ASimpleProject.cpp`. (We discuss the `.cpp` file extension shortly.) In Section 2.6, we modify this file to change the functionality of our application. We discuss some of the other files later in the book.

The plus and minus boxes to the left of the project and solution names expand and collapse the tree, respectively (similar to those in Windows Explorer). Click a plus box to display more options; click a minus box to collapse a tree that is already expanded. Users also can expand or collapse a tree by double-clicking the name of the folder. Many other Visual Studio .NET windows use the plus/minus boxes as well.

The **Solution Explorer** contains a toolbar (Fig. 2.11). The icon displays the **Property Pages** dialog for the selected (highlighted) item. The **Property Pages** dialog allows users to configure compilation options. If there are no open projects, selecting this icon opens the **Properties** window (Section 2.4.3).

2.4.2 Toolbox Window

The **Toolbox** (Fig. 2.12) contains reusable software components (called controls) that can be used to customize applications. Using *visual programming*, you can "drag and drop" controls onto a form (the application's window) instead of writing the actual code. Just as people do not need to know how to build an engine to drive a car, you do not need to build a control to use it. This allows you to concentrate on the big picture, rather than the complex details of every control. The wide variety of tools available to programmers is a powerful feature of Visual C++ .NET. We demonstrate the power of the controls in the **Toolbox** when we create our own Windows application later in the chapter. [*Note:* Many of the **Toolbox** features discussed in this section will not be available to you until a Windows application is created or loaded. These features will be viewable on the user's machine in Section 2.7, when a Windows application is created.]

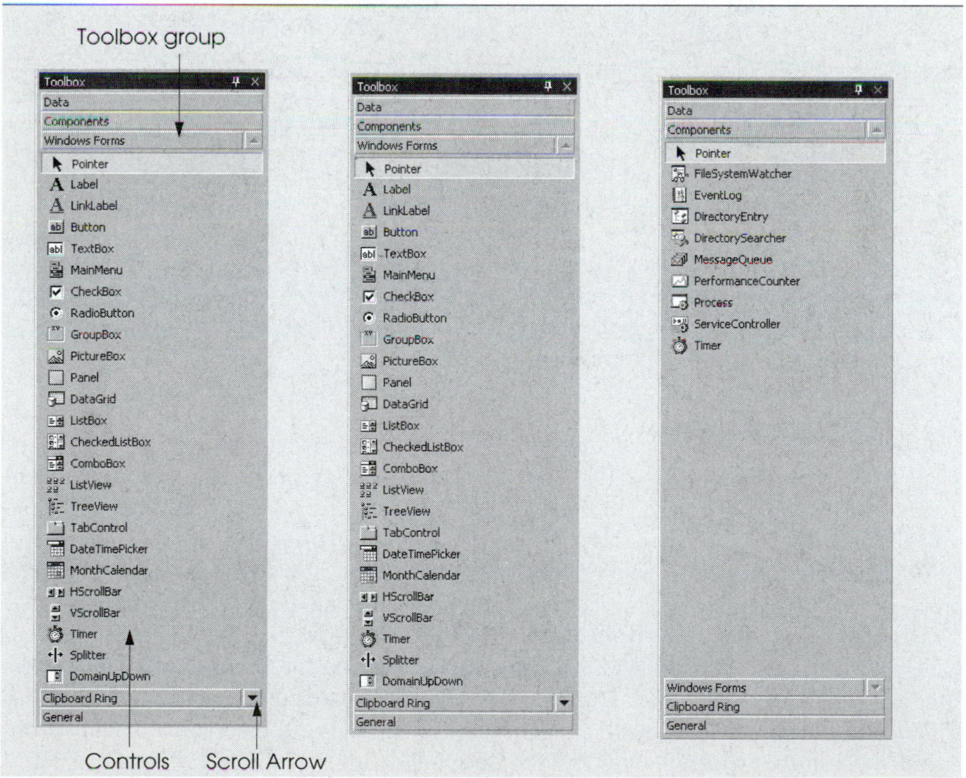

Fig. 2.12 **Toolbox** window.

The **Toolbox** contains groups of related components (e.g., **Data**, **Components**, **Windows Forms**). Expand the members of a group by clicking the name of the group. Users can scroll through the individual items by using the black scroll arrows on the right side of the **Toolbox**. The first item in the group is not a control—it is the mouse pointer. Clicking this icon allows the user to deselect the current control in the **Toolbox**. Note that there are no tool tips, because the **Toolbox** icons already are labelled with the names of the controls. In later chapters, we discuss many of these controls.

Initially, the **Toolbox** may be hidden, with only the name of the window showing on the side of the IDE (Fig. 2.13). Moving the mouse pointer over a window name opens this window. Moving the mouse pointer outside the window causes the window to disappear. This feature is known as *auto hide*. To "pin down" the **Toolbox** (i.e., disable auto hide), click the pin icon in the upper right corner of the window (see Fig. 2.13). To enable auto hide (if it previously has been disabled), click the pin icon again. Notice that when auto hide is enabled, the pin points to the left, as is shown in Fig. 2.13.

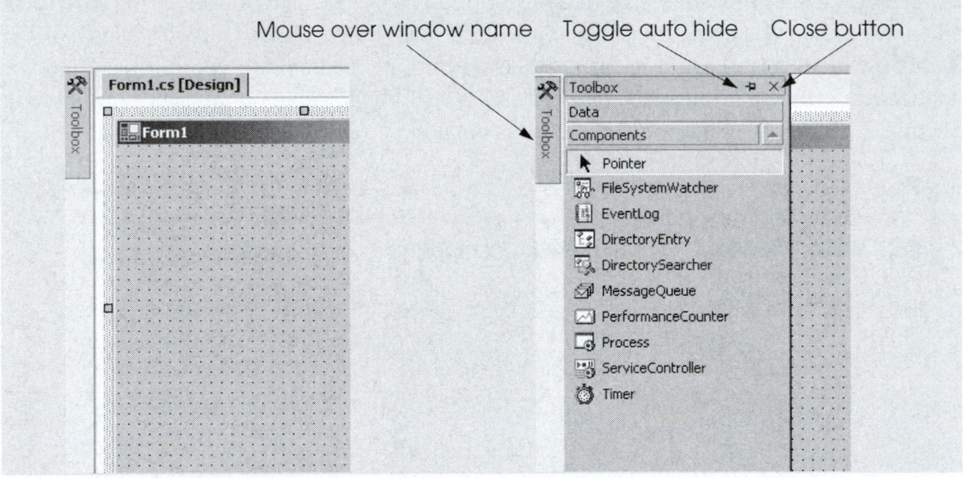

Fig. 2.13 Demonstrating window auto-hide.

2.4.3 Properties Window

The ***Properties*** window (Fig. 2.14) allows manipulation of the *properties* for a form or control. Properties specify information about a control, such as size, color and position. Each control has its own set of properties. The bottom of the **Properties** window contains a description of the selected property.The **Properties** window also allows manipulation of the properties for a project or a class, such as its full path name and its dependences (if any).

The left column of the **Properties** window lists the properties. The right column displays their current values. As with the **Solution Explorer**, the **Properties** window has a toolbar. Icons on this toolbar sort properties either alphabetically (by clicking the *alphabetic icon*) or categorically (by clicking the *categorized icon*). If there are too many properties to list in the window, a vertical scrollbar is provided by the IDE. Users can scroll through the list of properties by *dragging* the scrollbar *thumb*—the rectangle that represents the current position in the scrollbar—up or down (i.e., holding down the left mouse button

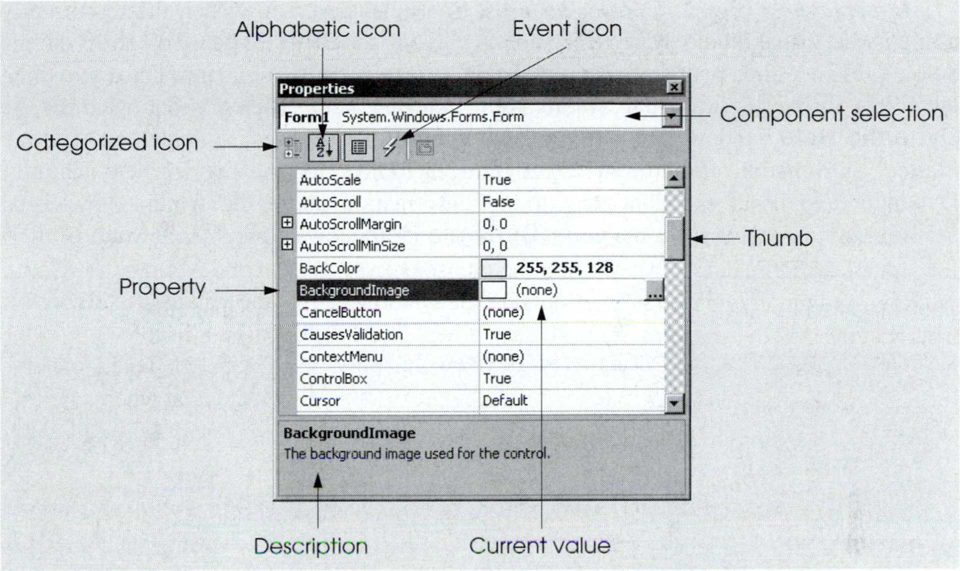

Fig. 2.14 **Properties** window.

while the mouse cursor is over the thumb, moving the mouse up or down and releasing the mouse button). The *event icon* allows the control or form to respond to certain user actions. We discuss events in Chapter 12, Graphical User Interface Concepts: Part 1. We show how to set individual properties later in this chapter and throughout the book.

The **Properties** window also is important to visual programming. Controls are usually customized after they are created from the **Toolbox**. The **Properties** window allows you to modify controls visually, without writing code. This setup has a number of benefits. First, you can see which properties are available for modification and what the possible values are; you do not have to look up or remember what settings a particular property can have. Second, the window displays a brief description of each property, allowing you to understand each property's purpose. Third, a property's value can be set quickly using the window; only a single click is required, and no code need be written. All these features are designed to help you program without performing many repetitive tasks.

At the top of the **Properties** window is a drop-down list called the *component selection*. This list shows the current component that is being altered. The programmer can use the list to choose which component to edit. For example, if a GUI contains several buttons, you can select the name of a specific button to configure.

2.5 Using Help

Visual Studio .NET has an extensive help mechanism. The ***Help*** *menu* contains a variety of options. The ***Contents*** *menu item* displays a categorized table of contents that lists available help topics. The ***Index*** *Menu item* displays an alphabetical index. The ***Search*** feature allows you to find particular help articles based on a few search words. Each of these features includes a subset of available topics, or filter, that can narrow the search to articles related only to Visual C++ .NET.

Dynamic help (Fig. 2.15) provides a list of articles based on what you are currently doing in the Visual Studio .NET IDE (such as viewing the **Start Page**). To open dynamic help (if it is not already open), select **Help > Dynamic Help** command. Once you click an object displayed in Visual Studio .NET, relevant help articles will appear in the **Dynamic Help** window. The window lists relevant help entries, samples and "Getting Started" information, in addition to providing a toolbar for the regular help features. Dynamic help is an excellent way to get information about the features of Visual Studio .NET. Note that for some users, **Dynamic Help** slows down Visual Studio.

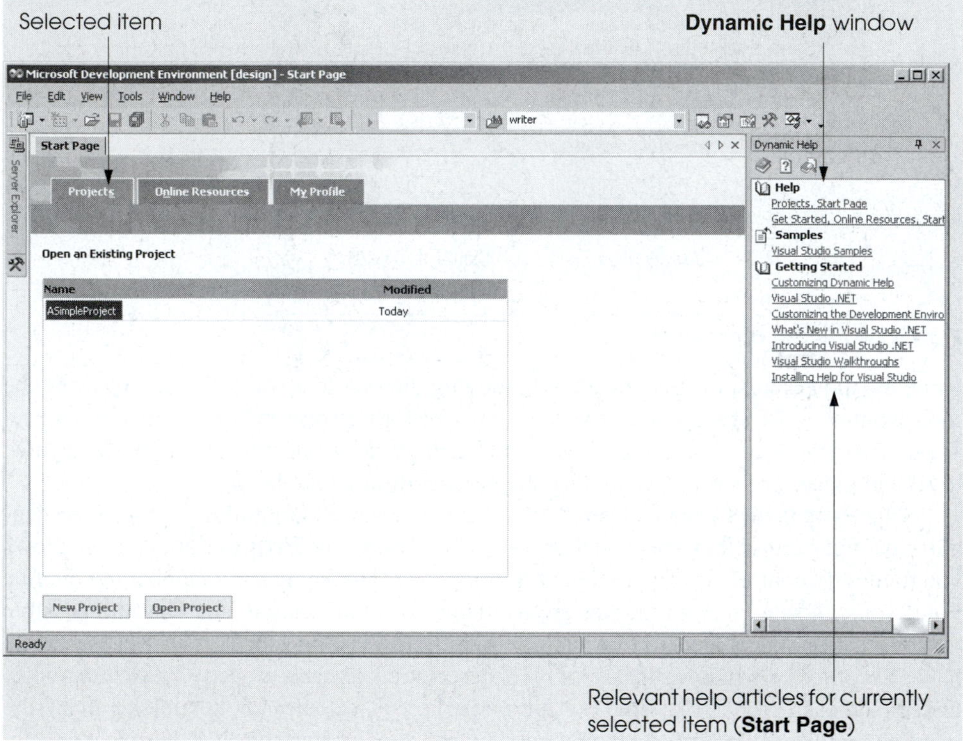

Fig. 2.15 **Dynamic Help** window.

Performance Tip 2.1

If you experience slow response times from Visual Studio, you can disable (i.e., close) **Dynamic Help** *by clicking the* **X** *in the upper-right corner of the* **Dynamic Help** *window.*

In addition to dynamic help, Visual Studio .NET provides *context-sensitive help*. Context-sensitive help is similar to dynamic help, except that context-sensitive help immediately brings up a relevant help article rather than presenting a list. To use context-sensitive help, select an item and press the *F1* key. Help can appear either *internally* or *externally*. With external help, a relevant article immediately pops up in a separate window, outside the IDE. With internal help, a help article appears as a tabbed window inside Visual Studio .NET. Help options can be set from the **My Profile** section of the **Start Page** as well as from the **Tools > Options > Environment > Help** menu item.

2.6 Simple Program: Displaying Text

In this section, we create a console application that prints the text "`Welcome to Visual C++ .NET!`" to the screen. The program consists of a single *.cpp* (the file extension for a MC++ program) file that displays a message. Figure 2.16 shows the program's output.

```
Welcome to Visual C++ .NET!
```

Fig. 2.16 Simple program as it executes.

To create, run and terminate this first program, perform the following steps:

1. *Create the new project.* If you have not yet created the project (`ASimpleProject` from Fig. 2.5), refer to Section 2.2 to create it. However, if another project is already open, first close it by selecting **File > Close Solution** from the menu. A dialog asking whether to save the current solution may appear. Save the solution to keep any unsaved changes. Then create `ASimpleProject`.

2. *Opening the generated code file.* To open the generated code file (`ASimpleProject.cpp`), first expand the **Source Files** folder in the **Solution Explorer** by clicking the plus sign next to it (if necessary). Next, double-click **ASimpleProject.cpp** under the expanded **Source Files** folder. The generated file, `ASimpleProject.cpp`, is shown in Fig. 2.17.

```
// This is the main project file for VC++ application project
// generated using an Application Wizard.

#include "stdafx.h"

#using <mscorlib.dll>

using namespace System;

int _tmain()
{
   // TODO: Please replace the sample code below with your own.
   Console::WriteLine(S"Hello World");
   return 0;
}
```

Fig. 2.17 Program file automatically generated by Visual Studio .NET.

3. *Modifying the program.* Notice that the program file generated by Visual Studio .NET contains code. We introduce the reader to program syntax in Chapter 3, Introduction to Visual C++ .NET Programming. For now, simply modify `ASimpleProject.cpp` so that it matches the program shown in Fig. 2.18. The program displays a message.

```
// Fig. 2.18: ASimpleProject.cpp
// Simple welcome program.

#include "stdafx.h"

#using <mscorlib.dll>

using namespace System;

int _tmain()
{
   Console::WriteLine( S"Welcome to Visual C++ .NET!" );

   return 0;
}
```

Fig. 2.18 Code for IDE demonstration.

4. *Save the project.* Select **File > Save All** to save the entire solution. To save an individual file, select it in the **Solution Explorer**, and select **File > Save** *Filename*, where *Filename* is the name of the file you wish to save. In this case, the IDE stores the source code in file `ASimpleProject.cpp`. The project file `ASimpleProject.vcproj` contains the names and locations of all the files in the project. Choosing **Save All** saves the project, the solution and the code file.

5. *Run the project.* Prior to this step, we have been working in the IDE *design mode* (i.e., the program being created is not executing). This mode is indicated by the text **Microsoft Visual C++ [design]** in the title bar. While in design mode, programmers have access to all the environment windows (e.g., **Toolbox** and **Properties**), menus, toolbars and so on. While in *run mode*, however, the program is executing, and users can interact with only a few IDE features. Features that are not available are disabled or grayed out. To execute or run the program, we first need to compile it, which is accomplished by clicking on the ***Build Solution*** command in the ***Build*** *menu* (or typing *Ctrl + Shift + B*). The program then can be executed by clicking the ***Start*** button (the blue triangle located in the toolbar), selecting the **Debug** menu's **Start** command or pressing the *F5* key. Figure 2.19 shows the IDE in run mode. Note that the IDE title bar displays **[run]** and that many toolbar icons are disabled. The console window closes as soon as the program finishes executing. To keep the console window open, users can select **Debug > Start Without Debugging** or press *Ctrl + F5*. This causes the console window to prompt the user to press a key after the program terminates, allowing the user to observe the program's output. Throughout this book, we execute console applications using the **Start Without Debugging** command so that the reader can see the output.

6. *Terminating execution.* To terminate the program, press any key or click the running application's close button (the **X** in the top-right corner). All these actions terminate program execution and return the IDE to design mode.

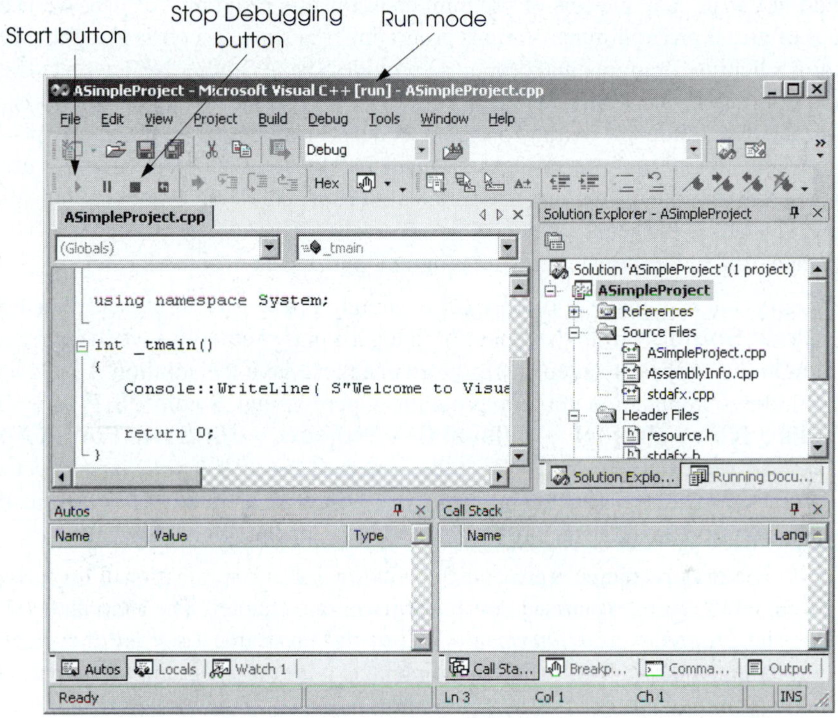

Fig. 2.19 IDE in run mode.

2.7 Simple Program: Displaying Text and an Image

In this section, we create a Windows application that displays the text **Welcome to Visual C++ .NET!** and an image. The program consists of a single form that uses a label to display text and a picture box to display an image. Figure 2.20 shows the program as it executes. The example is available on the included CD.

Fig. 2.20 Simple program as it executes.

We do not write a single line of program code for this program. Instead, we use the techniques of visual programming. Various programmer *gestures* (such as using the mouse for pointing, clicking, dragging and dropping) provide Visual Studio .NET with sufficient information for it to generate all or a major portion of the program code. In the next chapter, we begin our discussion of writing program code. Throughout the book, we produce increasingly substantial and powerful programs. Visual C++ .NET programming usually involves a combination of writing a portion of the program code and having Visual Studio .NET generate the remaining code.

To create, run and terminate this first program, perform the following steps:

1. *Create the new project.* If a project is already open, close it by selecting **File > Close Solution** from the menu. A dialog asking whether to save the current solution may appear to keep any unsaved changes. Save the solution. Create a new Windows application for our program. Open Visual Studio .NET, and select **File > New > Project... > Visual C++ Projects > Windows Forms Application (.NET)** (Fig. 2.21). Name the project `ASimpleProject2`, and select a directory in which to save the project. Click **OK**. Visual Studio .NET will load the new solution, and a form labelled **Form1** will appear (Fig. 2.22).

   The gray rectangle represents the window for our application. This rectangle is called the form, discussed briefly earlier in this chapter. The form and controls are the *graphical user interface* (*GUI*) of the program. They are the graphical components through which the user interacts with the program. Users enter data (*inputs*) into the program by entering information from the keyboard and by clicking the mouse buttons. The program displays instructions and other information (*outputs*) for users to read in the GUI.

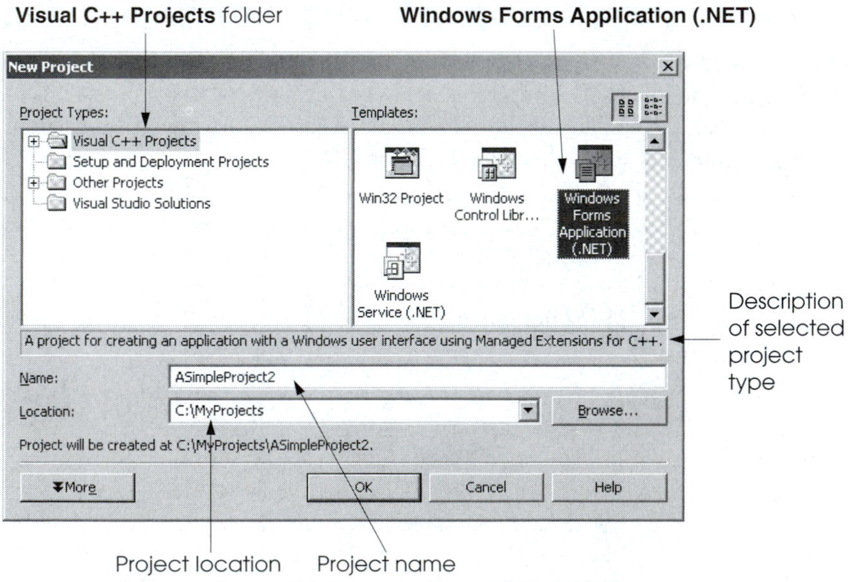

Fig. 2.21 **New Project** dialog.

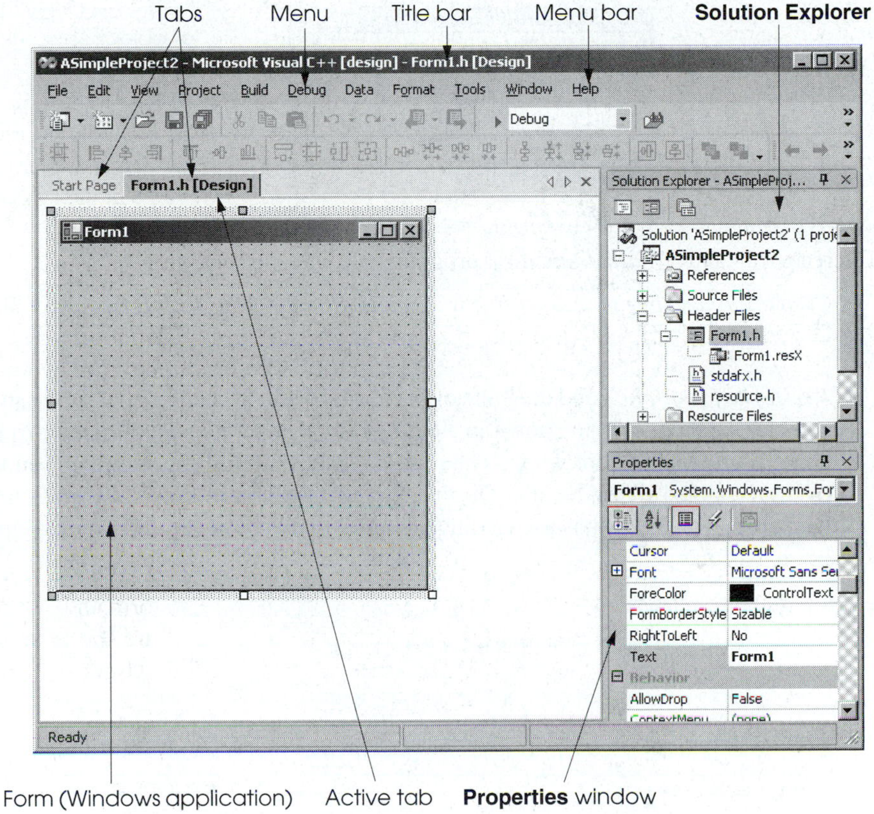

Fig. 2.22 Visual Studio .NET after a Windows application has been created.

Notice how a tab appears for each open document. In our case, the documents are the **Start Page** and **Form1.h [Design]**. To view a tabbed document, click the tab with the name of the document you wish to view. Tabbing saves space and allows easy access to multiple documents. The current tabbed document displays the **Form1.cs**, the default file created for Windows applications. The text **[Design]** following the name of the file means that we are designing the form visually, rather than programming it using code. If we had been writing code, the title bar would have contained only the text **Form1.h.**

2. *Set the form's title bar*. First, you will set the text that appears in the title bar. This text is determined by the form's `Text` property (Fig. 2.23). If the form's **Properties** window is not open, click the **Properties** icon in the toolbar or select the **View** menu's **Properties Window** command. Use the mouse to select the form; the **Properties** window shows information about the currently selected item. In the window, click in the box to the right of the **Text** property's box. To set a value for the **Text** property, type the value in the box. In this case, type `A Simple Program`, as in Fig. 2.23. Press the *Enter* key to update the form's title bar in the design area.

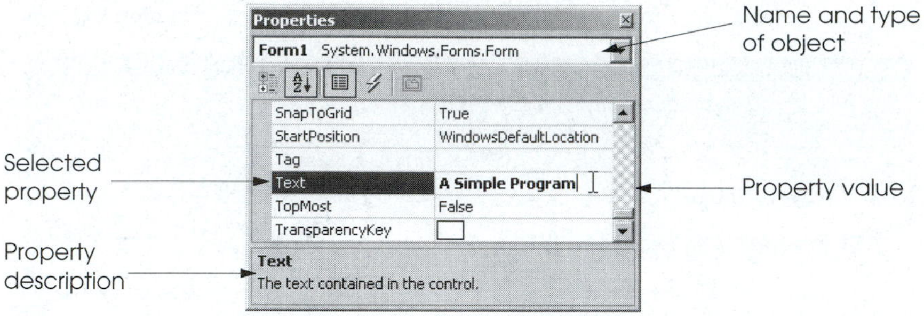

Fig. 2.23 Setting the form's `Text` property.

3. *Resize the form.* Click and drag one of the form's enabled *sizing handles* (the small squares around the form shown in Fig. 2.24) to change the size of the form. Enabled sizing handles are white. The mouse cursor changes appearance when it is over an enabled sizing handle. Disabled sizing handles are gray. The grid on the background of the form is used to align controls and does not appear when the program executes.

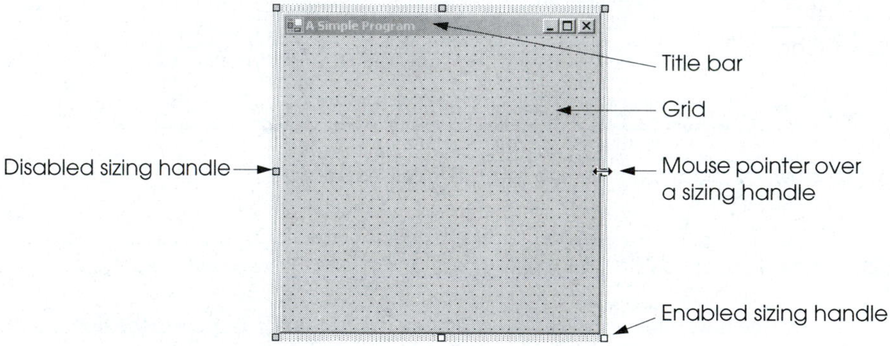

Fig. 2.24 Form with sizing handles.

4. *Change the form's background color.* The `BackColor` property specifies a form's or control's background color. Clicking `BackColor` in the **Properties** window causes a down-arrow button to appear next to the property value (Fig. 2.25). When clicked, the down arrow drops down to display other options. (The options vary, depending on the property.) In this case, it displays the tabs ***System*** (the default), ***Web*** and ***Custom***. Click the **Custom** tab to display the *palette* (a selection box of colors). Select the box that represents yellow. The palette will disappear, and the form's background color will change to yellow.

5. *Add a label control to the form.* Double-click the label control in the **Toolbox** (if it is not already open, the user can open the **Toolbox** by selecting **View > Toolbox**). This action creates a label with sizing handles in the upper-left corner of the form (Fig. 2.26). Double-clicking any **Toolbox** control places it on the form. Alternatively, programmers can "drag" controls from the **Toolbox** to the form. La-

bels display text; our label displays `label1` by default. Notice that our label is the same color as the form's background color. The form's background color is also the default background color of controls added to the form.

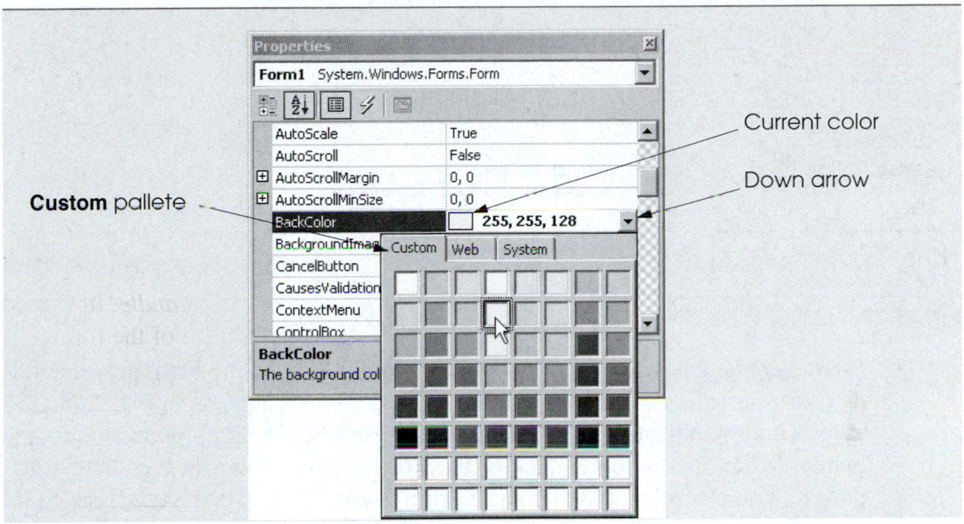

Fig. 2.25 Changing property `BackColor`.

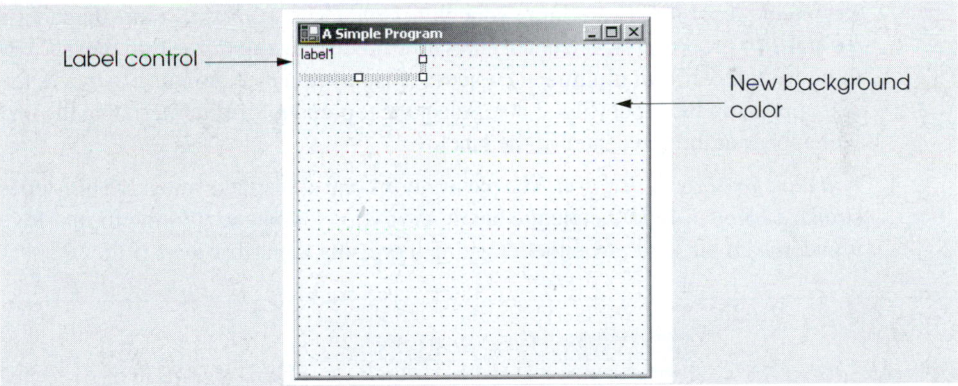

Fig. 2.26 Adding a new label to the form.

6. *Set the label's text.* Select the label so that its properties appear in the **Properties** window. The label's **Text** property determines the text (if any) that the label displays. The form and label each have their own **Text** property. Forms and controls can have the same types of properties without conflict. We will see that many controls have property names in common. Set the **Text** property of the label to `Welcome to Visual C++ .NET!` (Fig. 2.27). Resize the label (using the sizing handles) to make the text fit. Move the label to the top center of the form by dragging it or using the arrow keys. Alternatively, you can move the label by selecting **Format > Center In Form > Horizontally** from the menu bar.

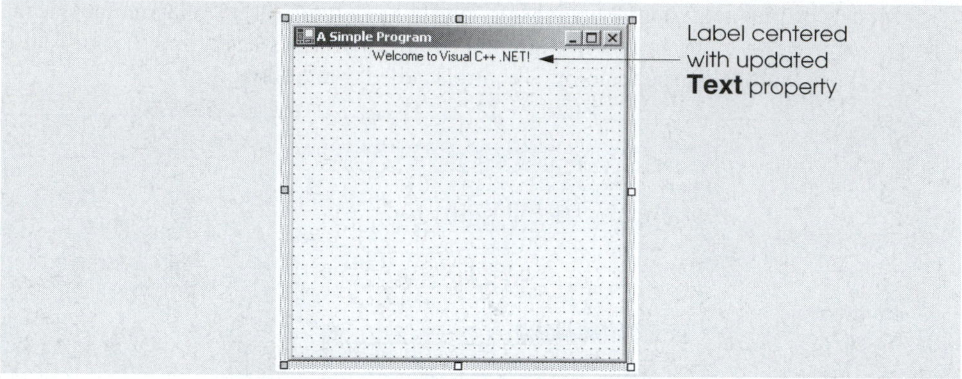

Fig. 2.27 Label in position with its `Text` property set.

7. *Set the label's font size and align the label's text.* Clicking the **Font** property value causes an *ellipsis* button (...) to appear next to the value, as in Fig. 2.28. The ellipsis button indicates that a dialog will appear when the programmer clicks the button. When the button is clicked, the ***Font*** *dialog* shown in Fig. 2.29 is displayed. You can select the font name (**Microsoft Sans Serif**, **Arial**, etc.), font style (**Regular**, **Bold**, etc.) and font size (**8**, **10**, etc.) in this window. The text in the ***Sample*** *area* displays the selected font. Under the **Size** category, select **24** and click **OK**. If the text does not fit on a single line, it will wrap to the next line. Resize the label if it is not large enough to hold the text. Next, select the label's ***TextAlign*** property, which determines how the text is aligned within the label. A three-by-three grid of alignment choices is displayed, corresponding to where the text appears in the label (Fig. 2.30). Select the top-center grid item, so that the text will appear at the top center of the label.

8. *Add a picture box to the form.* The picture-box control displays images. This step is similar to *Step 5*. Find the picture box in the toolbox, and add it to the form. Move it underneath the label, by either dragging it or using the arrow keys (Fig. 2.31).

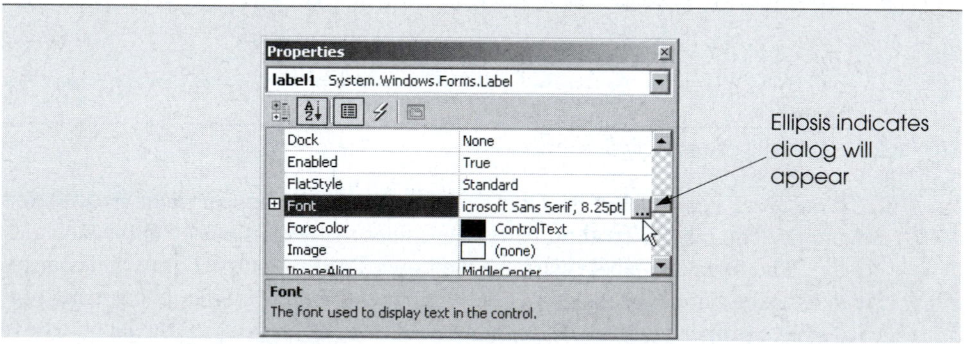

Fig. 2.28 **Properties** window displaying the label's properties.

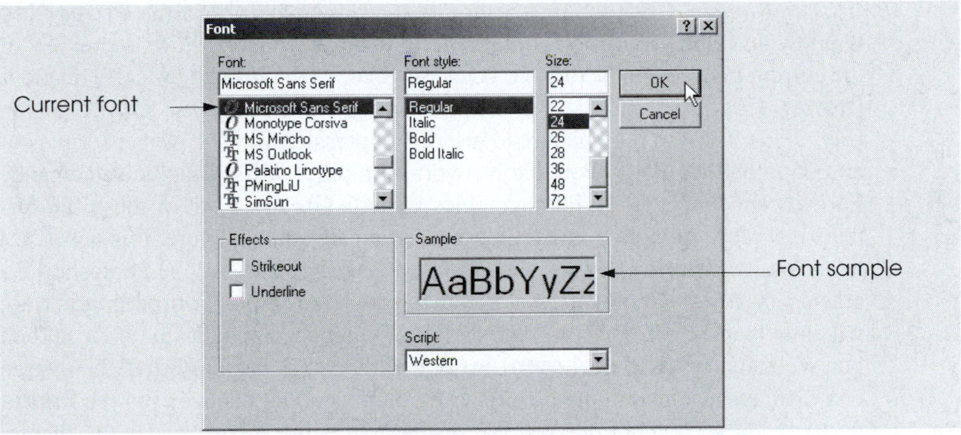

Fig. 2.29 **Font** window for selecting fonts, styles and sizes.

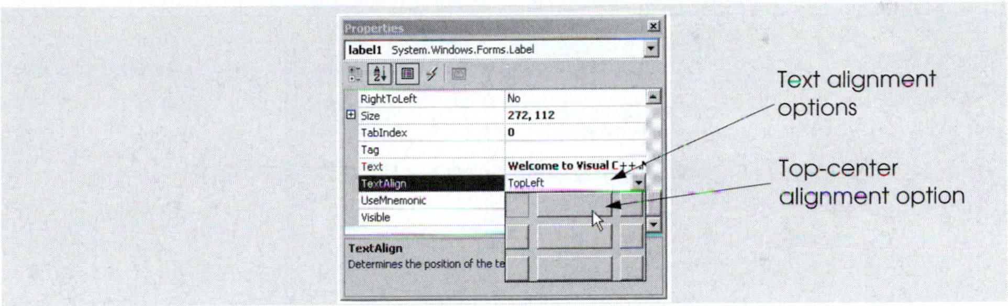

Fig. 2.30 Centering the text in the label.

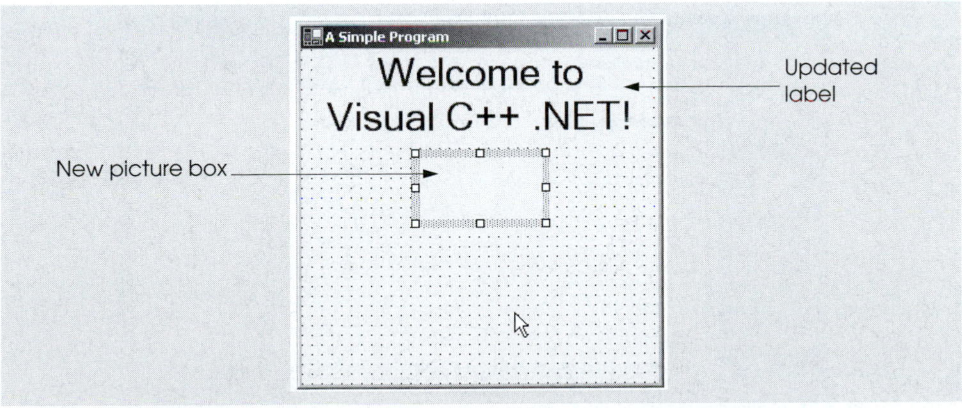

Fig. 2.31 Inserting and aligning the picture box.

9. *Insert an image*. Click the picture box to load its properties in the **Properties** window and find the ***Image** property*. The **Image** property shows a preview of the current picture. No picture has been assigned, so the **Image** property displays **(none)** (Fig. 2.32). Click the ellipsis button to display an **Open** dialog (Fig. 2.33). Browse for a picture to insert, and press *Enter*. The proper formats of an image include PNG (Portable Networks Graphic), GIF (Graphic Interchange Format) and JPEG (Joint Photographics Experts Group). Each of these file formats is widely supported on the Internet. To create a new picture, it is necessary to use image-editing software, such as Jasc Paint Shop Pro, Adobe Photoshop Elements or Microsoft Paint. We use the picture **ASimpleProgramImage.png**, which is located with this example on the CD that accompanies the book and on our Web site (**www.deitel.com**). After the image has been inserted, the picture box displays as much of the picture as it can (depending on size) and the **Image** property shows a small preview. To display the entire image, resize the picture box by dragging the picture box's handles (Fig. 2.34).

10. *Save the project*. Select **File > Save All** to save the entire solution.

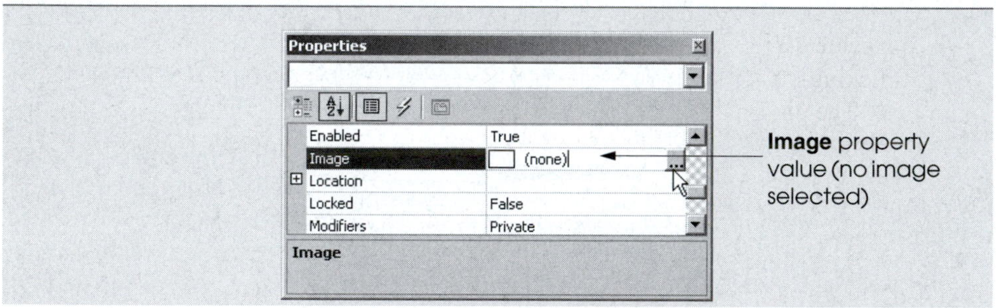

Fig. 2.32 `Image` property of the picture box.

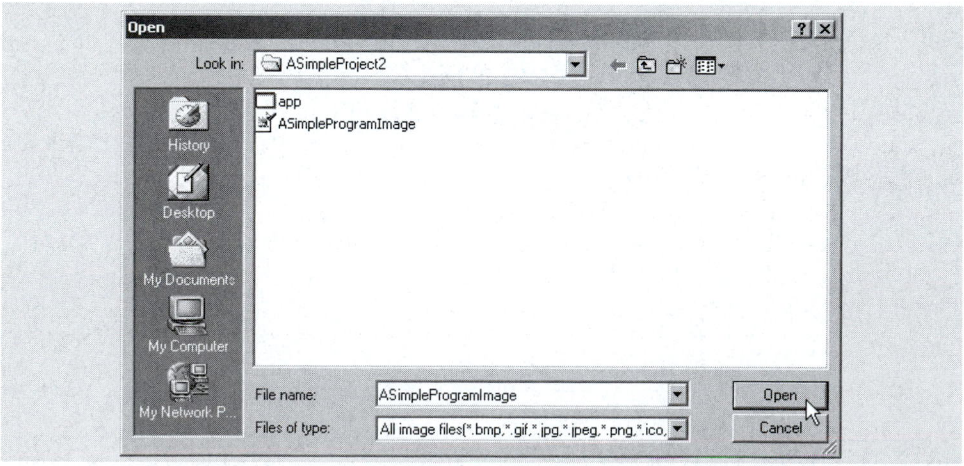

Fig. 2.33 Selecting an image for the picture box.

Fig. 2.34 Picture box after the image has been inserted.

11. *Run the project.* The text **Form1.h [Design]** in the title bar means that we are designing the form visually, rather than programming it using code. If we had been writing code, the title bar would have contained only the text **Form1.h**. To execute or run our program, we first need to compile it, which is accomplished by clicking on the **Build Solution** *option* in the **Build** *menu* (or type *Ctrl* + *Shift* + *B*). The program can then be executed by clicking the ***Start*** button (the blue triangle), selecting the **Debug** menu's **Start** command or pressing the *F5* key. The application should appear as in Fig. 2.20.

12. *Terminating execution.* To terminate the program, click the running application's ***Close*** button (the **X** in the top-right corner). Alternatively, click the ***End*** button (the blue square) in the toolbar. Either action stops program execution and puts the IDE into design mode.

We have just created a working Visual C++ .NET program without writing a single line of code. Visual programming allows us to create controls and set properties using windows, rather than lines of code. In Chapters 3–11, we use console applications to discuss nonvisual, or conventional, programming—we create a program using only code. Visual C++ .NET programming is a mixture of the two styles: Visual programming allows us to develop a GUI and avoid tedious tasks, while conventional programming specifies the behavior of our program. The most important part of an application is its behavior, which we explain how to program in the upcoming chapters. We will return to visual programming in Chapter 12, Graphical User Interface Concepts: Part 1. After that point, we will demonstrate creating applications that combine visual programming with conventional (also known as non-visual) programming.

Software Engineering Observation 2.1

Visual programming can be simpler and faster than writing code.

Software Engineering Observation 2.2

Most programs require more than visual programming. In such programs, some code must be written by hand. Examples include applications that use event handlers (used to respond to the user's actions), databases, security, networking, text editing, graphics and multimedia.

SUMMARY

- Visual Studio .NET is Microsoft's integrated development environment (IDE) for creating, running and debugging programs.
- When Visual Studio .NET is loaded for the first time, the **Start Page** is displayed. This page contains helpful links, such as recent projects, online newsgroups, downloads and user profile settings.
- The **Get Started** section contains links to recently opened projects.
- The **My Profile** page allows users to customize Visual Studio .NET.
- In the Visual Studio .NET IDE, users can browse the Web via Internet Explorer.
- Dialogs are windows that are used to communicate with users.
- Programs in Visual Studio .NET are organized into projects and solutions. A project is a group of related files. A solution is a group of projects that represent a complete application, or set of related applications.
- Console applications are applications that contain output consisting of text. Text output in a console application is displayed in a console window (also called a **Command Prompt**).
- Windows applications are programs that execute inside the Windows OS and appear in their own windows, like Microsoft Word, Internet Explorer and Visual Studio .NET. They contain controls—reusable graphical elements, such as buttons and labels—which the user uses to interact with the application.
- The title bar displays the name of the project, the programming language, the mode of the IDE, the file being viewed and the mode of the file being viewed.
- Menus contain groups of related commands that, when selected, cause the IDE to perform some action. Visual Studio .NET provides different modes for the user. Certain menu items appear only in some of these modes.
- The toolbar contains icons that represent menu items. To select an item, click the corresponding icon. Click the down arrow beside an icon to display other available items.
- Visual Studio .NET provides keyboard shortcuts (also called mnemonics) for some menu items, such as *Ctrl+Shift+N* for the **File > New > Project**... menu item. These keyboard shortcuts provide another way to access commonly used commands.
- Moving the mouse pointer over an icon highlights the icon and displays a tool tip.
- The **Solution Explorer** window lists all the files in the solution.
- The startup project of the solution is the project that executes when you execute the solution.
- The plus and minus boxes to the left of the project and solution names expand and collapse the tree, respectively.
- The **Toolbox** contains controls that customize forms.
- By using visual programming, programmers can "drag and drop" controls onto the form instead of writing the code themselves.
- Moving the mouse pointer over the label of a hidden window opens the window. Moving the mouse pointer outside the window causes the window to disappear. This feature is known as auto hide. To "pin down" the **Toolbox** window (i.e., to disable auto hide), click the pin icon in the upper-right corner.
- The **Properties** window displays the properties for a form or control. Properties are information about a control, such as size, color and position.
- Each type of control has its own set of properties.

- The **Help** menu contains several items. **Contents** displays a categorized table of contents of available help topics. **Index** displays an alphabetical index that can be browsed. **Search** allows users to find particular help articles, based on a few search words.
- Dynamic help is an excellent way to get information about the features of Visual Studio .NET.
- Dynamic help provides a list of articles, based on the current content (i.e., the location of the mouse cursor).
- Note that for some users, **Dynamic Help** slows down Visual Studio.
- Context-sensitive help is similar to dynamic help, except that context-sensitive help immediately brings up a relevant help article. To use context-sensitive help, select an item and press the *F1* key.
- To create a new console application, open Visual Studio .NET and select **File > New > Project… > Visual C++ Projects > Console Application (.NET)**. Name the project, select a directory, and click **OK**. Visual Studio .NET will load the new solution.
- When creating a project of type **Console Application (.NET)**, Visual Studio .NET generates a program file named *ProjectName*`.cpp`, where *ProjectName* is the name of the new project.
- Select **File > Save All** to save the entire solution. To save an individual file, select it in the **Solution Explorer** and select **File > Save**.
- The IDE design mode is indicated by the text **Microsoft Visual C++ .NET [design]** in the title bar.
- While in run mode, the program is executing, and users can interact with only a few IDE features.
- To execute or run a program, click the **Start** button (the blue triangle), or select **Debug > Start**. The IDE title bar displays **[run]**, and many toolbar icons are disabled.
- Terminate execution by clicking the **Close** button. Alternatively, click the **Stop Debugging** button (a blue square) in the toolbar.
- To create a new Windows Forms project, open Visual Studio .NET and select **File > New > Project… > Visual C++ Projects > Windows Forms Application (.NET)**. Name the project, and select a directory. Then click OK. Visual Studio .NET will load the new solution, and a blank form labelled `Form1` will appear.
- The text that appears on the top of the form (the title bar) is determined by the `Text` property of the form. To set a value for the property, simply type it in the space provided and press *Enter*.
- To resize the form, click and drag one of the form's enabled sizing handles (the small squares around the form). Enabled sizing handles are white; disabled sizing handles are gray.
- The grid on the background of the form is used to align controls and does not appear when the program is running.
- The `BackColor` property specifies a form's or control's background color. The form's background color is the default background color for any controls added to the form.
- Double-clicking any **Toolbox** control icon places a control of that type on the form. Alternatively, programmers can "drag" controls from the **Toolbox** to the form.
- The label's `Text` property determines the text (if any) that the label displays. The form and label each have their own `Text` property.
- When clicked, the ellipsis button displays a dialog.
- In the **Font** dialog users can select a font using the font name, font style and font size.
- The `TextAlign` property determines how the text is aligned within the label's boundaries.
- The picture-box control allows us to display an image on the form. The `Image` property shows a preview of the current picture. To select an image, click the ellipsis button, which displays an **Open** dialog. Browse for a picture to insert (of the proper format, such as PNG, GIF or JPEG), and then press *Enter*.

TERMINOLOGY

`Alignment` property
alphabetic icon
auto hide
`BackColor` property
background color
Build menu
Build Solution option
button
categorized icon
clicking
Close button icon
collapse a tree
Command Prompt
compile a program
console window
console application
Console Application (.NET) project type
context-sensitive help
control
customize Visual Studio .NET
Data menu
debug a program
Debug menu
design mode
dialog
double-clicking
down arrow
dynamic help
Dynamic Help window
Edit menu
event icon
expand a tree
external help
F1 help key
File menu
`Font` property
font size
font style
Font dialog
form
Format menu
Get Started link
GUI (Graphical User Interface)
Help menu
icon
IDE (integrated development environment)
`Image` property
input
internal help
Internet Explorer
label
menu
menu bar in Visual Studio .NET
mnemonic
mouse pointer
New Project dialog
new project in Visual Studio .NET
opening a project
output
palette
picture box
project
Project location
Project menu
Properties window
property
Property Pages dialog
recent project
right-clicking
Run menu
run mode
Save File As dialog
scrollbar thumb
Search feature
selecting
single-clicking with the left mouse button
single-clicking with the right mouse button
sizing handle
solution
Solution Explorer
Start button
Start Page
startup project
tabbed window
`Text` property
title bar
tool tip
toolbar
toolbar icon
Toolbox
Tools menu
View menu
Visual Studio .NET
Windows menu
Windows application
Windows Forms Application (.NET) project type

SELF-REVIEW EXERCISES

2.1 Fill in the blanks in each of the following statements:

a) The __________ contains pictures called icons that represent commands.
b) A(n) __________ is a group of files and objects that make up an application.
c) The __________ of the solution is the project that executes when you execute the solution.
d) A(n) __________ appears when the mouse cursor hovers over an icon.
e) The __________ window allows you to browse the files in your solution.
f) A plus icon indicates that the tree in the **Solution Explorer** can __________.
g) The **Properties** window can be sorted __________ or __________.
h) The __________ menu item displays a categorized table of contents.
i) The __________ feature allows users to find particular help articles based on a few search words.
j) __________ displays relevant help articles, based on the current context.

2.2 State whether each of the following is *true* or *false*. If *false*, explain why.

a) The title bar displays the mode of the IDE.
b) The **Online Resources** tab of the **Start Page** allows the user to customize the IDE.
c) The **XML Web Services** section allows the user to obtain updates and code samples.
d) The toolbar provides a convenient way to execute certain commands.
e) The toolbar contains icons representing GUI controls that can be added to a form.
f) Holding the mouse pointer over an icon on the toolbar displays a description of the icon called a tool tip.
g) While in run mode, the user can interact with only a few IDE features.
h) The **Contents** menu displays links to recently opened projects.
i) Buttons usually perform actions when clicked.
j) To execute or run a program, click the **Start** button.

ANSWERS TO SELF-REVIEW EXERCISES

2.1 a) toolbar. b) project. c) startup project. d) tool tip. e) **Solution Explorer**. f) expand. g) alphabetically, categorically. h) **Contents**. i) **Search**. j) Dynamic help.

2.2 a) True. b) False. The **My Profile** tab of the **Start Page** allows the user to customize the IDE. c) False. The **Downloads** section allows the user to obtain updates and code samples. d) True. e) False. The toolbar contains icons the represent menu commands. f) True. g) True. h) False. The **Get Started** section contains links to recently opened projects. i) True. j) True.

EXERCISES

2.3 Fill in the blanks in each of the following statements:

a) The **Properties** window allows manipulation of the properties for a(n) __________ or a(n) __________.
b) To save every file in a solution, select the __________ menu item from the menu.
c) __________ help immediately brings up a relevant article. It can be accessed by pressing the __________ key.
d) __________ provides a list of articles based on the current content.

2.4 State whether each of the following is *true* or *false*. If *false*, explain why.

a) Visual Studio .NET provides users with windows for exploring files.
b) Click a minus box to collapse a tree that is already expanded.

c) A person can browse the Internet from within Visual Studio .NET.
d) The `BackColor` property specifies a form's or control's background color.
e) Context-sensitive help provides a list of articles based on the current content.

2.5 Some features appear throughout Visual Studio .NET, performing similar actions in different contexts. Explain and give examples of how plus/minus icons, down arrows and tool tips act in this manner. Why do you think Visual Studio .NET was designed to be this way?

2.6 Fill in the blanks in each of the following statements:
a) The left column of the __________ window shows the properties.
b) A(n) ________ is a group of projects that are combined to solve a developer's problem.
c) The ________ menu contains items for arranging a form's controls.
d) The ________ menu contains items for compiling a program.

2.7 Briefly describe each of the following IDE features:
a) toolbar
b) menu bar
c) tooltip
d) icon
e) project
f) title bar

3

Introduction to Visual C++ .NET Programming

Objectives

- To write simple Visual C++ .NET programs.
- To use input and output statements.
- To become familiar with primitive data types.
- To understand basic memory concepts.
- To use arithmetic operators.
- To understand the precedence of arithmetic operators.
- To write decision-making statements.
- To use relational and equality operators.

Comment is free, but facts are sacred.
C. P. Scott

The creditor hath a better memory than the debtor.
James Howell

When faced with a decision, I always ask, "What would be the most fun?"
Peggy Walker

Equality, in a social sense, may be divided into that of condition and that of rights.
James Fenimore Cooper

Outline

3.1 Introduction

This chapter introduces the *Managed Extensions for C++ (MC++)* programming language. MC++ is an extension of traditional C++ that allows programmers to access and manipulate the .NET Framework. Throughout this book, we present examples that illustrate several important features of MC++. Examples are analyzed one line at a time. Beginning in this chapter, we provide a detailed treatment of program development and program control in Visual C++ .NET. We demonstrate important concepts using console applications that execute in a Command Prompt. Later in this text we will create Windows applications, which contain graphical user interfaces. We showed an example of both a console application and a Windows application in Chapter 2.

3.2 Simple Program: Printing a Line of Text

MC++ uses some notations that might appear strange to nonprogrammers or standard C++ programmers. We begin by considering a simple console application that displays a line of text. The program and its output are shown in Fig. 3.1. The program is followed by an output window that displays the program's results. When you execute this program, this output appears in a console window. [*Note:* Review Chapter 2, Introduction to the Visual Studio .NET IDE, for instructions on creating a console application.]

```
// Fig. 3.1: Welcome1.cpp
// A first program in Visual C++ .NET.

// includes contents of stdafx.h into this program file
#include "stdafx.h"

// references prepackaged Microsoft code
#using <mscorlib.dll>

// declares the use of namespace System
using namespace System;

int _tmain()
{
```

Fig. 3.1 Printing a line with Visual C++ .NET. (Part 1 of 2.)

```
15      // display the string between the two parentheses in the console window
16      Console::WriteLine( S"Welcome to Visual C++ .NET Programming!" );
17
18      return 0; // indicate that program ended successfully
19   } // end _tmain
```

```
Welcome to Visual C++ .NET Programming!
```

Fig. 3.1 Printing a line with Visual C++ .NET. (Part 2 of 2.)

This program illustrates several important features of MC++. All programs we present in this book will include line numbers for the reader's convenience; these line numbers are not part of the MC++ programs. Line 16 in Fig. 3.1 does the "real work" of the program, displaying the phrase `Welcome to Visual C++ .NET Programming!` on the screen.

Line 1 begins with `//`, indicating that the remainder of the line is a *comment*. Programmers insert comments to *document* and improve the readability of their code. Comments also help other programmers read and understand your programs. This comment simply indicates the figure number and file name for this program. In this case, we have named the file `Welcome1.cpp`. A comment that begins with `//` is called a *single-line comment*, because the comment terminates at the end of the line. Single-line comments can be placed almost anywhere in the program.

You can also write *multiple-line comments*, such as

```
/* This is a multiple-line
   comment. It can be
   split over many lines. */
```

that begin with *delimiter* `/*` and end with *delimiter* `*/`. All text between these delimiters is treated as a comment. In the Visual Studio .NET IDE, all comment text appears in green by default.[1] Comments of the form `//` and `/* … */` are ignored by the compiler—they do not cause the computer to perform any action when the program executes. Throughout this book, we use mostly single-line comments.

Common Programming Error 3.1

Forgetting one of the delimiters of a multiple-line comment is a syntax error. A syntax error *is caused when the compiler cannot recognize a statement. The compiler normally issues an error message to help the programmer locate and fix the incorrect statement. Syntax errors are violations of the language rules. Syntax errors are also called* compile errors, compile-time errors *or* compilation errors *because they are detected during the compilation phase. A program cannot compile or execute until all the syntax errors are corrected.*

Good Programming Practice 3.1

Every program should begin with one or more comments that describe the program's purpose.

Line 3 is a blank line. Programmers often use blank lines and space characters throughout a program to make the code easier to read. Blank lines, space characters, new-

1. Fonts and colors in Visual Studio .NET can be modified in the **Environment > Fonts and Colors** section of the **Tools > Options…** dialog.

line characters and tab characters are known collectively as *white space* (space characters and tabs are known specifically as *white-space characters*). The compiler ignores blank lines, tabs and extra spaces that separate language elements. Several conventions for using white-space characters are discussed in this and subsequent chapters.

Good Programming Practice 3.2

Use blank lines, space characters and tab characters in a program to enhance program readability.

Line 5 contains an *`#include` directive*, which instructs the compiler to treat the contents of a specified file as if they are inserted into the current file in place of the `#include` statement. In this case, line 5 specifies that we wish to "include" the contents of `stdafx.h` into our program file, `welcome1.cpp`. The file `stdafx.h`, which is generated by Visual Studio .NET, references useful preexisting code. We discuss the `#include` directive in more detail in Chapter 8, Object-Based Programming.

Line 8 (known as a *`#using` preprocessor directive*) references *`mscorlib.dll`*, a prepackaged unit of code. A `#using` preprocessor directive begins with the syntax `#using` and imports data, such as the information contained in a `.dll` file, into a program. We will discuss *`.dll` (dynamic link library)* files in further detail in Chapter 8.

The *`using` directive* in line 11 declares that the program uses features in *namespace `System`* (part of `mscorlib.dll`). A `using` directive (which is different from a `#using` preprocessor directive) begins with keyword `using` and declares the use of a namespace in a program. *Keywords*[2] (sometimes called *reserved words*) are reserved for use by Visual C++ .NET (we discuss the various keywords throughout the text). A *namespace* groups various MC++ features into related categories. One of the great strengths of MC++ is that programmers can use the rich set of namespaces provided by the .NET Framework. These namespaces contain code that programmers can reuse, rather than "reinventing the wheel." This makes programming easier and faster. The namespaces that are defined in the .NET Framework contain preexisting code known as the *.NET Framework Class Library*. An example of one of the features in namespace `System` is class `Console`, which we discuss momentarily. The various features are organized into namespaces that enable programmers to locate them easily. We discuss many namespaces and their features throughout the book.

Line 13 begins *`_tmain`*, which is known as the *entry point* of the program. The parentheses after `_tmain` indicate that `_tmain` is a program building block called a *function*. Functions can perform tasks and return information when these tasks complete. Information also can be passed (as *arguments*) to a function. This information may be necessary for the function to complete its task. Functions are explained in detail in Chapter 6, Functions. [*Note*: In Visual Studio .NET, functions are sometimes also referred to as *methods* or *subroutines*.]

For an MC++ application, exactly one function must define the entry point of the program; otherwise, the program is not executable. Throughout this book, we use function `_tmain` as the entry point of console applications and function *`_tWinMain`* as the entry point of *GUI* (*graphical user interface*) applications.[3] GUI applications are programs that display

---

2. The complete list of Visual C++ .NET keywords is shown in Fig. 4.2.
3. Functions `_tmain` and `_tWinMain` ensure that, if support is available, an application uses special strings known as Unicode® strings (which will be discussed later in this chapter); if Unicode is unavailable, the application still compiles and runs normally. For this reason, we use these functions as application entry points rather than more widely recognized entry points, such as `main`.

graphical elements, such as buttons and labels, with which the user interacts. We discuss GUI applications and function `_tWinMain` in more detail in Chapter 12, Graphical User Interface Concepts: Part 1.

The left brace (`{`) in line 14 begins the *body of the function definition* (the code which will be executed as a part of our program). A corresponding right brace (`}`) terminates the function definition's body (line 19). Notice that the lines in the body of the function are indented between these braces.

Good Programming Practice 3.3

Indent the entire body of each function definition one "level" of indentation between the left brace (`{`) and the right brace (`}`) that define the function body. This makes the structure of the function stand out, improving the function definition's readability.

Line 16 instructs the computer to perform an *action*, namely, to print a series of characters contained between the double quotation marks. Characters delimited in this manner are called *strings*, *character strings* or *string literals*. We refer to characters between double quotation marks generically as strings. White-space characters in strings are not ignored by the compiler.

The ***`Console`*** class enables programs to output information to the computer's *standard output* (usually the computer screen). *Classes* are logical groupings of members (e.g., functions, which are called methods when they appear in classes) that simplify program organization. Class `Console` provides methods, such as method ***`WriteLine`***, that allow MC++ programs to display strings and other types of information in the Windows console window.

Method ***`WriteLine`*** *displays* (or *prints*) a line of text in the console window. When `WriteLine` completes its task, it outputs a *newline character* to position the *output cursor* (the location where the next character will be displayed) at the beginning of the next line in the console window. (This is similar to pressing the *Enter* key when typing in a text editor—the cursor is repositioned at the beginning of the next line in the file.)

The entire line, including `Console::WriteLine`, its *argument* in the parentheses (`S"Welcome to Visual C++ .NET Programming!"`) and the *semicolon* (`;`), is called a *statement*. Every statement must end with a semicolon (known as the *statement terminator*). When this statement executes, it displays the message `Welcome to Visual C++ .NET Programming!`(Fig. 3.2) in the console window.

Common Programming Error 3.2

Omitting the semicolon at the end of a statement is a syntax error.

Error-Prevention Tip 3.1

When the compiler reports a syntax error, the error might not be on the line indicated by the error message. First, check the line where the error was reported. If that line does not contain a syntax error, check the lines that precede the one reported.

The ***`S`*** *prefix* in line 16 indicates that the string that follows is a string-literal in the Managed Extensions for C++ (MC++). Programmers can place strings on consecutive lines and the pieces will be *concatenated* (i.e., joined to form one string), as in:

```
Console::WriteLine( S"Welcome to Visual C++ .NET "
   S"Programming!" );
```

In MC++ statements, we normally precede each class name with its namespace name and the *scope resolution operator (::)*. For example, line 16 would normally be

```
System::Console::WriteLine(
   S"Welcome to Visual C++ .NET Programming!" );
```

for the program to compile successfully. The `using` directive in line 11 eliminates the need to precede every use of `Console` with `System::`. Notice, however, that we still must precede method `WriteLine` with its class name (`Console`) and the scope resolution operator (`::`). This specifies that we are referring to method `WriteLine` of class `Console`.

Line 18 introduces the `return` statement. Keyword `return` is one of several means we will use to *exit a function* (or method). When the `return` statement is used at the end of `_tmain` as shown here, the value `0` indicates that the program terminated successfully. In Chapter 6, Functions, we discuss the reasons for including this statement. For now, simply include this statement in each program, or the compiler might produce a warning on some systems. Figure 3.2 shows the result of executing the program.

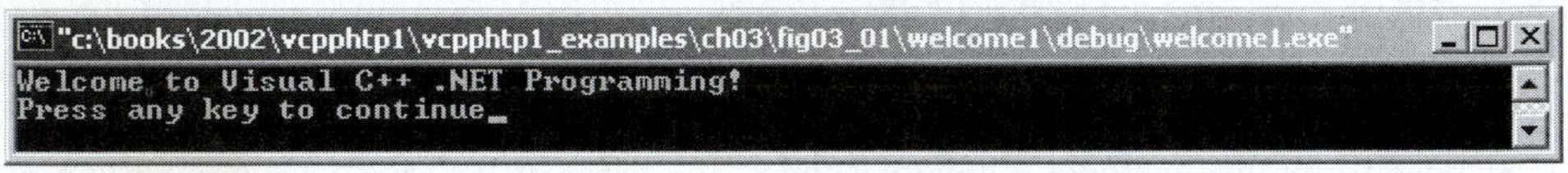

Fig. 3.2 Execution of the `Welcome1` program.

Displaying One Line of Text with Multiple Statements

The message `Welcome to Visual C++ .NET Programming!` can also be displayed via multiple method calls. File `Welcome2.cpp` of Fig. 3.3 uses two statements to produce the same output as Fig. 3.2.

```
// Fig. 3.3: Welcome2.cpp
// Printing a line with multiple statements.

#include "stdafx.h"

#using <mscorlib.dll>

using namespace System;

int _tmain()
{
   // use two Console statements to print a string
   Console::Write( S"Welcome to " );
   Console::WriteLine( S"Visual C++ .NET Programming!" );

   return 0;
} // end _tmain
```

```
Welcome to Visual C++ .NET Programming!
```

Fig. 3.3 Printing on one line with separate statements.

Lines 13–14 of Fig. 3.3 display one line in the console window. The first statement calls `Console` method *`Write`* to display a string. Unlike `WriteLine`, `Write` does not position the output cursor at the beginning of the next line in the console window after displaying its string. Rather, the cursor remains immediately after the last character displayed. This way, the next character displayed in the console window appears immediately after the last character displayed with `Write`. Thus, when line 14 executes, the first character displayed (`V`) appears immediately after the last character displayed with `Write` (i.e., the space character after the word `"to"` in line 13).

Displaying Multiple Lines of Text with a Single Statement

A single statement can display multiple lines by using newline characters. Newline characters indicate when to position the output cursor at the beginning of the next line in the console window to continue output. Figure 3.4 demonstrates using newline characters.

```
1  // Fig. 3.4: Welcome3.cpp
2  // Printing multiple lines with a single statement.
3
4  #include "stdafx.h"
5
6  #using <mscorlib.dll>
7
8  using namespace System;
9
10 int _tmain()
11 {
12    // use the new line character to display four lines of output
13    // with a single Console statement
14    Console::WriteLine( S"Welcome\nto\nVisual C++ .NET\nProgramming!" );
15
16    return 0;
17 } // end _tmain
```

```
Welcome
to
Visual C++ .NET
Programming!
```

Fig. 3.4 Printing on multiple lines with a single statement.

Line 14 produces four separate lines of text in the console window. Normally, the characters in a string are displayed exactly as they appear between the double quotes. However, notice that the two characters `"\"` and `"n"` do not appear on the screen. The *backslash* (\) is called an *escape character*. It indicates that a "special" character is to be output. When a backslash is encountered in a string of characters, the next character is combined with the backslash to form an *escape sequence*. This escape sequence `\n` is the *newline character*. It causes the cursor (i.e., the current screen position indicator) to move to the beginning of the next line in the console window. Some common escape sequences are listed in Fig. 3.5. Notice that Fig. 3.5 also contains escape sequences for the backslash character (\) and the double quote character ("). These are special characters, so programmers must use their respective escape sequences when including them in a string.

Escape sequence	Description
`\n`	Newline. Position the screen cursor to the beginning of the next line.
`\t`	Horizontal tab. Move the screen cursor to the next tab stop.
`\r`	Carriage return. Position the screen cursor to the beginning of the current line; do not advance to the next line. Any characters output after the carriage return overwrite the previous characters output on that line.
`\\`	Backslash. Used to print a backslash character.
`\"`	Double quote. Used to print a double quote (") character.

Fig. 3.5 Some common escape sequences.

Common Programming Error 3.3

Forgetting to precede a special character by the escape character (\) is a common mistake which can lead to incorrect output or even syntax errors.

3.3 Another Simple Program: Adding Integers

Our next application (Fig. 3.6) inputs two integers typed by a user at the keyboard, computes the sum of these values and displays the result. As the user types each integer and presses the *Enter* key, the integer is read into the program as a string, then converted to an integer for use in the addition calculation. Lines 1–2 are single-line comments stating the figure number, file name and purpose of the program.

```
1   // Fig. 3.6: Addition.cpp
2   // An addition program that adds two integers.
3
4   #include "stdafx.h"
5
6   #using <mscorlib.dll>
7
8   using namespace System;
9
10  int _tmain()
11  {
12     String *firstNumber,    // first user input
13            *secondNumber;   // second user input
14
15     int number1,   // first number
16         number2,   // second number
17         sum;       // sum of both numbers
18
19     // prompt first number
20     Console::Write( S"Please enter the first integer: " );
21
22     // obtain first number from user
23     firstNumber = Console::ReadLine();
```

Fig. 3.6 Addition program that adds two values entered by the user. (Part 1 of 2.)

```
24
25       // prompt second number
26       Console::Write( S"\nPlease enter the second integer: " );
27
28       // obtain second number from user
29       secondNumber = Console::ReadLine();
30
31       // convert numbers from type String * to type integer
32       number1 = Int32::Parse( firstNumber );
33       number2 = Int32::Parse( secondNumber );
34
35       // add numbers
36       sum = number1 + number2;
37
38       // display the sum as a string
39       Console::WriteLine( S"\nThe sum is {0}.", sum.ToString() );
40
41       return 0;
42    } // end _tmain
```

```
Please enter the first integer: 45

Please enter the second integer: 72

The sum is 117.
```

Fig. 3.6 Addition program that adds two values entered by the user. (Part 2 of 2.)

The program begins execution with function `_tmain` in line 10. The left brace (line 11) begins `_tmain`'s body and the corresponding right brace (line 42) terminates `_tmain`'s body.

Lines 12–17 are *declarations.* The words `firstNumber`, `secondNumber`, `number1`, `number2` and `sum` are the names of *variables.* A variable is a location in the computer's memory where a value can be stored for use by a program. All variables must be declared with a name and a type before they can be used in a program. There are certain types already defined in the .NET Framework, known as *built-in types* or *primitive types*. Types such as `int`, `double` and `__wchar_t` are examples of primitive types. Primitive type names are keywords. The primitive types are summarized in Chapter 4, Control Statements: Part 1.

A variable name can be any valid identifier, which is a series of characters consisting of letters, digits, and underscores (_). Identifiers cannot begin with a digit, cannot contain spaces, and cannot be a keyword. Examples of valid identifiers are `Welcome1`, `_value`, `m_inputField1` and `button7`. The name `7button` is not a valid identifier because it begins with a digit, and the name `input field` is not a valid identifier because it contains a space. MC++ is *case sensitive*—uppercase and lowercase letters are considered different letters, so `a1` and `A1` are different identifiers. Declarations end with a semicolon (`;`) and can be split over several lines with each variable in the declaration separated by a comma (i.e., a *comma-separated list* of variable names). Several variables of the same type may be declared in one or in multiple declarations. We could have written two declarations, one for each variable, but the preceding declaration is more concise. Notice the single-line comments at the end of each line. This is a common syntax used by programmers to indicate the purpose of each variable in the program.

Good Programming Practice 3.4

Choosing meaningful variable names helps a program to be "self-documenting" (i.e., easier to understand simply by reading it, rather than having to read manuals or use excessive comments).

Good Programming Practice 3.5

Variable-name identifiers should begin with a lowercase letter. Every word in the name after the first word should begin with a capital letter. For example, identifier `firstNumber` *has a capital* `N` *in its second word,* `Number`*. These practices make variable names easier to read.*

Good Programming Practice 3.6

Some programmers prefer to declare each variable on a separate line. This format allows for easy insertion of a comment that describes each variable.

Lines 12–13 declare that variables `firstNumber` and `secondNumber` are of data type `String *`, which means that these variables will hold string literals. The asterisk (*) that follows `String` will be discussed in Chapter 6, Functions. Lines 15–17 declare that variables `number1`, `number2` and `sum` are of data type `int`, which means that these variables will hold *integer* values (i.e., whole numbers such as –11, 0 and 31914). In contrast, the data types `float` and `double` specify real numbers (i.e., floating-point numbers with decimal points, such as 3.4, 0.0 and –11.19) and variables of type `__wchar_t` specify character data. A `__wchar_t` variable may hold only a single character, such as `x`, `$`, `7` or `*`, or an escape sequences (such as the newline character `\n`). Often in programs, characters are denoted in single quotes, such as `'x'`, `'$'`, `'7'`, `'*'` and `'\n'`. MC++ is also capable of representing all Unicode characters. *Unicode*® is an international *character set* (collection of characters) that enables the programmer to display letters in different languages, mathematical symbols and much more. For more information on this topic, see Appendix D, Unicode.

Lines 20 and 23 prompt the user to input an integer and read from the user a `String *` representing the first of the two integers that the program will add. The message output by line 20 is called a *prompt*, because it directs the user to take a specific action. Method `ReadLine` (line 23) causes the program to pause and wait for user input. The user types characters at the keyboard, then presses the *Enter* key to submit the string to the program.

Technically, the user can send anything to the program as input. For this program, if the user types a noninteger value, a *run-time logic error* (an error that has its effect at execution time) occurs. Chapter 11, Exception Handling, discusses how to make your programs more robust by handling such errors.

When the user types a number and presses *Enter*, the program assigns the string representation of this number to variable `firstNumber` (line 23) with the *assignment operator* `=`. The statement is read as, "`firstNumber` *gets* the value returned by method `ReadLine`." The `=` operator is a *binary operator*, because it has two *operands*—`firstNumber`, and the result of the expression `Console::ReadLine()`. The entire statement is an *assignment statement*, because it assigns a value to a variable. In an assignment statement, first the right side of the assignment is evaluated, then the result is assigned to the variable on the left side of the assignment. So, line 23 executes method `ReadLine`, then assigns the string value input to `firstNumber`.

Good Programming Practice 3.7

Place spaces on either side of a binary operator. This makes the operator stand out and makes the program more readable.

Lines 26 and 29 prompt the user to enter a second integer and read from the user a string representing the value. In MC++, users input data as strings (type `String *`). We must convert these strings to numeric values to perform integer arithmetic.

Lines 32–33 convert the two strings input by the user to `int` values that can be used in a calculation. Method *`Int32::Parse`* (a method of class `Int32`) converts its `String *` argument to an `int`. Class `Int32` is part of the `System` namespace. Line 32 assigns the integer that `Int32::Parse` returns to variable `number1`. Any subsequent references to `number1` in the program use this integer value. Line 33 assigns the integer that `Int32::Parse` returns to variable `number2`. Any subsequent references to `number2` in the program use this integer value.

Notice that we only use `String *` variables `firstNumber` and `secondNumber` to store the user input temporarily until the program converts these values to integers. Alternatively, you can eliminate the need for `String *` variables `firstNumber` and `secondNumber` by combining the input and conversion operations as follows:

```
Console::Write( S"Please enter the first integer: " );
number1 = Int32::Parse( Console::ReadLine() );

Console::Write( S"\nPlease enter the second integer: " );
number2 = Int32::Parse( Console::ReadLine() );
```

The preceding statements do not make use of the `String *` variables.

The assignment statement in line 36 calculates the sum of the variables `number1` and `number2` and assigns the result to variable `sum` by using the assignment operator `=`. The statement is read as, "`sum` *gets* the value of `number1` plus `number2`." Most calculations are performed in assignment statements.

After performing the calculation, line 39 displays the result of the addition. The syntax

```
sum.ToString()
```

first obtains the string representation of variable `sum` so that is can be used in the output. We obtain the string representation using method *`ToString`*. Notice that we invoke method `ToString` of variable `sum` using the *dot operator* (`.`) rather than the scope resolution operator (`::`). The dot operator accesses methods of an object rather than methods of a class. We discuss objects in more detail in Chapter 8, Object-Based Programming.

Once we have obtained the string representation of variable `sum`, we would like to output it with method `WriteLine` using a format string. Let us discuss how this is done.

The *comma-separated* arguments to `Console::WriteLine` in line 39

```
"\nThe sum is {0}.", sum.ToString()
```

use `{0}` to indicate a placeholder for a variable's value. If we assume that `sum` contains the value `117`, the expression evaluates as follows: Method `WriteLine` encounters a number in curly braces, `{0}`, known as a *format*. This indicates that the expression found after the string in the list of arguments (in this case, `sum.ToString()`) will be evaluated and incorporated into our string, in place of the format. The resulting string will be `"The sum is 117."` Similarly, in the statement

```
Console::WriteLine( "The numbers entered are {0} and {1}",
   number1.ToString(), number2.ToString() );
```

the value of `number1.ToString()` would replace `{0}` (because it is the first expression) and the value of `number2` would replace `{1}` (because it is the second expression). The resulting string would be `"The numbers entered are 45 and 72"`. More formats can be used (`{2}`, `{3}` etc.) if there are more values to display in the string.

Good Programming Practice 3.8

Place a space after each comma in a method's argument list to make programs more readable.

Note that to display a curly brace in a string containing formats, two of the desired curly braces must be used. This is similar to using an escape sequence. For example, if variable `sum` had the value `117`, the following statement

```
Console::WriteLine( S"{{ The sum is {{{0}}} }}", sum.ToString() );
```

would output `"{ The sum is {117} }"`. Notice that only one curly brace is output for every two braces that do not form a format.

Finally, note that lines 36 and 39 can be combined as follows:

```
Console::WriteLine( S"\nThe sum is {0}.",
   ( number1 + number2 ).ToString() );
```

In this case, the expression (number1 + number 2) is evaluated first, then its value is used in the output statement.

3.4 Memory Concepts

Variable names, such as `number1`, `number2` and `sum`, actually correspond to *locations* in the computer's memory. Every variable has a *name,* a *type,* a *size* and a *value.*

In the addition program in Fig. 3.6, the statement at line 32

```
number1 = Int32::Parse( firstNumber );
```

converts the string that the user entered to an `int`. This `int` is placed into a memory location to which the name `number1` has been assigned by the compiler. Suppose the user enters the string `45` as the value for `firstNumber`. The program converts `firstNumber` to an `int`, and the computer places the integer value `45` into location `number1`, as shown in Fig. 3.7.

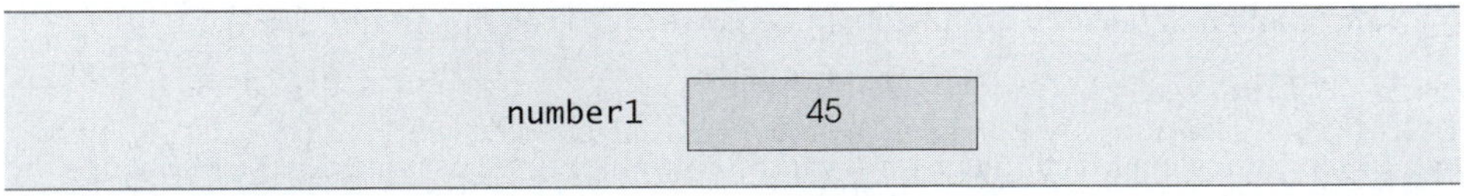

Fig. 3.7 Memory location showing name and value of variable `number1`.

When a value is placed in a memory location, this value replaces the previous value in that location. The previous value is lost (or destroyed).

When the statement at line 33

```
number2 = Int32::Parse( secondNumber );
```

executes, suppose the user types `72` as the value for `secondNumber`. The program converts `secondNumber` to an `int`, the computer places the integer value `72` into location `number2` and memory appears as shown in Fig. 3.8.

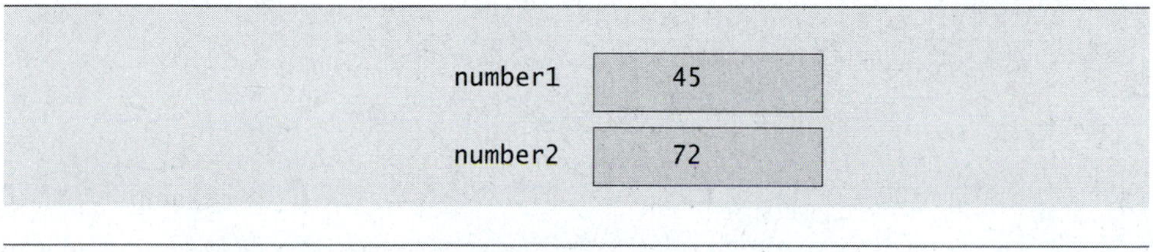

Fig. 3.8 Memory locations after values for variables `number1` and `number2` have been input.

Once the program has obtained values for `number1` and `number2`, it adds these values and places their total into variable `sum`. The statement

```
sum = number1 + number2;
```

performs the addition and replaces (i.e., destroys) `sum`'s previous value. After calculating the `sum`, memory appears as shown in Fig. 3.9. Note that the values of `number1` and `number2` appear exactly as they did before the calculation of `sum`. These values were used, but not destroyed, as the computer performed the calculation. Thus, when a value is read from a memory location, the process is *nondestructive.*

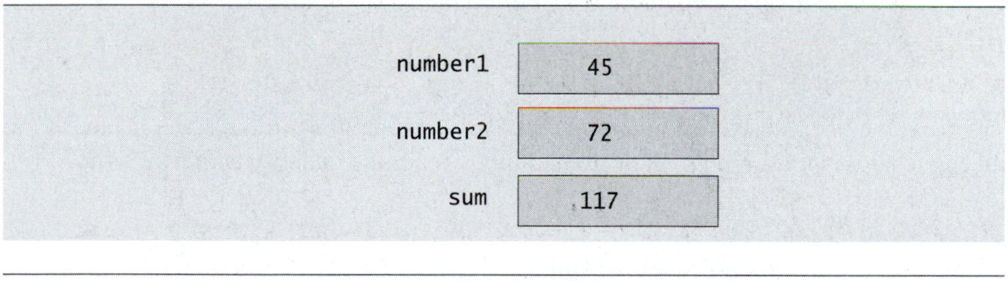

Fig. 3.9 Memory locations after a calculation.

3.5 Arithmetic

Most programs perform arithmetic calculations. Figure 3.10 summarizes the *arithmetic operators*. Note the use of various special symbols not used in algebra. The *asterisk* (`*`)[4] indicates multiplication, and the *percent sign* (`%`) represents the *modulus operator*, which is discussed shortly. The arithmetic operators in Fig. 3.10 are binary operators, because they each require two operands. For example, the expression `sum + value` contains the binary operator `+` and the two operands `sum` and `value`.

4. Not to be confused with the `*` in type `String *`, which will be discussed in Chapter 6, Functions.

MC++ operation	Arithmetic operator	Algebraic expression	MC++ expression
Addition	+	$f + 7$	`f + 7`
Subtraction	–	$p - c$	`p - c`
Multiplication	*	bm	`b * m`
Division	/	x / y or $\frac{x}{y}$ or $x \div y$	`x / y`
Modulus	%	r mod s	`r % s`

Fig. 3.10 Arithmetic operators.

Integer division contains two `int` operands. The result of this computation is an integer quotient; for example, the expression `7 / 4` evaluates to `1` and the expression `17 / 5` evaluates to `3`. Note that any fractional part in integer division is simply discarded (i.e., truncated)—no rounding occurs. MC++ provides the modulus operator, `%`, which yields the remainder after division. The expression `x % y` yields the remainder after `x` is divided by `y`. Thus, `7 % 4` yields `3` and `17 % 5` yields `2`. This operator is used most commonly with integral operands, but also can be used with other arithmetic types. In later chapters, we consider interesting applications of the modulus operator, such as determining whether one number is a multiple of another.

Arithmetic expressions in MC++ must be written in *straight-line form* to facilitate entering programs into a computer. Thus, expressions such as "a divided by b" must be written as `a / b` so that all constants, variables and operators appear in a straight line. The following algebraic notation generally is not acceptable to compilers:

$$\frac{a}{b}$$

Parentheses are used to group terms in MC++ expressions in the same manner as in algebraic expressions. For example, to multiply `a` times the quantity `b + c`, we write

```
a * ( b + c )
```

MC++ applies the operators in arithmetic expressions in a precise sequence, determined by the following *rules of operator precedence,* which are generally the same as those followed in algebra:

1. Multiplication, division and modulus operations are applied first. If an expression contains several multiplication, division and modulus operations, operators are applied from left to right. Multiplication, division and modulus are said to have the same level of precedence.

2. Addition and subtraction operations are applied next. If an expression contains several addition and subtraction operations, operators are applied from left to right. Addition and subtraction have the same level of precedence.

The rules of operator precedence enable MC++ to apply operators in the correct order. When we say operators are applied from left to right, we are referring to the *associativity* of the operators. If there are multiple operators, each with the same precedence, the associativity determines the order in which the operators are applied. We will see that some operators associate from right to left. Figure 3.11 summarizes the rules of operator precedence. This table will expand as we introduce additional MC++ operators in subsequent chapters. See Appendix A for a complete operator-precedence chart.

Operator(s)	Operation	Order of evaluation (precedence)

`*`
`/`
`%`
	Multiplication
	Division
	Modulus
		Evaluated first. If there are several such operators, they are evaluated left to right.

`+` `-`	Addition Subtraction	Evaluated next. If there are several such operators, they are evaluated left to right.

Fig. 3.11 Precedence of arithmetic operators.

Now, let us consider several expressions in light of the rules of operator precedence. Each example lists an algebraic expression and its MC++ equivalent. The following is an example of an arithmetic mean (average) of five terms:

Algebra: $m = \dfrac{a + b + c + d + e}{5}$

MC++: `m = ( a + b + c + d + e ) / 5;`

The parentheses are required because division has higher precedence than addition. The entire quantity `( a + b + c + d + e )` is to be divided by `5`. If the parentheses are erroneously omitted, we obtain `a + b + c + d + e / 5`, which evaluates as

$$a + b + c + d + \frac{e}{5}$$

The following is the equation of a straight line:

Algebra: $y = mx + b$

MC++: `y = m * x + b;`

No parentheses are required. The multiplication occurs first because multiplication has a higher precedence than addition. The assignment occurs last because it has a lower precedence than multiplication and addition.

The following example contains modulus (%), multiplication, division, addition and subtraction operations:

Algebra: $z = pr\%q + w/x - z$

MC++:
```
z  =  p  *  r  %  q  +  w  /  x  -  y;
   6     1     2     4     3     5
```

The circled numbers under the statement indicate the order in which MC++ applies the operators. The multiplication, modulus and division operators evaluate first in left-to-right order (i.e., they associate from left to right). The addition and subtraction evaluate next. These also are applied from left to right.

To develop a better understanding of the rules of operator precedence, consider how a second-degree polynomial ($y = ax^2 + bx + c$) is evaluated:

```
y  =  a  *  x  *  x  +  b  *  x  +  c;
  (6)   (1)   (2)   (4)   (3)   (5)
```

The circled numbers under the statement indicate the order in which MC++ applies the operators. There is no arithmetic operator for exponentiation in Visual C++ .NET; x^2 is represented as `x * x`. The .NET Framework Class Library also provides method `Math::Pow` for exponentiation. (Chapter 6, Functions, discusses how to perform exponentiation in MC++.)

Suppose `a`, `b`, `c` and `x` are initialized as follows: `a = 2`, `b = 3`, `c = 7` and `x = 5`. Figure 3.12 illustrates the order of evaluation of the operators.

Step 1. `y = 2 * 5 * 5 + 3 * 5 + 7;` *(Leftmost multiplication)*
`2 * 5 is 10`

Step 2. `y = 10 * 5 + 3 * 5 + 7;` *(Leftmost multiplication)*
`10 * 5 is 50`

Step 3. `y = 50 + 3 * 5 + 7;` *(Multiplication before addition)*
`3 * 5 is 15`

Step 4. `y = 50 + 15 + 7;` *(Leftmost addition)*
`50 + 15 is 65`

Step 5. `y = 65 + 7;` *(Last addition)*
`65 + 7 is 72`

Step 6. `y = 72;` *(Last operation—place 72 in y)*

Fig. 3.12 Order in which a second-degree polynomial is evaluated.

As in algebra, it is acceptable to place unnecessary parentheses in an expression to make the expression easier to read. Unnecessary parentheses are also called *redundant parentheses*. For example, the preceding assignment statement might be parenthesized as

```
y = ( a * x * x ) + ( b * x ) + c;
```

Good Programming Practice 3.9

Using parentheses for more complex arithmetic expressions, even when the parentheses are not necessary, can make the arithmetic expressions easier to read.

3.6 Decision Making: Equality and Relational Operators

This section introduces the `if` *statement*, which allows a program to make a decision based on whether a *condition* is true or false. If the condition is met (i.e., the condition is *true*), the statement in the body of the `if` statement executes. If the condition is not met (i.e., the condition is *false*), the body statement does not execute. Conditions in `if` statements can be formed by using the *equality operators* and *relational operators,* summarized in Fig. 3.13. The relational operators all have the same level of precedence and associate from left to right. The equality operators both have the same level of precedence, which is lower than the precedence of the relational operators. The equality operators also associate from left to right.

Standard algebraic equality or relational operator	MC++ equality or relational operator	Example of MC++ condition	Meaning of MC++ condition
Equality operators			
=	`==`	`x == y`	x is equal to y
≠	`!=`	`x != y`	x is not equal to y
Relational operators			
>	`>`	`x > y`	x is greater than y
<	`<`	`x < y`	x is less than y
≥	`>=`	`x >= y`	x is greater than or equal to y
≤	`<=`	`x <= y`	x is less than or equal to y

Fig. 3.13 Equality and relational operators.

Common Programming Error 3.4

It is a syntax error if the operators ==, !=, >= and<= contain spaces between their symbols (as in = =, ! =, > =, < =).

Common Programming Error 3.5

Reversing the operators >= and <= (as in => and =<) is a syntax error. Reversing the operator != (as in =!) is a logic error.

Common Programming Error 3.6

Confusing the equality operator == with the assignment operator = is a logic error. The equality operator should be read "is equal to," and the assignment operator should be read "gets" or "gets the value of." Some people prefer to read the equality operator as "double equals" or "equals equals."

The next example uses six `if` statements to compare two numbers input into a program by the user. If the condition in any of these `if` statements is true, the assignment statement associated with that `if` executes. The user inputs values that the program converts to integers and stores in variables `number1` and `number2`. The program compares the numbers and displays the results of the comparison in the command prompt. The program and sample outputs are shown in Fig. 3.14.

```
// Fig. 3.14: Comparison.cpp
// Using if statements, relational operators and equality
// operators.

#include "stdafx.h"

#using <mscorlib.dll>

using namespace System;

int _tmain()
{
   int number1,
       number2;

   Console::Write( S"Please enter first integer: " );
   number1 = Int32::Parse( Console::ReadLine() );

   Console::Write( S"Please enter second integer: " );
   number2 = Int32::Parse( Console::ReadLine() );

   if ( number1 == number2 )
      Console::WriteLine( S"\n{0} == {1}", number1.ToString()
         number2.ToString() );

   if ( number1 != number2 )
      Console::WriteLine( S"\n{0} != {1}", number1.ToString(),
         number2.ToString() );

   if ( number1 < number2 )
      Console::WriteLine( S"{0} < {1}", number1.ToString(),
         number2.ToString() );

   if ( number1 > number2 )
      Console::WriteLine( S"{0} > {1}", number1.ToString(),
         number2.ToString() );

   if ( number1 <= number2 )
      Console::WriteLine( S"{0} <= {1}", number1.ToString(),
         number2.ToString() );

   if ( number1 >= number2 )
      Console::WriteLine( S"{0} >= {1}", number1.ToString(),
         number2.ToString() );

```

Fig. 3.14 Using equality and relational operators. (Part 1 of 2.)

```
46      return 0;
47   } // end _tmain
```

```
Please enter first integer: 2000
Please enter second integer: 1000

2000 != 1000
2000 > 1000
2000 >= 1000
```

```
Please enter first integer: 1000
Please enter second integer: 2000

1000 != 2000
1000 < 2000
1000 <= 2000
```

```
Please enter first integer: 1000
Please enter second integer: 1000

1000 == 1000
1000 <= 1000
1000 >= 1000
```

Fig. 3.14 Using equality and relational operators. (Part 2 of 2.)

Function `_tmain` begins at line 11. Lines 13–14 declare the variables used in method `_tmain`. Note that there are two variables of type `int`. Remember that variables of the same type may be declared in one declaration or in multiple declarations. Also recall that, if more than one variable is placed in one declaration (lines 13–14), those variables are separated by commas (`,`).

Line 16 is called a prompts the user to take a specific action. Method *`ReadLine`* (line 17) causes the program to pause and wait for user input—a `String *` representing the first of the two integers that the program will compare. The user inputs characters from the keyboard, then presses the *Enter* key to submit the string to the program. Line 17 reads in the first number from the user, converts the `String *` to an `int` using method *`Parse`* of class *`System::Int32`* and stores the result in variable `number1`.

In MC++, type `int` is an alias for structure `Int32` (i.e., `int` is an alternative name for `Int32` and the two are interchangeable), a fundamental data type supplied by the .NET Framework.[5] Throughout this book, we use `int` rather than `Int32` for the convenience of standard C++ programmers. However, we use `Int32` explicitly when using methods or

5. *Structures*, which are defined with keyword `struct`, are aggregate data types built using elements of other types. Only `String` in Fig. 3.14 is a class rather than a `struct`. Structures are further explained in Chapter 15, Strings, Characters and Regular Expressions.

properties of Int32. Figure 3.15 lists some data types[6] supplied by the .NET Framework and their MC++ aliases.[7,8]

FCL Structure/ Class Name	Description	MC++ Type
Int16	16-bit signed (i.e., could be positive or negative) integer	**short**
Int32	32-bit signed integer	**int** or **long**
Int64	64-bit signed integer	**__int64**
Single	single-precision (32-bit) floating-point number	**float**
Double	double-precision (64-bit) floating-point number	**double**
Boolean	boolean value (**true** or **false**)	**bool**
Char	Unicode (16-bit) character	**wchar_t** or **__wchar_t**
String	immutable, fixed-length string of Unicode characters	String *

Fig. 3.15 Some data types supplied by the .NET Framework and their aliases.

Lines 17 and 20 obtain the user inputs, convert them to type int and assign the values to the appropriate variable. Notice that these statements can be combined with the variable declarations and placed on one line with statements of the form

```
int number1 = Int32::Parse( Console::ReadLine() );
```

which declares the variable, reads a string from the user, converts the string to an integer and stores the integer in the variable.

The if statement in lines 22–24 compares the values of the variables number1 and number2 for equality. If the values are equal, the program outputs the value of "{0} == {1}", where {0} corresponds to number1.ToString() and {1} corresponds to number2.ToString(). The {0} and {1} formats act as placeholders for two values.

As the program proceeds through the if statements, more strings will be output by these Console::WriteLine statements. For example, given the value 1000 for number1 and number2, the if conditions in lines 38 (<=) and 42 (>=) will also be true. Thus, the output displayed will be

```
1000 == 1000
1000 <= 1000
1000 >= 1000
```

6. The __wchar_t data type is a Microsoft-specific data type, and wchar_t is an standard C++ data type. For the Visual C++ .NET compiler to recognize the wchar_t data type, programmers must specify compiler option /Zc:wchar_t by setting **Project > Properties > Configuration Properties > C/C++ > Language > Treat wchar_t as Built-in Type** to **Yes**. For simplicity, we use the __wchar_t data type throughout this book.
7. For more information about the .NET data types, visit the site msdn.microsoft.com/library/en-us/cpguide/html/cpconthenetframeworkclasslibrary.asp.
8. String * is an MC++ alias for .NET's String class, so some sources tend to use these terms interchangeably, or to use one term and not the other. In this book, we will use String * to represent objects of type String * and String when referring to class String.

The third output window of Fig. 3.14 demonstrates this case. Notice the indentation in the `if` statements throughout the program. Such indentation enhances program readability.

Common Programming Error 3.7

Replacing operator == in the condition of an `if` statement, such as `if ( x == 1 )`, with operator =, as in `if ( x = 1 )`, is a logic error. Such a statement will actually perform the assignment and evaluate to true because any nonzero value is true in C++.

Good Programming Practice 3.10

Indent the statement in the body of an `if` statement to make the body of the structure stand out and to enhance program readability.

Good Programming Practice 3.11

Place only one statement per line in a program. This enhances program readability.

Common Programming Error 3.8

Forgetting the left and right parentheses for the condition in an `if` statement is a syntax error. The parentheses are required.

There is no semicolon (`;`) at the end of the first line of each `if` statement. Such a semicolon would result in a logic error at execution time. For example,

```
if ( number1 == number2 );
   Console::WriteLine( S"{0} == {1}", number1.ToString(),
      number2.ToString() );
```

would actually be interpreted by the compiler as

```
if ( number1 == number2 )
   ;

Console::WriteLine( S"{0} == {1}", number1.ToString(),
   number2.ToString() );
```

where the semicolon on the line by itself—called the *null statement* or *empty statement*—is the statement to execute if the condition is true. When the null statement executes, no task is performed. The program continues with the `Console::WriteLine` statement, which executes regardless of whether the condition is true or false.

Common Programming Error 3.9

Placing a semicolon immediately after the right parenthesis of the condition in an `if` statement is normally a logic error. The compiler generates a warning if it encounters an `if` statement with an empty body. The semicolon causes the body of the `if` statement to be empty, so the `if` statement performs no action, regardless of whether its condition is true. Worse, the intended body statement of the `if` statement becomes a statement in sequence after the `if` statement and always executes.

Notice the use of spacing in Fig. 3.14. Remember that the compiler normally ignores white-space characters, such as tabs, newlines and spaces. Statements may be split over several lines and may be spaced according to the programmer's preferences without affecting the meaning of a program. For example, line 20 (Fig. 3.14) could be changed to

```
number2 = Int32::Parse(
   Console::ReadLine() );
```

It is incorrect, however, to split identifiers and string literals. Ideally, statements should be kept small, but it is not always possible to do so.

Good Programming Practice 3.12

A lengthy statement may be spread over several lines. If a single statement must be split across lines, choose breaking points that make sense, such as after a comma in a comma-separated list or after an operator in a lengthy expression. If a statement is split across two or more lines, indent all subsequent lines by one level of indentation.

The chart in Fig. 3.16 shows the precedence of the operators introduced in this chapter. The operators are displayed from top to bottom in decreasing order of precedence. Notice that all these operators, with the exception of the assignment operator =, associate from left to right. Addition is left associative, so an expression such as `x + y + z` is evaluated as if it were written `(x + y) + z`. The assignment operator = associates from right to left, so an expression such as `x = y = 0` is evaluated as if it were written `x = (y = 0)`. The latter expression, `x = (y = 0)`, first assigns the value `0` to variable `y`, then assigns the result of that assignment, `0`, to `x`.

Operators	Associativity	Type
`::`	left to right	scope resolution
`*` `/` `%`	left to right	multiplicative
`+` `-`	left to right	additive
`<` `<=` `>` `>=`	left to right	relational
`==` `!=`	left to right	equality
`=`	right to left	assignment

Fig. 3.16 Precedence and associativity of operators discussed in this chapter.

Good Programming Practice 3.13

Refer to the operator-precedence chart when writing expressions containing many operators. Confirm that the operators in the expression are performed in the expected order. If you are uncertain about the order of evaluation in a complex expression, use parentheses to group expressions, as you would do in an algebraic expression. Remember that some operators, such as assignment (=), associate from right to left rather than from left to right.

In this chapter, we introduced important features of MC++, including displaying data on the screen, inputting data from the keyboard, performing calculations and making decisions. The next chapter demonstrates many similar techniques. We also introduce *structured programming* and familiarize the reader further with indentation techniques. We study how to specify and vary the order in which statements execute—this order is called *flow of control.*

SUMMARY

- Programmers insert comments to document programs and improve program readability. Every program should begin with a comment describing the purpose of the program.

- A comment that begins with // is called a single-line comment, because the comment terminates at the end of the current line. A // comment can begin in the middle of a line and continue until that line's end. Multiple-line comments begin with the delimiter /* and end with delimiter */. The compiler ignores all text between the delimiters of the comment.
- A namespace groups various MC++ features into related categories, providing programmers with the ability to locate these features quickly.
- An `#include` directive instructs the compiler to treat the contents of a specified file as if they are inserted into the current file in place of the `#include` statement.
- A `#using` preprocessor directive begins with the syntax `#using` and imports data, such as the information contained in a `.dll` file, into a program.
- A `using` directive (which is different from a `#using` preprocessing directive) begins with keyword `using` and declares the use of a namespace in a program.
- Blank lines, space characters and tab characters are known as white space. Such characters are ignored by the compiler and used to improve program readability.
- Function `_tmain` can be the entry point of an MC++ program.
- Functions can perform tasks and return information when these tasks complete. Information also can be passed to a function. This information may be necessary for the function to complete its task and is called an argument.
- A string is sometimes called a character string, a message or a string literal. White-space characters in strings are not ignored by the compiler. String contents must be delimited with double quotes.
- Every statement must end with a semicolon (the statement terminator). Omitting the semicolon at the end of a statement is a syntax error.
- A syntax error occurs when the compiler cannot recognize a statement. The compiler normally issues an error message to help the programmer locate and fix the incorrect statement. Syntax errors are violations of the language's rules.
- When the compiler reports a syntax error, the error might not be on the line indicated by the error message. First, check the line where the error was reported. If that line does not contain a syntax error, check the preceding lines in the program.
- A single output statement can display multiple lines by using newline characters.
- The backslash (\) is called an escape character. It indicates that a "special" character is to be output. When a backslash is encountered in a string of characters, the next character combined with the backslash forms an escape sequence.
- A variable is a location in memory where a value can be stored for use by a program.
- All variables must be declared with a name and a type before they can be used in a program.
- A variable name can be any valid identifier.
- A valid identifier is a series of characters consisting of letters, digits, and underscores (_). Identifiers cannot begin with numbers, contain spaces, or be a keyword.
- Whenever a value is placed in a memory location, this value replaces the previous value in that location. The previous value is destroyed (lost).
- When a value is read from a memory location, the process is nondestructive.
- Declarations end with a semicolon (`;`) and can be split over several lines, with each variable in the declaration separated by a comma.
- Several variables of the same type may be declared in either one declaration or separate declarations.
- The keywords `int`, `double` and `__wchar_t` are primitive types.

- Arithmetic expressions must be written in straight-line form to facilitate entering programs into the computer.
- Parentheses are used in MC++ expressions in the same manner as in algebraic expressions.
- MC++ applies the operators in arithmetic expressions in a precise sequence determined by the rules of operator precedence.
- As in algebra, it is acceptable to place unnecessary (redundant) parentheses in an expression to make the expression clearer.
- The `if` statement allows a program to make a decision based on whether a condition is true or false. If the condition is met (i.e., the condition is true), the statement in the body of the `if` statement executes. If the condition is not met (i.e., the condition is false), the body statement does not execute.
- Conditions in `if` statements can be formed by using equality operators and relational operators.

TERMINOLOGY

`!=` is-not-equal-to operator
`"` double quotation
`%` modulus operator
`*/` end a multiline comment
`/*` start a multiline comment
`//` single-line comment
`;` statement terminator
`\\` backslash escape sequence
`\n` newline escape sequence
`\r` carriage return escape sequence
`\t` tab escape sequence
`_` underscore
`{` left brace
`}` right brace
`<` is-less-than operator
`<=` is-less-than-or-equal-to operator
`=` assignment operator
`==` is-equal-to operator
`>` is-greater-than operator
`>=` is-greater-than-or-equal-to operator
algebraic notation
application
argument
arithmetic calculation
arithmetic operators
assignment statement
associativity of operators
asterisk (`*`) indicating multiplication
average
backslash (`\`)
binary operator
blank line
body of a function definition
built-in data type
carriage return
case sensitive
character set
character string
comma (`,`)
comma-separated list of variable names
comment
compiler
compile-time error
condition
`Console` class
`Console::ReadLine` method
`Console::Write` method
`Console::WriteLine` method
decision
declaration
display output
documentation
`double`
embedded parentheses
Enter key
entry point of a program
escape sequence
exponentiation
`float`
flow of control
format
identifier
`if` statement
indentation in `if` statements
indentation techniques
inputting data from the keyboard
`Int32::Parse` method
integer division
integer quotient
keyboard
keyword
left-to-right evaluation

location in the computer's memory
logic error
making decisions
matching left and right braces
multiple-line comment (/*... */)
name of a variable
namespace
null statement (;)
object
operand
operator precedence
output
parentheses ()
Parse method
performing a calculation
polynomial
precedence
primitive type
prompt
ReadLine method of class Console
real number
redundant parentheses
"reinventing the wheel"
reuse
run-time logic error
self-documenting code
single-line comment
size of a variable
space character
spacing convention
special character
standard output
statement
straight-line form
string
string literal
string of characters
String * type
structured programming
syntax error
System namespace
tab character
text editor
_tmain entry point
truncate
type of a variable
Unicode
#using preprocessor directive
using directive
value of a variable
variable
white-space character
Write method of class Console
WriteLine method of class Console

SELF-REVIEW EXERCISES

3.1 Fill in the blanks in each of the following statements:

a) The __________ and __________ begin and end every function body.
b) Every statement must end with a(n) __________ statement terminator.
c) The __________ statement is used to make decisions.
d) __________ begins a single-line comment.
e) __________, __________ and __________ are known as white-space characters.
f) A(n) __________ is an error that has its affect at execution time.
g) MC++ applications can begin execution at the __________ function.
h) Methods __________ and __________ display information in the console window.
i) An MC++ program includes __________ directives to indicate that we are incorporating classes from certain namespaces.
j) When a value is placed in a memory location, this value __________ the previous value in that location.
k) Saying that operators are applied from left to right refers to the __________ of the operators.
l) MC++'s if statement allows a program to make a decision based on whether a condition is __________ or __________.
m) Types such as int, float, double and __wchar_t are often called __________ types.
n) A variable is a location in the computer's __________ where a value can be stored.
o) The expression to the __________ of the assignment operator (=) is always evaluated first.
p) Data types __________ and __________ contain decimal points for storing numbers such as 3.44 or 1.20846.

q) Arithmetic expressions in MC++ must be written in __________ form to facilitate entering programs into the computer.

3.2 State whether each of the following is *true* or *false*. If *false*, explain why.

a) Comments cause the computer to print the text after the `//` on the screen when the program is executed.
b) All variables must be given a type when they are declared.
c) MC++ considers the variables `number` and `NuMbEr` to be identical.
d) The arithmetic operators `*`, `/`, `%`, `+` and `-` all have the same level of precedence.
e) Method `Int32::Parse` converts an integer to a `String`.
f) A comment that begins with `//` is called a single-line comment.
g) A string of characters contained between double quotation marks is called a phrase or phrase literal.
h) Blank lines, space characters, newline characters and tab characters outside of strings are ignored by the compiler.
i) Curly braces that define bodies of `if` statements need not occur in matching pairs.
j) MC++ applications begin executing at an entry point.
k) `class` statements identify namespaces referenced in an MC++ program.
l) Integer division yields an integer quotient.

ANSWERS TO SELF-REVIEW EXERCISES

3.1 a) Left brace (`{`), right brace (`}`). b) semicolon (`;`). c) `if`. d) `//`. e) Space characters, newline characters, tab characters. f) run-time error. g) `_tmain`. h) `Console::WriteLine`, `Console::Write`. i) `using`. j) replaces. k) associativity. l) true, false. m) primitive (or built-in). n) memory. o) right. p) `float`, `double`. q) straight-line.

3.2 a) False. Comments do not cause any action to be performed when the program is executed. They are used to document programs and improve their readability. b) True. c) False. MC++ is case sensitive, so these variables are distinct. d) False. The operators `*`, `/` and `%` are on the same level of precedence, and the operators `+` and `-` are on a lower level of precedence. e) False. Method `Int32::Parse` converts a `String` to an integer (`int`) value. f) True. g) False. A string of characters is called a string or string literal. h) True. i) False. Curly braces that do not match cause syntax errors. j) True. k) False. The compiler uses `using` directives to identify and load namespaces. l) True.

EXERCISES

3.3 Write MC++ statements that accomplish each of the following tasks:

a) Display the message `"Enter two numbers"`, in the console window.
b) Assign the product of variables `b` and `c` to variable `a`.
c) State that a program performs a sample payroll calculation (i.e., use text that helps to document a program).

3.4 What displays in the console window when each of the following MC++ statements is performed? Assume the value of `x` is 2 and the value of `y` is 3.

a)
```
Console::WriteLine( S"x = ", x.ToString() );
```
b)
```
Console::WriteLine( S"The value of x + x is {0}",
   ( x + x ).ToString() );
```
c)
```
Console::WriteLine( S"x =" );
```
d)
```
Console::WriteLine( S"{0} = {1}", ( x + y ).ToString(),
   ( y + x ).ToString() );
```

3.5 Given $y = ax^3 + 7$, which of the following are correct statements for this equation?

a)
```
y = a * x * x * x + 7;
```

b) `y = a * x * x * ( x + 7 );`
c) `y = ( a * x ) * x * ( x + 7 );`
d) `y = ( a * x ) * x * x + 7;`
e) `y = a * ( x * x * x ) + 7;`
f) `y = a * x * ( x * x + 7 );`

3.6 Indicate the order of evaluation of the operators in each of the following MC++ statements, and show the value of `x` after each statement is performed.
a) `x = 7 + 3 * 6 / 2 - 1;`
b) `x = 2 % 2 + 2 * 2 - 2 / 2;`
c) `x = ( 3 * 9 * ( 3 + ( 9 * 3 / ( 3 ) ) ) );`

3.7 Write an application that displays the numbers 1 to 4 on the same line with each pair of adjacent numbers separated by one space. Write the program using the following methods:
a) Use one `Console::Write` statement.
b) Use four `Console::Write` statements.

3.8 Write an application that asks the user to enter two numbers, obtains the two numbers from the user and prints the sum, product, difference and quotient of the two numbers.

3.9 Write an application that inputs from the user the radius of a circle and prints the circle's diameter, circumference and area. Use the following formulas (r is the radius): *diameter* = $2r$, *circumference* = $2\pi r$, *area* = πr^2. [*Hint*: `Math::PI` will return a double representation of π. For example, the following line will store π into the variable `myPI`:]

```
double myPI = Math::PI;
```

3.10 Write an application that displays in the console window a box, an oval, an arrow and a diamond, using asterisks (*) as follows:

```
*********      ***         *          *
*       *    *     *      ***        * *
*       *   *       *    *****      *   *
*       *   *       *      *       *     *
*       *   *       *      *      *       *
*       *   *       *      *       *     *
*       *   *       *      *        *   *
*       *    *     *       *         * *
*********      ***         *          *
```

3.11 What does the following code print?

```
Console::WriteLine( S"*\n**\n***\n****\n*****" );
```

3.12 What does the following code print?

```
Console::Write( S"*" );
Console::Write( S"***" );
Console::WriteLine( S"*****" );
Console::Write( S"****" );
Console::WriteLine( S"**" );
```

3.13 Write an application that reads in two integers and determines and prints whether the first is a multiple of the second. For example, if the user inputs 15 and 3, the first number is a multiple of the second. If the user inputs 2 and 4, the first number is not a multiple of the second. [*Hint*: Use the modulus operator.]

3.14 Here is a peek ahead. In this chapter, you learned about integers and the data type `int`. MC++ can also represent uppercase letters, lowercase letters and a considerable variety of special symbols. Every character has a corresponding integer representation. The set of characters a computer uses and the corresponding integer representations for those characters is called that computer's character set. You can indicate a character value in a program simply by enclosing that character in single quotes, as with `'A'`. You can determine the integer equivalent of a character by placing that character in parentheses preceded by **`static_cast< int >`**—this is called a cast. (We will say more about casts in Chapter 4.)

```
static_cast< int >( 'A' )
```

The following statement would output a character and its integer equivalent:

```
Console::WriteLine( S"The character A has the value {0}",
   ( static_cast< int >( 'A' ) ).ToString() );
```

When the preceding statement executes, it displays the character `A` and the value `65` (from the Unicode character set) as part of the string.

Write an application that displays the integer equivalents of some uppercase letters, lowercase letters, digits and special symbols. At a minimum, display the integer equivalents of the following: `A B C a b c 0 1 2 $ * + /` and the blank (" ") character.

3.15 Write an application that receives from the user one number consisting of five digits. Separate the number into its individual digits and print the digits separated from one another by three spaces each. For example, if the user types in the number `42339`, the program should print

```
4   2   3   3   9
```

[*Hint*: This exercise is possible with the techniques you learned in this chapter. You will need to use both division and modulus operations to "pick off" each digit.]

For the purpose of this exercise, assume that the user enters the correct number of digits. What happens when you execute the program and type a number with more than five digits? What happens when you execute the program and type a number with fewer than five digits?

3.16 Using only the programming techniques you learned in this chapter, write an application that calculates the squares and cubes of the numbers from 0 to 10 and prints the resulting values in table format, as follows:

```
number  square  cube
0       0       0
1       1       1
2       4       8
3       9       27
4       16      64
5       25      125
6       36      216
7       49      343
8       64      512
9       81      729
10      100     1000
```

[*Note*: This program does not require any input from the user.]

3.17 Write a program that reads a first name and a last name from the user as two separate inputs and concatenates the first name and last name, but separated by a space. Display the concatenated name at the command prompt.

4

Control Statements: Part 1

Objectives

- To understand basic problem-solving techniques of programming.
- To develop algorithms through the process of top-down, stepwise refinement.
- To use the `if` and `if...else` selection statements to choose among alternative actions.
- To use the `while` repetition statement to execute statements in a program repeatedly.
- To understand counter-controlled repetition and sentinel-controlled repetition.
- To use the increment, decrement and assignment operators.

Let's all move one place on.
Lewis Carroll

The wheel is come full circle.
William Shakespeare, *King Lear*

How many apples fell on Newton's head before he took the hint?
Robert Frost

Outline

4.1 Introduction

Before writing a program to solve a problem, it is essential to have a thorough understanding of the problem and a carefully planned approach to solving the problem. When writing a program, it is equally essential to understand the types of building blocks that are available and to employ proven program construction principles. In this chapter and the next, we discuss these issues in our presentation of the theory and principles of structured programming. The techniques you will learn are applicable to most high-level languages, including MC++. When we study object-based programming in more depth in Chapter 8, we will see that concepts presented here are helpful in building and manipulating objects.

4.2 Algorithms

Any computing problem can be solved by executing a series of actions in a specific order. A *procedure* for solving a problem in terms of

1. the *actions* to be executed and
2. the *order* in which these actions are to be executed

is called an *algorithm*. The example that follows demonstrates the importance of correctly specifying the order in which the actions are to be executed.

Consider the "rise-and-shine algorithm" followed by one junior executive for getting out of bed and going to work: (1) get out of bed, (2) take off pajamas, (3) take a shower, (4) get dressed, (5) eat breakfast, (6) carpool to work. This routine gets the executive to work well-prepared to make critical decisions.

Suppose that the same steps are performed in a slightly different order: (1) get out of bed, (2) take off pajamas, (3) get dressed, (4) take a shower, (5) eat breakfast, (6) carpool to work. In this case, our executive shows up for work soaking wet.

The importance of correctly specifying the order in which actions appear applies to computer programs, as well. *Program control* refers to the task of ordering a program's statements correctly. In this chapter, we begin to investigate the program control capabilities of MC++.

4.3 Pseudocode

Pseudocode is an artificial and informal language that helps programmers develop algorithms. The pseudocode we present is particularly useful for developing algorithms that will be converted to structured portions of MC++ programs. Pseudocode is similar to everyday English; it is convenient and user-friendly, and it is not an actual computer programming language.

Pseudocode is not executed on computers. Rather, pseudocode helps the programmer "think out" a program before attempting to write it in a programming language, such as MC++. In this chapter, we provide several examples of pseudocode algorithms.

Software Engineering Observation 4.1

Pseudocode helps the programmer conceptualize a program during the program design process. The pseudocode may then be converted to MC++.

The style of pseudocode that we present consists solely of characters; thus programmers may type pseudocode conveniently using an editor program. Programmers can convert carefully prepared pseudocode programs to corresponding MC++ programs easily. In many cases, this conversion takes place simply by replacing pseudocode statements with their MC++ equivalents.

Pseudocode normally describes only executable statements—the actions that are performed when the pseudocode is converted to MC++ and executed. Declarations are not executable statements. For example, the declaration

```
int integerValue;
```

tells the compiler variable `integerValue`'s type and instructs the compiler to reserve space in memory for the variable. This declaration does not cause any action, such as input, output or a calculation, to occur when the program executes. Some programmers choose to list variables and their purposes at the beginning of a pseudocode program.

4.4 Control Structures[1]

Normally, statements in a program execute one after the other in the order in which they appear in the program. This is called *sequential execution*. Various MC++ statements, which we will soon discuss, enable the programmer to specify that the next statement to

1. The term "control structures" comes from the field of computer science. When we introduce MC++'s implementations of control structures, we refer to them with the terminology of the Visual C++ .NET documentation, which refers to them as "statements."

execute may not be the next one in sequence. A *transfer of control* occurs when a statement other than the next one in the program executes.

During the 1960s, it became clear that the indiscriminate use of transfers of control was causing difficulty for software development groups. The problem was the *`goto` statement,* which, in some programming languages, allows the programmer to specify a transfer of control to one of a wide range of possible destinations in a program. This caused programs to become quite unstructured and hard to follow. The notion of *structured programming* became almost synonymous with "*`goto`* elimination."

The research of Bohm and Jacopini[2] demonstrated that all programs with `goto` statements could be written without them. The challenge of the era for programmers was to shift their styles to "`goto`-less programming." It was not until the 1970s that programmers started taking structured programming seriously. The results were impressive, as software development groups reported reduced development times, more frequent on-time delivery of systems and more frequent within-budget completion of software projects. The key to these successes was that structured programs were clearer, easier to debug and modify and more likely to be bug-free in the first place.

Bohm and Jacopini's work demonstrated that all programs could be written in terms of only three *control structures*, namely, the *sequence structure*, the *selection structure* and the *repetition structure*. The sequence structure is built into MC++. Unless directed otherwise, the computer executes MC++ statements one after the other in the order in which they appear in a program. The *flowchart* segment of Fig. 4.1 illustrates a typical sequence structure in which two calculations are performed in order.

A flowchart is a graphical representation of an algorithm or a portion of an algorithm. Flowcharts contain certain special-purpose symbols, such as rectangles, diamonds, ovals and small circles. These symbols are connected by arrows called *flowlines,* which indicate the order in which the actions of the algorithm execute. This order is known as the flow of control.

Like pseudocode, flowcharts often are useful for developing and representing algorithms, although pseudocode is preferred by many programmers. Flowcharts show clearly how control structures operate; that is all we use them for in this text. The reader should compare carefully the pseudocode and flowchart representations of each control structure.

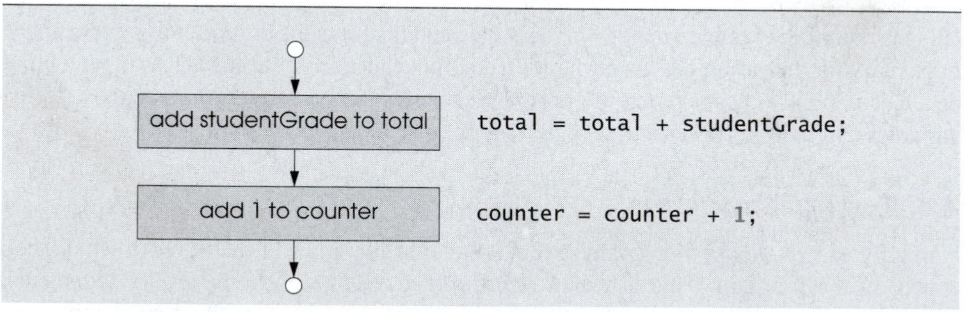

Fig. 4.1 Flowcharting Visual C++ .NET's sequence structure.

2. Bohm, C., and G. Jacopini, "Flow Diagrams, Turing Machines, and Languages with Only Two Formation Rules," *Communications of the ACM*, Vol. 9, No. 5, May 1966, pp. 336–371.

Consider the flowchart segment for the sequence structure in Fig. 4.1. We use the *rectangle symbol*, also called the *action symbol,* to indicate any type of action, including a calculation or an input/output operation. The flowlines in the figure indicate the order in which the actions are to be performed—first, `studentGrade` is to be added to `total`, then `1` is to be added to `counter`. We can have as many actions as we want in a sequence structure. Several actions may be placed anywhere in a sequence that a single action may be placed.

When drawing a flowchart that represents a complete algorithm, an *oval symbol* containing the word "Begin" is the first symbol used; an oval symbol containing the word "End" indicates where the algorithm ends. When drawing only a portion of an algorithm, as in Fig. 4.1, the oval symbols are omitted in favor of using *small circle symbols,* also called *connector symbols*.

Perhaps the most important flowcharting symbol is the *diamond symbol*, also called the *decision symbol,* which indicates that a decision is to be made. We discuss the diamond symbol in Section 4.5.

MC++ has only seven control structures—one *sequence structure* (sequential execution), three types of *selection structures* and three types of *repetition structures*. Each program is formed by combining as many of each type of control structure as is necessary.

In MC++, selection structures are created with *selection statements*. MC++ provides three types of selection statements, which we discuss in this chapter and the next. The `if` selection statement performs (selects) an action if a condition is true or skips the action if the condition is false. The `if...else` statement performs an action if a condition is true and performs a different action if the condition is false. The `switch` selection statement, discussed in Chapter 5, performs one of many actions, depending on the value of an expression.

The `if` statement is called a *single-selection structure* because it selects or ignores a single action (or a single group of actions). The `if...else` statement is called a *double-selection structure* because it selects between two different actions (or groups of actions). The `switch` statement is called a *multiple-selection structure* because it selects among many different actions (or groups of actions).

In MC++, repetition structures are created with *repetition statements*.[3] MC++ provides three repetition statements: `while`, `do...while` and `for`. The words `if`, `else`, `switch`, `while`, `do` and `for` are standard MC++ keywords. These words are used to implement various MC++ features, such as control structures. Keywords cannot be used as identifiers, such as for variable names. Figure 4.2 lists the keywords available to MC++ developers.[4] The first section displays the standard C++ keywords. The second section displays keywords added by Microsoft to the core C++ language. The third and final section lists the MC++ keywords. The keywords in the first two sections can be used for both managed and unmanaged code, whereas the keywords in the last section can be used only with managed code. MC++ applications can use all keywords listed in Fig. 4.2. Notice that many of the Microsoft-specific keywords are preceded by two underscores.

---

3. Repetition statements are also referred to as *iteration statements*. For more information about different types of statements, visit `msdn.microsoft.com/library/default.asp?url=/library/en-us/vclang/html/_pluslang_Statements.asp`.
4. For more information on keywords, visit `msdn.microsoft.com/library/default.asp?url=/library/en-us/vclang/html/_pluslang_c.2b2b_.keywords.asp`.

Visual C++ .NET Keywords

Standard C++ keywords

auto	bool	break	case
catch	char	class	const
const_cast	continue	default	delete
do	double	dynamic_cast	else
enum	explicit	extern	false
float	for	friend	goto
if	inline	int	long
mutable	namespace	new	operator
private	protected	public	register
reinterpret_cast	return	short	signed
sizeof	static	static_cast	struct
switch	template	this	throw
true	try	typedef	typeid
typename	union	unsigned	using
virtual	void	volatile	wchar_t
while			

Microsoft-specific keywords for C++

__alignof	__asm	__assume	__based
__cdecl	__declspec	deprecated	dllexport
dllimport	__event	__except	__fastcall
__finally	__forceinline	__hook	__identifier
__if_exists	__if_not_exists	__inline	__int8
__int16	__int32	__int64	__interface
__leave	__m64	__m128	__m128d
__m128i	__multiple_inheritance		naked
noinline	__noop	noreturn	nothrow
novtable	property	__raise	selectany
__single_inheritance		__stdcall	__super
thread	__try/__except	__try/__finally	__unhook
uuid	__uuidof	__virtual_inheritance	
__w64	__wchar_t		

MC++ keywords (also Microsoft-specific)

__abstract	__box	__delegate	__gc
__nogc	__pin	__property	__sealed
__try_cast	__value		

Fig. 4.2 Visual C++ .NET keywords.

Single-entry/single-exit control structures make it easy to build programs; the control structures are attached to one another by connecting the exit point of one control structure to the entry point of the next. This construction is similar to the stacking of building blocks; thus, we call it *control-structure stacking*. There is only one other way in which control structures may be connected, and that is through *control-structure nesting*, where one or more control structures can be placed inside another. Thus, algorithms in C++ programs are constructed from only seven different types of control structures, combined in only two ways.

4.5 `if` Selection Statement

In a program, a selection statement chooses among alternative courses of action. For example, suppose that the passing grade on an examination is 60 (out of 100). Then the pseudocode statement

If student's grade is greater than or equal to 60
Print "Passed"

determines if the condition "student's grade is greater than or equal to 60" is true or false. If the condition is true, then *Passed* is printed, and the next pseudocode statement in order is "performed." (Remember that pseudocode is not a real programming language.) If the condition is false, the print statement is ignored, and the next pseudocode statement in order is performed. Note that the second line of this selection structure is indented. Such indentation is optional, but it is highly recommended because it emphasizes the inherent structure of structured programs. The preceding pseudocode *If* statement may be written in MC++ as

```
if ( studentGrade >= 60 )
   Console::WriteLine( S"Passed" );
```

Notice that the MC++ code corresponds closely to the pseudocode, demonstrating how pseudocode can be useful as a program development tool. The statement in the body of the `if` statement outputs the character string `"Passed"` in the console window.

The flowchart in Fig. 4.3 illustrates the single-selection `if` statement. This flowchart contains the most important flowcharting symbol—the decision (or diamond) symbol, which indicates that a decision is to be made. The decision symbol contains a condition, that can be either true or false. The decision symbol has two flowlines emerging from it. One indicates the direction to be taken when the condition in the symbol is true; the other indicates the direction to be taken when the condition is false. A decision can be made on any expression that evaluates to a value of MC++'s *`bool`* type (i.e., any expression that evaluates to *`true`* or *`false`*). Note that any nonzero value evaluates to true and zero evaluates to false.

The `if` statement is a single-entry/single-exit structure. The flowcharts for the remaining control structures also contain (aside from small circle symbols and flowlines) only rectangle symbols, to indicate the actions to be performed, and diamond symbols, to indicate decisions to be made. This is the *action/decision model of programming* we have been emphasizing.

We can envision seven bins, each containing control statements for only one of the seven types. The control statements in each bin are empty; nothing is written in the rectangles or diamonds. The programmer's task is to assemble a program using as many control

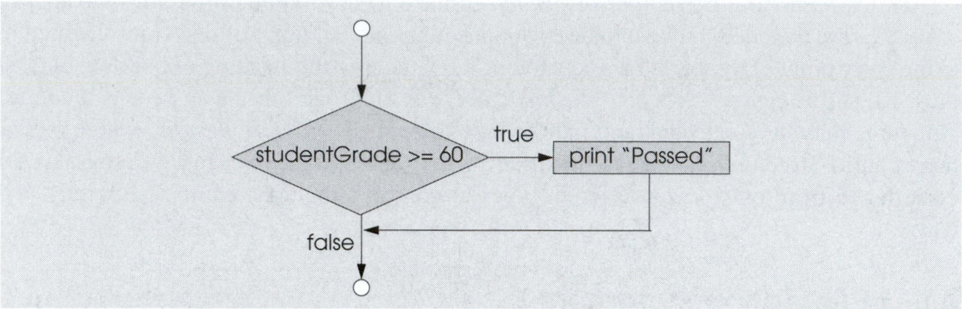

Fig. 4.3 Flowcharting a single-selection `if` statement.

statements as the algorithm demands, combining those control statements in only two possible ways (stacking or nesting), then filling in the actions and decisions in a manner appropriate for the algorithm. We will discuss the variety of ways in which actions and decisions may be written.

4.6 `if...else` Selection Statement

The `if` single-selection statement performs an indicated action only when the condition evaluates to true; otherwise, the action is skipped. The `if...else` selection statement allows the programmer to specify different actions to perform when the condition is true and when the condition is false. For example, the pseudocode statement

If student's grade is greater than or equal to 60
    Print "Passed"
Else
    Print "Failed"

prints *Passed* if the student's grade is greater than or equal to 60, and prints *Failed* if the student's grade is less than 60. In either case, after printing occurs, the next pseudocode statement in sequence is "performed." The preceding pseudocode *If...Else* statement may be written in MC++ as

```
if ( studentGrade >= 60 )
   Console::WriteLine( S"Passed" );
else
   Console::WriteLine( S"Failed" );
```

Good Programming Practice 4.1

Indent both body statements of an `if...else` statement.

Note that the body of the `else` also is indented. The indentation convention you choose should be applied carefully throughout your programs. It is difficult to read programs that do not use uniform spacing conventions.

The flowchart in Fig. 4.4 illustrates the flow of control in the `if...else` statement. Note that (besides small circles and arrows) the only symbols in the flowchart are rectangles (for actions) and a diamond (for a decision). We continue to emphasize this action/decision model of computing.

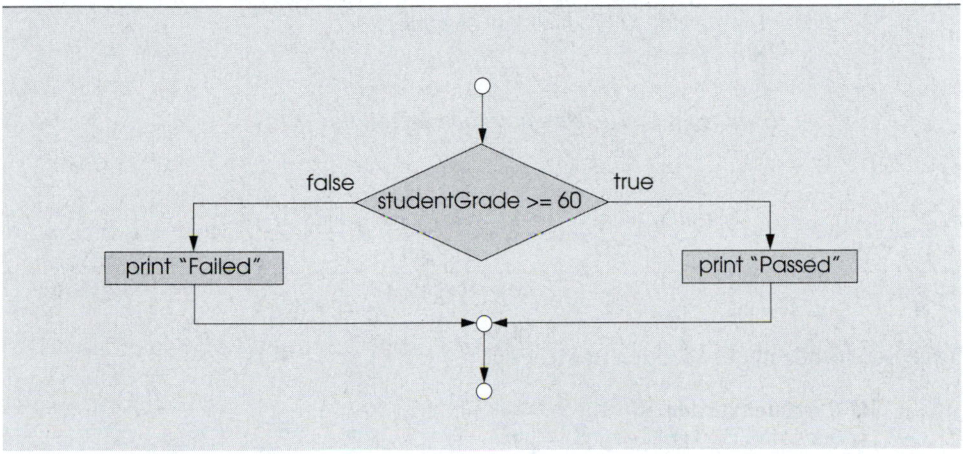

Fig. 4.4 Flowcharting a double-selection `if...else` statement.

The *conditional operator* (`?:`) is related closely to the `if...else` statement. The `?:` is MC++'s only *ternary operator*—it takes three operands. The operands and the `?:` form a *conditional expression*. The first operand is a *condition* (i.e., an expression that evaluates to a `bool` value), the second is the value for the conditional expression if the condition evaluates to true and the third is the value for the conditional expression if the condition evaluates to false. For example, the output statement

```
Console::WriteLine( studentGrade >= 60 ? S"Passed" : S"Failed" );
```

contains a conditional expression that evaluates to the string `"Passed"` if the condition `studentGrade >= 60` is true and evaluates to the string `"Failed"` if the condition is false.

The statement with the conditional operator performs in the same manner as the preceding `if...else`. The precedence of the conditional operator is low, so the entire conditional expression normally is placed in parentheses. Conditional expressions can be used in some situations where `if...else` cannot, such as the argument to the `WriteLine` method.

Good Programming Practice 4.2

Although the conditional operator provides a convenient alternative to the `if...else` *statement, it can sometimes make code less readable. Use the conditional operator only when performing simple, straight forward tasks.*

Nested `if...else` *statements* can test for multiple cases by placing `if...else` statements inside other `if...else` statements. For example, the following pseudocode statement will print `A` for exam grades greater than or equal to 90, `B` for grades in the range 80–89, `C` for grades in the range 70–79, `D` for grades in the range 60–69 and `F` for all other grades:

```
If student's grade is greater than or equal to 90
   Print "A"
Else
   If student's grade is greater than or equal to 80
      Print "B"
   Else
      If student's grade is greater than or equal to 70
         Print "C"
      Else
         If student's grade is greater than or equal to 60
            Print "D"
         Else
            Print "F"
```

This pseudocode may be written in MC++ as

```
if ( studentGrade >= 90 )
   Console::WriteLine( S"A" );
else
   if ( studentGrade >= 80 )
      Console::WriteLine( S"B" );
   else
      if ( studentGrade >= 70 )
         Console::WriteLine( S"C" );
      else
         if ( studentGrade >= 60 )
            Console::WriteLine( S"D" );
         else
            Console::WriteLine( S"F" );
```

If `studentGrade` is greater than or equal to 90, the first four conditions are true, but only the `Console::WriteLine` statement after the first test executes. After that particular `Console::WriteLine` executes, the program skips the `else` part of the "outer" `if...else` statement.

Good Programming Practice 4.3

If there are several levels of indentation, each level should be indented the same additional amount of space.

Most MC++ programmers prefer to write the preceding `if` statement as

```
if ( studentGrade >= 90 )
   Console::WriteLine( S"A" );
else if ( studentGrade >= 80 )
   Console::WriteLine( S"B" );
else if ( studentGradeS >= 70 )
   Console::WriteLine( S"C" );
else if ( studentGrade >= 60 )
   Console::WriteLine( S"D" );
else
   Console::WriteLine( S"F" );
```

Both forms are equivalent. The latter form is popular because it avoids the deep indentation of the code. Such indentation often leaves little room on a line, forcing lines to be split and decreasing program readability.

The MC++ compiler always associates an `else` with the previous `if`, unless told to do otherwise by the placement of braces (`{}`). This is referred to as the *dangling-else problem*. For example,

```
if ( x > 5 )
   if ( y > 5 )
      Console::WriteLine( S"x and y are > 5" );
else
   Console::WriteLine( S"x is <= 5" );
```

appears to indicate that if `x` is greater than `5`, the `if` statement in its body determines if `y` is also greater than `5`. If so, the string `"x and y are > 5"` is output. Otherwise, it *appears* that if `x` is not greater than `5`, the `else` part of the outer `if` statement outputs the string `"x is <= 5"`. However, the preceding nested `if` statement does not execute as its indentation implies. The compiler actually interprets the statement as

```
if ( x > 5 ) {
   if ( y > 5 )
      Console::WriteLine( S"x and y are > 5" );
   else
      Console::WriteLine( S"x is <= 5" );
}
```

in which the body of the first `if` statement is an `if...else` statement. This statement tests if `x` is greater than `5`. If so, execution continues by testing if `y` is also greater than `5`. If the second condition is true, the proper string—`"x and y are > 5"`—is displayed. However, if the second condition is false, the string `"x is <= 5"` is displayed, even though we know `x` is greater than `5`.

Error-Prevention Tip 4.1

The reader can use Visual Studio .NET to indent code properly. To check indentation, the reader should highlight the relevant code and press Ctrl-K *followed immediately by* Ctrl-F*. This applies proper indentation to the highlighted code.*

To force the preceding nested `if` statement to execute as it was originally intended, the statement must be written as follows:

```
if ( x > 5 ) {
   if ( y > 5 )
      Console::WriteLine( S"x and y are > 5" );
}
else
   Console::WriteLine( S"x is <= 5" );
```

The braces (`{}`) indicate to the compiler that the second `if` statement is in the body of the first `if` statement and that the `else` is matched with the first `if`.

The `if` selection statement normally expects only one statement in its body. To include several statements in the body of an `if`, enclose these statements in braces (`{` and `}`). A set of statements contained in a pair of braces is called a *block*.

Software Engineering Observation 4.2

A block can be placed anywhere in a program where a single statement can be placed.

The following example includes a block in the `else` part of an `if...else` statement:

```
if ( studentGrade >= 60 )
   Console::WriteLine( S"Passed" );
else {
   Console::WriteLine( S"Failed" );
   Console::WriteLine( S"You must take this course again." );
}
```

In this case, if `studentGrade` is less than 60, the program executes both statements in the body of the `else` and prints

```
Failed
You must take this course again.
```

Notice the braces surrounding the two statements in the `else` body. These braces are important. Without the braces, the statement

```
Console::WriteLine( S"You must take this course again." );
```

would be outside the body of the `else` and would execute regardless of whether the grade is less than 60.

Syntax errors, such as when one brace in a block is left out of the program, are caught by the compiler. A *logic error*, such as the error caused when both braces in a block are left out of the program, has its effect at execution time. A *fatal logic error* causes a program to fail and terminate prematurely. A *nonfatal logic error* allows a program to continue executing, but the program produces incorrect results.

Common Programming Error 4.1

Forgetting one of the braces that delimit a block can lead to syntax errors. Forgetting both of the braces that delimit a block can lead to syntax and/or logic errors.

Good Programming Practice 4.4

Always using braces in an `if...else` (or other) statement helps prevent their accidental omission, especially when adding statements to an `if` or `else` at a later time. To avoid omitting one or both of the braces, some programmers prefer to type the beginning and ending braces of blocks before typing the individual statements within the braces.

In this section, we introduced the notion of a block. A block may contain declarations. The declarations in a block commonly are placed first in the block before any action statements, but declarations may be intermixed with action statements.

Just as a block can be placed anywhere a single statement can be placed, it is also possible to have a null statement, which is represented by placing a semicolon (`;`) where a statement normally would be.

Common Programming Error 4.2

Placing a semicolon after the condition in an `if` or `if...else` statement leads to a logic error in single-selection `if` statements and a syntax error in double-selection `if...else` statements (when the `if` clause contains a non-null body statement).

4.7 `while` Repetition Statement

A *repetition statement* (also called an *iteration statement*) allows the programmer to specify that an action is to be repeated while a condition remains true. The pseudocode statement

While there are more items on my shopping list
Purchase next item and cross it off my list

describes the repetition that occurs during a shopping trip. The condition, "there are more items on my shopping list" may be true or false. If it is true, then the action, "Purchase next item and cross it off my list" is performed. This action executes repeatedly while the condition remains true. The statement(s) contained in the *While* statement constitute the body of the *While*. The *While* statement body may be a single statement or a block. Eventually, the condition becomes false (when the last item on the shopping list has been purchased and crossed off the list). At this point, the repetition terminates, and the first statement after the while statement executes.

As an example of a `while` statement, consider a program segment designed to find the first power of 2 larger than 1000. Suppose `int` variable `product` contains the value 2. When the following `while` statement finishes executing, `product` contains the first power of 2 larger than 1000.

```
int product = 2;

while ( product <= 1000 )
   product = 2 * product;
```

When the `while` statement begins executing, `product` is 2. Variable `product` is repeatedly multiplied by 2, taking on the values 4, 8, 16, 32, 64, 128, 256, 512 and 1024, successively. When `product` becomes 1024, the condition `product <= 1000` in the `while` statement becomes false. This terminates the repetition with 1024 as `product`'s final value. Execution continues with the next statement after the `while`. [*Note*: If a `while` statement's condition is initially false, the body statement(s) will never be executed.]

The flowchart in Fig. 4.5 illustrates the flow of control of the preceding `while` repetition statement. Once again, note that (besides small circles and arrows) the flowchart contains only a rectangle symbol and a diamond symbol.

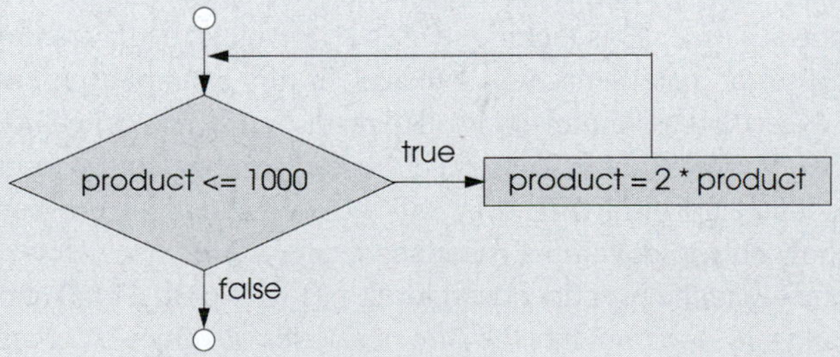

Fig. 4.5 Flowcharting the `while` statement.

Common Programming Error 4.3

Not providing in the body of a `while` *statement an action that eventually causes the condition to become false is a logic error. Normally, such a statement will never terminate, which is an error called an "infinite loop."*

Common Programming Error 4.4

Beginning the keyword `while` *with an uppercase* `W`*, as in* `While`*, is a syntax error. Remember that MC++ is a case-sensitive language. All MC++'s keywords—*`while`*,* `if`*,* `else`*, etc.—contain only lowercase letters.*

Error-Prevention Tip 4.2

Visual Studio .NET will not color a keyword properly unless that keyword is spelled correctly and with the correct case.

Imagine, again, a deep bin of empty `while` statements that may be stacked and nested with other control statements to form a structured implementation of an algorithm's flow of control. The empty rectangles and diamonds are filled with appropriate actions (such as `product = 2 * product`) and decisions (such as `product <= 1000`). The flowchart clearly shows the repetition. The flowline emerging from the rectangle indicates that program control continues with the decision, which is tested during each iteration of the loop until the decision eventually becomes false. At this point, the `while` statement terminates, and control passes to the next statement following the `while` statement in the program.

4.8 Formulating Algorithms: Case Study 1 (Counter-Controlled Repetition)

To illustrate how algorithms are developed, we solve two variations of a class-averaging problem. Consider the following problem statement:

> *A class of ten students took a quiz. The grades (integers in the range 0 to 100) for this quiz are available to you. Determine the class average on the quiz.*

The class average is equal to the sum of the grades divided by the number of students. The algorithm for solving this problem on a computer must input each of the grades, perform the averaging calculation and display the result.

Let us use pseudocode to list the actions to execute and to specify the order of execution. The number of grades is know in advance, so use *counter-controlled repetition* to input the grades one at a time. This technique uses a variable called a *counter* to control the number of times a set of statements will execute. In this example, repetition terminates when the counter exceeds 10. Counter-controlled repetition is also called *definite repetition* because the number of repetitions is known before the loop begins executing. This section presents a pseudocode algorithm (Fig. 4.6) and the corresponding program (Fig. 4.7). In Section 4.9, we show how to develop a pseudocode algorithm.

Note the references in the pseudocode algorithm (Fig. 4.6) to a total and a counter. The pseudocode variable *total* accumulates the sum of a series of values. A counter is a variable that counts—in this case, that counts the number of grades entered. Variables that store totals normally should be initialized to zero before being used in a program; otherwise, the sum would include the previous value stored in the memory location for the total.

Set total to zero
Set grade counter to one

While grade counter is less than or equal to ten
    Input the next grade
    Add the grade to the total
    Add one to the grade counter

Set the class average to the total divided by ten
Print the class average

Fig. 4.6 Pseudocode algorithm that uses counter-controlled repetition to solve the class-average problem.

```
// Fig. 4.7: Average1.cpp
// Class average with counter-controlled repetition.

#include "stdafx.h"

#using <mscorlib.dll>

using namespace System;

int _tmain()
{
   int total,           // sum of grades input by user
       gradeCounter,    // number of grade to be entered next
       gradeValue,      // grade value
       average;         // average of grades

   // initialization phase
   total = 0;           // initialize total
   gradeCounter = 1;    // initialize loop counter

   // processing phase
   while ( gradeCounter <= 10 ) {  // loop 10 times

      // prompt for input and read and convert grade from user
      Console::Write( S"Enter integer grade: " );
      gradeValue = Int32::Parse( Console::ReadLine() );

      total = total + gradeValue;        // add grade to total

      gradeCounter = gradeCounter + 1;   // increment counter
   } // end while

   // termination phase
   average = total / 10;   // integer division

```

Fig. 4.7 Class average program with counter-controlled repetition. (Part 1 of 2.)

```
36     // display average of exam grades
37     Console::WriteLine( S"\nClass average is {0}", average.ToString() );
38
39     return 0;
40  } // end _tmain
```

```
Enter integer grade: 100
Enter integer grade: 88
Enter integer grade: 93
Enter integer grade: 55
Enter integer grade: 68
Enter integer grade: 77
Enter integer grade: 83
Enter integer grade: 95
Enter integer grade: 73
Enter integer grade: 62

Class average is 79
```

Fig. 4.7 Class average program with counter-controlled repetition. (Part 2 of 2.)

Error-Prevention Tip 4.3

Initialize counters and totals.

Lines 12–15 (Fig. 4.7) declare variables `total`, `gradeCounter`, `gradeValue` and `average` to be of type `int`. Variable `gradeValue` will store the value the user inputs after the value is converted from a `String` to an `int`.

Good Programming Practice 4.5

Always place a blank line between a declaration and executable statements. This makes the declarations stand out in a program and contributes to program clarity.

Lines 18–19 are assignment statements that initialize `total` to `0` and `gradeCounter` to `1`. Variables `total` and `gradeCounter` are initialized before they are used in a calculation. Note that using uninitialized variables in calculations can cause incorrect results.

Line 22 indicates that the `while` statement should loop as long as the value of `gradeCounter` is less than or equal to 10. Lines 25 and 26 correspond to the pseudocode statement *"Input the next grade."* Line 25 displays the prompt `"Enter integer grade: "` on the screen. Line 26 reads the information entered by the user, converts it to an `int` and stores the value in `gradeValue`. Next, line 28 updates `total` with the new `gradeValue` by adding `gradeValue` to the previous value of `total` and assigning the result to `total`.

The program is now ready to increment the variable `gradeCounter` to indicate that a grade has been processed. Line 30 adds `1` to `gradeCounter`, so the condition in the `while` statement will eventually become false and terminate the loop. Line 34 assigns the results of the average calculation to variable `average`. Line 37 displays a message containing the string `"Class average is "` followed by the value of variable `average`.

Note that because two integers (`total` and `10`) are used in the averaging calculation, an integer result is produced (in this case, `79`). Actually, the sum of the grade values in this example is 794, which, when divided by 10, yields 79.4. Such numbers with a decimal point are called floating-point numbers; we discuss performing calculations with floating-point numbers in the next section.

4.9 Formulating Algorithms with Top-Down, Stepwise Refinement: Case Study 2 (Sentinel-Controlled Repetition)

Let us generalize the class-average problem. Consider the following problem:

> *Develop a class-averaging program that processes an arbitrary number of grades each time the program executes.*

In the first class-average example, the number of grades (10) was known in advance. In this example, no indication is given of how many grades are to be input. The program must process an arbitrary number of grades. How can the program determine when to stop the input of grades? How will it know when to calculate and print the class average?

One way to solve this problem is to use a special value called a *sentinel value* (also called a *signal value*, a *dummy value* or a *flag value*) to indicate "end of data entry." The user inputs all grades, then types the sentinel value to indicate that the last grade has been entered. Sentinel-controlled repetition is often called *indefinite repetition* because the number of repetitions is not known before the loop begins executing.

The sentinel value cannot be confused with an acceptable input value. Grades on a quiz are normally nonnegative integers, thus –1 is an acceptable sentinel value for this problem. A run of the class-average program might process a stream of inputs such as 95, 96, 75, 74, 89 and –1. The program would then compute and print the class average for the grades 95, 96, 75, 74 and 89. The sentinel value, –1, should not enter into the averaging calculation.

Common Programming Error 4.5

Choosing a sentinel value that is also a legitimate data value results in a logic error and may prevent a sentinel-controlled loop from terminating properly, a problem known as an infinite loop.

We approach the class-average program with *top-down, stepwise refinement*, a technique essential to the development of well-structured algorithms. We begin with a pseudocode representation of the *top*—a single statement that conveys the overall function of the program

> *Determine the class average for the quiz*

The top is, in effect, a complete representation of a program. Unfortunately, the top rarely conveys a sufficient amount of detail from which to write the MC++ algorithm. Therefore, we conduct the refinement process. We divide the top into a series of smaller tasks and list these in the order in which they must be performed. This results in the following *first refinement*:

> *Initialize variables*
> *Input, sum and count the quiz grades*
> *Calculate and print the class average*

Here, only the sequence structure has been used—the steps listed are to be executed in order, one after the other.

Software Engineering Observation 4.3

Each refinement, including the top, is a complete specification of the algorithm; only the level of detail in each refinement varies.

To proceed to the next level of refinement (i.e., the *second refinement*), we commit to specific variables. We need a running total of the numbers, a count of how many numbers have been processed, a variable to receive the value of each grade and a variable to hold the calculated average. The pseudocode statement

Initialize variables

may be refined as follows:

Initialize total to zero
Initialize counter to zero

Notice that only the variables *total* and *counter* are initialized before they are used; the variables *average* and *grade* (for the calculated average and the user input, respectively) need not be initialized because their values are determined as they are calculated or input.

The pseudocode statement

Input, sum and count the quiz grades

requires a repetition statement (i.e., a loop) that successively inputs each grade. We do not know how many grades are to be processed, thus we use sentinel-controlled repetition. The user types in legitimate grades one at a time. After the last legitimate grade is typed, the user types the sentinel value. The program tests for the sentinel value after each grade is input and terminates the loop when the user enters the sentinel value. The second refinement of the preceding pseudocode statement is then

Input the first grade (possibly the sentinel)

While the user has not as yet entered the sentinel
    Add this grade to the running total
    Add one to the grade counter
    Input the next grade (possibly the sentinel)

We do not use braces around the pseudocode that forms the body of the *While* statement. We simply indent the pseudocode under the *While* to show that it belongs to the *While* statement. Note that a grade is input both before reaching the loop and at the end of the loop's body. As we enter the loop, the grade input before the loop is tested to determine whether it is the sentinel. If so, the loop terminates; otherwise, the body of the loop executes. The body processes the grade, then inputs the next grade. Then, the new grade is tested at the top of the loop to determine if that grade is the sentinel.

The pseudocode statement

Calculate and print the class average

may be refined as follows:

If the counter is not equal to zero
    Set the average to the total divided by the counter
    Print the average
Else
    Print "No grades were entered"

We test for the possibility of division by zero—a logic error that, if undetected, would cause the program to fail. The complete second refinement of the pseudocode algorithm for the class-average problem is shown in Fig. 4.8.

```
Initialize total to zero
Initialize counter to zero

Input the first grade (possibly the sentinel)

While the user has not as yet entered the sentinel
    Add this grade to the running total
    Add one to the grade counter
    Input the next grade (possibly the sentinel)

If the counter is not equal to zero
    Set the average to the total divided by the counter
    Print the average
Else
    Print "No grades were entered"
```

Fig. 4.8 Pseudocode algorithm that uses sentinel-controlled repetition to solve the class-average problem.

Error-Prevention Tip 4.4

When performing division by an expression whose value could be zero, explicitly test for this case and handle it appropriately in your program, possibly printing an error message.

Good Programming Practice 4.6

Include blank lines in pseudocode for increased readability. The blank lines separate pseudocode control statements and the program's phases.

Software Engineering Observation 4.4

Many algorithms can be divided logically into three phases—an initialization phase that initializes the program variables, a processing phase that inputs data values and adjusts program variables accordingly and a termination phase that calculates and prints the results.

The pseudocode algorithm in Fig. 4.8 solves the more general class-averaging problem. This algorithm was developed after only two levels of refinement. Sometimes more levels are necessary.

Software Engineering Observation 4.5

The programmer terminates the top-down, stepwise refinement process when the pseudocode algorithm is specified in sufficient detail for the programmer to convert the pseudocode to an MC++ program. Then, implementing the MC++ program is normally a straightforward manner.

The MC++ program for this pseudocode is shown in Fig. 4.9. Notice from the output that each grade entered is an integer, although the averaging calculation is likely to produce a number with a decimal point. The type `int` cannot represent real numbers, so this program uses type *`double`* to handle floating-point numbers. The program also introduces the *cast operator* *`static_cast`* (line 40) to handle the type conversion for the averaging calculation. These features are explained in detail in our discussion of Fig. 4.9.

```
1  // Fig. 4.9: Average2.cpp
2  // Class average with sentinel-controlled repetition.
3
4  #include "stdafx.h"
5
6  #using <mscorlib.dll>
7
8  using namespace System;
9
10 int _tmain()
11 {
12    int total,          // sum of grades
13        gradeCounter,   // number of grades entered
14        gradeValue;     // grade value
15
16    double average;     // number with decimal point for average
17
18    // initialization phase
19    total = 0;
20    gradeCounter = 0;
21
22    // processing phase
23    // get first grade from user
24    Console::Write( S"Enter integer grade, -1 to Quit: " );
25    gradeValue = Int32::Parse( Console::ReadLine() );
26
27    // loop until sentinel value is read from user
28    while ( gradeValue != -1 ) {
29       total = total + gradeValue;
30
31       gradeCounter = gradeCounter + 1;  // increment counter
32
33       Console::Write( S"Enter integer grade, -1 to Quit: " );
34       gradeValue = Int32::Parse( Console::ReadLine() );
35    } // end while
36
37    // termination phase
38    // if user entered at least one grade...
39    if ( gradeCounter != 0 ) {
40       average = static_cast< double >( total ) / gradeCounter;
41       Console::WriteLine( S"\nClass average is {0}", average.ToString() );
42    } // end if
43    else
44       Console::WriteLine( S"No grades were entered." );
45
46    return 0;
47 } // end _tmain
```

Fig. 4.9 Class-average program with sentinel-controlled repetition. (Part 1 of 2.)

```
Enter integer grade, -1 to Quit: 97
Enter integer grade, -1 to Quit: 88
Enter integer grade, -1 to Quit: 72
Enter integer grade, -1 to Quit: -1

Class average is 85.6666666666667
```

Fig. 4.9 Class-average program with sentinel-controlled repetition. (Part 2 of 2.)

In this example, we examine how control statements may be stacked on top of one another, in sequence. The `while` statement (lines 28–35) is followed immediately by an `if...else` statement (lines 39–44). Much of the code in this program is identical to the code in Fig. 4.7, so we concentrate on the new features in this example.

Line 16 declares variable `average` to be of type `double`. This change allows us to store the result of the class-average calculation as a floating-point number. Line 20 initializes `gradeCounter` to `0` because no grades have been input yet—recall that this program uses sentinel-controlled repetition. To keep an accurate record of the number of grades entered, variable `gradeCounter` is incremented only when a valid grade value is input.

Notice the differences between sentinel-controlled repetition and the counter-controlled repetition of Fig. 4.7. In counter-controlled repetition, we read a value from the user during each iteration of the `while` statement for the specified number of iterations. In sentinel-controlled repetition, we read one value (line 25) before the program reaches the `while` statement. This value is used to determine if the program's flow of control should enter the body of the `while` statement. If the `while` statement condition is false (i.e., the user has entered the sentinel value), the body of the `while` statement does not execute (i.e., no grades were entered). If, on the other hand, the condition is true, the body begins execution, and the value input by the user is processed (added to the `total`). Then, the next value is input from the user (line 34) before the end of the `while` statement's body. When program control reaches the closing right brace (`}`) of the body (line 35), execution continues with the next test of the `while` statement condition. The new value input by the user determines whether the `while` statement's body should execute again. Notice that the next value is input from the user immediately before the `while` statement condition is evaluated (line 34). This allows the program to determine whether the value just input by the user is the sentinel value *before* the program processes that value as a valid grade. If the value entered is the sentinel value, the `while` statement terminates, and the sentinel value is not added to `total`.

Notice the block that composes the `while` loop in Fig. 4.9. Without the braces, the last three statements in the body of the loop would be outside the loop, causing the computer to interpret the code incorrectly, as follows:

```
while ( gradeValue != -1 )
   total = total + gradeValue;

gradeCounter = gradeCounter + 1; // increment counter

Console::Write( S"Enter Integer Grade, -1 to Quit: " );
gradeValue = Int32::Parse( Console::ReadLine() );
```

In this case, an infinite loop occurs in the program if the user fails to input the sentinel `-1` as the input value in line 25 (before the `while` statement).

Common Programming Error 4.6

Omitting the braces that delimit a block in a repetition statement can lead to logic errors, such as infinite loops.

Good Programming Practice 4.7

In a sentinel-controlled loop, the prompts requesting data entry should remind the user of the sentinel value.

Averages do not always evaluate to integer values. Often, an average is a value such as 3.333 or 2.7, that contains a fractional part. These values are floating-point numbers and are normally represented by the type `double`. We declare the variable `average` as type `double` to capture the fractional result of our calculation. However, the result of the calculation `total / gradeCounter` is an integer because `total` and `gradeCounter` are both integer variables. Dividing two integers results in *integer division*, in which any fractional part of the calculation is *truncated* and the result is a whole number. The calculation is performed first, thus the fractional part is lost before the result is assigned to `average`.

To produce a floating-point calculation with integer values, we must create temporary values that are floating-point numbers for the calculation. The `static_cast` operator (line 40) performs a conversion between data types. The value to cast (e.g., `total`) is contained in parentheses of the `static_cast` operator, and the desired type is contained in angle brackets (e.g., `< double >`). Line 40 explicitly casts (converts) a copy of the value of `total` to a `double` for use in the average calculation.

Common Programming Error 4.7

Assuming that integer division rounds (rather than truncates) can lead to incorrect results.

Common Programming Error 4.8

Using floating-point numbers in a manner that assumes that they are precisely represented real numbers can lead to incorrect results. Real numbers are represented only approximately by computers.

Good Programming Practice 4.8

Do not compare floating-point values for equality or inequality. Rather, test that the absolute value of the difference between two floating-point numbers is less than a specified small value.

Despite the fact that floating-point numbers are not always "100% precise," they have numerous applications. For example, when we speak of a "normal" body temperature of 98.6, we do not need to be precise to a large number of digits. When we view the temperature on a thermometer and read it as 98.6, it may actually be 98.5999473210643. Calling such a number simply 98.6 is fine for most applications.

Floating-point numbers also occur as a result of division. When we divide 10 by 3, the result is 3.3333333…, with the sequence of 3s repeating infinitely. The computer allocates only a fixed amount of space to hold such a value, so the stored floating-point value can be only an approximation.

Line 41 displays the value of `average` using method `WriteLine`. We convert the value to a `String` by specifying `average.ToString()` as the second argument to `WriteLine`.

4.10 Formulating Algorithms with Top-Down, Stepwise Refinement: Case Study 3 (Nested Control Structures)

Let us work through another complete problem. We will again formulate the algorithm using pseudocode and top-down, stepwise refinement; we will write a corresponding MC++ program.

Consider the following problem statement:

> *A college offers a course that prepares students for the state licensing exam for real estate brokers. Last year, several of the students who completed this course took the licensing examination. The college wants to know how well its students did on the exam. You have been asked to write a program to summarize the results. You have been given a list of the 10 students. Next to each name is written a 1 if the student passed the exam and a 2 if the student failed the exam. If more than 8 students passed the exam, print the message "Raise tuition."*

After reading the problem statement carefully, we make the following observations about the problem:

1. The program must process test results for 10 students. A counter-controlled loop will be used.
2. Each test result is a number—either a 1 or a 2. Each time the program reads a test result, the program must determine if the number is a 1 or a 2. We test for a 1 in our algorithm. If the number is not a 1, we assume that it is a 2. (An exercise at the end of the chapter considers the consequences of this assumption.)
3. Two counters keep track of the exam results—one to count the number of students who passed the exam and one to count the number of students who failed.
4. After the program processes all the results, it must decide if more than eight students passed the exam.

Let us proceed with top-down, stepwise refinement. We begin with a pseudocode representation of the top:

Analyze exam results and decide if tuition should be raised

Once again, it is important to emphasize that the top is a complete representation of the program, but several refinements are likely to be needed before the pseudocode can be evolved naturally into an MC++ program. Our first refinement is

Initialize variables
Input the ten exam grades and count passes and failures
Print a summary of the exam results and decide if tuition should be raised

Even though we have a complete representation of the entire program, further refinement is necessary. We must commit to specific variables. Counters are needed to record the passes and failures. A counter controls the looping process and a variable stores the user input. The pseudocode statement

Initialize variables

may be refined as follows:

Initialize passes to zero
Initialize failures to zero
Initialize student to one

Only the counters for the number of passes, number of failures and number of students are initialized. The pseudocode statement

Input the ten quiz grades and count passes and failures

requires a loop that successively inputs the result of each exam. Here, it is known in advance that there are precisely ten exam results, so counter-controlled repetition is appropriate. Inside the loop (i.e., *nested* within the loop) a double-selection structure determines whether each exam result is a pass or a failure, and the structure increments the appropriate counter accordingly. The refinement of the preceding pseudocode statement is

```
While student counter is less than or equal to ten
    Input the next exam result

    If the student passed
        Add one to passes
    Else
        Add one to failures

    Add one to student counter
```

Notice the use of blank lines to offset the *If...Else* control statement to improve program readability. The pseudocode statement

Print a summary of the exam results and decide if tuition should be raised

may be refined as follows:

```
Print the number of passes
Print the number of failures

If more than eight students passed
    Print "Raise tuition"
```

The complete second refinement appears in Fig. 4.10. Notice that blank lines also set off the *While* statement for program readability.

The pseudocode is now refined sufficiently for conversion to MC++. The MC++ program and sample executions are shown in Fig. 4.11.

Lines 12–15 declare the variables used in `_tmain` to process the examination results. We have taken advantage of an MC++ feature that incorporates variable initialization into declarations (`passes` is assigned `0`, `failures` is assigned `0` and `student` is assigned `1`). Notice the use of the nested `if...else` statement (lines 23–26) in the `while` statement's body. Lines 33–34 display the final values of `passes` and `failures`.

Software Engineering Observation 4.6

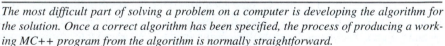

The most difficult part of solving a problem on a computer is developing the algorithm for the solution. Once a correct algorithm has been specified, the process of producing a working MC++ program from the algorithm is normally straightforward.

Software Engineering Observation 4.7

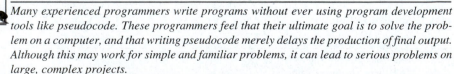

Many experienced programmers write programs without ever using program development tools like pseudocode. These programmers feel that their ultimate goal is to solve the problem on a computer, and that writing pseudocode merely delays the production of final output. Although this may work for simple and familiar problems, it can lead to serious problems on large, complex projects.

Initialize passes to zero
Initialize failures to zero
Initialize student to one

While student counter is less than or equal to ten
    Input the next exam result

    If the student passed
        Add one to passes
    Else
        Add one to failures

    Add one to student counter

Print the number of passes
Print the number of failures

If more than eight students passed
    Print "Raise tuition"

Fig. 4.10 Pseudocode for examination-results problem.

```
// Fig. 4.11: Analysis.cpp
// Analysis of examination results.

#include "stdafx.h"

#using <mscorlib.dll>

using namespace System;

int _tmain()
{
   int passes = 0,        // number of passes
       failures = 0,      // number of failures
       student = 1,       // student counter
       result;            // one exam result

   // process 10 students; counter-controlled loop
   while ( student <= 10 ) {
      Console::Write( S"Enter result (1=pass, 2=fail): " );
      result = Int32::Parse( Console::ReadLine() );

      // if result is 1, increment passes; if...else nested in while
      if ( result == 1 )
         passes = passes + 1;
      else
         failures = failures + 1;

      // increment student counter so loop eventually terminates
      student = student + 1;
   } // end while
```

Fig. 4.11 Examination-results problem. (Part 1 of 2.)

```

    // termination phase
    Console::WriteLine( S"\nPassed: {0}\nFailed: {1}",
       passes.ToString(), failures.ToString() );

    // determine whether more than 8 students passed
    if ( passes > 8 )
       Console::WriteLine( S"Raise Tuition\n" );

    return 0;
 }
```

```
Enter result (1=pass, 2=fail): 1
Enter result (1=pass, 2=fail): 2
Enter result (1=pass, 2=fail): 2
Enter result (1=pass, 2=fail): 2
Enter result (1=pass, 2=fail): 2
Enter result (1=pass, 2=fail): 2
Enter result (1=pass, 2=fail): 1
Enter result (1=pass, 2=fail): 1
Enter result (1=pass, 2=fail): 1
Enter result (1=pass, 2=fail): 1

Passed: 5
Failed: 5
```

Fig. 4.11 Examination-results problem. (Part 2 of 2.)

4.11 Assignment Operators

C++ provides several assignment operators for abbreviating assignment expressions. For example, the statement

```
c = c + 3;
```

can be abbreviated with the *addition assignment operator* += as

```
c += 3;
```

The += operator adds the value of the expression on the right of the operator to the value of the variable on the left of the operator and stores the result in the variable on the left of the operator. Any statement of the form

variable = *variable operator expression*;

where *operator* is one of the binary operators +, -, *, / or %, can be written in the form

variable operator= *expression*;

Figure 4.12 includes the arithmetic assignment operators, sample expressions using these operators and explanations.

Common Programming Error 4.9

Placing a space character between symbols that compose an arithmetic assignment operator is a syntax error.

Assignment operator	Sample expression	Explanation	Assigns
Assume: `int c = 3, d = 5, e = 4, f = 6, g = 12;`			
+=	`c += 7`	`c = c + 7`	10 to c
-=	`d -= 4`	`d = d - 4`	1 to d
*=	`e *= 5`	`e = e * 5`	20 to e
/=	`f /= 3`	`f = f / 3`	2 to f
%=	`g %= 9`	`g = g % 9`	3 to g

Fig. 4.12 Arithmetic assignment operators.

4.12 Increment and Decrement Operators

MC++ provides the unary *increment operator*, ++, and the unary *decrement operator*, --, which are summarized in Fig. 4.13. A *unary operator* is an operator that takes only one operand. In Chapter 3, we studied the binary arithmetic operators. Java also supports unary versions of the plus (+) and minus (-) operators, so the programmer can write expressions like -7 or +5. A program can increment the value of a variable called c by 1 using the increment operator, ++, rather than the expression c = c + 1 or c += 1. If an increment or decrement operator is placed before a variable, it is referred to as the *prefix increment* or *prefix decrement operator*, respectively. If an increment or decrement operator is placed after a variable, it is referred to as the *postfix increment* or *postfix decrement operator*, respectively.

Operator	Called	Sample expression	Explanation
++	prefix increment	++a	Increment a by 1, then use the new value of a in the expression in which a resides.
++	postfix increment	a++	Use the value of a in the expression in which a resides, then increment a by 1.
--	prefix decrement	--b	Decrement b by 1, then use the new value of b in the expression in which b resides.
--	postfix decrement	b--	Use the value of b in the expression in which b resides, then decrement b by 1.

Fig. 4.13 The increment and decrement operators.

Preincrementing (or predecrementing) a variable causes the variable to be incremented (or decremented) by 1, then the new value of the variable is used in the expression in which it appears. Postincrementing (or postdecrementing) the variable causes the value of the variable to be used in the expression in which it appears, then the variable value is incremented (or decremented) by 1.

The application in Fig. 4.14 demonstrates the difference between preincrementing and postincrementing with the ++ increment operator. Postincrementing the variable c causes it to be incremented after it is used in the `Console::WriteLine` method call (line 17). Preincrementing the variable `c` causes it to be incremented before it is used in the `Console::WriteLine` method call (line 25).

```
1  // Fig. 4.14: Increment.cpp
2  // Preincrementing and postincrementing.
3
4  #include "stdafx.h"
5
6  #using <mscorlib.dll>
7
8  using namespace System;
9
10 int _tmain()
11 {
12    int c;
13
14    // demostrate postincrement
15    c = 5;                       // assign 5 to c
16    Console::WriteLine( c );     // print 5
17    Console::WriteLine( c++ );   // print 5 then postincrement
18    Console::WriteLine( c );     // print 6
19
20    Console::WriteLine();        // skip a line
21
22    // demonstrate preincrement
23    c = 5;                       // assign 5 to c
24    Console::WriteLine( c );     // print 5
25    Console::WriteLine( ++c );   // preincrement then print 6
26    Console::WriteLine( c );     // print 6
27
28    return 0;
29 } // end _tmain
```

```
5
5
6

5
6
6
```

Fig. 4.14 Preincrementing and postincrementing variables.

The program displays the value of `c` before and after the `++` operator is used. The decrement operator (`--`) works similarly. Line 20 uses `Console::WriteLine` to output a blank line.

Good Programming Practice 4.9

For readability, unary operators should be placed next to their operands, with no intervening spaces.

It is important to note here that when incrementing or decrementing a variable in an expression or statement by itself, the preincrement and postincrement forms have the same effect, and the predecrement and postdecrement forms have the same effect. It is only when a variable appears in the context of a larger expression that preincrementing and postincrementing the variable have different effects (and similarly for predecrementing and postdecrementing).

Common Programming Error 4.10

Attempting to use the increment or decrement operator on an expression other than an lvalue *is a syntax error. An* lvalue *is a variable or expression that can appear on the left side of an assignment operation. For example, writing* `++(x + 1)` *is a syntax error, because* `(x + 1)` *is not an* lvalue.

Figure 4.15 shows the precedence and associativity of the operators introduced to this point. The operators are shown top to bottom in decreasing order of precedence. The second column describes the associativity of the operators at each level of precedence. Notice that the conditional operator (`?:`), the unary operators increment (`++`), decrement (`--`), plus (`+`), minus (`-`) and the assignment operators (`=`, `+=`, `-=`, `*=`, `/=` and `%=`) associate from right to left. All other operators in the operator precedence chart of Fig. 4.15 associate from left to right. The third column names the groups of operators.

Operators	Associativity	Type
`::`	left to right	scope resolution
`++` `--`	left to right	unary postfix
`static_cast< type >`	left to right	unary cast
`++` `--` `+` `-`	right to left	unary prefix
`*` `/` `%`	left to right	multiplicative
`+` `-`	left to right	additive
`<` `<=` `>` `>=`	left to right	relational
`==` `!=`	left to right	equality
`?:`	right to left	conditional
`=` `+=` `-=` `*=` `/=` `%=`	right to left	assignment

Fig. 4.15 Precedence and associativity of the operators discussed so far.

SUMMARY

- Any computing problem can be solved by executing a series of actions in a specific order.
- An algorithm is a procedure for solving a problem in terms of the actions to execute and the order in which these actions execute.
- Program control specifies the order in which statements execute in a computer program.
- Pseudocode is an artificial and informal language that helps programmers develop algorithms and "think out" a program during the program design process.
- MC++ code corresponds closely to pseudocode. This is a property of pseudocode that makes it a useful program development tool.

- Normally, statements in a program execute one after the other in the order in which they appear. This is called sequential execution.
- Various MC++ statements enable the programmer to specify that the next statement to execute may not be the next one in sequence. This is called transfer of control.
- Many programming complications in the 1960s were a result of misusing the `goto` statement, which allows the programmer to specify a transfer of control to one of a wide range of possible destinations in a program. The notion of structured programming became almost synonymous with "`goto` elimination."
- Bohm and Jacopini's work demonstrated that all programs could be written in terms of only three control structures—sequence, selection and repetition.
- The sequence structure is built into MC++. Unless directed otherwise, the computer executes MC++ statements one after the other in the order in which they appear.
- A flowchart is a graphical representation of an algorithm or a portion of an algorithm. Flowcharts are drawn using symbols, such as rectangles, diamonds, ovals and small circles; these symbols are connected by arrows called flowlines, which indicate the order in which the algorithm's actions execute.
- The `if` selection statement performs (selects) an action if a condition is true or skips the action if the condition is false.
- The `if...else` selection statement performs an action if a condition is `true` and performs a different action if the condition is `false`.
- A single-selection structure selects or ignores a single action.
- A double-selection structure selects between two actions.
- A multiple-selection structure selects among many actions.
- Keywords are reserved by the language to implement various features, such as MC++'s control statements. Keywords cannot be used as identifiers.
- Each program is formed by combining as many of each type of MC++'s seven control statements as is appropriate for the algorithm the program implements.
- Algorithms in MC++ programs are constructed from control statements combined in only two ways: control-structure stacking and control-structure nesting.
- Single-entry/single-exit control structures make it easy to build programs. The control structures are attached to one another by connecting the exit point of one control structure to the entry point of the next. This is called control-structure stacking.
- The decision symbol has two flowlines emerging from it. One indicates the direction to be taken when the expression in the symbol is true; the other indicates the direction to be taken when the expression is false.
- Control structure flowcharts contain (besides small circle symbols and flowlines) only rectangle symbols to indicate the actions to be performed and diamond symbols to indicate decisions to be made. This is the action/decision model of programming.
- The ternary conditional operator (`?:`) is closely related to the `if...else` statement. The operands and the `?:` form a conditional expression. The first operand is a condition that evaluates to a `bool` value, the second is the value for the conditional expression if the condition evaluates to `true` and the third is the value for the conditional expression if the condition evaluates to `false`.
- Nested `if...else` statements test for multiple cases by placing `if...else` statements inside other `if...else` statements.
- A set of statements in a pair of braces is called a block. A block can be placed anywhere in a program that a single statement can be placed.

- A syntax error is caught by the compiler at compile time, while a logic error has its effect during program execution.
- A fatal logic error causes a program to fail and terminate prematurely. A nonfatal logic error allows a program to continue executing, but the program produces incorrect results.
- A repetition statement repeats an action (or set of actions) while some condition remains true.
- Eventually, the condition in a `while` statement will become false. At this point, the repetition terminates, and the first statement after the `while` statement executes.
- A repetition statement that never terminates is an "infinite loop."
- Counter-controlled repetition is often called definite repetition because the number of repetitions is known before the loop begins executing. This technique uses a variable called a counter to control the number of times a set of statements will execute.
- Sentinel-controlled repetition is often called indefinite repetition because the number of repetitions is not known before the loop begins executing.
- The sentinel value (also called the signal value, dummy value or flag value) determines when to terminate a repetition statement.
- We approach programming problems with top-down, stepwise refinement—a technique that is essential to the development of well-structured algorithms.
- The top is a single statement that conveys the overall function of the program. As such, the top is a complete representation of a program.
- We divide the top into a series of smaller tasks and list these in the order in which they must be performed. Each refinement, including the top itself, is a complete specification of the algorithm; only the level of detail in each refinement varies.
- Many algorithms can be divided logically into three phases—an initialization phase that initializes the program variables, a processing phase that inputs data values and adjusts program variables accordingly and a termination phase that calculates and prints the results.
- The programmer terminates the top-down, stepwise refinement process when the pseudocode algorithm is specified in sufficient detail for the programmer to convert the pseudocode to an MC++ program.
- Dividing two integers results in integer division, in which any fractional part of the calculation is truncated.
- A unary operator is defined as an operator which takes only one operand.
- MC++ provides the unary increment operator, ++, and the unary decrement operator, `--`. These operators add 1 to or subtract 1 from their operand, respectively.
- If an increment or decrement operator is placed before a variable, it is referred to as the prefix increment or prefix decrement operator, respectively.
- If an increment or decrement operator is placed after a variable, it is referred to as the postfix increment or postfix decrement operator, respectively.

TERMINOLOGY

%= (modulus assignment operator)
*= (multiplication assignment operator)
`--` (unary decrement operator)
/= (division assignment operator)
; (null statement)
`?:` (conditional operator)
{ (open brace)
} (close brace)
++ (unary increment operator)
+= (addition assignment operator)
= (assignment operator)
-= (subtraction assignment operator)

abbreviating an assignment expression
action symbol
action/decision model of programming
algorithm
assignment operator (=)
block
body of the `while`
braces that delimit a block
building block
complete representation of a program
conditional expression
conditional operator (`?:`)
connector symbol
control structure
control-structure nesting
control-structure stacking
counter-controlled repetition
dangling-`else` problem
decision symbol
declaration
definite repetition
design phase
diamond symbol
division by zero
`do...while` repetition statement
`double`
double-selection structure
`else`
entry point of control structure
exit point of control structure
explicit conversion
`false`
fatal logic error
flag value
floating-point division
floating-point number
flow of control
flowchart
flowline
`for` repetition statement
fractional result
graphical representation of an algorithm
`if` selection statement
`if...else` selection statement
indefinite repetition
indentation convention
infinite loop
initialization phase
initialize a variable
input/output operation
integer division
keyword
loop
lvalue
multiple-selection structure
nonfatal logic error
oval symbol
postfix decrement operator (`--`)
postfix increment operator (++)
prefix decrement operator (`--`)
prefix increment operator (++)
procedure for solving a problem
processing phase
program control
program development tool
pseudocode
real number
rectangle symbol
refinement process
repetition structure
selection structure
sentinel value
sentinel-controlled repetition
sequence structure
sequential execution
signal value
single-entry/single-exit control structure
single-selection structure
small circle symbol
`static_cast` operator
structured programming
temporary value
termination phase
ternary operator (`?:`)
top-down, stepwise refinement
transfer of control
`true`
truncate
unary operator
`while` repetition statement

SELF-REVIEW EXERCISES

4.1 Fill in the blanks in each of the following statements:

a) All programs can be written in terms of three types of control structures: ________, ________ and ________.

b) The __________ selection statement executes one action when a condition is true and another action when a condition is false.
c) Repetition of a set of instructions a specific number of times is called __________ repetition.
d) When it is not known in advance how many times a set of statements will be repeated, a(n) __________ value can be used to terminate the repetition.
e) Specifying the order in which statements are to be executed in a computer program is called __________.
f) __________ is an artificial and informal language that helps programmers develop algorithms.
g) __________ are reserved by MC++ to implement various features, such as the language's control statements.
h) A(n) __________ statement specifying that no action is to be taken is indicated by placing a semicolon where a statement normally would be.
i) The increment operator (++) and decrement operator (--) increment and decrement a variable's value by __________.
j) Conversions between types can be performed with the __________ operator.

4.2 State whether each of the following is *true* or *false*. If *false*, explain why.
a) It is difficult to convert pseudocode into a working MC++ program.
b) Sequential execution refers to statements in a program that execute one after another.
c) It is recommended that MC++ programmers use `goto` statements.
d) The `if` statement is called a single-selection statement.
e) Structured programs are clear, easy to debug and modify and more likely than unstructured programs to be bug-free in the first place.
f) The sequence structure is not built into MC++.
g) Pseudocode usually resembles actual MC++ code.
h) Placing a semicolon after the condition in an `if` statement is a syntax error.
i) The `while` statement body may be a single statement or a block.

4.3 Write four different MC++ statements that each add 1 to integer variable `x` and store the result in `x`.

4.4 Write MC++ statements to accomplish each of the following:
a) Assign the sum of `x` and `y` to `z` then increment `x` by 1 after the calculation. Use only one statement.
b) Test if the value of the variable `count` is greater than 10. If it is, print `"Count is greater than 10"`.
c) Decrement the variable `x` by 1, then subtract it from the variable `total`. Use only one statement.
d) Calculate the remainder after `q` is divided by `divisor` and assign the result to `q`. Write this statement two different ways.

4.5 Write an MC++ statement to accomplish each of the following tasks:
a) Declare variables `sum` and `x` to be of type `int`.
b) Assign `1` to variable `x`.
c) Assign `0` to variable `sum`.
d) Add variable `x` to variable `sum` and assign the result to variable `sum`.
e) Print `"The sum is : "` followed by the value of variable `sum`.

4.6 Combine the statements that you wrote in Exercise 4.5 into an MC++ application that calculates and prints the sum of the integers from 1 to 10. Use the `while` statement to loop through the calculation and increment statements. The loop should terminate when the value of `x` becomes `11`.

4.7 Determine the values of each variable after the calculation is performed. Assume that when each statement begins executing, all variables have the integer value 5.

a) `product *= x++;`

b) `quotient /= ++x;`

4.8 Identify and correct the errors in each of the following:

a)
```
while ( c <= 5 ) {
   product *= c;
   ++c;
```

b)
```
if ( gender == 1 )
   Console::WriteLine( S"Woman" );
else;
   Console::WriteLine( S"Man" );
```

4.9 What is wrong with the following `while` repetition statement?

```
while ( z >= 0 )
   sum += z;
```

ANSWERS TO SELF-REVIEW EXERCISES

4.1 a) sequence, selection, repetition. b) `if...else`. c) counter-controlled or definite. d) sentinel, signal, flag or dummy. e) program control. f) Pseudocode. g) Keywords. h) null. i) one. j) `static_cast`.

4.2 a) False. Properly refined pseudocode converts easily into MC++ code. b) True. c) False. `goto` statements violate structured programming and cause considerable problems. d) True. e) True. f) False. The sequence structure is built into MC++; lines of code execute in the order in which they are written, unless explicitly directed to do otherwise. g) True. h) False. Placing a semicolon after the condition in an `if` statement is usually a logic error. i) True.

4.3
```
x = x + 1;
x += 1;
++x;
x++;
```

4.4 a) `z = y + x++;`

b)
```
if ( count > 10 )
   Console::WriteLine( S"Count is greater than 10" );
```

c) `total -= --x;`

d)
```
q %= divisor;
q = q % divisor;
```

4.5 a) `int sum, x;`

b) `x = 1;`

c) `sum = 0;`

d) `sum += x;` or `sum = sum + x;`

e) `Console::WriteLine( S"The sum is: {0}", sum.ToString() );`

4.6 Combine the statements that you wrote in Exercise 4.5 into an MC++ application that calculates and prints the sum of the integers from 1 to 10. Use the `while` statement to loop through the calculation and increment statements. The loop should terminate when the value of `x` becomes `11`.

```
// Calculate the sum of the integers from 1 to 10

#include "stdafx.h"

#using <mscorlib.dll>

using namespace System;

int _tmain()
{
   int sum, x;

   x = 1;
   sum = 0;

   while ( x <= 10 ) {
      sum += x;
      x++;
   } // end while

   Console::WriteLine( S"The sum is: {0}", sum.ToString() );

   return 0;
} // end _tmain
```

4.7 a) `product = 25, x = 6;`
b) `quotient = 0, x = 6;`

4.8 a) Error: Missing the closing right brace of the `while` body.
Correction: Add closing right brace after the statement `++c;`.
b) Error: Semicolon after `else` results in a logic error. The second output statement will always be executed.
Correction: Remove the semicolon after `else`.

4.9 The value of the variable `z` is never changed in the `while` statement. Therefore, if the loop-continuation condition `( z >= 0 )` is true, an infinite loop is created. To prevent the infinite loop, `z` must be decremented so that it eventually becomes less than 0.

EXERCISES

For Exercise 4.10 and Exercise 4.11, perform each of the following steps:

a) Read the problem statement.
b) Formulate the algorithm using pseudocode and top-down, stepwise refinement.
c) Write a Visual C++ .NET program.
d) Test, debug and execute the Visual C++ .NET program.
e) Process three complete sets of data.

4.10 Drivers are concerned with the mileage obtained by their automobiles. One driver has kept track of several tankfuls of gasoline by recording miles driven and gallons used for each tankful. Develop an MC++ program that will input the miles driven and gallons used (both as `int`s) for each tankful. The program should calculate and display the miles per gallon obtained for each tankful (as a `double`) and print the combined miles per gallon obtained for all tankfuls up to this point. All average calculations should produce floating-point results. [*Hint:* Use a sentinel value to determine when the user is finished entering input.]

```
Enter the number of miles traveled, -1 to quit: 50
Enter the number of gallons used: 3
Average miles / gallon: 16.6666666666667.
Combined miles / gallon: 16.6666666666667.
Enter the number of miles traveled, -1 to quit: 100
Enter the number of gallons used: 5
Average miles / gallon: 20
Combined miles / gallon: 18.75
Enter the number of miles traveled, -1 to quit: -1
```

4.11 Develop an MC++ application that will determine if a department store customer has exceeded the credit limit on a charge account. For each customer, the following facts are available:

a) Account number
b) Balance at the beginning of the month
c) Total of all items charged by this customer this month
d) Total of all credits applied to this customer's account this month
e) Allowed credit limit

Users should input as integers each of these facts, calculate the new balance (= *beginning balance + charges – credits*), display the new balance and determine if the new balance exceeds the customer's credit limit. For those customers whose credit limit is exceeded, the program should display the message, "Credit limit exceeded."

```
Enter account, -1 to quit: 153
Enter balance: 200
Enter charges: 300
Enter credits: 150
Enter credit limit: 400
New balance is 350.
Enter account, -1 to quit: 257
Enter balance: 200
Enter charges: 300
Enter credits: 50
Enter credit limit: 400
New balance is 450.

CREDIT LIMIT EXCEEDED
Enter account, -1 to quit: -1
```

4.12 Write an MC++ application that uses a loop to print the following table of values:

```
N       10*N     100*N    1000*N

1       10       100      1000
2       20       200      2000
3       30       300      3000
4       40       400      4000
5       50       500      5000
```

4.13 *(Dangling-Else Problem)* Determine the output for each of the following, when `x` is `9` and `y` is `11`, and when `x` is `11` and `y` is `9`. Note that the compiler ignores the indentation in an MC++ program. Also, the MC++ compiler always associates an `else` with the previous `if` unless told to do otherwise by the placement of braces (`{}`). On first glance, the programmer may not be sure which `if` and `else` match; this is referred to as the "dangling-else" problem. We have eliminated the indentation from the following code to make the problem more challenging. [*Hint*: Apply indentation conventions that you have learned.]

a)
```
if ( x < 10 )
if ( y > 10 )
Console::WriteLine( S"*****" );
else
Console::WriteLine( S"#####" );
Console::WriteLine( S"$$$$$" );
```

b)
```
if ( x < 10 ) {
if ( y > 10 )
Console::WriteLine( S"*****" );
}
else {
Console::WriteLine( S"#####" );
Console::WriteLine( S"$$$$$" );
}
```

4.14 A palindrome is a number or a text phrase that reads the same backwards as forwards. For example, each of the following five-digit integers are palindromes: 12321, 55555, 45554 and 11611. Write an application that reads in a five-digit integer and determines whether it is a palindrome. If the number is not five digits, display an error message indicating the problem to the user. Then allow the user to enter a new value.

4.15 A company wants to transmit data over the telephone, but the company is concerned that its phones may be tapped. All its data is transmitted as four-digit integers. The company has asked you to write a program that will encrypt its data so that it may be transmitted more securely. Your application should read a four-digit integer entered by the user and encrypt it as follows: Replace each digit by *(the sum of that digit plus 7) modulus 10*. Then swap the first digit with the third, and swap the second digit with the fourth. Print the encrypted integer. Write a separate application that inputs an encrypted four-digit integer and decrypts it to form the original number. [*Note:* For the encryption application, the encrypted integer may display with only three digits, as the first integer may be a `0`.]

4.16 The factorial of a positive integer n is written $n!$ (pronounced "n factorial") and is defined as follows:

$$n! = n \cdot (n - 1) \cdot (n - 2) \cdot \ldots \cdot 1 \quad \text{(for values of } n \text{ greater than or equal to 1)}$$

and

$$n! = 1 \quad (\text{for } n = 0).$$

For example, $5! = 5 \cdot 4 \cdot 3 \cdot 2 \cdot 1$, which is 120.

a) Write an application that reads a positive integer from an input dialog and computes and prints its factorial.

b) Write an application that estimates the value of the mathematical constant e by using the formula

$$e = 1 + \frac{1}{1!} + \frac{1}{2!} + \frac{1}{3!} + \ldots$$

c) Write an application that computes the value of e^x by using the formula

$$e^x = 1 + \frac{x}{1!} + \frac{x^2}{2!} + \frac{x^3}{3!} + \ldots$$

5

Control Statements: Part 2

Objectives

- To use the `for` and `do...while` repetition statements to execute statements in a program repeatedly.
- To understand multiple selection with `switch` selection statement.
- To use the `break` and `continue` program-control statements.
- To use the logical operators.

Who can control his fate?
William Shakespeare, *Othello*

The used key is always bright.
Benjamin Franklin

Man is a tool-making animal.
Benjamin Franklin

Intelligence … is the faculty of making artificial objects, especially tools to make tools.
Henri Bergson

Outline

5.1 Introduction

Chapter 4 began our introduction to the types of building blocks that are available for problem solving and used those building blocks to implement proven program-construction principles. In this chapter, we continue our presentation of the theory and principles of structured programming by introducing MC++'s remaining control statements. As in Chapter 4, the MC++ techniques you learn here are applicable to most high-level languages. When we begin our formal treatment of object-based programming in Chapter 8, we will see that the control statements we study in this chapter and in Chapter 4 are helpful in building and manipulating objects.

5.2 Essentials of Counter-Controlled Repetition

In the last chapter, we introduced the concept of counter-controlled repetition. In this section, we formalize the elements needed in counter-controlled repetition, namely:

1. The *name* of a *control variable* (or loop counter) used to determine whether the loop continues
2. The *initial value* of the control variable
3. The *increment* (or *decrement*) by which the control variable is modified each time through the loop (also known as *each iteration of the loop*)
4. The condition that tests for the *final value* of the control variable (i.e., whether looping should continue)

To see the four elements of counter-controlled repetition, consider the simple program in Fig. 5.1, which displays the digits 1–5.

```
// Fig. 5.1: WhileCounter.cpp
// Counter-controlled repetition.

```

Fig. 5.1 Counter-controlled repetition with `while` statement. (Part 1 of 2.)

```
4   #include "stdafx.h"
5
6   #using <mscorlib.dll>
7
8   using namespace System;
9
10  int _tmain()
11  {
12     int counter = 1; // initialization
13
14     while ( counter <= 5 ) { // repetition condition
15        Console::WriteLine( counter );
16        counter++; // increment
17     } // end while
18
19     return 0;
20  } // end _tmain
```

```
1
2
3
4
5
```

Fig. 5.1 Counter-controlled repetition with `while` statement. (Part 2 of 2.)

Line 12 *names* the control variable (`counter`), declares it to be an integer, reserves space for it in memory and sets it to an *initial value* of `1`. The declaration and initialization of `counter` could also have been accomplished with a separate declaration and initialization statement

```
int counter;   // declare counter
counter = 1;   // initialize counter to 1
```

The declaration is not executable, but the assignment statement is. We use both approaches to initialization throughout this book.

Lines 14–17 define the `while` statement. During each iteration of the loop, line 15 displays the current value of `counter`, and line 16 *increments* the control variable by `1` upon each iteration of the loop. The loop-continuation condition in the `while` statement tests whether the value of the control variable is less than or equal to `5` (the *final value* for which the condition is true). The body of this `while` is performed even when the control variable is `5`. The loop terminates when the control variable exceeds `5` (i.e., `counter` becomes `6`).

Good Programming Practice 5.1

Control counting loops with integer values.

Good Programming Practice 5.2

Place a blank line before and after each major control statement to make it stand out in the program.

Good Programming Practice 5.3

Vertical spacing above and below control statements, and indentation of the bodies of control statements within the control statements' headers, gives programs a two-dimensional appearance that enhances readability.

Notice that in line 15 we pass the value of variable `counter` to method `WriteLine` rather than the `String *` obtained from the expression `counter.ToString()`. This is possible because method `WriteLine` also accepts single numerical values, which it converts to strings implicitly by calling the variable's `ToString` method.

5.3 for Repetition Statement

The `for` repetition statement handles the details of counter-controlled repetition. To illustrate the power of `for`, let us rewrite the program in Fig. 5.1. The result is displayed in Fig. 5.2.

```
1  // Fig. 5.2: ForCounter.cpp
2  // Counter-controlled repetition with the for statement.
3
4  #include "stdafx.h"
5
6  #using <mscorlib.dll>
7
8  using namespace System;
9
10 int _tmain()
11 {
12    // initialization, repetition condition and incrementing
13    // are all included in the for statement
14    for ( int counter = 1; counter <= 5; counter++ ) {
15       Console::WriteLine( counter );
16    } // end for
17
18    return 0;
19 } // end _tmain
```

```
1
2
3
4
5
```

Fig. 5.2 Counter-controlled repetition with the `for` statement.

Function `_tmain` (lines 10–19) operates as follows: When the `for` statement (line 14) begins executing, the program initializes the control variable `counter` to `1` (the first two elements of counter-controlled repetition—control variable *name* and *initial value*). Next, the program tests the loop-continuation condition, `counter <= 5`. The initial value of `counter` is `1`; thus, the condition is true, so line 15 outputs the `counter`'s value. Then, the program increments variable `counter` in the expression `counter++`, and the next iteration of the loop begins with the loop-continuation test. The control variable is now equal to 2. This value does not exceed the final value, so the program executes the body statement again (i.e., performs the next iteration of the loop). This process continues until the control variable `counter` becomes 6, causing the loop-continuation test to fail and repetition to terminate. The program continues by performing the first statement after the `for` statement. (In this case, function `_tmain` terminates because the program reaches the `return` statement in line 18.)

Figure 5.3 takes a closer look at the `for` statement of Fig. 5.2. The first line of the `for` statement (including the keyword `for` and everything in parentheses after `for`) is sometimes called the *`for` statement header*. Notice that the `for` statement specifies each of the items needed for counter-controlled repetition with a control variable. If there is more than one statement in the body of the `for` statement, braces ({ and }) are required to define the loop's body.

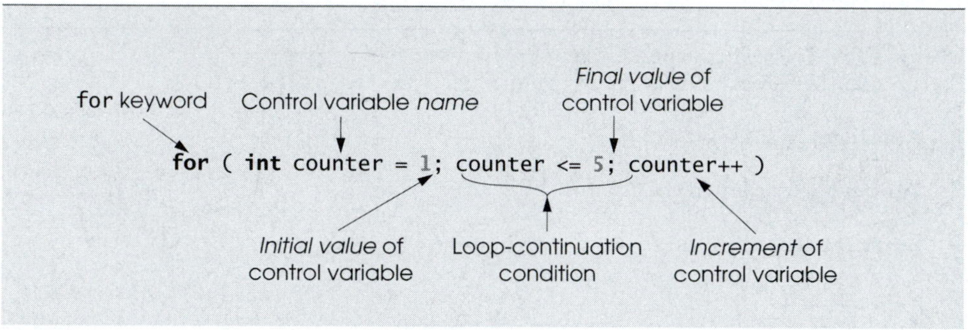

Fig. 5.3 Components of a typical `for` header.

Figure 5.2 uses the loop-continuation condition `counter <= 5`. If the programmer incorrectly writes `counter < 5` instead, the loop executes only four times. This common logic error is called an *off-by-one error*.

Common Programming Error 5.1

Using an incorrect relational operator or using an incorrect final value for a loop counter in the condition of a `while`, `for` or `do...while` statement (introduced in Section 5.6) can cause an off-by-one error.

Common Programming Error 5.2

Floating-point values may be approximate, so controlling counting loops with floating-point variables can result in imprecise counter values and inaccurate tests for termination.

Error-Prevention Tip 5.1

Using the final value in the condition of a `while` or `for` statement and using the `<=` relational operator will help avoid off-by-one errors. For a loop used to print the values from 1 to 10, for example, the loop-continuation condition should be `counter <= 10`, rather than `counter < 10` (which is an off-by-one error) or `counter < 11` (which also works). This approach is commonly known as one-based counting. *When we study arrays in Chapter 7, Arrays, we will see* zero-based counting, *in which to count 10 times through a loop, `counter` is initialized to zero and the loop-continuation test is `counter < 10`.*

The general format of the `for` statement is

```
for ( expression1; expression2; expression3 )
   statement;
```

where *expression1* names the loop's control variable and provides its initial value, *expression2* is the loop-continuation condition (containing the control variable's final value) and *expression3* usually increments or decrements the control variable. In most cases, the `for` statement can be represented with an equivalent `while` statement, with *expression1*, *expression2* and *expression3* placed as follows:

```
expression1;

while ( expression2 ) {
   statement
   expression3;
}
```

In Section 5.7, we discuss an exception to this rule.

Programmers can declare the control variable in *expression1* of the `for` statement header (i.e., the control variable's type is specified before the variable name), rather than earlier in the code. In Visual C++ .NET, this approach is equivalent to declaring the control variable immediately before the `for` statement. Therefore, the `for` statement

```
for ( int counter = 1; counter <= 5; counter++ )
   Console::WriteLine( counter );
```

is equivalent to

```
int counter;

for ( counter = 1; counter <= 5; counter++ )
   Console::WriteLine( counter );
```

Both code segments create variable `counter` with a *scope* that allows `counter` to be used after the `for` statement. The scope of a variable specifies where it can be used in a program. Scope is discussed in detail in Chapter 6, Functions. [*Note*: In standard C++, a variable declared in the `for` header can be used only in the `for` statement.[1]]

Good Programming Practice 5.4

When a control variable is declared in the initialization section (e.g., expression1*) of a* `for` *statement header, avoid declaring the control variable again after the* `for` *statement's body.*

expression1 and *expression3* in a `for` statement also can be comma-separated lists of expressions that enable the programmer to specify multiple initialization expressions or multiple increment (or decrement) expressions. For example, there may be several control variables in a single `for` statement that must be initialized and incremented or decremented.

1. You can simulate the behavior of standard C++ using the `/Zc:forScope` compiler option. This option can be set in the IDE by selecting **Project > Properties > Configuration Properties > C/C++ > Language**, and changing option **Force Conformance In For Loop Scope** to **Yes (/Zc:forScope)**.

Good Programming Practice 5.5

Place only expressions involving control variables in the initialization and increment or decrement sections of a `for` *statement. Manipulations of other variables should appear either before the loop (if they execute only once, like initialization statements) or in the loop body (if they execute once per iteration of the loop, like incrementing or decrementing statements).*

The three expressions in the `for` statement are optional, but the two semicolons are required. If *expression2* is omitted, MC++ assumes that the loop-continuation condition is always true, thus creating an infinite loop. A programmer might omit *expression1* if the program initializes the control variable before the loop. *expression3* might be omitted if statements in the body of the `for` calculate the increment or decrement, or if no increment or decrement is necessary. The increment (or decrement) expression in the `for` statement executes as if it is a standalone statement at the end of the `for` body. Therefore, the expressions

```
counter = counter + 1
counter += 1
++counter
counter++
```

are equivalent when used in *expression3*. Some programmers prefer the form `counter++`, because the `++` is at the end of the expression and the increment portion of a `for` loop executes after the body. For this reason, the postincrementing (or postdecrementing) form in which the variable is incremented after it is used seems more natural. The variable being either incremented or decremented does not appear in a larger expression, so preincrementing and postincrementing the variable have the same effect.

Common Programming Error 5.3

Using commas in a `for` *statement header instead of the two required semicolons is a syntax error.*

Common Programming Error 5.4

Placing a semicolon immediately to the right of a `for` *statement header's right parenthesis makes the body of that* `for` *statement a null statement. This is normally a logic error.*

The initialization, loop-continuation condition and increment or decrement portions of a `for` statement can contain arithmetic expressions. For example, assume that `x = 2` and `y = 10`. If `x` and `y` are not modified in the loop body, the statement

```
for ( int j = x; j <= 4 * x * y; j += y / x )
```

is equivalent to the statement

```
for ( int j = 2; j <= 80; j += 5 )
```

The "increment" of a `for` statement may be negative, in which case it is really a decrement and the loop actually counts downward.

If the loop-continuation condition in the `for` statement is initially false, the body of the `for` statement does not execute. Instead, execution proceeds with the statement that follows the `for` statement.

The control variable is frequently printed or used in calculations in the body of a `for` statement, but it does not have to be. Often the control variable simply controls repetition and is not mentioned in the body of the `for` statement.

Error-Prevention Tip 5.2

Avoid changing the value of the control variable in the body of a `for` *loop, to avoid subtle errors such as premature termination or an infinite loop.*

The `for` statement flowchart is similar to that of the `while` statement. For example, the flowchart of the `for` statement in Fig. 5.2 appears in Fig. 5.4. This flowchart clarifies that the initialization occurs only once, and that incrementing occurs each time *after* the body statement is performed. Note that (besides small circles and flowlines) the flowchart contains only rectangle symbols and a diamond symbol. The rectangles and diamonds are filled with actions and decisions appropriate to the algorithm.

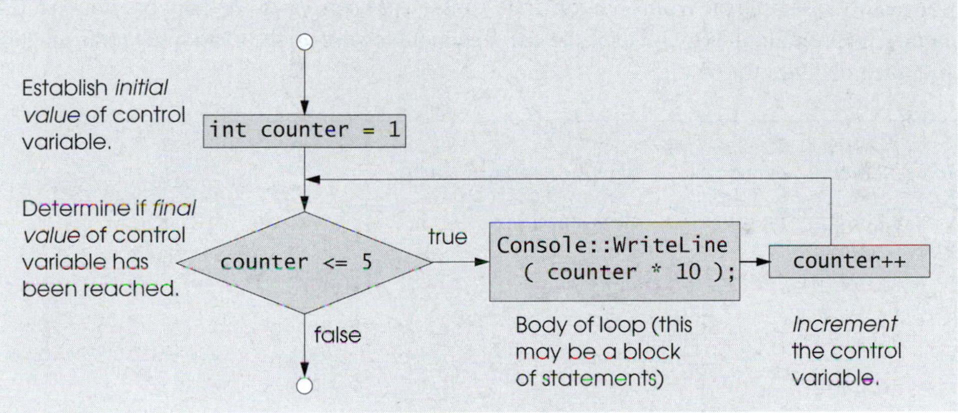

Fig. 5.4 Flowcharting a typical `for` repetition statement.

5.4 Examples Using the for Statement

The following examples demonstrate methods of varying the control variable in a `for` statement. In each case, we write the appropriate `for` header. Note the change in the relational operator for loops that decrement the control variable.

a) Vary the control variable from `1` to `100` in increments of `1`.

```
for ( int i = 1; i <= 100; i++ )
```

b) Vary the control variable from `100` to `1` in increments of `-1` (decrements of `1`).

```
for ( int i = 100; i >= 1; i-- )
```

c) Vary the control variable from `7` to `77` in steps of `7`.

```
for ( int i = 7; i <= 77; i += 7 )
```

d) Vary the control variable from `20` to `2` in steps of `-2`.

```
for ( int i = 20; i >= 2; i -= 2 )
```

e) Vary the control variable over the sequence of the following values: `2, 5, 8, 11, 14, 17, 20`.

```
for ( int j = 2; j <= 20; j += 3 )
```

f) Vary the control variable over the sequence of the following values: 99, 88, 77, 66, 55, 44, 33, 22, 11, 0.

```
for ( int j = 99; j >= 0; j -= 11 )
```

Common Programming Error 5.5

Not using the proper relational operator in the loop-continuation condition of a loop that counts downward (e.g., using `i <= 1` in a loop counting down to 1) is usually a logic error that will yield incorrect results (or an infinite loop) when the program runs.

Sum the Even Integers from 2 to 100

The next two sample programs demonstrate simple applications of the `for` repetition statement. The program in Fig. 5.5 uses the `for` statement to sum all the even integers from 2 to 100, then displays the result.

```
// Fig. 5.5: Sum.cpp
// Summation with the for statement.

#include "stdafx.h"

#using <mscorlib.dll>

using namespace System;

int _tmain()
{
   int sum = 0;

   for ( int number = 2; number <= 100; number += 2 )
      sum += number;

   Console::WriteLine( S"The sum is {0}", sum.ToString() );

   return 0;
} // end _tmain
```

```
The sum is 2550
```

Fig. 5.5 Summation using `for`.

The body of the `for` statement in Fig. 5.5 actually could be merged into the rightmost portion of the `for` header by using a *comma* as follows:

```
for ( int number = 2; number <= 100;
        sum += number, number += 2 )
   ; // null statement
```

Similarly, the initialization `sum = 0` could be merged into the initialization section of the `for` statement. Statements that precede a `for` and statements in the body of a `for` often can be merged into the `for` header. However, such merging decreases the readability of the program.

Good Programming Practice 5.6

Limit the size of control statement headers to a single line if possible.

Compound Interest Calculations

The next example uses a `for` statement to compute compound interest. Consider the following problem statement:

> *A person invests \$1000.00 in a savings account yielding 5% interest. Assuming that all interest is left on deposit, calculate and print the amount of money in the account at the end of each year for 10 years. To determine these amounts, use the following formula:*
>
> $$a = p\,(1 + r)^{n}$$
>
> *where*
>
> p is the original amount invested (i.e., the principal)
> r is the annual interest rate
> n is the number of years
> a is the amount on deposit at the end of the nth year.

This problem involves a loop that performs the indicated calculation for each of the 10 years that the money remains on deposit. A solution is the program shown in Fig. 5.6. Line 12 in function `_tmain` declares two *`Decimal`* variables—`amount` and `principal`—and initializes `principal` to `1000.00`. The type `Decimal` is used for monetary calculations (discussed shortly). Line 13 declares `double` variable `rate`, which we initialize to `.05`.

```
1  // Fig. 5.6: interest.cpp
2  // Calculating compound interest.
3
4  #include "stdafx.h"
5
6  #using <mscorlib.dll>
7
8  using namespace System;
9
10 int _tmain()
11 {
12    Decimal amount, principal = 1000.00;
13    double rate = .05;
14
15    Console::WriteLine( S"Year\tAmount on deposit" );
16
17    for ( int year = 1; year <= 10; year++ ) {
18       amount = principal * Math::Pow( 1.0 + rate, year );
19
20       Console::WriteLine( String::Concat( year.ToString(), S"\t",
21          amount.ToString( "C" ) ) );
22    } // end for
23
24    return 0;
25 } // end _tmain
```

Fig. 5.6 Calculating compound interest with `for`. (Part 1 of 2.)

```
Year    Amount on deposit
1       $1,050.00
2       $1,102.50
3       $1,157.63
4       $1,215.51
5       $1,276.28
6       $1,340.10
7       $1,407.10
8       $1,477.46
9       $1,551.33
10      $1,628.89
```

Fig. 5.6 Calculating compound interest with `for`. (Part 2 of 2.)

The `for` statement (lines 17–22) executes its body 10 times, varying control variable `year` from `1` to `10` in increments of `1`. Note that `year` represents n in the problem statement. MC++ does not have an exponentiation operator, so we use method `Pow` in class `Math` for this purpose. `Math::Pow( x, y )` calculates the value of `x` raised to the `y` power. Method `Math::Pow` takes two arguments of type `double` and returns a `double` value. Line 18 performs the calculation from the problem statement

$$a = p\,(1 + r)^{\,n}$$

where a is `amount`, p is `principal`, r is `rate` and n is `year`.

Lines 20–21 use method `Concat` of class `Sytem::String` to build an output `String`. Method *`Concat`* concatenates multiple `Strings` and returns a new `String` containing the combined characters from the original `Strings`. We discuss method `Concat` in more detail in Chapter 15, Strings, Characters and Regular Expressions.

Common Programming Error 5.6

Attempting to use + to concatenate `String *`s is a syntax error.

The concatenated text (lines 20–21) includes the current value of `year` (`year.ToString()`), a tab character (`\t`) to position to the second column, the amount on deposit (`amount.ToString( "C" )`) and a newline character to position the output cursor to the next line. Note that `ToString` call for `amount`, which converts `amount` to a `String *` and formats this `String *` as a monetary amount. The argument to method `ToString` specifies the formatting of the string and is referred to as the *formatting code*. In this case, we use formatting code `C` (for "currency"), which indicates that the string should be displayed as a monetary amount. There are several other formatting codes, which can be found in the MSDN documentation.[2] [*Note*: Method `ToString` uses .NET's string formatting codes to represent numeric and monetary values in a form that is appropriate to the execution environment. For example, U.S. dollars are represented as `$634,307.08`, whereas Malaysian ringgits are represented as `R634.307,08`.] Figure 5.7 shows several formatting codes. If no formatting code is specified (e.g., `year.ToString()`), the formatting code `G` is used.

---

2. For more information on string formatting, visit `msdn.microsoft.com/library/default.asp?url=/library/en-us/cpguide/html/cpconformattingtypes.asp`.

Format Code	Description
`C` or `c`	Formats the string as currency. Precedes the number with an appropriate currency symbol (`$` for U.S. settings). Separates digits with an appropriate separator character and sets the number of decimal places to two by default.
`D` or `d`	Formats the string as a decimal.
`N` or `n`	Formats the string with comma-separator characters and two decimal places.
`E` or `e`	Formats the string in scientific notation with a default of six decimal places (e.g., the value `27,900,000` becomes `2.790000E+007`).
`F` or `f`	Formats the string with a fixed number of decimal places (two by default).
`G` or `g`	Formats the string as decimal, using the `E` or `F` format code, whichever provides the most compact result.
`P` or `p`	Formats the string as a percentage. By default, the value is multiplied by 100, and a percent sign is appended to it.
`R` or `r`	Ensures that a value converted to a string can be converted back (e.g., using `Int32::Parse`) without loss of precision or data.
`X` or `x`	Formats the string as hexadecimal.

Fig. 5.7 Numeric formatting codes.

We declared variables `amount` and `principal` to be of type `Decimal` (line 12) because the program deals with fractional parts of dollars. In such cases, programs need a type that is not subject to round-off errors in monetary calculations. Here is a simple example of how round-off errors can occur when using `double` (or `float`) to represent dollar amounts (assuming that dollar amounts are displayed with two digits to the right of the decimal point): Two `double` dollar amounts stored in the machine could be 14.234 (which would normally be rounded to 14.23 for display purposes) and 18.673 (which would normally be rounded to 18.67 for display purposes). When these amounts are added, they produce the internal sum 32.907, which would normally be rounded to 32.91 for display purposes. Thus, your output could appear as

```
  14.23
+ 18.67
-------
  32.91
```

but a person adding the individual numbers as displayed would expect the sum to be 32.90. For this reason, programmers should use type `Decimal` to perform monetary calculations.

Good Programming Practice 5.7

Do not use variables of type `double` (or `float`) to perform precise monetary calculations. The imprecision of floating-point numbers can cause errors that will result in incorrect monetary values. Rather, type `Decimal` should be used to perform such calculations.

Variable `rate` is of type `double` because it is used in the calculation `1.0 + rate`, which appears as a `double` argument to method `Pow` of class `Math`. Note that the calculation `1.0 + rate` appears in the body of the `for` statement. The calculation produces the same result each time through the loop, so repeating the calculation is unnecessary. We only place `1.0 + rate` inside the loop for program clarity. However, for performance reasons, this calculation could be moved before the loop.

Performance Tip 5.1

Avoid placing expressions containing values that do not change inside a loop. Such expressions should be evaluated only once before the loop.

5.5 `switch` Multiple-Selection Statement

The previous chapter discussed the `if` single-selection and the `if...else` double-selection statements. Occasionally, an algorithm contains a series of decisions in which the algorithm tests a variable or expression separately for each *constant integral expression* the variable or expression may assume. A constant integral expression is any expression involving character and integer constants that evaluates to an integer value (e.g., values of type `int` or `__wchar_t`). The algorithm then takes different actions, based on those values. MC++ provides the *`switch` multiple-selection statement* to handle such decision making.

In the next example (Fig. 5.8), let us assume that a class of 10 students took an exam and that each student received a letter grade of A, B, C, D or F. The program will input the letter grades and summarize the results by using `switch` to count the number of each different letter grade that students earned on an exam.

```
// Fig. 5.8: switchTest.cpp
// Counting letter grades.

#include "stdafx.h"

#using <mscorlib.dll>

using namespace System;

int _tmain()
{
   __wchar_t grade;  // one grade
   int aCount = 0,   // number of As
      bCount = 0,    // number of Bs
      cCount = 0,    // number of Cs
      dCount = 0,    // number of Ds
      fCount = 0;    // number of Fs

   for ( int i = 1; i <= 10; i++ ) {
      Console::Write( S"Enter a letter grade: " );
      grade = Char::Parse( Console::ReadLine() );

      switch ( grade ) {
         case 'A':      // grade is uppercase A
         case 'a':      // or lowercase a
            ++aCount;
            break;
```

Fig. 5.8 `switch` multiple-selection statement. (Part 1 of 3.)

```

         case 'B':      // grade is uppercase B
         case 'b':      // or lowercase b
            ++bCount;
            break;

         case 'C':      // grade is uppercase C
         case 'c':      // or lowercase c
            ++cCount;
            break;

         case 'D':      // grade is uppercase D
         case 'd':      // or lowercase d
            ++dCount;
            break;

         case 'F':      // grade is upppercase F
         case 'f':      // or lowercase f
            ++fCount;
            break;

         default:       // processes all other characters
            Console::WriteLine(
               S"Incorrect letter grade entered."
               S"\nGrade not added to totals." );
            break;
      } // end switch
   } // end for

   Console::WriteLine(
      S"\nTotals for each letter grade are: \nA: {0} "
      S"\nB: {1}\nC: {2}\nD: {3}\nF: {4}", aCount.ToString(),
      bCount.ToString(), cCount.ToString(), dCount.ToString(),
      fCount.ToString() );

   return 0;
} // end _tmain
```

```
Enter a letter grade: a
Enter a letter grade: A
Enter a letter grade: c
Enter a letter grade: F
Enter a letter grade: z
Incorrect letter grade entered.
Grade not added to totals.
Enter a letter grade: D
Enter a letter grade: d
Enter a letter grade: B
Enter a letter grade: a
Enter a letter grade: C
```

Fig. 5.8 `switch` multiple-selection statement. (Part 2 of 3.)

```
Totals for each letter grade are:
A: 3
B: 1
C: 2
D: 2
F: 1
```

Fig. 5.8 `switch` multiple-selection statement. (Part 3 of 3.)

Line 12 declares variable `grade` as type `__wchar_t`. Lines 13–17 define counter variables that the program uses to count each letter grade (`aCount` will contain the amount of `A` grades, `bCount` will contain the amount of `B` grades, etc.). Line 19 begins a `for` statement that loops 10 times. At each iteration, line 20 prompts the user for the next grade, and line 21 invokes `Char` method `Parse` to read the user input as a `__wchar_t`. Recall that in MC++, `__wchar_t` is an alias for type `Char` (see Chapter 3). The `Char` structure represents Unicode characters. Nested in the body of the `for` statement is a `switch` statement (lines 23–54) that processes the letter grades. The `switch` statement consists of a series of *`case` labels* and an optional *`default` case*.

When the flow of control reaches the `switch` statement, the program evaluates the *controlling expression* (`grade` in this example) in the parentheses following keyword `switch`. The value of this expression is compared with each `case` label until a match occurs. Assume the user entered the letter `B` as the grade. `B` is compared to each `case` in the `switch`, until a match occurs in line 29 (`case 'B':`). When this happens, the statements for that `case` execute. For the letter `B`, line 31 increments the number of `B` grades stored in variable `bCount`, and the `switch` statement exits immediately with the `break` statement (line 32). The *`break` statement* causes program control to proceed with the first statement after the immediate control statement it occurs in. When this happens, we reach the end of the `for` statement's body, so control flows to the increment expression in the `for` statement header. The counter variable in the `for` statement is incremented, and the loop-continuation condition is evaluated to determine whether another iteration of the loop is necessary.

Good Programming Practice 5.8

Indent the body statements of each `case` in a `switch` statement.

If no match occurs between the controlling expression's value and a `case` label, the `default` case (line 49) executes. Lines 50–52 display an error message. Note that the `default` case is optional in the `switch` statement. If the controlling expression does not match a `case` and there is no `default` case, program control proceeds to the next statement after the `switch` statement.

Each `case` can contain multiple actions or no actions at all. A `case` with no statements is considered an *empty case*. The last `case` in a `switch` statement must not be an empty `case` or a syntax error occurs.

If the `case` label matches our controlling expression, and the case contains no `break` statement, *fall through* occurs. This means that the `switch` statement executes the statements in the matching case as well as those in the next case. If that `case` also contains no `break` statement, this process will continue until a `break` statement is found, or the statements for the last case are executed. This provides the programmer with a way to specify that statements should be executed for several `case`s. Figure 5.8 demonstrates this. Lines 26–27 execute for both cases in lines 24–25 (if the grade entered was either `A` or `a`), lines 31–32 execute for both cases in lines 29–30 (if the grade entered was either `B` or `b`) and so on. Furthermore, if all the `break` statements were removed from Figure 5.8, and the user entered the letter `A`, the statements for every `case` would execute (including the `default` case).

Common Programming Error 5.7

Not including a `break` statement at the end of each `case` in a `switch` statement can lead to logic errors. Only omit `break` statements from `case`s that should result in fall through.

Common Programming Error 5.8

Be sure to check all possible values when creating `case`s to confirm that no two `case`s in a `switch` statement are for the same integral value. If the values are the same, a compile-time error will occur.

Finally, it is important to notice that the `switch` statement is different than other control statements in that braces are not required around multiple statements in each `case`. [*Note*: One exception occurs when a `case` contains the declaration and initialization of a variable (e.g., `int x = 2;`). In this scenario, the `case` statements must be enclosed in braces.] The general `switch` statement (using a `break` in each `case`) is flowcharted in Fig. 5.9. Again, note that (besides small circles and flowlines) the flowchart contains only rectangle and diamond symbols. The programmer fills the rectangles and diamonds with actions and decisions appropriate to the algorithm. Although nested control statements are common, it is rare to find nested `switch` statements in a program.

Good Programming Practice 5.9

Provide a `default` case in every `switch` statement. Cases not explicitly tested in a `switch` that lacks a `default` case are ignored. Including a `default` case focuses the programmer on processing exceptional conditions. There are situations, however, in which no `default` processing is required.

Good Programming Practice 5.10

Although the `case`s in a `switch` statement can occur in any order, it is considered a good programming practice to order the `case`s in a logical manner.

When using the `switch` statement, remember that the expression after each `case` in a particular `switch` statement must be a constant integral expression, i.e., any combination of character constants and integer constants that evaluates to a constant integer value. A *character constant* is represented as a specific character in single quotes (such as `'A'`). An integer constant is simply an integer value. The expression after each `case` also can be a *constant*—a variable that contains a value that does not change throughout the entire program. Such a variable is declared with keyword *`const`* (discussed in Chapter 6, Functions).

When we discuss object-oriented programming in Chapter 10, we present a more elegant way of implementing `switch` logic. In that chapter, we use a technique called *polymorphism* to create programs that are clearer and easier to maintain and extend than programs that use `switch` logic.

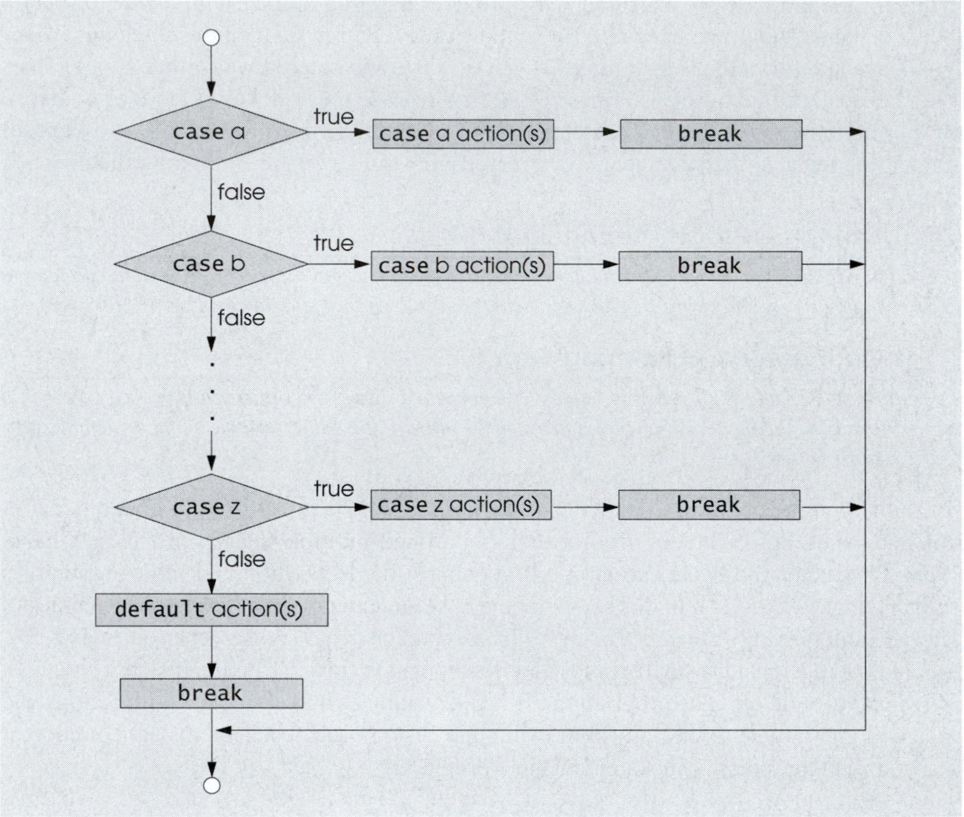

Fig. 5.9 Flowcharting the `switch` multiple-selection statement.

5.6 do...while Repetition Statement

The *do...while* repetition statement is similar to the `while` statement. In the `while` statement, the test of the loop-continuation condition occurs at the beginning of the loop, before the body of the loop executes. The `do...while` statement tests the loop-continuation condition *after* the loop body executes; therefore, *the loop body always executes at least once.* When a `do...while` statement terminates, execution continues with the statement after the `while` clause. The program in Fig. 5.10 uses a `do...while` statement to output the values 1–5.

```
// Fig. 5.10: DoWhileLoop.cpp
// The do...while repetition statement.

#include "stdafx.h"

#using <mscorlib.dll>

```

Fig. 5.10 do...while repetition statement. (Part 1 of 2.)

```
8   using namespace System;
9
10  int _tmain()
11  {
12     int counter = 1;
13
14     do {
15        Console::WriteLine( counter );
16        counter++;
17     } while ( counter <= 5 );
18
19     return 0;
20  } // end _tmain
```

```
1
2
3
4
5
```

Fig. 5.10 do...while repetition statement. (Part 2 of 2.)

Lines 14–17 demonstrate the `do...while` statement. When program execution reaches the `do...while` statement, the program executes lines 15–16, which display the value of `counter` (at this point, `1`) and increment `counter` by `1`. Then, the program evaluates the condition in line 17. At this point, variable `counter` is 2, which is less than or equal to 5, so the `do...while` statement's body executes again, and so on. The fifth time the `do...while` executes, line 15 outputs the value `5` and line 16 increments `counter` to `6`. Then the condition in line 17 evaluates to false and the `do...while` statement exits.

The `do...while` flowchart (Fig. 5.11) makes it clear that the loop-continuation condition does not execute until the body executes at least once. The flowchart contains only a rectangle and a diamond. The programmer fills the rectangle and diamond with actions and decisions appropriate to the algorithm.

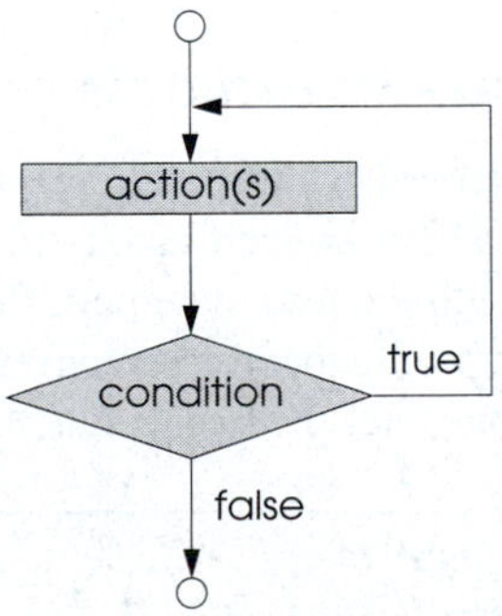

Fig. 5.11 Flowcharting the do...while repetition statement.

Note that it is not necessary to use braces in the `do...while` statement if there is only one statement in the body. However, the braces normally are included to avoid confusion between the `while` and `do...while` statements. For example,

```
while ( condition )
```

typically is the header to a `while` statement. A `do...while` with no braces around the single statement body appears as

```
do
   statement;
while ( condition );
```

which can be confusing. The last line—`while(` *condition* `);`—might be misinterpreted by the reader as a `while` statement containing a null statement (the semicolon by itself). Thus, the `do...while` with one statement is often written as follows to avoid confusion:

```
do
{
   statement;
} while ( condition );
```

Good Programming Practice 5.11

Some programmers always include braces in a `do...while` *statement, even when the braces are unnecessary. This helps eliminate ambiguity between a* `while` *statement and a* `do...while` *statement that contains only one statement.*

Common Programming Error 5.9

Infinite loops occur when the loop-continuation condition in a `while`, `for` *or* `do...while` *statement never becomes false. To prevent this, make sure there is no semicolon immediately after the header of a* `while` *or* `for` *statement. In a counter-controlled loop, make sure the control variable is incremented (or decremented) in the body of the loop. In a sentinel-controlled loop, make sure the* sentinel value *(i.e., the value indicating "end of data entry") eventually is input.*

Common Programming Error 5.10

Placing a semicolon immediately after the word `do` *in a* `do...while` *statement is a syntax error.*

5.7 break and continue Statements

The ***break*** and ***continue*** statements alter the flow of control. The `break` statement, when executed in a `while`, `for`, `do...while` or `switch` statement, causes immediate exit from that statement. Execution continues with the first statement that follows the control statement. Common uses of the `break` statement are to exit prematurely from a loop or to exit a `switch` (as in Fig. 5.8). Figure 5.12 demonstrates the `break` statement in a `for` statement.

```
// Fig. 5.12: BreakTest.cpp
// Using the break statement in a for statement.

```

Fig. 5.12 `break` statement in a `for` statement. (Part 1 of 2.)

```
4  #include "stdafx.h"
5
6  #using <mscorlib.dll>
7
8  using namespace System;
9
10 int _tmain()
11 {
12    int count;
13
14    for ( count = 1; count <= 10; count++ ) {
15
16       if ( count == 5 )
17          break;     // skip remaining code in loop if count == 5
18
19       Console::Write( String::Concat( count.ToString(), S" " ) );
20    } // end for
21
22    Console::WriteLine( S"\nBroke out of loop at count = {0}",
23       count.ToString() );
24
25    return 0;
26 } // end _tmain
```

```
1 2 3 4
Broke out of loop at count = 5
```

Fig. 5.12 `break` statement in a `for` statement. (Part 2 of 2.)

When the `if` statement in line 16 detects that `count` is `5`, `break` is executed. This terminates the `for` statement and the program proceeds to line 22 (immediately after the `for`). The output statement produces the string that is displayed in lines 22–23. The loop executes its body completely only four times.

The `continue` statement, when executed in a `while`, `for` or `do...while` statement, skips the remaining statements in the body of that control statement and proceeds with the next iteration of the loop. In `while` and `do...while` statements, the loop-continuation condition evaluates immediately after `continue` executes. In a `for` statement, the increment/decrement expression executes, then the loop-continuation test evaluates.

Recall from Section 5.3 that the `while` statement can replace the `for` statement in most cases. One exception occurs when the increment/decrement expression in the `while` statement follows the `continue` statement. In this case, the increment/decrement does not execute before the repetition-continuation condition is tested, and the `while` does not execute in the same manner as the `for`.

Figure 5.13 uses the `continue` statement in a `for` statement to skip the output statement in line 18 when the `if` statement (line 14) determines that the value of `count` is `5`. When the `continue` statement executes, program control continues with the increment of the control variable in the `for` statement.

```
// Figure 5.13: continueTest.cpp
// Using the continue statement in a for statement.

#include "stdafx.h"

#using <mscorlib.dll>

using namespace System;

int _tmain()
{
   for ( int count = 1; count <= 10; count++ ) {

      if ( count == 5 )
         continue;  // skip remaining code in loop
                    // only if count == 5

      Console::Write( String::Concat( count.ToString(), S" " ) );
   } // end for

   Console::WriteLine( S"\nUsed continue to skip printing 5" );

   return 0;
} // end _tmain
```

```
1 2 3 4 6 7 8 9 10
Used continue to skip printing 5
```

Fig. 5.13 `continue` statement in a `for` statement.

Performance Tip 5.2

When used properly, the `break` and `continue` statements perform faster than their corresponding structured techniques.

Software Engineering Observation 5.1

Some programmers believe that `break` and `continue` violate structured programming. The effects of these statements can be achieved by structured programming techniques, so these programmers avoid `break` and `continue`.

Software Engineering Observation 5.2

There is a debate between achieving quality software engineering and achieving the best performing software. Often, one of these goals is achieved at the expense of the other. For all but the most performance-intensive situations, apply the following "rule of thumb": First, make your code simple and correct; then make it fast and small, but only if necessary.

5.8 Logical Operators

So far, we have studied only *simple conditions,* such as `count <= 10`, `total > 1000` and `number != sentinelValue`. These conditions were expressed in terms of the relational operators >, <, >= and <= and the equality operators == and !=. Each decision tested one condition.

To test multiple conditions in the process of making a decision, we performed these tests in separate statements or in nested `if` or `if...else` statements.

MC++ provides several *logical operators* that may be used to form complex conditions by combining simple conditions. The operators are && (*logical AND*), || (*logical OR*) and ! (*logical NOT*, also called *logical negation*). We will consider examples using each of these operators.

Common Programming Error 5.11

Placing a space between the && or || operator results in a syntax error.

Suppose we wish to ensure that two conditions are *both* true in a program before we choose a certain path of execution. In this case, we can use the && (logical AND) operator as follows:

```
if ( gender == FEMALE && age >= 65 )
   ++seniorFemales;
```

This `if` statement contains two simple conditions. The condition `gender == FEMALE` is evaluated to determine whether a person is female. The condition `age >= 65` is evaluated to determine whether a person is a senior citizen. The two simple conditions are evaluated first, because the precedences of == and >= are both higher than the precedence of &&. The `if` statement then considers the combined condition

```
gender == FEMALE && age >= 65
```

This condition is true only if both the simple conditions are true. Finally, if this combined condition is true, the body statement increments the count of `seniorFemales` by `1`. If either or both of the simple conditions are false, the program skips the incrementing and proceeds to the statement that follows the `if` statement. The preceding combined condition can be made more readable by adding redundant parentheses:

```
( gender == FEMALE ) && ( age >= 65 )
```

The table in Fig. 5.14 summarizes the && operator. The table shows all four possible combinations of false and true values for *expression1* and *expression2*. Such tables often are called *truth tables*. MC++ evaluates to `true` or `false` expressions that include relational operators, equality operators and logical operators.

expression1	expression2	expression1 && expression2
`false`	`false`	`false`
`false`	`true`	`false`
`true`	`false`	`false`
`true`	`true`	`true`

Fig. 5.14 Truth table for the && (logical AND) operator.

Now let us consider the `||` (logical OR) operator. Suppose we wish to ensure that either *or* both of two conditions are true before we choose a certain path of execution. We use the `||` operator to test two simple conditions in the following program segment:

```
if ( semesterAverage >= 90 || finalExam >= 90 )
   Console::WriteLine( S"Student grade is A" );
```

The condition `semesterAverage >= 90` determines whether the student deserves an "A" in the course because of a solid performance throughout the semester. The condition `finalExam >= 90` determines whether the student deserves an "A" in the course because of an outstanding performance on the final exam. The `if` statement then considers the combined condition

```
semesterAverage >= 90 || finalExam >= 90
```

and awards the student an "A" if either or both of the simple conditions are true. Note that the message `"Student grade is A"` prints unless *both* of the simple conditions are false. Figure 5.15 is a truth table for the logical OR operator (`||`).

expression1	expression2	expression1 || expression2
`false`	`false`	`false`
`false`	`true`	`true`
`true`	`false`	`true`
`true`	`true`	`true`

Fig. 5.15 Truth table for the `||` (logical OR) operator.

The `&&` operator has a higher precedence than the `||` operator. Both operators associate from left to right. An expression containing `&&` or `||` operators is evaluated only until truth or falsity is known. Thus, evaluation of the expression

```
gender == FEMALE && age >= 65
```

stops immediately if `gender` is not equal to `FEMALE` (i.e., if one condition is `false`, then the entire expression is `false`) and continues if `gender` is equal to `FEMALE` (i.e., the entire expression could still be `true` if the condition `age >= 65` is `true`). This performance feature for the evaluation of logical AND and logical OR expressions is called *short-circuit evaluation.*

Performance Tip 5.3

In expressions using operator `&&`, if the separate conditions are independent of one another, make the condition most likely to be false the leftmost condition. In expressions using operator `||`, make the condition most likely to be true the leftmost condition. This use of short-circuit evaluation can reduce a program's execution time.

Short-circuit evaluation is useful in cases where one condition could cause an error in the program. For example, the expression

```
grades > 0 && ( total / grades > 60 )
```

stops immediately if `grades` is not greater than `0`; otherwise the expression evaluates the second condition. Notice that if we omit the first condition (`grades > 0`), and `grades` is `0`, the second condition (`total / grades > 60`) will attempt to divide `total` by `0`. This will result in a program error called an *exception*, which could cause the program to terminate. We discuss exceptions in detail in Chapter 11, Exception Handling.

MC++ provides the `!` (logical negation) operator to enable a programmer to "reverse" the meaning of a condition. Unlike the operators `&&` and `|`, which combine two conditions (binary operators), the logical negation operator has only a single condition as an operand (unary operator). The logical negation operator is placed before a condition to choose a path of execution if the original condition (without the logical negation operator) is false. This is demonstrated by the following program segment:

```
if ( !( grade == sentinelValue ) )
   Console::WriteLine( S"grade is {0}" + grade.ToString() );
```

The parentheses around the condition `grade == sentinelValue` are needed because the logical negation operator has a higher precedence than the equality operator. Figure 5.16 is a truth table for the logical negation operator.

expression	!expression
`false`	`true`
`true`	`false`

Fig. 5.16 Truth table for operator `!` (logical negation).

In most cases, the programmer can avoid using logical negation by expressing the condition differently with relational or equality operators. For example, the preceding statement may also be written as follows:

```
if ( grade != sentinelValue )
   Console::WriteLine( S"grade is {0}" + grade.ToString() );
```

This flexibility can help a programmer express a condition more naturally.

The application in Fig. 5.17 demonstrates the logical operators by displaying their truth tables in the console window.

```
// Fig. 5.17: LogicalOperators.cpp
// Demonstrating the logical operators.

#include "stdafx.h"

#using <mscorlib.dll>

using namespace System;

```

Fig. 5.17 Logical operators. (Part 1 of 2.)

```
10 int _tmain()
11 {
12    // testing the logical AND operator (&&)
13    Console::WriteLine( String::Concat(
14       S"Logical AND (&&)",
15       S"\nfalse && false: ", ( false && false ).ToString(),
16       S"\nfalse && true:  ", ( false && true ).ToString(),
17       S"\ntrue && false:  ", ( true && false ).ToString(),
18       S"\ntrue && true:   ", ( true && true ).ToString() ) );
19
20    // testing the logical OR operator (||)
21    Console::WriteLine( String::Concat(
22       S"\n\Logical OR (||)",
23       S"\nfalse || false: ", ( false || false ).ToString(),
24       S"\nfalse || true:  ", ( false || true ).ToString(),
25       S"\ntrue || false:  ", ( true || false ).ToString(),
26       S"\ntrue || true:   ", ( true || true ).ToString() ) );
27
28    // testing the logical NOT operator (!)
29    Console::WriteLine( String::Concat(
30       S"\n\nLogical NOT (!)",
31       S"\n!false: ", ( !false ).ToString(),
32       S"\n!true: ", ( !true ).ToString() ) );
33
34    return 0;
35 } // end _tmain
```

```
Logical AND (&&)
false && false: False
false && true:  False
true && false:  False
true && true:   True


Logical OR (||)
false || false: False
false || true:  True
true || false:  True
true || true:   True


Logical NOT (!)
!false: True
!true:  False
```

Fig. 5.17 Logical operators. (Part 2 of 2.)

Lines 13–18 demonstrate the && operator, lines 21–26 demonstrate the || operator and lines 29–32 demonstrate the ! operator. This application outputs the string representations of the expressions using method `ToString`.

Figure 5.18 shows the precedence and associativity of the MC++ operators that have been introduced thus far. The operators are shown from top to bottom in decreasing order of precedence.

Operators	Associativity	Type
`::`	left to right	scope resolution
`++ --`	left to right	unary postfix
static_cast< *type* >	left to right	unary cast
`++ -- + - !`	right to left	unary prefix
`* / %`	left to right	multiplicative
`+ -`	left to right	additive
`< <= > >=`	left to right	relational
`== !=`	left to right	equality
&&	left to right	logical AND
||	left to right	logical OR
`?:`	right to left	conditional
`= += -= *= /= %=`	right to left	assignment

Fig. 5.18 Precedence and associativity of the operators discussed so far.

5.9 Structured-Programming Summary

Just as architects design buildings by employing the collective wisdom of their profession, so should programmers design programs. Our field is younger than architecture is, and our collective wisdom is considerably sparser. We have learned that structured programming produces programs that are easier to understand, test, debug, modify and prove correct in a mathematical sense than unstructured programs.

Figure 5.19 summarizes MC++'s control statements. Small circles in the figure indicate the single entry point and the single exit point of each control statement. Connecting individual flowchart symbols arbitrarily can lead to unstructured programs. Therefore, the programming profession has chosen to combine flowchart symbols to form only a limited set of control statements and to build structured programs by combining control statements in only two simple ways.

For simplicity, only single-entry/single-exit control statements are used—there is only one way to enter and only one way to exit each control statement. To connect control statements in sequence to form structured programs, the exit point of one control statement is connected to the entry point of the next control statement (i.e., the control statements are simply placed one after another in a program). We call this process "control-structure stacking." The rules for forming structured programs also allow control structures to be nested. Figure 5.20 contains the rules for forming properly structured programs. The rules assume that you start with the simplest flowchart (Figure 5.21) and that the rectangle flowchart symbol can indicate any action, including input/output.

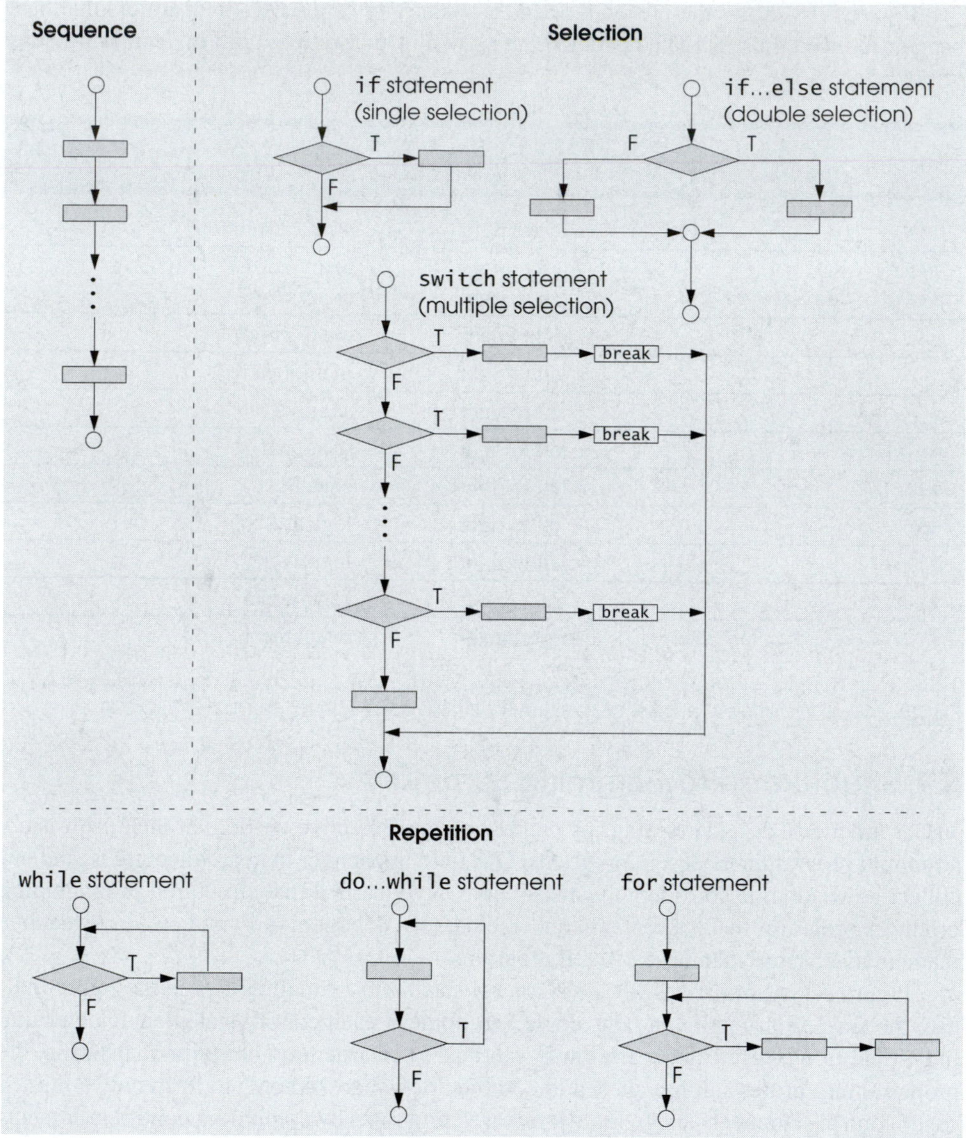

Fig. 5.19 Visual C++ .NET's single-entry/single-exit sequence, selection and repetition statements.

Rules for Forming Structured Programs	
1)	Begin with the "simplest flowchart" (Fig. 5.21).
2)	Any rectangle (action) can be replaced by two rectangles (actions) in sequence.

Fig. 5.20 Rules for forming structured programs. (Part 1 of 2.)

Rules for Forming Structured Programs

3) Any rectangle (action) can be replaced by any control statement (sequence, `if`, `if...else`, `switch`, `while`, `do...while` or `for`.
4) Rules 2 and 3 may be applied as often as you like and in any order.

Fig. 5.20 Rules for forming structured programs. (Part 2 of 2.)

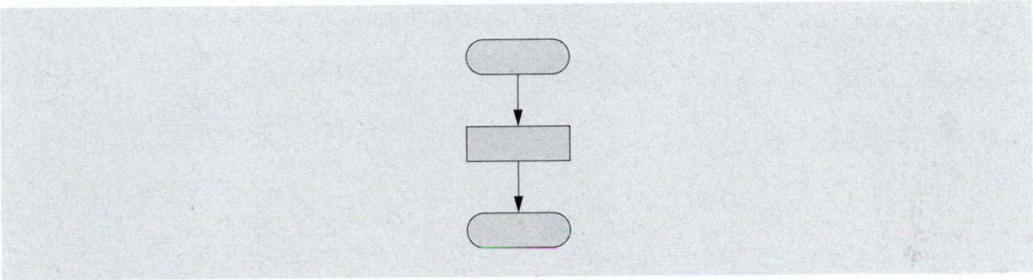

Fig. 5.21 Simplest flowchart.

Applying the rules of Fig. 5.20 always results in a structured flowchart with a neat, building-block appearance. For example, repeatedly applying rule 2 to the simplest flowchart results in a structured flowchart that contains many rectangles in sequence (Fig. 5.22). Notice that rule 2 generates a stack of control statements; therefore, we call rule 2 the *stacking rule*.

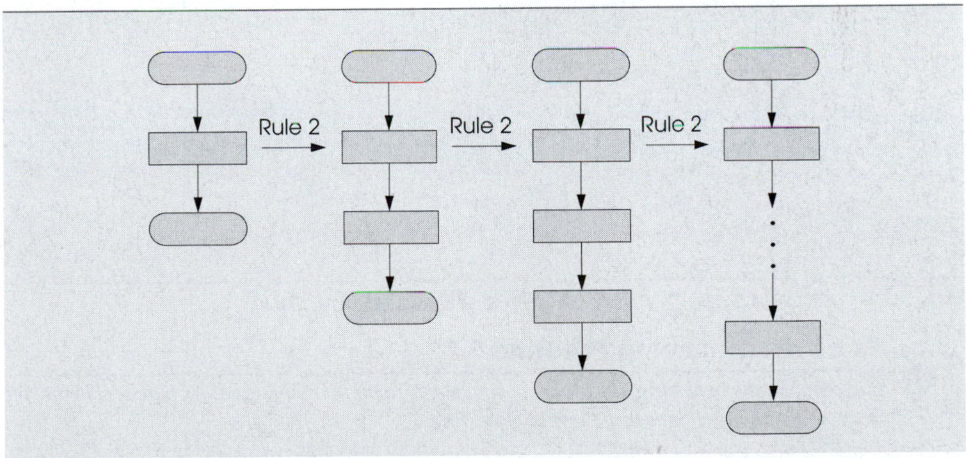

Fig. 5.22 Repeatedly applying rule 2 of Fig. 5.20 to the simplest flowchart.

Rule 3 is the *nesting rule*. Repeatedly applying rule 3 to the simplest flowchart results in a flowchart with neatly nested control statements. For example, in Fig. 5.23, the rectangle in the simplest flowchart first is replaced with a double-selection (`if...else`) statement. Then rule 3 is applied again to both rectangles in the double-selection statement, replacing each of the rectangles with a double-selection statement. The dashed boxes around each of the double-selection statements represent the rectangles that were replaced with these control statements.

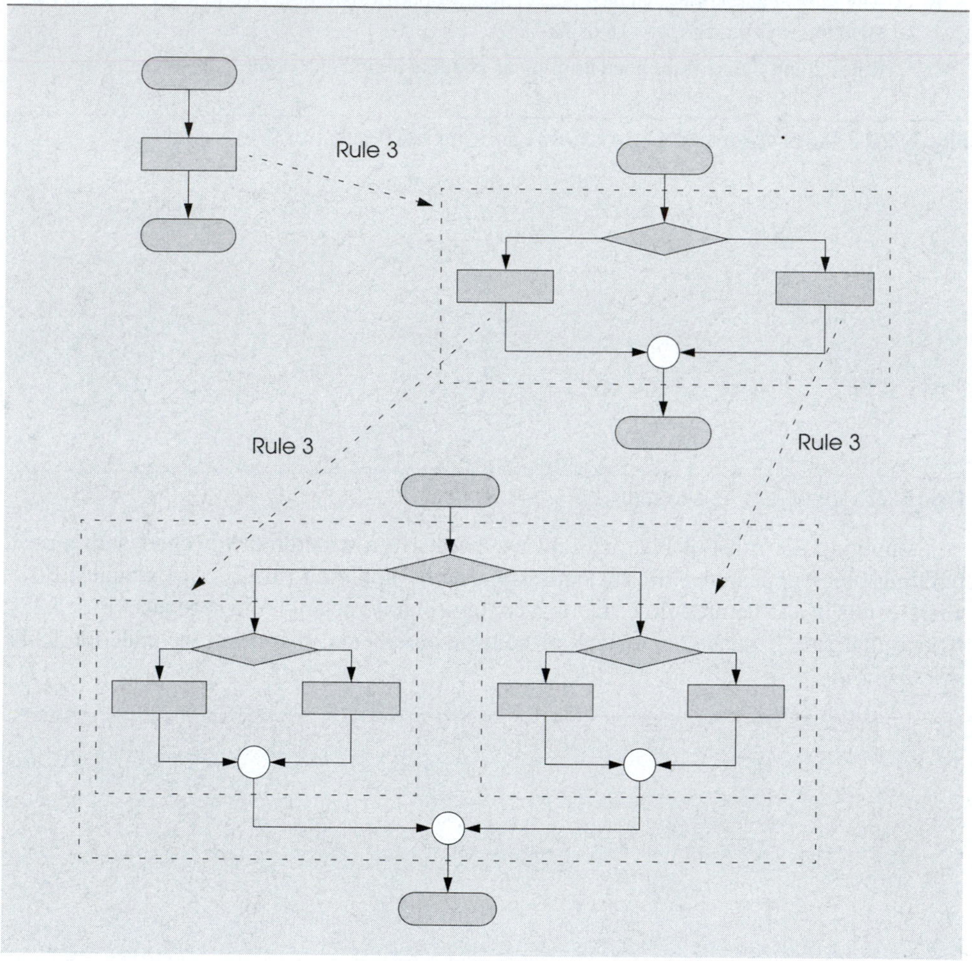

Fig. 5.23 Applying rule 3 of Fig. 5.20 to the simplest flowchart.

Good Programming Practice 5.12

Too many levels of nesting can make a program difficult to understand. As a general rule, try to avoid using more than three levels of nesting.

Rule 4 generates larger, more involved and deeply-nested statements. The flowcharts that emerge from applying the rules in Fig. 5.20 constitute the set of all possible structured flowcharts and the set of all possible structured programs. The structured approach has the advantage of using only eight simple single-entry/single-exit pieces and allowing us to assemble them in only two simple ways. Figure 5.24 shows the kinds of correctly stacked building blocks that emerge from applying rule 2 and the kinds of correctly nested building blocks that emerge from applying rule 3. The figure also shows the kind of overlapped building blocks that cannot occur in structured flowcharts (as a result of avoiding `goto` statements).

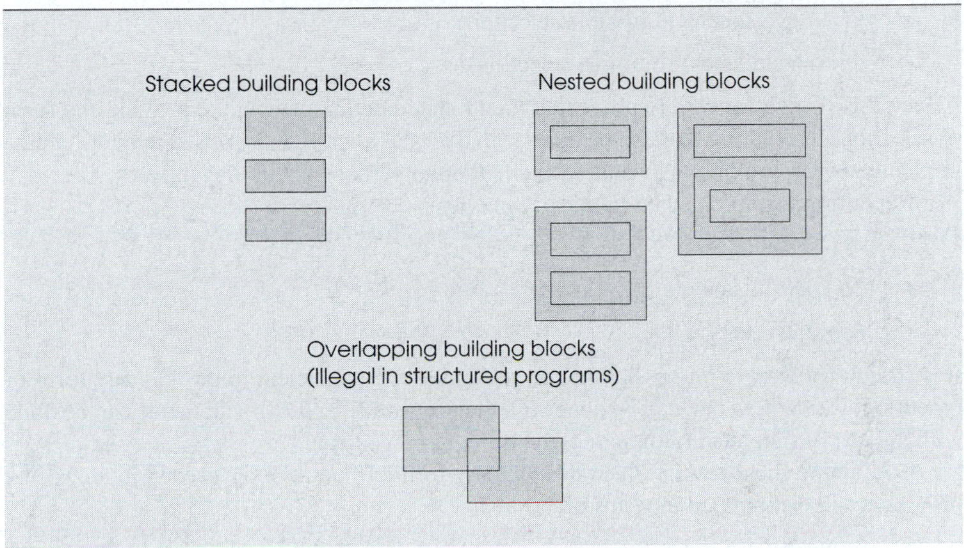

Fig. 5.24 Stacked, nested and overlapped building blocks.

If the rules in Fig. 5.20 are followed, an unstructured flowchart (such as that in Fig. 5.25) cannot be created. If you are uncertain about whether a particular flowchart is structured, apply the rules in Fig. 5.20 in reverse to try to reduce the flowchart to the simplest flowchart. If the flowchart can be reduced to the simplest flowchart, the original flowchart is structured; otherwise, it is not.

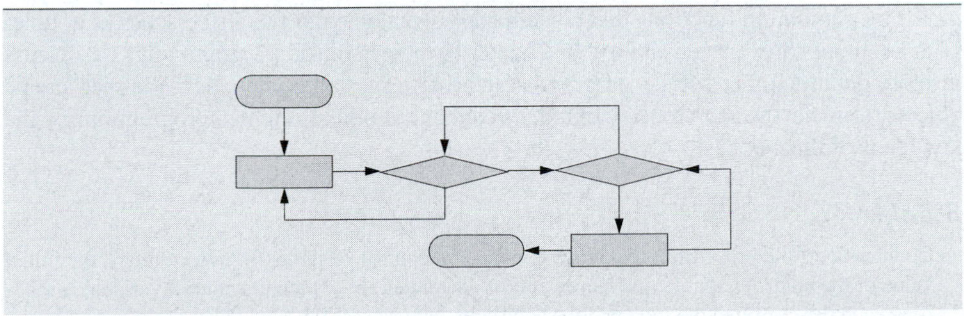

Fig. 5.25 Unstructured flowchart.

In summary, structured programming promotes simplicity. Bohm and Jacopini have found that only three forms of control are necessary:

- Sequence
- Selection
- Repetition

Sequence is trivial. Selection is implemented in one of three ways:

- `if` statement (single selection)
- `if...else` statement (double selection)
- `switch` statement (multiple selection)

In fact, it is straightforward to prove that the `if` statement is sufficient to provide any form of selection. Everything that can be done with the `if...else` and `switch` statements can be implemented by combining `if` statements (although perhaps not as elegantly).

Repetition is implemented in one of three ways:

- `while` statement
- `do...while` statement
- `for` statement

It is straightforward to prove that the `while` statement is sufficient to provide any form of repetition. Everything that can be done with the `do...while` and `for` statements can be done with the `while` statement (although perhaps not as elegantly).

Combining these results illustrates that any form of control ever needed in an MC++ program can be expressed in terms of:

- sequence
- `if` statement (selection)
- `while` statement (repetition)

These control statements can be combined in only two ways—stacking and nesting. Indeed, structured programming promotes simplicity.

In this chapter and the previous chapter, we discussed how to compose programs from control statements that contain actions and decisions. In Chapter 6, Functions, we introduce another program-structuring unit, called the *function*. We will learn to compose large programs by combining functions that contain control statements. We also discuss how functions promote software reusability. In Chapter 8, Object-Based Programming, we discuss in more detail another MC++ program-structuring unit, called the *class*. We then create objects from classes and proceed with our treatment of object-oriented programming—the key focus of this book.

SUMMARY

- Counter-controlled repetition requires the name of a control variable (or loop counter), the initial value of the control variable, the increment (or decrement) by which the control variable is modified each time through the loop and the condition that tests for the final value of the control variable (i.e., whether looping should continue).
- Declarations that include initialization are executable statements.
- Floating-point values may be approximate, so controlling counting loops with floating-point variables may result in imprecise counter values and inaccurate tests for termination.
- Using an incorrect relational operator or an incorrect final value of a loop counter in the condition of a `while`, `for` or `do...while` statement can cause an off-by-one error.
- A `for` statement is an example of a counter-controlled repetition statement. The general format of the `for` statement is

```
for ( expression1; expression2; expression3 )
    statement
```

where *expression1* names the loop's control variable and provides its initial value, *expression2* is the loop-continuation condition (containing the control variable's final value) and *expression3* increments the control variable.

- If there is more than one statement in the body of the `for`, the statements must appear in a block.
- The three expressions in the `for` statement are optional. The two semicolons in the `for` statement are required.
- If the loop-continuation condition is initially false, the body of the `for` statement does not execute.
- Changing the value of the control variable in the body of a `for` loop can lead to subtle errors.
- In most cases, the `for` statement can be represented with an equivalent `while` statement with *expression1*, *expression2* and *expression3* placed as follows:

```
expression1;

while ( expression2 ) {
    statement
    expression3;
}
```

- The scope of a variable specifies where the variable can be used in a program.
- Unlike standard C++, the `for` statement's control variable (when declared in the `for` statement's header) can be used outside of the `for` statement.
- Do not use variables of type `float` or `double` to perform precise monetary calculations. The imprecision of floating-point numbers can cause errors that will result in incorrect monetary values. Type `Decimal` is available for performing monetary calculations properly.
- The `switch` statement consists of a series of `case` labels and an optional `default` case.
- When the flow of control reaches the `switch` statement, the program evaluates the controlling expression in the parentheses following keyword `switch`. The value of this expression is compared with each `case` label until a match occurs.
- If no match occurs between the controlling expression's value and a `case` label, the `default` case executes. Note that the `default` case is optional in the `switch` statement. If the controlling expression does not match a `case` and there is no `default` case, program control proceeds to the next statement after the `switch` statement.
- Each `case` can contain multiple actions or no actions at all. A `case` with no statements is considered an empty `case`. The last `case` in a `switch` statement must not be an empty `case` or a syntax error occurs.
- If the `case` label matches the controlling expression, and the case contains no `break` statement, fall through occurs. This means that the `switch` statement executes the statements in the matching case as well as those in the next case. If that `case` also contains no `break` statement, this process will continue until a `break` statement is found, or the statements for the last case are executed. This provides the programmer with a way to specify that statements are executed for several `cases`.
- Not including a break statement at the end of each case in a switch statement can lead to logic errors. Only omit break statements from cases that should result in fall through.
- When using the `switch` statement, remember that the expression after each `case` must be a constant integral expression (i.e., any combination of character and integer constants that evaluates to a constant integer value).

- The do...while statement tests the loop-continuation condition after the loop body executes; therefore, the loop body always executes at least once.
- The break statement, when executed in a while, for, do...while or switch statement, causes immediate exit from that control statement. Execution continues with the first statement after the control statement.
- The continue statement, when executed in a while, for or do...while statement, skips the remaining statements in the body of that control statement and proceeds with the next iteration of the loop.
- MC++ uses logical operators to form complex conditions by combining simple ones.
- The logical operators are && (logical AND), || (logical OR) and ! (logical NOT, also called logical negation).
- The logical && operator ensures that two conditions are both true before we choose a certain path of execution.
- The logical || operator ensures that at least one of two conditions is true before we choose a certain path of execution.
- The ! (logical negation) operator "reverses" the meaning of a condition.
- Flowcharts graphically represent the flow of program control.
- In flowcharts, small circles indicate the single entry point and exit point of each control statement.
- Connecting individual flowchart symbols arbitrarily can lead to unstructured programs. Therefore, the programming profession has chosen to combine flowchart symbols to form a limited set of control statements and to build structured programs by properly combining control statements in two simple ways—stacking and nesting.
- Structured programming, which includes the repetition statements and conditional operators covered in this chapter, promotes simplicity.
- Bohm and Jacopini have given us the result that only three forms of control are needed—sequence, selection and repetition.
- Selection is implemented with one of three control statements—if, if...else and switch.
- Repetition is implemented with one of three control statements—while, do...while and for.
- The if statement is sufficient to provide any form of selection.
- The while statement is sufficient to provide any form of repetition.

TERMINOLOGY

! logical NOT
&& logical AND
|| logical OR
binary operator
body of a loop
bool values
braces ({ and })
break statement
case
constant integral expression
continue statement
control variable
controlling expression
control-structure nesting
control-structure stacking
counter variable
counter-controlled repetition
Decimal
decrement expression
default statement
do...while statement
double-selection statement
empty case
entry point of a control statement
fall through
for statement
for statement header
formatting code

`goto` statement
`if` statement
`if...else` statement
increment expression
initialization section of a `for` statement
labels in a `switch` statement
levels of nesting
logical AND operator (&&)
logical negation or logical NOT operator (`!`)
logical OR operator (`||`)
loop body
loop counter
loop-continuation condition
`Math` class
multiple-selection statement
nested building block
nested control statement
nesting rule
off-by-one error
one-based counting
optimization
`Pow` method of class `Math`
rectangle symbol
scope of a variable
short-circuit evaluation
simple condition
simplest flowchart
single-entry/single-exit control statement
stacking
stacking rule
`String` formatting codes
structured programming
`switch` statement
truth table
unary operator
zero-based counting

SELF-REVIEW EXERCISES

5.1 State whether each of the following is *true* or *false*. If *false*, explain why.

a) The `default` case is required in the `switch` selection statement.
b) If there is more than one statement in the body of the `for`, braces (`{` and `}`) are needed to define the body of the loop.
c) The expression `( x > y && a < b )` is true if either `x > y` is true or `a < b` is true.
d) An expression containing the `||` operator is true if either or both of its operands is true.
e) The expression `( x <= y && y > 4 )` is true if `x` is less than or equal to `y` or `y` is greater than 4.
f) A `for` loop requires two commas in its header.
g) Infinite loops are caused when the loop-termination condition is always `true`.
h) The following syntax continues iterating the loop while $10 < x < 100$:

```
while ( x > 10 && x < 100 )
```

i) The `break` statement, when executed in a repetition statement, causes immediate exit from the repetition statement.
j) The `||` operator has a higher precedence than the && operator.

5.2 Fill in the blanks in each of the following statements:

a) Specifying the order in which statements are to be executed in a computer program is called ________.
b) Placing a semicolon after a `for` statement typically results in a(n) ________ error.
c) A `for` loop should count with ________ values.
d) Using the < relational operator instead of <= in a `while`-repetition condition that should loop 10 times (as shown below) causes a(n) ________ error:

```
int x = 1;
while ( x < 10 ) ...
```

e) The ________ of a variable defines where the variable can be used in a program.
f) In a `for` loop, incrementing occurs ________ the body of the statement is performed each time.

g) Multiple initializations in the `for` statement header should be separated by _________.
h) The _________ format code formats a number using scientific notation.
i) The value in parentheses immediately following the keyword `switch` is called the _________.

5.3 Write a statement or a set of statements to accomplish each of the following tasks:
a) Sum the odd integers between 1 and 99, using a `for` statement. Assume that the integer variables `sum` and `count` have been declared, but are uninitialized.
b) Calculate the value of `2.5` raised to the power of 3, using the `Math::Pow` method.
c) Print the integers from 1 to 20, using a `while` loop and the counter variable `x`. Assume that the variable `x` has been declared, but not initialized. Print only five integers per line. [*Hint*: Use the calculation `x % 5`. When the value of this is 0, print a newline character; otherwise, print a tab character. Use the `Console::WriteLine()` method to output the newline character, and use the `Console::Write( '\t' )` method to output the tab character.]
d) Repeat part c, using a `for` statement.

ANSWERS TO SELF-REVIEW EXERCISES

5.1 a) False. The `default` case is optional. If no default action is required, then there is no need for a `default` case. b) True. c) False. Both of the relational expressions must be true for the entire expression to be true. d) True. e) False. The expression `( x <= y && y > 4 )` is true if `x` is less than or equal to `y` and `y` is greater than 4. f) False. A `for` loop requires two semicolons in its header. g) False. Infinite loops are caused when the loop-continuation condition is always `false`. h) True. i) True. j) False. The && operator has higher precedence than the `||` operator.

5.2 a) program control. b) logic. c) integer. d) off-by-one. e) scope. f) after. g) commas. h) E or e. i) controlling expression.

5.3 a)
```
sum = 0;
for ( count = 1; count <= 99; count += 2 )
      sum += count;
```
b)
```
Math::Pow( 2.5, 3 )
```
c)
```
x = 1;

while ( x <= 20 ) {
   Console::Write( x );

   if ( x % 5 == 0 )
      Console::WriteLine();
   else
      Console::Write( S"\t" );

   ++x;
}
```
d)
```
for ( x = 1; x <= 20; x++ ) {
   Console::Write( x );

   if ( x % 5 == 0 )
      Console::WriteLine();
   else
      Console::Write( S"\t" );
}
```

or

```
for ( x = 1; x <= 20; x++ )

   if ( x % 5 == 0 )
      Console::WriteLine( x );
   else
      Console::Write( S"{0}\t", x.ToString() );
```

EXERCISES

5.4 *Factorials* are used frequently in probability problems. The factorial of a positive integer *n* (written *n!* and pronounced "n factorial") is equal to the product of the positive integers from 1 to *n*. Write a program that evaluates the factorials of the integers from 1 to 20 with different integer data types. Display the results in a three-column output table. [*Hint*: create a console application, using two sets of loops to line up the columns correctly.] The first column should display the *n* values (1-20). The second column should display *n!*, calculated with `int` (`Int32`, a 32-bit integer value). The third column should display *n!*, calculated with `__int64` (`Int64`, a 64-bit integer value). What happens when `int` (`Int32`) is too small in size to hold the result of a factorial calculation?

5.5 Write two programs that each print a table of the binary, octal, and hexadecimal equivalents of the decimal numbers in the range 1–256. If you are not familiar with these number systems, read Appendix B, Number Systems, first.

a) For the first program, print the results to the console without using any `String` formats.
b) For the second program, print the results to the console using both the decimal and hexadecimal `String` formats (there are no formats for binary and octal in MC++).

5.6 (*Pythagorean Triples*) A right triangle can have sides that are all integers. A set of three integer values for the sides of a right triangle is called a Pythagorean triple. These three sides must satisfy the relationship that the sum of the squares of the two sides is equal to the square of the hypotenuse. Write a program to find all Pythagorean triples for `side1`, `side2` and `hypotenuse`, none larger than 30. Use a triple-nested `for` loop that tries all possibilities. This is an example of "brute force" computing. You will learn in more advanced computer science courses that there are several problems for which there is no other known algorithmic approach.

5.7 Write a program that displays the following patterns separately, one below the other. Use `for` loops to generate the patterns. All asterisks (*) should be printed by a single statement of the form `Console::Write( S"*" );` (this causes the asterisks to print side by side). A statement of the form `Console::WriteLine();` can be used to position to the next line. A statement of the form `Console::Write( " " );` can be used to display spaces for the last two patterns. There should be no other output statements in the program. [*Hint*: The last two patterns require that each line begin with an appropriate number of blanks.]

```
(A)             (B)             (C)             (D)

*               **********      **********               *
**              *********        *********              **
***             ********          ********             ***
****            *******            *******            ****
*****           ******              ******           *****
******          *****                *****          ******
*******         ****                  ****         *******
********        ***                    ***        ********
*********       **                      **       *********
**********      *                        *      **********
```

5.8 Modify Exercise 5.7 to combine your code from the four separate triangles of asterisks into a single program that prints all four patterns side by side, making clever use of nested `for` loops.

5.9 Write a program that prints the following diamond shape. You may use output statements that print a single asterisk (*), a single space or a single newline character. Maximize your use of repetition (with nested `for` statements) and minimize the number of output statements.

```
    *
   ***
  *****
 *******
*********
 *******
  *****
   ***
    *
```

5.10 Modify the program you wrote in Exercise 5.9 to read an odd number in the range from 1 to 19 to specify the number of rows in the diamond. Your program should then display a diamond of the appropriate size.

int Pal

Write "Please enter a 5 digit #
or -1 to exit"

Readline

While Pal != -1

if Pal[0] ==Pal[4] ;

if Pal[1] == P[3]

Write __________________

else

Write __________________

6

Functions

Objectives

- To construct programs modularly from small pieces called functions.
- To become familiar with the common math methods available in the Framework Class Library.
- To create functions.
- To understand the mechanisms for passing data between functions.
- To introduce simulation techniques that use random number generation.
- To understand how the visibility of identifiers is limited to specific regions of programs.
- To understand how to write and use functions that call themselves.

Form ever follows function.
Louis Henri Sullivan

E pluribus unum.
(One composed of many.)
Virgil

O! call back yesterday, bid time return.
William Shakespeare

Call me Ishmael.
Herman Melville

When you call me that, smile.
Owen Wister

Outline

6.1 Introduction

Most computer programs that solve real-world problems are much larger than the programs presented in the first few chapters of this text. Experience has shown that the best way to develop and maintain a large program is to construct it from small, simple pieces, or *modules*. This technique is known as *divide and conquer*. This chapter describes many key features of MC++ that facilitate the design, implementation, operation and maintenance of large programs.

6.2 Functions and Methods in Managed Extensions for C++

There are three kinds of modules in MC++—*functions*, *methods* and *classes*. MC++ programs are written by combining new functions, methods and classes that the programmer writes with "prepackaged" methods and classes available in the *.NET Framework Class Library* (*FCL*). In this chapter, we concentrate on functions and methods. We discuss classes in detail in Chapter 8, Object-Based Programming.

A *method* is a function that is a member of a class. The FCL provides a rich collection of classes and methods for performing common mathematical calculations, string manipulations, character manipulations, input/output operations, error checking and many other useful operations. This set of preexisting code makes the programmer's job easier by providing many capabilities that programmers need. The FCL methods are part of the .NET Framework, which includes the FCL classes `Console` and `String` used in earlier examples.

Software Engineering Observation 6.1

Familiarize yourself with the rich collection of classes and methods in the FCL (`msdn.microsoft.com/library/en-us/cpref/html/cpref_start.asp`).

Software Engineering Observation 6.2

When possible, use .NET Framework classes and methods instead of writing new classes and methods. This practice reduces both program development time and errors.

Programmers can write functions to define specific tasks that may be used at many points in a program. Such functions are known as *programmer-defined* (or *user-defined*) *functions.* The actual statements defining the function are written only once (but can be used many times) and are hidden from other functions.

A function is *invoked* (i.e., made to perform its designated task) by a *function call.* The function call specifies the name of the function and may provide information (as *arguments*) that the called function requires to perform its task. When the function call completes, the function either returns a result to the *calling function* (or *caller*) or simply returns control to the calling function. A common analogy for this is the hierarchical form of management. A boss (the caller) asks a worker (the *called function*) to perform a task and report back (i.e., *return*) the results after completing the task. The boss function does not know *how* the worker function performs its designated tasks. The worker may also call other worker functions, unbeknownst to the boss. This "hiding" of implementation details promotes good software engineering. Figure 6.1 shows the `boss` function communicating with several worker functions in a hierarchical manner. The `boss` function divides the responsibilities among the various `worker` functions. Note that `worker1` acts as a "boss function" to `worker4` and `worker5`. Relationships among functions may also be different from the hierarchical structure shown in this figure.

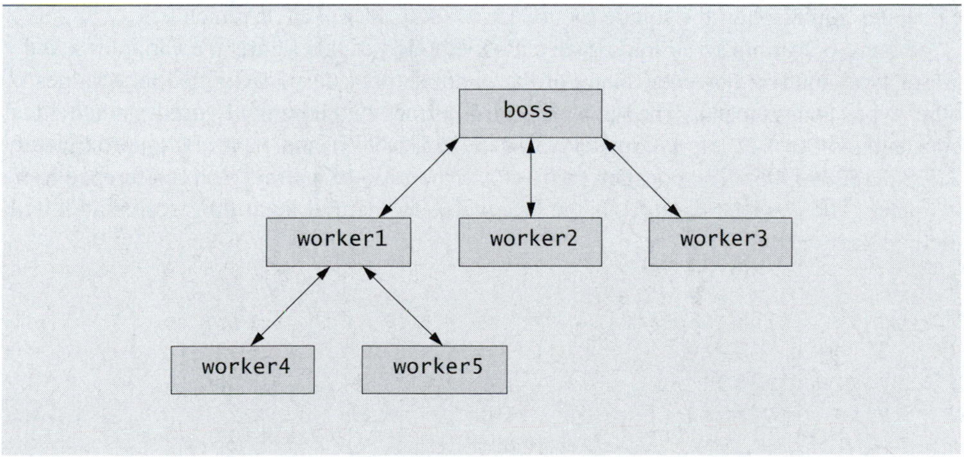

Fig. 6.1 Hierarchical boss function/worker function relationship.

6.3 Math Class Methods

Class `Math` provides a collection of methods that enable you to perform certain common mathematical calculations. We use various `Math` class methods to introduce the concept of functions in general. Throughout the book, we discuss many other methods from the classes of the Framework Class Library.

Methods (and functions) are called by writing the name of the method (or function), followed by a left parenthesis, the *argument* (or a comma-separated list of arguments) of the method (or function) and a right parenthesis. The parentheses may be empty, if we are calling a method (or function) that needs no information to perform its task. For example, a programmer wishing to calculate and print the square root of `900.0` might write

```
Console::WriteLine( Math::Sqrt( 900.0 ) );
```

When this statement executes, the method `Sqrt` of class `Math` calculates the square root of the number in parentheses (`900.0`). The number `900.0` is the argument to method `Math::Sqrt`. Method `Math::Sqrt` takes an argument of type `double` and returns a result of type `double`. The preceding statement uses the result of method `Math::Sqrt` as the argument to method `Console::WriteLine` and displays `30`. Note that all `Math` class methods must be invoked by preceding the method name with the class name `Math` and the scope resolution operator (`::`). This is because the methods of class `Math` are *`static` methods*. We discuss `static` methods in Chapter 8, Object-Based Programming.

Common Programming Error 6.1

Forgetting to invoke a `Math` class method by preceding the method name with the class name `Math` and a scope resolution (`::`) operator results in a compilation error.

Method arguments may be constants, variables or expressions. If `c = 13.0`, `d = 3.0` and `f = 4.0`, then the statement

```
Console::WriteLine( Math::Sqrt( c + d * f ) );
```

calculates and displays the square root of `13.0 + 3.0 * 4.0 = 25.0`, which is `5`.

Figure 6.2 summarizes some `Math` class methods.[1] In this figure, the variables `x` and `y` are of type `double`; however, many of the methods provide versions that take values of other types as arguments. The `Math` class also defines two commonly used mathematical constants—`Math::PI` (approximately 3.14159265358979) and `Math::E` (approximately 2.71828182845905). The constant `Math::PI` is the ratio of a circle's circumference to its diameter. The constant `Math::E` is the base value for natural logarithms (calculated with method `Math::Log`).

1. A complete list of the methods provided by class `Math` can be found at `msdn.microsoft.com/library/en-us/cpref/html/frlrfSystemMathMethodsTopic.asp`.

Method	Description	Example

`Abs( x )`	absolute value of *x*	`Abs( 23.7 )` is `23.7`
		`Abs( 0 )` is `0`
		`Abs( -23.7 )` is `23.7`

`Ceiling( x )`	rounds *x* to the smallest integer not less than *x*	`Ceiling( 9.2 )` is `10.0` `Ceiling( -9.8 )` is `-9.0`
`Cos( x )`	trigonometric cosine of *x* (*x* in radians)	`Cos( 0.0 )` is `1.0`
`Exp( x )`	exponential method e^x	`Exp( 1.0 )` is approximately `2.7182818284590451` `Exp( 2.0 )` is approximately `7.3890560989306504`
`Floor( x )`	rounds *x* to the largest integer not greater than *x*	`Floor( 9.2 )` is `9.0` `Floor( -9.8 )` is `-10.0`
`Log( x )`	natural logarithm of *x* (base *e*)	`Log( 2.71828182845905 )` is approximately `1.0` `Log( 7.38905609893065 )` is approximately `2.0`
`Max( x, y )`	larger value of *x* and *y* (also has versions for `float`, `int` and `long` values)	`Max( 2.3, 12.7 )` is `12.7` `Max( -2.3, -12.7 )` is `-2.3`
`Min( x, y )`	smaller value of *x* and *y* (also has versions for `float`, `int` and `long` values)	`Min( 2.3, 12.7 )` is `2.3` `Min( -2.3, -12.7 )` is `-12.7`
`Pow( x, y )`	*x* raised to power *y* (x^y)	`Pow( 2.0, 7.0 )` is `128.0` `Pow( 9.0, .5 )` is `3.0`
`Sin( x )`	trigonometric sine of *x* (*x* in radians)	`Sin( 0.0 )` is `0.0`
`Sqrt( x )`	square root of *x*	`Sqrt( 900.0 )` is `30.0` `Sqrt( 9.0 )` is `3.0`
`Tan( x )`	trigonometric tangent of *x* (*x* in radians)	`Tan( 0.0 )` is `0.0`

Fig. 6.2 Commonly used `Math` class methods.

6.4 Functions

Functions allow programmers to modularize programs. Variables declared in function definitions are *local variables*—only the function that defines them knows they exist. Most functions have a list of *parameters* that enable function calls to communicate information between functions. A function's parameters are also variables local to that function and are not visible in any other functions. Local variables are discussed in more detail in Section 6.15.

There are several motivations for modularizing a program with functions. The divide-and-conquer approach makes program development more manageable. Another motivation is *software reusability*—using existing functions as building blocks to create new programs. With proper function naming and definition, we can create programs from standardized functions, rather than building customized code. For example, we did not have to define how to convert `Strings` to integers—the .NET Framework Class Library already defines such a method for us (`Int32::Parse`). A third motivation is to avoid repeating code in a program. Packaging code as a function allows that code to be executed from several locations in a program—we simply have to call that function.

Good Programming Practice 6.1

Make good use of modularity to increase the clarity and organization of your program. This will not only help others understand your program, but it will also aid in program development, testing and debugging.

Software Engineering Observation 6.3

To promote reusability, each function should perform a single, well-defined task, and the name of the function should express that task effectively.

Software Engineering Observation 6.4

If you cannot choose a concise name that expresses what the function does, it is possible that your function is attempting to perform too many diverse tasks. Usually it is best to break such a function into several smaller functions.

6.5 Function Definitions

The programs presented up to this point each contained a function called `_tmain`. This function has called FCL methods to accomplish the program's tasks. We now consider how to write programmer-defined functions.

Consider a program that calculates the square of the integers from 1 to 10 (Fig. 6.3). The program invokes programmer-defined function `Square` in line 16. The parentheses, `()`, after `Square` represent the *function-call operator*. When the function call is evaluated, the program makes a copy of the value of `counter` (the argument to the function call), and program control transfers to function `Square` (defined in lines 22–25). Function `Square` receives the copy of the value of `counter` in the *parameter* `y`. Then `Square` calculates `y * y` in a ***`return`*** statement (line 24) to return (i.e., give back) the result of the calculation to the statement that invoked `Square` (located in line 16). Lines 15–16 display `"The square of"`, the value of `counter`, `" is "`, the value returned by the function call and a newline character to the console output. The `for` loop repeats this process 10 times. In line 16, note that the call to `Square` is immediately followed by `.ToString()`. This converts the value returned from `Square` to a `String *` for output purposes.

```
1  // Fig. 6.3: SquareInt.cpp
2  // Demonstrates a programmer-defined square function.
3
4  #include "stdafx.h"
5
6  #using <mscorlib.dll>
7
8  using namespace System;
```

Fig. 6.3 Using programmer-defined function `Square`. (Part 1 of 2.)

```
9
10  int Square( int );    // function prototype
11
12  int _tmain()
13  {
14     for ( int counter = 1; counter <= 10; counter++ )
15        Console::WriteLine( S"The square of {0} is {1}",
16           counter.ToString(), Square( counter ).ToString() );
17
18     return 0;
19  } // end _tmain
20
21  // function definition
22  int Square( int y )
23  {
24     return y * y;  // return square of y
25  } // end function Square
```

```
The square of 1 is 1
The square of 2 is 4
The square of 3 is 9
The square of 4 is 16
The square of 5 is 25
The square of 6 is 36
The square of 7 is 49
The square of 8 is 64
The square of 9 is 81
The square of 10 is 100
```

Fig. 6.3 Using programmer-defined function `Square`. (Part 2 of 2.)

The definition of `Square` (lines 22–25) shows that it uses integer parameter `y` to hold the value passed to `Square` as an argument. The parameter name provides access to the argument value, so that code in the function body can use the value. Keyword `int` preceding the function name indicates that `Square` returns an integer result. The `return` statement in `Square` (line 24) passes the result of the calculation `y * y` back to the calling statement.

Line 10 is the *function prototype* for function `Square`. The compiler uses function prototypes to validate function calls.[2] The type `int` in parentheses informs the compiler that function `Square` expects an integer value from the caller. The type `int` to the left of the function name informs the compiler that `Square` returns an integer result to the caller. The compiler refers to the function prototype[3] to check that calls to Square contain the correct number and types of arguments and that the arguments are in the correct order. In addition, the compiler uses the prototype to ensure that the type returned by the function can be used correctly in the expression that called the function. If the arguments passed to a function do not match the types specified in the function's prototype, the compiler attempts to convert

2. The compiler uses function *signatures* to distinguish different functions. We introduce this term and discuss this process in more detail in Section 6.19.
3. Function prototypes are usually placed in *header files*. We discuss header files in Chapter 8, Object-Based Programming.

the arguments to the types specified in the prototype. Section 6.19 discusses the rules for these conversions. Function prototypes are discussed in detail in Section 6.6.

Good Programming Practice 6.2

Place a blank line between function definitions to separate the functions and enhance program readability.

General Format of a Function Definition

The format of a function definition is

```
return-value-type function-name( parameter-list )
{
    declarations and statements
}
```

The first line is sometimes called the *function header*. The *function-name* is any valid identifier. The *return-value-type* is the type of the result that the function returns to its caller. The *return-value-type* `void` indicates that a function does not return a value. Functions can return at most one value.

Common Programming Error 6.2

Omitting the return-value-type *in a function definition is a syntax error. If a function does not return a value, the function's* return-value-type *must be* `void`*.*

Common Programming Error 6.3

Forgetting to return a value from a function that is supposed to return a value is a compilation error. If a return-value-type *other than* `void` *is specified, the function must contain a* `return` *statement that returns a value of type* return-value-type.

Common Programming Error 6.4

Returning a value from a function whose return type has been declared `void` *is a compilation error.*

The *parameter-list* is a comma-separated list in which the function declares each parameter's type and name. The function call must specify one argument for each parameter in the function definition and the arguments must appear in the same order as the parameters in the function definition. The arguments also must be compatible with the parameter's type. For example, a parameter of type `double` could receive values of 7.35, 22 or –.03546, but not `"hello"` because a `double` variable cannot contain a string value. If a function does not receive any values, the parameter list is empty (i.e., the function name is followed by an empty set of parentheses). Each parameter in a function's parameter list must have a type; otherwise, a syntax error occurs.

Common Programming Error 6.5

Declaring function parameters of the same type as `float x, y` *instead of* `float x, float y` *is a syntax error, because types are required for each parameter in the parameter list.*

Common Programming Error 6.6

Placing a semicolon after the right parenthesis enclosing the parameter list of a function definition is a syntax error.

Common Programming Error 6.7

Redeclaring a function parameter in the function's body is a compilation error.

Common Programming Error 6.8

Passing to a function an argument that is not compatible with the corresponding parameter's type is a compilation error.

Good Programming Practice 6.3

Choosing meaningful function names and parameter names makes programs more readable and helps avoid excessive use of comments.

Software Engineering Observation 6.5

A function requiring a large number of parameters may be performing too many tasks. Consider dividing the function into smaller functions that perform separate tasks. As a rule of thumb, the function header should fit on one line (if possible).

Software Engineering Observation 6.6

Generally, the number, type and order of arguments in a function call must exactly match those of the parameters in the corresponding function header.

The declarations and statements within braces form the *function body*. The function body is also referred to as a block. Variables can be declared in any block, and blocks can be nested.

Common Programming Error 6.9

Defining a function inside another function is a syntax error (i.e., functions cannot be nested).

There are three ways to return control to the point at which a function was invoked. If the function does not return a result (i.e., the function has a `void` return type), control returns when the program reaches the function-ending right brace or when the statement

```
return;
```

executes. If the function does return a result, the statement

`return` *expression*;

returns the value of *expression* to the caller. When a `return` statement executes, control returns immediately to the point at which the function was invoked.

Software Engineering Observation 6.7

As a rule of thumb, a function should be no longer than one page. Better yet, a function should be no longer than half a page. Regardless of how long a function is, it should perform one task well. Small functions promote software reusability.

Error-Prevention Tip 6.1

Small functions are easier to test, debug and understand than large functions.

Notice the syntax that invokes function `Square` in line 16 of Fig. 6.3—we use the function name, followed by the argument to the function in parentheses. There are four ways to call a function or a method with arguments, three of which we have already demonstrated—

by using a function name by itself (such as `Square( counter )`), by using the variable name for the object followed by the dot operator (`.`) and the function name (such as `counter.ToString()`) and by using a class name followed by the scope resolution operator and the method name (such as `Math::Sqrt( 9.0 )`. We discuss the fourth way to call a function or method in Section 6.12.

Programmer-Defined Method `Maximum`

The application in our next example (Fig. 6.4) uses programmer-defined function `Maximum` to determine and return the largest of three floating-point values input by the user.

```
// Fig. 6.4: MaximumValue.cpp
// Finding the maximum of three double values.

#include "stdafx.h"

#using <mscorlib.dll>

using namespace System;

double Maximum( double, double, double );  // function prototype

int _tmain()
{
   // get input and convert strings to doubles
   Console::Write( S"Enter first number: " );
   double number1 = Double::Parse( Console::ReadLine() );

   Console::Write( S"Enter second number: " );
   double number2 = Double::Parse( Console::ReadLine() );

   Console::Write( S"Enter third number: " );
   double number3 = Double::Parse( Console::ReadLine() );

   // invoke function Maximum to determine the largest value
   double max = Maximum( number1, number2, number3 );

   // display maximum value
   Console::WriteLine( S"Maximum is: {0}", max.ToString() );

   return 0;
} // end _tmain

// function Maximum definition
double Maximum( double x, double y, double z )
{
   return Math::Max( x, Math::Max( y, z ) );
}
```

```
Enter first number: 37.3
Enter second number: 99.32
Enter third number: 27.1928
Maximum is: 99.32
```

Fig. 6.4 Programmer-defined `Maximum` function.

Lines 16, 19 and 22 invoke `Double` method `Parse` on the user input. Line 25 then invokes our `Maximum` function, which returns the largest number. Line 25 stores the result in `double` variable `max`. Line 28 displays the result to the user.

Now let us examine the implementation of function `Maximum` (lines 34–37). The header indicates that the function returns a `double` value, that the function's name is `Maximum` and that the function takes three `double` parameters (`x`, `y` and `z`). The statement in the body of the function (line 36) returns the largest of the three floating-point values using two calls to method `Math::Max`. First, method `Math::Max` is invoked and passed the values of variables `y` and `z` to determine the larger of these two values. Next, the value of variable `x` and the result of the first call to `Math::Max` are passed to method `Math::Max`. Finally, the result of the second call to `Math::Max` is returned to the caller.

6.6 Argument Promotion

Argument promotion (or *coercion of arguments*) occurs when a function is called with an argument that does not match the type of the specified parameter. In this case, the compiler attempts to convert the argument to the specified parameter type. This process is commonly referred to as *implicit conversion*—a copy of the argument's value is converted to a different type without an explicit cast. *Explicit conversion* occurs when an explicit cast specifies that conversion is to occur. Such conversions can also be done with class `Convert` in namespace `System`. MC++ supports both widening and narrowing conversions—*widening conversion* occurs when a type is converted to a type that can store at least the same range of values, and *narrowing conversion* occurs when a type is converted to a type that can store a smaller range of values. Figure 6.5 provides size information for the various built-in types of .NET, and Fig. 6.6 shows safe widening conversions—widening conversions that do not result in the loss of data. Note that the types shown in Fig. 6.5–Fig. 6.6 are those provided by the .NET Framework.[4] Their MC++ aliases are shown in parentheses in the left column of Fig. 6.5.[5]

Type	Bits	Values	Standard
`Boolean` (**`bool`**)	8	`true` or `false`	
`Char` (**`__wchar_t`**)	16	`'\u0000'` to `'\uFFFF'`	(Unicode character set)
`Byte` (**`char`**)	8	0 to 255	(unsigned)
`SByte` (**`signed char`**)	8	–128 to +127	
`Int16` (**`short`**)	16	–32,768 to +32,767	

Fig. 6.5 Built-in types in the .NET Framework. (Part 1 of 2.)

4. For more information about type conversions in .NET, visit `msdn.microsoft.com/library/en-us/cpguide/html/cpcontypeconversiontables.asp`.
5. Each data type in Fig. 6.5 is listed with its size in bits (there are 8 bits to a byte) and its range of values. The architects of .NET wanted code to be portable; therefore, they chose to use internationally recognized standards for both character formats (Unicode) and floating-point numbers (IEEE 754). Unicode is discussed in Appendix D.

Type	Bits	Values	Standard
UInt16 (**unsigned short**)	16	0 to 65,535	(unsigned)
Int32 (**int** or **long**)	32	–2,147,483,648 to +2,147,483,647	
UInt32 (**unsigned int/long**)	32	0 to 4,294,967,295	(unsigned)
Int64 (**__int64**)	64	–9,223,372,036,854,775,808 to +9,223,372,036,854,775,807	
UInt64 (**unsigned __int64**)	64	0 to 18,446,744,073,709,551,615	(unsigned)
Decimal (**Decimal**)	96	$-7.9 \infty 10^{28}$ to $+7.9 \infty 10^{28}$	
Single (**float**)	32	$-3.4 \infty 10^{38}$ to $+3.4 \infty 10^{38}$	(IEEE 754 floating point)
Double (**double**)	64	$-1.7 \infty 10^{308}$ to $+1.7 \infty 10^{308}$	(IEEE 754 floating point)
Object (Object *)			
String (String *)			(Unicode character set)

Fig. 6.5 Built-in types in the .NET Framework. (Part 2 of 2.)

Type	Can be Safely Converted to Type(s)
Byte	UInt16, Int16, UInt32, Int32, UInt64, Int64, Single, Double or Decimal
SByte	Int16, Int32, Int64, Single, Double or Decimal
Int16	Int32, Int64, Single, Double or Decimal
UInt16	UInt32, Int32, UInt64, Int64, Single, Double or Decimal
Char	UInt16, UInt32, Int32, UInt64, Int64, Single, Double or Decimal
Int32	Int64, Double or Decimal
UInt32	Int64, Double or Decimal
Int64	Decimal
UInt64	Decimal
Single	Double

Fig. 6.6 Safe widening conversions.

As an example of an implicit conversion, method `Sqrt` of class `Math` can be called with an integer argument, even though the method is defined in class `Math` to receive a `double` argument. The statement

```
Console::WriteLine( Math::Sqrt( 4 ) );
```

correctly evaluates `Math::Sqrt( 4 )` and displays the value `2`. MC++ implicitly converts the `int` value `4` to the `double` value `4.0` before passing the value to `Math::Sqrt`. In many cases, MC++ applies implicit conversions to argument values that do not correspond precisely to the parameter types in the function definition. In some cases, attempting these conversions leads to compiler warnings because Visual C++ .NET uses conversion rules to determine when a widening conversion can occur. In our previous `Math::Sqrt` example, MC++ converts an `int` to a `double` without changing its value. However, converting a `double` to an `int` truncates the fractional part of the `double` value. Converting large integer types to small integer types (e.g., `int` to `short`) can also result in changed values. Such narrowing conversions, as well as some widening conversions, can result in a loss of information; therefore, the programmer could be forced to perform the conversion with a cast operation to avoid compiler warnings. The conversion rules apply to expressions containing values of two or more types (also referred to as *mixed-type expressions*) and to primitive-type values (i.e., values of a built-in type such as `int`) passed as arguments to functions. MC++ converts the type of each value in a mixed-type expression to the "highest" type (i.e., the type that can store the widest range of values) in the expression. MC++ creates a temporary copy of each value and uses it in the expression—the original values remain unchanged. A function argument's type can be promoted to any "higher" type. The table of Fig. 6.6 can be used to determine the highest type in an expression. For each type in the left column, the corresponding types in the right column are considered to be of higher type. For instance, types `Int64`, `Double` and `Decimal` are higher than type `Int32`.

Converting values to lower types can result in data loss. In cases where information could be lost through conversion, the compiler might issue a warning (although the program might still be runnable). Programmers can use a cast to force the conversion to occur and eliminate compiler warnings. Recall that our `Square` function (Fig. 6.3) expects an `int` argument. To call `Square` with the `double` variable `y`, the function call would be written as

```
int result = Square( static_cast< int >( y ) );
```

This statement explicitly casts (converts) a copy of the value of `y` to an integer for use in function `Square`. For example, if `y`'s value is `4.5`, function `Square` receives the value `4` and returns `16`, not `20.25`. [*Note*: To review the syntax of the `static_cast` operator, see Chapter 4.]

Common Programming Error 6.10

When performing a narrowing conversion (e.g., `double` *to* `int`*), converting a primitive-type value to another primitive type might result in a loss of data (such as truncating a* `double` *value).*

6.7 Namespaces in Managed Extensions for C++

As we have seen, MC++ contains many predefined classes that are grouped into namespaces. Collectively, we refer to this preexisting code as the .NET Framework Class Library (FCL). The actual code for the classes is located in `.dll` files called *assemblies*. Assemblies are the packaging units for applications. [*Note*: Assemblies can contain many different types of files.]

Throughout the text, `using` directives specify the namespaces we use in each program. For example, a program includes the directive

```
using namespace System;
```

to tell the compiler that we are using the `System` namespace. This `using` directive allows us to write `Console::WriteLine` rather than `System::Console::WriteLine` throughout the program.

We exercise a large number of the FCL classes in this book. Figure 6.7 lists a subset of the many namespaces in the FCL and provides a brief description of each. We use classes from these namespaces and others throughout the book. This table introduces readers to the variety of reusable components in the FCL. When learning MC++, spend time reading the documentation for FCL classes, to familiarize yourself with their capabilities.

Namespace	Description
`System`	Contains essential classes and types (`Int32`, `Char`, `String`, etc.).
`System::Data`	Contains classes that form ADO .NET, used for database access and manipulation.
`System::Drawing`	Contains classes used for drawing and graphics.
`System::IO`	Contains classes for the input and output of data, such as with files.
`System::Threading`	Contains classes for multithreading, used to run multiple parts of a program simultaneously.
`System::Windows::Forms`	Contains classes used to create graphical user interfaces.
`System::Xml`	Contains classes used to process XML data.

Fig. 6.7 Some namespaces in the Framework Class Library.

The set of namespaces available in the FCL is quite large. In addition to the namespaces summarized in Fig. 6.7, the FCL includes namespaces for complex graphics, advanced graphical user interfaces, printing, advanced networking, security, multimedia, accessibility (for people with disabilities) and much more. For an overview of the namespaces in the FCL, look up "Class Library" in the **Help** index or visit:

```
msdn.microsoft.com/library/default.asp?url=/library/en-us/cpref/
html/cpref_start.asp
```

6.8 Value Types and Reference Types

In Fig. 6.10, we will discuss how arguments are passed to functions in MC++. To understand this, we first need to discuss two categories of types in MC++—*value types* and *reference types*. A variable of a value type contains data of that type. A variable of a reference type, in contrast, contains the address of the location in memory where the data of that type is stored.

Value types are accessed directly; reference types are accessed through *pointers* or *references*, special variables that we discuss in the next section. Value types normally contain primitive-type data, such as `int` or `bool` values. Reference types, on the other hand, usually refer to objects. All non-value types are reference types. An example of a non-value type is `String *`. Programs use variables of reference types to refer to and manipulate objects. We discuss objects in detail in Chapters 8–10.

MC++ includes built-in value types and reference types. Figure 6.5 listed the .NET built-in types, which are building blocks for more complicated types.[6] Their MC++ aliases are shown in parentheses. The built-in value types are the *integral types* (`signed char`, `char`, `__wchar_t`, `short`, `unsigned short`, `int`, `unsigned int`, `long`, `unsigned long`, `__int64` and `unsigned __int64`), the *floating-point types* (`float` and `double`) and the types `Decimal` and `bool`. In MC++, these types map to types provided by the .NET Framework (`Int32`, `Char`, `Double`, etc.). The built-in reference types are `String *` and `Object *`. Programmers can create new value types and reference types; the reference types and value types that programmers can create include classes (Chapter 8), interfaces (Chapter 8) and delegates (Chapter 9). Like C and C++, MC++ requires all variables to have a type before they can be used in a program. For this reason, MC++ is referred to as a *strongly typed language*.

6.9 Pointers and References

In the last section, we discussed reference types. We now introduce you to *pointers* and *references*, which enable programs to manipulate objects of reference types via the objects' memory addresses. Why use pointers and references? Because certain types (such as strings) can become quite large in memory, which affects the performance of your programs when such objects must be passed between functions. On the other hand, memory addresses are small numeric values that can be passed between functions efficiently. As you will learn in Chapter 22, pointers also enable programs to create and manipulate dynamic data structures (i.e., data structures that can grow and shrink), such as linked lists, queues, stacks and trees.

Pointers and references are variables that contain memory addresses as their values. Normally, a variable directly contains a specific value. A pointer, on the other hand, contains the address of another variable that contains a specific value. In this sense, a variable *directly* references a value, and pointer *indirectly* references a value (Fig. 6.8). Referencing a value through a pointer is often called indirection. Note that diagrams typically represent a pointer as an arrow from the variable that contains an address to the variable located at that address in memory.

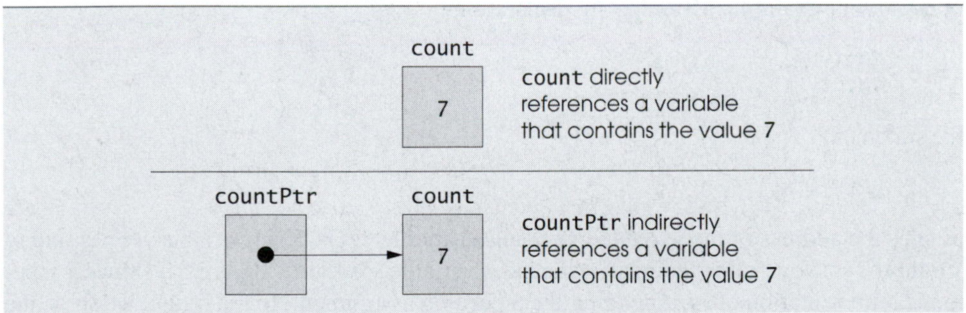

Fig. 6.8 Directly and indirectly referencing a variable.

6. For more information about data types provided by the .NET Framework (and their MC++ aliases), visit `msdn.microsoft.com/library/en-us/cpguide/html/cpconthenetframeworkclasslibrary.asp`.

Pointers

Pointers, like any other variables, must be declared before they can be used. For example, the declaration

```
int *countPtr, count;
```

declares the variable `countPtr` to be of type `int *` (i.e., a pointer to an `int` value) and is read "`countPtr` is a pointer to `int`." Also, variable `count` in the preceding declaration is declared to be an `int`, not a pointer to an `int`. The `*` in the declaration applies only to `countPtr`. Each variable being declared as a pointer must be preceded by an asterisk (*). For example, the declaration

```
double *xPtr, *yPtr;
```

indicates that both `xPtr` and `yPtr` are pointers to `double` values. When `*` appears in a declaration, it is not an operator; rather it indicates that the variable being declared is a pointer. Pointers can be declared to point to objects of any type.

Common Programming Error 6.11

*Assuming that the * used to declare a pointer distributes to all variable names in a declaration's comma-separated list of variables can lead to errors. Each pointer must be declared with the * prefixed to the name.*

Pointers should be initialized when they are declared or in an assignment statement before they are used. A pointer may be initialized to `0`, `NULL` or an address. A pointer with the value `0` or `NULL` points to nothing. Symbolic constant `NULL` is defined to represent the value `0`. Initializing a pointer to `NULL` is equivalent to initializing a pointer to 0, but in C++, `0` is used by convention. The value `0` is the only integer value that can be assigned directly to a pointer variable.

Error-Prevention Tip 6.2

Initialize pointers to prevent pointing to unknown or uninitialized areas of memory.

The *address-of operator* (&) is a unary operator that returns the memory address of its operand. For example, assuming the declarations

```
int y = 5;
int *yPtr;
```

the statement

```
yPtr = &y;
```

assigns the address of the variable y to pointer variable `yPtr`. Then variable `yPtr` is said to "point to" `y`. Now, `yPtr` indirectly references variable `y`'s value. Figure 6.9 shows a schematic representation of memory after the preceding assignment. In the figure, we show the "pointing relationship" by drawing an arrow from the box that represents the pointer `yPtr` in memory to the box that represents the variable `y` in memory.

Figure 6.10 shows another representation of the pointer in memory, assuming that integer variable `y` is stored at location `600000` and that pointer variable `yPtr` is stored at location `500000`. The operand of the address-of operator must be an *lvalue*; the address-of operator cannot be applied to constants or to expressions that do not result in references.

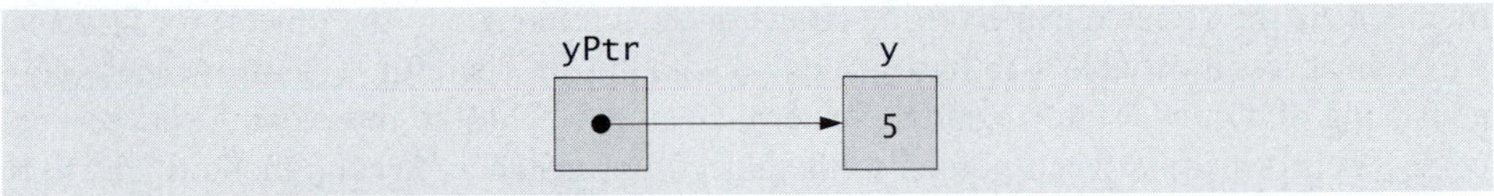

Fig. 6.9 Graphical representation of a pointer pointing to a variable in memory.

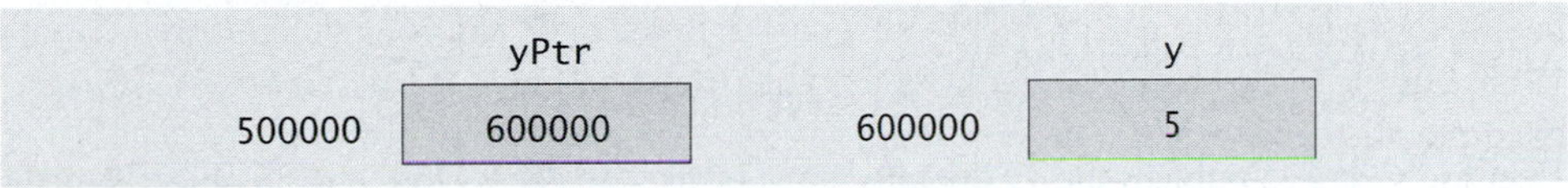

Fig. 6.10 Representation of y and yPtr in memory.

The * *operator*, commonly referred to as the *indirection operator* or *dereferencing operator*, returns an synonym (i.e., an alias or a nickname) for the object to which its operand (i.e., a pointer) points. For example, the statement

```
*yPtr = 9;
```

would assign 9 to y. The dereferenced pointer is an *lvalue*. Using * in this manner is called *dereferencing a pointer*. The value that yPtr is pointing to can be displayed as

```
Console::WriteLine( ( *yPtr ).ToString() );
```

The parentheses are needed because the dot operator has higher precedence than the * operator. If the parentheses were removed, the * operator would be applied to the return value of yPtr.ToString (which, as you will see shortly, is not a valid method call).

References

References provide functionality similar to that of pointers. Developers can use references to access and modify objects (just as with pointers), using a slightly different syntax. The following code

```
int count = 1;
int &cRef = count;
++cRef;
```

creates a reference cRef, which can be used as an alias for count. The third statement increments variable count by using its alias cRef. Reference variables must be initialized in their declarations and cannot be reassigned as aliases to other variables. Once a reference is declared as an alias for another variable, all operations performed on the reference are actually preformed on the original variable. The alias is simply another name for the original variable.

In most cases, you will not declare references locally in a function. Rather, references will be used as parameters in function definitions. Such references are initialized when the function is called. We demonstrate this use of references in Section 6.10.

Calling Methods Using Pointers and References

There are two different member access operators that can be used to call an object's methods—the *arrow operator* (->) and the *dot operator* (.). The dot operator accesses a class member via the variable name for the object or via a reference to the object; for instance, we often access a variable's `ToString` method with the dot operator. The arrow operator—consisting of a minus sign (-) and a greater than sign (>) with no intervening spaces—accesses a class member via a pointer to the object. For instance, `String` method ***EndsWith*** returns a boolean value indicating whether a `String *` ends with certain characters. Consider the statements

```
String *text = "hello";

if ( text->EndsWith( "lo" ) )
   Console::WriteLine( "{0} ends with lo", text );
```

Because `text` is a pointer, the `->` operator must be used to access the `String` object's methods. This method returns true (because the characters `"lo"` are found at the end of `"hello"`. The output from the if statement would be `"hello ends with lo"`.

To access an object's members using a dereferenced pointer, the dot (`.`) operator is used in place of the arrow (`->`) operator. Therefore, the call to `EndsWith` from above can also be written as

```
if ( ( *text ).EndsWith( "lo" ) )
   Console::WriteLine( "{0} ends with lo", text );
```

6.10 Passing Arguments: Pass-by-Value vs. Pass-by-Reference

Two ways to pass arguments to functions in many programming languages are *pass-by-value* and *pass-by-reference* (also referred to as *call-by-value* and *call-by-reference*). When an argument is passed by value, the called function receives a *copy* of the argument's value.

Performance Tip 6.1

One disadvantage of pass-by-value is that, if a large data item is being passed, copying that data can take a considerable amount of execution time and memory space.

Error-Prevention Tip 6.3

With pass-by-value, changes to the called function's copy do not affect the original variable's value. This prevents some possible side effects that hinder the development of correct and reliable software systems.

When an argument is passed by reference, the caller gives the function the ability to directly access and modify the caller's original data. Pass-by-reference can improve performance because it eliminates the overhead of copying large data items such as objects; however, pass-by-reference can weaken security because the called function can modify the caller's data.

In Section 6.8, we discussed value types and reference types. One of the major differences between the two types is that value-type variables are passed to functions by value and reference-type variables are passed to functions by reference. What if the programmer would like to pass a value type by reference? In this section, we introduce *reference parameters*, a means by which MC++ performs pass-by-reference.

A reference parameter is an alias for its corresponding argument. To indicate that a function parameter is passed by reference (using references), declare the parameter as a reference in the function prototype (for instance, if a `double` is being passed by reference, specify `double &`); use the same convention when declaring the parameter in the function header. In the function call, simply specify the name of a variable as the argument for the reference parameter and the variable will be passed by reference. The original variable in the calling function can be modified directly by the called function by using the reference parameter.

In this section we also demonstrate pass-by-reference using *pointer parameters*. To indicate that a function parameter is passed by reference using pointers, declare the parameter as a pointer in the function prototype (for instance, if a `double` is being passed by reference, specify type `double *`); use the same convention when declaring the parameter type in the function header. In the function call, pass the address of a variable (using the `&` operator) as the argument for the pointer parameter, and the variable will be passed by reference. The original variable in the calling function can be modified directly by dereferencing the pointer parameter in the called function. However, to access that variable's value in the called function, the parameter must be dereferenced, as it is a pointer.

Software Engineering Observation 6.8

When returning information from a function via a `return` *statement, value-type variables are always returned by value and reference-type variables are always returned by reference.*

Figure 6.11 compares pass-by-value with pass-by-reference (using both reference parameters and pointer parameters for pass-by-reference). Notice that the "styles" of the arguments in the calls to `SquareByValue` (lines 23) and `SquareByReference` (line 27) are identical—both variables are mentioned by name. However, the call to `SquareByPointer` (line 31) passes the address of the variable `z` using the `&` operator. Without checking the function prototypes or function definitions of `SquareByValue` and `SquareByReference`, it is not possible to determine from the calls alone whether either function can modify its arguments. In `SquareByReference` (lines 44–47), note that the parameter `cRef` is modified. Because `cRef` is actually an alias for variable `y` in `_tmain`, variable `y` is modified when line 46 executes in response to the call at line 27. In `SquareByPointer` (lines 50–53), `cPtr` must be dereferenced to access the value of variable `z` in `_tmain`. When line 52 executes in response to the call at line 31, the value at the location that `cRef` points to is multiplied by itself and stored in the same location in memory (i.e., variable `z`), thus modifying the value of `z`.

```
1   // Fig. 6.11: PassByReference.cpp
2   // Comparing pass-by-value and pass-by-reference.
3
4   #include "stdafx.h"
5
6   #using <mscorlib.dll>
7
8   using namespace System;
9
10  int SquareByValue( int );
11  void SquareByReference( int & );
12  void SquareByPointer( int * );
13
14  int _tmain()
15  {
16     int x = 2, y = 3, z = 4;
```

Fig. 6.11 Pass-by-reference demonstration. (Part 1 of 2.)

```

   Console::WriteLine( S"Original value of x: {0}", x.ToString() );
   Console::WriteLine( S"Original value of y: {0}", y.ToString() );
   Console::WriteLine( S"Original value of z: {0}", z.ToString() );

   Console::Write( S"Value of x after SquareByValue: " );
   SquareByValue( x );
   Console::WriteLine( x.ToString() );

   Console::Write( S"Value of y after SquareByReference: " );
   SquareByReference( y );
   Console::WriteLine( y.ToString() );

   Console::Write( S"Value of z after SquareByPointer: " );
   SquareByPointer( &z );
   Console::WriteLine( z.ToString() );

   return 0;
} // end _tmain

// function definition with the parameter passed by value
int SquareByValue( int a )
{
   return a * a;  // caller's argument not modified
}

// function definition with a reference parameter
void SquareByReference( int &cRef )
{
   cRef *= cRef;  // caller's argument modified
}

// function definition with a pointer parameter
void SquareByPointer( int *cPtr )
{
   *cPtr *= *cPtr; // caller's argument modified
}
```

```
Original value of x: 2
Original value of y: 3
Original value of z: 4
Value of x after SquareByValue: 2
Value of y after SquareByReference: 9
Value of z after SquareByPointer: 16
```

Fig. 6.11 Pass-by-reference demonstration. (Part 2 of 2.)

Common Programming Error 6.12

Reference parameters are mentioned only by name in the body of the called function, so the programmer might inadvertently treat reference parameters as pass-by-value parameters. This can cause unexpected side effects if the original copies of the variables are changed by the calling function.

6.11 Default Arguments

It is not uncommon for a program to invoke a function repeatedly with the same argument value for a particular parameter. In such cases, the programmer can specify that the parameter has a *default argument* and can provide the default value for that parameter. When a program omits a default argument in a function call, the compiler rewrites the function call and inserts the default value of that argument to be passed as an argument to the function call.

Default arguments must be the rightmost (trailing) arguments in a function's parameter list. When calling a function with two or more default arguments, if an omitted argument is not the rightmost argument in the argument list, then all arguments to the right of that argument also must be omitted. Default arguments should be specified with the first occurrence of the function name—typically, in the function prototype. Default values can be constants, global variables or function calls.

Figure 6.12 demonstrates using default arguments in calculating the volume of a box. The function prototype for `BoxVolume` (line 11) specifies that all three arguments have been given default values of `1`. Note that the default values should be defined only in the function prototype. Also note that we provided variable names in the function prototype for readability. As always, variable names are not required in function prototypes.

```
1  // Fig. 6.12 DefaultArguments.cpp
2  // Using default arguments
3
4  #include "stdafx.h"
5
6  #using <mscorlib.dll>
7
8  using namespace System;
9
10 // function prototype that specifies default arguments
11 int BoxVolume( int length = 1, int width = 1, int height = 1 );
12
13 int _tmain()
14 {
15    // no arguments--use default values for all dimensions
16    Console::WriteLine( S"The default box volume is: {0}",
17       BoxVolume().ToString() );
18
19    // specify length; default width and height
20    Console::WriteLine( S"\nThe volume of a box with length 10," );
21    Console::WriteLine( S"width 1 and height 1 is: {0}",
22       BoxVolume( 10 ).ToString() );
23
24    // specify length and width; default height
25    Console::WriteLine( S"\nThe volume of a box with length 10," );
26    Console::WriteLine( S"width 5 and height 1 is: {0}",
27       BoxVolume( 10, 5 ).ToString() );
28
29    // specify all arguments
30    Console::WriteLine( S"\nThe volume of a box with length 10," );
```

Fig. 6.12 Default arguments to a function. (Part 1 of 2.)

```
31      Console::WriteLine(
32         S"width 5 and height 2 is: {0}", BoxVolume( 10, 5, 2 ).ToString() );
33
34      return 0;
35   } // end _tmain
36
37   // function BoxVolume calculates the volume of a box
38   int BoxVolume( int length, int width, int height )
39   {
40      return length * width * height;
41   } // end function BoxVolume
```

```
The default box volume is: 1

The volume of a box with length 10,
width 1 and height 1 is: 10

The volume of a box with length 10,
width 5 and height 1 is: 50

The volume of a box with length 10,
width 5 and height 2 is: 100
```

Fig. 6.12 Default arguments to a function. (Part 2 of 2.)

The first call to `BoxVolume` (line 17) specifies no arguments, thus using all three default values. The second call (line 22) passes a `length` argument, thus using default values for the `width` and `height` arguments. The third call (line 27) passes arguments for `length` and `width`, thus using a default value for the `height` argument. The last call (line 32) passes arguments for `length`, `width` and `height`, thus using no default values. Note that any arguments passed to the function explicitly are assigned to the function's parameters from left to right. Therefore, when `BoxVolume` receives one argument, the function assigns the value of that argument to its `length` parameter (i.e., the leftmost parameter in the parameter list). When `BoxVolume` receives two arguments, the function assigns the values of those arguments to its `length` and `width` parameters in that order. Finally, when `BoxVolume` receives all three arguments, the function assigns the values of those arguments to its `length`, `width` and `height` parameters, respectively.

Good Programming Practice 6.4

Using default arguments can simplify writing function calls. However, some programmers feel that explicitly specifying all arguments is clearer. If the default values for a function change, the program may not yield the desired results.

Common Programming Error 6.13

Specifying and attempting to use a default argument that is not a rightmost (trailing) argument (while not simultaneously defaulting all the rightmost arguments) is a syntax error.

6.12 Random-Number Generation

We now take a brief and hopefully entertaining diversion into a popular programming application—simulation and game playing. In this section and the next, we develop a nicely structured game-playing program that includes multiple functions. The program uses most of the control statements we have studied to this point and also introduces several new concepts.

There is something in the air of a gambling casino that invigorates people—from the high rollers at the plush mahogany-and-felt craps tables to the quarter poppers at the one-armed bandits. It is the *element of chance,* the possibility that luck will convert a pocketful of money into a mountain of wealth. The element of chance can be introduced into computer applications with class *Random* (located in namespace System). Random numbers can be generated using an object of class Random (which is a reference type). The following statements create a Random object and use it to generate a random number:

```
Random *randomObject = new Random();
int randomNumber = randomObject->Next();
```

The first line uses *operator new* to create and allocate space in memory for an object of class Random. This is required for objects of reference types in MC++. Operator new will be discussed further in Chapter 8, Object-Based Programming. Variable randomObject is a pointer—randomObject contains the memory address where the newly created Random object is stored. The second line calls the *Next* method to generate a positive int value between zero and the constant *Int32::MaxValue*, which represents the largest possible Int32 value (i.e., 2,147,483,647).[7] If Next produces values at random, every value in this range has an equal *chance* (or *probability*) of being chosen when Next is called. Note that values returned by Next are actually *pseudo-random numbers*—a sequence of values produced by a complex mathematical calculation. A *seed* value is required in this mathematical calculation. When we create our Random object, we use the default seed. We could also supply a seed as an integral argument when creating the Random object (e.g., Random * randomObject = new Random(3)). A particular seed value produces the same series of random numbers each time the program executes. Programmers commonly use the current time of day as a seed value, since it changes each second and, therefore produces different random-number sequences each time the program executes. If no argument is specified when creating the Random object, a seed value based on the system's clock is used.

The range of values produced directly by Next is often different from the range of values required in a particular application. For example, a program that simulates coin-tossing might require only 0 for "heads" and 1 for "tails." A program that simulates rolling a six-sided die would require random integers in the range 1–6. A video-game program that randomly predicts the next type of spaceship (out of four possibilities) that will fly across the horizon might require random integers in the range 1–4.

The one-argument version of method Next returns values in the range from 0 up to (but not including) the value of that argument. For example,

```
value = randomObject->Next( 6 );
```

produces values from 0 through 5. This is called *scaling*, because the range of values produced has been scaled down from greater than two billion to only six. The number 6 is the *scaling factor.* The two-argument version of method Next allows us to *shift* and scale the range of numbers. For example, we can use method Next as follows

7. This method call demonstrates the final way of calling a function or method—by using a pointer to an object followed by the arrow operator (->) and the function or method name. The arrow operator is discussed further in Chapter 8, Object-Based Programming.

```
value = randomObject->Next( 1, 7 );
```

to produce integers in the range from 1 to 6. In this case, we have shifted the numbers to produce a range from 1 up to (but not including) 7.

The application of Fig. 6.13 simulates 20 rolls of a six-sided die and shows the integer value of each roll. The `for` loop on lines 15–27 repeatedly invokes method `Next` (line 18) of class `Random` to simulate rolling the die. (Note that we use the arrow operator to call `Next` because `randomInteger` is a pointer to a `Random` object.) Line 21 displays the value rolled. After every five rolls, line 25 moves the cursor to the next line to make the output more readable. Because the default seed based on the system clock is used, a different series of values will result each time the program is run. If a seed were provided in line 12, then the same sequence of values would result each time the program is run.

```
1  // Fig. 6.13: RandomInt.cpp
2  // Generating random integer values.
3
4  #include "stdafx.h"
5
6  #using <mscorlib.dll>
7
8  using namespace System;
9
10 int _tmain()
11 {
12    Random *randomInteger = new Random();
13
14    // loop 20 times
15    for ( int counter = 1; counter <= 20; counter++ ) {
16
17       // pick random integer between 1 and 6
18       int nextValue = randomInteger->Next( 1, 7 );
19
20       // output value
21       Console::Write( S"{0} ", nextValue.ToString() );
22
23       // add newline after every 5 values
24       if ( counter % 5 == 0 )
25          Console::WriteLine();
26
27    } // end for
28
29    return 0;
30 } // end _tmain
```

```
4 2 1 5 4
1 4 2 6 6
2 4 3 6 6
2 3 1 1 5
```

Fig. 6.13 Randomizing a die-rolling program.

Figure 6.14 demonstrates that class `Random` produces numbers with approximately equal likelihood by keep some simple statistics. This example builds upon the previous example by using a simulation of die rolling.

```
// Fig. 6.14: RollDie.cpp
// Rolling 12 dice with frequency chart.

#include "stdafx.h"

#using <mscorlib.dll>

using namespace System;

int _tmain()
{
   Random *randomNumber = new Random();
   int face;
   int ones = 0, twos = 0, threes = 0, fours = 0, fives = 0, sixes = 0;

   for ( int roll = 1; roll <= 6000; roll++ ) {
      face = randomNumber->Next( 1, 7 );

      // add one to frequency of current face
      switch ( face ) {
         case 1:
            ones++;
            break;

         case 2:
            twos++;
            break;

         case 3:
               threes++;
               break;

         case 4:
            fours++;
            break;

         case 5:
            fives++;
            break;

         case 6:
            sixes++;
            break;
       } // end switch
   } // end for loop

   double total = ones + twos + threes + fours + fives + sixes;

```

Fig. 6.14 Rolling 12 dice with frequency chart. (Part 1 of 2.)

```
49       // display the current frequency values
50       Console::WriteLine( S"Face\t\tFrequency\tPercent" );
51
52       Console::WriteLine( S"1\t\t{0}\t\t{1}%",
53          ones.ToString(), ( ones / total * 100 ).ToString() );
54       Console::WriteLine( S"2\t\t{0}\t\t{1}%",
55          twos.ToString(), ( twos / total * 100 ).ToString() );
56       Console::WriteLine( S"3\t\t{0}\t\t{1}%",
57          threes.ToString(), ( threes / total * 100 ).ToString() );
58       Console::WriteLine( S"4\t\t{0}\t\t{1}%",
59          fours.ToString(), ( fours / total * 100 ).ToString() );
60       Console::WriteLine( S"5\t\t{0}\t\t{1}%",
61          fives.ToString(), ( fives / total * 100 ).ToString() );
62       Console::WriteLine( S"6\t\t{0}\t\t{1}%",
63          sixes.ToString(), ( sixes / total * 100 ).ToString() );
64
65       return 0;
66    } // end _tmain
```

```
Face            Frequency       Percent
1               978             16.3%
2               1011            16.85%
3               981             16.35%
4               980             16.3333333333333%
5               1003            16.7166666666667%
6               1047            17.45%
```

```
Face            Frequency       Percent
1               971             16.1833333333333%
2               1027            17.1166666666667%
3               1021            17.0166666666667%
4               961             16.0166666666667%
5               1036            17.2666666666667%
6               984             16.4%
```

```
Face            Frequency       Percent
1               1020            17%
2               996             16.6%
3               1051            17.5166666666667%
4               994             16.5666666666667%
5               972             16.2%
6               967             16.1166666666667%
```

Fig. 6.14 Rolling 12 dice with frequency chart. (Part 2 of 2.)

The `for` loop in lines 16–45 simulates rolling a die 6000 times. The `switch` statement in lines 20–44 determines which face value was rolled and increments the frequency count for that value. Lines 47–63 then calculate the frequencies for each face and display the results. As the program output demonstrates, over a large number of die rolls, each of the possible faces from 1 through 6 appears with approximately equal likelihood (i.e., about one-sixth of the time). After studying arrays in Chapter 7, Arrays, we will show how to replace the entire `switch` statement in this program with a single-line statement.

6.13 Example: Game of Chance

One of the most popular games of chance is a dice game known as "craps," played in casinos and back alleys throughout the world. The rules of the game are straightforward:

> *A player rolls two dice. Each die has six faces. Each face contains 1, 2, 3, 4, 5 or 6 spots. After the dice have come to rest, the sum of the spots on the two upward faces is calculated. If the sum is 7 or 11 on the first throw, the player wins. If the sum is 2, 3 or 12 on the first throw (called "craps"), the player loses (i.e., the "house" wins). If the sum is 4, 5, 6, 8, 9 or 10 on the first throw, that sum becomes the player's "point." To win, players must continue rolling the dice until they "make their point" (i.e., roll their point value). The player loses by rolling a 7 before making the point.*

Figure 6.15 contains a program which simulates the game of craps.

Notice that the player rolls two dice on each roll. Function `RollDice` (lines 71–82) simulates the rolling of the two dice and returns their sum. The application displays the results of each roll. The sample outputs show the execution of several games.

```
1   // Fig. 6.15: CrapsGame.cpp
2   // Simulating the game of Craps.
3
4   #include "stdafx.h"
5
6   #using <mscorlib.dll>
7
8   using namespace System;
9
10  int RollDice( Random *randomNumber );
11
12  int _tmain()
13  {
14     int myPoint; // player's point value
15     int sum;
16
17     enum DiceNames
18     {
19        SNAKE_EYES = 2,
20        TREY = 3,
21        CRAPS = 7,
22        LUCKY_SEVEN = 7,
23        YO_LEVEN = 11,
24        BOX_CARS = 12,
25     };
26
27     enum Status { CONTINUE, WON, LOST };
28
29     Status gameStatus = CONTINUE;
```

Fig. 6.15 Craps game simulation. (Part 1 of 3.)

```
   Random *randomNumber = new Random();

   sum = RollDice( randomNumber );   // first roll of the dice

   switch ( sum ) {
      case LUCKY_SEVEN:
      case YO_LEVEN:
         gameStatus = WON;   // win on first roll
         break;

      case SNAKE_EYES:
      case TREY:
      case BOX_CARS:
         gameStatus = LOST;   // lose on first roll
         break;

      default:
         gameStatus = CONTINUE;
         myPoint = sum;   // remember point
         Console::WriteLine( S"Point is {0}", myPoint.ToString() );
         break;   // optional
   } // end switch

   while ( gameStatus == CONTINUE ) {   // keep rolling
      sum = RollDice( randomNumber );

      if ( sum == myPoint )   // win by making point
         gameStatus = WON;
      else
         if ( sum == CRAPS )   // lose by rolling 7
            gameStatus = LOST;

   } // end while

      Console::WriteLine(
         gameStatus == WON ? S"Player wins!" : S"Player loses" );

   return 0;
} // end _tmain

// roll dice, calculate sum and display results
int RollDice( Random *randomNumber )
{
   int die1, die2, workSum;

   die1 = randomNumber->Next( 1, 7 );
   die2 = randomNumber->Next( 1, 7 );
   workSum = die1 + die2;
   Console::WriteLine( S"Player rolled {0} + {1} = {2}",
      die1.ToString(), die2.ToString(), workSum.ToString() );

   return workSum;
} // end function RollDice
```

Fig. 6.15 Craps game simulation. (Part 2 of 3.)

```
Player rolled 6 + 1 = 7
Player wins!
```

```
Player rolled 5 + 3 = 8
Point is 8
Player rolled 6 + 2 = 8
Player wins!
```

```
Player rolled 6 + 3 = 9
Point is 9
Player rolled 3 + 3 = 6
Player rolled 2 + 5 = 7
Player loses
```

Fig. 6.15 Craps game simulation. (Part 3 of 3.)

The program declares two *enumerations* (lines 17–25 and line 27). An enumeration, introduced by the MC++ keyword `enum` and followed by a *type name*, is a value type that contains a set of constant integer values. The constant values, called *enumeration constants* or *enumerators*, start at `0`, unless specified otherwise, and are incremented by `1`. The identifiers in an `enum` must be unique, but separate enumerators can have the same integer value.

Good Programming Practice 6.5

Capitalize the first letter of an identifier used as a user-defined type name.

Common Programming Error 6.14

Assigning the integer equivalent of an enumerator to a variable of the enumeration type is a syntax error.

A popular enumeration is

```
enum Months {
   JAN = 1, FEB, MAR, APR, MAY, JUN, JUL, AUG, SEP, OCT, NOV, DEC };
```

which creates a user-defined type `Months` with enumerators representing the months of the year. The first value in the preceding enumeration is explicitly set to `1`, so the remaining values are incremented from `1`, resulting in the values `1` through `12`. Any enumerator can be assigned an integer value in the enumeration definition, and subsequent enumerators will each have a value 1 higher than the preceding constant.

Common Programming Error 6.15

After an enumerator has been defined, attempting to assign another value to the enumerator is a syntax error.

Good Programming Practice 6.6

Use only uppercase letters in the names of enumerators. This makes these constants stand out in a program and reminds the programmer that enumerators are not variables.

Good Programming Practice 6.7

Using enumerations rather than integer constants can make programs clearer.

An enumeration is a convenient way to define constant values used throughout a program. Lines 17–25 declare enumeration `DiceNames`. The identifiers `SNAKE_EYES`, `TREY`, `CRAPS`, `LUCKY_SEVEN`, `YO_LEVEN` and `BOX_CARS` represent significant values in craps. Enumeration `Status` (line 27) represents the possible outcomes of a dice roll. Using these identifiers makes the program more readable. Also, if we need to change one of these values, we can modify the enumeration instead of changing the values where they are used throughout the program. Variables of user-defined type `Status` (line 27) can only be assigned one of the three values declared in the `Status` enumeration (`CONTINUE`, `WON` or `LOST`).

Line 32 invokes function `RollDice` (defined on lines 71–82), which rolls the dice, displays the values and returns their sum. Lines 34–51 use a `switch` statement to determine whether the player won, lost or established a point value. If the player won by rolling `LUCKY_SEVEN` or `YO_LEVEN` (i.e., 7 or 11), lines 64–65 print `"Player wins"`. If the player lost by rolling `SNAKE_EYES`, `TREY` or `BOX_CARS` (i.e., 2, 3 or 12), lines 64–65 print `"Player loses"`.

After the first roll, if the game is not over, `sum` is saved in `myPoint` (line 48). Execution proceeds while `gameStatus` is equal to `CONTINUE`. During each iteration of the `while` loop (lines 53–62), function `RollDice` produces a new `sum`. If `sum` matches `myPoint`, the player wins. If `sum` equals 7 (`CRAPS`), the player loses. If neither happens, the dice are rolled again in the next iteration of the loop.

6.14 Duration of Variables

The attributes of variables include name, type, size and value. Each variable in a program has additional attributes, including *duration* and *scope*.

A variable's duration (also called its *lifetime*) is the period during which the variable exists in memory. Some variables exist briefly, some are created and destroyed repeatedly and others exist for the entire execution of a program.

A variable's *scope* is where the variable's identifier (i.e., name) can be referenced in a program. Some variables can be referenced throughout a program, while others can be referenced from limited portions of a program. This section discusses the duration of variables. Section 6.15 discusses the scope of identifiers.

Local variables in a function (i.e., parameters and variables declared in the function body) have *automatic duration*. Automatic duration variables are created when program control reaches their declaration; that is, they exist while the block in which they are declared is active, and they are destroyed when that block is exited. For the remainder of the text, we refer to variables of automatic duration as automatic variables, or local variables. Automatic variables must be initialized by the programmer before they can be used.

Variables of *static duration* exist from the time at which the block that defines them is loaded into memory. These variables then last until the program terminates. Their storage is allocated and initialized when their classes are loaded into memory. Static-duration variable names exist when their classes are loaded into memory, but this does not mean that these identifiers necessarily can be used throughout the program—their scopes may be limited. We discuss static variables more in the next section.

6.15 Scope Rules

The *scope* (sometimes called *declaration space*) of an identifier for a variable, pointer or function is the portion of the program in which the identifier can be accessed. A local variable or pointer declared in a block can be used only in that block or in blocks nested within that block. Four scopes for an identifier are *file scope*, *function scope*, *local scope* (also known as *block scope*) and *prototype scope*. In Chapter 8 we will see one more scope—*class scope*.

An identifier declared outside any function has *file scope*. Such an identifier is "known" in all functions from the point at which the identifier is declared until the end of the file. *Global variables* (i.e., variables that can be referenced anywhere in an application), function prototypes placed outside a function and function definitions have file scope.

Labels, identifiers followed by a colon (such as `start:`), are implementation details that functions hide from one another. Labels are the only identifiers with *function scope*. Labels can be used anywhere in the function in which they appear, but cannot be referenced outside the function body. Labels are used in `switch` statements (as `case` labels). Hiding implementation details—more formally called *information hiding*—is one of the fundamental principles of good software engineering.

Identifiers declared inside a block have *local scope* (*local-variable declaration space*). Local scope begins at the identifier's declaration and ends at the block's terminating right brace (`}`). Local variables of a function have local scope, as do function parameters, which are local variables of the function. Any block may contain variable declarations. When blocks are nested in a function's body and an identifier declared in an outer block has the same name as an identifier declared in an inner block, the identifier in the outer block is "hidden" until the inner block terminates. While executing, the inner block sees the value of its own local identifier and not the value of the identically named identifier in the enclosing block. In Chapter 8, Object-Based Programming, we discuss how to access such "hidden" variables. The reader should note that local scope also applies to functions and `for` statements. However, any variable declared in the initialization portion of the `for` header will still be in scope after that `for` statement terminates.[8] Refer to Chapter 5, Control Statements: Part 2, for a discussion of the scope of `for` statements.

Common Programming Error 6.16

Accidentally using the same name for the identifiers of both an inner block and an outer block, when in fact that programmer wants the identifier in the outer block to be active for the duration of the inner block, is normally a logic error.

Good Programming Practice 6.8

Avoid variable names that hide names in outer scopes.

The only identifiers with *prototype scope* are those used in the parameter list of a function prototype. Function prototypes do not require names in the parameter list—only types are required. If a name is used in the parameter list of a function prototype, the compiler ignores the name. For this reason, identifiers used in a function prototype can be redeclared and reused elsewhere in the program without ambiguity.

8. Recall from Chapter 5 that this behavior can be prevented by using compiler option `/Zc:forScope`.

The program in Fig. 6.16 demonstrates scoping issues with global variables, *automatic local variables* and `static` local variables. Automatic local variables are created when the block in which they are declared is entered, and they are destroyed when the block is exited. Local variables declared as `static` retain their values even when they are out of scope.

```
// Fig. 6.16: Scoping.cpp
// Demonstrating variable scope.

#include "stdafx.h"

#using <mscorlib.dll>

using namespace System;

void FunctionA();
void FunctionB();
void FunctionC();

int x = 1;    // global variable

int _tmain()
{
   int x = 5;    // local variable to _tmain

   Console::WriteLine( S"local x in outer scope of _tmain is {0}",
      x.ToString() );

   { // start new scope
      int x = 7;
      Console::WriteLine( S"local x in inner scope of _tmain is {0}",
         x.ToString() );
   } // end new scope

   Console::WriteLine( S"local x in outer scope of _tmain is {0}",
      x.ToString() );

   FunctionA();    // FunctionA has automatic local x
   FunctionB();    // FunctionB has static local x
   FunctionC();    // FunctionC uses global x
   FunctionA();    // FunctionA reinitializes automatic local x
   FunctionB();    // static local x retains its previous value
   FunctionC();    // global x also retains its value

   Console::WriteLine( S"\nlocal x in _tmain is {0}", x.ToString() );

   return 0;
} // end _tmain

void FunctionA()
{
   int x = 25;    // initialized each time FunctionA is called

```

Fig. 6.16 Scoping. (Part 1 of 3.)

```
   Console::WriteLine( S"\nlocal x in FunctionA is {0} {1}",
      x.ToString(), S"after entering FunctionA" );

   ++x; // increment local variable x

   Console::WriteLine( S"local x in FunctionA is {0} {1}",
      x.ToString(), S"before exiting FunctionA" );
} // end FunctionA

void FunctionB()
{
   static int x = 50;    // static initialization only
                         // first time FunctionB is called

   Console::WriteLine( S"\nlocal static x is {0} {1}",
      x.ToString(), S"on entering FunctionB" );

   ++x;

   Console::WriteLine( S"local static x is {0} {1}",
      x.ToString(), S"before exiting FunctionB" );
} // end FunctionB

void FunctionC()
{
   Console::WriteLine( S"\nglobal x is {0} {1}", x.ToString(),
      S"on entering FunctionC" );

   x *= 10;

   Console::WriteLine( S"global x is {0} {1}", x.ToString(),
      S"on exiting FunctionC" );
} // end FunctionC
```

```
local x in outer scope of _tmain is 5
local x in inner scope of _tmain is 7
local x in outer scope of _tmain is 5

local x in FunctionA is 25 after entering FunctionA
local x in FunctionA is 26 before exiting FunctionA

local static x is 50 on entering FunctionB
local static x is 51 before exiting FunctionB

global x is 1 on entering FunctionC
global x is 10 on exiting FunctionC

local x in FunctionA is 25 after entering FunctionA
local x in FunctionA is 26 before exiting FunctionA

local static x is 51 on entering FunctionB
local static x is 52 before exiting FunctionB
```

Fig. 6.16 Scoping. (Part 2 of 3.)

```
global x is 10 on entering FunctionC
global x is 100 on exiting FunctionC

local x in _tmain is 5
```

Fig. 6.16 Scoping. (Part 3 of 3.)

A global variable `x` is declared and initialized to `1` (line 14). This global variable is hidden in any block (or function) in which another variable `x` is declared. In `_tmain`, a local variable `x` is declared and initialized to `5` (line 18). This variable is printed to show that the global `x` is hidden in `_tmain`.

Next, a new block (lines 23–27) is defined in `_tmain`, with another local variable `x` initialized to `7` (line 24). This variable is printed to show that it hides `x` in the outer block `_tmain`. The variable `x` with value `7` is destroyed at the end of the block, and the local variable `x` in the outer block is printed to show that it is no longer hidden.

The program defines three functions—each takes no arguments and returns nothing. `FunctionA` (defined at lines 44–55) defines automatic variable `x` and initializes it to `25`. When `FunctionA` is called (lines 32 and 35), the variable `x` is printed, incremented and printed again before exiting the function. Each time this function is called, automatic variable `x` is recreated and initialized to `25`, so the function produces the same output each time it is called.

`FunctionB` (defined at lines 57–69) declares `static` variable `x` and initializes it to `50`. When `FunctionB` is called, `x` is printed, incremented and printed again before exiting the function. In the next call to this function, `static` local variable `x` will contain the value `51` because the `static` local variable `x` maintains its value between function calls.

`FunctionC` (defined at lines 71–80) does not declare any variables. Therefore, when it refers to variable `x`, the global `x` is used. When `FunctionC` is called, the global variable is printed, multiplied by `10` and printed again before exiting the function. The next time function `FunctionC` is called, the global variable has its modified value, `10`.

Finally, the program prints the local variable `x` in `_tmain` again to show that none of the function calls modified the value of `_tmain`'s local variable `x`, because the functions all referred to variables in other scopes.

6.16 Recursion

The programs we have discussed so far are structured as functions that call one another in a hierarchical manner. For some problems, it is useful to have a function call itself. A *recursive function* is a function that calls itself either directly, or indirectly through another function. Recursion is an important topic discussed at length in upper-level computer science courses. In this section and the next, we present two simple examples of recursion. We consider recursion conceptually first.

Recursive problem-solving approaches have a number of elements in common. A recursive function is called to solve a problem. When a recursive function is called to solve a problem, the function actually is capable of solving only the simplest case(s), or *base case(s)*. If the function is called with a base case, the function returns a result. If the function is called with a more complex problem, the function divides the problem into two conceptual pieces—a piece that the function knows how to perform (base case) and a piece that the function does not know how to perform. To make recursion feasible, the latter piece must resemble the original problem, but be a slightly simpler or smaller version of it. The function invokes (calls) a fresh copy of itself to work on the smaller problem—this call is referred to as a *recursive call*, or a *recursion step*. The recursion step also normally includes the keyword `return`, because its result will be combined with the portion of the problem that the function knew how to solve. Such a combination will form a result that will be passed back to the original caller.

The recursion step executes while the original call to the function is still "open" (i.e., it has not finished executing). The recursion step can result in many more recursive calls, as the function divides each new subproblem into two conceptual pieces. Each time the function calls itself with a slightly simpler version of the original problem, the sequence of smaller and smaller problems must converge on the base case, so the recursion can eventually terminate. At that point, the function recognizes the base case and returns a result to the previous copy of the function. A sequence of returns ensues up the line until the original function call returns the final result to the caller. As an example of these concepts, let us write a recursive program to perform a popular mathematical calculation.

Calculating Factorials Recursively

The factorial of a nonnegative integer *n*, written *n!* (and pronounced "*n* factorial"), is the product

$$n \cdot (n-1) \cdot (n-2) \cdot \ldots \cdot 1$$

with 1! equal to 1, and 0! defined as 1. For example, 5! is the product $5 \cdot 4 \cdot 3 \cdot 2 \cdot 1$, which is equal to 120.

The factorial of an integer `number` greater than or equal to 0 can be calculated *iteratively* (nonrecursively) using `for` as follows:

```
int factorial = 1;

for ( int counter = number; counter >= 1; counter-- )
   factorial *= counter;
```

We arrive at a recursive definition of the factorial function with the following relationship:

$$n! = n \cdot (n-1)!$$

For example, 5! is clearly equal to $5 \cdot 4!$, as shown by the following:

$$5! = 5 \cdot 4 \cdot 3 \cdot 2 \cdot 1$$
$$5! = 5 \cdot (4 \cdot 3 \cdot 2 \cdot 1)$$
$$5! = 5 \cdot (4!)$$

A recursive evaluation of 5! would proceed as shown in Fig. 6.17. Figure 6.17a shows how the succession of recursive calls proceeds until 1! is evaluated to be 1, which terminates the recursion. Each rectangle represents a function call. Figure 6.17 shows the values returned from each recursive call to its caller until the final value is calculated and returned.

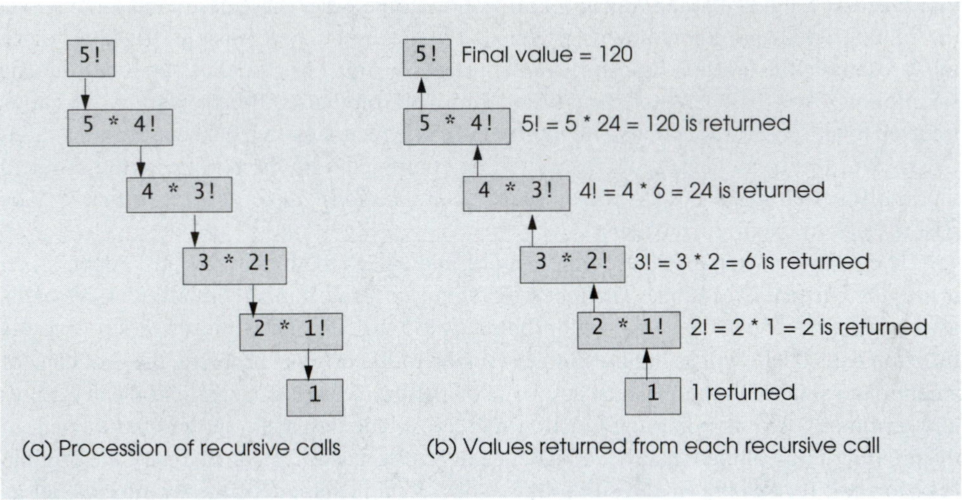

Fig. 6.17 Recursive evaluation of 5!.

Figure 6.18 uses recursion to calculate and print the factorials of the integers 0–10. The recursive function `Factorial` (lines 22–28) first determines whether its terminating condition is `true` (i.e., `number` is less than or equal to `1`). If `number` is less than or equal to `1`, `factorial` returns `1`, no further recursion is necessary and the function returns. If `number` is greater than `1`, line 27 expresses the problem as the product of `number` and a recursive call to `Factorial`, evaluating the factorial of `number - 1`. Note that `Factorial( number - 1 )` is a slightly simpler problem than the original calculation `Factorial( number )`.

```
1  // Fig. 6.18: FactorialTest.cpp
2  // Calculating factorials with recursion.
3
4  #include "stdafx.h"
5
6  #using <mscorlib.dll>
7
8  using namespace System;
9
10 int Factorial( int );
11
12 int _tmain()
13 {
14    for ( int i = 0; i <= 10; i++ )
15       Console::WriteLine( S"{0}! = {1}", i.ToString(),
16          Factorial( i ).ToString() );
17
18    return 0;
19 } // end _tmain
20
```

Fig. 6.18 Recursively calculating factorials. (Part 1 of 2.)

```
// recursive declaration of function factorial
int Factorial( int number )
{
   if ( number <= 1 )  // base case
      return 1;
   else
      return number * Factorial( number - 1 );  // recursive step
} // end function Factorial
```

```
0! = 1
1! = 1
2! = 2
3! = 6
4! = 24
5! = 120
6! = 720
7! = 5040
8! = 40320
9! = 362880
10! = 3628800
```

Fig. 6.18 Recursively calculating factorials. (Part 2 of 2.)

Function `Factorial` receives a parameter of type `int` and returns a result of type `int`. As seen in Fig. 6.18, factorial values become large quickly. Unfortunately, the `Factorial` function produces large values so quickly, type `int` and even `__int64` (a type which can hold larger integers than `int`) will not help us print many more factorial values before the size of such variables is exceeded.

This points to a weakness in most programming languages, namely, that the languages are not easily extended to handle the unique requirements of various applications. As we will see in our treatment of object-oriented programming beginning in Chapter 8 Object-Based Programming, MC++ is an extensible language—programmers with unique requirements can extend the language with new types (called classes). A programmer could create a `HugeInteger` class, for example, that would enable a program to calculate the factorials of arbitrarily large numbers.

Common Programming Error 6.17

Forgetting to return a value from a recursive function can result in syntax and/or logic errors.

Common Programming Error 6.18

Omitting the base case or writing the recursion step so that it does not converge on the base case will cause infinite recursion, eventually exhausting memory. Infinite recursion is analogous to the problem of an infinite loop in an iterative (nonrecursive) solution.

6.17 Example Using Recursion: The Fibonacci Series

The Fibonacci series

0, 1, 1, 2, 3, 5, 8, 13, 21, …

begins with 0 and 1 and has the property that each subsequent Fibonacci number is the sum of the previous two Fibonacci numbers.

The series occurs in nature and, in particular, describes a form of spiral. The ratio of successive Fibonacci numbers converges on a constant value of 1.618.... This number, too, repeatedly occurs in nature and has been called the *golden ratio* or the *golden mean.* Humans tend to find the golden mean aesthetically pleasing. Architects often design windows, rooms and buildings whose length and width are in the ratio of the golden mean. Postcards often are designed with a golden mean width-to-height ratio.

The recursive definition of the Fibonacci series is as follows:

$$Fibonacci(\ 0\ ) = 0$$
$$Fibonacci(\ 1\ ) = 1$$
$$Fibonacci(\ n\ ) = Fibonacci(\ n - 1\ ) + Fibonacci(\ n - 2\ )$$

Note that there are two base cases for the Fibonacci calculation—*Fibonacci(0)* evaluates to 0, and *Fibonacci(1)* evaluates to 1. The application in Fig. 6.19 calculates the ith Fibonacci number recursively using function `Fibonacci`. The user enters an integer indicating the ith Fibonacci number to calculate. In Fig. 6.19, the sample outputs show the results of calculating several Fibonacci numbers.

```
// Fig. 6.19: FibonacciTest.cpp
// Recursive fibonacci function.

#include "stdafx.h"

#using <mscorlib.dll>

using namespace System;

int Fibonacci( int );

int _tmain()
{
   int number, result;

   Console::Write( S"Enter an integer: " );
   number = Int32::Parse( Console::ReadLine() );
   result = Fibonacci( number );
   Console::WriteLine( S"Fibonacci({0}) = {1}",
      number.ToString(), result.ToString() );

   return 0;
} // end _tmain

// calculates Fibonacci number
int Fibonacci( int number )
{
   if ( number == 0 || number == 1 )
      return number;
```

Fig. 6.19 Recursively generating Fibonacci numbers. (Part 1 of 3.)

```
    else
       return Fibonacci( number - 1 ) + Fibonacci( number - 2 );
}
```

```
Enter an integer: 0
Fibonacci(0) = 0
```

```
Enter an integer: 1
Fibonacci(1) = 1
```

```
Enter an integer: 2
Fibonacci(2) = 1
```

```
Enter an integer: 3
Fibonacci(3) = 2
```

```
Enter an integer: 4
Fibonacci(4) = 3
```

```
Enter an integer: 5
Fibonacci(5) = 5
```

```
Enter an integer: 6
Fibonacci(6) = 8
```

```
Enter an integer: 10
Fibonacci(10) = 55
```

```
Enter an integer: 20
Fibonacci(20) = 6765
```

```
Enter an integer: 30
Fibonacci(30) = 832040
```

Fig. 6.19 Recursively generating Fibonacci numbers. (Part 2 of 3.)

```
Enter an integer: 35
Fibonacci(35) = 9227465
```

Fig. 6.19 Recursively generating Fibonacci numbers. (Part 3 of 3.)

The call to `Fibonacci` (line 18) is not a recursive call, but all subsequent calls to `Fibonacci` in line 31 are recursive. Each time `Fibonacci` is invoked, it immediately tests for the base case—that is, `number` equal to 0 or 1 (line 28). If this is true, `Fibonacci` returns `number` (*fibonacci(0)* is 0 and *fibonacci(1)* is 1). Interestingly, if `number` is greater than 1, the recursion step generates *two* recursive calls (line 31), each of which is for a slightly simpler problem than the original call to `Fibonacci`. Figure 6.20 shows how `Fibonacci(3)` evaluates.

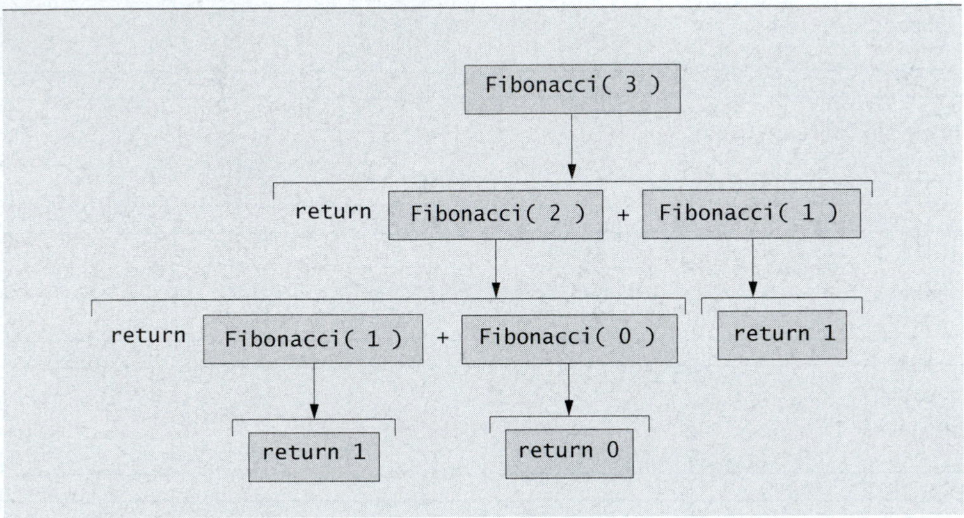

Fig. 6.20 Set of recursive calls to function `Fibonacci`.

This figure raises some issues about the order in which MC++ compilers will evaluate operands. Figure 6.20 shows that, during the evaluation of `Fibonacci(3)`, two recursive calls will be made—`Fibonacci(2)` and `Fibonacci(1)`. In what order will these calls be made? Most programmers assume the operands will be evaluated from left to right; in MC++ this is not necessarily true.

The C and C++ languages do not specify the order in which the operands of most operators (including `+`) are evaluated. Therefore, in Visual C++ .NET, the programmer can make no assumption about the order in which these calls execute. The calls could, in fact, execute `Fibonacci(2)`, then `Fibonacci(1)`, or they could execute in the reverse order (`Fibonacci(1)`, then `Fibonacci(2)`).

Good Programming Practice 6.9

Do not write expressions that depend on the order of evaluation of the operator's operands. Doing so often results in programs that are difficult to read, debug, modify and maintain.

A word of caution about using a recursive program to generate Fibonacci numbers: Each invocation of the `Fibonacci` function that does not match one of the base cases (i.e., 0 or 1) results in two recursive calls to the `Fibonacci` function. This quickly results in many function invocations. Calculating the Fibonacci value of 20 using the program in Fig. 6.19 requires 21,891 calls to the `Fibonacci` function; calculating the Fibonacci value of 30 requires 2,692,537 calls to the `Fibonacci` function.

As the programmer tries larger values, each consecutive Fibonacci number that the program is asked to calculate results in a substantial increase in the number of calls to the `Fibonacci` function and hence in calculation time. For example, the Fibonacci value 31 requires 4,356,617 calls, and the Fibonacci value of 32 requires 7,049,155 calls. As you can see, the number of calls to Fibonacci increases quickly—1,664,080 additional calls between the Fibonacci values of 30 and 31, and 2,692,538 additional calls between the Fibonacci values of 31 and 32. This difference in number of calls made between the Fibonacci values of 31 and 32 is more than 1.5 times the difference for Fibonacci values of 30 and 31. Problems of this nature humble even the world's most powerful computers! In the field called *complexity theory*, computer scientists determine how hard algorithms work to do their jobs. Complexity issues are discussed in detail in the upper-level computer science curriculum course generally called "Algorithms."

Performance Tip 6.2

Avoid Fibonacci-style recursive programs, which result in an exponential "explosion" of function calls.

6.18 Recursion vs. Iteration

In the previous sections, we studied two functions that can be implemented either recursively or iteratively. In this section, we compare the two approaches and discuss why the programmer might choose one approach over the other.

Both iteration and recursion are based on a control statement—iteration uses a repetition statement (such as `for`, `while` or `do...while`) and recursion uses a selection statement (such as `if`, `if...else` or `switch`). Both iteration and recursion involve repetition—iteration explicitly uses a repetition statement and recursion achieves repetition through repeated function calls. Iteration and recursion each involve a termination test—iteration terminates when the loop-continuation condition fails and recursion terminates when a base case is recognized. Iteration with counter-controlled repetition and recursion both gradually approach termination—iteration keeps modifying a counter until the counter assumes a value that makes the loop-continuation condition fail and recursion keeps producing simpler versions of the original problem until a base case is reached. Both iteration and recursion can execute infinitely—an infinite loop occurs with iteration if the loop-continuation test never becomes false and infinite recursion occurs if the recursion step does not reduce the problem in a manner that converges on a base case.

Recursion has many negatives. It repeatedly invokes the mechanism, and consequently the overhead, of function calls. This can be costly in both processor time and memory space. Each recursive call creates another copy of the function (actually, only the function's variables); this can consume considerable memory. Iteration normally occurs within a function, so the overhead of repeated function calls and extra memory assignment is omitted. Why then would a programmer choose recursion?

Software Engineering Observation 6.9

Any problem that can be solved recursively also can be solved iteratively (nonrecursively). A recursive approach normally is chosen in preference to an iterative approach when the recursive approach more naturally mirrors the problem and results in a program that is easier to understand and debug. Recursive solutions are also chosen when iterative solutions are not apparent.

Performance Tip 6.3

Avoid using recursion in performance situations. Recursive calls take time and consume additional memory.

Common Programming Error 6.19

Accidentally having a nonrecursive function call itself through another function can cause infinite recursion.

Most programming textbooks introduce recursion much later than we have done in this book. We feel that recursion is a sufficiently rich and complex topic that it is better to introduce it early and spread its examples over the remainder of the text.

6.19 Function Overloading

MC++ enables several functions of the same name to be defined in the same scope, as long as these functions have different sets of parameters (number of parameters, types of parameters or order of the parameters). This is called *function overloading*. When an overloaded function is called, the Visual C++ .NET compiler selects the proper function by examining the number, types and order of the call's arguments. Function overloading commonly is used to create several functions with the same name that perform similar tasks, but on different types. Figure 6.21 uses overloaded function `Square` to calculate the square of an `int` and a `double`.

```
// Fig. 6.21: FunctionOverload.cpp
// Using overloaded functions.

#include "stdafx.h"

#using <mscorlib.dll>

using namespace System;

int Square( int );
double Square( double );

int _tmain()
{
   Console::Write( S"The square of integer 7 is " );
   Console::WriteLine( Square( 7 ) );

   Console::Write( S"The square of double 7.5 is " );
   Console::WriteLine( Square( 7.5 ) );
```

Fig. 6.21 Function overloading. (Part 1 of 2.)

```
20
21      return 0;
22   } // end _tmain
23
24   // first version, takes one integer
25   int Square( int x )
26   {
27      return x * x;
28   }
29
30   // second version, takes one double
31   double Square( double y )
32   {
33      return y * y;
34   }
```

```
The square of integer 7 is 49
The square of double 7.5 is 56.25
```

Fig. 6.21 Function overloading. (Part 2 of 2.)

Good Programming Practice 6.10

Overloading functions that perform closely related tasks can make programs more readable and understandable.

The compiler distinguishes overloaded functions by their signatures. A function's *signature* is a combination of the function's name and parameter types. If the compiler looked only at function names during compilation, the code in Fig. 6.21 would be ambiguous—the compiler would not know how to distinguish the two `Square` functions. The compiler uses *overload resolution* to determine which function to call. This process first searches for all the functions that *can* be used in the context, based on the number and type of arguments that are present. It might seem that only one function would match, but recall that MC++ can convert argument values to other types implicitly. Once all matching functions are found, the closest match is chosen. This match is based on a "best-fit" algorithm, which analyzes the implicit conversions that will take place. If two or more functions match, the compiler generates an error message.

Let us look at an example. In Fig. 6.21, the compiler might use the logical name "`Square` of `int`" for the `Square` function that specifies an `int` parameter (line 10) and "`Square` of `double`" for the `Square` function that specifies a `double` parameter (line 11). If a function `Foo`'s definition begins as

```
void Foo( int a, float b )
```

the compiler might use the logical name "`Foo` of `int` and `float`." If the parameters are specified as

```
void Foo( float a, int b )
```

the compiler might use the logical name "`Foo` of `float` and `int`." The order of the parameters is important to the compiler; it considers the preceding two `Foo` functions distinct.

So far, the logical names of functions that have been used by the compiler have not mentioned the functions' return types. This is because function calls cannot be distinguished by return type. The program in Fig. 6.22 illustrates the syntax error that is generated when two functions have the same signature and different return types. Overloaded functions with different parameter lists can have different return types. Overloaded functions need not have the same number of parameters.

```
// Fig. 6.22: InvalidFunctionOverload.cpp
// Demonstrating incorrect function overloading.

#include "stdafx.h"

#using <mscorlib.dll>

using namespace System;

int Square( double x )
{
   return x * x;
} // end Square()

// ERROR! Second Square function takes same number, order
// and type of arguments.
double Square( double y )
{
   return y * y ;
} // end Square()
```

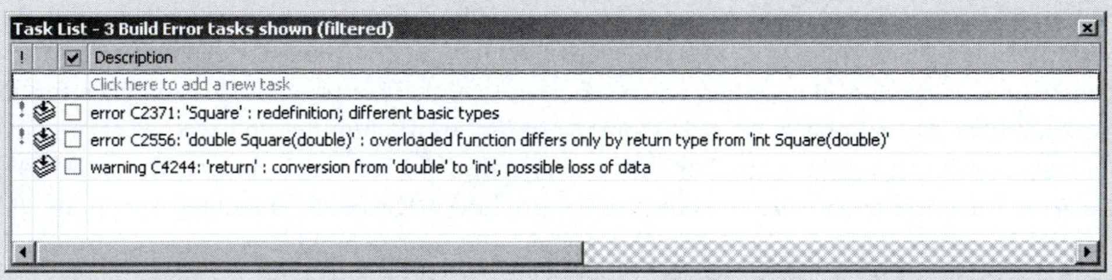
Task List - 3 Build Error tasks shown (filtered)
Description
Click here to add a new task
error C2371: 'Square' : redefinition; different basic types
error C2556: 'double Square(double)' : overloaded function differs only by return type from 'int Square(double)'
warning C4244: 'return' : conversion from 'double' to 'int', possible loss of data

Fig. 6.22 Incorrect function overloading.

Common Programming Error 6.20

Defining overloaded functions with identical parameter lists and different return types is a syntax error.

SUMMARY

- The best way to develop and maintain a large program is to construct it from small pieces, or modules. This technique is called divide and conquer.
- There are three kinds of modules in MC++—functions, methods and classes.
- Programs are written by combining new functions and classes that the programmer writes with "prepackaged" methods and classes in the .NET Framework Class Library (FCL), and in various other function and class libraries.

- The .NET Framework Class Library provides a rich collection of classes and methods for performing common mathematical calculations, string manipulations, character manipulations, input/output, error checking and other useful operations.
- The programmer can write functions to define specific tasks that may be used at many points in a program. These functions sometimes are referred to as programmer-defined functions.
- The actual statements defining the function are written only once and are hidden from other functions.
- Functions are called by writing the name of the function, followed by a left parenthesis, the function's argument (or a comma-separated list of arguments) and a right parenthesis.
- All variables declared in function definitions are local variables—they are known only in the function in which they are defined.
- Packaging code as a function allows that code to be executed from several locations in a program when the function is called.
- The `return` statement in a function passes the results of the function back to the calling function.
- The format of a function definition is

```
return-value-type function-name( parameter-list )
{
    declarations and statements
}
```

- The first line of a function definition is sometimes known as the function header. The attributes and modifiers in the function header are used to specify information about the function.
- The function *return-value-type* is the type of the result that is returned from the function to the caller. Functions can return one value at most.
- The *parameter-list* is a comma-separated list containing the declarations of the parameters received by the called function. There must be one argument in the function call for each parameter in the function definition.
- The declarations and statements within the braces that follow the function header form the function body.
- Variables can be declared in any block, and blocks can be nested.
- A function cannot be defined inside another function.
- In many cases, an argument value that does not correspond precisely to the parameter types in the function definition is converted to the proper type before the function is called.
- Types are either value types or reference types. A variable of a value type contains data of that type. A variable of a reference type, in contrast, contains the address of the location in memory where the data is stored.
- Value types are accessed directly and are passed by value; reference types are accessed through pointers or references and are passed by reference.
- Value types normally contain small pieces of data, such as `int` or `bool` values. Reference types, on the other hand, usually refer to objects.
- MC++ includes built-in value types and reference types. The built-in value types are the integral types (`signed char`, `char`, `__wchar_t`, `short`, `unsigned short`, `int`, `unsigned int`, `long`, `unsigned long`, `__int64` and `unsigned __int64`), the floating-point types (`float` and `double`) and the types `Decimal` and `bool`. In MC++, these types map to types provided by the .NET Framework (`Int32`, `Char`, `Double`, etc.). The built-in reference types are `String *` and `Object *`.

- Programmers can create new value types and reference types; the reference types and value types that programmers can create include classes, interfaces and delegates.
- Pointers enable programs to create and manipulate dynamic data structures (i.e., data structures that can grow and shrink), such as linked lists, queues, stacks and trees.
- A pointer contains the address of a variable that contains a specific value.
- The address-of operator (&) is a unary operator that returns the memory address of its operand.
- The * operator, commonly referred to as the indirection operator or dereferencing operator, returns an alias for the object to which its pointer operand points.
- Developers can use references to access and modify objects.
- The arrow operator—consisting of a minus sign (-) and a greater than sign (>) with no intervening spaces—accesses a class member via a pointer to the object.
- When an argument is passed by value, a copy of the argument's value is made and passed to the called function.
- With pass-by-reference, the caller enables the called function to access the caller's data directly and to modify that data if the called function chooses.
- It is not uncommon for a program to invoke a function repeatedly with the same argument value for a particular parameter. In such cases, the programmer can specify that the parameter has a default argument and can provide the default value for that parameter.
- Class `Random` can be used to generate random numbers.
- An enumeration, introduced by the MC++ keyword `enum` and followed by a type name, is a value type that contains a set of constant values. The constant values, called enumeration constants or enumerators, start at 0 (unless specified otherwise) and are incremented by 1.
- The identifiers in an `enum` must be unique, but separate enumerators can have the same integer value.
- An identifier's duration (its lifetime) is the period during which that identifier exists in memory.
- Identifiers that represent local variables in a function have automatic duration. Automatic-duration variables are created when program control reaches the variable's declaration. They exist while the block in which they are declared is active, and they are destroyed when the block in which they are declared is exited.
- The scope (sometimes called a declaration space) of an identifier for a variable, reference or function is the portion of the program in which that identifier can be referenced.
- A local variable or reference declared in a block can be used only in that block or in blocks nested within that block.
- A recursive function is one that calls itself either directly, or indirectly through another function.
- A recursive function is capable of solving only the simplest case(s), or base case(s). If the function is called with a base case, the function returns a result. If the function is called with a more complex problem, the function divides the problem into two conceptual pieces—a piece that the function knows how to solve (base case) and a piece that the function does not know how to solve.
- To make recursion feasible, the portion of the problem that the function does not know how to solve must resemble the original problem, but be a slightly simpler or smaller version.
- Certain recursive functions can lead to an exponential "explosion" of function calls.
- Both iteration and recursion are based on a control statement. Iteration uses a repetition statement (such as `for`, `while` or `do...while`); recursion uses a selection statement (such as `if`, `if...else` or `switch`).
- Both iteration and recursion involve repetition. Iteration explicitly uses a repetition statement; recursion achieves repetition through repeated function calls.

- Iteration and recursion each involve a termination test. Iteration terminates when the loop-continuation condition fails; recursion terminates when a base case is recognized.
- Both iteration and recursion can execute infinitely. An infinite loop occurs with iteration if the loop-continuation test never becomes false; infinite recursion occurs if the recursion step does not reduce the problem in a manner that converges on the base case.
- A recursive approach normally is chosen in preference to an iterative approach when the recursive approach more naturally mirrors the problem and results in a program that is easier to understand and debug.
- Several functions can have the same name, as long as these functions have different sets of parameters, in terms of number of parameters, types of the parameters and order of the parameters. This is called function overloading.
- Function overloading commonly is used to create several functions with the same name that perform similar tasks, but on different types.
- A function's signature is a combination of the function's name and parameter types.

TERMINOLOGY

address-of operator (&)
argument to a function call
arrow operator (->)
assembly
automatic duration
base case in recursion
calling function
cast operator
coercion of arguments
comma-separated list of arguments
complexity theory
constant variable
control statements in iteration
control statements in recursion
default argument
divide-and-conquer approach
duration of an identifier
enumeration
enumeration constant
enumerator
`enum` keyword
exhausting memory
exponential "explosion" of calls in recursion
factorial
Fibonacci series defined recursively
function
function body
function call
function header
function overloading
function prototype
golden ratio
indirection operator (*)
infinite loop
infinite recursion
invoke a function
lifetime of an identifier
local variable
method
mixed-type expression
modularizing a program with functions
nested block
`new` operator
overloaded function
parameter list
pass-by-reference
pass-by-value
pointer
programmer-defined function
promotions for primitive types
`Random` class
recursive function
reference
reference type
`return` keyword
return-value type
scaling factor
scope of an identifier
sequence of random numbers
signature of a function
simulation
software reusability
`static` duration
`static` method
static variable
termination test

user-defined function
value type

`void` return-value type

SELF-REVIEW EXERCISES

6.1 Fill in the blanks in each of the following statements:

a) Program modules in MC++ are called ________, ________ and ________.
b) A function is invoked with a(n) ________.
c) A variable known only within the function in which it is defined is called a(n) ________.
d) The ________ statement in a called function can be used to pass the value of an expression back to the calling function.
e) The keyword ________ is used in a function header to indicate that a function does not return a value.
f) The ________ of an identifier is the portion of the program in which the identifier can be used.
g) The three ways to return control from a called function to a caller are ________, ________ and ________.
h) The ________ method of class `Random` generates random numbers.
i) Variables declared in a block or in a function's parameter list are of ________ duration.
j) A function that calls itself either directly or indirectly is a(n) ________ function.
k) A recursive function typically has two components: one that provides a means for the recursion to terminate by testing for a(n) ________ case, and one that expresses the problem as a recursive call for a slightly simpler problem than the original call.
l) In MC++, it is possible to have various functions with the same name that operate on different types or numbers of arguments. This is called function ________.
m) Local variables declared in a function have ________ scope, as do function parameters, which are considered local variables of the function.
n) Iteration is based on a control statement. It uses a(n) ________ statement.
o) Recursion is based on a control statement. It uses a(n) ________ statement.
p) Recursion achieves repetition through repeated ________ calls.
q) The best way to develop and maintain a large program is to divide it into several smaller program ________, each of which is more manageable than the original program.
r) It is possible to define functions with the same ________, but different parameter lists.
s) Placing a semicolon after the right parenthesis that encloses the parameter list of a function definition is a(n) ________ error.
t) The ________ is a comma-separated list containing the declarations of the parameters received by the called function.
u) The ________ is the type of the result returned from a called function.

6.2 State whether each of the following is *true* or *false*. If *false*, explain why.

a) `Math` method `Abs` rounds its parameter to the smallest integer.
b) Variable type `float` can be promoted to type `double`.
c) Variable type `__wchar_t` cannot be promoted to type `int`.
d) A recursive function is one that calls itself.
e) When a function recursively calls itself, this call is known as the base case.
f) 0! is equal to 1.
g) Forgetting to return a value from a recursive function when one is needed results in a syntax error.
h) Infinite recursion occurs when a function converges on the base case.
i) A recursive implementation of the `Fibonacci` function is always efficient.
j) Any problem that can be solved recursively also can be solved iteratively.

6.3 Write an application that tests whether the examples of the `Math` class method calls shown in Fig. 6.2 actually produce the indicated results.

6.4 Give the function header for each of the following functions:

a) Function `hypotenuse`, which takes two double-precision, floating-point arguments `side1` and `side2` and returns a double-precision, floating-point result.
b) Function `smallest`, which takes three integers, `x`, `y`, `z`, and returns an integer.
c) Function `instructions`, which does not take any arguments and does not return a value. [*Note*: Such functions commonly are used to display instructions to a user.]
d) Function `intToFloat`, which takes an integer argument, `number`, and returns a floating-point result.

6.5 Find the error in each of the following program segments and explain how the error can be corrected:

a)
```
int g() {
   Console::WriteLine( S"Inside function g" );
   int h() {
      Console::WriteLine( S"Inside function h" );
   }
}
```
b)
```
int sum( int x, int y ) {
   int result;
   result = x + y;
}
```
c)
```
int sum( int n ) {
   if ( n == 0 )
      return 0;
   else
      n + sum( n - 1 );
}
```
d)
```
void f( float a ); {
   float a;
   Console::WriteLine( a );
}
```
e)
```
void product() {
   int a = 6, b = 5, c = 4, result;
   result = a * b * c;
   Console::WriteLine( S"Result is {0} ", result.ToString() );
   return result;
}
```

ANSWERS TO SELF-REVIEW EXERCISES

6.1 a) functions, methods, classes. b) function call. c) local variable. d) `return`. e) `void`. f) scope. g) `return;`, `return` *expression*;, encountering the closing right brace of a function. h) `Next`. i) automatic. j) recursive. k) base. l) overloading. m) block. n) repetition. o) selection. p) function. q) modules. r) name. s) syntax. t) parameter list. u) return-value-type.

6.2 a) False. `Math` method `Abs` returns the absolute value of a number. b) True. c) False. Type `__wchar_t` can be promoted to `int`, `float`, `__int64` and `double`. d) True. e) False. When a function recursively calls itself, it is known as the recursive call or recursion step. f) True. g) True. h) False. Infinite recursion will occur when a recursive function does not converge on the base case. i) False. Recursion repeatedly invokes the mechanism, and consequently, the overhead, of function calls. j) True.

6.3 The following code demonstrates the use of some `Math` class method calls:

```
// Exercise 6.3: MathMethods.cpp
// Demonstrates Math class methods.

#include "stdafx.h"

       <mscorlib.dll>

                System;

   _tmain()
{

   Console::WriteLine( S"Math::Abs( 23.7 ) = {0}",
      Math::Abs( 23.7 ).ToString() );
   Console::WriteLine( S"Math::Abs( 0.0 ) = {0}" ,
      Math::Abs( 0.0 ).ToString() );
   Console::WriteLine( S"Math::Abs( -23.7 ) = {0}",
      Math::Abs( -23.7 ).ToString() );
   Console::WriteLine( S"Math::Ceiling( 9.2 ) = {0}",
      Math::Ceiling( 9.2 ).ToString() );
   Console::WriteLine( S"Math::Ceiling( -9.8 ) = {0}",
      Math::Ceiling( -9.8 ).ToString() );
   Console::WriteLine( S"Math::Cos( 0.0 ) = {0}",
      Math::Cos( 0.0 ).ToString() );
   Console::WriteLine( S"Math::Exp( 1.0 ) = {0}",
      Math::Exp( 1.0 ).ToString() );
   Console::WriteLine( S"Math::Exp( 2.0 ) = {0}",
      Math::Exp( 2.0 ).ToString() );
   Console::WriteLine( S"Math::Floor( 9.2 ) = {0}",
      Math::Floor( 9.2 ).ToString() );
   Console::WriteLine( S"Math::Floor( -9.8 ) = {0}",
      Math::Floor( -9.8 ).ToString() );
   Console::WriteLine( S"Math::Log( 2.718282 ) = {0}",
      Math::Log( 2.718282 ).ToString() );
   Console::WriteLine( S"Math::Log( 7.389056 ) = {0}",
      Math::Log( 7.389056 ).ToString() );
   Console::WriteLine( S"Math::Max( 2.3, 12.7 ) = {0}",
      Math::Max( 2.3, 12.7 ).ToString() );
   Console::WriteLine( S"Math::Max( -2.3, -12.7 ) = {0}",
      Math::Max( -2.3, -12.7 ).ToString() );
   Console::WriteLine( S"Math::Min( 2.3, 12.7 ) = {0}",
      Math::Min( 2.3, 12.7 ).ToString() );
   Console::WriteLine( S"Math::Min( -2.3, -12.7 ) = {0}",
      Math::Min( -2.3, -12.7 ).ToString() );
   Console::WriteLine( S"Math::Pow( 2, 7 ) = {0}",
      Math::Pow( 2, 7 ).ToString() );
   Console::WriteLine( S"Math::Pow( 9, .5 ) = {0}",
      Math::Pow( 9, .5 ).ToString() );
   Console::WriteLine( S"Math::Sin( 0.0 ) = {0}",
      Math::Sin( 0.0 ).ToString() );
   Console::WriteLine( S"Math::Sqrt( 25.0 ) = {0}",
      Math::Sqrt( 25.0 ).ToString() );
   Console::WriteLine( S"Math::Tan( 0.0 ) = {0}",
      Math::Tan( 0.0 ).ToString() );

   return 0;
} // end _tmain
```

(Part 1 of 2.)

```
Math::Abs( 23.7 ) = 23.7
Math::Abs( 0.0 ) = 0
Math::Abs( -23.7 ) = 23.7
Math::Ceiling( 9.2 ) = 10
Math::Ceiling( -9.8 ) = -9
Math::Cos( 0.0 ) = 1
Math::Exp( 1.0 ) = 2.71828182845905
Math::Exp( 2.0 ) = 7.38905609893065
Math::Floor( 9.2 ) = 9
Math::Floor( -9.8 ) = -10
Math::Log( 2.718282 ) = 1.00000006310639
Math::Log( 7.389056 ) = 1.99999998661119
Math::Max( 2.3, 12.7 ) = 12.7
Math::Max( -2.3, -12.7 ) = -2.3
Math::Min( 2.3, 12.7 ) = 2.3
Math::Min( -2.3, -12.7 ) = -12.7
Math::Pow( 2, 7 ) = 128
Math::Pow( 9, .5 ) = 3
Math::Sin( 0.0 ) = 0
Math::Sqrt( 25.0 ) = 5
Math::Tan( 0.0 ) = 0
```

(Part 2 of 2.)

6.4 a) `double hypotenuse( double side1, double side2 )`
b) `int smallest( int x, int y, int z )`
c) `void instructions()`
d) `float intToFloat( int number )`

6.5 a) Error: Function `h` is defined in function `g`.
Correction: Move the definition of `h` out of the definition of `g`.
b) Error: The function is supposed to return an integer, but does not.
Correction: Delete variable `result` and place the following statement in the function:

```
return x + y;
```

or add the following statement at the end of the function body:

```
return result;
```

c) Error: The result of `n + sum(n - 1)` is not returned by this recursive function, resulting in a syntax error.
Correction: Rewrite the statement in the `else` clause as

```
return n + sum( n - 1 );
```

d) Error: The semicolon after the right parenthesis that encloses the parameter list, and the redefining of the parameter `a` in the function definition are both incorrect.
Correction: Delete the semicolon after the right parenthesis of the parameter list and delete the declaration `float a;`.
e) Error: The `void` function returns a value.
Correction: Change the return type to `int` or eliminate the `return` statement.

EXERCISES

6.6 What is the value returned by each of the following calls?
a) `Math::Abs( 7.5 );`
b) `Math::Floor( 7.5 );`
c) `Math::Abs( 0.0 );`

d) `Math::Ceiling( 0.0 );`
e) `Math::Abs( -6.4 );`
f) `Math::Ceiling( -6.4 );`
g) `Math::Ceiling( -Math::Abs( -8 + Math::Floor( -5.5 ) ) );`

6.7 A parking garage charges a $2.00 minimum fee to park for up to three hours. The garage charges an additional $0.50 per hour for each hour *or part thereof* in excess of three hours. The maximum charge for any given 24-hour period is $10.00. Assume that no car parks for longer than 24 hours at a time. Write a program that calculates and displays the parking charges for each customer who parked a car in this garage yesterday. You should enter the hours parked for each customer. The program should display the charge for the current customer. The program should use the function `CalculateCharges` to determine the charge for each customer.

6.8 Write a function `IntegerPower( base, exponent )` that returns the value of

$\texttt{base}^{\texttt{exponent}}$

For example, `IntegerPower( 3, 4 ) = 3 * 3 * 3 * 3`. Assume that `exponent` is a positive, nonzero integer, and `base` is an integer. Function `IntegerPower` should use `for` or `while` to control the calculation. Do not use any `Math` class methods. Incorporate this function into a program that reads integer values for `base` and `exponent` from the user and performs the calculation with the `IntegerPower` function.

6.9 Define a function `Hypotenuse` that calculates the length of the hypotenuse of a right triangle when the other two sides are given. The function should take two arguments of type `double` and return the hypotenuse as a `double`. Incorporate this function into a program that reads integer values for `side1` and `side2` from the user and performs the calculation with the `Hypotenuse` function. Determine the length of the hypotenuse for each of the triangles in Fig. 6.23:

Triangle	Side 1	Side 2
1	3.0	4.0
2	5.0	12.0
3	8.0	15.0

Fig. 6.23 Values for the sides of triangles in Exercise 6.9.

6.10 Write a function `SquareOfAsterisks` that displays a solid square of asterisks whose side is specified in integer parameter `side`. For example, if `side` is 4, the function displays

```
****
****
****
****
```

Incorporate this function into an application that reads an integer value for `side` from the user and performs the drawing with the `SquareOfAsterisks` function. This function should display the result based on input from the user.

6.11 Modify the function created in Exercise 6.10 to form the square out of whatever character is contained in character parameter `fillCharacter`. Thus, if `side` is `5` and `fillCharacter` is `'#'`, this function should print

```
#####
#####
#####
#####
#####
```

6.12 Write an application that simulates coin tossing. Let the program toss the coin until the user no longer wishes to continue. Count the number of times each side of the coin appears. Display the results. The program should call function `Flip` that takes no arguments and returns `false` for tails and `true` for heads. [*Note*: If the program realistically simulates the coin tossing, each side of the coin should appear approximately half of the time.]

6.13 Computers are playing an increasing role in education. Write a program that will help an elementary school student learn multiplication. Use the `Next` function from an object of type `Random` to produce two positive one-digit integers. It should print a question, such as

```
How much is 6 times 7?
```

The student should then type the answer. Your program should check the student's answer. If it is correct, print the string `"Very good!"`, then ask another multiplication question. If the answer is wrong, print the string `"No. Please try again."`, then let the student try the same question again until the student finally gets it right. A separate function should be used to generate each new question. This function should be called once when the program begins execution and each time the user answers the question correctly.

6.14 (*Towers of Hanoi*) Every budding computer scientist must grapple with certain classic problems and the Towers of Hanoi (Fig. 6.24) is one of the most famous. Legend has it that in a temple in the Far East, priests are attempting to move a stack of disks from one peg to another. The initial stack had 64 disks threaded onto one peg and arranged from bottom to top by decreasing size. The priests are attempting to move the stack from this peg to a second peg under the constraints that exactly one disk is moved at a time, and at no time may a larger disk be placed above a smaller disk. A third peg is available for temporarily holding disks. Supposedly, the world will end when the priests complete their task, so there is little incentive for us to facilitate their efforts.

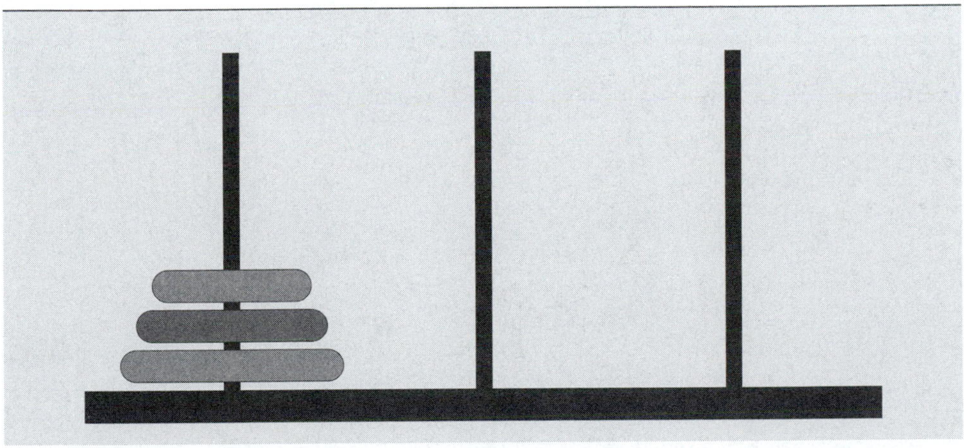

Fig. 6.24 The Towers of Hanoi for the case with three disks.

Let us assume that the priests are attempting to move the disks from peg 1 to peg 3. We wish to develop an algorithm that will print the precise sequence of peg-to-peg disk transfers.

If we were to approach this problem with conventional functions, we would find ourselves hopelessly knotted up in managing the disks. However, if we attack the problem with recursion in mind, it becomes tractable. Moving n disks can be viewed in terms of moving only $n - 1$ disks (and hence, the recursion) as follows:

a) Move $n - 1$ disks from peg 1 to peg 2, using peg 3 as a temporary holding area.
b) Move the last disk (the largest) from peg 1 to peg 3.
c) Move the $n - 1$ disks from peg 2 to peg 3, using peg 1 as a temporary holding area.

The process ends when the last task involves moving $n = 1$ disk (i.e., the base case). This is accomplished by trivially moving the disk without the need for a temporary holding area.

Write a program to solve the Towers of Hanoi problem. Allow the user to enter the number of disks. Use a recursive `Tower` function with four parameters:

a) The number of disks to be moved
b) The peg on which these disks are threaded initially
c) The peg to which this stack of disks is to be moved
d) The peg to be used as a temporary holding area

Your program should display the precise instructions for moving the disks from the starting peg to the destination peg. For example, to move a stack of three disks from peg 1 to peg 3, your program should print the following series of moves:

1 → 3 (This means move one disk from peg 1 to peg 3.)
1 → 2
3 → 2
1 → 3
2 → 1
2 → 3
1 → 3

6.15 The *greatest common divisor* of integers `x` and `y` is the largest integer that evenly divides both `x` and `y`. Write a recursive function `Gcd` that returns the greatest common divisor of `x` and `y`. The `Gcd` of `x` and `y` is defined recursively as follows: If `y` is equal to `0`, then `Gcd( x, y )` is `x`; otherwise, `Gcd( x, y )` is `Gcd( y, x % y )`, where `%` is the modulus operator.

7

Arrays

Objectives

- To become familiar with the array data structure.
- To understand how managed arrays store, sort and search lists and tables of values.
- To understand how to declare and initialize a managed array.
- To be able to refer to individual elements of a managed array.
- To understand how to pass managed arrays to functions.
- To understand basic sorting techniques.
- To be able to declare and manipulate multidimensional managed arrays.

With sobs and tears he sorted out
Those of the largest size …
Lewis Carroll

Attempt the end, and never stand to doubt;
Nothing's so hard, but search will find it out.
Robert Herrick

Now go, write it before them in a table,
and note it in a book.
Isaiah 30:8

'Tis in my memory lock'd,
And you yourself shall keep the key of it.
William Shakespeare

Outline

7.1 Introduction

This chapter serves as an introduction to data structures. *Arrays* are data structures consisting of data items of the same type. Arrays are "static" entities, in that they remain the same size once they are created. MC++ provides *managed arrays*. Managed arrays are actually objects of the `System::Array` class and can therefore use the various methods and properties provided by this class. We begin by learning how to create and access managed arrays, then use this knowledge for more complex array manipulations, including powerful searching and sorting techniques. Next, we demonstrate arrays that have multiple dimensions. Chapter 22, Data Structures and Collections, combines our discussion of data structures by introducing dynamic data structures such as lists, queues, stacks and trees that, unlike arrays, can grow and shrink as programs execute. Chapter 22 also introduces Visual C++ .NET's predefined data structures that enable the programmer to use existing data structures for lists, queues, stacks and trees, rather than having to "reinvent the wheel."

7.2 Arrays

An array is a named group of memory locations that all have the same type. To refer to a particular location or element in the array, we specify the name of the array and the *position number* (a value that indicates a specific location within the array) of the element to which we refer.

Figure 7.1 shows an integer array called `c`. This array contains 12 *elements*. A program can refer to any element of an array by giving the name of the array followed by the position number of the element in square brackets ([]). The first element in every array is referred to as the *zeroth element*. Thus, the first element of array c is referred to as c[0], the second element of array c is referred to as c[1], the seventh element of array c is referred to as c[6] and so on. In general, the *i*th element of array c is referred to as c[i - 1]. Array names follow the same conventions as other variable names, as discussed in Chapter 3.

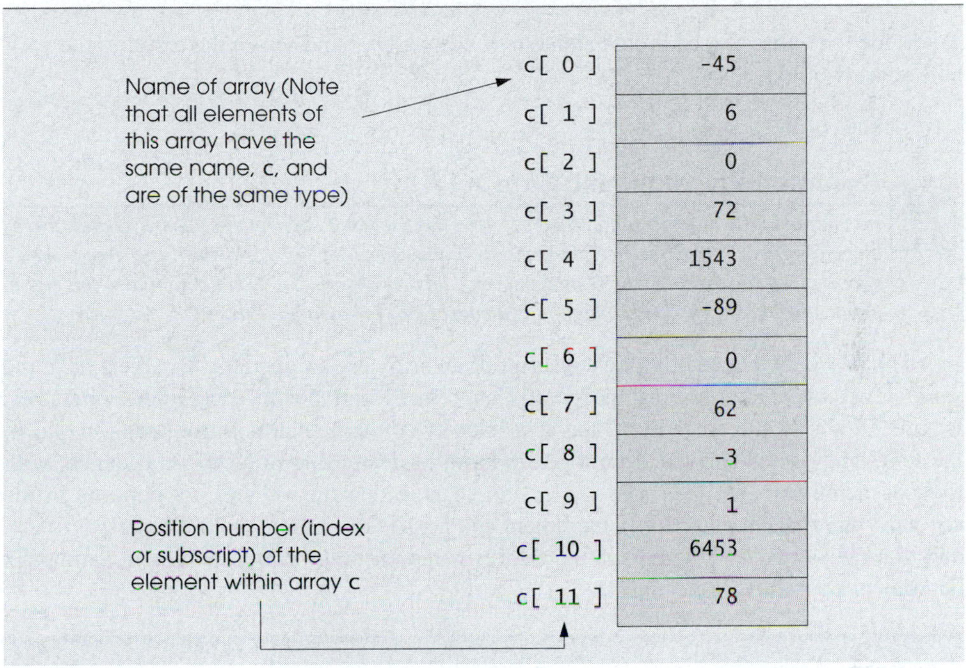

Fig. 7.1 12-element array.

The position number in square brackets is more formally called a *index* (or a *subscript*). An index must be an integer or an integer expression. If a program uses an expression as an index, the program evaluates the expression first to determine the index. For example, if variable a is equal to 5 and variable b is equal to 6, then the statement

```
c[ a + b ] += 2;
```

adds 2 to array element c[11]. Note that an indexed array name is an *lvalue*—it can be used on the left side of an assignment to place a new value into an array element.

Let us examine array c in Fig. 7.1 more closely. Every array in MC++ "knows" its own length. The length of array c is obtained by the expression:[1]

```
c->Length
```

1. Notice that we use the arrow operator (->) rather than the dot operator (.) to access members of an array. If the dot operator is used with the array name, the Visual Studio .NET compiler automatically replaces it with the arrow operator. We discuss member access operators in more detail in Chapter 8, Object-Based Programming.

The 12 elements of array `c` are referred to as `c[ 0 ]`, `c[ 1 ]`, `c[ 2 ]`, …, `c[ 11 ]`. The *value* of `c[ 0 ]` is `-45`, the value of `c[ 1 ]` is `6`, the value of `c[ 2 ]` is `0`, the value of `c[ 7 ]` is `62` and the value of `c[ 11 ]` is `78`. To calculate the sum of the values contained in the first three elements of array `c` and to store the result in variable `sum`, we would write

```
sum = c[ 0 ] + c[ 1 ] + c[ 2 ];
```

To divide the value of the seventh element of array `c` by `2` and assign the result to the variable `x`, we would write

```
x = c[ 6 ] / 2;
```

Common Programming Error 7.1

It is important to note the difference between the "seventh element of the array" and "array element seven." Array subscripts begin at 0, thus the "seventh element of the array" has a subscript of 6, while "array element seven" has a subscript of 7 and is actually the eighth element of the array. This confusion is a source of "off-by-one" errors.

The brackets that enclose the subscript of an array are an operator. Brackets have the same level of precedence as the postfix increment and postfix decrement operators. Figure 7.2 shows the precedence and associativity of the operators introduced thus far in the text. They are displayed from top to bottom in decreasing order of precedence, with their associativity and type. The reader should note that the `++` and `--` operators in the second row represent the postfix increment and postfix decrement operators, respectively, and that the `++` and `--` operators in the third row represent the prefix increment and prefix decrement operators, respectively.

<table>
<tr><th>Operators</th><th>Associativity</th><th>Type</th></tr>
<tr><td>::</td><td>left to right</td><td>scope resolution</td></tr>
<tr><td>[]   .   ->   ++   --
static_cast< type ></td><td>left to right
left to right</td><td>postfix
unary cast</td></tr>
<tr><td>++   --   +   -   !</td><td>right to left</td><td>prefix</td></tr>
<tr><td>&
*</td><td>right to left</td><td>address-of
dereference</td></tr>
<tr><td>*   /   %</td><td>left to right</td><td>multiplicative</td></tr>
<tr><td>+   -</td><td>left to right</td><td>additive</td></tr>
<tr><td><   <=   >   >=</td><td>left to right</td><td>relational</td></tr>
<tr><td>==   !=</td><td>left to right</td><td>equality</td></tr>
<tr><td>&&</td><td>left to right</td><td>logical AND</td></tr>
<tr><td>||</td><td>left to right</td><td>logical OR</td></tr>
<tr><td>?:</td><td>right to left</td><td>conditional</td></tr>
<tr><td>=   +=   -=   *=   /=   %=</td><td>right to left</td><td>assignment</td></tr>
</table>

Fig. 7.2 Precedence and associativity of the operators discussed so far.

7.3 Declaring and Allocating Arrays

Arrays occupy space in memory. The programmer specifies the type of the elements and uses *operator new* to allocate dynamically the number of elements required by each array. Arrays are allocated with new because arrays are objects and all objects must be created with new. We will see an exception to this rule shortly.

The declaration

```
int c __gc[] = new int __gc[ 12 ];
```

allocates 12 elements for integer array c. The preceding statement can also be performed in two steps as follows:

```
// declare managed array
int c __gc[];

// allocate space for array; set pointer to that space
c = new int __gc[ 12 ];
```

When managed arrays are allocated (such as the one allocated previously), the elements are initialized to zero for the numeric primitive-type variables, to false for bool variables and to 0 for pointers.

MC++ keyword *__gc* in the array declarations specifies that the arrays are *managed arrays.*[2] In general, keyword __gc declares a *managed type.*[3] Managed types are garbage collected (i.e., memory no longer in use is freed) and managed by the CLR[4] part of the .NET Framework that executes MC++ programs (also known as a *runtime environment*). Managed arrays (sometimes called __gc arrays) inherit from class System::Array. We discuss __gc classes and garbage collection in Chapter 8, Object-Based Programming and Chapter 9, Object-Oriented Programming: Inheritance.

Conversely, keyword *__nogc* declares an *unmanaged array*. Unmanaged arrays (sometimes called __nogc arrays) are standard C++ arrays and do not receive the benefits of managed arrays, such as garbage collection. Unmanaged arrays are also not considered objects in C++ as managed arrays are in MC++. Throughout this book, we will use managed arrays unless otherwise specified.

A single declaration may be used to reserve memory for several arrays. The following declaration reserves 100 elements for String * array b and 27 elements for String * array x:

```
String *b[] = new String*[ 100 ],
   *x[] = new String*[ 27 ];
```

Similarly, the following declaration reserves 10 elements for array1 and 20 elements for array2 (both of type double):

```
double array1 __gc[] = new double __gc[ 10 ],
   array2 __gc[] = new double __gc[ 20 ];
```

---

2. For more information about managed arrays, visit msdn.microsoft.com/library/default.asp?url=/library/en-us/vcmxspec/html/vcManagedExtensionsSpec_4_5.asp.
3. For more information about managed types, visit msdn.microsoft.com/library/default.asp?url=/library/en-us/vcmex/html/vclrf__gc.asp.
4. For more information about the CLR, visit msdn.microsoft.com/library/default.asp?url=/library/en-us/cpguide/html/cpconthecommonlanguageruntime.asp.

Notice that, in the `String *` array declaration, we have to prefix `x[]` with `*` to declare it as a `String *` array (in the same way that we prefix `b[]` with `*`). Also notice that we do not have to include keyword `__gc`. `String *` represents a pointer to a managed type (`System::String`), so arrays `b` and `x` are managed arrays by default. Keyword `__gc` is optional when declaring managed arrays a managed type (e.g., `Int32`, `Double`, `Boolean` and `String *`). However, `__gc` is required when using MC++ aliases (e.g, `int`, `double` and `bool`) to declare managed arrays. For example, we must use keyword `__gc` when declaring `array1` and `array2`, because `double` is an MC++ alias for .NET type `Double` (located in namespace `System`). If we replace `double` with `Double`, we can declare the arrays as follows:

```
Double array1[] = new Double[ 10 ],
   array2[] = new Double[ 20 ];
```

Refer to Fig. 6.5 to review types of the .NET Framework and their MC++ aliases.

Managed arrays may be declared to contain any managed type. In an array of value types, every element of the array contains one value of the declared type. For example, every element of an `int` array is an `int` value.

In an array of pointers, every element of the array points to an object of the type of the array. For example, every element of a `String *` array is a pointer to an object of class `String`.

7.4 Examples Using Arrays

This section presents several examples using arrays that demonstrate declaring arrays, allocating arrays, initializing arrays and manipulating array elements in various ways. For simplicity, most examples in this section use arrays that contain elements of type `int`. Please remember that a program can declare arrays of most types.

7.4.1 Allocating an Array and Initializing Its Elements

Figure 7.3 creates three integer arrays of 10 elements each and displays those arrays in tabular format. The program demonstrates several techniques for declaring and initializing arrays.

```
// Fig. 7.3: InitArray.cpp
// Different ways of initializing arrays.

#include "stdafx.h"

#using <mscorlib.dll>

using namespace System;

int _tmain()
{
   int x __gc[];                   // declare array x
   x = new int __gc[ 10 ];   // dynamically allocate array

```

Fig. 7.3 Initializing array elements in three different ways. (Part 1 of 2.)

```
15       // initializer list specifies value of each element in y; number of
16       // elements in array determined by number of initializer values
17       int y __gc[] = { 32, 27, 64, 18, 95, 14, 90, 70, 60, 37 };
18
19       const int ARRAY_SIZE = 10;    // named constant
20       int z __gc[];                 // declare array z
21
22       // allocate array of ARRAY_SIZE (i.e., 10) elements
23       z = new int __gc[ ARRAY_SIZE ];
24
25       // set the values in array z
26       for ( int i = 0; i < z->Length; i++ )
27          z[ i ] = 2 + 2 * i;
28
29       Console::WriteLine( S"Subscript\tArray x\t\tArray y\t\tArray z" );
30
31       // output values for each array
32       for ( int i = 0; i < ARRAY_SIZE; i++ )
33          Console::WriteLine( S"{0}\t\t{1}\t\t{2}\t\t{3}", i.ToString(),
34             x[ i ].ToString(), y[ i ].ToString(), z[ i ].ToString() );
35
36       return 0;
37    } // end _tmain
```

```
Subscript     Array x     Array y     Array z
0             0           32          2
1             0           27          4
2             0           64          6
3             0           18          8
4             0           95          10
5             0           14          12
6             0           90          14
7             0           70          16
8             0           60          18
9             0           37          20
```

Fig. 7.3 Initializing array elements in three different ways. (Part 2 of 2.)

Line 12 declares array `x` to be a managed array of `int` values. The name of an array (`x`) is actually a pointer to the array's first element. Each element in the array is of type `int`. The variable `x` is of type `int __gc[]`, which denotes a managed array whose elements are of type `int`. Line 13 allocates the 10 elements of the array with `new` and assigns the array to pointer `x`. Each element of this array has the default value `0`.

Line 17 creates another `int` array and initializes each element via an *initializer list*. In this case, the number of values in the initializer list determines the array's size. For example, line 17 creates a 10-element array with the indices `0–9` and the values specified in braces to the right of the =. Note that this declaration does not require the `new` operator to create the array object—the compiler allocates memory for the object when it encounters an array declaration that includes an initializer list.

On line 19, we create constant integer `ARRAY_SIZE`, using keyword *`const`*. *Constants* are values that cannot change during program execution. A constant must be initialized in the same statement where it is declared and cannot be modified thereafter. If an attempt is made to modify a `const` variable after it is declared, the compiler issues a compilation error. Constants are also called *named constants*. They are often used to make a program more readable and usually are denoted with variable names in all capital letters.

Common Programming Error 7.2

Assigning a value to a constant after the constant has been initialized is a compilation error.

Good Programming Practice 7.1

Using constants instead of literal constants (e.g., values such as 8) makes programs clearer. This technique is used to eliminate so-called magic numbers*; i.e., repeatedly mentioning the number 10, for example, as a counter for a loop gives the number 10 an artificial significance and could unfortunately confuse the reader when the program includes other 10s that have nothing to do with the counter.*

Line 23 creates integer array `z` of length 10, using the `ARRAY_SIZE` named constant to specify the number of elements in the array. The `for` statement in lines 26–27 initializes each element in array `z`. The loop uses the array's member `Length` to determine the number of elements in the array. Array `z` has access to property `Length` because, as a managed array, it is also an object of type `System::Array` (as are arrays `x` and `y`). Line 27 generates each initial value multiplying each successive value of the loop counter by `2` and adding `2` to the product. After this initialization, array `z` contains the even integers `2`, `4`, `6`, …, `20`.

The `for` statement in lines 32–34 displays the values in arrays `x`, `y` and `z`. Zero-based counting (remember, array subscripts start at 0) allows the loop to access every element of the array. The constant `ARRAY_SIZE` in the `for` statement condition (line 32) specifies the arrays' lengths.

7.4.2 Totaling the Elements of an Array

Often, the elements of an array represent a series of values to be used in calculations. For example, if the elements of an array represent total sales in different districts for a certain company, the company may wish to total the elements of the array to calculate the total sales in all the districts combined.

Figure 7.4 sums the values contained in the 10-element integer array `a` (declared, allocated and initialized on line 12). Line 16 in the body of the `for` loop performs the addition using the array element at position `i` during each loop iteration. [*Note:* The values being supplied as initializers for array `a` normally would be read into the program. For example, the user could enter the values through a GUI textbox or the values could be read from a file on disk. (See Chapter 17, Files and Streams.)]

```
1  // Fig. 7.4: SumArray.cpp
2  // Computing the sum of the elements in an array.
3
4  #include "stdafx.h"
5
6  #using <mscorlib.dll>
```

Fig. 7.4 Summing the elements of an array. (Part 1 of 2.)

```
using namespace System;

int _tmain()
{
   int a __gc[] = { 1, 2, 3, 4, 5, 6, 7, 8, 9, 10 };
   int total = 0;

   for ( int i = 0; i < a->Length; i++ )
      total += a[ i ];

   Console::WriteLine( S"Total of array elements: {0}",
      total.ToString() );

   return 0;
} // end _tmain
```

```
Total of array elements: 55
```

Fig. 7.4 Summing the elements of an array. (Part 2 of 2.)

7.4.3 Using Histograms to Display Array Data Graphically

Many programs present data to users in a graphical manner. For example, numeric values often are displayed as bars in a bar chart. In such a chart, longer bars represent larger numeric values. One simple way to display numeric data graphically is with a *histogram* that shows each numeric value as a bar of asterisks (*).

Our next application (Fig. 7.5) reads numbers from an array and graphs the information in the form of a bar chart, or histogram. The program displays each number followed by a bar consisting of a corresponding number of asterisks. The nested `for` loops (lines 17–25) append the bars to the output. Note the loop continuation condition of the inner `for` statement on line 21 (`j <= array[ i ]`). Each time the program reaches the inner `for` statement, the loop counts from `1` to `array[ i ]`, using a value in array `array` to determine the final value of the control variable `j` and the number of asterisks to display.

```
1  // Fig. 7.5: Histogram.cpp
2  // Using data to create a histogram.
3
4  #include "stdafx.h"
5
6  #using <mscorlib.dll>
7
8  using namespace System;
9
10 int _tmain()
11 {
12    int array __gc[] = { 19, 3, 15, 7, 11, 9, 13, 5, 17, 1 };
13
14    Console::WriteLine( S"Element\tValue\tHistogram" );
```

Fig. 7.5 Histogram-printing program. (Part 1 of 2.)

```

   // output histogram
   for ( int i = 0 ; i < array->Length; i++ )
      Console::Write(
         S"{0}\t{1}\t", i.ToString(), array[ i ].ToString() );

      for ( int j = 1; j <= array[ i ]; j++ ) // print a bar
         Console::Write( S"*" );

      Console::WriteLine(); // move cursor to next line
   } // end outer for loop

   return 0;
} // end _tmain
```

```
Element Value   Histogram
0       19      *******************
1       3       ***
2       15      ***************
3       7       *******
4       11      ***********
5       9       *********
6       13      *************
7       5       *****
8       17      *****************
9       1       *
```

Fig. 7.5 Histogram-printing program. (Part 2 of 2.)

7.4.4 Using the Elements of an Array as Counters

Sometimes programs use a series of counter variables to summarize data, such as the results of a survey. In Chapter 6, Functions, we used a series of counters in our dice-rolling program to track the number of occurrences of each side on a six-sided die as the program rolled 12 dice at a time. We also indicated that there is a more elegant technique than the one used in Fig. 6.14 for writing the dice-rolling program. An array version of this application is shown in Fig. 7.6.

The program in Fig. 7.6 uses the seven-element array `frequency` to count the occurrences of each side of the die. Line 19 replaces lines 20–44 of Fig. 6.14. Line 19 uses a random `face` value as the subscript for array `frequency` to determine which element should be incremented during each iteration of the loop. The random number calculation on line 18 produces numbers 1–6 (the values for a six-sided die); thus, the `frequency` array must be large enough to allow subscript values of 1–6. The smallest number of elements required for an array to have these subscript values is seven elements (subscript values 0–6). In this program, we ignore element 0 of array `frequency`. Lines 27–33 replace lines 50–63 from Fig. 6.14. We can loop through array `frequency`; therefore, we do not have to enumerate each line of text to display, as we did in Fig. 6.14.

```
// Fig. 7.6: RollDie.cpp
// Rolling 12 dice.

#include "stdafx.h"

#using <mscorlib.dll>

using namespace System;

int _tmain()
{
   Random *randomNumber = new Random();
   int face;
   int frequency __gc[] = new int __gc[ 7 ];
   double total;

   for ( int roll = 1; roll <= 6000; roll++ ) {
      face = randomNumber->Next( 1, 7 );
      ++frequency[ face ];
   } // end for loop

   total = 0;

   for ( int i = 1; i < 7; i++ )
      total += frequency[ i ];

   Console::WriteLine( S"Face\tFrequency\tPercent" );

   // output frequency values
   for ( int x = 1; x < frequency->Length; x++ )
      Console::WriteLine( S"{0}\t{1}\t\t{2}%", x.ToString(),
         frequency[ x ].ToString(),
         ( frequency[ x ] / total * 100 ).ToString( "N" ) );

   return 0;
} // end _tmain
```

```
Face    Frequency       Percent
1       988             16.47%
2       1010            16.83%
3       1060            17.67%
4       972             16.20%
5       1047            17.45%
6       923             15.38%
```

Fig. 7.6 Dice-rolling program using an array to eliminate a `switch` statement.

7.4.5 Using Arrays to Analyze Survey Results

Our next example uses arrays to summarize the results of data collected in a survey. Consider the following problem statement:

Forty students were asked to rate the quality of the food in the student cafeteria on a scale of 1 to 10, with 1 being awful and 10 being excellent. Place the 40 responses in an integer array and summarize the frequency for each rating.

This is a typical array processing application (Fig. 7.7). We wish to summarize the number of responses of each type (i.e., 1–10). The array `responses` is a 40-element integer array of the students' responses to the survey. We use an 11-element array `frequency` to count the number of occurrences of each response. We ignore the first element, `frequency[ 0 ]`, because it is more logical to have a response of `1` increment `frequency[ 1 ]` than `frequency[ 0 ]`. We can use each response directly as a subscript on the `frequency` array. Each element of the array is used as a counter for one of the survey responses.

Good Programming Practice 7.2

Strive for program clarity. It is sometimes worthwhile to trade off the most efficient use of memory or processor time for writing clearer programs.

The `for` loop (lines 19–20) takes the responses from the array `response` one at a time and increments one of the 10 counters in the `frequency` array (`frequency[ 1 ]` to `frequency[ 10 ]`). The key statement in the loop is in line 20, which increments the appropriate counter in the `frequency` array, depending on the value of element `responses[ answer ]`.

```
1  // Fig. 7.7: StudentPoll.cpp
2  // A student poll program.
3
4  #include "stdafx.h"
5
6  #using <mscorlib.dll>
7
8  using namespace System;
9
10 int _tmain()
11 {
12    int responses __gc[] = { 1, 2, 6, 4, 8, 5, 9, 7, 8, 10, 1,
13       6, 3, 8, 6, 10, 3, 8, 2, 7, 6, 5, 7, 6, 8, 6, 7, 5, 6, 6,
14       5, 6, 7, 5, 6, 4, 8, 6, 8, 10 };
15
16    int frequency __gc[] = new int __gc[ 11 ];
17
18    // increment the frequency for each response
19    for ( int answer = 0; answer < responses->Length; answer++ )
20       ++frequency[ responses[ answer ] ];
21
22    Console::WriteLine( S"Rating\tFrequency" );
23
24    // output results
25    for ( int rating = 1; rating < frequency->Length; rating++ )
26       Console::WriteLine( S"{0}\t{1}", rating.ToString(),
27          frequency[ rating ].ToString() );
28
```

Fig. 7.7 Student-poll analysis program. (Part 1 of 2.)

```
    return 0;
} // end _tmain
```

```
Rating  Frequency
1       2
2       2
3       2
4       2
5       5
6       11
7       5
8       7
9       1
10      3
```

Fig. 7.7 Student-poll analysis program. (Part 2 of 2.)

Let us consider several iterations of the `for` loop. When counter `answer` is `0`, `responses[ answer ]` is the value of the first element of array `responses` (i.e., `1`). In this case, the program interprets `++frequency[ responses[ answer ] ];` as `++frequency[ 1 ];`, which increments array element `1`. In evaluating the expression, start with the value in the innermost set of square brackets (`answer`). Once you know the value of `answer`, plug that value into the expression and evaluate the next outer set of square brackets (`responses[ answer ]`). Use that value as the subscript for the `frequency` array to determine which counter to increment.

When `answer` is `1`, `responses[ answer ]` is the value of the second element of array `responses` (i.e., `2`), so the program interprets

```
++frequency[ responses[ answer ] ];
```

as `++frequency[ 2 ];`, which increments array element 2 (the third element of the array). When `answer` is `2`, `responses[ answer ]` is the value of the third element of array `respons-es` (i.e., `6`), so the program interprets

```
++frequency[ responses[ answer ] ];
```

as `++frequency[ 6 ];`, which increments array element 6 (the seventh element of the array) and so on. Note that, regardless of the number of responses processed in the survey, only an 11-element array is required (ignoring element 0) to summarize the results, because all the response values are between 1 and 10, and the subscript values for an 11-element array are 0–10. The results are correct, because the elements of the `frequency` array were initialized to zero when the array was allocated with `new`.

If the data contained invalid values, such as 13, the program would attempt to add `1` to `frequency[ 13 ]`. This is outside the bounds of the array. In the C and C++ programming languages, no checks are performed to prevent programs from reading data outside the bounds of arrays. At execution time, the program would "walk" past the end of the array to where element number 13 would be located and add 1 to whatever data are stored at that location in memory. This could potentially modify another variable in the program or even result in premature program termination. The .NET framework provides exception handling mechanisms to prevent accessing elements outside the bounds of arrays. When an invalid array reference occurs, Visual C++ .NET generates an `IndexOutOfRangeException`, rather than performing the invalid array reference. We discuss exceptions in more detail in Chapter 11, Exception Handling.

Error-Prevention Tip 7.1

When a MC++ program executes, array subscripts are checked for validity (i.e., all subscripts must be greater than or equal to 0 and less than the length of the array).

Error-Prevention Tip 7.2

Exceptions indicate when errors occur in programs. Programmers can write code to recover from exceptions and continue program execution instead of terminating the program abnormally.

Common Programming Error 7.3

Referring to an element outside the array bounds generates an `IndexOutOfRangeException` *exception.*

Error-Prevention Tip 7.3

When looping through an array, the array subscript should never go below 0 and should always be less than the total number of elements in the array (one less than the length of the array). The loop-terminating condition should prevent accessing elements outside this range.

Error-Prevention Tip 7.4

Programs should validate the correctness of all input values to prevent erroneous information from affecting a program's calculations.

7.5 Passing Arrays to Functions

To pass an array argument to a function, specify the name of the array without using brackets. For example, if array `hourlyTemperatures` is declared as

```
int hourlyTemperatures __gc[] = new int __gc[ 24 ];
```

then the function call

```
ModifyArray( hourlyTemperatures );
```

passes array `hourlyTemperatures` (by reference) to function `ModifyArray`. Every array object "knows" its own size (via the `Length` property), so that, when we pass an array object into a function, we do not pass the size of the array as an additional argument.

Although entire arrays are passed by reference, individual array elements of primitive types are passed by value. (The objects referred to by individual elements of a non-primitive-type array are passed by reference.) Such simple single pieces of data are sometimes called *scalars* or *scalar quantities.* To pass an array element to a function, use the subscripted name of the array element as an argument in the function call; for example, the zeroth element of array `scores` is passed by value as `scores[ 0 ]`.

For a function to receive an array through a function call, the function's parameter list must specify that array will be received. For example, the function header for function `ModifyArray` might be written as

```
void ModifyArray( int b __gc[] )
```

indicating that `ModifyArray` expects to receive an integer array in parameter `b`. Arrays are passed by reference; when the called function uses the array parameter name `b`, this parameter name refers to the original array.

A programmer can return an array from a function by appending `__gc[]` to both the function prototype and function-definition header.[5] For instance, the following is the prototype for a function that returns a managed array of integers

`int` *FunctionName*`(` *parameter-list* `) __gc[];`

The `__gc[]` indicates that function *FunctionName* returns a managed array, and `int` indicates that the array returned is an integer array. The header of the function definition follows the same syntax, except without the semicolon. As with the declaration of managed arrays, the `__gc` is optional when the managed type aliases are not used. For instance,

`Int32` *FunctionName*`(` *parameter-list* `) [];`

would also declare a function that returns a managed array of integers.

The application in Fig. 7.8 demonstrates the difference between passing an entire array and passing an array element to a function. Lines 20–21 display the five elements of integer array `array1`. Line 23 invokes function `ModifyArray` and passes it the array `array1` as an argument. Function `ModifyArray` (lines 43–47) multiplies each element by 2. To illustrate that array `array1`'s elements were modified, lines 28–29 display the array elements again. As the output indicates, the elements of `array1` are modified by `ModifyArray`.

Lines 31–33 display the value of `array1[ 3 ]` (and other information) before the call to `ModifyElement`. Line 36 invokes function `ModifyElement` (defined in lines 50–59) with argument `array1[ 3 ]`. Remember that `array1[ 3 ]` is a single `int` value in the array `array1`. Also, remember that values of primitive types always are passed to functions by value (by default). Therefore, a copy of `array1[ 3 ]` is passed. Function `ModifyElement` multiplies its argument by 2 and stores the result in its parameter `element`. The parameter of `ModifyElement` is a local variable, so when the function terminates, the local variable is destroyed. Thus, when control is returned to `_tmain`, the unmodified value of `array1[ 3 ]` is displayed (lines 38–39).

```
1  // Fig. 7.8: PassArray.cpp
2  // Passing arrays and individual elements to functions.
3
4  #include "stdafx.h"
5
6  #using <mscorlib.dll>
7
8  using namespace System;
```

Fig. 7.8 Passing arrays and individual elements to functions. (Part 1 of 3.)

5. This is the syntax used to indicate that the function returns a one-dimensional array. We will discuss returning multidimensional arrays from functions in Section 7.8.

```

void ModifyArray( int __gc[] );
void ModifyElement( int );

int _tmain()
{
   int array1 __gc[] = { 1, 2, 3, 4, 5 };

   Console::WriteLine( S"Effects of passing entire array "
      S"pass-by-reference:\n\nOriginal array's values:" );

   for ( int i = 0; i < array1->Length; i++ )
      Console::Write( S"   {0}", array1[ i ].ToString() );

   ModifyArray( array1 );   // array is passed pass-by-reference

   Console::WriteLine( S"\nModified array's values:" );

   // display elements of array array1
   for ( int i = 0; i < array1->Length; i++ )
      Console::Write( S"   {0}", array1[ i ].ToString() );

   Console::Write( S"\n\nEffects of passing array "
      S"element pass-by-value:\n\narray1[ 3 ] before " );
   Console::Write( S"ModifyElement: {0}", array1[ 3 ].ToString() );

   // array element passed pass-by-value
   ModifyElement( array1[ 3 ] );

   Console::WriteLine( S"\narray1[ 3 ] after ModifyElement: {0}",
      array1[ 3 ].ToString() );
} // end _tmain

// function modifies the array it receives
void ModifyArray( int array2 __gc[] )
{
   for ( int j = 0; j < array2->Length; j++ )
      array2[ j ] *= 2;
} // end ModifyArray

// function modifies the integer passed to it, original not modified
void ModifyElement( int element )
{
   Console::WriteLine( S"\nvalue received in ModifyElement: {0}",
      element.ToString() );

   element *= 2;

   Console::WriteLine( S"value calculated in ModifyElement: {0}",
      element.ToString() );
} // end ModifyElement
```

Fig. 7.8 Passing arrays and individual elements to functions. (Part 2 of 3.)

```
Effects of passing entire array pass-by-reference:

Original array's values:
   1   2   3   4   5
Modified array's values:
   2   4   6   8   10

Effects of passing array element pass-by-value:

array1[ 3 ] before ModifyElement: 8
value received in ModifyElement: 8
value calculated in ModifyElement: 16

array1[ 3 ] after ModifyElement: 8
```

Fig. 7.8 Passing arrays and individual elements to functions. (Part 3 of 3.)

7.6 Sorting Arrays

Sorting data (i.e., arranging the data into some particular order, such as ascending or descending) is one of the most important computing applications. A bank sorts all checks by account number so that it can prepare individual bank statements at the end of each month. Telephone companies sort their lists of accounts by last name, and within that, by first name to make it easy to find phone numbers. Virtually every organization must sort some data, and in many cases, massive amounts of it. Sorting data is an intriguing problem that has attracted some of the most intense research efforts in the computer science field. In this section, we discuss one of the simplest sorting schemes. In the exercises, we investigate one of the more sophisticated sorting algorithms.

Performance Tip 7.1

Sometimes, the simplest algorithms perform poorly. Their virtue is that they are easy to write, test and debug. Complex algorithms are sometimes needed to realize maximum performance of a program.

Figure 7.9 sorts the values of the 10-element array `a` into ascending order. The technique we use is called the *bubble sort*, because smaller values gradually "bubble" their way to the top of the array (i.e., toward the first element) like air bubbles rising in water. The technique is sometimes called the *sinking sort*, because the larger values sink to the bottom of the array. Bubble sort uses nested loops to make several passes through the array. Each pass compares successive pairs of elements. If a pair is in increasing order (or the values are equal), the values remain in the same order. If a pair is in decreasing order, the bubble sort swaps the values in the array. The program contains functions `_tmain` (lines 13–32), `BubbleSort` (lines 35–43) and `Swap` (lines 46–53). Line 15 creates array `a`. Line 23 invokes function `BubbleSort` to sort array `a`. Line 42 in function `BubbleSort` calls function `Swap` to exchange two elements of the array.

Function `BubbleSort` receives the array as parameter `b`. The nested `for` loop in lines 37–42 performs the sort. The outer loop controls the number of passes of the array. The inner loop controls the comparisons per pass. If necessary, the `if` statement at lines 41–42 of the inner loop swaps adjacent elements that are out of order during each pass.

```
// Fig. 7.9: BubbleSorter.cpp
// Sorting an array's values into ascending order.

#include "stdafx.h"

#using <mscorlib.dll>

using namespace System;

void BubbleSort( int __gc[] );
void Swap( int __gc[], int );

int _tmain()
{
   int a __gc[] = { 2, 6, 4, 8, 10, 12, 89, 68, 45, 37 };

   Console::WriteLine( S"Data items in original order" );

   for ( int i = 0; i < a->Length; i++ )
      Console::Write( S"   {0}", a[ i ].ToString() );

   // sort elements in array a
   BubbleSort( a );

   Console::WriteLine( S"\nData items in ascending order" );

   for ( int i = 0; i < a->Length; i++ )
      Console::Write( S"   {0}", a[ i ].ToString() );
   Console::WriteLine();

   return 0;
} // end _tmain

// sort the elements of an array with bubble sort
void BubbleSort( int b __gc[] )
{
   for ( int pass = 1; pass < b->Length; pass++ ) // passes

      for ( int i = 0; i < b->Length - 1; i++ )   // one pass

         if ( b[ i ] > b[ i + 1 ] )       // one comparison
            Swap( b, i );           // one swap
} // end function BubbleSort

// swap two elements of an array
void Swap( int c __gc[], int first )
{
   int hold;      // temporary holding area for swap

   hold = c[ first ];
   c[ first ] = c[ first + 1 ];
   c[ first + 1 ] = hold;
} // end function Swap
```

Fig. 7.9 Sorting an array with bubble sort. (Part 1 of 2.)

```
Data items in original order
   2   6   4   8   10   12   89   68   45   37
Data items in ascending order
   2   4   6   8   10   12   37   45   68   89
```

Fig. 7.9 Sorting an array with bubble sort. (Part 2 of 2.)

Function `BubbleSort` first compares `b[ 0 ]` to `b[ 1 ]`, then `b[ 1 ]` to `b[ 2 ]`, then `b[ 2 ]` to `b[ 3 ]` and so on, until it completes the pass by comparing `b[ 8 ]` to `b[ 9 ]`. Although there are 10 elements, the comparison loop performs only nine comparisons. As a result of the way the successive comparisons are made, a large value may move down the array (sink) many positions (and sometimes all the way to the bottom of the array) on a single pass. However, a small value may move up (bubble) only one position. On the first pass, the largest value is guaranteed to sink to the bottom element of the array, `b[ 9 ]`. On the second pass, the second largest value is guaranteed to sink to `b[ 8 ]`. On the ninth pass, the ninth largest value sinks to `b[ 1 ]`. This leaves the smallest value in `b[ 0 ]`, so a maximum of nine passes are needed to sort a 10-element array.

If a comparison reveals that the two elements appear in descending order, `BubbleSort` calls `Swap` to exchange the two elements so they will be in ascending order in the array. Function `Swap` receives a pointer to the array (which it calls `c`) and one integer representing the subscript of the first element of the array to be exchanged. Three assignment statements in lines 50–52 perform the exchange, where the extra variable `hold` temporarily stores one of the two values being swapped. The swap cannot be performed with only the two assignment statements, such as

```
c[ first ] = c[ first + 1 ];
c[ first + 1 ] = c[ first ];
```

If `c[ first ]` is `7` and `c[ first + 1 ]` is `5`, after the first assignment, both elements of the array contain `5` and the value `7` is lost—hence, the need for the extra variable `hold`.

The advantage of the bubble sort is that it is easy to program. However, the bubble sort runs slowly, which becomes apparent when sorting large arrays. More advanced courses (often titled "Data Structures" or "Algorithms" or "Computational Complexity") investigate sorting and searching in greater depth. Note that the .NET framework includes a built-in array-sorting capability that implements a high-speed sort. To sort the array a in Fig. 7.9, you can use the statement[6]

```
Array::Sort( a );
```

7.7 Searching Arrays: Linear Search and Binary Search

Often, programmers work with large amounts of data stored in arrays. It might be necessary in this case to determine whether an array contains a value that matches a certain *key value*. The process of locating a particular element value in an array is called *searching*. In this section, we discuss two searching techniques—the simple *linear search* technique and the

6. More information about class `System::Array`, including method `Sort`, can be found in Chapter 22, Data Structures and Collections as well as at `msdn.microsoft.com/library/en-us/cpref/html/frlrfSystemArrayClassTopic.asp`.

more efficient *binary search* technique. Exercise 7.8 and Exercise 7.9 at the end of this chapter ask you to implement recursive versions of the linear and binary search.

7.7.1 Searching an Array with Linear Search

The application of Fig. 7.10 implements the linear search algorithm. In the program in Fig. 7.10, function `LinearSearch` (lines 32–41) uses a `for` statement containing an `if` statement to compare each element of an array with a *search key* (line 36). If the search key is found, the function returns the subscript value for the element to indicate the exact position of the search key in the array. If the search key is not found, the function returns `-1`. (The value `-1` is a good choice because it is not a valid subscript.) If the elements of the array being searched are not in any particular order, it is just as likely that the value will be found in the first element as in the last. On average, the program will have to compare the search key with half the elements of the array. The program contains a 25-element array filled with the even integers from 2 to 50, inclusive. The user enters the search key at the command prompt.

```
1  // Fig. 7.10: LinearSearcher.cpp
2  // Demonstrating linear searching of an array.
3
4  #include "stdafx.h"
5
6  #using <mscorlib.dll>
7
8  using namespace System;
9
10 int LinearSearch( int __gc[], int );
11
12 int _tmain()
13 {
14    int a __gc[] = { 2, 4, 6, 8, 10, 12, 14, 16, 18, 20, 22, 24,
15       26, 28, 30, 32, 34, 36, 38, 40, 42, 44, 46, 48, 50 };
16
17    Console::Write( S"Please enter a search key: " );
18    int searchKey = Int32::Parse( Console::ReadLine() );
19
20    int elementIndex = LinearSearch( a, searchKey );
21
22    if ( elementIndex != -1 )
23       Console::WriteLine( S"Found value in element {0}",
24          elementIndex.ToString() );
25    else
26       Console::WriteLine( S"Value not found" );
27
28    return 0;
29 } // end _tmain
30
31 // search array for the specified key value
32 int LinearSearch( int array __gc[], int key )
33 {
```

Fig. 7.10 Linear search of an array. (Part 1 of 2.)

```
   for ( int n = 0; n < array->Length; n++ ) {

      if ( array[ n ] == key )
         return n;
   } // end for

   return -1;
} // end function LinearSearch
```

```
Please enter a search key: 6
Found value in element 2
```

```
Please enter a search key: 15
Value not found
```

Fig. 7.10 Linear search of an array. (Part 2 of 2.)

7.7.2 Searching a Sorted Array with Binary Search

The linear search function works well for small or unsorted arrays. However, for large arrays, linear searching is inefficient. If the array is sorted, the high-speed *binary search* technique can be used. The binary search algorithm eliminates half of the elements in the array being searched after each comparison. The algorithm locates the middle array element and compares it with the search key. If they are equal, the search key has been found, and the subscript of that element is returned. Otherwise, the problem is reduced to searching half of the array. If the search key is less than the middle array element, the first half of the array is searched; otherwise, the second half of the array is searched. If the search key is not the middle element in the specified *subarray* (a piece of the original array), the algorithm is repeated in one quarter of the original array. The search continues until the search key is equal to the middle element of a subarray, or until the subarray consists of one element that is not equal to the search key (i.e., the search key is not found).

In a worst-case scenario, performing a binary search on an array of 1023 elements will take only 10 comparisons. Repeatedly dividing 1024 by 2 (after each comparison we eliminate from consideration half the array) yields the values 512, 256, 128, 64, 32, 16, 8, 4, 2 and 1. The number 1024 (2^{10}) is divided by 2 only ten times to get the value 1. Dividing by 2 is equivalent to one comparison in the binary search algorithm. An array of 1,048,576 (2^{20}) elements takes a maximum of 20 comparisons to find the key. An array of one billion elements takes a maximum of 30 comparisons to find the key. This is a tremendous increase in performance over the linear search, which required comparing the search key with an average of half the elements in the array. For a one-billion-element array, the difference is between an average of 500 million comparisons and a maximum of 30 comparisons! The maximum number of comparisons needed for the binary search of any sorted array is the exponent of the first power of 2 greater than the number of elements in the array.

Figure 7.11 presents the iterative version of function `BinarySearch` (lines 36–59). The function receives two arguments—an integer array called `array` (the array to search) and an integer `key` (the search key). Line 43 calculates the middle element of the array being searched by determining the number of elements in the current portion of the array and dividing this value by 2. Recall that using the / operator with integers performs an integer division, which truncates the result. So, when there is an even number of elements in the array there is no "middle" element—the middle of our array is actually between two elements. When this occurs, the calculation in line 43 returns the smaller index of the two middle elements.

```
1  // Fig. 7.11: BinarySearchTest.cpp
2  // Demonstrating a binary search of an array.
3
4  #include "stdafx.h"
5
6  #using <mscorlib.dll>
7
8  using namespace System;
9
10 int BinarySearch( int __gc[], int );
11 void ShowOutput( int __gc[], int, int, int );
12
13 int _tmain()
14 {
15    int a __gc[] = { 0, 2, 4, 6, 8, 10, 12, 14, 16,
16       18, 20, 22, 24, 26, 28 };
17
18    Console::Write( S"Please enter a search key: " );
19    int searchKey = Int32::Parse( Console::ReadLine() );
20
21    Console::WriteLine( S"\nPortions of array searched" );
22
23    // perform the binary search
24    int element = BinarySearch( a, searchKey );
25
26    if ( element != -1 )
27       Console::WriteLine( S"\nFound value in element {0}",
28           element.ToString() );
29    else
30       Console::WriteLine( S"\nValue not found" );
31
32    return 0;
33 } // end _tmain
34
35 // search array for specified key
36 int BinarySearch( int array __gc[], int key )
37 {
38    int low = 0; // low index
39    int high = array->Length - 1; // high index
40    int middle; // middle index
41
42    while ( low <= high ) {
43       middle = ( low + high ) / 2;
44
45       // the following line displays the portion
46       // of the array currently being manipulated during
```

Fig. 7.11 Binary search of a sorted array. (Part 1 of 3.)

```
      // each iteration of the binary search loop
      ShowOutput( array, low, middle, high );

      if ( key == array[ middle ] )   // match
         return middle;
      else if ( key < array[ middle ] )
         high = middle - 1;  // key less than middle, set new high
      else
         low = middle + 1; // key greater than middle, set new low
   } // end binary search

   return -1; // search key not found
} // end function BinarySearch

// show current part of array being processed
void ShowOutput( int array __gc[], int low, int mid, int high )
{
   for ( int i = 0; i < array->Length; i++ ) {

      if ( i < low || i > high )
         Console::Write( S"    " );

      // else mark middle element in output
      else if ( i == mid )
         Console::Write( S"{0}* ", array[ i ].ToString( "00" ) );
      else
         Console::Write( S"{0}  ", array[ i ].ToString( "00" ) );
   } // end for

   Console::WriteLine();
} // end function ShowOutput
```

```
Please enter a search key: 6

Portions of array searched
00  02  04  06  08  10  12  14* 16  18  20  22  24  26  28
00  02  04  06* 08  10  12

Found value in element 3
```

```
Please enter a search key: 8

Portions of array searched
00  02  04  06  08  10  12  14* 16  18  20  22  24  26  28
00  02  04  06* 08  10  12
                08  10* 12
                08*

Found value in element 4
```

Fig. 7.11 Binary search of a sorted array. (Part 2 of 3.)

```
Please enter a search key: 25

Portions of array searched
00  02  04  06  08  10  12  14* 16  18  20  22  24  26  28
                                16  18  20  22* 24  26  28
                                                24  26* 28
                                                24*

Value not found
```

Fig. 7.11 Binary search of a sorted array. (Part 3 of 3.)

If `key` matches the `middle` element of a subarray (line 50), `BinarySearch` returns `middle` (the index of the current element), indicating that the value was found and the search is complete. If `key` does not match the `middle` element of a subarray, `BinarySearch` adjusts the `low` index or `high` index (both declared in the function) so that a smaller subarray can be searched. If `key` is less than the middle element (line 52), the `high` index is set to `middle - 1`, and the search continues on the elements from `low` to `middle - 1`. If `key` is greater than the middle element (line 54), the `low` index is set to `middle + 1`, and the search continues on the elements from `middle + 1` to `high`. These comparisons occur in the nested `if...else` statement in lines 50–55.

The program uses a 15-element array. The first power of 2 greater than the number of array elements is 16 (2^4)—so at most four comparisons are required to find the `key`. To illustrate this concept, function `BinarySearch` calls function `ShowOutput` (lines 62–77) to output each subarray during the binary search process. `ShowOutput` marks the middle element in each subarray with an asterisk (*) to indicate the element with which the `key` is compared. Each search in this example results in a maximum of four lines of output—one per comparison. Note that the .NET framework includes a built-in array-searching capability that implements the binary-search algorithm. To search for the key 7 in the sorted array a in Fig. 7.11, you can use the statement

```
Array::BinarySearch( a, 7 );
```

7.8 Multidimensional Arrays

So far, we have studied *one-dimensional* (or *single-subscripted*) arrays—i.e., those that contain single lists of values. In this section, we introduce *multidimensional* (sometimes called *multiple-subscripted*) arrays. Such arrays require two or more subscripts to identify particular elements. Arrays that require two subscripts to identify a particular element commonly are called *two-dimensional arrays.* We concentrate on two-dimensional arrays (often called *double-subscripted arrays*). Multidimensional arrays with two dimensions often represent *tables* of values consisting of information arranged in *rows* and *columns*, where each row has the same number of columns. To identify a particular table element, we must specify two indices—by convention, the first identifies the element's row, the second the element's column. Multidimensional arrays can have two or more subscripts. Figure 7.12 illustrates a two-dimensional array, a, containing three rows and four columns (i.e., a 3-by-4 array). An array with *m* rows and *n* columns is called an *m-by-n array.*

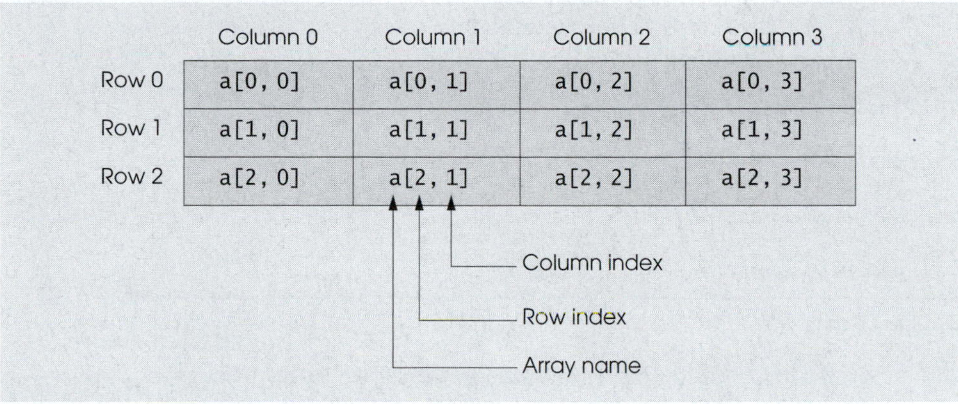

Fig. 7.12 Two-dimensional array with three rows and four columns.

Every element in array a is identified in Fig. 7.12 by an element name of the form `a[ i, j ]`, in which a is the name of the array and `i` and `j` are the subscripts that uniquely identify the row and column of each element in a. Notice that the names of the elements in the first row all have a first index of 0; the names of the elements in the fourth column all have a second index of 3.

Multidimensional arrays can be initialized in declarations like one-dimensional arrays. A two-dimensional array b with two rows and two columns could be declared and initialized with

```
int b __gc[,] = new int __gc[ 2, 2 ];

b[ 0, 0 ] = 1;
b[ 0, 1 ] = 2;
b[ 1, 0 ] = 3;
b[ 1, 1 ] = 4;
```

Method *GetLength* returns the length of a particular array dimension. In the preceding example, `b->GetLength( 0 )` returns the length of the zeroth dimension of b, which is 2. The number of dimensions in an array is called its *rank*. The rank of an array is one more than the number of commas used in its declaration. For example, array b is declared via the notation `[,]`, which contains one comma. Therefore, the rank of array b is 2. To declare a three-dimensional array, we would use the notation `[,,]`.

In Section 7.5, we discussed returning arrays from functions. Programmers can also specify multidimensional arrays to be returned, using the notation above. For instance, the programmer indicates that a function returns a two-dimensional array of integers using the following syntax:

```
int FunctionName( parameter-list ) __gc[,];
```

Two-Dimensional Array Example: Displaying Element Values

Figure 7.13 demonstrates the initialization of multidimensional arrays and the use of nested `for` loops to traverse the arrays (i.e., to manipulate each array element).

```
1  // Fig. 7.13: TwoDimensionalArrays.cpp
2  // Initializing two-dimensional arrays.
3
4  #include "stdafx.h"
5
6  #using <mscorlib.dll>
7
8  using namespace System;
9
10 void DisplayArray( int __gc[,] );
11
12 int _tmain()
13 {
14    // declaration and initialization of 2D array
15    int array __gc[,] = new int __gc[ 2, 3 ];
16
17    for ( int i = 0; i < array->GetLength( 0 ); i++ )
18
19       for ( int j = 0; j < array->GetLength( 1 ); j++ )
20          array[ i, j ] = ( i + 1 ) * ( j + 1 );
21
22    Console::WriteLine( S"Values in the array by row are" );
23
24    // display 2D array
25    DisplayArray( array );
26
27    return 0;
28 } // end _tmain
29
30 // display rows and columns of a 2D array
31 void DisplayArray( int array __gc[,] )
32 {
33    for ( int i = 0; i < array->GetLength( 0 ); i++ ) {
34
35       for ( int j = 0; j < array->GetLength( 1 ); j++ )
36          Console::Write( S"{0} ", array[ i, j ].ToString() );
37
38       Console::WriteLine();
39    } // end for
40 } // end function DisplayArray
```

```
Values in the array by row are
1 2 3
2 4 6
```

Fig. 7.13 Initializing two-dimensional arrays.

The declaration of `array` (line 15) creates a 2-by-3 managed array. Lines 17–20 populate the multidimensional array. The first row of the array has the values `1`, `2` and `3`. The second row of the array contains the values `2`, `4` and `6`.

Function `DisplayArray` (lines 31–40) displays the elements of `array`. Note the use of a nested `for` statement to output the rows of the two-dimensional array. In the nested `for` statements for `array`, we use method `GetLength` to determine the number of elements in each dimension of the array. Line 33 determines the number of rows in the array by invoking `array->GetLength( 0 )`; line 35 determines the number of columns by invoking `array->GetLength( 1 )`. Arrays with additional dimensions would require additional nested `for` loops.

Common Multidimensional-Array Manipulations Performed with `for` Statements

Many common array manipulations use `for` repetition statements. Imagine a multidimensional array a, which contains three rows. The following `for` statement sets all the elements in the third row of array a to zero:

```
for ( int column = 0; column < a->GetLength( 0 ); column++ )
   a[ 2, column ] = 0;
```

We specified the *third* row; therefore, we know that the first index is always `2`. (`0` specifies the first row, `1` the second row.) The `for` loop varies only the second index (i.e., the column subscript). Notice the use of `a->GetLength( 0 )` in the `for` statement's conditional expression. Assuming that this array contains four columns, the preceding `for` statement is equivalent to the assignment statements

```
a[ 2, 0 ] = 0;
a[ 2, 1 ] = 0;
a[ 2, 2 ] = 0;
a[ 2, 3 ] = 0;
```

The following nested `for` statement sums the elements in array `a`. We use `a->Length` in the conditional expression of the outer `for` statement to determine the number of rows (i.e., the number of subarrays) in `a`, in this case, 3:

```
int total = 0;

for ( int row = 0; row < a->GetLength( 0 ); row++ )

   for ( int column = 0; column < a->GetLength( 1 ); column++ )
      total += a[ row, column ];
```

The `for` statement totals the elements of the array one row at a time. The outer `for` statement begins by setting the `row` index to `0`, so the elements of the first row may be totaled by the inner `for` statement. Then the outer `for` statement increments `row` to `1`, so the second row can be totaled. Finally, the outer `for` statement increments `row` to 2, so the third row can be totaled. The result can be displayed when the nested `for` statement terminates.

Two-Dimensional Array Example: Summarizing Student's Exam Grades

The program in Fig. 7.14 performs several array manipulations on 3-by-4 array `grades`. Each row of the array represents a student, and each column represents a grade on one of the four exams that the student took during the semester. The array manipulations are performed by three functions. Function `Minimum` (lines 62–74) determines the lowest grade of any student for the semester. Function `Maximum` (lines 77–89) determines the highest grade of any student for the semester. Function `Average` (lines 92–100) determines a particular student's semester average.

```
// Fig. 7.14: DoubleArray.cpp
// Manipulating a double-subscripted array.

#include "stdafx.h"

#using <mscorlib.dll>

using namespace System;

int Minimum( int __gc[,], int, int );
int Maximum( int __gc[,], int, int );
double Average( int __gc *, int );

int _tmain()
{
   int grades[,] = new int __gc[ 3, 4 ];
   grades[ 0, 0 ] = 77;
   grades[ 0, 1 ] = 68;
   grades[ 0, 2 ] = 86;
   grades[ 0, 3 ] = 73;
   grades[ 1, 0 ] = 96;
   grades[ 1, 1 ] = 87;
   grades[ 1, 2 ] = 89;
   grades[ 1, 3 ] = 81;
   grades[ 2, 0 ] = 70;
   grades[ 2, 1 ] = 90;
   grades[ 2, 2 ] = 86;
   grades[ 2, 3 ] = 81;

   int students = grades->GetLength( 0 );  // number of students
   int exams = grades->GetLength( 1 );     // number of exams

   // line up column headings
   Console::Write( S"          " );

   // output the column headings
   for ( int i = 0; i < exams; i++ )
      Console::Write( S"[{0}]", i.ToString() );

   // output the rows
   for ( int i = 0; i < students; i++ ) {
      Console::Write( S"\ngrades[{0}]     ", i.ToString() );

      for ( int j = 0; j < exams; j++ )
         Console::Write( S"{0} ", grades[ i, j ].ToString() );
   } // end for

   Console::WriteLine( S"\n\nLowest grade: {0}\nHighest grade: {1}",
      Minimum( grades, students, exams ).ToString(),
      Maximum( grades, students, exams ).ToString() );

```

Fig. 7.14 Example using two-dimensional arrays. (Part 1 of 3.)

```
   for ( int i = 0; i < students; i++ )
      Console::Write( S"\nAverage for student {0} is {1}", i.ToString(),
         Average( &grades[ i, 0 ], exams ).ToString( ".00" ) );

   Console::WriteLine();

   return 0;
} // end _tmain

// find minimum grade in grades array
int Minimum( int grades __gc[,], int students, int exams )
{
   int lowGrade = 100;

   for ( int i = 0; i < students; i++ )

      for ( int j = 0; j < exams; j++ )

         if ( grades[ i, j ] < lowGrade )
            lowGrade = grades[ i, j ];

   return lowGrade;
} // end function Minimum

// find maximum grade in grades array
int Maximum( int grades __gc[,], int students, int exams )
{
   int highGrade = 0;

   for ( int i = 0; i < students; i++ )

      for ( int j = 0; j < exams; j++ )

         if ( grades[ i, j ] > highGrade )
            highGrade = grades[ i, j ];

   return highGrade;
} // end function Maximum

// determine average grade for a particular student
double Average( int __gc *setOfGrades, int grades )
{
   int total = 0;

   for ( int i = 0; i < grades; i++ )
      total += setOfGrades[ i ];

   return static_cast< double >( total ) / grades;
} // end function Average
```

Fig. 7.14 Example using two-dimensional arrays. (Part 2 of 3.)

```
              [0] [1] [2] [3]
grades[0]      77  68  86  73
grades[1]      96  87  89  81
grades[2]      70  90  86  81

Lowest grade: 68
Highest grade: 96

Average for student 0 is 76.00
Average for student 1 is 88.25
Average for student 2 is 81.75
```

Fig. 7.14 Example using two-dimensional arrays. (Part 3 of 3.)

Functions `Minimum` and `Maximum` use array `grades` and the variables `students` (number of rows in the array) and `exams` (number of columns in the array). Each function loops through array `grades` by using nested `for` statements. Consider the nested `for` statement (lines 66–71) from function `Minimum`. The outer `for` statement sets `i` (i.e., the row subscript) to `0` so the elements of the first row can be compared with variable `lowGrade` in the body of the inner `for` statement. The inner `for` statement loops through the four grades of a particular row and compares each grade with `lowGrade`. If a grade is less than `lowGrade`, then `lowGrade` is set to that grade. The outer `for` statement then increments the row subscript by `1`. The elements of the second row are compared with variable `lowGrade`. The outer `for` statement then increments the row subscript to `2`. The elements of the third row are compared with variable `lowGrade`. When execution of the nested statement is complete, `lowGrade` contains the smallest grade in the double-subscripted array. Function `Maximum` works similarly to function `Minimum`.

Function `Average` takes two arguments—a pointer to a one-dimensional array of test results for a particular student and the number of test results in the array. When `Average` is called (line 54), the argument `&grades[ i,0 ]` specifies that a particular row of the double-subscripted array `grades` is to be passed to `Average`. The argument `&grades[ i,0 ]` generates a managed integer pointer. For example, the argument `&grades[ 1,0 ]` represents the four values (a single-subscripted array of grades) stored in the second row of the double-subscripted array `grades`. Function `Average` calculates the sum of the array elements, divides the total by the number of test results and returns the floating-point result cast as a `double` value (line 99).

SUMMARY

- An array is a group of memory locations that all have the same name and type.
- Visual C++ .NET supports managed arrays. Managed arrays are allocated dynamically using keyword `new`.
- Managed arrays are "static" entities, in that they remain the same size once they are created.
- To refer to a particular location or element in an array, specify the name of the array and the position number of the element within the array.
- The first element in every array is the zeroth element (i.e., element 0).
- The position number in square brackets is more formally called an index (or a subscript). This number must be an integer or an integer expression.

- To reference the ith element of a single-dimensional array, use $i-1$ as the index.
- The brackets that enclose the subscript of an array are operators that have the same level of precedence as the postfix increment and postfix decrement operators.
- When arrays are allocated, the elements are initialized to 0 for the numeric primitive-data-type variables, to `false` for `bool` variables or to 0 for pointers.
- MC++ keyword `__gc` in the array declarations specifies that the arrays are managed arrays.
- In general, keyword `__gc` declares a managed type. Managed types are garbage collected (i.e., memory no longer in use is freed) and managed by the CLR, a runtime environment provided by the .NET Framework.
- Managed arrays (sometimes called `__gc` arrays) inherit from class `System::Array`.
- Keyword `__nogc` declares an unmanaged array. Unmanaged arrays (sometimes called `__nogc` arrays) are standard C++ arrays and do not receive the benefits of managed arrays, such as garbage collection.
- Managed arrays may be declared to contain any managed type.
- In an array of value types, every element of the array contains one value of the declared type. For example, every element of an `int` array is an `int` value.
- In an array of pointers, every element of the array points to an object of the type of the array. For example, every element of a `String *` array is a pointer to an object of class `String`; each of the `String *` objects points to an object containing the empty string by default.
- Constants are values that cannot change during program execution. A constant, declared with keyword `const`, must be initialized in the same statement where it is declared and cannot be modified thereafter.
- If an attempt is made to modify a `const` variable after it is declared, the compiler issues a compilation error.
- Constants are also called named constants.
- Unlike their predecessors C and C++, .NET-compliant languages, such as MC++, provide mechanisms to prevent accessing elements outside the bounds of the array.
- When a reference is made to a nonexistent element of an array, an `IndexOutOfRangeException` occurs.
- For a function to receive an array through a function call, the function's parameter list must specify that an array will be received. For example, the function header for function `ModifyArray` might be written as

```
void ModifyArray( int b __gc[] )
```

  indicating that `ModifyArray` expects to receive an integer array in parameter `b`.
- Arrays are passed by reference; when the called function uses the array parameter name `b`, it refers to the actual array in the caller.
- A programmer can return an array from a function by appending `__gc[]` to both the function prototype and function-definition header. For instance, the following is the general syntax for a function that returns an array of integers

```
int FunctionName( parameter-list ) __gc[];
```

  The `__gc[]` indicates that function *FunctionName* returns a managed array, and `int` indicates that the array returned is an integer array.

- To pass an array argument to a function, specify the name of the array without any brackets.
- Although entire arrays are passed by reference, individual array elements of primitive types are passed by value, as are simple variables.
- To pass an array element to a function, use the subscripted name of the array element as an argument in the function call.
- Sorting data (i.e., placing the data into a particular order, such as ascending or descending) is one of the most important computing applications.
- The chief virtue of the bubble sort is that it is easy to program. However, the bubble sort runs slowly, which becomes apparent when sorting large arrays.
- The linear search function works well for small or unsorted arrays. However, for large arrays, linear searching is inefficient.
- The binary search algorithm eliminates from consideration half the elements in the array being searched after each comparison. The maximum number of comparisons needed for the binary search of any sorted array is the exponent of the first power of 2 that is greater than the number of elements in the array.
- In general, an array with *m* rows and *n* columns is referred to as an *m*-by-*n* array.

TERMINOLOGY

`[]` (subscript operator)
array
array allocated with `new`
array automatically initialized to zeros
array bounds
`Array` class
array declaration
bar chart
binary search algorithm
bubble sort
column
`const`
constant variable
declare an array
double-subscripted array
element of an array
exception
histogram
index
`IndexOutOfRangeException`
initializer list
key value
length of an array
`Length` property
linear search
lvalue ("left value")
managed array
m-by-*n* array
multidimensional array
multiple-subscripted array
named constant
`new` operator
"off-by-one error"
one-dimensional array
pass of a bubble sort
passing array element to function
passing array to function
position number
runtime environment
searching
search key
single-subscripted array
sinking sort
size of an array
sorting
square brackets (`[]`)
subarray
sub-initializer list
subscript
swap
`System::Array` class
table
table element
two-dimensional array
"walk" past end of an array
zero-based counting
zeroth element

SELF-REVIEW EXERCISES

7.1 Fill in the blanks in each of the following statements:

a) Lists and tables of values can be stored in _________.
b) The elements of an array are related by the fact that they have the same _________ and _________.
c) The number that refers to a particular element of an array is called its _________.
d) The process of placing the elements of an array in order is called _________ the array.
e) Determining if an array contains a certain key value is called _________ the array.
f) Arrays that use two or more subscripts are referred to as _________ arrays.
g) A(n) _________ variable must be declared and initialized in the same statement, or a syntax error will occur.
h) Many common array manipulations use the _________ repetition statement.
i) When an invalid array reference is made, a(n) _________ is generated.

7.2 State whether each of the following is *true* or *false*. If *false*, explain why.

a) An array can store many different types of values at the same time.
b) An array index normally should be of type `float`.
c) An individual array element that is passed to a function and modified in that function will contain the modified value when the called function completes execution.
d) The maximum number of comparisons needed for the binary search of any sorted array is the exponent of the first power of 2 greater than the number of elements in the array.
e) After each comparison, the binary search algorithm eliminates from consideration one third of the elements in the portion of the array that is being searched.
f) To determine the number of elements in an array, we can use property `NumberOfElements`.
g) Linear search works well for small or unsorted arrays.
h) In an *m*-by-*n* array, the *m* stands for the number of columns and the *n* stands for the number of rows.

ANSWERS TO SELF-REVIEW EXERCISES

7.1 a) arrays. b) name, type. c) index, subscript or position number. d) sorting. e) searching. f) multidimensional or multiple-subscripted. g) `const`. h) `for`. i) `IndexOutofRangeException`.

7.2 a) False. An array can store only values of the same type. b) False. An array index must be an integer or an integer expression. c) False. For individual primitive-data-type elements of an array, they are passed by value. If a reference to an array element is passed, then modifications to that array element are reflected in the original. An individual element of a reference type is passed to a function by reference. d) True. e) False. After each comparison, the binary search algorithm eliminates from consideration half the elements in the portion of the array that is being searched. f) False. To determine the number of elements in an array, we can use property `Length`. g) True. h) False. In an *m*-by-*n* array, the *m* stands for the number of rows and the *n* stands for the number of columns.

EXERCISES

7.3 Write statements to accomplish each of the following tasks:

a) Display the value of the seventh element of character array `f`.
b) Initialize each of the five elements of one-dimensional integer array `g` to `8`.
c) Total the elements of floating-point array `c` of 100 elements.
d) Copy 11-element array `a` into the first portion of array `b` containing 34 elements.
e) Determine the smallest and largest values contained in 99-element floating-point array `w`.

7.4 Use a one-dimensional array to solve the following problem: A company pays its salespeople on a commission basis. The salespeople receive $200 per week, plus 9% of their gross sales for that week. For example, a salesperson who grosses $5000 in sales in a week receives $200 plus 9% of $5000, or a total of $650. Write a program (using an array of counters) that determines how many of the salespeople earned salaries in each of the following ranges (assume that each salesperson's salary is truncated to an integer amount):

a) $200–299
b) $300–399
c) $400–499
d) $500–599
e) $600–699
f) $700–799
g) $800–899
h) $900–999
i) $1000 and over

7.5 Use a one-dimensional array to solve the following problem: Read in 20 numbers, each of which is between 10 and 100, inclusive. As each number is read, print it only if it is not a duplicate of a number already read. Provide for the "worst case" (in which all 20 numbers are different). Use the smallest possible array to solve this problem.

7.6 (*Turtle Graphics*) The Logo language made famous the concept of *turtle graphics.* Imagine a mechanical turtle that walks around the room under the control of a program. The turtle holds a pen in one of two positions, up or down. While the pen is down, the turtle traces out shapes as it moves; while the pen is up, the turtle moves about without writing anything. In this problem, you will simulate the operation of the turtle and create a computerized sketchpad.

Use a 20-by-20 array `floor`, which is initialized to zeros. Read commands from an array that contains them. At all times, keep track of the current position and direction of the turtle and whether the pen is up or down. Assume that the turtle always starts at position 0, 0 of the floor with its pen up. The set of turtle commands your program must process are shown in Fig. 7.15.

Command	Meaning
`1`	Pen up
`2`	Pen down
`3`	Turn right
`4`	Turn left
`5,10`	Move forward 10 spaces (or a number other than 10)
`6`	Print the 20-by-20 array
`9`	End of data (sentinel)

Fig. 7.15 Turtle graphics commands.

Suppose that the turtle is somewhere near the center of the floor. The following "program" would draw and print a 12-by-12 square, leaving the pen in the up position:

```
2
5,12
3
```

```
5,12
3
5,12
3
5,12
1
6
9
```

As the turtle moves with the pen down, set the appropriate elements of array `floor` to `1`s. When the 6 command (print) is given, wherever there is a `1` in the array, print an asterisk or another character. Wherever there is a zero, print a blank. Write a program to implement the turtle graphics capabilities we have discussed. Write several turtle graphics programs to draw interesting shapes. Add commands to increase the power of your turtle graphics language.

SPECIAL SECTION: RECURSION EXERCISES

7.7 (*Palindromes*) A palindrome is a string that is spelled the same forward and backward. Some examples of palindromes are "radar," "able was i ere i saw elba" and, if blanks are ignored, "a man a plan a canal panama." Write a recursive function `TestPalindrome` that returns `true` if the string stored in the array is a palindrome and `false` otherwise. The function should ignore spaces and punctuation in the string.

7.8 (*Linear Search*) Modify Fig. 7.10 to use recursive function `LinearSearch` to perform a linear search of the array. The function should receive an integer array and the size of the array as arguments. If the search key is found, return the array subscript; otherwise, return –1.

7.9 (*Binary Search*) Modify the program in Fig. 7.11 to use a recursive function `BinarySearch` to perform the binary search of the array. The function should receive an integer array and the starting and ending subscript as arguments. If the search key is found, return the array subscript; otherwise, return –1.

7.10 (*Quicksort*) In this chapter, we discussed the sorting technique bubble sort. We now present the recursive sorting technique called Quicksort. The basic algorithm for a one-dimensional array of values is as follows:

a) *Partitioning Step.* Take the first element of the unsorted array and determine its final location in the sorted array (i.e., all values to the left of the element in the array are less than the element, and all values to the right of the element in the array are greater than the element). We now have one element in its proper location and two unsorted subarrays.
b) *Recursive Step.* Perform *Step 1* on each unsorted subarray.

Each time *Step 1* is performed on a subarray, another element is placed in its final location of the sorted array, and two unsorted subarrays are created. When a subarray consists of one element, it must be sorted; therefore, that element is in its final location.

The basic algorithm seems simple, but how do we determine the final position of the first element of each subarray? Consider the following set of values (partitioning element in bold—it will be placed in its final location in the sorted array):

37 2 6 4 89 8 10 12 68 45

a) Starting from the rightmost element of the array, compare each element to **37** until an element less than **37** is found, then swap **37** and that element. The first element less than **37** is 12, so **37** and 12 are swapped. The new array is

12 2 6 4 89 8 10 **37** 68 45

Element 12 is italicized to indicate that it was just swapped with **37**.

b) Starting from the left of the array, but beginning with the element after 12, compare each element to **37** until an element greater than **37** is found, then swap **37** and that element. The first element greater than **37** is 89, so **37** and 89 are swapped. The new array is

```
12  2  6  4  37  8  10  89  68  45
```

c) Starting from the right, but beginning with the element before 89, compare each element to **37** until an element less than **37** is found, then swap **37** and that element. The first element less than **37** is 10, so **37** and 10 are swapped. The new array is

```
12  2  6  4  10  8  37  89  68  45
```

d) Starting from the left, but beginning with the element after 10, compare each element to **37** until an element greater than **37** is found, then swap **37** and that element. There are no more elements greater than **37**, so when we compare **37** to itself, we know that **37** has been placed in its final location of the sorted array.

Once the partition has been applied to the previous array, there are two unsorted subarrays. The subarray with values less than 37 contains 12, 2, 6, 4, 10 and 8. The subarray with values greater than 37 contains 89, 68 and 45. The sort continues with both subarrays being partitioned in the same manner as the original array.

Using the preceding discussion, write recursive function `QuickSort` to sort a one-dimensional integer array. The function should receive as arguments an integer array, a starting subscript and an ending subscript. Function `Partition` should be called by `QuickSort` to perform the partitioning step.

7.11 (*Maze Traversal*) The following grid of #s and dots (`.`) is a two-dimensional array representation of a maze:

```
# # # # # # # # # # # #
# . . . # . . . . . . #
. . # . # . # # # # . #
# # # . # . . . . # . #
# . . . . # # # . # . .
# # # # . # . # . # . #
# . . # . # . # . # . #
# # . # . # . # . # . #
# . . . . . . . . # . #
# # # # # # . # # # . #
# . . . . . . # . . . #
# # # # # # # # # # # #
```

The #s represent the walls of the maze, and the dots represent squares in the possible paths through the maze. Moves can be made only to a location in the array that contains a dot.

There is a simple algorithm for walking through a maze that guarantees finding the exit (assuming there is an exit). If there is not an exit, you will arrive at the starting location again. Place your right hand on the wall to your right and begin walking forward. Never remove your hand from the wall. If the maze turns to the right, you follow the wall to the right. As long as you do not remove your hand from the wall, eventually you will arrive at the exit of the maze. There may be a shorter path than the one you have taken, but you are guaranteed to get out of the maze if you follow the algorithm.

Write recursive function `MazeTraverse` to walk through the maze. The function should receive as arguments a 12-by-12 character array representing the maze and the starting location of the maze. As `MazeTraverse` attempts to locate the exit from the maze, it should place the character `X` in each square in the path. The function should print the maze after each move so the user can watch as the maze is solved.

8

Object-Based Programming

Objectives

- To understand encapsulation and data hiding.
- To understand the concepts of data abstraction and abstract data types (ADTs).
- To create, use and destroy objects.
- To control access to data members and methods.
- To use properties to keep objects in consistent states.
- To understand the use of the `this` pointer.
- To understand namespaces and assemblies.
- To use the **Class View** in Visual Studio .NET.

My object all sublime
I shall achieve in time.
W. S. Gilbert

Is it a world to hide virtues in?
William Shakespeare

Your public servants serve you right.
Adlai Stevenson

This above all: to thine own self be true.
William Shakespeare

Outline

8.1 Introduction

In this chapter, we investigate object orientation in MC++. Some readers might ask, why have we deferred this topic until now? There are several reasons. First, the objects we build in this chapter are partially composed of structured program pieces. To explain the organization of objects, we needed to establish a basis in structured programming with control statements. We also wanted to study functions in detail before introducing object orientation.

Let us briefly overview some key concepts and terminology of object orientation. Object orientation uses classes to *encapsulate* (i.e., wrap together) data (*attributes*) and methods (*behaviors*). Objects have the ability to hide their implementation from other objects (this principle is called *information hiding*). Although some objects can communicate with one another across well-defined *interfaces* (just like the driver's interface to a car includes a steering wheel, accelerator pedal, brake pedal and gear shift), objects are unaware of how other objects are implemented (just as the driver is unaware of how the steering, engine, brake and transmission mechanisms are implemented). Normally, implementation details are hidden within the objects themselves. Surely, it is possible to drive a car effectively without knowing the details of how engines, transmissions and exhaust systems work. Later, we will see why information hiding is so crucial to good software engineering.

In *procedural programming languages* (like C), programming tends to be *action oriented.* MC++ programming, however, is *object oriented.* In C, the unit of programming is the *function*. In MC++, the unit of programming is the *class*. Objects eventually are *instan-*

tiated (i.e., created) from these classes, and functions are encapsulated within the "boundaries" of classes as *methods*.

C programmers concentrate on writing functions. They group actions that perform some task into a function, then group functions to form a program. Data are certainly important in C, but they exist primarily to support the actions that functions perform. C programmers use the *verbs* in a system-requirements document to determine the set of functions needed to implement a system.

By contrast, MC++ programmers concentrate on creating their own *user-defined types*, called *classes*. We also refer to classes as *programmer-defined types*. Each class contains both data and a set of methods that manipulate the data. The data components of a class are called *data members*, *member variables* or *instance variables* (many MC++ programmers prefer the term *fields*). Just as we call an instance of a built-in type—such as `int`—a *variable*, we call an instance of a programmer-defined type (i.e., a class) an *object*. In MC++, attention is focused on classes, rather than on functions. Whereas C programmers use the verbs in a system-requirements document, MC++ programmers use the *nouns*. These nouns can be used to determine an initial set of classes with which to begin the design process. Programmers use these classes to instantiate objects that work together to implement a system.

This chapter explains how to create and use classes and objects, a subject known as *object-based programming (OBP)*. Chapter 9 and Chapter 10 introduce *inheritance* and *polymorphism*—key technologies that enable *object-oriented programming (OOP)*.

8.2 Implementing a Time Abstract Data Type with a Class

Classes in MC++ facilitate the creation of *abstract data types (ADT)*, which hide their implementation from clients (or users of the class object). A problem in procedural programming languages is that client code is often dependent on implementation details of the data used in the code. This dependency might necessitate rewriting the client code if the data implementation changes. ADTs eliminate this problem by providing implementation-independent *interfaces* to their clients. The creator of a class can change the internal implementation of that class without affecting the clients of that class.

Software Engineering Observation 8.1

It is important to write programs that are understandable and easy to maintain. Change is the rule, rather than the exception. Programmers should anticipate that their code will be modified. As we will see, classes facilitate program modifiability.

Our first example consists of class `Time1` (Fig. 8.1 and Fig. 8.2) and the driver program `Time1Test.cpp` (Fig. 8.3), which we use to test the class. A *driver* is an application that is used to test software. Class `Time1` contains the time of day in 24-hour clock format. Program `Time1Test.cpp` contains function `_tmain`, which creates an instance of class `Time1` and demonstrates the features of that class.

```
// Fig. 8.1: Time1.h
// Demonstrating class Time1.

#pragma once
```

Fig. 8.1 Abstract data type `Time1` definition as a class. (Part 1 of 2.)

```

#using <mscorlib.dll>

using namespace System;

public __gc class Time1
{
public:
   Time1();   // constructor
   void SetTime( int, int, int ); // set method
   String *ToUniversalString();
   String *ToStandardString();

private:
   int hour;     // 0-23
   int minute;   // 0-59
   int second;   // 0-59
}; // end class Time1
```

Fig. 8.1 Abstract data type `Time1` definition as a class. (Part 2 of 2.)

```
// Fig. 8.2: Time1.cpp
// Implementing class Time1.

#include "stdafx.h"
#include "Time1.h"

// Time1 constructor initializes variables to
// zero to set default time to midnight
Time1::Time1()
{
   SetTime( 0, 0, 0 );
}

// set new time value in 24-hour format. Perform validity
// checks on the data. Set invalid value to zero.
void Time1::SetTime( int hourValue, int minuteValue, int secondValue )
{
   hour = ( hourValue >= 0 && hourValue < 24 ) ? hourValue : 0;
   minute = ( minuteValue >= 0 && minuteValue < 60 ) ? minuteValue : 0;
   second = ( secondValue >= 0 && secondValue < 60 ) ? secondValue : 0;
}

// convert time to universal-time (24 hour) format string
String *Time1::ToUniversalString()
{
   return String::Concat( hour.ToString( S"D2" ), S":",
      minute.ToString( S"D2" ), S":", second.ToString( S"D2" ) );
}

```

Fig. 8.2 Class `Time1` method definitions. (Part 1 of 2.)

```
// convert time to standard-time (12 hour) format string
String *Time1::ToStandardString()
{
   return String::Concat(
      ( ( hour == 12 || hour == 0 ) ? 12 : hour % 12 ).ToString(),
      S":", minute.ToString( S"D2" ), S":", second.ToString( S"D2" ),
      S" ", ( hour < 12 ? S"AM" : S"PM" ) );
}
```

Fig. 8.2 Class `Time1` method definitions. (Part 2 of 2.)

```
// Fig. 8.3: Time1Test.cpp
// Demonstrating class Time1.

#include "stdafx.h"
#include "Time1.h"

#using <mscorlib.dll>
#using <system.windows.forms.dll>

using namespace System;
using namespace System::Windows::Forms;

int _tmain()
{
   Time1 *time = new Time1(); // calls Time1 constructor
   String *output;

   // assign string representation of time to output
   output = String::Concat( S"Initial universal time is: ",
      time->ToUniversalString(), S"\nInitial standard time is: ",
      time->ToStandardString() );

   // attempt valid time settings
   time->SetTime( 13, 27, 6 );

   // append new string representations of time to output
   output = String::Concat( output,
      S"\n\nUniversal time after SetTime is: ",
      time->ToUniversalString(),
      S"\nStandard time after SetTime is: ",
      time->ToStandardString() );

   // attempt invalid time settings
   time->SetTime( 99, 99, 99 );

   output = String::Concat( output,
      S"\n\nAfter attempting invalid settings: ",
      S"\nUniversal time: ", time->ToUniversalString(),
      S"\nStandard time: ", time->ToStandardString() );

   MessageBox::Show( output, S"Testing Class Time1" );
```

Fig. 8.3 Using an abstract data type. (Part 1 of 2.)

```

    return 0;
} // end _tmain
```

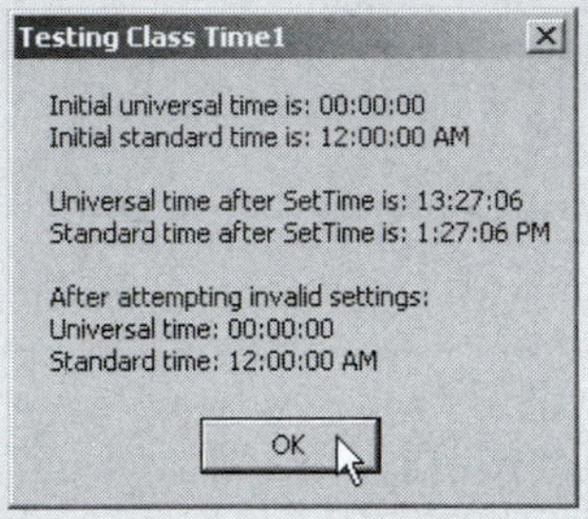

Fig. 8.3 Using an abstract data type. (Part 2 of 2.)

When building an MC++ application, each class definition (sometimes called the class declaration) normally is placed in a *header file,* and that class's method definitions (sometimes called the class's implementation) are placed in *source-code files* with the same name and the extension `.cpp`. A header file (extension `.h`) contains the prototypes of all methods (or *member functions*[1]), the names and types of all data members, and other information about the class needed by the compiler. The header files are included (via `#include`) in each file in which the class is used, and the source-code file is compiled and linked with the file containing the main program. The `#include` directive causes a copy of a specified file to be included in place of the directive. To create a new header file and add it to a currently open project in Visual Studio .NET, perform the following steps (these steps assume that you have already created a console application called `Time1Test` and that the code from Fig. 8.3 is included in `Time1Test.cpp`):

1. *Create the new header file.* Select **File > New > File...** to open a new file. In the **New File** dialog (Fig. 8.4), select the type of file needed and click **Open**. For this example, we select **Header File (.h)** from the **Visual C++** folder. Visual Studio .NET names the file `Header1` by default. If there is already a header file named `Header1`, the file will be named `Header2` by default, and so on until a name is found that is not already being used. This creates a new (blank) file. To rename the file, select **File > Save Header1 As...** and specify the filename (in this case, `Time1.h`) in the **Save File As** dialog (Fig. 8.5). Browse to the project folder and save the file in that folder by clicking **Save**. Note that the **File > Save Header1 As...** option appears only if the `Header1` text-editor window is the active window.

1. In C++, the methods of a class are usually referred to as member functions. However, in the .NET community, the term "methods" is the proper idiom. Therefore, we use "methods" throughout this book.

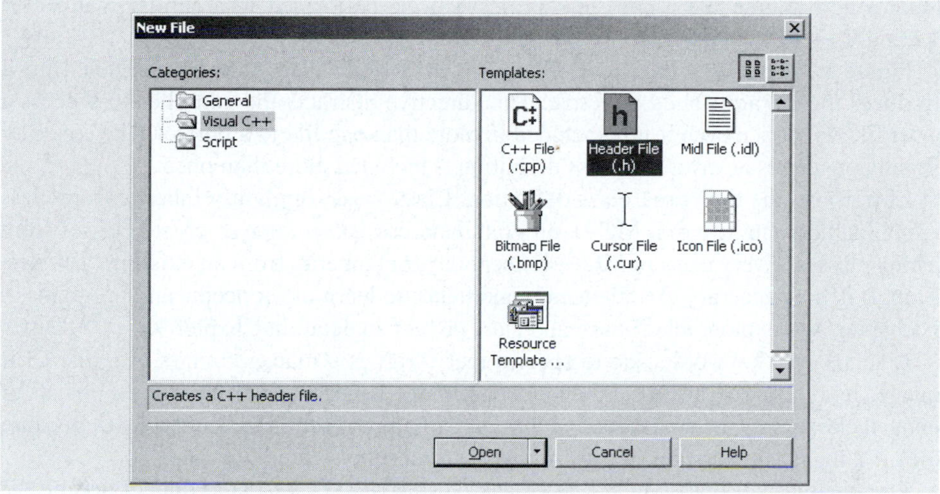

Fig. 8.4 Creating a new header file.

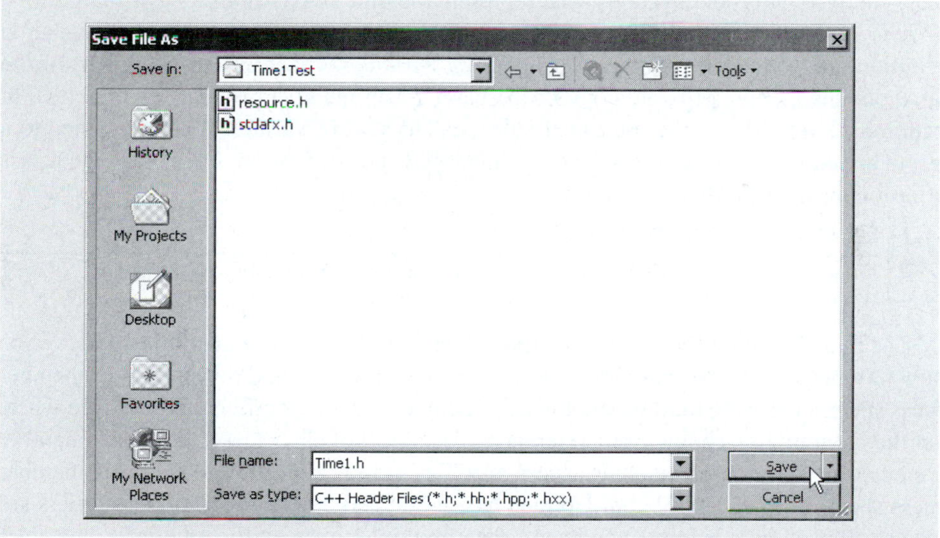

Fig. 8.5 Renaming a header file.

2. *Add the header file to the project.* Select **File > Move Time1.h into Project** (or right-click inside the editor and select **Move Time1.h into Project** from the context menu). The submenu that appears lists any open projects. Select **Time1Test** from this list. [*Note*: Some users prefer to combine *Steps* 1 and 2 by right-clicking **Header Files** in the **Solution Explorer** and selecting **Add > Add New Item**… from the context menu.]

If the header file already exists, you can simply right click **Header Files** in the **Solution Explorer** and select **Add > Add Existing Item**… from the popup menu. Note that adding a new source file (.cpp) to a project can be performed in a similar manner by selecting **C++ File (.cpp)** from the **New File** dialog.

Figure 8.1 consists of the header file Time1.h in which class Time1 is defined. Line 4 introduces the *#pragma once* directive. This directive instructs the compiler to process a header file only once even if it is included in more than one file in a project. The compiler normally generates an error if a class definition is included more than once.

Line 10 begins the Time1 class definition. Class Time1 implicitly inherits from class *Object* (namespace System). MC++ programmers use *inheritance* to create classes from existing classes. Every class in MC++ (except Object) inherits from an existing class definition. It is not necessary to understand inheritance to learn the concepts and programs in this chapter. We explore inheritance and class Object in detail in Chapter 9.

Line 10 uses keyword __gc to specify that Time1 is a managed class (i.e., the CLR manages its lifetime). The .NET Framework garbage collector destroys unused objects of managed classes in your programs. We discuss garbage collection in Section 8.10. Because Time1 is a managed class, all objects of this class must be created with new.

The opening left brace ({) at line 11 and closing right brace (}) at line 22 delimit the *body* of class Time1. Any information that we place in this body is said to be encapsulated (i.e., wrapped) in the class. For example, lines 19–21 of class Time1 declare three int variables—hour, minute and second—that represent the time of day in *universal-time* format (*24-hour clock* format). Variables declared in a class definition, but not inside a method definition, are called *data members* or *instance variables*—each instance (object) of the class contains its own separate copy of the class's data members (instance variables). In Section 8.22 we will see that other variables (called static variables) can be added to a class. The semicolon (;) at line 22 ends the managed class definition. Every managed class definition must end with a semicolon.

Common Programming Error 8.1

Failure to end a class definition with a semicolon is a syntax error.

The *public:* and *private:* labels (lines 12 and 18) are *member access specifiers* (also known as *member access modifiers*). Any data member or method declared after member access specifier public (and before the next member access specifier) is accessible wherever the program has a pointer or a reference to an object of class Time1. Any data member or method declared after member access specifier private (and up to the next member access specifier) is accessible only to methods of that class. Member access specifiers are always followed by a colon (:) and can appear multiple times and in any order in a class definition. For the remainder of the text, we will refer to the member access specifiers as public and private, without the colon. In Chapter 9, we introduce a third member access specifier, protected, as we study inheritance and the part it plays in object-oriented programming.

Good Programming Practice 8.1

Even though private *and* public *members can be intermixed, use each member access specifier only once in a class definition for clarity and readability. Place* public *members first so that they are easy to locate.*

The default member access for a class's members is private. Thus, if we did not provide any member access specifiers in Fig. 8.1, all the data members and methods of the class would be considered `private`. *Structures*, which are similar to classes, have default member access `public`. Structures are declared with keyword `struct`.[2]

The three integer members appear after the `private` member access specifier. Lines 19–21 declare each of the three `private int` data members—`hour`, `minute` and `second`—indicating that these data members of the class are accessible only to the methods of the class. (This is known as *data hiding*.) Normally, data members are declared `private`, and methods are declared `public`. However, it is possible to have `private` methods and `public` data members, as we will see later. Often, `private` methods are called *utility methods*, or *helper methods*, because they can be called only by other methods of that class. The purpose of utility methods is to support the operation of a class's other methods. Declaring data members and utility methods as `public` is a dangerous practice. —code in other classes could set `public` data members to invalid values, producing potentially disastrous results.

Software Engineering Observation 8.2

Declare all data members of a class as `private`. The architecture of accessing `private` data through `public` methods that first validate the data allows the developer to ensure that an object's data remains in a consistent state—that is, the data is always valid.

Software Engineering Observation 8.3

Make a class member `private` if there is no reason for that member to be accessed outside of the class.

Classes often include *accessor methods* (or more simply, *accessors*) that can read or display data. Another common use for accessor methods is to test the truth of conditions—such methods often are called *predicate methods*. For example, we could design predicate method `IsEmpty` for a *container class*—a class capable of holding many objects, such as a linked list, a stack or a queue. (These data structures are discussed in detail in Chapter 22, Data Structures and Collections.) `IsEmpty` would return `true` if the container is empty and `false` otherwise. A program might call `IsEmpty` before attempting to read another item from the container object. Similarly, a program might call another predicate method (e.g., `IsFull`) before attempting to insert an item into a container object.

Class `Time1` (Fig. 8.1) contains constructor `Time1` (line 13) and prototypes for the methods `SetTime` (line 14), `ToUniversalString` (line 15) and `ToStandardString` (line 16). These are the *`public` methods* (also called the *`public` services*, *`public` interface* or *`public` behaviors*) of the class. Clients of class `Time1`, such as class `Time1Test.cpp` (Fig. 8.3), use `Time1`'s `public` interface to manipulate the data stored in `Time1` objects or to cause class `Time1` to perform its services. The data members of the class support the delivery of the *services* the class provides to its clients.

The source-code file `Time1.cpp` (Fig. 8.2) defines the methods of class `Time1`. Line 5 uses `#include` to link to the class header file. The compiler uses the information in `Time1.h` to ensure that the method headers are defined correctly and that the methods use the class's data correctly. Lines 9–12 define the *constructor* of class `Time1`. A class's constructor initializes objects of that class. When a program creates an object of class `Time1` with operator `new`, the constructor is called to initialize the object. Line 11 of class `Time1`'s constructor

2. Structures are not discussed in this book. More information about structures can be found at `msdn.microsoft.com/library/default.asp?url=/library/en-us/vclang/html/vcsmpstruct.asp`.

calls method `SetTime` (lines 16–21) to initialize variables `hour`, `minute` and `second` to `0` (representing midnight). Constructors can take arguments, but cannot return values. As we will see, a class can have overloaded constructors. An important difference between constructors and other methods is that constructors cannot specify a return type. Generally, constructors are `public`. Note that the constructor name must have the exact same name as the class.

Common Programming Error 8.2

Attempting to `return` *a value from a constructor is a syntax error.*

Method `SetTime` (lines 16–21) is a `public` method that receives three `int` parameters and uses them to set the time. A conditional expression tests each argument to determine whether the value is in a specified range. For example, the `hour` value must be greater than or equal to 0 and less than 24, because universal-time format represents the hour as an integer from 0 to 23. Similarly, the minute and second values must be greater than or equal to 0 and less than 60. Any values outside these ranges are invalid values and are set to zero by default. Setting invalid values to 0 ensures that a `Time1` object always contains valid data (because, in this example, 0 is a valid value for `hour`, `minute` and `second`). Rather than simply assigning a default value, developers might want to indicate to the client that the time entered was invalid. In Chapter 11, we discuss exception handling, which can be used to indicate invalid initialization values.

Software Engineering Observation 8.4

Always define a class so that each of its variables contains valid values.

Method `ToUniversalString` (lines 24–28) takes no arguments and returns a `String *` in universal-time format, consisting of six digits—two for the hour, two for the minute and two for the second. For example, if the time were 1:30:07 PM, method `ToUniversalString` would return `13:30:07`. Lines 26–27 use `String` method `Concat` to configure the universal-time string. Method `ToString` is called on each integer with argument *`D2`* (a two-digit base 10-decimal number format) for display purposes. The `D2` format specification causes single-digit values to appear as two digits with a leading `0` (e.g., `8` would be represented as `08`). The colons separate the hour from the minute and the minute from the second in the resulting `String *` object.

Method `ToStandardString` (lines 31–37) takes no arguments and returns a `String *` object in standard-time format, consisting of the `hour`, `minute` and `second` values separated by colons and followed by an AM or a PM indicator (e.g., `1:27:06 PM`). Like method `ToUniversalString`, method `ToStandardString` uses `String` method `Concat` to format the `minute` and `second` as two-digit values with leading zeros if necessary. Line 34 determines the value for `hour` in the `String *` object—if the `hour` is `0` or `12` (AM or PM), the `hour` appears as 12; otherwise, the `hour` appears as a value from 1 to 11.

After defining the class, we can use it as a type in declarations such as

```
Time1 *sunset; // pointer to a Time1 object
```

which declares a pointer to a `Time1` object. The class name (`Time1`) is a type name. A class can yield many objects, just as a primitive data type, such as `int`, can yield many variables.

Programmers can create class types as needed; this is one reason why MC++ is known as an *extensible language.*

The driver program `Time1Test` (Fig. 8.3) demonstrates of class `Time1`. Note that line 5 uses `#include` to link to the class header file. This allows the driver to use our new type `Time1`.

Although all the programs in the previous chapters displayed output in the command prompt, most MC++ applications use windows or *dialogs* to display output. Dialogs are windows that typically display important messages to the user of an application. The .NET Framework Class Library includes class *`MessageBox`* for creating dialogs. Class `MessageBox` is defined in namespace *`System::Windows::Forms`* (referenced in line 11). The code defining this namespace is included into the application on line 8, as we will discuss shortly. The program in Fig. 8.3 displays its output in a message dialog using class `MessageBox`.

Function `_tmain` (lines 13–44) declares and initializes `Time1` pointer `time` (line 15) with an object of class `Time1`. When the object is instantiated, *operator `new`* allocates the memory in which the `Time1` object will be stored, then calls the `Time1` constructor (lines 9–12 of Fig. 8.2) to initialize the data members of the `Time1` object. As mentioned before, this constructor invokes method `SetTime` of class `Time1` to initialize each `private` variable to `0`. Operator `new` (line 15 of Fig. 8.3) then returns a pointer to the newly created object; this pointer is assigned to `time`.

Software Engineering Observation 8.5

Note the relationship between operator `new` and the constructor of a class. When operator `new` creates a pointer to an object of a class, that class's constructor is called to initialize the object's variables.

Line 16 declares `String` pointer `output` to store the `String` containing the results, which later will be displayed in a `MessageBox`. Lines 19–21 assign to `output` the time in universal-time format (by invoking method `ToUniversalString` of the `Time1` object) and standard-time format (by invoking method `ToStandardString` of the `Time1` object). Note the syntax of the method call in each case—the pointer `time` is followed by the member access operator (`->`) followed by the method name. Members of a class are accessed using the member access operators—the dot operator (`.`) and the arrow operator (`->`). The dot operator accesses a class member via the variable name for the object or via a reference to the object; for instance, we often access a variable's `ToString` method with the dot operator. The arrow operator—consisting of a minus sign (`-`) and a greater than sign (`>`) with no intervening spaces—accesses a class member via a pointer to the object.

Line 24 sets the time for the `Time1` object to which `time` points by passing valid hour, minute and second arguments to `Time1` method `SetTime`. Lines 27–31 append to `output` the new time in both universal and standard formats to confirm that the time was set correctly.

To illustrate that method `SetTime` validates the values passed to it, line 34 passes invalid time arguments to method `SetTime`. Lines 36–39 append to `output` the new time in both formats. All three values passed to `SetTime` are invalid, so variables `hour`, `minute` and `second` are set to `0`. Line 41 displays a `MessageBox` with the results of our program. Notice in the last two lines of the output window that the time was indeed set to midnight when invalid arguments were passed to `SetTime`.

Recall that the class declares data members `hour`, `minute` and `second` as `private`. Such variables are not accessible outside the class in which they are declared. A class's clients should not be concerned with the data representation of that class. Clients of a class should be interested only in the services provided by that class. For example, the class could represent the time internally as the number of seconds that have elapsed since the previous midnight. Suppose the data representation changes. Clients still are able to use the same `public` methods and obtain the same results without being aware of the change in internal representation. In this sense, the implementation of a class is said to be *hidden* from its clients.

Software Engineering Observation 8.6

Information hiding promotes program modifiability and simplifies the client's perception of a class.

Software Engineering Observation 8.7

Clients of a class can (and should) use the class without knowing the internal details of how the class is implemented. If the class implementation changes (to improve performance, for example), but the class interface remains constant, the client's source code need not change. This makes it much easier to modify systems.

In this program, the `Time1` constructor initializes the data members to `0` (the universal-time equivalent of 12 midnight) to ensure that the object is created in a *consistent state*—i.e., all data members have valid values. The data members of a `Time1` object cannot store invalid values, because the constructor, which calls `SetTime`, is called to initialize the data members when the `Time1` object is created. Method `SetTime` scrutinizes subsequent attempts by a client to modify the data members.

Normally, the data members of a class are initialized in that class's constructor, but they also can be initialized when they are declared in the class body. If a programmer does not initialize data members explicitly, the compiler implicitly initializes them. When this occurs, the compiler sets primitive numeric variables to `0`, `bool` values to `false` and pointers to `NULL`. [*Note*: Readers should recall that in MC++, `0` represents a null pointer. However, sometimes in this book, we use `NULL` in place of `0`. `NULL` is defined in a number of headers, including *`tchar.h`*, and is interchangeable with `0`.]

Note the use of *binary scope resolution operator (`::`)* in each method definition (lines 9, 16, 24 and 31 of Fig. 8.2). Once a class is defined and its methods are declared, the methods must be defined. For each method defined, the methods name is preceded by the class name and the binary scope resolution operator (`::`). This "ties" the method's name to the class name to uniquely identify the methods of a particular class.

Common Programming Error 8.3

When defining a class's methods outside that class, omitting the class name and scope resolution operator on the method name is an error.

Even though a method declared in a class definition may be defined outside that class definition (and "tied" to the class via the binary scope resolution operator), that method is still within that *class's scope*, i.e., its name is known only to other members of the class unless referred to via an object of the class, a reference to an object of the class or a pointer to an object of the class. We will say more about class scope shortly.

Methods `ToUniversalString` and `ToStandardString` take no arguments, because, by default, these methods manipulate the data members of the particular `Time1` object on which they are invoked. This often makes method calls more concise than conventional function calls in procedural programming languages. It also reduces the likelihood of passing the wrong arguments, the wrong types of arguments or the wrong number of arguments.

Software Engineering Observation 8.8

An object-oriented programming approach often simplifies method calls by reducing the number of arguments that must be passed. This benefit of object-oriented programming derives from the fact that encapsulation of data members and methods within an object gives the object's methods the right to access the object's data members.

Classes simplify programming, because the client need be concerned only with the `public` operations available for the object. Usually, such operations are designed to be client oriented, rather than implementation oriented. Clients are neither aware of, nor involved in, a class's implementation. Interfaces change less frequently than do implementations. When an implementation changes, implementation-dependent code must change accordingly. By hiding the implementation, we eliminate the possibility that other program parts will become dependent on a class's implementation details.

Often, programmers do not have to create classes "from scratch." Rather, they can derive classes from other classes that provide behaviors required by the new classes. Classes also can include pointers to objects as members. Such *software reuse* can greatly enhance programmer productivity. Chapter 9 discusses *inheritance*—the process by which new classes are derived from existing classes. Section 8.8 discusses *composition* (or *aggregation*), in which classes include as members objects or pointers to objects of other classes.

Many compiled classes in the .NET Framework Class Library (including `MessageBox`) need to be referenced before they can be used in a program. Depending on the type of application we create, classes may be compiled into files with an `.exe` (*executable*) extension, a `.dll` (*dynamic link library*) extension or one of several other extensions. Dynamic link libraries, which cannot be run as programs by themselves, contain executable code (e.g., functions and classes). Programs link to DLLs, which can be shared among several executing programs. DLLs are dynamically loaded at runtime. Executable files contain an application entry point (e.g., a `_tmain` function). Such files are called *assemblies* and are the packaging units for code in MC++. [*Note*: Assemblies can be comprised of files of different types, including `.h` and `.cpp` files.] The assembly is a package containing the Microsoft Intermediate Language (MSIL) code that a project has been compiled into, plus any other information that is needed for these classes. The assembly that we need to reference can be found in the Visual Studio .NET documentation for the class we wish to use. The easiest way to access this information is to go to the **Help** menu in Visual Studio .NET and choose **Index**. The reader then can type in the name of the class to access the documentation. Class `MessageBox` is located in assembly `System.Windows.Forms.dll` (referenced in line 8 of Fig. 8.3). Other classes that create GUI components will be described in Chapter 12 and Chapter 13.

In `_tmain`, line 41 calls method `Show` of class `MessageBox` (Fig. 8.3). This overloaded version of the method takes two strings as arguments. The first string (`output`) is the message to be displayed. The second string is the title of the message dialog (`"Testing Class Time1"`). If the second argument is omitted, the message dialog will have no title. Method `Show` is called a `static` *method*. Such methods always are called by using their class name (in this case, `MessageBox`) followed by the scope resolution operator (`::`) and the method name (in this case, `Show`). We discuss `static` methods in Section 8.11.

Line 41 displays the dialog shown in Fig. 8.6. The dialog includes an **OK** button that allows the user to *dismiss (close)* the dialog. Positioning the mouse cursor (also called the mouse pointer) over the **OK** button and clicking the mouse dismisses the dialog. The user can also close the dialog by clicking the close box in the upper-right corner of the dialog. Once this occurs, the program terminates, because the `_tmain` function terminates.

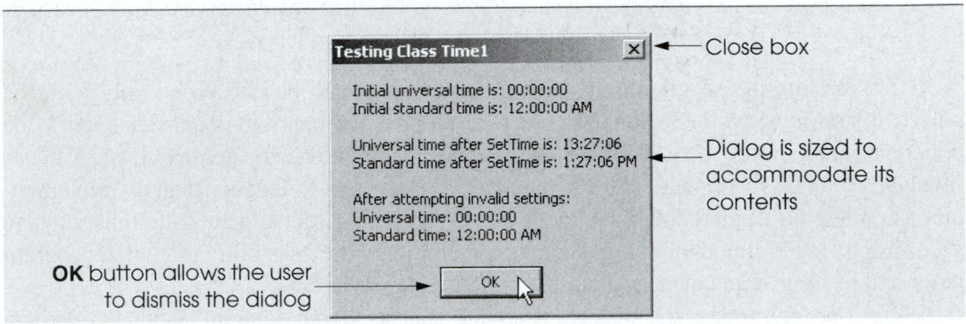

Fig. 8.6 Dialog displayed by calling `MessageBox::Show`.

8.3 Class Scope

In Section 6.15, we discussed method scope; now, we discuss *class scope*. A class's members belong to that class's scope. Within a class's scope, class members are immediately accessible to that class's methods and can be referenced by name. Outside a class's scope, class members cannot be referenced directly by name. Those class members that are visible (such as `public` members) can be accessed only through a "handle" such as a pointer to an object (via the format *pointerName->memberName*), a reference to an object (via the format *referenceName*`.`*memberName*) or the name of a value-type object (via the format *objectName*`.`*memberName*).

If a variable is defined in a method, only that method can access the variable (i.e., the variable is a local variable of that method). Such variables are said to have *local scope*, or *block scope*. If a method defines a variable that has the same name as a variable with class scope (i.e., a data member), the local-scope variable hides the class-scope variable in that method's scope. A hidden variable can be accessed in a method by preceding its name with the keyword *`this`* and the arrow member access operator, as in `this->hour`. We discuss keyword `this` in Section 8.9.

8.4 Controlling Access to Members

The member access specifiers `public` and `private` control access to a class's data and methods. (In Chapter 9, Object-Oriented Programming: Inheritance, we introduce another access specifier—`protected`.)

As previously stated, `public` methods present to the class's clients a view of the *services* that the class provides (i.e., the `public` interface of the class). Previously, we mentioned the merits of writing methods that perform only one task. If a method must execute other tasks to calculate its final result, these tasks should be performed by helper methods.

A client does not need to call these helper methods, nor does it need to be concerned with how the class uses its helper methods. For these reasons, helper methods are declared as `private` members of a class.

Common Programming Error 8.4

Attempting to access a `private` class member from outside that class is a compilation error.

The application of Fig. 8.7 (which uses the `Time1` class from Fig. 8.1–Fig. 8.2) demonstrates that `private` class members are not accessible outside the class. Lines 17–19 attempt to access the `private` variables `hour`, `minute` and `second` of the `Time1` object to which `time` points. When this program is compiled, the compiler reports errors stating that the `private` members `hour`, `minute` and `second` are not accessible.

```
1  // Fig. 8.7: RestrictedAccess.cpp
2  // Demonstrate compilation errors from attempt to access
3  // private class members.
4
5  #include "stdafx.h"
6  #include "Time1.h"
7
8  #using <mscorlib.dll>
9
10 using namespace System;
11
12 // main entry point for application
13 int _tmain()
14 {
15    Time1 *time = new Time1();
16
17    time->hour = 7;
18    time->minute = 15;
19    time->second = 30;
20
21    return 0;
22 } // end _tmain
```

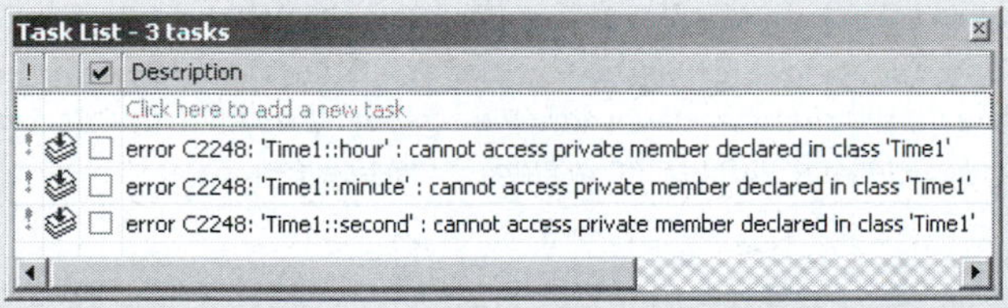
Task List - 3 tasks
Description
Click here to add a new task
error C2248: 'Time1::hour' : cannot access private member declared in class 'Time1'
error C2248: 'Time1::minute' : cannot access private member declared in class 'Time1'
error C2248: 'Time1::second' : cannot access private member declared in class 'Time1'

Fig. 8.7 Accessing `private` class members from client code generates compilation errors.

8.5 Initializing Class Objects: Constructors

When a program creates an instance of a class, the program invokes the class's constructor to initialize the class's data members. A class can contain overloaded constructors to provide multiple ways to initialize objects of that class.

Common Programming Error 8.5

Only `static` *variables can be initialized in their declarations in the body of a managed class (i.e., within the managed class but outside that class's methods). Attempting to initialize a non-*`static` *variable in its declaration in the body of a managed class is a syntax error. Non-*`static` *variables must be initialized in constructors.*

Regardless of whether data members receive explicit initialization values, the data members always are initialized. In such cases, data members receive their default values (`0` for primitive numeric type variables, `false` for `bool` variables and `0` for pointers).

Performance Tip 8.1

Data members always are initialized to default values by the runtime; therefore, avoid initializing data members to their default values in the constructor.

Software Engineering Observation 8.9

When appropriate, provide a constructor to ensure that every object is initialized with meaningful values.

When creating an object of a class, the programmer can provide *initializers* in parentheses to the right of the class name. These initializers are the arguments to the constructor. In general, an object can be created as follows

ClassName **objectPointer* = **new** *ClassName*(*arguments*);

where *objectPointer* is a pointer of the appropriate data type, `new` indicates that an object is being created, *ClassName* indicates the type of the new object (and the name of the constructor being called) and *arguments* specifies a comma-separated list of the values used by the constructor to initialize the object's data members.

If a class does not define any constructors, the compiler provides a *default* (*no-argument*) *constructor*. This compiler-provided default constructor does not contain code (i.e., the constructor has an empty body) and does not have parameters. The programmer also can provide a no-argument constructor, as we demonstrated in class `Time1` (Fig. 8.1 and Fig. 8.2). Programmer-provided no-argument constructors can have code in their bodies.

Common Programming Error 8.6

If a class has constructors, but none of the `public` *constructors is a default constructor, and a program attempts to call a no-argument constructor to initialize an object of the class, a compilation error occurs. A constructor can be called with no arguments only if there are no constructors for the class (in which case the compiler-provided default constructor is called) or if the class defines a* `public` *no-argument constructor.*

8.6 Using Overloaded Constructors

Like methods, constructors of a class can be overloaded. The `Time1` constructor in Fig. 8.2 initialized `hour`, `minute` and `second` to `0` (i.e., midnight in universal time) via a call to the method `SetTime`. However, class `Time2` (Fig. 8.8 and Fig. 8.9) overloads the constructor to provide a variety of ways to initialize `Time2` objects. Each constructor calls `Time2` method `SetTime`, which ensures that the object begins in a consistent state by setting out-of-range values to `0`. MC++ invokes the appropriate constructor by matching the number, types and order of arguments specified in the constructor call with the number, types and order of parameters specified in each constructor definition. Figure 8.8–Fig. 8.10 demonstrate using initializers and overloaded constructors.

```
// Fig. 8.8: Time2.h
// Class Time2 header file.

#pragma once

#using <mscorlib.dll>

using namespace System;

// Time2 class definition
public __gc class Time2
{
public:
   Time2();

   // overloaded constructors
   Time2( int );
   Time2( int, int );
   Time2( int, int, int );
   Time2( Time2 * );

   void SetTime( int, int, int );
   String *ToUniversalString();
   String *ToStandardString();

private:
   int hour;    // 0-23
   int minute;  // 0-59
   int second;  // 0-59
}; // end class Time2
```

Fig. 8.8 Overloaded constructors provide flexible object-initialization options.

```
// Fig. 8.9: Time2.cpp
// Class Time2 provides overloaded constructors.

#include "stdafx.h"
#include "Time2.h"

// Time2 constructor initializes variables to
// zero to set default time to midnight
Time2::Time2()
{
   SetTime( 0, 0, 0 );
}

```

Fig. 8.9 `Time2` class method definitions. (Part 1 of 2.)

```
// Time2 constructor: hour supplied, minute and second
// defaulted to 0
Time2::Time2( int hourValue )
{
   SetTime( hourValue, 0, 0 );
}

// Time2 constructor: hour and minute supplied, second
// defaulted to 0
Time2::Time2( int hourValue, int minuteValue )
{
   SetTime( hourValue, minuteValue, 0 );
}

// Time2 constructor: hour, minute, and second supplied
Time2::Time2( int hourValue, int minuteValue, int secondValue )
{
   SetTime( hourValue, minuteValue, secondValue);
}

// Time2 constructor: initialize using another Time2 object
Time2::Time2( Time2 *time )
{
   SetTime( time->hour, time->minute, time->second );
}

// set new time value in 24-hour format. Perform validity
// check on the data. Set invalid values to zero.
void Time2::SetTime( int hourValue, int minuteValue, int secondValue )
{
   hour = ( hourValue >= 0 && hourValue < 24 ) ? hourValue : 0;
   minute = ( minuteValue >= 0 && minuteValue < 60 ) ? minuteValue : 0;
   second = ( secondValue >= 0 && secondValue < 60 ) ? secondValue : 0;
}

// convert time to universal-time (24 hour) format string
String *Time2::ToUniversalString()
{
   return String::Concat( hour.ToString( S"D2" ), S":"
      minute.ToString( S"D2" ), S":", second.ToString( S"D2" ) );
}

// convert time to standard-time (12 hour) format string
String *Time2::ToStandardString()
{
   return String::Concat(
      ( ( hour == 12 || hour == 0 ) ? 12 : hour % 12 ).ToString(),
      S":", minute.ToString( S"D2" ), S":", second.ToString( S"D2" ),
      S" ", ( hour < 12 ? S"AM" : S"PM" ) );
}
```

Fig. 8.9 `Time2` class method definitions. (Part 2 of 2.)

Most of the code in class `Time2` is identical to that in class `Time1`, so this discussion concentrates only on the overloaded constructors. Lines 9–12 (of Fig. 8.9) define the no-argument constructor that sets the time to midnight. Lines 16–19 define a `Time2` constructor that receives a single `int` argument representing the `hour` and sets the time using the specified `hour` value and zero for `minute` and `second`. Lines 23–26 define a `Time2` constructor that receives two `int` arguments representing the `hour` and `minute` and sets the time using those values and zero for the `second`. Lines 29–32 define a `Time2` constructor that receives three `int` arguments representing the `hour`, `minute` and `second` and uses those values to set the time. Lines 35–38 define a `Time2` constructor that receives a pointer to another `Time2` object. When this last constructor is called, the values from the `Time2` argument are used to initialize the `hour`, `minute` and `second` values of the new `Time2` object. Even though class `Time2` declares `hour`, `minute` and `second` as `private` (lines 27–29 of Fig. 8.8), the `Time2` constructor can access these values in its `Time2` argument directly via the pointer `time` and the arrow operator using the expressions `time->hour`, `time->minute` and `time->second`.

Software Engineering Observation 8.10

When one object of a class has a pointer to another object of the same class, the first object can access all the second object's data and methods (including those that are `private`*).*

Notice that the second, third and fourth constructors (beginning in lines 16, 23 and 29 of Fig. 8.9) have some arguments in common and that those arguments are kept in the same order. For instance, the constructor that starts in line 23 has as its two arguments an integer representing the hour and an integer representing the minute. The constructor beginning in line 29 has these same two arguments in the same order, followed by its last argument (an integer representing the second).

Good Programming Practice 8.2

When defining overloaded constructors, keep the order of arguments as similar as possible; this makes client programming easier.

Common Programming Error 8.7

Unlike functions, constructors and methods cannot have default arguments. Attempting to specify a default value for a constructor or method argument generates a compilation error.

Constructors cannot specify return types; doing so results in syntax errors. Also, notice that each constructor receives a different number or different types of arguments. Even though only two of the constructors receive values for the `hour`, `minute` and `second`, each constructor calls `SetTime` with values for `hour`, `minute` and `second` (if necessary, uses zeros for the missing values) to satisfy `SetTime`'s requirement of three arguments.

Driver `Time2Test` (Fig. 8.10) demonstrates class `Time2`'s overloaded constructors. Line 16 declares six `Time2` pointers and lines 18–23 create `Time2` objects, using the overloaded constructors to initialize those objects. Line 18 invokes the no-argument constructor by placing an empty set of parentheses after the class name. Line 19 invokes the single-argument constructor that takes an `int` argument. Line 20 invokes the two-argument constructor. Lines 21–22 invoke the three-argument constructor. Line 23 invokes the single-argument constructor that receives a `Time2` pointer. To invoke the appropriate constructor, pass the proper number, types and order of arguments (specified by the constructor's definition) to that constructor. Lines 25–53 invoke methods `ToUniversalString` and `ToStan-`

dardString for each Time2 object to demonstrate that the constructors initialize the objects correctly.

```
// Fig. 8.10: Time2Test.cpp
// Using overloaded constructors.

#include "stdafx.h"
#include "Time2.h"

#using <system.dll>
#using <system.windows.forms.dll>

using namespace System;
using namespace System::Windows::Forms;

// main entry point for application
int _tmain()
{
   Time2 *time1, *time2, *time3, *time4, *time5, *time6;

   time1 = new Time2();                 // 00:00:00
   time2 = new Time2( 2 );              // 02:00:00
   time3 = new Time2( 21, 34 );         // 21:34:00
   time4 = new Time2( 12, 25, 42 );     // 12:25:42
   time5 = new Time2( 27, 74, 99 );     // 00:00:00
   time6 = new Time2( time4 );          // 12:25:42

   String *output = String::Concat( S"Constructed with: ",
      S"\ntime1: all arguments defaulted",
      S"\n\t", time1->ToUniversalString(),
      S"\n\t", time1->ToStandardString() );

   output = String::Concat( output,
      S"\ntime2: hour specified; minute and ",
      S"second defaulted", S"\n\t", time2->ToUniversalString(),
      S"\n\t", time2->ToStandardString() );

   output = String::Concat( output,
      S"\ntime3: hour and minute specified; ",
      S"second defaulted", S"\n\t", time3->ToUniversalString(),
      S"\n\t", time3->ToStandardString() );

   output = String::Concat( output,
      S"\ntime4: hour, minute and second specified", S"\n\t",
      time4->ToUniversalString(), S"\n\t",
      time4->ToStandardString() );

   output = String::Concat( output,
      S"\ntime5: all invalid values specified ",
      S"\n\t", time5->ToUniversalString(), S"\n\t",
      time5->ToStandardString() );
```

Fig. 8.10 Using overloaded constructors. (Part 1 of 2.)

```

   output = String::Concat( output,
      S"\ntime6: Time2 object time4 specified", S"\n\t",
      time6->ToUniversalString(), S"\n\t",
      time6->ToStandardString() );

   MessageBox::Show( output,  S"Demonstrating Overloaded Constructors" );

   return 0;
} // end _tmain
```

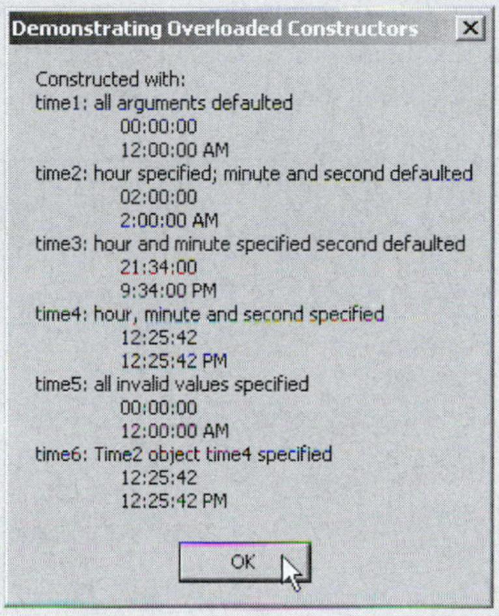

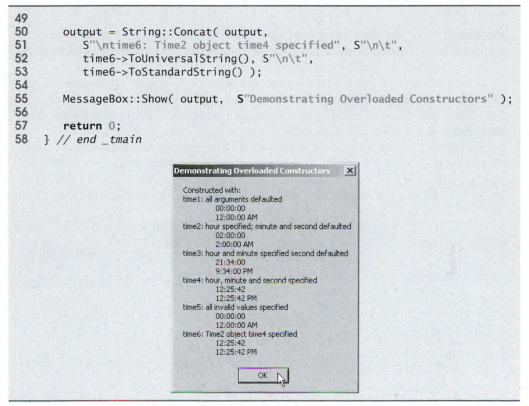

Fig. 8.10 Using overloaded constructors. (Part 2 of 2.)

Each `Time2` constructor could have been written to include a copy of the appropriate statements from method `SetTime`. This might be slightly more efficient, because it eliminates the extra call to `SetTime`. However, consider what would happen if the programmer were to change the representation of the time from three `int` values (requiring 12 bytes of memory) to a single `int` value representing the total number of seconds that have elapsed in the day (requiring 4 bytes of memory). Placing identical code in the `Time2` constructors and method `SetTime` makes such a change in the class definition more difficult, because every constructor's body would require modifications to manipulate the data as a single `int` rather than three `int`s. If the `Time2` constructors call `SetTime` directly, any changes to the implementation of `SetTime` must be made only once, in the body of `SetTime`. This reduces the likelihood of introducing a programming error when altering the implementation, because we make only one change in the class, rather than changing every constructor and method `SetTime`.

Software Engineering Observation 8.11

If a method of a class provides functionality required by a constructor (or other method) of the class, call that method from the constructor (or other method). This simplifies the maintenance of the code and reduces the likelihood of introducing errors into the code.

8.7 Properties

Methods of a class can manipulate that class's `private` data members. A typical manipulation might be the adjustment of a customer's bank balance—a `private` data member of a class `BankAccount`—by a `ComputeInterest` method.

Classes often provide `public` *properties* to allow clients to *set* (i.e., assign values to) or *get* (i.e., obtain the values of) `private` data members. Figure 8.11 enhances our `Time` class, now called `Time3`, to include three properties—`Hour`, `Minute` and `Second`—for the `private` data members `hour`, `minute` and `second`. Each property contains a *get method* (or *get accessor)* to retrieve the value, a *set method* (or *set accessor)* to modify the value or both. The *set* methods of these properties strictly control the setting of the data members to valid values. Each *get* method returns the appropriate data member's value. Figure 8.12 contains the method definitions for class `Time3`, and Fig. 8.13 demonstrates the `Time3` class.

```
// Fig. 8.11: Time3.h
// Class Time3 introduces properties.

#pragma once

#using <mscorlib.dll>

using namespace System;

// Time3 class definition
public __gc class Time3
{
public:
   Time3();
   Time3( int );
   Time3( int, int );
   Time3( int, int, int );
   Time3( Time3 * );
   void SetTime( int, int, int );

   // get method for property Hour
   __property int get_Hour()
   {
      return hour;
   }

   // set method for property Hour
   __property void set_Hour( int value )
   {
      hour = ( ( value >= 0 && value < 24 ) ? value : 0 );
   }

   // get method for property Minute
   __property int get_Minute()
   {
      return minute;
   }
```

Fig. 8.11 Properties provide controlled access to an object's data. (Part 1 of 2.)

```

   // set method for property Minute
   __property void set_Minute( int value )
   {
      minute = ( ( value >= 0 && value < 60 ) ? value : 0 );
   }

   // get method for property Second
   __property int get_Second()
   {
      return second;
   }

   // set method for property Second
   __property void set_Second( int value )
   {
      second = ( ( value >= 0 && value < 60 ) ? value : 0 );
   }

   String *ToUniversalString();
   String *ToStandardString();

private:
   int hour;   // 0-23
   int minute; // 0-59
   int second; // 0-59
}; // end class Time3
```

Fig. 8.11 Properties provide controlled access to an object's data. (Part 2 of 2.)

```
// Fig. 8.12: Time3.cpp
// Method definitions for class Time3.

#include "stdafx.h"
#include "Time3.h"

// Time3 constructor initializes variables to
// zero to set default time to midnight
Time3::Time3()
{
   SetTime( 0, 0, 0 );
}

// Time3 constructor: hour supplied, minute and second
// defaulted to 0
Time3::Time3( int hourValue )
{
   SetTime( hourValue, 0, 0 );
}

```

Fig. 8.12 `Time3` class method definitions. (Part 1 of 2.)

```
// Time3 constructor: hour and minute supplied, second
// defaulted to 0
Time3::Time3( int hourValue, int minuteValue )
{
   SetTime( hourValue, minuteValue, 0 );
}

// Time3 constructor: hour, minute and second supplied
Time3::Time3( int hourValue, int minuteValue, int secondValue )
{
   SetTime( hourValue, minuteValue, secondValue );
}

// Time3 constructor: intialize using another Time3 object
Time3::Time3( Time3 *time )
{
   SetTime( time->Hour, time->Minute, time->Second );
}

// set new time value in 24-hour format
void Time3::SetTime( int hourValue, int minuteValue, int secondValue )
{
   Hour = hourValue;
   Minute = minuteValue;
   Second = secondValue;
}

// convert time to universal-time (24 hour) format string
String *Time3::ToUniversalString()
{
   return String::Concat( Hour.ToString( S"D2" ), S":",
      Minute.ToString( S"D2" ), S":", Second.ToString( S"D2" ) );
}

// convert time to standard-time (12 hour) format string
String *Time3::ToStandardString()
{
   return String::Concat(
      ( ( Hour == 12 || Hour == 0 ) ? 12 : Hour % 12 ).ToString(),
      S":", Minute.ToString( S"D2" ), S":",
      Second.ToString( S"D2" ), S" ",
      ( Hour < 12 ? S"AM" : S"PM" ) );
}
```

Fig. 8.12 `Time3` class method definitions. (Part 2 of 2.)

Software Engineering Observation 8.12

Class designers need not provide set *or* get *methods for each* `private` *data member; these capabilities should be provided only when doing so makes sense.*

Error-Prevention Tip 8.1

Declaring the variables of a class as `private` *and the methods and properties of the class as* `public` *facilitates debugging, because problems with data manipulations are localized to the class methods that manipulate that data.*

Providing *set* and *get* capabilities appears to be the same as making the variables `public`. However, this is another one of MC++'s subtleties that makes it so attractive from a software-engineering standpoint. If a variable is `public`, the variable can be read or written to by any method or property in the program. If a variable is `private`, a `public` *get* method seems to allow other methods or properties to read the data at will. However, the *get* method can control the format in which the data is returned to the client code. For example, the time could be stored as the total number of seconds since midnight. In this case, the *get* method for the `hour` would calculate and return the hour value, rather than returning the total number of seconds since midnight. Similarly, a `public` *set* method can scrutinize attempts to modify the variable's value, thus ensuring that the new value is appropriate for that data member. For example, an attempt to *set* the day of the month to 37 would be rejected, and an attempt to *set* a person's weight to a negative value would be rejected. So, *set* and *get* methods can provide access to `private` data, but the implementation of these accessors controls what the client code can do to the data.

The declaration of variables as `private` does not guarantee their integrity. Programmers must provide validity checking—MC++ provides only the framework with which programmers can design better programs.

Error-Prevention Tip 8.2

Methods that set the values of `private` *data should verify that the intended new values are valid; if they are not, the methods should take appropriate action. The* set *methods could display an error message, they could place the* `private` *variables into an appropriate consistent state or they could retain the current values of the variables.*

The *set* methods of a property cannot return values indicating a failed attempt to assign invalid data to objects of the class. Such return values could be useful to a client of a class when handling errors. The client could take appropriate actions if the objects occupy invalid states. Chapter 11 presents exception handling—a mechanism that can be used to indicate attempts to set an object's members to invalid values.

Lines 22–55 (Fig. 8.11) define `Time3` properties `Hour`, `Minute` and `Second` by defining their *get* and *set* accessor methods. A property does not necessarily need both a *get* and a *set* method. A *set* method definition has the general form

```
__property void set_PropertyName( type value )
```

Its corresponding *get* accessor has the general form

```
__property type get_PropertyName()
```

Every property method name must be preceded by either `set_` or `get_`. The *PropertyName* portion of the method declaration specifies the name of the property.

The *get* methods are in lines 22–25, 34–37 and 46–49. These accessors return the `hour`, `minute` and `second`, respectively. The *set* methods are defined in lines 28–31, 40–43 and 52–55. The body of each *set* method performs the same conditional statement that was performed by method `SetTime` previously to set the `hour`, `minute` and `second`.

Common Programming Error 8.8

The methods of a property are prefixed with `get` *or* `set`*. If the* `get` *or* `set` *prefixes are omitted, a compilation error will occur.*

Method `SetTime` (lines 41–46 of Fig. 8.12) now uses properties `Hour`, `Minute` and `Second` to ensure that data members `hour`, `minute` and `second` have valid values. Properties `Hour`, `Minute` and `Second` are *scalar properties*. Scalar properties are properties that can be accessed like variables. We assign values to scalar properties using the = (assignment) operator. When this assignment occurs, the code in the *set* accessor for that property executes. Similarly, methods `ToUniversalString` (lines 49–53) and `ToStandardString` (lines 56–63) now use properties `Hour`, `Minute` and `Second` to obtain the values of data members `hour`, `minute` and `second`. Referencing the scalar property executes the *get* accessor for that property.

By using *set* and *get* methods throughout the constructors and other methods of class `Time3`, we minimize the changes that we must make to the class definition in the event that we alter the data representation from `hour`, `minute` and `second` to another representation (such as total elapsed seconds in the day). When such changes are made, we must provide only new *set* and *get* method bodies. Using this technique also enables programmers to change the implementation of a class without affecting the clients of that class (as long as all the `public` methods of the class still are called in the same way).

Software Engineering Observation 8.13

Accessing `private` data through set *and* get *methods not only protects the data members from receiving invalid values, but also hides the internal representation of the data members from that class's clients. Thus, if representation of the data changes (typically, to reduce the amount of required storage or to improve performance), only the method implementations need to change—the client implementations need not change, as long as the interface provided by the class's methods is preserved.*

`Time3Test.cpp` (Fig. 8.13) defines a console-based application for manipulating an object of class `Time3`. Line 13 creates an object of class `Time3` and assigns it to `time`. Line 15 creates bool variable `finished` and initializes it to `false` to indicate that the user is not finished with the program. The `while` loop (lines 18–77) executes until `finished` becomes `true`. Lines 21–24 use the `Time3` properties to display the `hour`, `minute` and `second` values. Lines 25–27 use `Time3` methods `ToUniversalString` and `ToStandardString` to display the universal- and standard-time representations.

```
1  // Fig. 8.13: Time3Test.cpp
2  // Demonstrating Time3 properties Hour, Minute and Second.
3
4  #include "stdafx.h"
5  #include "Time3.h"
6
7  #using <mscorlib.dll>
8
9  using namespace System;
10
11 int _tmain()
12 {
13    Time3 *time = new Time3();
14    int choice;
15    bool finished = false;
```

Fig. 8.13 Properties demonstration for class `Time3`. (Part 1 of 4.)

```

   // loop until user decides to quit
   while ( !finished ) {

      // display current time
      Console::WriteLine( String::Concat( S"\nHour: ",
         time->Hour.ToString(), S"; Minute: ",
         time->Minute.ToString(), S"; Second: ",
         time->Second.ToString() ) );
      Console::WriteLine( String::Concat( S"Standard time: ",
         time->ToStandardString(), S"\nUniversal time: ",
         time->ToUniversalString() ) );

      // display options
      Console::WriteLine( S"   1: Set Hour" );
      Console::WriteLine( S"   2: Set Minute" );
      Console::WriteLine( S"   3: Set Second" );
      Console::WriteLine( S"   4: Add 1 to Second" );
      Console::WriteLine( S"  -1: Quit" );
      Console::Write( S"=> " );
      choice = Int32::Parse( Console::ReadLine() );

      switch ( choice ) {

         // set Hour property
         case 1:
            Console::Write( S"New Hour: " );
            time->Hour = Int32::Parse( Console::ReadLine() );
            break;

         // set Minute property
         case 2:
            Console::Write( S"New Minute: " );
            time->Minute = Int32::Parse( Console::ReadLine() );
            break;

         // set Second property
         case 3:
            Console::Write( S"New Second: " );
            time->Second = Int32::Parse( Console::ReadLine() );
            break;

         // add one to Second property
         case 4:
            time->Second = ( time->Second + 1 ) % 60;

            if ( time->Second == 0 ) {
               time->Minute = ( time->Minute + 1 ) % 60;

               if ( time->Minute == 0 )
                  time->Hour = ( time->Hour + 1 ) % 24;
            } // end if
```

Fig. 8.13 Properties demonstration for class `Time3`. (Part 2 of 4.)

```

            break;

         // exit loop
         default:
            finished = true;
            break;
      } // end switch

   } // end while

   return 0;
} // end _tmain
```

```
Hour: 0; Minute: 0; Second: 0
Standard time: 12:00:00 AM
Universal time: 00:00:00
   1: Set Hour
   2: Set Minute
   3: Set Second
   4: Add 1 to Second
  -1: Quit
=> 1
New Hour: 23
```

```
Hour: 23; Minute: 0; Second: 0
Standard time: 11:00:00 PM
Universal time: 23:00:00
   1: Set Hour
   2: Set Minute
   3: Set Second
   4: Add 1 to Second
  -1: Quit
=> 2
New Minute: 59
```

```
Hour: 23; Minute: 59; Second: 0
Standard time: 11:59:00 PM
Universal time: 23:59:00
   1: Set Hour
   2: Set Minute
   3: Set Second
   4: Add 1 to Second
  -1: Quit
=> 3
New Second: 58
```

Fig. 8.13 Properties demonstration for class `Time3`. (Part 3 of 4.)

```
Hour: 23; Minute: 59; Second: 58
Standard time: 11:59:58 PM
Universal time: 23:59:58
   1: Set Hour
   2: Set Minute
   3: Set Second
   4: Add 1 to Second
  -1: Quit
=> 4
```

```
Hour: 23; Minute: 59; Second: 59
Standard time: 11:59:59 PM
Universal time: 23:59:59
   1: Set Hour
   2: Set Minute
   3: Set Second
   4: Add 1 to Second
  -1: Quit
=> 4
```

```
Hour: 0; Minute: 0; Second: 0
Standard time: 12:00:00 AM
Universal time: 00:00:00
   1: Set Hour
   2: Set Minute
   3: Set Second
   4: Add 1 to Second
  -1: Quit
=> -1
```

Fig. 8.13 Properties demonstration for class `Time3`. (Part 4 of 4.)

Lines 30–34 display a menu of options to the user. The `switch` statement (lines 38–75) executes statements corresponding to the user's choice. Choices `1`–`3` (lines 41–56) alter the values of a `Time3` property (`Hour`, `Minute` or `Second`). Choice `4` (lines 59–69) enables the user to increment the `second` value by `1`. Lines 60–67 use the `Time3` object's properties to determine and set the new time. For example, `23:59:59` becomes `00:00:00` when the user selects choice `4`. Any other choice (such as `-1`) sets `finished` to `false` and terminates the program.

Properties are not limited to accessing `private` data—properties also can be used to calculate values associated with an object. One example of this would be a `student` object with a property representing the student's GPA (called `GPA`).

8.8 Composition: Object Pointers as Data Members of Other Classes

In many situations, referencing existing objects is more convenient than rewriting the objects' code for new classes in new projects. Suppose that we were to implement an `AlarmClock` object that needs to know when to sound its alarm. Referencing an existing `Time` object (like those from earlier examples in this chapter) is easier than writing a new `Time` object. The use of pointers to objects of preexisting classes as members of new objects is called *composition* (or *aggregation*). [*Note:* A class's data members can also be value types. Most classes contain data members of both value types and reference types.]

Software Engineering Observation 8.14

One form of software reuse is composition, in which a class has as members pointers to objects of other classes.

The application of Fig. 8.14–Fig. 8.18 demonstrates composition. The program contains two classes. Class `Date` (Fig. 8.14 and Fig. 8.15) encapsulates information relating to a specific date. Class `Employee` (Fig. 8.16 and Fig. 8.17) encapsulates the name of the employee and two `Date` objects representing the `Employee`'s birthday and hire date. The main program `CompositionTest` (Fig. 8.18) creates an object of class `Employee` to demonstrate composition.

```
// Fig. 8.14: Date.h
// Date class definition encapsulates month, day and year.

#pragma once

#using <mscorlib.dll>

using namespace System;

// Date class definition
public __gc class Date
{
public:
   Date( int, int, int );
   String *ToDateString();

private:

   int CheckDay( int ); // utility method

   int month;  // 1-12
   int day;    // 1-31 based on month
   int year;   // any year
}; // end class Date
```

Fig. 8.14 `Date` class encapsulates day, month and year information.

```
// Fig. 8.15: Date.cpp
// Method definitions for class Date.

#include "stdafx.h"
#include "Date.h"

// constructor confirms proper value for month;
// call method CheckDay to confirm proper
```

Fig. 8.15 `Date` class method definitions. (Part 1 of 2.)

```
// value for day
Date::Date( int theMonth, int theDay, int theYear )
{
   // validate month
   if ( theMonth > 0 && theMonth <= 12 )
      month = theMonth;
   else {
      month = 1;
      Console::WriteLine( S"Month {0} invalid. Set to month 1.",
         theMonth.ToString() );
   } // end else

   year = theYear;              // could validate year
   day = CheckDay( theDay );   // validate day
} // end Date constructor

// utility method confirms proper day value
// based on month and year
int Date::CheckDay( int testDay )
{
   int daysPerMonth[] =
      { 0, 31, 28, 31, 30, 31, 30, 31, 31, 30, 31, 30, 31 };

   // check if day in range for month
   if ( testDay > 0 && testDay <= daysPerMonth[ month ] )
      return testDay;

   // check for leap year
   if ( month == 2 && testDay == 29 &&
      ( year % 400 == 0 ||
      ( year % 4 == 0 && year % 100 != 0 ) ) )
      return testDay;

   Console::WriteLine( S"Day {0} invalid. Set to day 1.",
      testDay.ToString() );

   return 1; // leave object in consistent state
} // end method CheckDay

// return date string as month/day/year
String *Date::ToDateString()
{
   return String::Concat( month.ToString(), S"/",
      day.ToString(), S"/", year.ToString() );
} // end method ToDateString
```

Fig. 8.15 `Date` class method definitions. (Part 2 of 2.)

```
// Fig. 8.16: Employee.h
// Employee class definition encapsulates employee's first name,
// last name, birthday and hire date.
```

Fig. 8.16 `Employee` class encapsulates employee name, birthday and hire date. (Part 1 of 2.)

```

#pragma once

#using <mscorlib.dll>

using namespace System;

#include "Date.h"

// Employee class definition
public __gc class Employee
{
public:
   Employee( String *, String *, int, int, int, int, int, int );
   String *ToEmployeeString();

private:
   String *firstName;
   String *lastName;
   Date *birthDate;   // pointer to a Date object
   Date *hireDate;    // pointer to a Date object
}; // end class Employee
```

Fig. 8.16 `Employee` class encapsulates employee name, birthday and hire date. (Part 2 of 2.)

```
// Fig. 8.17: Employee.cpp
// Method definitions for class Employee.

#include "stdafx.h"
#include "Employee.h"

// constructor initializes name, birthday and hire date
Employee::Employee( String *first, String *last, int birthMonth,
   int birthDay, int birthYear, int hireMonth, int hireDay, int hireYear )
{
   firstName = first;
   lastName = last;

   // create and initialize new Date objects
   birthDate = new Date( birthMonth, birthDay, birthYear );
   hireDate = new Date( hireMonth, hireDay, hireYear );
} // end Employee constructor

// return Employee as String * object
String *Employee::ToEmployeeString()
{
   return String::Concat( lastName, S", ", firstName,
      S" Hired: ", hireDate->ToDateString(), S" Birthday: ",
      birthDate->ToDateString() );
}
```

Fig. 8.17 `Employee` class method definitions.

```
// Fig. 8.18: CompositionTest.cpp
// Demonstrates an object with member object pointer.

#include "stdafx.h"
#include "Employee.h"

#using <mscorlib.dll>
#using <system.windows.forms.dll>

using namespace System;
using namespace System::Windows::Forms;

// main entry point for application
int _tmain()
{
   Employee *e = new Employee( S"Bob", S"Jones",
      7, 24, 1949, 3, 12, 1988 );

   MessageBox::Show( e->ToEmployeeString(), S"Testing Class Employee" );

   return 0;
} // end _tmain
```

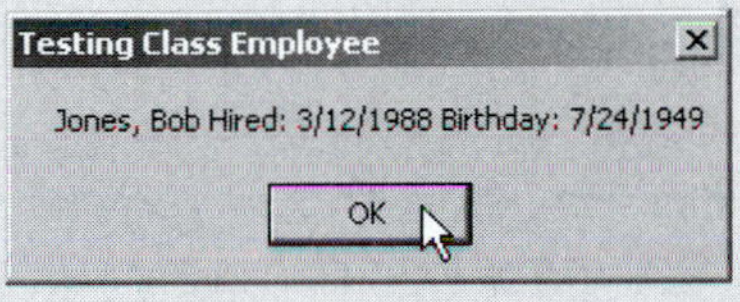
Testing Class Employee
Jones, Bob Hired: 3/12/1988 Birthday: 7/24/1949
OK

Fig. 8.18 Composition demonstration.

Class `Date` declares `int` variables `month`, `day` and `year` (lines 21–23 of Fig. 8.14). Lines 10–23 of Fig. 8.15 define the constructor, which receives values for `month`, `day` and `year` as arguments and assigns these values to the variables after ensuring that the values are in a consistent state. Note that lines 17–18 print an error message if the constructor receives an invalid month value. Ordinarily, rather than printing error messages, a constructor would "throw an exception." We discuss exceptions in Chapter 11. Method `ToDateString` (lines 49–53) returns the `String *` representation of a `Date`.

Class `Employee` encapsulates information relating to an employee's name, birthday and hire date (lines 21–24 of Fig. 8.16) using variables `firstName`, `lastName`, `birthDate` and `hireDate`. Members' `birthDate` and `hireDate` are pointers to `Date` objects, each of which contains variables `month`, `day` and `year`. In this example, class `Employee` is *composed of* two pointers of type `String` and two pointers of class `Date`. The `Employee` constructor (lines 8–17 of Fig. 8.17) takes eight arguments (`first`, `last`, `birthMonth`, `birthDay`, `birthYear`, `hireMonth`, `hireDay` and `hireYear`). Line 15 passes arguments `birthMonth`, `birthDay` and `birthYear` to the `Date` constructor to create the `birthDate` object. Similarly, line 16 passes arguments `hireMonth`, `hireDay` and `hireYear` to the `Date` constructor to create the `hireDate` object. Method `ToEmployeeString` (lines 20–25) returns a pointer to a string containing the name of the `Employee` and the string representations of the `Employee`'s `birthDate` and `hireDate`.

CompositionTest (Fig. 8.18) runs the application with function _tmain. Lines 16–17 instantiate an Employee object, and line 19 displays the string representation of the Employee to the user.

8.9 Using the this Pointer

Every object can access a pointer to itself, called the *this pointer*. The this pointer is used to implicitly reference the data members, properties and methods of an object from the properties and methods of that object; the this pointer can be used explicitly as well. Keyword this is commonly used within methods, where this is a pointer to the object on which the method is performing operations.

We now demonstrate implicit and explicit use of the this pointer to display the private data of a Time4 object. Class Time4 (Fig. 8.19 and Fig. 8.20) defines three private variables—hour, minute and second (lines 20–22 of Fig. 8.19). The constructor (lines 8–13 of Fig. 8.20) receives three int arguments to initialize a Time4 object. Note that, for this example, we have made the parameter names for the constructor (line 8) identical to the class's data member names (Fig. 8.19, lines 20–22). We did this to illustrate explicit use of the this pointer. If a method contains a local variable with the same name as an data member of that class, that method will refer to the local variable, rather than to the data member (i.e., the local variable hides the data member in that method's scope). However, the method can use the this pointer to refer to the hidden data members explicitly (lines 10–12 of Fig. 8.20).

```
1  // Fig. 8.19: Time4.h
2  // Class Time4 demonstrates the this pointer.
3
4  #pragma once
5
6  #using <mscorlib.dll>
7
8  using namespace System;
9
10 // Time4 class definition
11 public __gc class Time4
12 {
13 public:
14    Time4( int, int, int );
15
16    String *BuildString();
17    String *ToStandardString();
18
19 private:
20    int hour;      // 0-23
21    int minute;    // 0-59
22    int second;    // 0-59
23 }; // end class Time4
```

Fig. 8.19 this pointer used implicitly and explicitly to enable an object to manipulate its own data and invoke its own methods.

```
1  // Fig. 8.20: Time4.cpp
2  // Method definitions for class Time4.
3
4  #include "stdafx.h"
5  #include "Time4.h"
6
7  // constructor
8  Time4::Time4( int hour, int minute, int second )
9  {
10    this->hour = hour;
11    this->minute = minute;
12    this->second = second;
13 }
14
15 // create string using this and implicit pointers
16 String *Time4::BuildString()
17 {
18    return String::Concat(
19       S"this->ToStandardString(): ", this->ToStandardString(),
20       S"\n( *this ).ToStandardString(): ", ( *this ).ToStandardString(),
21       S"\nToStandardString(): ", ToStandardString() );
22 }
23
24 // convert time to standard-time (12 hour) format string
25 String *Time4::ToStandardString()
26 {
27    return String::Concat(
28       ( ( this->hour == 12 || this->hour == 0 ) ? S"12"
29       : ( this->hour % 12 ).ToString( S"D2" ) ), S":",
30       this->minute.ToString( S"D2" ), S":",
31       this->second.ToString( S"D2" ), S" ",
32       ( this->hour < 12 ? S"AM" : S"PM" ) );
33 }
```

Fig. 8.20 `Time4` class method definitions.

Recall from Chapter 7 that the dereferencing operator (*) can be applied to a pointer to refer to an object directly. Thus, the notation of line 10 (Fig. 8.20) is equivalent to

```
( *this ).hour = hour;
```

Note the parentheses around `*this` when used with the dot member selection operator (`.`). The parentheses are needed because the dot operator has higher precedence than the * operator. We demonstrate this alternative notation in method `BuildString`.

Method `BuildString` (lines 16–22) returns a pointer to a `String` created by a statement that uses the `this` pointer explicitly and implicitly. Lines 19 and 20 use the `this` pointer explicitly to call method `ToStandardString`, whereas line 21 uses the `this` pointer implicitly to call the same method. Note that lines 19, 20 and 21 all perform the same task. Therefore, programmers usually do not use the `this` pointer explicitly to reference methods within the current object.

Method `ToStandardString` (lines 25–33) builds and returns a pointer to a `String` that represents the specified time in 12-hour clock format.

Common Programming Error 8.9

For a method in which a parameter (or local variable) has the same name a data member, use pointer `this` *if you wish to access the data member; otherwise, the method parameter (or local variable) will be referenced.*

Error-Prevention Tip 8.3

Avoid parameter names (or local variable names) that conflict with data member names to prevent subtle, hard-to-trace bugs.

Good Programming Practice 8.3

The explicit use of the `this` *pointer can increase program clarity in some contexts where* `this` *is optional.*

Driver `ThisTest.cpp` (Fig. 8.21) runs the application that demonstrates explicit use of the `this` pointer. Line 15 instantiates an instance of class `Time4`. Lines 17–18 invoke method `BuildString` of the `Time4` object, then display the results to the user in a `MessageBox`.

```
1  // Fig. 8.21: ThisTest.cpp
2  // Using the this pointer.
3
4  #include "stdafx.h"
5  #include "Time4.h"
6
7  #using <mscorlib.dll>
8  #using <system.windows.forms.dll>
9
10 using namespace System;
11 using namespace System::Windows::Forms;
12
13 int _tmain()
14 {
15    Time4 *time = new Time4( 12, 30, 19 );
16
17    MessageBox::Show( time->BuildString(),
18       S"Demonstrating the \"this\" Pointer" );
19
20    return 0;
21 } // end _tmain
```

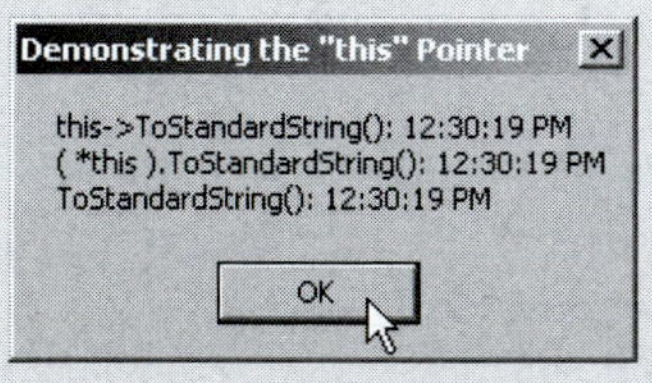
Demonstrating the "this" Pointer
this->ToStandardString(): 12:30:19 PM
(*this).ToStandardString(): 12:30:19 PM
ToStandardString(): 12:30:19 PM
OK

Fig. 8.21 `this` pointer demonstration.

The problem of parameters (or local variables) hiding data members can be solved by using properties. If we have a property `Hour` that accesses the `hour` data members, then we would not need to use `( *this ).hour` or `this->hour` to distinguish between a parameter (or local variable) `hour` and the data members `hour`—we would simply assign `hour` to the property `Hour`.

8.10 Garbage Collection

In previous examples, we have seen how a constructor initializes data in an object of a class after the object is created. Operator `new` allocates memory for the object, then calls that object's constructor. The constructor might acquire other system resources, such as network connections, databases or files. Objects must have a disciplined way to return memory and release resources when the program no longer uses those objects. Failure to release such resources causes *resource leaks*—potentially exhausting the pool of available resources that programs might need to continue executing.

Unlike C and standard C++, in which programmers must manage memory explicitly, managed C++ performs memory management internally. The .NET Framework performs *garbage collection* of memory to return to the system memory that is no longer needed. When the *garbage collector* executes, it locates objects for which the application has no references or pointers. Such objects can be collected at that time or during a subsequent execution of the garbage collector. Therefore, the *memory leaks* that are common in such languages as C and C++, where memory is not reclaimed by the runtime, are rare in managed C++.

Allocation and deallocation of other resources—such as network connections, database connections and files—must be handled explicitly by the programmer. One technique employed to handle these resources (in conjunction with the garbage collector) is to define a *destructor* that returns resources to the system. The garbage collector calls an object's destructor to perform *termination housekeeping* on that object just before the garbage collector reclaims the object's memory (called *finalization*).

Each class can contain only one destructor. The name of a destructor is formed by preceding the class name with a ~ character. For example, the destructor for class `Time` would be `~Time()`. Destructors do not receive arguments, so destructors cannot be overloaded. When the garbage collector is removing an object from memory, the garbage collector first invokes that object's destructor to clean up resources used by the object. However, we cannot determine exactly when the destructor is called, because we cannot determine exactly when garbage collection occurs.

8.11 `static` Class Members

Each object of a class has its own copy of all the data members of the class. However, in certain cases, all class objects should share only one copy of a particular variable. Such variables are called *`static` variables* (or *class variables*). A program contains only one copy of each of a class's `static` variables in memory, no matter how many objects of the class have been instantiated. A `static` variable represents *class-wide information*—all class objects share the same `static` data item.

The declaration of a `static` member begins with the keyword `static`. A `static` variable can be initialized in its declaration by following the variable name with an `=` and an initial value. In cases where a `static` variable requires more complex initialization, programmers can define a *`static` constructor* to initialize only the `static` members. Such constructors are optional and must be declared with the `static` keyword, followed by the name of the class. `static` constructors are called before any `static` members are used and before any class objects are instantiated.

We now consider a video-game example to justify the need for `static` class-wide data. Suppose that we have a video game involving `Martian`s and other space creatures. Each `Martian` tends to be brave and willing to attack other space creatures when the `Martian` is aware that there are at least four other `Martian`s present. If there are fewer than five `Martian`s present, each `Martian` becomes cowardly. For this reason, each `Martian` must know the `martianCount`. We could endow class `Martian` with `martianCount` as a data member. However, if we were to do this, then every `Martian` would have a separate copy of the data member, and every time we create a `Martian`, we would have to update the data member `martianCount` in every `Martian`. The redundant copies waste space, and updating those copies is time consuming. Instead, we declare `martianCount` to be `static` so that `martianCount` is class-wide data. Each `Martian` can see the `martianCount` as if it were a data member of that `Martian`, but only one copy of the `static` variable `martianCount` is actually maintained to save space. This technique also saves time; because there is only one copy, we do not have to increment separate copies of `martianCount` for each `Martian` object.

Performance Tip 8.2

When a single copy of the data will suffice, use `static` variables to save storage.

Although `static` variables might seem like *global variables* (variables that can be referenced anywhere in a program) in other programming languages, `static` variables need not be globally accessible. Static variables have class scope.

The `public static` data members of a class can be accessed from client code through the class name using the scope resolution operator (`::`) (e.g., `Math::PI`). The `private static` members can be accessed only through methods or properties of the class. Static members are available as soon as the class is loaded into memory at execution time and they exist for the duration of program execution, even when no objects of that class exist. To enable a client program to access a `private static` member when no objects of the class exist, the class must provide a `public static` method or property.

A `static` method cannot access non-`static` data members. Unlike non-`static` methods, a `static` method has no `this` pointer, because `static` variables and `static` methods exist even when there are no objects of that class in which the `static` members are defined.

Common Programming Error 8.10

Using the `this` pointer in a `static` method or `static` property results in a compilation error.

Common Programming Error 8.11

A call to an non-`static` method or an attempt to access a data member from a `static` method is a compilation error.

Class `Employee` (Fig. 8.22 and Fig. 8.23) demonstrates a `public static` property that enables a program to obtain the value of a `private static` variable. The `static` variable `count` (line 42 of Fig. 8.22) is not initialized explicitly, so it receives the value 0 by default. Class variable `count` maintains a count of the number of objects of class `Employee` that have been instantiated, including those objects that have already been marked for garbage collection, but have not yet been reclaimed by the garbage collector.

```
// Fig. 8.22: Employee.h
// Employee class contains static data and a static property.

#pragma once

#using <mscorlib.dll>

using namespace System;

// Employee class definition
public __gc class Employee
{
public:

   // constructor increments static Employee count
   Employee( String *fName, String *lName );

   // destructor decrements static Employee count
   ~Employee();

   // FirstName property
   __property String *get_FirstName()
   {
      return firstName;
   }

   // LastName property
   __property String *get_LastName()
   {
      return lastName;
   }

   // static Count property
   __property static int get_Count()
   {
      return count;
   }

private:
   String *firstName;
   String *lastName;
   static int count;    // Employee objects in memory
}; // end class Employee
```

Fig. 8.22 `static` members are accessible to all objects of a class.

```
// Fig. 8.23: Employee.cpp
// Method definitions for class Employee.

#include "stdafx.h"
#include "Employee.h"

```

Fig. 8.23 `Employee` class method definitions. (Part 1 of 2.)

```
7  // constructor increments static Employee count
8  Employee::Employee( String *fName, String *lName )
9  {
10    firstName = fName;
11    lastName = lName;
12
13    ++count;
14
15    Console::WriteLine( String::Concat(
16       S"Employee object constructor: ", firstName, S" ",
17       lastName, S"; count = ", Count.ToString() ) );
18 }
19
20 // destructor decrements static Employee count
21 Employee::~Employee()
22 {
23    --count;
24
25    Console::WriteLine( String::Concat(
26       S"Employee object destructor: ", firstName, S" ",
27       lastName, S"; count = ", Count.ToString() ) );
28 }
```

Fig. 8.23 `Employee` class method definitions. (Part 2 of 2.)

When objects of class `Employee` exist, `static` member `count` can be used in any method of an `Employee` object—in this example, the constructor (lines 8–18 of Fig. 8.23) increments `count`, and the destructor (lines 21–28) decrements `count`. If no objects of class `Employee` exist, the value of member `count` can be obtained through `static` property `Count` (Fig. 8.22, lines 34–37); this also works when there are `Employee` objects in memory.

Driver `StaticTest.cpp` (Fig. 8.24) runs the application that demonstrates the `static` members of class `Employee` (Fig. 8.22 and Fig. 8.23). Lines 14–16 use the `static` property `Count` of class `Employee` to obtain the current `count` value before the program creates `Employee` objects. Notice that the syntax used to access a `static` member is

ClassName::*StaticMember*

In line 16, *ClassName* is `Employee` and *StaticMember* is `Count`. Recall that we used this syntax in prior examples to call the `static` methods of class `Math` (e.g., `Math::Pow`, `Math::Abs`, etc.) and other methods, such as `Int32::Parse` and `MessageBox::Show`.

```
1 // Fig. 8.24: StaticTest.cpp
2 // Demonstrating static class members.
3
4 #include "stdafx.h"
5 #include "Employee.h"
6
7 #using <mscorlib.dll>
8
9 using namespace System;
```

Fig. 8.24 `static` member demonstration. (Part 1 of 2.)

```

// main entry point for application
int _tmain()
{
   Console::WriteLine( String::Concat(
      S"Employees before instantiation: ",
      Employee::Count.ToString(), S"\n" ) );

   // create two Employees
   Employee *employee1 = new Employee( S"Susan", S"Baker" );
   Employee *employee2 = new Employee( S"Bob", S"Jones" );

   Console::WriteLine( String::Concat(
      S"Employees after instantiation: ",
      Employee::Count.ToString(), S"\n" ) );

   // display Employees
   Console::WriteLine( String::Concat( S"Employee1: ",
      employee1->FirstName, S" ", employee1->LastName,
      S"\nEmployee2: ", employee2->FirstName, S" ",
      employee2->LastName, S"\n" ) );

   // remove references to objects to indicate that
   // objects can be garbage collected
   employee1 = 0;
   employee2 = 0;

   // force garbage collection
   GC::Collect();

   // wait until collection completes
   GC::WaitForPendingFinalizers();

   Console::WriteLine(
      String::Concat( S"\nEmployees after garbage collection: ",
      Employee::Count.ToString() ) );

   return 0;
} // end _tmain
```

```
Employees before instantiation: 0

Employee object constructor: Susan Baker; count = 1
Employee object constructor: Bob Jones; count = 2
Employees after instantiation: 2

Employee1: Susan Baker
Employee2: Bob Jones

Employee object destructor: Bob Jones; count = 1
Employee object destructor: Susan Baker; count = 0

Employees after garbage collection: 0
```

Fig. 8.24 `static` member demonstration. (Part 2 of 2.)

Next, lines 19–20 instantiate two `Employee` objects and assign them to pointers `employee1` and `employee2`. Each call to the `Employee` constructor increments the `count` value by `1`. Lines 22–30 display the value of `Count` as well as the names of the two employees. Note that the count is now 2. Lines 34–35 set pointers `employee1` and `employee2` to `0`, so they no longer point to the `Employee` objects. These were the only pointers in the program to the `Employee` objects, so those objects can now be garbage collected.

The garbage collector is not invoked directly by the program. Either the garbage collector reclaims the memory for objects when the runtime determines garbage collection is appropriate, or the operating system recovers the memory when the program terminates. However, it is possible to request that the garbage collector attempt to collect available objects. Line 38 uses `public static` method *`Collect`* from class *`GC`* (namespace `System`) to make this request. The garbage collector is not guaranteed to collect all objects that are currently available for collection. If the garbage collector decides to collect objects, the garbage collector first invokes the destructor of each object. It is important to understand that the garbage collector executes as an independent entity called a *thread*. (Threads are discussed in Chapter 14, Multithreading.) It is possible for multiple threads to execute in parallel on a multiprocessor system or to share a processor on a single-processor system. Thus, a program could run in parallel with garbage collection. For this reason, we call `static` method *`WaitForPendingFinalizers`* of class `GC` (line 41), which forces the program to wait until the garbage collector invokes the destructors for all objects that are ready for collection and reclaims those objects. When the program reaches lines 43–45, we are assured that both destructor calls completed and that the value of `count` has been decremented accordingly.

Software Engineering Observation 8.15

Programs normally do not call methods `GC::Collect` and `GC::WaitForPendingFinalizers` explicitly because they might decrease performance.

In this example, the output shows that the destructor was called for each `Employee`, which decrements the `count` value by two (once per `Employee` being collected). Lines 43–45 use property `Count` to obtain the value of `count` after invoking the garbage collector. If the objects had not been collected, the `count` would be greater than `0`.

Toward the end of the output, notice that the `Employee` object for `Bob Jones` was finalized before the `Employee` object for `Susan Baker`. However, the output of this program on your system could differ. The garbage collector is not guaranteed to collect objects in a specific order.

8.12 `const` Keyword and Read-Only Properties

MC++ allows programmers to create *constants* whose values cannot change during program execution.

Error-Prevention Tip 8.4

If a variable's value should never change, make it a constant. This helps eliminate errors that might occur if the value of the variable were to change.

To create a constant data member of a class, either declare that member using the *`const`* keyword or create a property for the data member and provide only a *get* method. In this section, we focus on constant data members that are also `static`. Data members declared as `static const` must be initialized in their declaration. Once they are initialized, `const` values cannot be modified.

Common Programming Error 8.12

Declaring a class data member as `static const`, but failing to initialize it in that class's declaration is a syntax error.

Common Programming Error 8.13

Assigning a value to a `const` data member after that data member has been initialized is a compilation error.

A read-only property provides only a *get* method. Without a *set* method, the property's value cannot be changed by client code. The property usually controls access to a `private` data member. The value of the data member can be changed within its class.

Members that are declared as `const` must be assigned values at compile time. Therefore, `const` members can be initialized only with other constant values, such as integers, string literals, characters and other `const` members. Constant members with values that cannot be determined at compile time must be declared as properties without *set* methods. The constant member then can be assigned a value in the constructor and the programmer can only retrieve the private constant data member's value using the *get* method.

The application of Fig. 8.25–Fig. 8.27 demonstrates constants. Class `Constants` defines constant `PI` (line 16 of Fig. 8.25), the source file implements the constructor (lines 7–10 of Fig. 8.26) and driver `UsingConst.cpp` (Fig. 8.27) demonstrates the constant in class `Constants`.

```
1  // Fig. 8.25: Constants.h
2  // Class Constants contains a const data member.
3
4  #pragma once
5
6  #using <mscorlib.dll>
7
8  using namespace System;
9
10 // Constants class definition
11 public __gc class Constants
12 {
13 public:
14
15    // create constant PI
16    static const double PI = 3.14159;
17
18    Constants( int );
19
20    // radius is readonly
21    __property int get_Radius()
22    {
23       return radius;
24    }
```

Fig. 8.25 `const` class member demonstration. (Part 1 of 2.)

```

private:
   int radius;
}; // end class Constants
```

Fig. 8.25 const class member demonstration. (Part 2 of 2.)

```
// Fig. 8.26: Constants.cpp
// Method definitions for class Constants.

#include "stdafx.h"
#include "Constants.h"

Constants::Constants( int radiusValue )
{
   radius = radiusValue;
}
```

Fig. 8.26 Constants class method definitions.

```
// Fig. 8.27: UsingConst.cpp
// Demonstrating constant values.

#include "stdafx.h"
#include "Constants.h"

#using <mscorlib.dll>
#using <system.windows.forms.dll>

using namespace System;
using namespace System::Windows::Forms;

// create Constants object and display its values
int _tmain()
{
   Random *random = new Random();

   Constants *constantValues = new Constants( random->Next( 1, 20 ) );

   String *output = String::Concat( S"Radius = ",
      constantValues->Radius.ToString(), S"\nCircumference = ",
      ( 2 * Constants::PI * constantValues->Radius ).ToString() );

   MessageBox::Show( output, S"Circumference" );

   return 0;
} // end _tmain
```

Fig. 8.27 Using const data members demonstration. (Part 1 of 2.)

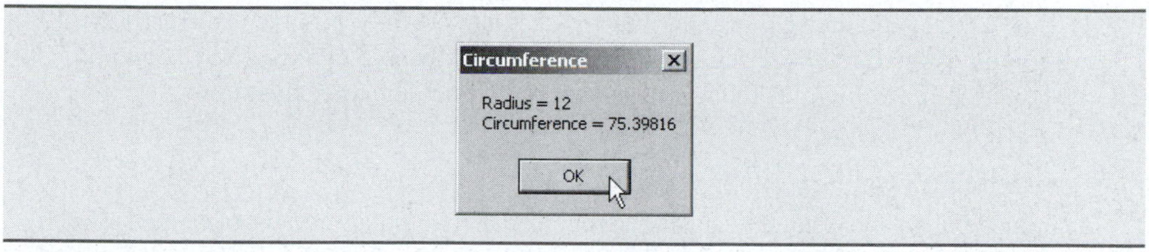

Fig. 8.27 Using `const` data members demonstration. (Part 2 of 2.)

Line 16 in class `Constants` (Fig. 8.25) creates constant `PI` using keyword `const` and initializes `PI` with the `double` value `3.14159`—an approximation of π that the program uses to calculate the circumference of a circle. Note that we could have used the predefined constant `PI` of class `Math` (`Math::PI`) as the value, but we wanted to demonstrate how to define a `const` member explicitly. The compiler must be able to determine a `const` variable's value at compile time; otherwise, a compilation error will occur. For example, if line 16 initialized `PI` with the expression

```
Double::Parse( S"3.14159" )
```

the compiler would generate an error. Although the expression uses `String *` literal `"3.14159"` (a constant value) as an argument, the compiler cannot evaluate the method call `Double::Parse` at compile time.

Variables that are declared `const` do not necessarily need to be declared `static`. We could have declared `PI` as a non-static const data member, by simply omitting the `static` keyword on line 16 of Fig. 8.25. Non-`static const` data members cannot be initialized when they are declared. To initialize such data members, we need to use a *member initializer list.* Member initializers appear between a constructor's parameter list and the left brace that begins the constructor's body. The member initializer list is separated from the parameter list with a colon (`:`). The following constructor initializes the non-`static const PI`:

```
Constants::Constants( int radiusValue )
   : PI( 3.14159 )
{
   // constructor body
}
```

Using this syntax, a `const` can be given a value based on arguments passed to the constructor. In the above code, `3.14159` could have been replaced with `radiusValue`. This enables the programmer to create a `const` that is specific to the class instance. The value for π is the same for each instance of class `Constants`, so we make `PI static` in Fig. 8.25.

Line 27 declares variable `radius`, but does not initialize it. Property `Radius` has only a *get* method (lines 21–24). Clients of the class can only read the value of the `private` data member `radius` after it has been initialized. The `Constants` constructor (lines 7–10 of Fig. 8.26) receives an `int` value and assigns it to `radius` when the program creates a `Constants` object. Note that `radius` also can be initialized with a more complex expression, such as a method call that returns an `int`.

Line 16 (Fig. 8.27) creates a `Random` object; line 18 uses method `Next` of class `Random` to generate a random `int` between `1` and `20` that corresponds to a circle's `radius`. Then, that value is passed to the `Constants` constructor to initialize the read-only variable `radius`.

Line 21 uses pointer `constantValues` to access read-only property `Radius`. Line 22 then computes the circle's circumference using `const` variable `Constants::PI` and property `Radius`. Line 24 outputs the radius and circumference in a `MessageBox`.

8.13 Indexed Properties

Sometimes a class encapsulates data that a program can manipulate as a list of elements. Such a class can define special properties called *indexed properties* that allow array-style indexed access to lists of elements. With "conventional" managed arrays, the subscript number must be an integer value. A benefit of indexed properties is that the programmer can define both integer subscripts and non-integer subscripts. For example, a programmer could allow client code to manipulate data using strings as subscripts that represent the data items' names or descriptions. When manipulating managed array elements, the array subscript operator always returns the same data type—i.e., the type of the array. Index properties are more flexible—they can return any data type, even one that is different from the type of the data in the list of elements. Although an indexed property's subscript operator is used like an array-subscript operator, indexed properties are defined as properties in a class.

Common Programming Error 8.14

Defining an indexed property as `static` *is a syntax error.*

The application of Fig. 8.28–Fig. 8.30 demonstrates indexed properties. Figure 8.28–Fig. 8.29 define class `Box`—a box with a length, a width and a height. Fig. 8.30 is the main entry point of the application that demonstrates class `Box`'s indexed properties.

```
// Fig. 8.28: Box.h
// Class Box represents a box with length,
// width and height dimensions.

#pragma once

#using <mscorlib.dll>

using namespace System;

public __gc class Box
{
public:

   // constructor
   Box( double, double, double );

   // access dimensions by index number
   __property double get_Dimension( int index )
   {
      return ( index < 0 || index > dimensions->Length ) ?
         -1 : dimensions[ index ];
   }
```

Fig. 8.28 Box class represents a box with length, width and height dimensions. (Part 1 of 2.)

```

   __property void set_Dimension( int index, double value )
   {
      if ( index >= 0 && index < dimensions->Length )
         dimensions[ index ] = value;

   } // end numeric indexed property

   // access dimensions by their names
   __property double get_Dimension( String *name )
   {
      // locate element to get
      int i = 0;

      while ( i < names->Length &&
         name->ToLower()->CompareTo( names[ i ] ) != 0 )
         i++;

      return ( i == names->Length ) ? -1 : dimensions[ i ];
   }

   __property void set_Dimension( String *name, double value )
   {
      // locate element to set
      int i = 0;

      while ( i < names->Length &&
         name->ToLower()->CompareTo( names[ i ] ) != 0 )
         i++;

      if ( i != names->Length )
         dimensions[ i ] = value;

   } // end String indexed property

private:
   static String *names[] = { S"length", S"width", S"height" };
   static double dimensions __gc[] = new double __gc[ 3 ];
}; // end class Box
```

Fig. 8.28 Box class represents a box with length, width and height dimensions. (Part 2 of 2.)

```
// Fig. 8.29: Box.cpp
// Method definitions for class Box.

#include "stdafx.h"
#include "Box.h"

Box::Box( double length, double width, double height )
{
   dimensions[ 0 ] = length;
```

Fig. 8.29 Box class method definition. (Part 1 of 2.)

```
    dimensions[ 1 ] = width;
    dimensions[ 2 ] = height;
}
```

Fig. 8.29 Box class method definition. (Part 2 of 2.)

The `private` data members of class `Box` are `String *` array `names` (Fig. 8.28, line 60), which contains the names (i.e., `"length"`, `"width"` and `"height"`) for the dimensions of a `Box`, and `double` array `dimensions` (line 61), which contains the size of each dimension. Each element in array `names` corresponds to an element in array `dimensions` (e.g., `dimensions[ 2 ]` contains the height of the `Box`).

`Box` defines two indexed properties (lines 19–30 and lines 33–57) that each return a `double` value representing the size of the dimension specified by the property's parameter. Indexed properties can be overloaded like methods. The first indexed property uses an `int` subscript to manipulate an element in the `dimensions` array. The second indexed property uses a `String *` subscript representing the name of the dimension to manipulate an element in the `dimensions` array. Unlike scalar properties, the *get* methods of indexed properties accept arguments. Each property in Fig. 8.28 returns `-1` if its *get* method encounters an invalid subscript. Each indexed property's *set* method assigns its `value` argument to the appropriate element of array `dimensions` only if the index is valid. Normally, the programmer would have an indexed property throw an exception if it received an invalid index.

Notice that the `String` indexed properties use `while` statements to search for a matching `String *` object in the `names` array. If a match is found, the indexed property manipulates the corresponding element in array `dimensions`.

```
// Fig. 8.30: BoxTest.cpp
// Indexed properties provide access to an object's members
// via a subscript operator.

#include "stdafx.h"
#include "Box.h"

#using <mscorlib.dll>

using namespace System;

void ShowValueAtIndex( Box *, String *, int );
void ShowValueAtIndex( Box *, String *, String * );

int _tmain()
{
   Box *box = new Box( 0.0, 0.0, 0.0 );
   int choice;
   bool finished = false;
   int index = 0;
   String *name = S"";

```

Fig. 8.30 Indexed properties provide subscripted access to an object's members. (Part 1 of 4.)

```
   // loop until user decides to quit
   while ( !finished ) {

      // display options
      Console::Write( S"\n   1: Get Value by Index\n"
         S"   2: Set Value by Index\n   3: Get Value by Name\n"
         S"   4: Set Value by Name\n  -1: Quit\n=> " );
      choice = Int32::Parse( Console::ReadLine() );

      switch ( choice ) {

         // get value at specified index
         case 1:
            Console::Write( S"Index to get: " );
            ShowValueAtIndex( box, S"get: ",
               Int32::Parse( Console::ReadLine() ) );
            break;

         // set value at specified index
         case 2:
            Console::Write( S"Index to set: " );
            index = Int32::Parse( Console::ReadLine() );
            Console::Write( S"Value to set: " );
            box->Dimension[ index ] = Double::Parse(
               Console::ReadLine() );

            ShowValueAtIndex( box, S"set: ", index );
            break;

         // get value with specified name
         case 3:
            Console::Write( S"Name to get: " );
            ShowValueAtIndex( box, S"get: ",
               Console::ReadLine() );
            break;

         // set value with specified name
         case 4:
            Console::Write( S"Name to set: " );
            name = Console::ReadLine();
            Console::Write( S"Value to set: " );
            box->Dimension[ name ] = Double::Parse(
               Console::ReadLine() );

            ShowValueAtIndex( box, S"set: ", name );
            break;

         // exit loop
         default:
            finished = true;
            break;
      } // end switch
```

Fig. 8.30 Indexed properties provide subscripted access to an object's members. (Part 2 of 4.)

```

      } // end while

      return 0;
   } // end _tmain

   // display value at specified index number
   void ShowValueAtIndex( Box *box, String *prefix, int index )
   {
      Console::WriteLine( String::Concat( prefix, S"box[ ",
         index.ToString(), S" ] = ", box->Dimension[ index ] ) );
   }

   // display value with specified name
   void ShowValueAtIndex( Box *box, String *prefix, String *name )
   {
      Console::WriteLine( String::Concat( prefix, S"box[ ",
         name, S" ] = ", box->Dimension[ name ] ) );
   }
```

```
   1: Get Value by Index
   2: Set Value by Index
   3: Get Value by Name
   4: Set Value by Name
  -1: Quit
=> 2
Index to set: 0
Value to set: 123.45
set: box[ 0 ] = 123.45
```

```
   1: Get Value by Index
   2: Set Value by Index
   3: Get Value by Name
   4: Set Value by Name
  -1: Quit
=> 3
Name to get: length
get: box[ length ] = 123.45
```

```
   1: Get Value by Index
   2: Set Value by Index
   3: Get Value by Name
   4: Set Value by Name
  -1: Quit
=> 4
Name to set: width
Value to set: 33.33
set: box[ width ] = 33.33
```

Fig. 8.30 Indexed properties provide subscripted access to an object's members. (Part 3 of 4.)

```
   1: Get Value by Index
   2: Set Value by Index
   3: Get Value by Name
   4: Set Value by Name
  -1: Quit
=> 1
Index to get: 1
get: box[ 1 ] = 33.33
```

Fig. 8.30 Indexed properties provide subscripted access to an object's members. (Part 4 of 4.)

`BoxTest.cpp` (Fig. 8.30) is a console-based application that manipulates the `private` data members of class `Box` through `Box`'s indexed properties. Figure 8.30 declares variable `box` and initializes its dimensions to `0.0` (line 17). The `while` loop in lines 24–76 executes until boolean variable `finished` becomes `true` (line 72). Lines 27–29 display a menu of options to the user. Choice `1` (lines 35–39) and choice `3` (lines 53–57) retrieve the value at the specified index or name, respectively. Choice `1` invokes method `ShowValueAtIndex` (lines 82–86) to retrieve the value at the specified index number. Similarly, choice `3` invokes method `ShowValueAtIndex` (lines 89–93) to retrieve the value with the specified name. Choice `2` (lines 42–50) and choice `4` (lines 60–68) set a value at the specified index or name, respectively. Any other choice (such as `-1`) sets `finished` to `false`, exiting the program.

8.14 Data Abstraction and Information Hiding

As we pointed out at the beginning of this chapter, classes normally hide the details of their implementation from their clients. This is called information hiding. As an example of information hiding, let us consider a data structure called a *stack.*

Readers can think of a stack as analogous to a pile of dishes. When a dish is placed on the pile, it is always placed at the top (referred to as *pushing* the dish onto the stack). Similarly, when a dish is removed from the pile, it is always removed from the top (referred to as *popping* the dish off the stack). Stacks are known as *last-in, first-out (LIFO) data structures*—the last item pushed (inserted) on the stack is the first item popped (removed) from the stack.

Stacks can be implemented with arrays and with other data structures, such as linked lists. (We discuss stacks and linked lists in Chapter 22, Data Structures and Collections.) A client of a stack class need not be concerned with the stack's implementation. The client knows only that when data items are placed in the stack, these items will be recalled in last-in, first-out order. The client cares about *what* functionality a stack offers, but not about *how* that functionality is implemented. This concept is referred to as *data abstraction.* Although programmers might know the details of a class's implementation, they should not write code that depends on these details. This enables a particular class (such as one that implements a stack and its operations, *push* and *pop*) to be replaced with another version without affecting the rest of the system. As long as the `public` services of the class do not change (i.e., every method still has the same name, return type and parameter list in the new class definition), the rest of the system is not affected.

Most programming languages emphasize actions. In these languages, data exist to support the actions that programs must take. Data are "less interesting" than actions. Data are "crude."

Only a few built-in data types exist, and it is difficult for programmers to create their own data types. MC++ and the object-oriented style of programming elevate the importance of data. The primary activities of object-oriented programming in MC++ is the creation of data types (i.e., classes) and the expression of the interactions among objects of those data types. To create languages that emphasize data, the programming-languages community needed to formalize some notions about data. The formalization we consider here is the notion of *abstract data types (ADTs)*. ADTs receive as much attention today as structured programming did decades earlier. ADTs, however, do not replace structured programming. Rather, they provide an additional formalization to improve the program-development process.

Consider built-in type `int`, which most people would associate with an integer in mathematics. Rather, an `int` is an abstract representation of an integer. Unlike mathematical integers, computer `int`s are fixed in size. For example, type `int` in .NET is limited approximately to the range –2 billion to +2 billion. If the result of a calculation falls outside this range, an error occurs, and the computer responds in some machine-dependent manner. It might, for example, "quietly" produce an incorrect result. Mathematical integers do not have this problem. Therefore, the notion of a computer `int` is only an approximation of the notion of a real-world integer. The same is true of `float` and other built-in types.

We have taken the notion of `int` for granted until this point, but we now consider it from a new perspective. Types like `int`, `float`, `__wchar_t` and others are all examples of abstract data types. These types are representations of real-world notions to some satisfactory level of precision within a computer system.

An ADT actually captures two notions: A *data representation* and the *operations* that can be performed on that data. For example, in MC++, an `int` contains an integer value (data) and provides addition, subtraction, multiplication, division and modulus operations; however, division by zero is undefined. MC++ programmers use classes to implement abstract data types.

Software Engineering Observation 8.16

Programmers can create types through the use of the class mechanism. These new types can be designed so that they are as convenient to use as the built-in types. This marks MC++ as an extensible language. *Although the language is easy to extend via new types, the programmer cannot alter the base language itself.*

Another abstract data type we discuss is a *queue*, which is similar to a "waiting line." Computer systems use many queues internally. A queue offers well-understood behavior to its clients: Clients place items in a queue one at a time via an *enqueue* operation, then get those items back one at a time via a *dequeue* operation. A queue returns items in *first-in, first-out (FIFO)* order, which means that the first item inserted in a queue is the first item removed. Conceptually, a queue can become infinitely long, but real queues are finite.

The queue hides an internal data representation that keeps track of the items currently waiting in line, and it offers a set of operations to its clients (*enqueue* and *dequeue*). The clients are not concerned about the implementation of the queue—clients simply depend upon the queue to operate "as advertised." When a client enqueues an item, the queue should accept that item and place it in some kind of internal FIFO data structure. Similarly, when the client wants the next item from the front of the queue, the queue should remove the item from its internal representation and deliver the item in FIFO order (i.e., the item that has been in the queue the longest should be the next one returned by the next dequeue operation).

The queue ADT guarantees the integrity of its internal data structure. Clients cannot manipulate this data structure directly—only the queue ADT has access to its internal data. Clients are able to perform only allowable operations on the data representation; the ADT rejects operations that its public interface does not provide.

8.15 Software Reusability

MC++ programmers concentrate both on crafting new classes and on reusing classes from the Framework Class Library (FCL), which contains thousands of predefined classes. Developers construct software by combining programmer-defined classes with well-defined, carefully tested, well-documented, portable and widely available FCL classes. This kind of software reusability speeds the development of powerful, high-quality software. *Rapid applications development (RAD)* is of great interest today.

The FCL allows MC++ programmers to achieve software reusability across platforms that support .NET and rapid applications development. MC++ programmers focus on the high-level programming issues and leave the low-level implementation details to classes in the FCL. For example, an MC++ programmer who writes a graphics program does not need to know the details of every .NET-platform graphics capability. Instead, MC++ programmers concentrate on learning and using the FCL's graphics classes.

The FCL enables MC++ developers to build applications faster by reusing preexisting, extensively tested classes. In addition to reducing development time, FCL classes also improve programmers' abilities to debug and maintain applications, because proven software components are being used. For programmers to take advantage of the FCL's classes, they must familiarize themselves with the FCL's rich set of capabilities.

Software reuse is not limited to Windows-application development. The FCL also includes classes for creating *Web services*, which are applications packaged as services that clients can access via the Internet. Any MC++ application is a potential Web service, so programmers can reuse existing applications as building blocks to form larger more sophisticated Web-enabled applications. Visual C++ .NET provides all the features necessary for creating scalable, robust Web services. We formally introduce Web services in Chapter 20, Web Services.

8.16 Namespaces and Assemblies

As we have seen in almost every example in the text, classes from preexisting libraries, such as the .NET Framework, must be imported into an MC++ program by adding a reference to the appropriate libraries (a process we demonstrated in Section 3.2). Remember that each class in the Framework Class Library belongs to a specific namespace. The preexisting code in the FCL facilitates software reuse.

Programmers should concentrate on making the software components they create reusable. However, doing so often results in *naming collisions*. For example, two classes defined by different programmers can have the same name. If a program needs both of those classes, the program must have a way to distinguish between the two classes in the code.

Common Programming Error 8.15

Attempting to compile code that contains naming collisions will generate compilation errors.

Namespaces help minimize this problem by providing a convention for *unique class names*. No two classes in a given namespace can have the same name, but different namespaces can contain classes of the same name. With hundreds of thousands of people writing MC++ programs, there is a good chance the names that one programmer chooses to describe classes will conflict with the names that other programmers choose for their classes.

We begin our discussion of reusing existing class definition in Fig. 8.31–Fig. 8.32, which provides the code for class `Time3` (originally defined in Fig. 8.11–Fig. 8.12). When reusing class definitions between programs, programmers create class libraries that can be imported for use in a program via a `#using` preprocessor directive (for instance, lines 7 and 8 of Fig. 8.3), or by using the IDE to *add a reference* to the class library (we will demonstrate how to do this shortly). Only `public` classes can be reused from class libraries. Non-`public` classes can be used only by other classes in the same assembly.

```
// Fig. 8.31: TimeLibrary.h
// Class Time3 is defined within namespace TimeLibrary.

#pragma once

using namespace System;

namespace TimeLibrary
{
   // Time3 class definition
   public __gc class Time3
   {
   public:
      Time3();
      Time3( int );
      Time3( int, int );
      Time3( int, int, int );
      Time3( Time3 * );
      void SetTime( int, int, int );

      __property int get_Hour()
      {
         return hour;
      }

      __property void set_Hour( int value )
      {
         hour = ( ( value >= 0 && value < 24 ) ? value : 0 );
      }

      __property int get_Minute()
      {
         return minute;
      }

      __property void set_Minute( int value )
      {
```

Fig. 8.31 Assembly `TimeLibrary` contains class `Time3`. (Part 1 of 2.)

```
         minute = ( ( value >= 0 && value < 60 ) ? value : 0 );
      }

      __property int get_Second()
      {
         return second;
      }

      __property void set_Second( int value )
      {
         second = ( ( value >= 0 && value < 60 ) ? value : 0 );
      }

      String *ToUniversalString();
      String *ToStandardString();

   private:
      int hour;   // 0-23
      int minute; // 0-59
      int second; // 0-59
   }; // end class Time3
} // end namespace TimeLibrary
```

Fig. 8.31 Assembly `TimeLibrary` contains class `Time3`. (Part 2 of 2.)

```
// Fig. 8.32: TimeLibrary.cpp
// Method definitions for class Time3.

#include "stdafx.h"

#include "TimeLibrary.h"

using namespace TimeLibrary;

// Time3 constructor initializes variables to
// zero to set default time to midnight
Time3::Time3()
{
   SetTime( 0, 0, 0 );
}

// Time3 constructor: hour supplied, minute and second
// defaulted to 0
Time3::Time3( int hourValue )
{
   SetTime( hourValue, 0, 0 );
}

// Time3 constructor: hour and minute supplied, second
// defaulted to 0
Time3::Time3( int hourValue, int minuteValue )
{
```

Fig. 8.32 `Time3` class method definitions. (Part 1 of 2.)

```
   SetTime( hourValue, minuteValue, 0 );
}

// Time3 constructor: hour, minute and second supplied
Time3::Time3( int hourValue, int minuteValue, int secondValue )
{
   SetTime( hourValue, minuteValue, secondValue );
}

// Time3 constructor: intialize using another Time3 object
Time3::Time3( Time3 *time )
{
   SetTime( time->Hour, time->Minute, time->Second );
}

// set new time value in 24-hour format
void Time3::SetTime(
   int hourValue, int minuteValue, int secondValue )
{
   Hour = hourValue;
   Minute = minuteValue;
   Second = secondValue;
}

// convert time to universal-time (24 hour) format string
String *Time3::ToUniversalString()
{
   return String::Concat( Hour.ToString( S"D2" ), S":",
      Minute.ToString( S"D2" ), S":", Second.ToString( S"D2" ) );
}

// convert time to standard-time (12 hour) format string
String *Time3::ToStandardString()
{
   return String::Concat(
      ( ( Hour == 12 || Hour == 0 ) ? 12 : Hour % 12 ).ToString(),
      S":", Minute.ToString( S"D2" ), S":",
      Second.ToString( S"D2" ), S" ",
      ( Hour < 12 ? S"AM" : S"PM" ) );
}
```

Fig. 8.32 `Time3` class method definitions. (Part 2 of 2.)

If a programmer does not specify the namespace for a class (as was the case in Fig. 8.11–Fig. 8.12), the class is placed in the *default namespace*, which includes the compiled classes in the current directory. The only difference between class `Time3` in this example and the version in Fig. 8.11 and Fig. 8.12 is that we define class `Time3` in namespace `TimeLibrary`. Each class library is defined in a namespace that contains all the classes in the library. We will demonstrate momentarily how to package class `Time3` into `TimeLibrary.dll`—the *dynamic link library* that we create for reuse in other programs. Programs can load dynamic link libraries at execution time to access common functionality that can be shared among many programs. A dynamic link library represents an assembly.

When a project uses a class library, the project must contain a reference to the assembly that defines the class library.

We now describe, step-by-step, how to create the class library `TimeLibrary` containing class `Time3`:

1. *Create a class library project.* First select **File > New > Project...**. In the **New Project** dialog, ensure that **Visual C++ Projects** is selected in the **Project Types** section and click **Class Library (.NET)**. Name the project **TimeLibrary** and choose the directory in which you would like to store the project. A simple class library will be created, as shown in Fig. 8.33. There are two important points to note about the generated code. The first is that the class does not contain a `_tmain` function. This indicates that the class in the class library cannot be used to begin the execution of an application. This class is designed to be used by other programs. Also notice that `Class1` is created as a `public` class. If another project uses this library, only the library's `public` classes are accessible. We created class `Time3` as `public` for this purpose (line 11 of Fig. 8.31) by renaming the class `Class1` (created by Visual Studio .NET as part of the project) to `Time3`.
2. *Add the code for class `Time3`.* Delete the code for `Class1` (lines 9–12 of Fig. 8.33). Replace this code with the `Time3` code (lines 10–58) from Fig. 8.31. Add the comments from lines 1, 2 and 59 of Fig. 8.31 to `TimeLibrary.h`. Likewise, replace the code in the `TimeLibrary.cpp` file with the code in Fig. 8.32.

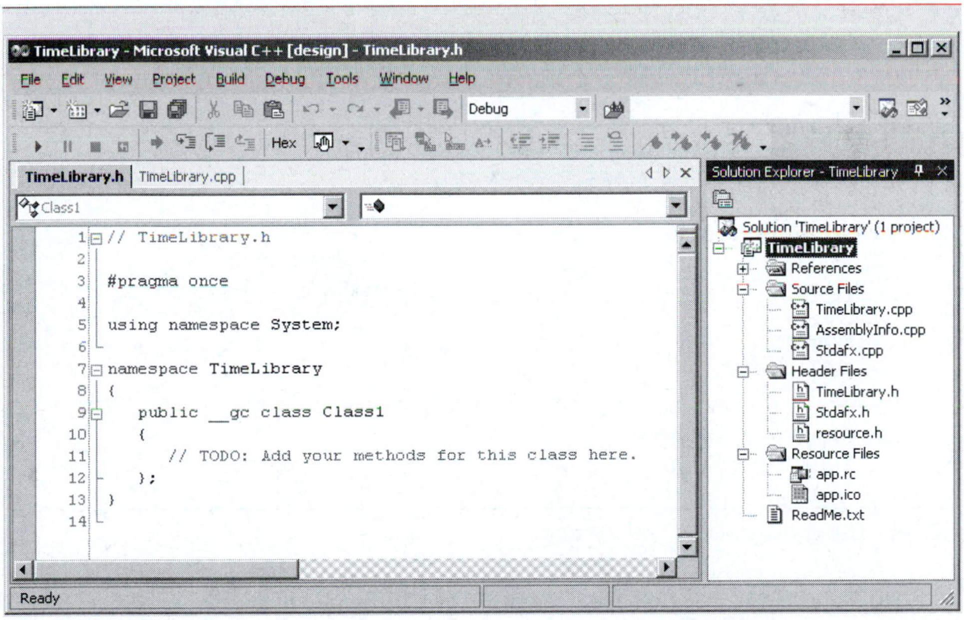

Fig. 8.33 Simple class library.

3. *Compile the code.* From the **Build** menu, choose option **Build Solution**. The code should compile successfully. Remember that this code cannot be executed—

there is no entry point into the program. In fact, if you try running the program by selecting **Debug > Start**, Visual Studio .NET prompts the programmer to locate the executable file.

Compiling the project creates an assembly (a dynamic link library) that represents the new class library. This assembly can be found in the `Debug` folder of the main project directory. By default, the assembly name will include the namespace name. (In this case, the name will be `TimeLibrary.dll`.) The assembly file contains class `Time3`, which other projects can use. Assembly files, which have file extensions `.dll` and `.exe` (as well as others), are integral to MC++ applications. The Windows operating system uses executable files (`.exe`) to run applications, whereas it uses library files (`.dll`, or *dynamic link library*) to represent code libraries that can be loaded dynamically by many applications and shared among those applications.

In Fig. 8.34, we define a console application (`AssemblyTest.cpp`) that uses class `Time3` in assembly `TimeLibrary.dll` to create a `Time3` object and display its standard and universal string formats.

```
1  // Fig. 8.34: AssemblyTest.cpp
2  // Using class Time3 from assembly TimeLibrary.
3
4  #include "stdafx.h"
5
6  #using <mscorlib.dll>
7
8  using namespace System;
9  using namespace TimeLibrary;
10
11 int _tmain()
12 {
13    Time3 *time = new Time3( 13, 27, 6 );
14
15    Console::WriteLine(
16       S"Standard time: {0}\nUniversal time: {1}\n",
17       time->ToStandardString(), time->ToUniversalString() );
18
19    return 0;
20 } // end _tmain
```

```
Standard time: 1:27:06 PM
Universal time: 13:27:06
```

Fig. 8.34 Using assembly `TimeLibrary`.

Before `AssemblyTest.cpp` can use class `Time3`, its project must have a reference to the `TimeLibrary` assembly. To add the reference, right click on project `AssemblyTest` in the **Solution Explorer** and select **Add Reference**.... Using the **Browse**... button, select `TimeLibrary.dll` (located in the `Debug` directory of the `TimeLibrary` project), then click **OK** to add the resource to the project. After adding the reference, add a `using` directive to inform the compiler that we will use classes from namespace `TimeLibrary` (line 9 in Fig. 8.34).

8.17 Class View

Now that we have introduced key concepts of object-based programming, we present a feature of Visual Studio .NET that facilitates the design of object-oriented applications—***Class View***.

The **Class View** displays the variables and methods for all classes in a project. To access this feature, select **View > Class View**. Figure 8.35 shows the **Class View** for the `Time1Test` project of Fig. 8.1, Fig. 8.2 and Fig. 8.3 (class `Time1`). The view follows a hierarchical structure, positioning the project name (`Time1Test`) as the root and including a series of nodes (e.g., classes, variables, methods, etc.). If a plus sign (+) appears to the left of a node, that node can be expanded to show other nodes. By contrast, if a minus sign (-) appears to the left of a node, that node has been expanded (and can be collapsed). According to the **Class View**, project `Time1Test` contains **Global Functions and Variables** and class `Time1` *children*. Class `Time1` contains methods `SetTime`, `Time1`, `ToStandardString` and `ToUniversalString` (indicated by purple boxes) and data members `hour`, `minute` and `second` (indicated by blue boxes). The lock icons, placed to the left of the blue-box icons for the data members, specify that the data members are `private`. Project `Time1Test` includes global functions and variables, such as the `_tmain` function. Note that class `Time1` contains the **Bases and Interfaces** node. If you expand this node, you will see class `Object`, because each class inherits from class `System::Object` (discussed in Chapter 9).

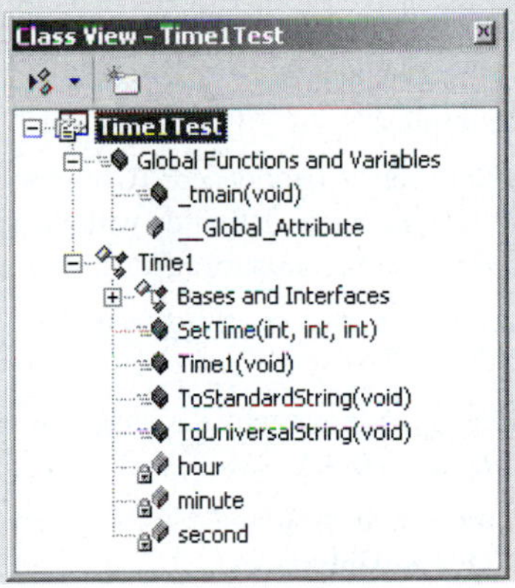

Fig. 8.35 **Class View** of class `Time1` (Fig. 8.1).

This chapter is the first in a series of three chapters that cover the fundamentals of object-based and object-oriented programming. In this chapter, we discussed how to create class definitions, how to control access to class members and several features commonly used to craft valuable classes for reuse by other programmers. Chapter 9 focuses on inheritance. In Chapter 9, you will learn how to build classes that inherit data and functionality from existing class definitions. You also will learn other MC++ features that are specific to the inheritance relationship between classes. These features serve as the basis for the object-oriented programming concept called polymorphism that we present in Chapter 10.

SUMMARY

- Object orientation uses classes to encapsulate (i.e., wrap together) data (attributes) and methods (behaviors).
- Objects have the ability to hide their implementation from other objects (this principle is called information hiding).
- MC++ programmers concentrate on creating their own programmer-defined types, called classes. Each class contains both data and a set of methods that manipulate the data.
- The data components, or data members, of a class are also called member variables, or instance variables.
- Keywords `public` and `private` are member access specifiers.
- Data members and methods that are declared with member access specifier `public` are accessible wherever the program has a handle (such as a pointer) to an object of that class.
- Data members and methods that are declared with member access specifier `private` are accessible only to non-`static` methods of the class in which the `private` members are defined.
- The `private` methods often are called utility methods, or helper methods, because they can be called only by other methods of that class and are used to support the operation of those methods.
- Classes simplify programming, because the client code need only be concerned with the `public` operations encapsulated in an object of the class.
- Access methods can read or display data. Another common use for access methods is to test the truth of conditions—such methods often are called predicate methods.
- A class's constructor is called when an object of that class is instantiated. It is common to have overloaded constructors for a class. Normally, constructors are `public`.
- If no constructors are defined for a class, a default constructor with no arguments and an empty body will be provided by the compiler.
- Methods and constructors of a class can be overloaded. To overload a method/constructor of a class, simply provide a separate method/constructor definition with the same name for each version of the method/constructor. Overloaded methods/constructors must have different parameter lists.
- Data members can be initialized by the class constructor, or they can be assigned values by the *set* method of a property.
- Data members that are not initialized explicitly by the programmer are initialized by the compiler. (Primitive numeric variables are set to `0`, `bool` values are set to `false` and pointers are set to `0`.)
- Every class in MC++, such as the classes from the .NET Framework, belongs to a namespace that contains a group of related classes and interfaces.
- If the programmer does not specify the namespace for a class, the class is placed in the default namespace, which includes the compiled classes in the current directory.
- Namespaces provide a mechanism for software reuse.
- Class `MessageBox` (from `System::Windows::Forms`) allows you to display a dialog containing information.
- Method `MessageBox::Show` is a `static` method of class `MessageBox`.
- `static` methods are called with their class name followed by a scope resolution operator (`::`) and the method name.
- A class's non-`static` variables and methods belong to that class's scope. Within a class's scope, class members are immediately accessible to all that class's non-`static` methods and can be referenced by name. Outside a class's scope, class members cannot be referenced directly by name.

- In certain cases, all objects of a class should share only one copy of a particular variable. Programmers use `static` variables for this and other reasons.
- A `static` variable represents class-wide information—all objects of the class share the same piece of data.
- The declaration of a `static` member begins with the keyword `static`. Such variables have class scope.
- A class's `public static` members can be accessed via the class name and the scope resolution operator (e.g., `Math::PI`).
- A class's `private static` members can be accessed only through methods or properties of the class.
- A method declared `static` cannot access non-`static` members.
- Many compiled classes in the .NET Framework Class Library (including `MessageBox`) need to be referenced before they can be used in a program.
- Depending on the type of application we create, classes may be compiled into files with an `.exe` (executable) extension, a `.dll` (or dynamic link library) extension or one of several other extensions.
- Dynamic link libraries, which cannot be run as programs by themselves, contain executable code (e.g., functions and classes). Programs link to DLLs, which can be shared among several executing programs. DLLs are loaded at runtime dynamically.
- Executable files contain an application entry point (e.g., a `_tmain` function). Such files are called assemblies and are the packaging units for code in MC++.
- The assembly is a package containing the Microsoft Intermediate Language (MSIL) code that a project has been compiled into, plus any other information that is needed for these classes.
- To allow clients to manipulate the value of `private` data, the class can provide a property definition, which will enable the user to access this `private` data in a safe way.
- A property definition contains methods that handle the details of modifying and returning data. A property definition can contain a *set* method, a *get* method or both.
- A *get* method enables the client to read the field's value, and the *set* method enables the client to modify the value.
- Although *set* and *get* methods can provide access to `private` data, the access is restricted by the programmer's implementation of those methods.
- Scalar properties are properties that can be accessed like data members or variables.
- Software reusability speeds the development of powerful, high-quality software. Rapid applications development (RAD) is of great interest today.
- One form of software reuse is composition, in which a class contains as members pointers to objects of other classes.
- Every object can access a pointer to itself, called the `this` pointer. The `this` pointer is used implicitly and explicitly to refer to the non-`static` members of an object.
- The .NET Framework performs automatic garbage collection.
- Every class can have a programmer-defined destructor that typically returns resources to the system. The destructor for an object is guaranteed to be called to perform termination housekeeping on the object just before the garbage collector reclaims the memory for the object (called finalization).
- To create a constant member of a class, the programmer must declare that member using keyword `const`.

- Members declared `static const` must be initialized in the declaration.
- Once they are initialized, `const` values cannot be modified.
- A class can define indexed properties to provide subscripted access to the data in an object of that class.
- Indexed properties can be defined to use any data type as the subscript.
- Each indexed property can define a *get* and *set* method.
- Indexed properties can be overloaded.
- The Visual Studio .NET **Class View** feature displays the variables and methods for all classes in a project. To access this feature, select **View > Class View**.

TERMINOLOGY

abstract data type (ADT)
accessor
action
action-oriented
aggregation
assembly
attribute (data)
behavior (method)
block scope
body of a class definition
built-in data types
class
class definition
class library
class scope
class-scope variable hidden by local variable
"class-wide" information
client of a class
compile a class
composition
consistent state
`const` keyword
constant
constructor
data abstraction
data integrity
data member
data representation of an abstract data type
default constructor
default namespace
dequeue operation
destructor
`.dll`
driver
dynamic link library
encapsulate
enqueue operation
`.exe`
explicit use of `this` pointer
extensible language
field
finalization
first-in, first-out (FIFO) data structure
garbage collector
get method of a property
helper method
hide a data member
hide implementation details
implementation
indexed property
indexed property *get* method
indexed property *set* method
information hiding
inheritance
initialize a class object
initialize a data member
initialize to default values
instance of a built-in type
instance of a user-defined type
instance variable
instantiate (or create) an object
interactions among objects
interface
internal data representation
last-in, first-out (LIFO) data structure
local scope
local variable
member access specifier
member variable
memory leak
`MessageBox` class
method overloading
namespace
`new` operator

no-argument constructor
object (or instance)
`Object` class
object-based programming (OBP)
object-oriented programming (OOP)
overloaded constructor
overloaded method
popping off a stack
predicate method
`private` member access specifier
procedural programming language
program-development process
programmer-defined type
`public` member access specifier
`public` method
`public` operations encapsulated in an object
`public` service
pushing onto a stack
queue
rapid applications development (RAD)
reclaim memory
resource leak
reusable software component
scalar property
scope resolution operator (`::`)
service of a class
set method of a property
software reuse
stack
standard-time format
`static` keyword
`static` variable
termination housekeeping
`this` keyword
universal-time format
user-defined type
utility method
validity checking

SELF-REVIEW EXERCISES

8.1 Fill in the blanks in each of the following statements:

a) Members of a class declared ________ are accessible only to members of the class in which those members are defined.
b) A(n) ________ initializes the data members of a class.
c) A property's ________ method is used to assign values to `private` data members of a class.
d) Methods of a class normally are declared ________, and data members of a class normally are declared ________.
e) A(n) ________ method of a property is used to retrieve values of `private` data of a class.
f) The keyword ________ specifies that a class is managed (i.e. the common language runtime manages its lifetime).
g) Members of a class declared ________ are accessible anywhere that an object of the class is in scope.
h) The ________ operator allocates memory dynamically for an object of a specified type and returns a(n) ________ to the newly created object.
i) A(n) ________ variable represents class-wide information.
j) The keyword ________ specifies that a data member must be initialized in its declaration and cannot be modified once it is initialized.
k) A method declared `static` cannot access ________ class members.

8.2 State whether each of the following is *true* or *false*. If *false* explain why.

a) If not initialized when an object of a class is instantiated, primitive numeric variables are set to `0`, `bool` values are set to `false` and pointers are set to `0`.
b) Constructors can have return values.
c) Properties must define *get* and *set* methods.
d) The `this` pointer of an object is a pointer to that object itself.
e) A `static` member can be referenced when no object of that type exists.

f) Variables declared `const` must be initialized either in a declaration or in the class constructor.
g) Different namespaces cannot have classes/methods with the same names.
h) Indexed properties can be overloaded like methods.
i) Indexed properties can return any type in Visual C++ .NET.

ANSWERS TO SELF-REVIEW EXERCISES

8.1 a) `private`. b) constructor. c) *set*. d) `public`, `private`. e) *get*. f) `_gc`. g) `public`. h) `new`, pointer. i) `static`. j) `const`. k) non-`static`.

8.2 a) True. b) False. Constructors are not permitted to return values. c) False. A property definition can specify a *set* method, a *get* method or both. d) True. e) True. f) False. Variables declared `const` must be initialized when they are declared. g) False. Different namespaces can have classes/methods with the same names. h) True. i) True.

EXERCISES

8.3 Create a class called `Complex` for performing arithmetic with complex numbers. Write a driver program to test your class.

Complex numbers have the form

```
realPart + imaginaryPart * i
```

where *i* is

$$\sqrt{-1}$$

Use floating-point variables to represent the `private` data of the class. Provide a constructor that enables an object of this class to be initialized when it is declared. Provide a no-argument constructor with default values in case no initializers are provided. Provide `public` methods for each of the following:

a) *Addition of two `Complex` numbers.* The real parts are added together and the imaginary parts are added together.
b) *Subtraction of two `Complex` numbers.* The real part of the right operand is subtracted from the real part of the left operand and the imaginary part of the right operand is subtracted from the imaginary part of the left operand.
c) *Printing of `Complex` numbers in the form `(a, b)`, where `a` is the real part and `b` is the imaginary part.*

8.4 Modify the `Date` class of Fig. 8.14–Fig. 8.15 to provide methods `NextDay`, `NextMonth` and `NextYear` to increment the day, month and year by one (respectively). The `Date` object should always remain in a consistent state. Write a program that tests these new methods to illustrate that the new methods works correctly. Be sure to test the following cases:

a) Incrementing the year.
b) Incrementing the month into the next year.
c) Incrementing the day into the next month.

8.5 Write a console application that implements a `Square` shape. Class `Square` should contain a property `Side` that has *get* and *set* methods to provide a controlled access to class `Square`'s `private` data. Provide two constructors: one that takes no arguments and another that takes a `side` length as a value. Write an application class that tests class `Square`'s functionality.

8.6 Create a `Date` class with the following capabilities:

a) Output the date in multiple formats such as

```
MM/DD/YYYY
June 14, 2001
DDD YYYY
```

where `DDD` is the number of days from the start of the year.

b) Use overloaded constructors to create `Date` objects initialized with dates of the formats in part a).

8.7 Create class `SavingsAccount`. Use `static` variable `annualInterestRate` to store the interest rate for all account holders. Each object of the class contains a `private` data member `savingsBalance` indicating the amount the saver currently has on deposit, and provide a property that will return that value. Provide method `CalculateMonthlyInterest` to calculate the monthly interest by multiplying the `savingsBalance` by `annualInterestRate` divided by 12; this interest should be added to `SavingsBalance`. Provide a `static` method `ModifyInterestRate` that sets the `annualInterestRate` to a new value. Write a driver program to test class `SavingsAccount`. Instantiate two `savingsAccount` objects, `saver1` and `saver2`, with balances of $2000.00 and $3000.00, respectively. Set `annualInterestRate` to 4%, then calculate the monthly interest and print the new balances for each of the savers. Then set the `annualInterestRate` to 5% and calculate the next month's interest and print the new balances for each of the savers.

8.8 Create a class `TicTacToe` that will enable you to write a complete program to play a console-based game of Tic-Tac-Toe. The class contains as `private` data a 3-by-3 two-dimensional array of characters. The constructor should initialize the empty board to all spaces, `' '`. Allow two players. Wherever the first player moves, place an `'X'` in the specified square; place an `'O'` wherever the second player moves. Each move must be to an empty square. After each move, determine whether the game has been won or if the game is a draw via a `gameStatus` method. [*Hint*: use an enumeration constant to maintain the following statuses: `WIN`, `DRAW`, `CONTINUE`.] Write program `TicTacToeTest` to test your class. If you feel ambitious, modify your program so that the computer makes the moves for one of the players automatically. Also, allow the player to specify whether he or she wants to go first or second. If you feel exceptionally ambitious, develop a program that will play three-dimensional Tic-Tac-Toe on a 4-by-4-by-4 board [*Note:* This is a challenging project that could take many weeks of effort!]

9

Object-Oriented Programming: Inheritance

Objectives

- To understand inheritance and software reusability.
- To understand the concepts of base classes and derived classes.
- To understand member access specifier `protected`.
- To understand the use of constructors and destructors in base classes and derived classes.
- To present a case study that demonstrates the mechanics of inheritance.

Say not you know another entirely, till you have divided an inheritance with him.
Johann Kasper Lavater

This method is to define as the number of a class the class of all classes similar to the given class.
Bertrand Russell

Good as it is to inherit a library, it is better to collect one.
Augustine Birrell

Outline

9.1 Introduction

In this chapter, we continue our discussion of *object-oriented programming (OOP)* by introducing one of its main features—*inheritance*. Inheritance is a form of software reusability in which classes are created by absorbing an existing class's data and behaviors and embellishing them with new capabilities. Software reusability saves time during program development. It also encourages the reuse of proven and debugged high-quality software, which increases the likelihood that a system will be implemented effectively.

When creating a class, instead of writing completely new data members and methods, the programmer can designate that the new class should *inherit* the data members, properties and methods of another class. The previously defined class is called the *base class*, and the new class is referred to as the *derived class*. (Other programming languages, such as Java, refer to the base class as the *superclass* and the derived class as the *subclass*.) Once created, each derived class can become the base class for future derived classes. A derived class—to which unique class variables, properties and methods normally are added—is often larger than its base class. Therefore, a derived class is more specific than its base class and represents a more specialized group of objects. Typically, the derived class contains the behaviors of its base class and additional behaviors. The *direct base class* is the base class from which the derived class explicitly inherits. An *indirect base class* is inherited from two or more levels up the *class hierarchy*. In the case of *single inheritance,* a class is derived from one base class. Unlike standard C++, MC++ does not support *multiple inheritance*, which occurs when a class is derived from more than one direct base class.

Every object of a derived class is also an object of that derived class's base class. However, base-class objects are not objects of their derived classes. For example, all cars are vehicles, but not all vehicles are cars. As we continue our study of object-oriented programming here and in Chapter 10, we take advantage of this relationship to perform some interesting manipulations.

Experience in building software systems indicates that significant amounts of code deal with closely related special cases. When programmers are preoccupied with special cases, the details can obscure the "big picture." With object-oriented programming, programmers focus on the commonalities among objects in the system, rather than on the special cases. This process is called *abstraction*.

In discussing inheritance, it is important to distinguish between the *"is-a" relationship* and the *"has-a" relationship*. "Is-a" represents inheritance. In an "is-a" relationship, an object of a derived class also can be treated as an object of its base class. For example, a car *is a* vehicle. By contrast, "has-a" stands for composition (composition is discussed in Chapter 8, Object-Based Programming). In a "has-a" relationship, a class object contains one or more objects (or pointers to objects) of other classes as members. For example, a car *has a* steering wheel.

Derived-class methods might require access to their base-class's data members, properties and methods. A derived class can access the non-`private` members of its base class. Base-class members that should be inaccessible to properties or methods of any of its derived classes are declared `private` in the base class. A derived class can effect state changes in `private` base-class members, but only through non-`private` methods and properties provided in the base class and inherited into the derived class.

Software Engineering Observation 9.1

Properties and methods defined in a derived class cannot directly access `private` *members of the base class.*

Software Engineering Observation 9.2

Hiding `private` *members helps programmers test, debug and correctly modify systems. If a derived class could access its base class's* `private` *members, classes that inherit from that derived class could access that data as well. This would propagate access to what should be* `private` *data, and the benefits of information hiding would be lost.*

One problem with inheritance is that a derived class can inherit properties and methods it does not need or should not have. It is the class designer's responsibility to ensure that the capabilities provided by a class are appropriate for future derived classes, as described in Section 9.4. Even when a base-class property or method is appropriate for a derived class, that derived class often requires the property or method to perform its task in a manner specific to the derived class. In such cases, the base-class property or method can be *overridden* (redefined) in the derived class with an appropriate implementation.

New classes can inherit from abundant *class libraries*. Organizations develop their own class libraries and can take advantage of other libraries available worldwide. Someday, the vast majority of new software likely will be constructed from *standardized reusable components*, as most hardware is constructed today. This will facilitate the development of more powerful and abundant software.

9.2 Base Classes and Derived Classes

Often, an object of one class "is an" object of another class, as well. For example, a rectangle *is a* quadrilateral (as are squares, parallelograms and trapezoids). Thus, class `Rectangle` can be said to *inherit* from class `Quadrilateral`. In this context, class `Quadrilateral` *is a* base class, and class `Rectangle` *is a* derived class. A rectangle *is a* specific type of quadrilateral, but it is incorrect to claim that a quadrilateral *is a* rectangle—the quadrilateral could be a parallelogram or some other type of quadrilateral. Figure 9.1 lists several simple examples of base classes and derived classes.

Every derived-class object "is an" object of its base class, and one base class can have many derived classes; therefore, the set of objects represented by a base class typically is larger than the set of objects represented by any of its derived classes. For example, the base class `Vehicle` represents all vehicles, including cars, trucks, boats, bicycles and so on. By contrast, derived-class `Car` represents only a small subset of all `Vehicles`.

Base class	Derived classes
`Student`	`GraduateStudent`, `UndergraduateStudent`
`Shape`	`Circle`, `Triangle`, `Rectangle`
`Loan`	`CarLoan`, `HomeImprovementLoan`, `MortgageLoan`
`Employee`	`FacultyMember`, `StaffMember`
`Account`	`CheckingAccount`, `SavingsAccount`

Fig. 9.1 Inheritance examples.

Inheritance relationships form tree-like hierarchical structures. A base class exists in a hierarchical relationship with its derived classes. Although classes can exist independently, once they are employed in inheritance arrangements, they become affiliated with other classes. A class becomes either a base class, supplying data and behaviors to other classes, or a derived class, inheriting its data and behaviors from other classes.

Let us develop a simple inheritance hierarchy. A university community has thousands of members. These members consist of employees, students and alumni. Employees are either faculty members or staff members. Faculty members are either administrators (such as deans and department chairpersons) or teachers. This organizational structure yields the inheritance hierarchy depicted in Fig. 9.2. Note that the inheritance hierarchy could contain many other classes. For example, students can be graduate or undergraduate students. Undergraduate students can be freshmen, sophomores, juniors and seniors. Each arrow in the hierarchy represents an "is-a" relationship. As we follow the arrows in this class hierarchy, we can state, "an `Employee` *is a* `CommunityMember`" and "a `Teacher` *is a* `Faculty` member." `CommunityMember` is the *direct base class* of `Employee`, `Student` and `Alumnus`. In addition, `CommunityMember` is an *indirect base class* of all the other classes in the hierarchy diagram.

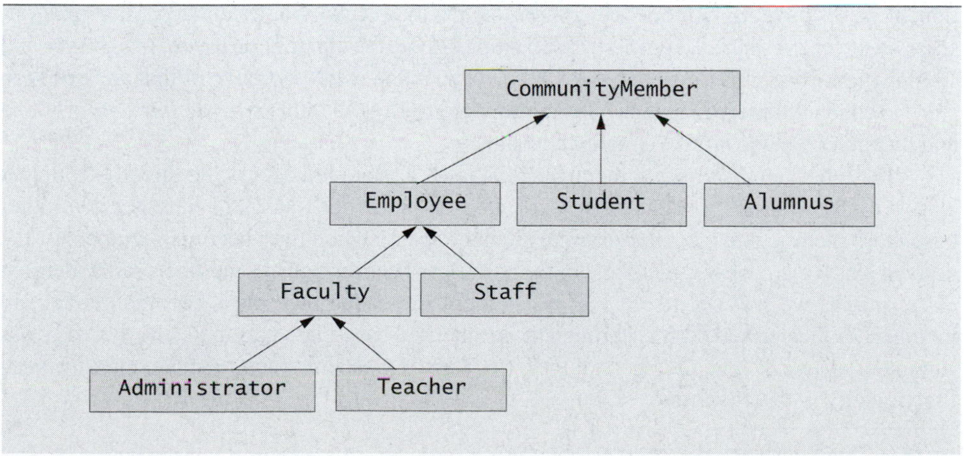

Fig. 9.2 Inheritance hierarchy for university `CommunityMembers`.

Starting from the bottom of the diagram, the reader can follow the arrows and apply the "is-a" relationship to the topmost base class. For example, an `Administrator` *is a* `Faculty` member, *is an* `Employee` and *is a* `CommunityMember`. In MC++, an `Administrator` also *is an* `Object`, because all classes[1] have `System::Object` as either a direct or indirect base class. Thus, all classes are connected via a hierarchical relationship in which they share the methods defined by class `Object` (there are eight such methods). We discuss some of these `Object` methods throughout the text.

Another inheritance hierarchy is the `Shape` hierarchy (Fig. 9.3). To specify that class `TwoDimensionalShape` is derived from (or inherits from) class `Shape`, class `TwoDimensionalShape` could be defined in MC++ as follows:

```
public __gc class TwoDimensionalShape : public Shape
```

Common Programming Error 9.1

When creating a new derived class, using the keyword `private` *or omitting the keyword* `public` *in front of the base class name leads to compilation errors because* `private` *inheritance for MC++ classes is strictly forbidden.*[2]

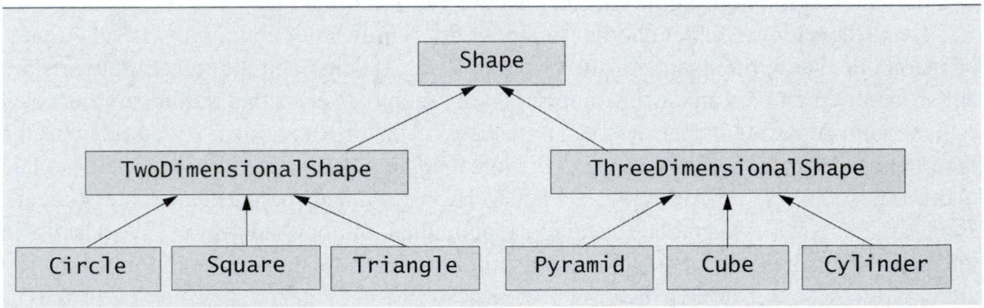

Fig. 9.3 Shape class hierarchy.

In Chapter 8, Object-Based Programming, we briefly discussed "has-a" relationships, in which classes have as members objects or pointers to objects of other classes. Such relationships create classes by *composition*. For example, given the classes `Employee`, `BirthDate` and `TelephoneNumber`, it is improper to say that an `Employee` *is a* `BirthDate` or that an `Employee` *is a* `TelephoneNumber`. However, it is appropriate to say that an `Employee` *has a* `BirthDate` and that an `Employee` *has a* `TelephoneNumber`.

With inheritance, `private` members of a base class are not accessible directly from that class's derived classes, but these `private` base-class members are still inherited. All other base-class members retain their original member access when they become members of the derived class (e.g., `public` members of the base class become `public` members of the derived class, and, as we will soon see, `protected` members of the base class become `protected` members of the derived class). Through these inherited base-class members, the derived class can manipulate `private` members of the base class (if these inherited members provide such functionality in the base class).

1. Throughout this book, when we use the general term *classes*, we refer to `__gc` managed classes, unless otherwise specified.
2. Currently, MC++ supports only `public` inheritance of a base class.

It is possible to treat base-class objects and derived-class objects similarly; their commonalities are expressed in the data members, properties and methods of the base class. Objects of all classes derived from a common base class can be treated as objects of that base class. In Chapter 10, Object-Oriented Programming: Polymorphism, we consider many examples that take advantage of this relationship.

Software Engineering Observation 9.3

Constructors are never inherited—they are specific to the class in which they are defined.

9.3 `protected` Members

Chapter 8, Object-Based Programming, discussed the `public` and `private` member access specifiers. A base class's `public` members are accessible anywhere that the program has a pointer to an object of that base class or one of its derived classes. A base class's `private` members are accessible only within the body of that base class. In this section, we introduce an additional member access specifier, ***`protected`***.

`Protected` access offers an intermediate level of protection between `public` and `private` access. A base class's `protected` members can be accessed only in that base class or in any classes derived from that base class.

Derived-class methods normally can refer to `public` and `protected` members of the base class simply using the member names. Note that `protected` data "breaks" encapsulation—a change to `protected` members of a base class may require modification of all derived classes.

9.4 Relationship Between Base Classes and Derived Classes

In this section, we use a point-circle hierarchy[3] to discuss the relationship between a base class and a derived class. We divide our discussion of the point–circle relationship into several parts. First, we create class `Point`, which directly inherits from class `System::Object` and contains as `private` data an *x-y* coordinate pair. Then, we create class `Circle`, which also directly inherits from class `System::Object` and contains as `private` data an *x-y* coordinate pair (representing the location of the center of the circle) and a radius. We do not use inheritance to create class `Circle`; rather, we construct the class by writing every line of code the class requires. Next, we create a `Circle2` class, which directly inherits from class `Point` (i.e., class `Circle2` *is a* `Point` that also contains a radius) and attempts to use the `private` members of class `Point`—this results in compilation errors, because the derived class does not have access to the base-class's `private` data. We then show that if `Point`'s data is declared as `protected`, a `Circle3` class that inherits from class `Point2` can access that data. Both the inherited and noninherited `Circle` classes contain identical functionality, but we show how the inherited `Circle3` class is easier to create and manage. After discussing the merits of using `protected` data, we set the `Point` data back to `private` (to enforce good software engineering), then show how a separate `Circle4` class (which inherits from class `Point3`) can use `Point3` methods and properties to manipulate `Point3`'s `private` data.

---

3. The point-circle relationship may seem unnatural when we discuss it in the context of a circle "is a" point. This example teaches what is sometimes called *structural inheritance*; the example focuses on the "mechanics" of inheritance and how a base class and a derived class relate to one another.

Creating and Using a `Point` class

Let us first examine class `Point` (Fig. 9.4–Fig. 9.5). The `public` services of class `Point` include two `Point` constructors (lines 14–15 of Fig. 9.4), properties `X` and `Y` (lines 18–37) and method `ToString` (line 39). The variables `x` and `y` of `Point` are specified as `private` (lines 41–42), so objects of other classes cannot access `x` and `y` directly. Technically, even if `Point`'s variables `x` and `y` were made `public`, `Point` can never maintain an inconsistent state, because the *x-y* coordinate plane is infinite in both directions, so `x` and `y` can hold any `int` value. In general, however, declaring data as `private`, while providing non-`private` properties to manipulate and perform validation checking on that data, enforces good software engineering.

```
1  // Fig. 9.4: Point.h
2  // Point class represents an x-y coordinate pair.
3
4  #pragma once
5
6  #using <mscorlib.dll>
7
8  using namespace System;
9
10 // Point class definition implicitly inherits from Object
11 public __gc class Point
12 {
13 public:
14    Point();                           // default constructor
15    Point( int, int );                 // constructor
16
17    // property X
18    __property int get_X()
19    {
20       return x;
21    }
22
23    __property void set_X( int value )
24    {
25       x = value;
26    }
27
28    // property Y
29    __property int get_Y()
30    {
31       return y;
32    }
33
34    __property void set_Y( int value )
35    {
36       y = value;
37    }
38
39    String *ToString();   // return string representation of Point
40
```

Fig. 9.4 `Point` class represents an *x-y* coordinate pair. (Part 1 of 2.)

```
private:
   int x, y;              // point coordinates
}; // end class Point
```

Fig. 9.4 `Point` class represents an *x-y* coordinate pair. (Part 2 of 2.)

```
1  // Fig. 9.5: Point.cpp
2  // Method definitions for class Point.
3
4  #include "stdafx.h"
5  #include "Point.h"
6
7  // default (no-argument) constructor
8  Point::Point()
9  {
10    // implicit call to Object constructor occurs here
11 }
12
13 // constructor
14 Point::Point( int xValue, int yValue )
15 {
16    // implicit call to Object constructor occurs here
17    x = xValue;
18    y = yValue;
19 }
20
21 // return string representation of Point
22 String *Point::ToString()
23 {
24    return String::Concat( S"[", x.ToString(), S", ",
25       y.ToString(), S"]" );
26 }
```

Fig. 9.5 `Point` class method definitions.

We mentioned in Section 9.2 that constructors are not inherited. Therefore, class `Point` does not inherit class `Object`'s constructor. However, class `Point`'s constructors (lines 8–19 of Fig. 9.5) call class `Object`'s constructor implicitly. In fact, the first task of any derived-class constructor is to call its direct base class's constructor, either implicitly or explicitly. (The syntax for calling a *base-class constructor* is discussed when we define class `Circle4` later in this section.) If the code does not include an explicit call to the base-class constructor, an implicit call is made to the base class's default (no-argument) constructor. The comments in lines 10 and 16 indicate where the implicit calls to the base-class `Object`'s default constructor occur. The driver (Fig. 9.6) executes the application.

Every `__gc` class in MC++ (such as class `Point`) inherits either directly or indirectly from class `System::Object`, which is the root of the class hierarchy.

Software Engineering Observation 9.4

The Visual C++ .NET compiler sets the base class of a derived class to `Object` when the program does not specify a base class explicitly.

As we mentioned previously, this means that every class inherits the eight methods defined by class `Object`. One of these methods is *`ToString`*, which returns a pointer to a `String` object. The default implementation of this method returns a string containing the object's type preceded by its namespace. Method `ToString` is sometimes called implicitly to obtain an object's string representation (such as when an object is concatenated to a string). Method `ToString` of class `Point` *overrides* the original `ToString` from class `Object`—when invoked, method `ToString` of class `Point` returns a string containing an ordered pair of the values `x` and `y` (lines 24–25 of Fig. 9.5). A derived class overrides a base class method when the derived class method requires different results from the base class method. To override a method, the derived class must define that method with the exact same header as the base class.

`PointTest` (Fig. 9.6) tests class `Point`. Line 16 instantiates an object of class `Point` and initializes the object with `72` as the *x*-coordinate value and `115` as the *y*-coordinate value. Lines 19–20 use properties `X` and `Y` to retrieve these values, then append the data to `output`. Lines 22–23 change the values of properties `X` and `Y` (implicitly invoking their *set* methods), and line 27 calls `Point`'s `ToString` method to obtain the `Point`'s string representation.

```
1  // Fig. 9.6: PointTest.cpp
2  // Testing class Point.
3
4  #include "stdafx.h"
5  #include "Point.h"
6
7  #using <mscorlib.dll>
8  #using <system.windows.forms.dll>
9
10 using namespace System;
11 using namespace System::Windows::Forms;
12
13 int _tmain()
14 {
15    // instantiate Point object
16    Point *point = new Point( 72, 115 );
17
18    // display point coordinates via X and Y properties
19    String *output = String::Concat( S"X coordinate is ",
20       point->X.ToString(), S"\nY coordinate is ", point->Y.ToString() );
21
22    point->X = 10;      // set x-coordinate via X property
23    point->Y = 10;      // set y-coordinate via Y property
24
25    // display new point value
26    output = String::Concat( output,
27       S"\n\nThe new location of point is ", point->ToString() );
28
29    MessageBox::Show( output, S"Demonstrating Class Point" );
30
31    return 0;
32 } // end _tmain
```

Fig. 9.6 `PointTest` demonstrates `Point` functionality. (Part 1 of 2.)

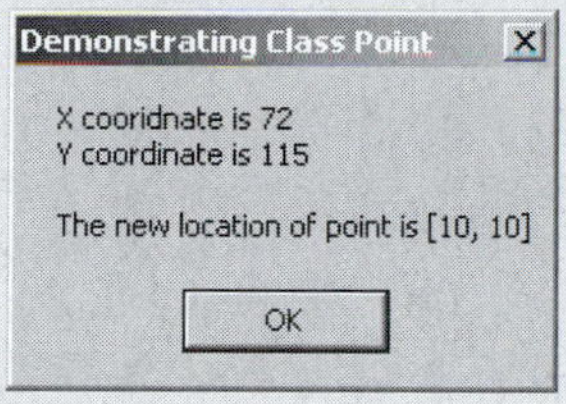

Fig. 9.6 `PointTest` demonstrates `Point` functionality. (Part 2 of 2.)

Creating a `Circle` Class without Using Inheritance

We now discuss the second part of our introduction to inheritance by creating and testing class `Circle` (Fig. 9.7–Fig. 9.8), which directly inherits from class `System::Object` and represents an *x*-*y* coordinate pair (representing the center of the circle) and a radius. Lines 58–59 (of Fig. 9.7) declare the variables `x`, `y` and `radius` as `private` data. The `public` services of class `Circle` include two `Circle` constructors (lines 14–15); properties `X`, `Y` and `Radius` (lines 18–49); and methods `Diameter`, `Circumference`, `Area` and `ToString` (lines 51–55). These properties and methods encapsulate all necessary features (i.e., the "analytic geometry") of a circle; in the next section, we show how this encapsulation enables us to reuse and extend this class. The constructor and method definitions appear in Fig. 9.8.

```
1  // Fig. 9.7: Circle.h
2  // Circle class contains x-y coordinates pair and radius.
3
4  #pragma once
5
6  #using <mscorlib.dll>
7
8  using namespace System;
9
10 // Circle class definition implicitly inherits from Object
11 public __gc class Circle
12 {
13 public:
14    Circle();                    // default constructor
15    Circle( int, int, double );  // constructor
16
17    // property X
18    __property int get_X()
19    {
20       return x;
21    }
22
23    __property void set_X( int value )
24    {
25       x = value;
26    }
```

Fig. 9.7 `Circle` class contains an *x*-*y* coordinate and a radius. (Part 1 of 2.)

```

   // property Y
   __property int get_Y()
   {
      return y;
   }

   __property void set_Y( int value )
   {
      y = value;
   }

   // property Radius
   __property double get_Radius()
   {
      return radius;
   }

   __property void set_Radius( double value )
   {
      if ( value >= 0 )    // validation needed
         radius = value;
   }

   double Diameter();      // calculate diameter
   double Circumference(); // calculate circumference
   double Area();          // calculate area

   String *ToString();     // return string representation of Circle

private:
   int x, y;               // coordinates of Circle's center
   double radius;          // Circle's radius
}; // end class Circle
```

Fig. 9.7 `Circle` class contains an *x-y* coordinate and a radius. (Part 2 of 2.)

```
// Fig. 9.8: Circle.cpp
// Method definitions for class Circle.

#include "stdafx.h"
#include "Circle.h"

// default constructor
Circle::Circle()
{
   // implicit call to Object constructor occurs here
}

// constructor
Circle::Circle( int xValue, int yValue, double radiusValue )
{
```

Fig. 9.8 `Circle` class method definitions. (Part 1 of 2.)

```
    // implicit call to Object constructor occurs here
    x = xValue;
    y = yValue;
    radius = radiusValue;
}

// calculate diameter
double Circle::Diameter()
{
    return radius * 2;
}

// calculate circumference
double Circle::Circumference()
{
    return Math::PI * Diameter();
}

// calculate area
double Circle::Area()
{
    return Math::PI * Math::Pow( radius, 2 );
}

// return string representation of Circle
String *Circle::ToString()
{
    return String::Concat( S"Center = [", x.ToString(),
        S", ", y.ToString(), S"]; Radius = ", radius.ToString() );
}
```

Fig. 9.8 `Circle` class method definitions. (Part 2 of 2.)

`CircleTest` (Fig. 9.9) tests class `Circle`. Line 16 instantiates an object of class `Circle` and initializes it with `37` as the *x*-coordinate value, `43` as the *y*-coordinate value and `2.5` as the radius value. Lines 19–22 use properties `X`, `Y` and `Radius` to retrieve these values, then concatenate the data to `output`. Lines 25–27 use `Circle`'s `X`, `Y` and `Radius` properties to change the *x*-*y* coordinates and the radius, respectively. Property `Radius` ensures that member variable `radius` cannot be assigned a negative value (lines 47–48 of Fig. 9.7). Lines 30–31 (of Fig. 9.9) call `Circle`'s `ToString` method to obtain the `Circle`'s string representation, and lines 34–43 call `Circle`'s `Diameter`, `Circumference` and `Area` methods.

```
1  // Fig. 9.9: CircleTest.cpp
2  // Testing class Circle.
3
4  #include "stdafx.h"
5  #include "Circle.h"
6
7  #using <mscorlib.dll>
8  #using <system.windows.forms.dll>
```

Fig. 9.9 `CircleTest` demonstrates `Circle` functionality. (Part 1 of 2.)

```
using namespace System;
using namespace System::Windows::Forms;

int _tmain()
{
   // instantiate Circle
   Circle *circle = new Circle( 37, 43, 2.5 );

   // get Circle's initial x-y coordinates and radius
   String *output = String::Concat( S"X coordinate is ",
      circle->X.ToString(), S"\nY coordinate is ",
      circle->Y.ToString(), S"\nRadius is ",
      circle->Radius.ToString() );

   // set Circle's x-y coordinates and radius to new values
   circle->X = 2;
   circle->Y = 2;
   circle->Radius = 4.25;

   // display Circle's string representation
   output = String::Concat( output, S"\n\nThe new location and "
      S"radius of circle are \n", circle->ToString(), S"\n" );

   // display diameter
   output = String::Concat( output, S"Diameter is ",
      circle->Diameter().ToString( S"F" ), S"\n" );

   // display circumference
   output = String::Concat( output, S"Circumference is ",
      circle->Circumference().ToString( S"F" ), S"\n" );

   // display area
   output = String::Concat( output, S"Area is ",
      circle->Area().ToString( S"F" ) );

   MessageBox::Show( output, S"Demonstrating Class Circle" );

   return 0;
} // end _tmain
```

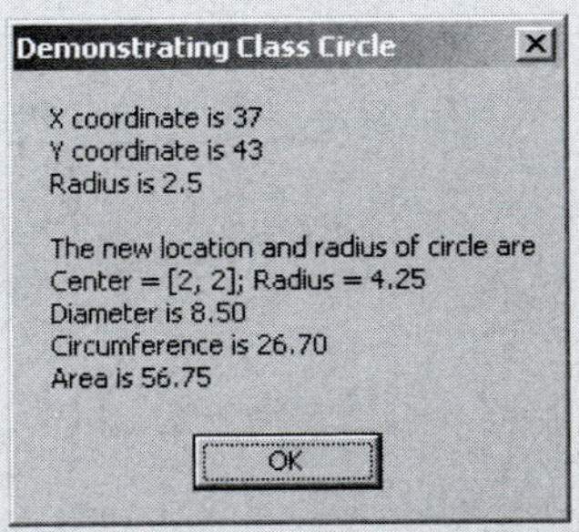

Demonstrating Class Circle
X coordinate is 37
Y coordinate is 43
Radius is 2.5
The new location and radius of circle are
Center = [2, 2]; Radius = 4.25
Diameter is 8.50
Circumference is 26.70
Area is 56.75
OK

Fig. 9.9 `CircleTest` demonstrates `Circle` functionality. (Part 2 of 2.)

After writing all the code for class `Circle` (Fig. 9.7–Fig. 9.8), we note that a major portion of the code in this class is similar, if not identical, to much of the code in class `Point`. For example, the declaration in `Circle` of `private` variables `x` and `y` and properties `X` and `Y` are identical to those of class `Point`. In addition, the class `Circle` constructors and method `ToString` are almost identical to those of class `Point`, except that they also supply `radius` information. The only other additions to class `Circle` are `private` data member `radius`, property `Radius` and methods `Diameter`, `Circumference` and `Area`.

It appears that we literally copied code from class `Point`, pasted this code in the code from class `Circle`, then modified class `Circle` to include a radius. This "copy-and-paste" approach is often error-prone and time-consuming. Worse yet, it can result in many physical copies of the code existing throughout a system, creating a code-maintenance "nightmare." Is there a way to "absorb" the attributes and behaviors of one class in a way that makes them part of other classes without duplicating code? In the next examples we answer that question, using a more elegant class construction approach emphasizing the benefits of inheritance.

`Point-Circle` Hierarchy Using Inheritance

Now, we create and test a class `Circle2` (Fig. 9.10–Fig. 9.11) that inherits variables `x` and `y` and properties `X` and `Y` from class `Point` (Fig. 9.4). This class `Circle2` *is a* `Point` (because inheritance absorbs the capabilities of class `Point`), but also contains its own member `radius` (line 34 of Fig. 9.10). The *colon (:) symbol* in the class declaration (line 9) indicates inheritance. As a derived class, `Circle2` inherits all the members of class `Point`, except for the constructors. Thus, the `public` services to `Circle2` include the two `Circle2` constructors (lines 12–13); the `public` methods inherited from class `Point`; property `Radius` (lines 16–25); and the `Circle2` methods `Diameter`, `Circumference`, `Area` and `ToString` (lines 27–31).

```
1  // Fig. 9.10: Circle2.h
2  // Circle2 class that inherits from class Point.
3
4  #pragma once
5
6  #include "Point.h"
7
8  // Circle2 class definition inherits from Point
9  public __gc class Circle2 : public Point
10 {
11 public:
12    Circle2();                          // default constructor
13    Circle2( int, int, double );        // constructor
14
15    // property Radius
16    __property double get_Radius()
17    {
18       return radius;
19    }
20
```

Fig. 9.10 `Circle2` class that inherits from class `Point`. (Part 1 of 2.)

```
   __property void set_Radius( double value )
   {
      if ( value >= 0 )
         radius = value;
   }

   double Diameter();
   double Circumference();
   double Area();

   String *ToString(); // return string representation of Circle2

private:
   double radius;      // Circle2's radius
}; // end class Circle2
```

Fig. 9.10 Circle2 class that inherits from class Point. (Part 2 of 2.)

```
// Fig. 9.11: Circle2.cpp
// Method definitions for class Circle2.

#include "stdafx.h"
#include "Point.h"
#include "Circle2.h"

// default constructor
Circle2::Circle2()
{
   // implicit call to Point constructor occurs here
}

// constructor
Circle2::Circle2( int xValue, int yValue, double radiusValue )
{
   // implicit call to Point constructor occurs here
   x = xValue;
   y = yValue;
   Radius = radiusValue;
}

// calculate diameter
double Circle2::Diameter()
{
   return radius * 2;
}

// calculate circumference
double Circle2::Circumference()
{
   return Math::PI * Diameter();
}
```

Fig. 9.11 Circle2 class method definitions. (Part 1 of 2.)

```
34
35 // calculate area
36 double Circle2::Area()
37 {
38    return Math::PI * Math::Pow( radius, 2 );
39 }
40
41 // return string representation of Circle2
42 String *Circle2::ToString()
43 {
44    return String::Concat( S"Center = [", x.ToString(),
45       y.ToString(), S"]; Radius = ", radius.ToString() );
46 }
```

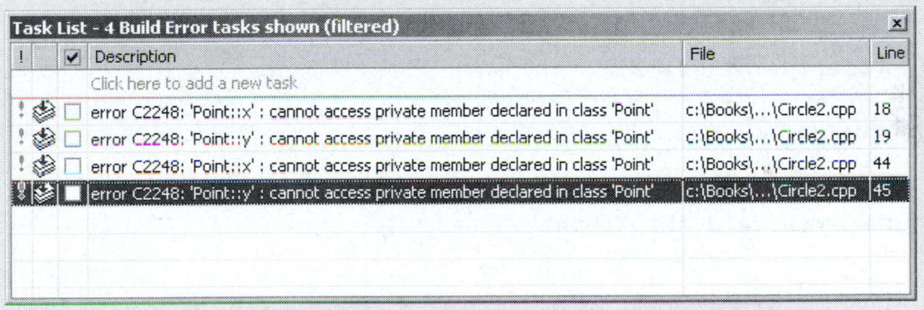

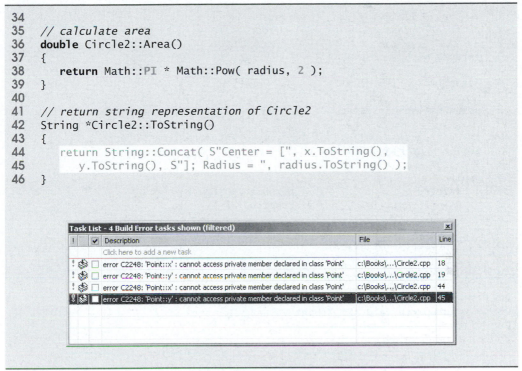

Fig. 9.11 `Circle2` class method definitions. (Part 2 of 2.)

Lines 11 and 17 of Fig. 9.11 demonstrate when the default `Point` constructor will be invoked, initializing the base-class portion (variables `x` and `y`, inherited from class `Point`) of a `Circle2` object to `0`. However, because the parameterized constructor (lines 15–21) should set the *x-y* coordinate to a specific value, lines 18–19 attempt to assign argument values to `x` and `y` directly. Even though lines 18–19 attempt to set `x` and `y` values explicitly, line 17 first calls the `Point` default constructor to initialize these variables to their default values. The compiler generates syntax errors for lines 18–19 (and lines 44–45, where `Circle2`'s method `ToString` attempts to use the values of `x` and `y` directly), because the derived class `Circle2` is not allowed to access the base class `Point`'s `private` members `x` and `y`. MC++ rigidly enforces restriction on accessing `private` data members, so that even a derived class (i.e., which is closely related to its base class) cannot access base-class `private` data.

`Point`-`Circle` Hierarchy Using `protected` Data

To enable class `Circle2` to access `Point` member variables `x` and `y` directly, we can declare those variables as `protected`. As we discussed in Section 9.3, a base class's `protected` members can be accessed only in that base class or in any classes derived from that base class. Our next example defines classes `Point2` and `Circle3`. Class `Point2` (Fig. 9.12–Fig. 9.13) modifies class `Point` (Fig. 9.4) to declare variables `x` and `y` as `protected` (Fig. 9.12, line 43) instead of `private`. Class `Circle3` (Fig. 9.14–Fig. 9.15) inherits from class `Point2`.

```
// Fig. 9.12: Point2.h
// Point2 class contains an x-y coordinate pair as protected data.

#pragma once

#using <mscorlib.dll>

using namespace System;

// Point2 class definition implicitly inherits from Object
public __gc class Point2
{
public:
   Point2();                  // default constructor
   Point2( int, int );        // constructor

   // property X
   __property int get_X()
   {
      return x;
   }

   __property void set_X( int value )
   {
      x = value;
   }

   // property Y
   __property int get_Y()
   {
      return y;
   }

   __property void set_Y( int value )
   {
      y = value;
   }

   // return string representation of Point2
   String *ToString();

protected:
   int x, y;                 // point coordinate
}; // end class Point2
```

Fig. 9.12 `Point2` class represents an *x*-*y*-coordinate pair as `protected` data.

```
// Fig. 9.13: Point2.cpp
// Method definitions for class Point2.

#include "stdafx.h"
#include "Point2.h"
```

Fig. 9.13 `Point2` class method definitions. (Part 1 of 2.)

```

// default constructor
Point2::Point2()
{
   // implicit call to Object constructor occurs here
}

// constructor
Point2::Point2( int xValue, int yValue )
{
   // implicit call to Object constructor occurs here
   x = xValue;
   y = yValue;
}

// return string representation of Point2
String *Point2::ToString()
{
   return String::Concat( S"[", x.ToString(),
      S", ", y.ToString(), S"]" );
}
```

Fig. 9.13 `Point2` class method definitions. (Part 2 of 2.)

Class `Circle3` (Fig. 9.14–Fig. 9.15) modifies class `Circle2` (Fig. 9.10–Fig. 9.11) to inherit from class `Point2` rather than inheriting from class `Point`. As a derived class of class `Point2`, class `Circle3` can access class `Point2`'s `protected` data members `x` and `y` directly. This shows the special privileges that a derived class is granted to access `protected` base-class data members. A derived class also can access its base class's `protected` properties and methods. The driver (Fig. 9.16) executes the application.

```
// Fig. 9.14: Circle3.h
// Circle2 class that inherits from class Point2.

#pragma once

#include "Point2.h"

public __gc class Circle3 : public Point2
{
public:
   Circle3();                        // default constructor
   Circle3( int, int, double );      // constructor

   // property Radius
   __property double get_Radius()
   {
      return radius;
   }

```

Fig. 9.14 `Circle3` class that inherits from `Point2`. (Part 1 of 2.)

```
   __property void set_Radius( double value )
   {
      if ( value >= 0 )
         radius = value;
   }

   double Diameter();            // calculate diameter
   double Circumference();       // calculate circumference
   double Area();                // calculate area

   // return string representation of Circle3
   String *ToString();

private:
   double radius;                // Circle3's radius
}; // end class Circle3
```

Fig. 9.14 `Circle3` class that inherits from `Point2`. (Part 2 of 2.)

```
// Fig. 9.15: Circle3.cpp
// Method definitions for class Circle3.

#include "stdafx.h"
#include "Circle3.h"

// default constructor
Circle3::Circle3()
{
   // implicit call to Point2 constructor occurs here
}

// constructor
Circle3::Circle3( int xValue, int yValue, double radiusValue )
{
   // implicit call to Point2 constructor occurs here
   x = xValue;
   y = yValue;
   Radius = radiusValue;
}

// calculate diameter
double Circle3::Diameter()
{
   return radius * 2;
}

// calculate circumference
double Circle3::Circumference()
{
   return Math::PI * Diameter();
}

```

Fig. 9.15 `Circle3` class method definitions. (Part 1 of 2.)

```
// calculate area
double Circle3::Area()
{
   return Math::PI * Math::Pow( radius, 2 );
}

// return string representation of Circle3
String *Circle3::ToString()
{
   return String::Concat( S"Center = [", x.ToString(),
      S", ", y.ToString(), S"]; Radius = ", radius.ToString() );
}
```

Fig. 9.15 `Circle3` class method definitions. (Part 2 of 2.)

```
// Fig. 9.16: CircleTest3.cpp
// Testing class Circle3.

#include "stdafx.h"
#include "Circle3.h"

#using <mscorlib.dll>
#using <system.windows.forms.dll>

using namespace System;
using namespace System::Windows::Forms;

int _tmain()
{
   // instantiate Circle3
   Circle3 *circle = new Circle3( 37, 43, 2.5 );

   // get Circle3's initial x-y coordinates and radius
   String *output = String::Concat( S"X coordinate is ",
      circle->X.ToString(), S"\nY coordinate is ",
      circle->Y.ToString(), S"\nRadius is ",
      circle->Radius.ToString() );

   // set Circle3's x-y coordinates and radius to new values
   circle->X = 2;
   circle->Y = 2;
   circle->Radius = 4.25;

   // display Circle3's string representation
   output = String::Concat( output, S"\n\n",
      S"The new location and radius of circle are\n",
      circle, S"\n" );

   // display diameter
   output = String::Concat( output, S"Diameter is ",
      circle->Diameter().ToString( S"F" ), S"\n" );

```

Fig. 9.16 `CircleTest3` demonstrates `Circle3` functionality. (Part 1 of 2.)

```
      // display circumference
      output = String::Concat( output, S"Circumference is ",
         circle->Circumference().ToString( S"F" ), S"\n" );

      // display area
      output = String::Concat( output, S"Area is ",
         circle->Area().ToString( S"F" ) );

      MessageBox::Show( output, S"Demonstrating Class Circle3" );

      return 0;
   } // end _tmain
```

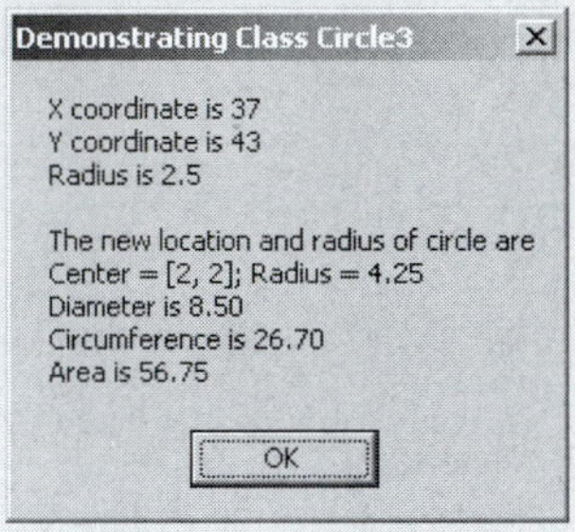
Demonstrating Class Circle3
X coordinate is 37
Y coordinate is 43
Radius is 2.5
The new location and radius of circle are
Center = [2, 2]; Radius = 4.25
Diameter is 8.50
Circumference is 26.70
Area is 56.75
OK

Fig. 9.16 `CircleTest3` demonstrates `Circle3` functionality. (Part 2 of 2.)

`CircleTest3` (Fig. 9.16) performs identical tests on class `Circle3` as `CircleTest` (Fig. 9.9) performed on class `Circle`. Note that the outputs of the two programs are identical. We created class `Circle` without using inheritance and created class `Circle3` using inheritance; however, both classes provide the same functionality. Also, there is now only one copy of the point functionality.

In the previous example, we declared the base-class data members as `protected`, so that a derived class could modify their values directly. The use of `protected` variables allows for a slight increase in performance, because we avoid incurring the overhead of a method call to a property's *set* or *get* method. However, in most MC++ applications in which user interaction comprises a large part of the execution time, the optimization offered through the use of `protected` variables is negligible.

Using `protected` data members creates two major problems. First, the derived-class object does not have to use a property to set the value of the base-class's `protected` data. Therefore, a derived-class object can easily assign an inappropriate value to the `protected` data, thus leaving the object in an inconsistent state. For example, if we were to declare `Circle3`'s data member `radius` as `protected`, a derived-class object (e.g., `Cylinder`) could then assign a negative value to `radius`. The second problem with using `protected` data is that derived-class methods are more likely to be written to depend on base-class implementation. In practice, derived classes should depend only on the base-class services (i.e., non-`private` methods and properties) and not on base-class implementation. With `protected` data in the base class, if the base-class implementation changes, we may need to modify all derived classes of that base class. For example, if for some reason we were to change the names of variables `x` and `y` to `xCoordinate` and `yCoordinate`, then we would have to do so for all occurrences in which a derived class references these base-class variables directly. In such a case, the software is said to be *fragile* or *brittle*. The programmer should be able to change the base-class implementation freely, while still providing the same services to derived classes. (Of course, if the base-class services change, we must reimplement our derived classes. However, good object-oriented design attempts to prevent this.)

Software Engineering Observation 9.5

The most appropriate time to use the `protected` *access specifier is when a base class should provide a service only to its derived classes (i.e., the base class should not provide the service to other clients).*

Software Engineering Observation 9.6

Declaring base-class data members `private` *(as opposed to declaring them* `protected`*) enables programmers to change base-class implementation without having to change derived-class implementations.*

Error-Prevention Tip 9.1

When possible, avoid including `protected` *data in a base class. Rather, include non-*`private` *properties and methods that access* `private` *data, ensuring that the object maintains a consistent state.*

`Point`-`Circle` *Hierarchy Using* `private` *Data*

We re-examine our point-circle hierarchy example once more; this time, we attempt to use the best software engineering techniques. We use `Point3` (Fig. 9.17–Fig. 9.18), which declares variables `x` and `y` as `private` and uses properties in method `ToString` to access these values. We show how derived class `Circle4` (Fig. 9.19–Fig. 9.20) can invoke non-`private` base-class methods and properties to manipulate these variables. The driver (Fig. 9.21) executes the application.

Software Engineering Observation 9.7

When possible, use properties to alter and obtain the values of member variables, even if those values can be modified directly. A property's set *method can prevent attempts to assign an inappropriate value to that member variable, and a property's* get *method can help control the presentation of the data to clients.*

Performance Tip 9.1

Using a property to access a variable's value is slightly slower than accessing the data directly. However, attempting to optimize programs by referencing data directly often is unnecessary, because the compiler optimizes the programs implicitly. Today's so-called "optimizing compilers" are carefully designed to perform many optimizations implicitly, even if the programmer does not write what appears to be the most optimal code. A good rule is, "Do not second-guess the compiler."

```
// Fig. 9.17: Point3.h
// Point3 class represents an x-y coordinate pair.

#pragma once

#using <mscorlib.dll>
```

Fig. 9.17 `Point3` class uses properties to manipulate `private` data. (Part 1 of 2.)

```

using namespace System;

public __gc class Point3
{
public:
   Point3();              // default constructor
   Point3( int, int );    // constructor

   // property X
   __property int get_X()
   {
      return x;
   }

   __property void set_X( int value )
   {
      x = value;
   }

   // property Y
   __property int get_Y()
   {
      return y;
   }

   __property void set_Y( int value )
   {
      y = value;
   }

   // return string representation of Point3
   String *ToString();

private:
   int x, y;              // point coordinate
}; // end class Point3
```

Fig. 9.17 Point3 class uses properties to manipulate private data. (Part 2 of 2.)

```
// Fig. 9.18: Point3.cpp
// Method definitions for class Point3.

#include "stdafx.h"
#include "Point3.h"

// default constructor
Point3::Point3()
{
   // implicit call to Object constructor occurs here
}

```

Fig. 9.18 Point3 class method definitions. (Part 1 of 2.)

```
// constructor
Point3::Point3( int xValue, int yValue )
{
   // implicit call to Object constructor occurs here
   x = xValue;              // use property X
   y = yValue;              // use property Y
}

// return string representation of Point3
String *Point3::ToString()
{
   return String::Concat( S"[", X.ToString(), S", ",
      Y.ToString(), S"]" );
}
```

Fig. 9.18 Point3 class method definitions. (Part 2 of 2.)

```
// Fig. 9.19: Circle4.h
// Circle4 class that inherits from class Point3.

#pragma once

#include "Point3.h"

// Circle4 class definition inherits from Point3
public __gc class Circle4 : public Point3
{
public:
   Circle4();                         // default constructor
   Circle4( int, int, double );       // constructor

   // property Radius
   __property double get_Radius()
   {
      return radius;
   }

   __property void set_Radius( double value )
   {
      if ( value >= 0 )               // validation needed
         radius = value;
   }

   double Diameter();              // calculate diameter
   double Circumference();         // calculate circumference
   double Area();                  // calculate area

   // return string representation of Circle4
   String *ToString();

```

Fig. 9.19 Circle4 class that inherits from Point3, which does not provide protected data. (Part 1 of 2.)

```
private:
   double radius;
}; // end class Circle4
```

Fig. 9.19 `Circle4` class that inherits from `Point3`, which does not provide `protected` data. (Part 2 of 2.)

```
// Fig. 9.20: Circle4.cpp
// Method definitions for class Circle4.

#include "stdafx.h"
#include "Circle4.h"

// default constructor
Circle4::Circle4()
{
   // implicit call to Point3 constructor occurs here
}

// constructor
Circle4::Circle4( int xValue, int yValue, double radiusValue )
   : Point3( xValue, yValue )
{
   Radius = radiusValue;
}

// calculate diameter
double Circle4::Diameter()
{
   return Radius * 2;    // use property Radius
}

// calculate circumference
double Circle4::Circumference()
{
   return Math::PI * Diameter();
}

// calculate area
double Circle4::Area()
{
   return Math::PI * Math::Pow( Radius, 2 ); // user property
}

// return string representation of Circle4
String *Circle4::ToString()
{
   // return Point3 string representation
   return String::Concat( S"Center= ", __super::ToString(),
      S"; Radius = ", Radius.ToString() ); //use property Radius
}
```

Fig. 9.20 `Circle4` class method definitions.

```
// Fig. 9.21: CircleTest4.cpp
// Testing class Circle4.

#include "stdafx.h"
#include "Circle4.h"

#using <mscorlib.dll>
#using <system.windows.forms.dll>

using namespace System;
using namespace System::Windows::Forms;

int _tmain()
{
   // instantiate Circle4
   Circle4 *circle = new Circle4( 37, 43, 2.5 );

   // get Circle4's initial x-y coordinates and radius
   String *output = String::Concat( S"X coordinate is ",
      circle->X.ToString(), S"\nY coordinate is ",
      circle->Y.ToString(), S"\nRadius is ",
      circle->Radius.ToString() );

   // set Circle4's x-y coordinates and radius to new values
   circle->X = 2;
   circle->Y = 2;
   circle->Radius = 4.25;

   // display Circle4's string representation
   output = String::Concat( output, S"\n\n",
      S"The new location and radius of circle are\n",
      circle, S"\n" );

   // display diameter
   output = String::Concat( output, S"Diameter is ",
      circle->Diameter().ToString( S"F" ), S"\n" );

   // display circumference
   output = String::Concat( output, S"Circumference is ",
      circle->Circumference().ToString( S"F" ), S"\n" );

   // display area
   output = String::Concat( output, S"Area is ",
      circle->Area().ToString( S"F" ) );

   MessageBox::Show( output, S"Demonstrating Class Circle4" );

   return 0;
} // end _tmain
```

Fig. 9.21 CircleTest4 demonstrates Circle4 functionality. (Part 1 of 2.)

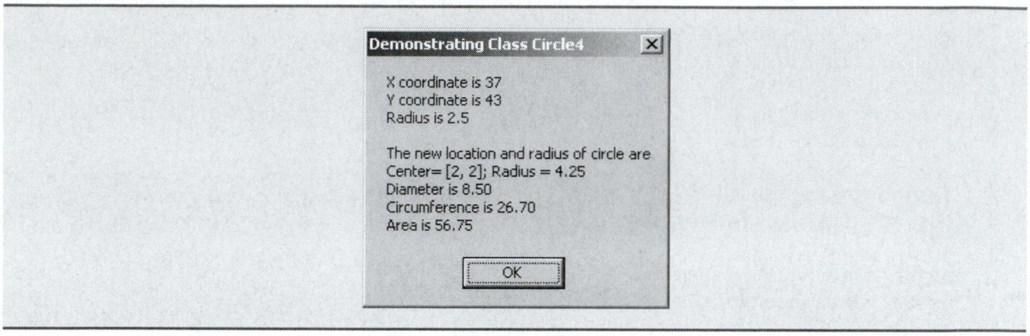
Demonstrating Class Circle4
X coordinate is 37
Y coordinate is 43
Radius is 2.5
The new location and radius of circle are
Center= [2, 2]; Radius = 4.25
Diameter is 8.50
Circumference is 26.70
Area is 56.75
OK

Fig. 9.21 `CircleTest4` demonstrates `Circle4` functionality. (Part 2 of 2.)

For the purpose of this example, to demonstrate both explicit and implicit calls to base-class constructors, we include a second constructor that calls the base-class constructor explicitly. Lines 14–18 (Fig. 9.20) declare the `Circle4` constructor that invokes the second `Point3` constructor explicitly (line 15 of Fig. 9.20). In this case, `xValue` and `yValue` are passed to initialize the `private` base-class members `x` and `y`. The colon symbol (`:`) followed by the class name calls the base-class constructor explicitly. By making this call, we can initialize `x` and `y` in the base class to specific values, rather than to `0`.

Class `Circle4`'s `ToString` method (lines 39–44 of Fig. 9.20) overrides class `Point3`'s `ToString` method (lines 22–26 of Fig. 9.18). Method `ToString` of class `Circle4` displays the `private` variables `x` and `y` of class `Point3` by calling the base class's `ToString` method (in this case, `Point3`'s `ToString` method). The call is made in line 42 of Fig. 9.20 via the expression `__super::ToString()` (discussed shortly) and causes the values of `x` and `y` to become part of the `Circle4`'s string representation. Proceeding the method name with `__super` and the scope resolution operator specifies that the base-class version of a method should be called. Using this approach is a good software engineering practice: class `Point3`'s `ToString` method performs part of the task that we would like class `Circle4`'s `ToString` method to perform, so we call `Point3`'s ToString from class `Circle4`'s `ToString` rather than duplicating the code. Note that the expression `__super::ToString()` is equivalent to `Point3::ToString()`. However, we do not use keyword `__super` in line 15 of Fig. 9.20; rather, we specify class `Point3` explicitly. This is because keyword `__super` can appear only in the body of a method.

Software Engineering Observation 9.8

Although method `ToString` certainly could be overridden to perform arbitrary actions, the general understanding in the .NET community is that method `ToString` should be overridden to obtain an object's string representation.

Common Programming Error 9.2

When a base-class method is overridden in a derived class, the derived-class version often calls the base-class version to do additional work. Failure to use the `__super` keyword followed by the binary resolution operator (`::`) when referencing the base class's method causes infinite recursion, because using the name of the method by itself would cause the derived-class method to call itself.

`CircleTest4` (Fig. 9.21) performs identical manipulations on class `Circle4` (Fig. 9.19–Fig. 9.20) as did classes `CircleTest` (Fig. 9.9) and `CircleTest3` (Fig. 9.16). Note that the outputs of all three examples are identical. Although each "circle" class behaves identically, class `Circle4` uses the best software engineering. Using inheritance, we have efficiently and effectively constructed a well-engineered class.

9.5 Example: Three-Level Inheritance Hierarchy

Let us consider a more substantial inheritance example involving a three-level point-circle-cylinder hierarchy. In Section 9.4, we developed classes `Point3` (Fig. 9.17–Fig. 9.18) and `Circle4` (Fig. 9.19–Fig. 9.20). Now, we present an example in which we derive class `Cylinder` from class `Circle4`.

The first class that we use in our example is class `Point3` (Fig. 9.17–Fig. 9.18). We declared `Point3`'s data members as `private`. Class `Point3` also contains properties `X` and `Y` for accessing `x` and `y`, and method `ToString` (which `Point3` overrides from class `Object`) for obtaining a string representation of the *x*-*y* coordinate pair.

We also created class `Circle4` (Fig. 9.19–Fig. 9.20), which inherits from class `Point3`. In addition, `Circle4` provides property `Radius` (which ensures that the `radius` data member cannot hold a negative value) and methods `Diameter`, `Circumference`, `Area` and `ToString`.

Figure 9.22–Fig. 9.23 presents class `Cylinder`, which inherits from class `Circle4` (line 9 of Fig. 9.22). Class `Cylinder`'s `public` services include the inherited `Circle4` methods `Diameter`, `Circumference`, `Area` and `ToString`; the inherited `Circle4` property `Radius`; the indirectly inherited `Point3` properties `X` and `Y`; the `Cylinder` constructor, property `Height` and method `Volume`.

Figure 9.23 shows class `Cylinder`'s method definitions. Method `Area` (lines 21–24) redefines method `Area` of class `Circle4` to calculate the surface area. Method `ToString` (lines 33–37 of Fig. 9.23) obtains a string representation for the cylinder. Class `Cylinder` also includes method `Volume` (lines 27–30 of Fig. 9.23) to calculate the cylinder's volume.

```
1  // Fig. 9.22: Cylinder.h
2  // Cylinder class that inherits from class Circle4.
3
4  #pragma once
5
6  #include "Circle4.h"
7
8  // Cylinder class definition inherits from Circle4
9  public __gc class Cylinder : public Circle4
10 {
11 public:
12    Cylinder();                                 // default constructor
13    Cylinder( int, int, double, double );      // constructor
14
15    // property Height
16    __property double get_Height()
17    {
18       return height;
19    }
```

Fig. 9.22 `Cylinder` class inherits from `Circle4` and overrides method `Area`. (Part 1 of 2.)

```
   __property void set_Height( double value )
   {
      if ( value >= 0 )       // validate height
         height = value;
   }

   // override Circle4 method Area to calculate Cylinder Area
   double Area();             // calculate area
   double Volume();           // calculate volume
   String *ToString();        // convert Cylinder to string

private:
   double height;
}; // end class Cylinder
```

Fig. 9.22 Cylinder class inherits from Circle4 and overrides method Area. (Part 2 of 2.)

```
// Fig. 9.23: Cylinder.cpp
// Method definitions for class Cylinder.

#include "stdafx.h"
#include "Cylinder.h"

// default constructor
Cylinder::Cylinder()
{
   // implicit call to Circle4 constructor occurs here
}

// constructor
Cylinder::Cylinder( int xValue, int yValue, double radiusValue,
   double heightValue ) : Circle4( xValue, yValue, radiusValue )
{
   height = heightValue;
}

// override Circle4 method Area to calculate Cylinder Area
double Cylinder::Area()
{
   return 2 * __super::Area() + __super::Circumference() * Height;
}

// calculate volume
double Cylinder::Volume()
{
   return __super::Area() * Height;
}

```

Fig. 9.23 Cylinder class method definitions. (Part 1 of 2.)

```
// convert Cylinder to string
String *Cylinder::ToString()
{
   return String::Concat( __super::ToString(),
      S"; Height = ", Height.ToString() );
}
```

Fig. 9.23 `Cylinder` class method definitions. (Part 2 of 2.)

`CylinderTest` (Fig. 9.24) tests class `Cylinder`. Line 16 instantiates an object of class `Cylinder`. Lines 19–23 use properties `X`, `Y`, `Radius` and `Height` to obtain information about the `Cylinder` object, because `CylinderTest` cannot reference the `private` data of class `Cylinder` directly. Lines 26–29 use properties `X`, `Y`, `Radius` and `Height` to reset the `Cylinder`'s *x-y* coordinates (we assume the cylinder's *x-y* coordinates specify its position on the *x-y* plane), radius and height. Class `Cylinder` can use class `Point3`'s `X` and `Y` properties, because class `Cylinder` inherits them indirectly from class `Point3`—class `Cylinder` inherits properties `X` and `Y` directly from class `Circle4`, which inherited them directly from class `Point3`. Line 33 invokes method `ToString` implicitly to obtain the string representation of the `Cylinder` object. Lines 36–41 invoke methods `Diameter` and `Circumference` that were inherited from `Circle4`. Lines 44–49 invoke methods `Area` and `Volume`. Class `Cylinder` redefines method `Area`, so class `Cylinder`'s version is called in line 45.

```
1  // Fig. 9.24: CylinderTest.cpp
2  // Tests class Cylinder.
3
4  #include "stdafx.h"
5  #include "Cylinder.h"
6
7  #using <mscorlib.dll>
8  #using <system.windows.forms.dll>
9
10 using namespace System;
11 using namespace System::Windows::Forms;
12
13 int _tmain()
14 {
15    // instantiate object of class Cylinder
16    Cylinder *cylinder = new Cylinder( 12, 23, 2.5, 5.7 );
17
18    // properties get initial x-y coordinates, radius and height
19    String *output = String::Concat( S"X coordinate is ",
20       cylinder->X.ToString(), S"\nY coordinate is ",
21       cylinder->Y.ToString(), S"\nRadius is ",
22       cylinder->Radius.ToString(), S"\nHeight is ",
23       cylinder->Height.ToString() );
24
25    // properties set new x-y coordinate, radius and height
26    cylinder->X = 2;
```

Fig. 9.24 `CylinderTest` demonstrates `Cylinder` functionality. (Part 1 of 2.)

```
   cylinder->Y = 2;
   cylinder->Radius = 4.25;
   cylinder->Height = 10;

   // get new x-y coordinate and radius
   output = String::Concat( output, S"\n\nThe new location, ",
      S"radius and height of cylinder are\n", cylinder, S"\n\n" );

   // display diameter
   output = String::Concat( output, S"Diameter is ",
      cylinder->Diameter().ToString( S"F" ), S"\n" );

   // display circumference
   output = String::Concat( output, S"Circumference is ",
      cylinder->Circumference().ToString( S"F" ), S"\n" );

   // display area
   output = String::Concat ( output, S"Area is ",
      cylinder->Area().ToString( S"F" ), S"\n" );

   // display volume
   output = String::Concat( output, S"Volume is ",
      cylinder->Volume().ToString( S"F" ) );

   MessageBox::Show( output, S"Demonstrating Class Cylinder" );

   return 0;
} // end _tmain
```

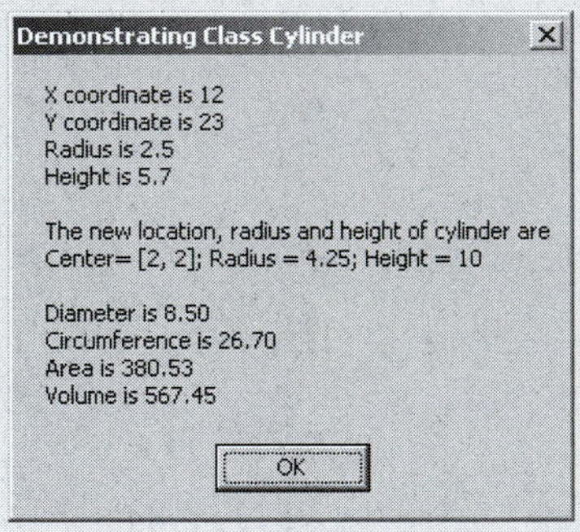

Demonstrating Class Cylinder
X coordinate is 12
Y coordinate is 23
Radius is 2.5
Height is 5.7
The new location, radius and height of cylinder are
Center= [2, 2]; Radius = 4.25; Height = 10
Diameter is 8.50
Circumference is 26.70
Area is 380.53
Volume is 567.45
OK

Fig. 9.24 `CylinderTest` demonstrates `Cylinder` functionality. (Part 2 of 2.)

Using the point-circle-cylinder example, we have shown the use and benefits of inheritance. We were able to develop classes `Circle4` and `Cylinder` using inheritance much faster than if we had developed these classes "from scratch." Inheritance avoids duplicating code and the associated code-maintenance problems.

9.6 Constructors and Destructors in Derived Classes

As we explained in the previous section, instantiating a derived-class object begins a chain of constructor calls in which the derived-class constructor, before performing its own tasks, invokes the base-class constructor either explicitly or implicitly. Similarly, if the base-class was derived from another class, the base-class constructor must invoke the constructor of the next class up in the hierarchy, and so on. The last constructor called in the chain is class `Object`'s constructor whose body actually finishes executing first—the original derived class constructor's body finishes executing last. Each base-class constructor initializes the base-class data members that the derived-class object inherits from that base class. For example, consider the `Point3`/`Circle4` hierarchy. When a program creates a `Circle4` object, one of the `Circle4` constructors is called. That constructor calls class one of `Point3`'s constructors, which in turn calls class `Object`'s constructor. When class `Object`'s constructor completes execution, it returns control to class `Point3`'s constructor, which initializes the *x*-*y* coordinates of the `Circle4` object. When class `Point3`'s constructor completes execution, it returns control to class `Circle4`'s constructor, which initializes the `Circle4` object's radius.

Software Engineering Observation 9.9

When a program creates a derived-class object, the derived-class constructor immediately calls the base-class constructor, the base-class constructor's body executes, then the derived-class constructor's body executes.

When the garbage collector removes a derived-class object from memory, the garbage collector calls that object's destructor. This begins a chain of destructor calls in which the derived-class destructor and the destructors of the direct and indirect base classes execute in the reverse order of the order in which the constructors executed. Executing the destructors should free all the resources the object acquired before the *garbage collector* reclaims the memory for that object. When the garbage collector calls a derived-class object's destructor, the destructor performs its task, then invokes the destructor of the base class. This process repeats until class `Object`'s destructor is called.

Software Engineering Observation 9.10

Like constructors, destructors are never inherited—they are specific to the class in which they are defined.

MC++ actually implements a class's destructor (such as `~Point`) using class `Object`'s *`Finalize`* method (one of the eight methods that every `__gc` class inherits). When compiling a class definition that contains a destructor, the compiler translates a destructor definition into a `Finalize` method that performs the destructor's tasks, then invokes the base-class `Finalize` method as the last statement in the derived-class `Finalize` method. As mentioned in Chapter 8, Object-Based Programming, we cannot determine exactly when the destructor call will occur, because we cannot determine exactly when garbage collection occurs. However, by defining a destructor, we can specify code to execute before the garbage collector removes an object from memory.

Our next example revisits the point-circle hierarchy by defining class `Point4` (Fig. 9.25–Fig. 9.26) and class `Circle5` (Fig. 9.27–Fig. 9.28) that contain constructors and destructors, each of which prints a message when it runs. We use these messages to demonstrate when constructors and destructors are called.

Class `Point4` (Fig. 9.25–Fig. 9.26) contains the features shown in Fig. 9.4 and Fig. 9.5. We modified the constructors (lines 8–21 of Fig. 9.26) to output a line of text when they are called and added a destructor (lines 24–27) that also outputs a line of text when it is called. Each output statement (lines 11, 20 and 26) adds pointer `this` to the output string. This implicitly invokes the class's `ToString` method to obtain the string representation of `Point4`'s coordinates.

```
// Fig. 9.25: Point4.h
// Point4 class represents an x-y coordinate pair.

#pragma once

#using <mscorlib.dll>

using namespace System;

// Point4 class definition
public __gc class Point4
{
public:
   Point4();                        // default constructor
   Point4( int, int );              // constructor
   ~Point4();                       // destructor

   // property X
   __property int get_X()
   {
      return x;
   }

   __property void set_X( int value )
   {
      x = value;
   }

   // property Y
   __property int get_Y()
   {
      return y;
   }

   __property void set_Y( int value )
   {
      y = value;
   }

   // return string representation of Point4
   String *ToString();

private:
   int x, y;                        // point coordinate
}; // end class Point4
```

Fig. 9.25 `Point4` base class contains constructors and destructor.

```
// Fig. 9.26: Point4.cpp
// Method definitions for class Point4.

#include "stdafx.h"
```

Fig. 9.26 `Point4` class method definitions. (Part 1 of 2.)

```
#include "Point4.h"

// default constructor
Point4::Point4()
{
   // implicit call to Object constructor occurs here
   Console::WriteLine( S"Point4 constructor: {0}", this );
}

// constructor
Point4::Point4( int xValue, int yValue )
{
   // implicit call to Object constructor occurs here
   x = xValue;
   y = yValue;
   Console::WriteLine( S"Point4 constructor: {0}", this );
}

// destructor
Point4::~Point4()
{
   Console::WriteLine( S"Point4 destructor: {0}", this );
}

// return string representation of Point4
String *Point4::ToString()
{
   return String::Concat( S"[", x.ToString(), S", ", y.ToString(), S"]" );
}
```

Fig. 9.26 `Point4` class method definitions. (Part 2 of 2.)

Class `Circle5` (Fig. 9.27–Fig. 9.28) contains the features of `Circle4` (Fig. 9.19–Fig. 9.20). We modified the two constructors (lines 8–20 of Fig. 9.28) to output a line of text when they are called. We also added a destructor (lines 23–26) that outputs a line of text when it is called. Each output statement (lines 11, 19 and 25) adds pointer `this` to the output string. This implicitly invokes the `Circle5`'s `ToString` method to obtain the string representation of `Circle5`'s coordinates and radius.

```
// Fig. 9.27: Circle5.h
// Circle5 class that inherits from class Point4.

#pragma once

#include "Point4.h"

// Circle5 class definition inherits from Point4
public __gc class Circle5 : public Point4
{
public:
   Circle5();                          // default constructor
```

Fig. 9.27 `Circle5` class inherits from `Point4` and declares a destructor. (Part 1 of 2.)

```
   Circle5( int, int, double );   // constructor
   ~Circle5();   // destructor

   // property Radius
   __property double get_Radius()
   {
      return radius;
   }

   __property void set_Radius( double value )
   {
      if ( value >= 0 )
         radius = value;
   }

   double Diameter();                  // calculate diameter
   double Circumference();             // calculate circumference
   double Area();                      // calculate area

   // return string representation of Circle5
   String *ToString();

private:
   double radius;
}; // end class Circle5
```

Fig. 9.27 `Circle5` class inherits from `Point4` and declares a destructor. (Part 2 of 2.)

```
// Fig. 9.28: Circle5.cpp
// Method definitions for class Circle5.

#include "stdafx.h"
#include "Circle5.h"

// default constructor
Circle5::Circle5()
{
   // implicit call to Point4 constructor occurs here
   Console::WriteLine( S"Circle5 constructor: {0}", this );
}

// constructor
Circle5::Circle5( int xValue, int yValue, double radiusValue )
   : Point4( xValue, yValue )
{
   Radius = radiusValue;
   Console::WriteLine( S"Circle5 constructor: {0}", this );
}

// destructor
Circle5::~Circle5()
{
```

Fig. 9.28 `Circle5` class method definitions. (Part 1 of 2.)

```
   Console::WriteLine( S"Circle5 destructor: {0}", this );
}

// calculate diameter
double Circle5::Diameter()
{
   return Radius * 2;
}

// calculate circumference
double Circle5::Circumference()
{
   return Math::PI * Diameter();
}

// calculate area
double Circle5::Area()
{
   return Math::PI * Math::Pow( Radius, 2 );
}

// return string representation of Circle5
String *Circle5::ToString()
{
   // return Point4 string
   return String::Concat( S"Center = ", __super::ToString(),
      S"; Radius = ", Radius.ToString() );
}
```

Fig. 9.28 `Circle5` class method definitions. (Part 2 of 2.)

Figure 9.29 demonstrates the order in which constructors and destructors are called for objects of classes that are part of an inheritance class hierarchy. Function `_tmain` (lines 12–30) begins by instantiating an object of class `Circle5`, then assigns it to pointer `circle1` (line 17). This invokes the `Circle5` constructor, which invokes the `Point4` constructor immediately. Then, the `Point4` constructor invokes the `Object` constructor. When the `Object` constructor (which does not print anything) returns control to the `Point4` constructor, the `Point4` constructor initializes the *x-y* coordinates, then outputs a string indicating that the `Point4` constructor was called. The output statement also calls method `ToString` implicitly (using pointer `this`) to obtain the string representation of the object being constructed. Then, control returns to the `Circle5` constructor, which initializes the radius and outputs the `Circle5`'s *x-y* coordinates and radius by calling method `ToString`.

```
1  // Fig. 9.29: ConstructorAndDestructor.cpp
2  // Display order in which base-class and derived-class
3  // constructors and destructors are called.
4
5  #include "stdafx.h"
6  #include "Circle5.h"
7
```

Fig. 9.29 Order in which constructors and destructors are called. (Part 1 of 2.)

```
8   #using <mscorlib.dll>
9
10  using namespace System;
11
12  int _tmain()
13  {
14     Circle5 *circle1, *circle2;
15
16     // instantiate Circle5 objects
17     circle1 = new Circle5( 72, 29, 4.5 );
18     circle2 = new Circle5( 5, 5, 10 );
19
20     Console::WriteLine();
21
22     // mark objects for garbage collection
23     circle1 = 0;
24     circle2 = 0;
25
26     // inform garbage collector to execute
27     GC::Collect();
28
29     return 0;
30  } // end _tmain
```

```
Point4 constructor: Center = [72, 29]; Radius = 0
Circle5 constructor: Center = [72, 29]; Radius = 4.5
Point4 constructor: Center = [5, 5]; Radius = 0
Circle5 constructor: Center = [5, 5]; Radius = 10

Circle5 destructor: Center = [5, 5]; Radius = 10
Point4 destructor: Center = [5, 5]; Radius = 10
Circle5 destructor: Center = [72, 29]; Radius = 4.5
Point4 destructor: Center = [72, 29]; Radius = 4.5
```

Fig. 9.29 Order in which constructors and destructors are called. (Part 2 of 2.)

Notice that the first two lines of the output from this program contain values for the *x*-*y* coordinates and the radius of `Circle5` object `circle1`. When constructing a `Circle5` object, the `this` pointer used in the body of both the `Circle5` and `Point4` constructors points to the `Circle5` object being constructed. When a program invokes method `ToString` on an object, the version of `ToString` that executes is always the version defined in that object's class. Pointer `this` points to the current `Circle5` object being constructed, so `Circle5`'s `ToString` method executes even when `ToString` is invoked from the body of class `Point4`'s constructor. [*Note*: This would not be the case if the `Point4` constructor were called to initialize an object that was actually a new `Point4` object.] When the `Point4` constructor invokes method `ToString` for the `Circle5` being constructed, the program displays `0` for the `radius` value, because the `Circle5` constructor's body has not yet initialized the `radius`. Remember that `0.0` (displayed as `0`) is the default value of a `double` variable. The second line of the output shows the proper `radius` value (`4.5`), because that line is output after the `radius` is initialized.

Line 18 of Fig. 9.29 instantiates another object of class `Circle5`, then assigns it to pointer `circle2`. Again, this begins the chain of constructor calls in which the `Circle5` constructor, the `Point4` constructor and the `Object` constructor are called. In the output, notice that the body of the `Point4` constructor executes before the body of the `Circle5` constructor. This demonstrates that objects are constructed "inside out" (i.e., the base-class constructor is called first).

Lines 23–24 set pointers `circle1` and `circle2` to `0`. This removes the only pointers to these `Circle5` objects in the program. Thus, the garbage collector can release the memory that these objects occupy. Remember that we cannot guarantee when the garbage collector will execute, nor can we guarantee that it will collect all available objects when it does execute. To demonstrate the destructor invocations for the two `Circle5` objects, line 27 invokes class `GC`'s method `Collect` to request the garbage collector to run. Notice that each `Circle5` object's destructor outputs information before calling class `Point4`'s destructor. Objects are destroyed "outside in" (i.e., the derived-class destructor completes its tasks before invoking the base-class destructor).

9.7 Software Engineering with Inheritance

In this section, we discuss the use of inheritance to customize existing software. When we use inheritance to create a new class from an existing one, the new class inherits the data members, properties and methods of the existing class. We can customize the new class to meet our needs by including additional data members, properties and methods, and by overriding base-class members.

Sometimes, it is difficult for readers to appreciate the scope of problems faced by designers who work on large-scale software projects in industry. People experienced with such projects say that effective software reuse improves the software-development process. Object-oriented programming facilitates software reuse, thus shortening development times.

Visual C++ .NET encourages software reuse by providing the .NET Framework Class Library (FCL), which delivers the maximum benefits of software reuse through inheritance. As interest in .NET grows, interest in the FCL *class libraries* also increases. There is a worldwide commitment to the continued evolution of the FCL class libraries for a wide variety of applications. The FCL will grow as .NET matures.

Software Engineering Observation 9.11

At the design stage in an object-oriented system, the designer often determines that certain classes are closely related. The designer should "factor out" common attributes and behaviors and place these in a base class, then use inheritance to form derived classes, endowing them with capabilities beyond those inherited from the base class.

Software Engineering Observation 9.12

The creation of a derived class does not affect its base class's source code. Inheritance preserves the integrity of a base class.

Software Engineering Observation 9.13

Just as designers of non-object-oriented systems should avoid proliferation of methods, designers of object-oriented systems should avoid proliferation of classes. Proliferation of classes creates management problems and can hinder software reusability, because it becomes difficult for a client to locate the most appropriate class to use. The alternative is to create fewer classes, in which each provides more substantial functionality, but such classes might provide too much functionality.

Performance Tip 9.2

If classes produced through inheritance are larger than they need to be (i.e., contain too much functionality), memory and processing resources might be wasted. Inherit from the class whose functionality is "closest" to what is needed.

Reading derived-class definitions can be confusing, because inherited members are not shown physically in the derived class, but nevertheless are present in the derived classes. A similar problem exists when documenting derived-class members.

In this chapter, we introduced inheritance—the ability to create classes by absorbing an existing class's data members and behaviors and embellishing these with new capabilities. In Chapter 10, we build upon our discussion of inheritance by introducing *polymorphism*—an object-oriented technique that enables us to write programs that handle, in a more general manner, a wide variety of classes related by inheritance. After studying Chapter 10, you will be familiar with encapsulation, inheritance and polymorphism—the most crucial aspects of object-oriented programming.

SUMMARY

- An "is-a" relationship represents inheritance. In an "is-a" relationship, an object of a derived class also can be treated as an object of its base class.
- A "has-a" relationship represents composition. In a "has-a" relationship, a class object has one or more objects or pointers to objects of other classes as members.
- Inheritance relationships form tree-like hierarchical structures. A class exists in a hierarchical relationship with its derived classes.
- The direct base class of a derived class is the base class from which the derived class inherits [via the colon (`:`) symbol]. An indirect base class of a derived class is two or more levels up the class hierarchy from that derived class.
- With single inheritance, a class is derived from one base class. Visual C++ .NET does not support multiple inheritance with managed classes.
- A derived class can include its own data members, properties and methods, so a derived class is often larger than its base class.
- A derived class is more specific than its base class and represents a smaller group of objects.
- Every object of a derived class is also an object of that class's base class. However, base-class objects are not objects of their derived classes.
- It is possible to treat base-class objects and derived-class objects similarly; the commonality shared between the object types is expressed in the data members, properties and methods of the base class.
- A derived class can access the `public` and `protected` members of its base class directly.
- A derived class cannot access `private` members of its base class directly.
- A base class's `public` members are accessible anywhere that the program has a handle to an object of that base class or to an object of one of that base class's derived classes.
- A base class's `private` members are accessible only within the definition of that base class.
- A base class's `protected` members have an intermediate level of protection between `public` and `private` access. A base class's `protected` members can be accessed only in that base class or in any classes derived from that base class.
- Visual C++ .NET rigidly enforces restrictions on accessing `private` data members, so that even derived classes cannot access their base-class `private` data.

- Declaring data members `private`, while providing non-`private` properties to manipulate and perform validation checking on this data, enforces good software engineering.
- When a base-class member is inappropriate for a derived class, that member can be overridden (redefined) in the derived class with an appropriate implementation.
- A derived class can redefine a base-class method using the same signature; this is called overriding that base-class method.
- When a method is overridden in a derived class and that method is called by a derived-class object, the derived-class version (not the base-class version) is called.
- When an object of a derived class is instantiated, the base class's constructor is called immediately (either explicitly or implicitly) to do any necessary initialization of the base-class data members in the derived-class object (before the derived classes data members are initialized).
- Base-class constructors and destructors are not inherited by derived classes.
- Software reusability reduces program-development time.
- If an object's method or property performs the actions needed by another object, call that method or property rather than duplicating its code body. Duplicated code creates code-maintenance problems.

TERMINOLOGY

abstraction
base class
base-class constructor
base-class default constructor
base-class destructor
base-class object
behavior
class hierarchy
class library
colon (`:`) to indicate inheritance
composition
constructor
default constructor
derived class
derived-class constructor
destructor
direct base class
`Finalize` method
garbage collector
"has-a" relationship
hierarchy diagram
indirect base class
information hiding
inheritance
inheritance hierarchy
"is-a" relationship
multiple inheritance
`Object` class
object of a base class
object of a derived class
object-oriented programming (OOP)
overloading
overriding
overriding a base-class method
`private` base-class member
`protected` member access specifier
`protected` base-class member
`public` base-class member
reusable component
single inheritance
software reuse
subclass
superclass

SELF-REVIEW EXERCISES

9.1 Fill in the blanks in each of the following statements:

a) ________ is a form of software reusability in which new classes absorb the data and behaviors of existing classes and embellish these classes with new capabilities.

b) A base class's ________ members can be accessed only in the base-class definition or in derived-class definitions.

c) In a(n) ________ relationship, an object of a derived class also can be treated as an object of its base class.
d) In a(n) ________ relationship, a class object has one or more references to objects of other classes as members.
e) A class exists in a(n) ________ relationship with its derived classes.
f) A base class's ________ members are accessible anywhere that the program has a reference to that base class or to one of its derived classes.
g) A base class's `protected` access members have a level of protection between those of `public` and ________ access.
h) The `public` and `protected` members of a base class can be referred to in a derived-class's definition by using their ________.
i) When an object of a derived class is instantiated, the base class's ________ is called implicitly or explicitly to do any necessary initialization of the base-class data members in the derived-class object.

9.2 State whether each of the following is *true* or *false*. If *false*, explain why.
a) It is possible to treat base-class objects and derived-class objects similarly.
b) Base-class constructors are not inherited by derived classes.
c) A "has-a" relationship is implemented via inheritance.
d) A derived class is often larger than its base class.
e) A derived class cannot access `private` members of its base class directly.
f) When a derived class redefines a base-class method having the same signature, the derived class is said to overload that base-class method.
g) A `Car` class has an "is-a" relationship with its `SteeringWheel` and `Brakes`.
h) Inheritance encourages the reuse of proven high-quality software.

ANSWERS TO SELF-REVIEW EXERCISES

9.1 a) Inheritance. b) `protected`. c) "is-a" or inheritance. d) "has-a," composition or aggregation. e) hierarchical. f) `public`. g) `private`. h) member names. i) constructor.

9.2 a) True. b) True. c) False. A "has-a" relationship is implemented via composition. An "is-a" relationship is implemented via inheritance. d) True. e) True. f) False. When a derived class redefines a base-class method having the same signature, the derived class overrides that base-class method. g) False. This is an example of a "has-a" relationship. Class `Car` has an "is-a" relationship with class `Vehicle`. h) True.

EXERCISES

9.3 Many programs written with inheritance could be written with composition instead, and vice versa. Rewrite classes `Point3`, `Circle4` and `Cylinder` to use composition, rather than inheritance. After you do this, assess the relative merits of the two approaches for both the `Point3`, `Circle4`, `Cylinder` problem, as well as for object-oriented programs in general. Which approach is more natural, why?

9.4 Some programmers prefer not to use `protected` access because it breaks the encapsulation of the base class. Discuss the relative merits of using `protected` access vs. insisting on using `private` access in base classes.

9.5 Rewrite the case study in Section 9.5 as a `Point`, `Square`, `Cube` program. Do this two ways—once via inheritance and once via composition.

9.6 Write an inheritance hierarchy for class `Quadrilateral`, `Trapezoid`, `Parallelogram`, `Rectangle` and `Square`. Use `Quadrilateral` as the base class of the hierarchy. Make the hierarchy as deep (i.e., as many levels) as possible. The `private` data of `Quadrilateral` should be the *x*-*y* coordinate pairs for the four endpoints of the `Quadrilateral`. Write a program that instantiates objects of each of the classes in your hierarchy and polymorphically outputs each object's dimensions and area.

9.7 Modify classes `Point3`, `Circle4` and `Cylinder` to contain destructors. Then, modify the program of Fig. 9.29 to demonstrate the order in which constructors and destructors are invoked in this hierarchy.

9.8 Write down all the shapes you can think of—both two-dimensional and three-dimensional—and form those shapes into a shape hierarchy. Your hierarchy should have base class `Shape` from which class `TwoDimensionalShape` and class `ThreeDimensionalShape` are derived. Once you have developed the hierarchy, define each of the classes in the hierarchy. We will use this hierarchy in the exercises of Chapter 10 to process all shapes as objects of base-class `Shape`. (This is a technique called polymorphism.)

10

Object-Oriented Programming: Polymorphism

Objectives

- To understand the concept of polymorphism.
- To understand how polymorphism makes systems extensible and maintainable.
- To understand the distinction between abstract classes and concrete classes.
- To learn how to create `__sealed` classes, interfaces and delegates.

One Ring to rule them all, One Ring to find them,
One Ring to bring them all and in the darkness bind them.
John Ronald Reuel Tolkien

General propositions do not decide concrete cases.
Oliver Wendell Holmes

A philosopher of imposing stature doesn't think in a vacuum. Even his most abstract ideas are, to some extent, conditioned by what is or is not known in the time when he lives.
Alfred North Whitehead

Outline

10.1 Introduction

The previous chapter's object-oriented programming (OOP) discussion focused on one of OOP's key component technologies, inheritance. In this chapter, we continue our study of OOP by explaining and demonstrating *polymorphism*. Both inheritance and polymorphism are crucial technologies in the development of complex software. Polymorphism enables us to write programs that handle a wide variety of related classes in a generic manner and facilitates adding new classes and capabilities to a system.

With polymorphism, it is possible to design and implement systems that are easily extensible. Programs can process objects of all classes in a class hierarchy generically as objects of a common base class. Furthermore, new classes can be added with little or no modification to the generic portions of the program, as long as those classes are part of the inheritance hierarchy that the program processes generically. The only parts of a program that must be altered to accommodate new classes are those program components that require direct knowledge of the new classes that the programmer adds to the hierarchy. In this chapter, we demonstrate two substantial class hierarchies and manipulate objects from those hierarchies polymorphically.

10.2 Derived-Class-Object to Base-Class-Object Conversion

In Chapter 9, we created a point-circle class hierarchy, in which class `Circle` inherited from class `Point`. The programs that manipulated objects of these classes always used `Point` pointers to refer to `Point` objects and `Circle` pointers to refer to `Circle` objects. In this section, we discuss the relationships between classes in a hierarchy that enable programs to assign derived-class objects to base-class pointers—a fundamental part of programs that process objects polymorphically. This section also discusses explicit casting between types in a class hierarchy.

An object of a derived class can be treated as an object of its base class. This enables various interesting manipulations. For example, a program can create an array of base-class pointers that refer to objects of many derived-class types. This is allowed despite the fact that the derived-class objects are of different data types. However, the reverse is not true—a base-class object is not an object of any of its derived classes. For example, a `Point` is not a `Circle` in the hierarchy defined in Chapter 9. If a base-class pointer refers to a derived-class object, it is possible to convert the base-class pointer to the object's actual data type and manipulate the object as that type.

The example in Fig. 10.1–Fig. 10.5 demonstrates assigning derived-class objects to base-class pointers and casting base-class pointers to derived-class pointers. Class `Point` (Fig. 10.1–Fig. 10.2), which we discussed in Chapter 9, represents an *x-y* coordinate pair. Class `Circle` (Fig. 10.3–Fig. 10.4), which we also discussed in Chapter 9, represents a circle and inherits from class `Point`. Each `Circle` object *is a* `Point` and also has a radius (represented via property `Radius`). `PointCircleTest.cpp` (Fig. 10.5) demonstrates the assignment and cast operations.

```
// Fig. 10.1: Point.h
// Point class represents an x-y coordinate pair.

#pragma once

#using <mscorlib.dll>

using namespace System;

// Point class definition implicitly inherits from Object
public __gc class Point
{
public:
   Point();                  // default constructor
   Point( int, int );        // constructor

   // property X
   __property int get_X()
   {
      return x;
   }

   __property void set_X( int value )
   {
      x = value;
   }

   // property Y
   __property int get_Y()
   {
      return y;
   }

   __property void set_Y( int value )
   {
      y = value;
   }

```

Fig. 10.1 `Point` class represents an *x-y* coordinate pair. (Part 1 of 2.)

```
   // return string representation of Point
   String *ToString();

private:
   int x, y;                    // point coordinate
}; // end class Point
```

Fig. 10.1 `Point` class represents an *x-y* coordinate pair. (Part 2 of 2.)

```
// Fig. 10.2: Point.cpp
// Method definitions for class Point.

#include "stdafx.h"
#include "Point.h"

// default constructor
Point::Point()
{
   // implicit call to Object constructor occurs here
}

// constructor
Point::Point( int xValue, int yValue )
{
   // implicit call to Object constructor occurs here
   X = xValue;
   Y = yValue;
}

// return string representation of Point
String *Point::ToString()
{
   return String::Concat( S"[", X.ToString(), S", ",
      Y.ToString(), S"]" );
}
```

Fig. 10.2 `Point` class method definitions.

```
// Fig. 10.3: Circle.h
// Circle class that inherits form class Point.

#pragma once

#include "Point.h"

// Circle class definition inherits from Point
public __gc class Circle : public Point
{
public:
   Circle();                    // default constructor
   Circle( int, int, double );  // constructor
```

Fig. 10.3 `Circle` class that inherits from class `Point`. (Part 1 of 2.)

```

   // property Radius
   __property double get_Radius()
   {
      return radius;
   }

   __property void set_Radius( double value )
   {
      if ( value >= 0 )              // validate radius
         radius = value;
   }

   double Diameter();
   double Circumference();
   virtual double Area();

   // return string representation of Circle
   String *ToString();

private:
   double radius;                 // Circle's radius
}; // end class Circle
```

Fig. 10.3 `Circle` class that inherits from class `Point`. (Part 2 of 2.)

```
// Fig. 10.4: Circle.cpp
// Method definitions for class Circle.

#include "stdafx.h"
#include "Circle.h"

// default constructor
Circle::Circle()
{
   // implicit call to Point constructor occurs here
}

// constructor
Circle::Circle( int xValue, int yValue, double radiusValue )
   : Point( xValue, yValue )
{
   Radius = radiusValue;
}

// calculate diameter
double Circle::Diameter()
{
   return Radius * 2;
}

```

Fig. 10.4 `Circle` class method definitions. (Part 1 of 2.)

```
// calculate circumference
double Circle::Circumference()
{
   return Math::PI * Diameter();
}

// calculate area
double Circle::Area()
{
   return Math::PI * Math::Pow( Radius, 2 );
}

// return string representation of Circle
String *Circle::ToString()
{
   return String::Concat( S"Center = ", __super::ToString(),
      S"; Radius = ", Radius.ToString() );
}
```

Fig. 10.4 `Circle` class method definitions. (Part 2 of 2.)

Notice that in class `Circle` (Fig. 10.3), method `Area` is declared *`virtual`* (line 29). *Virtual method. Virtual methods* allow programmers to design and implement systems that are more extensible. With virtual methods, programs can be written to process—as base-class objects—objects of all existing classes in a hierarchy.

To illustrate why `virtual` methods are useful, suppose a set of shape classes such as `Circle`, `Triangle`, `Rectangle`, `Square`, etc. derive from base class `Shape`. In object-oriented programming, each of these classes might be endowed with the ability to draw itself. Although each class has its own `Draw` method, the `Draw` method for each shape is quite different. When drawing a shape, whatever that shape may be, it would be nice to be able to treat all these shapes generically as objects of the base class `Shape`. Then to draw any shape, we could simply call method `Draw` of base class `Shape` and let the program determine dynamically (i.e., at run time) which derived class `Draw` method to use. To enable this kind of behavior, we declare `Draw` in the base class as a `virtual` method and we override `Draw` in each of the derived classes to draw the appropriate shape.

Method `ToString` of class `Object` is, in fact, declared `virtual`. To view the method header for `ToString`, select **Help > Index...**, and enter `Object.ToString method` (filtered by **.NET Framework**) in the search text box. The page displayed contains a description of method `ToString`, which includes the following header:

```
public: virtual String * ToString();
```

Any class can override class `Object`'s `ToString` method. We have, in fact, overridden `Object`'s `ToString` method in several classes already (as all classes in MC++ are derived from class `Object`). When an object of a derived class calls method `ToString`, the correct `ToString` implementation is called. If the derived class does not override `ToString`, the derived class inherits its immediate base class's version of the method. If the `Point` class did not override `ToString`, invoking method `ToString` on a `Point` object would call base class `Object`'s version of the method. We will see the benefits of using `virtual` methods shortly.

Software Engineering Observation 10.1

Once a method is declared `virtual`, it remains `virtual` for all derived classes in the inheritance hierarchy even if it is not declared `virtual` when a derived class overrides it.

Good Programming Practice 10.1

Even though certain methods are implicitly `virtual` because of a declaration in a base class, explicitly declare these methods `virtual` in every derived class to promote program clarity.

Software Engineering Observation 10.2

When a derived class chooses not to define a `virtual` method, the derived class simply inherits its immediate base class's `virtual` method definition.

Figure 10.5 demonstrates assigning derived-class pointers to base-class pointers and casting base-class pointers to derived-class pointers. Lines 15–16 declare a `Point` pointer (`point1`) and a `Circle` pointer (`circle1`) and initializes these pointers with new `Point` and `Circle` objects, respectively. Lines 18–19 append string representations of each object to `output` to show the values used to initialize these objects. `point1` is a pointer to a `Point` object, so the call to method `ToString` for `point1` returns the string representation of the `Point` object. Similarly, `circle1` is pointer to a `Circle` object, so the call to method `ToString` for `circle1` returns the string representation of the `Circle` object.

```
1  // Fig. 10.5: PointCircleTest.cpp
2  // Demonstrating inheritance and polymorphism.
3
4  #include "stdafx.h"
5  #include "Circle.h"
6
7  #using <mscorlib.dll>
8  #using <system.windows.forms.dll>
9
10 using namespace System;
11 using namespace System::Windows::Forms;
12
13 int _tmain()
14 {
15    Point *point1 = new Point( 30, 50 );
16    Circle *circle1 = new Circle( 120, 89, 2.7 );
17
18    String *output = String::Concat( S"Point point1: ",
19       point1->ToString(), S"\nCircle circle1: ", circle1->ToString() );
20
21    // use 'is a' relationship to assign
22    // Circle *circle1 to Point pointer
23    Point *point2 = circle1;
24
25    output = String::Concat( output, S"\n\n",
26       S"Circle circle1 (via point2): ", point2->ToString() );
27
```

Fig. 10.5 Derived-class pointers assigned to base-class pointers. (Part 1 of 2.)

```
28     // downcast point2 to Circle *circle2
29     Circle *circle2 = __try_cast< Circle * >( point2 );
30
31     output = String::Concat( output, S"\n\n",
32        S"Circle circle1 (via circle2): ", circle2->ToString() );
33
34     output = String::Concat( output,
35        S"\nArea of circle1 (via circle2): ",
36        circle2->Area().ToString( "F" ) );
37
38     // attempt to assign point1 object to Circle pointer
39     if ( point1->GetType() == __typeof( Circle ) ) {
40        circle2 = __try_cast< Circle * >( point1 );
41        output = String::Concat( output, S"\n\ncast successful" );
42     } // end if
43     else {
44        output = String::Concat( output,
45           S"\n\npoint1 does not refer to a Circle" );
46     } // end else
47
48     MessageBox::Show( output, S"Demonstrating the 'is a' relationship" );
49
50     return 0;
51  } // end _tmain
```

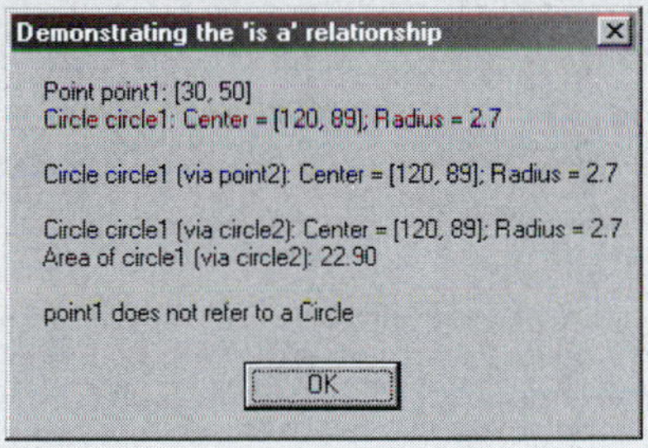
Demonstrating the 'is a' relationship
Point point1: [30, 50]
Circle circle1: Center = [120, 89]; Radius = 2.7
Circle circle1 (via point2): Center = [120, 89]; Radius = 2.7
Circle circle1 (via circle2): Center = [120, 89]; Radius = 2.7
Area of circle1 (via circle2): 22.90
point1 does not refer to a Circle
OK

Fig. 10.5 Derived-class pointers assigned to base-class pointers. (Part 2 of 2.)

Line 23 (Fig. 10.5) assigns `circle1` (a pointer to a derived-class object) to `point2` (a base-class pointer). This assignment is acceptable because of the inheritance "is a" relationship. Class `Circle` inherits from class `Point`, so a `Circle` *is a* `Point` (in a structural sense, at least). However, assigning a base-class pointer to a derived-class pointer is potentially dangerous and is not allowed without an explicit cast (as we will discuss).

Lines 25–26 invoke `point2->ToString` and append the result to `output`. When a `virtual` method invocation is encountered, the compiler determines which version of the method to call from the type of the object on which the method is called, not the type of the pointer that refers to the object. In this case, `point2` points to a `Circle` object, so `Circle` method `ToString` is called, rather than `Point` method `ToString` (as one might have expected because the `point2` pointer was declared as type `Point *`). The decision about which method to call is an example of *polymorphism*, a concept that we discuss in detail throughout this chapter. Note that if `point2` pointed to a `Point` object rather than a `Circle` object, `Point`'s `ToString` method would have been invoked instead.

Previous chapters used methods such as `Int32::Parse` and `Double::Parse` to convert between various built-in types. Now, this example converts between object pointers of programmer-defined types. We use explicit casts to perform these conversions. Managed C++ supports five cast operators—`static_cast`, `dynamic_cast`, `reinterpret_cast`, `const_cast` and `__try_cast`. Operator `static_cast` performs a conversion between most fundamental data types at compile time. Operator `dynamic_cast` performs conversions of base-class objects to derived-class objects at runtime. If the cast is valid, the `dynamic_cast` operator returns a pointer to the derived-class object. However, if the cast is invalid, the operator returns `0` to indicate that a base-class object cannot be converted to the specified derived-class object. The *`reinterpret_cast`* operator performs *nonstandard casts* (e.g., casting from one pointer type to a different, unrelated pointer type). The `reinterpret_cast` operator can convert between pointer types not related by a hierarchy. Operator `reinterpret_cast` cannot be used to perform standard casts (i.e., `double` to `int`, etc.). The `const_cast` operator can be used to cast away (i.e., remove) a `const` or `volatile`[1] attribute of an object or pointer. Operator *`__try_cast`*, a new feature of MC++, is similar to `dynamic_cast` except that if the cast is invalid, the operator throws an *`InvalidCastException`*, which indicates that the cast operation is not allowed. Because of this inherent feature, we generally use operator `__try_cast` in our examples rather than `dynamic_cast`. Exceptions are discussed in detail in Chapter 11, Exception Handling.

Line 29 casts `point2`, which currently points to a `Circle` object (`circle1`), to a `Circle *` and assigns the result to `circle2`. As we discuss momentarily, this cast would be dangerous if `point2` pointed to a `Point` object. Lines 31–32 invoke method `ToString` of the `Circle` object to which `circle2` now points (note that the third line of text in the output window demonstrates that `Circle`'s `ToString` method is called). Lines 34–36 calculate and output `circle2`'s `Area` to demonstrate that we are able to access other methods of class `Circle` through the `Circle2` pointer.

Common Programming Error 10.1

Assigning a base-class object (or a base-class pointer) to a derived-class pointer (without an explicit cast) is a compilation error.

Software Engineering Observation 10.3

If a derived-class object has been assigned to a pointer of one of its direct or indirect base classes, it is acceptable to cast that base-class pointer back to a pointer of the derived-class type. In fact, this must be done to send that object messages (i.e., invoke methods or use properties) that do not appear in the base class.

Line 40 explicitly casts pointer `point1` to a `Circle *`. This is a dangerous operation, because `point1` points to a `Point` object, and a `Point` is not a `Circle *`. Objects can be cast only to their own type or to their base-class types. If this statement were to execute, the CLR would determine that `point1` points to a `Point` object, recognize the cast to `Circle` as dangerous and indicate an improper cast with an `InvalidCastException` message. However, we prevent this statement from executing by including an `if...else` statement (lines 39–46). The condition (line 39) uses the `GetType` method and `__typeof` keyword to deter-

1. The `volatile` type qualifier is applied to a definition of a variable that may be altered from outside the program (i.e., the variable is not completely under the control of the program and may be altered by the operating system, hardware, etc.).

mine whether the object to which `point1` points *is a* `Circle`. Method *`GetType`*, one of the eight methods inherited from `System::Object`, returns the type of an object. Similarly, the *`__typeof`* keyword returns the type of a managed class, value class or managed interface. In our example, `GetType` returns `Point` and `__typeof` returns `Circle`. As a `Point` object is not a `Circle` object, the condition fails, and lines 44–45 append to `output` a string that indicates the result. Note that the `if` condition will be `true` if the left operand is a pointer to an instance of the right operand or if the left operand is a pointer to an instance of a class that is derived from the right operand.

Common Programming Error 10.2

Using the `__try_cast` operator when attempting to cast a base-class pointer to a derived-class type causes an `InvalidCastException` if the pointer points to a base-class object rather than an appropriate derived-class object.

If we remove the `if` test and execute the program, a `MessageBox` similar to the one in Fig. 10.6 is displayed. We discuss how to deal with such situations in Chapter 11, Exception Handling.

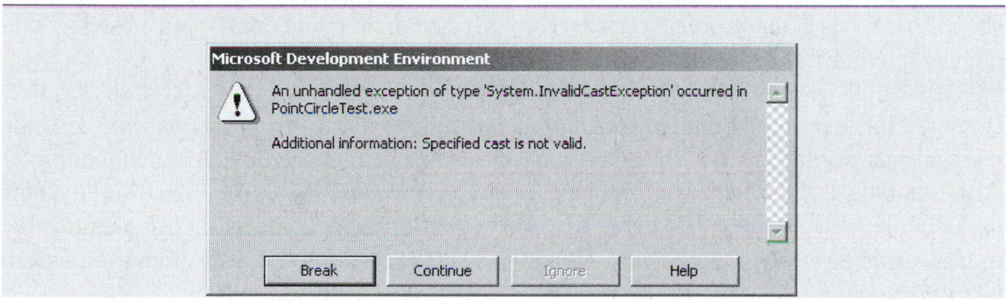

Fig. 10.6 `System.InvalidCastException` error message.

Despite the fact that a derived-class object also *is a* base-class object, the derived-class and base-class objects are different. As we have discussed previously, derived-class objects can be treated as if they were base-class objects. This is a logical relationship, because the derived class contains members that correspond to all members in the base class, but the derived class can have additional members. For this reason, assigning a base-class object's address to a derived-class pointer is not allowed without an explicit cast. Such an assignment would leave the pointer pointing to an object that does not have the additional derived-class members.

There are four ways to mix base-class pointers and derived-class pointers with base-class objects and derived-class objects:

1. Referring to a base-class object with a base-class pointer is straightforward.
2. Referring to a derived-class object with a derived-class pointer is straightforward.
3. Referring to a derived-class object with a base-class pointer is safe, because the derived-class object *is an* object of its base class. However, this pointer can refer only to base-class members of the object. If this code refers to derived-class-only members through the base-class pointer, the compiler reports an error.

4. Referring to a base-class object with a derived-class pointer generates a compiler error. To avoid this error, the derived-class pointer first must be cast to a base-class pointer explicitly. In this cast, the derived-class pointer must point to a derived-class object, or the .NET runtime generates a runtime error.

Common Programming Error 10.3

After assigning a derived-class object to a base-class pointer, attempting to reference derived-class-only members with the base-class pointer is a compilation error.

Common Programming Error 10.4

Treating a base-class object as a derived-class object can cause errors.

10.3 Type Fields and `switch` Statements

One way to determine the type of an object that is incorporated in a larger program is to use a `switch` statement. This allows us to distinguish among object types, then invoke an appropriate action for a particular object. For example, in a hierarchy of shapes in which each shape object has a `ShapeType` property, a `switch` statement could employ the object's `ShapeType` to determine which `Print` method to call.

However, using `switch` logic exposes programs to several of potential problems. For example, the programmer might forget to include a type test when one is warranted, or the programmer might forget to test all possible cases in a `switch` statement. When modifying a `switch`-based system by adding new types, the programmer might forget to insert the new cases in all relevant `switch` statements. Every addition or deletion of a class requires the modification of every `switch` statement in the system; tracking these statements down can be time consuming and error prone.

Software Engineering Observation 10.4

Polymorphic programming can eliminate the need for unnecessary `switch` *logic. Using the polymorphism mechanism to perform the equivalent logic, programmers can avoid the kinds of errors typically associated with* `switch` *logic.*

Error-Prevention Tip 10.1

An interesting consequence of using polymorphism is that programs take on a simplified appearance. They contain less branching logic and more simple, sequential code. This simplification facilitates testing, debugging and program maintenance.

10.4 Polymorphism Examples

In this section, we discuss several examples of polymorphism. If class `Rectangle` is derived from class `Quadrilateral`, then a `Rectangle` object is a more specific version of a `Quadrilateral` object. Any operation (such as calculating the perimeter or the area) that can be performed on an object of class `Quadrilateral` also can be performed on an object of class `Rectangle`. Such operations also can be performed on other kinds of `Quadrilaterals`, such as `Squares`, `Parallelograms` and `Trapezoids`. When a program invokes a derived-class method through a base-class (i.e., `Quadrilateral`) pointer, the compiler polymorphically chooses the correct overriding method in the derived class from which the object was instantiated. We investigate this behavior in later examples.

Suppose that we design a video game that manipulates objects of many different types, including objects of classes `Martian`, `Venutian`, `Plutonian`, `SpaceShip` and `LaserBeam`. Also, imagine that each of these classes inherits from the common base class called `SpaceObject`, which contains method `DrawYourself`. Each derived class implements this method. A screen-manager program would maintain a container (such as a `SpaceObject` array) of pointers to objects of the various classes. To refresh the screen, the screen manager would periodically send each object the same message—namely, `DrawYourself`. However, each object responds in a unique way. For example, a `Martian` object would draw itself in red with the appropriate number of antennae. A `SpaceShip` object would draw itself as a bright silver flying saucer. A `LaserBeam` object would draw itself as a bright red beam across the screen. Thus, the same message sent to a variety of objects would have "many forms" of results—hence, the term *polymorphism.*

A polymorphic screen manager facilitates adding new classes to a system with minimal modifications to the system's code. Suppose that we want to add class `Mercurians` to our video game. To do so, we must build a class `Mercurian` that inherits from `SpaceObject`, but provides its own definition of method `DrawYourself`. Then, when objects of class `Mercurian` appear in the container, the programmer does not need to modify the code for the screen manager. The screen manager invokes method `DrawYourself` on every object in the container, regardless of the object's type, so the new `Mercurian` objects simply "plug right in." Thus, without modifying the system (other than to build and include the classes themselves), programmers can use polymorphism to include additional types of classes that were not envisioned when the system was created.

With polymorphism, one method can cause different actions to occur, depending on the type of the object on which the method is invoked. This gives the programmer tremendous expressive capability. In the next several sections, we provide examples that demonstrate polymorphism.

Software Engineering Observation 10.5

With polymorphism, the programmer can deal in generalities and let the execution-time environment concern itself with the specifics. The programmer can command a wide variety of objects to behave in manners appropriate to those objects, even if the programmer does not know the objects' types.

Software Engineering Observation 10.6

Polymorphism promotes extensibility. Software used to invoke polymorphic behavior is written to be independent of the types of the objects to which messages (i.e., method calls) are sent. Thus, programmers can include into a system additional types of objects that respond to existing messages and can do this without modifying the base system.

10.5 Abstract Classes

When we think of a class as a type, we assume that programs will create objects of that type. However, there are cases in which it is useful to define classes for which the programmer never intends to instantiate any objects. Such classes are called *abstract classes*. The purpose of an abstract class is to provide an appropriate base class from which other classes may inherit. We refer to such classes as *abstract base classes,* because such classes normally are used as base classes in inheritance hierarchies. These classes cannot be used to instantiate objects, since abstract classes are incomplete. Derived classes must define the "missing pieces." Abstract classes normally contain one or more *pure* `virtual` *methods* (sometimes called *abstract methods*), which we will discuss shortly. Derived classes must override inherited pure `virtual` methods and properties to enable objects of those derived classes to be instantiated. We discuss abstract classes extensively in Sections 10.6 and 10.8.

Classes from which objects can be instantiated are called *concrete classes*. Such classes provide implementations of every method and property they define. We could have an abstract base class `TwoDimensionalObject` and derive such concrete classes as `Square`, `Circle` and `Triangle`. We could also have an abstract base class `ThreeDimensionalObject` and derive such concrete classes as `Cube`, `Sphere` and `Cylinder`. Abstract base classes are too generic to define real objects; we need to be more specific before we can think of instantiating objects. For example, if someone tells you to "draw the shape," what shape would you draw? Concrete classes provide the specifics that make it reasonable to instantiate objects.

A class is made abstract by using the keyword `__abstract`, or by declaring one or more of its `virtual` methods to be "pure." A *pure `virtual` method* is one with an *initializer* of `= 0` in its declaration as in

```
virtual double earnings() = 0; // pure virtual
```

We can also declare the *get* and *set* methods of properties as pure `virtual` methods as in

```
__property virtual String *get_Name() = 0; // pure virtual
```

For clarity, we explicitly declare abstract classes with the keyword `__abstract`. However, the `__abstract` keyword is optional if a `__gc` class contains one or more pure `virtual` methods. Declaring an abstract class with keyword `__abstract` does not affect the methods or properties of the class. It simply ensures that the class cannot be instantiated. Methods and properties of `__abstract` classes are not implicitly `virtual`.

An inheritance hierarchy does not need to contain any abstract classes, but, as we will see, many good object-oriented systems have class hierarchies headed by abstract base classes. In some cases, abstract classes constitute the top few levels of the hierarchy. A good example of this is the shape hierarchy in Fig. 9.3. The hierarchy begins with abstract base-class `Shape`. On the next level of the hierarchy, we have two more abstract base classes, namely `TwoDimensionalShape` and `ThreeDimensionalShape`. The next level of the hierarchy would define concrete classes for two-dimensional shapes, such as `Circle` and `Square`, and for three-dimensional shapes, such as `Sphere` and `Cube`.

Software Engineering Observation 10.7

An abstract class defines a common set of `public` methods and properties for the various members of a class hierarchy. An abstract class typically contains one or more pure `virtual` methods that derived classes will override. All classes in the hierarchy can use this common set of `public` methods and properties.

Abstract classes must specify prototypes for their methods and properties. Concrete derived classes may override the virtual methods and properties of an abstract class and provide concrete implementations of those methods or properties. However, to be concrete, derived classes must override all pure `virtual` methods of an abstract class.

Common Programming Error 10.5

Attempting to instantiate an object of an abstract class results in a compilation error.

Common Programming Error 10.6

Failure to override a pure `virtual` method in a derived class is a compilation error, unless the derived class also is an abstract class.

Software Engineering Observation 10.8

An abstract class can have instance data and non-virtual methods (including constructors), which are subject to the normal rules of inheritance by derived classes.

Software Engineering Observation 10.9

Concrete classes that indirectly inherit from an abstract class do not necessarily have to override the pure `virtual` methods of the abstract class. If any class higher in the hierarchy has already provided an overridden version of a pure `virtual` method, the current class inherits that version and does not have to provide a separate implementation.

Although we cannot instantiate objects of abstract base classes, we *can* use abstract base classes to declare pointers; these pointers can point to objects of any concrete classes derived from the abstract class. Programs can use such pointers to manipulate instances of the derived classes polymorphically.

Let us consider another application of polymorphism. A screen manager needs to display a variety of objects, including new types of objects that the programmer will add to the system after writing the screen manager. The system might need to display various shapes, such as `Circle`, `Triangle` or `Rectangle`, which are derived from abstract class `Shape`. The screen manager uses base-class pointers of type `Shape` to manage the objects that are displayed. To draw any object (regardless of the level at which that object's class appears in the inheritance hierarchy), the screen manager uses a base-class pointer to the object to invoke the object's `Draw` method. Method `Draw` is declared as pure `virtual` method in __`abstract` class `Shape`; therefore, each derived class should implement method `Draw`. Each `Shape` object in the inheritance hierarchy knows how to draw itself. The screen manager does not have to worry about the type of each object or whether the screen manager has ever encountered objects of that type.

Polymorphism is particularly effective for implementing layered software systems. In operating systems, for example, each type of physical device could operate quite differently from the others. Even so, commands to *read* or *write* data from and to devices may have a certain uniformity. The write message sent to a device-driver object needs to be interpreted specifically in the context of that device driver and how that device driver manipulates devices of a specific type. However, the write call itself really is no different from the write to any other device in the system—place some number of bytes from memory onto that device. An object-oriented operating system might use an abstract base class to provide an interface appropriate for all device drivers. Then, through inheritance from that abstract base class, derived classes are formed that all operate similarly. The capabilities (i.e., the `public` services) offered by the device drivers are provided as pure `virtual` methods in the abstract base class. The implementations of these pure `virtual` methods are provided in the derived classes that correspond to the specific types of device drivers.

It is common in object-oriented programming to define an *iterator class* that can traverse all the objects in a container (such as an array). For example, a program can print a list of objects in a linked list by creating an iterator object, then using the iterator to obtain the next element of the list each time the iterator is called. Iterators often are used in polymorphic programming to traverse an array or a linked list of objects from various levels of a hierarchy. The pointers in such a list are all base-class pointers. (See Chapter 22, Data Structures and Collections, to learn more about linked lists and iterators.) A list of objects of base class `TwoDimensionalShape` could contain objects from classes `Square`, `Circle`, `Triangle` and so on. Using polymorphism to send a `Draw` message to each object in the list would draw each object correctly on the screen.

10.6 Case Study: Inheriting Interface and Implementation

Our next example (Fig. 10.7–Fig. 10.15) reexamines the `Point`, `Circle`, `Cylinder` hierarchy that we explored in Chapter 9. In this example, the hierarchy begins with abstract base class `Shape` (Fig. 10.7–Fig. 10.8). This hierarchy mechanically demonstrates the power of polymorphism.

```
// Fig. 10.7: Shape.h
// Demonstrate a shape hierarchy using an abstract base class.

#pragma once

#using <mscorlib.dll>

using namespace System;

// __abstract classes cannot be instantiated
__abstract __gc class Shape
{
public:
   virtual double Area();
   virtual double Volume();

   // property Name's get method is a pure virtual method
   __property virtual String *get_Name() = 0;
}; // end class Shape
```

Fig. 10.7 Shape abstract base class.

```
// Fig. 10.8: Shape.cpp
// Method definitions for class Shape.

#include "stdafx.h"
#include "Shape.h"

// return area
double Shape::Area()
{
   return .00;
}

// return volume
double Shape::Volume()
{
   return 0.0;
}
```

Fig. 10.8 Shape class method definitions.

Abstract class Shape defines two virtual methods and one pure virtual method. All shapes in this hierarchy have an area and a volume, so we include virtual methods Area (line 14 of Fig. 10.7) and Volume (line 15), which return the shape's area and volume, respectively. The volume of two-dimensional shapes is always zero, whereas three-dimensional shapes have a positive, nonzero volume. In class Fig. 10.8, methods Area and Volume are defined to return zero, by default. Programmers can override these methods in derived classes when those classes should have different area calculations or different volume calculations. Read-only property Name (line 18 of Fig. 10.7) is declared as a pure virtual method, so derived classes must implement this method to become concrete classes. This method is pure virtual because class Shape does not contain enough information to determine a Shape's name. This information will be provided by the concrete subclasses of Shape.

Class Point2 (Fig. 10.9–Fig. 10.10) inherits from __abstract class Shape and overrides the property Name, which makes Point2 a concrete class. A point's area and volume are zero, so class Point2 does not override base-class methods Area and Volume. Lines 39–42 (Fig. 10.9) implement property Name. If we did not provide this implementation, class Point2 would be an abstract class (despite that fact that it is not declared as abstract) and we would not be able to instantiate Point2 objects.

```
1  // Fig. 10.9: Point2.h
2  // Point2 inherits from abstract class Shape and represents
3  // an x-y coordinate pair.
4
5  #pragma once
6
7  #include "Shape.h"
8
9  // Point2 inherits from abstract class Shape
10 public __gc class Point2: public Shape
11 {
12 public:
13    Point2();                    // default constructor
14    Point2( int, int );          // constructor
15
16    // property X
17    __property int get_X()
18    {
19       return x;
20    }
21
22    __property void set_X( int value )
23    {
24       x = value;
25    }
26
27    // property Y
28    __property int get_Y()
29    {
30       return y;
31    }
```

Fig. 10.9 Point2 class inherits from abstract class Shape. (Part 1 of 2.)

```

   __property void set_Y( int value )
   {
      y = value;
   }

   // implement property Name of class Shape
   __property virtual String *get_Name()
   {
      return S"Point2";
   }

   String *ToString();

private:
   int x, y;                        // Point2 coordinates
}; // end class Point2
```

Fig. 10.9 Point2 class inherits from abstract class Shape. (Part 2 of 2.)

```
// Fig. 10.10: Point2.cpp
// Method definitions for class Point2.

#include "stdafx.h"
#include "Point2.h"

// default constructor
Point2::Point2()
{
   // implicit call to Object constructor occurs here
}

// constructor
Point2::Point2( int xValue, int yValue )
{
   X = xValue;
   Y = yValue;
}

// return string representation of Point2 object
String *Point2::ToString()
{
   return String::Concat( S"[", X.ToString(),
      S", ", Y.ToString(), S"]" );
}
```

Fig. 10.10 Point2 class method definitions.

Figure 10.11 defines class Circle2, which inherits from class Point2. Class Circle2 contains property Radius (lines 16–27) for accessing the circle's radius. A circle has zero volume, so we do not override base-class method Volume. Rather, Circle2 inherits Volume from class Point2, which inherited the method from Shape. A circle does have an area, so Circle2 overrides Shape method Area (lines 32–35 of Fig. 10.12). Property Name (lines 30–33 of Fig. 10.11) overrides property Name of class Point2. If Circle2 did not override property Name, the class would inherit the Point2 version of property Name. In that case, Circle2's Name property would erroneously return "Point2."

```
1  // Fig. 10.11: Circle2.h
2  // Circle2 inherits from class Point2 and overrides key members.
3
4  #pragma once
5
6  #include "Point2.h"
7
8  // Circle2 inherits from class Point2
9  public __gc class Circle2 : public Point2
10 {
11 public:
12    Circle2();                           // default constructor
13    Circle2( int, int, double );         // constructor
14
15    // property Radius
16    __property double get_Radius()
17    {
18       return radius;
19    }
20
21    __property void set_Radius( double value )
22    {
23
24       // ensure non-negative radius value
25       if ( value >= 0 )
26          radius = value;
27    }
28
29    // override property Name of class Point2
30    __property virtual String *get_Name()
31    {
32       return S"Circle2";
33    }
34
35    double Diameter();
36    double Circumference();
37    double Area();
38    String *ToString();
39
40 private:
41    double radius;                      // Circle2 radius
42 }; // end class Circle2
```

Fig. 10.11 Circle2 class that inherits from class Point2.

```
// Fig. 10.12: Circle2.cpp
// Method definitions for class Circle2.

#include "stdafx.h"
#include "Circle2.h"

// default constructor
Circle2::Circle2()
{
   // implicit call to Point2 constructor occurs here
}

Circle2::Circle2( int xValue, int yValue, double radiusValue )
   : Point2( xValue, yValue )
{
   Radius = radiusValue;
}

// calculate diameter
double Circle2::Diameter()
{
   return Radius * 2;
}

// calculate circumference
double Circle2::Circumference()
{
   return Math::PI * Diameter();
}

// calculate area
double Circle2::Area()
{
   return Math::PI * Math::Pow( Radius, 2 );
}

// return string representation of Circle2 object
String *Circle2::ToString()
{
   return String::Concat( S"Center = ",
      __super::ToString(), S"; Radius = ", Radius.ToString() );
}
```

Fig. 10.12 `Circle2` class method definitions.

Figure 10.13 defines class `Cylinder2`, which inherits from class `Circle2`. Class `Cylinder2` contains property `Height` (lines 16–27) for accessing the cylinder's height. A cylinder has different area and volume calculations from those of a circle, so this class overrides method `Area` (lines 20–23 of Fig. 10.14) to calculate the cylinder's surface area and overrides method `Volume` (lines 26–29). Property `Name` (lines 30–33 of Fig. 10.13) overrides property `Name` of class `Circle2`. If this class did not override property `Name`, the class would inherit property `Name` of class `Circle2`, and this property would erroneously return "`Circle2`."

```
// Fig. 10.13: Cylinder2.h
// Cylinder2 inherits from class Circle2 and overrides key members.

#pragma once

#include "Circle2.h"

// Cylinder2 inherits from class Circle2
public __gc class Cylinder2 : public Circle2
{
public:
   Cylinder2();                              // default constructor
   Cylinder2( int, int, double, double );   // constructor

   // property Height
   __property double get_Height()
   {
      return height;
   }

   __property void set_Height( double value )
   {

      // ensure non-negative height value
      if ( value >= 0 )
         height = value;
   }

   // override property Name of class Circle2
   __property virtual String *get_Name()
   {
      return S"Cylinder2";
   }

   double Area();
   double Volume();
   String *ToString();

private:
   double height;          // Cylinder2 height
}; // end class Cylinder2
```

Fig. 10.13 `Cylinder2` class inherits from class `Circle2`.

```
// Fig. 10.14: Cylinder2.cpp
// Cylinder2 inherits from class Circle2 and overrides key members.

#include "stdafx.h"
#include "Cylinder2.h"

```

Fig. 10.14 `Cylinder2` class method definitions. (Part 1 of 2.)

```
Cylinder2::Cylinder2()
{
   // implicit call to Circle2 constructor occurs here
}

// constructor
Cylinder2::Cylinder2( int xValue, int yValue, double radiusValue,
   double heightValue ) : Circle2( xValue, yValue, radiusValue )
{
   Height = heightValue;
}

// calculate area
double Cylinder2::Area()
{
   return 2 * __super::Area() + __super::Circumference() * Height;
}

// calculate volume
double Cylinder2::Volume()
{
   return __super::Area() * Height;
}

// return string representation of Circle2 object
String *Cylinder2::ToString()
{
   return String::Concat( __super::ToString(), S"; Height = ",
      Height.ToString() );
}
```

Fig. 10.14 `Cylinder2` class method definitions. (Part 2 of 2.)

`AbstractShapesTest.cpp` (Fig. 10.15), creates an object of each of the three concrete classes and manipulates those objects polymorphically using an array of `Shape` pointers. Lines 16–18 instantiate a `Point2` object, a `Circle2` object and a `Cylinder2` object, respectively. Next, line 21 allocates array `arrayOfShapes`, which contains three `Shape` pointers. Line 24 assigns pointer `point` to the array element `arrayOfShapes[ 0 ]`, line 27 assigns pointer `circle` to the array element `arrayOfShapes[ 1 ]` and line 30 assigns pointer `cylinder` to the array element `arrayOfShapes[ 2 ]`. These assignments are possible because a `Point2` is a `Shape`, a `Circle2` is a `Shape` and a `Cylinder2` is a `Shape`. Therefore, we can assign pointers of derived classes `Point2`, `Circle2` and `Cylinder2` to base-class `Shape` pointers.

Lines 32–34 access property `Name` and invoke method `ToString` (implicitly) for objects `point`, `circle` and `cylinder`. Property `Name` returns the object's class name and method `ToString` returns the object's string representation (i.e., *x-y* coordinate pair, radius and height, depending on each object's type). Note that lines 32–34 use derived-class pointers to invoke each derived-class object's methods and properties.

```
// Fig. 10.15: AbstractShapesTest.cpp
// Demonstrates polymorphism in Point-Circle-Cylinder hierarchy.

#include "stdafx.h"
#include "Cylinder2.h"

#using <mscorlib.dll>
#using <system.windows.forms.dll>

using namespace System;
using namespace System::Windows::Forms;

int _tmain()
{
   // instantiates Point2, Circle2, Cylinder2 objects
   Point2 *point = new Point2( 7, 11 );
   Circle2 *circle = new Circle2( 22, 8, 3.5 );
   Cylinder2 *cylinder = new Cylinder2( 10, 10, 3.3, 10 );

   // create empty array of Shape base-class pointers
   Shape *arrayOfShapes[] = new Shape *[ 3 ];

   // arrayOfShapes[ 0 ] points to Point2 object
   arrayOfShapes[ 0 ] = point;

   // arrayOfShapes[ 1 ] points to Circle2 object
   arrayOfShapes[ 1 ] = circle;

   // arrayOfShapes[ 2 ] points to Cylinder2 object
   arrayOfShapes[ 2 ] = cylinder;

   String *output = String::Concat( point->Name, S": ", point,
      S"\n", circle->Name, S": ", circle, S"\n",
      cylinder->Name, S": ", cylinder );

   // display Name, Area and Volume for each object
   // in arrayOfShapes polymorphically
   Shape *shape;

   for ( int i = 0; i < arrayOfShapes->Length; i++ ) {

      output = String::Concat( output, S"\n\n", arrayOfShapes[ i ]->Name,
         S": ", arrayOfShapes[ i ], S"\nArea = ",
         arrayOfShapes[ i ]->Area().ToString( S"F" ), S"\nVolume = ",
         arrayOfShapes[ i ]->Volume().ToString( S"F" ) );
   } // end for

   MessageBox::Show( output, S"Demonstrating Polymorphism" );

   return 0;
} // end _tmain
```

Fig. 10.15 AbstractShapesTest demonstrates polymorphism in point-circle-cylinder hierarchy. (Part 1 of 2.)

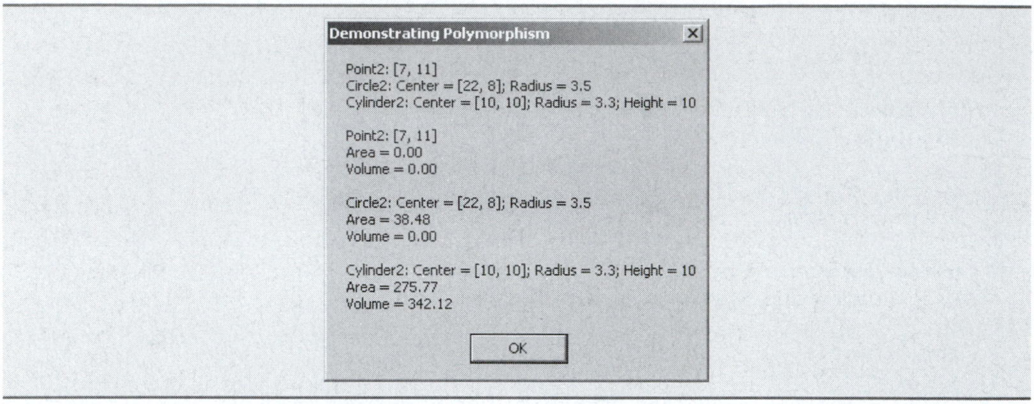

Fig. 10.15 `AbstractShapesTest` demonstrates polymorphism in point-circle-cylinder hierarchy. (Part 2 of 2.)

By contrast, the `for` statement (lines 40–46) uses base-class `Shape` pointers to invoke each derived-class object's methods and properties. The `for` statement uses property `Name` and calls methods `ToString`, `Area` and `Volume` for each `Shape` pointer in `arrayOfShapes`. The property and methods are invoked on each object in `arrayOfShapes`. When the compiler looks at each method/property call, the compiler determines whether each `Shape` pointer (in `arrayOfShapes`) can make these calls. This is the case for property `Name` and methods `Area` and `Volume`, because they are defined in class `Shape`. However, class `Shape` does not define method `ToString`. For this method, the compiler proceeds to `Shape`'s base class (class `Object`) and determines that `Shape` inherited a no-argument `ToString` method from class `Object`. Once the compiler has determined that the `Name` property and methods `ToString`, `Area` and `Volume` can be called for all `Shape`s, the program can compile successfully. At runtime, however, the correct version of the `Name` property and methods `ToString`, `Area` and `Volume` will be called based on the type of the object (i.e., `Point2`, `Circle2` or `Cylinder2`).

The screen capture of Fig. 10.15 illustrates that the "appropriate" property `Name` and methods `ToString`, `Area` and `Volume` were invoked for each type of object in `arrayOfShapes`. By "appropriate," we mean that each property and method call is mapped to the proper object. For example, in the `for` statement's first iteration, pointer `arrayOfShapes[ 0 ]` (which is a pointer to type `Shape`) points to the same object as `point` (which points to a `Point2` object). Class `Point2` overrides property `Name` and method `ToString`, and inherits method `Area` and `Volume` from class `Shape`. At runtime, `arrayOfShapes[ 0 ]` accesses property `Name` and invokes methods `ToString`, `Area` and `Volume` of the `Point2` object. The compiler determines the correct object type, then uses that type to determine the appropriate version of each method to invoke. Through polymorphism, the call to property `Name` returns the string `"Point2:"`; the call to method `ToString` returns the string representation of `point`'s *x*-*y* coordinate pair; and methods `Area` and `Volume` each return `0.00` (as shown in the second group of outputs in Fig. 10.15).

Polymorphism occurs in the next two iterations of the `for` statement as well. Pointer `arrayOfShapes[ 1 ]` points to the same object as `circle` (which points to a `Circle2` object). Class `Circle2` provides implementations for property `Name`, method `ToString` and method `Area`, and inherits method `Volume` from class `Point2` (which, in turn, inherited method

Volume from class Shape). The compiler associates property Name and methods ToString, Area and Volume of the Circle2 object to pointer arrayOfShapes[1]. As a result, property Name returns the string "Circle2:"; method ToString returns the string representation of circle's *x-y* coordinate pair and radius; method Area returns the area (38.48); and method Volume returns 0.00.

For the final iteration of the for statement, pointer arrayOfShapes[2] points to the same object as cylinder (which points to a Cylinder2 object). Class Cylinder2 provides its own implementations for property Name and for methods ToString, Area and Volume. The compiler associates property Name and methods ToString, Area and Volume of the Cylinder2 object to pointer arrayOfShapes[2]. Property Name returns the string "Cylinder2:"; method ToString returns the string representation of cylinder's *x-y* coordinate pair, radius and height; method Area returns the cylinder's surface area (275.77); and method Volume returns the cylinder's volume (342.12).

10.7 __sealed Classes and Methods

The keyword *__sealed* is applied to methods and classes to prevent overriding and inheritance, respectively. A method that is declared __sealed cannot be overridden in a derived class.

Performance Tip 10.1

If the correct command line options are specified, the compiler can decide to inline a __sealed method call and will do so for small, simple __sealed methods. Inlining does not violate encapsulation or information hiding (but does improve performance, because it eliminates the overhead of making a method call).

Performance Tip 10.2

Pipelined processors can improve performance by executing portions of the next several instructions simultaneously, but not if those instructions follow a method call. Inlining (which the compiler can perform on a __sealed method) can improve performance in these processors as it eliminates the out-of-line transfer of control associated with a method call.

Software Engineering Observation 10.10

A class that is declared __sealed cannot be a base class (i.e., a class cannot inherit from a __sealed class). All methods in a __sealed class are __sealed implicitly.

Using the __sealed keyword with classes allows other runtime optimizations. For example, virtual method calls can be transformed into non-virtual method calls.

A __sealed class cannot have any derived classes. A class cannot be declared both __sealed and __abstract.

10.8 Case Study: Payroll System Using Polymorphism

Let us use __abstract classes and polymorphism to perform payroll calculations for various types of employees. We begin by creating abstract base class Employee. The derived classes of Employee are Boss (paid a fixed weekly salary, regardless of the number of hours worked), CommissionWorker (paid a flat base salary plus a percentage of the worker's sales), PieceWorker (paid a flat fee per item produced) and HourlyWorker (paid by the hour with "time-and-a-half" for overtime).

The application must determine the weekly earnings for all types of employees, so each class derived from `Employee` requires method `Earnings`. However, each derived class uses a different calculation to determine earnings for each specific type of employee. Therefore, we declare method `Earnings` as a pure `virtual` method in `Employee` and declare `Employee` to be an `__abstract` class. Each derived class overrides this method to calculate earnings for that employee type.

To calculate any employee's earnings, the program can use a base-class pointer to a derived-class object and invoke method `Earnings`. A real payroll system might reference the various `Employee` objects with individual elements in an array of `Employee` pointers. The program would traverse the array one element at a time, using the `Employee` pointers to invoke the appropriate `Earnings` method of each object.

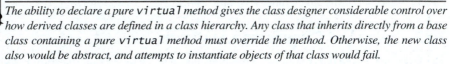

Software Engineering Observation 10.11

The ability to declare a pure `virtual` method gives the class designer considerable control over how derived classes are defined in a class hierarchy. Any class that inherits directly from a base class containing a pure `virtual` method must override the method. Otherwise, the new class also would be abstract, and attempts to instantiate objects of that class would fail.

Let us consider class `Employee` (Fig. 10.16–Fig. 10.17). The `public` members include a constructor (lines 8–12 of Fig. 10.17) that takes as arguments the employee's first and last names; properties `FirstName` (lines 16–24 of Fig. 10.16) and `LastName` (lines 27–35); method `ToString` (lines 15–18 of Fig. 10.17), which returns the first name and last name separated by a space; and a pure `virtual` method `Earnings` (line 38 of Fig. 10.16). The `__abstract` keyword (line 10) indicates that class `Employee` is abstract; thus, it cannot be used to instantiate `Employee` objects. Method `Earnings` is defined as a pure `virtual` method, so the class does not provide a method implementation. All classes derived directly from class `Employee`—except for abstract derived classes—must implement this method. Method `Earnings` is defined as a `virtual` method in `Employee`, because we cannot calculate the earnings for a generic employee. To determine earnings, we first must know of the *type* of the employee. By declaring this method as a pure `virtual` method, we indicate that we will provide an implementation in each concrete derived class, but not in the base class itself.

```
1  // Fig. 10.16: Employee.h
2  // Abstract base class for company employees.
3
4  #pragma once
5
6  #using <mscorlib.dll>
7
8  using namespace System;
9
10 __abstract __gc class Employee
11 {
12 public:
13    Employee( String *, String * );        // constructor
14
```

Fig. 10.16 `Employee` abstract base class definition. (Part 1 of 2.)

```
   // property FirstName
   __property String *get_FirstName()
   {
      return firstName;
   }

   __property void set_FirstName( String *value )
   {
      firstName = value;
   }

   // property LastName
   __property String *get_LastName()
   {
      return lastName;
   }

   __property void set_LastName( String *value )
   {
      lastName = value;
   }

   String *ToString();
   virtual Decimal Earnings() = 0;        // pure virtual method

private:
   String *firstName;
   String *lastName;
}; // end class Employee
```

Fig. 10.16 Employee abstract base class definition. (Part 2 of 2.)

```
// Fig. 10.17: Employee.cpp
// Method definitions for class Employee.

#include "stdafx.h"
#include "Employee.h"

// constructor
Employee::Employee( String *firstNameValue, String *lastNameValue )
{
   FirstName = firstNameValue;
   LastName = lastNameValue;
}

// return string representation of Employee
String *Employee::ToString()
{
   return String::Concat( FirstName, S" ", LastName );
}
```

Fig. 10.17 Employee class method definitions.

Class Boss (Fig. 10.18–Fig. 10.19) inherits from Employee. Class Boss's constructor (lines 8–13 of Fig. 10.19) receives as arguments a first name, a last name and a salary. The constructor passes the first name and last name to the Employee constructor (line 10), which initializes the FirstName and LastName members of the base-class part of the derived-class object. Other public methods in class Boss include method Earnings (lines 16–19), which defines the calculation of a boss's earnings, and method ToString (lines 22–25), which returns a string that indicates the type of employee (i.e., "Boss: ") and the boss's name. Class Boss also includes property WeeklySalary (lines 14–24 of Fig. 10.18), which manipulates the value for member variable salary. Note that this property ensures only that salary cannot hold a negative value—in a real payroll system, this validation would be more extensive and carefully controlled.

```
1   // Fig. 10.18: Boss.h
2   // Boss class derived from Employee.
3
4   #pragma once
5
6   #include "Employee.h"
7
8   public __gc class Boss: public Employee
9   {
10  public:
11     Boss( String *, String *, Decimal );     // constructor
12
13     // property WeeklySalary
14     __property Decimal get_WeeklySalary()
15     {
16        return salary;
17     }
18
19     __property void set_WeeklySalary( Decimal value )
20     {
21        // ensure positive salary value
22        if ( value >= 0 )
23           salary = value;
24     }
25
26     Decimal Earnings();
27     String *ToString();
28
29  private:
30     Decimal salary; // Boss's salary
31  }; // end class Boss
```

Fig. 10.18 Boss class inherits from class Employee.

```
1   // Fig. 10.19: Boss.cpp
2   // Method definitions for class Boss.
3
4   #include "stdafx.h"
```

Fig. 10.19 Boss class method definitions. (Part 1 of 2.)

```
#include "Boss.h"

// constructor
Boss::Boss( String *firstNameValue, String *lastNameValue,
   Decimal salaryValue )
   : Employee ( firstNameValue, lastNameValue )
{
   WeeklySalary = salaryValue;
}

// override base-class method to calculate Boss's earnings
Decimal Boss::Earnings()
{
   return WeeklySalary;
}

// return string representation of Boss
String *Boss::ToString()
{
   return String::Concat( S"Boss: ", __super::ToString() );
}
```

Fig. 10.19 `Boss` class method definitions. (Part 2 of 2.)

Class `CommissionWorker` (Fig. 10.20–Fig. 10.21) also inherits from class `Employee`. The constructor for this class (lines 8–16 of Fig. 10.21) receives as arguments a first name, a last name, a salary, a commission and a quantity of items sold. Line 11 passes the first name and last name to the base-class `Employee` constructor. Class `CommissionWorker` also provides properties `WeeklySalary` (lines 14–24 of Fig. 10.20), `Commission` (lines 27–37) and `Quantity` (lines 40–50); method `Earnings` (lines 20–23 of Fig. 10.21), which calculates the worker's wages; and method `ToString` (lines 26–29), which returns a string that indicates the employee type (i.e., "`CommissionWorker: `") and the worker's name.

```
1  // Fig. 10.20: CommissionWorker.h
2  // CommissionWorker class derived from Employee.
3
4  #pragma once
5
6  #include "Employee.h"
7
8  public __gc class CommissionWorker : public Employee
9  {
10 public:
11    CommissionWorker( String *, String *, Decimal, Decimal, int );
12
13    // property WeeklySalary
14    __property Decimal get_WeeklySalary()
15    {
16       return salary;
17    }
```

Fig. 10.20 `CommissionWorker` class inherits from class `Employee`. (Part 1 of 2.)

```

   __property void set_WeeklySalary( Decimal value )
   {
      // ensure non-negative salary value
      if ( value >= 0 )
         salary = value;
   }

   // property Commission
   __property Decimal get_Commission()
   {
      return commission;
   }

   __property void set_Commission( Decimal value )
   {
      // ensure non-negative salary value
      if ( value >= 0 )
         commission = value;
   }

   // property Quantity
   __property int get_Quantity()
   {
      return quantity;
   }

   __property void set_Quantity( int value )
   {
      // ensure non-negative salary value
      if ( value >= 0 )
         quantity = value;
   }

   Decimal Earnings();
   String *ToString();

private:
   Decimal salary;        // base weekly salary
   Decimal commission;    // amount paid per item sold
   int quantity;          // total items sold
}; // end class CommissionWorker
```

Fig. 10.20 `CommissionWorker` class inherits from class `Employee`. (Part 2 of 2.)

```
// Fig. 10.21: CommissionWorker.cpp
// Method definitions for class Employee.

#include "stdafx.h"
#include "CommissionWorker.h"

```

Fig. 10.21 `CommissionWorker` class method definitions. (Part 1 of 2.)

```
// constructor
CommissionWorker::CommissionWorker( String *firstNameValue,
   String *lastNameValue, Decimal salaryValue,
   Decimal commissionValue, int quantityValue )
   : Employee( firstNameValue, lastNameValue )
{
   WeeklySalary = salaryValue;
   Commission = commissionValue;
   Quantity = quantityValue;
}

// override base-class method to calculate
// CommissionWorker's earnings
Decimal CommissionWorker::Earnings()
{
   return WeeklySalary + Commission * Quantity;
}

// return string representation of CommissionWorker
String *CommissionWorker::ToString()
{
   return String::Concat( S"CommissionWorker: ", __super::ToString() );
}
```

Fig. 10.21 `CommissionWorker` class method definitions. (Part 2 of 2.)

Class `PieceWorker` (Fig. 10.22–Fig. 10.23) inherits from class `Employee`. The constructor for this class (lines 8–14 of Fig. 10.23) receives as arguments a first name, a last name, a wage per piece and a quantity of items produced. Line 10 then passes the first name and last name to the base-class `Employee` constructor. Class `PieceWorker` also provides properties `WagePerPiece` (lines 14–24 of Fig. 10.22) and `Quantity` (lines 27–37); method `Earnings` (lines 17–20 of Fig. 10.23), which calculates a piece worker's earnings; and method `ToString` (lines 23–26), which returns a string that indicates the type of the employee (i.e., "`PieceWorker: `") and the piece worker's name.

```
1  // Fig. 10.22: PieceWorker.h
2  // PieceWorker class derived from Employee.
3
4  #pragma once
5
6  #include "Employee.h"
7
8  public __gc class PieceWorker : public Employee
9  {
10 public:
11    PieceWorker( String *, String *, Decimal, int );
12
13    // property WagePerPiece
14    __property Decimal get_WagePerPiece()
15    {
```

Fig. 10.22 `PieceWorker` class inherits from class `Employee`. (Part 1 of 2.)

```
         return wagePerPiece;
      }

      __property void set_WagePerPiece( Decimal value )
      {
         // ensure non-negative salary value
         if ( value >= 0 )
            wagePerPiece = value;
      }

      // property Quantity
      __property int get_Quantity()
      {
         return quantity;
      }

      __property void set_Quantity( int value )
      {
         // ensure non-negative salary value
         if ( value >= 0 )
            quantity = value;
      }

      Decimal Earnings();
      String *ToString();

   private:
      Decimal wagePerPiece;  // wage per piece produced
      int quantity;          // quantity of pieces produced
   }; // end class PieceWorker
```

Fig. 10.22 `PieceWorker` class inherits from class `Employee`. (Part 2 of 2.)

```
// Fig. 10.23: PieceWorker.cpp
// Method definitions for class PieceWorker.

#include "stdafx.h"
#include "PieceWorker.h"

// constructor
PieceWorker::PieceWorker( String *firstNameValue,
   String *lastNameValue, Decimal wagePerPieceValue,
   int quantityValue ) : Employee( firstNameValue, lastNameValue )
{
   WagePerPiece = wagePerPieceValue;
   Quantity = quantityValue;
}

// override base-class method to calculate PieceWorker's earnings
Decimal PieceWorker::Earnings()
{
```

Fig. 10.23 `PieceWorker` class method definitions. (Part 1 of 2.)

```
      return Quantity * WagePerPiece;
   }

   // return string representation of PieceWorker
   String *PieceWorker::ToString()
   {
      return String::Concat( S"PieceWorker: ", __super::ToString() );
   }
```

Fig. 10.23 `PieceWorker` class method definitions. (Part 2 of 2.)

Class `HourlyWorker` (Fig. 10.24–Fig. 10.25) also inherits from class `Employee`. The constructor for this class (lines 8–14 of Fig. 10.25) receives as arguments a first name, a last name, a wage and the number of hours worked. Line 10 passes the first name and last name to the base-class `Employee` constructor. Class `HourlyWorker` also provides properties `Wage` (lines 14–24 of Fig. 10.24) and `HoursWorked` (lines 27–37); method `Earnings` (lines 17–33 of Fig. 10.25), which calculates an hourly worker's earnings; and method `ToString` (lines 36–39), which returns a string that indicates the type of the employee (i.e., `"HourlyWorker:"`) and the hourly worker's name. Note that hourly workers are paid "time-and-a-half" for "overtime" (i.e., hours worked in excess of 40 hours).

```
1  // Fig. 10.24: HourlyWorker.h
2  // HourlyWorker class derive from Employee.
3
4  #pragma once
5
6  #include "Employee.h"
7
8  public __gc class HourlyWorker : public Employee
9  {
10 public:
11    HourlyWorker( String *, String *, Decimal, double );
12
13    // property Wage
14    __property Decimal get_Wage()
15    {
16       return wage;
17    }
18
19    __property void set_Wage( Decimal value )
20    {
21       // ensure non-negative wage value
22       if ( value >= 0)
23          wage = value;
24    }
25
26    // property HoursWorked
27    __property double get_HoursWorked()
28    {
```

Fig. 10.24 `HourlyWorker` class inherits from class `Employee`. (Part 1 of 2.)

```
      return hoursWorked;
   }

   __property void set_HoursWorked( double value )
   {
      // ensure non-negative hoursWorked value
      if ( value >= 0 )
         hoursWorked = value;
   }

   Decimal Earnings();
   String *ToString();

private:
   Decimal wage;          // wage per hour of work
   double hoursWorked;    // hours worked during week
   static const int STANDARD_HOURS = 40;
}; // end class HourlyWorker
```

Fig. 10.24 HourlyWorker class inherits from class Employee. (Part 2 of 2.)

```
// Fig. 10.25: HourlyWorker.cpp
// Method definitions for class HourlyWorker.

#include "stdafx.h"
#include "HourlyWorker.h"

// constructor
HourlyWorker::HourlyWorker( String *firstNameValue,
   String *lastNameValue, Decimal wageValue, double hoursWorkedValue )
   : Employee( firstNameValue, lastNameValue )
{
   Wage = wageValue;
   HoursWorked = hoursWorkedValue;
}

// override base-class method to calculate HourlyWorker earnings
Decimal HourlyWorker::Earnings()
{
   // compensate for overtime (paid "time-and-a-half")
   if ( HoursWorked <= STANDARD_HOURS ) {
      return Wage * static_cast< Decimal >( HoursWorked );
   } // end if

   else {
      // calculate base and overtime pay
      Decimal basePay = Wage *
         static_cast< Decimal >( STANDARD_HOURS );
      Decimal overtimePay = Wage * 1.5 *
         static_cast< Decimal >( HoursWorked - STANDARD_HOURS );

```

Fig. 10.25 HourlyWorker class method definitions. (Part 1 of 2.)

```
         return basePay + overtimePay;
      } // end else
   } // end method Earnings

   // return string representation of HourlyWorker
   String *HourlyWorker::ToString()
   {
      return String::Concat( S"HourlyWorker: ", __super::ToString() );
   }
```

Fig. 10.25 `HourlyWorker` class method definitions. (Part 2 of 2.)

Function `_tmain` (lines 20–60) of class `EmployeesTest` (Fig. 10.26) declares `Employee` pointer `employee` (line 33). Each employee type is handled similarly in `_tmain`, so we discuss only the manipulations of the `Boss` object.

```
1  // Fig. 10.26: EmployeesTest.cpp
2  // Domesticates polymorphism by displaying earnings
3  // for various Employee types.
4
5  #include "stdafx.h"
6  #include "PieceWorker.h"
7  #include "CommissionWorker.h"
8  #include "HourlyWorker.h"
9  #include "Boss.h"
10
11 #using <mscorlib.dll>
12 #using <system.windows.forms.dll>
13
14 using namespace System;
15 using namespace System::Windows::Forms;
16
17 // return string that contains Employee information
18 String *GetString( Employee *worker );
19
20 int _tmain()
21 {
22    Boss *boss = new Boss( S"John", S"Smith", 800 );
23
24    CommissionWorker *commissionWorker =
25       new CommissionWorker( S"Sue", S"Jones", 400, 3, 150 );
26
27    PieceWorker *pieceWorker = new PieceWorker( S"Bob", S"Lewis",
28       static_cast< Decimal >( 2.5 ), 200 );
29
30    HourlyWorker *hourlyWorker = new HourlyWorker( S"Karen",
31       S"Price", static_cast< Decimal >( 13.75 ), 50 );
32
33    Employee *employee = boss;
34
35    String *output = String::Concat( GetString( employee ), boss,
36       S" earned ", boss->Earnings().ToString( "C" ), S"\n\n" );
```

Fig. 10.26 `EmployeesTest` class tests the `Employee` class hierarchy. (Part 1 of 2.)

```
37
38     employee = commissionWorker;
39
40     output = String::Concat( output, GetString( employee ),
41        commissionWorker, S" earned ",
42        commissionWorker->Earnings().ToString( "C" ), S"\n\n" );
43
44     employee = pieceWorker;
45
46     output = String::Concat( output, GetString( employee ),
47        pieceWorker, S" earned ",
48        pieceWorker->Earnings().ToString( "C" ), S"\n\n" );
49
50     employee = hourlyWorker;
51
52     output = String::Concat( output, GetString( employee ),
53        hourlyWorker, S" earned ",
54        hourlyWorker->Earnings().ToString( "C" ), S"\n\n" );
55
56     MessageBox::Show( output, S"Demonstrating Polymorphism",
57        MessageBoxButtons::OK, MessageBoxIcon::Information );
58
59     return 0;
60  } // end _tmain
61
62  // return string that contains Employee information
63  String *GetString( Employee *worker )
64  {
65     return String::Concat( worker->ToString(), S" earned ",
66        worker->Earnings().ToString( "C" ), S"\n" );
67  } // end function GetString
```

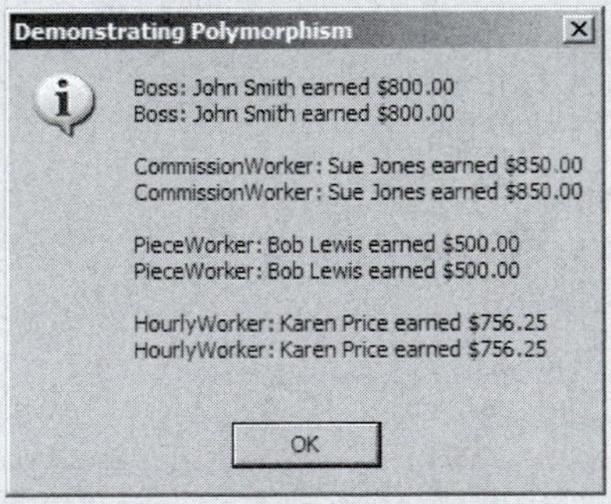
Demonstrating Polymorphism
Boss: John Smith earned $800.00
Boss: John Smith earned $800.00
CommissionWorker: Sue Jones earned $850.00
CommissionWorker: Sue Jones earned $850.00
PieceWorker: Bob Lewis earned $500.00
PieceWorker: Bob Lewis earned $500.00
HourlyWorker: Karen Price earned $756.25
HourlyWorker: Karen Price earned $756.25
OK

Fig. 10.26 `EmployeesTest` class tests the `Employee` class hierarchy. (Part 2 of 2.)

Line 22 creates a new `Boss` object and passes to its constructor the boss's first name ("`John`"), last name ("`Smith`") and fixed weekly salary (`800`). Line 33 assigns the derived-class pointer `boss` to the base-class `Employee` pointer `employee`, so we can demonstrate the polymorphic determination of `boss`'s earnings. Lines 35–36 pass pointer `employee` as an argument to function `GetString` (lines 63–67), which polymorphically invokes methods `ToString` and `Earnings` on the `Employee` object the method receives as an argument. So lines 65–66 invoke `Boss` methods `ToString` and `Earnings` through the `Employee` pointer. These are classic examples of polymorphic behavior.

Method `Earnings` returns a `Decimal` object on which line 66 then calls method `ToString`. In this case, the string `"C"`, which is passed to an overloaded version of `Decimal` method `ToString`, stands for currency, and `ToString` formats the string as a currency amount.

When function `GetString` returns to `_tmain`, lines 35–36 explicitly invoke methods `ToString` and `Earnings` through derived-class `Boss` pointer `boss` to show the method invocations that do not use polymorphic processing. The output generated in lines 35–36 is identical for the method calls made both through the base class `Employee` pointer and the derived class `Boss` pointer, which verifies that the polymorphic method calls performed on method `GetString` invoke the appropriate methods in derived class `Boss`.

To prove that the base-class pointer `employee` can invoke the proper derived-class versions of methods `ToString` and `Earnings` for the other types of employees, lines 38, 44 and 50 assign to base-class pointer `employee` a different type of `Employee` object (`CommissionWorker`, `PieceWorker` and `HourlyWorker`, respectively). After each assignment, the application calls method `GetString` to return the results via the base-class pointer. Then the application calls methods `ToString` and `Earnings` through each derived-class pointer to show that the compiler correctly associates each method call to its corresponding derived-class object.

10.9 Case Study: Creating and Using Interfaces

We now present two more examples of polymorphism using *interfaces* that specify sets of `public` services (i.e., methods and properties) that classes must implement. An interface is used when there is no default implementation to inherit (i.e., no data members and no default-method implementations). Whereas an abstract class is best used for providing data and services for objects in a hierarchical relationship, an interface can be used for providing services that "bring together" disparate objects that relate to one another only through that interface.

An interface definition begins with the keyword `__interface` and contains a list of `public` methods and properties. All methods and properties of an interface are pure `virtual` methods and are `public`. Interfaces cannot contain data members. Interfaces can inherit from other interfaces, but not from classes. To use an interface, a class must specify that it implements the interface (also referred to as "inheriting the interface") and must provide implementations for every method and property specified in the interface definition. A class that implements an interface effectively signs a contract with the compiler that states, "this class will define all the methods and properties specified by the interface."

Software Engineering Observation 10.12

All methods and properties of an interface are both `public` and pure `virtual`; as a result, the `public` and `virtual` keywords may be omitted, as well as the "= 0" initializer for the method.

Common Programming Error 10.7

When a non-abstract class implements an `__interface`, leaving even a single `__interface` method or property undefined is an error. The class must define every method and property in the `__interface`.

Interfaces provide uniform sets of methods and properties for objects of disparate classes. These methods and properties enable programs to process the objects of those disparate classes polymorphically. For example, consider disparate objects that represent a person, a tree, a car and a file. These objects have "nothing to do" with one another—a person has a first name and last name; a tree has a trunk, a set of branches and a bunch of leaves; a car has wheels, gears and several other mechanisms that enable the car to move; and a file contains data. Due to the lack of commonality among these classes, modeling them via an inheritance hierarchy with a common base class seems illogical. However, these objects certainly have at least one common characteristic—an age. A person's age is represented by the number of years since that person was born; a tree's age is represented by the number of rings in its trunk; a car's age is represented by its manufacture date; and file's age is represented by its creation date. We can use an interface that provides a method or property that objects of these disparate classes can implement to return each object's age.

Inheriting the `IAge` Interface

In this example, we use interface `IAge` (Fig. 10.27) to return the age information for classes `Person` (Fig. 10.28–Fig. 10.29) and `Tree` (Fig. 10.30–Fig. 10.31). The definition of interface `IAge` begins in line 10 with `public __gc __interface` and ends in line 15 with a closing curly brace. Lines 13–14 specify read-only properties `Age` and `Name`, for which every class that implements interface `IAge` must provide implementations. Declaring read-only properties is not required—an interface can also provide methods, write-only properties and properties with both *get* and *set* methods. By specifying these property declarations, interface `IAge` provides an opportunity for an object that implements `IAge` to return its age and name, respectively. Classes implementing interface `IAge` are required to provide implementations for the interface's properties.

```
1  // Fig. 10.27: IAge.h
2  // Interface IAge declares property for setting and getting age.
3
4  #pragma once
5
6  #using <mscorlib.dll>
7
8  using namespace System;
9
10 public __gc __interface IAge
11 {
12 public:
13    __property int get_Age() = 0;
14    __property String *get_Name() = 0;
15 }
```

Fig. 10.27 `IAge` interface for returning age of objects of disparate classes.

Good Programming Practice 10.2

By convention, begin the name of each interface with "I."

Line 8 (Fig. 10.28) uses MC++'s inheritance notation (i.e., *ClassName* : *InterfaceName*) to indicate that class `Person` implements interface `IAge`. In this example, class `Person` implements only one interface. A class can implement any number of interfaces in addition to inheriting from one class. To implement more than one interface or to implement interfaces in addition to inheriting from one class, the class definition must provide a comma-separated list of names after the semicolon such as

```
public __gc class MyClass2 : public IFace1, public IFace2,
   public MyClass1
```

Class `Person` (Fig. 10.28) has `private` data members `firstName`, `lastName` and (lines 26–28), for which the constructor (lines 8–19 of Fig. 10.29) sets values. Class `Person` (Fig. 10.28) implements interface `IAge`, so class `Person` must implement properties `Age` and `Name`—defined in lines 14–17 and lines 20–23, respectively. Property `Age` allows the client to obtain the person's age, and property `Name` returns a string containing `firstName` and `lastName`. Note that property `Age` calculates the person's age by subtracting `yearBorn` from the current year (via property `Year` of property `DateTime::Now`, which returns the current date). These properties satisfy the implementation requirements defined in interface `IAge`, so class `Person` has fulfilled its "contract" with the compiler.

```
1  // Fig. 10.28: Person.h
2  // Class Person has a birthday.
3
4  #pragma once
5
6  #include "IAge.h"
7
8  public __gc class Person : public IAge
9  {
10 public:
11    Person( String *, String *, int );
12
13    // property Age implementation of interface IAge
14    __property int get_Age()
15    {
16       return DateTime::Now.Year - yearBorn;
17    }
18
19    // property Name implementation of interface IAge
20    __property String *get_Name()
21    {
22       return String::Concat( firstName, S" ", lastName );
23    }
24
25 private:
26    String *firstName;
27    String *lastName;
28    int yearBorn;
29 }; // end class Person
```

Fig. 10.28 `Person` class implements `IAge` interface.

```
1  // Fig. 10.29: Person.cpp
2  // Method definitions of class Person.
3
4  #include "stdafx.h"
```

Fig. 10.29 `Person` class method definitions. (Part 1 of 2.)

```
#include "Person.h"

// constructor
Person::Person( String *firstNameValue, String *lastNameValue,
   int yearBornValue )
{
   firstName = firstNameValue;
   lastName = lastNameValue;

   if ( ( yearBornValue > 0 ) &&
      ( yearBornValue <= DateTime::Now.Year ) )
         yearBorn = yearBornValue;
   else
      yearBorn = DateTime::Now.Year;
}
```

Fig. 10.29 Person class method definitions. (Part 2 of 2.)

Class `Tree` (Fig. 10.30–Fig. 10.31) also implements interface `IAge`. Class `Tree` has `private` data member `rings` (line 27 of Fig. 10.30), which represents the number of rings inside the tree's trunk—this variable corresponds directly to the tree's age. The `Tree` constructor (lines 8–16 of Fig. 10.31) receives as an argument an `int` that specifies in which year the tree was planted. Class `Tree` also includes method `AddRing` (lines 19–22), which enables a program to increment the number of rings in the tree. Class `Tree` implements interface `IAge`, so class `Tree` (Fig. 10.30) must implement properties `Age` and `Name`—defined in lines 15–18 and lines 21–24, respectively. Property `Age` returns the value of `rings`, and property `Name` returns `"Tree"`.

```
1  // Fig. 10.30: Tree.h
2  // Class Tree contains number of rings corresponding to its age.
3
4  #pragma once
5
6  #include "IAge.h"
7
8  public __gc class Tree : public IAge
9  {
10 public:
11    Tree( int );                   // constructor
12    void AddRing();
13
14    // property Age implementation of interface IAge
15    __property int get_Age()
16    {
17       return rings;
18    }
19
20    // property Name implementation of interface IAge
21    __property String *get_Name()
22    {
23       return "Tree";
24    }
```

Fig. 10.30 Tree class implements IAge interface. (Part 1 of 2.)

```

private:
   int rings;      // number of rings in tree trunk
}; // end class Tree
```

Fig. 10.30 Tree class implements IAge interface. (Part 2 of 2.)

```
// Fig. 10.31: Tree.cpp
// Method definitions for class Tree.

#include "stdafx.h"
#include "Tree.h"

// constructor
Tree::Tree( int yearPlanted )
{
   if ( yearPlanted >= 0 && yearPlanted <= DateTime::Now.Year )

      // count number of rings in Tree
      rings = DateTime::Now.Year - yearPlanted;
   else
      rings = 0;
}

// increment rings
void Tree::AddRing()
{
   rings++;
}
```

Fig. 10.31 Tree class method definitions.

InterfacesTest.cpp (Fig. 10.32) demonstrates polymorphism on the objects of disparate classes Person and Tree. Line 16 instantiates pointer tree of type Tree *, and line 17 instantiates pointer person of type Person *. Line 20 declares iAgeArray—an array of two pointers to IAge objects. Lines 23 and 26 assign the address of tree and person to the first and second pointers in iAgeArray, respectively. Lines 29–30 invoke method ToString on tree, then invoke its properties Age and Name to return age and name information for object tree. Lines 33–34 invoke method ToString on person, then invoke its properties Age and Name to return age and name information for person. Next, we manipulate these objects polymorphically through the iAgeArray array of pointers to IAge objects. Lines 39–44 define a for statement that uses properties Age and Name to obtain age and name information for each IAge pointer in iAgeArray. Note that a program also can invoke class Object's public methods (e.g., ToString) using any interface pointer. This is possible because every object inherits directly or indirectly from class Object. Therefore, every object is guaranteed to have the class Object's public methods.

Software Engineering Observation 10.13

In MC++, an interface pointer may invoke methods and properties that the interface declares and the public *methods of class* Object*.*

Software Engineering Observation 10.14

In MC++, an interface provides only those `public` *services declared in the interface, whereas an abstract class provides the* `public` *services defined in the abstract class and those members inherited from the abstract class's base class.*

```
// Fig. 10.32: InterfacesTest.cpp
// Demonstrating polymorphism with interfaces.

#include "stdafx.h"
#include "Person.h"
#include "Tree.h"

#using <mscorlib.dll>
#using <system.windows.forms.dll>

using namespace System;
using namespace System::Windows::Forms;

int _tmain()
{
   Tree *tree = new Tree( 1978 );
   Person *person = new Person( S"Bob", S"Jones", 1971 );

   // create array of IAge pointers
   IAge *iAgeArray[] = new IAge *[ 2 ];

   // IAgeArray[ 0 ] points to Tree object
   iAgeArray[ 0 ] = tree;

   // IAgeArray[ 1 ] points to Person object
   iAgeArray[ 1 ] = person;

   // display tree information
   String *output = String::Concat( tree, S": ", tree->Name,
      S"\nAge is ", tree->Age, S"\n\n" );

   // display person information
   output = String::Concat( output, person, S": ", person->Name,
      S"\nAge is ", person->Age, S"\n\n" );

   // display name and age for each IAge object in iAgeArray
   IAge *agePtr;

   for ( int i = 0; i < iAgeArray->Length; i++ ) {
      agePtr = iAgeArray[ i ];

      output = String::Concat( output, agePtr->Name,
         S": Age is ", agePtr->Age.ToString(), S"\n" );
   } // end for

   MessageBox::Show( output, S"Demonstrating Polymorphism" );
```

Fig. 10.32 Polymorphism demonstrated on objects of disparate classes. (Part 1 of 2.)

```

   return 0;
} // end _tmain
```

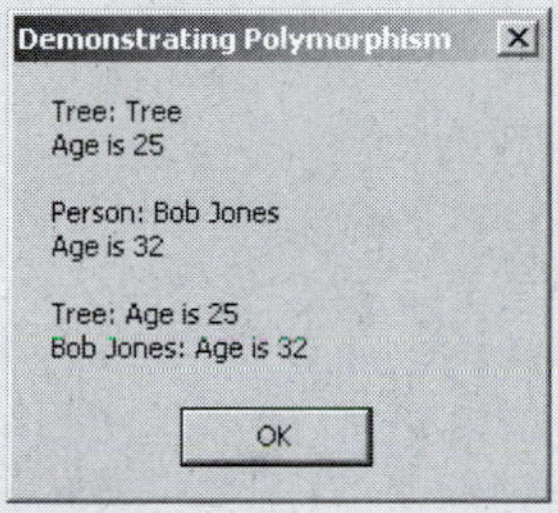
Demonstrating Polymorphism
Tree: Tree
Age is 25
Person: Bob Jones
Age is 32
Tree: Age is 25
Bob Jones: Age is 32
OK

Fig. 10.32 Polymorphism demonstrated on objects of disparate classes. (Part 2 of 2.)

Implementing the `Point-Circle-Cylinder` Hierarchy Using an Interface

Our next example reexamines the `Point-Circle-Cylinder` hierarchy using an interface, rather than using an abstract class, to describe the common methods and properties of the classes in the hierarchy. We now show how a class can implement an interface, then act as a base class for derived classes to inherit the implementation. We create interface `IShape` (Fig. 10.33), which specifies methods `Area` and `Volume` and property `Name` (lines 14, 15, and 16). Every class that implements interface `IShape` must provide implementations for these two methods and this read-only property. Note that, even though the methods in this example interface do not receive arguments, interface methods can receive arguments (just as regular methods can receive arguments).

```
1  // Fig. 10.33: IShape.h
2  // Interface IShape for Point, Circle, Cylinder Hierarchy.
3
4  #pragma once
5
6  #using <mscorlib.dll>
7
8  using namespace System;
9
10 public __gc __interface IShape
11 {
12    // classes that implement IShape must implement these methods
13    // and this property
14    double Area();
15    double Volume();
16    __property String *get_Name();
17 }; // end interface IShape
```

Fig. 10.33 `IShape` interface provides methods `Area` and `Volume` and property `Name`.

Class `Point3` (Fig. 10.34–Fig. 10.35) implements interface `IShape`; therefore, class `Point3` must implement all three `IShape` members. Lines 28–31 (Fig. 10.35) implement method `Area`, which returns `0`, because points have an area of zero. Lines 34–37 implement method `Volume`, which also returns `0`, because points have a volume of zero. Lines 43–46 (Fig. 10.34) implement read-only property `Name`, which returns the class name, or `"Point3"`.

```
// Fig. 10.34: Point3.h
// Point3 implements interface IShape and represents
// an x-y coordinate pair.

#pragma once

#include "IShape.h"

// Point3 implements IShape
public __gc class Point3 : public IShape
{
public:
   Point3();                          // default constructor
   Point3( int, int );                // constructor

   // property X
   __property int get_X()
   {
      return x;
   }

   __property void set_X( int value )
   {
      x = value;
   }

   // property Y
   __property int get_Y()
   {
      return y;
   }

   __property void set_Y( int value )
   {
      y = value;
   }

   String *ToString();
   virtual double Area();
   virtual double Volume();

   // property Name
   __property virtual String *get_Name()
   {
      return S"Point3";
   }

private:
   int x, y;                          // Point3 coordinates
}; // end class Point3
```

Fig. 10.34 `Point3` class implements interface `IShape`.

```
// Fig. 10.35: Point3.cpp
// Method definitions for class Point3.

#include "stdafx.h"
#include "Point3.h"

// default constructor
Point3::Point3()
{
   // implicit call to Object constructor occurs here
}

// constructor
Point3::Point3( int xValue, int yValue )
{
   X = xValue;
   Y = yValue;
}

// return string representation of Point3 object
String *Point3::ToString()
{
   return String::Concat( S"[", X.ToString(), S", ",
      Y.ToString(), S"]" );
}

// implement interface IShape method Area
double Point3::Area()
{
   return 0;
}

// implement interface IShape method Volume
double Point3::Volume()
{
   return 0;
}
```

Fig. 10.35 `Point3` class method definitions.

When a class implements an interface, the class enters the same kind of "is-a" relationship that inheritance establishes. In our example, class `Point3` implements interface `IShape`. Therefore, a `Point3` object *is an* `IShape`, and objects of any class that inherits from `Point3` are also `IShape`s. For example, class `Circle3` (Fig. 10.36–Fig. 10.37) inherits from class `Point3`; thus, a `Circle3` *is an* `IShape`. Class `Circle3` implements interface `IShape` implicitly and inherits the `IShape` methods that class `Point` implemented. Circles do not have volume, so class `Circle3` does not override class `Point3`'s `Volume` method, which returns zero. However, we do not want to use the class `Point3` method `Area` or property `Name` for class `Circle3`. Class `Circle3` should provide its own implementation for these, because the area and name of a circle differ from those of a point. Lines 33–36 (Fig. 10.37) override method `Area` to return the circle's area, and lines 35–38 (Fig. 10.36) override property `Name` to return `"Circle3"`.

```
// Fig. 10.36: Circle3.h
// Circle3 inherits from class Point3 and overrides key members.

#pragma once

#include "Point3.h"

// Circle3 inherits from class Point3
public __gc class Circle3 : public Point3
{
public:
   Circle3();                          // default constructor
   Circle3( int, int, double );        // constructor

   // property Radius
   __property double get_Radius()
   {
      return radius;
   }

   __property void set_Radius( double value )
   {

      // ensure non-negative radius value
      if ( value >= 0 )
         radius = value;
   }

   double Diameter();
   double Circumference();
   double Area();
   String *ToString();

   // override property Name from class Point3
   __property String *get_Name()
   {
      return S"Circle3";
   }

private:
   double radius;                      // Circle3 radius
}; // end class Circle3
```

Fig. 10.36 Circle3 class inherits from class Point3.

```
// Fig. 10.37: Circle3.cpp
// Method definitions for class Circle3.

#include "stdafx.h"
#include "Circle3.h"

// default constructor
Circle3::Circle3()
```

Fig. 10.37 Circle3 class method definitions. (Part 1 of 2.)

```
{
   // implicit call to Point3 constructor occurs here
}

// constructor
Circle3::Circle3( int xValue, int yValue, double radiusValue )
   : Point3( xValue, yValue )
{
   Radius = radiusValue;
}

// calculate diameter
double Circle3::Diameter()
{
   return Radius * 2;
}

// calculate circumference
double Circle3::Circumference()
{
   return Math::PI * Diameter();
}

// calculate area
double Circle3::Area()
{
   return Math::PI * Math::Pow( Radius, 2 );
}

// return string representation of Circle3 object
String *Circle3::ToString()
{
   return String::Concat( S"Center = ", __super::ToString(),
      S"; Radius = ", Radius.ToString() );
}
```

Fig. 10.37 `Circle3` class method definitions. (Part 2 of 2.)

Class `Cylinder3` (Fig. 10.38–Fig. 10.39) inherits from class `Circle3`. `Cylinder3` implements interface `IShape` implicitly, because `Cylinder3` indirectly derives from `Point3`, which implements interface `IShape`. `Cylinder3` inherits method `Area` and property `Name` from `Circle3` and method `Volume` from `Point3`. However, `Cylinder3` overrides property `Name` and methods `Area` and `Volume` to perform `Cylinder3`-specific operations. Lines 21–24 (Fig. 10.39) override method `Area` to return the cylinder's surface area, lines 27–30 override method `Volume` to return the cylinder's volume, and lines 34–37 (Fig. 10.38) override property `Name` to return `"Cylinder3"`.

```
1  // Fig. 10.38: Cylinder3.h
2  // Cylinder3 inherits from class Circle3 and overrides key members.
3
```

Fig. 10.38 `Cylinder3` class inherits from class `Circle3`. (Part 1 of 2.)

```
#pragma once

#include "Circle3.h"

// Cylinder3 inherits from class Circle3
public __gc class Cylinder3 : public Circle3
{
public:
   Cylinder3();                                    // default constructor
   Cylinder3( int, int, double, double ); // constructor

   // property Height
   __property double get_Height()
   {
      return height;
   }

   __property void set_Height( double value )
   {

      // ensure non-negative height value
      if ( value >= 0 )
         height = value;
   }

   double Area();                                  // calculate area
   double Volume();                                // calculate volume
   String *ToString();

   // override property Name from class Cylinder3
   __property String *get_Name()
   {
      return S"Cylinder3";
   }

private:
   double height;                                  // Cylinder3 height
}; // end class Cylinder3
```

Fig. 10.38 `Cylinder3` class inherits from class `Circle3`. (Part 2 of 2.)

```
// Fig. 10.39: Cylinder3.cpp
// Method definitions for class Cylinder3.

#include "stdafx.h"
#include "Cylinder3.h"

// default constructor
Cylinder3::Cylinder3()
{
   // implicit call to Circle3 constructor occurs here
}
```

Fig. 10.39 `Cylinder3` class method definitions. (Part 1 of 2.)

```

// constructor
Cylinder3::Cylinder3( int xValue, int yValue, double radiusValue,
   double heightValue ) : Circle3( xValue, yValue, radiusValue )
{
   Height = heightValue;
}

// calculate area
double Cylinder3::Area()
{
   return 2 * __super::Area() + __super::Circumference() * Height;
}

// calculate volume
double Cylinder3::Volume()
{
   return __super::Area() * Height;
}

// return string representation of Circle3 object
String *Cylinder3::ToString()
{
   return String::Concat( __super::ToString(),
      S"; Height = ", Height.ToString() );
}
```

Fig. 10.39 `Cylinder3` class method definitions. (Part 2 of 2.)

`Interfaces2Test.cpp` (Fig. 10.40) demonstrates our point-circle-cylinder hierarchy that uses interfaces. Figure 10.40 is almost identical to the example in Fig. 10.15, which tested the class hierarchy created from the `__abstract` base class `Shape`. In Fig. 10.40, line 22 declares `arrayOfShapes` as an array of `IShape` interface pointers, rather than `Shape` base-class pointers.

```
1  // Fig. 10.40: Interfaces2Test.cpp
2  // Demonstrating polymorphism with interfaces in
3  // Point-Circle-Cylinder hierarchy.
4
5  #include "stdafx.h"
6  #include "Cylinder3.h"
7
8  #using <mscorlib.dll>
9  #using <system.windows.forms.dll>
10
11 using namespace System;
12 using namespace System::Windows::Forms;
13
14 int _tmain()
15 {
```

Fig. 10.40 `Interfaces2Test` uses interfaces to demonstrate polymorphism in point-circle-cylinder hierarchy. (Part 1 of 2.)

```
   // instantiate Point3, Circle3 and Cylinder3 objects
   Point3 *point = new Point3( 7, 11 );
   Circle3 *circle = new Circle3( 22, 8, 3.5 );
   Cylinder3 *cylinder = new Cylinder3( 10, 10 , 3.3, 10 );

   // create array of IShape pointers
   IShape *arrayOfShapes[] = new IShape*[ 3 ];

   // arrayOfShapes[ 0 ] points to Point3 object
   arrayOfShapes[ 0 ] = point;

   // arrayOfShapes[ 1 ] points to Circle3 object
   arrayOfShapes[ 1 ] = circle;

   // arrayOfShapes[ 2 ] points to Cylinder3 object
   arrayOfShapes[ 2 ] = cylinder;

   String *output = String::Concat( point->Name, S": ",
      point->ToString(), S"\n", circle->Name,
      S": ", circle, S"\n", cylinder->Name,
      S": ", cylinder->ToString() );

   IShape *shape;

   for ( int i = 0; i < arrayOfShapes->Length; i++ ) {

      output = String::Concat( output, S"\n\n",
         arrayOfShapes[ i ]->Name, S": ", arrayOfShapes[ i ],
         S"\nArea = ", arrayOfShapes[ i ]->Area().ToString( S"F" ),
         S"\nVolume = ", arrayOfShapes[ i ]->Volume().ToString( S"F" ) );
   } // end for

   MessageBox::Show( output, S"Demonstrating Polymorphism" );

   return 0;
} // end _tmain
```

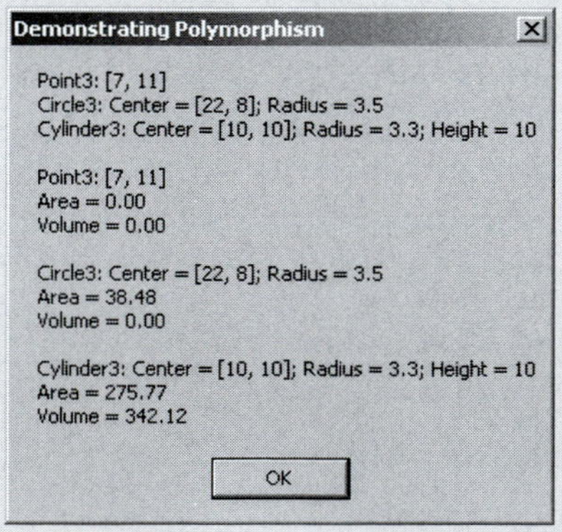

Fig. 10.40 `Interfaces2Test` uses interfaces to demonstrate polymorphism in point-circle-cylinder hierarchy. (Part 2 of 2.)

10.10 Delegates

In Chapter 9, we discussed how objects can pass member variables as arguments to methods. However, sometimes, it is beneficial for objects to pass methods as arguments to other methods. For example, suppose that you wish to sort a series of values in ascending and descending order. Rather than provide separate ascending and descending sorting methods (one for each type of comparison), we could provide a single method that receives as an argument a pointer to the comparison method to use. To perform an ascending sort, we could pass to the sorting method the pointer to the ascending-sort-comparison method; to perform a descending sort, we could pass to the sorting method the pointer to the descending-sort-comparison method. The sorting method then would use this comparison method to sort the list—the sorting method would not need to know whether it is performing an ascending or a descending sort, or how the comparison method is implemented.

MC++ does not allow the passing of method pointers directly as arguments to other methods, but does provide *delegates*, which are classes that encapsulate sets of pointers to methods. A delegate object that contains method pointers can be passed to another method. Rather than send method pointers directly, objects can send delegate instances, which contain the pointers to the methods that we would like to send. The method that receives the pointer to the delegate then can invoke the methods the delegate contains.

A delegate can contain one or several methods, and is created or derived from class *`MulticastDelegate`* (which, in turn, is derived from class *`Delegate`*). Both delegate classes belong to namespace `System`.

To use a delegate, we first must declare one. The delegate's declaration specifies a method prototype (parameters and return value). When the application is compiled, the delegate's declaration is used to create a managed class that inherits from class `MulticastDelegate`. This class will have the same name as the delegate itself. Methods whose pointers will be contained within a delegate object must have the same signature as that defined in the delegate declaration. We then create methods that have this signature. The next step is to create a delegate instance (using the generated class) that contains a pointer to that method. The delegate always accepts two parameters—a pointer to an object that encapsulates the method definition and a pointer to the method. After we create the delegate instance, we can invoke the method pointer that it contains. We show this process in our next example.

Software Engineering Observation 10.15

Delegates may not be overloaded.

Class `DelegateBubbleSort` (Fig. 10.41–Fig. 10.42) uses delegates to sort an integer array in ascending or descending order. Line 13 (Fig. 10.41) provides the declaration for delegate `Comparator`. To declare a delegate, we declare a prototype of a method—keyword `__delegate`, followed by the return type, the delegate name and parameter list. Delegate `Comparator` defines a method signature for methods that receive two `int` arguments and return a `bool`. Note that the body of delegate `Comparator` is not defined in Fig. 10.42. As we soon demonstrate, class `BubbleSort` (Fig. 10.43–Fig. 10.44) implements methods that adhere to delegate `Comparator`'s signature, then passes these methods (as arguments of type `Comparator`) to method `SortArray`. The declaration of a delegate does not define its intended role or implementation; our application uses this particular delegate when comparing two `int`s, but other applications might use it for different purposes.

```
// Fig. 10.41: DelegateBubbleSort.h
// Demonstrating delegates for sorting numbers.

#pragma once

#using <mscorlib.dll>

using namespace System;

public __gc class DelegateBubbleSort
{
public:
   __delegate bool Comparator( int, int );

   // sort array using Comparator delegate
   static void SortArray( int __gc[], Comparator * );

private:

   // swap two elements
   static void Swap( int __gc *, int __gc * );
}; // end class DelegateBubbleSort
```

Fig. 10.41 Delegates used in a bubble-sort program.

```
// Fig. 10.42: DelegateBubbleSort.cpp
// Method definitions for class DelegateBubbleSort.

#include "stdafx.h"
#include "DelegateBubbleSort.h"

// sort array using Comparator delegate
void DelegateBubbleSort::SortArray( int array __gc[],
   Comparator *Compare )
{
   for ( int pass = 0; pass < array->Length; pass++ )

      for ( int i = 0; i < array->Length - 1; i++ )

         if ( Compare( array[ i ], array [ i + 1 ] ) )
            Swap( &array[ i ], &array[ i + 1 ] );
}

// swap two elements
void DelegateBubbleSort::Swap( int __gc *firstElement,
   int __gc *secondElement )
{
   int hold = *firstElement;
   *firstElement = *secondElement;
   *secondElement = hold;
}
```

Fig. 10.42 `DelegateBubbleSort` class method definitions.

Lines 8–17 (Fig. 10.42) define method `SortArray`, which takes an array and a pointer to a `Comparator` delegate object as arguments. Recall that a class with the same name as the delegate (`Comparator`) will be created when the application is compiled. This is why we can create objects of type `Comparator`. Method `SortArray` modifies the array by sorting its contents. Line 15 uses the delegate method to determine how to sort the array. Line 15 invokes the method enclosed within the delegate object by treating the delegate pointer as the method that the delegate object contains. MC++ invokes the enclosed method pointer directly, passing it parameters `array[ i ]` and `array[ i + 1 ]`. The `Comparator` determines the sorting order for its two arguments. If the `Comparator` returns `true`, the two elements are out of order, so line 16 invokes method `Swap` (lines 20–26) to swap the elements. If the `Comparator` returns `false`, the two elements are in the correct order. To sort in ascending order, the `Comparator` returns `true` when the first element being compared is greater than the second element being compared. Similarly, to sort in descending order, the `Comparator` returns `true` when the first element being compared is less than the second element being compared.

Class `BubbleSort` (Fig. 10.43–Fig. 10.44) maintains the array to be sorted (line 23 of Fig. 10.43). The constructor (lines 7–10 of Fig. 10.44) calls method `PopulateArray` (lines 25–34), which fills the array with random integer values.

```
1  // Fig. 10.43: BubbleSort.h
2  // Demonstrates bubble sort using delegates to determine
3  // the sort order.
4
5  #pragma once
6
7  #include "DelegateBubbleSort.h"
8
9  public __gc class BubbleSort
10 {
11 public:
12    BubbleSort();   // constructor
13
14    void PopulateArray();
15
16    // sort the array
17    void SortArrayAscending();
18    void SortArrayDescending();
19
20    String *ToString();
21
22 private:
23    static int elementArray __gc[] = new int __gc[ 10 ];
24
25    // delegate implementation for ascending sort
26    bool SortAscending( int, int );
27
28    // delegate implementation for descending sort
29    bool SortDescending( int, int );
30 }; // end class BubbleSort
```

Fig. 10.43 `BubbleSort` class uses delegates to determine the sort order.

```
// Fig. 10.44: BubbleSort.cpp
// Method definitions for class BubbleSort.

#include "stdafx.h"
#include "BubbleSort.h"

BubbleSort::BubbleSort()
{
   PopulateArray();
}

// delegate implementation for ascending sort
bool BubbleSort::SortAscending( int element1, int element2 )
{
   return element1 > element2;
}

// delegate implementation for descending sort
bool BubbleSort::SortDescending( int element1, int element2 )
{
   return element1 < element2;
}

// populate the array with random numbers
void BubbleSort::PopulateArray()
{

   // create random-number generator
   Random *randomNumber = new Random();

   // populate elementArray with random integers
   for ( int i = 0; i < elementArray->Length; i++ )
      elementArray[ i ] = randomNumber->Next( 100 );
} // end method PopulateArray

// sort randomly generated numbers in ascending order
void BubbleSort::SortArrayAscending()
{
   DelegateBubbleSort::SortArray( elementArray,
      new DelegateBubbleSort::Comparator(
      this, SortAscending ) );
}

// sort randomly generated numbers in descending order
void BubbleSort::SortArrayDescending()
{
   DelegateBubbleSort::SortArray( elementArray,
      new DelegateBubbleSort::Comparator(
      this, SortDescending ) );
}

// return the contents of the array
String *BubbleSort::ToString()
```

Fig. 10.44 `BubbleSort` class method definitions. (Part 1 of 2.)

```
54 {
55    String *contents;
56
57    for( int i = 0; i < elementArray->Length; i++ ) {
58       contents = String::Concat( contents,
59          elementArray[ i ].ToString(), S" " );
60    } // end for
61
62    return contents;
63 } // end method ToString
```

Fig. 10.44 `BubbleSort` class method definitions. (Part 2 of 2.)

Methods `SortAscending` (lines 13–16 of Fig. 10.44) and `SortDescending` (lines 19–22) each have a signature that corresponds with the prototype defined by the `Comparator` delegate declaration (i.e., each receives two `int`s and returns a `bool`). As we will see, the program passes to `DelegateBubbleSort` method `SortArray` delegates containing pointers to methods `SortAscending` and `SortDescending`, which will specify class `DelegateBubbleSort`'s sorting behavior.

Methods `SortArrayAscending` (lines 37–42) and `SortArrayDescending` (lines 45–50) sort the array in ascending and descending order, respectively. Method `SortArrayAscending` passes to `DelegateBubbleSort` method `SortArray` array `elementArray` and a pointer to method `SortAscending`. The syntax in lines 40–41

```
new DelegateBubbleSort::Comparator( this, SortAscending )
```

creates a `Comparator` delegate that contains a pointer to method `SortAscending`.

Figure 10.45 demonstrates class `BubbleSort` and displays the results in a `MessageBox`. We continue to explain and use delegates throughout the book.

```
// Fig. 10.45: DelegatesTest.cpp
// Demonstrates bubble-sort program.

#include "stdafx.h"
#include "BubbleSort.h"

#using <mscorlib.dll>
#using <system.windows.forms.dll>

using namespace System;
using namespace System::Windows::Forms;

int _tmain()
{
   BubbleSort *sortPtr = new BubbleSort();

   String *output = String::Concat( S"Unsorted array:\n",
      sortPtr->ToString() );

   sortPtr->SortArrayAscending();
   output = String::Concat( output, S"\n\nSorted ascending:\n",
      sortPtr->ToString() );
```

Fig. 10.45 Bubble-sort application demonstrates delegates. (Part 1 of 2.)

```

   sortPtr->SortArrayDescending();
   output = String::Concat( output, S"\n\nSorted descending:\n",
      sortPtr->ToString() );

   MessageBox::Show( output, S"Demonstrating delegates" );

   return 0;
} // end _tmain
```

Demonstrating delegates
Unsorted array:
73 17 59 31 9 46 90 62 98 27
Sorted ascending:
9 17 27 31 46 59 62 73 90 98
Sorted descending:
98 90 73 62 59 46 31 27 17 9
OK

Fig. 10.45 Bubble-sort application demonstrates delegates. (Part 2 of 2.)

10.11 Operator Overloading

Manipulations on class objects are accomplished by sending messages (in the form of method calls) to the objects. This method-call notation is cumbersome for certain kinds of classes, especially mathematical classes. For these classes, it would be convenient to use MC++'s rich set of built-in operators to specify object manipulations. In this section, we show how to enable MC++'s operators to work with class objects—via a process called *operator overloading*.

Software Engineering Observation 10.16

Use operator overloading when using an operator makes a program clearer than accomplishing the same operations with explicit method calls.

Software Engineering Observation 10.17

Avoid excessive or inconsistent use of operator overloading, as this can make a program cryptic and difficult to read.

MC++ enables the programmer to overload most operators to make them sensitive to the context in which they are used. Some operators are overloaded frequently, especially the assignment operator and various arithmetic operators, such as + and -. The job performed by overloaded operators also can be performed by explicit method calls, but operator notation often is more natural. The next several figures provide an example of using operator overloading with a complex-number class.

Class `ComplexNumber` (Fig. 10.46–Fig. 10.47) overloads the plus (+), minus (-) and multiplication (*) operators to enable programs to add, subtract and multiply instances of class `ComplexNumber` using common mathematical notation.

```
// Fig. 10.46: Comp lexNumber.h
// Class that overloads operators for adding, subtracting
// and multiplying complex numbers.
```

Fig. 10.46 Overloading operators for complex numbers. (Part 1 of 2.)

```

#pragma once

#using <mscorlib.dll>

using namespace System;

public __value class ComplexNumber
{
public:
   ComplexNumber();                    // default constructor
   ComplexNumber( int, int );          // constructor
   String *ToString();

   // property Real
   __property int get_Real()
   {
      return real;
   }

   __property void set_Real( int value )
   {
      real = value;
   }

   // property Imaginary
   __property int get_Imaginary()
   {
      return imaginary;
   }

   __property void set_Imaginary ( int value )
   {
      imaginary = value;
   }

   // overload the addition operator
   static ComplexNumber op_Addition( ComplexNumber,
      ComplexNumber );

   // overload the subtraction operator
   static ComplexNumber op_Subtraction( ComplexNumber,
      ComplexNumber );

   // overload the multiplication operator
   static ComplexNumber op_Multiply( ComplexNumber,
      ComplexNumber );

private:
   int real;
   int imaginary;
}; // end class ComplexNumber
```

Fig. 10.46 Overloading operators for complex numbers. (Part 2 of 2.)

```
// Fig. 10.47: ComplexNumber.cpp
// Method definitions for class ComplexNumber.

#include "stdafx.h"
#include "ComplexNumber.h"

// default constructor
ComplexNumber::ComplexNumber() {}

// constructor
ComplexNumber::ComplexNumber( int a, int b )
{
   Real = a;
   Imaginary = b;
}

// return string representation of ComplexNumber
String *ComplexNumber::ToString()
{
   return String::Concat( S"( ", real.ToString(),
      ( imaginary < 0 ? S" - " : S" + " ),
      ( imaginary < 0 ? ( imaginary * -1 ).ToString() :
      imaginary.ToString() ), S"i )" );
}

// overload the addition operator
ComplexNumber ComplexNumber::op_Addition( ComplexNumber x,
   ComplexNumber y )
{
   return ComplexNumber( x.Real + y.Real,
      x.Imaginary + y.Imaginary );
}

// overload the subtraction operator
ComplexNumber ComplexNumber::op_Subtraction( ComplexNumber x,
   ComplexNumber y )
{
   return ComplexNumber( x.Real - y.Real,
      x.Imaginary - y.Imaginary );
}

// overload the multiplication operator
ComplexNumber ComplexNumber::op_Multiply( ComplexNumber x,
   ComplexNumber y )
{
   return ComplexNumber(
      x.Real * y.Real - x.Imaginary * y.Imaginary,
      x.Real * y.Imaginary + y.Real * x.Imaginary );
}
```

Fig. 10.47 `ComplexNumber` class method definitions.

Line 11 of Fig. 10.46 demonstrates the `__value` keyword. Unlike `__gc` classes, which are reference types, `__value` classes are value types.[2] For small objects with a short lifetime, creating `__value` classes improves program execution, because the overhead of passing objects (or classes) by reference is reduced. Using `__value` classes rather than `__gc` classes also allows us to access the objects directly, rather than using pointers. Members of `__value` classes are accessed using the dot operator (`.`). We will see the benefit of overloading operators in `__value` classes shortly.

Lines 27–32 (Fig. 10.47) overload the addition operator (+) to perform addition of `ComplexNumbers`. In MC++, specific method names are used to indicate overloaded operators. Method name `op_Addition` (line 27) indicates that a method will overload the addition operator. Similarly, method names `op_Subtraction` (line 35) and `op_Multiply` (line 43) indicate overloaded subtraction and multiplication operators, respectively.[3]

Methods that overload binary operators must take two arguments. The first argument is the left operand, and the second argument is the right operand. Class `ComplexNumber`'s overloaded addition operator takes two `ComplexNumbers` as arguments and returns a `ComplexNumber` that represents the sum of the arguments. Note that this method is marked `public` and `static` (Fig. 10.46, lines 13 and 41), which is required for overloaded operators. The body of the method (lines 30–31 of Fig. 10.47) performs the addition and returns the result as a new `ComplexNumber`. Lines 35–49 provide similar overloaded operators for subtracting and multiplying `ComplexNumbers`.

Software Engineering Observation 10.18

Overload operators to perform the same function or similar functions on class objects as the operators perform on objects of built-in types. Avoid non-intuitive use of operators.

Software Engineering Observation 10.19

At least one argument of an operator overload method must refer to an object of the class in which the operator is overloaded. This prevents programmers from changing how operators work on built-in types. (For example, if we were to define method `op_Addition` with two `int` arguments, we would be changing how the + operator works for `int` types.)

`ComplexNumberTest.cpp` (Fig. 10.48) demonstrates adding, subtracting and multiplying `ComplexNumbers`. Lines 16–22 create two `ComplexNumbers` and add their string representations to the output. Lines 25–26 perform an addition of the two `ComplexNumbers` using overloaded operator `op_Addition`. Because `x` and `y` are value types, rather than reference types, line 26 can use the familiar syntax of `( x + y )` to invoke method `op_Addition`. This syntax is equivalent to invoking method `op_Addition` directly (e.g., `ComplexNumber::op_Addition( x, y )`). Lines 29–34 perform similar operations for subtraction and multiplication of the two `ComplexNumbers`. Line 36 displays the results in a `MessageBox`.

---

2. More information about value types and reference types can be found in Chapter 6, Functions.
3. For more operator method names, visit `msdn.microsoft.com/library/default.asp?url=/library/en-us/cpgenref/html/cpconoperatoroverloadingusageguidelines.asp`.

```
// Fig. 10.48: ComplexNumberTest.cpp
// Example that uses operator overloading.

#include "stdafx.h"
#include "ComplexNumber.h"

#using <mscorlib.dll>
#using <system.windows.forms.dll>

using namespace System;
using namespace System::Windows::Forms;

int _tmain()
{
   // create two ComplexNumbers
   ComplexNumber x = ComplexNumber( 1, 2 );
   String *output = String::Concat(
      S"First Complex Number is: ", x.ToString() );

   ComplexNumber y = ComplexNumber( 5, 9 );
   output = String::Concat( output,
      S"\nSecond Complex Number is: ", y.ToString() );

   // perform addition
   output = String::Concat( output, S"\n\n",
      x.ToString(), S" + ", y.ToString(), S" = ", ( x + y ) );

   // perform subtraction
   output = String::Concat( output, S"\n",
      x.ToString(), S" - ", y.ToString(), S" = ", ( x - y ) );

   // perform multiplication
   output = String::Concat( output, S"\n",
      x.ToString(), S" * ", y.ToString(), S" = ", ( x * y ) );

   MessageBox::Show( output, S"Operator Overloading" );

   return 0;
} // end _tmain
```

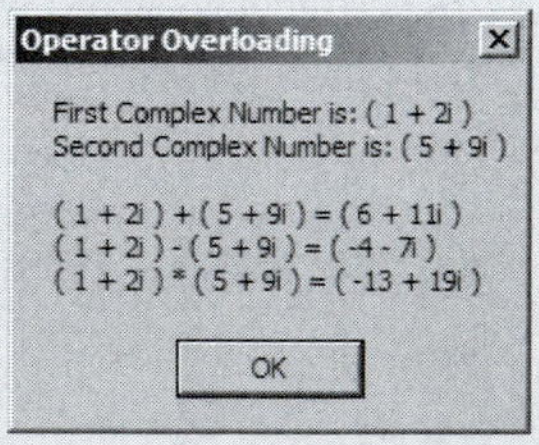
Operator Overloading
First Complex Number is: (1 + 2i)
Second Complex Number is: (5 + 9i)
(1 + 2i) + (5 + 9i) = (6 + 11i)
(1 + 2i) - (5 + 9i) = (-4 - 7i)
(1 + 2i) * (5 + 9i) = (-13 + 19i)
OK

Fig. 10.48 `ComplexNumberTest` demonstrates operator overloading.

We now discuss operator overloading in `__gc` classes. If `ComplexNumber` was a `__gc` class, we would have to use pointers to refer to `ComplexNumbers` (i.e., `x` and `y` would be of type `ComplexNumber *`). In this case, we would have to invoke method `op_Addition` as `( *x + *y )` and modify `op_Addition` to accept and return references as

```
ComplexNumber& ComplexNumber::op_Addition( ComplexNumber &x,
   ComplexNumber &y )
{
   return *( new ComplexNumber( x.Real + y.Real,
      x.Imaginary + y.Imaginary ) );
}
```

Note that `op_Addition` returns a reference to a `__gc` type. Therefore, we would have to explicitly call method `ToString` (e.g., `( *x + *y ).ToString()`) in the call to `String::Concat`.[4]

SUMMARY

- Polymorphism enables us to write programs in a general fashion to handle a wide variety of existing and future related classes.
- One means of processing objects of many different types is to use a `switch` statement to perform an appropriate action on each object based on that object's type. Polymorphic programming can eliminate the need for `switch` logic.
- When we override a base class's method in a derived class, we hide the base class's implementation of that method.
- With polymorphism, new types of objects not even envisioned when a system is created may be added without modification to the system (other than the new class itself).
- Polymorphism allows one method call to perform different actions, depending on the type of the object receiving the call. The same message assumes "many forms"—hence, the term polymorphism.
- With polymorphism, the programmer can deal in generalities and let the executing program concern itself with the specifics.
- A method that is not declared `virtual` cannot be overridden in a derived class. Methods that are declared `static` and or `private` are implicitly non-virtual.
- A class is made abstract by using the keyword `__abstract`, or by declaring one or more of its `virtual` methods to be "pure."
- A program cannot instantiate objects of abstract classes, but can declare pointers to abstract classes. Such pointers can manipulate polymorphically instances of the derived classes.
- A `__sealed` class cannot be a base class (i.e., a class cannot inherit from a `__sealed` class).
- An interface is used when there is no default implementation to inherit (i.e., no data members and no default-method implementations). Whereas an abstract class is best used for providing data and services for objects in a hierarchical relationship, an interface can be used for providing services that "bring together" disparate objects that relate to one another only through that interface.
- An interface definition begins with the keyword `__interface` and contains a list of `public` methods and properties.
- To use an interface, a class must specify that it implements the interface and must provide implementations for every method and property specified in the interface definition. A class that implements an interface effectively signs a contract with the compiler that states, "this class will define all the methods and properties specified by the interface."
- In MC++, it is impossible to pass a method pointer directly as an argument to another method. To address this problem, MC++ allows the creation of delegates, which are classes that encapsulate a set of pointers to methods.

4. It is possible to avoid this by having method `op_Addition` return a `ComplexNumber *`. However, it is preferable to have such overloaded operators return the same type as their arguments.

- MC++ enables the programmer to overload most operators to make them sensitive to the context in which they are used.
- Methods that overload binary operators must take two arguments. The first argument is the left operand, and the second argument is the right operand.
- Method name `op_Addition` indicates that a method will overload the addition operator. Similarly, method names `op_Subtraction` and `op_Multiply` indicate overloaded subtraction and multiplication operators, respectively.

TERMINOLOGY

abstract base class
`__abstract` class
abstract method
casting
class hierarchy
concrete class
delegate
`__delegate` keyword
`GetType` method of class `Object`
information hiding
inheritance
inheritance hierarchy
interface
`__interface` keyword
`InvalidCastException`
iterator class
method pointer
object-oriented programming (OOP)
`op_Addition` method
`op_Multiply` method
`op_Subtraction` method
operator overloading
polymorphic programming
polymorphism
pure `virtual` method
reference type
`reinterpret_cast` operator
`__sealed` keyword
`switch` logic
`__try_cast` operator
`__typeof` keyword
`__value` keyword
`virtual` method

SELF-REVIEW EXERCISES

10.1 Fill in the blanks in each of the following statements:
a) Treating a base-class object as a(n) ________ can cause errors.
b) Polymorphism helps eliminate unnecessary ________ logic.
c) If a class contains one or more pure `virtual` methods, it is a(n) ________ class.
d) Classes from which objects can be instantiated are called ________ classes.
e) Classes declared with keyword ________ cannot be inherited.
f) An attempt to cast an object to one of its derived types can cause a(n) ________.
g) Polymorphism involves using a base-class reference to manipulate ________.
h) Abstract classes are declared with the ________ keyword.
i) ________ are classes that encapsulate pointers to methods.

10.2 State whether each of the following is *true* or *false*. If *false*, explain why.
a) Referring to a derived-class object with a base-class pointer is dangerous.
b) A class with a pure `virtual` method must be declared `__abstract`.
c) Classes declared with the `__sealed` keyword cannot be base classes.
d) Polymorphism allows programmers to manipulate derived classes with references to base-class pointers.
e) Polymorphic programming can eliminate the need for unnecessary `switch` logic.
f) Methods of `__abstract` classes are implicitly `virtual`.
g) The delegate's declaration must specify its implementation.

ANSWERS TO SELF-REVIEW EXERCISES

10.1 a) derived-class object. b) `switch`. c) abstract. d) concrete. e) `__sealed`. f) `InvalidCastException`. g) derived-class objects. h) `__abstract`. i) Delegates.

10.2 a) False. Referring to a base-class object with a derived-class pointer is dangerous. b) False. A class with a pure `virtual` method is implicitly abstract. c) True. d) True. e) True. f) False. Methods of `__abstract` classes are not implicitly `virtual`. g) False. The delegate's declaration specifies only a method signature (method name, parameters and return value).

EXERCISES

10.3 How is it that polymorphism enables you to program "in the general" rather than "in the specific"? Discuss the key advantages of programming "in the general."

10.4 Discuss the problems of programming with `switch` logic. Explain why polymorphism can be an effective alternative to using `switch` logic.

10.5 Distinguish between inheriting services and inheriting implementation. How do inheritance hierarchies designed for inheriting services differ from those designed for inheriting implementation?

10.6 Modify the payroll system of Fig. 10.16–Fig. 10.26 to add `private` variable `birthDate` (use class `Date` from Fig. 8.14–Fig. 8.15) to class `Employee`. Assume that payroll is processed once per month. Create an array of `Employee` references to store the various employee objects. In a loop, calculate the payroll for each `Employee` (polymorphically) and add a $100.00 bonus to the person's payroll amount if this is the month in which the `Employee`'s birthday occurs.

10.7 Implement the `Shape` hierarchy shown in Fig. 9.3. Each `TwoDimensionalShape` should contain method `Area` to calculate the area of the two-dimensional shape. Each `ThreeDimensionalShape` should have methods `Area` and `Volume` to calculate the surface area and volume of the three-dimensional shape, respectively. Create a program that uses an array of `Shape` references to objects of each concrete class in the hierarchy. The program should output the string representation of each object in the array. Also, in the loop that processes all the shapes in the array, determine whether each shape is a `TwoDimensionalShape` or a `ThreeDimensionalShape`. If a shape is a `TwoDimensionalShape`, display its `Area`. If a shape is a `ThreeDimensionalShape`, display its `Area` and `Volume`.

10.8 Reimplement the program of Exercise 10.7 such that classes `TwoDimensionalShape` and `ThreeDimensionalShape` implement an `IShape` interface, rather than extending `abstract` class `Shape`.

11

Exception Handling

Objectives

- To understand exceptions and error handling.
- To use `try` blocks to delimit code in which exceptions may occur.
- To `throw` exceptions.
- To use `catch` blocks to specify exception handlers.
- To use the `__finally` block to release resources.
- To understand the .NET exception-class hierarchy.
- To create programmer-defined exceptions.

It is common sense to take a method and try it. If it fails, admit it frankly and try another. But above all, try something.
Franklin Delano Roosevelt

O! throw away the worser part of it,
And live the purer with the other half.
William Shakespeare

If they're running and they don't look where they're going
I have to come out from somewhere and catch them.
Jerome David Salinger

And oftentimes excusing of a fault
Doth make the fault the worse by the excuse.
William Shakespeare

I never forget a face, but in your case I'll make an exception.
Groucho (Julius Henry) Marx

Outline

11.1 Introduction

In this chapter, we introduce *exception handling*. An *exception* is an indication of a problem that occurs during a program's execution. The name "exception" comes from the fact that although a problem can occur, the problem occurs infrequently—if the "rule" is that a statement normally executes correctly, then the "exception to the rule" is that a problem occurs. Exception handling enables programmers to create applications that can resolve (or handle) exceptions. In many cases, handling an exception allows a program to continue executing as if no problem was encountered. A more severe problem may prevent a program from continuing normal execution, instead requiring the program to notify the user of the problem, then terminate in a controlled manner. The features presented in this chapter enable programmers to write clear, robust and more *fault-tolerant programs*.

The style and details of exception handling in MC++ are based in part on the work of Andrew Koenig and Bjarne Stroustrup, as presented in their paper, "Exception Handling for C++ (revised)."[1] MC++ designers extended the exception-handling mechanism used in standard C++.

This chapter begins with an overview of exception-handling concepts, then demonstrates basic exception-handling techniques. The chapter continues with an overview of the .NET exception class hierarchy. Programs typically request and release resources (such as files on disk) during program execution. Often, these resources are in limited supply or can be used by only one program at a time. We demonstrate a part of the exception-handling mechanism that enables a program to use a resource, then guarantees that the program releases the resource for use by other programs. The chapter continues with an example that demonstrates several properties of class `System::Exception` (the base class of all exception classes), followed by an example that shows programmers how to create and use their own exception classes.

11.2 Exception Handling Overview

The logic of the program frequently tests conditions that determine how program execution proceeds. We begin by performing a task. We then test whether that task executed correctly.

---

1. Koenig, A. and B. Stroustrup, "Exception Handling for C++ (revised)," *Proceedings of the Usenix C++ Conference*, San Francisco, April 1990, 149–176.

If not, we perform error processing. Otherwise we continue with the next task. Although this form of error-handling logic works, intermixing the logic of the program with the error-handling logic can make the program difficult to read, modify, maintain and debug—especially in large applications. In fact, if many of the potential problems occur infrequently, intermixing program logic and error handling can degrade the performance of the program, because the program must test extra conditions to determine whether the next task can be performed.

Exception handling enables the programmer to remove error-handling code (i.e., the code that resolves the error) from the "main line" of the program's execution. This improves program clarity and enhances modifiability. Programmers can decide to handle whatever exceptions they choose—all types of exceptions, all exceptions of a certain type or all exceptions of a group of related types. Such flexibility reduces the likelihood that errors will be overlooked and thereby increases a program's robustness.

Error-Prevention Tip 11.1

Exception handling helps improve a program's fault tolerance. When it is easy to write error-processing code, programmers are more likely to use it.

Software Engineering Observation 11.1

Although it is possible to do so, do not use exception handling for conventional flow of control. It is difficult to keep track of a larger number of exception cases, and programs with a large number of exception cases are hard to read and maintain.

Exception handling is designed to process *synchronous errors*—errors that occur during the normal program flow of control. Common examples of these errors are out-of-range array subscripts, arithmetic overflow (i.e., a value outside the representable range of values), division by zero, invalid method parameters and running out of available memory. Exception handling also can process certain *asynchronous* events, such as disk I/O completions.

Good Programming Practice 11.1

Avoid using exception handling for purposes other than error handling, because this can reduce program clarity.

With programming languages that do not support exception handling, programmers often delay the writing of error-processing code and sometimes simply forget to include it. This results in less robust software products. MC++ enables the programmer to deal with exception handling easily from the inception of a project. Still, the programmer must put considerable effort into incorporating an exception-handling strategy into software projects.

Software Engineering Observation 11.2

Try to incorporate the exception-handling strategy into a system from the inception of the design process. Adding effective exception handling after a system has been implemented can be difficult.

Software Engineering Observation 11.3

In the past, programmers used many techniques to implement error-processing code. Exception handling provides a single, uniform technique for processing errors. This helps programmers working on large projects to understand each other's error-processing code.

The exception-handling mechanism also is useful for processing problems that occur when a program interacts with software elements such as methods, constructors, assemblies and classes. Rather than internally handling problems that occur, such software elements often use exceptions to notify programs when problems occur. This enables programmers to implement customized error handling for each application.

Common Programming Error 11.1

Aborting a program component could leave a resource—such as file stream or I/O device—in a state in which other programs are unable to acquire the resource. This is known as a "resource leak."

Performance Tip 11.1

When no exceptions occur, exception-handling code incurs little performance penalties. Thus, programs that implement exception handling operate more efficiently than programs that perform error handling throughout the program logic.

Performance Tip 11.2

Exception handling should be used only for problems that occur infrequently. As a "rule of thumb," if a problem occurs at least 30% of the time when a particular statement executes, the program should test for the error inline; otherwise, the overhead of exception handling will cause the program to execute more slowly.[2]

Software Engineering Observation 11.4

Methods with common error conditions should return a null pointer (or another appropriate value) rather than throwing exceptions. A program calling such a method simply can check the return value to determine success or failure of the method call.[3]

Complex applications normally consist of predefined software components (such as those defined in the .NET Framework) and components specific to the application that use the predefined components. When a predefined component encounters a problem, that component needs a mechanism to communicate the problem to the application-specific component—the predefined component cannot know in advance how each application will process a problem that occurs. Exception handling simplifies combining software components and having them work together effectively by enabling predefined components to communicate problems that occur to application-specific components, which can then process the problems in an application-specific manner.

Exception handling is geared to situations in which the method or function that detects an error is unable to handle it. Such a method or function *throws an exception*. There is no guarantee that there will be an *exception handler*—code that executes when the program detects an exception—to process that kind of exception. If there is, the exception will be *caught* and *handled*. The result of an *uncaught exception* depends on whether the program executes in debug mode or standard execution mode. In debug mode, when the program detects an uncaught exception, a dialog box appears that enables the programmer to view the problem in the debugger or continue program execution by ignoring the problem that occurred. In standard execution mode, a Windows application presents a dialog that enables the user to continue or terminate program execution, and a console application presents a dialog that enables the user to open the program in the debugger or terminate program execution.

---

2. "Best Practices for Handling Exceptions," *.NET Framework Developer's Guide*, Visual Studio .NET Online Help. `<msdn.microsoft.com/library/default.asp?url=/library/en-us/cpguide/html/cpconbestpracticesforhandlingexceptions.asp>`
3. "Best Practices for Handling Exceptions."

MC++ uses *`try` blocks* to enable exception handling. A `try` block consists of keyword `try` followed by braces (`{}`) that define a block of code in which exceptions may occur. The `try` block encloses statements that might cause exceptions and any statements that should not execute if an exception occurs. Immediately following the `try` block are zero or more *`catch` blocks* (also called *`catch` handlers*). Each `catch` handler specifies in parentheses an exception parameter that represents the type of exception the `catch` handler can handle. If an exception parameter includes an optional parameter name, the `catch` handler can use that parameter name to interact with a caught exception object. Optionally, programmers can include a *parameterless `catch` handler* (also called a "catch-all" handler) that catches all exception types. After the last `catch` handler, an optional *`__finally` block* contains code that always executes (provided that program execution entered the `try` block), regardless of whether an exception occurs. A `try` block must be followed by at least one `catch` block or a `__finally` block.

Common Programming Error 11.2

The parameterless `catch` handler must be the last `catch` handler following a particular `try` block; otherwise, a syntax error occurs.

When a method or function called in a program detects an exception or when the CLR (Common Language Runtime) detects a problem, the method/function or CLR *throws an exception*. The point in the program at which an exception occurs is called the *throw point*—an important location for debugging purposes (as we demonstrate in Section 11.6). Exceptions are objects of classes that extend class *`Exception`* of namespace `System`. If an exception occurs in a `try` block, the `try` block *expires* (i.e., terminates immediately) and program control transfers to the first `catch` handler (if there is one) following the `try` block. MC++ is said to use the *termination model of exception handling*, because the `try` block enclosing a thrown exception expires immediately when that exception occurs.[4] As with any other block of code, when a `try` block terminates, local variables defined in the block go out of scope. Next, the CLR searches for the first `catch` handler that can process the type of exception that occurred. The CLR locates the matching `catch` by comparing the thrown exception's type to each `catch`'s exception-parameter type until the CLR finds a match. A match occurs if the types are identical or if the thrown exception's type is a derived class of the exception-parameter type. When a `catch` handler finishes processing, local variables defined within the `catch` handler (including the `catch` parameter) go out of scope. If a match occurs, code contained within the matching `catch` handler executes. All remaining `catch` handlers that correspond to the `try` block are ignored and execution resumes at the first line of code after the `try...catch` sequence.

If no exceptions occur in a `try` block, the CLR ignores the exception handlers for that block. Program execution resumes with the next statement after the `try...catch` sequence. If an exception that occurs in a `try` block has no matching `catch` handler, or if an exception occurs in a statement that is not in a `try` block, the method or function containing that statement terminates immediately and the CLR attempts to locate an enclosing `try` block in a calling method or function. This process is called *stack unwinding* (discussed in Section 11.6).

---

4. Some languages use the *resumption model of exception handling*, in which, after the handling of the exception, control returns to the point at which the exception was thrown and execution resumes from that point.

11.3 Example: DivideByZeroException

Let us consider a simple example of exception handling. The application in Fig. 11.1 uses `try` and `catch` to specify a block of code that might throw exceptions and to handle those exceptions if they occur. The application prompts the user to enter two integers. The program converts the input values to type `int` and divides the first number (`numerator`) by the second number (`denominator`). Assuming that the user provides integers as input and does not specify 0 as the denominator for the division, line 24 displays the division result. However, if the user inputs a non-integer value or supplies 0 as the denominator, an exception occurs. This program demonstrates how to catch these exceptions.

```
1  // Fig. 11.1: DivideByZero.cpp
2  // Divide-by-zero exception handling.
3
4  #include "stdafx.h"
5
6  #using <mscorlib.dll>
7
8  using namespace System;
9
10 int _tmain()
11 {
12    try {
13       Console::Write( S"Enter an integral numerator: " );
14
15       int numerator = Convert::ToInt32( Console::ReadLine() );
16
17       Console::Write( S"Enter an integral denominator: " );
18       int denominator = Convert::ToInt32( Console::ReadLine() );
19
20       // division generates DivideByZeroException if
21       // denominator is 0
22       int result = numerator / denominator;
23
24       Console::WriteLine( result );
25    } // end try
26
27    // process invalid number format
28    catch ( FormatException * ) {
29       Console::WriteLine( S"You must enter two integers." );
30    } // end catch
31
32    // user attempted to divide by zero
33    catch ( DivideByZeroException *divideByZeroException ) {
34       Console::WriteLine( divideByZeroException->Message );
35    } // end catch
36
37    return 0;
38 } // end _tmain
```

Fig. 11.1 Divide-by-zero exception handling example. (Part 1 of 2.)

```
Enter an integral numerator: 100
Enter an integral denominator: 7
14
```

```
Enter an integral numerator: 10
Enter an integral denominator: hello
You must enter two integers.
```

```
Enter an integral numerator: 100
Enter an integral denominator: 0
Attempted to divide by zero.
```

Fig. 11.1 Divide-by-zero exception handling example. (Part 2 of 2.)

Before we discuss the program details, consider the sample outputs in Fig. 11.1. The first output shows a successful calculation in which the user inputs the numerator `100` and the denominator `7`. Note that the result (`14`) is an integer, because integer division always yields integer results. The second output shows the result of inputting a non-integer value—in this case, the user input `"hello"` at the second prompt. The program attempts to convert the string the user input into an `int` value with method `Convert::ToInt32`. If the argument to `Convert::ToInt32` is not a valid representation of an integer (in this case a valid string representation of an integer, such as `"14"`), a *`FormatException`* (namespace `System`) is generated. The program detects the exception and displays an error message, indicating that the user must enter two integers. The last output demonstrates the result after an attempt to divide by zero. In integer arithmetic, the CLR tests for division by zero and generates a *`DivideByZeroException`* (namespace `System`) if the denominator is zero. The program detects the exception and displays an error-message, indicating an attempt to divide by zero.[5]

Let us consider the user interactions and flow of control that yield the results shown in the sample outputs. Lines 12–25 define a `try` block that encloses the code that can throw exceptions, as well as the code that should not execute if an exception occurs. For example, the program should not display a new result (line 24) unless the calculation (line 22) completes successfully. Remember that the `try` block terminates immediately if an exception occurs, so the remaining code in the `try` block will not execute.

The two statements that read the integers (lines 15 and 18) each call method `Convert::ToInt32` to convert strings to `int` values. This method throws a `FormatException` if it cannot convert its `String *` argument to an integer. If lines 15 and 18 properly convert the values (i.e., no exceptions occur), then line 22 divides the `numerator` by the `denomi-`

5. The CLR allows floating-point division by zero, which produces a positive or negative infinity result, depending on whether the numerator is positive or negative. Dividing zero by zero is a special case that results in a value called "not a number." Programs can test for these results using constants for positive infinity (*`PositiveInfinity`*), negative infinity (*`NegativeInfinity`*) and not a number (*`NaN`*) that are defined in structures `Double` (for `double` calculations) and `Single` (for `float` calculations).

nator and assigns the result to variable result. If the denominator is zero, line 22 causes the CLR to throw a DivideByZeroException. If line 22 does not cause an exception, then line 24 displays the result of the division. If no exceptions occur in the try block, the program successfully completes the try block and ignores the catch handlers in lines 28–30 and 33–35—the program execution continues with the first statement following the try...catch sequence.

Immediately following the try block are two catch handlers (also called *catch blocks* or *exception handlers*)—lines 28–30 define the exception handler for a FormatException, and lines 33–35 define the catch handler for the DivideByZeroException. Each catch handler begins with keyword catch followed by an exception parameter in parentheses that specifies the type of exception handled by the catch handler. The exception-handling code appears in the catch handler. In general, when an exception occurs in a try block, a catch handler catches the exception and handles it. In Fig. 11.1, the first catch handler specifies that it catches the type FormatExceptions (thrown by method Convert::ToInt32), and the second catch handler specifies that it catches type DivideByZeroExceptions (thrown by the CLR). Only the matching catch handler executes if an exception occurs. Both of the exception handlers in this example display an error-message to the user. When program control reaches the end of a catch handler, the program considers the exception as having been handled, and program control continues with the first statement after the try...catch sequence (the return statement of function _tmain in this example).

In the second sample output, the user input hello as the denominator. When line 18 executes, Convert::ToInt32 cannot convert this string to an int, so Convert::ToInt32 throws a FormatException object to indicate that the method was unable to convert the String * to an int. When an exception occurs, the try block expires (terminates). Any local variables defined in the try block go out of scope; therefore, those variables (numerator, denominator and result in this example) are not available to the exception handlers. Next, the CLR attempts to locate a matching catch handler, starting with the catch in line 28. The program compares the type of the thrown exception (FormatException) with the type in parentheses following keyword catch (also FormatException). A match occurs, so that exception handler executes and the program ignores all other exception handlers following the corresponding try block. Once the catch handler finishes processing, local variables defined within the catch handler go out of scope. If a match did not occur, the program compares the type of the thrown exception with the next catch handler in sequence and repeats the process until a match is found.

Software Engineering Observation 11.5

Enclose in a try block a significant logical section of the program in which several statements can throw exceptions, rather than using a separate try block for every statement that throws an exception. However, for proper exception-handling granularity, each try block should enclose a section of code small enough that when an exception occurs, the specific context is known and the catch handlers can process the exception properly.

Common Programming Error 11.3

Attempting to access a try block's local variables in one of that try block's associated catch handlers is an error. Before a corresponding catch handler can execute, the try block expires, and its local variables go out of scope.

Common Programming Error 11.4

Specifying a comma-separated list of exception parameters in a catch handler is a syntax error. Each catch can have only one exception parameter.

In the third sample output, the user input 0 as the denominator. When line 22 executes, the CLR throws a DivideByZeroException object to indicate an attempt to divide by zero. Once again, the try block terminates immediately upon encountering the exception, and the program attempts to locate a matching catch handler, starting from the catch handler in line 28. The program compares the type of the thrown exception (DivideByZeroException) with the type in parentheses following keyword catch (FormatException). In this case, there is no match, because they are not the same exception types and because FormatException is not a base class of DivideByZeroException. So the program proceeds to line 33 and compares the type of the thrown exception (DivideByZeroException) with the type in parentheses following keyword catch (also DivideByZeroException). A match occurs, so that exception handler executes. Line 34 in this handler uses property *Message* of class Exception to display the error message to the user. If there were additional catch handlers, the program would ignore them.

Notice that the catch handler that begins in line 33 specifies parameter name divideByZeroException. Line 34 uses this parameter (of type DivideByZeroException *) to interact with the caught exception and access its Message property. Meanwhile, the catch handler that begins in line 28 does not specify a parameter name. Thus, this catch handler cannot interact with the caught exception object.

11.4 .NET Exception Hierarchy

The exception-handling mechanism allows only objects of class Exception and its derived classes to be thrown and caught.[6] This section overviews several of the .NET Framework's exception classes. In addition, we discuss how to determine whether a particular method throws exceptions.

Class Exception of namespace System is the base class of the .NET Framework exception hierarchy. Two of the most important derived classes of Exception are *ApplicationException* and *SystemException*. ApplicationException is a base class that programmers can extend to create exception data types that are specific to their applications. We discuss creating programmer-defined exception classes in Section 11.7. Programs can recover from most ApplicationExceptions and continue execution.

The CLR can generate SystemExceptions at any point during the execution of the program. Many of these exceptions can be avoided by coding properly. These are called *runtime exceptions* and they derive from class SystemException. For example, if a program attempts to access an out-of-range array subscript, the CLR throws an exception of type IndexOutOfRangeException (a class derived from SystemException). Similarly, a runtime exception occurs when a program attempts to use a null pointer to manipulate an object. Attempting to use such a null pointer causes a *NullReferenceException* (another type of SystemExcep-

6. Actually, it is possible to catch exceptions of types that are not derived from class Exception using the parameterless catch handler. This is useful for handling exceptions from code written in other languages that do not require all exception types to derive from class Exception in the .NET framework.

tion). For a complete list of derived classes of Exception, look up "Exception class" in the **Index** of the Visual Studio .NET online documentation.

A benefit of using the exception-class hierarchy is that a catch handler can catch exceptions of a particular type or can use a base-class type to catch exceptions in a hierarchy of related exception types. For example, a catch handler that specifies an exception parameter of type Exception also can catch exceptions of all classes that extend Exception, because Exception is the base class of all exception classes. This allows for polymorphic processing of related exceptions. The benefit of the latter approach is that the exception handler can use the exception parameter to manipulate the caught exception. If the exception handler does not need access to the caught exception, the exception parameter may be omitted. If no exception type is specified, the catch handler will catch all exceptions. [*Note:* In such cases, the catch handler's parameter is specified as an ellipse (...). You will learn more about the ellipse in Section 11.5.]

Using inheritance with exceptions enables an exception handler to catch related exceptions with a concise notation. An exception handler certainly could catch each derived-class exception type individually, but catching the base-class exception type is more concise. However, this makes sense only if the handling behavior is the same for a base class exception and its derived exception classes. Otherwise, catch each derived-class exception individually.

At this point, we know that there are many different exception types. We also know that methods and the CLR can both throw exceptions. But, how do we determine that an exception could occur in a program? For methods in the .NET Framework classes, we can look at the detailed description of the methods in the online documentation. If a method throws an exception, its description contains a section called "Exceptions" that specifies the types of exceptions thrown by the method and briefly describes potential causes for the exceptions. For example, look up "Convert.ToInt32 method" in the index of the Visual Studio .NET online documentation. In the document that describes the method, click the link "public: static int ToInt32(String *);." In the document that appears, the "Exceptions" section indicates that method Convert.ToInt32 throws three exception types—ArgumentException, FormatException and OverflowException—and describes the conditions under which each exception type occurs.

Good Programming Practice 11.2

Inserting a comment header for each method that lists the explicit exceptions that the method can throw makes future maintenance of the code easier.

Software Engineering Observation 11.6

If a method is capable of throwing exceptions, statements that invoke that method should be placed in try *blocks and those exceptions should be caught and handled.*

11.5 __finally Block

Programs frequently request and release resources dynamically (i.e., at execution time). For example, a program that reads a file from disk first attempts to open the file. If that request succeeds, the program reads the contents of the file. Operating systems typically prevent more than one program from manipulating a file at once. Therefore, when a program finishes processing a file, the program normally closes the file (i.e., releases the resource).

This enables other programs to use the file. Closing the file helps prevent the *resource leak*, in which the file resource is unavailable to other programs because a program using the file never closed it. Programs that obtain certain types of resources (such as files) must return those resources explicitly to the system to avoid resource leaks.

In programming languages, like C and C++, in which the programmer is responsible for dynamic memory management, the most common type of resource leak is a *memory leak*. This happens when a program allocates memory (as we do with operator `new`), but does not deallocate the memory when the memory is no longer needed in the program. In MC++, this normally is not an issue, because the CLR performs "garbage collection" of memory no longer needed by an executing program. However, other kinds of resource leaks (such as the unclosed file mentioned previously) can occur in MC++.

Error-Prevention Tip 11.2

The CLR does not completely eliminate memory leaks. The CLR will not garbage-collect an object until the program has no more pointers to that object. In addition, the CLR cannot reclaim unmanaged memory. Thus, memory leaks can occur if programmers erroneously keep pointers to unwanted objects.

Most resources that require explicit release have potential exceptions associated with the processing of the resource. For example, a program that processes a file might receive `IOException`s during the processing. For this reason, file-processing code normally appears in a `try` block. Regardless of whether a program successfully processes a file, the program should close the file when the file is no longer needed. Suppose that a program places all resource-request and resource-release code in a `try` block. If no exceptions occur, the `try` block executes normally and releases the resources after using them. However, if an exception occurs, the `try` block may expire before the resource-release code can execute. We could duplicate all resource-release code in the `catch` handlers, but this makes the code more difficult to modify and maintain.

The exception-handling mechanism provides the *`__finally`* block, which is guaranteed to execute if program control enters the corresponding `try` block. The `__finally` block executes regardless of whether that `try` block executes successfully or an exception occurs. This guarantee makes the `__finally` block an ideal location to place resource deallocation code for resources acquired and manipulated in the corresponding `try` block. If the `try` block executes successfully, the `__finally` block executes immediately after the `try` block terminates. If an exception occurs in the `try` block, the `__finally` block executes immediately after a `catch` handler completes exception handling. If the exception is not caught by a `catch` handler associated with that `try` block or if a `catch` handler associated with that `try` block throws an exception, the `__finally` block executes, then the exception is processed by the next enclosing `try` block (if there is one).

Error-Prevention Tip 11.3

A `__finally` block typically contains code to release resources acquired in the corresponding `try` block; this makes the `__finally` block an effective way to eliminate resource leaks.

Error-Prevention Tip 11.4

The only reason a `__finally` block will not execute if program control entered the corresponding `try` block is that the application terminates before `__finally` can execute.

Performance Tip 11.3

As a rule, resources should be released as soon as it is apparent that they are no longer needed in a program, to make those resources immediately available for reuse, thus enhancing resource utilization in the program.

If one or more `catch` handlers follow a `try` block, the `__finally` block is optional. If no `catch` handlers follow a `try` block, a `__finally` block must appear immediately after the `try` block. If any `catch` handlers follow a `try` block, the `__finally` block appears after the last `catch`. Only white space and comments can separate the blocks in a `try...catch...__finally` sequence.

Common Programming Error 11.5

Placing the `__finally` block before a `catch` handler is a syntax error.

The MC++ application in Fig. 11.2 demonstrates that the `__finally` block always executes, even if no exception occurs in the corresponding `try` block. The program contains four functions that `_tmain` invokes to demonstrate `__finally`—`DoesNotThrowException` (lines 62–81), `ThrowExceptionWithCatch` (lines 84–107), `ThrowExceptionWithoutCatch` (lines 110–128) and `ThrowExceptionCatchRethrow` (lines 131–160).

```
1  // Fig. 11.2: UsingExceptionTest.cpp
2  // Demonstrating __finally blocks.
3
4  #include "stdafx.h"
5
6  #using <mscorlib.dll>
7
8  using namespace System;
9
10 void DoesNotThrowException();
11 void ThrowExceptionWithCatch();
12 void ThrowExceptionWithoutCatch();
13 void ThrowExceptionCatchRethrow();
14
15 // main entry point for application
16 int _tmain()
17 {
18    // Case 1: no exceptions occur in called function
19    Console::WriteLine( S"Calling DoesNotThrowException" );
20    DoesNotThrowException();
21
22    // Case 2: exception occurs and is caught
23    Console::WriteLine( S"\nCalling ThrowExceptionWithCatch" );
24    ThrowExceptionWithCatch();
25
26    // Case 3: exception occurs, but not caught
27    // in called function, because no catch handlers
```

Fig. 11.2 Demonstrating that `__finally` blocks always execute regardless of whether an exception occurs. (Part 1 of 4.)

```
   Console::WriteLine(
      S"\nCalling ThrowExceptionWithoutCatch" );

   // calls ThrowExceptionWithoutCatch
   try {
      ThrowExceptionWithoutCatch();
   } // end try

   // process exception returned from ThrowExceptionWithoutCatch
   catch ( ... ) {
      Console::WriteLine( S"Caught exception from: "
         S"ThrowExceptionWithoutCatch in _tmain" );
   } // end catch

   // Case 4: exception occurs and is caught
   // in called function, then rethrown to caller
   Console::WriteLine(
      S"\nCalling ThrowExceptionCatchRethrow" );

   // call ThrowExceptionCachRethrow
   try {
      ThrowExceptionCatchRethrow();
   } // end try

   // process exception returned from ThrowExceptionCatchRethrow
   catch (...) {
      Console::WriteLine( String::Concat ( S"Caught exception from ",
         S"ThrowExceptionCatchRethrow in _tmain" ) );
   } // end catch

   return 0;
} // end _tmain

// no exception thrown
void DoesNotThrowException()
{
   // try block does not throw any exceptions
   try {
      Console::WriteLine( S"In DoesNotThrowException" );
   } // end try

   // this catch never executes
   catch ( ... ) {
      Console::WriteLine( S"This catch never executes" );
   } // end catch

   // __finally executes because corresponding try executed
   __finally {
      Console::WriteLine(
         S"Finally executed in DoesNotThrowException" );
   } // end finally

```

Fig. 11.2 Demonstrating that `__finally` blocks always execute regardless of whether an exception occurs. (Part 2 of 4.)

```
   Console::WriteLine( S"End of DoesNotThrowException" );
} // end function DoesNotThrowException

// throw exception and catches it locally
void ThrowExceptionWithCatch()
{
   // try block throws exception
   try {
      Console::WriteLine( S"In ThrowExceptionWithCatch" );

      throw new Exception(
         S"Exception in ThrowExceptionWithCatch" );
   } // end try

   // catch exception thrown in try block
   catch ( Exception *error ) {
      Console::WriteLine( String::Concat( S"Message: ",
         error->Message ) );
   } // end catch

   // __finally executes because of corresponding try executed
   __finally {
      Console::WriteLine(
         S"Finally executed in ThrowExceptionWithCatch" );
   } // end finally

   Console::WriteLine( S"End of ThrowExceptionWithCatch" );
} // end function ThrowExceptionWithCatch

// throw exception and does not catch it locally
void ThrowExceptionWithoutCatch()
{
   // throw exception, but do not catch it
   try {
      Console::WriteLine( S"In ThrowExceptionWithoutCatch" );

      throw new Exception(
         S"Exception in ThrowExceptionWithoutCatch" );
   }// end try

   // __finally executes because of corresponding try executed
   __finally {
      Console::WriteLine( String::Concat( S"Finally executed in ",
        S"ThrowExceptionWithoutCatch" ) );
   } // end finally

   // unreachable code; would generate logic error
   Console::WriteLine( S"This will never be printed" );
} // end function ThrowExceptionWithoutCatch
```

Fig. 11.2 Demonstrating that `__finally` blocks always execute regardless of whether an exception occurs. (Part 3 of 4.)

```
// throws exception, catches it and rethrows it
void ThrowExceptionCatchRethrow()
{
   // try block throws exception
   try {
      Console::WriteLine( S"In ThrowExceptionCatchRethrow" );

      throw new Exception(
         S"Exception in ThrowExceptionCatchRethrow" );
   } // end try

   // catch any exception, place in object error
   catch ( Exception *error ) {
      Console::WriteLine( String::Concat( S"Message: ",
         error->Message ) );

      // rethrow exception for further processing
      throw error;

      // unreachable code; would generate logic error
   } // end catch

   // __finally executes because of corresponding try executed
   __finally {
      Console::WriteLine( String::Concat( S"Finally executed in ",
        S"ThrowExceptionCatchRethrow" ) );
   }  // end finally

   // unreachable code; would generate logic error
   Console::WriteLine( S"This will never be printed" );
} // end function ThrowExceptionCatchRethrow
```

```
Calling DoesNotThrowException
In DoesNotThrowException
Finally executed in DoesNotThrowException
End of DoesNotThrowException

Calling ThrowExceptionWithCatch
In ThrowExceptionWithCatch
Message: Exception in ThrowExceptionWithCatch
Finally executed in ThrowExceptionWithCatch
End of ThrowExceptionWithCatch

Calling ThrowExceptionWithoutCatch
In ThrowExceptionWithoutCatch
Finally executed in ThrowExceptionWithoutCatch
Caught exception from: ThrowExceptionWithoutCatch in _tmain

Calling ThrowExceptionCatchRethrow
In ThrowExceptionCatchRethrow
Message: Exception in ThrowExceptionCatchRethrow
Finally executed in ThrowExceptionCatchRethrow
Caught exception from ThrowExceptionCatchRethrow in _tmain
```

Fig. 11.2 Demonstrating that `__finally` blocks always execute regardless of whether an exception occurs. (Part 4 of 4.)

Line 20 invokes function `DoesNotThrowException` (lines 62–81). The `try` block (lines 65–67) begins by outputting a message (line 66). The `try` block does not throw any exceptions, so program control reaches the closing brace of the `try` block. The program skips the `catch` handler (lines 70–72), because no exception is thrown; instead, the program executes the `__finally` block (lines 75–78), which outputs a message. At this point, program control continues with the first statement after the `__finally` block (line 80), which outputs a message indicating that the end of the function has been reached. Then, program control returns to `_tmain`. Notice that line 70 specifies the parameterless `catch` handler by placing an ellipsis (...) within the parentheses following keyword `catch`. Recall that the parameterless `catch` handler matches any exception.

Line 24 of `_tmain` invokes function `ThrowExceptionWithCatch` (lines 84–107), which begins in its `try` block (lines 87–92) by outputting a message. Next, the `try` block creates a new `Exception` object and uses a *`throw` statement* to throw the exception object (lines 90–91). The string passed to the constructor becomes the exception object's error message. When a `throw` statement executes in a `try` block, the `try` block expires immediately, and program control continues at the first `catch` (lines 95–98) following this `try` block. In this example, the type thrown (`Exception`) matches the type specified in the `catch`, so lines 96–97 output a message indicating the exception that occurred. Then, the `finally` block (lines 101–104) executes and outputs a message. At this point, program control continues with the first statement after the `__finally` block (line 106), which outputs a message indicating that the end of the function has been reached, then program control returns to `_tmain`. Note that, in line 97, we use the exception object's `Message` property to access the error message associated with the exception—(the message passed to the `Exception` constructor). Section 11.6 discusses several properties of class `Exception`.

Common Programming Error 11.6

In MC++, the expression in a `throw` statement—an exception object—must be of either class `Exception` or one of its derived classes.

Lines 32–34 of `_tmain` define a `try` block in which `_tmain` invokes function `ThrowExceptionWithoutCatch` (lines 110–128). The `try` block enables `_tmain` to catch any exceptions thrown by `ThrowExceptionWithoutCatch`. The `try` block in lines 113–118 of `ThrowExceptionWithoutCatch` begins by outputting a message. Next, the `try` block throws an `Exception` (lines 116–117), and the `try` block expires immediately. Normally, program control would continue at the first `catch` following the `try` block. However, this `try` block does not have any corresponding `catch` handlers. Therefore, the exception is not caught in function `ThrowExceptionWithoutCatch`. Normal program control cannot continue until that exception is caught and processed. Thus, the CLR will terminate `ThrowExceptionWithoutCatch` and program control will return to `_tmain`. Before control returns to `_tmain`, the `__finally` block (lines 121–124) executes and outputs a message. At this point, program control returns to `_tmain`—any statements appearing after the `__finally` block would not execute. In this example, because the exception thrown in lines 116–117 is not caught, function `ThrowExceptionWithoutCatch` always terminates after the `__finally` block executes. In `_tmain`, the `catch` handler in lines 37–40 catches the exception and displays a message indicating that the exception was caught in `_tmain`.

Lines 48–50 of `_tmain` define a `try` block in which `_tmain` invokes function `ThrowExceptionCatchRethrow` (lines 131–160). The `try` block enables `_tmain` to catch any exceptions thrown by `ThrowExceptionCatchRethrow`. The `try` block in lines 134–139 of `ThrowExceptionCatchRethrow` begins by outputting a message (line 135), then throwing an `Exception` (lines 137–138). The `try` block expires immediately, and program control continues at the first `catch` (lines 142–150) following the `try` block. In this example, the type thrown (`Exception`) matches the type specified in the `catch`, so lines 143–144 output a message indicating the exception that occurred. Line 147 uses the `throw` statement to *rethrow* the exception. This indicates that the `catch` handler performed partial processing (or no processing) of the exception and is now passing the exception back to the calling function (in this case `_tmain`) for further processing. Note that the expression in the `throw` statement is the pointer to the exception that was caught. When rethrowing the original exception, you can also use the statement

```
throw;
```

with no expression. Section 11.6 discusses the `throw` statement with an expression. Such a `throw` statement enables programmers to catch an exception, create an exception object, then throw a different type of exception from the `catch` handler. Class library designers often do this to customize the exception types thrown from methods in their class libraries or to provide additional debugging information.

Software Engineering Observation 11.7

Whenever possible, a method should handle exceptions that are thrown in that method, rather than passing the exceptions to another region of the program.

Software Engineering Observation 11.8

Before throwing an exception to a calling method, the method that throws the exception should release any resources acquired within the method before the exception occurred.[7]

The exception handling in function `ThrowExceptionCatchRethrow` did not complete, because the program cannot run code in the `catch` handler placed after the invocation of the `throw` statement (line 147). Therefore, function `ThrowExceptionCatchRethrow` will terminate and return control to `_tmain`. Once again, the `__finally` block (lines 153–156) will execute and output a message before control returns to `_tmain`. When control returns to `_tmain`, the `catch` handler in lines 53–56 catches the exception and displays a message indicating that the exception was caught.

Note that the point at which program control continues after the `__finally` block executes depends on the exception-handling state. If the `try` block successfully completes or if a `catch` handler catches and handles an exception, control continues with the next statement after the `__finally` block. If an exception is not caught or if a `catch` handler rethrows an exception, program control continues in the next enclosing `try` block. The enclosing `try` may be in the calling function or one of its callers. Nesting a `try...catch` sequence in a `try` block is also possible, in which case the outer `try` block's catch handlers would process any exceptions that were not caught in the inner `try...catch` sequence. If a `try` block has a corresponding `__finally` block, the `__finally` block executes even if the `try` block terminates due to a `return` statement; then the `return` occurs.

7. "Best Practices for Handling Exceptions."

Common Programming Error 11.7

Throwing an exception from a `__finally` block can be dangerous. If an uncaught exception is awaiting processing when the `__finally` block executes and the `__finally` block throws a new exception that is not caught in the `__finally` block, the first exception is lost, and the new exception is the one passed to the next enclosing `try` block.

Error-Prevention Tip 11.5

When placing code that can throw an exception in a `__finally` block, always enclose that code in a `try...catch` sequence that catches the appropriate exception types. This prevents losing uncaught and rethrown exceptions that occur before the `__finally` block executes.

Performance Tip 11.4

Adding an excessive number of `try-catch-__finally` blocks in your code can result in reduced performance.

11.6 `Exception` Properties

As we discussed in Section 11.4, exception data types derive from class `Exception`, which has several properties. These properties frequently are used to formulate error messages for a caught exception. Two important properties are `Message` and `StackTrace`. Property `Message` stores the error message associated with an `Exception` object. This message may be a default message associated with the exception type or a customized message passed to an exception object's constructor when the exception object is constructed. Property `StackTrace` contains a string that represents the *method call stack*. The runtime environment keeps a list of method calls that have been made up to a given moment. The `StackTrace` string represents this sequential list of methods that had not finished processing at the time the exception occurred. The exact location at which the exception occurs in the program is called the exception's *throw point*.

Error-Prevention Tip 11.6

A stack trace shows the complete method call stack at the time an exception occurred. This lets the programmer view the series of method calls that led to the exception. Information in the stack trace includes names of the methods on the call stack at the time of the exception, names of the classes in which those methods are defined, names of the namespaces in which those classes are defined and line numbers. The first line number in the stack trace indicates the throw point. Subsequent line numbers indicate the locations from which each method in the stack trace was called.

Another property used frequently by class library programmers is `InnerException`. Typically, programmers use this property to "wrap" exception objects caught in their code, then throw new exception types that are specific to their libraries. For example, a programmer implementing an accounting system might have some account-number processing code in which account numbers are input as strings, but represented with integers in the code. As you know, a program can convert strings to `Int32` values with `Convert::ToInt32`, which throws a `FormatException` when it encounters an invalid number format. When an invalid account-number format occurs, the accounting-system programmer might wish either to indicate an error message different from the default one supplied by `FormatException` or to indicate a new exception type, such as `InvalidAccountNumberFormatException`. In these cases, the programmer would provide code to catch the `FormatException`, then create an exception object in the `catch` handler, passing the original exception as one of the constructor arguments. The original exception object becomes the `InnerException` of the new exception object. When an `InvalidAccountNumberFormatException` occurs in code that uses the accounting-system library, the `catch` handler that catches the exception can view the original exception via the property `InnerException`. Thus, the exception indicates that an invalid account number was specified and that the particular problem was an invalid number format.

Our next example (Fig. 11.3–Fig. 11.5) demonstrates properties `Message`, `StackTrace` and `InnerException`, as well as method `ToString`. In addition, this example demonstrates *stack unwinding*—the process that attempts to locate an appropriate `catch` handler for an uncaught exception. As we discuss this example, we keep track of the methods on the call stack, so we can discuss property `StackTrace` and the stack-unwinding mechanism.

```
// Fig. 11.3: Properties.h
// Stack unwinding and Exception class properties.

#pragma once

#using <mscorlib.dll>

using namespace System;

// demonstrates using the Message, StackTrace and
// InnerException properties
public __gc class Properties
{
public:
   static void Method1();
   static void Method2();
   static void Method3();
}; // end class Properties
```

Fig. 11.3 `Exception` properties and stack unwinding.

```
// Fig. 11.4: Properties.cpp
// Method definitions for class Properties.

#include "stdafx.h"
#include "Properties.h"

// calls Method2
void Properties::Method1()
{
   Method2();
} // end method Method1

// calls Method3
void Properties::Method2()
{
```

Fig. 11.4 `Properties` class method definitions. (Part 1 of 2.)

```
    Method3();
} // end method Method2

// throws an Exception containing an InnerException
void Properties::Method3()
{
   // attempt to convert non-integer string to int
   try {
      Convert::ToInt32( S"Not an integer" );
   } // end try

   // catch FormatException and wrap it in new Exception
   catch ( FormatException *error ) {
      throw new Exception( S"Exception occurred in Method3", error );
   } // end try
} // end method Method3
```

Fig. 11.4 `Properties` class method definitions. (Part 2 of 2.)

```
// Fig. 11.5: PropertiesTest.cpp
// PropertiesTest demonstrates stack unwinding.

#include "stdafx.h"
#include "Properties.h"

#using <mscorlib.dll>

using namespace System;

// entry point for application
int _tmain()
{
   // calls Method1, any Exception it generates will be
   // caught in the catch handler that follows
   try {
      Properties::Method1();
   } // end try

   // output string representation of Exception, then
   // output values of InnerException, Message,
   // and StackTrace properties
   catch( Exception *exception ) {
      Console::WriteLine( S"exception->ToString(): \n{0}\n",
         exception->ToString() );

      Console::WriteLine( S"exception->Message: \n{0}\n",
         exception->Message );

      Console::WriteLine( S"exception->StackTrace: \n{0}\n",
         exception->StackTrace );

```

Fig. 11.5 `PropertiesTest` demonstrates stack unwinding. (Part 1 of 2.)

```
33        Console::WriteLine( S"exception->InnerException: \n{0}",
34           exception->InnerException );
35     } // end catch
36
37     return 0;
38  } // end _tmain
```

```
exception->ToString():
System.Exception: Exception occurred in Method3 ---> System.FormatException:
Input string was not in a correct format.
   at System.Number.ParseInt32(String s, NumberStyles style,
      NumberFormatInfo info)
   at System.Convert.ToInt32(String value)
   at Properties.Method3() in c:\books\2003\vcpphtp1\vcpphtp1_examples\ch11\
      fig11_03-05\propertiestest\properties.cpp:line 24
   --- End of inner exception stack trace ---
   at Properties.Method3() in c:\books\2003\vcpphtp1\vcpphtp1_examples\ch11\
      fig11_03-05\propertiestest\properties.cpp:line 29
   at Properties.Method2() in c:\books\2003\vcpphtp1\vcpphtp1_examples\ch11\
      fig11_03-05\propertiestest\properties.cpp:line 16
   at Properties.Method1() in c:\books\2003\vcpphtp1\vcpphtp1_examples\ch11\
      fig11_03-05\propertiestest\properties.cpp:line 10
   at main() in c:\books\2003\vcpphtp1\vcpphtp1_examples\ch11\
      fig11_03-05\propertiestest\propertiestest.cpp:line 17

exception->Message:
Exception occurred in Method3

exception->StackTrace:
   at Properties.Method3() in c:\books\2003\vcpphtp1\vcpphtp1_examples\ch11\
      fig11_03-05\propertiestest\properties.cpp:line 29
   at Properties.Method2() in c:\books\2003\vcpphtp1\vcpphtp1_examples\ch11\
      fig11_03-05\propertiestest\properties.cpp:line 16
   at Properties.Method1() in c:\books\2003\vcpphtp1\vcpphtp1_examples\ch11\
      fig11_03-05\propertiestest\properties.cpp:line 10
   at main() in c:\books\2003\vcpphtp1\vcpphtp1_examples\ch11\
      fig11_03-05\propertiestest\propertiestest.cpp:line 17

exception->InnerException:
System.FormatException: Input string was not in a correct format.
   at System.Number.ParseInt32(String s, NumberStyles style,
      NumberFormatInfo info)
   at System.Convert.ToInt32(String value)
   at Properties.Method3() in c:\books\2003\vcpphtp1\vcpphtp1_examples\ch11\
      fig11_03-05\propertiestest\properties.cpp:line 24
```

Fig. 11.5 `PropertiesTest` demonstrates stack unwinding. (Part 2 of 2.)

Program execution begins with the invocation of `_tmain` (Fig. 11.5), which becomes the first method on the method call stack (`_tmain` is actually a function, but both functions and methods can be added to the method call stack). Line 17 of the `try` block in `_tmain` invokes `Method1` (lines 8–11 of Fig. 11.4), which becomes the second method on the stack. If `Method1` throws an exception, the `catch` handler in lines 23–35 (Fig. 11.5) handles the exception and outputs information about the exception that occurred. Line 10 of `Method1` (Fig. 11.4) invokes `Method2` (lines 14–17), which becomes the third method on the stack. Then line 16 of `Method2` invokes `Method3` (defined in lines 20–31), which becomes the fourth method on the stack.

Error-Prevention Tip 11.7

When reading a stack trace, start from the top of the stack trace and read the error message first. Then, read the remainder of the stack trace, looking for the first line that indicates code that you wrote in your program. Normally, this is the location that caused the exception.

At this point, the method call stack for the program is

```
Method3
Method2
Method1
_tmain
```

with the last method called (`Method3`) at the top and the first method called (`_tmain`) at the bottom. The `try` block (lines 23–25 of Fig. 11.4) in `Method3` invokes method `Convert::ToInt32` (line 24) and attempts to convert a string to an `int`. At this point, `Convert::ToInt32` becomes the fifth and final method on the call stack.

The argument to `Convert::ToInt32` is not in integer format, so line 24 of Fig. 11.4 throws a `FormatException` that is caught in line 28 in `Method3`. The exception terminates the call to `Convert::ToInt32`, so the method is removed from the method-call stack. The `catch` handler creates an `Exception` object, then throws it. The first argument to the `Exception` constructor is the custom error message for our example, `"Exception occurred in Method3"`. The second argument is the `InnerException` object—the `FormatException` that was caught. Note that the `StackTrace` for this new exception object will reflect the point at which the exception was thrown (line 29). Now, `Method3` terminates, because the exception thrown in the `catch` handler is not caught in the method body. Thus, control will be returned to the statement that invoked `Method3` in the prior method in the call stack (`Method2`). This *unwinds* (removes) `Method3` from the method-call stack.

Good Programming Practice 11.3

When catching and rethrowing an exception, provide additional debugging information in the rethrown exception. To do so, create an `Exception` *object with more specific debugging information and pass the original caught exception to the new exception object's constructor to initialize the* `InnerException` *property.*[8]

When control returns to line 16 in `Method2`, the CLR determines that line 16 is not in a `try` block. Therefore, the exception cannot be caught in `Method2`, and `Method2` terminates. This unwinds `Method2` from the method-call stack and returns control to line 10 in `Method1`. Here again, line 10 is not in a `try` block, so the exception cannot be caught in `Method1`. The method terminates and unwinds from the call stack, returning control to line 17 in `_tmain` (Fig. 11.5), which is in a `try` block. The `try` block in `_tmain` expires, and the `catch` handler in lines 23–35 catches the exception. The `catch` handler uses method

8. "InnerException Property," *.NET Framework Developer's Guide*, Visual Studio .NET Online Help. `<msdn.microsoft.com/library/default.asp?url=/library/en-us/cpref/html/frlrfsystemexceptionclassinnerexceptiontopic.asp>`

`ToString` and properties `Message`, `StackTrace` and `InnerException` to produce the output. Note that stack unwinding continues until either a `catch` handler catches the exception or the program terminates.

The first block of output (reformatted for readability) in Fig. 11.5 shows the exception's string representation returned from method `ToString`. This begins with the name of the exception class followed by the `Message` property value. The next eight lines show the string representation of the `InnerException` object. The remainder of that block of output shows the `StackTrace` for the exception thrown in `Method3`. Note that the `StackTrace` represents the state of the method-call stack at the throw point of the exception, not at the point where the exception eventually is caught. Each of the `StackTrace` lines that begins with `"at"` represents a method on the call stack. These lines indicate the method in which the exception occurred, the file in which that method resides and the line number in the file. Also, note that the stack trace includes the inner-exception stack trace. [*Note:* File and line number information is not shown for FCL classes and methods.]

The next block of output (two lines) simply displays the `Message` property (`Exception occurred in Method3`) of the exception thrown in `Method3`.

The third block of output displays the `StackTrace` property of the exception thrown in `Method3`. Note that the `StackTrace` property includes the stack trace starting from line 29 in `Method3`, because that is the point at which the `Exception` object was created and thrown. The stack trace always begins from the exception's throw point.

Finally, the last block of output displays the `ToString` representation of the `InnerException` property, which includes the namespace and class names of that exception object, its `Message` property and its `StackTrace` property.

11.7 Programmer-Defined Exception Classes

In many cases, programmers can use existing exception classes from the .NET Framework to indicate exceptions that occur in their programs. However, in some cases, programmers may wish to create exception types that are more specific to the problems that occur in their programs. *Programmer-defined exception classes* should derive directly or indirectly from class `ApplicationException` of namespace `System`.

Good Programming Practice 11.4

Associating each type of malfunction with an appropriately named exception class improves program clarity.

Software Engineering Observation 11.9

Before creating programmer-defined exception classes, investigate the existing exception classes in the .NET Framework to determine whether an appropriate exception type already exists.

Software Engineering Observation 11.10

Programmers should create exception classes only if they need to catch and handle the new exceptions differently from other existing exception types.

Software Engineering Observation 11.11

Always catch any exception class that you create and throw.

Good Programming Practice 11.5

Only handle one problem per exception class. Never overload an exception class to deal with several exceptions.

Good Programming Practice 11.6

Use significant and meaningful names for exception classes.

Figures 11.6–11.8 demonstrate defining and using a programmer-defined exception class. Class `NegativeNumberException` (Fig. 11.6–Fig. 11.7) is a programmer-defined exception class representing exceptions that occur when a program performs an illegal operation on a negative number, such as the square root of a negative number.

```
// Fig. 11.6: NegativeNumberException.h
// NegativeNumberException represents exceptions caused by illegal
// operations performed on negative numbers.

#pragma once

#using <mscorlib.dll>

using namespace System;

// NegativeNumberException represents exceptions caused by
// illegal operations performed on negative numbers
public __gc class NegativeNumberException : public ApplicationException
{
public:
   NegativeNumberException();
   NegativeNumberException( String * );
   NegativeNumberException( String *, Exception * );
}; // end class NegativeNumberException
```

Fig. 11.6 `ApplicationException` subclass thrown when a program performs illegal operations on negative numbers.

```
// Fig. 11.7: NegativeNumberException.cpp
// Method definitions for class NegativeNumberException.

#include "stdafx.h"
#include "NegativeNumberException.h"

// default constructor
NegativeNumberException::NegativeNumberException()
   : ApplicationException( S"Illegal operation for a negative number" )
{
}

```

Fig. 11.7 `NegativeNumberException` class method definitions. (Part 1 of 2.)

```
// constructor for customizing error message
NegativeNumberException::NegativeNumberException( String *message )
   : ApplicationException( message )
{
}

// constructor for customizing error message and
// specifying inner exception object
NegativeNumberException::NegativeNumberException( String *message,
   Exception *inner ) : ApplicationException( message, inner )
{
}
```

Fig. 11.7 NegativeNumberException class method definitions. (Part 2 of 2.)

Programmer-defined exceptions should extend class ApplicationException, should have a class name that ends with "Exception" and should define three constructors—a default constructor, a constructor that receives a string argument (the error message) and a constructor that receives a string argument and an Exception argument (the error message and the inner-exception object).[9]

NegativeNumberExceptions most likely occur during arithmetic operations, so it seems logical to derive class NegativeNumberException from class ArithmeticException. However, class ArithmeticException derives from class SystemException—the category of exceptions thrown by the CLR. ApplicationException specifically is the base class for exceptions thrown by a user program, not by the CLR.

Figure 11.8 demonstrates our programmer-defined exception class. The application enables the user to input a numeric value, then invokes function FindSquareRoot (lines 41–50) to calculate the square root of that value. For this purpose, FindSquareRoot invokes class Math's *Sqrt* method, which receives a positive double value as its argument. If the argument is negative, method Sqrt normally returns constant NaN—"not a number"—from class Double. In this program, we would like to prevent the user from calculating the square root of a negative number. If the numeric value received from the user is negative, FindSquareRoot throws a NegativeNumberException (lines 45–46). Otherwise, FindSquareRoot invokes class Math's *Sqrt* method to compute the square root.

```
1  // Fig. 11.8: SquareRoot.cpp
2  // Demonstrating a programmer-defined exception class.
3
4  #include "stdafx.h"
5  #include "NegativeNumberException.h"
6
7  #using <mscorlib.dll>
8
9  using namespace System;
10
```

Fig. 11.8 FindSquareRoot function throws exception if error occurs when calculating square root. (Part 1 of 2.)

9. "Best Practices for Handling Exceptions."

```
double FindSquareRoot( double );

// obtain user input, convert to double and calculate square root
int _tmain()
{
   // catch any NegativeNumberExceptions thrown
   try {
      Console::Write( S"Please enter a number: " );

      double result =
         FindSquareRoot( Double::Parse( Console::ReadLine() ) );

      Console::WriteLine( result );
   } // end try

   // process invalid number format
   catch ( FormatException *notInteger ) {
      Console::WriteLine( notInteger->Message );
   } // end catch

   // display message if negative number input
   catch ( NegativeNumberException *error ) {
      Console::WriteLine( error->Message );
   } // end catch

   return 0;
} // end _tmain

// computes the square root of its parameter; throws
// NegativeNumberException if parameter is negative
double FindSquareRoot( double operand )
{
   // if negative operand, throw NegativeNumberException
   if ( operand < 0 )
      throw new NegativeNumberException(
         S"Square root of negative number not permitted." );

   // compute the square root
   return Math::Sqrt( operand );
} // end function FindSquareRoot
```

```
Please enter a number: 33
5.74456264653803
```

```
Please enter a number: hello
Input string was not in a correct format.
```

```
Please enter a number: -12.45
Square root of negative number not permitted.
```

Fig. 11.8 `FindSquareRoot` function throws exception if error occurs when calculating square root. (Part 2 of 2.)

The `try` block (lines 17–24) attempts to invoke `FindSquareRoot` with the value input by the user. If the user input is not a valid number, a `FormatException` occurs, and the `catch` handler in lines 27–29 processes the exception. If the user inputs a negative number, function `FindSquareRoot` throws a `NegativeNumberException` (lines 45–46). The `catch` handler in lines 32–33 catches and handles that exception.

SUMMARY

- An exception is an indication of a problem that occurs during a program's execution.
- Exception handling enables programmers to create applications that can resolve exceptions, often allowing a program to continue execution as if no problems were encountered.
- Exception handling enables programmers to write clear, robust and more fault-tolerant programs.
- Exception handling enables programmers to remove error-handling code from the "main line" of the program's execution. This improves program clarity and enhances modifiability.
- Exception handling is designed to process synchronous errors, such as out-of-range array subscripts, arithmetic overflow, division by zero, invalid method parameters and memory exhaustion, and asynchronous events, such as disk I/O completion.
- When a method called in a program or the CLR detects a problem, the method or CLR throws an exception. The point in the program at which an exception occurs is called the throw point.
- There is no guarantee that there will be an exception handler to process that kind of exception. If there is, the exception will be caught and handled.
- A `try` block consists of keyword `try` followed by braces (`{}`) that delimit a block of code in which exceptions could occur.
- Immediately following the `try` block are zero or more `catch` handlers. Each `catch` specifies in parentheses an exception parameter representing the exception type the `catch` can handle.
- If an exception parameter includes an optional parameter name, the `catch` handler can use that parameter name to interact with a caught exception object.
- There can be one parameterless `catch` handler that catches all exception types.
- After the last `catch` handler, an optional `__finally` block contains code that always executes, regardless of whether an exception occurs.
- MC++ uses the termination model of exception handling. If an exception occurs in a `try` block, the block expires and program control transfers to the first `catch` handler following the `try` block that can process the type of exception that occurred.
- The appropriate handler is the first one in which the thrown exception's type matches, or is derived from, the exception type specified by the `catch` handler's exception parameter.
- If no exceptions occur in a `try` block, the CLR ignores the exception handlers for that block.
- If no exceptions occur or if an exception is caught and handled, the program resumes execution with the next statement after the `try...catch...__finally` sequence.
- If an exception occurs in a statement that is not in a `try` block, the method containing that statement terminates immediately—a process called stack unwinding.
- The MC++ exception-handling mechanism allows only objects of class `Exception` and its derived classes to be thrown and caught. Class `Exception` of namespace `System` is the base class of the .NET Framework exception hierarchy.
- Exceptions are objects of classes that inherit directly or indirectly from class `Exception`.

TERMINOLOGY

ApplicationException class
arithmetic overflow
call stack
catch all exception types
catch block (or handler)
disk I/O completion
divide by zero
DivideByZeroException class
Double class
eliminate resource leaks
error-processing code
exception
Exception class
exception handler
fault-tolerant program
__finally block
FormatException class
IndexOutOfRangeException class
inheritance with exceptions
InnerException property of Exception
memory leak
Message property of class Exception
method call stack
NaN constant of class Double
negative infinity
NullReferenceException
out-of-range array subscript
overflow
OverflowException class
polymorphic processing of related exceptions
positive infinity
programmer-defined exception classes
release a resource
resource leak
result of an uncaught exception
resumption model of exception handling
rethrow an exception
runtime exception
stack unwinding
StackTrace property of Exception
synchronous error
SystemException class
termination model of exception handling
throw an exception
throw point
throw statement
ToInt32 method of Convert
try block
uncaught exception

SELF-REVIEW EXERCISES

11.1 Fill in the blanks in each of the following statements:

a) A method ________ an exception when that method detects that a problem occurred.
b) The ________ block associated with a try block always executes.
c) Exception classes in MC++ are derived from class ________.
d) The statement that throws an exception is called the ________ of the exception.
e) A(n) ________ block encloses code that might throw an exception and code that should not execute if an exception occurs
f) If the catch-all exception handler is declared before another exception handler, a(n) ________ occurs.
g) An uncaught exception in a method causes that method to ________ from the method-call stack.
h) Method Convert::ToInt32 can throw a(n) ________ exception if its argument is not a valid integer value.
i) Runtime exceptions derive from class ________.
j) The ________ property of class Exception represents the state of the method-call stack at the throw point of an exception.

11.2 State whether each of the following is *true* or *false*. If *false*, explain why.

a) Exceptions always are handled in the method that initially detects the exception.
b) Programmer-defined exception classes should extend class SystemException.
c) Accessing an out-of-bounds array subscript causes the CLR to throw an exception.
d) A __finally block is optional after a try block.

e) If a `__finally` block appears in a method, that `__finally` block is guaranteed to execute.
f) Returning to the throw point of an exception using keyword `return` is possible.
g) Exceptions can be rethrown.
h) MC++ exceptions are objects of classes that inherit directly or indirectly from class `Exception`.
i) Property `Message` of class `Exception` returns a `String *` indicating the method from which the exception was thrown.
j) Exceptions can be thrown only by methods explicitly called in a `try` block.

ANSWERS TO SELF-REVIEW EXERCISES

11.1 a) throws. b) `__finally`. c) `Exception`. d) throw point. e) `try`. f) syntax error. g) unwind. h) `FormatException`. i) `SystemException`. j) `StackTrace`.

11.2 a) False. Exceptions are handled by the first matching `catch` handler, which could follow an enclosing `try` block. b) False. Programmer-defined exception classes should extend class `ApplicationException`. c) True. d) False. The `__finally` block is an option *only* if there is at least one `catch` handler. If there are no `catch` handlers, the `__finally` block is *required.* e) False. The `__finally` block will execute only if program control enters the corresponding `try` block. f) False. Keyword `return` causes control to `return` to the calling method. g) True. h) True. i) False. Property `Message` returns a `String *` representing the error message. j) False. Exceptions can be thrown by any method, called from a `try` block or not. Also, the CLR can throw exceptions.

EXERCISES

11.3 Use inheritance to create an exception base class and various exception-derived classes. Write a program to demonstrate that the `catch` specifying the base class catches derived-class exceptions.

11.4 Write an MC++ program that demonstrates how various exceptions are caught with

```
catch ( Exception *exception )
```

11.5 Write an MC++ program that shows the importance of the order of exception handlers. Write two programs: One with the correct order of `catch` handlers, and one with an incorrect order (i.e., place the base class exception handler before the derived-class exception handlers). Show that if you attempt to catch a base-class exception type before a derived-class exception type, the derived-class exceptions are not invoked (which potentially yield logical errors in routine). Explain why these errors occur.

11.6 Exceptions can be used to indicate problems that occur when an object is being constructed. Write an MC++ program that shows a constructor passing information about constructor failure to an exception handler that occurs after a `try` block. The exception thrown also should contain the arguments sent to the constructor.

11.7 Write an MC++ program that demonstrates rethrowing an exception.

11.8 Write an MC++ program that shows that a method with its own `try` block does not have to `catch` every possible exception that occurs within the `try` block. Some exceptions can slip through to, and be handled in, other scopes.

12

Graphical User Interface Concepts: Part 1

Objectives

- To understand the design principles of graphical user interfaces.
- To understand, use and create event handlers.
- To understand the namespaces containing graphical user interface components and event-handling classes and interfaces.
- To create graphical user interfaces.
- To create and manipulate buttons, labels, lists, text boxes and panels.
- To be able to use mouse and keyboard events.

... the wisest prophets make sure of the event first.
Horace Walpole

...The user should feel in control of the computer; not the other way around. This is achieved in applications that embody three qualities: responsiveness, permissiveness, and consistency.
Inside Macintosh, Volume 1
Apple Computer, Inc. 1985

All the better to see you with, my dear.
The Big Bad Wolf to Little Red Riding Hood

Outline

12.1 Introduction

A *graphical user interface* (*GUI*) allows users to interact with a program visually. A GUI (pronounced "GOO-EE") gives a program a distinctive "look" and "feel." By providing different applications with a consistent set of intuitive user-interface components, GUIs allow users to spend less time trying to remember which keystroke sequences perform what functions and spend more time using the program in a productive manner.

Look-and-Feel Observation 12.1

Consistent user interfaces enable users to learn new applications faster.

As an example of a GUI, Fig. 12.1 contains an Internet Explorer window with some of its *GUI components* labeled. In the window, there is a *menu bar* containing *menus*, including **File**, **Edit**, **View**, **Favorites**, **Tools** and **Help**. Below the menu bar is a set of *buttons*; each has a defined task in Internet Explorer. Below the buttons is a *text box,* in which the user can type the location of a World Wide Web site to visit. To the left of the text box is a *label* that indicates the text box's purpose. On the far right and bottom there are *scrollbars*. Scrollbars are used when there is more information in a window than can be displayed at once. By moving the scrollbars back and forth, the user can view different portions of the Web page. The menus, buttons, text boxes, labels and scrollbars are part of Internet Explorer's GUI. They form a user-friendly interface through which the user interacts with the Internet Explorer Web browser.

GUIs are built from *GUI components*. A GUI component is an object with which the user interacts via the mouse or keyboard. Several common .NET GUI component classes are listed in Fig. 12.2. In the sections that follow, we discuss these GUI components in detail. In the next chapter, we discuss more advanced GUI components.

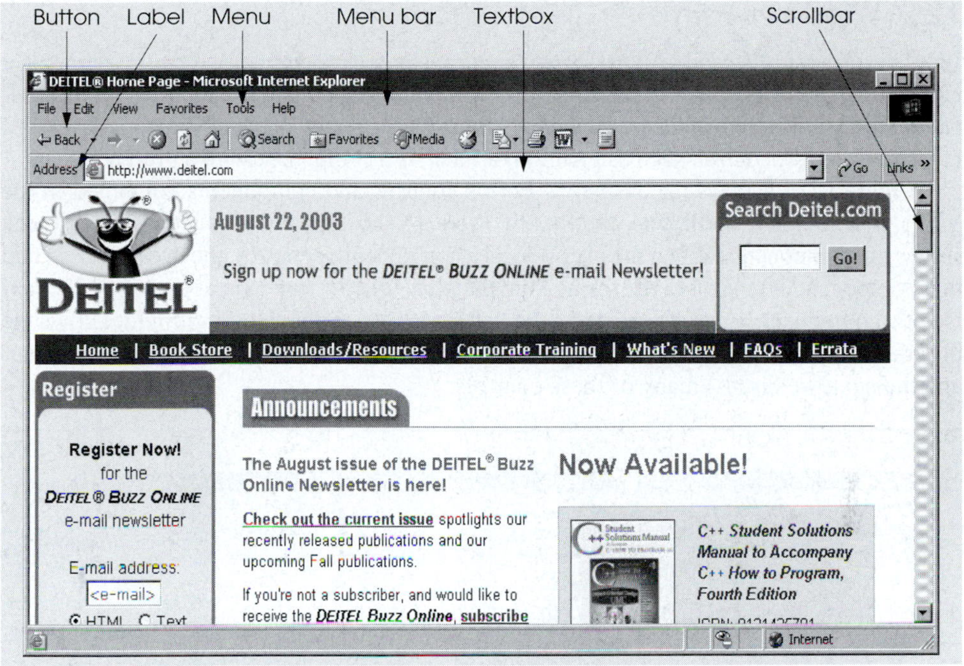

Fig. 12.1 Sample Internet Explorer window with GUI components.

Control	Description
`Label`	An area in which icons or uneditable text can be displayed.
`TextBox`	An area in which the user inputs data from the keyboard. The area also can display information.
`Button`	An area that triggers an event when clicked.
`CheckBox`	A GUI control that is either selected or not selected.
`ComboBox`	A drop-down list of items from which the user can make a selection, by clicking an item in the list or by typing into a box, if permitted.
`ListBox`	An area in which a list of items is displayed from which the user can make a selection by clicking once on any element. Multiple elements can be selected.
`Panel`	A container in which components can be placed.
`HScrollBar`	A horizontal scrollbar. Allows the user to access a data that cannot normally fit in its container horizontally.
`VScrollBar`	A vertical scrollbar. Allows the user to access data that cannot normally fit in its container vertically.

Fig. 12.2 Some basic GUI components.

12.2 Windows Forms

Windows Forms (also called *WinForms*) create GUIs for programs. A form is a graphical element that appears on the desktop. A form can be a dialog, an *SDI window* (*single document interface window*) or an *MDI window* (*multiple document interface window*, discussed in Chapter 13). A *control*, such as a button or label, is a component with a graphical part.

Figure 12.3 displays the Windows Forms controls and components contained in the Visual Studio .NET **Toolbox**—the first two screens show the controls and the last screen shows the components. When the user selects a component or control, the user then can add that component or control to the form. Note that the **Pointer** (the icon at the top of the list) is not a component; rather it represents the default mouse action. Highlighting it allows the programmer to use the mouse cursor instead of adding an item to the form. In this chapter and the next, we discuss many of these controls.

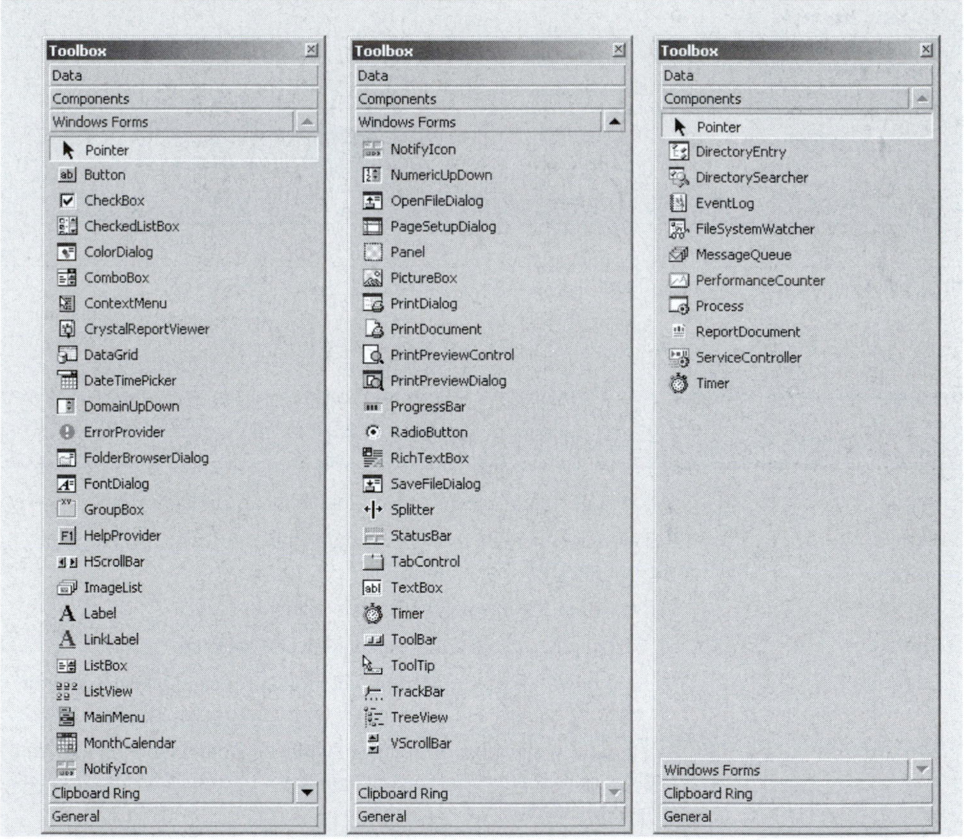

Fig. 12.3 Components and controls for Windows Forms.

When interacting with windows, we say that the *active window* has the *focus*. The active window is the frontmost window and has a highlighted title bar. A window becomes the active window when the user clicks somewhere inside it. When a window has focus, the operating system directs user input from the keyboard and mouse to that application.

The form acts as a *container* for components and controls. Controls must be added to the form using code. When the user interacts with a control by using the mouse or keyboard, events (discussed in Section 12.3) are generated, and *event handlers* process those events. Events typically cause something to happen in response to a user interaction. For example, clicking the **OK** button in a `MessageBox` generates an event. An event handler in class `MessageBox` closes the `MessageBox` in response to this event.

Each .NET Framework class we present in this chapter is located in the *`System::Windows::Forms` namespace*. Class `Form`, the basic window used by Windows applications, is fully qualified as `System::Windows::Forms::Form`. Likewise, class `Button` is actually `System::Windows::Forms::Button`.

The general design process for creating Windows applications requires creating a Windows Form, setting its properties, adding controls, setting their properties and implementing the event handlers. Figure 12.4 lists common `Form` properties and events.

Form Properties and Events	Description / Delegate and Event Arguments
Common Properties	
`AcceptButton`	Specifies which button will be clicked when the user presses *Enter*.
`AutoScroll`	Specifies whether scrollbars appear when needed (if the data fills more than one screen).
`CancelButton`	Specifies which button is clicked when the user presses *Escape*.
`FormBorderStyle`	Specifies the border of the form (e.g., `none`, `single`, `3D`, `sizable`).
`Font`	Specifies the font of text displayed on the form, as well as the default font of controls added to the form.
`Text`	Specifies the text in the form's title bar.
Common Methods	
`Close`	Closes form and releases all resources. A closed form cannot be reopened.
`Hide`	Hides form (does not release resources).
`Show`	Displays a hidden form.
Common Events	*(Delegate `EventHandler`, event arguments `EventArgs`)*
`Load`	Occurs before a form is shown.

Fig. 12.4 Common `Form` properties and events.

Visual Studio .NET generates most GUI-related code when we create controls and event handlers. Programmers can use Visual Studio .NET to perform most of these tasks graphically, by dragging and dropping components onto the form and setting properties in the **Properties** window. In visual programming, the IDE generally maintains GUI-related code, and the programmer writes the bodies of the event handlers that specify how the application responds to user interactions.

12.3 Event-Handling Model

GUIs are *event driven* (i.e., they generate *events* when the program's user interacts with the GUI). Typical interactions include moving the mouse, clicking the mouse, clicking a button, typing in a text box, selecting an item from a menu and closing a window. Event handlers are methods that process events and perform tasks. For example, consider a form that changes color when a button is clicked. When clicked, the button generates an event and passes it to the event handler, and the event-handler code changes the form's color.

Each control that can generate events has an associated delegate that defines the signature for that control's event handlers. Recall from Chapter 10 that delegates are objects that contain pointers to methods. Event delegates are *multicast* (class `MulticastDelegate`)—they contain lists of method pointers. Each method must have the same *signature* (i.e., the same list of parameters). In the event-handling model, delegates act as intermediaries between objects that generate events and methods that handle those events (Fig. 12.5).

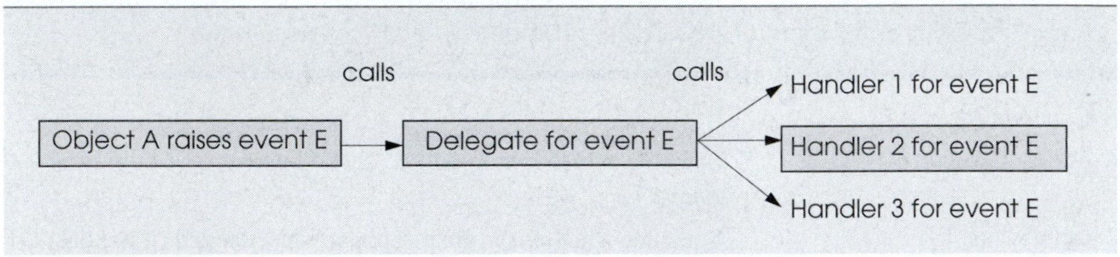

Fig. 12.5 Event-handling model using delegates.

Software Engineering Observation 12.1

Delegates enable classes to specify methods that will not be named or implemented until the class is instantiated. This is extremely helpful in creating event handlers. For instance, the creator of the `Form` *class does not need to name or define the method that will be invoked when a control is clicked. Using delegates, the class can specify when such an event handler would be called. Programmers that create their own forms then can name and define the event handlers. As long as an event handler is registered with a proper delegate, the event handler will be called at the proper time.*

Once an event is raised, every method that the delegate references is called. Every method in the delegate must have the same signature, because they are all passed the same information.

12.3.1 Basic Event Handling

In most cases, we do not have to create our own events. Instead, we can just handle the events generated by .NET controls. These controls already have delegates for every event they can raise. The programmer creates the event handler and registers it with the delegate—Visual Studio .NET helps with this task. In the following example, we create a form that displays a message box when clicked. Afterwards, we will analyze the event code that Visual Studio .NET generates.

First, create a new project of type **Windows Forms Application (.NET)** and call it `SimpleEventTest`. When you create this type of application, a blank form will be created. To register and define an event handler for this form, click the **Events** icon (the yellow lightning bolt) and click the **Alphabetic** icon (to get listings as in Fig. 12.6) in the form's **Properties** window (Fig. 12.6). This window allows the programmer to access, modify and create event handlers for a control. The left panel lists the events that the object can generate. The right panel lists the registered event handlers for the corresponding event; this list is initially empty. The drop-down button indicates that multiple handlers can be registered for one event. A brief description of the event appears on the bottom of the window.

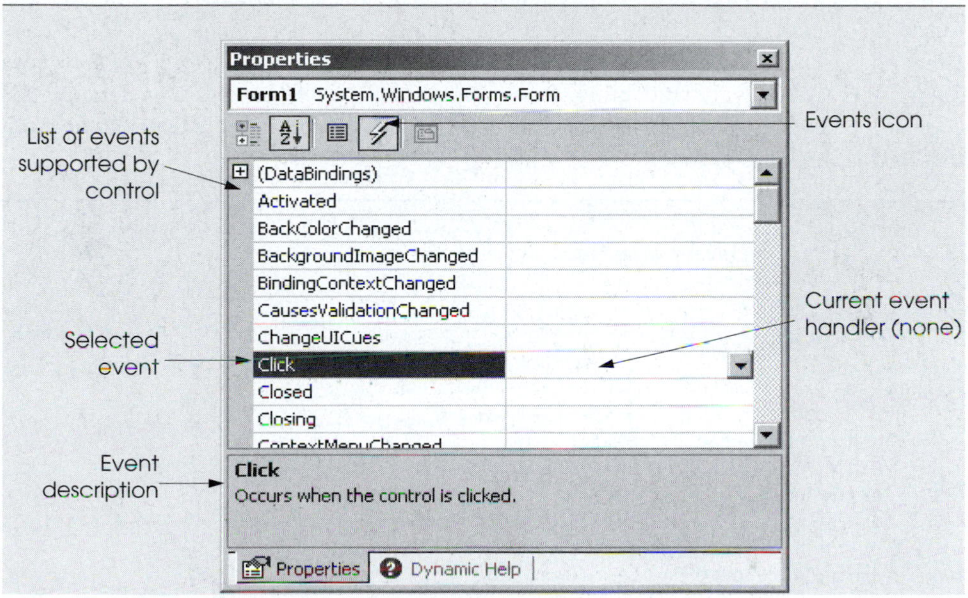

Fig. 12.6 Events section of the **Properties** window.

In this example, the form will perform an action when clicked. Double-click the **Click** event in the **Properties** window to create an empty event handler in the program code. Visual Studio .NET inserts code of the format:

```
private: System::Void FormName_Click(System::Object *sender,
            System::EventArgs *e)
         {
         }
```

This is the method that will be called when the form is clicked. As a response, we will have the form display a message box. To do this, insert the statement

```
MessageBox::Show( S"Form was pressed" );
```

the body of the event handler.

We can now discuss the details of the program, which appears in Fig. 12.8. Class `Form1` (the default name chosen by Visual Studio .NET) inherits from class `Form` (which represents a form) in the .NET Framework Class Library's `System::Windows::Form` namespace (line 26 of Fig. 12.7). A key benefit of inheriting from class `Form` is that someone else has previously defined "what it means to be a `Form`." The Windows operating system expects every form (e.g., window) to have certain attributes and behaviors. However, because class `Form` already provides those capabilities, programmers do not need to "reinvent the wheel" by defining all those capabilities themselves. Class `Form` has over 400 methods! Extending class `Form` enables programmers to create forms quickly.

In this example, whenever the form is clicked, a message box appears. First, we view the event handler (lines 53–57 of Fig. 12.7) that was inserted by Visual Studio .NET. Every event handler must have the signature that the corresponding event delegate specifies. Event handlers are passed two object references. The first is a pointer to the object that raised the event (`sender`), and the second is a pointer to an `EventArgs` object (`e`). Class `EventArgs` is the base class for objects that contain event information. [*Note*: We split lines 53–54 over two lines for readability. However, when the event handler is generated, this code will take up only one line. The source code provided on this book's CD does not split these generated lines of code.]

```
1  // Fig. 12.7: Form1.h
2  // Creating an event handler.
3
4  #pragma once
5
6
7  namespace SimpleEventTest
8  {
9     using namespace System;
10    using namespace System::ComponentModel;
11    using namespace System::Collections;
12    using namespace System::Windows::Forms;
13    using namespace System::Data;
14    using namespace System::Drawing;
15
16    /// <summary>
17    /// Summary for Form1
18    ///
19    /// WARNING: If you change the name of this class, you will need to
20    ///          change the 'Resource File Name' property for the managed
21    ///          resource compiler tool associated with all .resx files
22    ///          this class depends on.  Otherwise, the designers will not
23    ///          be able to interact properly with localized resources
24    ///          associated with this form.
25    /// </summary>
26    public __gc class Form1 : public System::Windows::Forms::Form
27    {
28    public:
29       Form1(void)
30       {
31          InitializeComponent();
32       }
33
34    protected:
35       void Dispose(Boolean disposing)
36       {
37          if (disposing && components)
38          {
```

Fig. 12.7 `SimpleEvent` demonstrates event handling. (Part 1 of 2.)

```
            components->Dispose();
         }
         __super::Dispose(disposing);
      }

   private:
      /// <summary>
      /// Required designer variable.
      /// </summary>
      System::ComponentModel::Container * components;

   // Visual Studio .NET generated GUI code

   // display a MessageBox when the user clicks the form
   private: System::Void Form1_Click(System::Object *  sender,
               System::EventArgs *  e)
            {
               MessageBox::Show( S"Form was pressed" );
            }

   };
}
```

Fig. 12.7 `SimpleEvent` demonstrates event handling. (Part 2 of 2.)

Figure 12.8 presents function `_tWinMain` (lines 10–19), which is the entry point for GUI programs. The arguments on lines 10–13 can be used to specify information about the current application, such as how the form should be shown (e.g., maximized or hidden). We do not make use of these arguments in this text. Lines 15–16 (also added by the IDE) enable users of your program to interact with the Windows clipboard for cut, copy and paste operations, and allow .NET Windows applications to make use of older windows technologies such as *COM* (*Component Object Model*) and ActiveX. We do not discuss COM or ActiveX technologies in this text.

```
 1  // Fig. 12.8: Form1.cpp
 2  // Demonstrating an event handler.
 3
 4  #include "stdafx.h"
 5  #include "Form1.h"
 6  #include <windows.h>
 7
 8  using namespace SimpleEventTest;
 9
10  int APIENTRY _tWinMain(HINSTANCE hInstance,
11                         HINSTANCE hPrevInstance,
12                         LPTSTR    lpCmdLine,
13                         int       nCmdShow)
14  {
15     System::Threading::Thread::CurrentThread->ApartmentState =
16        System::Threading::ApartmentState::STA;
17     Application::Run(new Form1());
```

Fig. 12.8 Event-handling demonstration. (Part 1 of 2.)

```
18     return 0;
19  }
```

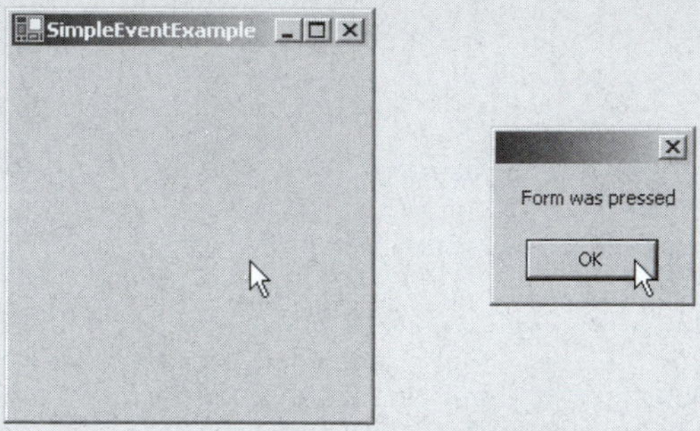

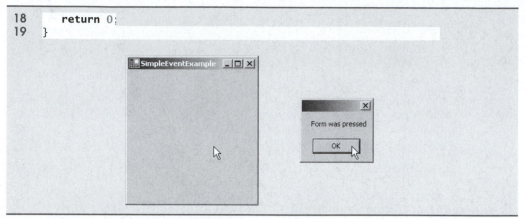

Fig. 12.8 Event-handling demonstration. (Part 2 of 2.)

Function `_tWinMain` associates a *message loop* with the current application, which will be handled in this application by class `Form`. Namespace `System::Windows::Form` includes class *`Application`*. Class `Application` contains `static` methods used to managed Windows applications. Method `Run` (line 17) displays the Windows form and starts the message loop. Windows applications communicate using *messages*—event descriptions. The message loop places each message on a queue and removes one at a time to forward it to the appropriate event handler. The .NET Framework hides the details of complex message processing from programmers for their convenience. Method `Run` also adds an event handler for the `Closed` event, which occurs when the user closes the window or the program calls method `Close`.

To create the event handler, we double-click an event name in the **Properties** window. This causes Visual Studio .NET to create a method with the proper signature (specified by the event's delegate). The naming convention used in the Visual Studio .NET generated code is *ControlName_EventName*; in our case the event handler is `Form1_Click`. [*Note:* The developer can use the **Properties** window to determine a control's events, or can view more information about the event by looking up the event argument's class. Consult the documentation index under *ControlName* `class` (i.e., `Form class`) and click the `events` section (Fig. 12.9). This displays a list of all the events the class can generate. Click the name of an event to bring up its delegate, event argument type and a description (Fig. 12.10).]

The format of this event-handling method is, in general,

```
private: System::Void ControlName_EventName(System::Object *sender,
            System::EventArgs *e)
         {
            event-handling code
         }
```

where the name of the event handler is by default the name of the control, followed by an underscore (_) and the name of the event. Event handlers have return type `System::Void` (the FCL structure equivalent to return type `void`). The differences between the various `EventArgs` classes are discussed in the following sections.

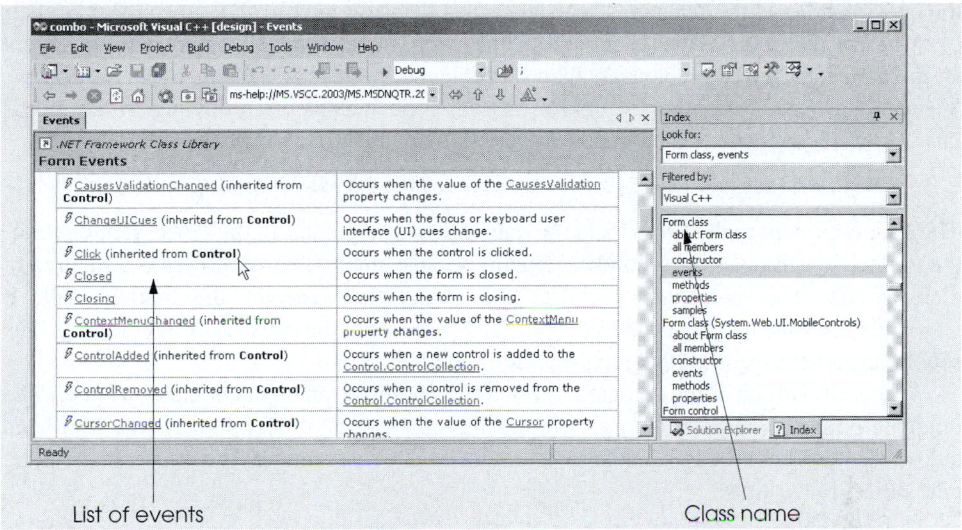

Fig. 12.9 List of `Form` events.

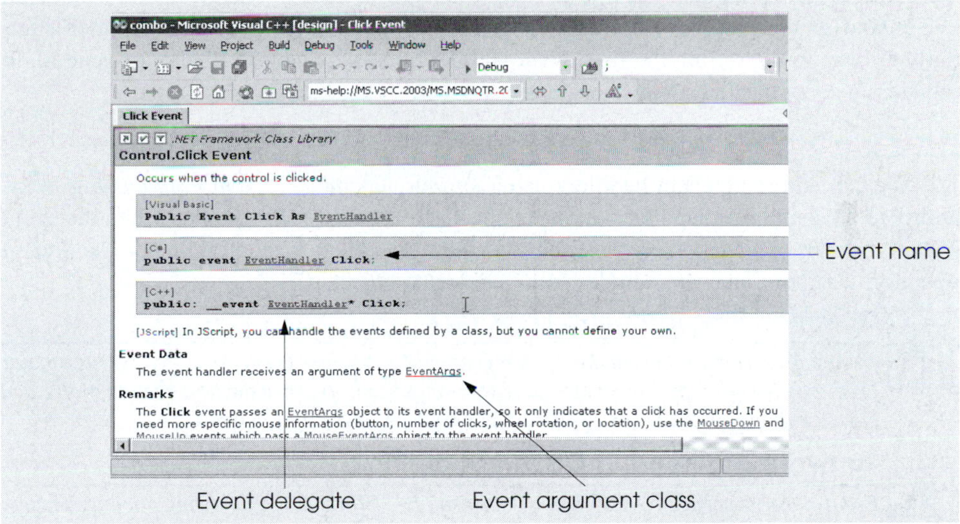

Fig. 12.10 Details of `Click` event.

Good Programming Practice 12.1

Use the event-handler naming convention ControlName_EventName *to keep methods organized. This tells a user which event a method handles, and for which control. Visual Studio .NET uses this naming convention when creating event handlers from the* **Properties** *window.*

After creating the event handler, we must *register* it with the delegate, which contains a list of event handlers to call. Registering an event handler with a delegate involves adding the event handler to the delegate's invocation list. Controls have a *delegate* for each of their events—the delegate has the same name as the event. For example, if we are handling event *EventName* for object `myControl`, then the delegate pointer is `myControl->`*EventName*. Visual Studio .NET registers events for us with code such as the following from method `InitializeComponent` (which is generated automatically):

```
this->Click += new System::EventHandler( this, Form1_Click );
```

The first argument to the `EventHandler` constructor is a pointer to the object that contains the method specified as the second argument, because method `Form1_Click` is a method of class `Form1`. This parameter specifies the object that receives the method call. If `Form1_Click` were a `static` method, the first parameter to the constructor would be `0`. The second argument specifies the event-handling method to call.

The lefthand side is the delegate `Click`. (`this` points to an object of class `MyForm`.) The delegate pointer is initially empty—we must assign to it an object pointer (the righthand side). We must create a new delegate object for each event handler. We create a new delegate object by writing

```
new System::EventHandler( this, methodName )
```

which returns a delegate object initialized with method *methodName*. The *methodName* is the name of the event handler, in our case it is `MyForm_Click`. The `+=` operator adds an `EventHandler` delegate to the current delegate's invocation list. The delegate pointer is initially empty, so registering the first event handler creates a delegate object. In general, to register an event handler, write

```
objectName->EventName += new System::EventHandler( this, MyEventHandler );
```

We can add more event handlers using similar statements. *Event multicasting* is the ability to have multiple handlers for one event. Each event handler is called when the event occurs, but the order in which the event handlers are called is indeterminate. Use the `-=` operator to remove an event handler from a delegate object.

Common Programming Error 12.1

Assuming that multiple event handlers registered for the same event are called in a particular order can lead to logic errors. If the order is important, register the first event handler and have it call the others in order, passing the sender and event arguments.

Software Engineering Observation 12.2

Events for prepackaged .NET components usually conform to the following naming scheme: If the event is named `EventName`, its delegate is `EventNameEventHandler`, and the event arguments class is `EventNameEventArgs`. Events that use class `EventArgs` usually use delegate `EventHandler`.

To review: The information needed to register an event is the `EventArgs` class (a parameter for the event handler) and the `EventHandler` delegate (to register the event handler). Visual Studio .NET can create this code for us. For simple events and event handlers it is often easier to allow Visual Studio .NET to generate this code. For more complicated solutions, registering your own event handlers might be necessary. In the upcoming sections, we will indicate the `Event-Args` class and the `EventHandler` delegate for each event we cover. To find more information about a particular type of event, search the help documentation for *ClassName* **class**; the events will be described with the class's other members.

12.4 Control Properties and Layout

This section overviews properties that are common to many controls. Controls derive from class `Control` (namespace `System::Windows::Forms`). Figure 12.11 contains a list of common properties and events for class `Control`. The `Text` property specifies the text that appears on a control, which may vary depending on the context. For example, the text of a Windows form appears in its title bar, and the text of a button appears on its face. The *`Focus`* method transfers the focus to a control. When the focus is on a control, it becomes the active control. When the *Tab* key is pressed, the *`TabIndex`* property determines the order in which controls are given focus. This is helpful for users with disabilities who cannot use a mouse and for the user who enters information in many different locations—the user can enter information and quickly select the next control by pressing the *Tab* key. The *`Enabled`* property indicates whether the control can be used. Programs can set property `Enabled` to `false` when an option is unavailable to the user. In most cases, the control's text will appear gray (rather than black), when a control is disabled. Without having to disable a control, the control can be hidden from the user by setting the *`Visible`* property to `false` or by calling method `Hide`. When a control's `Visible` property is set to `false`, the control still exists, but it is not shown on the form.

Control Properties and Methods	Description
Common Properties	
`BackColor`	Background color of the control.
`BackgroundImage`	Background image of the control.
`Enabled`	Specifies whether the control is enabled (i.e., if the user can interact with it). A disabled control will still be displayed, but "grayed-out"—portions of the control will become gray.
`Focused`	Specifies whether the control has focus.
`Font`	Font used to display control's `Text`.
`ForeColor`	Foreground color of the control. This is usually the color used to display the control's `Text` property.
`TabIndex`	Tab order of the control. When the *Tab* key is pressed, the focus is moved to controls in increasing tab order. This order can be set by the programmer if the `TabStop` property is true.
`TabStop`	If `true` (the default value), user can use the *Tab* key to select the control.
`Text`	Text associated with the control. The location and appearance varies with the type of control.
`TextAlign`	The alignment of the text on the control. One of three horizontal positions (left, center or right) and one of three vertical positions (top, middle or bottom).
`Visible`	Specifies whether the control is visible.

Fig. 12.11 `Control` class properties and methods. (Part 1 of 2.)

`Control` Properties and Methods	Description
Common Methods	
`Focus`	Transfers the focus to the control.
`Hide`	Hides the control (equivalent to setting `Visible` to `false`).
`Show`	Shows the control (equivalent to setting `Visible` to `true`).

Fig. 12.11 `Control` class properties and methods. (Part 2 of 2.)

Visual Studio .NET allows the programmer to *anchor* and *dock* controls, which helps to specify the layout of controls inside a container (such as a form). Anchoring allows controls to stay a fixed distance from the sides of the container, even when the control is resized. Docking allows controls to extend themselves along the sides of their containers.

A user may want a control to appear in a certain position (top, bottom, left or right) in a form even when that form is resized. The user can specify this by *anchoring* the control to a side (top, bottom, left or right). The control then maintains a fixed distance from the side to its parent container. In most cases, the parent container is a form; however, other controls can act as a parent container.

When parent containers are resized, all controls move. Unanchored controls move relative to their original position on the form, while anchored controls move so that they will be the same distance from each side that they are anchored to. For example, in Fig. 12.12, the topmost button is anchored to the top and left sides of the parent form. When the form is resized, the anchored button moves so that it remains a constant distance from the top and left sides of the form (its parent). The unanchored button changes position as the form is resized.

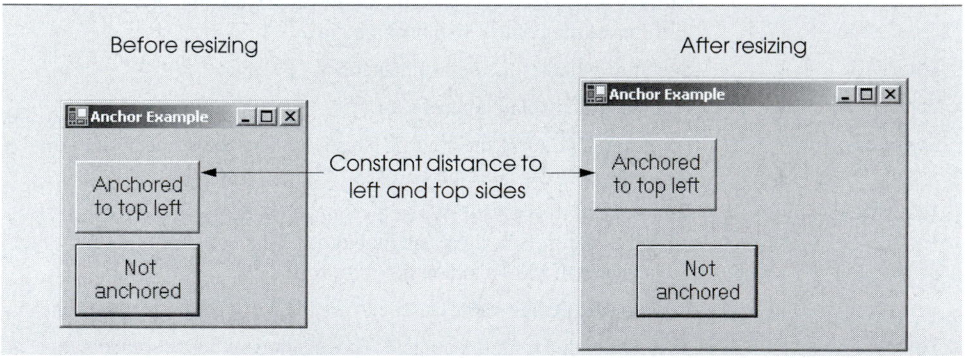

Fig. 12.12 Anchoring demonstration.

Create a simple **Windows Forms Application(.NET)** that contains two controls (such as the two button controls in Fig. 12.12). Controls can be added to the form by double-clicking a control in the **Toolbox**, or selecting a control in the **Toolbox** and (while holding the mouse down) dragging the control onto the form. The control can be placed at a specific location on the form by dragging the control with the mouse. The control's properties can be set using the **Properties** window. To display a control's properties, select the control. If the control's events are currently being displayed in the **Properties** window, select the alphabetic or categorized icon.

Anchor one control to the right side by setting the ***Anchor*** property as shown in Fig. 12.13. Leave the other control unanchored. Now, resize the form by dragging the right side farther to the right. (You can resize many controls in this manner, or by modifying the control's `Size` property.) Notice that both controls move. The anchored control moves so that it is always the same distance to the right wall. The unanchored control moves so that it is in the same place on the form, relative to each side. This control will continue to be somewhat closer to whatever sides it was originally close to, but will still reposition itself when the user resizes the application window.

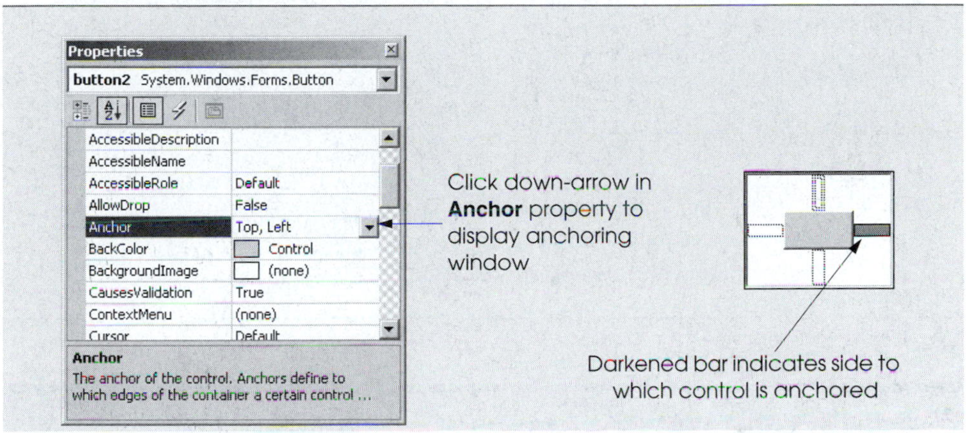

Fig. 12.13 Manipulating the **Anchor** property of a control.

Sometimes a programmer wants a control to span the entire side of the form, even when the form is resized. This is useful when we want one control to remain prevalent on the form, such as the status bar that might appear at the bottom of a program. *Docking* allows a control to spread itself along an entire side (left, right, top or bottom) of its parent container. When the parent is resized, the docked control resizes as well. In Fig. 12.14, a button is docked to the top of the form. (It lays across the top portion.) When the form is resized, the button is resized as well—the button always fills the entire top portion of the form. The *`Fill`* dock option effectively docks the control to all sides of its parent, which causes it to fill its entire parent. Windows forms contain property *`DockPadding`*, which sets the distance from docked controls to the edge of the form. The default value is zero, causing the controls to attach to the edge of the form. The control layout properties are summarized in Fig. 12.15.

The docking and anchoring options refer to the parent container, which may or may not be the form. (We learn about other parent containers later this chapter.) The minimum and maximum form sizes can be set using properties `MinimumSize` and `MaximumSize`, respectively. Both properties use the `Size` structure, which has properties `Height` and `Width`, specifying the size of the form. These properties allow the programmer to design the GUI layout for a given size range. To set a form to a fixed size, set its minimum and maximum size to the same value.

Look-and-Feel Observation 12.2

Allow Windows forms to be resized—this enables users with limited screen space or multiple applications running at once to use the application more easily. Check that the GUI layout appears consistent for all permissible form sizes.

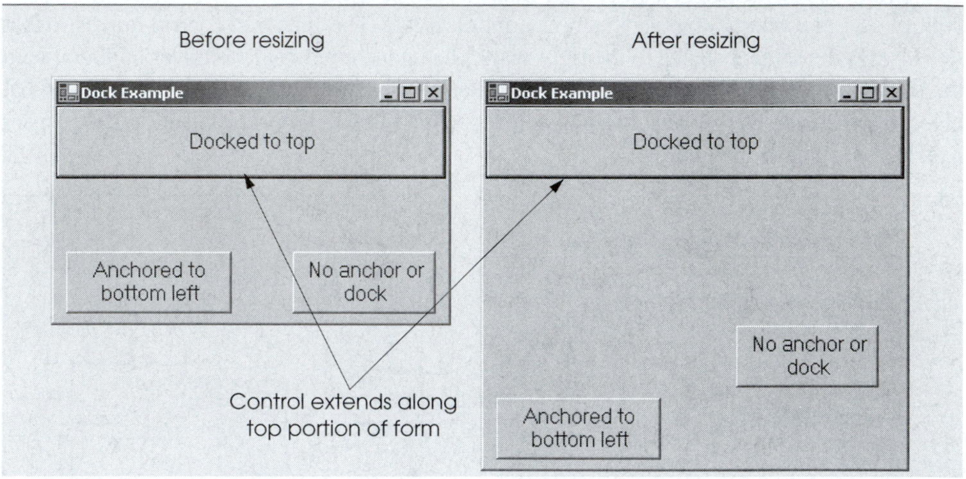

Fig. 12.14 Docking demonstration.

Common Layout Properties	Description
Common Properties	
`Anchor`	Side of parent container at which to anchor control—values can be combined, such as `Top`, `Left`.
`Dock`	Side of parent container to dock control—values cannot be combined.
`DockPadding` (for containers)	Sets the dock spacing for controls inside the container. Default is zero, so controls appear flush against the side of the container.
`Location`	Location of the upper left corner of the control, relative to its container.
`Size`	Size of the control. Takes a `Size` structure, which has properties `Height` and `Width`.
`MinimumSize`, `MaximumSize` (for Windows Forms)	The minimum and maximum size of the form.

Fig. 12.15 `Control` class layout properties.

12.5 `Label`s, `TextBox`es and `Button`s

Labels provide text instructions or information about the program. Labels are defined with class `Label`, which derives from class `Control`. A label displays *read-only text*, or text that the user cannot modify. Once labels are created, programs rarely change their contents. Figure 12.16 lists common `Label` properties.

`Label` Properties	**Description / Delegate and Event Arguments**
Common Properties	
`Font`	Font used by the text on the label.
`Text`	Text to appear on the label.
`TextAlign`	Alignment of the label's text on the control. One of three horizontal positions (`left`, `center` or `right`) and one of three vertical positions (`top`, `middle` or `bottom`).

Fig. 12.16 `Label` properties.

A *text box* (class `TextBox`) is an area in which text can be either input by the user from the keyboard or displayed. The programmer can also make a text box read only. The user may read, select and copy text from a read-only text box, but the user cannot alter the text. A *password text box* is a text box that hides what the user entered. As the user types in characters, the password text box displays only a certain character (usually *). Altering the `PasswordChar` property of a text box makes it a password text box and sets the appropriate character to be displayed. Figure 12.17 lists the common properties and events of text boxes.

`TextBox` Properties and Events	**Description / Delegate and Event Arguments**
Common Properties	
`AcceptsReturn`	If `true`, pressing *Enter* creates a new line in text box, if that text box spans multiple lines. If `false`, pressing *Enter* clicks the default button of the form.
`Multiline`	If `true`, text box can span multiple lines. Default is `false`.
`PasswordChar`	Single character to display instead of typed text, making the text box a password box. If no character is specified, text box displays the typed text.
`ReadOnly`	If `true`, text box has a gray background and its text cannot be edited. Default is `false`.
`ScrollBars`	For multiline text boxes, indicates which scrollbars appear (`none`, `horizontal`, `vertical` or `both`).
`Text`	Text to be displayed in the text box.
Common Events	*(Delegate `EventHandler`, event arguments `EventArgs`)*
`TextChanged`	Raised when text changes in text box (the user added or deleted characters).

Fig. 12.17 `TextBox` properties and events.

A *button* is a control that the user clicks to trigger a specific action. A program can use several other types of buttons, such as *checkboxes* and *radio buttons*. All the button types are derived from `ButtonBase` (namespace `System::Windows::Forms`), which defines common button features. In this section, we concentrate on class `Button`, which is often used to initiate a command. The other button types are covered in subsequent sections. The text on the face of a `Button` is called a *button label*. Figure 12.18 lists the common properties and events of buttons.

Button properties and events	Description / Delegate and Event Arguments
Common Properties	
`Text`	Text displayed on the button face.
Common Events	*(Delegate* `EventHandler`*, event arguments* `EventArgs`*)*
`Click`	Raised when user clicks the control.

Fig. 12.18 `Button` properties and events.

Look-and-Feel Observation 12.3

Although labels, text boxes and other controls can respond to mouse-button clicks, buttons naturally convey this meaning. Use buttons (e.g., **OK***), rather than other types of controls, to initiate user actions.*

The program in Fig. 12.19–Fig. 12.20 uses a text box, a button and a label. The user enters text into a password box and clicks the button. The text then appears in the label. Normally, we would not display this text—the purpose of password text boxes is to hide the text being entered by the user from anyone who may be looking over a person's shoulder.

```
// Fig. 12.19: Form1.h
// Using a Textbox, Label and Button to display
// the hidden text in a password field.

#pragma once


namespace LabelTextBoxButtonTest
{
   using namespace System;
   using namespace System::ComponentModel;
   using namespace System::Collections;
   using namespace System::Windows::Forms;
   using namespace System::Data;
   using namespace System::Drawing;

   /// <summary>
   /// Summary for Form1
```

Fig. 12.19 Using a password field. (Part 1 of 3.)

```
   ///
   /// WARNING: If you change the name of this class, you will need to
   ///          change the 'Resource File Name' property for the managed
   ///          resource compiler tool associated with all .resx files
   ///          this class depends on.  Otherwise, the designers will not
   ///          be able to interact properly with localized resources
   ///          associated with this form.
   /// </summary>
   public __gc class Form1 : public System::Windows::Forms::Form
   {
   public:
      Form1(void)
      {
         InitializeComponent();
      }

   protected:
      void Dispose(Boolean disposing)
      {
         if (disposing && components)
         {
            components->Dispose();
         }
         __super::Dispose(disposing);
      }
   private: System::Windows::Forms::Button *  displayPasswordButton;
   private: System::Windows::Forms::TextBox *  inputPasswordTextBox;
   private: System::Windows::Forms::Label *  displayPasswordLabel;

   private:
      /// <summary>
      /// Required designer variable.
      /// </summary>
      System::ComponentModel::Container * components;

      /// <summary>
      /// Required method for Designer support - do not modify
      /// the contents of this method with the code editor.
      /// </summary>
      void InitializeComponent(void)
      {
         this->displayPasswordButton =
            new System::Windows::Forms::Button();
         this->inputPasswordTextBox =
            new System::Windows::Forms::TextBox();
         this->displayPasswordLabel =
            new System::Windows::Forms::Label();
         this->SuspendLayout();
         //
         // displayPasswordButton
         //
         this->displayPasswordButton->Location =
            System::Drawing::Point(96, 96);
```

Fig. 12.19 Using a password field. (Part 2 of 3.)

```
            this->displayPasswordButton->Name = S"displayPasswordButton";
            this->displayPasswordButton->Size =
               System::Drawing::Size(96, 24);
            this->displayPasswordButton->TabIndex = 1;
            this->displayPasswordButton->Text = S"Show Me";
            this->displayPasswordButton->Click += new System::EventHandler(
               this, displayPasswordButton_Click);
            //
            // inputPasswordTextBox
            //
            this->inputPasswordTextBox->Location =
               System::Drawing::Point(16, 16);
            this->inputPasswordTextBox->Name = S"inputPasswordTextBox";
            this->inputPasswordTextBox->PasswordChar = '*';
            this->inputPasswordTextBox->Size =
               System::Drawing::Size(264, 20);
            this->inputPasswordTextBox->TabIndex = 0;
            this->inputPasswordTextBox->Text = S"";
            //
            // displayPasswordLabel
            //
            this->displayPasswordLabel->BorderStyle =
               System::Windows::Forms::BorderStyle::Fixed3D;
            this->displayPasswordLabel->Location =
               System::Drawing::Point(16, 48);
            this->displayPasswordLabel->Name = S"displayPasswordLabel";
            this->displayPasswordLabel->Size =
               System::Drawing::Size(264, 23);
            this->displayPasswordLabel->TabIndex = 2;
            //
            // Form1
            //
            this->AutoScaleBaseSize = System::Drawing::Size(5, 13);
            this->ClientSize = System::Drawing::Size(296, 133);
            this->Controls->Add(this->displayPasswordLabel);
            this->Controls->Add(this->inputPasswordTextBox);
            this->Controls->Add(this->displayPasswordButton);
            this->Name = S"Form1";
            this->Text = S"LabelTextBoxButtonTest";
            this->ResumeLayout(false);

         }

      // display user input on label
      private: System::Void displayPasswordButton_Click(
                  System::Object *  sender, System::EventArgs *  e)
               {
                  displayPasswordLabel->Text = inputPasswordTextBox->Text;
               }

      };
}
```

Fig. 12.19 Using a password field. (Part 3 of 3.)

```
// Fig. 12.20: Form1.cpp
// Displaying the hidden text in a password field.

#include "stdafx.h"
#include "Form1.h"
#include <windows.h>

using namespace LabelTextBoxButtonTest;

int APIENTRY _tWinMain(HINSTANCE hInstance,
                       HINSTANCE hPrevInstance,
                       LPTSTR    lpCmdLine,
                       int       nCmdShow)
{
   System::Threading::Thread::CurrentThread->ApartmentState =
      System::Threading::ApartmentState::STA;
   Application::Run(new Form1());
   return 0;
}
```

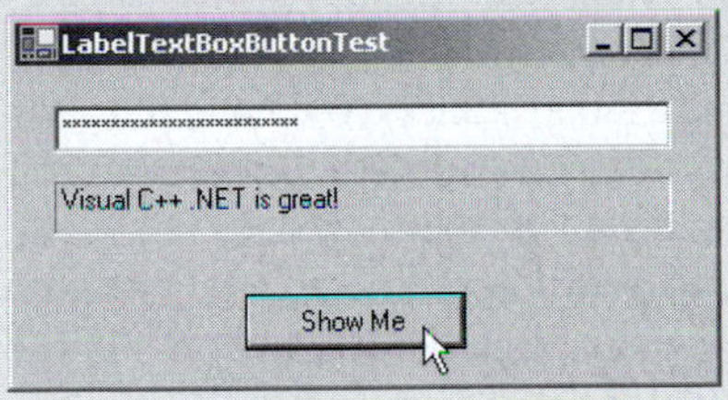

Fig. 12.20 Displaying the hidden text in a password field.

To build this application, create a new project of type **Windows Forms Application (.NET)** and call it `LabelTextBoxButtonTest`. Create the GUI by dragging the components (a button, a label and a text box) from the **Toolbox** onto the form. Once the components are positioned, use each control's `Name` property to change their names in the **Properties** window from the default values—`textBox1`, `label1`, `button1`—to the more descriptive `displayPasswordLabel`, `inputPasswordTextBox` and `displayPasswordButton`. Change the title of the form to display `LabelTextBoxButtonTest` by setting the form's `Text` property in the **Properties** window. Visual Studio .NET creates the code and places it inside method `InitializeComponent`.

Set `displayPasswordButton`'s `Text` property to "`Show Me`" and clear the `Text` of `displayPasswordLabel` and `inputPasswordTextBox` so that they are initially blank when the program runs. Set the `BorderStyle` property of `displayPasswordLabel` to `Fixed3D`, to give the `Label` a three-dimensional appearance. Notice that text boxes have their `BorderStyle` property set to `Fixed3D` by default. Set the password character by assigning the asterisk character (`*`) to the `PasswordChar` property of `inputPasswordTextBox`. This property can take only one character.

Examine the code that Visual Studio .NET generates by right-clicking the design and selecting `View Code`. This is important because not every change can be made in the `Properties` window.

We have learned in previous chapters that Visual Studio .NET adds comments to our code. These comments appear throughout the code, such as in lines 17–26 of Fig. 12.19. In future examples we remove some of these generated comments to make programs more concise and readable (unless they illustrate a capability we have not yet covered). The complete code for each program is located on the CD that accompanies the book.

Visual Studio .NET inserts declarations for the controls we add to the form (lines 44–46), namely, the label, text box and button. The IDE manages these declarations for us, making it easy to add and remove controls. Line 52 declares pointer `components`—an array to hold the components that we add. We are not using any components in this program (only controls), so the reference is `null`.

The constructor for our form is created for us—it calls method `InitializeComponent`. Method `InitializeComponent` creates the components and controls in the form and sets their properties. The usual "to do" comments generated by Visual Studio .NET have been removed, because there is no more code that needs to be added to the constructor. When the code contains such comments, they appear as reminders in the **Task List** window of Visual Studio .NET. Method `Dispose` cleans up allocated resources, but is not called explicitly in our programs.

Method `InitializeComponent` (lines 58–113) sets the properties of the controls added to the form (the text box, label and button). The code shown here is generated as you add controls to the form and set their properties. Lines 60–66 create new objects for the controls we add (a button, a text box and a label). Lines 84–85 and 89 set the `Name`, `PasswordChar` and `Text` properties for `inputPasswordTextBox`. The `TabIndex` property is initially set by Visual Studio .NET, but can be changed by the developer.

The comment in lines 54–57 advises us not to modify the contents of method `InitializeComponent`. We have altered it slightly for formatting purposes in this book, but this is not recommended. We have done this only so that the reader is able to see the important portions of the code. Visual Studio .NET examines this method to create the design view of the code. If we change this method, Visual Studio .NET might not recognize our modifications and might show the design improperly. It is important to note that the design view is based on the code, and not vice versa.

Error-Prevention Tip 12.1

To keep the design view accurate, do not modify the code in method `InitializeComponent`*. Make changes in the design window or property window.*

The `Click` event is triggered when a control is clicked. We create the handler using the procedure described in Section 12.3.1. We want to respond to the `Click` event of `displayPasswordButton`, so we first display the events for `displayPasswordButton` in the **Properties** window, then double click to the right of the `Click` event listing. (Alternately, we could simply have double-clicked `displayPasswordButton` in design view.) This creates an empty event handler named `displayPasswordButton_Click` (line 116). Visual Studio .NET also registers the event handler for us (lines 77–78). It adds the event handler to the `Click` event, using the `EventHandler` delegate. We must then implement the body of the event handler. Whenever `displayPasswordButton` is clicked, this event handler is called and displays `inputPasswordTextBox`'s text on `displayPasswordLabel`. Even though `inputPasswordTextBox` displays all asterisks, it still retains its input text in its `Text` property. To show the text, we set `displayPasswordLabel`'s `Text` to `inputPasswordTextBox`'s `Text` (line 119). You must program this line manually. When `display-`

PasswordButton is clicked, the Click event is triggered, and the event handler displayPasswordButton_Click runs (updating displayPasswordLabel).

Visual Studio .NET generated most of the code in this program. Visual Studio .NET simplifies tasks such as creating controls, setting their properties and registering event handlers. However, we should be aware of how these tasks are accomplished—in several programs we may set properties ourselves, using code.

12.6 GroupBoxes and Panels

Group boxes (class *GroupBox*) and panels (class *Panel*) arrange components on a GUI. For example, buttons related to a particular task can be placed inside a group box or panel. All these buttons move together when the group box or panel is moved.

The main difference between the two classes is that group boxes can display a caption, and panels can have scrollbars. The scrollbars allow the user to view additional controls inside the panel by scrolling the visible area. Group boxes have thin borders by default, but panels can be set to have borders by changing their BorderStyle property.

Look-and-Feel Observation 12.4

Panels and group boxes can contain other panels and group boxes.

Look-and-Feel Observation 12.5

Organize the GUI by anchoring and docking controls (of similar function) inside a group box or panel. The group box or panel then can be anchored or docked inside a form. This divides controls into functional "groups" that can be arranged easily.

To create a group box, drag it from the toolbar and place it on a form. Create new controls and place them inside the group box, causing them to become part of this class. These controls are added to the group box's Controls property. The group box's Text property determines its caption. The following tables list the common properties of GroupBoxes (Fig. 12.21) and Panels (Fig. 12.22).

GroupBox Properties	Description
Common Properties	
Controls	Controls that the group box contains.
Text	Text displayed on the top portion of the group box (its caption).

Fig. 12.21 GroupBox properties.

Panel Properties	Description
Common Properties	
AutoScroll	Specifies whether scrollbars appear when the panel is too small to hold its controls. Default is false.

Fig. 12.22 Panel properties. (Part 1 of 2.)

Panel Properties	Description
`BorderStyle`	Border of the panel (default `None`; other options are `Fixed3D` and `FixedSingle`).
`Controls`	Controls that the panel contains.

Fig. 12.22 `Panel` properties. (Part 2 of 2.)

To create a panel, drag it onto the form and add components to it. To enable the scrollbars, set the `Panel`'s `AutoScroll` property to `true` in the **Properties** window. If the panel is resized and cannot hold its controls, scrollbars appear (Fig. 12.23). These scrollbars then can be used to view all the components in the panel (both when running and designing the form). This allows the programmer to see the GUI exactly as it appears to the client.

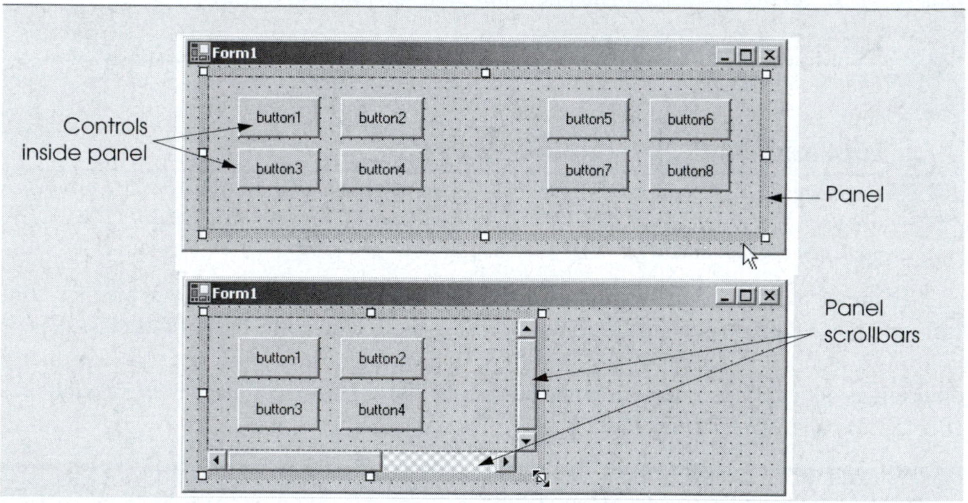

Fig. 12.23 Creating a panel with scrollbars.

Look-and-Feel Observation 12.6

Use panels with scrollbars to avoid cluttering a GUI and to reduce the GUI's size.

The program in Fig. 12.24–Fig. 12.25 uses a groupbox and a panel to arrange buttons. These buttons change the text on a label.

```
// Fig. 12.24: Form1.h
// Using GroupBoxes and Panels to hold buttons.

#pragma once
```

Fig. 12.24 `GroupBox` and `Panel` used to hold buttons. (Part 1 of 3.)

```
namespace GroupBoxPanelTest
{
   using namespace System;
   using namespace System::ComponentModel;
   using namespace System::Collections;
   using namespace System::Windows::Forms;
   using namespace System::Data;
   using namespace System::Drawing;

   /// <summary>
   /// Summary for Form1
   ///
   /// WARNING: If you change the name of this class, you will need to
   ///          change the 'Resource File Name' property for the managed
   ///          resource compiler tool associated with all .resx files
   ///          this class depends on.  Otherwise, the designers will not
   ///          be able to interact properly with localized resources
   ///          associated with this form.
   /// </summary>
   public __gc class Form1 : public System::Windows::Forms::Form
   {
   public:
      Form1(void)
      {
         InitializeComponent();
      }

   protected:
      void Dispose(Boolean disposing)
      {
         if (disposing && components)
         {
            components->Dispose();
         }
         __super::Dispose(disposing);
      }
   private: System::Windows::Forms::Label *  messageLabel;
   private: System::Windows::Forms::Button *  byeButton;
   private: System::Windows::Forms::GroupBox *  mainGroupBox;
   private: System::Windows::Forms::Button *  hiButton;
   private: System::Windows::Forms::Panel *  mainPanel;
   private: System::Windows::Forms::Button *  rightButton;
   private: System::Windows::Forms::Button *  leftButton;

   private:
      /// <summary>
      /// Required designer variable.
      /// </summary>
      System::ComponentModel::Container * components;
```

Fig. 12.24 GroupBox and Panel used to hold buttons. (Part 2 of 3.)

```
    // Visual Studio .NET generated GUI code

    // event handlers to change messageLabel

    // event handler for hi button
    private: System::Void hiButton_Click(System::Object *  sender,
                System::EventArgs *  e)
             {
                messageLabel->Text = S"Hi pressed";
             }

    // event handler for bye button
    private: System::Void byeButton_Click(System::Object *  sender,
                System::EventArgs *  e)
             {
                messageLabel->Text = S"Bye pressed";
             }

    // event handler for far left button
    private: System::Void leftButton_Click(System::Object *  sender,
                System::EventArgs *  e)
             {
                messageLabel->Text = S"Far left pressed";
             }

    // event handler for far right button
    private: System::Void rightButton_Click(System::Object *  sender,
                System::EventArgs *  e)
             {
                messageLabel->Text = S"Far right pressed";
             }
    };
}
```

Fig. 12.24 `GroupBox` and `Panel` used to hold buttons. (Part 3 of 3.)

```
// Fig. 12.25: Form1.cpp
// GroupBox and Panel demonstration.

#include "stdafx.h"
#include "Form1.h"
#include <windows.h>

using namespace GroupBoxPanelTest;

int APIENTRY _tWinMain(HINSTANCE hInstance,
                       HINSTANCE hPrevInstance,
                       LPTSTR    lpCmdLine,
                       int       nCmdShow)
{
   System::Threading::Thread::CurrentThread->ApartmentState =
      System::Threading::ApartmentState::STA;
```

Fig. 12.25 `GroupBox` and `Panel` demonstration. (Part 1 of 2.)

```
17      Application::Run(new Form1());
18      return 0;
19   }
```

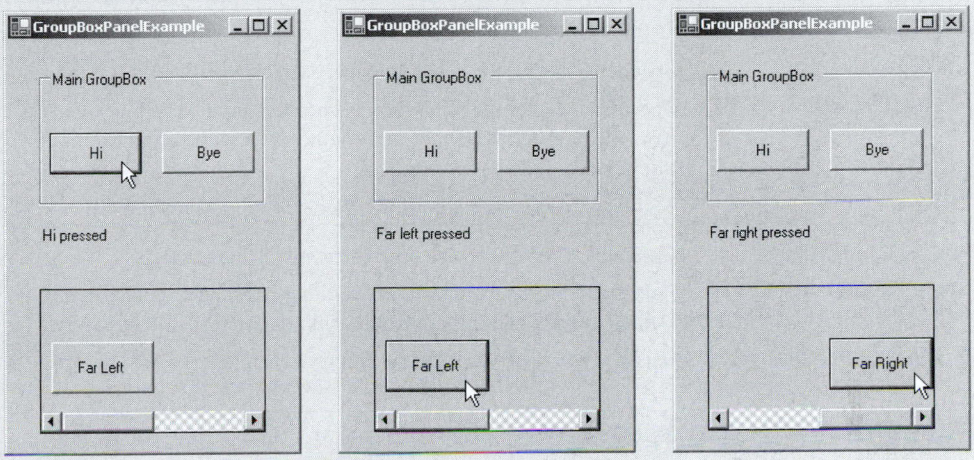

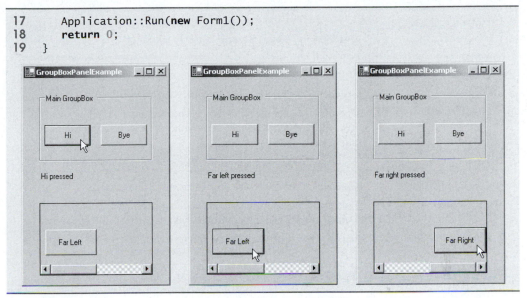

Fig. 12.25 `GroupBox` and `Panel` demonstration. (Part 2 of 2.)

The group box (named `mainGroupBox`) has two buttons, `hiButton` (labeled **Hi**) and `byeButton` (labeled **Bye**). The panel (named `mainPanel`) has two buttons as well, `left-Button` (labeled **Far Left**) and `rightButton` (labeled **Far Right**). The `mainPanel` control also has its `AutoScroll` property set to `True`, allowing scrollbars to appear if needed (i.e., if the contents of the panel take up more space than the panel itself). The label (named `mes-sageLabel`) is initially blank.

The event handlers for the four buttons are located in lines 62–87 of Fig. 12.24. To create an empty `Click` event handler, double click the button in design mode (instead of using the `Events` window). We add a line in each handler to change the text of `messageLabel` (lines 65, 72, 79 and 86). Notice that in this code example, we have replaced much of the generated code with a comment (line 57). Once again we have done this to make the code more concise and readable, but we have not modified the code provided on the book's CD.

12.7 CheckBoxes and RadioButtons

MC++ has two types of *state buttons*—check boxes (class *`CheckBox`*) and radio buttons (class *`RadioButton`*)—that can be in the on/off or true/false state. Classes `CheckBox` and `RadioButton` are derived from class `ButtonBase`. A group of check boxes allow the user to select combinations of choices. A radio button is different from a check box in that there are normally several radio buttons grouped together, and only one of the radio buttons in the group can be selected (true) at any time.

A checkbox is a small white square that can be blank, can contain a checkmark or can be dimmed (i.e., the checkbox's state is indeterminate). When a checkbox is selected, a black checkmark appears in the box. There are no restrictions on how checkboxes are used: Any number may be selected at a time. The text that appears alongside a checkbox is referred to as the *checkbox label*. A list of common and events of class `Checkbox` appears in Fig. 12.26.

CheckBox events and properties	Description / Delegate and Event Arguments
Common Properties	
`Checked`	Specifies whether the check box has been checked.
`CheckState`	Specifies whether the check box is checked (contains a black checkmark) or unchecked (blank). An enumeration with values `Checked`, `Unchecked` or `Indeterminate`.
`Text`	Text displayed to the right of the check box (called the label).
Common Events	*(Delegate `EventHandler`, event arguments `EventArgs`)*
`CheckedChanged`	Raised every time the check box is either checked or unchecked. Default event when this control is double clicked in the designer.
`CheckStateChanged`	Raised when the `CheckState` property changes.

Fig. 12.26 CheckBox properties and events.

The program in Fig. 12.27–Fig. 12.28 allows the user to select a check box to change the font style of a label. One check box applies a bold style, the other an italic style. If both checkboxes are selected, the style of the font is bold and italic. When the program initially executes, neither check box is checked.

```
// Fig. 12.27: Form1.h
// Using CheckBoxes to toggle italic and bold styles.

#pragma once


namespace CheckBoxTest
{
   using namespace System;
   using namespace System::ComponentModel;
   using namespace System::Collections;
   using namespace System::Windows::Forms;
   using namespace System::Data;
   using namespace System::Drawing;

   /// <summary>
   /// Summary for Form1
   ///
   /// WARNING: If you change the name of this class, you will need to
   ///          change the 'Resource File Name' property for the managed
   ///          resource compiler tool associated with all .resx files
   ///          this class depends on.  Otherwise, the designers will not
   ///          be able to interact properly with localized resources
   ///          associated with this form.
   /// </summary>
```

Fig. 12.27 Using CheckBoxes to toggle italic and bold styles. (Part 1 of 2.)

```
   public __gc class Form1 : public System::Windows::Forms::Form
   {
   public:
      Form1(void)
      {
         InitializeComponent();
      }

   protected:
      void Dispose(Boolean disposing)
      {
         if (disposing && components)
         {
            components->Dispose();
         }
         __super::Dispose(disposing);
      }
   private: System::Windows::Forms::CheckBox *  boldCheckBox;
   private: System::Windows::Forms::Label *  outputLabel;
   private: System::Windows::Forms::CheckBox *  italicCheckBox;

   private:
      /// <summary>
      /// Required designer variable.
      /// </summary>
      System::ComponentModel::Container * components;

   // Visual Studio .NET generated GUI code

   // make text bold if not bold, if already bold make not bold
   private: System::Void boldCheckBox_CheckedChanged(
               System::Object *  sender, System::EventArgs *  e)
            {
               outputLabel->Font = new Drawing::Font(
                  outputLabel->Font->Name, outputLabel->Font->Size,
                  static_cast< FontStyle >(
                  outputLabel->Font->Style ^ FontStyle::Bold ) );
            }

   // make text italic if not italic, if already italic make not italic
   private: System::Void italicCheckBox_CheckedChanged(
               System::Object *  sender, System::EventArgs *  e)
            {
               outputLabel->Font = new Drawing::Font(
                  outputLabel->Font->Name, outputLabel->Font->Size,
                  static_cast< FontStyle >(
                  outputLabel->Font->Style ^ FontStyle::Italic ) );
            }
   };
}
```

Fig. 12.27 Using CheckBoxes to toggle italic and bold styles. (Part 2 of 2.)

```
// Fig. 12.28: Form1.cpp
// CheckBox demonstration.

#include "stdafx.h"
#include "Form1.h"
#include <windows.h>

using namespace CheckBoxTest;

int APIENTRY _tWinMain(HINSTANCE hInstance,
                       HINSTANCE hPrevInstance,
                       LPTSTR    lpCmdLine,
                       int       nCmdShow)
{
   System::Threading::Thread::CurrentThread->ApartmentState =
      System::Threading::ApartmentState::STA;
   Application::Run(new Form1());
   return 0;
}
```

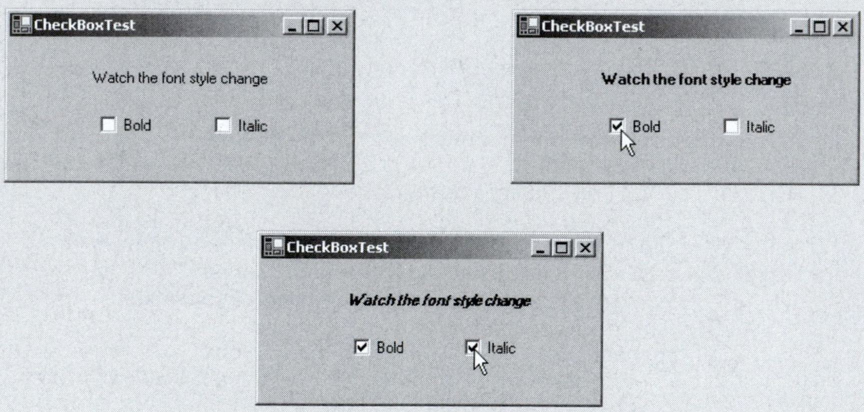

Fig. 12.28 CheckBox demonstration.

The first check box, named `boldCheckBox`, has its `Text` property set to `Bold`. The other check box is named `italicCheckBox` and has its `Text` property set to `Italic`. The label, named `outputLabel`, is labeled **Watch the font style change**.

After creating the components, we define their event handlers. To understand the code added to the event handler, we first discuss `outputLabel`'s `Font` property. To change the font, the `Font` property must be set to a `Font` object. The `Font` constructor we use takes the font name, size and style. The first two arguments make use of `outputLabel`'s `Font` object, namely, `outputLabel->Font->Name` and `outputLabel->Font->Size` (line 60 of Fig. 12.27). The third argument specifies the font style. The style is a member of the *`FontStyle`* enumeration, which contains the font styles `Regular`, `Bold`, `Italic`, `Strikeout` and `Underline`. (The `Strikeout` style displays text with a line through it, the `Underline` style displays text with a line below it.) A `Font` object's *`Style`* property is set when the `Font` object is created—the `Style` property itself is read-only.

Styles can be combined using *bitwise operators*, or operators that perform manipulation on bits. All data are represented on the computer as a series of 0's and 1's. Each 0 or 1 is called a bit. Actions are taken and data are modified using these bit values. In this program, we need to set the font style so that the text will appear bold if it was not bold originally, and vice versa. Notice that in line 62 we use the *bitwise XOR operator* (`^`) to do this. Applying this operator to two bits does the following: If exactly one of the corresponding bits is 1, set the result to 1. By using the `^` operator as we did in line 62, we are setting the bit values for bold in the same way. The operand on the right (`FontStyle::Bold`) always has bit values set to bold. The operand on the left (`outputLabel->Font->Style`) must not be bold for the resulting style to be bold. (Remember for XOR, if one value is set to 1, the other must be 0, or the result will not be 1.) If `outputLabel->Font->Style` is bold, then the resulting style will not be bold. This operator also allows us to combine the styles. For instance, if the text were originally italicized, it would now be italicized and bold, rather than just bold.

We could have explicitly tested for the current style and changed it according to what we needed. For example, in the method `boldCheckBox_CheckChanged` we could have tested for the regular style, made it bold, tested for the bold style, made it regular, tested for the italic style, made it bold italic, or the italic bold style and made it italic. However, this method has a drawback—for every new style we add, we double the number of combinations. To add a checkbox for underline, we would have to test for eight possible styles. To add a checkbox for strikeout as well, we would have 16 tests in each event handler. By using the bitwise XOR operator, we save ourselves from this trouble. Each new style needs only a single statement in its event handler. In addition, styles can be removed easily, removing their handler. If we tested for every condition, we would have to remove the handler and all the unnecessary test conditions in the other handlers.

Radio buttons are similar to checkboxes, because they also have two states—*selected* and *not selected* (also called *deselected*). However, radio buttons normally appear as a *group* in which only one radio button can be selected at a time. Selecting a different radio button in the group forces all other radio buttons in the group to be deselected. Radio buttons represent a set of *mutually exclusive* options (i.e., a set in which multiple options cannot be selected at the same time).

Look-and-Feel Observation 12.7

Use radio buttons when the user should choose only one option in a group.

Look-and-Feel Observation 12.8

Use check boxes when the user should be able to choose many options in a group.

All radio buttons added to a container (such as a form) become part of the same group. To create new groups, radio buttons must be added to other containers such as group boxes or panels. The common properties and events of class `RadioButton` are listed in Fig. 12.29.

Software Engineering Observation 12.3

Forms, group boxes, and panels can act as logical groups for radio buttons. The radio buttons within each group will be mutually exclusive to each other, but not to radio buttons in different groups.

RadioButton properties and events	Description / Delegate and Event Arguments
Common Properties	
`Checked`	Specifies whether the radio button is checked.
`Text`	Text displayed to the right of the radio button (called the label).
Common Events	*(Delegate* `EventHandler`*, event arguments* `EventArgs`*)*
`Click`	Raised when user clicks the control.
`CheckedChanged`	Raised every time the radio button is checked or unchecked.

Fig. 12.29 `RadioButton` properties and events.

The program in Fig. 12.30–Fig. 12.31 uses radio buttons to select the options for a `MessageBox`. Users select the attributes they want then press the display button, which causes the `MessageBox` to appear. A label in the lower-left corner shows the result of the `MessageBox` (**Yes**, **No**, **Cancel**, etc.). The different `MessageBox` icon and button types have been displayed in tables in Chapter 8, Object-Based Programming.

```
// Fig. 12.30: Form1.h
// Using RadioButtons to set message window options.

#pragma once


namespace RadioButtonTest
{
   using namespace System;
   using namespace System::ComponentModel;
   using namespace System::Collections;
   using namespace System::Windows::Forms;
   using namespace System::Data;
   using namespace System::Drawing;

   /// <summary>
   /// Summary for Form1
   ///
   /// WARNING: If you change the name of this class, you will need to
   ///          change the 'Resource File Name' property for the managed
   ///          resource compiler tool associated with all .resx files
   ///          this class depends on.  Otherwise, the designers will not
   ///          be able to interact properly with localized resources
   ///          associated with this form.
   /// </summary>
   public __gc class Form1 : public System::Windows::Forms::Form
   {
   public:
```

Fig. 12.30 Using `RadioButtons` to set message window options. (Part 1 of 4.)

```
      Form1(void)
      {
         InitializeComponent();
      }

   protected:
      void Dispose(Boolean disposing)
      {
         if (disposing && components)
         {
            components->Dispose();
         }
         __super::Dispose(disposing);
      }
   private: System::Windows::Forms::GroupBox *  buttonTypeGroupBox;
   private: System::Windows::Forms::RadioButton *  retryCancelButton;
   private: System::Windows::Forms::RadioButton *  yesNoButton;
   private: System::Windows::Forms::RadioButton *  yesNoCancelButton;
   private: System::Windows::Forms::RadioButton *  abortRetryIgnoreButton;
   private: System::Windows::Forms::RadioButton *  okCancelButton;
   private: System::Windows::Forms::RadioButton *  okButton;
   private: System::Windows::Forms::GroupBox *  iconTypeGroupBox;
   private: System::Windows::Forms::RadioButton *  questionButton;
   private: System::Windows::Forms::RadioButton *  informationButton;
   private: System::Windows::Forms::RadioButton *  exclamationButton;
   private: System::Windows::Forms::RadioButton *  errorButton;
   private: System::Windows::Forms::Label *  displayLabel;
   private: System::Windows::Forms::Button *  displayButton;
   private: System::Windows::Forms::Label *  promptLabel;

   private: static MessageBoxIcon iconType = MessageBoxIcon::Error;
   private: static MessageBoxButtons buttonType = MessageBoxButtons::OK;

   private:
      /// <summary>
      /// Required designer variable.
      /// </summary>
      System::ComponentModel::Container * components;

   // Visual Studio .NET generated GUI code

   // change button based on option chosen by sender
   private: System::Void buttonType_CheckedChanged(
               System::Object *  sender, System::EventArgs *  e)
            {
               if ( sender == okButton ) // display OK button
                  buttonType = MessageBoxButtons::OK;

               // display OK and Cancel buttons
               else if ( sender == okCancelButton )
                  buttonType = MessageBoxButtons::OKCancel;

```

Fig. 12.30 Using `RadioButtons` to set message window options. (Part 2 of 4.)

```
           // display Abort, Retry and Ignore buttons
           else if ( sender == abortRetryIgnoreButton )
              buttonType = MessageBoxButtons::AbortRetryIgnore;

           // display Yes, No and Cancel buttons
           else if ( sender == yesNoCancelButton )
              buttonType = MessageBoxButtons::YesNoCancel;

           // display Yes and No buttons
           else if ( sender == yesNoButton )
              buttonType = MessageBoxButtons::YesNo;

           // only one option left--display Retry and Cancel buttons
           else
              buttonType = MessageBoxButtons::RetryCancel;
         } // end method buttonType_CheckedChanged

   // change icon based on option chosen by sender
   private: System::Void iconType_CheckedChanged(
           System::Object *  sender, System::EventArgs *  e)
         {
           if ( sender == errorButton ) // display error icon
              iconType = MessageBoxIcon::Error;

           // display exclamation point
           else if ( sender == exclamationButton )
              iconType = MessageBoxIcon::Exclamation;

           // display information icon
           else if ( sender == informationButton )
              iconType = MessageBoxIcon::Information;

           else // only one option left--display question mark
              iconType = MessageBoxIcon::Question;
         } // end method iconType_CheckedChanged

   // display MessageBox and button user pressed
   private: System::Void displayButton_Click(
           System::Object *  sender, System::EventArgs *  e)
         {
           DialogResult = MessageBox::Show(
              S"This is Your Custom MessageBox.",
              S"Custom MessageBox", buttonType, iconType );

           // check for dialog result and display it in label
           switch ( DialogResult ) {

              case DialogResult::OK:
                 displayLabel->Text = S"OK was pressed.";
                 break;

```

Fig. 12.30 Using `RadioButtons` to set message window options. (Part 3 of 4.)

```
                    case DialogResult::Cancel:
                       displayLabel->Text = S"Cancel was pressed.";
                       break;

                    case DialogResult::Abort:
                       displayLabel->Text = S"Abort was pressed.";
                       break;

                    case DialogResult::Retry:
                       displayLabel->Text = S"Retry was pressed.";
                       break;

                    case DialogResult::Ignore:
                       displayLabel->Text = S"Ignore was pressed.";
                       break;

                    case DialogResult::Yes:
                       displayLabel->Text = S"Yes was pressed.";
                       break;

                    case DialogResult::No:
                       displayLabel->Text = S"No was pressed.";
                       break;
                 } // end switch
              } // end method displayButton_Click
   };
}
```

Fig. 12.30 Using RadioButtons to set message window options. (Part 4 of 4.)

```
// Fig. 12.31: Form1.cpp
// RadioButton demonstration.

#include "stdafx.h"
#include "Form1.h"
#include <windows.h>

using namespace RadioButtonTest;

int APIENTRY _tWinMain(HINSTANCE hInstance,
                       HINSTANCE hPrevInstance,
                       LPTSTR    lpCmdLine,
                       int       nCmdShow)
{
   System::Threading::Thread::CurrentThread->ApartmentState =
      System::Threading::ApartmentState::STA;
   Application::Run(new Form1());
   return 0;
}
```

Fig. 12.31 RadioButton demonstration. (Part 1 of 2.)

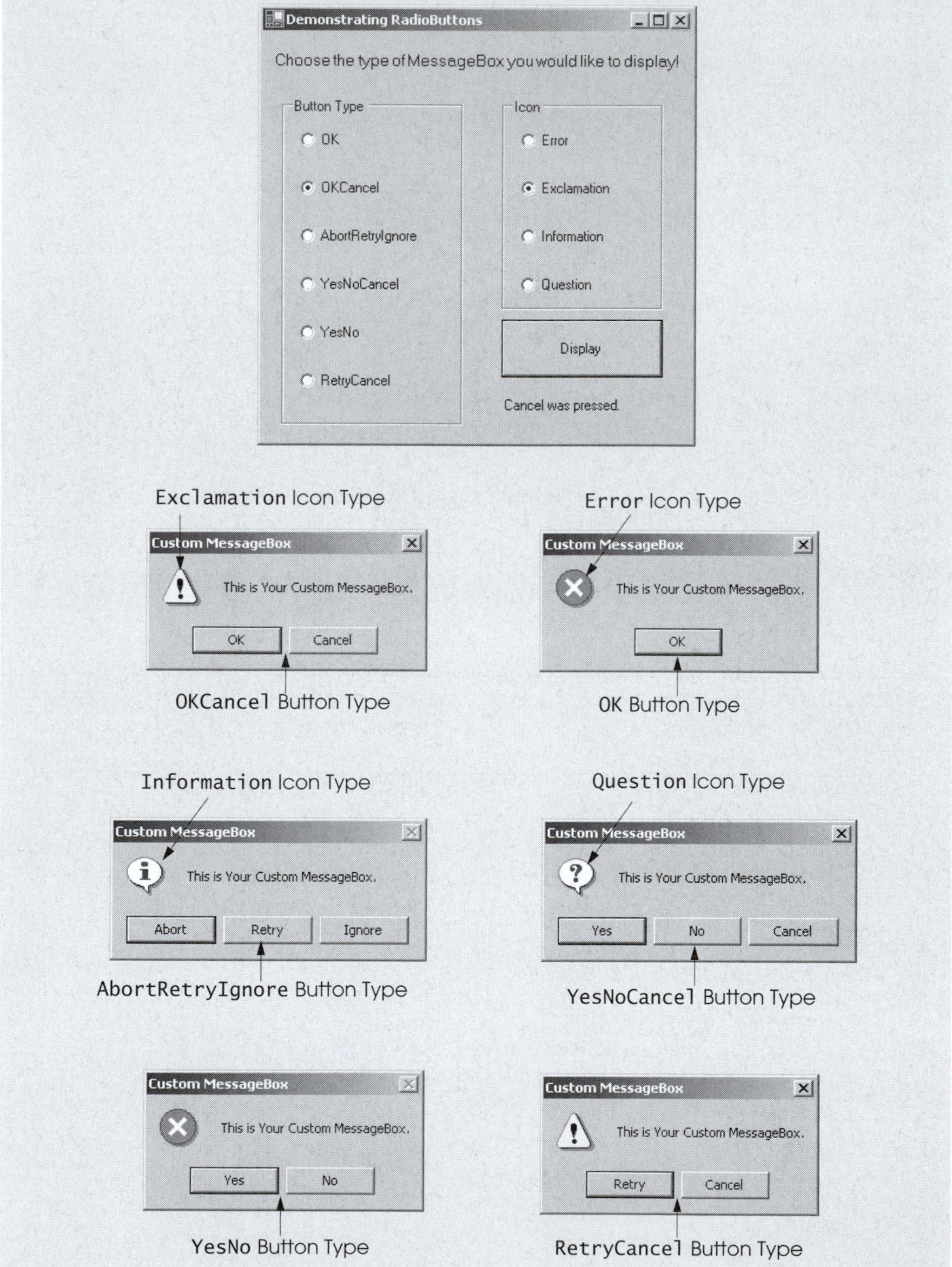

Fig. 12.31 `RadioButton` demonstration. (Part 2 of 2.)

To store the user's choice of options, the objects `iconType` and `buttonType` are created and initialized (lines 59–60 of Fig. 12.30). Object `iconType` can be assigned an enumeration `MessageBoxIcon` value—`Asterisk`, `Error`, `Exclamation`, `Hand`, `Information`, `Question`, `Stop` or `Warning`. In this example, we use only `Error`, `Exclamation`, `Information` and `Question`.

Object `buttonType` can be assigned an enumeration `MessageBoxButton` value—`AbortRetryIgnore`, `OK`, `OKCancel`, `RetryCancel`, `YesNo` or `YesNoCancel`. The name indicates which buttons will appear in the `MessageBox`. In this example, we use all `MessageBoxButton` enumeration values.

Radio buttons (lines 44–49 and 51–54 of Fig. 12.30) are created for the enumeration options, with their labels set appropriately. The radio buttons are grouped; thus, only one option can be selected from each group box. Two group boxes are created (lines 43 and 50), one for each enumeration. Their captions are **Button Type** and **Icon**. One label is used to prompt the user (`promptLabel`), while the other is used to display which button was pressed, once the custom `MessageBox` has been displayed (`displayLabel`). There is also a button (`displayButton`) that displays the text **Display**.

For event handling, one event handler exists for all the radio buttons in `buttonTypeGroupBox` and another for all the radio buttons in `iconTypeGroupBox`. Each radio button generates a `CheckedChanged` event when clicked. Each radio button that lists a button-type option is associated with `buttonType_CheckedChanged` (lines 71–96), while the ones that list the icon types are associated with `iconType_CheckedChanged` (lines 99–115).

Remember, to set the event handler for an event, use the events section of the **Properties** window. Create a new `CheckedChanged` event handler for one of the radio buttons in `buttonTypeGroupBox` and rename it `buttonType_CheckedChanged`. Then set the `CheckedChanged` event handlers for all the radio buttons in `buttonTypeGroupBox` to method `buttonType_CheckedChanged`. Create a second `CheckedChanged` event handler for a radio button in `iconTypeGroupBox` and rename it `iconType_CheckedChanged`. Finally, set the `CheckedChanged` event handlers for the radio buttons in `iconTypeGroupBox` to method `iconType_CheckedChanged`.

Both handlers compare the `sender` object with every radio button to determine which button was selected. Notice that each radio button is referred to by the identifier assigned to its `Name` property when it is compared to the `sender` object (e.g., line 74). Depending on the radio button selected, either `iconType` or `buttonType` changes.

Method `displayButton_Click` (lines 118–156) creates a `MessageBox` (lines 121–123). Some of the `MessageBox` options are set by `iconType` and `buttonType`. The result of the message box is a `DialogResult` enumeration value—`Abort`, `Cancel`, `Ignore`, `No`, `None`, `OK`, `Retry` or `Yes`. The `switch` statement (lines 126–155) tests for the result and sets `displayLabel->Text` appropriately.

12.8 PictureBoxes

A picture box (class *`PictureBox`*) displays an image. The image, set by an object of class *`Image`*, can be in a bitmap (`.bmp`), `.gif`, `.jpg`, `.jpeg`, icon or metafile format (e.g., `.emf` or `.mwf`). (Images and multimedia are discussed in Chapter 16, Graphics and Multimedia.) *GIF (Graphics Interchange Format)* and *JPEG (Joint Photographic Expert Group)* files are widely used image file formats.

The *Image* property of class `PictureBox` sets the `Image` object to display, and the *SizeMode* property sets how the image is displayed (`Normal`, `StretchImage`, `AutoSize` or `CenterImage`). Figure 12.32 describes the important properties and events of class `PictureBox`.

`PictureBox` **properties and events**	**Description / Delegate and Event Arguments**
Common Properties	
`Image`	Image to display in the picture box.
`SizeMode`	Gets value from enumeration `PictureBoxSizeMode` that controls image sizing and positioning. Values `Normal` (default), `StretchImage`, `AutoSize` and `CenterImage`. `Normal` puts image in top-left corner of picture box, and `CenterImage` puts image in middle. (Both cut off image if too large.) `StretchImage` resizes image to fit in picture box. `AutoSize` resizes picture box to hold image.
Common Events	*(Delegate* `EventHandler`*, event arguments* `EventArgs`*)*
`Click`	Raised when user clicks the control.

Fig. 12.32 `PictureBox` properties and events.

The program in Fig. 12.33–Fig. 12.34 uses picture box `imagePictureBox` to display one of three bitmap images—`image0`, `image1` or `image2`. They are located in the directory `images` of our project folder. Whenever the `imagePictureBox` is clicked, the image changes. The label (named `promptLabel`) on the top of the form includes the instructions **Click On Picture Box to View Images**.

```
// Fig. 12.33: Form1.h
// Using a PictureBox to display images.

#pragma once


namespace PictureBoxTest
{
   using namespace System;
   using namespace System::ComponentModel;
   using namespace System::Collections;
   using namespace System::Windows::Forms;
   using namespace System::Data;
   using namespace System::Drawing;
   using namespace System::IO;

```

Fig. 12.33 Using a `PictureBox` to display images. (Part 1 of 2.)

```
   /// <summary>
   /// Summary for Form1
   ///
   /// WARNING: If you change the name of this class, you will need to
   ///          change the 'Resource File Name' property for the managed
   ///          resource compiler tool associated with all .resx files
   ///          this class depends on.  Otherwise, the designers will not
   ///          be able to interact properly with localized resources
   ///          associated with this form.
   /// </summary>
   public __gc class Form1 : public System::Windows::Forms::Form
   {
   public:
      Form1(void)
      {
         InitializeComponent();
      }

   protected:
      void Dispose(Boolean disposing)
      {
         if (disposing && components)
         {
            components->Dispose();
         }
         __super::Dispose(disposing);
      }
   private: System::Windows::Forms::Label *  promptLabel;
   private: System::Windows::Forms::PictureBox *  imagePictureBox;

   private: static int imageNum = -1;

   private:
      /// <summary>
      /// Required designer variable.
      /// </summary>
      System::ComponentModel::Container * components;

   // Visual Studio .NET generated GUI code

   // change image whenever PictureBox clicked
   private: System::Void imagePictureBox_Click(
               System::Object *  sender,System::EventArgs *  e)
            {
               imageNum = ( imageNum + 1 ) % 3; // imageNum from 0 to 2

               // create Image object from file, display on PictureBox
               imagePictureBox->Image = Image::FromFile( String::Concat(
                  Directory::GetCurrentDirectory(), S"\\images\\image",
                  imageNum.ToString(), S".bmp" ) );
            }
   };
}
```

Fig. 12.33 Using a `PictureBox` to display images. (Part 2 of 2.)

```
// Fig. 12.34: Form1.cpp
// PictureBox demonstration.

#include "stdafx.h"
#include "Form1.h"
#include <windows.h>

using namespace PictureBoxTest;

int APIENTRY _tWinMain(HINSTANCE hInstance,
                       HINSTANCE hPrevInstance,
                       LPTSTR    lpCmdLine,
                       int       nCmdShow)
{
   System::Threading::Thread::CurrentThread->ApartmentState =
      System::Threading::ApartmentState::STA;
   Application::Run(new Form1());
   return 0;
}
```

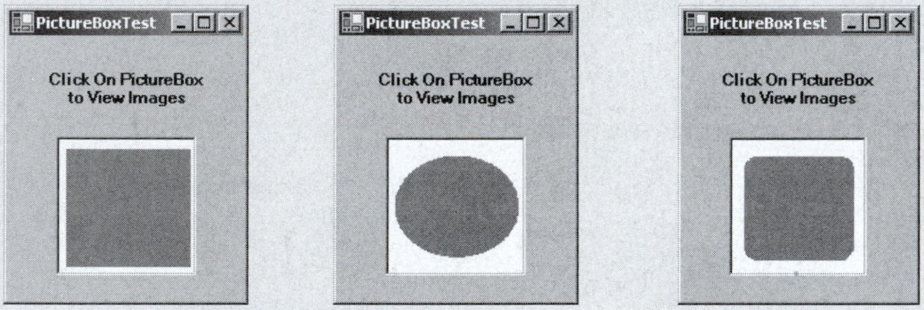

Fig. 12.34 `PictureBox` demonstration.

To respond to the user's clicks, we must handle the `Click` event (lines 58–67 of Fig. 12.33). Inside the event handler, we use an integer (`imageNum`) to store an integer representing the image we want to display. We then set the `Image` property of `imagePictureBox` to an `Image`. Class `Image` is discussed in Chapter 16, Graphics and Multimedia, but here we overview method *`FromFile`*, which takes a pointer to a `String` (the path to the image file) and creates an `Image` object.

To find the images, we use class *`Directory`* (namespace `System::IO`, specified in line 15 of Fig. 12.33) method *`GetCurrentDirectory`* (line 65 of Fig. 12.33). This returns the current directory of the executable file (usually `bin\Debug`) as a `String` pointer. To access the `images` subdirectory, we take the current directory and append `"\\images"` followed by `"\\"` and the file name. We use a double slash because an escape sequence is needed to represent a single slash in a string. We use `imageNum` to append the proper number, so we can load either `image0`, `image1` or `image2`. Integer `imageNum` stays between `0` and `2`, due to the modulus calculation (line 61). Finally, we append `".bmp"` to the filename. Thus, if we want to load `image0`, the string becomes "*CurrentDir*\ `images\image0.bmp`", where *CurrentDir* is the directory of the executable.

12.9 Mouse Event Handling

This section explains how to handle *mouse events,* such as *clicks, presses* and *moves.* Mouse events are generated when the mouse interacts with a control. They can be handled for any GUI control that derives from class `System::Windows::Forms::Control`. Mouse event information is passed using class *`MouseEventArgs`*, and the delegate to create the mouse event handlers is *`MouseEventHandler`*. Each mouse event-handling method must take an `object` and a `MouseEventArgs` object as arguments. The `Click` event, which we covered earlier, uses delegate `EventHandler` and event arguments `EventArgs`.

Class `MouseEventArgs` contains information about the mouse event, such as the *x*- and *y*-coordinates of the mouse pointer, the mouse button pressed, the number of clicks and the number of notches through which the mouse wheel turned. Note that the *x*- and *y*-coordinates of the `MouseEventArgs` object are relative to the control that raised the event. Point (0,0) is at the upper-left corner of the control. The various mouse events are described in Fig. 12.35.

Mouse Events, Delegates and Event Arguments	
Mouse Events (Delegate `EventHandler`, event arguments `EventArgs`)	
`MouseEnter`	Raised if the mouse cursor enters the area of the control.
`MouseLeave`	Raised if the mouse cursor leaves the area of the control.
Mouse Events (Delegate `MouseEventHandler`, event arguments `MouseEventArgs`)	
`MouseDown`	Raised if the mouse button (either mouse button) is pressed while its cursor is over the area of the control.
`MouseHover`	Raised if the mouse cursor hovers over the area of the control.
`MouseMove`	Raised if the mouse cursor is moved while in the area of the control.
`MouseUp`	Raised if the mouse button (either mouse button) is released when the cursor is over the area of the control.
Class `MouseEventArgs` Properties	
`Button`	Mouse button that was pressed (`left`, `right`, `middle` or `none`).
`Clicks`	The number of times the mouse button (either mouse button) was clicked.
`X`	The *x*-coordinate of the event, relative to the control.
`Y`	The *y*-coordinate of the event, relative to the control.

Fig. 12.35 Mouse events, delegates and event arguments.

The program of Fig. 12.36–Fig. 12.37 uses mouse events to draw on the form. Whenever the user drags the mouse (i.e., moves the mouse while holding down a button), the color blue-violet is drawn on the form.

Figure 12.36 (line 44) declares variable `shouldPaint`, which determines whether we should draw on the form. We want to draw only while the mouse button is pressed down. In the event handler for event `MouseDown`, `shouldPaint` is set to `true` (line 58 of

Fig. 12.36). As soon as the mouse button is released the program should stop drawing; so the `MouseUp` event handler sets `shouldPaint` to `false` (line 65).

```
1  // Fig. 12.36: Form1.h
2  // Using the mouse to draw on a form.
3
4  #pragma once
5
6
7  namespace PainterTest
8  {
9     using namespace System;
10    using namespace System::ComponentModel;
11    using namespace System::Collections;
12    using namespace System::Windows::Forms;
13    using namespace System::Data;
14    using namespace System::Drawing;
15
16    /// <summary>
17    /// Summary for Form1
18    ///
19    /// WARNING: If you change the name of this class, you will need to
20    ///          change the 'Resource File Name' property for the managed
21    ///          resource compiler tool associated with all .resx files
22    ///          this class depends on.  Otherwise, the designers will not
23    ///          be able to interact properly with localized resources
24    ///          associated with this form.
25    /// </summary>
26    public __gc class Form1 : public System::Windows::Forms::Form
27    {
28    public:
29       Form1(void)
30       {
31          InitializeComponent();
32       }
33
34    protected:
35       void Dispose(Boolean disposing)
36       {
37          if (disposing && components)
38          {
39             components->Dispose();
40          }
41          __super::Dispose(disposing);
42       }
43
44    private: static bool shouldPaint = false; // whether to paint
45
46    private:
47       /// <summary>
48       /// Required designer variable.
49       /// </summary>
```

Fig. 12.36 Mouse event handling. (Part 1 of 2.)

```
        System::ComponentModel::Container * components;

    // Visual Studio .NET generated GUI code

    // should paint after mouse button has been pressed
    private: System::Void Form1_MouseDown(System::Object *  sender,
                System::Windows::Forms::MouseEventArgs *  e)
             {
                shouldPaint = true;
             }

    // stop painting when mouse button released
    private: System::Void Form1_MouseUp(System::Object *  sender,
                System::Windows::Forms::MouseEventArgs *  e)
             {
                shouldPaint = false;
             }

    // draw circle whenever mouse button moves (and mouse is down)
    private: System::Void Form1_MouseMove(System::Object *  sender,
                System::Windows::Forms::MouseEventArgs *  e)
             {
                if ( shouldPaint ) {
                   Graphics *graphics = CreateGraphics();
                   graphics->FillEllipse( new SolidBrush(
                      Color::BlueViolet ), e->X, e->Y, 4, 4 );
                } // end if
             }
    };
}
```

Fig. 12.36 Mouse event handling. (Part 2 of 2.)

```
// Fig. 12.37: Form1.cpp
// Mouse event handling demonstration.

#include "stdafx.h"
#include "Form1.h"
#include <windows.h>

using namespace PainterTest;

int APIENTRY _tWinMain(HINSTANCE hInstance,
                       HINSTANCE hPrevInstance,
                       LPTSTR    lpCmdLine,
                       int       nCmdShow)
{
   System::Threading::Thread::CurrentThread->ApartmentState =
      System::Threading::ApartmentState::STA;
   Application::Run(new Form1());
   return 0;
}
```

Fig. 12.37 Mouse event handling demonstration. (Part 1 of 2.)

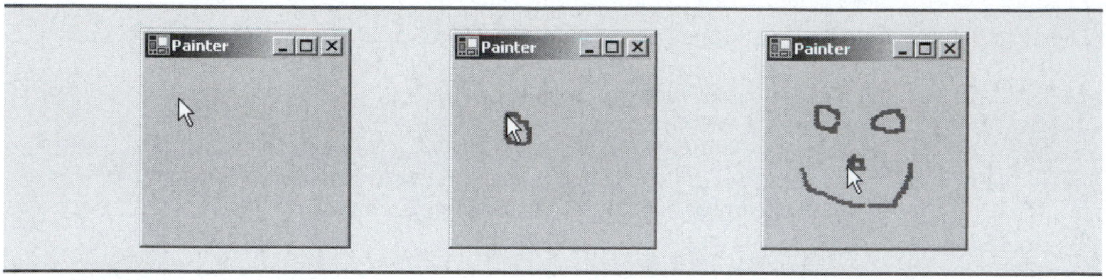

Fig. 12.37 Mouse event handling demonstration. (Part 2 of 2.)

Whenever the mouse moves while the button is pressed down, the MouseMove event is generated. The event will be generated repeatedly. Inside the Form1_MouseMove event handler (lines 69–77 of Fig. 12.36), the program draws only if shouldPaint is true (indicating that the mouse button is down). Line 73 creates a *Graphics* object for the form, which provides methods for drawing various shapes. Method *FillEllipse* (lines 74–75) draws a circle at every point the mouse cursor moves over (while the mouse button is pressed). The first parameter to method FillEllipse is a *SolidBrush* object, which determines the color of the shape drawn. We create a new SolidBrush object by passing the constructor a *Color* value. Structure Color contains numerous predefined color constants—we selected Color::BlueViolet (line 75). The SolidBrush fills an elliptical region, which lies inside a bounding rectangle. The bounding rectangle is specified by the *x*- and *y*-coordinates of its upper-left corner, its height and its width. These four parameters are the final four arguments to method FillEllipse. The *x*- and *y*-coordinates are the location of the mouse event: They can be taken from the mouse event arguments (e->X and e->Y). To draw a circle, we set the height and width of the bounding rectangle equal—in this case, they are each four pixels.

12.10 Keyboard Event Handling

This section explains how to handle *key events*. Key events are generated when keys on the keyboard are pressed and released. These events can be handled by any control that inherits from System::Windows::Forms::Control. There are three key events. The first is event *KeyPress*, which fires when a key representing an ASCII character is pressed (determined by *KeyPressEventArgs* property *KeyChar*). ASCII is a 128-character set of alphanumeric symbols. (The full listing can be found in Appendix C, ASCII Character Set.)

Using the KeyPress event, we cannot determine whether *modifier keys* (such as *Shift*, *Alt* and *Control*) were pressed. To determine such actions, handle the two remaining key events—*KeyUp* or *KeyDown*. Class *KeyEventArgs* contains information about special modifier keys. The key's *Key enumeration* value can be returned, giving information about a wide range of non-ASCII keys. Modifier keys are often used in conjunction with the mouse to select or highlight information. The delegates for the two classes are *KeyPressEventHandler* (event argument class KeyPressEventArgs) and *KeyEventHandler* (event argument class KeyEventArgs). Figure 12.38 lists important information about key events.

The program of Fig. 12.39–Fig. 12.40 demonstrates using the key event handlers to display the key that was pressed. The program's form contains two labels. It displays the key pressed on one label and modifier information on the other. The two labels (named charLabel and keyInfoLabel) are initially empty. The KeyDown and KeyPress events convey different information; thus, the form (KeyDemo) handles them both.

Keyboard Events, Delegates and Event Arguments	
Key Events (Delegate `KeyEventHandler`*, event arguments* `KeyEventArgs`*)*	
`KeyDown`	Raised when key is initially pushed down.
`KeyUp`	Raised when key is released.
Key Events (Delegate `KeyPressEventHandler`*, event arguments* `KeyPressEventArgs`*)*	
`KeyPress`	Raised when key is pressed. Occurs repeatedly while key is held down, at a rate specified by the operating system.
Class `KeyPressEventArgs` *Properties*	
`KeyChar`	Returns the ASCII character for the key pressed.
`Handled`	Indicates whether the `KeyPress` event was handled (i.e., has an event handler associated with it).
Class `KeyEventArgs` *Properties*	
`Alt`	Indicates whether the *Alt* key was pressed.
`Control`	Indicates whether the *Control* key was pressed.
`Shift`	Indicates whether the *Shift* key was pressed.
`Handled`	Indicates whether the event was handled (i.e., has an event handler associated with it).
`KeyCode`	Returns the key code for the key, as a `Keys` enumeration. This does not include modifier key information. Used to test for a specific key.
`KeyData`	Returns the key code as a `Keys` enumeration, combined with modifier information. Used to determine all information about the key pressed.
`KeyValue`	Returns the key code as an `int`, rather than as a `Keys` enumeration. Used to obtain a numeric representation of the key pressed.
`Modifiers`	Returns a `Keys` enumeration for any modifier keys pressed (*Alt*, *Control* and *Shift*). Used to determine modifier key information only.

Fig. 12.38 Keyboard events, delegates and event arguments.

```
// Fig. 12.39: Form1.h
// Displaying information about the key the user pressed.

#pragma once


namespace KeyDemoTest
{
   using namespace System;
   using namespace System::ComponentModel;
   using namespace System::Collections;
   using namespace System::Windows::Forms;
   using namespace System::Data;
```

Fig. 12.39 Keyboard event handling. (Part 1 of 3.)

```
   using namespace System::Drawing;

   /// <summary>
   /// Summary for Form1
   ///
   /// WARNING: If you change the name of this class, you will need to
   ///          change the 'Resource File Name' property for the managed
   ///          resource compiler tool associated with all .resx files
   ///          this class depends on.  Otherwise, the designers will not
   ///          be able to interact properly with localized resources
   ///          associated with this form.
   /// </summary>
   public __gc class Form1 : public System::Windows::Forms::Form
   {
   public:
      Form1(void)
      {
         InitializeComponent();
      }

   protected:
      void Dispose(Boolean disposing)
      {
         if (disposing && components)
         {
            components->Dispose();
         }
         __super::Dispose(disposing);
      }
   private: System::Windows::Forms::Label *  charLabel;
   private: System::Windows::Forms::Label *  keyInfoLabel;

   private:
      /// <summary>
      /// Required designer variable.
      /// </summary>
      System::ComponentModel::Container * components;

   // Visual Studio .NET generated GUI code

   // display the name of the pressed key
   private: System::Void Form1_KeyPress(System::Object *  sender,
               System::Windows::Forms::KeyPressEventArgs *  e)
            {
               charLabel->Text = String::Concat( S"Key pressed: ",
                  ( e->KeyChar ).ToString() );
            }

   // display modifier keys, key code, key data and key value
   private: System::Void Form1_KeyDown(System::Object *  sender,
               System::Windows::Forms::KeyEventArgs *  e)
            {
```

Fig. 12.39 Keyboard event handling. (Part 2 of 3.)

```
            keyInfoLabel->Text = String::Concat(
               S"Alt: ", ( e->Alt ? S"Yes" : S"No" ), S"\n",
               S"Shift: ", ( e->Shift ? S"Yes" : S"No" ), S"\n",
               S"Ctrl: ", ( e->Control ? S"Yes" : S"No" ), S"\n",
               S"KeyCode: ", __box( e->KeyCode ), S"\n",
               S"KeyData: ", __box( e->KeyData ), S"\n",
               S"KeyValue: ", e->KeyValue );
         }

   // clear labels when key released
   private: System::Void Form1_KeyUp(System::Object *  sender,
            System::Windows::Forms::KeyEventArgs *  e)
         {
            keyInfoLabel->Text = S"";
            charLabel->Text = S"";
         }
   };
}
```

Fig. 12.39 Keyboard event handling. (Part 3 of 3.)

```
// Fig. 12.40: Form1.cpp
// Keyboard event handling demonstration.

#include "stdafx.h"
#include "Form1.h"
#include <windows.h>

using namespace KeyDemoTest;

int APIENTRY _tWinMain(HINSTANCE hInstance,
                       HINSTANCE hPrevInstance,
                       LPTSTR    lpCmdLine,
                       int       nCmdShow)
{
   System::Threading::Thread::CurrentThread->ApartmentState =
      System::Threading::ApartmentState::STA;
   Application::Run(new Form1());
   return 0;
}
```

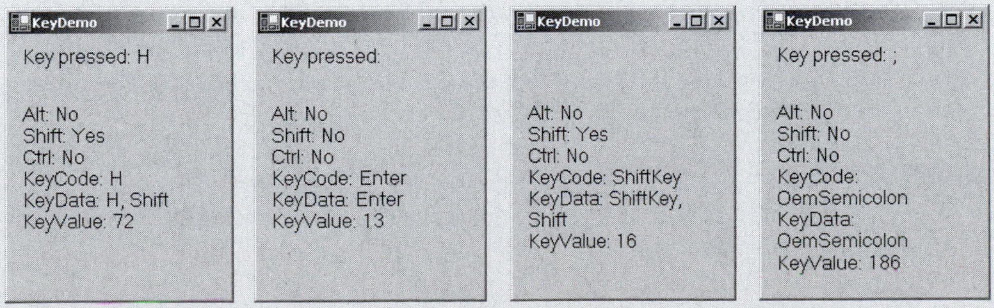

Fig. 12.40 Keyboard event handling demonstration.

The KeyPress event handler (lines 55–60 of Fig. 12.39) accesses the KeyChar property of the KeyPressEventArgs object. This returns the key pressed as a __wchar_t and displays it in charLabel (lines 58–59). If the key pressed was not an ASCII character, then the KeyPress event will not fire and charLabel remains empty. ASCII is a common encoding format for letters, numbers, punctuation marks and other characters. It does not support keys such as the *function keys* (like *F1*) or the modifier keys (*Alt*, *Control* and *Shift*).

The KeyDown event handler (lines 63–73) displays more information, all from its KeyEventArgs object. It tests for the *Alt*, *Shift* and *Control* keys (lines 67–69), using the Alt, Shift and Control properties, each of which returns bool. It then displays the KeyCode, KeyData and KeyValue properties.

The KeyCode property returns a Keys enumeration, which is converted to a string. The KeyCode property returns the key that was pressed, but does not provide any information about modifier keys. Thus, both a capital and a lowercase "a" are represented as the *A* key.

The KeyData property returns a Keys enumeration value as well, but includes data about modifier keys. Thus, if "A" is input, the KeyData shows that the *A* key and the *Shift* key were pressed. Lastly, KeyValue returns the key code for the key that was pressed as an integer. This integer is the *Windows virtual key code*, which provides an integer value for a wide range of keys and for mouse buttons. The Windows virtual key code is useful when testing for non-ASCII keys (such as *F12*).

Enumeration Keys is a value type. Method String::Concat (lines 66–72) expects to receive managed objects as its parameters. To use values from enumeration Keys enumeration (e.g., KeyCode) we need to convert the value types into reference types, or __gc objects.[1] We achieve this by *boxing* the values (lines 70–71). Boxing converts a value type into a managed object. Keyword __box creates a managed object, copies the value type's data into the new managed object and returns the address of the managed object.

Common Programming Error 12.2

The pointer returned by __box *points to a copy of the original value. Modifying the boxed value does not alter the original unboxed object.*

The KeyUp event handler clears both labels when the key is released (lines 79–80). As we can see from the output, non-ASCII keys are not displayed in the upper charLabel because the KeyPress event was not generated. The KeyDown event is still raised, and keyInfoLabel displays information about the key. The Keys enumeration can be used to test for specific keys by comparing the key pressed to a specific KeyCode. The Visual Studio. NET documentation has a complete list of the Keys enumerations.

Software Engineering Observation 12.4

To cause a control to react when a certain key is pressed (such as Enter*), handle a key event and test for the key pressed. To cause a button to be clicked when the* Enter *key is pressed on a form, set the form's* AcceptButton *property.*

SUMMARY

- A graphical user interface (GUI) presents a pictorial interface to a program. A GUI (pronounced "GOO-EE") gives a program a distinctive "look" and "feel."

1. More information about value types and reference types can be found in Chapter 6.

- By providing different applications with a consistent set of intuitive user interface components, GUIs allow the user to concentrate on using programs productively.
- GUIs are built from GUI components (sometimes called controls). A GUI control is a visual object with which the user interacts via the mouse or keyboard.
- Windows Forms create GUIs. A form is a graphical element that appears on the desktop. A form can be a dialog or a window.
- A control is a graphical component, such as a button. Components that are not visible usually are referred to simply as components.
- The active window has the focus. It is the frontmost window and has a highlighted title bar.
- A form acts as a container for components.
- When the user interacts with a control, an event is generated. This event can trigger methods that respond to the user's actions.
- All forms, components and controls are classes.
- The general design process for creating Windows applications involves creating a Windows Form, setting its properties, adding controls, setting their properties and configuring event handlers.
- GUIs are event driven. When a user interaction occurs, an event is generated. The event information then is passed to event handlers.
- Events are based on the notion of delegates. Delegates act as an intermediate step between the object creating (raising) the event and the method handling it.
- In many cases, the programmer will handle events generated by prepackaged controls. In this case, all the programmer needs to do is create and register the event handler.
- The information we need to register an event is the `EventArgs` class (to define the event handler) and the `EventHandler` delegate (to register the event handler).
- Labels (class `Label`) display read-only text instructions or information on a GUI.
- A text box is a single-line area in which text can be entered. A password text box displays only a certain character (such as *) when text is input.
- A button is a control that the user clicks to trigger a specific action. Buttons typically respond to the `Click` event.
- Group boxes and panels help arrange components on a GUI. The main difference between the classes is that group boxes can display text, and panels can have scrollbars.
- Visual C++ .NET has two types of state buttons—check boxes and radio buttons—that have on/off or true/false values.
- A checkbox is a small white square that can be blank or contain a checkmark.
- Use the bitwise XOR operator (^) to combine or negate a font style.
- Radio buttons (class `RadioButton`) have two states—selected and not selected. Radio buttons appear as a group in which only one radio button can be selected at a time. To create new groups, radio buttons must be added to group boxes or panels. Each group box or panel is a group.
- Radio buttons and checkboxes use the `CheckChanged` event.
- A picture box (class `PictureBox`) displays an image (set by an object of class `Image`).
- Mouse events (clicks, presses and moves) can be handled for any GUI control that derives from `System::Windows::Forms::Control`. Mouse events use class `MouseEventArgs` (`MouseEventHandler` delegate) and `EventArgs` (`EventHandler` delegate).
- Class `MouseEventArgs` contains information about the *x*- and *y*-coordinates, the button used, the number of clicks and the number of notches through which the mouse wheel turned.

- Key events are generated when keyboard's keys are pressed and released. These events can be handled by any control that inherits from System::Windows::Forms::Control.
- Event KeyPress can return a __wchar_t for any ASCII character pressed. One cannot determine if special modifier keys (such as *Shift*, *Alt* and *Control*) were pressed.
- Events KeyUp and KeyDown test for special modifier keys (using KeyEventArgs). The delegates are KeyPressEventHandler (KeyPressEventArgs) and KeyEventHandler (KeyEventArgs).
- Class KeyEventArgs has properties KeyCode, KeyData and KeyValue.
- Property KeyCode returns the key pressed, but does not give any information about modifier keys.
- The KeyData property includes data about modifier keys.
- The KeyValue property returns the key code for the key pressed as an integer.

TERMINOLOGY

active window
Alt property of class KeyEventArgs
anchoring a control
ASCII character
autoscaling
background color
bitwise operator
bitwise XOR operator (^)
__box keyword
boxing values
button
Button class
button label
checkbox
CheckBox class
checkbox label
CheckedChanged event
click a button
click a mouse button
Click event
component
container
control
Control property of class KeyEventArgs
delegate
deselected radio button
docking a control
drag and drop
Enabled property of class Control
Enter mouse event
event
event argument
event delegate
event driven
event handler
event multicasting
EventArgs class
event-handling model
focus
Font property of class Control
Font property of class Form
Font property of class Label
font style
FontStyle enumeration
form
Form class
function key
GetCurrentDirectory method of Directory
graphical user interface (GUI)
GroupBox
GUI component
handle event
Hide method of class Control
Hide method of class Form
Image property of class PictureBox
InitializeComponent method
key code
key data
key event
key value
keyboard
KeyDown event
KeyEventArgs class
KeyEventHandler delegate
KeyPress event
KeyPressEventArgs class
KeyPressEventHandler delegate
KeyUp event
label
Label class
list
menu

menu bar
modifier key
mouse
mouse click
mouse event
mouse move
mouse press
`MouseDown` event
`MouseEnter` event
`MouseEventArgs` class
`MouseEventHandler` delegate
`MouseHover` event
`MouseLeave` event
`MouseMove` event
`MouseUp` event
`MouseWheel` event
moving the mouse
multicast
`MulticastDelegate` class
mutually exclusive
`Name` property of class `Control`
panel
`Panel` class
password text box
`PasswordChar` property of class `TextBox`
picture box
`PictureBox` class
radio button
`RadioButton` class
radio-button group
raise an event
read-only text
register an event handler
`ResumeLayout` method of class `Control`
scrollbar
scrollbar in panel
selecting an item from a menu
`Shift` property of class `KeyEventArgs`
`SizeMode` property of class `PictureBox`
standard calling convention
`__stdcall` keyword
`SuspendLayout` method of class `Control`
`System::Windows::Forms` namespace
`TabIndex` property of class `Control`
text box
`Text` property of class `Button`
`Text` property of class `CheckBox`
`Text` property of class `Control`
`Text` property of class `Form`
`Text` property of class `GroupBox`
`Text` property of class `Label`
`Text` property of class `RadioButton`
`Text` property of class `TextBox`
`TextBox` class
`TextChanged` event
trigger an event
virtual key code
`Visible` property of class `Control`
visual programming
Windows Form
WinForm
`_tWinMain` function
XOR

SELF-REVIEW EXERCISES

12.1 State whether each of the following is *true* or *false*. If *false*, explain why.

a) A GUI is a pictorial interface to a program.
b) Windows Forms commonly are used to create GUIs.
c) A control is a nonvisible component.
d) All forms, components and controls are classes.
e) In the event-handling model, properties act as intermediaries between objects that generate events and methods that handle those events.
f) Class `Label` is used to provide read-only text instructions or information.
g) Button presses raise events.
h) Checkboxes in the same group are mutually exclusive.
i) Scrollbars allow the user to maximize or minimize a set of data.
j) All mouse events use the same event arguments class.
k) Key events are generated when keys on the keyboard are pressed and released.

12.2 Fill in the blanks in each of the following statements:

a) The active window is said to have the ________.
b) The form acts as a(n) ________ for the components that are added.

c) GUIs are ________ driven.
d) Every method that handles the same event must have the same ________.
e) The information required when registering an event handler is the ________ class and the ________.
f) A(n) ________ text box displays only a single character (such as an asterisk) as the user types.
g) Class ________ and class ________ help arrange components on a GUI and provide logical group for radio buttons.
h) Typical mouse events include ________, ________ and ________.
i) ________ events are generated when a key on the keyboard is pressed or released.
j) The modifier keys are ________, ________ and ________.
k) A(n) ________ event or delegate can call multiple methods.

ANSWERS TO SELF-REVIEW EXERCISES

12.1 a) True. b) True. c) False. A control is a visible component. d) True. e) False. In the event-handling model, delegates act as intermediaries between objects that generate events and methods that handle those events. f) True. g) True. h) False. Radio buttons in the same group are mutually exclusive. i) False. Scrollbars allow the user to view data that normally cannot fit in its container. j) False. Some mouse events use `EventArgs`, while others use `MouseEventArgs`. k) True.

12.2 a) focus. b) container. c) event. d) signature. e) event arguments, delegate. f) password. g) `GroupBox`, `Panel`. h) mouse clicks, mouse presses, mouse moves. i) Key. j) *Shift*, *Control*, *Alt*. k) multicast.

EXERCISES

12.3 Extend the program in Fig. 12.27–Fig. 12.28 to include a check box for every font style option. [*Hint*: Use XOR rather than testing for every bit explicitly.]

12.4 Create the GUI in Fig. 12.41. You do not have to provide any functionality.

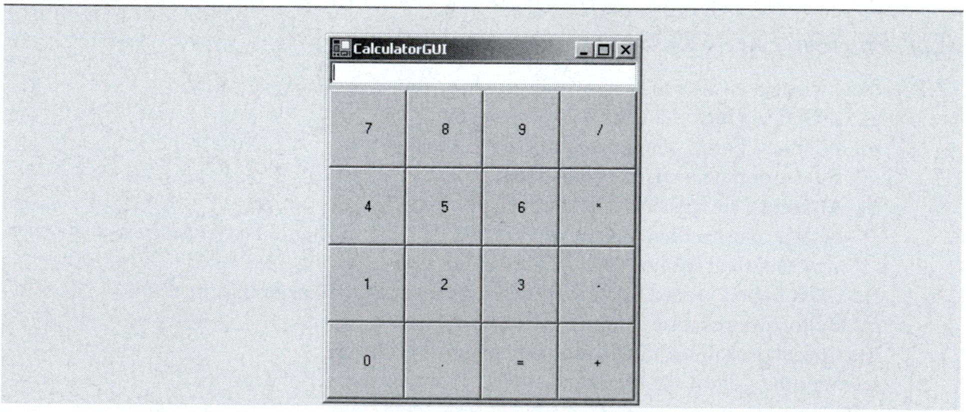

Fig. 12.41 GUI for Exercise 12.4.

12.5 Create the GUI in Fig. 12.42. You do not have to provide any functionality.

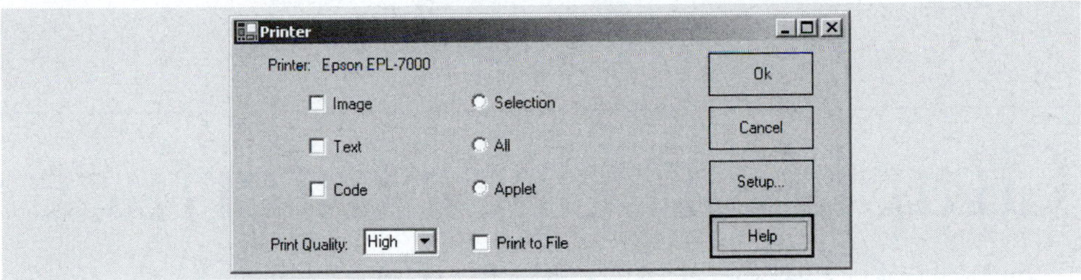

Fig. 12.42 GUI for Exercise 12.5.

12.6 Extend the program of Fig. 12.36–Fig. 12.37 to include options for changing the size and color of the lines drawn. Create a GUI similar to the one in Fig. 12.43. [*Hint*: Have variables to keep track of the currently selected size (`int`) and color (`Color` object). Set them using the event handlers for the radio buttons. For the color, use the various `Color` constants (such as `Color::Blue`). When responding to the mouse moves, simply use the size and color variables to determine the proper size and color.]

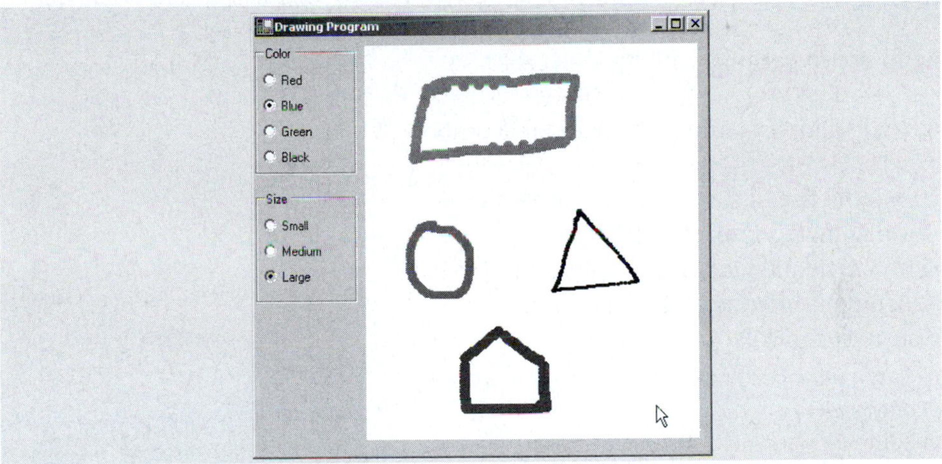

Fig. 12.43 GUI for Exercise 12.6.

12.7 Write a program that plays "guess the number" as follows: Your program chooses the number to be guessed by selecting an integer at random in the range 1–1000. The program then displays the following text in a label:

```
I have a number between 1 and 1000—can you guess my number?
Please enter your first guess.
```

A text box should be used to input the guess. As each guess is input, the background color should change to either red or blue. Red indicates that the user is getting "warmer," and blue indicates that the user is getting "colder." A label should display either `"Too High"` or `"Too Low"` to help the user choose a number closer toward the correct answer. When the user obtains the correct answer, `"Correct!"` should be displayed. The background should become green and the text box used for input should become uneditable. Provide a button that allows the user to play the game again. When the button is clicked, generate a new random number, change the background to the default color and reset the input text box to editable.

13

Graphical User Interface Concepts: Part 2

Objectives

- To be able to use hyperlinks with the `LinkLabel` control.
- To be able to display lists using list boxes and combo boxes.
- To understand the use of the `ListView` and `TreeView` controls for displaying information.
- To be able to create menus, window tabs and multiple-document-interface (MDI) programs.
- To create custom controls.

I claim not to have controlled events, but confess plainly that events have controlled me.
Abraham Lincoln

A good symbol is the best argument, and is a missionary to persuade thousands.
Ralph Waldo Emerson

Capture its reality in paint!
Paul Cézanne

But, soft! what light through yonder window breaks?
It is the east, and Juliet is the sun!
William Shakespeare

An actor entering through the door, you've got nothing. But if he enters through the window, you've got a situation.
Billy Wilder

Outline

13.1 Introduction

This chapter continues our study of GUIs. We begin our discussion of more advanced topics with a commonly used GUI component, the *menu*, which presents a user with several logically organized options. We introduce `LinkLabels`, powerful GUI components that enable the user to click the mouse to be taken to one of several destinations.

We consider GUI components that encapsulate smaller GUI components. We demonstrate how to manipulate a list of values via a list box and how to combine several checkboxes in a `CheckedListBox`. We also create drop-down lists using combo boxes and display data hierarchically with a `TreeView` control. We present two important GUI components—tab controls and multiple-document-interface (MDI) windows. These components enable developers to create real-world programs with sophisticated graphical user interfaces.

Most GUI components used in this book are included with Visual Studio .NET. We show how to design custom controls and add those controls to the Toolbox. The techniques in this chapter provide the background you need to create complex GUIs and custom controls.

13.2 Menus

Menus provide groups of related commands for Windows applications. Although these commands depend on the program, some—such as **Open** and **Save**—are common to many applications. Menus are an integral part of GUIs, because they make user actions possible without unnecessary "cluttering" of GUIs.

In Fig. 13.1, an expanded menu lists various commands (called *menu items*), plus *submenus* (menus within a menu). Notice that the top-level menus appear in the left portion of the figure, whereas any submenus are displayed to the right. A menu item that contains a submenu is considered to be the *parent menu* of that submenu.

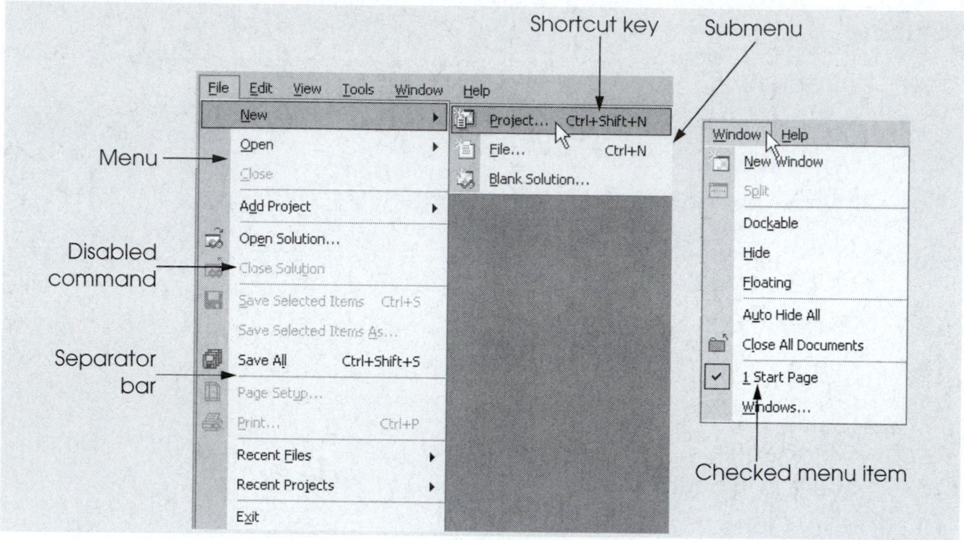

Fig. 13.1 Expanded and checked menus.

All menu items can have *Alt* key shortcuts (also called *access shortcuts* or *hot keys*), which are accessed by pressing *Alt* and the underlined letter (for example, *Alt* + *F* retrieves the **File** menu). This behavior can be established with property *`Mnemonic`* (Fig. 13.3). Property `Mnemonic` is read only, and the hot key is specified by inserting an ampersand before the character in the menu item's `Text` property. Menus that are not top-level menus can have shortcut keys as well (combinations of *Ctrl*, *Shift*, *Alt*, *F1*, *F2*, letter keys, etc.). Shortcut keys can be set with property *`ShortCut`*. Some menu items display checkmarks, usually indicating that multiple options on the menu can be selected at once.

To create a menu, open the **Toolbox**, and drag a *`MainMenu`* control onto the form. This creates a menu bar on the top of the form and places a `MainMenu` icon underneath it. To select the `MainMenu`, click the icon. This setup is known as the Visual Studio .NET **Menu Designer**, which allows the user to create and edit menus. Menus are like other controls; they have properties and events, which can be accessed through the **Properties** window or the **Menu Designer** (Fig. 13.2).

Look-and-Feel Observation 13.1

`Buttons` also can have access shortcuts. Place the & symbol just before the shortcut character in the button's `Text` property. To click the button, the user then presses Alt *and the underlined character.*

To add entries to the menu, click the **Type Here** textbox and type the text that should appear in the menu. Each entry in the menu is of type *`MenuItem`* from the `System::Windows::Forms` namespace. The menu itself is of type `MainMenu`. After the programmer presses the *Enter* key, the menu item is added. Then, more **Type Here** textboxes appear, allowing us to add items underneath or to the side of the original menu item (Fig. 13.2). To create an access shortcut, type an ampersand (&) in front of the character to be underlined. For example, to create the **File** menu item, type `&File`. The actual ampersand character is

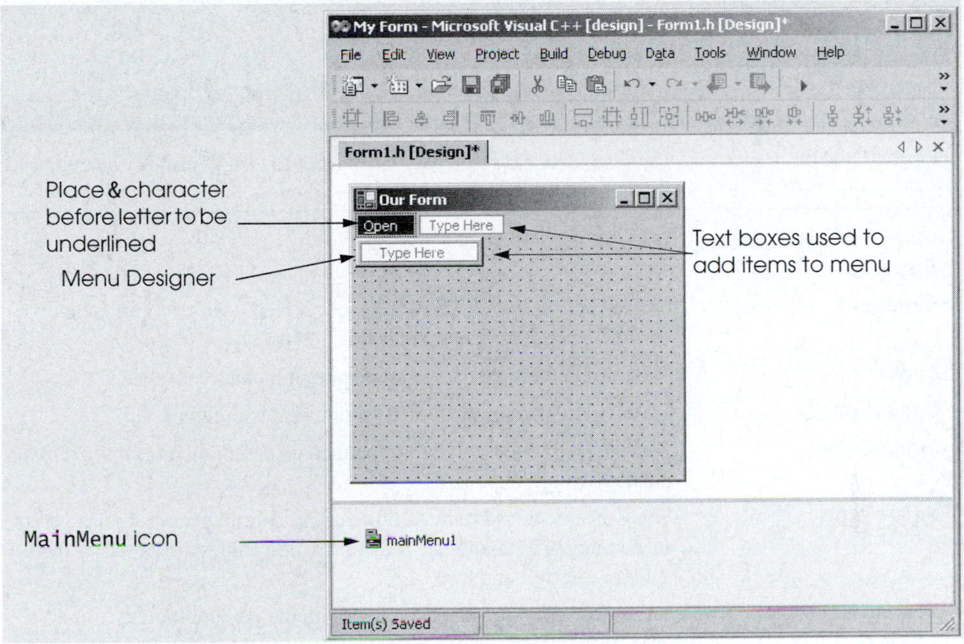

Fig. 13.2 Visual Studio .NET **Menu Designer**.

displayed by typing &&. To add other shortcut keys (such as *Ctrl* + *F9*), set the `Shortcut` property of the `MenuItem`.

Programmers can remove a menu item by selecting it with the mouse and pressing the *Delete* key. Separator bars are inserted by right-clicking the menu and selecting `Insert Separator` or by typing "-" as the menu text.

Menu items generate a `Click` event when selected. To create an empty event handler, double click on the `MenuItem` in design view. Menus can also display the names of open windows in multiple-document-interface (MDI) forms (see Section 13.9). Menu properties and events are summarized in Fig. 13.3.

Look-and-Feel Observation 13.2

It is conventional to place an ellipsis (...) after a menu item that brings up a dialog (such as **Save As...***). Menu items that produce an immediate action without prompting the user (such as* **Save***) should not have an ellipsis following their name.*

`MainMenu` and `MenuItem` events and properties	Description/Delegate and Event Arguments
Common `MainMenu` Properties	
`MenuItems`	Represents the `MenuItems` that are contained in the `MainMenu`.

Fig. 13.3 `MainMenu` and `MenuItem` properties and events. (Part 1 of 2.)

MainMenu and MenuItem events and properties	Description/Delegate and Event Arguments
RightToLeft	Causes menu text to display from right to left. Useful for languages that are read from right to left.
Common MenuItem Properties	
Checked	Indicates whether a menu item is checked. Default false, meaning that the menu item is not checked.
Index	Specifies an item's position in its parent menu.
MenuItems	Lists the submenu items for a particular menu item.
MergeOrder	Sets the position of a menu item when its parent menu is merged with another menu.
MergeType	Takes a value of the MenuMerge enumeration. Specifies how a parent menu merges with another menu. Possible values are Add, MergeItems, Remove and Replace.
Mnemonic	Indicates the character associated with the menu item (e.g., *Alt* + specified character is equivalent to clicking the item). Provides only a *get* method; set mnemonic character by preceding it with an ampersand (&) in menu item's Text property.
RadioCheck	Indicates whether a selected menu item appears as a radio button (black circle) or displays a checkmark. true creates radio button, false displays checkmark; default false.
Shortcut	Specifies the shortcut key for the menu item (e.g., *Ctrl* + *F9* can be equivalent to clicking a specific item).
ShowShortcut	Indicates whether a shortcut key is shown beside menu item text. Default is true, which displays the shortcut key.
Text	Specifies the text to appear in the menu item. To create an *Alt* access shortcut, precede a character with & (e.g., &File for **File**).
Common MainMenu and MenuItem Event	*(Delegate EventHandler, event arguments EventArgs)*
Click	Generated when a menu or menu item is clicked, or when a shortcut key is used.

Fig. 13.3 MainMenu and MenuItem properties and events. (Part 2 of 2.)

Class Form1 (beginning in line 26 of Fig. 13.4) creates a simple menu on a form. The form has a top-level **File** menu with menu items **About** (displays a message box) and **Exit** (terminates the program).The menu also includes a **Format** menu, which changes the text on a label. The **Format** menu has submenus **Color** and **Font**, which change the color and font of the text on a label. Function _tWinMain (Fig. 13.5) defines the entry point for the GUI application.

Look-and-Feel Observation 13.3

Using common Windows shortcuts (such as Ctrl+F for Find operations and Ctrl+S for Save operations) decreases the user's learning curve for a new application.

```
// Fig. 13.4: Form1.h
// Using menus to change font colors and styles.

#pragma once


namespace MenuTest
{
   using namespace System;
   using namespace System::ComponentModel;
   using namespace System::Collections;
   using namespace System::Windows::Forms;
   using namespace System::Data;
   using namespace System::Drawing;

   /// <summary>
   /// Summary for Form1
   ///
   /// WARNING: If you change the name of this class, you will need to
   ///          change the 'Resource File Name' property for the managed
   ///          resource compiler tool associated with all .resx files
   ///          this class depends on.  Otherwise, the designers will not
   ///          be able to interact properly with localized resources
   ///          associated with this form.
   /// </summary>
   public __gc class Form1 : public System::Windows::Forms::Form
   {
   public:
      Form1(void)
      {
         InitializeComponent();
      }

   protected:
      void Dispose(Boolean disposing)
      {
         if (disposing && components)
         {
            components->Dispose();
         }
         __super::Dispose(disposing);
      }

   // display label
   private: System::Windows::Forms::Label *  displayLabel;

   // main menu (contains file and format menu)
   private: System::Windows::Forms::MainMenu *  mainMenu;
```

Fig. 13.4 Menus for changing text and font color. (Part 1 of 5.)

```

      // file menu
      private: System::Windows::Forms::MenuItem *  fileMenuItem;
      private: System::Windows::Forms::MenuItem *  aboutMenuItem;
      private: System::Windows::Forms::MenuItem *  exitMenuItem;

      // format menu
      private: System::Windows::Forms::MenuItem *  formatMenuItem;

      // color submenu
      private: System::Windows::Forms::MenuItem *  colorMenuItem;
      private: System::Windows::Forms::MenuItem *  blackMenuItem;
      private: System::Windows::Forms::MenuItem *  blueMenuItem;
      private: System::Windows::Forms::MenuItem *  redMenuItem;
      private: System::Windows::Forms::MenuItem *  greenMenuItem;

      // font submenu
      private: System::Windows::Forms::MenuItem *  fontMenuItem;
      private: System::Windows::Forms::MenuItem *  timesMenuItem;
      private: System::Windows::Forms::MenuItem *  courierMenuItem;
      private: System::Windows::Forms::MenuItem *  comicMenuItem;
      private: System::Windows::Forms::MenuItem *  separatorMenuItem;
      private: System::Windows::Forms::MenuItem *  boldMenuItem;
      private: System::Windows::Forms::MenuItem *  italicMenuItem;

      private:
         /// <summary>
         /// Required designer variable.
         /// </summary>
         System::ComponentModel::Container * components;

      // Visual Studio .NET generated GUI code

      // display MessageBox
      private: System::Void aboutMenuItem_Click(System::Object *  sender,
                  System::EventArgs *  e)
               {
                  MessageBox::Show( S"This is an example\nof using menus.",
                     S"About", MessageBoxButtons::OK,
                     MessageBoxIcon::Information );
               } // end method aboutMenuItem_Click

      // exit program
      private: System::Void exitMenuItem_Click(System::Object *  sender,
                  System::EventArgs *  e)
               {
                  Application::Exit();
               } // end method exitMenuItem_Click

      // reset color
      private: void ClearColor()
               {
```

Fig. 13.4 Menus for changing text and font color. (Part 2 of 5.)

```
            // clear all checkmarks
            blackMenuItem->Checked = false;
            blueMenuItem->Checked = false;
            redMenuItem->Checked = false;
            greenMenuItem->Checked = false;
         } // end method ClearColor

   // update menu state and color display black
   private: System::Void blackMenuItem_Click(System::Object *  sender,
            System::EventArgs *  e)
         {
            // reset checkmarks for color menu items
            ClearColor();

            // set color to black
            displayLabel->ForeColor = Color::Black;
            blackMenuItem->Checked = true;
         } // end method blackMenuItem_Click

   // update menu state and color display blue
   private: System::Void blueMenuItem_Click(System::Object *  sender,
            System::EventArgs *  e)
         {
            // reset checkmarks for color menu items
            ClearColor();

            // set color to blue
            displayLabel->ForeColor = Color::Blue;
            blueMenuItem->Checked = true;
         } // end method blueMenuItem_Click

   // update menu state and color display red
   private: System::Void redMenuItem_Click(System::Object *  sender,
            System::EventArgs *  e)
         {
            // reset checkmarks for color menu items
            ClearColor();

            // set color to red
            displayLabel->ForeColor = Color::Red;
            redMenuItem->Checked = true;
         } // end method redMenuItem_Click

   // update menu state and color display green
   private: System::Void greenMenuItem_Click(System::Object *  sender,
            System::EventArgs *  e)
         {
            // reset checkmarks for color menu items
            ClearColor();

            // set color to green
            displayLabel->ForeColor = Color::Green;
```

Fig. 13.4 Menus for changing text and font color. (Part 3 of 5.)

```
               greenMenuItem->Checked = true;
            } // end method greenMenuItem_Click

   // reset font types
   private: void ClearFont()
            {
               // clear all checkmarks
               timesMenuItem->Checked = false;
               courierMenuItem->Checked = false;
               comicMenuItem->Checked = false;
            } // end method ClearFont

   // update menu state and set font to Times
   private: System::Void timesMenuItem_Click(System::Object *  sender,
               System::EventArgs *  e)
            {
               // reset checkmarks for font menu items
               ClearFont();

               // set Times New Roman font
               timesMenuItem->Checked = true;
               displayLabel->Font = new Drawing::Font(
                  S"Times New Roman", 14, displayLabel->Font->Style );
            } // end method timesMenuItem_Click

   // update menu state and set font to Courier
   private: System::Void courierMenuItem_Click(System::Object *  sender,
               System::EventArgs *  e)
            {
               // reset checkmarks for font menu items
               ClearFont();

               // set Courier font
               courierMenuItem->Checked = true;
               displayLabel->Font = new Drawing::Font(
                  S"Courier New", 14, displayLabel->Font->Style );
            } // end method courierMenuItem_Click

   // update menu state and set font to Comic Sans MS
   private: System::Void comicMenuItem_Click(System::Object *  sender,
               System::EventArgs *  e)
            {
               // reset checkmarks for font menu items
               ClearFont();

               // set Comic Sans font
               comicMenuItem->Checked = true;
               displayLabel->Font = new Drawing::Font(
                  S"Comic Sans MS", 14, displayLabel->Font->Style );
            } // end method comicMenuItem_Click

```

Fig. 13.4 Menus for changing text and font color. (Part 4 of 5.)

```
   // toggle checkmark and toggle bold style
   private: System::Void boldMenuItem_Click(System::Object *  sender,
               System::EventArgs *  e)
            {
               // toggle checkmark
               boldMenuItem->Checked = !boldMenuItem->Checked;

               // use Xor to toggle bold, keep all other styles
               displayLabel->Font = new Drawing::Font(
                  displayLabel->Font->FontFamily, 14,
                  static_cast< FontStyle >
                  ( displayLabel->Font->Style ^ FontStyle::Bold ) );
            } // end method boldMenuItem_Click

   // toggle checkmark and toggle italic style
   private: System::Void italicMenuItem_Click(System::Object *  sender,
               System::EventArgs *  e)
            {
               // toggle checkmark
               italicMenuItem->Checked = !italicMenuItem->Checked;

               // use Xor to toggle bold, keep all other styles
               displayLabel->Font = new Drawing::Font(
                  displayLabel->Font->FontFamily, 14,
                  static_cast< FontStyle >
                  ( displayLabel->Font->Style ^ FontStyle::Italic ) );
            } // end method italicMenuItem_Click
   };
}
```

Fig. 13.4 Menus for changing text and font color. (Part 5 of 5.)

```
// Fig. 13.5: Form1.cpp
// Demonstrating menus.

#include "stdafx.h"
#include "Form1.h"
#include <windows.h>

using namespace MenuTest;

int APIENTRY _tWinMain(HINSTANCE hInstance,
                       HINSTANCE hPrevInstance,
                       LPTSTR    lpCmdLine,
                       int       nCmdShow)
{
   System::Threading::Thread::CurrentThread->ApartmentState =
      System::Threading::ApartmentState::STA;
   Application::Run(new Form1());
   return 0;
} // end _tWinMain
```

Fig. 13.5 Menu demonstration. (Part 1 of 2.)

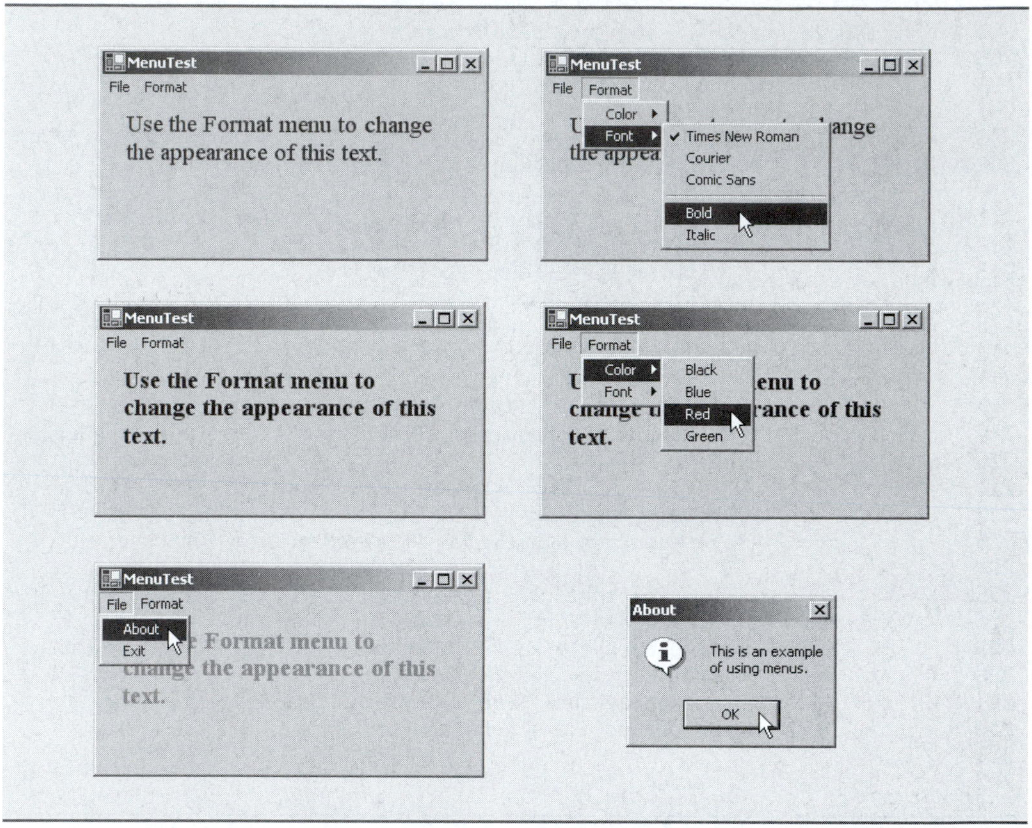

Fig. 13.5 Menu demonstration. (Part 2 of 2.)

We begin by dragging the `MainMenu` from the `ToolBox` onto the form. We then create our entire menu structure, using the **Menu Designer**. The **File** menu has items **About** (`aboutMenuItem`, line 52) and **Exit** (`exitMenuItem`, line 53); the **Format** menu (`formatMenu`, line 56) has two submenus. The first submenu, **Color** (`colorMenuItem`, line 59), contains menu items **Black** (`blackMenuItem`, line 60), **Blue** (`blueMenuItem`, line 61), **Red** (`redMenuItem`, line 62) and **Green** (`greenMenuItem`, line 63). The second submenu, **Font** (`fontMenuItem`, line 66), contains menu items **Times New Roman** (`timesMenuItem`, line 67), **Courier** (`courierMenuItem`, line 68), **Comic Sans** (`comicMenuItem`, line 69), a separator bar (`separatorMenuItem`, line 70), **Bold** (`boldMenuItem`, line 71) and **Italic** (`italicMenuItem`, line 72).

The **About** menu item in the **File** menu displays a `MessageBox` when clicked (lines 83–89). The **Exit** menu item closes the application by calling `static` method `Exit` of class `Application` (line 95). Class `Application` contains `static` methods used to control program execution.

We made the items in the **Color** submenu (**Black**, **Blue**, **Red** and **Green**) mutually exclusive—the user can select only one at a time (we explain how we did this shortly). To indicate this behavior to the user, we set the menu item's `RadioCheck` properties to `True`. This causes a radio button to appear (instead of a checkmark) when a user selects a color-menu item.

Each **Color** menu item has its own event handler. The event handler for color **Black** is `blackMenuItem_Click` (lines 109–118). The event handlers for colors **Blue**, **Red** and **Green** are `blueMenuItem_Click` (lines 121–130), `redMenuItem_Click` (lines 133–142) and `greenMenuItem_Click` (lines 145–154), respectively. Each event handler uses the *`Color`* structure to assign a new value to `displayLabel`'s `ForeColor` property (lines 116, 128, 140, and 152). The `Color` structure (located in namespace `System::Drawing`) contains several pre-defined colors as members. For instance, the color red can be specified using `Color::Red`. The `Color` structure will be discussed in more detail in Chapter 16, Graphics and Multimedia. Each **Color** menu item must be mutually exclusive, so each event handler calls method `ClearColor` (lines 99–106) before setting its corresponding `Checked` property to `true`. Method `ClearColor` sets the `Checked` property of each color `MenuItem` to `false`, effectively preventing more than one menu item from being checked at a time.

Software Engineering Observation 13.1

The mutual exclusion of menu items is not enforced by the `MainMenu`, even when property `RadioCheck` is `true`. We must program this behavior.

The **Font** menu contains three menu items for font types (**Courier**, **Times New Roman** and **Comic Sans**) and two menu items for font styles (**Bold** and **Italic**). We add a separator bar between the font-type and font-style menu items to indicate the distinction: Font types are mutually exclusive; font styles are not. This means that a `Font` object can specify only one font face at a time, but can set multiple styles at once (e.g., a font can be both bold and italic). The font-type menu items display checks. As with the **Color** menu, we also must enforce mutual exclusion in our event handlers.

Event handlers for font-type menu items **TimesRoman**, **Courier** and **ComicSans** are `timesMenuItem_Click` (lines 166–176), `courierMenuItem_Click` (lines 179–189) and `comicMenuItem_Click` (lines 192–202), respectively. These event handlers behave in a manner similar to that of the event handlers for the **Color** menu items. Each event handler clears the `Checked` properties for all font-type menu items by calling method `ClearFont` (lines 157–163), then sets the `Checked` property of the menu item that generated the event to `true`. This enforces the mutual exclusion of the font-type menu items.

The event handlers for the **Bold** and **Italic** menu items (lines 205–230) use the bitwise XOR operator. For each font style, the exclusive OR operator (`^`) changes the text to include the style or, if that style is already applied, to remove it. The toggling behavior provided by the XOR operator was explained in Chapter 12, Graphical User Interface Concepts: Part 1. As explained in Chapter 12, this program's event-handling structure allows us to add and remove menu entries while making minimal structural changes to the code.

13.3 `LinkLabel`s

The *`LinkLabel`* control displays links to other objects, such as files or Web pages (Fig. 13.6). A `LinkLabel` appears as underlined text (colored blue by default). When the mouse moves over the link, the pointer changes to a hand; this is similar to the behavior of a hyperlink in a Web page. The link can change color to indicate whether the link is new, visited or active. When clicked, the `LinkLabel` generates a *`LinkClicked`* event. Class `LinkLabel` is derived from class `Label` and therefore inherits all class `Label`'s functionality. Common `LinkLabel` properties and events are shown in Fig. 13.7.

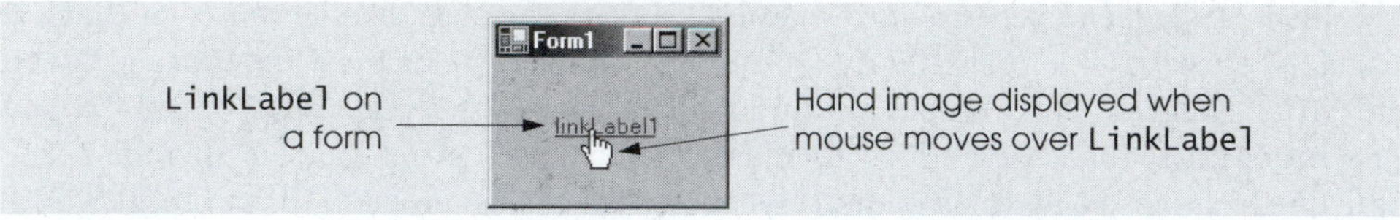

Fig. 13.6 LinkLabel control in running program.

LinkLabel properties and events	Description / Delegate and Event Arguments
Common Properties	
ActiveLinkColor	Specifies the color of the active link when clicked. Default is red.
LinkArea	Specifies which portion of text in the LinkLabel is treated as part of the link.
LinkBehavior	Specifies the link's behavior, such as how the link appears when the mouse is placed over it.
LinkColor	Specifies the original color of all links before they have been visited. Default is blue.
Links	Lists the LinkLabel::Link objects, which are the links contained in the LinkLabel.
LinkVisited	If true, link appears as if it were visited. (Its color is changed to that specified by property VisitedLinkColor.) Default false.
Text	Specifies the text to appear on the control.
UseMnemonic	If true, & character in Text property acts as a shortcut (similar to the *Alt* shortcut in menus).
VisitedLinkColor	Specifies the color of visited links. Default is purple.
Common Event	*(Delegate LinkLabelLinkClickedEventHandler, event arguments LinkLabelLinkClickedEventArgs)*
LinkClicked	Generated when link is clicked.

Fig. 13.7 LinkLabel properties and events.

The Form1 class in Fig. 13.8 uses three LinkLabels to link to the C:\ drive, the Deitel Web page (www.deitel.com) and the Notepad application, respectively. The Text properties of the LinkLabels driveLinkLabel (line 45 of Fig. 13.8), deitelLinkLabel (lines 46) and notepadLinkLabel (line 47) are set to describe each link's purpose. Function _tWinMain (Fig. 13.9) defines the entry point for the application.

Look-and-Feel Observation 13.4

Although other controls can perform actions similar to those of a LinkLabel (such as the opening of a Web page), LinkLabels indicate that a link can be followed—a regular label or button does not necessarily convey that idea.

```
// Fig. 13.8: Form1.h
// Using LinkLabels to create hyperlinks.

#pragma once


namespace LinkLabelTest
{
   using namespace System;
   using namespace System::ComponentModel;
   using namespace System::Collections;
   using namespace System::Windows::Forms;
   using namespace System::Data;
   using namespace System::Drawing;

   /// <summary>
   /// Summary for Form1
   ///
   /// WARNING: If you change the name of this class, you will need to
   ///          change the 'Resource File Name' property for the managed
   ///          resource compiler tool associated with all .resx files
   ///          this class depends on.  Otherwise, the designers will not
   ///          be able to interact properly with localized resources
   ///          associated with this form.
   /// </summary>
   public __gc class Form1 : public System::Windows::Forms::Form
   {
   public:
      Form1(void)
      {
         InitializeComponent();
      }

   protected:
      void Dispose(Boolean disposing)
      {
         if (disposing && components)
         {
            components->Dispose();
         }
         __super::Dispose(disposing);
      }

   // linklabels to C: drive, www.deitel.com and Notepad
   private: System::Windows::Forms::LinkLabel *  driveLinkLabel;
   private: System::Windows::Forms::LinkLabel *  deitelLinkLabel;
   private: System::Windows::Forms::LinkLabel *  notepadLinkLabel;

   private:
      /// <summary>
      /// Required designer variable.
      /// </summary>
```

Fig. 13.8 LinkLabels used to link to a folder, a Web page and an application. (Part 1 of 3.)

```
      System::ComponentModel::Container * components;

   // Visual Studio .NET generated GUI code

   // browse C:\ drive
   private: System::Void driveLinkLabel_LinkClicked(
               System::Object *  sender,
               System::Windows::Forms::LinkLabelLinkClickedEventArgs *  e)
            {
               driveLinkLabel->LinkVisited = true;

               try {
                  Diagnostics::Process::Start( S"C:\\" );
               } // end try
               catch ( ... ) {
                  MessageBox::Show( S"Error", S"No C:\\ drive" );
               } // end catch
            } // end method driveLinkLabel_LinkClicked

   // load www.deitel.com in Web broswer
   private: System::Void deitelLinkLabel_LinkClicked(
               System::Object *  sender,
               System::Windows::Forms::LinkLabelLinkClickedEventArgs *  e)
            {
               deitelLinkLabel->LinkVisited = true;

               try {
                  Diagnostics::Process::Start( S"IExplore",
                     S"http://www.deitel.com" );
               } // end try
               catch ( ... ) {
                  MessageBox::Show( S"Error",
                     S"Unable to open Internet Explorer" );
               } // end catch
            } // end method deitelLinkLabel_LinkClicked

   // run application Notepad
   private: System::Void notepadLinkLabel_LinkClicked(
               System::Object *  sender,
               System::Windows::Forms::LinkLabelLinkClickedEventArgs *  e)
            {
               notepadLinkLabel->LinkVisited = true;

               try {

                  // program called as if in run
                  // menu and full path not needed
                  Diagnostics::Process::Start( S"notepad" );
               } // end try
               catch ( ... ) {
                  MessageBox::Show( S"Error",
                     S"Unable to start Notepad" );
```

Fig. 13.8 LinkLabels used to link to a folder, a Web page and an application. (Part 2 of 3.)

```
            } // end catch
         } // end method notepadLinkLabel_LinkClicked
   };
}
```

Fig. 13.8 `LinkLabels` used to link to a folder, a Web page and an application. (Part 3 of 3.)

```
// Fig. 13.9: Form1.cpp
// LinkLabel demonstration.

#include "stdafx.h"
#include "Form1.h"
#include <windows.h>

using namespace LinkLabelTest;

int APIENTRY _tWinMain(HINSTANCE hInstance,
                     HINSTANCE hPrevInstance,
                     LPTSTR    lpCmdLine,
                     int       nCmdShow)
{
   System::Threading::Thread::CurrentThread->ApartmentState =
      System::Threading::ApartmentState::STA;
   Application::Run(new Form1());
   return 0;
} // end _tWinMain
```

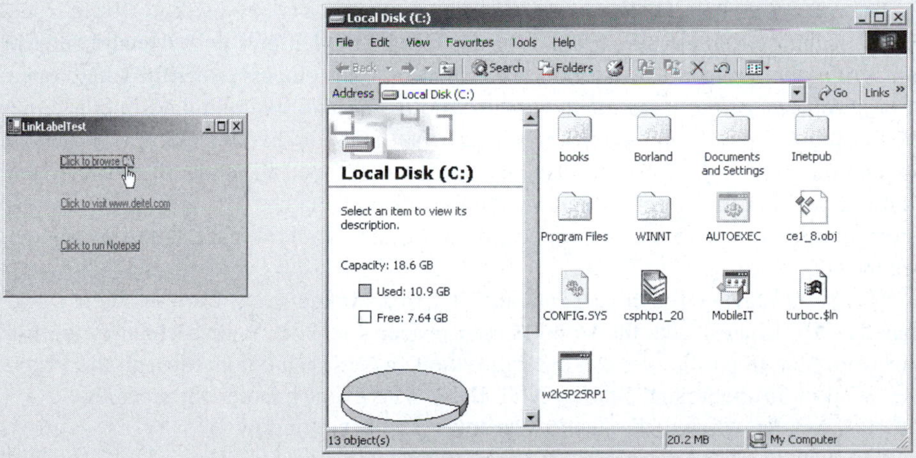

Fig. 13.9 `LinkLabel` demonstration. (Part 1 of 2.)

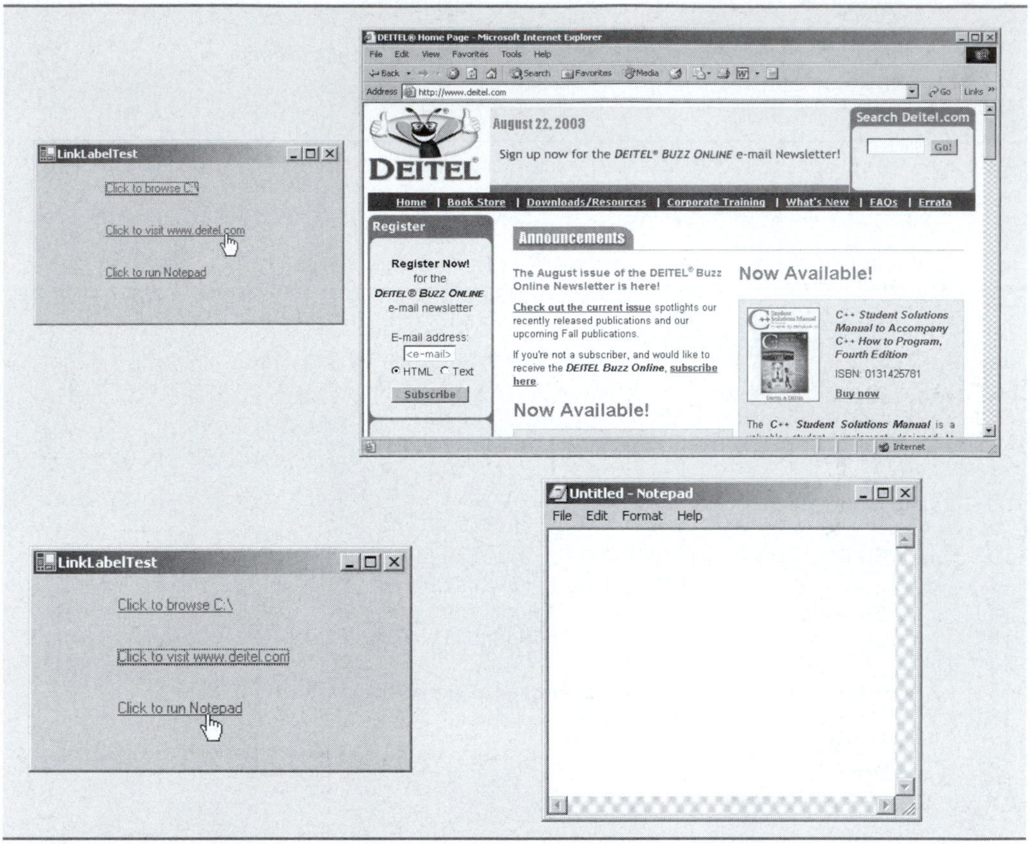

Fig. 13.9 `LinkLabel` demonstration. (Part 2 of 2.)

The event handlers for the `LinkLabel` instances call `static` method *`Start`* of class *`Process`* (namespace *`System::Diagnostics`*). This method allows us to execute other programs from our application. Method `Start` can take as arguments either the file to open (a `String *` object) or the name of the application to run and its command-line arguments (two `String *` objects). Method `Start`'s arguments can be in the same form as if they were provided for input to the **Run** command in Windows. To open a file that has a file type that Windows recognizes, simply insert the file's full path name. The Windows operating system should be able to use the application associated with the given file's extension to open the file.

The event handler for `driveLinkLabel`'s `LinkClicked` event browses the `C:\` drive (lines 58–70). Line 62 sets the `LinkVisited` property to `true`, which changes the link's color from blue to purple (we can configure the `LinkVisited` colors through the `Properties` window in the Visual Studio .NET IDE). The event handler then passes `"C:\"` to method `Start` line 65, which opens a **Windows Explorer** window.

The event handler for `deitelLinkLabel`'s `LinkClicked` events (lines 73–87) opens the Web page `www.deitel.com` in Internet Explorer. We achieve this by passing the string `"IExplore"` and the Web page address (lines 80–81), which opens Internet Explorer. Line 77 sets the `LinkVisited` property to `true`.

The event handler for `notepadLinkLabel`'s `LinkClicked` events opens the Notepad application (lines 90–106). Line 94 sets the link to appear as a visited link. Line 100 passes the argument `"notepad"` to method `Start`, which calls `notepad.exe`. Note that, in line 100, the `.exe` extension is not required—Windows can determine whether the argument given to method `Start` is an executable file.

13.4 ListBoxes and CheckedListBoxes

The list box control (class ***ListBox***) allows the user to view and select from multiple items in a list. (Users can select multiple items simultaneously from a list box, but not by default.) The ***CheckedListBox*** control extends a list box by including checkboxes next to each item in the list. This allows users to place checks on multiple items at once, as is possible with `CheckBox` controls. Figure 13.10 displays a sample list box and a sample `CheckedListBox`. In both controls, scrollbars appear if the number of items is too large to be displayed simultaneously in the component. Figure 13.11 lists common `ListBox` properties, methods and events.

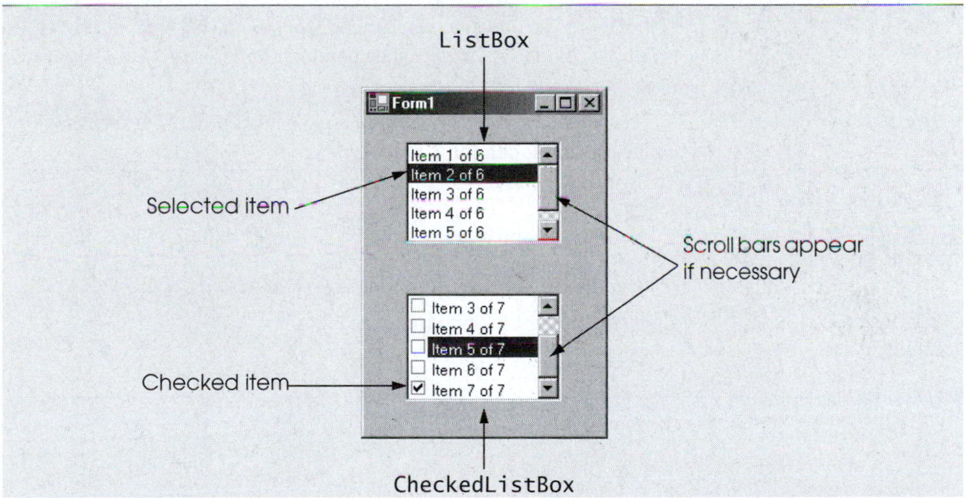

Fig. 13.10 `ListBox` and `CheckedListBox` on a form.

The ***SelectionMode*** property determines the number of items that can be selected. This property has the possible values ***None***, ***One***, ***MultiSimple*** and ***MultiExtended*** (from the ***SelectionMode enumeration***)—the differences among these settings are explained in Fig. 13.11. The ***SelectedIndexChanged*** event occurs when the user selects a new item.

Both the `ListBox` and `CheckedListBox` have properties `Items`, `SelectedItem` and `SelectedIndex`. Property `Items` returns all the objects in the list as a collection. Collections are a common way of exposing lists of `Objects` in the .NET Framework. Many .NET GUI controls (e.g., list boxes) use collections to expose lists of internal objects (e.g., items contained within a list box). We discuss collections further in Chapter 22, Data Structures and Collections. Property `SelectedItem` returns the currently selected item. If the user can

ListBox properties, methods and events	Description / Delegate and Event Arguments
Common Properties	
Items	Lists the items within the list box.
MultiColumn	Indicates whether the list box can break a list into multiple columns. Multiple columns are used to make vertical scrollbars unnecessary.
SelectedIndex	Returns the index of the currently selected item. If no items have been selected, the method returns -1.
SelectedIndices	Returns the indices of all currently selected items.
SelectedItem	Returns a pointer to the currently selected item. (If multiple items are selected, it returns the item with the lowest index number.)
SelectedItems	Returns the currently selected item(s).
SelectionMode	Determines the number of items that can be selected and the means through which multiple items can be selected. Values None, One, MultiSimple (multiple selection allowed) and MultiExtended (multiple selection allowed via a combination of arrow keys, mouse clicks and *Shift* and *Control* buttons).
Sorted	Indicates whether items appear in alphabetical order. true causes alphabetization; default is false.
Common Method	
GetSelected	Takes an index and returns true if the corresponding item is selected.
Common Event	*(Delegate EventHandler, event arguments EventArgs)*
SelectedIndex-Changed	Generated when selected index changes.

Fig. 13.11 ListBox properties, methods and events.

select multiple items, use collection SelectedItems to return all the selected items as a collection. Property SelectedIndex returns the index of the selected item—if there could be more than one, use property SelectedIndices. If no items are selected, property SelectedIndex returns -1. Method GetSelected takes an index and returns true if the corresponding item is selected.

To add items to the list box or the CheckedListBox, we must add objects to its Items collection. This can be accomplished by invoking method Add to add a String * to the ListBox's or CheckedListBox's Items collection. For example, we could write

```
myListBox->Items->Add( "myListItem" )
```

to add String * *myListItem* to list box *myListBox*. To add multiple objects, programmers can either use method Add multiple times or use method AddRange to add an array of objects. Classes ListBox and CheckedListBox use the ToString method of each object added to determine the label for the corresponding object's entry in the list. This allows developers to add different objects to a list box or a `CheckedListBox` that later can be returned through properties `SelectedItem` and `SelectedItems`.

Alternatively, we can add items to list boxes and `CheckedListBoxes` visually by examining the `Items` property in the `Properties` window. Clicking the ellipsis opens the **String Collection Editor**, a text area in which we can type the items to add; each item should appear on a separate line (Fig. 13.12). Visual Studio .NET then adds these `Strings` to the `Items` collection inside method `InitializeComponent`.

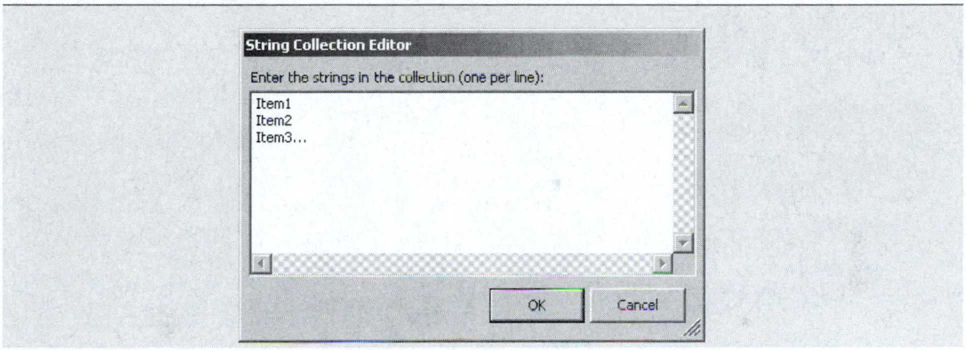

Fig. 13.12 String Collection Editor.

13.4.1 ListBoxes

The program of Fig. 13.13 (class `Form1`) and Fig. 13.14 enables the user to add, remove and clear items from list box `displayListBox` (line 45 of Fig. 13.13). This class uses `inputTextBox` (line 48) to allow the user to type in a new item. When the user clicks button `addButton` (line 51), the new item appears in `displayListBox`. Similarly, if the user selects an item and clicks `removeButton` (line 52), the item is deleted. Control `clearButton` (line 53) deletes all entries in `displayListBox`. The user terminates the application by clicking button `exitButton` (line 54).

```
1  // Fig. 13.13: Form1.h
2  // Program to add, remove and clear list box items.
3
4  #pragma once
5
6
7  namespace ListBoxTest
8  {
9     using namespace System;
10    using namespace System::ComponentModel;
11    using namespace System::Collections;
12    using namespace System::Windows::Forms;
13    using namespace System::Data;
14    using namespace System::Drawing;
15
```

Fig. 13.13 `ListBox` used in a program to add, remove and clear items. (Part 1 of 3.)

```
/// <summary>
/// Summary for Form1
///
/// WARNING: If you change the name of this class, you will need to
///          change the 'Resource File Name' property for the managed
///          resource compiler tool associated with all .resx files
///          this class depends on.  Otherwise, the designers will not
///          be able to interact properly with localized resources
///          associated with this form.
/// </summary>
public __gc class Form1 : public System::Windows::Forms::Form
{
public:
   Form1(void)
   {
      InitializeComponent();
   }

protected:
   void Dispose(Boolean disposing)
   {
      if (disposing && components)
      {
         components->Dispose();
      }
      __super::Dispose(disposing);
   }

// contains user-input list of elements
private: System::Windows::Forms::ListBox *  displayListBox;

// user input textbox
private: System::Windows::Forms::TextBox *  inputTextBox;

// add, remove, clear and exit command buttons
private: System::Windows::Forms::Button *  addButton;
private: System::Windows::Forms::Button *  removeButton;
private: System::Windows::Forms::Button *  clearButton;
private: System::Windows::Forms::Button *  exitButton;

private:
   /// <summary>
   /// Required designer variable.
   /// </summary>
   System::ComponentModel::Container * components;

// Visual Studio .NET generated code

// add new item (text from input box) and clear input box
private: System::Void addButton_Click(System::Object *  sender,
            System::EventArgs *  e)
         {
            if ( inputTextBox->Text->Length > 0 ) {
```

Fig. 13.13 `ListBox` used in a program to add, remove and clear items. (Part 2 of 3.)

```
               displayListBox->Items->Add( inputTextBox->Text );
               inputTextBox->Clear();
            } // end if
         } // end method addButton_Click

   // remove item if one selected
   private: System::Void removeButton_Click(System::Object *  sender,
            System::EventArgs *  e)
         {
            // remove only if item selected
            if ( displayListBox->SelectedIndex != -1 )
               displayListBox->Items->RemoveAt(
               displayListBox->SelectedIndex );
         } // end method removeButton_Click

   // clear all items
   private: System::Void clearButton_Click(System::Object *  sender,
            System::EventArgs *  e)
         {
            displayListBox->Items->Clear();
         } // end method clearButton_Click

   // exit application
   private: System::Void exitButton_Click(System::Object *  sender,
            System::EventArgs *  e)
         {
            Application::Exit();
         } // end method exitButton_Click
   };
}
```

Fig. 13.13 `ListBox` used in a program to add, remove and clear items. (Part 3 of 3.)

```
// Fig. 13.14: Form1.cpp
// List box demonstration.

#include "stdafx.h"
#include "Form1.h"
#include <windows.h>

using namespace ListBoxTest;

int APIENTRY _tWinMain(HINSTANCE hInstance,
                       HINSTANCE hPrevInstance,
                       LPTSTR    lpCmdLine,
                       int       nCmdShow)
{
   System::Threading::Thread::CurrentThread->ApartmentState =
      System::Threading::ApartmentState::STA;
   Application::Run(new Form1());
   return 0;
} // end _tWinMain
```

Fig. 13.14 `ListBox` demonstration. (Part 1 of 2.)

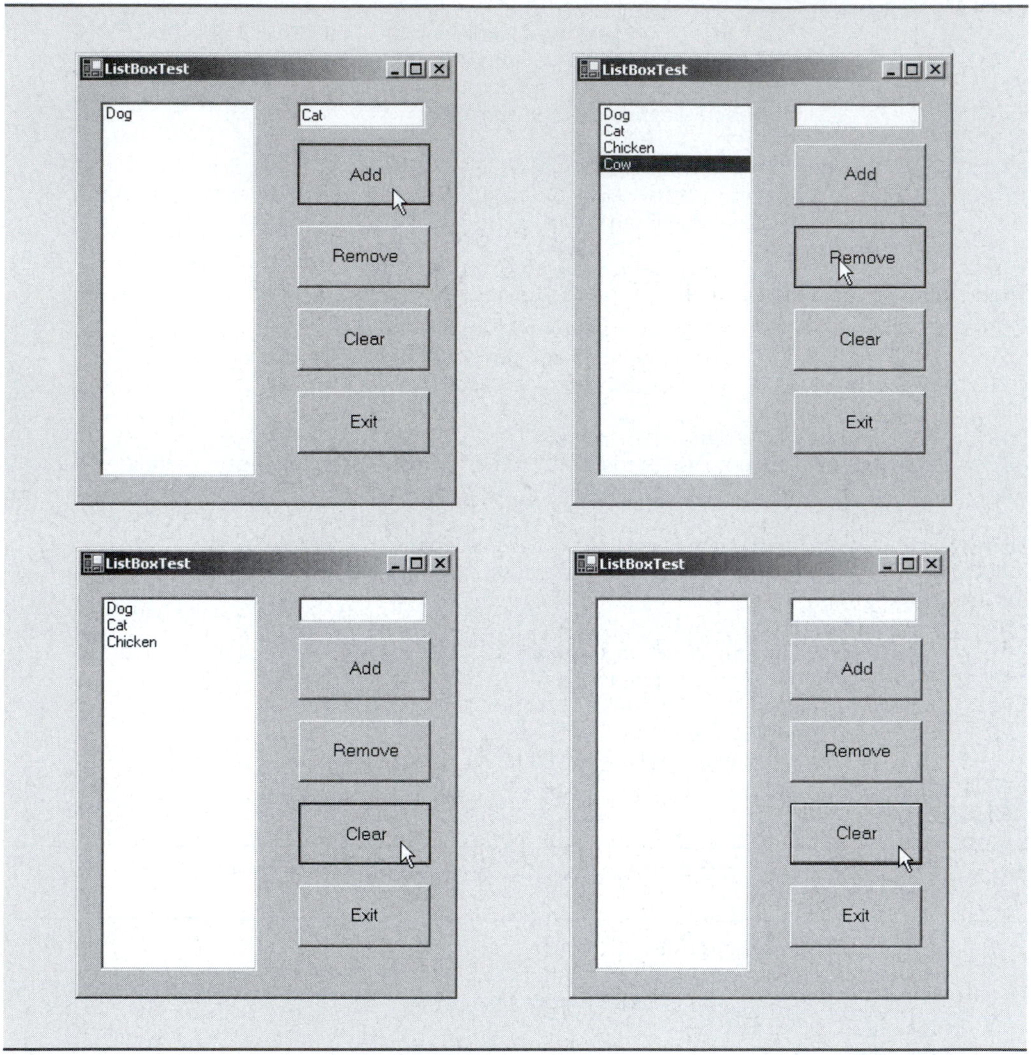

Fig. 13.14 `ListBox` demonstration. (Part 2 of 2.)

The `addButton_Click` event handler (lines 65–72) calls method `Add` of the `Items` collection in the list box. This method takes a `String *` to add to `displayListBox`. In this case, the `String *` is the user-input text, or `inputTextBox->Text` (line 69). After the item is added, `inputTextBox->Text` is cleared (line 70).

The `removeButton_Click` event handler (lines 75–82) calls method *`Remove`* of the `Items` collection to remove an item from the list box. Event handler `removeButton_Click` first uses property `SelectedIndex` to check which index is selected. Unless `SelectedIndex` is `-1` (line 79), the handler removes the item that corresponds to the selected index.

The event handler for `clearButton_Click` (lines 85–89) calls method *`Clear`* of the `Items` collection (line 88). This removes all the entries in `displayListBox`. Finally, event handler `exitButton_Click` (lines 92–96) terminates the application, using method `Application::Exit` (line 95).

13.4.2 CheckedListBoxes

The `CheckedListBox` control derives from class `ListBox` and includes a checkbox next to each item in the list. `CheckedListBoxes` imply that multiple items can be selected, and the only possible values for the `SelectionMode` property are `SelectionMode::None` and `SelectionMode::One`. `SelectionMode::One` allows multiple selection, because checkboxes imply that there are no logical restrictions on the items—the user can select as many items as required. Thus, the only choice is whether to give the user multiple selection or no selection at all. This keeps the `CheckedListBox`'s behavior consistent with that of `CheckBoxes`. The programmer should not use the last two `SelectionMode` values, `MultiSimple` and `MultiExtended`, because the only logical selection modes are handled by `None` and `One`. Common properties and events of `CheckedListBoxes` appear in Fig. 13.15.

Common Programming Error 13.1

If the programmer attempts to set the `SelectionMode` property to `MultiSimple` or `MultiExtended` for a `CheckedListBox`, a runtime error occurs.

`CheckedListBox` properties, methods and events	Description / Delegate and Event Arguments
Common Properties	*(All the `ListBox` properties and events are inherited by `CheckedListBox`.)*
`CheckedItems`	Lists the collection of items that are checked. This is distinct from the selected items, which are highlighted (but not necessarily checked). [*Note*: *There can be at most one selected item at any given time.*]
`CheckedIndices`	Returns indices for the items that are checked. Not the same as the selected indices.
`CheckOnClick`	If `true`, items can be checked and unchecked with a single mouse click. If `false`, items must be checked and unchecked with a double mouse click (the first click selects the item, the second click checks/unchecks the item).
`SelectionMode`	Determines how many items can be checked. Only possible values are `One` (allows multiple checks to be placed) or `None` (does not allow any checks to be placed).
Common Method	
`GetItemChecked`	Takes an index, and returns `true` if corresponding item is checked.
Common Event	*(Delegate `ItemCheckEventHandler`, event arguments `ItemCheckEventArgs`)*
`ItemCheck`	Generated when an item is checked or unchecked.
`ItemCheckEventArgs` Properties	
`CurrentValue`	Indicates whether current item is checked or unchecked. Possible values are `Checked`, `Unchecked` and `Indeterminate`.

Fig. 13.15 `CheckedListBox` properties, methods and events. (Part 1 of 2.)

CheckedListBox properties, methods and events	Description / Delegate and Event Arguments
`Index`	Returns index of the item that changed.
`NewValue`	Specifies the new state of the item after the event was raised.

Fig. 13.15 `CheckedListBox` properties, methods and events. (Part 2 of 2.)

Event `ItemCheck` is generated whenever a user checks or unchecks a `CheckedListBox` item. Event argument properties `CurrentValue` and `NewValue` return `CheckState` values for the current (i.e., the state before the event) and the new state of the item, respectively. Enumeration `CheckState` specifies the possible states of a `CheckedListBox` item (i.e., `Checked`, `Indeterminate`, `Unchecked`). A comparison of these values allows us to determine whether the `CheckedListBox` item was checked or unchecked. The `CheckedListBox` control retains the `SelectedItems` and `SelectedIndices` properties. (It inherits them from class `ListBox`.) However, it also includes properties `CheckedItems` and `CheckedIndices`, which return information about the checked items and indices.

The program of Fig. 13.16 and Fig. 13.17 uses a `CheckedListBox` and a list box to display a user's selection of books. The `CheckedListBox` named `inputCheckedListBox` (line 45 of Fig. 13.16) allows the user to select multiple titles. Items were added for some Deitel books: C++, Java, VB, Internet & WWW, Perl, Python, Wireless Internet and Advanced Java (the abbreviation HTP stands for "How to Program"). The `CheckedListBox`'s `CheckOnClick` property is set to `true`, so that items can be checked or unchecked with a single click. The list box, named `displayListBox` (line 48), displays the user's selection. In the screen shots accompanying this example, the `CheckedListBox` appears to the left, the list box to the right.

```
1  // Fig. 13.16: Form1.h
2  // Using the checked list boxes to add items to a list box.
3
4  #pragma once
5
6
7  namespace CheckedListBoxTest
8  {
9     using namespace System;
10    using namespace System::ComponentModel;
11    using namespace System::Collections;
12    using namespace System::Windows::Forms;
13    using namespace System::Data;
14    using namespace System::Drawing;
15
16    /// <summary>
```

Fig. 13.16 `CheckedListBox` and `ListBox` used in a program to display a user selection. (Part 1 of 3.)

```
   /// Summary for Form1
   ///
   /// WARNING: If you change the name of this class, you will need to
   ///          change the 'Resource File Name' property for the managed
   ///          resource compiler tool associated with all .resx files
   ///          this class depends on.  Otherwise, the designers will not
   ///          be able to interact properly with localized resources
   ///          associated with this form.
   /// </summary>
   public __gc class Form1 : public System::Windows::Forms::Form
   {
   public:
      Form1(void)
      {
         InitializeComponent();
      }

   protected:
      void Dispose(Boolean disposing)
      {
         if (disposing && components)
         {
            components->Dispose();
         }
         __super::Dispose(disposing);
      }

   // list of available book titles
   private: System::Windows::Forms::CheckedListBox *  inputCheckedListBox;

   // user selection list
   private: System::Windows::Forms::ListBox *  displayListBox;

   private:
      /// <summary>
      /// Required designer variable.
      /// </summary>
      System::ComponentModel::Container * components;

   // Visual Studio .NET generated GUI code

   // item about to change, add or remove from displayListBox
   private: System::Void inputCheckedListBox_ItemCheck(
               System::Object *  sender,
               System::Windows::Forms::ItemCheckEventArgs *  e)
            {
               // obtain pointer of selected item
               String *item =
                  inputCheckedListBox->SelectedItem->ToString();

               // if item checked add to listbox
               // otherwise remove from listbox
```

Fig. 13.16 CheckedListBox and ListBox used in a program to display a user selection. (Part 2 of 3.)

```
            if ( e->NewValue == CheckState::Checked )
               displayListBox->Items->Add( item );
            else
               displayListBox->Items->Remove( item );
         } // end method inputCheckedListBox_ItemCheck
   };
}
```

Fig. 13.16 `CheckedListBox` and `ListBox` used in a program to display a user selection. (Part 3 of 3.)

```
// Fig. 13.17: Form1.cpp
// Checked list boxes demonstration.

#include "stdafx.h"
#include "Form1.h"
#include <windows.h>

using namespace CheckedListBoxTest;

int APIENTRY _tWinMain(HINSTANCE hInstance,
                       HINSTANCE hPrevInstance,
                       LPTSTR    lpCmdLine,
                       int       nCmdShow)
{
   System::Threading::Thread::CurrentThread->ApartmentState =
      System::Threading::ApartmentState::STA;
   Application::Run(new Form1());
   return 0;
} // end _tWinMain
```

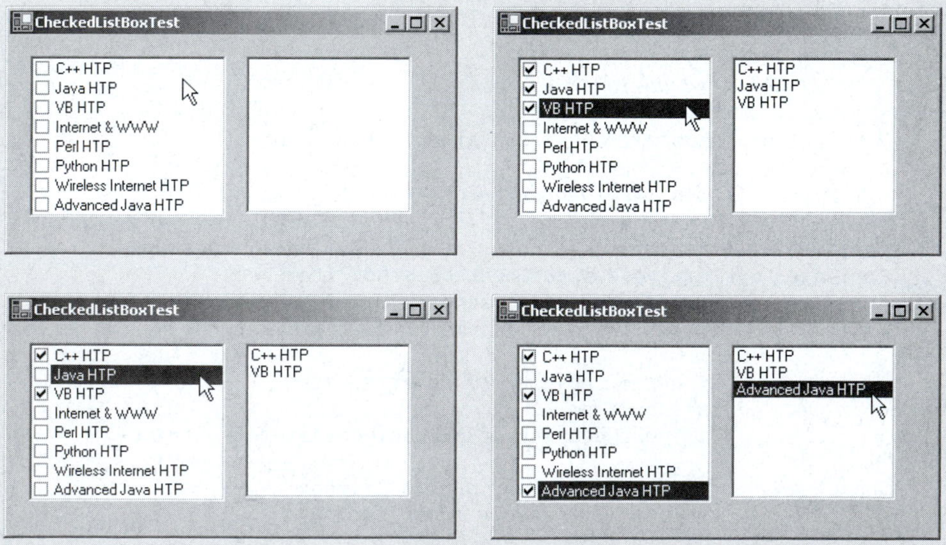

Fig. 13.17 `CheckedListBox` demonstration.

When the user checks or unchecks an item in CheckedListBox inputCheckedListBox, the system generates an ItemCheck event. Event handler inputCheckedListBox_ItemCheck (lines 59–73) handles the event. Lines 69–72 determine whether the user checked or unchecked an item in the CheckedListBox. Line 69 uses the NewValue property to test for whether the item is being checked (CheckState::Checked). If the user checks an item, line 70 adds the checked entry to the list box displayListBox. If the user unchecks an item, line 72 removes the corresponding item from displayListBox.

13.5 ComboBoxes

The *combo box* control (class *ComboBox*) control combines TextBox features with a *drop-down list*. A drop-down list is a GUI component that contains a list from which values can be chosen. It usually appears as a textbox with a down arrow to its right. By default, the user can enter text into the textbox or click the down arrow to display a list of predefined items. If a user chooses an element from this list, that element is displayed in the textbox. If the list contains more elements than can be displayed in the drop-down list, a scrollbar appears. The maximum number of items that a drop-down list can display at one time is set by property *MaxDropDownItems*. Figure 13.18 shows a sample combo box in three different states.

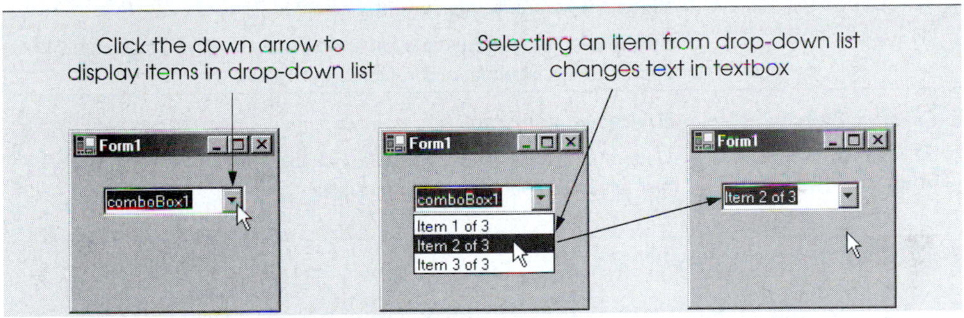

Fig. 13.18 ComboBox demonstration.

As with the list box control, the developer can add objects to collection Items programmatically, using methods Add and AddRange, or visually, with the **String Collection Editor**. Figure 13.19 lists common properties and events of class ComboBox.

Property *DropDownStyle* determines the type of combo box. Style *Simple* does not display a drop-down arrow. Instead, a scrollbar appears next to the control, allowing the user to select a choice from the list. The user can also type in a selection. Style *DropDown* (the default) displays a drop-down list when the down arrow is clicked (or the down arrow key is pressed). With this style the user can also enter text into the combo box, similar to entering text into a text box. The last style is DropDownList, which displays a drop-down list, but does not allow the user to enter a new item. Drop-down lists save room, so a combo box should be used when GUI space is limited.

The combo box control has properties Items (a collection), SelectedItem and SelectedIndex, which are similar to the corresponding properties in ListBox. Users can select only one item at a time in a combo box (if zero, then SelectedIndex is -1). When the selected item changes, event SelectedIndexChanged is generated.

ComboBox events and properties	Description / Delegate and Event Arguments
Common Properties	
`DropDownStyle`	Determines the type of combo box. Assigned a value from enumeration *`ComboBoxStyle`*. Value `Simple` means that the text portion is editable and the list portion is always visible. Value `DropDown` (the default) means that the text portion is editable, but the user must click an arrow button to see the list portion. Value `DropDownList` means that the text portion is not editable and the user must click the arrow button to see the list portion.
`Items`	The collection of items in the combo box control.
`MaxDropDownItems`	Specifies the maximum number of items (between `1` and `100`) that can display in the drop-down list. If the number of items exceeds the maximum number of items to display, a scroll bar appears.
`SelectedIndex`	Returns index of currently selected item. If there is no currently selected item, `-1` is returned.
`SelectedItem`	Returns a pointer to the currently selected item.
`Sorted`	Specifies whether items in a list are alphabetized. If `true`, items appear in alphabetical order. Default is `false`.
Common Event	*(Delegate `EventHandler`, event arguments `EventArgs`)*
`SelectedIndex-Changed`	Generated when the selected index changes (such as when a checkbox has been checked or unchecked).

Fig. 13.19 ComboBox properties and events.

The program of Fig. 13.20–Fig. 13.21 allows users to select a shape to draw—an empty or filled circle, ellipse, square or pie—by using a combo box. The combo box in this example is uneditable, so the user cannot input a custom item.

Look-and-Feel Observation 13.5

Make lists (such as combo boxes) editable only if the program is designed to accept user-submitted elements. Otherwise, the user might enter a custom item that is invalid.

```
// Fig. 13.20: Form1.h
// Using ComboBox to select shape to draw

#pragma once


namespace ComboBoxTest
{
   using namespace System;
   using namespace System::ComponentModel;
   using namespace System::Collections;
```

Fig. 13.20 ComboBox used to draw a selected shape. (Part 1 of 4.)

```
using namespace System::Windows::Forms;
using namespace System::Data;
using namespace System::Drawing;

/// <summary>
/// Summary for Form1
///
/// WARNING: If you change the name of this class, you will need to
///          change the 'Resource File Name' property for the managed
///          resource compiler tool associated with all .resx files
///          this class depends on.  Otherwise, the designers will not
///          be able to interact properly with localized resources
///          associated with this form.
/// </summary>
public __gc class Form1 : public System::Windows::Forms::Form
{
public:
   Form1(void)
   {
      InitializeComponent();
   }

protected:
   void Dispose(Boolean disposing)
   {
      if (disposing && components)
      {
         components->Dispose();
      }
      __super::Dispose(disposing);
   }

// contains shape list (circle, square, ellipse, pie)
private: System::Windows::Forms::ComboBox *  imageComboBox;

private:
   /// <summary>
   /// Required designer variable.
   /// </summary>
   System::ComponentModel::Container * components;

// Visual Studio .NET generated GUI code

// get selected index, draw shape
private: System::Void imageComboBox_SelectedIndexChanged(
            System::Object *  sender, System::EventArgs *  e)
         {
            // create graphics Object*, pen and brush
            Graphics *myGraphics = CreateGraphics();

            // create Pen using color DarkRed
            Pen *myPen = new Pen( Color::DarkRed );

```

Fig. 13.20 ComboBox used to draw a selected shape. (Part 2 of 4.)

```
         // create SolidBrush using color DarkRed
         SolidBrush *mySolidBrush =
            new SolidBrush( Color::DarkRed );

         // clear drawing area setting it to color White
         myGraphics->Clear( Color::White );

         // find index, draw proper shape
         switch ( imageComboBox->SelectedIndex ) {

            // case circle is selected
            case 0:
               myGraphics->DrawEllipse( myPen, 50, 50, 150, 150 );
               break;

            // case rectangle is selected
            case 1:
               myGraphics->DrawRectangle( myPen,
                  50, 50, 150, 150 );
               break;

            // case ellipse is selected
            case 2:
               myGraphics->DrawEllipse( myPen, 50, 85, 150, 115 );
               break;

            // case pie is selected
            case 3:
               myGraphics->DrawPie( myPen,
                  50, 50, 150, 150, 0, 45 );
               break;

            // case filled circle is selected
            case 4:
               myGraphics->FillEllipse( mySolidBrush,
                  50, 50, 150, 150 );
               break;

            // case filled rectangle is selected
            case 5:
               myGraphics->FillRectangle( mySolidBrush,
                  50, 50, 150, 150 );
               break;

            // case filled ellipse is selected
            case 6:
               myGraphics->FillEllipse( mySolidBrush,
                  50, 85, 150, 115 );
               break;

            // case filled pie is selected
            case 7:
```

Fig. 13.20 ComboBox used to draw a selected shape. (Part 3 of 4.)

```
                            myGraphics->FillPie( mySolidBrush,
                               50, 50, 150, 150, 0, 45 );
                            break;

                         // good programming practice to include a default case
                         default:
                            break;
                      } // end switch
                   } // end method imageComboBox_SelectedIndexChanged
   };
}
```

Fig. 13.20 ComboBox used to draw a selected shape. (Part 4 of 4.)

```
// Fig. 13.21: Form1.cpp
// ComboBox demonstration.

#include "stdafx.h"
#include "Form1.h"
#include <windows.h>

using namespace ComboBoxTest;

int APIENTRY _tWinMain(HINSTANCE hInstance,
                       HINSTANCE hPrevInstance,
                       LPTSTR    lpCmdLine,
                       int       nCmdShow)
{
   System::Threading::Thread::CurrentThread->ApartmentState =
      System::Threading::ApartmentState::STA;
   Application::Run(new Form1());
   return 0;
} // end _tWinMain
```

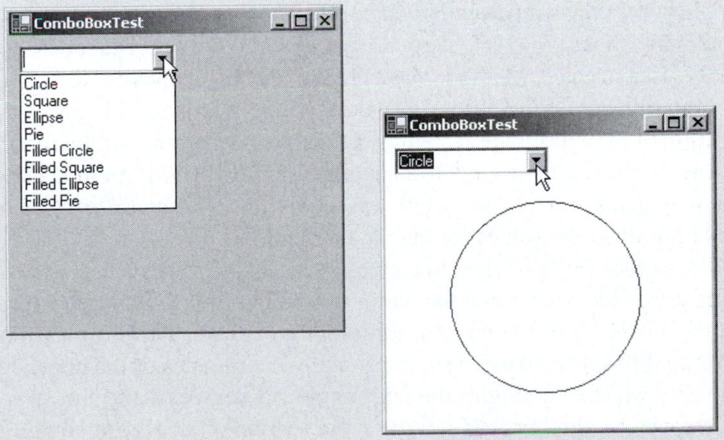

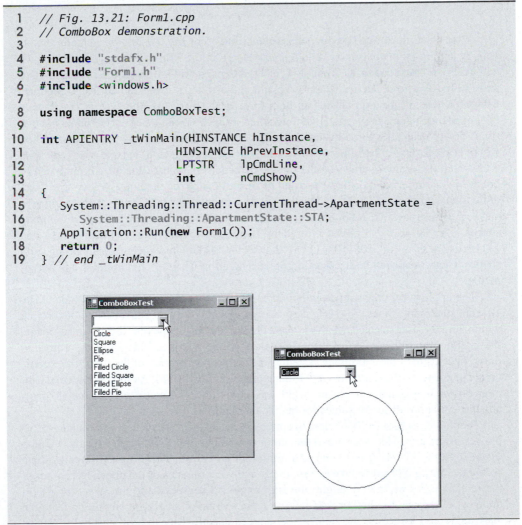

Fig. 13.21 ComboBox demonstration. (Part 1 of 2.)

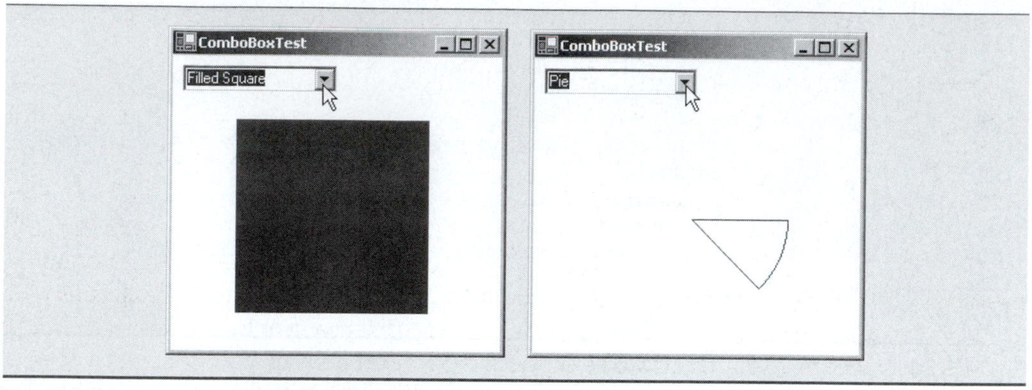

Fig. 13.21 ComboBox demonstration. (Part 2 of 2.)

After creating combo box `imageComboBox` (line 45 of Fig. 13.20), we make it uneditable by setting its `DropDownStyle` to `DropDownList` in the **Properties** window. Next, we add items `Circle`, `Square`, `Ellipse`, `Pie`, `Filled Circle`, `Filled Square`, `Filled Ellipse` and `Filled Pie` to collection `Items`. We added these items using the **String Collection Editor**. Whenever the user selects an item from `imageComboBox`, the system generates a `SelectedIndexChanged` event. Event handler `imageComboBox_SelectedIndexChanged` (lines 56–125) handles these events. Line 70 colors the entire form `White`, using method *`Clear`* of class *`Graphics`*. Lines 60–67 create a `Graphics` object, a *`Pen`* and a *`SolidBrush`*, with which the program draws on the form. The `Graphics` object (line 60) allows a pen or brush to draw on a component, using one of several `Graphics` methods. A `Pen` object can draw lines and curves. The `Pen` object is used by methods `DrawEllipse`, `DrawRectangle` and `DrawPie` (lines 77, 82–83, 88, and 93–94) to draw the outlines of their corresponding shapes. The `SolidBrush` object is used by methods `FillEllipse`, `FillRectangle` and `FillPie` (lines 99–100, 105–106, 111–112 and 117–118) to draw their corresponding solid shapes. Class `Graphics` is discussed in greater detail in Chapter 16, Graphics and Multimedia.

The application draws a particular shape specified by the selected item's index. The `switch` statement (lines 73–124) uses `imageComboBox->SelectedIndex` to determine which item the user selected. Method *`DrawEllipse`* of class `Graphics` (line 77) takes a `Pen`, the *x*- and *y*-coordinates of the ellipse's center and the width and height of the ellipse to draw. The origin of the coordinate system is in the upper-left corner of the form; the *x*-coordinate increases to the right, the *y*-coordinate increases downward. A circle is a special case of an ellipse in which the height and width are equal. Line 77 draws a circle. Line 88 draws an ellipse that has different values for height and width.

Method *`DrawRectangle`* of class `Graphics` (lines 82–83) takes a `Pen`, the *x*- and *y*-coordinates of the upper-left corner and the width and height of the rectangle to draw. Method *`DrawPie`* (lines 93–94) draws a pie as a portion of an ellipse. The ellipse is bounded by a rectangle. Method `DrawPie` takes a `Pen`, the *x*- and *y*-coordinates of the upper-left corner of the rectangle, its width and height, the start angle (in degrees), and the *sweep angle* (in degrees) of the pie. Method `DrawPie` draws a pie section of an ellipse beginning from the start angle and sweeping the number of degrees specified by the sweep angle. Angles increase clockwise. The *`FillEllipse`* (lines 99–100 and 111–112), *`FillRectangle`* (lines

105–106) and `FillPie` (lines 117–118) methods are similar to their unfilled counterparts, except that they take a `SolidBrush` instead of a `Pen`. Some of the drawn shapes are illustrated in the screen shots at the bottom of Fig. 13.21.

13.6 TreeViews

The *TreeView* control displays *nodes* hierarchically on a *tree*. Traditionally, nodes are objects that contain values and can refer to other nodes. A *parent node* contains *child nodes*, and the child nodes can be parents to other nodes. Each child has only one parent. Two child nodes that have the same parent node are considered *sibling nodes*. A tree is a collection of nodes, usually organized in a hierarchical manner. The first parent node of a tree is the *root* node (a `TreeView` control can have multiple roots). For example, the file system of a computer can be represented as a tree. The top-level directory (perhaps `C:`) would be the root, each subfolder of `C:` would be a child node and each child folder could have its own children. `TreeView` controls are useful for displaying hierarchical information, such as the file structure that we just mentioned. We cover nodes and trees in greater detail in Chapter 22, Data Structures and Collections.

Figure 13.22 displays a sample `TreeView` control on a form. A parent node can be expanded or collapsed by clicking the plus or minus box to its left. Nodes without children do not have an expand or collapse box.

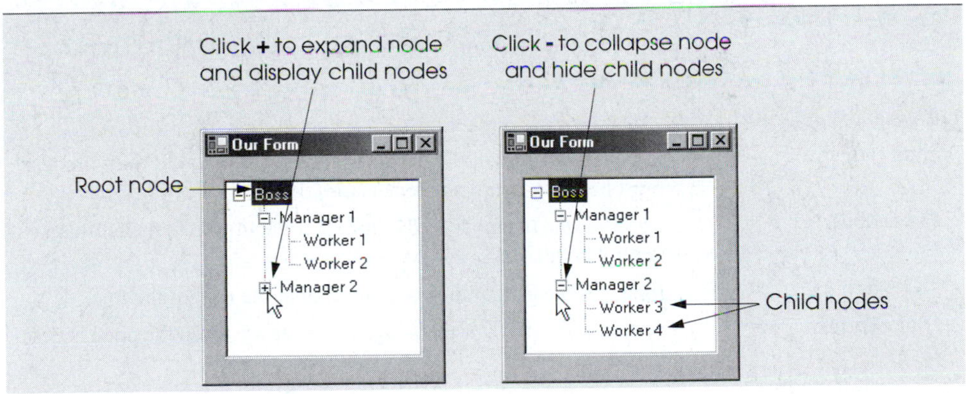

Fig. 13.22 `TreeView` displaying a sample tree.

The nodes displayed in a `TreeView` are instances of class *TreeNode*. Each `TreeNode` has a *Nodes* collection (type *TreeNodeCollection*), which contains a list of other `TreeNodes`—its children. The *Parent* property returns a pointer to the parent node (or `0` if the node is a root node). Figure 13.23 and Figure 13.24 list the common properties of `TreeViews` and `TreeNodes` and an event of `TreeViews`.

To add nodes to the `TreeView` visually, click the ellipsis by the `Nodes` property in the **Properties** window. This opens the **TreeNode Editor**, which displays an empty tree representing the `TreeView` (Fig. 13.25). There are buttons to create a root, and to add or delete a node.

TreeView properties and events	Description / Delegate and Event Arguments
Common Properties	
`CheckBoxes`	Indicates whether checkboxes appear next to nodes. If `true`, checkboxes are displayed. Default is `false`.
`ImageList`	Indicates the `ImageList` used to display icons by the nodes. An *`ImageList`* is a collection that contains a number of `Image` objects.
`Nodes`	Lists the collection of `TreeNodes` in the control. Contains methods `Add` (adds a `TreeNode` object), `Clear` (deletes the entire collection) and `Remove` (deletes a specific node). Removing a parent node deletes all its children.
`SelectedNode`	Currently selected node.
Common Event	*(Delegate `TreeViewEventHandler`, event arguments `TreeViewEventArgs`)*
`AfterSelect`	Generated after selected node changes.

Fig. 13.23 `TreeView` properties and events.

TreeNode properties and methods	Description / Delegate and Event Arguments
Common Properties	
`Checked`	Indicates whether the `TreeNode` is checked. (`CheckBoxes` property must be set to `true` in parent `TreeView`.)
`FirstNode`	Specifies the first node in the `Nodes` collection (i.e., first child in of current node).
`FullPath`	Indicates the path of the node, starting at the root of the tree.
`ImageIndex`	Specifies the index of the image to be shown when the node is deselected.
`LastNode`	Specifies the last node in the `Nodes` collection (i.e., last child in of current node).
`NextNode`	Next sibling node.
`Nodes`	The `TreeNodes` collection contained in the current node (i.e., the children of the current node). Contains methods `Add` (adds a `TreeNode` object), `Clear` (deletes the entire collection) and `Remove` (deletes a specific node). Removing a parent node deletes all its children.
`PrevNode`	Indicates the previous sibling node.
`SelectedImageIndex`	Specifies the index of the image to use when the node is selected.
`Text`	Specifies the text to display in the `TreeView`.

Fig. 13.24 `TreeNode` properties and methods. (Part 1 of 2.)

TreeNode properties and methods	Description / Delegate and Event Arguments
Common Methods	
`Collapse`	Collapses a node.
`Expand`	Expands a node.
`ExpandAll`	Expands all the children of a node.
`GetNodeCount`	Returns the number of child nodes.

Fig. 13.24 `TreeNode` properties and methods. (Part 2 of 2.)

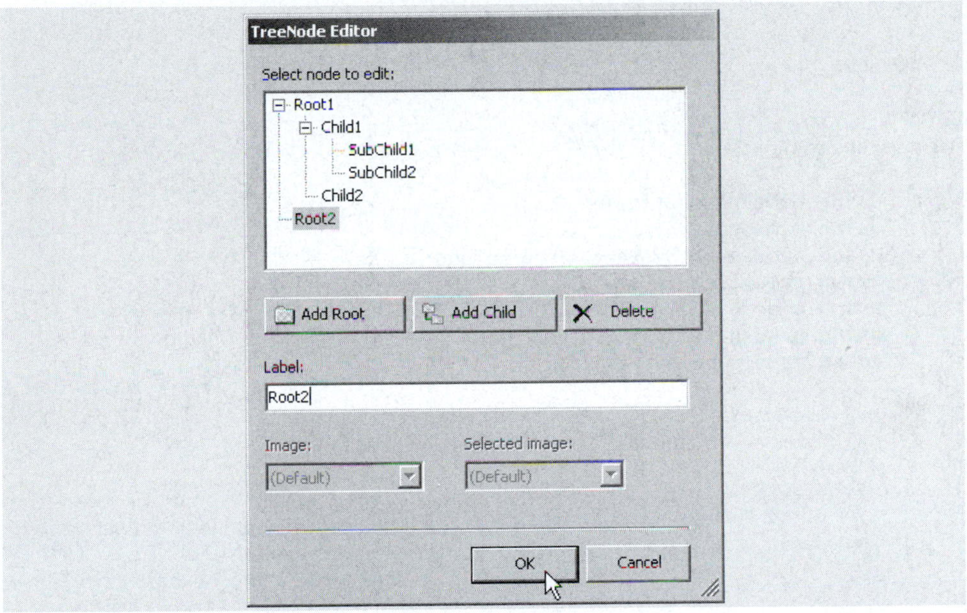

Fig. 13.25 TreeNode Editor.

To add nodes through code, we first must create a root node. Make a new `TreeNode` object and pass it a `String *` to display. Then use method `Add` to add this new `TreeNode` to the `TreeView`'s `Nodes` collection. Thus, to add a root node to `TreeView` *myTreeView*, write

myTreeView`->Nodes->Add(` **`new`** `TreeNode(` *RootLabel* `) )`

where *myTreeView* is the `TreeView` to which we are adding nodes and *RootLabel* is the text to display in *myTreeView*. To add children to a root node, add new `TreeNodes` to its `Nodes` collection. We select the appropriate root node from the `TreeView` by writing

myTreeView`->Nodes->GetItem(` *myIndex* `)`

where *myIndex* is the root node's index in *myTreeView*'s `Nodes` collection. We add nodes to child nodes through the same process by which we added root nodes to *myTreeView*. To add a child to the root node at index *myIndex*, write

```
myTreeView->Nodes->GetItem( myIndex )->Nodes->Add(
   new TreeNode( ChildLabel ) )
```

The program of Fig. 13.26–Fig. 13.27 uses a `TreeView` to display the directory file structure on a computer. The root node is the `C:` drive, and each subfolder of `C:` becomes a child. This layout is similar to that used in **Windows Explorer**. Folders can be expanded or collapsed by clicking the plus or minus boxes that appear to their left. Figure 13.27 presents the application's entry point.

```
// Fig. 13.26: Form1.h
// Using TreeView to display directory structure.

#pragma once


namespace TreeViewDirectoryStructureTest
{
   using namespace System;
   using namespace System::ComponentModel;
   using namespace System::Collections;
   using namespace System::Windows::Forms;
   using namespace System::Data;
   using namespace System::Drawing;
   using namespace System::IO;

   /// <summary>
   /// Summary for Form1
   ///
   /// WARNING: If you change the name of this class, you will need to
   ///          change the 'Resource File Name' property for the managed
   ///          resource compiler tool associated with all .resx files
   ///          this class depends on.  Otherwise, the designers will not
   ///          be able to interact properly with localized resources
   ///          associated with this form.
   /// </summary>
   public __gc class Form1 : public System::Windows::Forms::Form
   {
   public:
      Form1(void)
      {
         InitializeComponent();
      }

   protected:
      void Dispose(Boolean disposing)
      {
         if (disposing && components)
         {
```

Fig. 13.26 `TreeView` used to display directories. (Part 1 of 3.)

```
            components->Dispose();
         }
         __super::Dispose(disposing);
      }

   // contains view of C: drive directory structure
   private: System::Windows::Forms::TreeView *  directoryTreeView;

   private:
      /// <summary>
      /// Required designer variable.
      /// </summary>
      System::ComponentModel::Container * components;

   // Visual Studio .NET generated GUI code

   // populate treeview with subdirectories
   private: void PopulateTreeView( String *directoryValue,
               TreeNode *parentNode )
            {
               // populate current node with subdirectories
               String *directoryArray[] =
                  Directory::GetDirectories( directoryValue );

               // for every subdirectory, create new TreeNode,
               // add as child of current node and recursively
               // populate child nodes with subdirectories
               for ( int i = 0; i < directoryArray->Length; i++ ) {

                  try {

                     // create TreeNode for current directory
                     TreeNode *myNode = new TreeNode(
                        directoryArray[ i ] );

                     // add current directory node to parent node
                     parentNode->Nodes->Add( myNode );

                     // recursively populate every subdirectory
                     PopulateTreeView( directoryArray[ i ], myNode );
                  } // end try
                  catch ( UnauthorizedAccessException *exception ) {
                     parentNode->Nodes->Add( String::Concat(
                        S"Access denied\n", exception->Message ) );
                  } // end catch

               } // end for
            } // end method PopulateTreeView

   // called by system when form loads
   private: System::Void Form1_Load(System::Object *  sender,
               System::EventArgs *  e)
            {
```

Fig. 13.26 `TreeView` used to display directories. (Part 2 of 3.)

```
93                  // add c:\ drive to directoryTreeView
94                  // and insert its subfolders
95                  directoryTreeView->Nodes->Add( S"C:\\" );
96                  PopulateTreeView( S"C:\\",
97                     directoryTreeView->Nodes->Item[ 0 ] );
98               } // end method Form1_Load
99       };
100 }
```

Fig. 13.26 `TreeView` used to display directories. (Part 3 of 3.)

When `TreeViewDirectoryStructureTest` (Fig. 13.26) loads, the system generates a `Load` event, which is handled by event handler `Form1_Load` (lines 90–98). Line 95 adds a root node (`C:`) to our `TreeView`, named `directoryTreeView`. `C:` is the root folder for the entire directory structure. Lines 96–97 call method `PopulateTreeView` (lines 57–87), which takes a directory (a `String *`) and a parent node. Method `PopulateTreeView` then creates child nodes corresponding to the subdirectories of the directory that was passed to it.

```
// Fig. 13.27: Form1.cpp
// TreeView demonstration.

#include "stdafx.h"
#include "Form1.h"
#include <windows.h>

using namespace TreeViewDirectoryStructureTest;

int APIENTRY _tWinMain(HINSTANCE hInstance,
                       HINSTANCE hPrevInstance,
                       LPTSTR    lpCmdLine,
                       int       nCmdShow)
{
   System::Threading::Thread::CurrentThread->ApartmentState =
      System::Threading::ApartmentState::STA;
   Application::Run(new Form1());
   return 0;
} // end _tWinMain
```

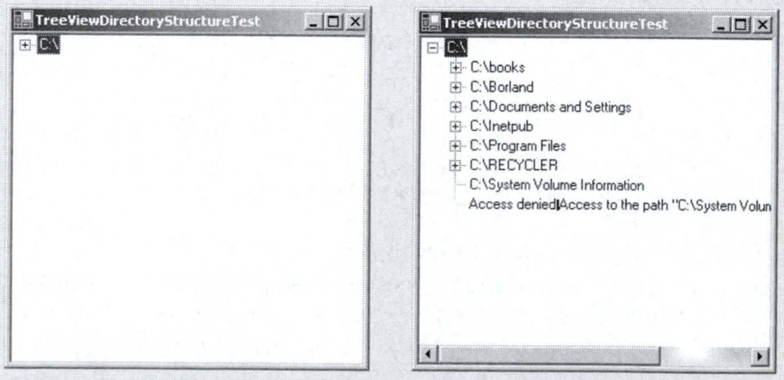

Fig. 13.27 `TreeView` demonstration. (Part 1 of 2.)

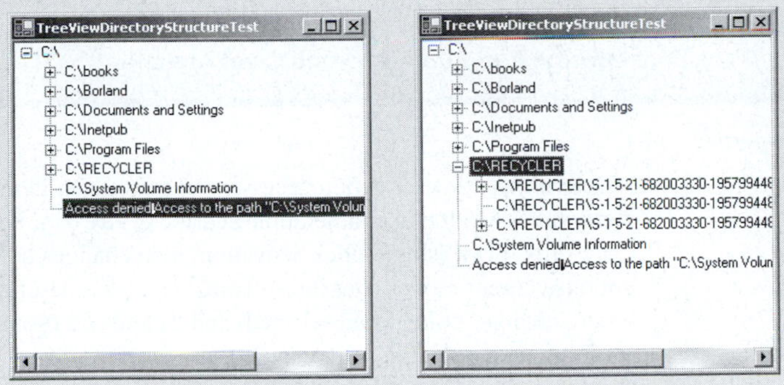

Fig. 13.27 `TreeView` demonstration. (Part 2 of 2.)

Method `PopulateTreeView` (lines 57–87) obtains a list of subdirectories, using method ***`GetDirectories`*** of class `Directory` (namespace `System::IO`) in line 62. Method `GetDirectories` takes a `String *` (the current directory) and returns an array of `String *` objects (the subdirectories), which is assigned to array `directoryArray`. If the specified directory is not accessible for security reasons, an `UnauthorizedAccessException` is thrown. Lines 81–84 catch this exception and add a node containing `"Access Denied"` instead of displaying the contents of the inaccessible directory. Note that the `try` and `catch` blocks are contained within the `for` loop; after an exception is handled, the `for` loop continues executing.

If there are accessible subdirectories, each `String *` in the `directoryArray` is used to create a new child node (lines 72–73). We use method `Add` (line 76) to add each child node to the parent. Then method `PopulateTreeView` is called recursively on every subdirectory (line 79) and eventually populates the entire directory structure. Our recursive algorithm causes our program to have a lengthy initial delay when it loads—it must create a tree for the entire `C:` drive. However, once the drive folder names are added to the appropriate `Nodes` collection, they can be expanded and collapsed without delay. In the next section, we present an alternative algorithm to solve this problem.

13.7 ListViews

The ***`ListView`*** control is similar to a list box, in that both display lists from which the user can select one or more items of type ***`ListViewItem`*** (to see an example of a `ListView` control, look ahead to the output of Fig. 13.31). The important difference between the two classes is that a `ListView` can display icons alongside the list items in a variety of ways (controlled by its `ImageList` property). Property ***`MultiSelect`*** (a boolean) determines whether multiple items can be selected. Checkboxes can be included by setting property `CheckBoxes` (a boolean) to `true`, making the `ListView`'s appearance similar to that of a `CheckedListBox`. Property ***`View`*** specifies the layout of the list box. Property ***`Activation`*** determines the method by which the user selects a list item. The details of these properties are explained in Fig. 13.28.

ListView events and properties	Description / Delegate and Event Arguments
Common Properties	
Activation	Determines the user action necessary to activate an item. This property takes a value in enumeration ItemActivation. Possible values are OneClick (single-click activation, item changes color when mouse cursor moves over item), TwoClick (double-click activation, item changes color when selected) and Standard (double-click activation, no associated color change).
CheckBoxes	Indicates whether items appear with checkboxes. If true, checkboxes are displayed. Default is false.
LargeImageList	Indicates the ImageList used when displaying large icons.
Items	Returns the collection of ListViewItems in the control.
MultiSelect	Determines whether multiple selection is allowed. Default is true, which enables multiple selection.
SelectedItems	Lists the collection of currently selected items.
SmallImageList	Specifies the ImageList used when displaying small icons.
View	Determines appearance of ListViewItems. Enumeration View values LargeIcon (large icon displayed, items can be in multiple columns), SmallIcon (small icon displayed), List (small icons displayed, items appear in a single column) and Details (like List, but multiple columns of information can be displayed per item).
Common Event	*(Delegate EventHandler, event arguments EventArgs)*
ItemActivate	Generated when an item in the ListView is activated. Does not specify which item is activated.

Fig. 13.28 ListView properties and events.

ListView allows us to define the images used as icons for ListView items. To display images, we must use an ImageList component. Create one by dragging it onto a form from the **ToolBox**. Then, click the Images collection in the **Properties** window to display the **Image Collection Editor** (Fig. 13.29). Here, developers can browse for images that they wish to add to the ImageList, which contains an array of Images. Once the images have been defined, set property SmallImageList of the ListView to the new ImageList object. Property SmallImageList specifies the image list for the small icons. Property LargeImageList sets the ImageList for large icons. Icons for the ListView items are selected by setting the item's ImageIndex property to the appropriate array index.

Class Form1 (Fig. 13.30) displays files and folders in a ListView, along with small icons representing each file or folder. If a file or folder is inaccessible because of permission settings, a message box appears. The program scans the contents of the directory as it browses, rather than indexing the entire drive at once. Function _tWinMain (Fig. 13.31) contains the entry point for ListViewTest.]

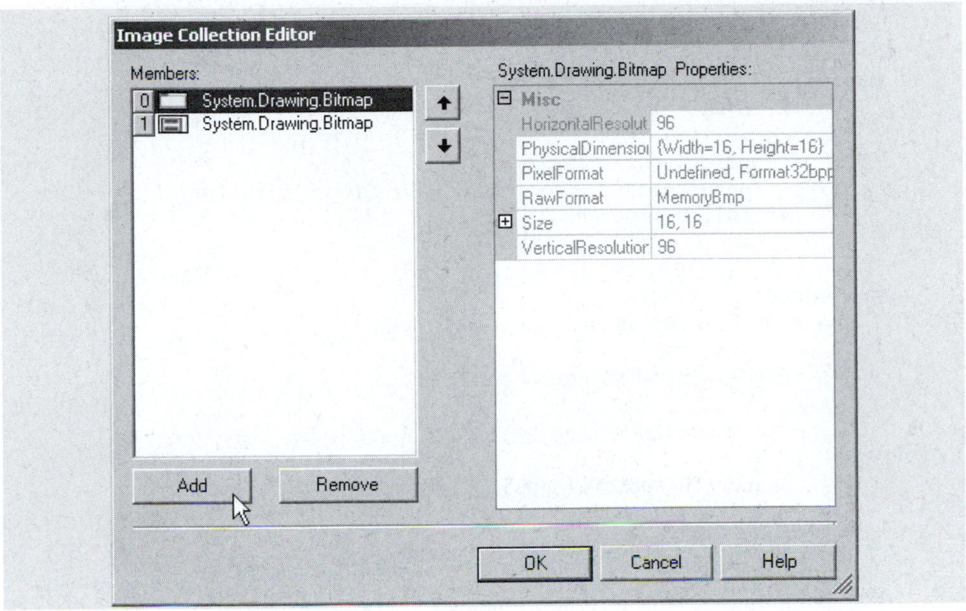

Fig. 13.29 Image Collection Editor window for an `ImageList` component.

```
// Fig. 13.30: Form1.h
// Displaying directories and their contents in ListView.

#pragma once


namespace ListViewTest
{
   using namespace System;
   using namespace System::ComponentModel;
   using namespace System::Collections;
   using namespace System::Windows::Forms;
   using namespace System::Data;
   using namespace System::Drawing;
   using namespace System::IO;

   /// <summary>
   /// Summary for Form1
   ///
   /// WARNING: If you change the name of this class, you will need to
   ///          change the 'Resource File Name' property for the managed
   ///          resource compiler tool associated with all .resx files
   ///          this class depends on.  Otherwise, the designers will not
   ///          be able to interact properly with localized resources
   ///          associated with this form.
   /// </summary>
```

Fig. 13.30 `ListView` displaying files and folders. (Part 1 of 5.)

```
public __gc class Form1 : public System::Windows::Forms::Form
{
public:
   Form1(void)
   {
      // get current directory
      currentDirectory = Directory::GetCurrentDirectory();
      InitializeComponent();
   }

protected:
   void Dispose(Boolean disposing)
   {
      if (disposing && components)
      {
         components->Dispose();
      }
      __super::Dispose(disposing);
   }

// displays labels for current location in directory tree
private: System::Windows::Forms::Label *  currentLabel;
private: System::Windows::Forms::Label *  displayLabel;

// display contents of current directory
private: System::Windows::Forms::ListView *  browserListView;

// specifies images for file icons and folder icons
private: System::Windows::Forms::ImageList *  fileFolder;

// get current directory
private: String *currentDirectory;

private:
   /// <summary>
   /// Required designer variable.
   /// </summary>
   System::ComponentModel::Container * components;

// Visual Studio .NET generated GUI Code

// display files/subdirectories of current directory
private: void LoadFilesInDirectory( String *currentDirectoryValue )
         {
            // load directory information and display
            try {

               // clear ListView and set first item
               browserListView->Items->Clear();
               browserListView->Items->Add( S"Go Up One Level" );

               // update current directory
               currentDirectory = currentDirectoryValue;
```

Fig. 13.30 `ListView` displaying files and folders. (Part 2 of 5.)

```
               DirectoryInfo *newCurrentDirectory =
                  new DirectoryInfo( currentDirectory );

               // put files and directories into arrays
               DirectoryInfo *directoryArray[] =
                  newCurrentDirectory->GetDirectories();

               FileInfo *fileArray[] =
                  newCurrentDirectory->GetFiles();

               DirectoryInfo *dir;

               // add directory names to ListView
               for ( int i = 0; i < directoryArray->Length; i++ ) {
                  dir = directoryArray[ i ];

                  // add directory to ListView
                  ListViewItem *newDirectoryItem =
                     browserListView->Items->Add( dir->Name );

                  // set directory image
                  newDirectoryItem->ImageIndex = 0;
               } // end for

               FileInfo *file;

               // add file names to ListView
               for ( i = 0; i < fileArray->Length; i++ ) {
                  file = fileArray[ i ];

                  // add file to ListView
                  ListViewItem *newFileItem =
                     browserListView->Items->Add( file->Name );

                  newFileItem->ImageIndex = 1;  // set file image
               } // end for
            } // end try

            // access denied
            catch ( UnauthorizedAccessException * ) {
               MessageBox::Show( String::Concat(
                  S"Warning: Some fields may not be ",
                  S"visible due to permission settings.\n" ),
                  S"Attention", MessageBoxButtons::OK,
                  MessageBoxIcon::Warning );
            } // end catch
         } // end method LoadFilesInDirectory

   // browse directory user clicked or go up one level
   private: System::Void browserListView_Click(System::Object *  sender,
               System::EventArgs *  e)
         {
```

Fig. 13.30 `ListView` displaying files and folders. (Part 3 of 5.)

```
            // ensure item selected
            if ( browserListView->SelectedItems->Count != 0 ) {

               // if first item selected, go up one level
               if ( browserListView->Items->Item[ 0 ]->Selected ) {

                  // create DirectoryInfo object for directory
                  DirectoryInfo *directoryObject =
                     new DirectoryInfo( currentDirectory );

                  // if directory has parent, load it
                  if ( directoryObject->Parent != 0 )
                     LoadFilesInDirectory(
                        directoryObject->Parent->FullName );
               } // end if

               // selected directory or file
               else {

                  // directory or file chosen
                  String *chosen =
                     browserListView->SelectedItems->Item[ 0 ]->Text;

                  // if item selected is directory
                  if ( Directory::Exists( String::Concat(
                     currentDirectory, S"\\", chosen ) ) ) {

                     // load subdirectory
                     // if in c:\, do not need '\',
                     // otherwise we do
                     if ( currentDirectory->Equals( "c:\\" ) )
                        LoadFilesInDirectory( String::Concat(
                           currentDirectory, chosen ));
                     else
                        LoadFilesInDirectory( String::Concat(
                        currentDirectory, S"\\", chosen ) );
                  } //end if
               } // end else

               // update displayLabel
               displayLabel->Text = currentDirectory;
            } // end if
         } // end method browserListView_Click

// handle load event when Form displayed for first time
private: System::Void Form1_Load(System::Object *  sender,
            System::EventArgs *  e)
         {
            // set image list
            Image *folderImage = Image::FromFile( String::Concat(
               currentDirectory, S"\\images\\folder.bmp" ) );

```

Fig. 13.30 `ListView` displaying files and folders. (Part 4 of 5.)

```
            Image *fileImage = Image::FromFile( String::Concat(
               currentDirectory, S"\\images\\file.bmp" ));

            fileFolder->Images->Add( folderImage );
            fileFolder->Images->Add( fileImage );

            // load current directory into browserListView
            LoadFilesInDirectory( currentDirectory );
            displayLabel->Text = currentDirectory;
         } // end method Form1_Load
   };
}
```

Fig. 13.30 `ListView` displaying files and folders. (Part 5 of 5.)

```
// Fig. 13.31: Form1.cpp
// ListView demonstration.

#include "stdafx.h"
#include "Form1.h"
#include <windows.h>

using namespace ListViewTest;

int APIENTRY _tWinMain(HINSTANCE hInstance,
                       HINSTANCE hPrevInstance,
                       LPTSTR    lpCmdLine,
                       int       nCmdShow)
{
   System::Threading::Thread::CurrentThread->ApartmentState =
      System::Threading::ApartmentState::STA;
   Application::Run(new Form1());
   return 0;
} // end _tWinMain
```

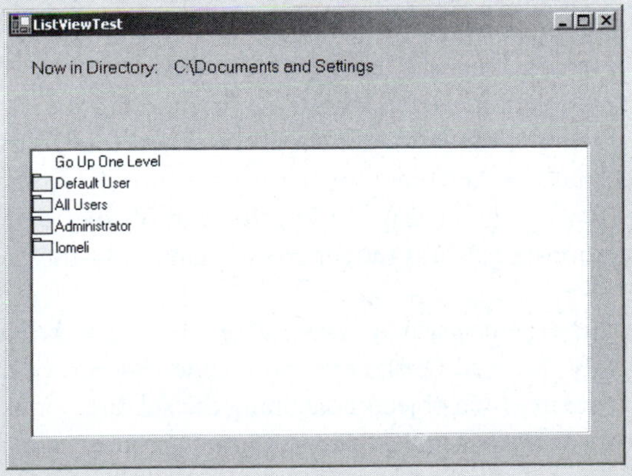

Fig. 13.31 `ListView` demonstration. (Part 1 of 2.)

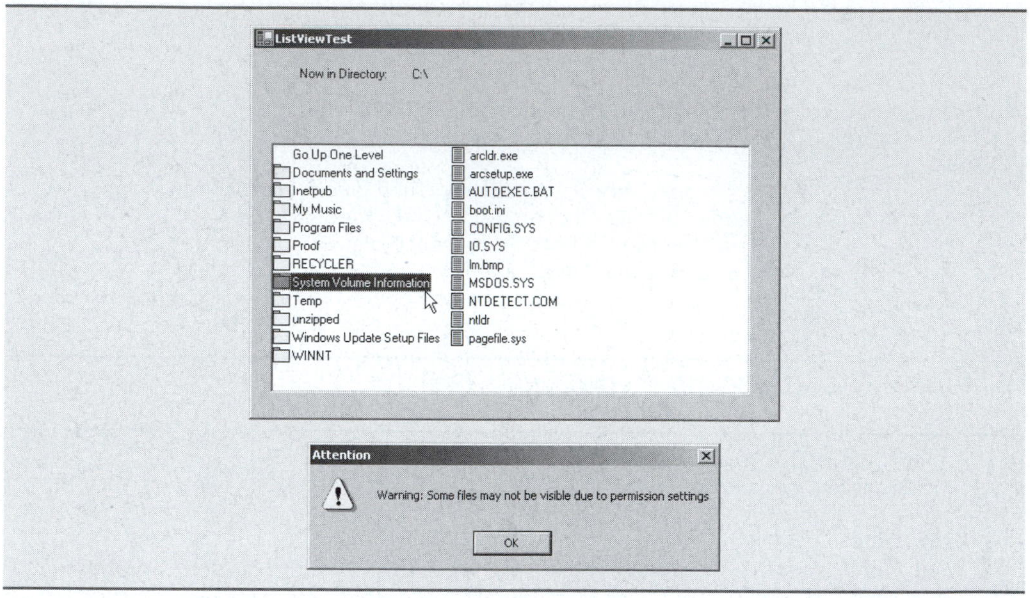

Fig. 13.31 `ListView` demonstration. (Part 2 of 2.)

To display icons beside list items, we must create an `ImageList` for the `ListView` `browserListView` (line 52 of Fig. 13.30). First, drag and drop an `ImageList` onto the form and open the **Image Collection Editor**. Create two simple bitmap images—one for a folder (array index 0) and another for a file (array index 1). Then, set the object `browserListView` property `SmallImageList` to the new `ImageList` in the **Properties** window. Developers can create such icons with any image software, such as Adobe® Photoshop™, Jasc® Paint Shop Pro™[1] or Microsoft® Paint. Developers can create bitmap images using Visual Studio. First, select **File > New > File...** which displays the **New File** dialog. Select **Bitmap File (.bmp)** which is listed in the **Visual C++** folder.

Method `LoadFilesInDirectory` (lines 69–126) is used to populate `browserListView` with the contents of the directory passed to it (`currentDirectoryValue`). It clears `browserListView` and adds the element `"Go Up One Level"`. When the user clicks this element, the program attempts to move up one level. (We see how shortly.) The method then creates a `DirectoryInfo` object initialized with the string `currentDirectory` (lines 80–81). If permission is not given to browse the directory, an exception is thrown (caught in lines 119–125). Method `LoadFilesInDirectory` works differently from method `PopulateTreeView` in the previous program (Fig. 13.26). Instead of loading all the folders in the entire hard drive, method `LoadFilesInDirectory` loads only the folders in the current directory.

Class *`DirectoryInfo`* (namespace `System::IO`) enables us to browse or manipulate the directory structure easily. Method `GetDirectories` (lines 84–85) of class `DirectoryInfo` returns an array of `DirectoryInfo` objects containing the subdirectories of the current directory. Similarly, method *`GetFiles`* (lines 87–88) returns an array of class *`FileInfo`* objects

---

1. Information about Adobe products can be found at `www.adobe.com`. Information about Jasc products and free trial downloads of the company's products are available at `www.jasc.com`.

containing the files in the current directory. Property *Name* (of both class `DirectoryInfo` and class `FileInfo`) contains only the directory or file name, such as `temp` instead of `C:\myfolder\temp`. To access the full name (i.e., the full path of the file or directory), use property *FullName* of class `FileSystemInfo`, a base class of `DirectoryInfo`.

Lines 93–102 and lines 107–115 iterate through the subdirectories and files of the current directory and add them to `browserListView`. Lines 101 and 114 set the `ImageIndex` properties of the newly created items. If an item is a directory, we set its icon to a directory icon (index `0`); if an item is a file, we set its icon to a file icon (index `1`).

Method `browserListView_Click` (lines 129–174) responds when the user clicks control `browserListView`. Line 133 determines whether anything is selected. If a selection has been made, line 136 determines whether the user chose the first item in `browserListView`. The first item in `browserListView` is always **Go up one level**; if it is selected, the program attempts to go up a level. Lines 139–140 create a `DirectoryInfo` object for the current directory. Line 143 tests property `Parent` to ensure that the user is not at the root of the directory tree. Property *Parent* indicates the parent directory as a `DirectoryInfo` object; if there is no parent directory, `Parent` returns the value `0`. If a parent directory exists, then lines 144–145 pass the full name of the parent directory to method `LoadFilesIn-Directory`.

If the user did not select the first item in `browserListView`, lines 149–173 allow the user to continue navigating through the directory structure. Lines 152–153 create `String * chosen`, which receives the text of the selected item (the first item in collection `Selected-Items`). Lines 156–157 test whether the user's selection exists as valid directory (rather than a file). The program combines variables `currentDirectory` and `chosen` (the new directory), separated by a backslash (\), and passes this value to class `Directory`'s method *Exists*. Method `Exists` returns `true` if its `String *` parameter is a directory. If this is true, the program passes the `String *` to method `LoadFilesInDirectory`. Notice that a backslash is not needed when the current directory is the C drive, as this drive is represented by `C:\` and already contains a backslash (lines 163–164). However, other directories must include the backslash (lines 166–167). Finally, `displayLabel` is updated with the new directory (line 172).

This program loads quickly, because it retrieves only the file names for the current directory. This means that, rather than having a large delay when the program begins executing, a small delay occurs whenever a new directory is loaded. In addition, changes in the directory structure can be shown by reloading a directory. This program (Fig. 13.30–Fig. 13.31) needs to be restarted to reflect any changes in the directory structure. This type of trade-off is typical in the software world. When designing applications that run for long periods of time, developers might choose a large initial delay to improve performance throughout the rest of the program. However, when creating applications that run for only short periods of time, developers often prefer fast initial loading times and a small delay after each action.

13.8 Tab Control

The *TabControl* creates tabbed windows, such as those we have seen in the Visual Studio .NET IDE (Fig. 13.32). This allows the programmer to design user interfaces that fit a large number of controls or a large amount of data without using valuable screen "real estate." `Tab-Controls` contain *TabPage* objects, which are similar to `Panels` and `GroupBoxes`. The programmer adds controls to the `TabPage` objects and adds the `TabPages` to the `TabControl`. Only one `TabPage` is displayed at a time. Figure 13.33 depicts a sample `TabControl`.

Programmers can add `TabControls` visually by dragging and dropping them onto a form in design mode. To add `TabPages` in the Visual Studio .NET designer, right-click the `TabControl` and select **Add Tab** (Fig. 13.34). Alternatively, click the `TabPages` collection in the **Properties** window and add tabs in the dialog that appears. To change a tab label, set the `Text` property of the `TabPage`.

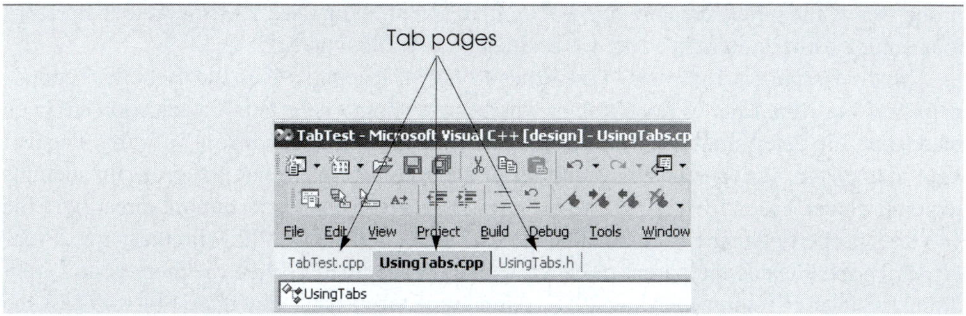

Fig. 13.32 Tabbed pages in Visual Studio .NET.

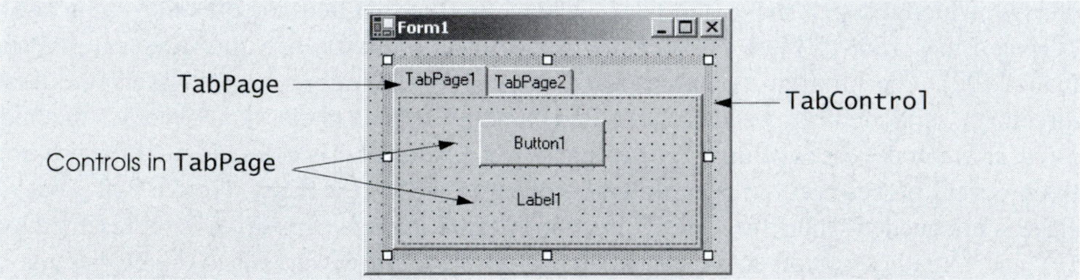

Fig. 13.33 `TabControl` with `TabPages` example.

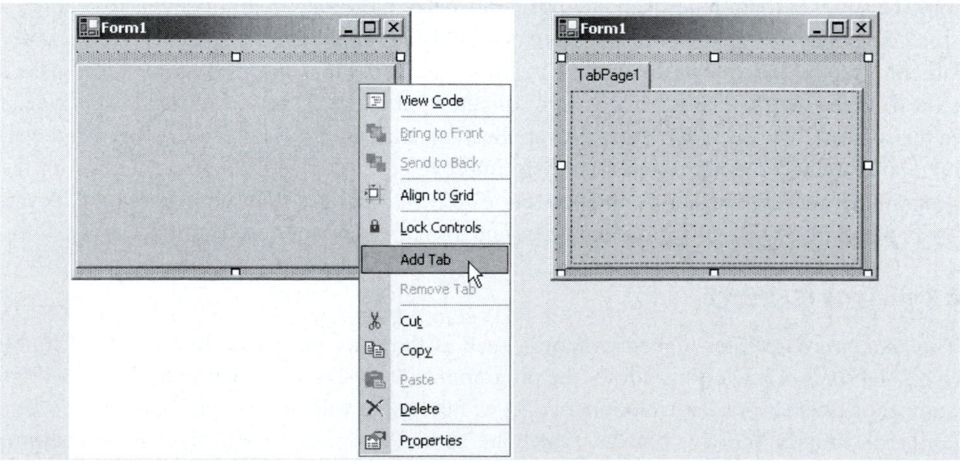

Fig. 13.34 `TabPages` added to a `TabControl`.

Note that clicking the tabs selects the TabControl—to select the TabPage, click the control area underneath the tabs. To view different TabPages, click the appropriate tab. Common properties and events of TabControls are described in Fig. 13.35.

TabControl properties and events	Description / Delegate and Event Arguments
Common Properties	
ImageList	Specifies images to be displayed on a tab.
ItemSize	Specifies tab size.
MultiLine	Indicates whether multiple rows of tabs can be displayed.
SelectedIndex	Indicates index of TabPage that is currently selected.
SelectedTab	Indicates the TabPage that is currently selected.
TabCount	Returns the number of tabs.
TabPages	Gets the collection of TabPages within a TabControl.
Common Event	*(Delegate* EventHandler*, event arguments* EventArgs*)*
SelectedIndexChanged	Generated when SelectedIndex changes (i.e., another TabPage is selected).

Fig. 13.35 TabControl properties and events.

Each TabPage generates its own Click event when its tab is clicked. Remember, events for controls can be handled by any event handler that is registered with the control's event delegate. This also applies to controls contained in a TabPage. For convenience, Visual Studio .NET generates the empty event handlers for these controls contained in a TabPage in the class in which we are currently working.

Class Form1 (Fig. 13.36) uses a TabControl to display various options relating to the text on a label (**Color**, **Size** and **Message**). The last TabPage displays an **About** message, which describes the use of TabControls. Function _tWinMain (Fig. 13.37) contains the entry point for UsingTabs.

```
// Fig. 13.36: Form1.h
// Using TabControl to display various font settings.

#pragma once


namespace UsingTabs
{
   using namespace System;
   using namespace System::ComponentModel;
   using namespace System::Collections;
   using namespace System::Windows::Forms;
   using namespace System::Data;
```

Fig. 13.36 TabControl used to display various font settings. (Part 1 of 4.)

```
using namespace System::Drawing;

/// <summary>
/// Summary for Form1
///
/// WARNING: If you change the name of this class, you will need to
///          change the 'Resource File Name' property for the managed
///          resource compiler tool associated with all .resx files
///          this class depends on.  Otherwise, the designers will not
///          be able to interact properly with localized resources
///          associated with this form.
/// </summary>
public __gc class Form1 : public System::Windows::Forms::Form
{
public:
   Form1(void)
   {
      InitializeComponent();
   }

protected:
   void Dispose(Boolean disposing)
   {
      if (disposing && components)
      {
         components->Dispose();
      }
      __super::Dispose(disposing);
   }
private: System::Windows::Forms::Label *  displayLabel;

// tab control containing table pages colorTabPage,
// sizeTabPage, messageTabPage and aboutTabPage
private: System::Windows::Forms::TabControl *  optionsTabControl;

// tab page containing color options
private: System::Windows::Forms::TabPage *  colorTabPage;
private: System::Windows::Forms::RadioButton *  greenRadioButton;
private: System::Windows::Forms::RadioButton *  redRadioButton;
private: System::Windows::Forms::RadioButton *  blackRadioButton;

// tab page containing font size options
private: System::Windows::Forms::TabPage *  sizeTabPage;
private: System::Windows::Forms::RadioButton *  size20RadioButton;
private: System::Windows::Forms::RadioButton *  size16RadioButton;
private: System::Windows::Forms::RadioButton *  size12RadioButton;

// tab page containing text display options
private: System::Windows::Forms::TabPage *  messageTabPage;
private: System::Windows::Forms::RadioButton *  goodByeRadioButton;
private: System::Windows::Forms::RadioButton *  helloRadioButton;

```

Fig. 13.36 `TabControl` used to display various font settings. (Part 2 of 4.)

```
   // tab page containing about message
   private: System::Windows::Forms::TabPage *  aboutTabPage;
   private: System::Windows::Forms::Label *  messageLabel;

   private:
      /// <summary>
      /// Required designer variable.
      /// </summary>
      System::ComponentModel::Container * components;

   // Visual Studio .NET generated GUI code

   // event handler for black color radio button
   private: System::Void blackRadioButton_CheckedChanged(
            System::Object *  sender, System::EventArgs *  e)
         {
            displayLabel->ForeColor = Color::Black;
         }

   // event handler for red color radio button
   private: System::Void redRadioButton_CheckedChanged(
            System::Object *  sender, System::EventArgs *  e)
         {
            displayLabel->ForeColor = Color::Red;
         }

   // event handler for green color radio button
   private: System::Void greenRadioButton_CheckedChanged(
            System::Object *  sender, System::EventArgs *  e)
         {
            displayLabel->ForeColor = Color::Green;
         }

   // event handler for size 12 radio button
   private: System::Void size12RadioButton_CheckedChanged(
            System::Object *  sender, System::EventArgs *  e)
         {
            displayLabel->Font =
               new Drawing::Font( displayLabel->Font->Name, 12 );
         }

   // event handler for size 16 radio button
   private: System::Void size16RadioButton_CheckedChanged(
            System::Object *  sender, System::EventArgs *  e)
         {
            displayLabel->Font =
               new Drawing::Font( displayLabel->Font->Name, 16 );
         }

   // event handler for size 20 radio button
   private: System::Void size20RadioButton_CheckedChanged(
            System::Object *  sender, System::EventArgs *  e)
         {
```

Fig. 13.36 `TabControl` used to display various font settings. (Part 3 of 4.)

```
119                 displayLabel->Font =
120                    new Drawing::Font( displayLabel->Font->Name, 20 );
121              }
122
123     // event handler for message "Hello!" radio button
124     private: System::Void helloRadioButton_CheckedChanged(
125                 System::Object *  sender, System::EventArgs *  e)
126              {
127                 displayLabel->Text = S"Hello!";
128              }
129
130     // event handler for message "Goodbye!" radio button
131     private: System::Void goodByeRadioButton_CheckedChanged(
132                 System::Object *  sender, System::EventArgs *  e)
133              {
134                 displayLabel->Text = S"Goodbye!";
135              }
136     };
137  }
```

Fig. 13.36 `TabControl` used to display various font settings. (Part 4 of 4.)

Objects `optionsTabControl` (line 47 of Fig. 13.36) and `colorTabPage` (line 50), `sizeTabPage` (line 56), `messageTabPage` (line 62) and `aboutTabPage` (line 67) are created in the designer (as described previously). Object `colorTabPage` contains three radio buttons for colors green (`greenRadioButton`, line 51), red (`redRadioButton`, line 52) and black (`blackRadioButton`, line 53). The `CheckChanged` event handler for each button updates the color of the text in `displayLabel` (lines 82, 89, and 96). Object `sizeTabPage` has three radio buttons, corresponding to font sizes 20 (`size20RadioButton`, line 57), 16 (`size16RadioButton`, line 58) and 12 (`size12RadioButton`, line 59), which change the font size of `displayLabel`—

```
// Fig. 13.37: Form1.cpp
// TabControl demonstration.

#include "stdafx.h"
#include "Form1.h"
#include <windows.h>

using namespace UsingTabs;

int APIENTRY _tWinMain(HINSTANCE hInstance,
                       HINSTANCE hPrevInstance,
                       LPTSTR    lpCmdLine,
                       int       nCmdShow)
{
   System::Threading::Thread::CurrentThread->ApartmentState =
      System::Threading::ApartmentState::STA;
   Application::Run(new Form1());
   return 0;
} // end _tWinMain
```

Fig. 13.37 `TabTest` demonstration. (Part 1 of 2.)

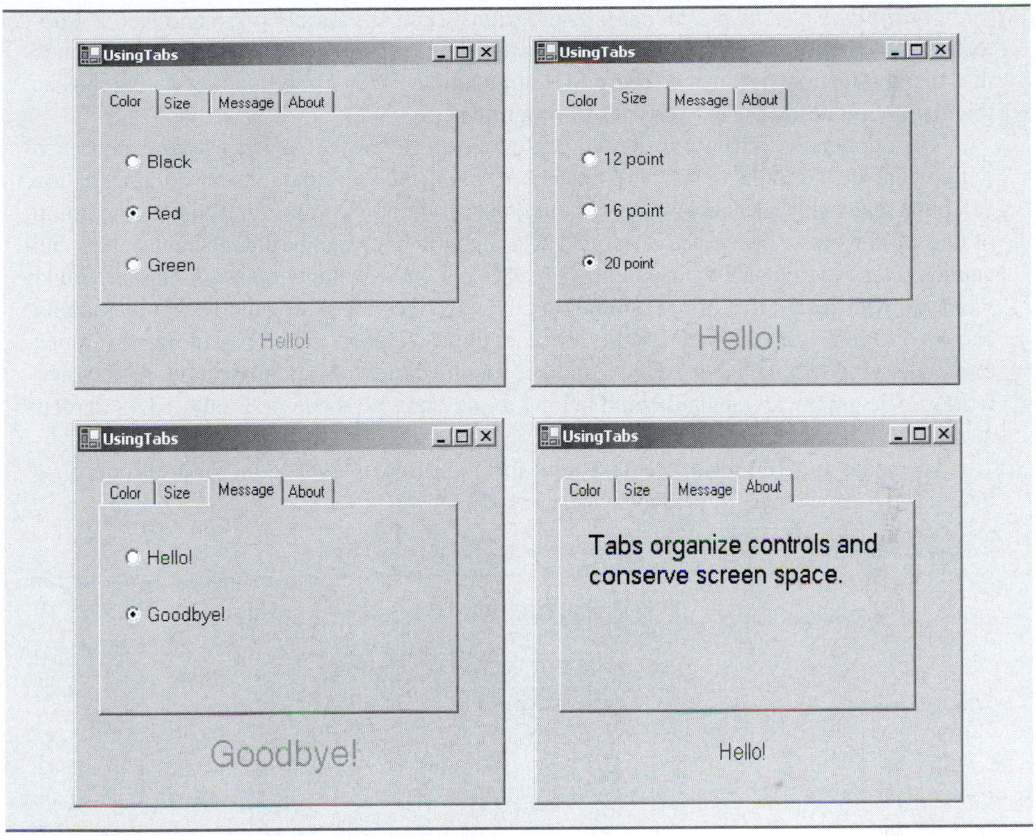

Fig. 13.37 `TabTest` demonstration. (Part 2 of 2.)

lines 103–104, 111–112 and 119–120, respectively. Object `messageTabPage` contains two radio buttons—for the messages **Goodbye!** (`goodbyeRadioButton`, line 63) and **Hello!** (`helloRadioButton`, line 64). The two radio buttons determine the text on `displayLabel` (lines 127 and 134).

Software Engineering Observation 13.2

A `TabPage` can act as a container for a single logical group of radio buttons and enforces their mutual exclusivity. To place multiple radio-button groups inside a single `TabPage`, programmers should group radio buttons within `Panels` or `GroupBoxes` contained within the `TabPage`.

The last `TabPage` (`aboutTabPage`, line 67 of Fig. 13.36) contains a `Label` (`messageLabel`, line 68) that describes the purpose of `TabControls`.

13.9 Multiple-Document-Interface (MDI) Windows

In previous chapters, we have built only *single-document-interface (SDI)* applications. Such programs (including Notepad or Paint) support only one open window or document at a time. To edit multiple documents, the user must create additional instances of the SDI application.

Multiple-document interface (MDI) programs (such as PaintShop Pro and Adobe Photoshop) enable users to edit multiple documents at once. Until now, we had not mentioned that the applications we created were SDI applications. We define this here to emphasize the distinction between the two types of programs.

The application window of an MDI program is called the *parent window*, and each window inside the application is referred to as a *child window*. Although an MDI application can have many child windows, each has only one parent window. Furthermore, a maximum of one child window can be active at once. Child windows cannot be parents themselves and cannot be moved outside their parent. Otherwise, a child window behaves like any other window (with regard to closing, minimizing, resizing etc.). A child window's functionality can be different from the functionality of other child windows of the parent. For example, one child window might edit images, another might edit text and a third might display network traffic graphically, but all could belong to the same MDI parent. Figure 13.38 depicts a sample MDI application.

To create an MDI form, create a new form and set its `IsMDIContainer` property to `true`. The form changes appearance, as in Fig. 13.39.

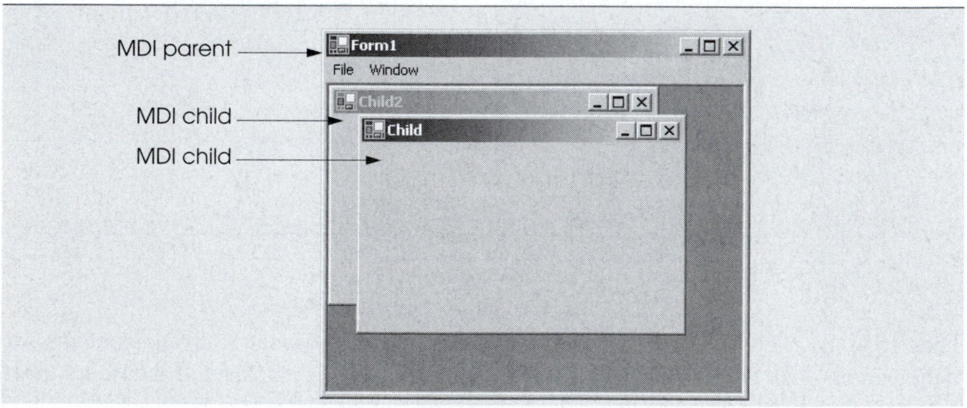

Fig. 13.38 MDI parent window and MDI child windows.

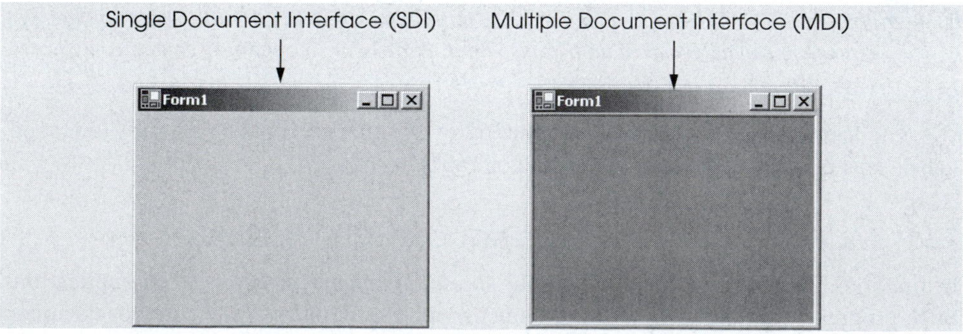

Fig. 13.39 SDI and MDI forms.

Next, create a child form class to be added to the form. To do this, right-click the project in the **Solution Explorer**, select **Add Windows Form**... and name the file. To add the child form to the parent, we must create a new child form object, set its `MdiParent` property to the parent form and call method `Show`. In general, to add a child form to a parent, write the following code in the parent form's class:

```
ChildFormClass *frmChild = new ChildFormClass();
frmChild->MdiParent = frmParent;
frmChild->Show();
```

The code to create a child usually appears in an event handler, which creates a new window in response to a user action. Menu selections (such as **File** followed by a submenu option of **New** followed by a submenu option of **Window**) are commonly used to create new child windows.

`Form` property *`MdiChildren`* is an array of child `Form` pointers. This is useful if the parent window wants to check the status of all its children (such as to ensure that all are saved before the parent closes). Property *`ActiveMdiChild`* returns a pointer to the active child window; it returns `0` if there are no active child windows. Other features of MDI windows are described in Fig. 13.40.

MDI Form events and properties	Description / Delegate and Event Arguments
Common MDI Child Properties	
`IsMdiChild`	Indicates whether the `Form` is an MDI child. If `true`, `Form` is an MDI child (read-only property).
`MdiParent`	Specifies the MDI parent `Form` of the child.
Common MDI Parent Properties	
`ActiveMdiChild`	Returns the `Form` that is the currently active MDI child (returns null reference if no children are active).
`IsMdiContainer`	Indicates whether a `Form` can be an MDI. If `true`, the `Form` can be an MDI parent. Default is `false`.
`MdiChildren`	Returns the MDI children as an array of `Form`s.
Common Method	
`LayoutMdi`	Determines the display of child forms on an MDI parent. Takes as a parameter an `MdiLayout` enumeration with possible values `ArrangeIcons`, `Cascade`, `TileHorizontal` and `TileVertical`. Figure 13.43 depicts the effects of these values.
Common Event	*(Delegate `EventHandler`, event arguments `EventArgs`)*
`MdiChildActivate`	Generated when an MDI child is closed or activated.

Fig. 13.40 MDI parent and MDI child events and properties.

Child windows can be minimized, maximized and closed independently of each other and of the parent window. Figure 13.41 shows two images, one containing two minimized child windows and a second containing a maximized child window. When the parent is minimized or closed, the child windows are minimized or closed as well. Notice that the title bar in the second image of Fig. 13.41 is **Parent Window - [Child]**. When a child window is maximized, its title bar is inserted into the parent window's title bar. When a child window is minimized or maximized, its title bar displays a restore icon, which returns the child window to its previous size (its size before it was minimized or maximized).

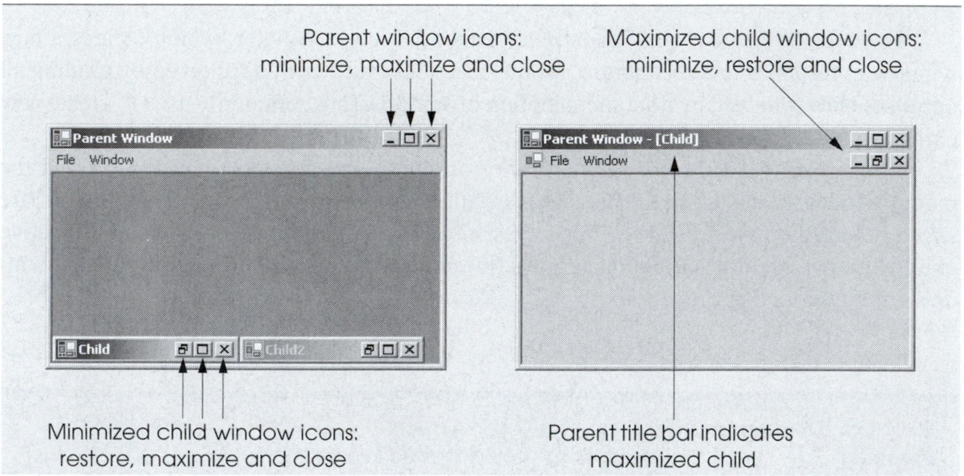

Fig. 13.41 Minimized and maximized child windows.

The parent and child forms can have different menus, which are merged whenever a child window is selected. To specify how the menus merge, programmers can set the *MergeOrder* and the *MergeType* properties for each `MenuItem` (see Fig. 13.3). `MergeOrder` determines the order in which `MenuItems` appear when two menus are merged. `MenuItems` with a lower `MergeOrder` value will appear first. For example, if `Menu1` has items **File**, **Edit** and **Window** (and their orders are 0, 10 and 20) and `Menu2` has items **Format** and **View** (and their orders are 7 and 15), then the merged menu contains menu items **File**, **Format**, **Edit**, **View** and **Window**, in that order.

Each `MenuItem` instance has its own `MergeOrder` property. It is likely that, at some point in an application, two `MenuItems` with the same `MergeOrder` value will merge. Property `MergeType` specifies the manner in which this conflict is resolved.

Property `MergeType` takes a *MenuMerge* enumeration value and determines which menu items will be displayed when two menu items with the same `MergeOrder` are merged. A menu item with value *Add* is added to its parent's menu as a new menu on the menu bar. (The parent's menu items come first.) If a child form's menu item has value *Replace*, it attempts to take the place of its parent form's corresponding menu item during merging. A menu with value *MergeItems* combines its items with that of its parent's corresponding menu. (If parent and child menus originally occupy the same space, their submenus will be brought together as one large menu.) A child's menu item with value *Remove* disappears when the menu is merged with that of its parent.

The .NET Framework provides a property that enables you to track which child windows are opened in an MDI container. Property `MdiList` (a boolean) of class `MenuItem` determines whether a `MenuItem` displays a list of open child windows. The list appears at the bottom of the menu following a separator bar (first screen in Fig. 13.42). When a new child window is opened, an entry is added to the list. By default, if nine or more child windows are open, the list includes the option **More Windows...**, which allows the user to select a window from a list, using a scrollbar. Multiple `MenuItem`s can have their `MdiList` property set; each displays a list of open child windows.

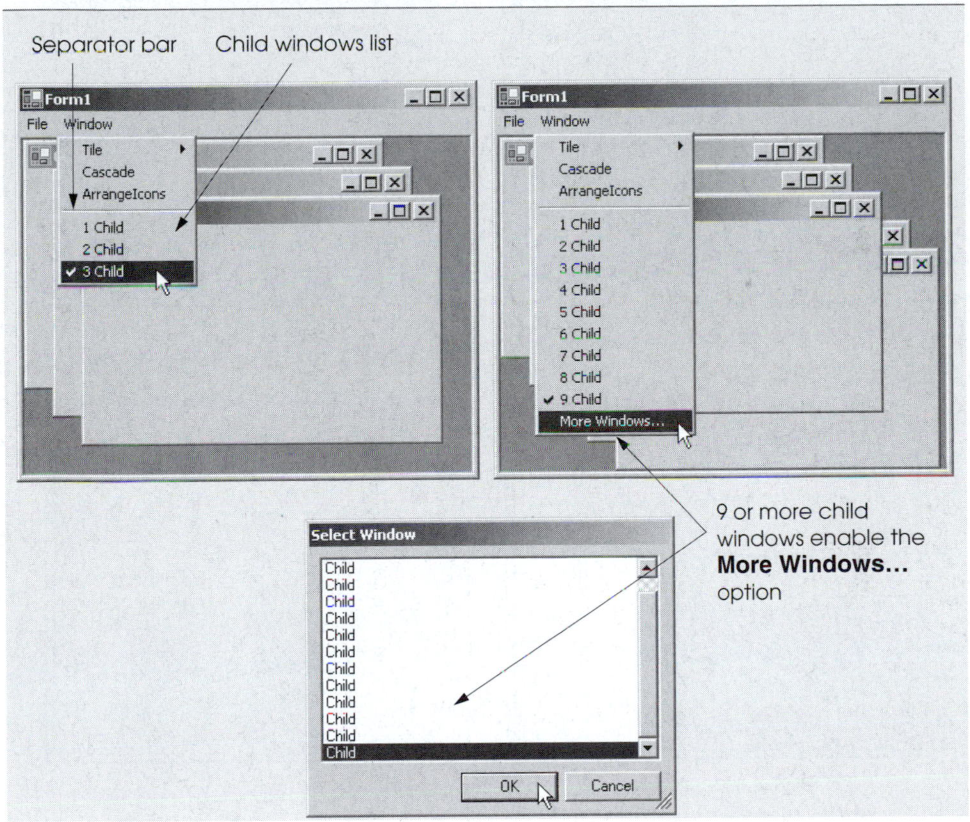

Fig. 13.42 `MenuItem` property `MdiList` example.

Good Programming Practice 13.1

When creating MDI applications, include a menu item with its `MdiList` *property set to* `true`*. This helps the user select a child window quickly, rather than having to search for it in the parent window. This feature normally appears in the* **Window** *menu.*

MDI containers allow developers to organize child window placement. The child windows in an MDI application can be arranged by calling method `LayoutMdi` of the parent form. Method `LayoutMdi` takes an `MdiLayout` enumeration value—`ArrangeIcons`, `Cascade`, `TileHorizontal` or `TileVertical`. *Tiled windows* completely fill the parent and do not overlap; such windows can be arranged horizontally (value `TileHorizontal`) or vertically (value `TileVertical`). *Cascaded windows* (value `Cascade`) overlap—each is the same size and displays a visible title bar, if possible. Value `ArrangeIcons` arranges the icons for any minimized child windows. If minimized windows are scattered around the parent window, value `ArrangeIcons` orders them neatly at the bottom-left corner of the parent window. Figure 13.43 illustrates the values of the `MdiLayout` enumeration.

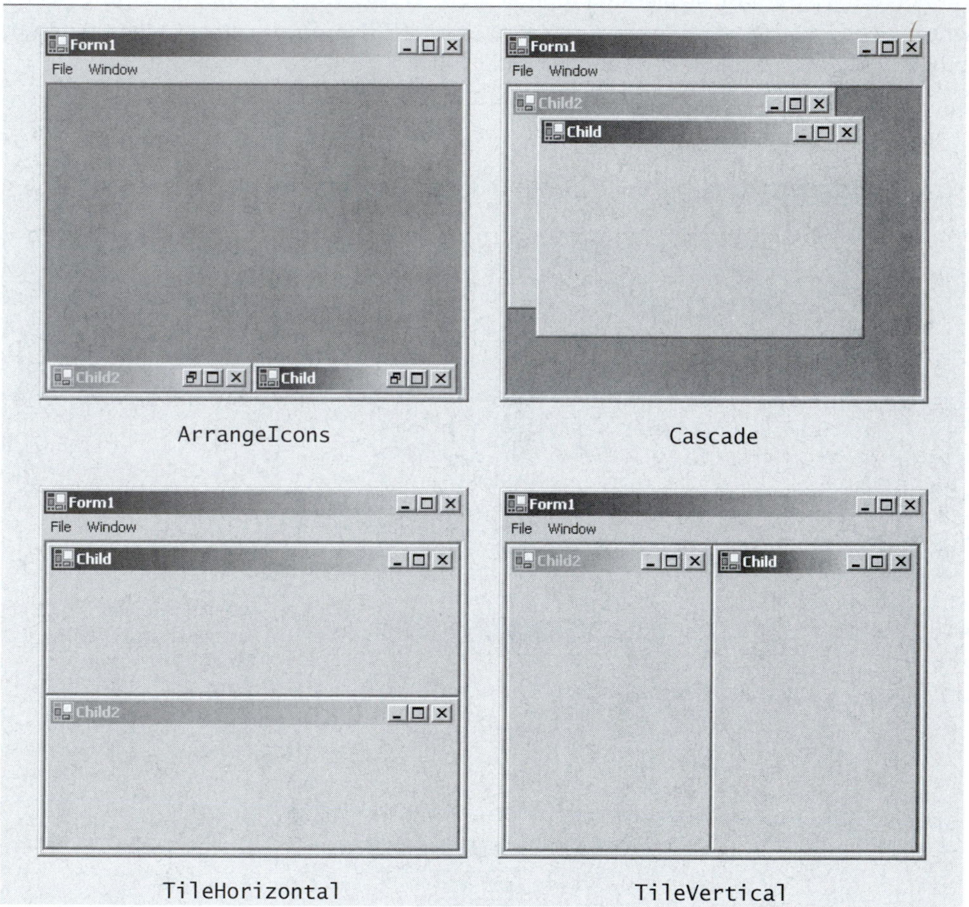

Fig. 13.43 `MdiLayout` enumeration values.

The next application demonstrates MDI windows. The application contains classes `Child` (Fig. 13.44) and `Form1` (Fig. 13.45). Class `Form1` uses three instances of class `Child`, each of which contains a `PictureBox` and an image. The parent MDI form contains a menu that enables users to create and arrange child forms.

The MDI parent form contains two top-level menus. The first of these menus, **File** (`fileMenuItem`, line 45 of Fig. 13.45), contains both a **New** submenu (`newMenuItem`, line 46) and an **Exit** item (`exitMenuItem`, line 50). The second menu, **Format** (`formatMenu-Item`, line 51), provides options for laying out the MDI children, plus a list of the active MDI children.

```
// Fig. 13.44: Child.h
// Child window of MDI parent.

#pragma once

using namespace System;
using namespace System::ComponentModel;
using namespace System::Collections;
using namespace System::Windows::Forms;
using namespace System::Data;
using namespace System::Drawing;
using namespace System::IO;

namespace UsingMDI
{
   /// <summary>
   /// Summary for Form1
   ///
   /// WARNING: If you change the name of this class, you will need to
   ///          change the 'Resource File Name' property for the managed
   ///          resource compiler tool associated with all .resx files
   ///          this class depends on.  Otherwise, the designers will not
   ///          be able to interact properly with localized resources
   ///          associated with this form.
   /// </summary>
   public __gc class Child : public System::Windows::Forms::Form
   {
   public:
      Child( String *title, String *fileName )
      {
         this->pictureBox = new PictureBox();
         Text = title;  // set title text

         InitializeComponent();

         // set image to display in pictureBox
         pictureBox->Image = Image::FromFile( String::Concat(
            Directory::GetCurrentDirectory(), fileName ) );
      }

   protected:
      void Dispose(Boolean disposing)
      {
         if (disposing && components)
         {
            components->Dispose();
         }
         __super::Dispose(disposing);
      }
   private: System::Windows::Forms::PictureBox *  pictureBox;

   private:
      /// <summary>
```

Fig. 13.44 Child window of MDI parent. (Part 1 of 2.)

```
      /// Required designer variable.
      /// </summary>
      System::ComponentModel::Container* components;

   // Visual Studio .NET generated GUI code
   };
}
```

Fig. 13.44 Child window of MDI parent. (Part 2 of 2.)

```
// Fig. 13.45: Form1.h
// Demonstrating use of MDI parent and child windows.

#pragma once

#include "Child.h"

namespace UsingMDI
{
   using namespace System;
   using namespace System::ComponentModel;
   using namespace System::Collections;
   using namespace System::Windows::Forms;
   using namespace System::Data;
   using namespace System::Drawing;

   /// <summary>
   /// Summary for Form1
   ///
   /// WARNING: If you change the name of this class, you will need to
   ///          change the 'Resource File Name' property for the managed
   ///          resource compiler tool associated with all .resx files
   ///          this class depends on.  Otherwise, the designers will not
   ///          be able to interact properly with localized resources
   ///          associated with this form.
   /// </summary>
   public __gc class Form1 : public System::Windows::Forms::Form
   {
   public:
      Form1(void)
      {
         InitializeComponent();
      }

   protected:
      void Dispose(Boolean disposing)
      {
         if (disposing && components)
         {
            components->Dispose();
         }
```

Fig. 13.45 Demonstrating use of MDI parent and child windows. (Part 1 of 3.)

```
         __super::Dispose(disposing);
      }
   private: System::Windows::Forms::MainMenu *  mainMenu1;
   private: System::Windows::Forms::MenuItem *  fileMenuItem;
   private: System::Windows::Forms::MenuItem *  newMenuItem;
   private: System::Windows::Forms::MenuItem *  child1MenuItem;
   private: System::Windows::Forms::MenuItem *  child2MenuItem;
   private: System::Windows::Forms::MenuItem *  child3MenuItem;
   private: System::Windows::Forms::MenuItem *  exitMenuItem;
   private: System::Windows::Forms::MenuItem *  formatMenuItem;
   private: System::Windows::Forms::MenuItem *  cascadeMenuItem;
   private: System::Windows::Forms::MenuItem *  tileHorizontalMenuItem;
   private: System::Windows::Forms::MenuItem *  tileVerticalMenuItem;

   private:
      /// <summary>
      /// Required designer variable.
      /// </summary>
      System::ComponentModel::Container * components;

   // Visual Studio .NET generated GUI code

   // create Child 1 when menu clicked
   private: System::Void child1MenuItem_Click(
               System::Object *  sender, System::EventArgs *  e)
            {
               // create new child
               Child *formChild = new Child( S"Child 1",
                  S"\\images\\csharphtp1.jpg" );
               formChild->MdiParent = this;   // set parent
               formChild->Show();             // display child
            } // end method child1MenuItem_Click

   // create Child 2 when menu clicked
   private: System::Void child2MenuItem_Click(
               System::Object *  sender, System::EventArgs *  e)
            {
               // create new child
               Child *formChild = new Child( S"Child 2",
                  S"\\images\\pythonhtp1.jpg" );
               formChild->MdiParent = this;   // set parent
               formChild->Show();             // display child
            } // end method child2MenuItem_Click

   // create Child 3 when menu clicked
   private: System::Void child3MenuItem_Click(
               System::Object *  sender, System::EventArgs *  e)
            {
               // create new child
               Child *formChild = new Child( S"Child 3",
                  S"\\images\\vbnethtp2.jpg" );
               formChild->MdiParent = this;   // set parent
```

Fig. 13.45 Demonstrating use of MDI parent and child windows. (Part 2 of 3.)

```
            formChild->Show();          // display child
         } // end method child3MenuItem_Click

   // exit application
   private: System::Void exitMenuItem_Click(
            System::Object *  sender, System::EventArgs *  e)
         {
            Application::Exit();
         } // end method exitMenuItem_Click

   // set cascade layout
   private: System::Void cascadeMenuItem_Click(
            System::Object *  sender, System::EventArgs *  e)
         {
            this->LayoutMdi( MdiLayout::Cascade );
         } // end method cascadeMenuItem_Click

   // set TileHorizontal layout
   private: System::Void tileHorizontalMenuItem_Click(
            System::Object *  sender, System::EventArgs *  e)
         {
            this->LayoutMdi( MdiLayout::TileHorizontal );
         } // end method tileHorizontalMenuItem_Click

   // set TileVertical layout
   private: System::Void tileVerticalMenuItem_Click(
            System::Object *  sender, System::EventArgs *  e)
         {
            this->LayoutMdi( MdiLayout::TileVertical );
         } // end method tileVerticalMenuItem_Click
   };
}
```

Fig. 13.45 Demonstrating use of MDI parent and child windows. (Part 3 of 3.)

```
// Fig. 13.46: Form1.cpp
// Main application.

#include "stdafx.h"
#include "Form1.h"
#include <windows.h>

using namespace UsingMDI;

int APIENTRY _tWinMain(HINSTANCE hInstance,
                       HINSTANCE hPrevInstance,
                       LPTSTR    lpCmdLine,
                       int       nCmdShow)
{
   System::Threading::Thread::CurrentThread->ApartmentState =
      System::Threading::ApartmentState::STA;
   Application::Run(new Form1());
```

Fig. 13.46 MDI demonstration. (Part 1 of 3.)

```
    return 0;
} // end _tWinMain
```

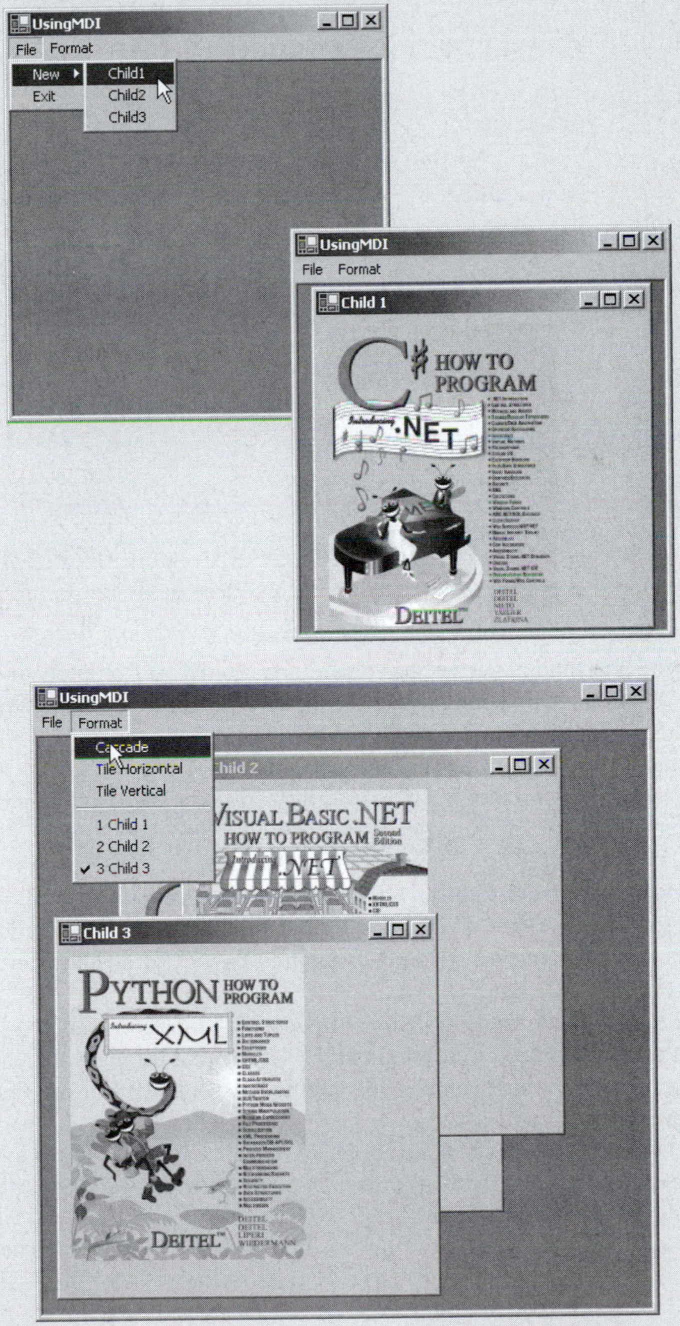

Fig. 13.46 MDI demonstration. (Part 2 of 3.)

Fig. 13.46 MDI demonstration. (Part 3 of 3.)

In the **Properties** window, we set the `Form`'s `IsMdiContainer` property to `True`, making the `Form` an MDI parent. In addition, we set `formatMenuItem` property `MdiList` to `True`. This enables `formatMenuItem` to list the active child MDI windows.

The **Cascade** menu item (`cascadeMenuItem`, line 52 of Fig. 13.45) has an event handler (`cascadeMenuItem_Click`, lines 105–109) that arranges the child windows in a cascading manner. The event handler calls method `LayoutMdi` with the argument `MdiLayout::Cascade` (line 108).

The **Tile Horizontal** menu item (`tileHorizontalMenuItem`, line 53) has an event handler (`tileHorizontalMenuItem_Click`, lines 112–116) that arranges the child windows in a horizontal manner. The event handler calls method `LayoutMdi` with the argument `MdiLayout::TileHorizontal` (line 115).

Finally, the **Tile Vertical** menu item (`tileVerticalMenuItem`, line 54 has an event handler (`tileVerticalMenuItem_Click`, lines 119–123) that arranges the child windows in a vertical manner. The event handler calls method `LayoutMdi` with the argument `MdiLayout::TileVertical` (line 122).

To define the child class for the MDI application, right-click the project in the **Solution Explorer** and select **Add** then **Add New Item**.... Select **Windows Form (.NET)** template and name the new class `Child` (Fig. 13.44).

Next, we add a `PictureBox` (`picDisplay`, line 31) to form `Child`. The constructor invokes method `InitializeComponent` (line 34) and initializes the form's title (line 32) and the image to display in the `PictureBox` (lines 37–38).

The parent MDI form (Fig. 13.45 and Fig. 13.46) creates new instances of class `Child` each time the user selects a new child window from the **File** menu. The event handlers in lines 65–95 of Fig. 13.45 create new child forms that each contain an image. Each event handler creates a new instance of the child form, sets its `MdiParent` property to the parent form and calls method `Show` to display the child.

13.10 Visual Inheritance

In Chapter 9, we discussed how to create classes by inheriting from other classes. We also can use inheritance to create `Form`s that display a GUI, because `Form`s are classes that derive from class `System::Windows::Forms::Form`. Visual inheritance allows us to create a new `Form` by inheriting from another `Form`. The derived `Form` class contains the functionality of its `Form` base class, including any base-class properties, methods, variables and controls. The derived class also inherits all visual aspects—such as sizing, component layout, spacing between GUI components, colors and fonts—from its base class.

Visual inheritance enables developers to achieve visual consistency across applications by reusing code. For example, a company could define a base form that contains a product's logo, a static background color, a predefined menu bar and other elements. Programmers then could use the base form throughout an application for purposes of uniformity and product branding.

Class `VisualInheritance` (Fig. 13.47) is a form that we use as a base class for demonstrating visual inheritance. The GUI contains two labels (one with text **Bugs, Bugs, Bugs** and one with **Copyright 2004, by Bug2Bug.com.**) and one button (displaying the text **Learn More**). When a user presses the **Learn More** button, method `learnMoreButton_Click` (lines 57–64) is invoked. This method displays a message box that provides some informative text.

To allow another form to inherit from class `VisualInheritance`, we must package the class in a DLL. Create a project of type **Class Library (.NET)** called `VisualInheritance`. Next, right click on `VisualInheritance.h` and `VisualInheritance.cpp` in the **Solution Explorer** and select **Remove**. Also, delete these files from the project folder. Then, right click on the `VisualInheritance` project in the **Solution Explorer** and select **Add > Add New Item**…. Add a **Windows Form (.NET)** called `VisualInheritance` to the project. Modify the form using the Form Designer to match Fig. 13.47. Then, build the project to produce the assembly `VisualInheritance.dll` that contains the `VisualInheritance` class.

```
1  // Fig. 13.47: VisualInheritance.h
2  // Base Form for use with visual inheritance.
3
4  #pragma once
5
6  using namespace System;
7  using namespace System::ComponentModel;
8  using namespace System::Collections;
9  using namespace System::Windows::Forms;
10 using namespace System::Data;
11 using namespace System::Drawing;
```

Fig. 13.47 Class `VisualInheritance`, which inherits from class `Form`, contains a button (**Learn More**). (Part 1 of 3.)

```
namespace VisualInheritance
{

   /// <summary>
   /// Summary for VisualInheritance
   ///
   /// WARNING: If you change the name of this class, you will need to
   ///          change the 'Resource File Name' property for the managed
   ///          resource compiler tool associated with all .resx files
   ///          this class depends on.  Otherwise, the designers will not
   ///          be able to interact properly with localized resources
   ///          associated with this form.
   /// </summary>
   public __gc class VisualInheritance :
      public System::Windows::Forms::Form
   {
   public:
      VisualInheritance(void)
      {
         InitializeComponent();
      }

   protected:
      void Dispose(Boolean disposing)
      {
         if (disposing && components)
         {
            components->Dispose();
         }
         __super::Dispose(disposing);
      }
   private: System::Windows::Forms::Label *  bugsLabel;
   private: System::Windows::Forms::Button *  learnMoreButton;
   private: System::Windows::Forms::Label *  label1;

   private:
      /// <summary>
      /// Required designer variable.
      /// </summary>
      System::ComponentModel::Container * components;

   // Visual Studio .NET generated GUI code

   private: System::Void learnMoreButton_Click(
               System::Object *  sender, System::EventArgs *  e)
         {
            MessageBox::Show(
               S"Bugs, Bugs, Bugs is a product of Bug2Bug.com.",
               S"Learn More", MessageBoxButtons::OK,
               MessageBoxIcon::Information );
```

Fig. 13.47 Class `VisualInheritance`, which inherits from class `Form`, contains a button (**Learn More**). (Part 2 of 3.)

```
            } // end method learnMoreButton_Click
    };
}
```

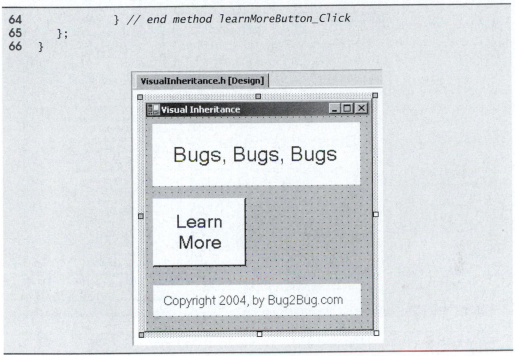

Fig. 13.47 Class `VisualInheritance`, which inherits from class `Form`, contains a button (**Learn More**). (Part 3 of 3.)

To create the derived form through visual inheritance, create a new project of type **Windows Forms Application (.NET)** called `VisualInheritanceTest`. Before the project's form can inherit from class `VisualInheritance`, it must have a reference to the `VisualInheritance` assembly. To add the reference, right click on the `VisualInheritanceTest` project in the **Solution Explorer** and select **Add Reference**.... Using the **Browse**... button, locate and select `VisualInheritance.dll` (in the `Debug` directory of the `VisualInheritance` project), then click **OK** to add the resource to the project. After adding the reference, add a `using` directive to inform that compiler that we will use classes from namespace `VisualInheritance` (line 15 of Fig. 13.49). Then, modify the line of code

```
public __gc class Form1 : public System::Windows::Forms::Form
```

to the following

```
public __gc class Form1 : public VisualInheritance
```

to specify that class `Form1` directly inherits from class `VisualInheritance`. Fig. 13.48 shows how the inherited form appears in the Form Designer after these changes have been made. Notice that inherited components are tagged with small arrows.

Class `Form1` of Fig. 13.49 derives from class `VisualInheritance`. The GUI contains those components derived from class `VisualInheritance`, plus a button with text **Learn The Program** that we added to class `Form1`. When a user presses this button, method `learnProgramButton_Click` (lines 55–62 of Fig. 13.49) is invoked. This method displays a simple message box.

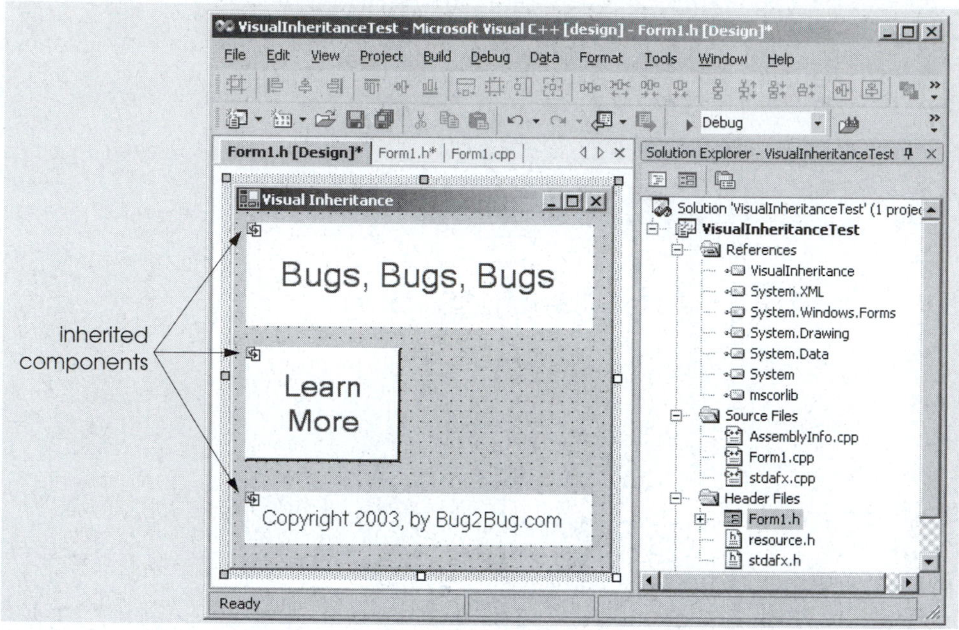

Fig. 13.48 Visual Inheritance displayed in the Form Designer.

```
// Fig. 13.49: Form1.h
// Derived Form using visual inheritance.

#pragma once


namespace VisualInheritanceTest
{
   using namespace System;
   using namespace System::ComponentModel;
   using namespace System::Collections;
   using namespace System::Windows::Forms;
   using namespace System::Data;
   using namespace System::Drawing;
   using namespace VisualInheritance;

   /// <summary>
   /// Summary for Form1
   ///
   /// WARNING: If you change the name of this class, you will need to
   ///          change the 'Resource File Name' property for the managed
   ///          resource compiler tool associated with all .resx files
   ///          this class depends on.  Otherwise, the designers will not
   ///          be able to interact properly with localized resources
   ///          associated with this form.
```

Fig. 13.49 Class `Form1`, which inherits from class `VisualInheritance`, contains an additional button. (Part 1 of 2.)

```
    /// </summary>
    public __gc class Form1 : public VisualInheritance
    {
    public:
       Form1(void)
       {
          InitializeComponent();
       }

    protected:
       void Dispose(Boolean disposing)
       {
          if (disposing && components)
          {
             components->Dispose();
          }
          __super::Dispose(disposing);
       }
    private: System::Windows::Forms::Button *  learnProgramButton;

    private:
       /// <summary>
       /// Required designer variable.
       /// </summary>
       System::ComponentModel::Container * components;

    // Visual Studio .NET generated GUI code

    // invoke when user clicks Learn the Program Button
    private: System::Void learnProgramButton_Click(
                System::Object *  sender, System::EventArgs *  e)
             {
                MessageBox::Show(
                   S"This program was created by Deitel & Associates.",
                   S"Learn the Program", MessageBoxButtons::OK,
                   MessageBoxIcon::Information );
             } // end method learnProgramButton_Click
    };
}
```

Fig. 13.49 Class `Form1`, which inherits from class `VisualInheritance`, contains an additional button. (Part 2 of 2.)

Figure 13.50 demonstrates that the components, their layouts and the functionality of the base class `VisualInheritance` (Fig. 13.47) are inherited by `Form1`. If a user clicks button **Learn More**, the base-class event handler `learnMoreButton_Click` displays a `MessageBox`.

```
// Fig. 13.50: Form1.cpp
// Entry point for application.

```

Fig. 13.50 Visual inheritance demonstration. (Part 1 of 2.)

```
#include "stdafx.h"
#include "Form1.h"
#include <windows.h>

using namespace VisualInheritanceTest;

int APIENTRY _tWinMain(HINSTANCE hInstance,
                       HINSTANCE hPrevInstance,
                       LPTSTR    lpCmdLine,
                       int       nCmdShow)
{
   System::Threading::Thread::CurrentThread->ApartmentState =
      System::Threading::ApartmentState::STA;
   Application::Run(new Form1());
   return 0;
} // end _tWinMain
```

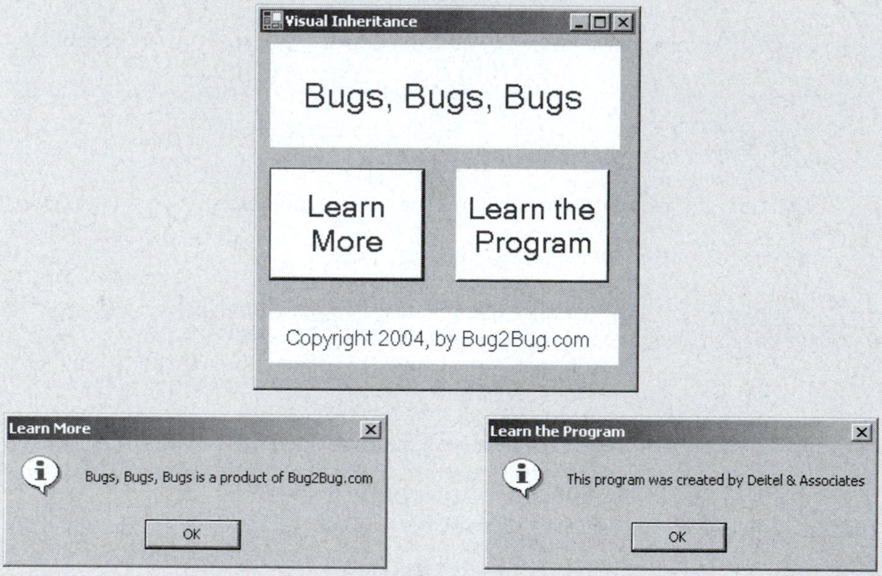

Fig. 13.50 Visual inheritance demonstration. (Part 2 of 2.)

13.11 User-Defined Controls

The .NET Framework allows programmers to create *custom controls* that can appear in the user's **Toolbox** and be added to `Forms`, `Panels` or `GroupBoxes` in the same way that we add `Buttons`, `Labels` and other predefined controls. The simplest way to create a custom control is to derive a class from an existing Windows Forms control, such as a `Label`. This is useful if the programmer wants to include functionality of an existing control, rather than having to reimplement the existing control in addition to including the desired new functionality. For example, we can create a new type of label that behaves like a normal `Label` but has a different appearance. We accomplish this by inheriting from class `Label` and overriding method `OnPaint`.

Look-and-Feel Observation 13.6

To change the appearance of any control, override method `OnPaint`.

All controls contain method *`OnPaint`*, which the system calls to redraw a component, which occurs in several cases, such as when a component is resized. Method `OnPaint` is passed a *`PaintEventArgs`* object, which contains graphics information—property *`Graphics`* is the graphics object used to draw on the control and property *`ClipRectangle`* defines the rectangular boundary of the control. Whenever the system generates the `Paint` event (e.g., method `OnPaint` is invoked), our control's base class catches the event. Event *`Paint`* is generated when a control is redrawn. Through polymorphism, our control's `OnPaint` method is called. If the new control requires code from the base class's `OnPaint` to execute, the new control's `OnPaint` must call the base class's version explicitly. This is normally the first statement in the overridden `OnPaint`.

To create a new control composed of existing controls, use class *`UserControl`*. Controls added to a custom control are called *constituent controls*. For example, a programmer could create a `UserControl` composed of a button, a label and a textbox, each associated with some functionality (such as that the button sets the label's text to that contained in the text box). The `UserControl` acts as a container for the controls added to it. The `UserControl` cannot determine how its constituent controls are drawn. Method `OnPaint` cannot be overridden in these custom controls—their appearance can be modified only by handling each constituent control's `Paint` event. The `Paint` event handler is passed a `PaintEventArgs` object, which can be used to draw graphics (lines, rectangles etc.) on the constituent controls.

A programmer can also create a brand-new control by inheriting from class `Control`. This class does not define any specific behavior; that task is left to the programmer. Instead, class `Control` handles the items associated with all controls, such as events and sizing handles. Method `OnPaint` should contain a call to the base class's `OnPaint` method, which calls the `Paint` event handlers. The programmer must then add code for custom graphics inside the overridden `OnPaint` method. This technique allows for the greatest flexibility, but also requires the most planning. All three approaches are summarized in Fig. 13.51.

Custom Control Techniques and `PaintEventArgs` Properties	Description
Inherit from Windows Forms control	Add functionality to a preexisting control. If overriding method `OnPaint`, call base class `OnPaint`. Can only add to the original control appearance, not redesign it.
Create a `UserControl`	Create a `UserControl` composed of multiple preexisting controls (and combine their functionality). Cannot override `OnPaint` methods of custom controls. Instead, add drawing code to a `Paint` event handler. Can only add to the original constituent control's appearance, not redesign it.

Fig. 13.51 Custom control creation. (Part 1 of 2.)

Custom Control Techniques and `PaintEventArgs` Properties	Description
Inherit from class `Control`	Define a brand-new control. Override `OnPaint` method, call base-class method `OnPaint` and include methods to draw the control. Can customize control appearance and functionality.
`PaintEventArgs` Properties	Use this object inside method `OnPaint` or `Paint` to draw on the control.
`Graphics`	Indicates the graphics object of control. Used to draw on control.
`ClipRectangle`	Specifies the rectangle indicating boundary of control.

Fig. 13.51 Custom control creation. (Part 2 of 2.)

We create a "clock" control in Fig. 13.55. This is a `UserControl` composed of a label and a timer—whenever the timer generates an event, the label is updated to reflect the current time.

A ***`Timer`*** (namespace `System::Windows::Forms`) is an invisible component that resides on a form and generates ***`Tick`*** events at a set interval. This interval is set by the `Timer`'s ***`Interval`*** property, which defines the number of milliseconds (thousandths of a second) between events. By default, a timer is disabled (i.e., it is not running).

We also create a `Form` that displays our custom control, `ClockControl` (Fig. 13.55). To create a `UserControl` that can be exported to other solutions, do the following:

1. Create a new project of type **Windows Control Library (.NET)**.
2. In the project, add controls and functionality to the `UserControl` (Fig. 13.52).

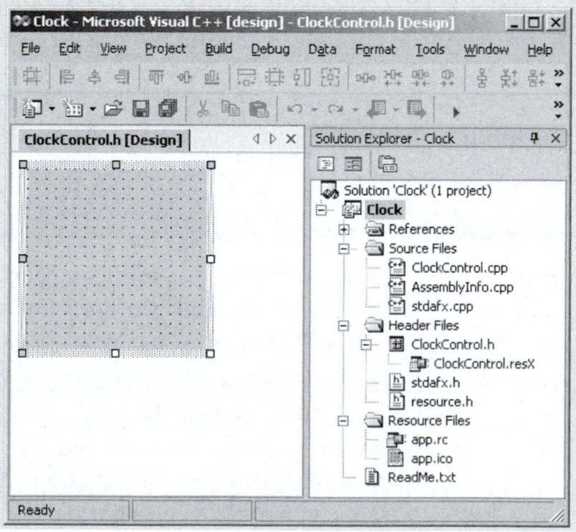

Fig. 13.52 Custom-control creation.

3. Build the project. Visual Studio .NET creates a `.dll` file for the `UserControl` in the project's `Debug` directory.
4. Create a new project of type **Windows Forms Application (.NET)**.
5. Import the `UserControl`. In the new project, right click the **ToolBox** and select **Add/Remove Items…**. In the dialog that appears, select the **.NET Framework Components** tab. Browse for the `.dll` file that contains the desired `UserControl`. Ensure that the checkbox next to the control is checked and click **OK** (Fig. 13.53).

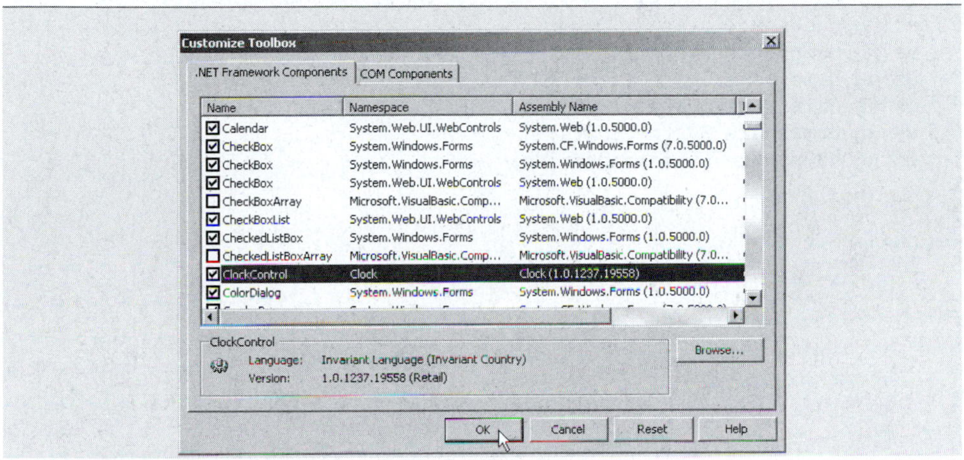

Fig. 13.53 Adding a custom control to the **ToolBox**.

6. The `UserControl` appears on the **ToolBox** and can be added to the form like any other control (Fig. 13.54).

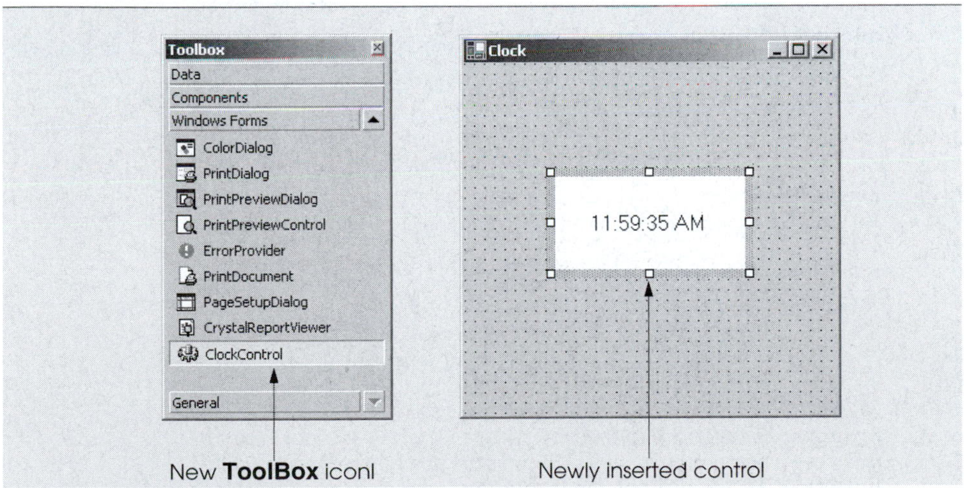

Fig. 13.54 Custom control added to the **ToolBox** and a `Form`.

Fig. 13.55 contains the code for our custom control, `ClockControl` (created using the previously described process) as well as the output of a simple **Windows Forms Application (.NET)** project (not shown) that demonstrates our `ClockControl`.

```
// Fig. 13.55: ClockControl.h
// User-defined control with a timer and a label.

#pragma once

using namespace System;
using namespace System::ComponentModel;
using namespace System::Collections;
using namespace System::Windows::Forms;
using namespace System::Data;
using namespace System::Drawing;


namespace Clock
{
   /// <summary>
   /// Summary for ClockControl
   /// </summary>
   ///
   /// WARNING: If you change the name of this class, you will need to
   ///          change the 'Resource File Name' property for the managed
   ///          resource compiler tool associated with all .resx files
   ///          this class depends on.  Otherwise, the designers will not
   ///          be able to interact properly with localized resources
   ///          associated with this form.
   /// </summary>
   public __gc class ClockControl :
      public System::Windows::Forms::UserControl
   {
   public:
      ClockControl(void)
      {
         InitializeComponent();
      }

   protected:
      void Dispose(Boolean disposing)
      {
         if (disposing && components)
         {
            components->Dispose();
         }
         __super::Dispose(disposing);
      }
   private: System::Windows::Forms::Timer *  clockTimer;
   private: System::Windows::Forms::Label *  displayLabel;
   private: System::ComponentModel::IContainer *  components;

```

Fig. 13.55 Programmer-defined control that displays the current time. (Part 1 of 2.)

```
49       private:
50          /// <summary>
51          /// Required designer variable.
52          /// </summary>
53
54       // Visual Studio .NET generated GUI code
55
56       // update label at every tick
57       private: System::Void clockTimer_Tick(
58                   System::Object *  sender, System::EventArgs *  e)
59                {
60                   // get current time (Now), convert to string
61                   displayLabel->Text = DateTime::Now.ToLongTimeString();
62                } // end method clockTimer_Tick
63       };
64    }
```

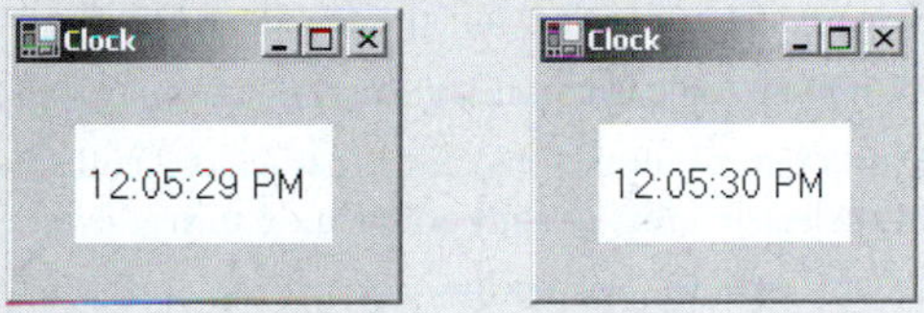

Fig. 13.55 Programmer-defined control that displays the current time. (Part 2 of 2.)

When designing our `ClockControl`, we can treat it like a Windows `Form` in the Form Designer, so we can add controls (using the **ToolBox**) and set properties (using the **Properties** window). However, instead of creating an application, we are simply creating a new control composed of existing controls. We add a `Timer` (`clockTimer`, line 45) and a `Label` (`displayLabel`, line 46) to the `UserControl`. We set the `Timer` interval to 1000 milliseconds and update `displayLabel`'s text with each event (lines 57–62). Note that `clockTimer` must be enabled by setting property `Enabled` to `True` in the **Properties** window.

Structure *`DateTime`* (namespace `System`) contains member `Now`, which is the current time. Method *`ToLongTimeString`* converts `Now` to a `String *` that contains the current hour, minute and second in 12-hour clock format. We use this to set `displayLabel`'s `Text` property in line 61. The `ClockControl` object has a white background to make it stand out in the form.

Many of today's most successful commercial programs provide GUIs that are easy to use and manipulate. Due to this demand for user-friendly GUIs, the ability to design sophisticated GUIs is an essential programming skill. In the last two chapters, we presented the techniques required to add various GUI components to a program. The next chapter explores *multithreading*. In many programming languages, the programmer can create multiple *threads*, enabling several parts of a program to share a single processor, or possibly to execute in parallel on a computer with multiple processors at once. Threads enable programmers to create robust applications that often use the processor more efficiently.

SUMMARY

- Menus provide groups of related commands for Windows applications. Menus are an integral part of GUIs, because they enable user–application interaction without unnecessarily "cluttering" the GUI.
- Window's top-level menus appear on the left of the screen—any submenus or menu items are indented. All menu items can have *Alt* key shortcuts (also called access shortcuts or hot keys).
- Non-top-level menus can have shortcut keys (combinations of *Ctrl*, *Shift*, *Alt,* function keys *F1*, *F2*, letter keys etc.).
- Menus generate a `Click` event when selected.
- The `LinkLabel` control is used to display links to other objects, such as files or Web pages. The links can change color to reflect whether each link is new, visited or active.
- When clicked, a `LinkLabel` generates a `LinkClicked` event.
- The list box control allows the user to view and select multiple items from a list.
- The `CheckedListBox` control extends a list box by accompanying each item in the list with a checkbox. This allows multiple items to be selected with no logical restriction.
- The `SelectionMode` property determines how many items in a `CheckedListBox` can be selected.
- The `SelectedIndexChanged` event occurs when the user selects a new item in a `CheckedListBox`.
- `CheckBox`'s property `Items` returns all the objects in the list as a collection. Property `Selected-Item` returns the currently selected item. `SelectedIndex` returns the index of the selected item.
- Method `GetSelected` takes an index and returns `true` if the corresponding item is selected.
- `CheckedListBox`es imply that multiple items can be selected—the `SelectionMode` property can only have values `None` or `One`. `One` allows multiple selection.
- Event `ItemCheck` is generated whenever a `CheckedListBox` item is about to change.
- The combo box control combines `TextBox` features with a drop-down list. The user can either select an option from the list or type one in (if allowed by the programmer). If the number of elements exceeds the maximum that can be displayed in the drop-down list, a scrollbar appears.
- Property `DropDownStyle` determines the type of combo box.
- The combo box control has properties `Items` (a collection), `SelectedItem` and `SelectedIn-dex`, which are similar to the corresponding properties in `ListBox`.
- When the selected item changes, event `SelectedIndexChanged` is generated.
- The `TreeView` control can display nodes hierarchically on a tree.
- A node is an element that contains a value and references to other nodes.
- A parent node contains child nodes, and the child nodes can be parents themselves.
- A tree is a collection of nodes, usually organized in some manner. The first parent node of a tree is often called the root node.
- Each node has a `Nodes` collection, which contains a list of the `Node`'s children.
- The `ListView` control is similar to a list box—it displays a list from which the user can select one or more items. However, a `ListView` can display icons alongside the list items in a variety of ways.
- A `ListView` control could be used to list directories and files.
- Class `DirectoryInfo` (namespace `System::IO`) allows us to browse or manipulate the directory structure easily. Method returns an array of `DirectoryInfo` objects containing the subdirectories of the current directory. Method `GetFiles` returns an array of class `FileInfo` objects containing the files in the current directory.

- The TabControl control creates tabbed windows. This allows the programmer to provide large quantities of information while saving screen space.
- TabControls contain TabPage objects, which can contain controls.
- Each TabPage generates its own Click event when its tab is clicked. Events for controls inside the TabPage are still handled by the form.
- Single-document-interface (SDI) applications can support only one open window or document at a time. Multiple-document-interface (MDI) programs allows users to edit multiple documents at a time.
- Each window inside an MDI application is called a child window, and the application window is called the parent window.
- To create an MDI form, set the form's IsMDIContainer property to True.
- The parent and child windows of an application can have different menus, which are merged (combined) whenever a child window is selected.
- Class MenuItem property MdiList (a boolean) allows a menu item to contain a list of open child windows.
- The child windows in an MDI application can be arranged by calling method LayoutMdi of the parent form.
- The .NET Framework allows the programmer to create customized controls. The most basic way to create a customized control is to derive a class from an existing Windows Forms control. If we inherit from an existing Windows Forms control, we can add to its appearance, but not redesign it. To create a new control composed of existing controls, use class UserControl. To create a new control from the ground up, inherit from class Control.

TERMINOLOGY

& (menu access shortcut)
access shortcut
Activation property of class ListView
ActiveLinkColor property of class LinkLabel
ActiveMdiChild property of class Form
Add member of enumeration MenuMerge
Add method of TreeNodeCollection
AfterSelect event of class TreeView
ArrangeIcons value in LayoutMdi enumeration
Cascade value in LayoutMdi enumeration
CheckBoxes property of class ListView
CheckBoxes property of class TreeView
Checked property of class MenuItem
Checked property of class TreeNode
CheckedIndices property of CheckedListBox
CheckedItems property of CheckedListBox
CheckedListBox class
CheckOnClick property of CheckedListBox
child node
child window
Clear method of class TreeNodeCollection
Click event of class MenuItem
ClipRectangle property of PaintEventArgs
Collapse method of class TreeNode
collapsing a node
combo box control
ComboBox class
control boundary
CurrentValue event of class CheckedListBox
custom control
DateTime structure
DirectoryInfo class
draw on a control
DrawEllipse method of class Graphics
DrawPie method of class Graphics
DrawRectangle method of class Graphics
drop-down list
DropDown style for ComboBox
DropDownList style for ComboBox
DropDownStyle property of ComboBox
events at an interval
Exit method of class Application
Expand method of class TreeNode
ExpandAll method of class TreeNode
expanding a node
FillEllipse method of class Graphics
FillPie method of class Graphics
FillRectangle method of class Graphics

FirstNode property of class TreeNode
FullName property of FileSystemInfo class
FullPath property of class TreeNode
GetDirectories method of class Directory
GetDirectories method of DirectoryInfo
GetFiles method of class DirectoryInfo
GetItemChecked method of CheckedListBox
GetNodeCount method of class TreeNode
GetSelected method of class ListBox
Graphics class
Graphics property of class PaintEventArgs
hot key
ImageIndex property of class ListViewItem
ImageIndex property of class TreeNode
ImageList class
ImageList property of class TabControl
ImageList property of class TreeView
Index event of class CheckedListBox
Index property of class MenuItem
inherit from a Windows Form control
Interval property of class Timer
IsMdiChild property of class Form
IsMdiContainer property of class Form
ItemActivate event of class ListView
ItemCheck event of class CheckedListBox
ItemCheckEventArgs of CheckedListBox
Items property of class ComboBox
Items property of class ListBox
Items property of class ListView
ItemSize property of class TabControl
LargeImageList property of class ListView
LastNode property of class TreeNode
LayoutMdi method of class Form
LinkArea property of class LinkLabel
LinkBehavior property of class LinkLabel
LinkClicked event of class LinkLabel
LinkColor property of class LinkLabel
LinkLabel class
Links property of class LinkLabel
LinkVisited property of class LinkLabel
list box control
ListBox class
ListView class
MaxDropDownItems property of ComboBox
MDI form
MDI parent-window class
MDI title bar
MdiChildActivate event of class Form
MdiChildren property of class Form
MdiLayout enumeration
MdiList property of class MenuItem
MdiParent property of class Form
menu
menu item
menu, expanded and checked
menu-access shortcut
MenuItem class
MenuItems property of class MainMenu
MenuItems property of class MenuItem
MenuMerge enumeration
MergeItems member of MenuMerge
MergeOrder property of class MenuItem
MergeType property of class MenuItem
MultiColumn property of class ListBox
MultiExtended value of SelectionMode
MultiLine property of class TabControl
multiple-document interface (MDI)
MultiSelect property of class ListView
MultiSimple value of SelectionMode
Name property of class DirectoryInfo
Name property of class FileInfo
NewValue event of CheckedListBox
NextNode property of class TreeNode
Nodes property of class TreeNode
Nodes property of class TreeView
None value of SelectionMode
Now property of structure DateTime
One value of SelectionMode
OnPaint method of class Control
PaintEventArgs class
parent menu
parent node
parent window
PictureBox class
PrevNode property of class TreeNode
Process class
RadioCheck property of class MenuItem
Remove member of enumeration MenuMerge
Remove method of class TreeNodeCollection
Replace member of enumeration MenuMerge
RightToLeft property of class MainMenu
root node
SelectedImageIndex property of TreeNode
SelectedIndex property of class ComboBox
SelectedIndex property of class ListBox
SelectedIndex property of class TabControl
SelectedIndexChanged event of ComboBox
SelectedIndexChanged event of ListBox
SelectedIndexChanged event of TabControl
SelectedIndices property of class ListBox

SelectedItem property of class ComboBox
SelectedItem property of class ListBox
SelectedItems property of class ListBox
SelectedItems property of class ListView
SelectedNode property of class TreeView
SelectedTab property of class TabControl
SelectionMode enumeration
SelectionMode property of CheckedListBox
SelectionMode property of class ListBox
separator bar
shortcut key
Shortcut property of class MenuItem
Show method of class Form
ShowShortcut property of class MenuItem
Simple style for ComboBox
single-document interface (SDI)
SmallImageList property of class ListView
Sorted property of class ComboBox
Sorted property of class ListBox
Start method of class Process
submenu
TabControl class
TabCount property of class TabControl
TabPage class
TabPages property of class TabControl
Text property of class LinkLabel
Text property of class MenuItem
Text property of class TreeNode
Tick event of class Timer
TileHorizontal value of LayoutMdi
TileVertical value of LayoutMdi
tree
TreeNode class
TreeView class
UseMnemonic property of class LinkLabel
UserControl class
user-defined control
View property of class ListView
VisitedLinkColor property of LinkLabel

SELF-REVIEW EXERCISES

13.1 State whether each of the following is *true* or *false*. If *false*, explain why.

a) Menus provide groups of related classes.
b) Menu items can display radio buttons, checkmarks and access shortcuts.
c) The list box control allows only single selection (like a radio button), whereas the CheckedListBox allows multiple selection (like a check box).
d) The combo box control has a drop-down list.
e) Deleting a parent node in a TreeView control deletes its child nodes.
f) The user can select only one item in a ListView control.
g) A TabPage can act as a logical group for radio buttons.
h) An MDI child window can have MDI children.
i) MDI child windows cannot be maximized (enlarged) inside their parent.
j) There are two basic ways to create a customized control.

13.2 Fill in the blanks in each of the following statements:

a) Method ________ of class Process can open files and Web pages, much as can the Run menu in Windows.
b) If more elements appear in a combo box than can fit, a(n) ________ appears.
c) The top-level node in a TreeView is the ________ node.
d) An ImageList is used to display icons in a(n) ________.
e) The MergeOrder and MergeType properties determine how ________ merge.
f) The ________ property allows a menu to display a list of active child windows.
g) An important feature of the ListView control is the ability to display ________.
h) Class ________ allows the programmer to combine several controls into a single, custom control.
i) The ________ saves space by layering TabPages on top of each other.
j) The ________ window layout option makes all windows the same size and layers them so every title bar is visible (if possible).
k) ________ are typically used to display hyperlinks to other objects, files or Web pages.

ANSWERS TO SELF-REVIEW EXERCISES

13.1 a) False. Menus provide groups of related commands. b) True. c) False. Both controls can have single or multiple selection. d) True. e) True. f) False. The user can select one or more items. g) True. h) False. Only an MDI parent window can have MDI children. An MDI parent window cannot be an MDI child. i) False. MDI child windows can be maximized inside of their parent windows. j) False. There are three ways: 1) Derive from an existing control, 2) use a `UserControl` or 3) derive from `Control` and create a control from scratch.

13.2 a) `Start`. b) scrollbar. c) root. d) `ListView`. e) menus. f) `MdiList`. g) icons. h) `UserControl`. i) `TabControl`. j) `Cascade`. k) `LinkLabels`.

EXERCISES

13.3 Write a program that displays the names of 15 states in a combo box. When an item is selected from the combo box, remove it.

13.4 Modify your solution to Exercise 13.3 to add a list box. When the user selects an item from the combo box, remove the item from the combo box, and add it to the list box. Your program should check to ensure that the combo box contains at least one item. If it does not, print a message in a message box, and terminate program execution.

13.5 Write a program that allows the user to enter strings in a `TextBox`. Each string input is added to a list box. As each string is added to the list box, ensure that the strings are in sorted order. Any sorting method may be used.

13.6 Create a file browser (similar to Windows Explorer) based on the programs in Fig. 13.8–Fig. 13.9, Fig. 13.26–Fig. 13.27 and Fig. 13.30–Fig. 13.31. The file browser should have a `TreeView`, which allows the user to browse directories. There should also be a `ListView`, which displays the contents (all subdirectories and files) of the directory being browsed. Double-clicking a file in the `ListView` should open it, and double-clicking a directory in either the `ListView` or the `TreeView` should browse it. If a file or directory cannot be accessed, because of its permission settings, notify the user.

13.7 Create an MDI text editor. Each child window should contain a multiline `TextBox`. The MDI parent should have a `Format` menu, with submenus to control the size, font and color of the text in the active child window. Each submenu should have at least three options. In addition, the parent should have a `File` menu with menu items `New` (create a new child), `Close` (close the active child) and `Exit` (exit the application). The parent should have a `Window` menu to display a list of the open child windows and their layout options.

13.8 Create a `UserControl` called `LoginPasswordUserControl`. The `LoginPasswordUserControl` contains a `Label` (`loginLabel`) that displays `string "Login:"`, a `TextBox` (`loginTextBox`) where the user inputs a login name, a `Label` (`passwordLabel`) that displays the `string "Password:"` and finally, a `TextBox` (`passwordTextBox`) where a user inputs a password (do not forget to set property `PasswordChar` to `"*"`). `LoginPasswordUserControl` must provide public read-only properties `Login` and `Password` that allow an application to retrieve the user input from `loginTextBox` and `passwordTextBox`. The `UserControl` must be exported to an application that displays the values input by the user in `LoginPasswordUserControl`.

14

Multithreading

Objectives

- To understand the concept of multithreading.
- To appreciate how multithreading can improve program performance.
- To understand how to create, manage and destroy threads.
- To understand the life cycle of a thread.
- To understand thread synchronization.
- To understand thread priorities and scheduling.

The spider's touch, how exquisitely fine!
Feels at each thread, and lives along the line.
Alexander Pope

A person with one watch knows what time it is; a person with two watches is never sure.
Proverb

Learn to labor and to wait.
Henry Wadsworth Longfellow

The most general definition of beauty…Multeity in Unity.
Samuel Taylor Coleridge

Outline

14.1 Introduction

It would be nice if we could perform one action at a time and perform it well, but that is usually difficult to do. The human body performs a great variety of operations *in parallel*—or, as we will say throughout this chapter, *concurrently*. Respiration, blood circulation and digestion, for example, can occur concurrently. All the senses—sight, touch, smell, taste and hearing—can occur at once. Computers, too, can perform operations concurrently. It is common for desktop personal computers to be compiling a program, sending a file to a printer and receiving electronic mail messages over a network concurrently.

In the past, most programming languages did not enable programmers to specify concurrent activities. Rather, programming languages generally provided only a simple set of control statements that enabled programmers to perform one action at a time, proceeding to the next action after the previous one has finished. Historically, the type of concurrency that computers perform today generally has been implemented as operating system "primitives" available only to highly experienced "systems programmers."

The Ada programming language, developed by the United States Department of Defense, made concurrency primitives widely available to defense contractors building military command-and-control systems. However, Ada has not been widely used in universities and commercial industry.

The .NET FCL makes concurrency primitives available to the applications programmer. The programmer specifies that applications contain "threads of execution," each thread designating a portion of a program that may execute concurrently with other threads. This capability is called *multithreading*. Multithreading is available to all .NET programming languages, including MC++, C# and Visual Basic .NET. The .NET Framework Class Library includes multithreading capabilities in namespace `System::Threading`.

There are many applications of concurrent programming. For example, when programs download large files, such as audio clips or video clips from the World Wide Web, users do not want to wait until an entire clip downloads before starting the playback. To solve this problem, we can put multiple threads to work—one thread downloads a clip, and another plays the clip. These activities, or *tasks*, then may proceed concurrently. To avoid choppy playback, we *synchronize* the threads so that the player thread does not begin playing until there is a sufficient amount of the clip in memory to keep the player thread busy.

Another example of multithreading is MC++'s automatic *garbage collection*. C and traditional (unmanaged) C++ require the programmer to reclaim dynamic memory. The CLR provides a *garbage-collector thread* that reclaims dynamically allocated memory that is no longer needed.

Performance Tip 14.1

One of the reasons for the popularity of C and C++ over the years was that their memory-management techniques were more efficient than those of languages that used garbage collectors. In fact, memory management in managed C++ often is faster than in C or unmanaged C++.[1]

Good Programming Practice 14.1

Set an object pointer to `0` *(or* `NULL`*) when the program no longer needs that object. This enables the garbage collector to determine at the earliest possible moment that the object can be garbage collected. If such an object has other pointers to it, that object cannot be collected.*

Writing multithreaded programs can be tricky. Although the human mind can perform functions concurrently, people find it difficult to jump between parallel "trains of thought." To see why multithreading can be difficult to program and understand, try the following experiment: Open three books to page 1, and try reading the books concurrently. Read a few words from the first book, then read a few words from the second book, then read a few words from the third book, then loop back and read the next few words from the first book, etc. After this experiment, you will appreciate the challenges of multithreading—switching between books, reading briefly, remembering your place in each book, moving the book you are reading closer so you can see it, pushing books you are not reading aside—and amidst all this chaos, trying to comprehend the content of the books!

Performance Tip 14.2

A problem with single-threaded applications is that lengthy activities must complete before other activities can begin. In a multithreaded application, threads can share a processor (or set of processors), so that multiple tasks are performed in parallel.

14.2 Thread States: Life Cycle of a Thread

At any time, a thread is said to be in one of several *thread states* (illustrated in Fig. 14.1). This section discusses these states and the transitions between states. This section also discusses several methods of classes *`Thread`* and *`Monitor`* (each from namespace `System::Threading`) that cause state transitions.

A `Thread` object begins its life cycle in the *Unstarted* state when the program creates the object and passes a *`ThreadStart`* delegate to the object's constructor. The `ThreadStart` delegate, which specifies the actions the thread will perform during its life cycle, must be a method that returns `void` and takes no arguments. The thread remains in the *Unstarted* state until the program calls the `Thread`'s *`Start`* method, which places the thread in the *Running* state and immediately returns control to the part of the program that called `Start`. Then the newly *Running* thread and any other threads in the program can execute concurrently on a multiprocessor system or share the processor on a system with a single processor.

---

1. E. Schanzer, "Performance Considerations for Run-Time Technologies in the .NET Framework," August 2001 <`http://msdn.microsoft.com/library/default.asp?url=/library/en-us/dndotnet/html/dotnetperftechs.asp`>.

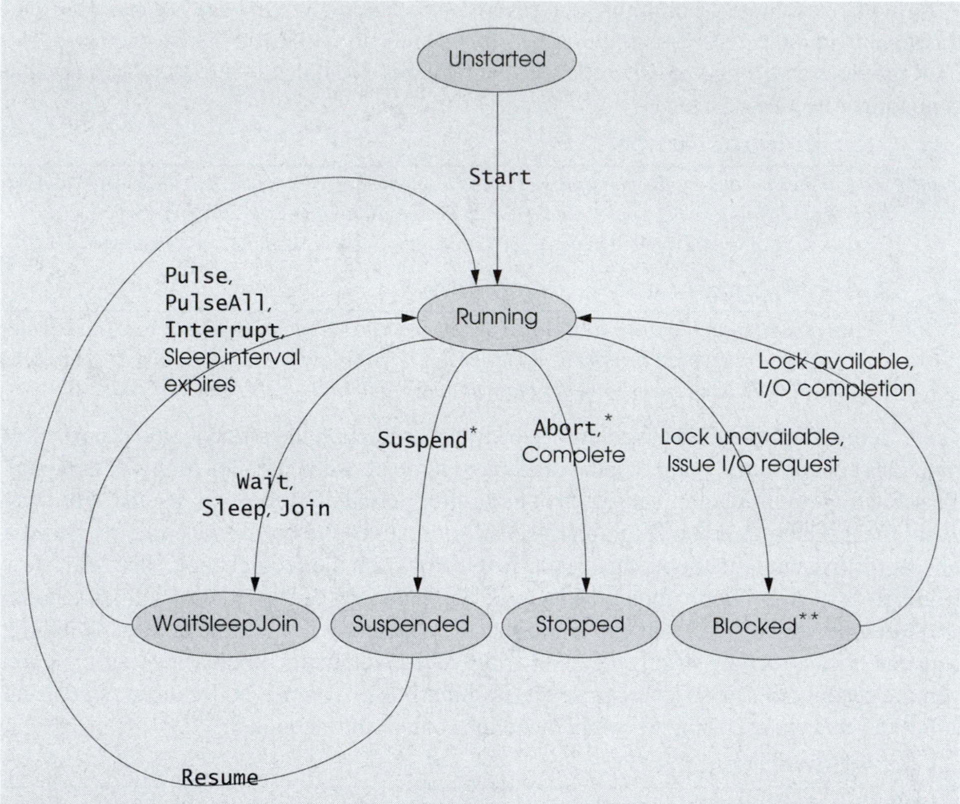

*A thread's **Suspend** and **Abort** methods may be called even if the thread is not in the *Running* state.

**The *Blocked* state is not an actual state in .NET. It is a conceptual state that describes a thread that is not *Running*. We discuss blocked threads in more detail later in this section.

Fig. 14.1 Thread life cycle.

While in the *Running* state, the thread may not actually be executing all the time. The thread executes in the *Running* state only when the operating system assigns a processor to the thread. (Section 14.3 discusses when different threads will be assigned the processor.) When a *Running* thread receives a processor for the first time, the thread begins executing its `ThreadStart` delegate.

A *Running* thread enters the *Stopped* (or *Aborted*) state when its `ThreadStart` delegate terminates. Note that a program can force a thread into the *Stopped* state by calling `Thread` method *`Abort`* on the appropriate `Thread` object. Method `Abort` throws a *`ThreadAbortException`* in the thread, normally causing the thread to terminate. When a thread is in the *Stopped* state and there are no pointers to the thread object, the garbage collector can remove the thread object from memory. [*Note*: Internally, when a thread's `Abort` method is called, the thread actually enters the *AbortRequested* state before entering the *Stopped* state. The thread remains in the *AbortRequested* state while waiting to receive the pending `ThreadAbortException`. When `Abort` is called, if the thread is in the *WaitSleepJoin*, *Sus-*

pended or *Blocked* state, the thread resides in its current state and the *AbortRequested* state, and cannot receive the `ThreadAbortException` until it leaves its current state.]

A thread is considered to be *blocked* if it is unable to use a processor, even if there is a processor available. For example, a thread becomes blocked when the thread issues an input/output request. The operating system blocks the thread from executing until the operating system can complete the I/O for which the thread is waiting. At that point, the thread returns to the *Running* state so it can resume execution. Another case in which a thread becomes blocked is in thread synchronization (Section 14.8). A thread being synchronized must acquire a lock on an object by calling `Monitor` method *`Enter`*.[2] If a lock is not available, the thread is blocked until the desired lock becomes available.

There are three ways by which a *Running* thread can enter the *WaitSleepJoin* state. If a thread encounters code that it cannot execute yet (normally because a condition is not satisfied), the thread can call `Monitor` method *`Wait`* to enter the *WaitSleepJoin* state. Once in this state, a thread returns to the *Running* state only when another thread invokes `Monitor` method *`Pulse`* or *`PulseAll`*. Method `Pulse` moves the next waiting thread back to the *Running* state. Method `PulseAll` moves all waiting threads back to the *Running* state.

A *Running* thread can call `Thread` method *`Sleep`* to enter the *WaitSleepJoin* state for a period of milliseconds specified as the argument to `Sleep`. A sleeping thread returns to the *Running* state when the designated sleep time expires. A sleeping thread cannot use a processor, even if one is available.

Any thread that enters the *WaitSleepJoin* state by calling `Monitor` method `Wait` or by calling `Thread` method `Sleep` can leave the *WaitSleepJoin* state and return to the *Running* state if that `Thread`'s *`Interrupt`* method is called by another thread in the program.

If a thread should not continue executing (we will call this the dependent thread) unless another thread terminates, the dependent thread calls the other thread's *`Join`* method to "join" the two threads and enters the *WaitSleepJoin* state. When two threads are "joined," the dependent thread leaves the *WaitSleepJoin* state when the other thread finishes execution (i.e., when it enters the *Stopped* state).

If a *Running* `Thread`'s *`Suspend`* method is called, the *Running* thread enters the *Suspended* state. A *Suspended* thread returns to the *Running* state when another thread in the program invokes the *Suspended* thread's *`Resume`* method. [*Note*: Internally, when a thread's `Suspend` method is called, the thread actually enters the *SuspendRequested* state before entering the *Suspended* state. The thread remains in the *SuspendRequested* state while waiting to respond to the `Suspend` request. If the thread is in the *WaitSleepJoin* state or is blocked when its `Suspend` method is called, the thread resides in its current state and the *SuspendRequested* state, and cannot respond to the `Suspend` request until it leaves its current state.]

If a thread's *`IsBackground`* property is set to `true`, the thread resides in the *Background* state (not shown in Fig. 14.1). A thread can reside in the *Background* state and any other state simultaneously. A process must wait for all *Foreground threads* (threads not in the *Background* state) to finish executing and enter the *Stopped* state before the process can terminate. However, if the only threads remaining in a process are *Background threads*, the CLR terminates those threads by invoking their `Abort` method and the process terminates.

---

2. Class `Monitor` is used to synchronize threads (see Section 14.5).

14.3 Thread Priorities and Thread Scheduling

Every thread has a priority in the range between `ThreadPriority::Lowest` to `ThreadPriority::Highest`. These two values come from the `ThreadPriority` enumeration (namespace `System::Threading`). The enumeration consists of the values `Lowest`, `BelowNormal`, `Normal`, `AboveNormal` and `Highest`. By default, each thread has priority `Normal`.

The Windows operating system supports a concept, called *timeslicing,* that enables threads of equal priority to share a processor. Without timeslicing, each thread in a set of equal-priority threads runs to completion (unless the thread leaves the *Running* state and becomes blocked) before the thread's peers get a chance to execute. With timeslicing, each thread receives a brief burst of processor time, called a *quantum* or *time slice*, during which the thread can execute. At the completion of the quantum, even if the thread has not finished executing, the processor is taken away from that thread and given to the next thread of equal priority, if one is available.

The job of the thread scheduler is to keep the highest-priority thread running at all times and, if there is more than one highest-priority thread, to ensure that all such threads execute for a quantum in round-robin fashion. Figure 14.2 illustrates the multilevel priority queue for threads. In Fig. 14.2, assuming a single-processor computer, threads A and B each execute for a quantum in round-robin fashion until both threads complete execution. This means that A gets a quantum of time to run. Then B gets a quantum. Then A gets another quantum. Then B gets another quantum. This continues until one thread completes. The processor then devotes all its power to the thread that remains (unless another thread of that priority is executing). Next, thread C runs to completion. Threads D, E and F each execute for a quantum in round-robin fashion until they all complete execution. This process continues until all threads run to completion. Note that, depending on the operating system, new higher-priority threads could postpone—possibly indefinitely—the execution of lower-priority threads. Such *indefinite postponement* often is referred to more colorfully as *starvation*. In Windows, the thread scheduler will, over time, increase the priority of a starving thread, such that the thread will execute for one quantum. Once that quantum expires (and if the thread has not run to completion), the thread is returned to its original priority. The thread scheduler may repeat this action if the thread continues to suffer from indefinite postponement.

A thread's priority can be adjusted with the `Priority` property, which accepts values from the `ThreadPriority` enumeration. If the argument is not one of the valid thread-priority constants, an `ArgumentException` occurs.

A thread executes until it dies; becomes blocked for input/output (or some other reason); calls `Sleep`, `Join` or `Monitor` method `Wait`; is preempted by a thread of higher priority or has its quantum expire. A thread with a higher priority than the executing thread can start executing (and, hence, preempt the previously executing thread) if a sleeping thread wakes up, if I/O completes for a thread that blocked for that I/O, if either `Pulse` or `PulseAll` is called on an object on which `Wait` was called, or if a thread to which the high-priority thread was `Join`ed completes.

14.4 Creating and Executing Threads

Figure 14.3–Fig. 14.5 demonstrate basic threading techniques, including the construction of a `Thread` object and using the `Thread` class's `static` method `Sleep`. The program creates

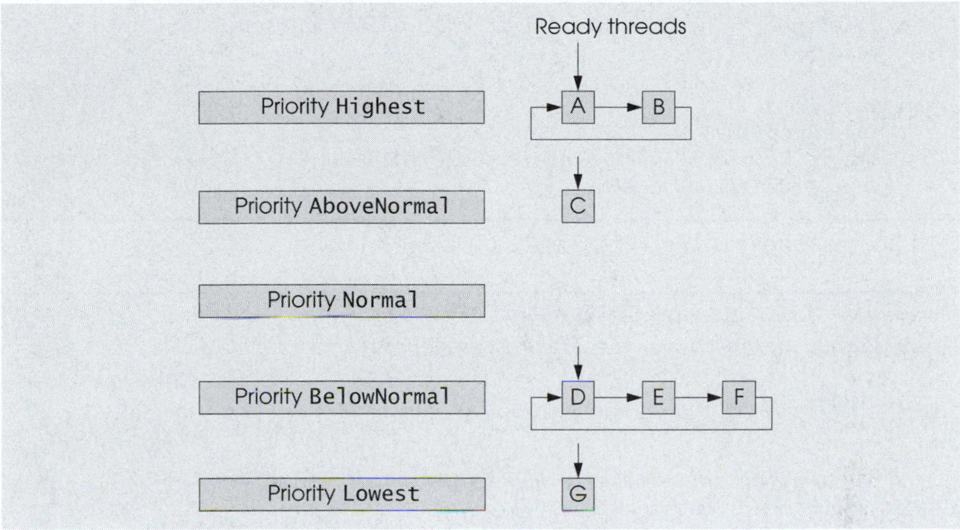

Fig. 14.2 Thread-priority scheduling.

three threads of execution, each with the default priority `Normal`. Each thread displays a message indicating that it is going to sleep for a random amount of time from 0 to 5000 milliseconds, then goes to sleep. When each thread awakens, the thread displays its name, indicates that it is done sleeping, terminates and enters the *Stopped* state. You will see that function `_tmain` (i.e., the *main thread of execution*) terminates before the application terminates. The application consists of class `MessagePrinter` (Fig. 14.3–Fig. 14.4), which defines a `Print` method containing the actions each thread will perform, and main program `ThreadTester` (Fig. 14.5), which creates three threads.

```
// Fig. 14.3: MessagePrinter.h
// Multiple threads printing at different intervals.

#pragma once

#using <mscorlib.dll>

using namespace System;
using namespace System::Threading;

// Print method of this class used to control threads
public __gc class MessagePrinter
{
public:

   // constructor to initialize a MessagePrinter object
   MessagePrinter();

```

Fig. 14.3 `MessagePrinter`. (Part 1 of 2.)

```
   // method Print controls thread that prints messages
   void Print();

private:
   int sleepTime;
   static Random *random = new Random();
}; // end class MessagePrinter
```

Fig. 14.3 MessagePrinter. (Part 2 of 2.)

```
// Fig. 14.4: MessagePrinter.cpp
// Method definitions for class MessagePrinter.

#include "stdafx.h"
#include "MessagePrinter.h"

// constructor to initialize a MessagePrinter object
MessagePrinter::MessagePrinter()
{
   // pick random sleep time between 0 and 5 seconds
   sleepTime = random->Next( 5001 );
}

// method Print controls thread that prints messages
void MessagePrinter::Print()
{
   // obtain pointer to currently executing thread
   Thread *current = Thread::CurrentThread;

   // put thread to sleep for sleepTime amount of time
   Console::WriteLine( String::Concat( current->Name,
      S" going to sleep for ", sleepTime.ToString() ) );

   Thread::Sleep( sleepTime );

   // print thread name
   Console::WriteLine( S"{0} done sleeping", current->Name );
} // end method Print
```

Fig. 14.4 MessagePrinter class method definitions.

```
// Fig. 14.5: ThreadTester.cpp
// Main program for MessagePrinter.

#include "stdafx.h"
#include "MessagePrinter.h"

#using <mscorlib.dll>

using namespace System;

```

Fig. 14.5 ThreadTester demonstrates class MessagePrinter. (Part 1 of 2.)

```
int _tmain()
{
   // Create and name each thread.  Use MessagePrinter's
   // Print method as argument to ThreadStart delegate
   MessagePrinter *printer1 = new MessagePrinter();
   Thread *thread1 = new Thread ( new ThreadStart( printer1,
      &MessagePrinter::Print ) );
   thread1->Name = S"thread1";

   MessagePrinter *printer2 = new MessagePrinter();
   Thread *thread2 = new Thread ( new ThreadStart( printer2,
      &MessagePrinter::Print ) );
   thread2->Name = S"thread2";

   MessagePrinter *printer3 = new MessagePrinter();
   Thread *thread3 = new Thread ( new ThreadStart( printer3,
      &MessagePrinter::Print ) );
   thread3->Name = S"thread3";

   Console::WriteLine( S"Starting threads" );

   // call each thread's Start method to place each
   // thread in Running state
   thread1->Start();
   thread2->Start();
   thread3->Start();

   Console::WriteLine( S"Threads started\n" );

   return 0;
} // end _tmain
```

```
Starting threads
Threads started

thread1 going to sleep for 2109
thread2 going to sleep for 2372
thread3 going to sleep for 4154
thread1 done sleeping
thread2 done sleeping
thread3 done sleeping
```

```
Starting threads
Threads started

thread1 going to sleep for 1271
thread2 going to sleep for 1083
thread3 going to sleep for 919
thread3 done sleeping
thread2 done sleeping
thread1 done sleeping
```

Fig. 14.5 `ThreadTester` demonstrates class `MessagePrinter`. (Part 2 of 2.)

Objects of class MessagePrinter (Fig. 14.3–Fig. 14.4) control the life cycle of each of the three threads that function _tmain creates. Class MessagePrinter consists of variable sleepTime (line 23 of Fig. 14.3), static variable random (line 24), a constructor (lines 8–12 of Fig. 14.4) and a Print method (lines 15–28). The MessagePrinter constructor (lines 8–12) initializes sleepTime to a random integer from 0 up to, but not including, 5001 (i.e., from 0 to 5000). Each thread controlled by a MessagePrinter object sleeps for the amount of time specified by the corresponding MessagePrinter object's sleepTime.

Method Print begins by obtaining a pointer to the currently executing thread (line 18) via class Thread's static property *CurrentThread*. The currently executing thread is the one that invokes method Print. Next, lines 21–22 display a message indicating the name of the currently executing thread and stating that the thread is going to sleep for a certain number of milliseconds. Note that line 21 uses the currently executing thread's *Name* property to obtain the thread's name (set in function _tmain when each thread is created). Line 24 invokes static Thread method Sleep to place the thread into the *WaitSleepJoin* state. At this point, the thread loses the processor and the system allows another thread to execute. When the thread awakens, it reenters the *Running* state again and waits until the system assigns a processor to the thread. When the MessagePrinter object begins executing again, line 27 displays the thread's name in a message that indicates the thread is done sleeping, and method Print terminates.

Function _tmain (Fig. 14.5) creates three objects of class MessagePrinter, in lines 15, 20 and 25, respectively. Lines 16–17, 21–22 and 26–27 create and initialize three Thread objects. Lines 18, 23 and 28 set each Thread's Name property, which we use for output purposes. Note that each Thread's constructor receives a ThreadStart delegate as an argument. Remember that a ThreadStart delegate specifies the actions a thread performs during its life cycle. Lines 16–17 specify that the delegate for thread1 will be printer1's Print method. When thread1 enters the *Running* state for the first time and begins executing, thread1 will invoke printer1's Print method to perform the tasks specified in method Print's body. Thus, thread1 will print its name, display the amount of time for which it will go to sleep, sleep for that amount of time, wake up and display a message indicating that the thread is done sleeping. At that point, method Print will terminate. A thread completes its task when the method specified by a Thread's ThreadStart delegate terminates, placing the thread in the *Stopped* state. When thread2 and thread3 enter the *Running* state for the first time and begin executing, they invoke the Print methods of printer2 and printer3, respectively. Threads thread2 and thread3 perform the same tasks as thread1 by executing the Print methods of the objects to which printer2 and printer3 point (each of which has its own randomly chosen sleep time).

Error-Prevention Tip 14.1

Naming threads helps in the debugging of a multithreaded program. Visual Studio .NET's debugger provides a **Threads** *window that displays the name of each thread and enables you to view the execution of any thread in the program.*

Lines 34–36 invoke each Thread's Start method to place the threads in the *Running* state (sometimes called *launching a thread*). Method Start returns immediately from each invocation, then line 38 outputs a message indicating that the threads were started, and the main thread of execution terminates. The program itself does not terminate, however, because there are still threads that are alive (i.e., threads that were started have not reached the *Stopped* state yet). The program will not terminate until its last thread dies. When the system assigns a processor to a thread, the thread starts executing and calls the method specified by the thread's `ThreadStart` delegate. In this program, each thread invokes method `Print` of the appropriate `MessagePrinter` object to perform the tasks discussed previously.

Note that the program's sample outputs show each thread and its sleep time as the thread goes to sleep. The thread with the shortest sleep time normally awakens first, then indicates that it is done sleeping and terminates. In Section 14.8, we discuss multithreading issues that could prevent the thread with the shortest sleep time from awakening first.

14.5 Thread Synchronization and Class `Monitor`

Often, multiple threads of execution manipulate shared data. If threads with access to shared data simply read that data, then there is no need to prevent the data from being accessed by more than one thread at a time. However, when multiple threads share data and that data is modified by one or more of those threads, then indeterminate results may occur. If one thread is in the process of updating the data and another thread tries to update it also, the data will reflect the update that occurs second. If the data is an array or other data structure in which the threads could update separate parts of the data concurrently, it is possible that part of the data will reflect the information from one thread while another part of the data will reflect information from a different thread. When this happens, the program has difficulty determining when the data has been updated properly.

The problem can be solved by giving one thread at a time exclusive access to code that manipulates the shared data. During that time, other threads desiring to manipulate the data should be kept waiting. When the thread with exclusive access to the data completes its manipulation of the data, one of the threads waiting to manipulate the data should be allowed to proceed. In this fashion, each thread accessing the shared data excludes all other threads from doing so simultaneously. This is called *mutual exclusion* or *thread synchronization*.

MC++ uses the .NET Framework's monitors[3] to perform synchronization. Class `Monitor` provides the methods for *locking objects* to implement synchronized access to shared data. Locking an object means that only one thread can access that object at a time. When a thread wishes to acquire exclusive control over an object, the thread invokes `Monitor` method *`Enter`* to acquire the lock on that data object. After acquiring the lock for an object, a thread can manipulate that object's data. While the object is locked, all other threads attempting to acquire the lock on that object are blocked from acquiring the lock. When the thread that locked the shared object no longer requires the lock, that thread invokes `Monitor` method *`Exit`* to release the lock. At this point, if there is a thread that was previously blocked from acquiring the lock on the shared object, that thread acquires the lock to begin its processing of the object. If all threads with access to an object attempt to acquire the object's lock before manipulating the object, only one thread at a time will be allowed to manipulate the object. This helps ensure the integrity of the data.

---

3. Hoare, C. A. R., Monitors: An Operating System Structuring Concept, *Communications of the ACM*. Vol. 17, No. 10, October 1974: 549–557. *Corrigendum, Communications of the ACM*. Vol. 18, No. 2, February 1975: 95.

Good Programming Practice 14.2

Make sure that all code that updates a shared object locks the object before doing so. Otherwise, a thread calling a method that does not lock the object can make the object unstable even when another thread has acquired the lock for the object.

Performance Tip 14.3

Placing the fewest number of statements necessary to update a shared object between calls to `Monitor` methods `Enter` and `Exit` minimizes the time that other threads must wait before updating the same object.

Common Programming Error 14.1

Deadlock occurs when a waiting thread (let us call this thread1*) cannot proceed because it is waiting for another thread (let us call this* thread2*) to proceed. Similarly,* thread2 *cannot proceed because it is waiting for* thread1 *to proceed. The two threads are waiting for each other; therefore, the actions that would enable each thread to continue execution never occur. The document at `ms-help://MS.VSCC/MS.MSDNVS/cpguide/html/cpconthreading.htm` provides links to more information about threading and resolving deadlocks.*

If a thread determines that it cannot perform its task on a locked object, the thread can call `Monitor` method `Wait` and pass as an argument the object on which the thread will wait until the thread can perform its task. Invoking `Monitor::Wait` places that thread into the *WaitSleepJoin* state for that object. A thread in the *WaitSleepJoin* state for an object leaves the *WaitSleepJoin* state when a separate thread invokes `Monitor` method `Pulse` or `PulseAll` with the object as an argument. Method `Pulse` transitions the object's first waiting thread from the *WaitSleepJoin* state to the *Running* state. Method `PulseAll` transitions all threads in the object's *WaitSleepJoin* state to the *Running* state. The transition to the *Running* state enables the thread (or threads) to get ready to continue executing.

Notice the difference between calling `Monitor` method `Enter` when a lock is not available and calling `Monitor` method `Wait`. Threads that call `Monitor` method `Wait` with the object as an argument wait in that object's *WaitSleepJoin* state. Threads that call `Monitor` method `Enter` while a lock is unavailable become blocked and wait there until the object's lock becomes available. Then, one of the blocked threads can acquire the object's lock.

`Monitor` methods `Enter`, `Exit`, `Wait`, `Pulse` and `PulseAll` all take a pointer to an object—usually the `this` pointer—as their argument.

Common Programming Error 14.2

A thread placed in the WaitSleepJoin *state by a call to method `Wait` cannot reenter the* Running *state to continue execution until a separate thread invokes `Monitor` method `Pulse` or `PulseAll` with the appropriate object as an argument or invokes `Thread` method `Interrupt` on the thread. If this does not occur, the waiting thread will wait forever and might cause deadlock.*

Error-Prevention Tip 14.2

When multiple threads manipulate a shared object, using monitors, ensure that if one thread calls `Monitor` method `Wait` to enter the WaitSleepJoin *state for the shared object, a separate thread eventually will call `Monitor` method `Pulse` to transition the thread waiting on the shared object back to the* Running *state. If multiple threads may be waiting for the shared object, a separate thread can call `Monitor` method `PulseAll` as a safeguard to ensure that all waiting threads have another opportunity to perform their tasks.*

Performance Tip 14.4

Synchronization to achieve correctness in multithreaded programs can make programs run more slowly, as a result of monitor overhead and the frequent transitioning of threads among the Running *and* WaitSleepJoin *states. There is not much to say, however, for highly efficient, incorrect multithreaded programs!*

14.6 Producer/Consumer Relationship without Thread Synchronization

In a *producer/consumer relationship*, the *producer* portion of an application generates data and the *consumer* portion of an application uses that data. In a multithreaded producer/consumer relationship, a *producer thread* calls a *produce method* to generate data and place it into a shared region of memory, called a *buffer*. A *consumer thread* calls a *consume method* to read that data from the buffer. If the producer waiting to put the next data into the buffer determines that the consumer has not yet read the previous data from the buffer, the producer thread should call `Wait`; otherwise, the consumer never sees the previous data and that data is lost to that application. When the consumer thread reads the message, it should call `Pulse` to allow a waiting producer to proceed. If a consumer thread finds the buffer empty or finds that the previous data has already been read, the consumer should call `Wait`; otherwise, the consumer might read "garbage" from the buffer or the consumer might process a previous data item more than once—each of these possibilities results in a logic error in the application. When the producer places the next data into the buffer, the producer should call `Pulse` to allow the consumer thread to proceed.

Let us consider how logic errors can arise if we do not synchronize access among multiple threads manipulating shared data. Consider a producer/consumer relationship in which a producer thread writes a sequence of numbers (we use 1–4) into a *shared buffer*—a memory location shared between multiple threads. The consumer thread reads this data from the shared buffer then displays the data. We display in the program's output the values that the producer writes (produces) and that the consumer reads (consumes). The next application demonstrates a producer and a consumer accessing a single shared cell (`int` variable `buffer`) of memory without any synchronization. Both the consumer and the producer threads access this single cell: The producer thread writes to the cell; the consumer thread reads from it. We would like each value the producer thread writes to the shared cell to be consumed exactly once by the consumer thread. However, the threads in this example are not synchronized. Therefore, data can be lost if the producer places new data into the buffer before the consumer consumes the previous data. Also, data can be incorrectly repeated if the consumer consumes data again before the producer produces the next item. To show these possibilities, the consumer thread in the following example keeps a total of all the values it reads. The producer thread produces values from 1 to 4. If the consumer reads each value produced once and only once, the total would be 10. However, if you execute this program several times, you will see that the total is rarely, if ever, 10. Also, to emphasize our point, the producer and consumer threads in the example each sleep for random intervals of up to three seconds between performing their tasks. Thus, we do not know exactly when the producer thread will attempt to write a new value, nor do we know when the consumer thread will attempt to read a value.

The program consists of three classes—`HoldIntegerUnsynchronized` (Fig. 14.6), `Producer` (Fig. 14.7–Fig. 14.8) and `Consumer` (Fig. 14.9–Fig. 14.10)—and function `_tmain` (Fig. 14.11).

Class `HoldIntegerUnsynchronized` (Fig. 14.6) consists of a no-argument constructor (lines 17–20), variable `buffer` (line 42) and property `Buffer` (lines 23–37), which provides both *get* and *set* methods. Variable `buffer` is initialized using the constructor's member initializer list (line 18). Property `Buffer`'s methods do not synchronize access to variable `buffer`. Note that each method uses class `Thread`'s `static` property `CurrentThread` to obtain a pointer to the currently executing thread, then uses that thread's property `Name` to obtain the thread's name.

```
1  // Fig. 14.6: Unsynchronized.h
2  // Showing multiple threads modifying a shared object without
3  // synchronization.
4
5  #pragma once
6
7  #using <mscorlib.dll>
8
9  using namespace System;
10 using namespace System::Threading;
11
12 // represents a single shared int
13 public __gc class HoldIntegerUnsynchronized
14 {
15 public:
16
17    HoldIntegerUnsynchronized() :
18       buffer( -1 )
19    {
20    }
21
22    // property Buffer
23    __property int get_Buffer()
24    {
25       Console::WriteLine( S"{0} reads {1}",
26          Thread::CurrentThread->Name, buffer.ToString() );
27
28       return buffer;
29    }
30
31    __property void set_Buffer( int value )
32    {
33       Console::WriteLine( S"{0} writes {1}",
34          Thread::CurrentThread->Name, value.ToString() );
35
36       buffer = value;
37    }
38
```

Fig. 14.6 `HoldIntegerUnsynchronized` class modifies as object without using synchronization. (Part 1 of 2.)

```
private:

   // buffer shared by producer and consumer threads
   int buffer;
}; // end class HoldIntegerUnsynchronized
```

Fig. 14.6 `HoldIntegerUnsynchronized` class modifies as object without using synchronization. (Part 2 of 2.)

Class `Producer` (Fig. 14.7–Fig. 14.8) consists of variable `sharedLocation` (line 20 of Fig. 14.7), variable `randomSleepTime` (line 21), a constructor (lines 8–12 of Fig. 14.8) to initialize the variables and a `Produce` method (lines 15–26). The constructor initializes variable `sharedLocation` to point to the `HoldIntegerUnsynchronized` object received from function `_tmain` as the argument `shared`. The producer thread in this program executes the tasks specified in method `Produce` of class `Producer`. Method `Produce` contains a `for` statement (lines 19–22) that loops four times. Each iteration of the loop first invokes `Thread` method `Sleep` to place producer thread into the *WaitSleepJoin* state for a random time interval between 0 and 3000 milliseconds. When the thread awakens, line 21 assigns the value of control variable `count` to the `HoldIntegerUnsynchronized` object's `Buffer` property, which causes the *set* method of `HoldIntegerUnsynchronized` to modify the `buffer` variable of the `HoldIntegerUnsynchronized` object. When the loop completes, lines 24–25 display a line of text in the console window indicating that the thread finished producing data and that the thread is terminating, then the `Produce` method terminates, causing the producer thread to enter the *Stopped* state.

```
1  // Fig. 14.7: Producer.h
2  // Class Producer's Produce method controls a thread that
3  // stores values from 1 to 4 in sharedLocation.
4
5  #pragma once
6
7  #include "Unsynchronized.h"
8
9  public __gc class Producer
10 {
11 public:
12
13    // constructor
14    Producer( HoldIntegerUnsynchronized *, Random * );
15
16    // store values 1-4 in object sharedLocation
17    void Produce();
18
19 private:
20    HoldIntegerUnsynchronized *sharedLocation;
21    Random *randomSleepTime;
22 }; // end class Producer
```

Fig. 14.7 `Producer` class controls a thread that stores values in `sharedLocation`.

```
// Fig. 14.8: Producer.cpp
// Method definitions for class Producer.

#include "stdafx.h"
#include "Producer.h"

// constructor
Producer::Producer( HoldIntegerUnsynchronized *shared, Random *random )
{
   sharedLocation = shared;
   randomSleepTime = random;
}

// store values 1-4 in object sharedLocation
void Producer::Produce()
{
   // sleep for random interval up to 3000 milliseconds
   // then set sharedLocation's Buffer property
   for ( int count = 1; count <= 4; count++ ) {
      Thread::Sleep( randomSleepTime->Next( 1, 3000 ) );
      sharedLocation->Buffer = count;
   } // end for

   Console::WriteLine( S"{0} done producing.\nTerminating {0}.",
      Thread::CurrentThread->Name );
} // end method Produce
```

Fig. 14.8 Producer class method definitions.

Class `Consumer` (Fig. 14.9–Fig. 14.10) consists of variable `sharedLocation` (line 20 of Fig. 14.9), variable `randomSleepTime` (line 21), a constructor (lines 8–12 of Fig. 14.10) to initialize the variables and a `Consume` method (lines 15–29). The constructor initializes `sharedLocation` to point to the `HoldIntegerUnsynchronized` object received from `_tmain` as the argument `shared`. The consumer thread in this program performs the tasks specified in class `Consumer`'s `Consume` method. The method contains a `for` statement (lines 21–24) that loops four times. Each iteration of the loop invokes `Thread` method `Sleep` to put the consumer thread into the *WaitSleepJoin* state for a random time interval between 0 and 3000 milliseconds. Next, line 23 gets the value of the `HoldIntegerUnsynchronized` object's `Buffer` property and adds the value to the variable `sum`. When the loop completes, lines 26–28 display a line in the console window indicating the sum of all values read, then the `Consume` method terminates, causing the consumer thread to enter the *Stopped* state.

```
1  // Fig. 14.9: Consumer.h
2  // Class Consumer's Consume method controls a thread that
3  // loops four times and reads a value from sharedLocation.
4
5  #pragma once
6
7  #include "Unsynchronized.h"
8
```

Fig. 14.9 Consumer class that reads a value from sharedLocation. (Part 1 of 2.)

```
public __gc class Consumer
{
public:

   // constructor
   Consumer( HoldIntegerUnsynchronized *, Random * );

   // read sharedLocation's value four times
   void Consume();

private:
   HoldIntegerUnsynchronized *sharedLocation;
   Random *randomSleepTime;
}; // end class Consumer
```

Fig. 14.9 `Consumer` class that reads a value from `sharedLocation`. (Part 2 of 2.)

```
// Fig. 14.10: Consumer.cpp
// Method definitions for class consumer.

#include "stdafx.h"
#include "Consumer.h"

// constructor
Consumer::Consumer( HoldIntegerUnsynchronized *shared, Random *random )
{
   sharedLocation = shared;
   randomSleepTime = random;
}

// read sharedLocation's value four times
void Consumer::Consume()
{
   int sum = 0;

   // sleep for random interval up to 3000 milliseconds
   // then add sharedLocation's Buffer property value to sum
   for ( int count = 1; count <= 4; count++ ) {
      Thread::Sleep( randomSleepTime->Next( 1, 3000 ) );
      sum += sharedLocation->Buffer;
   } // end for

   Console::WriteLine(
      S"{0} read values totaling: {1}.\nTerminating {0}.",
      Thread::CurrentThread->Name, sum.ToString() );
} // end method Consume
```

Fig. 14.10 `Consumer` class method definitions.

[*Note*: We use method `Sleep` in this example to emphasize the fact that, in multithreaded applications, it is unclear when each thread will perform its task and for how long it will perform that task when it has the processor. Normally, these thread-scheduling issues are the job of the computer's operating system. In this program, our thread's tasks are quite simple—for the producer, loop four times, and perform an assignment statement; for the consumer, loop four times, and add a value to variable `sum`. Without the `Sleep` method call, and if the producer executes first, the producer would complete its task before the consumer ever gets a chance to execute. If the consumer executes first, it would consume `-1` four times, then terminate before the producer can produce the first real value.]

Function `_tmain` (lines 13–41 of Fig. 14.11) instantiates a shared `HoldIntegerUnsynchronized` object (lines 16–17) and a `Random` object (line 20) for generating random sleep times and uses them as arguments to the constructors for the objects of classes `Producer` (lines 23) and `Consumer` (lines 24). The `HoldIntegerUnsynchronized` object contains the data that will be shared between the producer and consumer threads. Lines 28–30 create and name the `producerThread`. The `ThreadStart` delegate for `producerThread` specifies that the thread will execute method `Produce` of object `producer`. Lines 32–34 create and name the `consumerThread`. The `ThreadStart` delegate for the `consumerThread` specifies that the thread will execute method `Consume` of object `consumer`. Finally, lines 37–38 place the two threads in the *Running* state by invoking each thread's `Start` method. Function `_tmain` then terminates.

```
1  // Fig. 14.11: SharedCell.cpp
2  // Create and start producer and consumer threads.
3
4  #include "stdafx.h"
5  #include "Unsynchronized.h"
6  #include "Producer.h"
7  #include "Consumer.h"
8
9  #using <mscorlib.dll>
10
11 using namespace System;
12
13 int _tmain()
14 {
15    // create shared object used by threads
16    HoldIntegerUnsynchronized *holdInteger =
17       new HoldIntegerUnsynchronized();
18
19    // Random object used by each thread
20    Random *random = new Random();
21
22    // create Producer and Consumer objects
23    Producer *producer = new Producer( holdInteger, random );
24    Consumer *consumer = new Consumer( holdInteger, random );
25
26    // create threads for producer and consumer and set
27    // delegates for each thread
28    Thread *producerThread = new Thread( new ThreadStart(
29       producer, Producer::Produce ) );
30    producerThread->Name = S"Producer";
31
```

Fig. 14.11 `SharedCell` demonstrates accessing a shared object without synchronization. (Part 1 of 2.)

```
      Thread *consumerThread = new Thread( new ThreadStart(
         consumer, Consumer::Consume ) );
      consumerThread->Name = S"Consumer";

      // start each thread
      producerThread->Start();
      consumerThread->Start();

      return 0;
   } // end _tmain
```

```
Consumer reads -1
Consumer reads -1
Producer writes 1
Consumer reads 1
Consumer reads 1
Consumer read values totaling: 0.
Terminating Consumer.
Producer writes 2
Producer writes 3
Producer writes 4
Producer done producing.
Terminating Producer.
```

```
Producer writes 1
Producer writes 2
Consumer reads 2
Consumer reads 2
Producer writes 3
Consumer reads 3
Producer writes 4
Producer done producing.
Terminating Producer.
Consumer reads 4
Consumer read values totaling: 11.
Terminating Consumer.
```

```
Producer writes 1
Consumer reads 1
Producer writes 2
Consumer reads 2
Consumer writes 3
Consumer reads 3
Producer writes 4
Producer done producing.
Terminating Producer.
Consumer reads 4
Consumer read values totaling: 10.
Terminating Consumer.
```

Fig. 14.11 `SharedCell` demonstrates accessing a shared object without synchronization. (Part 2 of 2.)

Ideally, we would like every value produced by the `Producer` object to be consumed exactly once by the `Consumer` object. However, when we study the first output of Fig. 14.11, we see that the consumer retrieved a value (`-1`) before the producer ever placed a value in the shared buffer and that the value `1` was consumed twice. The consumer finished executing before the producer had an opportunity to produce the values `2`, `3` and `4`. Therefore, those three values were lost. In the second output, we see that the value `1` was lost, because the values `1` and `2` were produced before the consumer thread could read the value `1`. Also, the value `2` was consumed twice. The last sample output demonstrates that it is possible, with some luck, to get a proper output in which each value the producer produces is consumed once and only once by the consumer. This example clearly demonstrates that access to shared data by concurrent threads must be controlled carefully; otherwise, a program might produce incorrect results.

To solve the problems of lost data and data consumed more than once in the previous example, we will (in Fig. 14.12–Fig. 14.18) synchronize access of the concurrent producer and consumer threads to the code that manipulates the shared data by using `Monitor` class methods `Enter`, `Wait`, `Pulse` and `Exit`. When a thread uses synchronization to access a shared object, the object is *locked*, so no other thread can acquire the lock for that shared object at the same time.

14.7 Producer/Consumer Relationship with Thread Synchronization

Figure 14.12–Fig. 14.18 demonstrate a producer and a consumer accessing a shared cell of memory with synchronization, so that the consumer consumes only after the producer produces a value and the producer produces a new value only after the consumer consumes the previous value produced. Classes `Producer` (Fig. 14.14–Fig. 14.15) and `Consumer` (Fig. 14.16–Fig. 14.17) and function `_tmain` (Fig. 14.18) are identical to Fig. 14.6–Fig. 14.11, except that they use the class `HoldIntegerSynchronized` instead of `HoldIntenterUnsynchronized`.

Class `HoldIntegerSynchronized` (Fig. 14.12–Fig. 14.13) contains two variables—`buffer` (line 113 of Fig. 14.12) and `occupiedBufferCount` (line 116), which are initialized in the constructor's member initializer list (line 18). Also, property `Buffer`'s *get* (lines 23–69) and *set* (lines 72–105) methods now use methods of class `Monitor` to synchronize access to property `Buffer`. Variable `occupiedBufferCount` is known as a *condition variable*—property `Buffer`'s methods use this `int` in conditions to determine whether it is the producer's turn to perform a task or the consumer's turn to perform a task. If `occupiedBufferCount` is `0`, property `Buffer`'s *set* method can place a value into variable `buffer`, because the variable currently does not contain information. However, this means that property `Buffer`'s *get* method currently cannot read the value of `buffer`. If `occupiedBufferCount` is `1`, the `Buffer` property's *get* method can read a value from variable `buffer`, because the variable currently does contain information. In this case, property `Buffer`'s *set* method currently cannot place a value into `buffer`.

```
1  // Fig. 14.12: Synchronized.h
2  // Showing multiple threads modifying a shared object with
3  // synchronization.
```

Fig. 14.12 `HoldIntegerSynchronized` synchronizes access to an object. (Part 1 of 4.)

```

#pragma once

#using <mscorlib.dll>

using namespace System;
using namespace System::Threading;

// this class synchronizes access to an integer
public __gc class HoldIntegerSynchronized
{
public:

   HoldIntegerSynchronized :
      buffer( -1 ), occupiedBufferCount( 0 )
   {
   }

   // property get_Buffer
   __property int get_Buffer()
   {
      // obtain lock on this object
      Monitor::Enter( this );

      // if there is no data to read, place invoking
      // thread in WaitSleepJoin state
      if ( occupiedBufferCount == 0 ) {
         Console::WriteLine( S"{0} tries to read.",
            Thread::CurrentThread->Name );

         DisplayState( String::Concat( S"Buffer empty. ",
            Thread::CurrentThread->Name, S" waits." ) );

         Monitor::Wait( this );
      } // end if

      // indicate that producer can store another value
      // because a consumer just retrieved buffer value
      occupiedBufferCount--;

      DisplayState( String::Concat(
         Thread::CurrentThread->Name, S" reads ",
         buffer.ToString() ) );

      // tell waiting thread (if there is one) to
      // become ready to execute (Running state)
      Monitor::Pulse( this );

      // Get copy of buffer before releasing lock.
      // It is possible that the producer could be
      // assigned the processor immediately after the
      // monitor is released and before the return
      // statement executes.  In this case, the producer
```

Fig. 14.12 `HoldIntegerSynchronized` synchronizes access to an object. (Part 2 of 4.)

```
         // would assign a new value to buffer before the
         // return statement returns the value to the
         // consumer.  Thus, the consumer would receive the
         // new value.  Making a copy of buffer and
         // returning the copy ensures that the
         // consumer receives the proper value.
         int bufferCopy = buffer;

         // release lock on this object
         Monitor::Exit( this );

         return bufferCopy;
      } // end property get_Buffer

      // property set_Buffer
      __property void set_Buffer( int value )
      {
         // acquire lock for this object
         Monitor::Enter( this );

         // if there are no empty locations, place invoking
         // thread in WaitSleepJoin state
         if ( occupiedBufferCount == 1 ) {
            Console::WriteLine( S"{0} tries to write.",
               Thread::CurrentThread->Name );

            DisplayState( String::Concat( S"Buffer full. ",
               Thread::CurrentThread->Name, S" waits." ) );

            Monitor::Wait( this );
         } // end if

         // set new buffer value
         HoldIntegerSynchronized::buffer = value;

         // indicate producer cannot store another value
         // until consumer retrieves current buffer value
         occupiedBufferCount++;

         DisplayState( String::Concat( Thread::CurrentThread->Name,
            S" writes ", buffer.ToString() ) );

         // tell waiting thread (if there is one) to
         // become ready to execute (Running state)
         Monitor::Pulse( this );

         // release lock on this object
         Monitor::Exit( this );
      } // end property set_Buffer

      // display current operation and buffer state
      void DisplayState( String * );

```

Fig. 14.12 HoldIntegerSynchronized synchronizes access to an object. (Part 3 of 4.)

```
110 private:
111
112    // buffer shared by producer and consumer threads
113    int buffer;
114
115    // occupiedBufferCount maintains count of occupied buffers
116    int occupiedBufferCount;
117 }; // end class HoldIntegerSynchronized
```

Fig. 14.12 `HoldIntegerSynchronized` synchronizes access to an object. (Part 4 of 4.)

```
1  // Fig. 14.13: Synchronized.cpp
2  // Method definitions for class HoldIntegerSynchronized
3
4  #include "stdafx.h"
5  #include "Synchronized.h"
6
7  // display current operation and buffer state
8  void HoldIntegerSynchronized::DisplayState( String *operation )
9  {
10    Console::WriteLine( S"{0,-35}{1,-9}{2}\n", operation,
11       buffer.ToString(), occupiedBufferCount.ToString() );
12 } // end method DisplayState
```

Fig. 14.13 `HoldIntegerSynchronized` class method definitions.

The producer thread performs the tasks specified in the `producer` object's `Produce` method. When line 21 (Fig. 14.15) sets the value of `HoldIntegerSynchronized` property `Buffer`, the producer thread invokes the *set* method in lines 72–105 (Fig. 14.12). Line 75 (Fig. 14.12) invokes `Monitor` method `Enter` to acquire the lock on the `HoldIntegerSynchronized` object (`this`). The `if` statement in lines 79–87 determines whether `occupiedBufferCount` is 1. If this condition is `true`, lines 80–81 output a message indicating that the producer thread tries to write a value, and lines 83–84 invoke method `DisplayState` (defined on line 8 Fig. 14.13) to output another message indicating that the buffer is full and that the producer thread waits. Line 86 (Fig. 14.12) invokes `Monitor` method `Wait` to place the calling thread (i.e., the producer) in the *WaitSleepJoin* state for the `HoldIntegerSynchronized` object and releases the lock on the object. Now another thread can invoke an accessor method of the `HoldIntegerSynchronized` object's `Buffer` property.

```
// Fig. 14.14: Producer.h
// Class Producer's Produce method controls a thread that
// stores values from 1 to 4 in sharedLocation.

#pragma once

#include "Synchronized.h"

```

Fig. 14.14 `Producer` class controls a thread that stores values in `sharedLocation`. (Part 1 of 2.)

```
public __gc class Producer
{
public:

   // constructor
   Producer( HoldIntegerSynchronized *, Random * );

   // store values 1 - 4 in object sharedLocation
   void Produce();

private:
   HoldIntegerSynchronized *sharedLocation;
   Random *randomSleepTime;
}; // end class Producer
```

Fig. 14.14 `Producer` class controls a thread that stores values in `sharedLocation`. (Part 2 of 2.)

```
// Fig. 14.15: Producer.cpp
// Method definitions for class Producer.

#include "stdafx.h"
#include "Producer.h"

// constructor
Producer::Producer( HoldIntegerSynchronized *shared, Random *random )
{
   sharedLocation = shared;
   randomSleepTime = random;
}

// store values 1 - 4 in object sharedLocation
void Producer::Produce()
{
   // sleep for random interval up to 3000 milliseconds
   // then set sharedLocation's Buffer property
   for ( int count = 1; count <= 4 ; count++ ) {
      Thread::Sleep( randomSleepTime->Next( 1, 3000 ) );
      sharedLocation->Buffer = count;
   } // end for

   Console::WriteLine( S"{0} done producing.\nTerminating {0}.",
      Thread::CurrentThread->Name );
} // end method Produce
```

Fig. 14.15 `Producer` class method definitions.

The producer thread remains in the *WaitSleepJoin* state until the thread is notified that it may proceed—at which point the thread returns to the *Running* state and waits for the system to assign a processor to the thread. When the thread begins executing, the thread implicitly reacquires the lock on the `HoldIntegerSynchronized` object and the *set* method continues executing with the next statement after `Wait`. Line 90 (Fig. 14.12) assigns `value` to `buffer`. Line 94 increments the `occupiedBufferCount` to indicate that the shared buffer now contains a value (i.e., a consumer can read the value, and a producer cannot yet put another value there). Lines 96–97 invoke method `DisplayState` to output a line to the console window indicating that the producer is writing a new value into the `buffer`. Line 101 invokes `Monitor` method `Pulse` with the `HoldIntegerSynchronized` object as an argument. If there are any waiting threads, the first waiting thread enters the *Running* state, indicating that the thread can now attempt its task again (as soon as the thread is assigned a processor). The `Pulse` method returns immediately. Line 104 invokes `Monitor` method `Exit` to release the lock on the `HoldIntegerSynchronized` object, and the *set* method returns to its caller.

Common Programming Error 14.3

Failure to release the lock on an object when that lock is no longer needed is a logic error. This will prevent the threads in your program that require the lock from acquiring the lock to proceed with their tasks. These threads will be forced to wait (unnecessarily, because the lock is no longer needed). Such waiting can lead to deadlock and indefinite postponement.

The *get* and *set* methods are implemented similarly. The consumer thread performs the tasks specified in the `consumer` object's `Consume` method. The consumer thread gets the value of the `HoldIntegerSynchronized` object's `Buffer` property (line 26 of Fig. 14.17) by invoking the *get* method in Fig. 14.12. Line 26 (Fig. 14.12) invokes `Monitor` method `Enter` to acquire the lock on the `HoldIntegerSynchronized` object.

```
// Fig. 14.16: Consumer.h
// Class Consumer's Consume method controls a thread that
// loops four times and reads a value from sharedLocaton.

#pragma once

#include "Synchronized.h"

public __gc class Consumer
{
public:

   // constructor
   Consumer( HoldIntegerSynchronized *, Random * );

   // read sharedLocation's value four times
   void Consume();

private:
   HoldIntegerSynchronized *sharedLocation;
   Random *randomSleepTime;
}; // end class Consumer
```

Fig. 14.16 `Consumer` class reads values from `sharedLocation`.

```
1  // Fig. 14.17: Consumer.cpp
2  // Method definitions for class Consumer.
3
```

Fig. 14.17 `Consumer` class method definitions. (Part 1 of 2.)

```
#include "stdafx.h"
#include "Consumer.h"

// constructor
Consumer::Consumer( HoldIntegerSynchronized *shared, Random *random )
{
   sharedLocation = shared;
   randomSleepTime = random;
}

// read sharedLocation's value four times
void Consumer::Consume()
{
   int sum = 0;

   // get current thread
   Thread *current = Thread::CurrentThread;

   // sleep for random interval up to 3000 milliseconds
   // then add sharedLocation's Buffer property value to sum
   for ( int count = 1; count <= 4; count++ ) {
      Thread::Sleep( randomSleepTime->Next( 1, 3000 ) );
      sum += sharedLocation->Buffer;
   } // end for

   Console::WriteLine(
      S"{0} read values totaling: {1}.\n"Terminating {0}.",
      Thread::CurrentThread->Name, sum.ToString() );
} // end method Consume
```

Fig. 14.17 `Consumer` class method definitions. (Part 2 of 2.)

The `if` statement in lines 30–38 of Fig. 14.12 determines whether `occupiedBufferCount` is `0`. If this condition is `true`, lines 31–32 output a message indicating that the consumer thread tries to read a value, and lines 34–35 invoke method `DisplayState` to output another message indicating that the buffer is empty and that the consumer thread waits. Line 37 invokes `Monitor` method `Wait` to place the calling thread (i.e., the consumer) in the *WaitSleepJoin* state for the `HoldIntegerSynchronized` object and releases the lock on the object. Now another thread can invoke an accessor method of the `HoldIntegerSynchronized` object's `Buffer` property.

The consumer thread object remains in the *WaitSleepJoin* state until the thread is notified that it may proceed—at which point, the thread returns to the *Running* state and waits for the system to assign a processor to the thread. When the thread begins executing, the thread implicitly reacquires the lock on the `HoldIntegerSynchronized` object, and the *get* method continues executing with the next statement after `Wait`. Line 42 of Fig. 14.12 decrements `occupiedBufferCount` to indicate that the shared buffer is now empty (i.e., a consumer cannot read the value, but a producer can place another value into the shared buffer), lines 44–46 output a line to the console window indicating the value the consumer is reading and line 50 invokes `Monitor` method `Pulse` with the `HoldIntegerSynchronized` object as an argument. If there are any waiting threads, the first waiting thread enters the *Running* state, indicating that the thread can now attempt its task again (as soon as the thread is assigned a processor). The `Pulse` method returns immediately. Line 63 gets a copy of `buffer` before releasing the lock. It is possible that the producer could be assigned the processor immediately after the lock is released (line 66) and before the `return` statement executes (line 68). In this case, the producer would assign a new value to `buffer` before the `return` statement returns the value to the consumer. Thus, the consumer would receive the new value. Making a copy of `buffer` and returning the copy ensures that the consumer receives the proper value. Line 66 invokes `Monitor` method `Exit` to release the lock on the `HoldIntegerSynchronized` object, and the *get* method returns `bufferCopy` to its caller.

Study the outputs in Fig. 14.18. Observe that every integer produced is consumed exactly once—no values are lost, and no values are consumed more than once. This occurs because the producer and consumer cannot perform tasks unless it is "their turn." The producer must go first; the consumer must wait if the producer has not produced since the consumer last consumed; and the producer must wait if the consumer has not yet consumed the value the producer most recently produced. Execute this program several times to confirm that every integer produced is consumed exactly once.

```
// Fig. 14.18: SharedCell.cpp
// Creates and starts producer and consumer threads.

#include "stdafx.h"
#include "Synchronized.h"
#include "Producer.h"
#include "Consumer.h"

#using <mscorlib.dll>

using namespace System;

int _tmain()
{
   // create shared object used by threads
   HoldIntegerSynchronized *holdInteger =
      new HoldIntegerSynchronized();

   // Random object used by each thread
   Random *random = new Random();

   // create Producer and Consumer objects
   Producer *producer = new Producer( holdInteger, random );
   Consumer *consumer = new Consumer( holdInteger, random );

   // output column heads and initial buffer state
   Console::WriteLine( S"{0,-35}{1,-9}{2}\n", S"Operation",
      S"Buffer", S"Occupied Count" );
   holdInteger->DisplayState( S"Initial state" );
```

Fig. 14.18 `SharedCell` demonstrates the uses of classes `Producer` and `Consumer`. (Part 1 of 3.)

```

   // create threads for producer and consumer and set
   // delegates for each thread
   Thread *producerThread = new Thread( new ThreadStart(
      producer, Producer::Produce ) );
   producerThread->Name = S"Producer";

   Thread *consumerThread = new Thread( new ThreadStart(
      consumer, Consumer::Consume ) );
   consumerThread->Name = S"Consumer";

   // start each thread
   producerThread->Start();
   consumerThread->Start();

   return 0;
} // end _tmain
```

```
Operation                              Buffer   Occupied Count

Initial state                          -1       0

Producer writes 1                      1        1

Consumer reads 1                       1        0

Producer writes 2                      2        1

Producer tries to write.
Buffer full. Producer waits.           2        1

Consumer reads 2                       2        0

Producer writes 3                      3        1

Consumer reads 3                       3        0

Consumer tries to read.
Buffer empty. Consumer waits.          3        0

Producer writes 4                      4        1

Producer done producing.
Terminating Producer.

Consumer reads 4                       4        0

Consumer read values totaling: 10.
Terminating Consumer.
```

Fig. 14.18 SharedCell demonstrates the uses of classes Producer and Consumer. (Part 2 of 3.)

Operation	Buffer	Occupied Count
Initial state	-1	0
Consumer tries to read. Buffer empty. Consumer waits.	-1	0
Producer writes 1	1	1
Consumer reads 1	1	0
Consumer tries to read. Buffer empty. Consumer waits.	1	0
Producer writes 2	2	1
Consumer reads 2	2	0
Producer writes 3	3	1
Consumer reads 3	3	0
Producer writes 4	4	1
Producer done producing. Terminating Producer.		
Consumer reads 4	4	0
Consumer read values totaling: 10. Terminating Consumer.		

Fig. 14.18 `SharedCell` demonstrates the uses of classes `Producer` and `Consumer`. (Part 3 of 3.)

14.8 Producer/Consumer Relationship: Circular Buffer

Figure 14.12–Fig.14.18 used thread synchronization to guarantee that two threads manipulated data in a shared buffer correctly. However, the application may not perform optimally. If the two threads operate at different speeds, one of the threads will spend more (or most) of its time waiting. For example, in Fig. 14.12–Fig. 14.18 we shared a single integer between the two threads. If the producer thread produces values faster than the consumer can consume those values, then the producer thread waits for the consumer, because there are no other locations in memory to place the next value. Similarly, if the consumer consumes faster than the producer can produce values, the consumer waits until the producer places the next value into the shared location in memory. Even when we have threads that operate at the same relative speeds, over a period of time, those threads may become "out of sync," causing one of the threads to wait for the other. We cannot make assumptions about the relative speeds of asynchronous concurrent threads. There are too many interactions that occur with the operating system, the network, the user and other components, which can cause the threads to operate at different speeds. When this happens, threads wait.

When threads wait, programs become less productive, user-interactive programs become less responsive and network applications suffer longer delays because the processor is not used efficiently.

To minimize the waiting for threads that share resources and operate at the same relative speeds, we can implement a *circular buffer* that provides extra buffers into which the producer can place values and from which the consumer can retrieve those values. Let us assume that the buffer is implemented as an array. The producer and consumer work from the beginning of the array. When either thread reaches the end of the array, it simply returns to the first element of the array to perform its next task. If the producer temporarily produces values faster than the consumer can consume them, the producer can write additional values into the extra buffers (if cells are available). This enables the producer to perform its task even though the consumer is not ready to receive the current value being produced. Similarly, if the consumer consumes faster than the producer produces new values, the consumer can read additional values from the buffer (if there are any). This enables the consumer to perform its task even though the producer is not ready to produce additional values.

Note that the circular buffer would be inappropriate if the producer and consumer operate at different speeds. If the consumer always executes faster than the producer, then a buffer of one location is enough. Additional locations would waste memory. If the producer always executes faster, a buffer with an infinite number of locations would be required to absorb the extra production.

The key to using a circular buffer is to define it with enough extra cells to handle the anticipated "extra" production. If, over a period of time, we determine that the producer often produces as many as three more values than the consumer can consume, we can define a buffer of at least three cells to handle the extra production. We do not want the buffer to be too small, because that would cause threads to wait more. On the other hand, we do not want the buffer to be too large, because that would waste memory.

Performance Tip 14.5

Even when using a circular buffer, it is possible that a producer thread could fill the buffer, which would force the producer thread to wait until a consumer consumes a value to free an element in the buffer. Similarly, if the buffer is empty at any given time, the consumer thread must wait until the producer produces another value. The key to using a circular buffer is optimizing the buffer size to minimize the amount of thread-wait time.

Figure 14.19–Fig. 14.26 demonstrate a producer and a consumer accessing a circular buffer (in this case, a shared array of three cells) with synchronization. In this version of the producer/consumer relationship, the consumer consumes a value only when the array is not empty and the producer produces a value only when the array is not full. This program is implemented as a Windows application that sends its output to a `TextBox`. Classes `Producer` (Fig. 14.21–Fig. 14.22) and `Consumer` (Fig. 14.23–Fig. 14.24) perform the same tasks as in the previous examples, except that they output messages to the `TextBox` in the application window. The statements that created and started the thread objects in function `_tmain` of `SharedCell.cpp` in Fig. 14.11 and Fig. 14.18 now appear in class `Form1` (Fig. 14.25), where the `Load` event handler (lines 57–89) performs these tasks.

The most significant changes from Fig. 14.12–Fig. 14.18 occur in class `HoldIntegerSynchronized` (Fig. 14.19–Fig. 14.20), which now contains five variables. Array `buffers` is a three-element integer array that represents the circular buffer. Variable `occupied-`

BufferCount is the condition variable that can be used to determine whether a producer can write into the circular buffer (i.e., occupiedBufferCount is less than the number of elements in array buffers) and whether a consumer can read from the circular buffer (i.e., occupiedBufferCount is greater than 0). Variable readLocation indicates the position from which the next value can be read by a consumer. Variable writeLocation indicates the next location in which a value can be placed by a producer. The program displays output in outputTextBox.

```
// Fig. 14.19: HoldIntegerSynchronized.h
// Implementing the producer/consumer relationship with a
// circular buffer.

#pragma once

#using <mscorlib.dll>
#using <system.drawing.dll>
#using <system.windows.forms.dll>

using namespace System;
using namespace System::Drawing;
using namespace System::Windows::Forms;
using namespace System::Threading;

// implement the shared integer with synchronization
public __gc class HoldIntegerSynchronized
{
public:
   HoldIntegerSynchronized( TextBox * );    // constructor

   // property Buffer
   __property int get_Buffer()
   {
      // lock this object while getting value
      // from buffers array
      Monitor::Enter( this );

      // if there is no data to read, place invoking
      // thread in WaitSleepJoin state
      if ( occupiedBufferCount == 0 ) {
         outputTextBox->AppendText( String::Concat(
            S"\r\nAll buffers empty. ",
            Thread::CurrentThread->Name, S" waits." ) );

         Monitor::Wait( this );
      } // end if

      // obtain value at current readLocation, then
      // add string indicating consumed value to output
      int readValue = buffers[ readLocation ];

```

Fig. 14.19 HoldIntegerSynchronized class accesses threads through a circular buffer. (Part 1 of 3.)

```
         outputTextBox->AppendText( String::Concat(
            S"\r\n", Thread::CurrentThread->Name, S" reads ",
            buffers[ readLocation ].ToString(), S" " ) );

         // just consumed a value, so decrement number of
         // occupied buffers
         occupiedBufferCount--;

         // update readLocation for future read operation,
         // then add current state to output
         readLocation = ( readLocation + 1 ) % buffers->Length;
         outputTextBox->AppendText( CreateStateOutput() );

         // return waiting thread (if there is one)
         // to Running state
         Monitor::Pulse( this );

         Monitor::Exit( this ); // end lock

         return readValue;      // end lock
      } // end property get_Buffer

      // property set_Buffer
      __property void set_Buffer( int value )
      {
         // lock this object while setting value
         // in buffers array
         Monitor::Enter( this );

         // if there are no empty locations, place invoking
         // thread in WaitSleepJoin state
         if ( occupiedBufferCount == buffers->Length ) {
            outputTextBox->AppendText( String::Concat(
               S"\r\nAll buffers full. ",
               Thread::CurrentThread->Name, S" waits." ) );

            Monitor::Wait( this );
         } // end if

         // place value in writeLocation of buffers, then
         // add string indicating produced value to output
         buffers[ writeLocation ] = value;

         outputTextBox->AppendText( String::Concat(
            S"\r\n", Thread::CurrentThread->Name, S" writes ",
            buffers[ writeLocation ].ToString(), S" " ) );

         // just produced a value, so increment number of
         // occupied buffers
         occupiedBufferCount++;

```

Fig. 14.19 `HoldIntegerSynchronized` class accesses threads through a circular buffer. (Part 2 of 3.)

```
        // update writeLocation for future write operation,
        // then add current state to output
        writeLocation = ( writeLocation + 1 ) % buffers->Length;
        outputTextBox->AppendText( CreateStateOutput() );

        // return waiting thread (if there is one)
        // to Running state
        Monitor::Pulse( this );

        Monitor::Exit( this );     // end lock
     } // end property set_Buffer

     // create state output
     String *CreateStateOutput();

  private:

     // each array element is a buffer
     int buffers __gc[];

     // occupiedBufferCount maintains count of occupied buffers
     int occupiedBufferCount;

     // variable that maintains read and write buffer locations
     int readLocation, writeLocation;

     // GUI component to display output
     TextBox *outputTextBox;
  }; // end class HoldIntegerSynchronized
```

Fig. 14.19 HoldIntegerSynchronized class accesses threads through a circular buffer. (Part 3 of 3.)

```
// Fig. 14.20: HoldIntegerSynchronized.cpp
// Method definitions for class HoldIntegerSynchronized.

#include "stdafx.h"
#include "HoldIntegerSynchronized.h"

// constructor
HoldIntegerSynchronized::HoldIntegerSynchronized( TextBox *output ) :
   occupiedBufferCount( 0 ), readLocation( 0 ), writeLocation( 0 )
{

   buffers = new int __gc[ 3 ];

   for ( int i = 0; i < buffers->Length; i++ )
      buffers[ i ] = -1;

   outputTextBox = output;
}

```

Fig. 14.20 HoldIntegerSynchronized class method definitions. (Part 1 of 2.)

```
// create state output
String *HoldIntegerSynchronized::CreateStateOutput()
{

   // display first line of state information
   String *output = String::Concat ( S"(buffers occupied: ",
      occupiedBufferCount.ToString(), S")\r\nbuffers: " );

   for ( int i = 0; i < buffers->Length; i++ )
      output = String::Concat( output, S" ",
         buffers[ i ].ToString(), S"  " );

   output = String::Concat( output, S"\r\n" );

   // display second line of state information
   output = String::Concat( output, S"          " );

   for ( int i = 0; i < buffers->Length; i++ )
      output = String::Concat( output, S"---- " );

   output = String::Concat( output, S"\r\n" );

   // display third line of state information
   output = String::Concat( output, S"          " );

   // display readLocation (R) and writeLocation (W)
   // indicators below appropriate buffer locations
   for ( int i = 0; i < buffers->Length; i++ )
      if ( ( i == writeLocation ) &&
         ( writeLocation == readLocation ) )
            output = String::Concat( output, S" WR  " );
      else if ( i == writeLocation )
         output = String::Concat( output, S" W   " );
      else if ( i == readLocation )
         output = String::Concat( output, S"  R  " );
      else
         output = String::Concat( output, S"     " );

   output = String::Concat( output, S"\r\n" );

   return output;
} // end method CreateStateOutput
```

Fig. 14.20 `HoldIntegerSynchronized` class method definitions. (Part 2 of 2.)

The *set* method (lines 66–104 of Fig. 14.19) of property `Buffer` performs the same tasks that it did in Fig. 14.6, with a few modifications. As program control calls `Monitor` method `Enter` (line 70), the currently executing thread acquires the lock (assuming the lock is currently available) on the `HoldIntegerSynchronized` object (i.e., `this`). The `if` statement (lines 74–80) determines whether the producer must wait (i.e., all buffers are full). If the producer thread must wait, lines 75–77 append text to the `outputTextBox` indicating that the producer is waiting to perform its task, and line 79 invokes `Monitor` method `Wait` to place the producer thread in the *WaitSleepJoin* state of the `HoldIntegerSynchronized` object. When execution continues in line 84 after the `if` statement, the value written by the producer is placed in the circular buffer at location `writeLocation`. Next, lines 86–88 append a message containing the value produced to the `TextBox`. Line 92 increments `occupiedBufferCount`, because there is now at least one value in the buffer that the consumer can read. Then line 96 updates `writeLocation` for the next call to the *set* method of property `Buffer`. The output continues in line 97 by invoking method `CreateStateOutput` (lines 21–61 of Fig. 14.20), which outputs the number of occupied buffers, the contents of the buffers and the current `writeLocation` and `readLocation`. Line 101 (Fig. 14.19) invokes `Monitor` method `Pulse` to indicate that a thread waiting on the `HoldIntegerSynchronized` object (if there is a waiting thread) should transition to the *Running* state. Finally, line 103 invokes `Monitor` method `Exit`, causing the thread to release the lock on the `HoldIntegerSynchronized` object.

Error-Prevention Tip 14.3

When using class `Monitor`'s `Enter` and `Exit` methods to manage an object's lock, `Exit` must be called explicitly to release the lock. If an exception occurs in a method before `Exit` can be called and that exception is not caught, the method could terminate without calling `Exit`. If so, the lock is not released. To avoid this error, place code that could throw exceptions in a `try` block, and place the call to `Exit` in the corresponding `__finally` block to ensure that the lock is released.

The *get* method (lines 23–63 of Fig. 14.19) of property `Buffer` also performs the same tasks in this example that it did in Fig. 14.6, with a few minor modifications. Line 27 invokes `Monitor` method `Enter` to acquire the lock (assuming the lock is currently available). The `if` statement in lines 31–37 in the *get* method determines whether the consumer must wait (i.e., all buffers are empty). If the consumer thread must wait, lines 32–34 append text to the `outputTextBox` indicating that the consumer is waiting to perform its task, and line 36 invokes `Monitor` method `Wait` to place the consumer thread in the *WaitSleepJoin* state of the `HoldIntegerSynchronized` object. When execution continues at line 41 after the `if` statement, `readValue` is assigned the value at location `readLocation` in the circular buffer. Lines 43–45 append the value consumed to the `TextBox`. Line 49 decrements the `occupiedBufferCount`, because there is at least one open position in the buffer in which the producer thread can place a value. Then line 53 updates `readLocation` for the next call to the *get* method of `Buffer`. Line 54 invokes method `CreateStateOutput` to output the number of occupied buffers, the contents of the buffers and the current `writeLocation` and `readLocation`. Line 58 invokes method `Pulse` to transition the next thread waiting for the `HoldIntegerSynchronized` object into the *Running* state. Finally, line 60 invokes `Monitor` method `Exit`, causing the thread to release the lock on the `HoldIntegerSynchronized` object, and line 62 returns the consumed value to the calling method.

```
// Fig. 14.21: Producer.h
// Produce the integers from 11 to 20 and place them in buffer.

#pragma once

#include "HoldIntegerSynchronized.h"

```

Fig. 14.21 `Producer` class places integers in a circular buffer. (Part 1 of 2.)

```
public __gc class Producer
{
public:

   // constructor
   Producer( HoldIntegerSynchronized *, Random *, TextBox * );

   // produce values from 11-20 and place them in
   // sharedLocation's buffer
   void Produce();

private:
   HoldIntegerSynchronized *sharedLocation;
   TextBox *outputTextBox;
   Random *randomSleepTime;
}; // end class Producer
```

Fig. 14.21 `Producer` class places integers in a circular buffer. (Part 2 of 2.)

```
// Fig. 14.22: Producer.cpp
// Method definitions for class Producer.

#include "stdafx.h"
#include "Producer.h"

// constructor
Producer::Producer( HoldIntegerSynchronized *shared,
   Random *random, TextBox *output )
{
   sharedLocation = shared;
   outputTextBox = output;
   randomSleepTime = random;
}

// produce values from 11-20 and place them in
// sharedLocation's buffer
void Producer::Produce()
{

   // sleep for random interval up to 3000 milliseconds
   // then set sharedLocation's Buffer property
   for ( int count = 11; count <= 20; count++ ) {
      Thread::Sleep( randomSleepTime->Next( 1, 3000 ) );
      sharedLocation->Buffer = count;
   } // end for

   String *name = Thread::CurrentThread->Name;

   outputTextBox->AppendText( String::Concat(
      S"\r\n", name, S" done producing.\r\n", name,
      S" terminated.\r\n" ) );
} // end method Produce
```

Fig. 14.22 `Producer` class method definitions.

```
// Fig. 14.23: Consumer.h
// Consume the integers 1 to 10 from circular buffer.

#pragma once

#include "HoldIntegerSynchronized.h"

public __gc class Consumer
{
public:

   // constructor
   Consumer( HoldIntegerSynchronized *, Random *, TextBox * );

   // consume 10 integers from buffer
   void Consume();

private:
   HoldIntegerSynchronized *sharedLocation;
   TextBox *outputTextBox;
   Random *randomSleepTime;
}; // end class Consumer
```

Fig. 14.23 `Consumer` class to consume integers from circular buffer.

```
// Fig. 14.24: Consumer.cpp
// Method definitions for class Consumer.

#include "stdafx.h"
#include "Consumer.h"

// constructor
Consumer::Consumer( HoldIntegerSynchronized *shared,
   Random *random, TextBox *output )
{
   sharedLocation = shared;
   outputTextBox = output;
   randomSleepTime = random;
}

// consume 10 integers from buffer
void Consumer::Consume()
{
   int sum = 0;

   // loop 10 times and sleep for random interval up to
   // 3000 milliseconds then add sharedLocation's
   // Buffer property value to sum
   for ( int count = 1; count <= 10; count++ ) {
      Thread::Sleep( randomSleepTime->Next( 1, 3000 ) );
      sum += sharedLocation->Buffer;
   } // end for
```

Fig. 14.24 `Consumer` class method definitions. (Part 1 of 2.)

```

   String *name = Thread::CurrentThread->Name;

   outputTextBox->AppendText( String::Concat(
      S"\r\nTotal ", name, S" consumed: ", sum.ToString(),
      S".\r\n", name, S" terminated.\r\n" ) );
} // end method Consume
```

Fig. 14.24 `Consumer` class method definitions. (Part 2 of 2.)

```
// Fig. 14.25: Form1.h
// Implementing the producer/consumer
// relationship with a circular buffer.

#pragma once

#include "Producer.h"
#include "Consumer.h"

namespace CircularBuffer
{
   using namespace System;
   using namespace System::ComponentModel;
   using namespace System::Collections;
   using namespace System::Windows::Forms;
   using namespace System::Data;
   using namespace System::Drawing;

   /// <summary>
   /// Summary for Form1
   ///
   /// WARNING: If you change the name of this class, you will need to
   ///          change the 'Resource File Name' property for the managed
   ///          resource compiler tool associated with all .resx files
   ///          this class depends on.  Otherwise, the designers will not
   ///          be able to interact properly with localized resources
   ///          associated with this form.
   /// </summary>
   public __gc class Form1 : public System::Windows::Forms::Form
   {
   public:
      Form1(void)
      {
         InitializeComponent();
      }

   protected:
      void Dispose(Boolean disposing)
      {
```

Fig. 14.25 `CircularBuffer::Form1` class starts the producer and consumer threads. (Part 1 of 2.)

```
            if (disposing && components)
            {
               components->Dispose();
            }
            __super::Dispose(disposing);
         }
      private: System::Windows::Forms::TextBox *  outputTextBox;

      private:
         /// <summary>
         /// Required designer variable.
         /// </summary>
         System::ComponentModel::Container * components;

      // Visual Studio .NET generated GUI code

      // start producer and consumer
      private: System::Void Form1_Load(
                  System::Object *  sender, System::EventArgs *  e)
               {
                  // create shared object
                  HoldIntegerSynchronized *sharedLocation =
                     new HoldIntegerSynchronized( outputTextBox );

                  // display sharedLocation state before producer
                  // and consumer threads begin execution
                  outputTextBox->Text = sharedLocation->CreateStateOutput();

                  // Random object used by each thread
                  Random *random = new Random();

                  // create Producer and Consumer objects
                  Producer *producer =
                     new Producer( sharedLocation, random, outputTextBox );
                  Consumer *consumer =
                     new Consumer( sharedLocation, random, outputTextBox );

                  // create and name threads
                  Thread *producerThread = new Thread( new ThreadStart(
                     producer, Producer::Produce ) );
                  producerThread->Name = S"Producer";

                  Thread *consumerThread = new Thread( new ThreadStart(
                     consumer, Consumer::Consume ) );
                  consumerThread->Name = S"Consumer";

                  // start threads
                  producerThread->Start();
                  consumerThread->Start();
               } // end method Form1_Load
      };
   }
```

Fig. 14.25 `CircularBuffer::Form1` class starts the producer and consumer threads. (Part 2 of 2.)

In Fig. 14.26, the outputs include the current `occupiedBufferCount`, the contents of the buffers and the current `writeLocation` and `readLocation`. In the output, the letters `W` and `R` represent the current `writeLocation` and `readLocation`, respectively. Notice that, after the third value is placed in the third element of the buffer, the fourth value is inserted at the beginning of the array. This provides the circular buffer effect.

```
// Fig. 14.26: Form1.cpp
// Entry point of CircularBuffer application.

#include "stdafx.h"
#include "Form1.h"
#include <windows.h>

using namespace CircularBuffer;

int APIENTRY _tWinMain(HINSTANCE hInstance,
                       HINSTANCE hPrevInstance,
                       LPTSTR    lpCmdLine,
                       int       nCmdShow)
{
   System::Threading::Thread::CurrentThread->ApartmentState =
      System::Threading::ApartmentState::STA;
   Application::Run(new Form1());
   return 0;
} // end _tWinMain
```

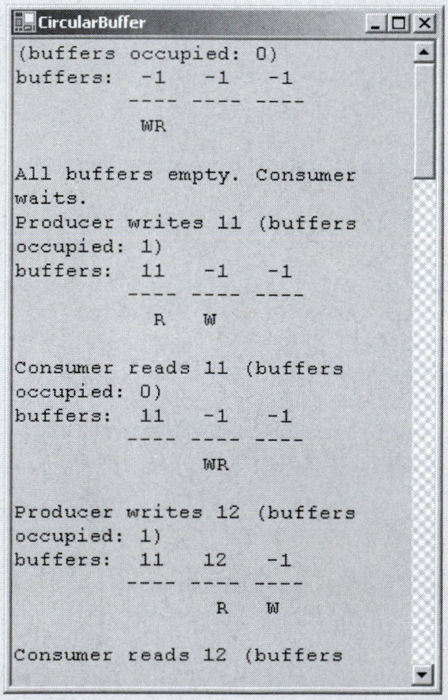

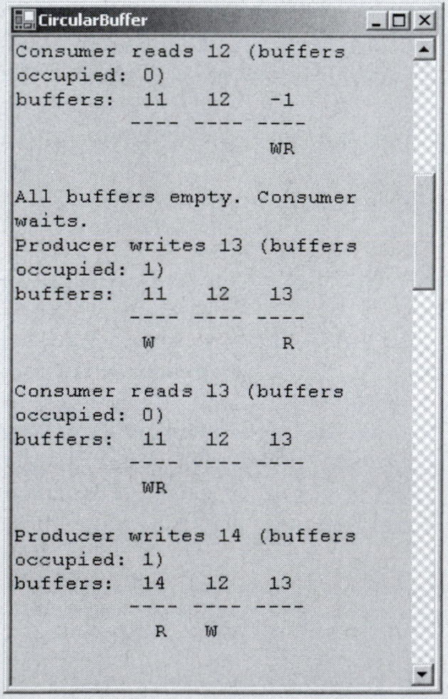

Fig. 14.26 Circular buffer demonstration. (Part 1 of 2.)

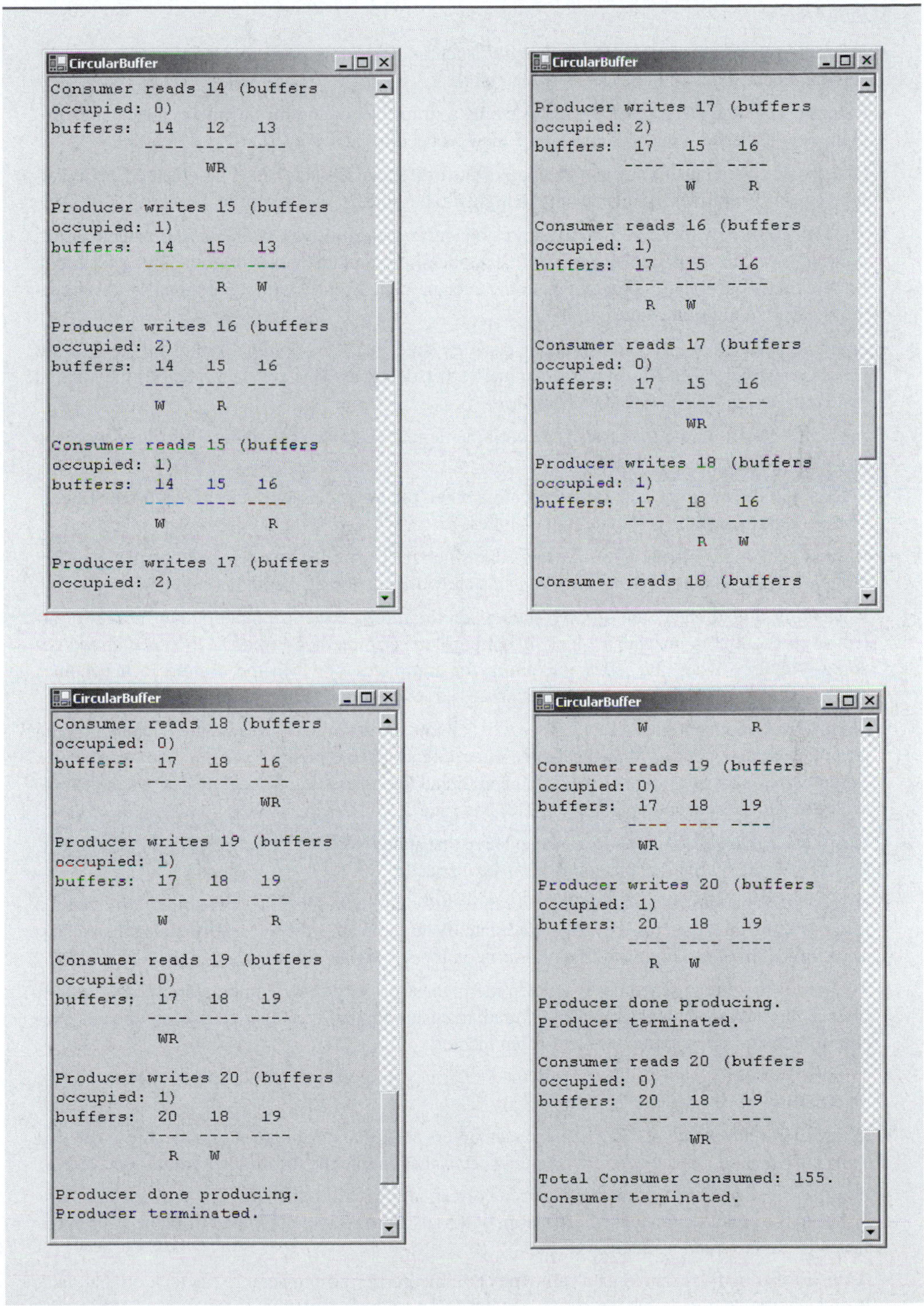

Fig. 14.26 Circular buffer demonstration. (Part 2 of 2.)

SUMMARY

- Computers perform operations concurrently, such as compiling programs, printing files and receiving electronic mail messages over a network.
- Programming languages generally provide only a simple set of control statements that enable programmers to perform one action at a time then proceed to the next action.
- Historically, the concurrency that computers perform generally has been implemented as operating system "primitives" available only to highly experienced "systems programmers."
- The .NET Framework Class Library makes concurrency primitives available to the applications programmer. The programmer specifies that applications contain threads of execution, each thread designating a portion of a program that may execute concurrently with other threads—this capability is called multithreading.
- A thread that was just created is in the *Unstarted* state. A thread is initialized using the `Thread` class's constructor, which receives a `ThreadStart` delegate. This delegate specifies the method that contains the tasks a thread will perform.
- A thread remains in the *Unstarted* state until the thread's `Start` method is called; this causes the thread to enter the *Running* state.
- A thread in the *Running* state starts executing when the system assigns a processor to the thread. The system assigns the processor to the highest-priority *Running* thread.
- A thread enters the *Stopped* (or *Aborted*) state when its `ThreadStart` delegate completes or terminates. A thread is forced into the *Stopped* state when its `Abort` method is called.
- A *Running* thread enters the *Blocked* state when the thread issues an input/output request or attempts to acquire an unavailable lock by calling `Monitor` method `Enter`. A *Blocked* thread becomes *Running* when the I/O it is waiting for completes or when the desired lock becomes available. A *Blocked* thread cannot use a processor, even if one is available.
- If a thread cannot continue executing (we will call this the dependent thread) unless another thread terminates, the dependent thread calls the other thread's `Join` method to "join" the two threads. When two threads are "joined," the dependent thread leaves the *WaitSleepJoin* state when the other thread finishes execution (enters the *Stopped* state).
- Any thread in the *WaitSleepJoin* state can leave that state if another thread invokes `Thread` method `Interrupt` on the thread in the *WaitSleepJoin* state.
- If `Thread` method `Suspend` is called on a thread (by the thread itself or by another thread in the program), the thread enters the *Suspended* state. A thread leaves the *Suspended* state when a separate thread invokes `Thread` method `Resume` on the suspended thread.
- The job of the thread scheduler is to keep the highest-priority thread running at all times and, if there is more than one highest-priority thread, to ensure that all equally high-priority threads execute for a quantum at a time in round-robin fashion.
- A thread's priority can be adjusted with the `Priority` property, which accepts an argument from the `ThreadPriority` enumeration.
- In thread synchronization, when a thread encounters code that it cannot yet run, the thread can call `Monitor` method `Wait` until certain actions occur that enable the thread to continue executing.
- If a thread called `Monitor` method `Wait`, a corresponding call to the `Monitor` method `Pulse` or `PulseAll` by another thread in the program will transition the original thread from the *WaitSleepJoin* state to the *Running* state.
- A thread that updates shared data calls `Monitor` method `Enter` to acquire the lock on that data. It updates the data and calls `Monitor` method `Exit` upon completion of the update. While that data is locked, all other threads attempting to acquire the lock on that data must wait.

TERMINOLOGY

Abort method of class Thread
Aborted state
AbortRequested state
Background state
background thread
Blocked state
Blocked thread
buffer
circular buffer
concurrency
concurrent programming
condition variable
consumer
CurrentThread property of class Thread
Enter method of class Monitor
Exit method of class Monitor
foreground thread
garbage collection
garbage-collector thread
indefinite postponement
Interrupt method of class Thread
IsBackground property of class Thread
Join method of class Thread
launching a thread
locking objects
main thread of execution
Monitor class
multilevel priority queue
multithreading
mutual exclusion
Name property of class Thread
Priority property of class Thread
producer
producer/consumer relationship
Pulse method of class Monitor
PulseAll method of class Monitor
quantum
Resume method of class Thread
Running state
shared buffer
Sleep method of class Thread
Start method of class Thread
starvation
Stopped state
Suspend method of class Thread
Suspended state
SuspendRequested state
synchronized block of code
System::Threading namespace
task
Thread class
thread of execution
thread state
thread synchronization
ThreadAbortException
ThreadPriority enumeration
ThreadStart delegate
timeslicing
Unstarted state
Wait method of class Monitor
WaitSleepJoin state

SELF-REVIEW EXERCISES

14.1 Fill in the blanks in each of the following statements:

a) Monitor methods ________ and ________ acquire and release the lock on an object.
b) Among a group of equal-priority threads, each thread receives a brief burst of time called a(n) ________, during which the thread has the processor and can perform its tasks.
c) The CLR provides a(n) ________ thread that reclaims dynamically allocated memory.
d) Four reasons a thread that is alive is not in the *Running* state are ________, ________, ________ and ________.
e) A thread enters the ________ state when the method that controls the thread's life cycle terminates.
f) A thread's priority must be one of the ThreadPriority constants ________, ________, ________, ________ and ________.
g) To wait for a designated number of milliseconds then resume execution, a thread should call the ________ method of class Thread.

h) Method ________ of class `Monitor` transitions a thread in the *WaitSleepJoin* state to the *Running* state.
i) Class `Monitor` provides methods that help ________ access to shared data.

14.2 State whether each of the following is *true* or *false*. If *false*, explain why.
a) A thread cannot execute if it is in the *Stopped* state.
b) A higher priority thread entering (or reentering) the *Running* state will preempt threads of lower priority.
c) The code that a thread executes is defined in its `main` method.
d) A thread in the *WaitSleepJoin* state always returns to the *Running* state when `Monitor` method `Pulse` is called.
e) Method `Sleep` of class `Thread` does not consume processor time while a thread sleeps.
f) A blocked thread can be placed in the *Running* state by `Monitor` method `Pulse`.
g) Class `Monitor`'s `Wait`, `Pulse` and `PulseAll` methods can be used in any block of code.
h) A thread cannot invoke its own `Abort` method.
i) When `Monitor` class method `Wait` is called after calling `Monitor` class method `Enter`, the lock for that block is released and the thread that called `Wait` is placed in the *WaitSleepJoin* state.

ANSWERS TO SELF-REVIEW EXERCISES

14.1 a) `Enter`, `Exit`. b) timeslice or quantum. c) garbage collector. d) waiting, sleeping, suspended, blocked. e) *Stopped*. f) `Lowest`, `BelowNormal`, `Normal`, `AboveNormal`, `Highest`. g) `Sleep`. h) `Pulse`. i) synchronize.

14.2 a) True. b) True. c) False. The code that a thread executes is defined in the method specified by the thread's `ThreadStart` delegate. d) False. A thread may be in the *WaitSleepJoin* state for several reasons. Calling `Pulse` moves a thread from the *WaitSleepJoin* state to the *Running* state only if the thread entered the *WaitSleepJoin* state as the result of a call to `Monitor` method `Wait`. e) True. f) False. A thread is blocked by the operating system and returns to the *Running* state when the operating system determines that the thread can continue executing (e.g., when an I/O request completes or when a lock the thread attempted to acquire becomes available). g) False. Class `Monitor` methods can be called only if the thread performing the call currently owns the lock on the object each method receives as an argument. h) False. A thread is forced into the *Stopped* state when its `Abort` method is called by itself or by another thread. i) True.

EXERCISES

14.3 The code that manipulates the circular buffer in Section 14.8 will work with a buffer of two or more elements. Try changing the buffer size to see how it affects the producer and consumer threads. In particular, notice that the producer waits to produce less frequently as the buffer grows in size.

14.4 Write a program to demonstrate that, as a high-priority thread executes, it will delay the execution of all lower-priority threads.

14.5 Write a program that demonstrates timeslicing among several equal-priority threads. Show that a lower-priority thread's execution is deferred by the timeslicing of the higher-priority threads.

14.6 Write a program that demonstrates a high-priority thread using `Sleep` to give lower-priority threads a chance to run.

14.7 Two problems that can occur that allow threads to wait are deadlock, in which one or more threads will wait forever for an event that cannot occur, and indefinite postponement, in which one or more threads will be delayed for some unpredictably long time but may eventually complete. Give an example of how each of these problems can occur in a multithreaded MC++ program.

14.8 *(Readers and Writers)* This exercise asks you to develop a MC++ monitor to solve a famous problem in concurrency control. This problem was first discussed and solved by P. J. Courtois, F. Heymans and D. L. Parnas in their research paper, "Concurrent Control with Readers and Writers," *Communications of the ACM*, Vol. 14, No. 10, October 1971, pp. 667–668. The interested student might also want to read C. A. R. Hoare's seminal research paper on monitors, "Monitors: An Operating System Structuring Concept," *Communications of the ACM*, Vol. 17, No. 10, October 1974, pp. 549–557. *Corrigendum, Communications of the ACM*, Vol. 18, No. 2, February 1975, p. 95. [The readers and writers problem is discussed at length in Chapter 5 of the author's book: Deitel, H. M., *Operating Systems*, Reading, MA: Addison-Wesley, 1990.]

With multithreading, many threads can access shared data; as we have seen, access to shared data needs to be synchronized to avoid corrupting the data.

Consider an airline-reservation system in which many clients are attempting to book seats on particular flights between particular cities. All the information about flights and seats is stored in a common database in memory. The database consists of many entries, each representing a seat on a particular flight for a particular day between particular cities. In a typical airline-reservation scenario, the client will probe the database looking for the "optimal" flight to meet that client's needs. A client may probe the database many times before trying to book a particular flight. A seat that was available during this probing phase could easily be booked by someone else before the client has a chance to book it after deciding on it. In that case, when the client attempts to make the reservation, the client will discover that the data has changed and the flight is no longer available.

The client probing the database is called a *reader.* The client attempting to book the flight is called a *writer.* Any number of readers can be probing shared data at once, but each writer needs exclusive access to the shared data to prevent the data from being corrupted.

Write a multithreaded MC++ program that launches multiple reader threads and multiple writer threads, each attempting to access a single reservation record. A writer thread has two possible transactions, `makeReservation` and `cancelReservation`. A reader has one possible transaction, `queryReservation`.

First, implement a version of your program that allows unsynchronized access to the reservation record. Show how the integrity of the database can be corrupted. Next, implement a version of your program that uses MC++ monitor synchronization with `Wait` and `Pulse` to enforce a disciplined protocol for readers and writers accessing the shared reservation data. In particular, your program should allow multiple readers to access the shared data simultaneously when no writer is active—but, if a writer is active, then no reader should be allowed to access the shared data.

Be careful. This problem has many subtleties. For example, what happens when there are several active readers and a writer wants to write? If we allow a steady stream of readers to arrive and share the data, they could indefinitely postpone the writer (who might become tired of waiting and take his or her business elsewhere). To solve this problem, you might decide to favor writers over readers. But here, too, there is a trap, because a steady stream of writers could then indefinitely postpone the waiting readers, and they, too, might choose to take their business elsewhere! Implement your monitor with the following methods: `startReading`, which is called by any reader who wants to begin accessing a reservation; `stopReading`, to be called by any reader who has finished reading a reservation; `startWriting`, to be called by any writer who wants to make a reservation; and `stopWriting`, to be called by any writer who has finished making a reservation.

15

Strings, Characters and Regular Expressions

Objectives

- To create and manipulate immutable character string objects of class `String`.
- To create and manipulate mutable character string objects of class `StringBuilder`.
- To use regular expressions in conjunction with classes `Regex` and `Match`.

The chief defect of Henry King
Was chewing little bits of string.
Hilaire Belloc

Vigorous writing is concise. A sentence should contain no unnecessary words, a paragraph no unnecessary sentences.
William Strunk, Jr.

I have made this letter longer than usual, because I lack the time to make it short.
Blaise Pascal

The difference between the almost-right word and the right word is really a large matter—it's the difference between the lightning bug and the lightning.
Mark Twain

Mum's the word.
Miguel de Cervantes

Outline

15.1 Introduction

In this chapter, we introduce the Framework Class Library's string and character processing capabilities and demonstrate the use of regular expressions to search for patterns in text. The techniques presented in this chapter can be employed to develop text editors, word processors, page-layout software, computerized typesetting systems and other kinds of text-processing software. Previous chapters have already presented several string-processing capabilities. In this chapter, we expand on this information by detailing the capabilities of class `String` and type `Char` from the `System` namespace, class `StringBuilder` from the `System::Text` namespace and classes `Regex` and `Match` from the `System::Text:: RegularExpressions` namespace.

15.2 Fundamentals of Characters and Strings

Characters are the fundamental building blocks of MC++ source code. Every program is composed of characters that, when grouped together meaningfully, create a sequence that the compiler interprets as a series of instructions that describe how to accomplish a task. In addition to normal characters, a program also can contain *character constants.* A character constant is a character that is represented as an integer value, called a *character code*. For example, the integer value `122` corresponds to the character constant `'z'`. The integer value `10` corresponds to the newline character `'\n'`. In Windows NT-based systems (Windows NT, 2000 and XP), character constants are established according to the *Unicode character set*, an international character set that contains many more symbols and letters than does the ASCII character set (see Appendix C). To learn more about Unicode, see Appendix D.

A string is a series of characters treated as a single unit. These characters can be uppercase letters, lowercase letters, digits and various *special characters*, such as +, -, *, /, `$` and others. In MC++, a string is an object of class `String` in the `System` namespace. `Strings` are a reference type, so MC++ programs use `String *` pointers to manipulate objects of type `String`. We write *string literals*, or *string constants* (often called *literal* `Strings`), as sequences of characters in double quotation marks, as follows:

```
"John Q. Doe"
"9999 Main Street"
"Waltham, Massachusetts"
"(201) 555-1212"
```

A declaration can assign a `String` literal to a `String` pointer. The declaration

```
String *color = "blue";
```

initializes `String` pointer `color` to point to the `String` literal object `"blue"`.

In MC++, `String` literals can also be prefixed by the letter `S` (e.g., `S"blue"`). `String` literals preceded by `S` are called managed `String` literals. Managed `String` literals are useful because they offer better performance than non-managed `String` literals.

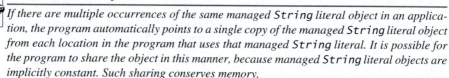

Performance Tip 15.1

If there are multiple occurrences of the same managed `String` literal object in an application, the program automatically points to a single copy of the managed `String` literal object from each location in the program that uses that managed `String` literal. It is possible for the program to share the object in this manner, because managed `String` literal objects are implicitly constant. Such sharing conserves memory.

Notice, however, that when we assign `"blue"` to `String` pointer `color` (above), we do not prefix it with the letter `S`. Thus, we are not creating a managed `String` literal. `Strings` without prefixes are standard C++ `String` literals.

`String` literals prefixed by the letter `L` (e.g., `L"String literal"`) are standard C++ *wide-character string literals*. Wide-character `String` literals have a different internal representation than regular C++ `String` literals.[1] In MC++, both standard C++ `String` literals (with no prefix) and wide-character `String` literals (prefixed by `L`) may be assigned to `String` pointers without casting.

Only managed `String` literals (prefixed by `S`) and standard C++ wide-character `String` literals (prefixed by `L`) can be used where `System::String` types are expected. Managed `String` literals cannot be used where standard C++ string types are expected.

15.3 `String` Constructors

Class `String` provides eight constructors for initializing `Strings` in various ways. Figure 15.1 demonstrates the use of three of the constructors.

1. For more information about standard C++ string literals, visit `www.zib.de/benger/C++/clause2.html#s2.13.4` and `www.tempest-sw.com/cpp/ch01.html`.

```
1  // Fig. 15.1: StringConstructor.cpp
2  // Demonstrating String class constructors.
3
4  #include "stdafx.h"
5
6  #using <mscorlib.dll>
7  #using <system.windows.forms.dll>
8
9  using namespace System;
10 using namespace System::Windows::Forms;
11
12 int _tmain()
13 {
14    String *output;
15    String *originalString;
16    String *string1, *string2, *string3, *string4;
17
18    __wchar_t characterArray __gc[] =
19       { 'b', 'i', 'r', 't', 'h', 'd', 'a', 'y' };
20
21    // string initialization
22    originalString = S"Welcome to Visual C++ .NET programming!";
23    string1 = originalString;
24    string2 = new String( characterArray );
25    string3 = new String( characterArray, 5, 3 );
26    string4 = new String( 'C', 5 );
27
28    output = String::Concat( S"string1 = ", S"\"", string1,
29       S"\"\n", S"string2 = ", S"\"", string2, S"\"\n",
30       S"string3 = ", S"\"", string3, S"\"\n",
31       S"string4 = ", S"\"", string4, S"\"\n" );
32
33    MessageBox::Show( output, S"String Class Constructors",
34       MessageBoxButtons::OK, MessageBoxIcon::Information );
35
36    return 0;
37 } // end _tmain
```

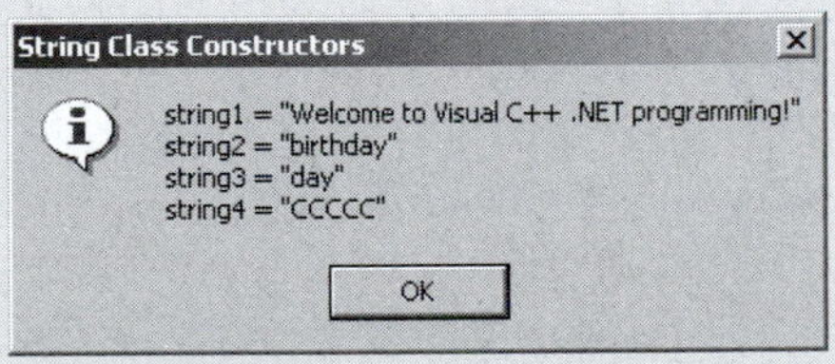
String Class Constructors
string1 = "Welcome to Visual C++ .NET programming!"
string2 = "birthday"
string3 = "day"
string4 = "CCCCC"
OK

Fig. 15.1 String constructors.

Lines 14–16 declare String pointers output, originalString, string1, string2, string3 and string4. Lines 18–19 allocate the __wchar_t array characterArray, which contains eight characters. Recall from Chapter 3 that __wchar_t is an MC++ alias for .NET type Char and that we use MC++ aliases for the convenience of standard C++ programmers. We discuss type Char in detail in Section 15.13.

Line 22 assigns managed `String` literal `"Welcome to Visual C++ .NET programming!"` to `String` pointer `originalString`. Line 23 sets `string1` to point to the same `String` literal.

Line 24 assigns to `string2` a new `String`, using the `String` constructor that takes a `__wchar_t __gc` array (a managed character array) as an argument. The new `String` contains a copy of the characters in array `characterArray`.

Software Engineering Observation 15.1

In most cases, it is not necessary to make a copy of an existing `String`. All `Strings` are immutable—their character contents cannot be changed after they are created. Also, if there are one or more pointers to a `String` (or any object for that matter), the object cannot be reclaimed by the garbage collector.

Line 25 assigns to `string3` a new `String`, using the `String` constructor that takes a managed `__wchar_t` array and two `int` arguments. The second argument specifies the starting index position (the *offset*) from which characters in the array are copied. The third argument specifies the number of characters (the *count*) to be copied from the specified starting position in the array. The new `String` contains a copy of the specified characters in the array. If the specified offset or count indicates that the program should access an element outside the bounds of the character array, an *`ArgumentOutOfRangeException`* is thrown.

Line 26 assigns to `string4` a new `String`, using the `String` constructor that takes as arguments a character and an `int` specifying the number of times to repeat that character in the `String`.

15.4 `String` Chars Property, Length Property and CopyTo Method

The application in Fig. 15.2 presents the `String` indexed property (*`Chars`*), which is used to retrieve any character in a `String`, and the `String` property *`Length`*, which returns the length of the `String`. The `String` method *`CopyTo`* copies a specified number of characters from a `String` into a `__wchar_t` array. This example determines the length of a `String`, prints the characters in the `String` in reverse order and copies a series of characters from the `String` into a character array.

```
// Fig. 15.2: StringMethods.cpp
// Using String property Chars, property Length and method CopyTo.

#include "stdafx.h"

#using <mscorlib.dll>
#using <system.windows.forms.dll>

using namespace System;
using namespace System::Windows::Forms;

int _tmain()
{
```

Fig. 15.2 `String` Chars property, Length property and CopyTo method. (Part 1 of 2.)

```
14    String *string1, *output;
15    __wchar_t characterArray __gc[];
16
17    string1 = S"hello there";
18    characterArray = new __wchar_t __gc[ 5 ];
19
20    // output string
21    output = String::Concat( S"string1: \"", string1, S"\"" );
22
23    // test Length property
24    output = String::Concat( output, S"\nLength of string1: ",
25       string1->Length.ToString() );
26
27    // loop through character in string1 and display reversed
28    output = String::Concat( output,
29       S"\nThe string reversed is: " );
30
31    for ( int i = string1->Length - 1; i >= 0; i-- )
32       output = String::Concat( output,
33          string1->Chars[ i ].ToString() );
34
35    // copy characters from string1 into characterArray
36    string1->CopyTo( 0, characterArray, 0, 5 );
37    output = String::Concat( output,
38       S"\nThe character array is: " );
39
40    for ( int i = 0; i < characterArray->Length; i++ )
41       output = String::Concat( output,
42          characterArray[ i ].ToString() );
43
44    String *output2 = String::Concat( S"Demonstrating the String",
45       S" Chars Property, Length Property and CopyTo method" );
46
47    MessageBox::Show( output, output2, MessageBoxButtons::OK,
48       MessageBoxIcon::Information );
49
50    return 0;
51 } // end _tmain
```

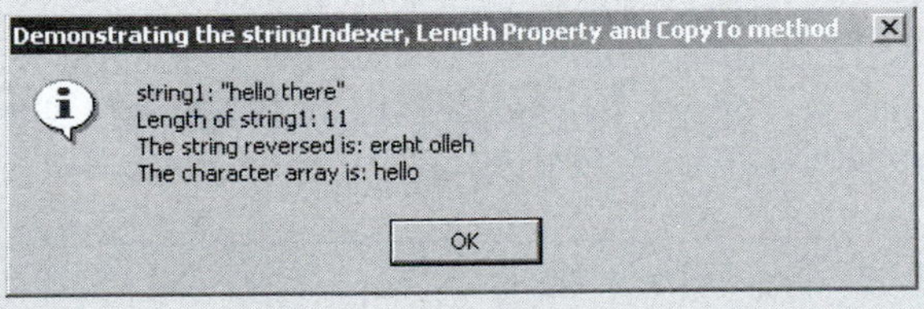
Demonstrating the stringIndexer, Length Property and CopyTo method
string1: "hello there"
Length of string1: 11
The string reversed is: ereht olleh
The character array is: hello
OK

Fig. 15.2 `String` `Chars` property, `Length` property and `CopyTo` method. (Part 2 of 2.)

Lines 24–25 of Fig. 15.2 use `String` property `Length` to determine the number of characters in the string pointed to by `string1`. Like arrays, `String`s always know their own size. Notice that in line 25, we use method `ToString` to convert the numerical length to a

`String *` to be displayed. This is because method `String::Concat` does not automatically convert its arguments to `String` objects. We discuss method `Concat` in Section 15.9.

Lines 31–33 append to `output` the characters of the `string1` in reverse order. Indexed property `Chars` (of class `String`) returns the character at a specific position in the `String`. Property `Chars` is accessed as an array of `__wchar_ts`. The indexed property receives an integer argument as the *position number* and returns the character at that position. As with arrays, the first element of a `String` is considered to be at position 0.

Common Programming Error 15.1

Attempting to access a character that is outside the bounds of a `String` (i.e., an index less than 0 or an index greater than or equal to the `String`'s length) results in an `IndexOutOfRangeException`.

Line 36 uses `String` method `CopyTo` to copy the characters of `string1` into `characterArray`. The first argument given to method `CopyTo` is the index from which the method begins copying characters in `string1`. The second argument is the character array into which the characters are copied. The third argument is the index specifying the location at which the method places the copied characters in the character array. The last argument is the number of characters that the method will copy from `string1`. Lines 40–42 append the `__wchar_t` array contents to `output` one character at a time.

15.5 Comparing `String`s

The next two examples demonstrate the methods that MC++ provides for comparing `String`s. To understand how one `String` can be "greater than" or "less than" another `String`, consider the process of alphabetizing a series of last names. The reader would, no doubt, place `"Jones"` before `"Smith"`, because the first letter of `"Jones"` comes before the first letter of `"Smith"` in the alphabet. The alphabet is more than just a set of 26 letters—it is an ordered list of characters in which each letter occurs in a specific position. For example, `Z` is more than just a letter of the alphabet; `Z` is specifically the twenty-sixth letter of the alphabet.

Computers can order characters alphabetically because the characters are represented internally as numeric codes. When comparing two `String`s, MC++ simply compares the numeric codes of the characters in the `String`s.

Demonstrating `Equals`, `CompareTo` and ==

Class `String` provides several ways to compare `String`s. Figure 15.3 demonstrates the use of method *`Equals`*, method *`CompareTo`* and the equality operator (==).

```
// Fig. 15.3: StringCompare.cpp
// Comparing strings.

#include "stdafx.h"

#using <mscorlib.dll>
#using <system.windows.forms.dll>

```

Fig. 15.3 `String` test to determine equality. (Part 1 of 3.)

```
using namespace System;
using namespace System::Windows::Forms;

int _tmain()
{
   String *string1 = S"hello";
   String *string2 = S"goodbye";
   String *string3 = S"Happy Birthday";
   String *string4 = S"happy birthday";
   String *output;

   // output values of four strings
   output = String::Concat( S"string1 = \"", string1, S"\"",
      S"\nstring2 = \"", string2, S"\"", S"\nstring3 = \"",
      string3, S"\"", S"\nstring4 = \"", string4, S"\"\n\n" );

   // test for equality using Equals method
   if ( string1->Equals( S"hello" ) )
      output = String::Concat( output,
         S"string1 equals \"hello\"\n" );
   else
      output = String::Concat( output,
         S"string1 does not equal \"hello\"\n" );

   // test for equality with ==
   if ( string1 == S"hello" )
      output = String::Concat( output,
         S"string1 equals \"hello\"\n" );
   else
      output = String::Concat( output,
         S"string1 does not equal \"hello\"\n" );

   // test for equality comparing case
   if ( String::Equals( string3, string4 ) )
      output = String::Concat( output,
         S"string3 equals string4\n" );
   else
      output = String::Concat( output,
         S"string3 does not equal string4\n" );

   // test CompareTo
   output = String::Concat( output,
      S"\nstring1->CompareTo( string2 ) is ",
      string1->CompareTo( string2 ).ToString(), S"\n",
      S"string2->CompareTo( string1 ) is ",
      string2->CompareTo( string1 ), S"\n",
      S"string1->CompareTo( string1 ) is ",
      string1->CompareTo( string1 ), S"\n",
      S"string3->CompareTo( string4 ) is ",
      string3->CompareTo( string4 ), S"\n",
      S"string4->CompareTo( string3 ) is ",
      string4->CompareTo( string3 ), S"\n" );
```

Fig. 15.3 String test to determine equality. (Part 2 of 3.)

```
62     MessageBox::Show( output, S"Demonstrating String Comparisons",
63        MessageBoxButtons::OK, MessageBoxIcon::Information );
64
65     return 0;
66  } // end _tmain
```

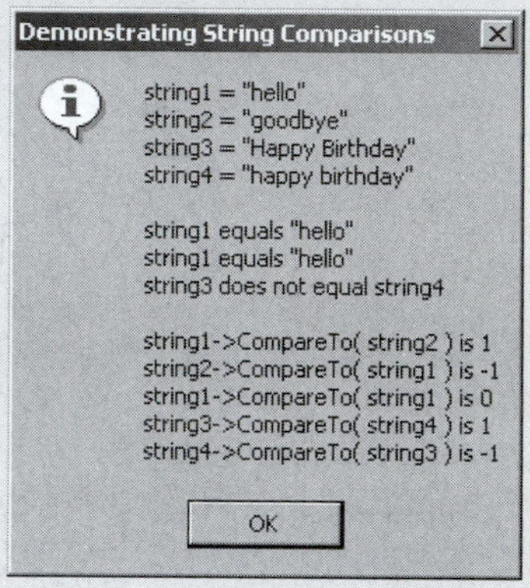
Demonstrating String Comparisons
string1 = "hello"
string2 = "goodbye"
string3 = "Happy Birthday"
string4 = "happy birthday"
string1 equals "hello"
string1 equals "hello"
string3 does not equal string4
string1->CompareTo(string2) is 1
string2->CompareTo(string1) is -1
string1->CompareTo(string1) is 0
string3->CompareTo(string4) is 1
string4->CompareTo(string3) is -1
OK

Fig. 15.3 `String` test to determine equality. (Part 3 of 3.)

The condition in the `if` statement (line 26) uses instance method `Equals` to compare `string1` and literal `String` `"hello"` to determine whether they are equal in content. Method `Equals` (inherited by `String` from class `Object`) tests any two objects for equality (i.e., checks whether the objects have identical contents). The method returns `true` if the objects are equal and `false` otherwise. In this instance, the preceding condition returns `true`, because `string1` points to `String` literal object `"hello"`. Method `Equals` uses a *lexicographical comparison*—the integer Unicode values that represent each character in each `String` are compared. Method `Equals` compares the numeric Unicode values that represent the characters in each `String`. A comparison of the `String` `"hello"` with the `String` `"HELLO"` would return `false`, because the numeric representations of lowercase letters are different from the numeric representations of corresponding uppercase letters.

The condition in the second `if` statement (line 34) uses the equality operator (==) to compare `string1` with the managed literal `"hello"` for equality. In MC++, the equality operator compares the pointers of two `String`s. Thus, the condition in the `if` statement evaluates to `true`, because `string1` points to managed literal `String` `"hello"`. If the pointers point to different string objects this condition will be `false`.

We present the test for `String` equality between `string3` and `string4` (line 42) to illustrate that comparisons are indeed case sensitive. Here `static` method `Equals` (as opposed to the instance method in line 26) is used to compare the values of two `String`s. `"Happy Birthday"` does not equal `"happy birthday"`, so the condition of the `if` statement fails, and the message `"string3 does not equal string4"` is added to the output message (lines 46–47).

Lines 50–60 use the `String` method `CompareTo` to compare `String`s. Method `CompareTo` returns `0` if the `String`s are equal, a `-1` if the `String` that invokes `CompareTo` is less than the `String` that is passed as an argument and a `1` if the `String` that invokes `CompareTo` is greater than the `String` that is passed as an argument. Method `CompareTo` uses a lexicographical (alphabetic) comparison.

Demonstrating `StartsWith` and `EndsWith`

The application in Fig. 15.4 shows how to test whether a `String` instance begins or ends with a given string. Method *`StartsWith`* determines whether a `String` instance starts with the `String` literal passed to it as an argument. Method *`EndsWith`* determines whether a `String` instance ends with the `String` literal passed to it as an argument. Application `StringStartEnd`'s `_tmain` function defines an array of `String` pointers (called `strings`), which contains `"started"`, `"starting"`, `"ended"` and `"ending"`. The remainder of function `_tmain` tests the elements of the array to determine whether they start or end with a particular set of characters.

```
// Fig. 15.4: StringStartEnd.cpp
// Demonstrating StartsWith and EndsWith methods.

#include "stdafx.h"

#using <mscorlib.dll>
#using <system.windows.forms.dll>

using namespace System;
using namespace System::Windows::Forms;

int _tmain()
{
   String *strings[] =
      { S"started", S"starting", S"ended", S"ending" };

   String *output = S"";

   // test every string to see if it starts with "st"
   for ( int i = 0; i < strings->Length; i++ )

      if ( strings[ i ]->StartsWith( S"st" ) )
         output = String::Concat( output, S"\"",
            strings[ i ], S"\" starts with \"st\"\n" );

   output = String::Concat( output, S"\n" );

   // test every string to see if it ends with "ed"
   for ( int i = 0; i < strings->Length; i++ )

      if ( strings[ i ]->EndsWith( S"ed" ) )
         output = String::Concat( output, S"\"",
            strings[ i ], S"\" ends with \"ed\"\n" );

   MessageBox::Show( output,
      S"Demonstrating StartsWith and EndsWith methods",
      MessageBoxButtons::OK, MessageBoxIcon::Information );

   return 0;
} // end _tmain
```

Fig. 15.4 `StartsWith` and `EndsWith` methods demonstrated. (Part 1 of 2.)

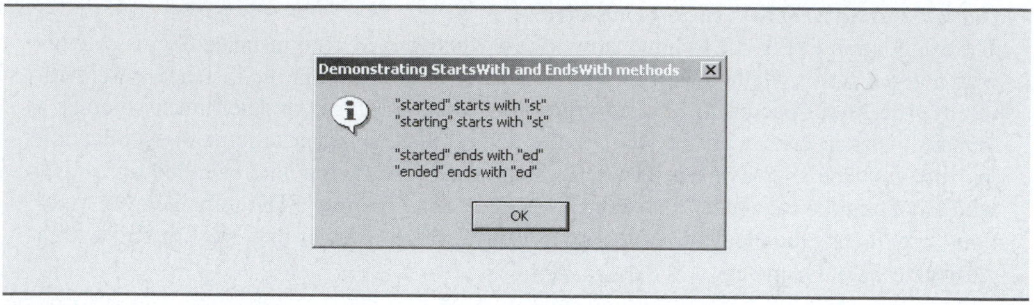

Fig. 15.4 `StartsWith` and `EndsWith` methods demonstrated. (Part 2 of 2.)

Line 22 uses method `StartsWith`, which takes a `String *` argument. The condition in the `if` statement determines whether the `String *` at index `i` of the array starts with the characters `"st"`. If so, the method returns `true` and appends `strings[ i ]` to `output` for display purposes.

Line 31 uses method `EndsWith`, which also takes a `String *` argument. The condition in the `if` statement determines whether the `String *` at index `i` of the array ends with the characters `"ed"`. If so, the method returns `true`, and `strings[ i ]` is appended to `output` for display purposes.

15.6 Locating Characters and Substrings in `Strings`

In many applications, it is necessary to search for a character or set of characters in a `String`. For example, a programmer creating a word processor would want to provide capabilities for searching through documents. Figure 15.5 demonstrates some of the many versions of `String` methods *`IndexOf`*, *`IndexOfAny`*, *`LastIndexOf`* and *`LastIndexOfAny`*, which search for a specified character or substring in a `String`. This example performs all searches on the `String` pointer `letters` (initialized with `"abcdefghijklmabcdefghijklm"`) located in function `_tmain`.

Lines 20, 23, and 26 of Fig. 15.5 use method `IndexOf` to locate the first occurrence of a character or substring in a `String`. If `IndexOf` finds a character, `IndexOf` returns the index of the specified character in the `String`; otherwise, `IndexOf` returns `-1`. The expression in line 23 uses a version of method `IndexOf` that takes two arguments—the character to search for and the starting index at which the search of the `String` should begin. The method does not examine any characters that occur prior to the starting index (in this case `1`). The expression in line 26 uses another version of method `IndexOf` that takes three arguments—the character to search for, the index at which to start searching and the number of characters to search.

Common Programming Error 15.2

Mixing up the order of arguments to `String` methods is a common logic error.

Common Programming Error 15.3

Be careful when specifying indices to `String` methods. Specifying values that are off by one number is a common logic error.

```
// Fig. 15.5: StringIndexMethods.cpp
// Using String searching methods.

#include "stdafx.h"

#using <mscorlib.dll>
#using <system.windows.forms.dll>

using namespace System;
using namespace System::Windows::Forms;

int _tmain()
{
   String *letters = S"abcdefghijklmabcdefghijklm";
   String *output = S"";
   __wchar_t searchLetters __gc[] = { 'c', 'a', '$' };

   // test IndexOf to locate a character in a string
   output = String::Concat( output, S"'c' is located at index ",
      letters->IndexOf( 'c' ).ToString() );

   output = String::Concat( output, S"\n'a' is located at index ",
      letters->IndexOf( 'a', 1 ).ToString() );

   output = String::Concat( output, S"\n'$' is located at index ",
      letters->IndexOf( '$', 3, 5 ).ToString() );

   // test LastIndexOf to find a character in a string
   output = String::Concat( output, S"\n\nlast 'c' is located at ",
      S"index ", letters->LastIndexOf( 'c' ).ToString() );

   output = String::Concat( output,
      S"\nLast 'a' is located at index ",
      letters->LastIndexOf( 'a', 25 ).ToString() );

   output = String::Concat( output,
      S"\nLast '$' is located at index ",
      letters->LastIndexOf( '$', 15, 5 ).ToString() );

   // test IndexOf to locate a substring in a string
   output = String::Concat( output,
      S"\n\n\"def\" is located at index ",
      letters->IndexOf( "def" ).ToString() );

   output = String::Concat( output,
      S"\n\"def\" is located at index ",
      letters->IndexOf( "def", 7 ).ToString() );

   output = String::Concat( output,
      S"\n\"hello\" is located at index ",
      letters->IndexOf( "hello", 5, 15 ).ToString() );

```

Fig. 15.5 `StringIndexMethods` demonstrates `String` searching capabilities. (Part 1 of 3.)

```
      // test LastIndexOf to find a substring in a string
      output = String::Concat( output,
         S"\n\nLast \"def\" is located at index ",
         letters->LastIndexOf( "def" ).ToString() );

      output = String::Concat( output,
         S"\nLast \"def\" is located at index ",
         letters->LastIndexOf( "def", 25 ).ToString() );

      output = String::Concat( output,
         S"\nLast \"hello\" is located at index ",
         letters->LastIndexOf( "hello", 20, 15 ).ToString() );

      // test IndexOfAny to find first occurrence of character
      // in array
      output = String::Concat( output,
         S"\n\nFirst occurrence of 'c', 'a', '$' is ",
         S"located at ",
         letters->IndexOfAny( searchLetters ).ToString() );

      output = String::Concat( output,
         S"\nFirst occurrence of 'c', 'a' or '$' is ",
         S"located at ",
         letters->IndexOfAny( searchLetters, 7 ).ToString() );

      output = String::Concat( output,
         S"\nFirst occurrence of 'c', 'a' or '$' is ",
         S"located at ",
         letters->IndexOfAny( searchLetters, 20, 5 ).ToString() );

      // test LastIndexOfAny to find last occurrence of character
      // in array
      output = String::Concat( output,
         S"\n\nLast occurrence of 'c', 'a' or '$' is ",
         S"located at ",
         letters->LastIndexOfAny( searchLetters ).ToString() );

      output = String::Concat( output,
         S"\nLast occurrence of 'c', 'a' or '$' is ",
         S"located at ",
         letters->LastIndexOfAny( searchLetters, 1 ).ToString() );

      output = String::Concat( output,
         S"\nLast occurrence of 'c', 'a' or '$' is located at ",
         letters->LastIndexOfAny( searchLetters, 25, 5 ).ToString() );

      MessageBox::Show( output,
         S"Demonstrating class index methods",
         MessageBoxButtons::OK, MessageBoxIcon::Information );

      return 0;
   } // end _tmain
```

Fig. 15.5 `StringIndexMethods` demonstrates `String` searching capabilities. (Part 2 of 3.)

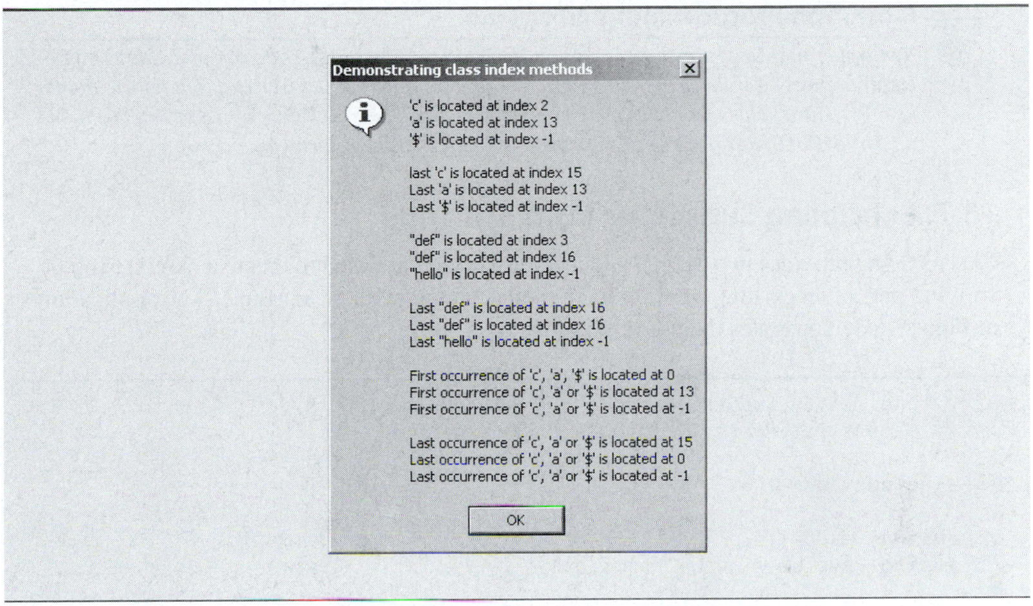

Demonstrating class index methods
'c' is located at index 2
'a' is located at index 13
'$' is located at index -1
last 'c' is located at index 15
Last 'a' is located at index 13
Last '$' is located at index -1
"def" is located at index 3
"def" is located at index 16
"hello" is located at index -1
Last "def" is located at index 16
Last "def" is located at index 16
Last "hello" is located at index -1
First occurrence of 'c', 'a', '$' is located at 0
First occurrence of 'c', 'a' or '$' is located at 13
First occurrence of 'c', 'a' or '$' is located at -1
Last occurrence of 'c', 'a' or '$' is located at 15
Last occurrence of 'c', 'a' or '$' is located at 0
Last occurrence of 'c', 'a' or '$' is located at -1
OK

Fig. 15.5 `StringIndexMethods` demonstrates `String` searching capabilities. (Part 3 of 3.)

Lines 30, 34, and 38 use method `LastIndexOf` to locate the last occurrence of a character in a `String`. Method `LastIndexOf` performs the search from the end of the `String` toward the beginning of the `String`. If method `LastIndexOf` finds the character, `LastIndexOf` returns the index of the specified character in the `String`; otherwise, `LastIndexOf` returns `-1`. There are three versions of `LastIndexOf` that search for characters in a `String`. The expression in line 30 uses the version of method `LastIndexOf` that takes as an argument the character for which to search. The expression in line 34 uses the version of method `LastIndexOf` that takes two arguments—the character for which to search and the highest index from which to begin searching backward for the character. The expression in line 38 uses a third version of method `LastIndexOf` that takes three arguments—the character for which to search, the starting index from which to start searching backward and the number of characters (the portion of the `String`) to search.

Lines 43–64 use versions of `IndexOf` and `LastIndexOf` that take a `String *` instead of a character as the first argument. These versions of the methods perform identically to those described earlier, except that they search for sequences of characters (or substrings) that are specified by their `String *` arguments.

Lines 71–97 use methods `IndexOfAny` and `LastIndexOfAny`, which take an array of characters as the first argument. These versions of the methods also perform identically to those just described, except that they return the index of the first occurrence of any of the characters in the character array argument.

Common Programming Error 15.4

In the overloaded methods `LastIndexOf` *and* `LastIndexOfAny` *that take three parameters, the second argument must always be greater than or equal to the third argument. This might seem counterintuitive, but remember that the search moves from the end of the string toward the start of the string.*

Common Programming Error 15.5

Remember that `String` methods `IndexOf`, `IndexOfAny`, `LastIndexOf` and `LastIndexOfAny` return `-1` if the specified characters are not found in the `String`. Therefore, do not use the return values from these methods to directly access members of a `String`. To avoid an `IndexOutOfRangeException`, always check that the return value is not `-1` first.

15.7 Extracting Substrings from Strings

Class `String` provides two ***`Substring`*** methods, which are used to create a new `String` by copying part of an existing `String`. Each method returns a new `String *`. The application in Fig. 15.6 demonstrates the use of both methods.

```
// Fig. 15.6: SubString.cpp
// Demonstrating the String Substring method.

#include "stdafx.h"

#using <mscorlib.dll>
#using <system.windows.forms.dll>

using namespace System;
using namespace System::Windows::Forms;

int _tmain()
{
   String *letters = S"abcdefghijklmabcdefghijklm";
   String *output = S"";

   // invoke Substring method and pass it one parameter
   output = String::Concat( output,
      S"Substring from index 20 to end is \"",
      letters->Substring( 20 ), S"\"\n" );

   // invoke Substring method and pass it two parameters
   output = String::Concat( output,
      S"Substring from index 0 to 6 is \"",
      letters->Substring( 0, 6 ), S"\"" );

   MessageBox::Show( output,
      S"Demonstrating String method Substring",
      MessageBoxButtons::OK, MessageBoxIcon::Information );

   return 0;
} // end _tmain
```

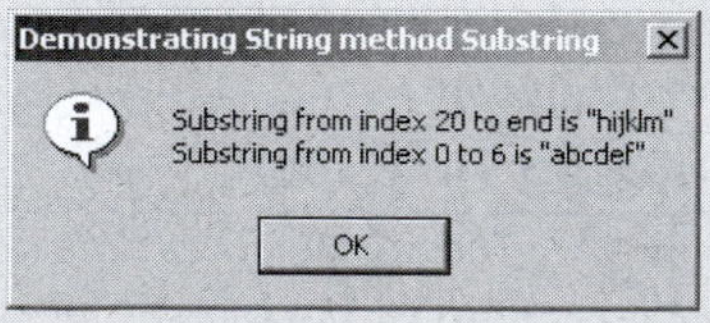
Demonstrating String method Substring
Substring from index 20 to end is "hijklm"
Substring from index 0 to 6 is "abcdef"
OK

Fig. 15.6 Substrings generated from `Strings`.

The statement in line 20 uses method `SubString` that takes one `int` argument. The argument specifies the starting index from which the method copies characters in the original `String`. The substring returned contains a copy of the characters from the starting index to the end of the `String`. If the index specified in the argument is outside the bounds of the `String`, the program throws an `ArgumentOutOfRangeException`.

The second version of method `SubString` (line 25) takes two `int` arguments. The first argument specifies the starting index from which the method copies characters from the original `String`. The second argument specifies the length of the substring to be copied. The substring returned contains a copy of the specified characters from the original `String`.

15.8 Miscellaneous `String` Methods

Class `String` provides several methods that return modified copies of `String`s. The application in Fig. 15.7 demonstrates the use of these methods, which include `String` methods *`Replace`*, *`ToLower`*, *`ToUpper`*, *`Trim`* and *`ToString`*.

```
// Fig. 15.7: StringMiscellaneous2.cpp
// Demonstrating String methods Replace, ToLower, ToUpper, Trim
// and ToString.

#include "stdafx.h"

#using <mscorlib.dll>
#using <system.windows.forms.dll>

using namespace System;
using namespace System::Windows::Forms;

int _tmain()
{
   String *string1 = S"cheers!";
   String *string2 = S"GOOD BYE ";
   String *string3 = S"   spaces   ";
   String *output;

   output = String::Concat( S"string1 = \"", string1,
      S"\"\n", S"string2 = \"", string2, S"\"\n",
      S"string3 = \"", string3, S"\"" );

   // call method Replace
   output = String::Concat( output,
      S"\n\nReplacing \"e\" with \"E\" in string1: \"",
      string1->Replace( 'e', 'E' ), S"\"" );

   // call methods ToLower and ToUpper
   output = String::Concat( output,
      S"\n\nstring1->ToUpper() = \"", string1->ToUpper(),
      S"\"\nstring2->ToLower() = \"", string2->ToLower(), S"\"" );
```

Fig. 15.7 `String` methods `Replace`, `ToLower`, `ToUpper`, `Trim` and `ToString`. (Part 1 of 2.)

```
33
34     // call method Trim
35     output = String::Concat( output,
36        S"\n\nstring3 after trim = \"", string3->Trim(), S"\"" );
37
38     // call method ToString
39     output = String::Concat( output, S"\n\nstring1 = \"",
40        string1->ToString(), S"\"" );
41
42     MessageBox::Show( output,
43        S"Demonstrating various String methods",
44        MessageBoxButtons::OK, MessageBoxIcon::Information );
45
46     return 0;
47  } // end _tmain
```

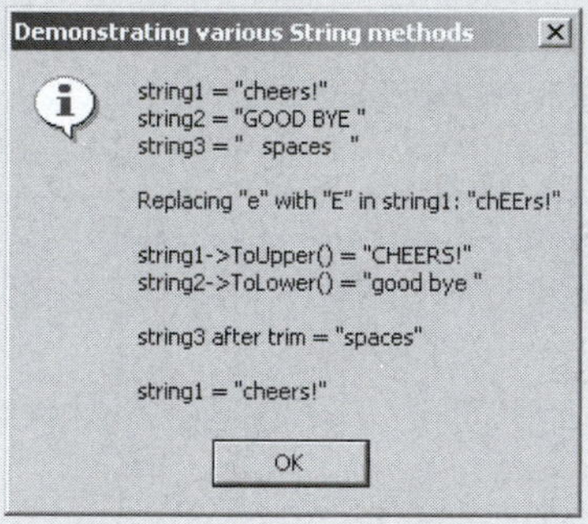
Demonstrating various String methods
string1 = "cheers!"
string2 = "GOOD BYE "
string3 = "   spaces   "
Replacing "e" with "E" in string1: "chEErs!"
string1->ToUpper() = "CHEERS!"
string2->ToLower() = "good bye "
string3 after trim = "spaces"
string1 = "cheers!"
OK

Fig. 15.7 `String` methods `Replace`, `ToLower`, `ToUpper`, `Trim` and `ToString`. (Part 2 of 2.)

Line 27 uses `String` method `Replace` to return a new `String *`, replacing every occurrence in `string1` of character `'e'` with character `'E'`. Method `Replace` takes two arguments—a character for which to search and another character with which to replace all matching occurrences of the first argument. There is another version of method `Replace` that takes `String` pointers instead of characters. The original `String` remains unchanged. If there are no occurrences of the first argument in the `String`, the method returns the original `String`.

`String` method `ToUpper` generates a new `String` (line 31) that replaces any lowercase letters in `string1` with their uppercase equivalent. The method returns a new `String *` containing the converted `String`; the original `String` remains unchanged. If there are no characters to convert to uppercase, the method returns the original `String *`. Line 32 uses `String` method `ToLower` to return a new `String *` in which any uppercase letters in `string2` are replaced by their lowercase equivalents. The original `String` is unchanged. As with `ToUpper`, if there are no characters to convert to lowercase, method `ToLower` returns the original `String *`.

Line 36 uses `String` method `Trim` to remove all white space characters that appear at the beginning and end of a `String`. Without otherwise altering the original `String`, the method returns a new `String *` with the leading or trailing white-space characters removed. Another version of method `Trim` takes a character array and returns a `String *` that does not contain the characters in the array argument.

Lines 39–40 use class `String`'s method `ToString` to show that the various other methods employed in this application have not modified `String1`. Why is the `ToString` method provided for class `String`? In MC++, all classes are derived from class `Object`, which defines `virtual` method `ToString`. Thus, method `ToString` can be called to obtain a `String` representation of any object. If a class that inherits from `Object` (such as `String`) does not override method `ToString`, the class uses the default version from class `Object`, which returns a `String *` consisting of the object's class name. Classes usually override method `ToString` to express the contents of an object as text. Class `String` overrides method `ToString` so that, instead of returning the class name, it simply returns the `String *`.

15.9 Class `StringBuilder`

The `String` class provides many capabilities for processing `String`s. However, a `String`'s contents can never change. Operations that seem to concatenate `String`s are in fact creating new `String`s.

The next several sections discuss the features of class *`StringBuilder`* (namespace `System::Text`), used to create and manipulate dynamic string information—i.e., *mutable* strings. Every `StringBuilder` object can store a certain number of characters, specified by its capacity. Exceeding the capacity of a `StringBuilder` causes the capacity to expand to accommodate the additional characters. As we will see, members of class `StringBuilder`, such as methods `Append` and `AppendFormat`, can be used for concatenation like method `Concat` for class `String`.

Software Engineering Observation 15.2

Objects of class `String` are constant (immutable) strings, whereas objects of class `String-Builder` are mutable strings. MC++ can perform certain optimizations involving managed `String`s (such as the sharing of one `String` among multiple pointers), because it knows these objects will not change.

Performance Tip 15.2

When given the choice between using a `String` to represent a string and using a `String-Builder` object to represent that string, always use a `String` if the contents of the object will not change. When appropriate, using `String`s instead of `StringBuilder` objects improves performance.

Class `StringBuilder` provides six overloaded constructors. Application `String-BuilderConstructor` (Fig. 15.8) demonstrates the use of three of these constructors.

```
// Fig. 15.8: StringBuilderConstructor.cpp
// Demonstrating StringBuilder class constructors.

#include "stdafx.h"

#using <mscorlib.dll>
#using <system.windows.forms.dll>

```

Fig. 15.8 `StringBuilder` class constructors. (Part 1 of 2.)

```
9  using namespace System;
10 using namespace System::Windows::Forms;
11 using namespace System::Text;
12
13 int _tmain()
14 {
15    StringBuilder *buffer1, *buffer2, *buffer3;
16    String *output;
17
18    buffer1 = new StringBuilder();
19    buffer2 = new StringBuilder( 10 );
20    buffer3 = new StringBuilder( S"hello" );
21
22    output = String::Concat( S"buffer = \"", buffer1, S"\"\n" );
23    output = String::Concat( output, S"buffer2 = \"", buffer2, S"\"\n" );
24    output = String::Concat( output, S"buffer3 = \"", buffer3, S"\"\n" );
25
26    MessageBox::Show( output,
27       S"Demonstrating StringBuilder class constructors",
28       MessageBoxButtons::OK, MessageBoxIcon::Information );
29
30    return 0;
31 } // end _tmain
```

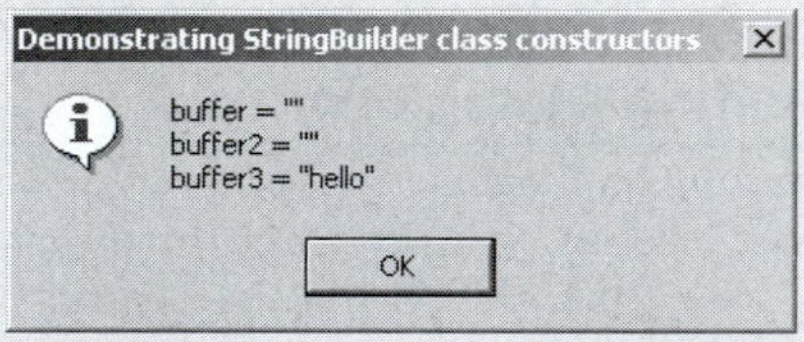

Fig. 15.8 `StringBuilder` class constructors. (Part 2 of 2.)

Line 18 uses the no-argument `StringBuilder` constructor to create a `StringBuilder` that contains no characters and has the default initial capacity (16 characters). Line 19 uses the `StringBuilder` constructor that takes an `int` argument to create a `StringBuilder` that contains no characters and has the initial capacity specified in the `int` argument (i.e., `10`). Line 20 uses the `StringBuilder` constructor that takes a `String *` argument to create a `StringBuilder` containing the characters referenced by the `String *` argument. The initial capacity is the smallest power of two greater than the number of characters in the `String` referenced by the `String *` argument. In this case, the capacity is eight, because eight is the smallest power of two greater than five, the number of characters in `"hello"`.

Lines 22–24 append the `StringBuilders` to the output `String`. Notice that we do not need to use `StringBuilder` method `ToString` to obtain a `String *` representation of the `StringBuilders`' contents (e.g., `buffer1->ToString`). This is because `String::Concat` can accept `StringBuilders` as arguments. Lines 26–28 display a message box containing the output string.

15.10 StringBuilder Length and Capacity Properties, and EnsureCapacity Method

Class StringBuilder provides the *Length* and *Capacity* properties to return the number of characters currently in a StringBuilder and the number of characters that a StringBuilder can store without allocating more memory, respectively. These properties can also be used to increase or decrease the length or the capacity of the StringBuilder.

Method *EnsureCapacity* allows programmers to guarantee that a StringBuilder has a capacity that is larger than or equal to a specified value. This method can be helpful in reducing the number of times the capacity must be increased. Method EnsureCapacity takes an integer value and, if that value is larger than the StringBuilder's current capacity, increases the StringBuilder's capacity to a value that is larger than or equal to the specified value. If the StringBuilder's capacity is already greater than or equal to the specified capacity, no change is made. The program in Fig. 15.9 demonstrates the use of these methods and properties.

Good Programming Practice 15.1

Accidentally specifying a Capacity below the StringBuilder's current Length will result in an ArgumentOutOfRangeException exception. Always use EnsureCapacity to alter the Capacity property of a StringBuilder object.

```
// Fig. 15.9: StringBuilderFeatures.cpp
// Demonstrating some features of class StringBuilder.

#include "stdafx.h"

#using <mscorlib.dll>
#using <system.windows.forms.dll>

using namespace System;
using namespace System::Windows::Forms;
using namespace System::Text;

int _tmain()
{
   StringBuilder *buffer = new StringBuilder( S"Hello, how are you?" );

   // use Length and Capacity properties
   String *output = String::Concat( S"buffer = ",
      buffer, S"\nLength = ", buffer->Length.ToString(),
      S"\nCapacity = ", buffer->Capacity.ToString() );

   // use EnsureCapacity method
   buffer->EnsureCapacity( 75 );

   output = String::Concat( output, S"\n\nNew capacity = ",
      buffer->Capacity.ToString() );

   // truncate StringBuilder by setting Length property
   buffer->Length = 10;
```

Fig. 15.9 StringBuilder size manipulation. (Part 1 of 2.)

```
30
31       output = String::Concat( output, S"\n\nNew length = ",
32          buffer->Length.ToString(), S"\nbuffer = " );
33
34       // use StringBuilder indexed property
35       for ( int i = 0; i < buffer->Length; i++ )
36          output = String::Concat( output, buffer->Chars[ i ].ToString() );
37
38       MessageBox::Show( output, S"StringBuilder features",
39          MessageBoxButtons::OK, MessageBoxIcon::Information );
40
41       return 0;
42    } // end _tmain
```

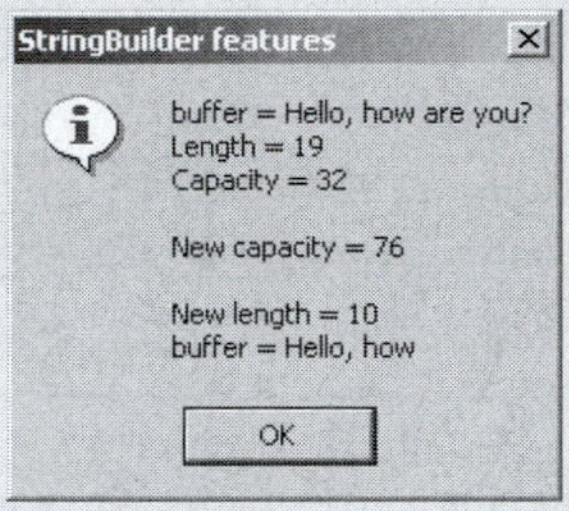

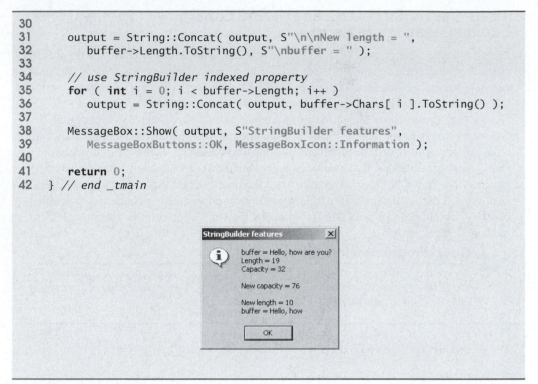

Fig. 15.9 `StringBuilder` size manipulation. (Part 2 of 2.)

The program contains one `StringBuilder`, called `buffer`. Line 15 of the program use the `StringBuilder` constructor that takes a `String *` argument to instantiate the `StringBuilder` and initialize its value to `"Hello, how are you?"`. Lines 18–20 append to `output` the content, length and capacity of the `StringBuilder`. In the output window, notice that the capacity of the `StringBuilder` is initially 16. Remember, the `StringBuilder` constructor that takes a `String *` argument creates a `StringBuilder` object with an initial capacity that is the smallest power of two greater than the number of characters in the `String *` passed as an argument.

Line 23 expands the capacity of the `StringBuilder` to a minimum of 76 characters, which is greater than or equal to the specified capacity (`75`). If new characters are added to a `StringBuilder` so that its length exceeds its capacity, the capacity grows to accommodate the additional characters.

Line 29 uses `Length`'s *set* method to set the length of the `StringBuilder` to `10`. If the specified length is less than the current number of characters in the `StringBuilder`, the contents of `StringBuilder` are truncated to the specified length (i.e., the program discards all characters in the `StringBuilder` that occur after the specified length). If the specified length is greater than the number of characters currently in the `StringBuilder`, null characters (that signal the end of a `String`) are appended to the `StringBuilder` until the total number of characters in the `StringBuilder` is equal to the specified length. Null characters have the numeric representation `0` and character constant representation `'\0'` (backslash followed by zero).

Common Programming Error 15.6

Assigning NULL *to a* String *pointer can lead to logic errors.* NULL *represents a null pointer, not a* String*. Do not confuse* NULL *with the empty string,* "" *(the* String *that is of length 0 and contains no characters).*

15.11 StringBuilder Append and AppendFormat Methods

Class StringBuilder provides 19 overloaded *Append* methods that allow various data-type values to be added to the end of a StringBuilder. MC++ provides versions for each of the primitive data types and for character arrays, String pointers and Object pointers. Each of the methods takes an argument, converts it to a String and appends it to the StringBuilder. Figure 15.10 demonstrates several Append methods.

```
// Fig. 15.10: StringBuilderAppend.cpp
// Demonstrating StringBuilder Append methods.

#include "stdafx.h"

#using <mscorlib.dll>
#using <system.windows.forms.dll>

using namespace System;
using namespace System::Windows::Forms;
using namespace System::Text;

int _tmain()
{
   Object *objectValue = S"hello";
   String *stringValue = S"goodbye";
   __wchar_t characterArray __gc[] = { 'a', 'b', 'c', 'd', 'e', 'f' };

   bool booleanValue = true;
   __wchar_t characterValue = 'Z';
   int integerValue = 7;
   long longValue = 1000000;
   float floatValue = 2.5;
   double doubleValue = 33.333;

   StringBuilder *buffer = new StringBuilder();

   // use method Append to add values to buffer
   buffer->Append( objectValue );
   buffer->Append( S"  " );
   buffer->Append( stringValue );
   buffer->Append( S"  " );
   buffer->Append( characterArray );
   buffer->Append( S"  " );
   buffer->Append( characterArray, 0, 3 );
   buffer->Append( S"  " );
   buffer->Append( booleanValue );
   buffer->Append( S"  " );
```

Fig. 15.10 Append methods of StringBuilder. (Part 1 of 2.)

```
39      buffer->Append( characterValue );
40      buffer->Append( S"  " );
41      buffer->Append( integerValue );
42      buffer->Append( S"  " );
43      buffer->Append( longValue );
44      buffer->Append( S"  " );
45      buffer->Append( floatValue );
46      buffer->Append( S"  " );
47      buffer->Append( doubleValue );
48      buffer->Append( S"  " );
49
50      MessageBox::Show( String::Concat( S"buffer = ", buffer ),
51         S"Demonstrating StringBuilder Append method",
52         MessageBoxButtons::OK, MessageBoxIcon::Information );
53
54      return 0;
55   } // end _tmain
```

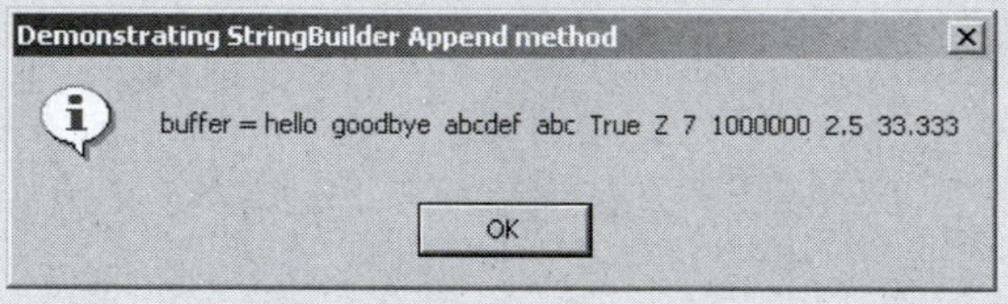
Demonstrating StringBuilder Append method
buffer = hello goodbye abcdef abc True Z 7 1000000 2.5 33.333
OK

Fig. 15.10 Append methods of `StringBuilder`. (Part 2 of 2.)

Lines 29–48 use ten different overloaded `Append` methods to attach the values assigned in lines 15–24 to the end of the `StringBuilder`. `Append` behaves similarly to the `Concat` method, which is used with `String`s.

Class `StringBuilder` also provides method *`AppendFormat`*, which converts a `String` to a specified format, then appends it to the `StringBuilder`. The example in Fig. 15.11 demonstrates the use of this method.

```
// Fig. 15.11: StringBuilderAppendFormat.cpp
// Demonstrating method AppendFormat.

#include "stdafx.h"

#using <mscorlib.dll>
#using <system.windows.forms.dll>

using namespace System;
using namespace System::Windows::Forms;
using namespace System::Text;

int _tmain()
{
   StringBuilder *buffer = new StringBuilder();
   String *string1, *string2;

```

Fig. 15.11 `StringBuilder`'s `AppendFormat` method. (Part 1 of 2.)

```
18      // formatted string
19      string1 = S"This {0} costs: {1:C}.\n";
20
21      // string1 argument array
22      Object *objectArray[] = new Object*[ 2 ];
23
24      objectArray[ 0 ] = S"car";
25      objectArray[ 1 ] = __box( 1234.56 );
26
27      // append to buffer formatted string with argument
28      buffer->AppendFormat( string1, objectArray );
29
30      // formatted string
31      string2 = String::Concat( S"Number: {0:d3}.\n",
32         S"Number right aligned with spaces:{0, 4}.\n",
33         S"Number left aligned with spaces:{0, -4}." );
34
35      // append to buffer formatted string with argument
36      buffer->AppendFormat( string2, __box( 5 ) );
37
38      // display formatted strings
39      MessageBox::Show( buffer->ToString(), S"Using AppendFormat",
40         MessageBoxButtons::OK, MessageBoxIcon::Information );
41
42      return 0;
43   } // end _tmain
```

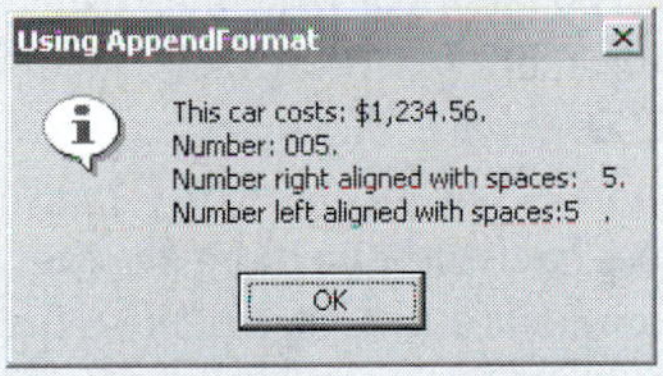
Using AppendFormat
This car costs: $1,234.56.
Number: 005.
Number right aligned with spaces: 5.
Number left aligned with spaces:5   .
OK

Fig. 15.11 `StringBuilder`'s `AppendFormat` method. (Part 2 of 2.)

Line 19 creates a `String *` that contains formatting information. The information enclosed within the braces determines how to format a specific piece of information. Formats have the form `{X[,Y][:FormatString]}`, where `X` is the number of the argument to be formatted, counting from zero. `Y` is an optional argument, which can be positive or negative, indicating how many characters should be in the result of formatting. If the resulting `String` is less than the number `Y`, the `String` will be padded with spaces to make up for the difference. A positive integer aligns the `String` to the right; a negative integer aligns it to the left. The optional `FormatString` applies a particular format to the argument (e.g., currency, decimal, scientific, etc.), `{0}` means the first argument will be printed out. `{1:C}` specifies that the second argument will be formatted as a currency value.

Line 22 creates array `objectArray`, and lines 24–25 insert two items into the `Object` array. Notice that line 25 must first use MC++ keyword `__box` to convert the value type (`1234.56`) to a managed `Object`. Refer to Chapter 12, Graphical User Interface Concepts: Part 1, for a discussion of keyword `__box`.

Line 28 shows a version of `AppendFormat`, which takes two parameters—a `String *` specifying the format and an array of objects to serve as the arguments to the format `String`. The argument indicated by `{0}` is in the object array at index `0`, and so on.

Lines 31–33 define another `String *` used for formatting. The first format `{0:d3}` specifies that the first argument will be formatted as a three-digit decimal, meaning any number that has fewer than three digits will have leading zeros placed in front to make up the difference. The next format `{0, 4}` specifies that the formatted `String` should have four characters and should be right aligned. The third format `{0, -4}` specifies that the `Strings` should be aligned to the left. For more formatting options, please refer to the documentation.

Line 36 uses a version of `AppendFormat` that takes two parameters: a `String *` containing a format and an object to which the format is applied. In this case, the object is the number `5`. The output of Fig. 15.11 displays the result of applying these two versions of `AppendFormat` with their respective arguments.

15.12 `StringBuilder` `Insert`, `Remove` and `Replace` Methods

Class `StringBuilder` provides 18 overloaded *`Insert`* methods to allow various data-type values to be inserted at any position in a `StringBuilder`. The class provides versions for each of the primitive data types and for character arrays, `String` pointers and `Object` pointers. Each version of `Insert` takes its second argument, converts it to a `String` and inserts the `String` into the `StringBuilder` in front of the index specified by the first argument. The index specified by the first argument must be greater than or equal to `0` and less than the length of the `StringBuilder`; otherwise, the program throws an `ArgumentOutOfRangeException`.

Class `StringBuilder` also provides method *`Remove`* for deleting any portion of a `StringBuilder`. Method `Remove` takes two arguments—the index at which to begin deletion and the number of characters to delete. The sum of the starting subscript and the number of characters to be deleted must always be less than the length of the `StringBuilder`; otherwise, the program throws an `ArgumentOutOfRangeException`. The `Insert` and `Remove` methods are demonstrated in Fig. 15.12.

```
// Fig. 15.12: StringBuilderInsertRemove.cpp
// Demonstrating methods Insert and Remove of the
// StringBuilder class.

#include "stdafx.h"

#using <mscorlib.dll>
#using <system.windows.forms.dll>

```

Fig. 15.12 `StringBuilder` text insertion and removal. (Part 1 of 3.)

```
using namespace System;
using namespace System::Windows::Forms;
using namespace System::Text;

int _tmain()
{
   Object *objectValue = S"hello";
   String *stringValue = S"good bye";
   __wchar_t characterArray __gc[] = { 'a', 'b', 'c', 'd', 'e', 'f' };
   bool booleanValue = true;
   __wchar_t characterValue = 'K';
   int integerValue = 7;
   long longValue = 10000000;
   float floatValue = 2.5;
   double doubleValue = 46.789;

   StringBuilder *buffer = new StringBuilder();
   String *output;

   // insert value into buffer
   buffer->Insert( 0, objectValue );
   buffer->Insert( 0, "  " );
   buffer->Insert( 0, stringValue );
   buffer->Insert( 0, "  " );
   buffer->Insert( 0, characterArray );
   buffer->Insert( 0, "  " );
   buffer->Insert( 0, booleanValue );
   buffer->Insert( 0, "  " );
   buffer->Insert( 0, characterValue );
   buffer->Insert( 0, "  " );
   buffer->Insert( 0, integerValue );
   buffer->Insert( 0, "  " );
   buffer->Insert( 0, longValue );
   buffer->Insert( 0, "  " );
   buffer->Insert( 0, floatValue );
   buffer->Insert( 0, "  " );
   buffer->Insert( 0, doubleValue );
   buffer->Insert( 0, "  " );

   output = String::Concat( S"buffer after inserts: \n",
      buffer, S"\n\n" );

   buffer->Remove( 10, 1 );  // delete 2 in 2.5
   buffer->Remove( 2, 4 );   // delete 46.7 in 46.789

   output = String::Concat( output, S"buffer after Removes:\n", buffer );

   MessageBox::Show( output,
      S"Demonstrating StringBuilder Insert and Remove methods",
      MessageBoxButtons::OK, MessageBoxIcon::Information );

   return 0;
} // end _tmain
```

Fig. 15.12 `StringBuilder` text insertion and removal. (Part 2 of 3.)

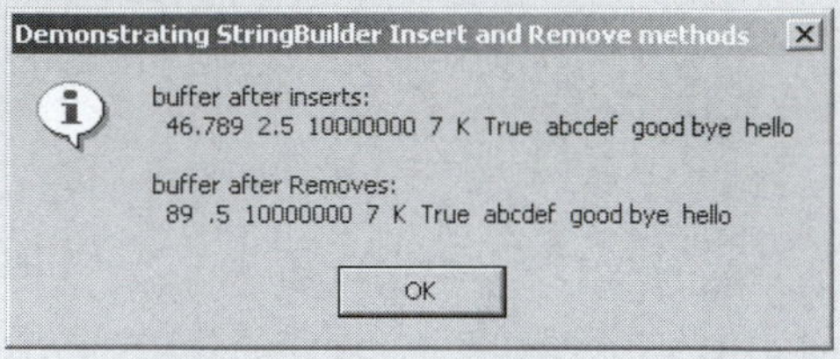

Fig. 15.12 `StringBuilder` text insertion and removal. (Part 3 of 3.)

Another useful method included with `StringBuilder` is ***Replace***, which searches for a specified `String` or character and substitutes another `String` or character in its place. Figure 15.13 demonstrates this method.

Line 21 of Fig. 15.13 uses method `Replace` to replace all instances of the `String` `"Jane"` with the `String` `"Greg"` in `builder1`. Another overload of this method takes two characters as parameters and replaces each occurrence of the first with one of the second. Line 22 uses an overload of `Replace` that takes four parameters, the first two of which are

```
1  // Fig. 15.13: StringBuilderReplace.cpp
2  // Demonstrating method Replace.
3
4  #include "stdafx.h"
5
6  #using <mscorlib.dll>
7  #using <system.windows.forms.dll>
8
9  using namespace System;
10 using namespace System::Windows::Forms;
11 using namespace System::Text;
12
13 int _tmain()
14 {
15    StringBuilder *builder1 = new StringBuilder( S"Happy Birthday Jane" );
16    StringBuilder *builder2 = new StringBuilder( S"goodbye greg" );
17
18    String *output = String::Concat( S"Before replacements:\n",
19       builder1, S"\n", builder2 );
20
21    builder1->Replace( S"Jane", S"Greg" );
22    builder2->Replace( 'g', 'G', 0, 5 );
23
24    output = String::Concat( output, S"\n\nAfter replacements:\n",
25       builder1, S"\n", builder2 );
26
27    MessageBox::Show( output, S"Using StringBuilder method Replace",
28       MessageBoxButtons::OK, MessageBoxIcon::Information );
29
30    return 0;
31 } // end _tmain
```

Fig. 15.13 `StringBuilder` text replacement. (Part 1 of 2.)

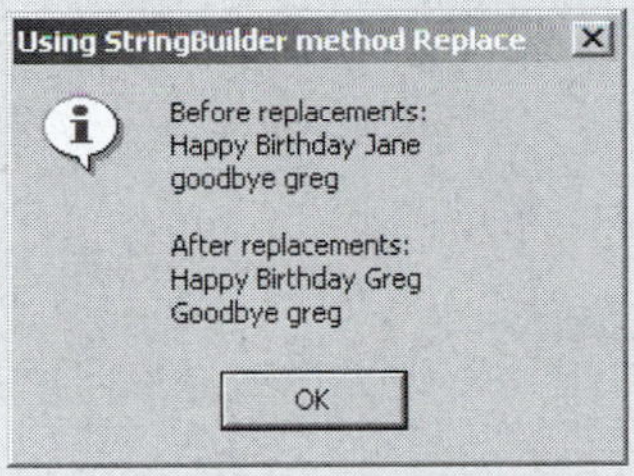

Fig. 15.13 `StringBuilder` text replacement. (Part 2 of 2.)

characters and the second two of which are `int`s. The method replaces all instances of the first character with the second, beginning at the index specified by the first `int` and continuing for a count specified by the second. Thus, in this case, `Replace` looks through only five characters starting with the character at index `0`. As the outputs illustrates, this version of `Replace` replaces `g` with `G` in the word `"goodbye"`, but not in `"greg"`. This is because the `g`s in `"greg"` do not fall in the range indicated by the `int` arguments (i.e., between indexes `0` and `4`).

15.13 Char Methods

MC++ provides a data type, called a *structure*, that is similar to a class. Like classes, structures include methods and properties. Both use the same specifiers (such as `public`, `private` and `protected`) and access members via the member access operator (`.`), the arrow member access operator (`->`) and the scope resolution operator (`::`). However, the default access specifier for classes is `private`, while the default access specifier for structures is `public`. Classes are created by using the keyword `class`, but structures are created using the keyword *`struct`*.

As discussed earlier in the book, many of the primitive data types that we have used in this book are actually aliases for structures. For instance, in MC++, an `int` is defined by structure `System::Int32`, a `bool` by `System::Boolean`, and so on. These structures are derived from class *`ValueType`*, which in turn is derived from class `Object`. In this section, we present structure *`Char`*, which is the structure for characters. Recall that in MC++, `__wchar_t` is an alias for `Char`.

Most `Char` methods are `static`, take at least one character argument and perform either a test or a manipulation on the character. We present several of these methods in the next example. Figures 15.14–15.15 demonstrate `static` methods that test characters to determine whether they are of a specific character type and `static` methods that perform case conversions on characters.

```
// Fig. 15.14: Form1.h
// Demonstrating static character testing methods
// from Char structure.
```

Fig. 15.14 `Char`'s `static` character-testing methods and case-conversion methods. (Part 1 of 3.)

```
#pragma once


namespace StaticCharMethods
{
   using namespace System;
   using namespace System::ComponentModel;
   using namespace System::Collections;
   using namespace System::Windows::Forms;
   using namespace System::Data;
   using namespace System::Drawing;

   /// <summary>
   /// Summary for Form1
   ///
   /// WARNING: If you change the name of this class, you will need to
   ///          change the 'Resource File Name' property for the managed
   ///          resource compiler tool associated with all .resx files
   ///          this class depends on.  Otherwise, the designers will not
   ///          be able to interact properly with localized resources
   ///          associated with this form.
   /// </summary>
   public __gc class Form1 : public System::Windows::Forms::Form
   {
   public:
      Form1(void)
      {
         InitializeComponent();
      }

   protected:
      void Dispose(Boolean disposing)
      {
         if (disposing && components)
         {
            components->Dispose();
         }
         __super::Dispose(disposing);
      }
   private: System::Windows::Forms::Label *  enterLabel;
   private: System::Windows::Forms::TextBox *  inputTextBox;
   private: System::Windows::Forms::Button *  analyzeButton;
   private: System::Windows::Forms::TextBox *  outputTextBox;

   private:
      /// <summary>
      /// Required designer variable.
      /// </summary>
      System::ComponentModel::Container * components;

```

Fig. 15.14 `Char`'s `static` character-testing methods and case-conversion methods. (Part 2 of 3.)

```
      // Visual Studio .NET generated GUI code

      // handle analyzeButton_Click
      private: System::Void analyzeButton_Click(
                  System::Object *  sender, System::EventArgs *  e)
               {
                  __wchar_t character =
                     Convert::ToChar( inputTextBox->Text );
                  BuildOutput( character );
               } // end method analyzeButton_Click

      // display character information in outputTextBox
      private: void BuildOutput( __wchar_t inputCharacter )
               {
                  String *output;

                  output = String::Concat( S"is digit: ",
                     Char::IsDigit( inputCharacter ).ToString(), S"\r\n" );

                  output = String::Concat( output, S"is letter: ",
                     Char::IsLetter( inputCharacter ).ToString(), S"\r\n" );

                  output = String::Concat( output, S"is letter or digit: ",
                     Char::IsLetterOrDigit( inputCharacter ).ToString(),
                     S"\r\n" );

                  output = String::Concat( output, S"is lower case: ",
                     Char::IsLower( inputCharacter ).ToString(), S"\r\n" );

                  output = String::Concat( output, S"is upper case: ",
                     Char::IsUpper( inputCharacter ).ToString(), S"\r\n" );

                  output = String::Concat( output, S"to upper case: ",
                     Char::ToUpper( inputCharacter ).ToString(), S"\r\n" );

                  output = String::Concat( output, S"to lower case: ",
                     Char::ToLower( inputCharacter ).ToString(), S"\r\n" );

                  output = String::Concat( output, S"is punctuation: ",
                     Char::IsPunctuation( inputCharacter ).ToString(),
                     S"\r\n" );

                  output = String::Concat( output, S"is symbol: ",
                     Char::IsSymbol( inputCharacter ).ToString() );

                  outputTextBox->Text = output;
               } // end method BuildOutput
   };
}
```

Fig. 15.14 Char's static character-testing methods and case-conversion methods. (Part 3 of 3.)

```
// Fig. 15.15: Form1.cpp
// Demonstrates Char methods.

#include "stdafx.h"
#include "Form1.h"
#include <windows.h>

using namespace StaticCharMethods;

int APIENTRY _tWinMain(HINSTANCE hInstance,
                       HINSTANCE hPrevInstance,
                       LPTSTR    lpCmdLine,
                       int       nCmdShow)
{
   System::Threading::Thread::CurrentThread->ApartmentState =
      System::Threading::ApartmentState::STA;
   Application::Run(new Form1());
   return 0;
} // end _tWinMain
```

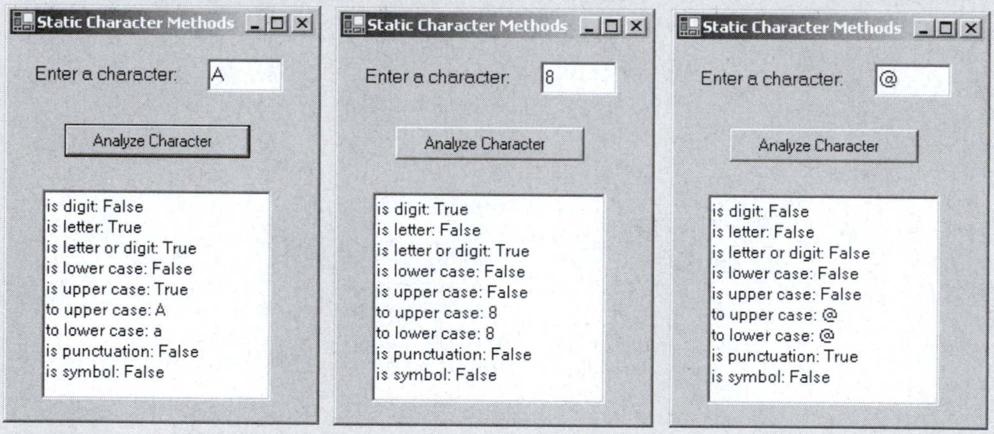

Fig. 15.15 `Char` methods demonstration.

This Windows application contains a prompt, a `TextBox` into which the user can input a character, a button that the user can press after entering a character and a second `TextBox` that displays the output of our analysis. When the user clicks the **Analyze Character** button, event handler `analyzeButton_Click` (lines 58–64 of Fig. 15.14) is invoked. This method converts the entered data from a `String *` to a `Char`, using method `Convert::ToChar` (line 62). Line 63 calls method `BuildOutput`, which is defined in lines 67–101.

Each of the methods that have names that have names that begin with `"Is"` return `true` or `false`. Line 72 uses `Char` method ***`IsDigit`*** to determine whether character `inputCharacter` is defined as a digit. Line 75 uses `Char` method ***`IsLetter`*** to determine whether character `inputCharacter` is a letter. Line 78 uses `Char` method ***`IsLetterOrDigit`*** to determine whether character `inputCharacter` is a letter or a digit. Line 82 uses `Char` method ***`IsLower`*** to determine whether character `inputCharacter` is a lowercase letter. Line 85 uses

Char method *IsUpper* to determine whether character inputCharacter is an uppercase letter. Line 88 uses Char method *ToUpper* to convert the character inputCharacter to its uppercase equivalent. The method returns the converted character if the character 91 an uppercase equivalent; otherwise, the method returns its original argument. Line 91 uses Char method *ToLower* to convert the character inputCharacter to its lowercase equivalent. The method returns the converted character if the character has a lowercase equivalent; otherwise, the method returns its original argument. Line 94 uses Char method *IsPunctuation* to determine whether character inputCharacter is a punctuation mark. Line 98 uses Char method *IsSymbol* to determine whether character inputCharacter is a symbol.

Structure Char also contains other methods not shown in this example. Many of the static methods are similar; for instance, *IsWhiteSpace* is used to determine whether a certain character is a white-space character (e.g., newline, tab or space). The structure also contains several public instance methods; many of these, such as methods ToString and Equals, are methods that we have seen before in other classes. This group includes method *CompareTo*, which is used to compare two character values with one another.

15.14 Card Shuffling and Dealing Simulation

In this section, we use random-number generation to develop a program that simulates the shuffling and dealing of cards. Once created, this program can be implemented in other applications that imitate specific card games.

Class Card (Fig. 15.16–Fig. 15.17) contains two String * variables—face and suit—that store the face name and suit name of a specific card. The constructor for the class receives two String pointers that it uses to initialize face and suit. Method ToString (lines 14–17 of Fig. 15.17) creates a String * consisting of the face of the card and the suit of the card.

```
// Fig. 15.16: Card.h
// Stores suit and face information of each card.

#pragma once

#using <mscorlib.dll>

using namespace System;

// representation of a card
public __gc class Card
{
public:
   Card( String *, String * );
   String *ToString();

private:
   String *face, *suit;
}; // end class Card
```

Fig. 15.16 Card class stores suit and face information.

```
// Fig. 15.17: Card.cpp
// Method definitions for class Card.

#include "stdafx.h"
#include "Card.h"

Card::Card( String *faceValue, String *suitValue )
{
   face = faceValue;
   suit = suitValue;
}

// override ToString
String *Card::ToString()
{
   return String::Concat( face, S" of ", suit );
} // end method ToString
```

Fig. 15.17 Card class method definitions.

The application in Fig. 15.18–Fig. 15.19 creates a deck of 52 playing cards, using `Card` objects. Users can deal each card by clicking the **Deal Card** button. Each dealt card is displayed in a `Label`. Users can also shuffle the deck at any time by clicking the **Shuffle Cards** button.

```
// Fig. 15.18: Form1.h
// Simulates card drawing and shuffling.

#pragma once

#include "Card.h"

namespace DeckOfCards
{
   using namespace System;
   using namespace System::ComponentModel;
   using namespace System::Collections;
   using namespace System::Windows::Forms;
   using namespace System::Data;
   using namespace System::Drawing;

   /// <summary>
   /// Summary for Form1
   ///
   /// WARNING: If you change the name of this class, you will need to
   ///          change the 'Resource File Name' property for the managed
   ///          resource compiler tool associated with all .resx files
   ///          this class depends on.  Otherwise, the designers will not
   ///          be able to interact properly with localized resources
   ///          associated with this form.
   /// </summary>
```

Fig. 15.18 `DeckOfCards::Form1` class simulates card drawing and shuffling. (Part 1 of 4.)

```
   public __gc class Form1 : public System::Windows::Forms::Form
   {
   public:
      Form1(void)
      {
         InitializeComponent();
      }

   protected:
      void Dispose(Boolean disposing)
      {
         if (disposing && components)
         {
            components->Dispose();
         }
         __super::Dispose(disposing);
      }
   private: System::Windows::Forms::Button *  dealButton;
   private: System::Windows::Forms::Button *  shuffleButton;
   private: System::Windows::Forms::Label *  displayLabel;
   private: System::Windows::Forms::Label *  statusLabel;

   private: static Card *deck[] = new Card *[ 52 ];
   private: int currentCard;

   private:
      /// <summary>
      /// Required designer variable.
      /// </summary>
      System::ComponentModel::Container * components;

   // Visual Studio .NET generated GUI code

   // handles form at load time
   private: System::Void Form1_Load(
               System::Object *  sender, System::EventArgs *  e)
            {
               String *faces[] = { S"Ace", S"Deuce", S"Three", S"Four",
                  S"Five", S"Six", S"Seven", S"Eight", S"Nine", S"Ten",
                  S"Jack", S"Queen", S"King" };

               String *suits[] = { S"Hearts", S"Diamonds", S"Clubs",
                  S"Spades" };

               // no cards have been drawn
               currentCard = -1;

               // initialize deck
               for ( int i = 0; i < deck->Length; i++ )
                  deck[ i ] = new Card( faces[ i % 13 ], suits[ i % 4 ] );
            } // end method Form1_Load

```

Fig. 15.18 `DeckOfCards::Form1` class simulates card drawing and shuffling. (Part 2 of 4.)

```
    // handles dealButton_Click
    private: System::Void dealButton_Click(
                System::Object *  sender, System::EventArgs *  e)
            {
                Card *dealt = DealCard();

                // if dealt card is null, then no cards left
                // player must shuffle cards
                if ( dealt != NULL ) {
                   displayLabel->Text = dealt->ToString();
                   statusLabel->Text = String::Concat( S"Card #: ",
                      currentCard.ToString() );
                } // end if
                else  {
                   displayLabel->Text = S"NO MORE CARDS TO DEAL";
                   statusLabel->Text = S"Shuffle cards to continue";
                } // end else
            } // end method dealButton_Click

    // shuffle cards
    private: void Shuffle()
            {
                Random *randomNumber = new Random();
                Card *temporaryValue;

                currentCard = -1;

                // swap each card with random card
                for ( int i = 0; i < deck->Length; i++ ) {
                   int j = randomNumber->Next( 52 );

                   // swap cards
                   temporaryValue = deck[ i ];
                   deck[ i ] = deck[ j ];
                   deck[ j ] = temporaryValue;
                } // end for

                dealButton->Enabled = true;
            } // end method Shuffle

    // deal the cards
    private: Card *DealCard()
            {
                // if there is a card to deal, then deal it;
                // otherwise, signal that cards need to be shuffled by
                // disabling dealButton and returning null
                if ( currentCard + 1 < deck->Length ) {
                   currentCard++;
                   return deck[ currentCard ];
                } // end if
                else {
                   dealButton->Enabled = false;
```

Fig. 15.18 DeckOfCards::Form1 class simulates card drawing and shuffling. (Part 3 of 4.)

```
131                 return NULL;
132              } // end else
133           } // end method DealCard
134
135     // handles shuffleButton_Click
136     private: System::Void shuffleButton_Click(
137              System::Object *  sender, System::EventArgs *  e)
138           {
139              displayLabel->Text = S"SHUFFLING...";
140              Shuffle();
141              displayLabel->Text = S"DECK IS SHUFFLED";
142              statusLabel->Text = S"";
143           } // end method shuffleButton_Click
144     };
145  }
```

Fig. 15.18 `DeckOfCards::Form1` class simulates card drawing and shuffling. (Part 4 of 4.)

Event handler `Form1_Load` (lines 61–77 of Fig. 15.18) uses the `for` statement (lines 75–76) to fill the `deck` array with `Card`s. Note that each `Card` is instantiated and initialized with two `String` pointers—one from the `faces` array (`"Ace"` through `"King"`) and one from the `suits` array (`"Hearts"`, `"Diamonds"`, `"Clubs"` or `"Spades"`). The calculation `i % 13` always results in a value from `0` to `12` (the thirteen subscripts of the `faces` array), and the calculation `i % 4` always results in a value from `0` to `3` (the four subscripts in the `suits` array). The initialized `deck` array contains the cards with faces ace through king for each suit.

When users click the **Deal Card** button, event handler `dealButton_Click` (lines 80–96) invokes method `DealCard` (defined in lines 120–133) to get the next card in the `deck` array. If the deck is not empty, the method returns a `Card` object pointer; otherwise, it returns `NULL`. If the pointer is not `NULL`, lines 88–90 display the `Card` in `displayLabel` and display the card number in the `statusLabel`.

If `DealCard` returns a `NULL` pointer, the `String` `"NO MORE CARDS TO DEAL"` is displayed in `displayLabel`, and the `String` `"Shuffle cards to continue"` is displayed in `statusLabel` (lines 93–94).

When users click the **Shuffle Cards** button, its event-handling method `shuffleButton_Click` (lines 136–143) invokes method `Shuffle` (defined on lines 99–117) to shuffle the cards. The method loops through all 52 cards (array subscripts `0`–`51`). For each card, the method randomly picks a number between `0` and `51`. Then the current `Card` object and the randomly selected `Card` object are swapped in the array. To shuffle the cards, method `Shuffle` makes a total of only 52 swaps during a single pass of the entire array. When the shuffling is complete, `displayLabel` displays the `String` `"DECK IS SHUFFLED"`. Figure 15.19 executes the application.

```
// Fig. 15.19: Form1.cpp
// Demonstrates card-shuffling program.

#include "stdafx.h"
```

Fig. 15.19 Card-shuffling demonstration. (Part 1 of 2.)

```
#include "Form1.h"
#include <windows.h>

using namespace DeckOfCards;

int APIENTRY _tWinMain(HINSTANCE hInstance,
                       HINSTANCE hPrevInstance,
                       LPTSTR    lpCmdLine,
                       int       nCmdShow)
{
   System::Threading::Thread::CurrentThread->ApartmentState =
      System::Threading::ApartmentState::STA;
   Application::Run(new Form1());
   return 0;
} // end _tWinMain
```

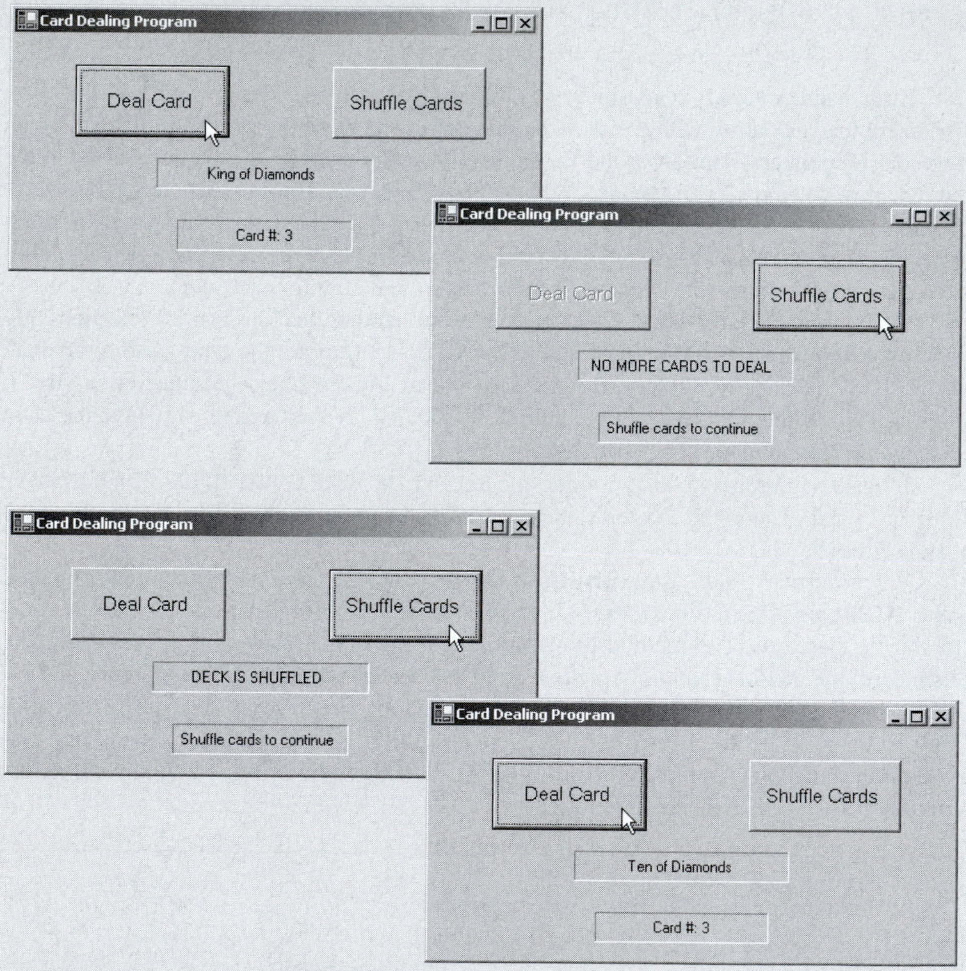

Fig. 15.19 Card-shuffling demonstration. (Part 2 of 2.)

15.15 Regular Expressions and Class Regex

Regular expressions are specially formatted `Strings` used to find patterns in text and can be useful during information validation, to ensure that data are in a particular format. For example, a ZIP code must consist of five digits, and a last name must start with a capital letter.

The .NET Framework provides several classes to help developers recognize and manipulate regular expressions. Class ***`Regex`*** (`System::Text::RegularExpressions` namespace) represents an immutable regular expression. It contains static methods that allow programs to use class `Regex` without explicitly instantiating objects of that class. Class ***`Match`*** represents the results of a regular expression matching operation.

Class `Regex` provides method ***`Match`***, which returns an object of class `Match` that represents a single regular expression match. `Regex` also provides method ***`Matches`***, which finds all matches of a regular expression in an arbitrary `String` and returns a ***`MatchCollection`*** object—i.e., a set of `Matches`.

Common Programming Error 15.7

When using regular expressions, do not confuse class `Match` with the method `Match`, which belongs to class `Regex`.

Character Classes

The table in Fig. 15.20 specifies some *character classes* that can be used with regular expressions. A character class is an escape sequence that represents a group of characters.

Character	Matches	Character	Matches
`\d`	any digit	`\D`	any non-digit
`\w`	any word character	`\W`	any non-word character
`\s`	any white space	`\S`	any non-white space

Fig. 15.20 Character classes.

Common Programming Error 15.8

Be sure to use the correct case when specifying a character class. Mixing up the case of character classes will cause a search for the exact opposite of what you are trying to find.

A *word character* is any alphanumeric character or underscore. A *white space* character is a space, a tab, a carriage return, a newline or a form feed. A *digit* is any numeric character. Regular expressions are not limited to these character classes, however. The expressions employ various operators and other forms of notation to search for complex patterns. We discuss several of these techniques in the context of the next few examples.

Using Method `Matches`

Figure 15.21 presents a simple example that employs regular expressions. This program takes birthdays and tries to match them to a regular expression. The expression matches only birthdays that do not occur in April and that belong to people whose names begin with `"J"`.

Line 18 creates an instance of class `Regex` and defines the regular expression pattern for which `Regex` will search. The first character in the regular expression, `"J"`, is treated as

```
// Fig. 15.21: RegexMatches.cpp
// Demonstrating Class Regex.

#include "stdafx.h"

#using <system.dll>
#using <system.windows.forms.dll>

using namespace System;
using namespace System::Windows::Forms;
using namespace System::Text::RegularExpressions;

int _tmain()
{
   String *output = "";

   // create regular expression
   Regex *expression = new Regex( S"(J.*\\d[0-35-9]-\\d\\d-\\d\\d)" );

   String *string1 = String::Concat(
      S"Jane's Birthday is 05-12-75\n",
      S"Dave's Birthday is 11-04-68\n",
      S"John's Birthday is 04-28-73\n",
      S"Joe's Birthday is 12-17-77" );

   // declare an object of Match
   Match *myMatch = 0;

   // match regular expression to string and
   // print out all matches
   for ( int i = 0; i < expression->Matches( string1 )->Count; i++ ) {
         myMatch = expression->Matches( string1 )->Item[ i ];
         output = String::Concat( output, myMatch->ToString(), S"\n" );
   } // end for

   MessageBox::Show( output, S"Using class Regex",
      MessageBoxButtons::OK, MessageBoxIcon::Information );

   return 0;
} // end _tmain
```

Using class Regex
Jane's Birthday is 05-12-75
Joe's Birthday is 12-17-77
OK

Fig. 15.21 Regular expressions used to check birthdays.

a literal character. This means that any `String` matching this regular expression is required to start with `"J"`.

In a regular expression, the dot character `"."` matches any single character except a newline character. However, when the dot character is followed by an asterisk, as in the expression ".*", it matches any number of unspecified characters. In general, when the operator "*" is applied to any expression, the expression will match zero or more occurrences of the expression. By contrast, the application of the operator "+" to an expression causes the expression to match one or more occurrences of that expression. For example, both "A*" and "A+" will match "A", but only "A*" will match an empty String.

As indicated in Fig. 15.20, "\d" matches any numeric digit. Notice that to specify character classes in the String * passed to the Regex constructor, we must precede each class (e.g., \d) with the escape character (\). To specify sets of characters other than those that have a character class, characters can be listed in square brackets, []. For example, the pattern "[aeiou]" can be used to match any vowel. Ranges of characters can be represented by placing a dash (-) between two characters. In the example, "[0-35-9]" matches only digits in the ranges specified by the pattern. In this case, the pattern matches any digit between 0 and 3 or between 5 and 9; therefore, it matches any digit except 4. If the first character in the brackets is the "^", the expression accepts any character other than those indicated. However, it is important to note that "[^4]" is not the same as "[0-35-9]"; the former matches any nondigit, in addition to the digits other than 4.

Although the "-" character indicates a range when it is enclosed in square brackets, instances of the "-" character outside grouping expressions are treated as literal characters. Thus, the regular expression in line 18 searches for a String that starts with the letter "J", followed by any number of characters, followed by a two-digit number (of which the second digit cannot be 4), followed by a dash, another two-digit number, a dash and another two-digit number.

Lines 31–34 use a for loop to iterate through each Match obtained from expression->Matches, which used string1 as an argument. The output in Fig. 15.21 indicates the two matches that were found in string1. Notice that both matches conform to the pattern specified by the regular expression.

Validating Input Using Quantifiers

The asterisk (*) and plus (+) in the previous example are called *quantifiers*. Quantifiers can be used to match a number of instances of a pattern, rather than just one instance of a pattern. Figure 15.22 lists various quantifiers and their uses.

Common Programming Error 15.9

Be sure to use the correct quantifier in a regular expression. Mixing up quantifiers is a common mistake, and using the incorrect quantifier may produce undesirable results.

Quantifier	Matche
*	Matches zero or more occurrences of the pattern.
+	Matches one or more occurrences of the pattern.
?	Matches zero or one occurrences of the pattern.
{n}	Matches exactly n occurrences.
{n,}	Matches at least n occurrences.
{n,m}	Matches between n and m (inclusive) occurrences.

Fig. 15.22 Quantifiers used in regular expressions.

We have already discussed how the asterisk (*) and plus (+) work. The question mark (?) matches zero or one occurrences of the expression that it quantifies. A set of braces containing one number ({n}) matches exactly n occurrences of the expression it quantifies. We demonstrate this quantifier in the next example. Including a comma after the number enclosed in braces matches at least n occurrences of the quantified expression. The set of braces containing two numbers ({n,m}), matches between n and m occurrences of the expression that it qualifies. All the quantifiers are *greedy*. This means that they will match as many occurrences as they can as long as the match is successful. However, if any of these quantifiers is followed by a question mark (?), the quantifier becomes *lazy*. It then will match as few occurrences as possible as long as the match is successful.

The Windows application in Fig. 15.23–Fig. 15.24 presents a more involved example that validates user input via regular expressions.

```
// Fig. 15.23: Form1.h
// Using regular expressions to validate user information.

#pragma once


namespace Validate
{
   using namespace System;
   using namespace System::ComponentModel;
   using namespace System::Collections;
   using namespace System::Windows::Forms;
   using namespace System::Data;
   using namespace System::Drawing;
   using namespace System::Text::RegularExpressions;

   /// <summary>
   /// Summary for Form1
   ///
   /// WARNING: If you change the name of this class, you will need to
   ///          change the 'Resource File Name' property for the managed
   ///          resource compiler tool associated with all .resx files
   ///          this class depends on.  Otherwise, the designers will not
   ///          be able to interact properly with localized resources
   ///          associated with this form.
   /// </summary>
   public __gc class Form1 : public System::Windows::Forms::Form
   {
   public:
      Form1(void)
      {
         InitializeComponent();
      }

   protected:
      void Dispose(Boolean disposing)
      {
```

Fig. 15.23 Validating user information using regular expressions. (Part 1 of 4.)

```
         if (disposing && components)
         {
            components->Dispose();
         }
         __super::Dispose(disposing);
      }
   private: System::Windows::Forms::Label *  phoneLabel;
   private: System::Windows::Forms::Label *  zipLabel;
   private: System::Windows::Forms::Label *  stateLabel;
   private: System::Windows::Forms::Label *  cityLabel;
   private: System::Windows::Forms::Label *  addressLabel;
   private: System::Windows::Forms::Label *  firstLabel;
   private: System::Windows::Forms::Label *  lastLabel;
   private: System::Windows::Forms::Button *  OkButton;
   private: System::Windows::Forms::TextBox *  phoneTextBox;
   private: System::Windows::Forms::TextBox *  zipTextBox;
   private: System::Windows::Forms::TextBox *  stateTextBox;
   private: System::Windows::Forms::TextBox *  cityTextBox;
   private: System::Windows::Forms::TextBox *  addressTextBox;
   private: System::Windows::Forms::TextBox *  firstTextBox;
   private: System::Windows::Forms::TextBox *  lastTextBox;

   private:
      /// <summary>
      /// Required designer variable.
      /// </summary>
      System::ComponentModel::Container * components;

   // Visual Studio .NET generated GUI code

   // handles OkButton_Click event
   private: System::Void OkButton_Click(
            System::Object *  sender, System::EventArgs *  e)
         {
            // ensures no textboxes are empty
            if ( lastTextBox->Text->Equals( String::Empty ) ||
               firstTextBox->Text->Equals( String::Empty ) ||
               addressTextBox->Text->Equals( String::Empty ) ||
               cityTextBox->Text->Equals( String::Empty ) ||
               stateTextBox->Text->Equals( String::Empty ) ||
               zipTextBox->Text->Equals( String::Empty ) ||
               phoneTextBox->Text->Equals( String::Empty ) ) {

               // display popup box
               MessageBox::Show( S"Please fill in all fields.",
                  S"Error", MessageBoxButtons::OK,
                  MessageBoxIcon::Error );

               // set focus to lastTextBox
               lastTextBox->Focus();

               return;
            } // end if
```

Fig. 15.23 Validating user information using regular expressions. (Part 2 of 4.)

```
         // if last name format invalid show message
         if ( !Regex::Match( lastTextBox->Text,
            S"^[A-Z][a-zA-Z]+$" )->Success ) {

            // last name was incorrect
            MessageBox::Show( S"Invalid Last Name", S"Message",
               MessageBoxButtons::OK, MessageBoxIcon::Error );
            lastTextBox->Focus();

            return;
         } // end if

         // if first name format invalid show message
         if ( !Regex::Match( firstTextBox->Text,
            S"^[A-Z][a-zA-Z]+$" )->Success ) {

            // first name was incorrect
            MessageBox::Show( S"Invalid First Name", S"Message",
               MessageBoxButtons::OK, MessageBoxIcon::Error );
            firstTextBox->Focus();

            return;
         } // end if

         // if address format invalid show message
         if ( !Regex::Match( addressTextBox->Text, String::Concat(
            S"^[0-9]+\\s+([a-zA-Z]+|[a-zA-Z]+",
            S"\\s[a-zA-Z]+)$" ) )->Success ) {

            // address was incorrect
            MessageBox::Show( S"Invalid Address", S"Message",
               MessageBoxButtons::OK, MessageBoxIcon::Error );
            addressTextBox->Focus();

            return;
         } // end if

         // if city format invalid show message
         if ( !Regex::Match( cityTextBox->Text,
            S"^([a-zA-Z]+|[a-zA-Z]+\\s[a-zA-Z]+)$" )->Success ) {

            // city was incorrect
            MessageBox::Show( S"Invalid City", S"Message",
               MessageBoxButtons::OK, MessageBoxIcon::Error );
            cityTextBox->Focus();

            return;
         } // end if

         // if state format invalid show message
         if ( !Regex::Match( stateTextBox->Text,
            S"^([a-zA-Z]+|[a-zA-Z]+\\s[a-zA-Z]+)$" )->Success ) {
```

Fig. 15.23 Validating user information using regular expressions. (Part 3 of 4.)

```

            // state was incorrect
            MessageBox::Show( S"Invalid State", S"Message",
              MessageBoxButtons::OK, MessageBoxIcon::Error );
            stateTextBox->Focus();

            return;
          } // end if

          // if zip code format invalid show message
          if ( !Regex::Match( zipTextBox->Text,
            S"^\\d{5}$" )->Success ) {

            // zip was incorrect
            MessageBox::Show( S"Invalid Zip Code", S"Message",
              MessageBoxButtons::OK, MessageBoxIcon::Error );
            zipTextBox->Focus();

            return;
          } // end if

          // if phone number format invalid show message
          if ( !Regex::Match( phoneTextBox->Text,
            S"^[1-9]\\d{2}-[1-9]\\d{2}-\\d{4}$" )->Success ) {

            // phone number was incorrect
            MessageBox::Show( S"Invalid Phone Number", S"Message",
              MessageBoxButtons::OK, MessageBoxIcon::Error );
            phoneTextBox->Focus();

            return;
          } // end if

          // information is valid, signal user and exit application
          this->Hide();
          MessageBox::Show( S"Thank You!", S"Information Correct",
            MessageBoxButtons::OK, MessageBoxIcon::Information );

          Application::Exit();
        } // end method OkButton_Click
  };
}
```

Fig. 15.23 Validating user information using regular expressions. (Part 4 of 4.)

```
// Fig. 15.24: Form1.cpp
// Demonstrates validation of user information.

#include "stdafx.h"
#include "Form1.h"
#include <windows.h>

```

Fig. 15.24 Demonstrating validation of user information. (Part 1 of 3.)

```
using namespace Validate;

int APIENTRY _tWinMain(HINSTANCE hInstance,
                       HINSTANCE hPrevInstance,
                       LPTSTR    lpCmdLine,
                       int       nCmdShow)
{
   System::Threading::Thread::CurrentThread->ApartmentState =
      System::Threading::ApartmentState::STA;
   Application::Run(new Form1());
   return 0;
} // end _tWinMain
```

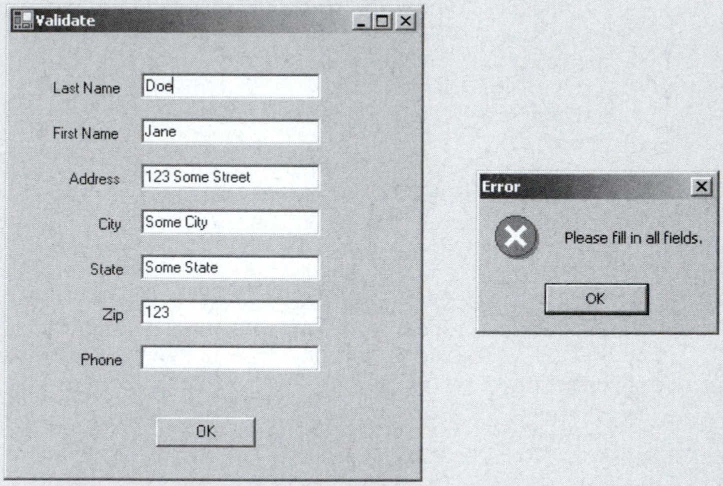

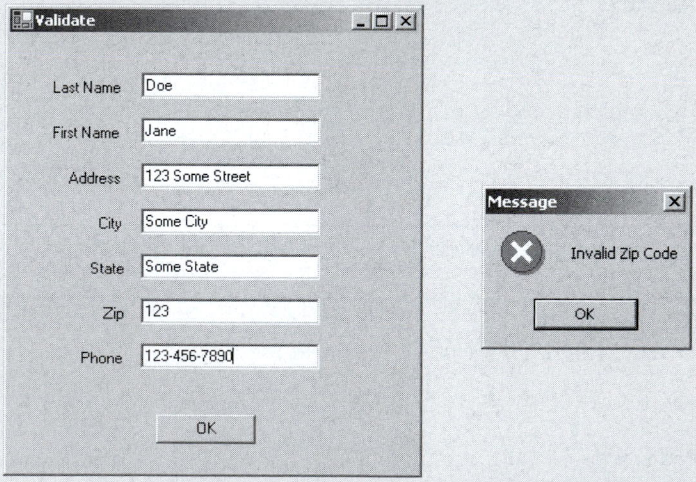

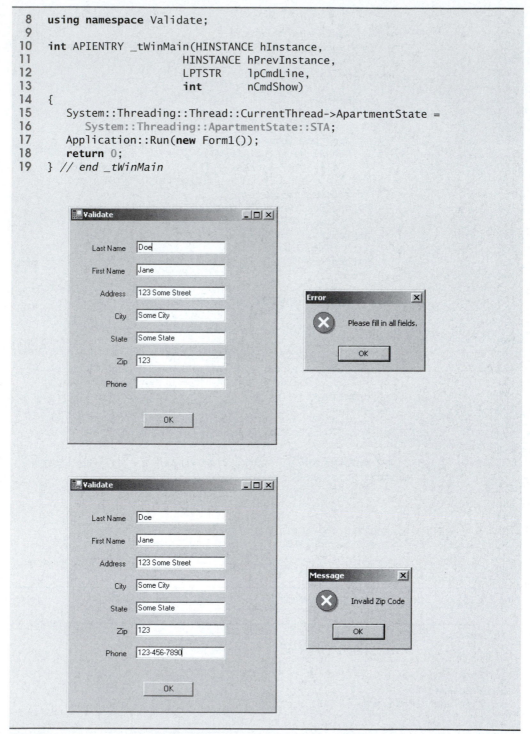

Fig. 15.24 Demonstrating validation of user information. (Part 2 of 3.)

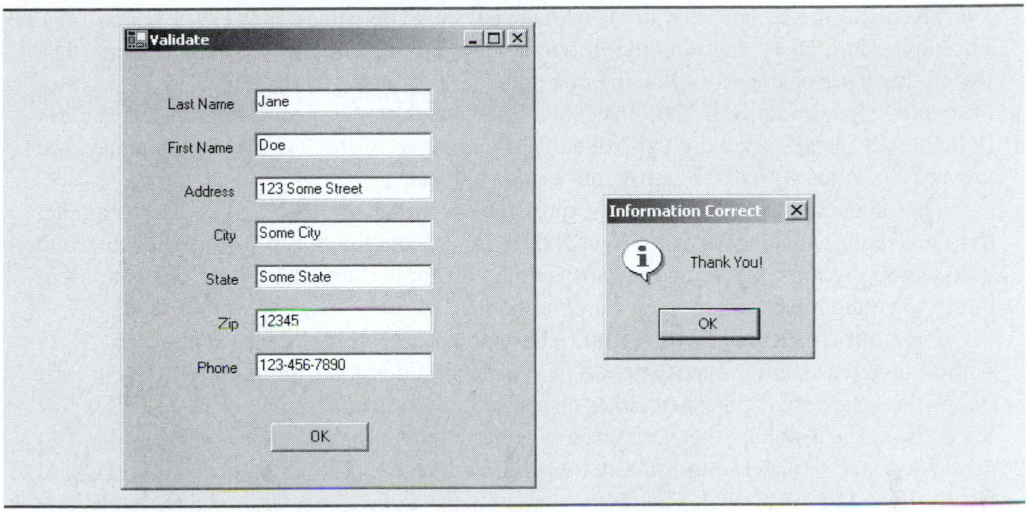

Fig. 15.24 Demonstrating validation of user information. (Part 3 of 3.)

When a user clicks the **OK** button, the program uses `String` field *`Empty`* to ensure that none of the fields are empty (lines 73–79 of Fig. 15.23). `String::Empty` is a read-only field that has the value of the empty string, `""`. We could replace each instance of `String::Empty` with the empty string itself, and the program would still function in the same way.

If one or more fields are empty, the program signals the user that all fields must be filled before the program can validate the input information (lines 82–84). Line 87 calls instance method *`Focus`* of class `TextBox`. Method `Focus` places the cursor within the text box that called `Focus` (in this case, `lastTextBox`). The program then exits the event handler (line 89). If there are no empty fields, the user input is validated. The **Last Name** is validated first (lines 93–94). If it passes the test (i.e., if the *`Success`* property of the `Match` instance is `true`), control moves on to validate the **First Name** (lines 105–106). This process continues until all `TextBox`es are validated or until a test fails (`Success` is `false`) and the program sends an appropriate error message. If all fields contain valid information, success is signaled, and the program quits.

In the previous example, we searched for substrings that matched a regular expression. In this example, we want to check whether an entire `String` conforms to a regular expression. For example, we want to accept `"Smith"` as a last name, but not `"9@Smith#"`. We achieve this effect by beginning each regular expression with a `"^"` character and ending it with a `"$"` character. The `"^"` and `"$"` characters match the positions at the beginning and end of a `String`, respectively. This forces the regular expression to evaluate the entire `String` and not return a match if a substring matches successfully.

In this program, we use the `static` version of `Regex` method `Match`, which takes an additional parameter specifying the regular expression that we are trying to match. The expression in line 94 (of Fig. 15.23) uses the square bracket and range notation to match an uppercase first letter, followed by letters of any case—`a-z` matches any lowercase letter, and `A-Z` matches any uppercase letter. The `+` quantifier signifies that the second range of characters might occur one or more times in the `String`. Thus, this expression matches any `String` consisting of one uppercase letter, followed by one or more additional letters.

The notation `\s` matches a single white-space character (lines 118–119, 131 and 143). The expression `\d{5}`, used in the **Zip** (zip code) field, matches any five digits (line 155). Recall that a set of braces containing one number (`{n}`) matches exactly `n` occurrences of the expression it quantifies. Thus, the expression `\d` with a positive integer `x` in curly braces (`\d{x}`) will match any `x` digits. (Notice the importance of the `"^"` and `"$"` characters to prevent zip codes with extra digits from being validated.)

The character `"|"` matches the expression to its left or to its right. For example, `Hi (John|Jane)` matches both `Hi John` and `Hi Jane`. Note the use of parentheses to group parts of the regular expression. Quantifiers may be applied to patterns enclosed in parentheses to create more complex regular expressions.

The **Last Name** and **First Name** fields both accept `String`s of any length, that begin with an uppercase letter. The **Address** field matches at least one digit, followed by at least one white-space character, then either one or more letters or else one or more letters followed by a space and another series of one or more letters (lines 117–119). Therefore, `"10 Broadway"` and `"10 Main Street"` are both valid addresses. The **City** (lines 130–131) and **State** (lines 142–143) fields match any word of at least one character or, alternatively, any two words of at least one character if the words are separated by a single space. This means both `Waltham` and `West Newton` would match. As previously stated, the **Zip** code must be a five-digit number (lines 154–155). The **Phone** number must be of the form `xxx-yyy-yyyy`, where the `x`s represent the area code and `y`s the number (lines 166–167). The first `x` and the first `y` cannot be zero.

Replacing Substrings and Splitting Strings

Sometimes it is useful to replace parts of a `String` with another, or split a `String` according to a regular expression. For this purpose, the `Regex` class provides `static` and instance versions of methods *`Replace`* and *`Split`*, which are demonstrated in Fig. 15.25.

```
// Fig. 15.25: RegexSubstitution.cpp
// Using Regex method Replace.

#include "stdafx.h"

#using <system.dll>
#using <system.windows.forms.dll>

using namespace System;
using namespace System::Windows::Forms;
using namespace System::Text::RegularExpressions;

int _tmain()
{
   String *testString1 = S"This sentence ends in 5 stars *****";
   String *testString2 = S"1, 2, 3, 4, 5, 6, 7, 8";
   Regex *testRegex1 = new Regex( S"stars" );
   Regex *testRegex2 = new Regex( S"\\d" );
   String *results[];
   String *output = String::Concat( S"Original String 1\t\t\t",
      testString1 );
```

Fig. 15.25 `Regex` methods `Replace` and `Split`. (Part 1 of 2.)

```

   testString1 = Regex::Replace( testString1, S"\\*", S"^" );

   output = String::Concat( output, S"\n^ substituted for ",
      S"*\t\t\t",testString1 );

   testString1 = testRegex1->Replace( testString1, S"carets" );

   output = String::Concat( output, S"\n\"carets\" ",
      S"substituted for \"stars\"\t", testString1 );

   output = String::Concat( output, S"\nEvery word replaced ",
      S"by \"word\"\t", Regex::Replace(
      testString1, S"\\w+", S"word" ) );

   output = String::Concat( output, S"\n\nOriginal ",
      S"String 2\t\t\t", testString2 );

   output = String::Concat( output, S"\nFirst 3 digits ",
      S"replaced by \"digit\"\t", testRegex2->Replace(
      testString2, S"digit", 3 ) );

   output = String::Concat( output, S"\nString split at ",
      S"commas\t\t[" );

   results = Regex::Split( testString2, S",\\s*" );

   String *resultString;

   for ( int i = 0; i < results->Length; i++ ) {
      resultString = results->Item[ i ]->ToString();
      output = String::Concat( output, S"\"", resultString, S"\", " );
   } // end if

   output = String::Concat( output->Substring( 0,
      output->Length - 2 ), S"]" );

   MessageBox::Show( output, S"Substitution Using Regular Expressions" );

   return 0;
} // end _tmain
```

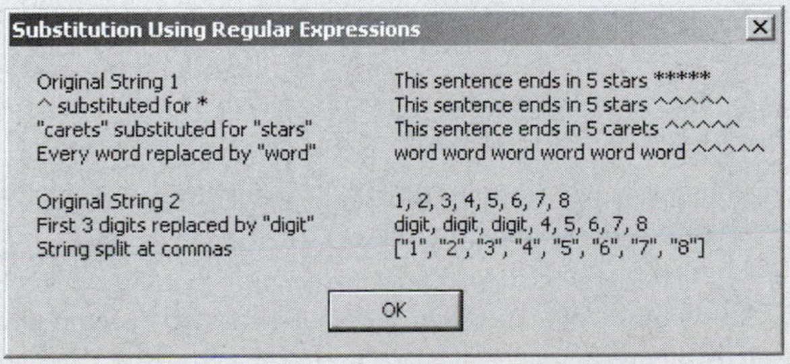
Substitution Using Regular Expressions
Original String 1
^ substituted for *
"carets" substituted for "stars"
Every word replaced by "word"
This sentence ends in 5 stars *****
This sentence ends in 5 stars ^^^^^
This sentence ends in 5 carets ^^^^^
word word word word word word ^^^^^
Original String 2
First 3 digits replaced by "digit"
String split at commas
1, 2, 3, 4, 5, 6, 7, 8
digit, digit, digit, 4, 5, 6, 7, 8
["1", "2", "3", "4", "5", "6", "7", "8"]
OK

Fig. 15.25 Regex methods `Replace` and `Split`. (Part 2 of 2.)

Method Replace replaces text in a String with new text wherever the original String matches a regular expression. We present two versions of this method in Fig. 15.25. The first version (line 23) is static and takes three parameters—a pointer to the String to modify, the String * containing the regular expression to match and a pointer to the replacement String. Here Replace replaces every instance of "*" in testString1 with "^". Notice that the regular expression ("*") precedes character * with a backslash, \. Normally, * is a quantifier indicating that a regular expression should match any number of occurrences of a preceding pattern. However, in line 23, we want to find all occurrences of the literal character *; to do this, we must escape character * with character \. By escaping a special regular expression character with a \, we inform the regular-expression matching engine to find the actual character, as opposed to what it represents in a regular expression. The second version of method Replace (line 28) is an instance method that uses the regular expression passed to the constructor for testRegex1 (line 17) to perform the replacement operation. In this case, every match for the regular expression "stars" in testString1 is replaced with "carets". Notice that we have now supplied two arguments to method Replace—a pointer to the String to modify and a pointer to the replacement String. The regular expression to match is provided by testRegex1, which calls the method.

Line 18 instantiates testRegex2 with argument "\\d". This call to instance method Replace in lines 41–42 takes three arguments—a pointer to the String to modify, the String * containing the replacement text and an int specifying the number of replacements to make. In other words, this version of Replace replaces the first three instances of a digit ("\d") in testString2 with the text "digit" (lines 41–42). Lines 56–57 remove the final space and quote, and add a closing brace, signifying the end of the list of digits.

Method Split divides a String into several substrings. The original String is broken in any location that matches a specified regular expression. Method Split returns an array containing the substrings between matches for the regular expression. In line 47, we use the static version of method Split to separate a String of comma-separated integers. The first argument is a pointer to the String to split; the second argument is the regular expression. In this case, we use the regular expression ",\\s*" to separate the substrings wherever a comma occurs. By matching any white-space characters, we eliminate extra spaces from the resulting substrings.

SUMMARY

- Characters are the fundamental building blocks of Visual C++ .NET program code. Every program is composed of a sequence of characters that is interpreted by the compiler as a series of instructions used to accomplish a task.
- A String is a series of characters treated as a single unit. A String may include uppercase letters, lowercase letter, digits and various special characters, such as +, -, *, /, $ and others.
- All characters correspond to numeric codes. When the computer compares two Strings, it actually compares the numeric codes of the characters in the Strings.
- Method Equals uses a lexicographical comparison, meaning that if a certain String has a higher value than another String, it would be found later in a dictionary. Method Equals compares the integer Unicode values that represent each character in each String.
- Method CompareTo returns 0 if the Strings are equal, a –1 if the String that invokes CompareTo is less than the String passed as an argument, a 1 if the String that invokes CompareTo

is greater than the String passed as an argument. Method CompareTo uses a lexicographical comparison.

- A hash table stores information, using a special calculation on the object to be stored that produces a hash code. The hash code is used to choose the location in the table at which to store the object.
- Class String provides two Substring methods to enable a new String to be created by copying part of an existing String.
- String method IndexOf locates the first occurrence of a character or a substring in a String. Method LastIndexOf locates the last occurrence of a character or a substring in a String.
- String method StartsWith determines whether a String starts with the characters specified as an argument. String method EndsWith determines whether a String ends with the characters specified as an argument.
- The String class provides many capabilities for processing Strings.
- Methods IndexOf, LastIndexOf, StartsWith, EndsWith, Concat, Replace, ToUpper, ToLower, Trim and Remove are provided for String manipulation.
- However, once a String is created, its contents can never change.
- Class StringBuilder is available for creating and manipulating dynamic Strings, i.e., Strings that can change.
- Class StringBuilder provides Length and Capacity properties to return the number of characters currently in a StringBuilder and the number of characters that can be stored in a StringBuilder without allocating more memory, respectively. These properties also can be used to increase or decrease the length or the capacity of the StringBuilder.
- Method EnsureCapacity allows programmers to guarantee that a StringBuilder has a capacity that is larger than or equal to a specified value. This method can be helpful in reducing the number of times the capacity must be increased.
- Class StringBuilder provides 19 overloaded Append methods to allow various data-type values to be added to the end of a StringBuilder. Versions are provided for each of the primitive data types and for character arrays, String pointers and Object pointers.
- The braces in a format String specify how to format a specific piece of information. Formats have the form {X[,Y][:FormatString]}, where X is the number of the argument to be formatted, counting from zero. Y is an optional argument, which can be positive or negative. Y indicates how many characters should be in the result of formatting; if the resulting String is less than this number, it will be padded with spaces to make up for the difference. A positive integer means the String will be right-aligned; a negative one means it will be left-aligned. The optional FormatString indicates what kind of formatting should be applied to the argument: currency, decimal, or scientific, among others.
- Class StringBuilder provides 18 overloaded Insert methods to allow various data-type values to be inserted at any position in a StringBuilder. Versions are provided for each of the primitive data types and for character arrays, String pointers and Object pointers.
- Class StringBuilder provides method Remove for deleting any portion of a StringBuilder.
- Another useful method included with StringBuilder is Replace. Replace searches for a specified String or character and substitutes another in its place.
- MC++ provides a data type, called a structure, that is similar to a class.
- Like classes, structures include methods and properties. Both use the same specifiers (such as public, private and protected) and access members via the member access operator (.), the arrow member access operator (->) and the scope resolution operator (::). However, the default access specifier for classes is private, while the default access specifier for structures is public.

- Classes are created by using keyword `class`. Structures are created by using keyword `struct`.
- Many of the primitive data types that we have been using are actually aliases for different structures. These structures are derived from class `ValueType`, which in turn is derived from class `Object`.
- Regular expressions find patterns in text.
- The .NET Framework provides class `Regex` to aid developers in recognizing and manipulating regular expressions. `Regex` provides method `Match`, which returns an object of class `Match`. This object represents a single match in a regular expression. `Regex` also provides the method `Matches`, which finds all matches of a regular expression in an arbitrary `String` and returns a `MatchCollection`—a set of `Matches`.
- Both classes `Regex` and `Match` are in namespace `System::Text::RegularExpressions`.

TERMINOLOGY

+ operator
== comparison operator
alphabetizing
`Append` method of class `StringBuilder`
`AppendFormat` method of `StringBuilder`
`ArgumentOutOfRangeException`
`Capacity` property of class `StringBuilder`
`Char` structure
character
character class
`Chars` property of class `String`
`CompareTo` method of class `String`
`CompareTo` method of structure `Char`
`CopyTo` method of class `String`
`Enabled` property of class `Control`
`EndsWith` method of class `String`
`EnsureCapacity` method of `StringBuilder`
`Equals` method of class `String`
format string
garbage collector
greedy quantifier
hash code
hash table
immutable `String`
`IndexOf` method of class `String`
`IndexOfAny` method of class `String`
`IsDigit` method of structure `Char`
`IsLetter` method of structure `Char`
`IsLetterOrDigit` method of structure `Char`
`IsLower` method of structure `Char`
`IsPunctuation` method of structure `Char`
`IsSymbol` method of structure `Char`
`IsUpper` method of structure `Char`
`IsWhiteSpace` method of structure `Char`
`LastIndexOf` method of class `String`
`LastIndexOfAny` method of class `String`
lazy quantifier
`Length` property of class `String`
`Length` property of class `StringBuilder`
lexicographical comparison
literal strings
`Match` class
`MatchCollection` class
page-layout software
`Parse` method of structure `Char`
quantifier
random-number generation
`Regex` class
`Remove` method of class `StringBuilder`
`Replace` method of class `Regex`
`Replace` method of class `String`
`Replace` method of class `StringBuilder`
special characters
`Split` method of class `Regex`
`StartsWith` method of class `String`
`String` class
string literal
`String` reference
`StringBuilder` class
`struct` keyword
structure
`Substring` method of class `String`
`Success` property of class `Match`
`System` namespace
`System::Text` namespace
`System::Text::RegularExpressions` namespace
text editor
`ToLower` method of class `String`
`ToLower` method of structure `Char`
`ToString` method of class `String`
`ToString` method of `StringBuilder`
`ToUpper` method of class `String`
`ToUpper` method of structure `Char`

trailing white-space characters
Trim method of class String
Unicode character set
ValueType class
white-space characters
word character

SELF-REVIEW EXERCISES

15.1 State whether each of the following is *true* or *false*. If *false*, explain why.

a) When String *s are compared with ==, the result is *true* if the String *s point to the same objects.
b) A String can be modified after it is created.
c) Class String has no ToString method.
d) StringBuilder method EnsureCapacity sets the StringBuilder instance's capacity to the argument's value.
e) Method Trim removes all white space at the beginning and the end of a String.
f) A regular expression matches a String to a pattern.
g) Class StringBuilder provides property Length to return the number of characters that can be stored in a StringBuilder without allocating more memory.
h) Class String method ToUpper capitalizes just the first letter of the String.
i) The expression \d in a regular expression denotes all letters.

15.2 Fill in the blanks in each of the following statements:

a) To concatenate two Strings, use String method ________.
b) Method Compare of class String uses a(n) ________ comparison of Strings.
c) Class Regex is located in namespace ________.
d) StringBuilder method ________ first formats the specified String, then concatenates it to the end of the StringBuilder.
e) If the arguments to a Substring method call are out of range, a(n) ________ exception is thrown.
f) Regex method ________ changes all occurrences of a pattern in a String to a specified String.
g) StringBuilder method ________ allows various data-type values to be inserted at any position in a StringBuilder.
h) Regular expression quantifier ________ matches zero or more occurrences of an expression.
i) Regular expression operator ________ inside square brackets will not match any of the characters in that set of brackets.

ANSWERS TO SELF-REVIEW EXERCISES

15.1 a) True. b) False. Strings are immutable and cannot be modified after they are created. StringBuilder objects can be modified after they are created. c) False. Class String overriddes the ToString method of class Object. d) False. StringBuilder method EnsureCapacity sets the StringBuilder instance's capacity to a value that is larger than or equal to the argument's value. e) True. f) True. g) False. Class StringBuilder provides property Capacity to return the number of characters that can be stored in a StringBuilder without allocating more memory. h) False. Class String method ToUpper capitalizes all letters in the String. i) False. The expression \d denotes all digits in a regular expression.

15.2 a) Concat. b) lexicographical. c) System::Text::RegularExpressions. d) AppendFormat. e) ArgumentOutOfRangeException. f) Replace. g) Insert. h) *. i) ^.

EXERCISES

15.3 Modify the program in Fig. 15.16–Fig. 15.19 so that the card-dealing method deals a five-card poker hand. Then write the following additional methods:

a) Determine if the hand contains a pair.
b) Determine if the hand contains two pairs.
c) Determine if the hand contains three of a kind (e.g., three jacks).
d) Determine if the hand contains four of a kind (e.g., four aces).
e) Determine if the hand contains a flush (i.e., all five cards of the same suit).
f) Determine if the hand contains a straight (i.e., five cards of consecutive face values).
g) Determine if the hand contains a full house (i.e., two cards of one face value and three cards of another face value).

15.4 Use the methods developed in Exercise 15.3 to write a program that deals two five-card poker hands, evaluates each hand and determines which is the better hand.

15.5 Write an application that uses `String` method `CompareTo` to compare two `Strings` input by the user. Output whether the first `String` is less than, equal to or greater than the second.

15.6 Write an application that uses random-number generation to create sentences. Use four arrays of `Strings`, called `article`, `noun`, `verb` and `preposition`. Create a sentence by selecting a word at random from each array in the following order: `article`, `noun`, `verb`, `preposition`, `article` and `noun`. As each word is picked, concatenate it to the previous words in the sentence. The words should be separated by spaces. When the final sentence is output, it should start with a capital letter and end with a period. The program should generate random sentences and output them to a text area.

The arrays should be filled as follows: The `article` array should contain the articles `"the"`, `"a"`, `"one"`, `"some"` and `"any"`; the `noun` array should contain the nouns `"boy"`, `"girl"`, `"dog"`, `"town"` and `"car"`; the `verb` array should contain the past-tense verbs `"drove"`, `"jumped"`, `"ran"`, `"walked"` and `"skipped"`; the `preposition` array should contain the prepositions `"to"`, `"from"`, `"over"`, `"under"` and `"on"`.

After the preceding program is written, modify the program to produce a short story consisting of several of these sentences. (How about the possibility of a random term-paper writer!)

15.7 (*Pig Latin*) Write an application that encodes English language phrases into pig Latin. Pig Latin is a form of coded language often used for amusement. Many variations exist in the methods used to form pig Latin phrases. For simplicity, use the following algorithm:

To translate each English word into a pig Latin word, place the first letter of the English word at the end of the word and add the letters "`ay`." Thus, the word "`jump`" becomes "`umpjay`," the word "`the`" becomes "`hetay`" and the word "`computer`" becomes "`omputercay`." Blanks between words remain as blanks. Assume the following: The English phrase consists of words separated by blanks, there are no punctuation marks and all words have two or more letters. Enable the user to input a sentence. Use techniques discussed in this chapter to divide the sentence into separate words. Method `GetPigLatin` should translate a single word into pig Latin. Keep a running display of all the converted sentences in a text area.

15.8 Write a program that reads a five-letter word from the user and produces all possible three-letter words that can be derived from the letters of the five-letter word. For example, the three-letter words produced from the word "bathe" include the commonly used words "ate," "bat," "bet," "tab," "hat," "the" and "tea." For the purposes of this exercise, you do not need to determine if the three-letter combination is an actual word. Therefore, "bathe" should also produce "ath", "het", etc.

16

Graphics and Multimedia

Objectives

- To understand graphics contexts and graphics objects.
- To manipulate colors and fonts.
- To understand and be able to use GDI+ `Graphics` methods to draw lines, rectangles, `Strings` and images.
- To use class `Image` to manipulate and display images.
- To draw complex shapes from simple shapes with class `GraphicsPath`.
- To use Windows Media Player and Microsoft Agent in an MC++ application.

One picture is worth ten thousand words.
Chinese proverb

Treat nature in terms of the cylinder, the sphere, the cone, all in perspective.
Paul Cezanne

Nothing ever becomes real till it is experienced—even a proverb is no proverb to you till your life has illustrated it.
John Keats

A picture shows me at a glance what it takes dozens of pages of a book to expound.
Ivan Sergeyevich

Outline

16.1 Introduction

In this chapter, we overview Visual C++ .NET's tools for drawing two-dimensional shapes and for controlling colors and fonts. Visual C++ .NET supports graphics that enable programmers to enhance their Windows applications visually. The FCL contains many sophisticated drawing capabilities as part of namespace *System::Drawing* and the other namespaces that make up the .NET resource *GDI+*. GDI+, an extension of the Graphical Device Interface, is an application programming interface (API) that provides classes for creating two-dimensional vector graphics (a way of describing graphics so that they may be easily manipulated with high-performance techniques), manipulating fonts and inserting images. GDI+ expands GDI by simplifying the programming model and introducing several new features, such as graphics paths, extended image-file format support and *alpha blending* (see Section 16.3). Using the GDI+ API, programmers can create images without worrying about the platform-specific details of their graphics hardware.

We begin with an introduction to the .NET framework's drawing capabilities. We then present more powerful drawing capabilities, such as changing the styles of lines used to draw shapes and controlling the colors and patterns of filled shapes.

Figure 16.1 depicts a portion of the `System::Drawing` and the *`System::Drawing::Drawing2D`* namespaces, which include several of the basic graphics classes and structures covered in this chapter. The most commonly used components of GDI+ reside in the `System::Drawing` and `System::Drawing::Drawing2D` namespaces.

Class *`Graphics`* contains methods used for drawing `Strings`, lines, rectangles and other shapes on a `Control`. The drawing methods of class `Graphics` usually require a *`Pen`* or *`Brush`* object to render a specified shape. The `Pen` draws shape outlines; the `Brush` draws solid objects.

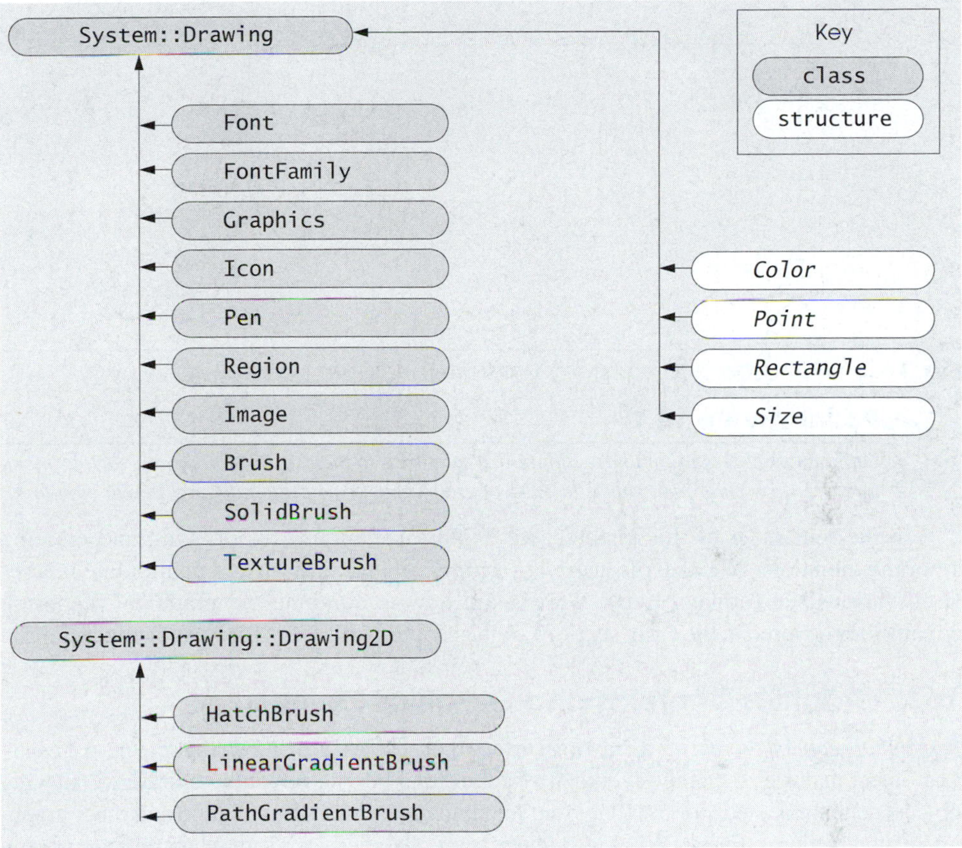

Fig. 16.1 `System::Drawing` namespace's classes and structures.

Structure *`Color`* contains numerous `static` properties (which can be used to set the colors of various graphical components) plus methods that allow users to create new colors. Class *`Font`* contains properties that define unique fonts. Class *`FontFamily`* contains methods for obtaining font information.

To begin drawing in MC++, we first must understand GDI+'s *coordinate system* (Fig. 16.2), a scheme for identifying every point on the screen. By default, the upper-left corner of a GUI component (such as a `Panel` or a `Form`) has the coordinates (0, 0). A coordinate pair has both an *x-coordinate* (the *horizontal coordinate*) and a *y-coordinate* (the *vertical coordinate*). The *x*-coordinate is the horizontal distance (to the right) from the upper-left corner. The *y*-coordinate is the vertical distance (downward) from the upper-left corner. The *x-axis* defines every horizontal coordinate, and the *y-axis* defines every vertical coordinate. Programmers position text and shapes on the screen by specifying their (*x*, *y*) coordinates. Coordinate units are measured in *pixels* ("picture elements"), which are the smallest units of resolution on a display monitor.

The `System::Drawing` namespace provides structures `Rectangle` and `Point`. The *`Rectangle` structure* defines rectangular shapes and dimensions. The *`Point` structure* represents the (*x*,*y*) coordinates of a point on a two-dimensional plane.

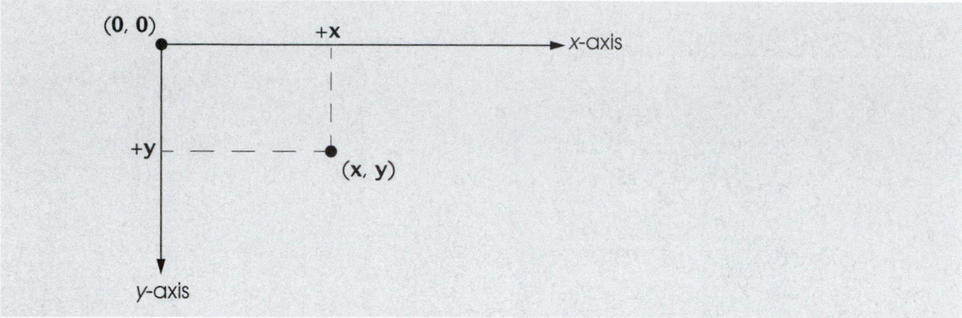

Fig. 16.2 GDI+ coordinate system. Units are measured in pixels.

Portability Tip 16.1

Different display monitors have different resolutions, so the density of pixels on various monitors will vary. This might cause the sizes of graphics to appear different on different monitors.

In the remainder of this chapter, we explore techniques for drawing and creating smooth animations. We also discuss class `Image`, which can store and manipulate images from various file formats. Later, we explain how to combine the graphical rendering capabilities covered in the early sections of the chapter with those for image manipulation.

16.2 Graphics Contexts and Graphics Objects

A *graphics context* represents a drawing surface that enables drawing on the screen. A `Graphics` object manages a graphics context by controlling how information is drawn. `Graphics` objects contain methods for drawing, font manipulation, color manipulation and other graphics-related actions. Every Windows application that derives from class `System::Windows::Forms::Form` inherits a `virtual` *`OnPaint`* event handler, where most graphics operations are performed. The arguments to the `OnPaint` method include a `PaintEventArgs *` object from which we can obtain a `Graphics` object for the control. We must obtain the `Graphics` object on each call to the method, because the properties of the graphics context that the graphics object represents could change. The `OnPaint` method triggers the `Control`'s *`Paint`* event, which indicates that a control is being drawn or redrawn.

When displaying graphical information on a `Form`'s client area, programmers can override the `OnPaint` method to retrieve a `Graphics` object from argument `PaintEventArgs *` or to create a new `Graphics` object associated with the appropriate surface. We demonstrate these techniques of drawing later in the chapter.

Every overridden `OnPaint` method should call the `OnPaint` method of its base class (`__super`). Therefore, the first statement in the overridden `OnPaint` method should be:

```
__super::OnPaint( e );
```

Next, extract the incoming `Graphics` object from the `PaintEventArgs` argument:

```
Graphics *graphicsObject = e->Graphics;
```

Variable `graphicsObject` now is available to draw shapes and `Strings` on the form.

Programmers seldom call the `OnPaint` method directly, because drawing graphics is an *event-driven process*. An event—such as the covering, uncovering or resizing of a window—

calls the `OnPaint` method of that form. Similarly, when any control (such as a `TextBox` or `Label`) is displayed, the program calls that control's `Paint` method.

If programmers need to cause method `OnPaint` to run explicitly, they should not call method `OnPaint`. Rather, they can call the ***`Invalidate`*** method (inherited from `Control`). This method refreshes a control's client area and implicitly invokes method `OnPaint`. Several overloaded `Invalidate` methods exist that allow programmers to update portions of the client area.

Common Programming Error 16.1

Forgetting to call the `OnPaint` method of the base class in the `OnPaint` method of a derived class can cause errors. Specifically, the `Paint` event may not be raised.

Performance Tip 16.1

Calling the `Invalidate` method to refresh a `Control` often is inefficient. Instead, call `Invalidate` with a `Rectangle` parameter to refresh only the area designated by the rectangle. This improves drawing performance.

Calling the `OnPaint` method raises the `Paint` event. Programmers can add an event handler for the `Paint` event instead of overriding the `OnPaint` method. The form of a `Paint` event handler is:

```
void className::controlName_Paint( Object *sender, PaintEventArgs *e )
```

where *controlName* is the name of the control for which we are defining a `Paint` event handler. Using `OnPaint` allows the `Paint` event to be handled without having to register the method via a delegate.

When any control (such as a `TextBox` or `Label`) is displayed, the program calls that control's `Paint` event handler. Thus, if we wish to define a method that only updates a certain control (rather than the entire `Form`, such as method `OnPaint`), we can simply provide an event handler for that control's `Paint` event. We demonstrate this in later examples.

Controls, such as `Labels` and `Buttons`, do not have their own graphics contexts (i.e., they normally cannot be drawn on), but one can be created. To draw on a control, first create its graphics object by invoking the ***`CreateGraphics`*** method:

```
Graphics *graphicsObject = controlName->CreateGraphics();
```

where *graphicsObject* represents an instance of class `Graphics` and *controlName* is any control. Now, a programmer can use the methods provided in class `Graphics` to draw on the control.

16.3 Color Control

Colors can enhance a program's appearance and help convey meaning. For example, a red traffic light indicates stop, yellow indicates caution and green indicates go.

Structure `Color` defines methods and constants used to manipulate colors. `Color` is a lightweight object that performs only a handful of operations and stores `static` fields, so it is implemented as a structure, rather than as a class.

Every color can be created from a combination of alpha, red, green and blue components. Together, these components are called *ARGB values*. All four ARGB components are `bytes` that represent integer values in the range from 0 to 255. The alpha value determines the opacity of the color. For example, the alpha value 0 specifies a transparent color, the value 255 an opaque color. Alpha values between 0 and 255 (inclusive) result in a weighted blending effect of the color's RGB value with that of any background color, causing a semitransparent effect. The first number in the RGB value defines the amount of red in the color, the second defines the amount of green and the third defines the amount of blue. The larger the value, the greater the amount of that particular color. Visual C++ .NET enables programmers to choose from almost 17 million colors. If a particular computer cannot display all these colors, it will display the color closest to the one specified or attempt to emulate it using *dithering* (using small dots of existing colors to form a pattern that simulates the desired color). Figure 16.3 summarizes some predefined `Color` constants, and Fig. 16.4 describes several `Color` methods and properties.

Constants in structure `Color` (all are `public static`)	RGB value	Constants in structure `Color` (all are `public static`)	RGB value
`Orange`	255, 200, 0	`White`	255, 255, 255
`Pink`	255, 175, 175	`Gray`	128, 128, 128
`Cyan`	0, 255, 255	`DarkGray`	64, 64, 64
`Magenta`	255, 0, 255	`Red`	255, 0, 0
`Yellow`	255, 255, 0	`Green`	0, 255, 0
`Black`	0, 0, 0	`Blue`	0, 0, 255

Fig. 16.3 `Color` structure `static` constants and their RGB values.

Structure `Color` methods and properties	Description
Common Methods	
`static FromArgb`	Creates a color based on red, green and blue values expressed as `int`s from 0 to 255. Overloaded version allows specification of alpha, red, green and blue values.
`static FromName`	Creates a color from a name, passed as a pointer to a `String`.
Common Properties	
`A`	`byte` between 0 and 255 (inclusive), representing the alpha component.
`R`	`byte` between 0 and 255 (inclusive), representing the red component.
`G`	`byte` between 0 and 255 (inclusive), representing the green component.
`B`	`byte` between 0 and 255 (inclusive), representing the blue component.

Fig. 16.4 `Color` structure members.

The table in Fig. 16.4 describes two *FromArgb* method calls. One takes three `int` arguments and one takes four `int` arguments (all argument values must be between 0 and 255, inclusive). Both take `int` arguments specifying the amount of red, green and blue. The overloaded version takes four arguments and allows the user to specify the alpha component; the three-argument version defaults the alpha to 255. Both methods return a `Color` object representing the specified values. `Color` properties *A*, *R*, *G* and *B* return `bytes` that represent `int` values from 0 to 255, corresponding to the amounts of alpha, red, green and blue, respectively. Methods in structure `Color` do not allow programmers to change the characteristics of the current color. To use a different color, create a new `Color` object.

Programmers draw shapes and `Strings` with `Brushes` and `Pens`. A `Pen`, which functions similarly to the way an ordinary pen does, is used to draw lines. Most drawing methods require a `Pen` object. The overloaded `Pen` constructors allow programmers to specify the colors and widths of the lines that they wish to draw. The `System::Drawing` namespace also provides a `Pens` collection containing predefined `Pens`.

All classes derived from abstract class `Brush` define objects that color the interiors of graphical shapes; for example, the `SolidBrush` constructor takes a `Color` object—the color to draw. In most `Fill` methods, `Brushes` fill a space with a color, pattern or image. Figure 16.5 summarizes various `Brushes` and their functions.

Class	Description
`HatchBrush`	Uses a rectangular brush to fill a region with a pattern. The pattern is defined by a member of the `HatchStyle` enumeration, a foreground color (with which the pattern is drawn) and a background color.
`LinearGradientBrush`	Fills a region with a gradual blend of one color into another. Linear gradients are defined along a line. They can be specified by the two colors, the angle of the gradient and either the width of a rectangle or two points.
`SolidBrush`	Fills a region with one color. Defined by a `Color` object.
`TextureBrush`	Fills a region by repeating a specified `Image` across the surface.

Fig. 16.5 Classes that derive from class `Brush`.

The application in Fig. 16.6–Fig. 16.7 demonstrates several of the methods and properties described in Fig. 16.4. It displays two overlapping rectangles, allowing the user to experiment with color values and color names. The color names entered should be the names of the predefined colors in the `Color` structure.

```
// Fig. 16.6: Form1.h
// Using different colors in Visual C++ .NET.

#pragma once


```

Fig. 16.6 Color value and alpha demonstration. (Part 1 of 4.)

```
namespace ShowColors
{
   using namespace System;
   using namespace System::ComponentModel;
   using namespace System::Collections;
   using namespace System::Windows::Forms;
   using namespace System::Data;
   using namespace System::Drawing;

   /// <summary>
   /// Summary for Form1
   ///
   /// WARNING: If you change the name of this class, you will need to
   ///          change the 'Resource File Name' property for the managed
   ///          resource compiler tool associated with all .resx files
   ///          this class depends on.  Otherwise, the designers will not
   ///          be able to interact properly with localized resources
   ///          associated with this form.
   /// </summary>
   public __gc class Form1 : public System::Windows::Forms::Form
   {
   public:
      Form1(void)
      {
         this->frontColor = Color::FromArgb( 100, 0 , 0, 255 );
         this->behindColor = Color::Wheat;
         InitializeComponent();
      }

   protected:
      void Dispose(Boolean disposing)
      {
         if (disposing && components)
         {
            components->Dispose();
         }
         __super::Dispose(disposing);
      }

   // color for back rectangle
   private: Color behindColor;

   // color for front rectangle
   private: Color frontColor;

   private: System::Windows::Forms::GroupBox *  nameGroup;
   private: System::Windows::Forms::GroupBox *  colorValueGroup;
   private: System::Windows::Forms::TextBox *  colorNameTextBox;
   private: System::Windows::Forms::TextBox *  alphaTextBox;
   private: System::Windows::Forms::TextBox *  redTextBox;
   private: System::Windows::Forms::TextBox *  greenTextBox;
   private: System::Windows::Forms::TextBox *  blueTextBox;
   private: System::Windows::Forms::Button *  colorValueButton;
```

Fig. 16.6 Color value and alpha demonstration. (Part 2 of 4.)

```
   private: System::Windows::Forms::Button *  colorNameButton;

   private:
      /// <summary>
      /// Required designer variable.
      /// </summary>
      System::ComponentModel::Container * components;

   // Visual Studio .NET generated GUI code

   protected:

      // override Form OnPaint method
      void OnPaint( PaintEventArgs *paintEvent )
      {
         __super::OnPaint( paintEvent ); // call base OnPaint method

         Graphics *graphicsObject = paintEvent->Graphics; // get graphics

         // create text brush
         SolidBrush *textBrush = new SolidBrush( Color::Black );

         // create solid brush
         SolidBrush *brush = new SolidBrush( Color::White );

         // draw white background
         graphicsObject->FillRectangle( brush, 4, 4, 275, 180 );

         // display name of behindColor
         graphicsObject->DrawString( this->behindColor.Name, Font,
            textBrush, 40, 5 );

         // set brush color and display back rectangle
         brush->Color = this->behindColor;

         graphicsObject->FillRectangle( brush, 45, 20, 150, 120 );

         // display ARGB values of front color
         graphicsObject->DrawString( String::Concat(
            S"Alpha: ", frontColor.A.ToString(),
            S" Red: ", frontColor.R.ToString(),
            S" Green: ", frontColor.G.ToString(),
            S" Blue: ", frontColor.B.ToString() ),
            Font, textBrush, 55, 165 );

         // set brush color and display front rectangle
         brush->Color = frontColor;

         graphicsObject->FillRectangle( brush, 65, 35, 170, 130 );
      } // end method OnPaint

```

Fig. 16.6 Color value and alpha demonstration. (Part 3 of 4.)

```
   // handle colorValueButton click event
   private: System::Void colorValueButton_Click(
               System::Object *  sender, System::EventArgs *  e)
            {
               try {

                  // obtain new front color from text boxes
                  frontColor = Color::FromArgb(
                     Convert::ToInt32( alphaTextBox->Text ),
                     Convert::ToInt32( redTextBox->Text ),
                     Convert::ToInt32( greenTextBox->Text ),
                     Convert::ToInt32( blueTextBox->Text ) );

                  // refresh Form
                  Invalidate( Rectangle( 4, 4, 275, 180 ) );
               } // end try
               catch ( FormatException *formatException ) {
                  MessageBox::Show( formatException->Message, S"Error",
                     MessageBoxButtons::OK, MessageBoxIcon::Error );
               } // end catch
               catch ( ArgumentException *argumentException ) {
                  MessageBox::Show( argumentException->Message, S"Error",
                     MessageBoxButtons::OK, MessageBoxIcon::Error );
               } // end catch
            } // end method colorValueButton_Click

   // handle colorNameButton click event
   private: System::Void colorNameButton_Click(
               System::Object *  sender, System::EventArgs *  e)
            {
               // set behindColor to color specified in text box
               behindColor = Color::FromName( colorNameTextBox->Text );

               Invalidate( Rectangle( 4, 4, 275, 180 ) ); // refresh Form
            } // end method colorNameButton_Click
   };
}
```

Fig. 16.6 Color value and alpha demonstration. (Part 4 of 4.)

```
// Fig. 16.7: Form1.cpp
// Entry point for application.

#include "stdafx.h"
#include "Form1.h"
#include <windows.h>

using namespace ShowColors;

```

Fig. 16.7 Color demonstration entry point. (Part 1 of 2.)

```
int APIENTRY _tWinMain(HINSTANCE hInstance,
                       HINSTANCE hPrevInstance,
                       LPTSTR    lpCmdLine,
                       int       nCmdShow)
{
   System::Threading::Thread::CurrentThread->ApartmentState =
      System::Threading::ApartmentState::STA;
   Application::Run(new Form1());
   return 0;
} // end _tWinMain
```

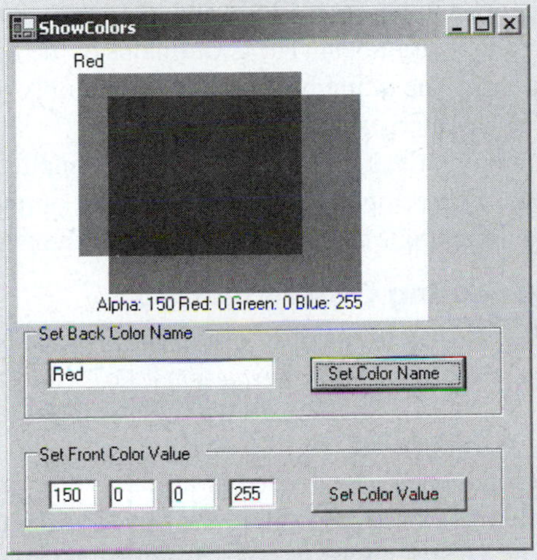

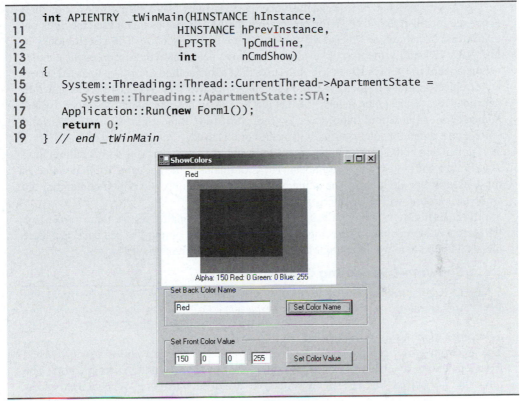

Fig. 16.7 Color demonstration entry point. (Part 2 of 2.)

When the application begins its execution, it calls the class's `OnPaint` method to paint the window. Line 75 invokes `__super::OnPaint( paintEvent )` (as discussed in Section 16.2). Line 77 (of Fig. 16.6) gets a pointer to `PaintEventArgs e`'s `Graphics` object and assigns it to `graphicsObject`. Lines 80 and 83 create black and white `SolidBrushes` for drawing on the form. Class `SolidBrush` derives from abstract base class `Brush`; programmers can draw solid shapes with the `SolidBrush`.

`Graphics` method ***`FillRectangle`*** draws a rectangle that is filled with the color or pattern of the `Brush` passed as its first argument. Line 86 calls method `FillRectangle` with `brush` as the first argument, specifying that we want a solid white rectangle to be drawn. Other parameters passed to this method are the *x*- and *y*-coordinates of a point and the width and height of the rectangle to draw. The point represents the upper-left corner of the rectangle. Lines 89–90 display the name of the `Brush`'s `Color` property with the `Graphics` ***`DrawString`*** method. The programmer has access to several overloaded `DrawString` methods; the version demonstrated in lines 89–90 takes a pointer to the `String` to display, the display `Font`, a `Brush` and the x- and y-coordinates of the location for the `String`'s first character.

Lines 31–32 assign `Color` value `behindColor`, which is initialized to `Color::Wheat` in line 32, to the `Brush`'s `Color` property and display a rectangle. Lines 98–103 extract and display the ARGB values of `Color frontColor` and lines 106 and 108 display a filled rectangle that overlaps the first.

Button event handler colorValueButton_Click (lines 112–135) uses Color method FromArgb to construct a new Color object from the ARGB values that a user specifies via text boxes. It then assigns the newly created Color to frontColor. The catch blocks in lines 127–134 notify the user if invalid values have been entered. Button event handler colorNameButton_Click (lines 138–145) uses the Color method FromName to create a new Color object from the colorName that a user enters in a text box. This Color is assigned to behindColor. Valid color names for method FromName are any name described by the *KnownColor* enumeration[1] (namespace System::Drawing). If the user does not enter a valid color name, a default color with ARGB values of 0 is used.

Notice that both colorValueButton_Click and colorNameButton_Click call method Invalidate with a Rectangle argument. The coordinates of the Rectangle are the same as those used in line 86 to draw the white background. Thus, only the region containing the white background will be updated each time.

If the user assigns an alpha value between 0 and 255 (inclusive) for the frontColor, the effects of alpha blending are apparent. In the screenshot output, the red back rectangle blends with the blue front rectangle to create purple where the two overlap.

Software Engineering Observation 16.1

Methods in structure Color do not allow programmers to change the characteristics of the current color. To use a different color, create a new Color object.

Selecting Colors Using ColorDialog

The predefined GUI component *ColorDialog* is a dialog box that allows users to select from a palette of available colors. It also offers the option of creating custom colors. The program in Fig. 16.8–Fig. 16.9 demonstrates the use of such a dialog. When a user selects a color and presses **OK**, the application retrieves the user's selection via the ColorDialog's *Color* property.

The GUI for this application contains two Buttons. The top one, backgroundColorButton, allows the user to change the form and button background colors. The bottom one, textColorButton, allows the user to change the button text colors.

```
// Fig. 16.8: Form1.h
// Change the background and text colors of a form.

#pragma once


namespace ShowColorsComplex
{
   using namespace System;
   using namespace System::ComponentModel;
   using namespace System::Collections;
   using namespace System::Windows::Forms;
```

Fig. 16.8 Change the background and text colors of a form. (Part 1 of 3.)

1. A list of colors defined by the KnownColor enumeration can be found at msdn.microsoft.com/library/default.asp?url=/library/en-us/cpref/html/frlrfsystemdrawingknowncolorclasstopic.asp.

```
using namespace System::Data;
using namespace System::Drawing;

/// <summary>
/// Summary for Form1
///
/// WARNING: If you change the name of this class, you will need to
///          change the 'Resource File Name' property for the managed
///          resource compiler tool associated with all .resx files
///          this class depends on.  Otherwise, the designers will not
///          be able to interact properly with localized resources
///          associated with this form.
/// </summary>
public __gc class Form1 : public System::Windows::Forms::Form
{
public:
   Form1(void)
   {
      InitializeComponent();
   }

protected:
   void Dispose(Boolean disposing)
   {
      if (disposing && components)
      {
         components->Dispose();
      }
      __super::Dispose(disposing);
   }
private: System::Windows::Forms::Button *  backgroundColorButton;
private: System::Windows::Forms::Button *  textColorButton;

private:
   /// <summary>
   /// Required designer variable.
   /// </summary>
   System::ComponentModel::Container * components;

// Visual Studio .NET generated GUI code

// change text color
private: System::Void textColorButton_Click(
            System::Object *  sender, System::EventArgs *  e)
         {
            // create ColorDialog object
            ColorDialog *colorChooser = new ColorDialog();
            Windows::Forms::DialogResult result;

            // get chosen color
            result = colorChooser->ShowDialog();

```

Fig. 16.8 Change the background and text colors of a form. (Part 2 of 3.)

```
            if ( result == DialogResult::Cancel )
               return;

            // assign forecolor to result of dialog
            this->ForeColor = colorChooser->Color;
         } // end method textColorButton_Click

   // change background color
   private: System::Void backgroundColorButton_Click(
            System::Object *  sender, System::EventArgs *  e)
         {
            // create ColorDialog object
            ColorDialog *colorChooser = new ColorDialog();
            Windows::Forms::DialogResult result;

            // show ColorDialog and get result
            colorChooser->FullOpen = true;
            result = colorChooser->ShowDialog();

            if ( result == DialogResult::Cancel )
               return;

            // set background color
            this->BackColor = colorChooser->Color;
         } // end method backgroundColorButton_Click
   };
}
```

Fig. 16.8 Change the background and text colors of a form. (Part 3 of 3.)

```
// Fig. 16.9: Form1.cpp
// Entry point for application.

#include "stdafx.h"
#include "Form1.h"
#include <windows.h>

using namespace ShowColorsComplex;

int APIENTRY _tWinMain(HINSTANCE hInstance,
                     HINSTANCE hPrevInstance,
                     LPTSTR    lpCmdLine,
                     int       nCmdShow)
{
   System::Threading::Thread::CurrentThread->ApartmentState =
      System::Threading::ApartmentState::STA;
   Application::Run(new Form1());
   return 0;
} // end _tWinMain
```

Fig. 16.9 Background and text colors entry point. (Part 1 of 2.)

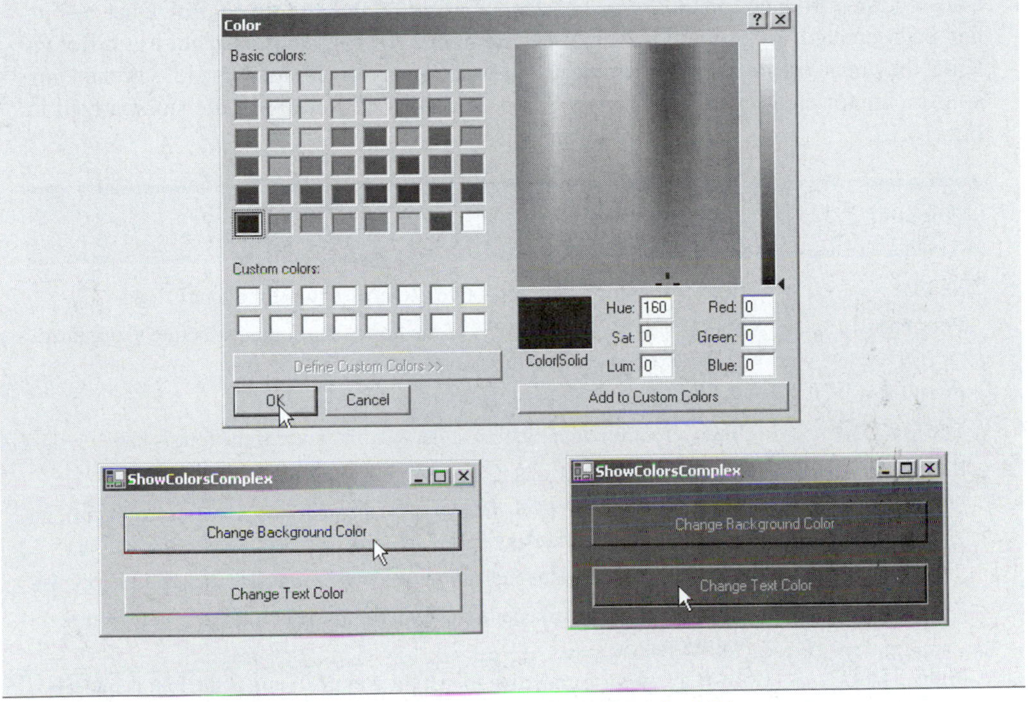

Fig. 16.9 Background and text colors entry point. (Part 2 of 2.)

Lines 55–70 (of Fig. 16.8) define the event handler that is called when the user clicks `Button textColorButton`. The event handler creates a new `ColorDialog` named `colorChooser` and invokes its *`ShowDialog`* method, which displays the window. Method `ShowDialog` returns a `DialogResult` (`result`) specifying whether the user selected **OK** (`DialogResult::OK`) or **Cancel** (`DialogResult::Cancel`). If the user selects **OK** after choosing a color, line 69 sets the text color of the form (including both buttons) to the selected color. Property `Color` of `colorChooser` stores the selected color.

Lines 73–89 define the event handler for button `backgroundColorButton`. The method modifies the background color of the form by setting `BackColor` equal to the dialog's `Color` property. The method creates a new `ColorDialog` and sets the dialog's *`FullOpen`* property to `true`. The dialog now displays all available colors, as shown in the screen capture in Fig. 16.9. We open the dialog to all available colors, so that the user can easily specify any color. The regular color display does not show the right-hand portion of the screen.

Users are not restricted to the `ColorDialog`'s 48 colors. To create a custom color, users can click anywhere in the `ColorDialog`'s large rectangle—this displays the various color shades. Adjust the slider, hue and other features to refine the color. When finished, click the **Add to Custom Colors** button, which adds the custom color to a square in the custom colors section of the dialog. Clicking **OK** sets the `Color` property of the `ColorDialog` to that color. Selecting a color and pressing the dialog's **OK** button causes the application's background color to change.

16.4 Font Control

This section introduces methods and constants that are related to font control. Once a `Font` has been created, its properties cannot be modified. If programmers require a different `Font`, they must create a new `Font` object—there are many overloaded versions of the `Font` constructor for creating custom `Fonts`. Some properties of class `Font` are summarized in Fig. 16.10.

Property	Description
`Bold`	Tests a font for a bold font style. Returns `true` if the font is bold.
`FontFamily`	Represents the `FontFamily` of the `Font` (a grouping structure to organize fonts and define their similar properties).
`Height`	Represents the height of the font.
`Italic`	Tests a font for an italic font style. Returns `true` if the font is italic.
`Name`	Represents the font's name as a `String` pointer.
`Size`	Returns a `float` value indicating the current font size measured in design units (*design units* are any specified units of measurement for the font).
`SizeInPoints`	Returns a `float` value indicating the current font size measured in points.
`Strikeout`	Tests a font for a strikeout font style. Returns `true` if the font is in strikeout format.
`Underline`	Tests a font for a underline font style. Returns `true` if the font is underlined.

Fig. 16.10 `Font` class read-only properties.

Note that the `Size` property returns the font size as measured in design units, whereas `SizeInPoints` returns the font size as measured in points (a more common measurement). When we say that the `Size` property measures the size of the font in design units, we mean that the font size can be specified in a variety of ways, such as inches or millimeters. Some versions of the `Font` constructor accept a *`GraphicsUnit`* argument—an enumeration that allows users to specify the unit of measurement employed to describe the font size. Members of the `GraphicsUnit` enumeration include *`Point`* (1/72 inch), *`Display`* (1/75 inch), *`Document`* (1/300 inch), *`Millimeter`*, *`Inch`* and *`Pixel`*. If this argument is provided, the `Size` property contains the size of the font as measured in the specified design unit, and the `SizeInPoints` property converts the size of the font into points. For example, if we create a `Font` having size `1` and specify that `GraphicsUnit::Inch` be used to measure the font, the `Size` property will be `1`, and the `SizeInPoints` property will be `72`. If we employ a constructor that does not accept a member of `GraphicsUnit`, the default measurement for the font size is `GraphicsUnit::Point` (thus, the `Size` and `SizeInPoints` properties will be equal).

Class `Font` has a number of constructors. Most require a *font name*, which is a `String *` representing a font currently supported by the system. Common fonts include Microsoft *SansSerif* and *Serif*. Constructors also usually require the *font size* as an argument. Lastly, `Font` constructors usually require a *font style*, specified by the *`FontStyle`* enumeration: *`Bold`*, *`Italic`*, *`Regular`*, *`Strikeout`* and *`Underline`*. Font styles can be combined via the '+' operator (for example, `FontStyle::Italic + FontStyle::Bold` makes a font both italic and bold).

Common Programming Error 16.2

Specifying a font that is not available on a system is a logic error. If this occurs, that system's default font will be used instead.

Figure 16.11–Fig. 16.12 display text in four different fonts, each of a different size. The program uses the `Font` constructor to initialize `Font` objects (lines 63–81 of Fig. 16.11). Each call to the `Font` constructor passes a font name (e.g., Arial, Times New Roman, Courier New or Tahoma) as a `String *`, a font size (a `float`) and a `FontStyle` object (`style`). `Graphics` method `DrawString` sets the font and draws the text at the specified location. Line 60 creates a `DarkBlue SolidBrush` object (`brush`), causing all `Strings` drawn with that brush to appear in `DarkBlue`. Lines 73–74 set the font style to both bold and italic using the + operator. Notice that we must cast the result of this operation to a `FontStyle` object before using it.

```
1  // Fig. 16.11: Form1.h
2  // Demonstrating various font settings.
3
4  #pragma once
5
6
7  namespace UsingFonts
8  {
9     using namespace System;
10    using namespace System::ComponentModel;
11    using namespace System::Collections;
12    using namespace System::Windows::Forms;
13    using namespace System::Data;
14    using namespace System::Drawing;
15
16    /// <summary>
17    /// Summary for Form1
18    ///
19    /// WARNING: If you change the name of this class, you will need to
20    ///          change the 'Resource File Name' property for the managed
21    ///          resource compiler tool associated with all .resx files
22    ///          this class depends on.  Otherwise, the designers will not
23    ///          be able to interact properly with localized resources
24    ///          associated with this form.
25    /// </summary>
26    public __gc class Form1 : public System::Windows::Forms::Form
27    {
28    public:
29       Form1(void)
30       {
31          InitializeComponent();
32       }
33
```

Fig. 16.11 `Fonts` and `FontStyles`. (Part 1 of 3.)

```
    protected:
        void Dispose(Boolean disposing)
        {
            if (disposing && components)
            {
                components->Dispose();
            }
            __super::Dispose(disposing);
        }

    private:
        /// <summary>
        /// Required designer variable.
        /// </summary>
        System::ComponentModel::Container * components;

    // Visual Studio .NET generated GUI code

    protected:

        // demonstrate various font and style settings
        void OnPaint( PaintEventArgs *paintEvent )
        {
            __super::OnPaint( paintEvent ); // call base OnPaint method

            Graphics *graphicsObject = paintEvent->Graphics;
            SolidBrush *brush = new SolidBrush( Color::DarkBlue );

            // arial, 12 pt bold
            FontStyle style = FontStyle::Bold;
            Drawing::Font *arial =
                new Drawing::Font( S"Arial", 12, style );

            // times new roman, 12 pt regular
            style = FontStyle::Regular;
            Drawing::Font *timesNewRoman =
                new Drawing::Font( S"Times New Roman", 12, style );

            // courier new, 16 pt bold and italic
            style = static_cast< FontStyle >( FontStyle::Bold +
                FontStyle::Italic );
            Drawing::Font *courierNew =
                new Drawing::Font( S"Courier New", 16, style );

            // tahoma, 18 pt strikeout
            style = FontStyle::Strikeout;
            Drawing::Font *tahoma =
                new Drawing::Font( S"Tahoma", 18, style );

            graphicsObject->DrawString( String::Concat( arial->Name,
                S" 12 point bold." ), arial, brush, 10, 10 );

```

Fig. 16.11 Fonts and FontStyles. (Part 2 of 3.)

```
         graphicsObject->DrawString( String::Concat(
            timesNewRoman->Name, S" 12 point plain." ),
            timesNewRoman, brush, 10, 30 );

         graphicsObject->DrawString( String::Concat( courierNew->Name,
            S" 16 point bold and italic." ), courierNew,
            brush, 10, 54 );

         graphicsObject->DrawString( String::Concat( tahoma->Name,
            S" 18 point strikeout." ), tahoma, brush, 10, 75 );
      } // end method OnPaint
   };
}
```

Fig. 16.11 Fonts and FontStyles. (Part 3 of 3.)

```
// Fig. 16.12: Form1.cpp
// Entry point for application.

#include "stdafx.h"
#include "Form1.h"
#include <windows.h>

using namespace UsingFonts;

int APIENTRY _tWinMain(HINSTANCE hInstance,
                      HINSTANCE hPrevInstance,
                      LPTSTR    lpCmdLine,
                      int       nCmdShow)
{
   System::Threading::Thread::CurrentThread->ApartmentState =
      System::Threading::ApartmentState::STA;
   Application::Run(new Form1());
   return 0;
} // end _tWinMain
```

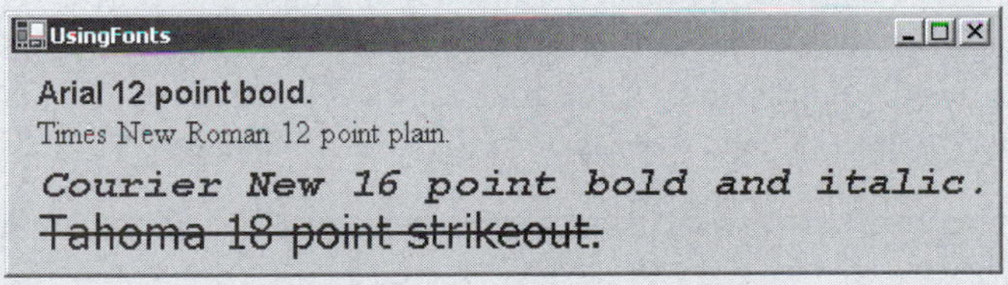

Fig. 16.12 Fonts and FontStyles entry point.

When creating a Font object, programmers can specify precise information about a font's *metrics* (or properties), such as *height*, *descent* (the amount that characters dip below the baseline), *ascent* (the amount that characters rise above the baseline) and *leading* (the difference between the ascent of one line and the descent of the previous line). Figure 16.13 illustrates these properties. Programmers can also use these properties to determine the metrics of a previously created Font object.

Fig. 16.13 Illustration of font metrics.

Class *FontFamily* defines characteristics common to a group of related fonts. Class `FontFamily` provides several methods used to determine the font metrics that are shared by members of a particular family. These methods are summarized in Fig. 16.14.

Method	Description
`GetCellAscent`	Returns an `int` representing the ascent of a font as measured in design units.
`GetCellDescent`	Returns an `int` representing the descent of a font as measured in design units.
`GetEmHeight`	Returns an `int` representing the height of a font as measured in design points.
`GetLineSpacing`	Returns an `int` representing the distance between two consecutive lines of text as measured in design units.

Fig. 16.14 `FontFamily` methods that return font-metric information.

Figure 16.15–Fig. 16.16 display the metrics of two fonts. Line 63 (Fig. 16.15) creates `Font arial` and sets it to 12-point Arial font. Line 64 uses `Font` property `FontFamily` to obtain object `arial`'s `FontFamily` object. Lines 69–70 output the `String` representation of the font. Lines 72–86 then use methods of class `FontFamily` to return integers specifying the ascent, descent, height and leading of the font. Lines 89–108 repeat this process for font `sansSerif`, a `Font` object derived from the MS Sans Serif `FontFamily`.

```
1  // Fig. 16.15: Form1.h
2  // Displaying font metric information.
3
4  #pragma once
5
6
7  namespace UsingFontMetrics
8  {
9     using namespace System;
10    using namespace System::ComponentModel;
11    using namespace System::Collections;
```

Fig. 16.15 `FontFamily` class used to obtain font-metric information. (Part 1 of 3.)

```
using namespace System::Windows::Forms;
using namespace System::Data;
using namespace System::Drawing;

/// <summary>
/// Summary for Form1
///
/// WARNING: If you change the name of this class, you will need to
///          change the 'Resource File Name' property for the managed
///          resource compiler tool associated with all .resx files
///          this class depends on.  Otherwise, the designers will not
///          be able to interact properly with localized resources
///          associated with this form.
/// </summary>
public __gc class Form1 : public System::Windows::Forms::Form
{
public:
   Form1(void)
   {
      InitializeComponent();
   }

protected:
   void Dispose(Boolean disposing)
   {
      if (disposing && components)
      {
         components->Dispose();
      }
      __super::Dispose(disposing);
   }

private:
   /// <summary>
   /// Required designer variable.
   /// </summary>
   System::ComponentModel::Container * components;

// Visual Studio .NET generated GUI code

protected:

   // displays font information
   void OnPaint( PaintEventArgs *paintEvent )
   {
      __super::OnPaint( paintEvent ); // call base OnPaint method

      Graphics *graphicsObject = paintEvent->Graphics;
      SolidBrush *brush = new SolidBrush( Color::DarkBlue );

      // Arial font metrics
      Drawing::Font *arial = new Drawing::Font( S"Arial", 12 );
      FontFamily *family = arial->FontFamily;
```

Fig. 16.15 `FontFamily` class used to obtain font-metric information. (Part 2 of 3.)

```
         Drawing::Font *sanSerif = new Drawing::Font(
            S"Microsoft Sans Serif", 14, FontStyle::Italic );

         // display Arial font metrics
         graphicsObject->DrawString( String::Concat
            ( S"Current Font: ", arial ), arial, brush, 10, 10 );

         graphicsObject->DrawString( String::Concat( S"Ascent: ",
            family->GetCellAscent( FontStyle::Regular ).ToString() ),
            arial, brush, 10, 30 );

         graphicsObject->DrawString( String::Concat( S"Descent: ",
            family->GetCellDescent( FontStyle::Regular ).ToString() ),
            arial, brush, 10, 50 );

         graphicsObject->DrawString( String::Concat( S"Height: ",
            family->GetEmHeight( FontStyle::Regular ).ToString() ),
            arial, brush, 10, 70 );

         graphicsObject->DrawString( String::Concat( S"Leading: ",
            family->GetLineSpacing( FontStyle::Regular ).ToString() ),
            arial, brush, 10, 90 );

         // display Sans Serif font metrics
         family = sanSerif->FontFamily;

         graphicsObject->DrawString( String::Concat( S"Current Font: ",
            sanSerif ), sanSerif, brush, 10, 130 );

         graphicsObject->DrawString( String::Concat( S"Ascent: ",
            family->GetCellAscent( FontStyle::Regular ).ToString() ),
            sanSerif, brush, 10, 150 );

         graphicsObject->DrawString( String::Concat( S"Descent: ",
            family->GetCellDescent( FontStyle::Regular ).ToString() ),
            sanSerif, brush, 10, 170 );

         graphicsObject->DrawString( String::Concat( S"Height: ",
            family->GetEmHeight( FontStyle::Regular ).ToString() ),
            sanSerif, brush, 10, 190 );

         graphicsObject->DrawString( String::Concat( S"Leading: ",
            family->GetLineSpacing( FontStyle::Regular ).ToString() ),
            sanSerif, brush, 10, 210 );
      } // end method OnPaint
   };
}
```

Fig. 16.15 `FontFamily` class used to obtain font-metric information. (Part 3 of 3.)

```
// Fig. 16.16: Form1.cpp
// Entry point for application.
```

Fig. 16.16 `UsingFontMetrics` entry point. (Part 1 of 2.)

```

#include "stdafx.h"
#include "Form1.h"
#include <windows.h>

using namespace UsingFontMetrics;

int APIENTRY _tWinMain(HINSTANCE hInstance,
                       HINSTANCE hPrevInstance,
                       LPTSTR    lpCmdLine,
                       int       nCmdShow)
{
   System::Threading::Thread::CurrentThread->ApartmentState =
      System::Threading::ApartmentState::STA;
   Application::Run(new Form1());
   return 0;
} // end _tWinMain
```

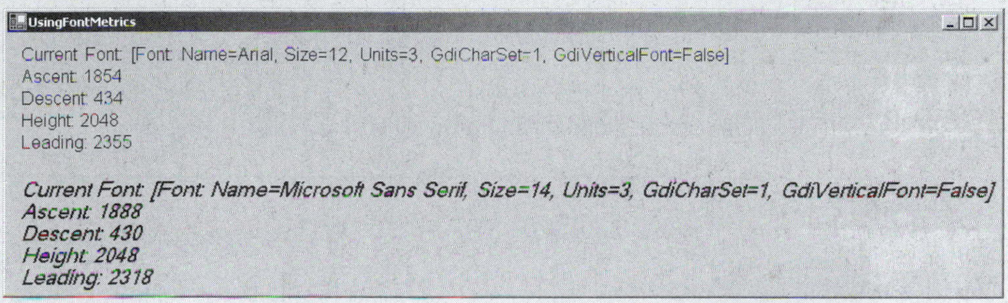
UsingFontMetrics
Current Font: [Font: Name=Arial, Size=12, Units=3, GdiCharSet=1, GdiVerticalFont=False]
Ascent: 1854
Descent: 434
Height: 2048
Leading: 2355
Current Font: [Font: Name=Microsoft Sans Serif, Size=14, Units=3, GdiCharSet=1, GdiVerticalFont=False]
Ascent: 1888
Descent: 430
Height: 2048
Leading: 2318

Fig. 16.16 `UsingFontMetrics` entry point. (Part 2 of 2.)

16.5 Drawing Lines, Rectangles and Ovals

This section presents `Graphics` methods for drawing lines, rectangles and ovals. Each of the drawing methods has several overloaded versions. When drawing lines, we specify four `int`s (for the coordinates of where the line starts and ends). When employing methods that draw shape outlines, we use versions that take a `Pen` and four `int`s; when employing methods that draw solid shapes, we use versions that take a `Brush` and four `int`s. In both instances, the first two `int` arguments represent the coordinates of the upper-left corner of the shape or its enclosing area, and the last two `int`s indicate the shape's width and height. Figure 16.17 summarizes various `Graphics` methods and their parameters.

Graphics Drawing Methods and Descriptions.
Note: Many of these methods are overloaded—consult the documentation for a full listing.
`DrawLine( Pen *p, int x1, int y1, int x2, int y2 )` Draws a line from (`x1`, `y1`) to (`x2`, `y2`). The `Pen` determines the color, style and width of the line.

Fig. 16.17 `Graphics` methods that draw lines, rectangles and ovals. (Part 1 of 2.)

Graphics Drawing Methods and Descriptions.
`DrawRectangle( Pen *p, int x, int y, int width, int height )` Draws a rectangle of the specified width and height. The top-left corner of the rectangle is at point (x, y). The `Pen` determines the color, style, and border width of the rectangle.
`FillRectangle( Brush *b, int x, int y, int width, int height )` Draws a solid rectangle of the specified width and height. The top-left corner of the rectangle is at point (`x`, `y`). The `Brush` determines the fill pattern inside the rectangle.
`DrawEllipse( Pen *p, int x, int y, int width, int height )` Draws an ellipse inside a rectangle. The width and height of the rectangle are as specified, and its top-left corner is at point (`x`, `y`). The `Pen` determines the color, style and border width of the ellipse.
`FillEllipse( Brush *b, int x, int y, int width, int height )` Draws a filled ellipse inside a rectangle. The width and height of the rectangle are as specified, and its top-left corner is at point (`x`, `y`). The `Brush` determines the pattern inside the ellipse.

Fig. 16.17 `Graphics` methods that draw lines, rectangles and ovals. (Part 2 of 2.)

The application in Fig. 16.18–Fig. 16.19 draws lines, rectangles and ellipses. In this application, we also demonstrate methods that draw filled and unfilled shapes.

```
// Fig. 16.18: Form1.h
// Demonstrating lines, rectangles and ovals.

#pragma once


namespace LinesRectanglesOvals
{
   using namespace System;
   using namespace System::ComponentModel;
   using namespace System::Collections;
   using namespace System::Windows::Forms;
   using namespace System::Data;
   using namespace System::Drawing;

   /// <summary>
   /// Summary for Form1
   ///
   /// WARNING: If you change the name of this class, you will need to
   ///          change the 'Resource File Name' property for the managed
   ///          resource compiler tool associated with all .resx files
   ///          this class depends on.  Otherwise, the designers will not
   ///          be able to interact properly with localized resources
   ///          associated with this form.
   /// </summary>
   public __gc class Form1 : public System::Windows::Forms::Form
   {
```

Fig. 16.18 Demonstration of methods that draw lines, rectangles and ellipses. (Part 1 of 3.)

```
   public:
      Form1(void)
      {
         InitializeComponent();
      }

   protected:
      void Dispose(Boolean disposing)
      {
         if (disposing && components)
         {
            components->Dispose();
         }
         __super::Dispose(disposing);
      }

   private:
      /// <summary>
      /// Required designer variable.
      /// </summary>
      System::ComponentModel::Container * components;

   // Visual Studio .NET generated GUI code

   protected:

      void OnPaint( PaintEventArgs *paintEvent )
      {
         __super::OnPaint( paintEvent ); // call base OnPaint method

         // get graphics object
         Graphics *graphicsObject = paintEvent->Graphics;
         SolidBrush *brush = new SolidBrush( Color::Blue );
         Pen *pen = new Pen( Color::AliceBlue );

         // create filled rectangle
         graphicsObject->FillRectangle( brush, 90, 30, 150, 90 );

         // draw lines to connect rectangles
         graphicsObject->DrawLine( pen, 90, 30, 110, 40 );
         graphicsObject->DrawLine( pen, 90, 120, 110, 130 );
         graphicsObject->DrawLine( pen, 240, 30, 260, 40 );
         graphicsObject->DrawLine( pen, 240, 120, 260, 130 );

         // draw top rectangle
         graphicsObject->DrawRectangle( pen, 110, 40, 150, 90 );

         // set brush to red
         brush->Color = Color::Red;

         // draw base Ellipse
         graphicsObject->FillEllipse( brush, 280, 75, 100, 50 );
```

Fig. 16.18 Demonstration of methods that draw lines, rectangles and ellipses. (Part 2 of 3.)

```
80
81             // draw connecting lines
82             graphicsObject->DrawLine( pen, 380, 55, 380, 100 );
83             graphicsObject->DrawLine( pen, 280, 55, 280, 100 );
84
85             // draw Ellipse outline
86             graphicsObject->DrawEllipse( pen, 280, 30, 100, 50 );
87          } // end method OnPaint
88       };
89    }
```

Fig. 16.18 Demonstration of methods that draw lines, rectangles and ellipses. (Part 3 of 3.)

```
// Fig. 16.19: Form1.cpp
// Entry point for application.

#include "stdafx.h"
#include "Form1.h"
#include <windows.h>

using namespace LinesRectanglesOvals;

int APIENTRY _tWinMain(HINSTANCE hInstance,
                       HINSTANCE hPrevInstance,
                       LPTSTR    lpCmdLine,
                       int       nCmdShow)
{
   System::Threading::Thread::CurrentThread->ApartmentState =
      System::Threading::ApartmentState::STA;
   Application::Run(new Form1());
   return 0;
} // end _tWinMain
```

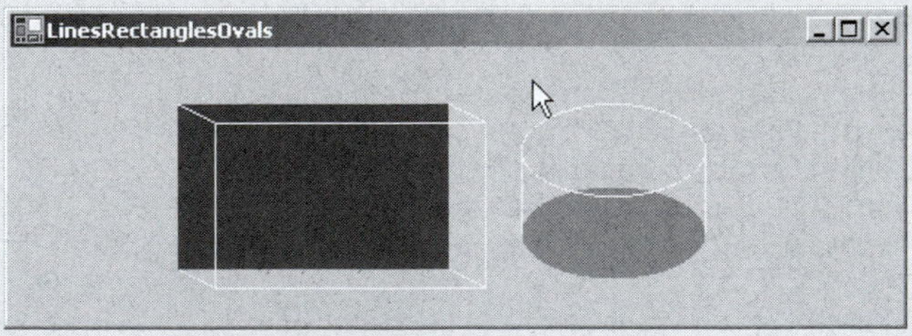

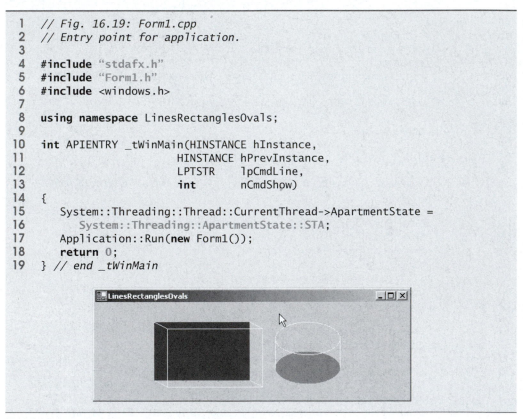

Fig. 16.19 `LinesRectanglesOvals` entry point.

Methods *`FillRectangle`* and *`DrawRectangle`* (lines 64 and 73 of Fig. 16.18) draw rectangles on the screen. For each method, the first argument specifies the drawing object to use. The `DrawRectangle` method uses a `Pen` object, whereas the `FillRectangle` method uses a `Brush` object (in this case, an instance of `SolidBrush`, which derives from `Brush`). The next two arguments specify the coordinates of the upper-left corner of the *bounding rectangle*, which represents the area in which the rectangle will be drawn. The fourth and fifth arguments specify the rectangle's width and height. Method `DrawLine` (lines 67–70) takes a `Pen` and two pairs of `ints`, specifying the startpoint and endpoint of the line. The method then draws a line, using the `Pen` object passed to it.

Methods `FillEllipse` and `DrawEllipse` (lines 79 and 86 of Fig. 16.18) each provide overloaded versions that take five arguments. In both methods, the first argument specifies the drawing object to use. The next two arguments specify the upper-left coordinates of the bounding rectangle representing the area in which the ellipse will be drawn. The last two arguments specify the bounding rectangle's width and height, respectively.

Figure 16.20 depicts an ellipse bounded by a rectangle. The ellipse touches the midpoint of each of the four sides of the bounding rectangle. The bounding rectangle is not displayed on the screen.

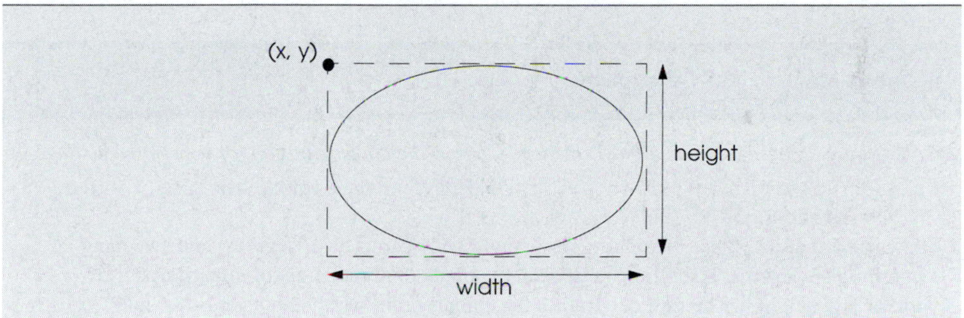

Fig. 16.20 Ellipse bounded by a rectangle.

16.6 Drawing Arcs

Arcs are portions of ellipses and are measured in degrees, beginning at a *starting angle* and continuing for a specified number of degrees called the *arc angle*. An arc is said to *sweep* (traverse) its arc angle, beginning from its starting angle. Arcs that sweep in a clockwise direction are measured in positive degrees; arcs that sweep in a counterclockwise direction are measured in negative degrees. Figure 16.21 depicts two arcs. Note that the arc in the left portion of the figure sweeps downward from zero degrees to approximately 110 degrees. Similarly, the arc in the right portion of the figure sweeps upward from zero degrees to approximately –110 degrees.

Notice the dashed boxes around the arcs in Fig. 16.21. We draw each arc as part of an oval (the rest of which is not visible). When drawing an oval, we specify the oval's dimensions in the form of a bounding rectangle that encloses the oval. The boxes in Fig. 16.21 correspond to these bounding rectangles. The `Graphics` methods used to draw arcs—`DrawArc`, `DrawPie` and `FillPie`—are summarized in Fig. 16.22.

The application in Fig. 16.23–Fig. 16.24 draws six images (three arcs and three filled pie slices) to demonstrate the arc methods listed in Fig. 16.22. To illustrate the bounding rectangles that determine the sizes and locations of the arcs, the arcs are displayed inside red rectangles that have the same *x*-coordinates, *y*-coordinates and width and height arguments as those that define the bounding rectangles for the arcs.

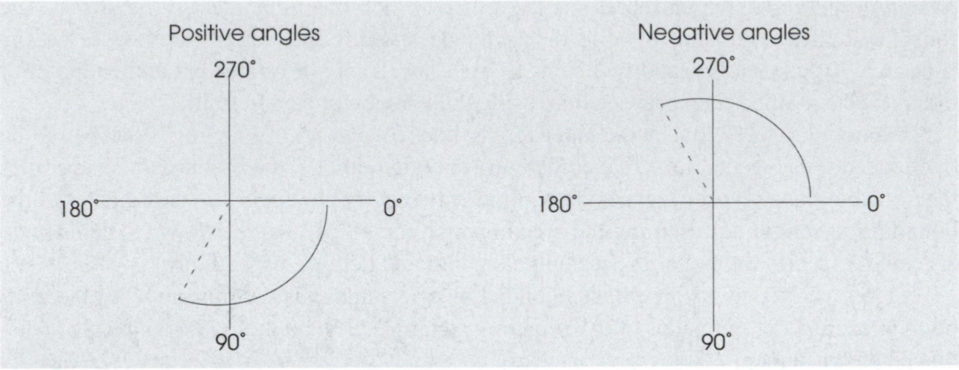

Fig. 16.21 Positive and negative arc angles.

Graphics Methods And Descriptions

Note: Many of these methods are overloaded—consult the documentation for a complete listing.

`DrawArc( Pen *p, int x, int y, int width, int height, int startAngle, int sweepAngle )`

Draws an arc of an ellipse, beginning from angle `startAngle` (in degrees) and sweeping `sweepAngle` degrees. The ellipse is defined by a bounding rectangle of upper-left corner (`x`, `y`), width `w` and height `h`. The `Pen` determines the color, border width and style of the arc.

`DrawPie( Pen *p, int x, int y, int width, int height, int startAngle, int sweepAngle )`

Draws a pie section of an ellipse, beginning from angle `startAngle` (in degrees) and sweeping `sweepAngle` degrees. The ellipse is defined by a bounding rectangle of upper-left corner (`x`, `y`), width `w` and height `h`. The `Pen` determines the color, border width and style of the arc.

`FillPie( Brush *b, int x, int y, int width, int height, int startAngle, int sweepAngle )`

Functions similarly to `DrawPie`, except draws a solid arc (i.e., a sector). The `Brush` determines the fill pattern for the solid arc.

Fig. 16.22 `Graphics` methods for drawing arcs.

```
// Fig. 16.23: Form1.h
// Drawing various arcs on a form.

#pragma once


namespace DrawArcs
{
   using namespace System;
   using namespace System::ComponentModel;
   using namespace System::Collections;
```

Fig. 16.23 Arc-method demonstration. (Part 1 of 3.)

```
using namespace System::Windows::Forms;
using namespace System::Data;
using namespace System::Drawing;

/// <summary>
/// Summary for Form1
///
/// WARNING: If you change the name of this class, you will need to
///          change the 'Resource File Name' property for the managed
///          resource compiler tool associated with all .resx files
///          this class depends on.  Otherwise, the designers will not
///          be able to interact properly with localized resources
///          associated with this form.
/// </summary>
public __gc class Form1 : public System::Windows::Forms::Form
{
public:
   Form1(void)
   {
      InitializeComponent();
   }

protected:
   void Dispose(Boolean disposing)
   {
      if (disposing && components)
      {
         components->Dispose();
      }
      __super::Dispose(disposing);
   }

private:
   /// <summary>
   /// Required designer variable.
   /// </summary>
   System::ComponentModel::Container * components;

// Visual Studio .NET generated code

protected:

   void OnPaint( PaintEventArgs *paintEvent )
   {
      __super::OnPaint( paintEvent ); // call base OnPaint method

      // get graphics object
      Graphics *graphicsObject = paintEvent->Graphics;
      Rectangle rectangle1 = Rectangle( 15, 35, 80, 80 );
      SolidBrush *brush1 = new SolidBrush( Color::Firebrick );
      Pen *pen1 = new Pen( brush1, 1 );
      SolidBrush *brush2 = new SolidBrush( Color::DarkBlue );
      Pen *pen2 = new Pen( brush2, 1 );
```

Fig. 16.23 Arc-method demonstration. (Part 2 of 3.)

```

         // start at 0 and sweep 360 degrees
         graphicsObject->DrawRectangle( pen1, rectangle1 );
         graphicsObject->DrawArc( pen2, rectangle1, 0, 360 );

         // start at 0 and sweep 110 degrees
         rectangle1.Location = Point( 100, 35 );
         graphicsObject->DrawRectangle( pen1, rectangle1 );
         graphicsObject->DrawArc( pen2, rectangle1, 0, 110 );

         // start at 0 and sweep -270 degrees
         rectangle1.Location = Point( 185, 35 );
         graphicsObject->DrawRectangle( pen1, rectangle1 );
         graphicsObject->DrawArc( pen2, rectangle1, 0, -270 );

         // start at 0 and sweep 360 degrees
         rectangle1.Location = Point( 15, 120 );
         rectangle1.Size = Drawing::Size( 80, 40 );
         graphicsObject->DrawRectangle( pen1, rectangle1 );
         graphicsObject->FillPie( brush2, rectangle1, 0, 360 );

         // start at 270 and sweep -90 degrees
         rectangle1.Location = Point( 100, 120 );
         graphicsObject->DrawRectangle( pen1, rectangle1 );
         graphicsObject->FillPie( brush2, rectangle1, 270, -90 );

         // start at 0 and sweep -270 degrees
         rectangle1.Location = Point( 185, 120 );
         graphicsObject->DrawRectangle( pen1, rectangle1 );
         graphicsObject->FillPie( brush2, rectangle1, 0, -270 );
      } // end method OnPaint
   };
}
```

Fig. 16.23 Arc-method demonstration. (Part 3 of 3.)

```
// Fig. 16.24: Form1.cpp
// Entry point for application.

#include "stdafx.h"
#include "Form1.h"
#include <windows.h>

using namespace DrawArcs;

int APIENTRY _tWinMain(HINSTANCE hInstance,
                       HINSTANCE hPrevInstance,
                       LPTSTR    lpCmdLine,
                       int       nCmdShow)
{
   System::Threading::Thread::CurrentThread->ApartmentState =
      System::Threading::ApartmentState::STA;
```

Fig. 16.24 DrawArcs entry point. (Part 1 of 2.)

```
    Application::Run(new Form1());
    return 0;
} // end _tWinMain
```

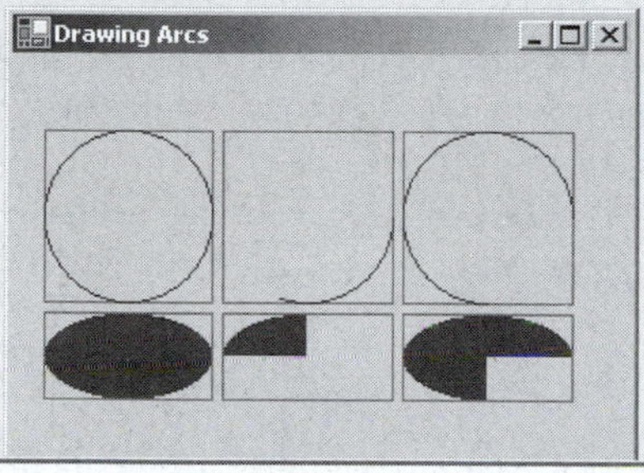

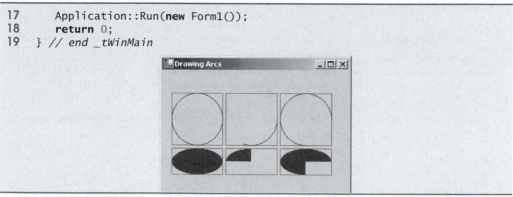

Fig. 16.24 `DrawArcs` entry point. (Part 2 of 2.)

Lines 59–64 (Fig. 16.23) create the objects that we need to draw various arcs: `Graphics` objects, `Rectangles`, `SolidBrushes` and `Pens`. Lines 67–68 draw a rectangle and an arc inside the rectangle. The arc sweeps 360 degrees, forming a circle. Line 71 changes the location of the `Rectangle` by setting its `Location` property to a new `Point`. The `Point` constructor takes the *x*- and *y*-coordinates of the new point. The `Location` property determines the upper-left corner of the `Rectangle`. After drawing the rectangle, the program draws an arc that starts at 0 degrees and sweeps 110 degrees. Angles in Visual C++ .NET increase in a clockwise direction, so the arc sweeps downward.

Lines 76–78 perform similar functions, except that the specified arc sweeps –270 degrees. The `Size` property of a `Rectangle` determines the arc's height and width. Line 82 sets the `Size` property to a new `Size` object, which changes the size of the rectangle.

The remainder of the program is similar to the portions described above, except that a `SolidBrush` is used with method `FillPie`, and the bounding rectangle has a different size. The resulting arcs, which are filled, can be seen in the bottom half of the screenshot in Fig. 16.24.

16.7 Drawing Polygons and Polylines

Polygons are multisided shapes. There are several `Graphics` methods used to draw polygons: ***`DrawLines`*** draws a series of connected points, ***`DrawPolygon`*** draws a closed polygon and ***`FillPolygon`*** draws a solid polygon. These methods are described in Fig. 16.25. The program in Fig. 16.26–Fig. 16.27 allows users to draw polygons and connected lines via the methods listed in Fig. 16.25.

Graphics Methods And Descriptions
Note: Many of these methods are overloaded—consult the documentation for a complete listing.
`DrawLines( Pen *p, Point[] )` Draws a series of connected lines. The coordinates of each point are specified in an array of `Points`. If the last point is different from the first point, the figure is not closed.

Fig. 16.25 `Graphics` methods for drawing polygons. (Part 1 of 2.)

Graphics Methods And Descriptions
`DrawPolygon( Pen *p, Point[] )` Draws a polygon. The coordinates of each point are specified in an array of `Point` objects. This method draws a closed polygon, even if the last point is different from the first point.
`FillPolygon( Brush *b, Point[] )` Draws a solid polygon. The coordinates of each point are specified in an array of `Points`. This method draws a closed polygon, even if the last point is different from the first point.

Fig. 16.25 `Graphics` methods for drawing polygons. (Part 2 of 2.)

To allow the user to specify a variable number of points, line 52 (Fig. 16.26) declares *ArrayList* `points` as a container for our `Point` objects. Class `ArrayList` (namespace `System::Collections`) mimics the functionality of conventional arrays, yet provides dynamic resizing of the collection through the class's methods. `ArrayLists` store pointers to `Objects`. All classes derive from class `Object`, so an `ArrayList` can contain objects of any type. In this example, we use class `ArrayList` to store `Point` objects. We discuss class `ArrayList` in more detail in Chapter 22, Data Structures and Collections.

Lines 55–56 declare the `Pen` and `Brush` used to color our shapes. The `MouseDown` event handler (lines 67–73 of Fig. 16.26) for `Panel drawPanel` stores mouse-click locations in the `points ArrayList` using method *Add*. `ArrayList` method `Add` appends a new element at the end of an `ArrayList`.

```
1  // Fig. 16.26: Form1.h
2  // Demonstrating polygons.
3
4  #pragma once
5
6
7  namespace DrawPolygons
8  {
9     using namespace System;
10    using namespace System::ComponentModel;
11    using namespace System::Collections;
12    using namespace System::Windows::Forms;
13    using namespace System::Data;
14    using namespace System::Drawing;
15
16    /// <summary>
17    /// Summary for Form1
18    ///
19    /// WARNING: If you change the name of this class, you will need to
20    ///          change the 'Resource File Name' property for the managed
21    ///          resource compiler tool associated with all .resx files
22    ///          this class depends on.  Otherwise, the designers will not
23    ///          be able to interact properly with localized resources
24    ///          associated with this form.
25    /// </summary>
```

Fig. 16.26 Polygon-drawing demonstration. (Part 1 of 4.)

```
   public __gc class Form1 : public System::Windows::Forms::Form
   {
   public:
      Form1(void)
      {
         InitializeComponent();
      }

   protected:
      void Dispose(Boolean disposing)
      {
         if (disposing && components)
         {
            components->Dispose();
         }
         __super::Dispose(disposing);
      }
   private: System::Windows::Forms::Button *  colorButton;
   private: System::Windows::Forms::Button *  clearButton;
   private: System::Windows::Forms::GroupBox *  typeGroup;
   private: System::Windows::Forms::RadioButton *  filledPolygonOption;
   private: System::Windows::Forms::RadioButton *  lineOption;
   private: System::Windows::Forms::RadioButton *  polygonOption;
   private: System::Windows::Forms::Panel *  drawPanel;

   // contains list of polygon vertices
   private: static ArrayList *points = new ArrayList();

   // initialize default pen and brush
   private: static Pen *pen = new Pen( Color::DarkBlue );
   private: static SolidBrush *brush = new SolidBrush( Color::DarkBlue );

   private:
      /// <summary>
      /// Required designer variable.
      /// </summary>
      System::ComponentModel::Container * components;

   // Visual Studio .NET generated GUI code

   // draw panel mouse down event handler
   private: System::Void drawPanel_MouseDown(System::Object *  sender,
               System::Windows::Forms::MouseEventArgs *  e)
            {
               // add mouse position to vertex list
               points->Add( __box( Point( e->X, e->Y ) ) );
               drawPanel->Invalidate(); // refresh panel
            } // end method drawPanel_MouseDown

   private: System::Void drawPanel_Paint(System::Object *  sender,
               System::Windows::Forms::PaintEventArgs *  e)
            {
```

Fig. 16.26 Polygon-drawing demonstration. (Part 2 of 4.)

```
            // get graphics object for panel
            Graphics *graphicsObject = e->Graphics;

            // if arraylist has 2 or more points, display shape
            if ( points->Count > 1 ) {

               // create array of points
               Point pointArray[] = new Point[ points->Count ];

               // add each point to the array
               for( int i = 0; i < points->Count; i++ )
                  pointArray[ i ] = *(
                  dynamic_cast< Point* >( points->Item[ i ] ) );

               if ( polygonOption->Checked )

                  // draw polygon
                  graphicsObject->DrawPolygon( pen, pointArray );

               else if ( lineOption->Checked )

                  // draw lines
                  graphicsObject->DrawLines( pen, pointArray );

               else if ( filledPolygonOption->Checked )

                  // draw filled
                  graphicsObject->FillPolygon( brush, pointArray );
            } //end if
         } // end method drawPanel_Paint

   // handle clearButton click event
   private: System::Void clearButton_Click(
            System::Object *  sender, System::EventArgs *  e)
         {
            points = new ArrayList(); // remove points

            drawPanel->Invalidate(); // refresh panel
         } // end method clearButton_Click

   // handle polygon radio button CheckedChanged event
   private: System::Void polygonOption_CheckedChanged(
            System::Object *  sender, System::EventArgs *  e)
         {
            drawPanel->Invalidate(); // refresh panel
         } // end method polygonOption_CheckedChanged

   // handle line radio button CheckedChanged event
   private: System::Void lineOption_CheckedChanged(
            System::Object *  sender, System::EventArgs *  e)
         {
            drawPanel->Invalidate(); // refresh panel
         } // end method lineOption_CheckedChanged
```

Fig. 16.26 Polygon-drawing demonstration. (Part 3 of 4.)

```
   // handle filled polygon radio button CheckedChanged event
   private: System::Void filledPolygonOption_CheckedChanged(
               System::Object *  sender, System::EventArgs *  e)
            {
               drawPanel->Invalidate(); // refresh panel
            } // end method filledPolygonOption_CheckedChanged

   // handle colorButton click event
   private: System::Void colorButton_Click(
               System::Object *  sender, System::EventArgs *  e)
            {
               // create new color dialog
               ColorDialog *dialogColor = new ColorDialog();

               // show dialog and obtain result
               Windows::Forms::DialogResult result =
                  dialogColor->ShowDialog();

               // return if user cancels
               if ( result == DialogResult::Cancel )
                  return;

               pen->Color = dialogColor->Color;   // set pen to color
               brush->Color = dialogColor->Color; // set brush
               drawPanel->Invalidate();           // refresh panel;
            } // end method colorButton_Click
   };
}
```

Fig. 16.26 Polygon-drawing demonstration. (Part 4 of 4.)

```
// Fig. 16.27: Form1.cpp
// Entry point for application.

#include "stdafx.h"
#include "Form1.h"
#include <windows.h>

using namespace DrawPolygons;

int APIENTRY _tWinMain(HINSTANCE hInstance,
                       HINSTANCE hPrevInstance,
                       LPTSTR    lpCmdLine,
                       int       nCmdShow)
{
   System::Threading::Thread::CurrentThread->ApartmentState =
      System::Threading::ApartmentState::STA;
   Application::Run(new Form1());
   return 0;
} // end _tWinMain
```

Fig. 16.27 `PolygonForm` entry point. (Part 1 of 2.)

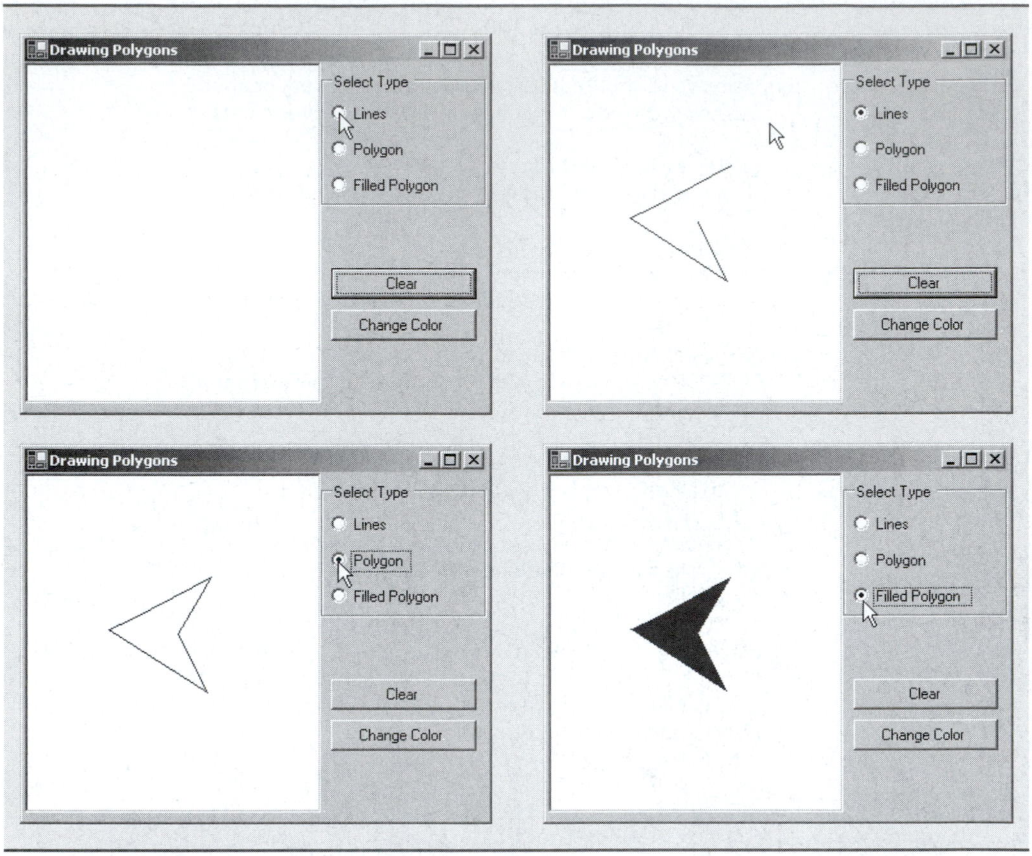

Fig. 16.27 `PolygonForm` entry point. (Part 2 of 2.)

Line 72 then calls method `Invalidate` of `drawPanel` to ensure that the panel refreshes to accommodate the new point. Notice that we call `Invalidate` of `drawPanel` rather than the entire `Form` because we only wish to update the `drawPanel`. Method `drawPanel_Paint` (lines 75–107) handles the `Panel`'s `Paint` event. It obtains the panel's `Graphics` object (line 79) and, if the `ArrayList points` contains two or more `Points`, displays the polygon with the method that the user selected via the GUI radio buttons (lines 82–106). In lines 85–90, we extract the `Point` objects from the `ArrayList` using indexed property *`Item`*. `ArrayList` elements are accessed by following the `ArrayList` indexed property `Item` with the array subscript operator (`[]`) and the desired index of the element (e.g., `points->Item[i]`). However, notice that line 90 uses `dynamic_cast` to cast the returned item to type `Point *`. This is necessary because `ArrayLists` only store and return pointers to `Objects`. Thus, the `Object *` returned from indexed property `Item` must be cast to type `Point *` (line 90).

Method `clearButton_Click` (lines 110–116) handles the **Clear** button's click event, creates an empty `ArrayList` (causing the old list to be erased) and refreshes the display. Lines 119–137 define the event handlers for the radio buttons' `CheckedChanged` event. Each method refreshes `Panel drawPanel` to ensure that the panel display reflects the selected drawing type. Event method `colorButton_Click` (140–157) allows the user to select a new drawing color with a `ColorDialog`, using the same technique demonstrated in Fig. 16.9.

16.8 Advanced Graphics Capabilities

.NET offers many additional graphics capabilities. The `Brush` hierarchy, for example, also includes *`HatchBrush`*, *`LinearGradientBrush`*, *`PathGradientBrush`* and *`TextureBrush`*.

Figure 16.28–Fig. 16.29 demonstrate several graphics features, such as dashed lines, thick lines and the ability to fill shapes with patterns. These represent just a few of the additional capabilities of the `System::Drawing` namespace.

```
// Fig. 16.28: Form1.h
// Drawing various shapes on a form.

#pragma once


namespace DrawShapes
{
   using namespace System;
   using namespace System::ComponentModel;
   using namespace System::Collections;
   using namespace System::Windows::Forms;
   using namespace System::Data;
   using namespace System::Drawing;
   using namespace System::Drawing::Drawing2D;

   /// <summary>
   /// Summary for Form1
   ///
   /// WARNING: If you change the name of this class, you will need to
   ///          change the 'Resource File Name' property for the managed
   ///          resource compiler tool associated with all .resx files
   ///          this class depends on.  Otherwise, the designers will not
   ///          be able to interact properly with localized resources
   ///          associated with this form.
   /// </summary>
   public __gc class Form1 : public System::Windows::Forms::Form
   {
   public:
      Form1(void)
      {
         InitializeComponent();
      }

   protected:
      void Dispose(Boolean disposing)
      {
         if (disposing && components)
         {
```

Fig. 16.28 Shapes drawn on a form. (Part 1 of 3.)

```
            components->Dispose();
         }
         __super::Dispose(disposing);
      }

   private:
      /// <summary>
      /// Required designer variable.
      /// </summary>
      System::ComponentModel::Container * components;

   // Visual Studio .NET generated GUI code

   protected:

      // draw various shapes on form
      void OnPaint( PaintEventArgs *paintEvent )
      {
         __super::OnPaint( paintEvent ); // call base OnPaint method

         // pointer to object we will use
         Graphics *graphicsObject = paintEvent->Graphics;

         // ellipse rectangle and gradient brush
         Rectangle drawArea1 = Rectangle( 5, 35, 30, 100 );
         LinearGradientBrush *linearBrush =
            new LinearGradientBrush( drawArea1, Color::Blue,
            Color::Yellow, LinearGradientMode::ForwardDiagonal );

         // pen and location for red outline rectangle
         Pen *thickRedPen = new Pen( Color::Red, 10 );
         Rectangle drawArea2 = Rectangle( 80, 30, 65, 100 );

         // bitmap texture
         Bitmap *textureBitmap = new Bitmap( 10, 10 );

         // get bitmap graphics
         Graphics *graphicsObject2 = Graphics::FromImage( textureBitmap );

         // brush and pen used throughout program
         SolidBrush *solidColorBrush = new SolidBrush( Color::Red );
         Pen *coloredPen = new Pen( solidColorBrush );

         // draw ellipse filled with a blue-yellow gradient
         graphicsObject->FillEllipse( linearBrush, 5, 30, 65, 100 );

         // draw thick rectangle outline in red
         graphicsObject->DrawRectangle( thickRedPen, drawArea2 );

         // fill textureBitmap with yellow
         solidColorBrush->Color = Color::Yellow;
         graphicsObject2->FillRectangle( solidColorBrush, 0, 0, 10, 10 );

```

Fig. 16.28 Shapes drawn on a form. (Part 2 of 3.)

```
         // draw small black rectangle in textureBitmap
         coloredPen->Color = Color::Black;
         graphicsObject2->DrawRectangle( coloredPen, 1, 1, 6, 6 );

         // draw small blue rectangle in textureBitmap
         solidColorBrush->Color = Color::Blue;
         graphicsObject2->FillRectangle( solidColorBrush, 1, 1, 3, 3 );

         // draw small red square in textureBitmap
         solidColorBrush->Color = Color::Red;
         graphicsObject2->FillRectangle( solidColorBrush, 4, 4, 3, 3 );

         // create textured brush and
         // display textured rectangle
         TextureBrush *texturedBrush = new TextureBrush( textureBitmap );
         graphicsObject->FillRectangle( texturedBrush, 155, 30, 75, 100 );

         // draw pie-shaped arc in white
         coloredPen->Color = Color::White;
         coloredPen->Width = 6;
         graphicsObject->DrawPie( coloredPen, 240, 30, 75, 100, 0, 270 );

         // draw lines in green and yellow
         coloredPen->Color = Color::Green;
         coloredPen->Width = 5;
         graphicsObject->DrawLine( coloredPen, 395, 30, 320, 150 );

         // draw a rounded, dashed yellow line
         coloredPen->Color = Color::Yellow;
         coloredPen->DashCap = DashCap::Round;
         coloredPen->DashStyle = DashStyle::Dash;
         graphicsObject->DrawLine( coloredPen, 320, 30, 395, 150 );
      } // end method OnPaint
   };
}
```

Fig. 16.28 Shapes drawn on a form. (Part 3 of 3.)

```
// Fig. 16.29: Form1.cpp
// Entry point for application.

#include “stdafx.h”
#include “Form1.h”
#include <windows.h>

using namespace DrawShapes;

int APIENTRY _tWinMain(HINSTANCE hInstance,
                     HINSTANCE hPrevInstance,
                     LPTSTR    lpCmdLine,
                     int       nCmdShow)
{
```

Fig. 16.29 DrawShapes entry point. (Part 1 of 2.)

```
    System::Threading::Thread::CurrentThread->ApartmentState =
       System::Threading::ApartmentState::STA;
    Application::Run(new Form1());
    return 0;
 } // end _tWinMain
```

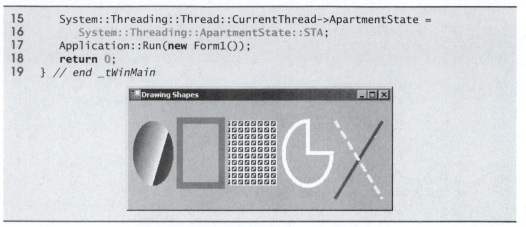

Fig. 16.29 DrawShapes entry point. (Part 2 of 2.)

Lines 56–125 (Fig. 16.28) define method `OnPaint` for our form. Lines 65–67 create `LinearGradientBrush` object `linearBrush`, which resides in namespace `System::Drawing::Drawing2D`. A `LinearGradientBrush` enables users to draw with a color gradient. The `LinearGradientBrush` used in this example takes four arguments: A `Rectangle`, two `Colors` and a member of enumeration *`LinearGradientMode`*. In Visual C++ .NET, all linear gradients are defined along a line that determines the gradient endpoint. This line can be specified either by starting and ending points or by the diagonal of a rectangle. The first argument, `Rectangle drawArea1`, specifies the defining line for `LinearGradientBrush linearBrush`. This `Rectangle` argument represents the endpoints of the linear gradient—the upper-left corner is the starting point, and the bottom-right corner is the ending point. The second and third arguments specify the colors that the gradient will use. In this case, the color of the ellipse will gradually change from `Color::Blue` to `Color::Yellow`. The last argument, a type from the enumeration *`LinearGradientMode`*, specifies the linear gradient's direction. In our case, we use *`LinearGradientMode::ForwardDiagonal`*, which creates a gradient from the upper-left to the lower-right corner. We then use `Graphics` method `FillEllipse` in line 84 to draw an ellipse with `linearBrush`; the color gradually changes from blue to yellow, as described above.

In line 70, we create a `Pen` object `thickRedPen`. We pass to `thickRedPen`'s constructor `Color::Red` and the `int` argument `10`, indicating that we want `thickRedPen` to draw red lines that are 10 pixels wide.

Line 74 creates a new *`Bitmap`* image, which initially is empty. Class `Bitmap` can produce images in color and gray scale; this particular `Bitmap` is 10 pixels wide and 10 pixels tall. Method *`FromImage`* (line 77) is a `static` member of class `Graphics` and retrieves the `Graphics` object associated with an `Image`, which can be used to draw on an image. Lines 94–108 draw on the `Bitmap` a pattern consisting of black, blue, red and yellow rectangles and lines. A `TextureBrush` is a brush that fills the interior of a shape with an image, rather than with a solid color. In lines 107–108, `TextureBrush` object `textureBrush` fills a rectangle with our `Bitmap`. The `TextureBrush` constructor version that we use takes as an argument an image that defines its texture.

Next, we draw a pie-shaped arc with a thick white line. Lines 111–112 set `coloredPen`'s color to `White` and modify its width to be six pixels. We then draw the pie on the form by specifying the `Pen`, the *x*-coordinate, *y*-coordinate, length and width of the bounding rectangle and the start angle and sweep angle.

Finally, lines 122–123 make use of `System::Drawing::Drawing2D` enumerations *`DashCap`* and *`DashStyle`* to draw a diagonal dashed line. Line 122 sets the *`DashCap`* property of `coloredPen` (not to be confused with the `DashCap` enumeration) to a member of the `DashCap` enumeration. The `DashCap` enumeration specifies the styles for the start and end of a dashed line. In this case, we want both ends of the dashed line to be rounded, so we use *`DashCap::Round`*. Line 123 sets the *`DashStyle`* property of `coloredPen` (not to be confused with the `DashStyle` enumeration) to *`DashStyle::Dash`*, indicating that we want our line to consist entirely of dashes.

General Paths

Our next example demonstrates the use of a *general path*. A general path is a shape constructed from straight lines and complex curves. An object of class *`GraphicsPath`* (`System::Drawing::Drawing2D` namespace) represents a general path. The `GraphicsPath` class provides functionality that enables the creation of complex shapes from vector-based primitive graphics objects. A `GraphicsPath` object consists of figures defined by simple shapes. The start point of each vector-graphics object (such as a line or arc) that is added to the path is connected by a straight line to the end point of the previous object. When called, `GraphicsPath` method *`CloseFigure`* method attaches the final vector-graphic object endpoint to the initial starting point for the current figure by a straight line, then starts a new figure. `GraphicsPath` method *`StartFigure`* begins a new figure within the path without closing the previous figure.

Figure 16.30–Fig. 16.31 draw general paths in the shape of five-pointed stars. Line 72 (Fig. 16.30) sets the origin of the `Graphics` object. The arguments to method *`TranslateTransform`* indicate that the origin should be translated to the coordinates (150, 150). Lines 65–66 define two `int` arrays, representing the *x*- and *y*-coordinates of the points in the star, and line 69 defines `GraphicsPath` object `star`. A `for` loop then creates lines to connect the points of the star and adds these lines to `star`. We use `GraphicsPath` method *`AddLine`* to append a line to the shape. The arguments of `AddLine` specify the coordinates for the line's endpoints; each new call to `AddLine` adds a line from the previous point to the current point. Line 80 uses `GraphicsPath` method `CloseFigure` to complete the shape.

```
1  // Fig. 16.30: Form1.h
2  // Using paths to draw stars on the form.
3
4  #pragma once
5
6
7  namespace DrawStars
8  {
9     using namespace System;
10    using namespace System::ComponentModel;
11    using namespace System::Collections;
12    using namespace System::Windows::Forms;
13    using namespace System::Data;
14    using namespace System::Drawing;
```

Fig. 16.30 Paths used to draw stars on a form. (Part 1 of 3.)

```
   using namespace System::Drawing::Drawing2D;

   /// <summary>
   /// Summary for Form1
   ///
   /// WARNING: If you change the name of this class, you will need to
   ///          change the 'Resource File Name' property for the managed
   ///          resource compiler tool associated with all .resx files
   ///          this class depends on.  Otherwise, the designers will not
   ///          be able to interact properly with localized resources
   ///          associated with this form.
   /// </summary>
   public __gc class Form1 : public System::Windows::Forms::Form
   {
   public:
      Form1(void)
      {
         InitializeComponent();
      }

   protected:
      void Dispose(Boolean disposing)
      {
         if (disposing && components)
         {
            components->Dispose();
         }
         __super::Dispose(disposing);
      }

   private:
      /// <summary>
      /// Required designer variable.
      /// </summary>
      System::ComponentModel::Container * components;

   // Visual Studio .NET generated GUI code

   protected:

      // create path and draw stars along it
      void OnPaint( PaintEventArgs *paintEvent )
      {
         __super::OnPaint( paintEvent ); // call base OnPaint method

         Graphics *graphicsObject = paintEvent->Graphics;
         Random *random = new Random();
         SolidBrush *brush = new SolidBrush( Color::DarkMagenta );

         // x and y points of the path
         int xPoints[] = { 55, 67, 109, 73, 83, 55, 27, 37, 1, 43 };
         int yPoints[] = { 0, 36, 36, 54, 96, 72, 96, 54, 36, 36 };

```

Fig. 16.30 Paths used to draw stars on a form. (Part 2 of 3.)

```
        // create graphics path for star;
        GraphicsPath *star = new GraphicsPath();

        // translate the origin to (150, 150)
        graphicsObject->TranslateTransform( 150, 150 );

        // create star from series of points
        for ( int i = 0; i <= 8; i += 2 )
           star->AddLine( xPoints[ i ], yPoints[ i ],
              xPoints[ i + 1 ], yPoints[ i + 1 ] );

        // close the shape
        star->CloseFigure();

        // rotate the origin and draw stars in random colors
        for ( int i = 1; i <= 18; i++ ) {
           graphicsObject->RotateTransform( 20 );

           brush->Color = Color::FromArgb(
              random->Next( 200, 256 ), random->Next( 256 ),
              random->Next( 256 ), random->Next( 256 ) );

           graphicsObject->FillPath( brush, star );
        } // end for
     } // end method OnPaint
  };
}
```

Fig. 16.30 Paths used to draw stars on a form. (Part 3 of 3.)

```
// Fig. 16.31: Form1.cpp
// Entry point for application.

#include "stdafx.h"
#include "Form1.h"
#include <windows.h>

using namespace DrawStars;

int APIENTRY _tWinMain(HINSTANCE hInstance,
                       HINSTANCE hPrevInstance,
                       LPTSTR    lpCmdLine,
                       int       nCmdShow)
{
   System::Threading::Thread::CurrentThread->ApartmentState =
      System::Threading::ApartmentState::STA;
   Application::Run(new Form1());
   return 0;
} // end _tWinMain
```

Fig. 16.31 DrawStars entry point. (Part 1 of 2.)

Fig. 16.31 `DrawStars` entry point. (Part 2 of 2.)

The `for` statement in lines 83–91 of Fig. 16.30 draws the `star` 18 times, rotating it around the origin. Line 84 uses `Graphics` method ***`RotateTransform`*** to move to the next position on the form; the argument specifies the rotation angle in degrees. `Graphics` method `FillPath` (line 90) then draws a filled version of the `star` with the `Color` created in lines 86–88. The application determines the `SolidBrush`'s color randomly, using `Random` method `Next`.

16.9 Introduction to Multimedia

Visual C++ .NET offers many convenient ways to include images and animations in programs. People who entered the computing field decades ago used computers primarily to perform arithmetic calculations. As the discipline evolves, we are beginning to realize the importance of computers' data-manipulation capabilities. There are many exciting three-dimensional applications. Multimedia programming is an entertaining and innovative field, but one that presents many challenges.

Multimedia applications demand extraordinary computing power. Until recently, affordable computers with this amount of power were not available. However, today's ultrafast processors are making multimedia-based applications commonplace. As the market for multimedia explodes, users are purchasing the faster processors, larger memories and wider communications bandwidths needed to support multimedia applications. This benefits the computer and communications industries, which provide the hardware, software and services fueling the multimedia revolution.

In the remaining sections of this chapter, we introduce the use and manipulation of images and other multimedia features and capabilities. Section 16.10 discusses how to load, display and scale images; Section 16.11 demonstrates image animation; Section 16.12 presents the video capabilities of the Windows Media Player control; and Section 16.13 explores Microsoft Agent technology.

16.10 Loading, Displaying and Scaling Images

Visual C++ .NET's multimedia capabilities include graphics, images, animations and video. Previous sections demonstrated vector-graphics capabilities; this section concentrates on image manipulation. The Windows form that we create in Fig. 16.32–Fig. 16.33 demonstrates the loading of an `Image` (`System::Drawing` namespace). The application allows users to enter a desired height and width for the `Image`, which then is displayed in the specified size.

```
// Fig. 16.32: Form1.h
// Displaying and resizing an image.

#pragma once


namespace DisplayLogo
{
   using namespace System;
   using namespace System::ComponentModel;
   using namespace System::Collections;
   using namespace System::Windows::Forms;
   using namespace System::Data;
   using namespace System::Drawing;

   /// <summary>
   /// Summary for Form1
   ///
   /// WARNING: If you change the name of this class, you will need to
   ///          change the 'Resource File Name' property for the managed
   ///          resource compiler tool associated with all .resx files
   ///          this class depends on.  Otherwise, the designers will not
   ///          be able to interact properly with localized resources
   ///          associated with this form.
   /// </summary>
   public __gc class Form1 : public System::Windows::Forms::Form
   {
   public:
      Form1(void)
      {
         InitializeComponent();
      }

   protected:
      void Dispose(Boolean disposing)
      {
         if (disposing && components)
         {
            components->Dispose();
         }
         __super::Dispose(disposing);
      }
   private: System::Windows::Forms::Button *  setButton;
   private: System::Windows::Forms::TextBox *  heightTextBox;
   private: System::Windows::Forms::Label *  heightLabel;
   private: System::Windows::Forms::TextBox *  widthTextBox;
   private: System::Windows::Forms::Label *  widthLabel;

```

Fig. 16.32 Image resizing. (Part 1 of 2.)

```
      private: static Image *image = Image::FromFile( S"images/Logo.gif" );

      private:
         /// <summary>
         /// Required designer variable.
         /// </summary>
         System::ComponentModel::Container * components;

      // Visual Studio .NET generated GUI code

      private: System::Void setButton_Click(
                     System::Object *  sender, System::EventArgs *  e)
               {
                  int width, height;

                  try {

                     // get user input
                     width = Convert::ToInt32( widthTextBox->Text );
                     height = Convert::ToInt32( heightTextBox->Text );
                  } // end try
                  catch ( FormatException *formatException ) {
                     MessageBox::Show( formatException->Message, S"Error",
                        MessageBoxButtons::OK, MessageBoxIcon::Error );

                     return;
                  } // end catch
                  catch ( OverflowException *overflowException ) {
                     MessageBox::Show( overflowException->Message, S"Error",
                        MessageBoxButtons::OK, MessageBoxIcon::Error );

                     return;
                  } // end catch

                  // if dimensions specified are too large
                  // display problem
                  if ( width > 375 || height > 225 ) {
                     MessageBox::Show( S"Height or Width too large" );

                     return;
                  } // end if

                  // obtain graphics object
                  Graphics *graphicsObject = this->CreateGraphics();

                  // clear Windows Form
                  graphicsObject->Clear( this->BackColor );

                  // draw image
                  graphicsObject->DrawImage( image, 5, 5, width, height );
               } // end method setButton_Click
   };
}
```

Fig. 16.32 Image resizing. (Part 2 of 2.)

```
// Fig. 16.33: Form1.cpp
// Entry point for application.

#include "stdafx.h"
#include "Form1.h"
#include <windows.h>

using namespace DisplayLogo;

int APIENTRY _tWinMain(HINSTANCE hInstance,
                       HINSTANCE hPrevInstance,
                       LPTSTR    lpCmdLine,
                       int       nCmdShow)
{
   System::Threading::Thread::CurrentThread->ApartmentState =
      System::Threading::ApartmentState::STA;
   Application::Run(new Form1());
   return 0;
} // end _tWinMain
```

Fig. 16.33 `DisplayLogoForm` class entry point.

Line 49 (Fig. 16.32) declares `Image` pointer `image`. The `static` `Image` method *`FromFile`* then retrieves an image stored on disk and assigns it to `image` (line 49). Notice that we use a forward slash (/) as a separator character rather than two backslash characters (\\). We discuss separator characters in Chapter 17, Files and Streams.

Line 92 (Fig. 16.32) uses `Form` method `CreateGraphics` to create a `Graphics` object associated with the `Form`; we use this object to draw on the `Form`. Method `CreateGraphics` is inherited from class `Control`; all Windows controls, such as `Buttons` and `Panels`, also provide this method. When users click **Set**, the width and height parameters are parsed from the `TextBoxes` (lines 67–68). The `catch` blocks in lines 70–81 inform the user if invalid values have been entered.

Line 85 then ensures that the dimensions are not too large. If the parameters are valid, line 95 calls `Graphics` method *`Clear`* to paint the entire `Form` in the current background color. Line 98 calls `Graphics` method *`DrawImage`* with the following parameters: the image to draw, the *x*-coordinate of the upper-left corner, the *y*-coordinate of the upper-left corner, the width of the image and the height of the image. If the width and height do not correspond to the image's original dimensions, the image is scaled to fit the new specifications.

16.11 Animating a Series of Images

The next example animates a series of images stored in an array. The application uses the same techniques to load and display `Images` as those illustrated in Fig. 16.32. The images were created with Adobe Photoshop.

The animation in Fig. 16.34–Fig. 16.35 uses a `PictureBox`, which contains the images that we animate. We use a `Timer` to cycle through the images, causing a new image to display every 50 milliseconds. Variable `count` keeps track of the current image number and increases by one every time we display a new image. The array includes 30 images (numbered 0–29); when the application reaches image 29, it returns to image 0. The 30 images were prepared in advance and placed in the `images` folder inside the directory of the project.

```
// Fig. 16.34: Form1.h
// Program that animates a series of images.

#pragma once


namespace LogoAnimator
{
   using namespace System;
   using namespace System::ComponentModel;
   using namespace System::Collections;
   using namespace System::Windows::Forms;
   using namespace System::Data;
   using namespace System::Drawing;

   /// <summary>
   /// Summary for Form1
   ///
   /// WARNING: If you change the name of this class, you will need to
   ///          change the 'Resource File Name' property for the managed
   ///          resource compiler tool associated with all .resx files
   ///          this class depends on.  Otherwise, the designers will not
   ///          be able to interact properly with localized resources
```

Fig. 16.34 Animation of a series of images. (Part 1 of 3.)

```
   ///          associated with this form.
   /// </summary>
   public __gc class Form1 : public System::Windows::Forms::Form
   {
   public:
      Form1(void)
      {
         InitializeComponent();

         for ( int i = 0; i < 30; i++ )
            images->Add( Image::FromFile( String::Concat(
            S"images/deitel", i.ToString(), S".gif" ) ) );

         // load first image
         logoPictureBox->Image =
            dynamic_cast< Image* >( images->Item[ 0 ] );

         // set PictureBox to be the same size as Image
         logoPictureBox->Size = logoPictureBox->Image->Size;
      }

   protected:
      void Dispose(Boolean disposing)
      {
         if (disposing && components)
         {
            components->Dispose();
         }
         __super::Dispose(disposing);
      }
   private: System::Windows::Forms::PictureBox *  logoPictureBox;
   private: System::Windows::Forms::Timer *  timer;
   private: System::ComponentModel::IContainer *  components;

   private: static ArrayList *images = new ArrayList();
   private: static int count = -1;

   private:
      /// <summary>
      /// Required designer variable.
      /// </summary>

   // Visual Studio .NET generated GUI code

   private: System::Void timer_Tick(
               System::Object *  sender, System::EventArgs *  e)
            {
               // increment counter
               count = ( count + 1 ) % 30;

               // load next image
               logoPictureBox->Image =
                  dynamic_cast< Image* >( images->Item[ count ] );
```

Fig. 16.34 Animation of a series of images. (Part 2 of 3.)

```
77             } // end method timer_Tick
78    };
79 }
```

Fig. 16.34 Animation of a series of images. (Part 3 of 3.)

```
// Fig. 16.35: Form1.cpp
// Entry point for application.

#include "stdafx.h"
#include "Form1.h"
#include <windows.h>

using namespace LogoAnimator;

int APIENTRY _tWinMain(HINSTANCE hInstance,
                       HINSTANCE hPrevInstance,
                       LPTSTR    lpCmdLine,
                       int       nCmdShow)
{
   System::Threading::Thread::CurrentThread->ApartmentState =
      System::Threading::ApartmentState::STA;
   Application::Run(new Form1());
   return 0;
} // end _tWinMain
```

Fig. 16.35 `LogoAnimator` class entry point.

Lines 33–35 (Fig. 16.34) load each of 30 images and place them in an `ArrayList`. Lines 34–35 use `ArrayList` method `Add` to add each `Image`. Lines 38–39 retrieve the first image using `ArrayList` indexed property `Item` then place it in the `PictureBox`. Line 42 modifies the size of the `PictureBox` so that it is equal to the size of the `Image` it is displaying. The event handler for `timer`'s `Tick` event (lines 68–77) then displays the next image from the `ArrayList`.

Collision Detection and Regional Invalidation

The following chess example demonstrates the capabilities of GDI+ as they pertain to a chess-game application. These capabilities include techniques for two-dimensional *collision detection* and *regional invalidation* (refreshing only the required parts of the screen) to increase performance. Two-dimensional collision detection is the detection of an overlap between two shapes. In the next example, we demonstrate the simplest form of collision detection, which determines whether a point (the mouse-click location) is contained within a rectangle (a chess-piece image).

Class `ChessPiece` (Fig. 16.36) is a container class for the individual chess pieces. Lines 22–30 creates public enumeration `Types`. This enumeration identifies each chess-piece type and also serves to identify the location of each piece in the chess-piece image file. For more information about enumerations, review Chapter 6. Notice that we use MC++ keyword `__value` when declaring enumeration `Types` to ensure that the enumeration is a value type. For more information about keyword `__value`, refer to Chapter 10.

```
1  // Fig. 16.36: ChessPiece.h
2  // Storage class for chess piece attributes.
3
4  #pragma once
5
6
7  #using <mscorlib.dll>
8  #using <system.dll>
9  #using <system.drawing.dll>
10 #using <system.windows.forms.dll>
11
12 using namespace System;
13 using namespace System::Drawing;
14 using namespace System::Collections;
15 using namespace System::Windows::Forms;
16
17 public __gc class ChessPiece
18 {
19 public:
20
21    // define chess-piece type constants (values 0-5)
22    __value enum Types
23    {
24       KING,
25       QUEEN,
26       BISHOP,
27       KNIGHT,
28       ROOK,
29       PAWN
30    };
31
32    ChessPiece( int, int, int, Bitmap * );
33    void Draw( Graphics * );
34    Rectangle GetBounds();
35    void SetLocation( int , int );
36
37 private:
38    int currentType;             // this object's type
39    Bitmap *pieceImage;          // this object's image
40    Rectangle targetRectangle; // default display location
41 }; // end class ChessPiece
```

Fig. 16.36 Container class for chess pieces.

`Rectangle` object `targetRectangle` (line 14 of Fig. 16.37) identifies the image location on the chess board. The `x` and `y` properties of the rectangle are assigned in the `ChessPiece` constructor, and all chess-piece images have width and height `75`.

```
1  // Fig. 16.37: ChessPiece.cpp
2  // Method definitions for class ChessPiece.
3
4  #include "stdafx.h"
5  #include "ChessPiece.h"
6
7  // construct piece
8  ChessPiece::ChessPiece( int type, int xLocation,
9     int yLocation, Bitmap *sourceImage )
10 {
11    currentType = type; // set current type
12
13    // set current location
14    targetRectangle = Rectangle( xLocation, yLocation, 75, 75 );
15
16    // obtain pieceImage from section of sourceImage
17    pieceImage = sourceImage->Clone( Rectangle( type * 75, 0, 75, 75 ),
18       Drawing::Imaging::PixelFormat::DontCare );
19 } // end constructor
20
21 // draw chess piece
22 void ChessPiece::Draw( Graphics *graphicsObject )
23 {
24    graphicsObject->DrawImage( pieceImage, targetRectangle );
25 } // end method Draw
26
27 // obtain this piece's location rectangle
28 Rectangle ChessPiece::GetBounds()
29 {
30    return targetRectangle;
31 } // end method GetBounds
32
33 // set this piece's location
34 void ChessPiece::SetLocation( int xLocation, int yLocation )
35 {
36    targetRectangle.X = xLocation;
37    targetRectangle.Y = yLocation;
38 } // end method SetLocation
```

Fig. 16.37 `ChessPiece` class method definitions.

The `ChessPiece` constructor (lines 8–19) requires that the calling class define a chess-piece type, its `x` and `y` location and the `Bitmap` containing all chess-piece images. Rather than loading the chess-piece image within the class, we allow the calling class to pass the image. This avoids the image-loading overhead for each piece. It also increases the flexibility of the class by allowing the user to change images; for example, in this case, we use the class for both black and white chess-piece images. Lines 17–18 extract a sub-image that contains only the current piece's bitmap data. Our chess-piece images are defined in a specific manner: One image contains six chess-piece images, each defined within a 75-pixel block, resulting in a total image size of 450 by 75. We obtain a single image via `Bitmap`'s *`Clone`* method, which allows us to specify a rectangle image location and the desired pixel format. The location is a 75-by-75 pixel block with its upper-left corner x equal to 75 * type and the corresponding y equal to 0. For the pixel format, we specify constant DontCare, causing the format to remain unchanged.

Method Draw (lines 22–25) causes the ChessPiece to draw pieceImage in targetRectangle on the passed Graphics object. Method GetBounds returns the object targetRectangle for use in collision detection, and SetLocation allows the calling class to specify a new piece location.

Class Form1 in Fig. 16.38 defines the game and graphics code for our chess game. Lines 51–62 define class-scope variables the program requires. ArrayList chessTile (line 51) stores the board tile images. It contains four images: Two light tiles and two dark tiles (to increase board variety). ArrayList chessPieces (line 54) stores all active ChessPiece objects and int selectedIndex (line 57) identifies the index in chessPieces of the currently selected piece. The board (line 59) is an 8-by-8, two-dimensional int array corresponding to the squares of a chess board. Each board element is an integer from 0 to 3 that corresponds to an index in chessTile and is used to specify the chess-board-square image. const int TILESIZE (line 62) defines the size of each tile in pixels.

```
1  // Fig. 16.38: Form1.h
2  // Chess Game graphics code.
3
4  #pragma once
5
6
7  #include "ChessPiece.h"
8
9  namespace ChessGame
10 {
11    using namespace System;
12    using namespace System::ComponentModel;
13    using namespace System::Collections;
14    using namespace System::Windows::Forms;
15    using namespace System::Data;
16    using namespace System::Drawing;
17
18    /// <summary>
19    /// Summary for Form1
20    ///
21    /// WARNING: If you change the name of this class, you will need to
22    ///          change the 'Resource File Name' property for the managed
23    ///          resource compiler tool associated with all .resx files
24    ///          this class depends on.  Otherwise, the designers will not
25    ///          be able to interact properly with localized resources
26    ///          associated with this form.
27    /// </summary>
28    public __gc class Form1 : public System::Windows::Forms::Form
29    {
30    public:
31       Form1(void)
32       {
33          InitializeComponent();
34       }
```

Fig. 16.38 Chess-game code. (Part 1 of 7.)

```
   protected:
      void Dispose(Boolean disposing)
      {
         if (disposing && components)
         {
            components->Dispose();
         }
         __super::Dispose(disposing);
      }
   private: System::Windows::Forms::PictureBox *  pieceBox;
   private: System::Windows::Forms::MainMenu *  GameMenu;
   private: System::Windows::Forms::MenuItem *  gameItem;
   private: System::Windows::Forms::MenuItem *  newGameItem;

   // ArrayList for board tile images
   private: static ArrayList *chessTile = new ArrayList();

   // ArrayList for chess pieces
   private: static ArrayList *chessPieces = new ArrayList();

   // define index for selected piece
   private: static int selectedIndex = -1;

   private: static int board[,] = new int __gc[ 8, 8 ]; // board array

   // define chess tile size in pixels
   private: static const int TILESIZE = 75;

   private:
      /// <summary>
      /// Required designer variable.
      /// </summary>
      System::ComponentModel::Container * components;

   // Visual Studio .NET generated GUI code

   // load tile bitmaps and reset game
   private: System::Void Form1_Load(
               System::Object *  sender, System::EventArgs *  e)
            {
               // load chess board tiles
               chessTile->Add( Bitmap::FromFile( S"lightTile1.png" ) );
               chessTile->Add( Bitmap::FromFile( S"lightTile2.png" ) );
               chessTile->Add( Bitmap::FromFile( S"darkTile1.png" ) );
               chessTile->Add( Bitmap::FromFile( S"darkTile2.png" ) );

               ResetBoard(); // initialize board
               Invalidate(); // refresh form
            } // end method Form1_Load

   private:
```

Fig. 16.38 Chess-game code. (Part 2 of 7.)

```
      // initialize pieces to start and rebuild board
      void ResetBoard()
      {
         int current = -1;
         ChessPiece *piece;
         Random *random = new Random();
         bool light = true;
         int type;

         // ensure empty arraylist
         chessPieces = new ArrayList();

         // load whitepieces image
         Bitmap *whitePieces =
            dynamic_cast < Bitmap * >(
               Image::FromFile( S"whitePieces.png" ) );

         // load blackpieces image
         Bitmap *blackPieces =
            dynamic_cast < Bitmap * >(
               Image::FromFile( S"blackPieces.png" ) );

         // set whitepieces drawn first
         Bitmap *selected = blackPieces;

         // traverse board rows in outer loop
         for ( int row = 0; row <= board->GetUpperBound( 0 ); row++ ) {

            // if at bottom rows, set to black pieces images
            if ( row > 5 )
               selected = whitePieces;

            // traverse board columns in inner loop
            for ( int column = 0;
               column <= board->GetUpperBound( 1 ); column++ ) {

               // if first or last row, organize pieces
               if ( row == 0 || row == 7 ) {

                  switch ( column ) {
                     case 0:
                     case 7: // set current piece to rook
                        current = ChessPiece::Types::ROOK;
                        break;

                     case 1:
                     case 6: // set current piece to knight
                        current = ChessPiece::Types::KNIGHT;
                        break;

                     case 2:
                     case 5: // set current piece to bishop
                        current = ChessPiece::Types::BISHOP;
```

Fig. 16.38 Chess-game code. (Part 3 of 7.)

```
                    break;

                 case 3: // set current piece to queen
                    current = ChessPiece::Types::QUEEN;
                    break;

                 case 4: // set current piece to king
                    current = ChessPiece::Types::KING;
                    break;

                 default:
                    break;
              } // end switch

              // create current piece at start position
              piece = new ChessPiece( current, column * TILESIZE,
                 row * TILESIZE, selected );

              // add piece to arraylist
              chessPieces->Add( piece );
           } // end if

           // if second or seventh row, organize pawns
           if ( row == 1 || row == 6 ) {
              piece = new ChessPiece( ChessPiece::Types::PAWN,
                 column * TILESIZE, row * TILESIZE, selected );

              // add piece to arraylist
              chessPieces->Add( piece );
           } // end if

           // determine board piece type
           type = random->Next( 0, 2 );

           if ( light ) {

              // set light tile
              board[ row, column ] = type;
              light = false;
           } // end if
           else {

              // set dark tile
              board[ row, column ] = type + 2;
              light = true;
           } // end else
        } // end inner for

        // account for new row tile color switch
        light = !light;
     } // end outer for
  } // end method ResetBoard

```

Fig. 16.38 Chess-game code. (Part 4 of 7.)

```
   protected:

      // display board in OnPaint method
      void OnPaint( PaintEventArgs *e )
      {
         __super::OnPaint( e ); // call base OnPaint method

         // obtain graphics object
         Graphics *graphicsObject = e->Graphics;

         for ( int row = 0; row <= board->GetUpperBound( 0 ); row++ ) {

            for ( int column = 0;
               column <= board->GetUpperBound( 1 ); column++ ) {

               // draw image specified in board array
               graphicsObject->DrawImage(
                  dynamic_cast < Image * >(
                  chessTile->Item[ board[ row, column ] ] ),
                  Point( TILESIZE * column, TILESIZE * row ) );
            } // end inner for
         } // end outer for
      } // end method OnPaint

   private:

      // return index of piece that intersects point
      // optionally exclude a value
      int CheckBounds( Point point, int exclude )
      {
         Rectangle rectangle; // current bounding rectangle

         for ( int i = 0; i < chessPieces->Count; i++ ) {

            // get piece rectangle
            rectangle = GetPiece( i )->GetBounds();

            // check if rectangle contains point
            if ( rectangle.Contains( point ) && i != exclude )
               return i;
         } // end for
         return -1;
      } // end method CheckBounds

   // handle pieceBox paint event
   private: System::Void pieceBox_Paint(System::Object *  sender,
               System::Windows::Forms::PaintEventArgs *  e)
            {
               // draw all pieces
               for ( int i = 0; i < chessPieces->Count; i++ )
                  GetPiece( i )->Draw( e->Graphics );
            } // end method pieceBox_Paint

```

Fig. 16.38 Chess-game code. (Part 5 of 7.)

```
    private: System::Void pieceBox_MouseDown(System::Object *  sender,
                System::Windows::Forms::MouseEventArgs *  e)
             {
                // determine selected piece
                selectedIndex = CheckBounds( Point( e->X, e->Y ), -1 );
             } // end method pieceBox_MouseDown

    // if piece is selected, move it
    private: System::Void pieceBox_MouseMove(System::Object *  sender,
                System::Windows::Forms::MouseEventArgs *  e)
             {
                if ( selectedIndex > -1 ) {
                   Rectangle region = Rectangle(
                      e->X - TILESIZE * 2, e->Y - TILESIZE * 2,
                      TILESIZE * 4, TILESIZE * 4 );

                   // set piece center to mouse
                   GetPiece( selectedIndex )->SetLocation(
                      e->X - TILESIZE / 2, e->Y - TILESIZE / 2 );

                   // refresh immediate are
                   pieceBox->Invalidate( region );
                } // end if
             } // end method pieceBox_MouseMove

    // on mouse up deselect piece and remove taken piece
    private: System::Void pieceBox_MouseUp(System::Object *  sender,
                System::Windows::Forms::MouseEventArgs *  e)
             {
                int remove = -1;
                int maxLocation = 7 * TILESIZE;

                //if chess piece was selected
                if ( selectedIndex > -1 ) {
                   Point current = Point( e->X, e->Y );
                   Point newPoint = Point(
                      current.X - ( current.X % TILESIZE ),
                      current.Y - ( current.Y % TILESIZE ) );

                   // ensure that new point is within bounds of board
                   if ( newPoint.X < 0 )
                      newPoint.X = 0;
                   else if ( newPoint.X > maxLocation )
                      newPoint.X = maxLocation;

                   if ( newPoint.Y < 0 )
                      newPoint.Y = 0;
                   else if ( newPoint.Y > maxLocation )
                      newPoint.Y = maxLocation;

                   // check bounds with point, exclude selected piece
                   remove = CheckBounds( newPoint, selectedIndex );

```

Fig. 16.38 Chess-game code. (Part 6 of 7.)

```
300                      // snap piece into center of closest square
301                      GetPiece( selectedIndex )->SetLocation( newPoint.X,
302                         newPoint.Y );
303
304                      // deselect piece
305                      selectedIndex = -1;
306
307                      // remove taken piece
308                      if ( remove > -1 )
309                         chessPieces->RemoveAt( remove );
310                   } // end if
311
312                   // refresh pieceBox to ensure artifact removal
313                   pieceBox->Invalidate();
314                } // end method pieceBox_MouseUp
315
316    private:
317
318       // helper method to convert ArrayList object to ChessPiece
319       ChessPiece* GetPiece( int i )
320       {
321          return dynamic_cast < ChessPiece* >( chessPieces->Item[ i ] );
322       } // end method GetPiece
323
324    // handle NewGame menu option click
325    private: System::Void newGameItem_Click(
326                   System::Object *  sender, System::EventArgs *  e)
327                {
328                   ResetBoard(); // reinitialize board
329                   Invalidate(); // refresh form
330                } // end method newGameItem_Click
331    };
332 }
```

Fig. 16.38 Chess-game code. (Part 7 of 7.)

The chess game GUI consists of `Form Form1`, the area in which we draw the tiles; `PictureBox pieceBox`, the window in which we draw the pieces (note that `pieceBox` background color is set to `"transparent"`); and a `Menu` that allows the user to begin a new game. Although the pieces and tiles could have been drawn on the same form, doing so would decrease performance. We would be forced to refresh the board as well as the pieces every time we refreshed the control.

The `Form1 Load` event (lines 73–84 of Fig. 16.38) loads each tile image into `chessTile`. It then calls method `ResetBoard` to refresh the `Form` and begin the game. Method `ResetBoard` (lines 89–192) assigns `chessPieces` to a new `ArrayList`, loading images for both the black and the white chess-piece sets, and creates `Bitmap selected` to define the currently selected `Bitmap` set. Lines 114–191 loop through the 64 positions on the chess board, setting the tile color and piece for each tile. Lines 117–118 cause the currently selected image to switch to the `whitePieces` after the fifth row. If the row counter is on the first or last row, lines 125–161 add a new piece to `chessPieces`. The type of the piece is based on the current column we are initializing. Pieces in chess are positioned in the following order, from left to right: rook, knight, bishop, queen, king, bishop, knight and rook. Lines 164–170 add a new pawn at the current location if the current `row` is second or seventh (`1` or `6`).

A chess board is defined by alternating light and dark tiles across a row in a pattern where the color that starts each row is equal to the color of the last tile of the previous row. Lines 175–186 assign the current board-tile color as an index in the `board` array. Based on the alternating value of `bool` variable `light` and the results of the random operation in line 173, `0` and `1` are light tiles, whereas `2` and `3` are dark tiles. Line 190 inverts the value of `light` at the end of each row to maintain the staggered effect of a chess board.

Method `OnPaint` (lines 197–216) handles this class `Form`'s `Paint` event and draws the tiles according to their values in the board array. Method `pieceBox_Paint` (lines 239–245), which handles the `pieceBox Panel Paint` event, iterates through each element of the `chessPiece ArrayList` and calls its `Draw` method.

The `MouseDown` event handler (lines 247–252) calls method `CheckBounds` (lines 222–236) with the location of the user's click to determine whether the user selected a piece. `CheckBounds` returns an integer locating a collision from a given point.

The `MouseMove` event handler (lines 255–270) moves the currently selected piece with the mouse. Lines 264–265 set the selected piece location to the mouse-cursor position, adjusting the location by up to half a tile to center the image on the mouse. Line 268 defines and refreshes a region of the `Panel` that spans two tiles in every direction from the mouse. As mentioned earlier in the chapter, the `Invalidate` method is slow. This means that the `MouseMove` event handler might be called again several times before the `Invalidate` method completes. If a user working on a slow computer moves the mouse quickly, the application could leave behind *artifacts*. An artifact is any unintended visual abnormality in a graphical program. By causing the program to refresh a two-square rectangle, which should suffice in most cases, we achieve a significant performance enhancement over an entire component refresh during each `MouseMove` event.

Lines 273–314 define the `MouseUp` event handler. If a piece has been selected, lines 280–310 determine the index in `chessPieces` of any piece collision, remove the collided piece, snap (align) the current piece into a valid location and deselect the piece. We check for piece collisions to allow the chess piece to "take" other chess pieces. Lines 287–295 begin by checking whether the current position exists on the game board. If the current position is not in the valid range (`0` to `TILESIZE * 7`), the position is modified to fit within the bounds of the board. Line 298 then checks whether any piece (excluding the currently selected piece) is beneath the new location. If a collision is detected, the returned piece index is assigned to `int remove`. Lines 301–302 determine the closest valid chess tile and "snap" the selected piece to that location. If `remove` contains a positive value, line 309 removes the object at that index from the `chessPieces ArrayList`. Finally, the entire `Panel` is `Invalidated` in line 313 to display the new piece location and remove any artifacts created during the move.

Method `CheckBounds` (lines 222–236) is a collision-detection helper method; it iterates through the `chessPieces ArrayList` and returns the index of any piece rectangle containing the point value passed to the method (the mouse location, in this example). Method `CheckBounds` optionally can exclude a single piece index (to ignore the selected index in the `MouseUp` event handler, in this example).

Lines 319–322 define method `GetPiece`, which simplifies the conversion from `Objects` in `ArrayList chessPieces` to `ChessPiece` types. The `newGameItem_Click` method handles the NewGame menu item click event, calls RefreshBoard to reset the game and Invalidates the entire form. Figure 16.39 executes the chess application.

```
// Fig. 16.39: Form1.cpp
// Entry point for application.

#include "stdafx.h"
#include "Form1.h"
#include <windows.h>

using namespace ChessGame;

int APIENTRY _tWinMain(HINSTANCE hInstance,
                       HINSTANCE hPrevInstance,
                       LPTSTR    lpCmdLine,
                       int       nCmdShow)
{
   System::Threading::Thread::CurrentThread->ApartmentState =
      System::Threading::ApartmentState::STA;
   Application::Run(new Form1());
   return 0;
} // end _tWinMain
```

Fig. 16.39 Chess-game demonstration. (Part 1 of 3.)

Fig. 16.39 Chess-game demonstration. (Part 2 of 3.)

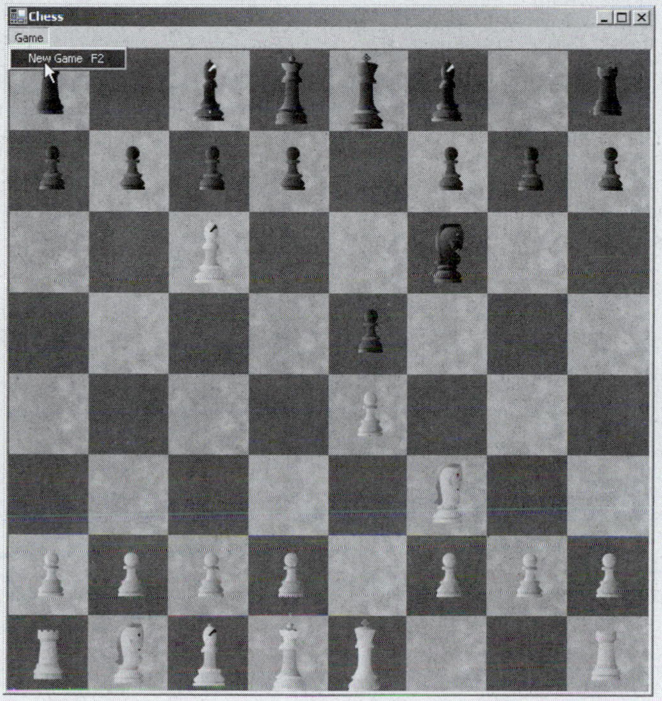

Fig. 16.39 Chess-game demonstration. (Part 3 of 3.)

16.12 Windows Media Player

The Windows Media Player control enables an application to play video and sound in many multimedia formats. These include *MPEG (Motion Pictures Experts Group)* audio and video, *AVI (audio-video interleave)* video, *WAV (Windows wave-file format)* audio and *MIDI (Musical Instrument Digital Interface)* audio. Users can find preexisting audio and video on the Internet, or they can create their own files, using available sound and graphics packages.

The Windows Media Player control is an *ActiveX control*. ActiveX controls are reusable GUI components in Windows. Windows comes with a number of pre-installed ActiveX controls, such as the Windows Media Player control.

To add the Windows Media Player control to a form, first add it to the **Toolbox**. To do this, right-click the **Toolbox** and select **Add/Remove Items**…. In the **COM Components** tab of the **Customize Toolbox** dialog, check the box next to the **Windows Media Player** component located at `c:\winnt\system32\msdxm.ocx` (or `c:\Windows\system32\msdxm.ocx`) and click **OK** (Fig. 16.40).[2] The **Windows Media Player** component will now appear in the **Toolbox** and can be added to the form in the same manner as other components. Figure 16.41–Fig. 16.42 demonstrate the Windows Media Player control.

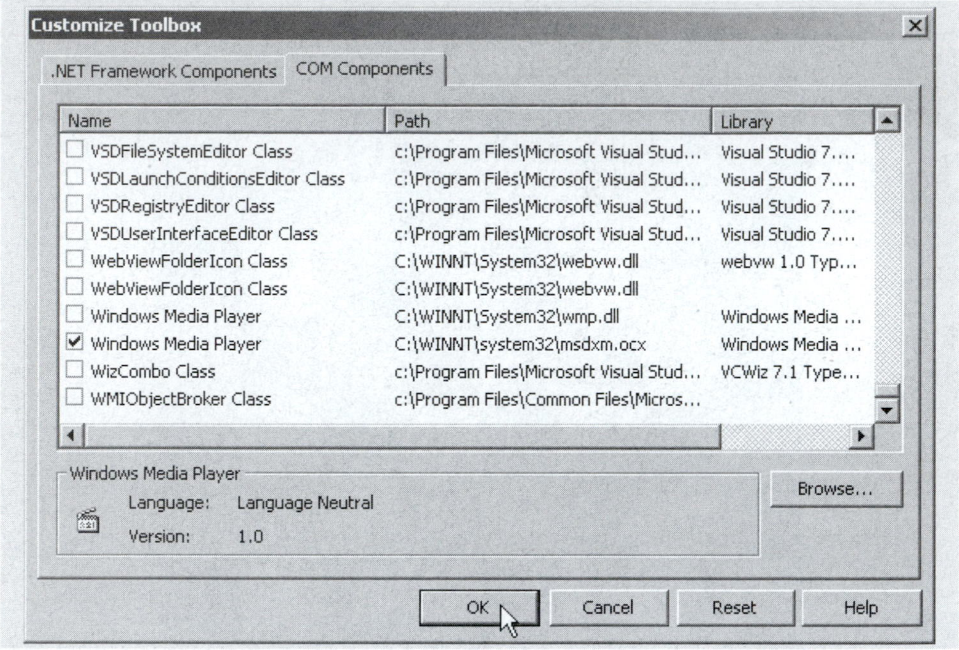

Fig. 16.40 Adding an ActiveX control to the **Toolbox**.

Line 49 declares a Windows Media Player control object of type `AxMediaPlayer`. The Windows Media Player control provides several buttons that allow the user to play the current file, pause, stop, play the previous file, rewind, forward and play the next file. The control also includes a volume control and trackbars to select a specific position in the media file.

The application provides a `MainMenu`, which includes **File** and **About** menus. The **File** menu contains the **Open** and **Exit** menu items; the **About** menu contains the **About Windows Media Player** menu item.

```
1  // Fig. 16.41: Form1.h
2  // Demonstrates the Windows Media Player control.
3
4  #pragma once
5
6
```

Fig. 16.41 Windows Media Player demonstration. (Part 1 of 3.)

2. You may need to register the ActiveX control (`msdxm.ocx`) with your system. To do this, select **Start > Run** and enter `Regsvr32.exe C:\WINNT\system32\msdxm.ocx` at the prompt (you may need to replace `WINNT` with `Windows`). Once you have done this, open a **Command Prompt** to the `C:\Program Files\Microsoft Visual Studio .NET 2003\SDK\v1.1\Bin` directory. Type `AxImp C:\WINNT\system32\msdxm.ocx` or `AxImp C:\Windows\system32\msdxm.ocx`. This command creates `.dll` files that you can use to add the ActiveX control to your application.

```
namespace MyMediaPlayer
{
   using namespace System;
   using namespace System::ComponentModel;
   using namespace System::Collections;
   using namespace System::Windows::Forms;
   using namespace System::Data;
   using namespace System::Drawing;

   /// <summary>
   /// Summary for Form1
   ///
   /// WARNING: If you change the name of this class, you will need to
   ///          change the 'Resource File Name' property for the managed
   ///          resource compiler tool associated with all .resx files
   ///          this class depends on.  Otherwise, the designers will not
   ///          be able to interact properly with localized resources
   ///          associated with this form.
   /// </summary>
   public __gc class Form1 : public System::Windows::Forms::Form
   {
   public:
      Form1(void)
      {
         InitializeComponent();
      }

   protected:
      void Dispose(Boolean disposing)
      {
         if (disposing && components)
         {
            components->Dispose();
         }
         __super::Dispose(disposing);
      }
   private: System::Windows::Forms::MainMenu *  applicationMenu;
   private: System::Windows::Forms::MenuItem *  fileItem;
   private: System::Windows::Forms::MenuItem *  openItem;
   private: System::Windows::Forms::MenuItem *  exitItem;
   private: System::Windows::Forms::MenuItem *  aboutItem;
   private: System::Windows::Forms::MenuItem *  aboutMessageItem;
   private: AxInterop::MediaPlayer::AxMediaPlayer *  player;
   private: System::Windows::Forms::OpenFileDialog *  openMediaFileDialog;

   private:
      /// <summary>
      /// Required designer variable.
      /// </summary>
      System::ComponentModel::Container * components;

   // Visual Studio .NET generated GUI code

```

Fig. 16.41 Windows Media Player demonstration. (Part 2 of 3.)

```
    // open new media file in Windows Media Player
    private: System::Void openItem_Click(
                System::Object *  sender, System::EventArgs *  e)
             {
                openMediaFileDialog->ShowDialog();

                player->FileName = openMediaFileDialog->FileName;

                // adjust the size of the Media Player control and
                // the Form according to the size of the image
                player->Size.Width = player->ImageSourceWidth;
                player->Size.Height = player->ImageSourceHeight;

                this->Size.Width = player->Size.Width + 20;
                this->Size.Height = player->Size.Height + 60;
             } // end method openItem_Click

    private: System::Void exitItem_Click(
                System::Object *  sender, System::EventArgs *  e)
             {
                Application::Exit();
             } // end method exitItem_Click

    private: System::Void aboutMessageItem_Click(
                System::Object *  sender, System::EventArgs *  e)
             {
                player->AboutBox();
             } // end method aboutMessageItem_Click
    };
}
```

Fig. 16.41 Windows Media Player demonstration. (Part 3 of 3.)

```
// Fig. 16.42: Form1.cpp
// Entry point for application.

#include "stdafx.h"
#include "Form1.h"
#include <windows.h>

using namespace MyMediaPlayer;

int APIENTRY _tWinMain(HINSTANCE hInstance,
                       HINSTANCE hPrevInstance,
                       LPTSTR    lpCmdLine,
                       int       nCmdShow)
{
   System::Threading::Thread::CurrentThread->ApartmentState =
      System::Threading::ApartmentState::STA;
   Application::Run(new Form1());
   return 0;
} // end _tWinMain
```

Fig. 16.42 `MyMediaPlayer` entry point. (Part 1 of 2.)

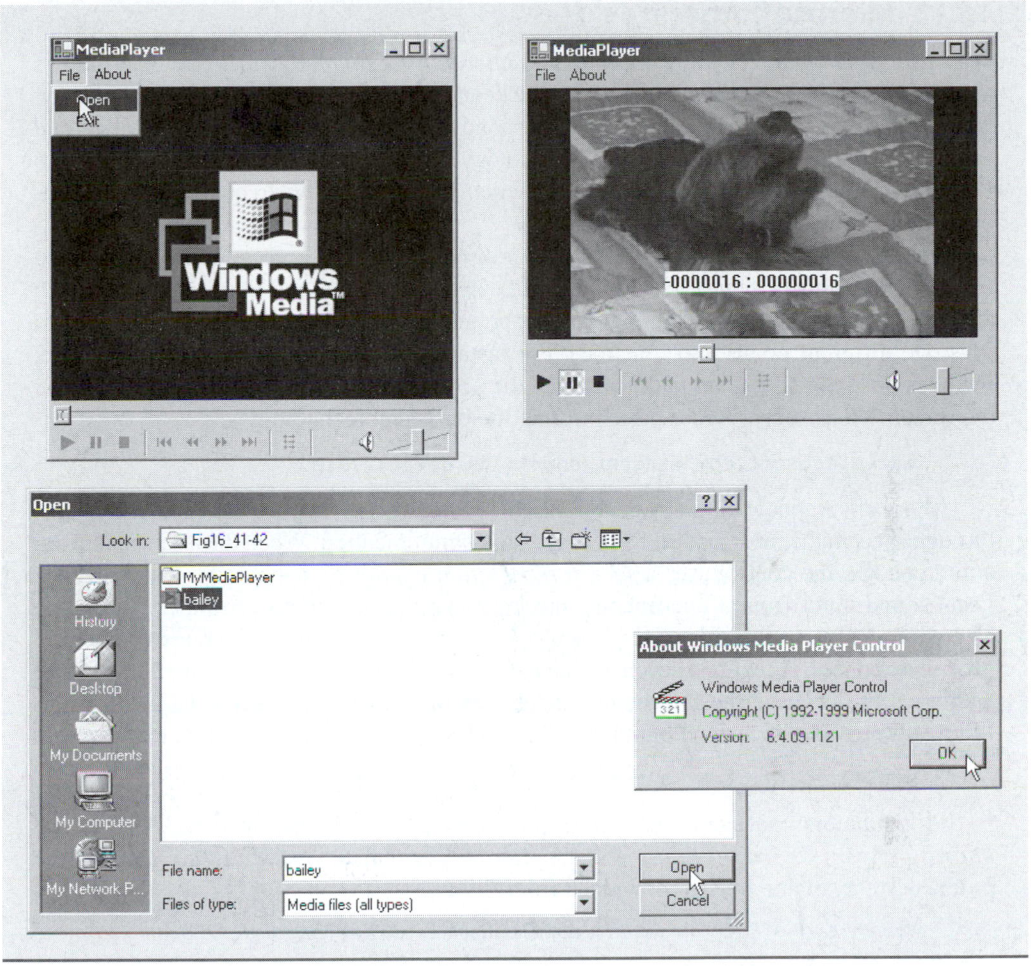

Fig. 16.42 `MyMediaPlayer` entry point. (Part 2 of 2.)

When a user chooses **Open** from the **File** menu, event handler `openItem_Click` (lines 61–75 of Fig. 16.41) executes. Line 64 invokes *`OpenFileDialog`* method *`ShowDialog`*. Class `OpenFileDialog` represents a dialog box that allows a user to select a file; Method `ShowDialog` displays the dialog box.

The program then sets the *`FileName`* property of the `player` (the Windows Media Player control object of type `AxMediaPlayer`) to the name of the file chosen by the user. The `FileName` property specifies the file that Windows Media Player currently is using. Lines 70–74 adjust the size of `player` and the application to reflect the size of the media contained in the file.

The event handler that executes when the user selects **Exit** from the **File** menu (lines 77–81) simply calls `Application::Exit` to terminate the application. The event handler that executes when the user chooses **About Windows Media Player** from the **About** menu (lines 83–87) calls the *`AboutBox`* method of the player. `AboutBox` simply displays a preset message box containing information about Windows Media Player.

16.13 Microsoft Agent

Microsoft Agent is a technology used to add *interactive animated characters* to Windows applications or Web pages. Interactivity is the key function of Microsoft Agent technology: Microsoft Agent characters can speak and respond to user input via speech recognition and synthesis. Microsoft employs its Agent technology in applications such as Word, Excel and PowerPoint. Agents in these programs aid users in finding answers to questions and in understanding how the applications function.

The Microsoft Agent control provides programmers with access to four predefined characters—*Genie* (a genie), *Merlin* (a wizard), *Peedy* (a parrot) and *Robby* (a robot). Each character has a unique set of animations that programmers can use in their applications to illustrate different points and functions. For instance, the Peedy character-animation set includes different flying animations, which the programmer might use to move Peedy on the screen. Microsoft provides basic information on Agent technology at

`www.microsoft.com/msagent/downloads/default.asp`

Microsoft Agent technology enables users to interact with applications and Web pages through speech, the most natural form of human communication. When the user speaks into a microphone, the control uses a *speech recognition engine,* an application that translates vocal sound input from a microphone into language that the computer understands. The Microsoft Agent control also uses a *text-to-speech engine*, which generates characters' spoken responses. A text-to-speech engine is an application that translates typed words into audio sound that users hear through headphones or speakers connected to a computer. Microsoft provides speech recognition and text-to-speech engines for several languages at

`www.microsoft.com/msagent/downloads/user.asp`

Programmers can even create their own animated characters with the help of the *Microsoft Agent Character Editor* and the *Microsoft Linguistic Sound Editing Tool*. These products are available free for download from

`www.microsoft.com/msagent/downloads/developer.asp`

This section introduces the basic capabilities of the Microsoft Agent control. For complete details on downloading this control, visit

`www.microsoft.com/msagent/downloads/default.asp`

The following example, Peedy's Pizza Palace, was developed by Microsoft to illustrate the capabilities of the Microsoft Agent control. Peedy's Pizza Palace is an online pizza shop where users can place their orders via voice input. The Peedy character interacts with users by helping them choose toppings, then calculating the totals for their orders.

Readers can view this example at

`agent.microsoft.com/agent2/sdk/samples/html/peedypza.htm`

To run this example, students must download the Peedy character file, a text-to-speech engine and a speech-recognition engine. When the page loads, the browser prompts for these downloads. Follow the directions provided by Microsoft to complete installation.

When the window opens, Peedy introduces himself (Fig. 16.43), and the words he speaks appear in a cartoon bubble above his head. Notice that Peedy's animations correspond to the words he speaks.

Programmers can synchronize character animations with speech output to illustrate a point or to convey a character's mood. For instance, Fig. 16.44 depicts Peedy's *Pleased* animation. The Peedy character-animation set includes eighty-five different animations, each of which is unique to the Peedy character.

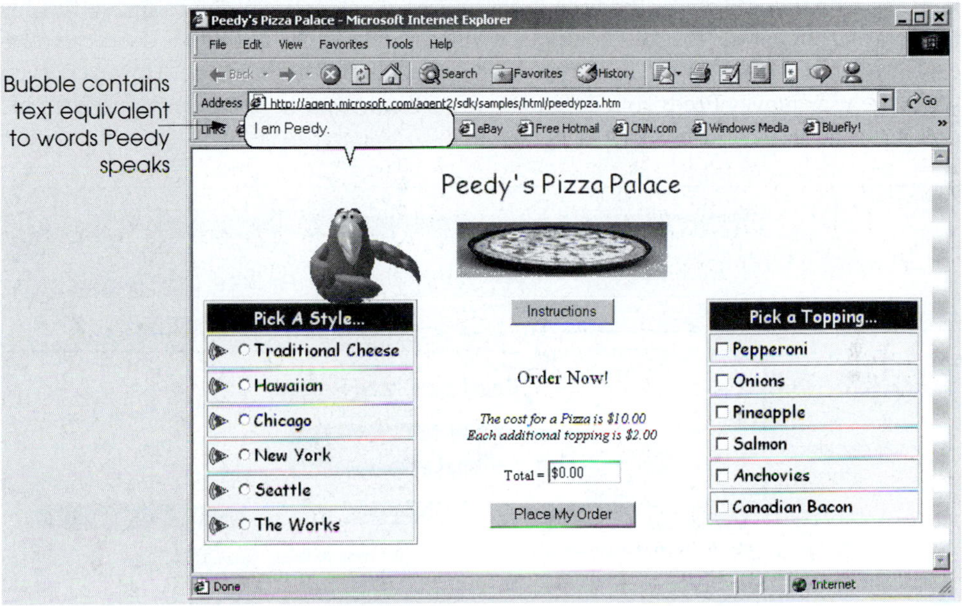

Fig. 16.43 Peedy introducing himself when the window opens.

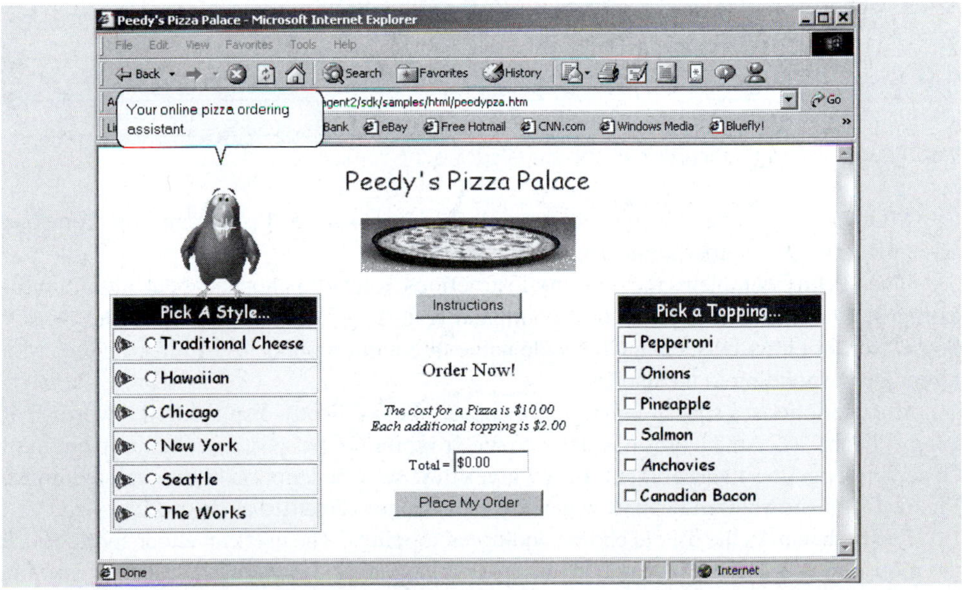

Fig. 16.44 Peedy's *Pleased* animation.

Look-and-Feel Observation 16.1

Agent characters remain on top of all active windows while a Microsoft Agent application is running. Their motions are not limited to the boundaries of the browser or application window.

Peedy also responds to input from the keyboard and mouse. Figure 16.45 shows what happens when a user clicks Peedy with the mouse pointer. Peedy jumps up, ruffles his feathers and exclaims, "Hey that tickles!" or, "Be careful with that pointer!" Users can relocate Peedy on the screen by clicking and dragging him with the mouse. However, even when the user moves Peedy to a different part of the screen, he continues to perform his preset animations and location changes.

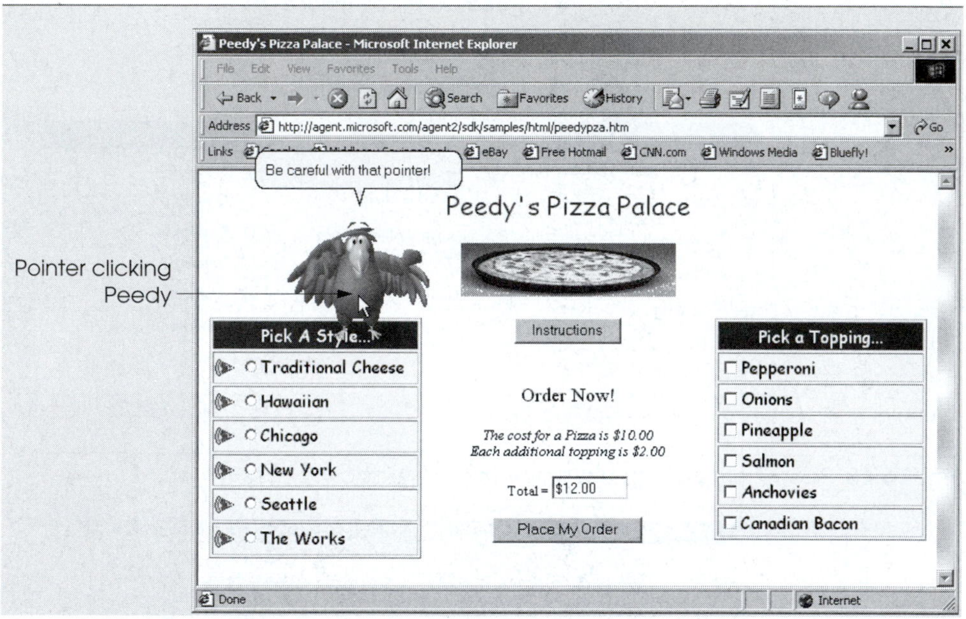

Fig. 16.45 Peedy's reaction when he is clicked.

Many location changes involve animations. For instance, Peedy can hop from one screen location to another, or he can fly (Fig. 16.46).

Once Peedy completes the ordering instructions, a text box appears beneath him indicating that he is listening for a voice command (Fig. 16.47). A user can enter the type of pizza to order either by speaking the style name into a microphone or by clicking the radio button corresponding to the choice.

If a user chooses speech input, a box appears below Peedy displaying the words that Peedy "heard" (i.e., the words translated to the program by the speech-recognition engine). Once he recognizes the user input, Peedy gives the user a description of the selected pizza. Figure 16.48 shows what happens when the user chooses **Seattle** as the pizza style.

Peedy then asks the user to choose additional toppings. The user can either speak or use the mouse to make a selection. Check boxes corresponding to toppings that come with the selected pizza style are checked for the user. Figure 16.49 shows what happens when a user chooses anchovies as an additional topping. Peedy makes a wisecrack about the user's choice.

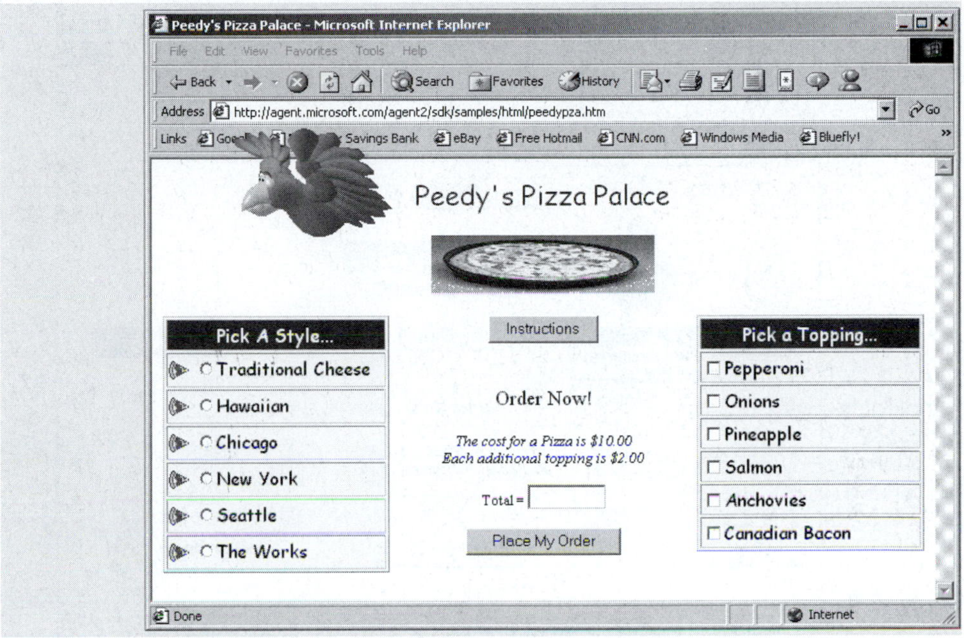

Fig. 16.46 Peedy flying animation.

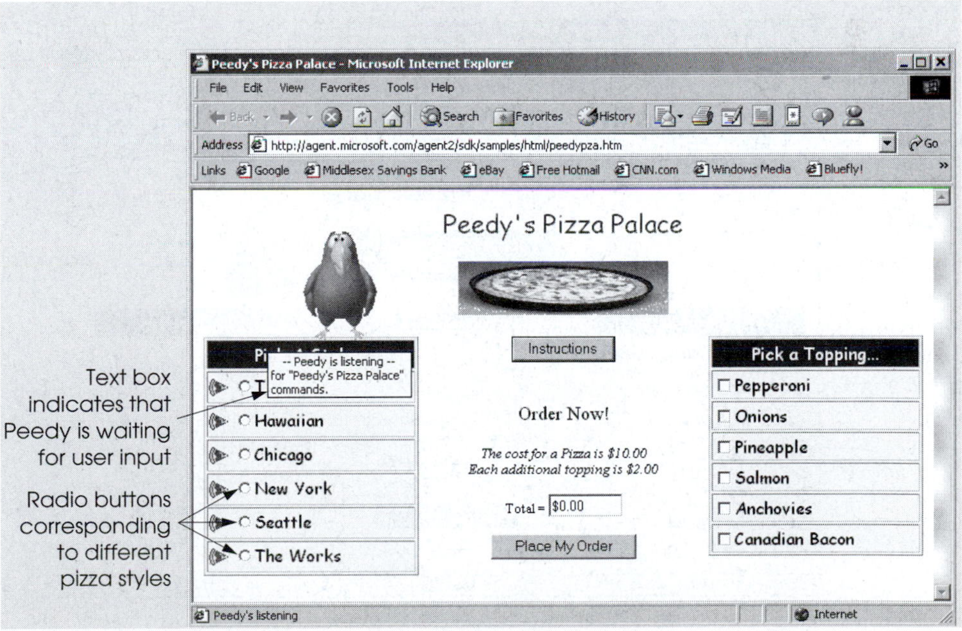

Fig. 16.47 Peedy waiting for speech input.

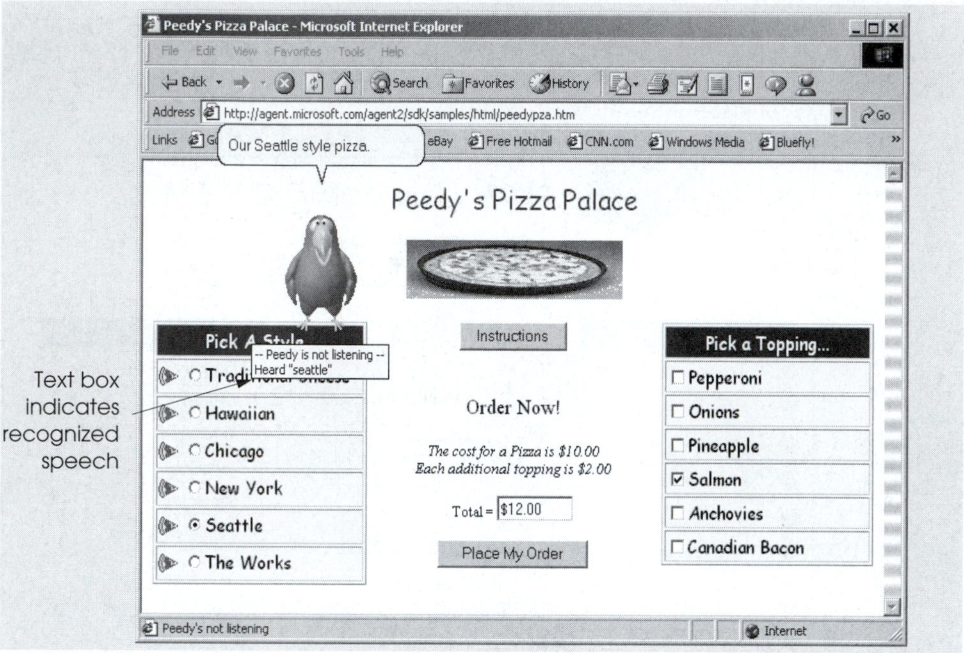

Fig. 16.48 Peedy repeating the user's request for Seattle-style pizza.

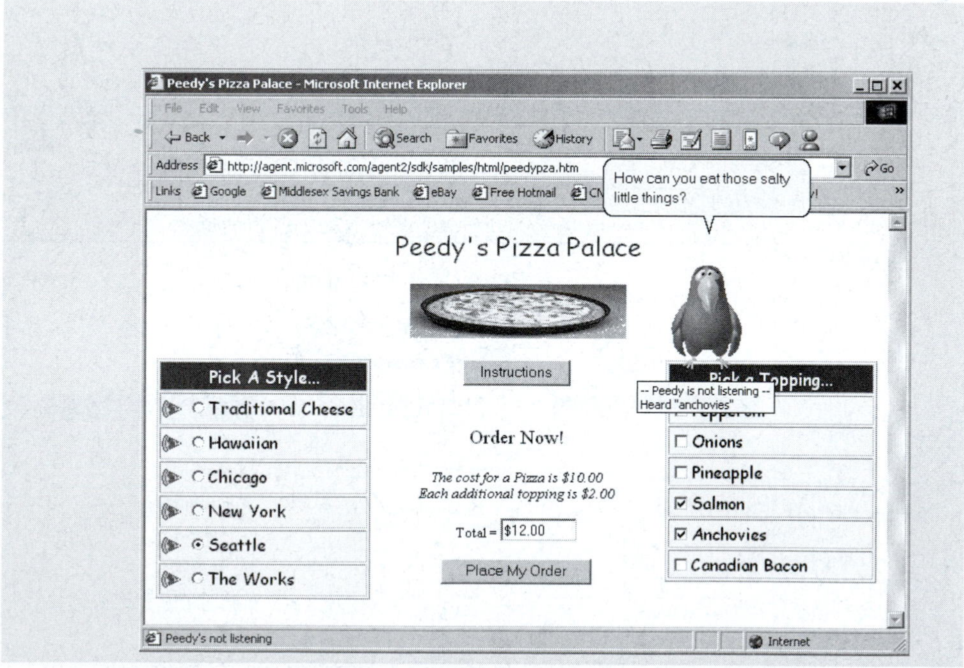

Fig. 16.49 Peedy repeating the user's request for anchovies as an additional topping.

The user can submit the order either by pressing the **Place My Order** button or by speaking "Place order" into the microphone. Peedy recounts the order while writing down the order items on his notepad (Fig. 16.50). He then calculates the figures on his calculator and reports the total to the user (Fig. 16.51).

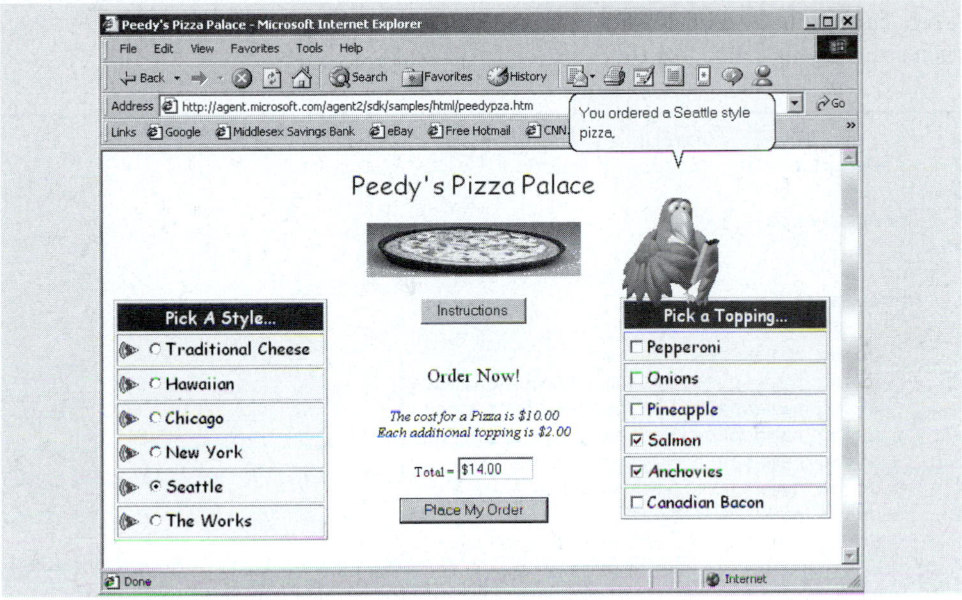

Fig. 16.50 Peedy recounting the order.

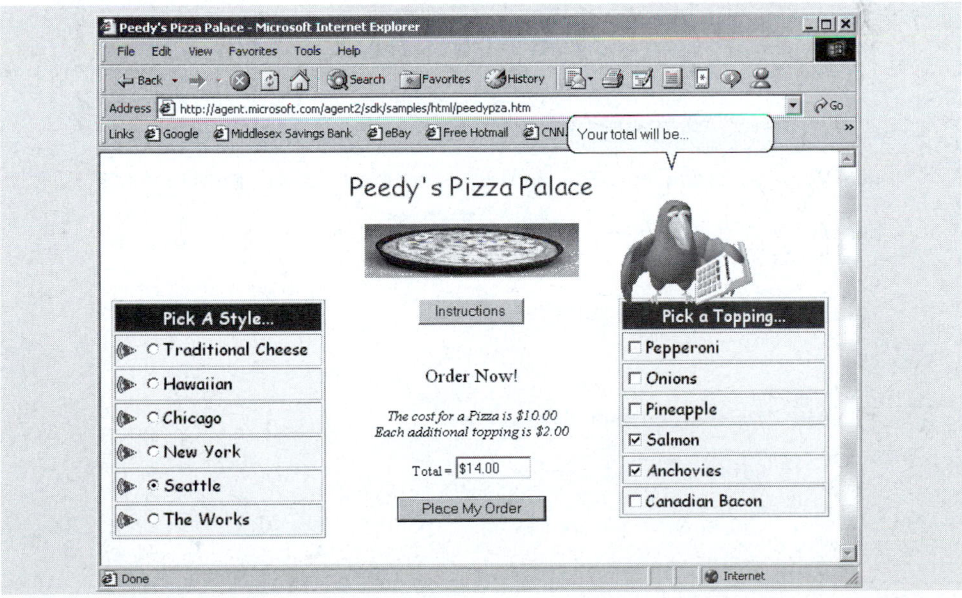

Fig. 16.51 Peedy calculating the total.

Figure 16.52–Fig. 16.53 demonstrate how to build a simple application with the Microsoft Agent control. This application contains two drop-down lists from which the user can choose an Agent character and a character animation. When the user chooses from these lists, the chosen character appears and performs the chosen animation. The application uses speech recognition and synthesis to control the character animations and speech: Users can tell the character which animation to perform by pressing the *Scroll Lock* key, then speaking the animation name into a microphone.

```
// Fig. 16.52: Form1.h
// Demonstrates Microsoft Agent.

#pragma once


namespace MicrosoftAgent
{
   using namespace System;
   using namespace System::ComponentModel;
   using namespace System::Collections;
   using namespace System::Windows::Forms;
   using namespace System::Data;
   using namespace System::Drawing;
   using namespace System::IO;
   using namespace System::Threading;

   /// <summary>
   /// Summary for Form1
   ///
   /// WARNING: If you change the name of this class, you will need to
   ///          change the 'Resource File Name' property for the managed
   ///          resource compiler tool associated with all .resx files
   ///          this class depends on.  Otherwise, the designers will not
   ///          be able to interact properly with localized resources
   ///          associated with this form.
   /// </summary>
   public __gc class Form1 : public System::Windows::Forms::Form
   {
   public:
      Form1(void)
      {
         InitializeComponent();
      }

   protected:
      void Dispose(Boolean disposing)
      {
         if (disposing && components)
         {
            components->Dispose();
         }
```

Fig. 16.52 Microsoft Agent demonstration. (Part 1 of 5.)

```
            __super::Dispose(disposing);
        }

    private: System::Windows::Forms::ComboBox *  actionsCombo;
    private: System::Windows::Forms::ComboBox *  characterCombo;

    private: System::Windows::Forms::Button *  speakButton;
    private: System::Windows::Forms::GroupBox *  characterGroup;
    private: AxInterop::AgentObjects::AxAgent *  mainAgent;

    private: System::Windows::Forms::TextBox *  speechTextBox;
    private: System::Windows::Forms::TextBox *  locationTextBox;

    private: Interop::AgentObjects::IAgentCtlCharacter *speaker;

    private:
        /// <summary>
        /// Required designer variable.
        /// </summary>
        System::ComponentModel::Container * components;

    // Visual Studio .NET generated GUI code

    // KeyDown event handler for locationTextBox
    private: System::Void locationTextBox_KeyDown(System::Object *  sender,
                System::Windows::Forms::KeyEventArgs *  e)
            {
                if ( e->KeyCode == Keys::Enter ) {

                    // set character location to text box value
                    String *location = locationTextBox->Text;

                    // initialize the characters
                    try {

                        // load characters into agent object
                        mainAgent->Characters->Load( S"Genie",
                           String::Concat( location, S"Genie.acs" ) );

                        mainAgent->Characters->Load( S"Merlin",
                           String::Concat( location, S"Merlin.acs" ) );

                        mainAgent->Characters->Load( S"Peedy",
                           String::Concat( location, S"Peedy.acs" ) );

                        mainAgent->Characters->Load( S"Robby",
                           String::Concat( location, S"Robby.acs" ) );

                        // disable TextBox for entering the location
                        // and enable other controls
                        locationTextBox->Enabled = false;
                        speechTextBox->Enabled = true;
                        speakButton->Enabled = true;
```

Fig. 16.52 Microsoft Agent demonstration. (Part 2 of 5.)

```
                  characterCombo->Enabled = true;
                  actionsCombo->Enabled = true;

                  // set current character to Genie and show him
                  speaker = mainAgent->Characters->Item[ S"Genie" ];

                  // obtain an animation name list
                  GetAnimationNames();
                  speaker->Show( 0 );
               } // end try
               catch( FileNotFoundException * ) {
                  MessageBox::Show( S"Invalid character location",
                     S"Error", MessageBoxButtons::OK,
                     MessageBoxIcon::Error );
               } // end catch
            } // end if
         } // end method locationTextBox_KeyDown

private: System::Void speakButton_Click(
            System::Object *  sender, System::EventArgs *  e)
         {
            // if textbox is empty, have the character ask
            // user to type the words into textbox, otherwise
            // have character say the words in textbox
            if ( speechTextBox->Text->Equals( S"" ) )
               speaker->Speak(
                  S"Please, type the words you want me to speak",
                  S"" );
            else
               speaker->Speak( speechTextBox->Text, S"" );

         } // end method speakButton_Click

// click event for agent
private: System::Void mainAgent_ClickEvent(System::Object *  sender,
            AxInterop::AgentObjects::_AgentEvents_ClickEvent *  e)
         {
            speaker->Play( S"Confused" );
            speaker->Speak( S"Why are you poking me?", S"" );
            speaker->Play( S"RestPose" );
         } // end method mainAgent_ClickEvent

// combobox changed event, switch active agent
private: System::Void characterCombo_SelectedIndexChanged(
            System::Object *  sender, System::EventArgs *  e)
         {
            ChangeCharacter( characterCombo->Text );
         } // end method characterCombo_SelectedIndexChanged

private:

   void ChangeCharacter( String *name )
   {
```

Fig. 16.52 Microsoft Agent demonstration. (Part 3 of 5.)

```
         speaker->Hide( 0 );
         speaker = mainAgent->Characters->Item[ name ];

         // regenerate animation name list
         GetAnimationNames();
         speaker->Show( 0 );
      } // end method ChangeCharacter

   private:

      // get animation names and store in arraylist
      void GetAnimationNames()
      {
         Monitor::Enter( this );  // ensure thread safety

         // get animation names
         IEnumerator *enumerator = mainAgent->Characters->Item[
            speaker->Name ]->AnimationNames->GetEnumerator();

         String *voiceString;

         // clear actionsCombo
         actionsCombo->Items->Clear();
         speaker->Commands->RemoveAll();

         // copy enumeration to ArrayList
         while ( enumerator->MoveNext() ) {

            //remove underscores in speech string
            voiceString = __try_cast< String * >( enumerator->Current );
            voiceString = voiceString->Replace( S"_", S"underscore" );

            actionsCombo->Items->Add( enumerator->Current );

            // add all animations as voice enabled commands
            speaker->Commands->Add(
               __try_cast< String * >( enumerator->Current ),
               enumerator->Current, voiceString,
               __box( true ), __box( false ) );
         } // end while

         // add custom command
         speaker->Commands->Add(
            S"MoveToMouse", S"MoveToMouse", S"MoveToMouse",
            __box( true ), __box( true ) );

         Monitor::Exit( this );
      } // end method GetAnimationNames

   // user selects new action
   private: System::Void actionsCombo_SelectedIndexChanged(
            System::Object *  sender, System::EventArgs *  e)
         {
```

Fig. 16.52 Microsoft Agent demonstration. (Part 4 of 5.)

```
                  speaker->StopAll( S"Play" );
                  speaker->Play( actionsCombo->Text );
                  speaker->Play( S"RestPose" );
               } // end method actionsCombo_SelectedIndexChanged

      // handles agent commands
      private: System::Void mainAgent_Command(System::Object *  sender,
                  AxInterop::AgentObjects::_AgentEvents_CommandEvent *  e)
               {
                  // get UserInput object
                  Interop::AgentObjects::IAgentCtlUserInput *command =
                     __try_cast<Interop::AgentObjects::IAgentCtlUserInput *>
                     ( e->userInput );

                  // change character if user speaks character name
                  if ( command->Voice->Equals( S"Peedy" ) ||
                     command->Voice->Equals( S"Robby" ) ||
                     command->Voice->Equals( S"Merlin" ) ||
                     command->Voice->Equals( S"Genie" ) ) {
                     ChangeCharacter( command->Voice );

                     return;
                  } // end if

                  // send agent to mouse
                  if ( command->Voice->Equals( S"MoveToMouse" ) ) {
                     speaker->MoveTo(
                        Convert::ToInt16( Cursor->Position.X - 60 ),
                        Convert::ToInt16( Cursor->Position.Y - 60 ),
                        __box( 5 ) );

                     return;
                  }

                  // play new animation
                  speaker->StopAll( S"Play" );
                  speaker->Play( command->Name );
               } // end method mainAgent_Command
      };
   }
```

Fig. 16.52 Microsoft Agent demonstration. (Part 5 of 5.)

```
// Fig. 16.53: Form1.cpp
// Entry point for application.

#include "stdafx.h"
#include "Form1.h"
#include <windows.h>

using namespace MicrosoftAgent;

```

Fig. 16.53 `MicrosoftAgent` entry point. (Part 1 of 3.)

```
int APIENTRY _tWinMain(HINSTANCE hInstance,
                       HINSTANCE hPrevInstance,
                       LPTSTR    lpCmdLine,
                       int       nCmdShow)
{
   System::Threading::Thread::CurrentThread->ApartmentState =
      System::Threading::ApartmentState::STA;
   Application::Run(new Form1());
   return 0;
} // end _tWinMain
```

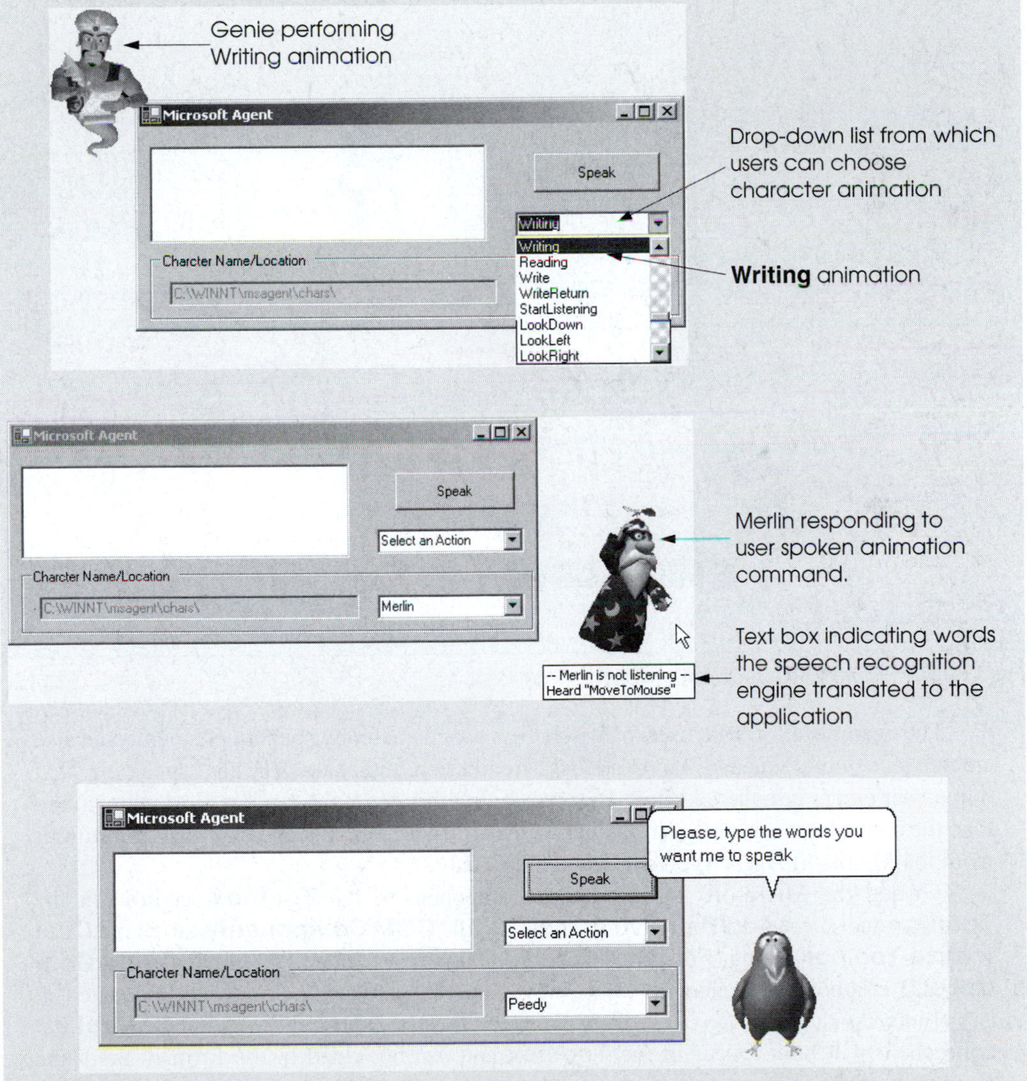

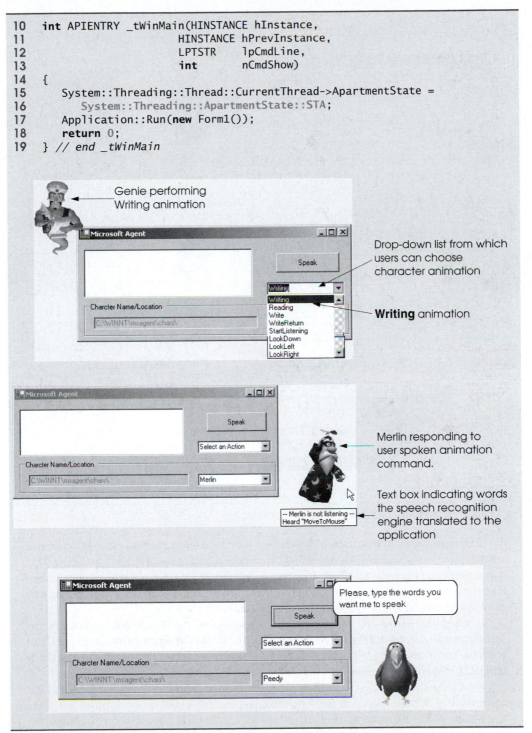

Fig. 16.53 `MicrosoftAgent` entry point. (Part 2 of 3.)

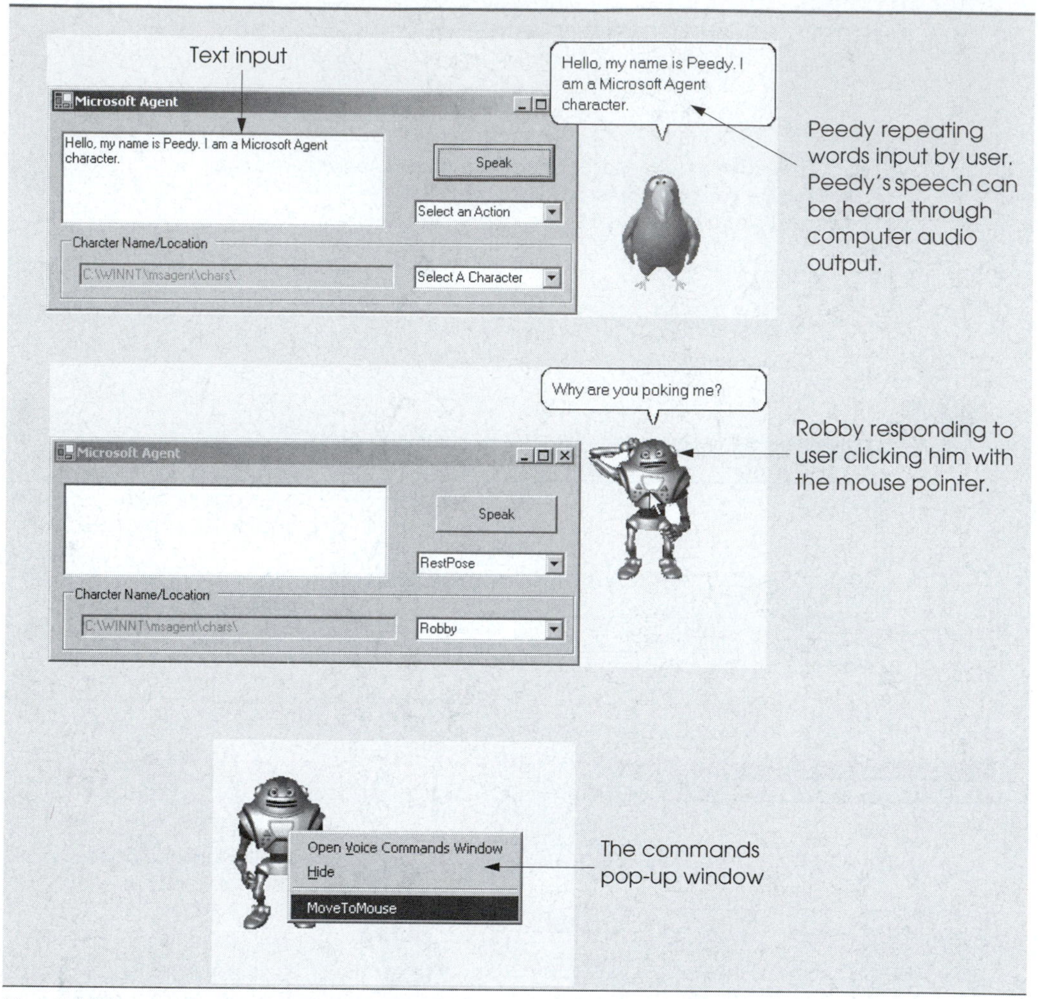

Fig. 16.53 `MicrosoftAgent` entry point. (Part 3 of 3.)

The example allows the user to switch to a new character by speaking its name and also creates a custom command, `MoveToMouse`. In addition, the characters also speak any text that a user enters into the text box. Before running this example, readers first must download the control, speech-recognition engine, text-to-speech engine and character definitions from the Microsoft Agent Web site listed previously.

To add the Microsoft Agent control component to the **Toolbox**, right-click the **Toolbox** and select **Add/Remove Items…**. In the **COM Components** tab of the **Customize Toolbox** dialog (Fig. 16.40), check the box next to the **Microsoft Agent Control 2.0** component located at `C:\winnt\msagent\agentctl.dll` (possibly located at `C:\Windows\msagent\agentctl.dll`) and click **OK**. The **Microsoft Agent Control 2.0** component will now appear in the **Toolbox** and can be added to the form in the same manner as other components. Fig. 16.54 shows a Microsoft Agent control component added to a form.

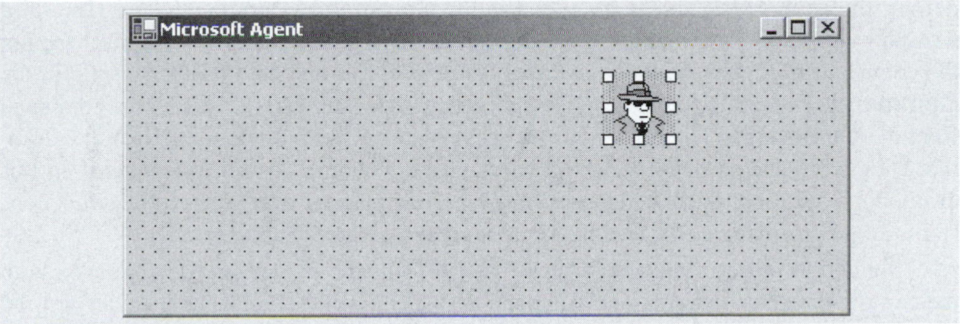

Fig. 16.54 Microsoft Agent Control 2.0 component added to a form.

Line 51 declares Microsoft Agent object (of type *AxAgent*) `mainAgent`. In addition to the Microsoft Agent object `mainAgent`, which manages all the characters, we also need an object of type *IAgentCtlCharacter* (located in namespace *Interop::AgentObjects*) to represent the current character. We declare this object, named `speaker`, in line 56.

When the program begins, the only enabled control is the `locationTextBox`. This text box contains the default location for the character files, but the user can change this location if the files are located elsewhere on the user's computer. Once the user presses *Enter* in the `TextBox`, event handler `locationTextBox_KeyDown` (lines 67–112 of Fig. 16.42) executes. Lines 79–89 load the character descriptions for the predefined animated characters. If the specified location of the characters is incorrect, or if any character is missing, a `FileNotFoundException` is thrown.

Lines 93–97 disable `locationTextBox` and enable the rest of the controls. Lines 100–104 set Genie as the default character, obtain all animation names via method `GetAnimationNames`, then call `IAgentCtlCharacter` method *Show* to display the character. We access characters through property *Characters* of `mainAgent`, which contains all characters that have been loaded. We use the indexer of the `Characters` property to specify the name of the character that we wish to load (`"Genie"`).

When a user pokes the character (i.e., clicks it with the mouse), event handler `mainAgent_ClickEvent` (lines 130–136) executes. First, `speaker` method *Play* plays an animation. This method accepts as an argument a `String *` representing one of the predefined animations for the character. (A list of animations for each character is available at the Microsoft Agent Web site; each character provides over 70 animations.) In our example, the argument to `Play` is `"Confused"`—this animation is defined for all four characters, each of which expresses this emotion in a unique way. The character then speaks, `"Why are you poking me?"` via a call to method *Speak*. Finally, the *RestPose* animation is played, which returns the character to its neutral, resting pose.

The list of valid commands for a character is contained in property *Commands* of the `IAgentCtlCharacter` object (`speaker`, in this example). The commands for an Agent character can be viewed in the **Commands** pop-up window, which displays when the user right-clicks an Agent character (the last screenshot in Fig. 16.53). Method *Add* (line 184–187) adds a new command to the command list. Method `Add` takes three `String *` arguments and two `bool` arguments. The first `String *` argument identifies the name of the command, which we use to identify the command programmatically. The second `String *` defines the command name as it appears in the **Commands** pop-up window. The third String * defines the voice input that triggers the command. The first bool specifies whether the command is active; the second bool indicates whether the command is visible in the **Commands** pop-up window. A command is triggered when the user selects the command from the **Commands** pop-up window or speaks the voice input into a microphone. Command logic is handled in the *Command* event of the AxAgent control (mainAgent, in this example). In addition, Agent defines several global commands that have predefined functions (for example, speaking a character name causes that character to appear).

Method GetAnimationNames (lines 160–196) fills the actionsCombo ComboBox with the current character's animation listing and defines the valid commands that can be used with the character. The method uses methods Monitor::Enter (line 162) and Monitor::Exit (line 195) to prevent errors resulting from rapid character changes.

Lines 165–166 obtain the current character's animations using interface *IEnumerator* (sometimes called an *enumerator* or an *iterator*). Interface IEnumerator (namespace System::Collections) can be used to iterate (traverse) through items in a collection one element at a time. After lines 171–172 clear the existing items in the ComboBox and character's Commands property, lines 175–188 iterate through all items in the animation-name enumerator. For each animation, in line 178, we assign the animation name to String * voiceString. Line 179 removes any underscore characters (_) and replaces them with the string "underscore"; this changes the string so that a user can pronounce and employ it as a command activator. The Add method (lines 184–187) adds a new command to the current character. The Add method adds all animations as commands by providing the following arguments: The animation name as the new command's name and caption, and voiceString for the voice activation string. The method's bool arguments enable the command, but make it unavailable in the **Commands** pop-up window. Thus, the command can be activated only by voice input. Lines 191–193 create a new command, named MoveToMouse, which is visible in the **Commands** pop-up window.

After the GetAnimationNames method has been called, the user can select a value from the actionsCombo ComboBox. Event handler actionsCombo_SelectedIndexChanged (lines 199–205) stops any current animation, then displays the animation that the user selected from the ComboBox.

The user also can type text into the TextBox and click **Speak**. This causes event handler speakButton_Click (line 114–127) to call speaker's method Speak, supplying as an argument the text in speechTextBox. If the user clicks **Speak** without providing text, the character speaks, "Please, type the words you want me to speak".

At any point in the program, the user can choose to display a different character from the ComboBox. When this happens, the SelectedIndexChanged event handler for characterCombo (lines 139–143) executes. The event handler calls method ChangeCharacter (lines 147–155) with the text in the characterCombo ComboBox as an argument. Method ChangeCharacter calls the Hide method of speaker (line 149) to remove the current character from view. Line 150 assigns the newly selected character to speaker, line 153 generates the character's animation names and commands, and line 154 displays the character via a call to method Show.

Each time a user presses the *Scroll Lock* key and speaks into a microphone or selects a command from the **Commands** pop-up window, event handler mainAgent_Command (lines 208–239) is called. This method is passed an argument of type AxAgent-

Objects::_AgentEvents_CommandEvent, which contains a single property, userInput. The userInput property returns an Object that can be converted to type *AgentObjects::IAgentCtlUserInput*, an interface that represents user input. The userInput object is assigned to a IAgentCtlUserInput object command, which is used to identify the command, then take appropriate action. Lines 217–224 use method ChangeCharacter to change the current Agent character if the user speaks a character name. Microsoft Agent always will show a character when a user speaks its name; however, by controlling the character change, we can ensure that only one Agent character is displayed at a time. Lines 227–234 move the character to the current mouse location if the user invokes the MoveToMouse command. The Agent method *MoveTo* takes *x*- and *y*-coordinate arguments and moves the character to the specified screen position, applying appropriate movement animations. For all other commands, we Play the command name as an animation in line 238.

In this chapter, we explored various graphics capabilities of GDI+, including pens, brushes and images, and some multimedia capabilities of the .NET Framework Class Library. In the next chapter, we cover the reading, writing and accessing of sequential- and random-access files. We also explore several types of streams included in Visual Studio .NET.

SUMMARY

- A coordinate system is used to identify every possible point on the screen.
- The upper-left corner of a GUI component has coordinates (0, 0). A coordinate pair is composed of an *x*-coordinate (the horizontal coordinate) and a *y*-coordinate (the vertical coordinate).
- Coordinate units are measured in pixels, which are the smallest units of resolution on a display monitor.
- A graphics context represents a drawing surface on the screen. A Graphics object provides access to the graphics context of a control.
- Graphics objects contain methods for drawing, font manipulation, color manipulation and other graphics-related actions.
- An instance of the Pen class is used to draw lines.
- An instance of one of the classes that derive from abstract class Brush is used to draw solid shapes.
- The Point structure can be used to represent a point in a two-dimensional plane.
- Method OnPaint normally is called in response to an event, such as the uncovering of a window. This method, in turn, triggers a Paint event.
- Structure Color defines constants for manipulating colors in a program. Color properties R, G and B return int values from 0–255, representing the amounts of red, green and blue, respectively, that exist in a Color. The larger the value, the greater the amount of that particular color.
- Visual C++ .NET provides class ColorDialog to display a dialog that allows users to select colors.
- Component property BackColor (one of the many Component properties that can be called on most GUI components) changes the component's background color.
- Class Font's constructors all take at least three arguments—the font name, the font size and the font style. The font name is any font currently supported by the system. The font style is a member of the FontStyle enumeration.
- Class FontMetrics defines several methods for obtaining font metrics.
- Class Font provides the Bold, Italic, Strikeout and Underline properties, which return true if the font is bold, italic, strikeout or underlined, respectively.

- Class Font provides the Name property, which returns a String * representing the name of the font.
- Class Font provides the Size and SizeInPoints properties, which return the size of the font in design units and in points, respectively.
- The FontFamily class provides information about such font metrics as the family's spacing and height.
- The FontFamily class provides the GetCellAscent, GetCellDescent, GetEmHeight and GetLineSpacing methods, which return the ascent of a font, the descent of a font, the font's height in points and the distance between two consecutive lines of text, respectively.
- Class Graphics provides methods DrawLine, DrawRectangle, DrawEllipse, DrawArc, DrawLines, DrawPolygon and DrawPie, which draw lines and shape outlines.
- Class Graphics provides methods FillRectangle, FillEllipse, FillPolygon and FillPie, which draw solid shapes.
- Classes HatchBrush, LinearGradientBrush, PathGradientBrush and TextureBrush all derive from class Brush and represent shape-filling styles.
- Graphics method FromImage retrieves the Graphics object associated with the image file that is its argument.
- The DashStyle and DashCap enumerations define the style of dashes and their ends, respectively.
- Class GraphicsPath represents a shape constructed from straight lines and curves.
- GraphicsPath method AddLine appends a line to the shape that is encapsulated by the object.
- GraphicsPath method CloseFigure completes the shape that is represented by the GraphicsPath object.
- Class Image is used to manipulate images.
- Class Image provides method FromFile to retrieve an image stored on disk and load it into an instance of class Image.
- Graphics method Clear paints the entire Control with the color that the programmer provides as an argument.
- Graphics method DrawImage draws the specified Image on the Control.
- Using Visual Studio .NET and MC++, programmers can create applications that use components, such as Windows Media Player and Microsoft Agent.
- The Windows Media Player allows programmers to create applications that can play multimedia files.
- Microsoft Agent is a technology that allows programmers to include interactive animated characters in their applications.

TERMINOLOGY

AboutBox method of AxMediaPlayer
Add method of class ArrayList
AddLine method of class GraphicsPath
animated characters
animating a series of images
animation
arc angle
arc method
ARGB values
ArrayList class
ascent of a font
audio-video interleave (AVI)
AxAgent class
AxMediaPlayer class
bandwidth
Bitmap class
Bold property of class Font
bounding rectangle for an oval
Brush class
Characters property of class AxAgent

`Point` structure
rectangle
`Rectangle` structure
`Regular` member of enumeration `FontStyle`
resolution
RGB values
Robby the Robot `Microsoft Agent` character
`RotateTransform` method of class `Graphics`
sector
`Show` method of `IAgentCtlCharacter`
`Size` property of class `Font`
`SizeInPoints` property of class `Font`
solid arc
solid polygon
solid rectangle
`SolidBrush` class
straight line
`Strikeout` member of `FontStyle`
`Strikeout` property of class `Font`
style of a font
`System::Drawing` namespace
`System::Drawing::Drawing2D` namespace
`TextureBrush` class
three-dimensional application
`Tick` event of class `Timer`
`Timer` class
`TranslateTransform` method of `Graphics`
two-dimensional shape
`Underline` property of class `Font`
upper-left corner of a GUI component
vertical coordinate
WAV
Windows Media Player
Windows wave file format (WAV)
x-axis
x-coordinate
y-axis
y-coordinate

SELF-REVIEW EXERCISES

16.1 State whether each of the following is *true* or *false*. If *false*, explain why.

a) A `Font` object's size can be changed by setting its `Size` property.
b) In the GDI+ coordinate system, *x*-values increase from left to right.
c) Method `FillPolygon` draws a solid polygon with a specified `Brush`.
d) Method `DrawArc` allows negative arc angles.
e) `Font` property `Size` returns the size of the current font in centimeters.
f) Pixel coordinate (0, 0) is located at the exact center of the monitor.
g) A `HatchBrush` is used to draw lines.
h) `Color` method `FromPredefinedName` creates a color from a name, passed as a pointer to a `String`.
i) Every `Control` has an associated `Graphics` object.
j) Method `OnPaint` is inherited by every `Form`.

16.2 Fill in the blanks in each of the following statements:

a) Class ________ is used to draw lines of various colors and thicknesses.
b) Classes ________ and ________ define the fill for a shape in such a way that the fill gradually changes from one color to another.
c) The ________ method of class `Graphics` draws a line between two points.
d) ARGB is short for ________, ________, ________ and ________.
e) Font sizes usually are measured in units called ________.
f) Class ________ fills a shape using a pattern drawn in a `Bitmap`.
g) The ________ allows an application to play multimedia files.
h) Class ________ defines a path consisting of lines and curves.
i) The FCL's drawing capabilities are part of the namespaces ________ and ________.
j) Method ________ loads an image from a disk into an `Image` object.

ANSWERS TO SELF-REVIEW EXERCISES

16.1 a) False. `Size` is a read-only property. b) True. c) True. d) True. e) False. It returns the size of the current `Font` in design units. f) False. The coordinate (0,0) corresponds to the upper-left corner of a GUI component on which drawing occurs. g) False. A `Pen` is used to draw lines, a `HatchBrush` fills a shape with a hatch pattern. h) False. `Color` method `FromName` creates a color from a name, passed as a pointer to a `String`. i) True. j) True.

16.2 a) `Pen`. b) `LinearGradientBrush`, `PathGradientBrush`. c) `DrawLine`. d) alpha, red, green, blue. e) points. f) `TextureBrush`. g) Windows Media Player. h) `GraphicsPath` i) `System::Drawing`, `System::Drawing::Drawing2D`. j) `FromFile`.

EXERCISES

16.3 Write a program that draws a four-sided pyramid. Use class `GraphicsPath` and method `DrawPath`.

16.4 Write a program that allows the user to draw "free-hand" images with the mouse in a `PictureBox`. Allow the user to change the drawing color and width of the pen. Provide a button that allows the user to clear the `PictureBox`.

16.5 Write a program that repeatedly flashes an image on the screen. Do this by interspersing the image with a plain background-color image.

16.6 If you want to emphasize an image, you might place a row of simulated light bulbs around the image. Write a program by which an image is emphasized this way. You can let the light bulbs flash in unison or you can let them fire on and off in sequence, one after another.

16.7 (*Eight Queens*) A puzzler for chess buffs is the Eight Queens problem. Simply stated: Is it possible to place eight queens on an empty chessboard so that no queen is "attacking" any other (i.e., so that no two queens are in the same row, in the same column or along the same diagonal)?

Create a GUI that allows the user to drag-and-drop each queen on the board. Use the graphical features of Fig. 16.39. Provide eight queen images to the right of the board (Fig. 16.55), which the user can drag-and-drop onto the board. When a queen is dropped on the board, its corresponding image to the right should not be visible. If a queen is in conflict with another queen when placed on the board, display a message box and remove that queen from the board.

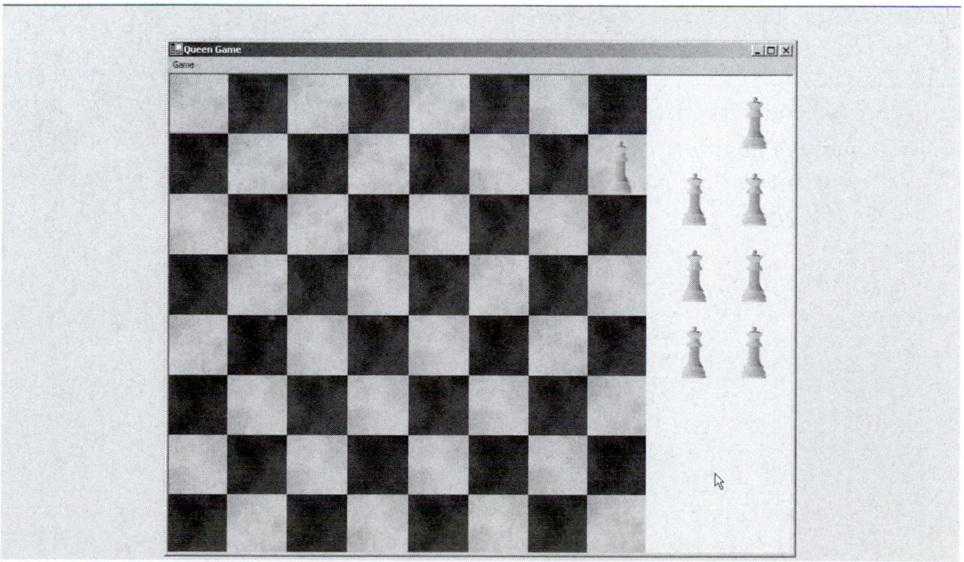

Fig. 16.55 GUI for Eight Queens exercise.

17

Files and Streams

Objectives

- To create, read, write and update files.
- To understand the streams class hierarchy in the .NET Framework.
- To use classes `File` and `Directory`.
- To use the `FileStream` and `BinaryFormatter` classes to read objects from, and write objects to, files.
- To become familiar with sequential-access and random-access file processing.

I can only assume that a "Do Not File" document is filed in a "Do Not File" file.
Senator Frank Church
Senate Intelligence Subcommittee Hearing, 1975

Consciousness … does not appear to itself chopped up in bits. … A "river" or a "stream" are the metaphors by which it is most naturally described.
William James

I read part of it all the way through.
Samuel Goldwyn

Outline

17.1 Introduction

Variables and arrays offer only temporary storage of data—the data are lost when an object is garbage collected or when the program terminates. By contrast, *files* are used for long-term storage of data and can retain data even after the program that created the data terminates. Data maintained in files often are called *persistent data*. Computers can store files on *secondary storage devices*, such as magnetic disks, optical disks and magnetic tapes. In this chapter, we explain how to create, update and process data files in MC++ programs. We consider both "sequential-access" files and "random-access" files, indicating the kinds of applications for which each is best suited. We have two goals in this chapter: To introduce the sequential-access and random-access file-processing paradigms and to provide the reader with sufficient stream-processing capabilities to support the networking features that we introduce in Chapter 21, Networking: Streams-Based Sockets and Datagrams.

File processing is one of a programming language's most important capabilities, because it enables a language to support commercial applications that typically process massive amounts of persistent data. This chapter discusses the .NET Framework's powerful and abundant file-processing and stream-input/output features.

17.2 Data Hierarchy

Ultimately, all data items processed by a computer are reduced to combinations of zeros and ones. This is because it is simple and economical to build electronic devices that can assume two stable states—`0` represents one state, and `1` represents the other. It is remarkable that the impressive functions performed by computers involve only the most fundamental manipulations of `0`s and `1`s.

The smallest data items that computers support are called *bits* (short for "*binary digit*"—a digit that can assume one of two values). Each data item, or bit, can assume either the value `0` or the value `1`. Computer circuitry performs various simple bit manipulations, such as examining the value of a bit, setting the value of a bit and reversing a bit (from 1 to 0 or from 0 to 1).

Programming with data in the low-level form of bits is cumbersome. It is preferable to program with data in forms such as *decimal digits* (i.e., 0, 1, 2, 3, 4, 5, 6, 7, 8 and 9), *letters* (i.e., A through Z and a through z) and *special symbols* (i.e., $, @, %, &, *, (,), -, +, ", :, ?, / and many others). Digits, letters and special symbols are referred to as *characters*. The set of all characters used to write programs and represent data items on a particular computer is called that computer's *character set*. Computers can process only `1`s and `0`s, so every character in a computer's character set is represented as a pattern of `1`s and `0`s. *Bytes* are composed of eight bits. For example, characters in `System::String` objects are *Unicode* characters, which are composed of 2 bytes, or 16 bits. Programmers create programs and data items with characters; computers manipulate and process these characters as patterns of bits. More information about Unicode can be found in Appendix D, Unicode.

The various kinds of data items processed by computers can form a *data hierarchy* (Fig. 17.1) in which data items become larger and more complex in structure as we progress from bits, to characters, to fields (discussed momentarily) and up to larger data structures. [*Note*: The structure we suggest in this section is not the only structure a file may have. We only supply this structure as an example that we can build upon throughout the chapter.]

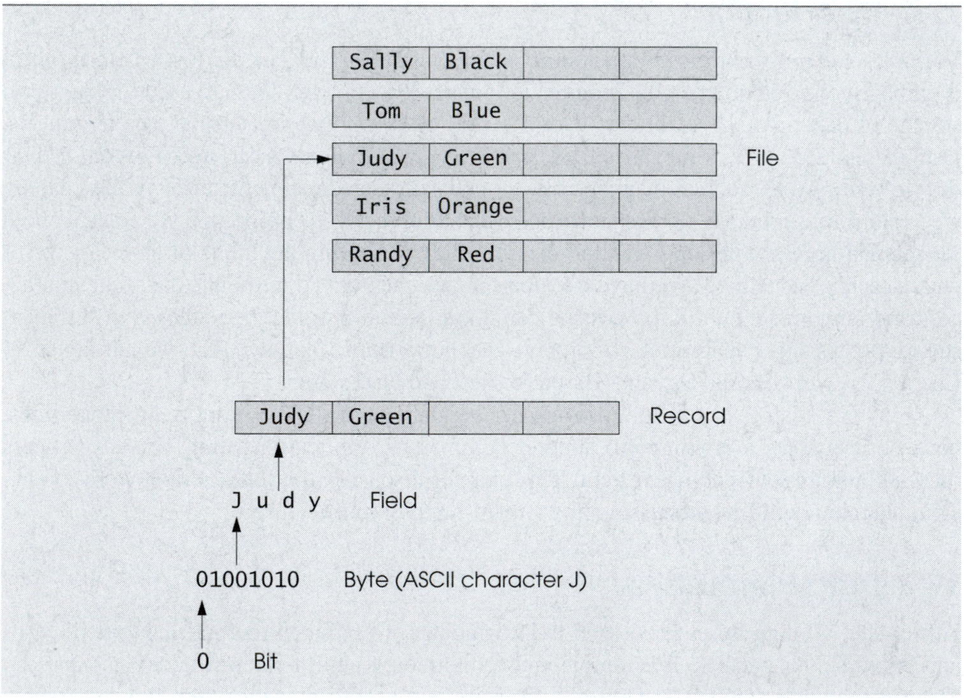

Fig. 17.1 Data hierarchy.

In the same way that characters are composed of bits, *fields* are composed of characters. A field is a group of characters that conveys some meaning. For example, a field consisting of uppercase and lowercase letters can represent a person's name.

Typically, a *record* is composed of several fields. In a payroll system, for example, a record for a particular employee might include the following fields:

1. Employee identification number
2. Name
3. Address
4. Hourly pay rate
5. Number of exemptions claimed
6. Year-to-date earnings
7. Amount of taxes withheld

Thus, a record is a group of related fields. In the preceding example, each field is associated with the same employee. A group of related records compose a *file*.[1] A company's payroll file normally contains one record for each employee. Thus, a payroll file for a small company might contain only 22 records, whereas a payroll file for a large company might contain 100,000 records. It is not unusual for a company to have many files, some containing millions, billions or even trillions of bits of information.

To facilitate the retrieval of specific records from a file, at least one field in each record is chosen as a unique *record key*. A record key identifies a record as belonging to a particular person or entity and distinguishes that record from all other records. In the payroll record described previously, the employee identification number normally would be chosen as the record key.

There are many ways of organizing records in a file. The most common type of organization is called a *sequential file*, in which records typically are stored in order by the record-key field. In a payroll file, records usually are placed in order by employee-identification numbers. The first employee record in the file contains the lowest employee-identification number, and subsequent records contain increasingly higher employee-identification numbers.

Most businesses use many different files to store data. For example, a company might have payroll files, accounts receivable files (listing money due from clients), accounts payable files (listing money due to suppliers), inventory files (listing facts about all the items handled by the business) and many other types of files. Sometimes, a group of related files is called a *database*. A collection of programs designed to create and manage databases is called a *database management system* (DBMS). We discuss databases in detail in Chapter 19, Database, SQL and ADO .NET.

17.3 Files and Streams

The .NET Framework views each file as a sequential *stream* of bytes (Fig. 17.2). Each file ends either with an *end-of-file marker* or at a specific byte number that is recorded in a system-maintained administrative data structure. When a file is *opened*, the Common Language

1. More generally, a file can contain arbitrary data in arbitrary formats. In most operating systems, a file is viewed as nothing more than a collection of bytes. In such an operating system, any organization of the bytes in a file (such as organizing the data into records) is a view created by the applications programmer.

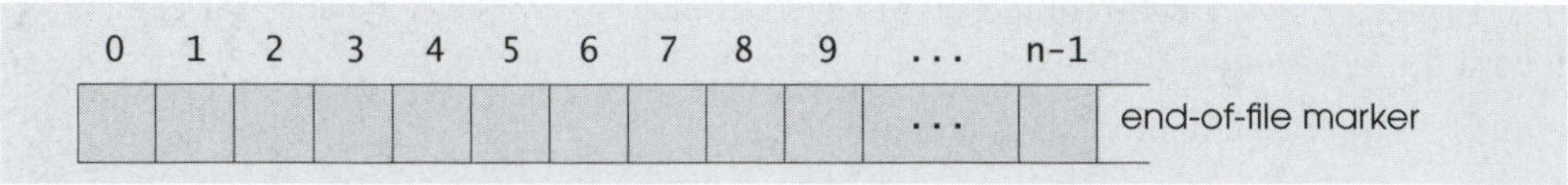

Fig. 17.2 .NET Framework's view of an *n*-byte file.

Runtime (CLR) creates an object, then associates a stream with that object. The runtime environment creates three stream objects upon program execution, which are accessible via properties `Console::Out`, `Console::In` and `Console::Error`, respectively. These objects facilitate communication between a program and a particular file or device. Property `Console::In` returns the *standard input stream object*, which enables a program to input data from the keyboard. Property `Console::Out` returns the *standard output stream object*, which enables a program to output data to the screen. Property `Console::Error` returns the *standard error stream object*, which enables a program to output error messages to the screen. We have been using `Console::Out` and `Console::In` in our console applications—`Console` methods `Write` and `WriteLine` use `Console::Out` to perform output, and methods `Read` and `ReadLine` use `Console::In` to perform input. To perform file processing in MC++, namespace `System::IO` must be referenced. This namespace includes definitions for such stream classes as *`StreamReader`* (for text input from a stream), *`StreamWriter`* (for text output to a stream) and *`FileStream`* (for both input from and output to a file). Files are opened by creating objects of these stream classes, which inherit from `abstract` classes *`TextReader`*, *`TextWriter`* and *`Stream`*, respectively. Actually, properties `In` and `Out` of class `Console` are a `TextReader` and `TextWriter`, respectively.

The .NET Framework provides class *`BinaryFormatter`*, which is used in conjunction with a `Stream` object to perform input and output of objects. *Serialization* involves converting an object into a format that can be written to a file without losing any of that object's data. *Deserialization* consists of reading this format from a file and reconstructing the original object from it. A `BinaryFormatter` can serialize objects to, and deserialize objects from, a specified `Stream`.

Abstract class *`Stream`* (namespace `System::IO`) provides functionality for representing streams as bytes. Classes *`FileStream`*, *`MemoryStream`* and *`BufferedStream`* (all from namespace `System::IO`) inherit from class `Stream`. Later in the chapter, we use `FileStream` to read data to, and write data from, sequential-access and random-access files. Class `MemoryStream` enables transfers of data directly to and from memory, which is much faster than are other types of data transfer (e.g., to and from disk). Class `BufferedStream` uses *buffering* to transfer data to or from a stream. Buffering is a performance-enhancement technique in which each I/O operation is directed to a region in memory, called a *buffer*, that is large enough to hold the data from many I/O operations. When performing output, the actual transfer to the output device is performed in one large *physical output operation* each time the buffer fills. The output operations directed to the output buffer in memory often are called *logical output operations*.

The .NET Framework offers many classes for performing input and output. In this chapter, we use several key stream classes to implement a variety of file-processing programs that create, manipulate and destroy sequential-access files and random-access files. In Chapter 21, Networking: Streams-Based Sockets and Datagrams, we use stream classes extensively to implement networking applications.

17.4 Classes File and Directory

Information on computers is stored in files, which are organized in directories. Class *File* is provided for manipulating files, and class *Directory* is provided for manipulating directories. Class File cannot write to or read from files directly; we discuss methods for reading and writing files in subsequent sections.

Note that the \ *separator character* separates directories and files in a path on Windows systems. On UNIX systems, the separator character is /. In Visual C++ .NET, both characters are actually processed identically in a path name. This means that, if we specified the path c:\visual_cpp/README, which uses one of each separator character, the file would still be processed properly. [*Note*: Remember that when specifying the path in a String, it is necessary to escape the backslash character (e.g., c:\\visual_cpp/README).]

Figure 17.3 lists some methods contained in class File for manipulating and determining information about particular files. Class File contains only static methods—you cannot instantiate objects of type File. We use several of these methods in the example of Fig. 17.5–Fig. 17.6.

static Method	Description
AppendText	Returns a StreamWriter that appends to an existing file or creates a file if one does not exist.
Copy	Copies a file to a new file.
Create	Creates a file and returns its associated FileStream.
CreateText	Creates a text file and returns its associated StreamWriter.
Delete	Deletes the specified file.
Exists	Returns true if the specified file exists (and the caller has the correct permissions); otherwise, it returns false.
GetCreationTime	Returns a DateTime object representing the time that the file was created.
GetLastAccessTime	Returns a DateTime object representing the time that the file was last accessed.
GetLastWriteTime	Returns a DateTime object representing the time that the file was last modified.
Move	Moves the specified file to a specified location.
Open	Returns a FileStream associated with the specified file and equipped with the specified read/write permissions.
OpenRead	Returns a read-only FileStream associated with the specified file.
OpenText	Returns a StreamReader associated with the specified file.
OpenWrite	Returns a read/write FileStream associated with the specified file.

Fig. 17.3 File class methods (partial list).

Class Directory provides capabilities for manipulating and iterating directories. Figure 17.4 lists some methods that can be used for directory manipulation. We employ several of these methods in the example of Fig. 17.5–Fig. 17.6.

static Method	Description
CreateDirectory	Creates a directory and returns its associated DirectoryInfo.
Delete	Deletes the specified directory.
Exists	Returns true if the specified directory exists; otherwise, it returns false.
GetLastWriteTime	Returns a DateTime object representing the time that the directory was last modified.
GetDirectories	Returns a String * array representing the names of the subdirectories in the specified directory.
GetFiles	Returns a String * array representing the names of the files in the specified directory.
GetCreationTime	Returns a DateTime object representing the time that the directory was created.
GetLastAccessTime	Returns a DateTime object representing the time that the directory was last accessed.
Move	Moves the specified directory to a specified location.
SetCreationTime	Sets the DateTime object representing the time that the directory was created.
SetLastAccessTime	Sets the DateTime object representing the time that the directory was last accessed.
SetLastWriteTime	Sets the DateTime object representing the time that items were last written to the directory.

Fig. 17.4 Directory class methods (partial list).

Determining Information About Files and Directories

The *DirectoryInfo* object returned by method CreateDirectory contains information about a directory. Much of the information contained in this class can also be accessed via the methods of class Directory. Class Form1 (Fig. 17.5) uses methods described in Fig. 17.3 and Fig. 17.4 to access file and directory information. The inputTextBox (line 46 of Fig. 17.5) enables the user to input a file or directory name. For each key that the user presses in the text box, the program calls method inputTextBox_KeyDown (lines 57–121 of Fig. 17.5). If the user presses the *Enter* key (line 61), this method displays either the file or directory contents, depending the text the user input in the TextBox. (Note that, if the user does not press the *Enter* key, this method returns without displaying any content.) Line 69 uses method Exists of class File to determine whether the user-specified text is a name of an existing file. If the user specifies an existing file, line 73 invokes private method GetInformation (lines 126–146), which calls methods GetCreationTime (line 134), GetLastWriteTime (line 138) and GetLastAccessTime (line 142) of class File to access file information. When method GetInformation returns, lines 79–80 instantiate a StreamReader for reading text from the file. The StreamReader constructor takes as an argument a String * containing the name of the file to open. Lines 81–82 call method *ReadToEnd* of the StreamReader to read the contents of the file, which are then displayed in the outputTextBox.

```
// Fig. 17.5: Form1.h
// Using classes File and Directory.

#pragma once


namespace FileTest
{
   using namespace System;
   using namespace System::ComponentModel;
   using namespace System::Collections;
   using namespace System::Windows::Forms;
   using namespace System::Data;
   using namespace System::Drawing;
   using namespace System::IO;

   /// <summary>
   /// Summary for Form1
   ///
   /// WARNING: If you change the name of this class, you will need to
   ///          change the 'Resource File Name' property for the managed
   ///          resource compiler tool associated with all .resx files
   ///          this class depends on.  Otherwise, the designers will not
   ///          be able to interact properly with localized resources
   ///          associated with this form.
   /// </summary>
   public __gc class Form1 : public System::Windows::Forms::Form
   {
   public:
      Form1(void)
      {
         InitializeComponent();
      }

   protected:
      void Dispose(Boolean disposing)
      {
         if (disposing && components)
         {
            components->Dispose();
         }
         __super::Dispose(disposing);
      }
   private: System::Windows::Forms::TextBox *  outputTextBox;
   private: System::Windows::Forms::Label *  directionsLabel;
   private: System::Windows::Forms::TextBox *  inputTextBox;

   private:
      /// <summary>
      /// Required designer variable.
      /// </summary>
      System::ComponentModel::Container * components;

```

Fig. 17.5 FileTest class demonstrates classes File and Directory. (Part 1 of 3.)

```
      // Visual Studio .NET generated GUI code

      // invoked when user presses key
      private: System::Void inputTextBox_KeyDown(System::Object *  sender,
                  System::Windows::Forms::KeyEventArgs *  e)
               {
                  // determine whether user pressed Enter key
                  if ( e->KeyCode == Keys::Enter ) {

                     String *fileName; // name of file or directory

                     // get user-specified file or directory
                     fileName = inputTextBox->Text;

                     // determine whether fileName is a file
                     if ( File::Exists( fileName ) ) {

                        // get file's creation date,
                        // modification date, etc.
                        outputTextBox->Text = GetInformation( fileName );

                        // display file contents through StreamReader
                        try {

                           // obtain reader and file contents
                           StreamReader *stream =
                              new StreamReader( fileName );
                           outputTextBox->Text = String::Concat(
                              outputTextBox->Text, stream->ReadToEnd() );
                        } // end try

                        // handle exception if StreamReader is unavailable
                        catch ( IOException * ) {
                           MessageBox::Show( S"File Error", S"File Error",
                              MessageBoxButtons::OK, MessageBoxIcon::Error );
                        } // end catch
                     } // end if

                     // determine whether fileName is a directory
                     else if ( Directory::Exists( fileName ) ) {

                        // get directory's creation date,
                        // modification date, etc.
                        outputTextBox->Text = GetInformation( fileName );

                        // obtain file/directory list of specified directory
                        String *directoryList[] =
                           Directory::GetDirectories( fileName );

                        outputTextBox->Text =
                           String::Concat( outputTextBox->Text,
                           S"\r\n\r\nDirectory contents:\r\n" );

```

Fig. 17.5 `FileTest` class demonstrates classes `File` and `Directory`. (Part 2 of 3.)

```
                    // output directoryList contents
                    for ( int i = 0; i < directoryList->Length; i++ )
                       outputTextBox->Text =
                          String::Concat( outputTextBox->Text,
                          directoryList[ i ], S"\r\n" );
                 } // end if
                 else {

                    // notify user that neither file nor directory exists
                    MessageBox::Show( String::Concat( inputTextBox->Text,
                       S" does not exist" ), S"File Error",
                       MessageBoxButtons::OK, MessageBoxIcon::Error );
                 } // end else
              } // end if
           } // end method inputTextBox_KeyDown

   private:

      // get information on file or directory
      String *GetInformation( String *fileName )
      {
         // output that file or directory exists
         String *information =
            String::Concat( fileName, S" exists\r\n\r\n" );

         // output when file or directory was created
         information = String::Concat( information, S"Created: ",
            ( File::GetCreationTime( fileName ) ).ToString(), S"\r\n" );

         // output when file or directory was last modified
         information = String::Concat( information, S"Last modified: ",
            ( File::GetLastWriteTime( fileName ) ).ToString(), S"\r\n" );

         // output when file or directory was last accessed
         information = String::Concat( information, S"Last accessed: ",
            ( File::GetLastAccessTime( fileName ) ).ToString(),
            S"\r\n\r\n" );

         return information;
      } // end method GetInformation
   };
}
```

Fig. 17.5 FileTest class demonstrates classes File and Directory. (Part 3 of 3.)

```
// Fig. 17.6: Form1.cpp
// Entry point for application.

#include "stdafx.h"
#include "Form1.h"
#include <windows.h>

```

Fig. 17.6 FileTest entry point. (Part 1 of 2.)

```
using namespace FileTest;

int APIENTRY _tWinMain(HINSTANCE hInstance,
                       HINSTANCE hPrevInstance,
                       LPTSTR    lpCmdLine,
                       int       nCmdShow)
{
   System::Threading::Thread::CurrentThread->ApartmentState =
      System::Threading::ApartmentState::STA;
   Application::Run(new Form1());
   return 0;
} // end _tWinMain
```

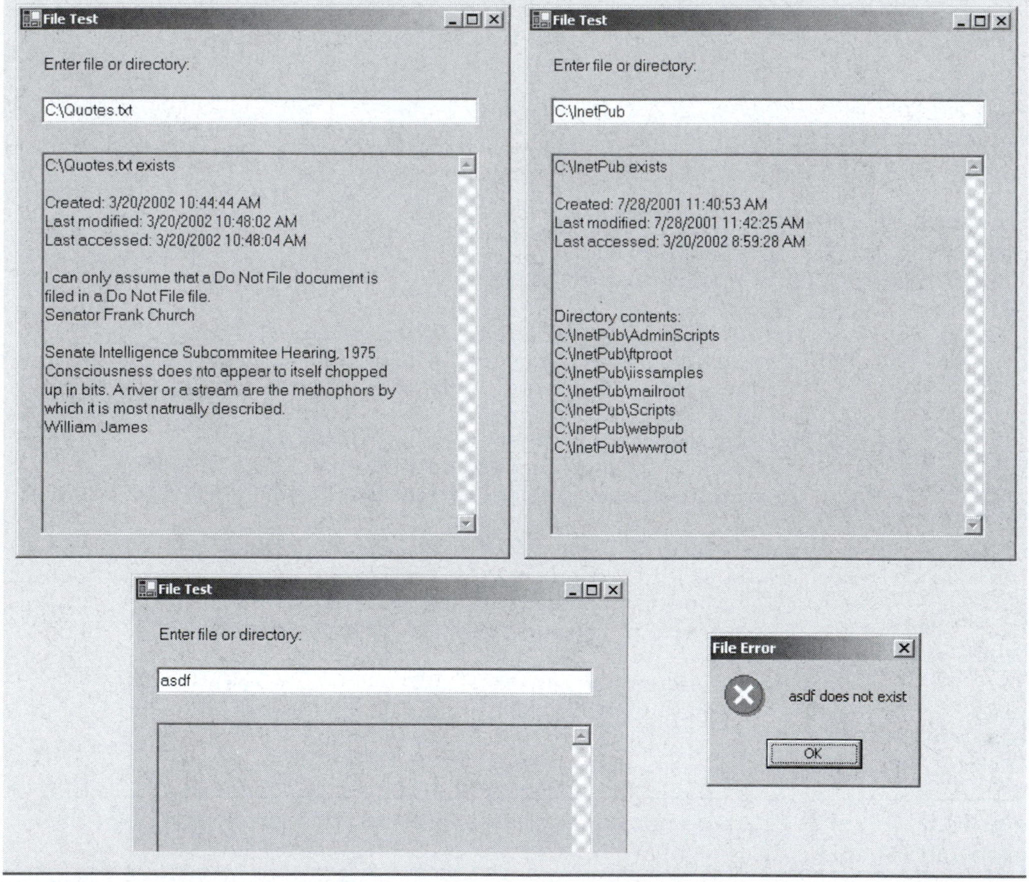

Fig. 17.6 `FileTest` entry point. (Part 2 of 2.)

If line 69 of Fig. 17.5 determines that the user-specified text is not a file, line 93 determines whether it is a directory, using method `Exists` of class `Directory`. If the user specified an existing directory, line 97 invokes method `GetInformation` to access the directory information. Line 101 calls method `GetDirectories` of class `Directory` to obtain a `String *` array containing the names of subdirectories in the specified directory. Lines 108–111 display each element in the `String *` array. Note that, if the user-specified text is neither a file nor a directory, lines 116–118 notify the user (via a `MessageBox`) that the file or directory does not exist.

Working With File Extensions

We now consider another example that uses the .NET Framework's file- and directory-manipulation capabilities. Class `Form1` (Fig. 17.7) uses classes `File` and `Directory` in conjunction with classes for performing regular expressions to report the number of files of each file type that exist in the specified directory path. The program also serves as a "clean-up" utility—when the program encounters a file that has the `.bak` extension (i.e., a backup file), the program displays a `MessageBox` asking whether that file should be removed, then responds appropriately to the user's input.

```
// Fig. 17.7: Form1.h
// Using regular expressions to determine file types.

#pragma once


namespace FileSearch
{
   using namespace System;
   using namespace System::ComponentModel;
   using namespace System::Collections;
   using namespace System::Windows::Forms;
   using namespace System::Data;
   using namespace System::Drawing;
   using namespace System::IO;
   using namespace System::Text::RegularExpressions;
   using namespace System::Collections::Specialized;

   /// <summary>
   /// Summary for Form1
   ///
   /// WARNING: If you change the name of this class, you will need to
   ///          change the 'Resource File Name' property for the managed
   ///          resource compiler tool associated with all .resx files
   ///          this class depends on.  Otherwise, the designers will not
   ///          be able to interact properly with localized resources
   ///          associated with this form.
   /// </summary>
   public __gc class Form1 : public System::Windows::Forms::Form
   {
   public:
      Form1(void)
      {
         found = new NameValueCollection();
         InitializeComponent();
      }

   protected:
```

Fig. 17.7 Using regular expressions to determine file types. (Part 1 of 5.)

```
      void Dispose(Boolean disposing)
      {
         if (disposing && components)
         {
            components->Dispose();
         }
         __super::Dispose(disposing);
      }
   private: System::Windows::Forms::TextBox *  outputTextBox;
   private: System::Windows::Forms::TextBox *  inputTextBox;
   private: System::Windows::Forms::Button *  searchButton;
   private: System::Windows::Forms::Label *  directionsLabel;
   private: System::Windows::Forms::Label *  directoryLabel;

   private: String *searchDirectory;

   // store extensions found and number found
   private: NameValueCollection *found;

   private:
      /// <summary>
      /// Required designer variable.
      /// </summary>
      System::ComponentModel::Container * components;

   // Visual Studio .NET generated GUI code

   // invoked when user types in text box
   private: System::Void inputTextBox_KeyDown(System::Object *  sender,
               System::Windows::Forms::KeyEventArgs *  e)
            {
               // determine whether user pressed Enter
               if ( e->KeyCode == Keys::Enter )
                  searchButton_Click( sender, e );
            } // end method inputTextBox_KeyDown

   // invoked when user clicks "Search Directory" button
   private: System::Void searchButton_Click(
               System::Object *  sender, System::EventArgs *  e)
            {
               // check for user input; default is current directory
               if ( inputTextBox->Text != S"" ) {

                  // verify that user input is valid directory name
                  if ( Directory::Exists( inputTextBox->Text ) ) {
                     searchDirectory = inputTextBox->Text;

                     // reset input text box and update display
                     directoryLabel->Text = String::Concat(
                        S"Current Directory:\r\n", searchDirectory );
                  } // end if
                  else {

```

Fig. 17.7 Using regular expressions to determine file types. (Part 2 of 5.)

```
                  // show error if invalid directory
                  MessageBox::Show( S"Invalid Directory", S"Error",
                     MessageBoxButtons::OK, MessageBoxIcon::Error );

                  return;
               } // end else
            } // end if

            // clear text boxes
            inputTextBox->Text = S"";
            outputTextBox->Text = S"";

            Cursor::Current = Cursors::WaitCursor; // set wait cursor

            SearchDirectory( searchDirectory ); // search directory

            Cursor::Current = Cursors::Default; // set default cursor

            // summarize and print results
            for ( int current = 0;
               current < found->Count; current++ ) {
               outputTextBox->AppendText( String::Concat(
                  S"* Found ", found->Get( current ), S" ",
                  found->GetKey( current ), S" files.\r\n" ) );
            } // end for

            // clear output for new search
            found->Clear();
         } // end method searchButton_Click

private:

   // search directory using regular expression
   void SearchDirectory( String *currentDirectory )
   {
      // for file name without directory path
      try {
         String *fileName = S"";

         // regular expression for extensions matching pattern
         Regex *regularExpression = new Regex(
            S"[a-zA-Z0-9]+\\.(?<extension>\\w+)" );

         // stores regular-expression-match result
         Match *matchResult;

         String *fileExtension; // holds file extensions

         // number of files with given extension in directory
         int extensionCount;

         // get directories
```

Fig. 17.7 Using regular expressions to determine file types. (Part 3 of 5.)

```
String *directoryList[] =
   Directory::GetDirectories( currentDirectory );

// get list of files in current directory
String *fileArray[] =
   Directory::GetFiles( currentDirectory );

// iterate through list of files
for ( int myFile = 0; myFile < fileArray->Length; myFile++ ) {

   // remove directory path from file name
   fileName = fileArray[ myFile ]->Substring(
      fileArray[ myFile ]->LastIndexOf( S"\\" ) + 1 );

   // obtain result for regular-expression search
   matchResult = regularExpression->Match( fileName );

   // check for match
   if ( matchResult->Success )
      fileExtension = matchResult->Result( S"${extension}" );
   else
      fileExtension = S"[no extension]";

   // store value from container
   if ( !( found->Get( fileExtension ) ) )
      found->Add( fileExtension, S"1" );
   else {
      extensionCount = Int32::Parse(
         found->Get( fileExtension ) ) + 1;

      found->Set( fileExtension, extensionCount.ToString() );
   } // end else

   // search for backup(.bak) files
   if ( fileExtension->Equals( S"bak" ) ) {

      // prompt user to delete (.bak) file
      Windows::Forms::DialogResult result = MessageBox::Show(
         String::Concat( S"Found backup file ", fileName,
         S". Delete?" ), S"Delete Backup",
         MessageBoxButtons::YesNo, MessageBoxIcon::Question );

      // delete file if user clicked 'yes'
      if ( result == DialogResult::Yes ) {
         File::Delete( fileArray[ myFile ] );

         extensionCount =
            Int32::Parse( found->Get( S"bak" ) ) - 1;

         found->Set( S"bak", extensionCount.ToString() );
      } // end inner if
   } // end outer if
} // end for
```

Fig. 17.7 Using regular expressions to determine file types. (Part 4 of 5.)

```
197
198                 // recursive call to search files in subdirectory
199                 for ( int i = 0; i < directoryList->Length; i++ )
200                    SearchDirectory( directoryList[ i ] );
201              } // end try
202
203              // handle exception if files have unauthorized access
204              catch ( UnauthorizedAccessException * ) {
205                 MessageBox::Show( String::Concat(
206                    S"Some files may not be visible due to permission ",
207                    S"settings\n" ), S"Warning",
208                    MessageBoxButtons::OK, MessageBoxIcon::Information );
209              } // end catch
210           } // end method SearchDirectory
211        };
212     }
```

Fig. 17.7 Using regular expressions to determine file types. (Part 5 of 5.)

When the user presses the *Enter* key or clicks the **Search Directory** button, the program invokes method `searchButton_Click` (lines 76–120 of Fig. 17.7), which searches recursively through the directory path that the user provides. If the user inputs text in the `TextBox`, line 83 calls method `Exists` of class `Directory` to determine whether that text indicates a valid directory. If the user specifies an invalid directory, lines 93–94 notify the user of the error and line 96 `returns` from the method.

If the directory is valid, lines 101–102 clear the `TextBoxes`. Line 104 then changes the user's mouse cursor using class *`Cursor`* (located in namespace `System::Windows::Forms`). Class `Cursor` represents the image used as the mouse cursor. Class *`Cursors`* (also located in namespace `System::Windows::Forms`), contains several `Cursor` objects that programmers can use. Line 104 sets `Cursor` property `Current` to `Cursors::`*`WaitCursor`*, which is a `Cursor` object that represents the *wait cursor*—usually an hourglass symbol. Thus, while the program searches, an hourglass symbol will be used as the mouse cursor.[2] This is demonstrated in the screen captures at the end of Fig. 17.8.

```
// Fig. 17.8: Form1.cpp
// Entry point for application.

#include "stdafx.h"
#include "Form1.h"
#include <windows.h>

using namespace FileSearch;

```

Fig. 17.8 `FileSearch` entry point. (Part 1 of 2.)

2. For more information about changing the mouse cursor, visit `msdn.microsoft.com/library/default.asp?url=/library/en-us/cpref/html/frlrfSystemWindowsFormsCursorClassTopic.asp`.

```
int APIENTRY _tWinMain(HINSTANCE hInstance,
                       HINSTANCE hPrevInstance,
                       LPTSTR    lpCmdLine,
                       int       nCmdShow)
{
   System::Threading::Thread::CurrentThread->ApartmentState =
      System::Threading::ApartmentState::STA;
   Application::Run(new Form1());
   return 0;
} // end _tWinMain
```

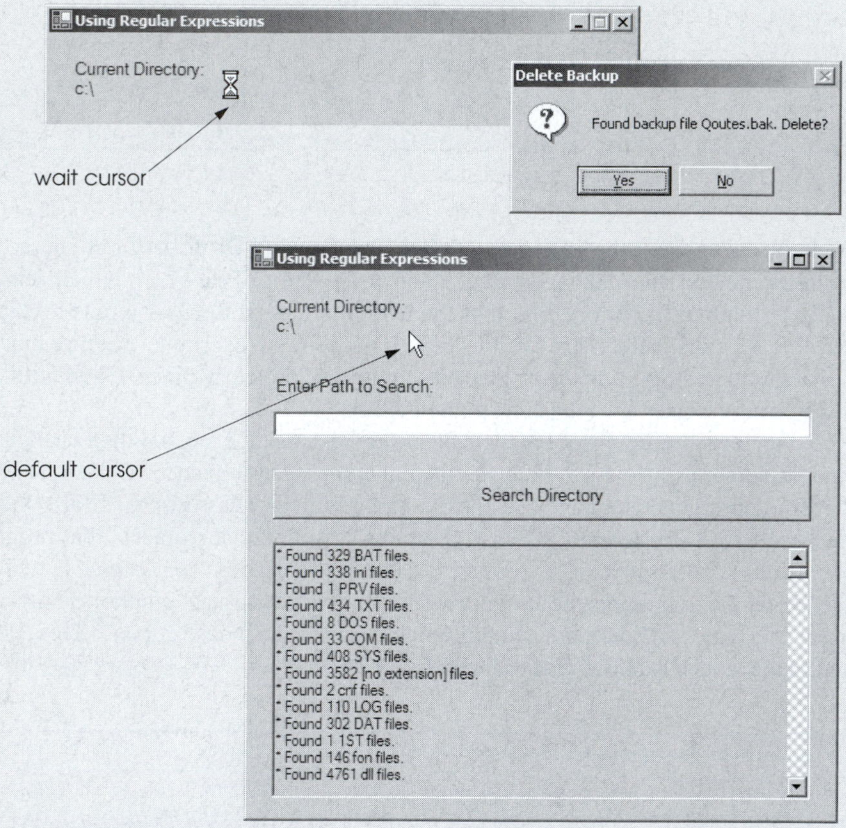

Fig. 17.8 `FileSearch` entry point. (Part 2 of 2.)

Line 106 then passes the directory name as an argument to `private` method `SearchDirectory` (lines 125–210). This method locates files that match the regular expression defined in lines 132–133, which matches any sequence of numbers or letters followed by a period and one or more letters. Notice the substring of format `(?<extension>`*regular-expression*`)` in the argument to the `Regex` constructor (line 133). This causes the portion of a `String` that matches *regular-expression* to be stored in a variable with the identifier `extension`. In this program, we assign to the variable `extension` any `String` matching one or more characters (i.e., `\w+`). The matched `String` can then be accessed later.

Lines 144–145 call method GetDirectories of class Directory to retrieve the names of all subdirectories that belong to the current directory. Lines 148–149 call method GetFiles of class Directory to store in String * array fileArray the names of files in the current directory. The for loop in lines 152–196 analyzes each file in the current directory; it then calls SearchDirectory recursively for each subdirectory in the current directory. Lines 155–156 eliminate the directory path, so the program can test only the file name when using the regular expression. Line 159 uses method Match of the Regex object to match the regular expression with the file name, then returns the result to object matchResult of type Match. If the match is successful, line 163 use method Result of object matchResult to store the extension variable from object matchResult in fileExtension (recall that line 133 stores the String that will contain the current file's extension in variable extension). The syntax for retrieving a variable using method Result is ${*variable-name*} (e.g., ${extension}). If the match is unsuccessful, line 165 sets fileExtension to hold the value "[no extension]".

Class Form1 uses an instance of class *NameValueCollection* (created in line 34 of Fig. 17.7) to store each file-extension type and the number of files for each type. A NameValueCollection contains a collection of key/value pairs, each of which is a String *, and provides method *Add* to add a key/value pair. The indexer for this pair can index according to the order that the items were added or according to the entry key. Line 168 (Fig. 17.7) uses NameValueCollection found to determine whether this is the first occurrence of the file extension. If so, line 169 adds that extension to found as a key with the value 1. If the extension is in found already, lines 171–174 increment the value associated with the extension in found to indicate another occurrence of that file extension.

Line 178 determines whether fileExtension equals "bak"—i.e., whether the file is a backup file. If so, lines 181–184 prompt the user to indicate whether the file should be removed; if the user clicks **Yes** (line 187), lines 188–193 delete the file and decrement the value for the "bak" file type in found.

Line 200 calls method SearchDirectory for each subdirectory. Using recursion, we ensure that the program performs the same logic for finding bak files on each subdirectory. After each subdirectory has been analyzed, method SearchDirectory completes. Line 108 then restores the user's mouse cursor to the *default cursor*—usually an arrow symbol—using class Cursors::*Default*. Finally, lines 111–115 display the search results in outputTextBox.

17.5 Creating a Sequential-Access File

The .NET Framework imposes no structure on files (i.e., concepts like that of a "record" do not exist). This means that the programmer must structure files to meet the requirements of applications. In the next example, we use text and special characters to organize our own concept of a "record."

The following examples demonstrate file processing in a bank-account maintenance application. These programs have similar user interfaces, so we created class BankUIForm (Fig. 17.9) to encapsulate a base-class GUI. (See the screen capture in Fig. 17.9.) Class BankUIForm contains four Labels (lines 43, 46, 49 and 52 of Fig. 17.9) and four TextBoxes (lines 44, 47, 50 and 53). Methods ClearTextBoxes (lines 79–92 of Fig. 17.9), SetTextBoxValues (lines 95–115) and GetTextBoxValues (lines 118–129) clear, set the values of, and get the values of the text in the TextBoxes, respectively.

```
// Fig. 17.9: BankUIForm.h
// A reusable windows form for the examples in this chapter.

#pragma once

using namespace System;
using namespace System::ComponentModel;
using namespace System::Collections;
using namespace System::Windows::Forms;
using namespace System::Data;
using namespace System::Drawing;


namespace BankLibrary
{
   /// <summary>
   /// Summary for BankUIForm
   ///
   /// WARNING: If you change the name of this class, you will need to
   ///          change the 'Resource File Name' property for the managed
   ///          resource compiler tool associated with all .resx files
   ///          this class depends on.  Otherwise, the designers will not
   ///          be able to interact properly with localized resources
   ///          associated with this form.
   /// </summary>
   public __gc class BankUIForm : public System::Windows::Forms::Form
   {
   public:
      BankUIForm(void)
      {
         InitializeComponent();
      }

   protected:
      void Dispose(Boolean disposing)
      {
         if (disposing && components)
         {
            components->Dispose();
         }
         __super::Dispose(disposing);
      }
   public: System::Windows::Forms::Label *  accountLabel;
   public: System::Windows::Forms::TextBox *  accountTextBox;

   public: System::Windows::Forms::Label *  firstNameLabel;
   public: System::Windows::Forms::TextBox *  firstNameTextBox;

   public: System::Windows::Forms::Label *  lastNameLabel;
   public: System::Windows::Forms::TextBox *  lastNameTextBox;

   public: System::Windows::Forms::Label *  balanceLabel;
   public: System::Windows::Forms::TextBox *  balanceTextBox;
```

Fig. 17.9 Base class for GUIs in our file-processing applications. (Part 1 of 3.)

```

   protected: static int TextBoxCount = 4; // number of TextBoxes on Form

   public:

      // enumeration constants specify TextBox indices
      __value enum TextBoxIndices
      {
         ACCOUNT,
         FIRST,
         LAST,
         BALANCE
      }; // end enum

   private:
      /// <summary>
      /// Required designer variable.
      /// </summary>
      System::ComponentModel::Container* components;

   // Visual Studio .NET generated GUI code

   public:

      // clear all TextBoxes
      void ClearTextBoxes()
      {
         // iterate through every Control on form
         for ( int i = 0; i < Controls->Count; i++ ) {
            Control *myControl = Controls->Item[ i ]; // get control

            // determine whether Control is TextBox
            if ( myControl->GetType() == __typeof( TextBox ) ) {

               // clear Text property (set to empty string)
               myControl->Text = S"";
            } // end if
         } // end for
      } // end method ClearTextBoxes

      // set text box values to String array values
      void SetTextBoxValues( String *values[] )
      {
         // determine whether String array has correct length
         if ( values->Length != TextBoxCount ) {

            // throw exception if not correct length
            throw ( new ArgumentException( String::Concat(
               S"There must be ", ( TextBoxCount + 1 ).ToString(),
               S" strings in the array" ) ) );
         } // end if

```

Fig. 17.9 Base class for GUIs in our file-processing applications. (Part 2 of 3.)

```
106          // set array values if array has correct length
107          else {
108
109             // set array values to text box values
110             accountTextBox->Text = values[ TextBoxIndices::ACCOUNT ];
111             firstNameTextBox->Text = values[ TextBoxIndices::FIRST ];
112             lastNameTextBox->Text = values[ TextBoxIndices::LAST ];
113             balanceTextBox->Text = values[ TextBoxIndices::BALANCE ];
114          } // end else
115       } // end method SetTextBoxValues
116
117       // return text box values as string array
118       String *GetTextBoxValues() []
119       {
120          String *values[] = new String*[ TextBoxCount ];
121
122          // copy text box fields to string array
123          values[ TextBoxIndices::ACCOUNT ] = accountTextBox->Text;
124          values[ TextBoxIndices::FIRST ] = firstNameTextBox->Text;
125          values[ TextBoxIndices::LAST ] = lastNameTextBox->Text;
126          values[ TextBoxIndices::BALANCE ] = balanceTextBox->Text;
127
128          return values;
129       } // end method GetTextBoxValues
130    };
131 }
```

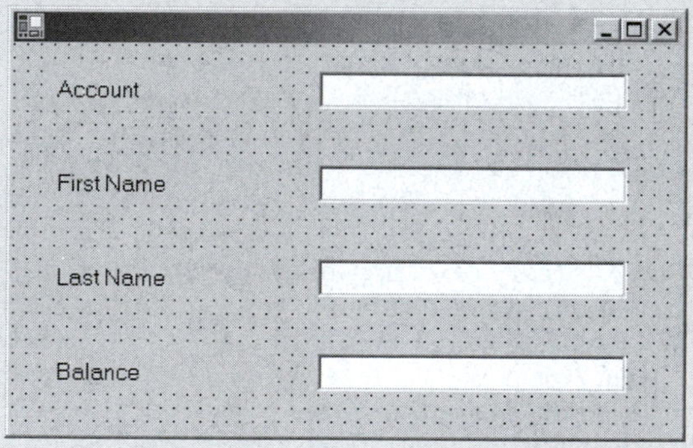

Fig. 17.9 Base class for GUIs in our file-processing applications. (Part 3 of 3.)

Notice that line 128 of method `GetTextBoxValues` returns a managed array of `String *` objects (`values`). Recall from Chapter 4 that any method that returns a managed array must suffix its definition with the dimensions of the array. For this reason, line 118 declares method `GetTextBoxValues` as

```
String *GetTextBoxValues() []
```

The `[]` notation indicates that method `GetTextBoxValues` will return a managed array with one dimension.

To reuse class `BankUIForm`, we compile the GUI into a DLL (dynamic link library) by creating a project of type **Managed C++ Class Library**. (The DLL we create is called

BankLibrary.dll.) This library can be found on the CD at the back of this book. See Section 8.16 for information on how to create and reuse dynamic link libraries.

Figure 17.10–Fig. 17.11 contain class Record, which Fig. 17.12–Fig. 17.13, Fig. 17.15–Fig. 17.16 and Fig. 17.17–Fig. 17.18 use for reading records from, and writing records to, a file sequentially. This class also belongs to the BankLibrary DLL, so it is located in the same project as is class BankUIForm.

```
// Fig. 17.10: Record.h
// Serializable class that represents a data record.

#pragma once

#using <mscorlib.dll>

using namespace System;

namespace BankLibrary
{
   [Serializable]
   public __gc class Record
   {
   public:

      // default constructor sets members to default values
      Record();
      Record( int, String *, String *, double );

      // set method for property Account
      __property void set_Account( int value )
      {
         account = value;
      }

      // get method for property Account
      __property int get_Account()
      {
         return account;
      }

      // set method for property FirstName
      __property void set_FirstName( String *value )
      {
         firstName = value;
      }

      // get method for property FirstName
      __property String *get_FirstName()
      {
         return firstName;
      }

```

Fig. 17.10 Serializable class that represents a data record. (Part 1 of 2.)

```
      // set method for property LastName
      __property void set_LastName( String *value )
      {
         lastName = value;
      }

      // get method for property LastName
      __property String *get_LastName()
      {
         return lastName;
      }

      // set method for property Balance
      __property void set_Balance( double value )
      {
         balance = value;
      }

      // get method for property Balance
      __property double get_Balance()
      {
         return balance;
      }

   private:
      int account;
      String *firstName;
      String *lastName;
      double balance;
   }; // end class Record
} // end namespace BankLibrary
```

Fig. 17.10 Serializable class that represents a data record. (Part 2 of 2.)

```
// Fig. 17.11: Record.cpp
// Method definitions for class Record.

#include "stdafx.h"
#include "Record.h"

using namespace BankLibrary;

// default constructor sets members to default values
Record::Record()
{
   Account = 0;
   FirstName = S"";
   LastName = S"";
   Balance = 0.0;
}

```

Fig. 17.11 Record class method definitions. (Part 1 of 2.)

```
18  // overloaded constructor sets members to parameter values
19  Record::Record( int accountValue, String *firstNameValue,
20     String *lastNameValue, double balanceValue )
21  {
22     Account = accountValue;
23     FirstName = firstNameValue;
24     LastName = lastNameValue;
25     Balance = balanceValue;
26  } // end constructor
```

Fig. 17.11 Record class method definitions. (Part 2 of 2.)

The *Serializable* attribute (line 12 of Fig. 17.10) indicates to the compiler that objects of class Record can be *serialized*—written to or read from a stream as objects. Objects that we wish to write to or read from a stream must include this attribute in their class definitions. Conversely, attribute *NonSerialized* can be used to indicate certain fields that should not be serialized.[3] *Attributes* are identifers (within square brackets) that specify additional information in a declaration. Attributes are used to define the underlying behavior of classes, methods or variables. The code that defines an attribute is applied at runtime.

Class Record contains private data members account, firstName, lastName and balance (lines 70–73), which collectively represent all information necessary to store record data. The default constructor (lines 10–16 of Fig. 17.11) sets these members to their default (i.e., empty) values, and the overloaded constructor (lines 19–26) sets these members to specified parameter values. Class Record also provides properties Account (lines 22–31 of Fig. 17.10), FirstName (lines 34–43), LastName (lines 46–55) and Balance (lines 58–67) for accessing the account number, first name, last name and balance of each customer, respectively.

Class Form1 (Fig. 17.12) uses instances of class Record to create a sequential-access file that might be used in an accounts receivable system—a program that organizes data regarding money owed by a company's credit clients. For each client, the program obtains an account number and the client's first name, last name and balance (i.e., the amount of money that the client owes to the company for previously received goods or services). The data obtained for each client constitutes a record for that client. In this application, the account number represents the record key—files are created and maintained in account-number order. This program assumes that the user enters records in account-number order. However, a comprehensive accounts receivable system would provide a sorting capability. The user could enter the records in any order, and the records then could be sorted and written to the file in order. (Note that all outputs in this chapter should be read row by row, from left to right in each row.)

```
// Fig. 17.12: Form1.h
// Creating a sequential-access file.

```

Fig. 17.12 CreateSequentialAccessFile program. (Part 1 of 5.)

3. For more information about serialization in .NET, visit www.msdnaa.net/interchange/preview.asp?PeerID=1399.

```
#pragma once


namespace CreateSequentialAccessFile
{
   using namespace System;
   using namespace System::ComponentModel;
   using namespace System::Collections;
   using namespace System::Windows::Forms;
   using namespace System::Data;
   using namespace System::Drawing;
   using namespace System::IO;
   using namespace System::Runtime::Serialization;
   using namespace System::Runtime::Serialization::Formatters::Binary;
   using namespace BankLibrary;   // Deitel namespace

   /// <summary>
   /// Summary for Form1
   ///
   /// WARNING: If you change the name of this class, you will need to
   ///          change the 'Resource File Name' property for the managed
   ///          resource compiler tool associated with all .resx files
   ///          this class depends on.  Otherwise, the designers will not
   ///          be able to interact properly with localized resources
   ///          associated with this form.
   /// </summary>
   public __gc class Form1 : public BankUIForm
   {
   public:
      Form1(void)
      {
         InitializeComponent();
      }

   protected:
      void Dispose(Boolean disposing)
      {
         if (disposing && components)
         {
            components->Dispose();
         }
         __super::Dispose(disposing);
      }
   private: System::Windows::Forms::Button *  saveButton;
   private: System::Windows::Forms::Button *  enterButton;
   private: System::Windows::Forms::Button *  exitButton;

   // serializes Record in binary format
   private: static BinaryFormatter *formatter = new BinaryFormatter();

   // stream through which serializable data is written to file
   private: FileStream *output;

```

Fig. 17.12 CreateSequentialAccessFile program. (Part 2 of 5.)

```
      private:
         /// <summary>
         /// Required designer variable.
         /// </summary>
         System::ComponentModel::Container * components;

      // Visual Studio .NET generated GUI code

      // invoked when user clicks Save button
      private: System::Void saveButton_Click(
                  System::Object *  sender, System::EventArgs *  e)
               {
                  // create dialog box enabling user to save file
                  SaveFileDialog *fileChooser = new SaveFileDialog();

                  Windows::Forms::DialogResult result =
                     fileChooser->ShowDialog();

                  String *fileName; // name of file to save data

                  // allow user to create file
                  fileChooser->CheckFileExists = false;

                  // exit event handler if user clicked "Cancel"
                  if ( result == DialogResult::Cancel )
                     return;

                  // get specified file name
                  fileName = fileChooser->FileName;

                  // show error if user specified invalid file
                  if ( ( fileName->Equals( S"" ) ) )
                     MessageBox::Show( S"Invalid File Name", S"Error",
                        MessageBoxButtons::OK, MessageBoxIcon::Error );
                  else {

                     // save file via FileStream if user specified valid file
                     try {

                        // open file with write access
                        output = new FileStream( fileName,
                           FileMode::OpenOrCreate, FileAccess::Write );

                        // disable Save As button and enable Enter button
                        saveButton->Enabled = false;
                        enterButton->Enabled = true;
                     } // end try

                     // handle exception if file does not exist
                     catch ( FileNotFoundException * ) {

```

Fig. 17.12 `CreateSequentialAccessFile` program. (Part 3 of 5.)

```
                     // notify user if file does not exist
                     MessageBox::Show( S"File Does Not Exist", S"Error",
                        MessageBoxButtons::OK, MessageBoxIcon::Error );
                  } // end catch
               } // end else
            } // end method saveButton_Click

   // invoke when user clicks Enter button
   private: System::Void enterButton_Click(
               System::Object *  sender, System::EventArgs *  e)
            {
               // store TextBox values string array
               String *values[] = GetTextBoxValues();

               // Record containing TextBox values to serialize
               Record *record = new Record();

               // determine whether TextBox account field is empty
               if ( values[ TextBoxIndices::ACCOUNT ] != S"" ) {

                  // store TextBox values in Record and serialize Record
                  try {

                     // get account number value from TextBox
                     int accountNumber = Int32::Parse(
                        values[ TextBoxIndices::ACCOUNT ] );

                     // determine whether accountNumber is valid
                     if ( accountNumber > 0 ) {

                        // store TextBox fields in Record
                        record->Account = accountNumber;
                        record->FirstName =
                           values[ TextBoxIndices::FIRST ];
                        record->LastName =
                           values[ TextBoxIndices::LAST ];
                        record->Balance = Double::Parse(
                           values[ TextBoxIndices::BALANCE ] );

                        // write Record to FileStream (serialize object)
                        formatter->Serialize( output, record );
                     } // end if
                     else {

                        // notify user if invalid account number
                        MessageBox::Show(
                           S"Invalid Account Number", S"Error",
                           MessageBoxButtons::OK, MessageBoxIcon::Error );
                     } // end else
                  } // end try

```

Fig. 17.12 CreateSequentialAccessFile program. (Part 4 of 5.)

```
159                  // notify user if error occurs in serialization
160                  catch ( SerializationException * ) {
161                     MessageBox::Show( S"Error Writing to File", S"Error",
162                        MessageBoxButtons::OK, MessageBoxIcon::Error );
163                  } // end catch
164
165                  // notify user if error occurs from parameter format
166                  catch( FormatException * ) {
167                     MessageBox::Show( S"Invalid Format", S"Error",
168                        MessageBoxButtons::OK, MessageBoxIcon::Error );
169                  } // end catch
170               } // end if
171
172               ClearTextBoxes(); // clear TextBox values
173            } // end method enterButton_Click
174
175      // invoked when user clicks Exit button
176      private: System::Void exitButton_Click(
177               System::Object *  sender, System::EventArgs *  e)
178            {
179               // determine whether file exists
180               if ( output != 0 ) {
181
182                  // close file
183                  try {
184                     output->Close();
185                  } // end try
186
187                  // notify user of error closing file
188                  catch ( IOException * ) {
189                     MessageBox::Show( S"Cannot close file", S"Error",
190                        MessageBoxButtons::OK, MessageBoxIcon::Error );
191                  } // end catch
192               } // end if
193
194               Application::Exit();
195            } // end method exitButton_Click
196      };
197   }
```

Fig. 17.12 `CreateSequentialAccessFile` program. (Part 5 of 5.)

Figure 17.12 contains the code for class `Form1`, which either creates or opens a file (depending on whether one exists), then allows the user to write bank information to that file. Line 18 imports the `BankLibrary` namespace; this namespace contains class `BankUIForm`, from which class `Form1` inherits (line 30). Because of this inheritance relationship, the `Form1` GUI is similar to that of class `BankUIForm` (shown in the Fig. 17.13 output), except that the inherited class contains buttons **Save As**, **Enter** and **Exit**. Review Section 13.10 for more information about visual inheritance.

When the user clicks the **Save As** button, the program invokes method `saveButton_Click` (lines 66–113 of Fig. 17.12). Line 70 instantiates an object of class *`SaveFileDialog`*, which belongs to the `System::Windows::Forms` namespace. Objects of this class are used for selecting files (as shown in the second image in Fig. 17.13). Line 73 calls method *ShowDialog* of the `SaveFileDialog` object to display the `SaveFileDialog`. When displayed, a `SaveFileDialog` prevents the user from interacting with any other window in the program until the user closes the `SaveFileDialog` by clicking either **Save** or **Cancel**. Dialogs that behave in this fashion are called *modal dialogs*. The user selects the appropriate drive, directory and file name, then clicks **Save**. Method `ShowDialog` returns an integer specifying which button (**Save** or **Cancel**) the user clicked to close the dialog. In this example, the `Form` property `DialogResult` receives this integer. Line 81 tests for whether the user clicked **Cancel** by comparing the value returned by property `DialogResult` to constant *DialogResult::Cancel*. If the values are equal, method `saveButton_Click` returns (line 82). If the values are unequal (i.e., the user clicked **Save**, instead of clicking **Cancel**), line 85 uses property *FileName* of class `SaveFileDialog` to obtain the user-selected file.

```
// Fig. 17.13: Form1.cpp
// Entry point for application.

#include "stdafx.h"
#include "Form1.h"
#include <windows.h>

using namespace CreateSequentialAccessFile;

int APIENTRY _tWinMain(HINSTANCE hInstance,
                       HINSTANCE hPrevInstance,
                       LPTSTR    lpCmdLine,
                       int       nCmdShow)
{
   System::Threading::Thread::CurrentThread->ApartmentState =
      System::Threading::ApartmentState::STA;
   Application::Run(new Form1());
   return 0;
} // end _tWinMain
```

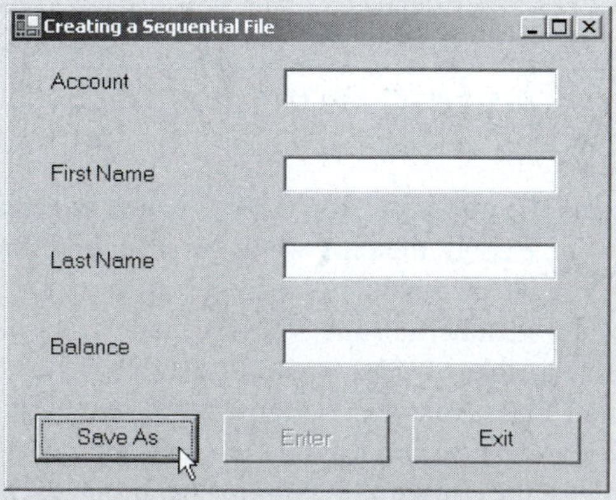

Fig. 17.13 `CreateSequentialAccessFile` entry point. (Part 1 of 3.)

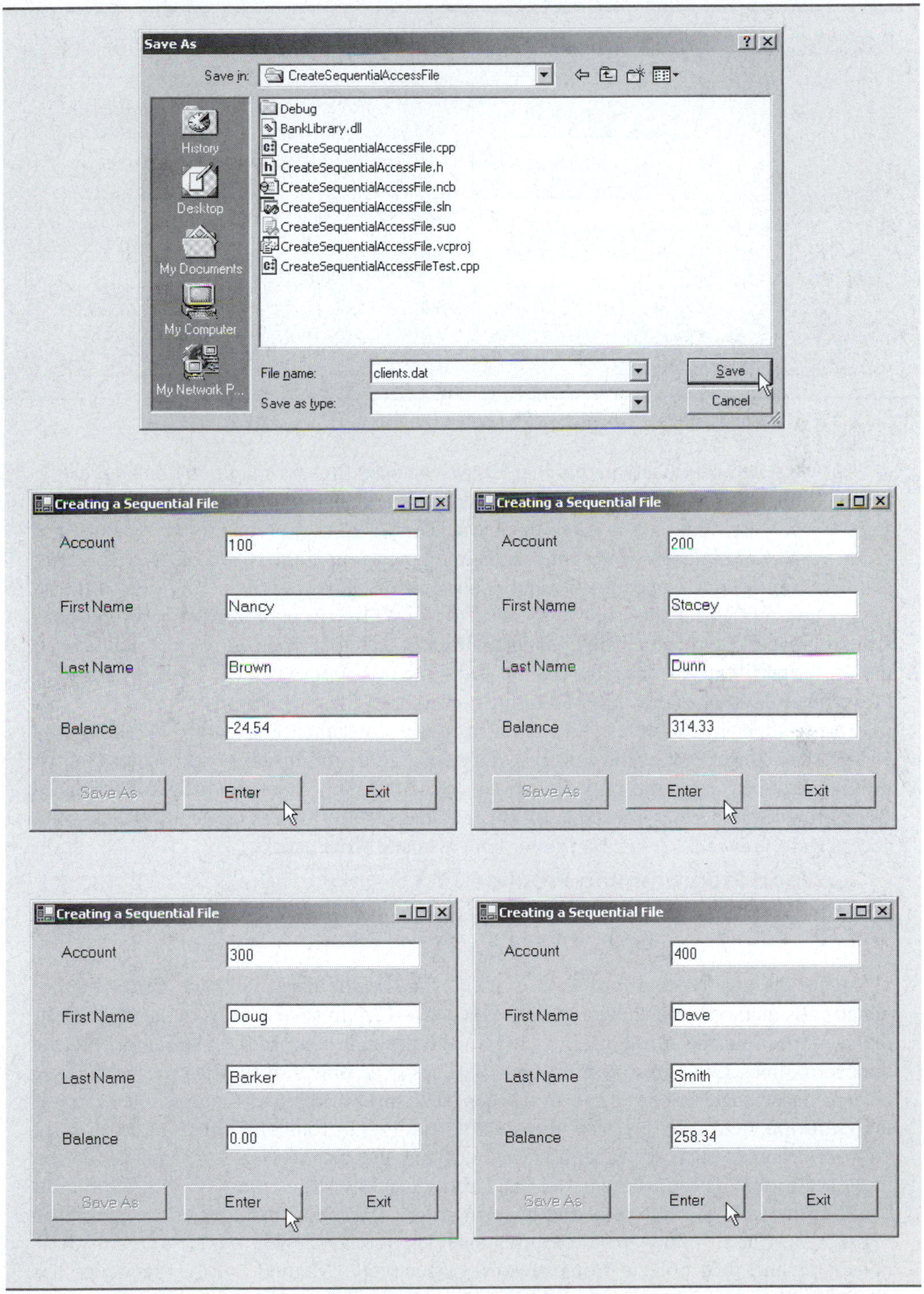

Fig. 17.13 `CreateSequentialAccessFile` entry point. (Part 2 of 3.)

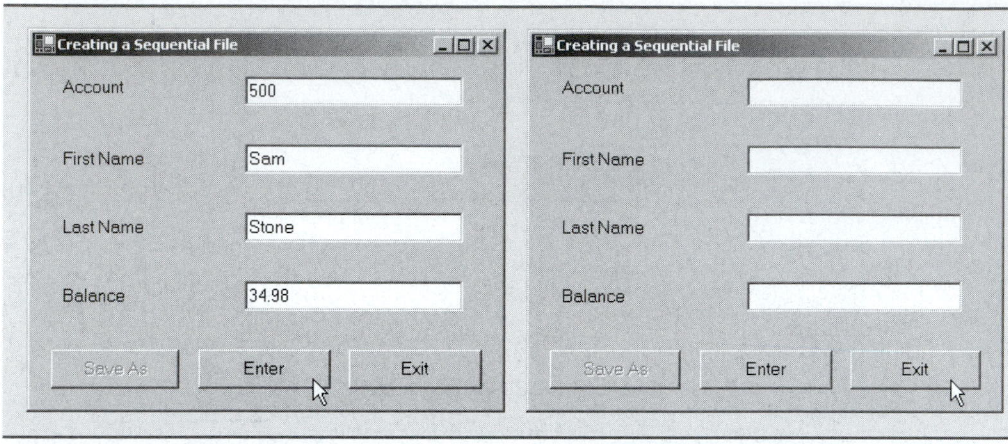

Fig. 17.13 `CreateSequentialAccessFile` entry point. (Part 3 of 3.)

As we stated previously in this chapter, we can open files for manipulation by creating objects of classes `FileStream`. In this example, we want the file to be opened for output, so lines 97–98 instantiate a `FileStream` object. The `FileStream` constructor that we use receives three arguments—a `String *` containing the name of the file to be opened, a constant describing how to open the file and a constant describing the file permissions. Line 98 passes constant `FileMode::OpenOrCreate` to the `FileStream` constructor as the constructor's second argument. This constant indicates that the `FileStream` object should open the file if the file exists or create the file if the file does not exist. The .NET Framework offers other `FileMode` constants describing how to open files; we introduce these constants as we use them in examples. Line 98 also passes constant `FileAccess::Write` to the `FileStream` constructor as the constructor's third argument. This constant ensures that the program can perform write-only operations on the `FileStream` object. The .NET Framework provides two other constants for this parameter—`FileAccess::Read` for read-only access and `FileAccess::ReadWrite` for both read and write access.

Good Programming Practice 17.1

When opening files, use the `FileAccess` enumeration to control user access to these files.

After the user types information in each `TextBox`, the user clicks the **Enter** button, which calls method `enterButton_Click` (lines 116–173) to save data from the `TextBox` in the user-specified file. If the user entered a valid account number (i.e., an integer greater than zero), lines 139–145 store the `TextBox` values in an object of type `Record`. If the user entered invalid data in one of the `TextBoxes` (such as entering non-numeric characters in the **Balance** field), the program throws a `FormatException`. The `catch` block in lines 166–169 handles such an exception by notifying the user (via a `MessageBox`) of the improper format. If the user entered valid data, line 148 writes the record to the file by invoking method `Serialize` of the `BinaryFormatter` object (instantiated in line 52 of Fig. 17.12). Class `BinaryFormatter` uses methods *`Serialize`* and *`Deserialize`* to write objects to and read objects from streams, respectively. Method `Serialize` writes the object's representation to a stream. Method `Deserialize` reads this representation from a stream and reconstructs the original object. Both methods throw a `SerializationExcep-`

`tion` if an error occurs during serialization or deserialization (errors result when the methods attempt to access streams or records that do not exist). Both methods `Serialize` and `Deserialize` require a `Stream` object (e.g., the `FileStream`) as a parameter so that the `BinaryFormatter` can access the correct file. Class `BinaryFormatter` belongs to the *`System::Runtime::Serialization::Formatters::Binary`* namespace.

Common Programming Error 17.1

Failure to open a file before attempting to reference it in a program is a logic error.

When the user clicks the **Exit** button, the program invokes method `exitButton_Click` (lines 176–195 of Fig. 17.12) to exit the application. Line 184 closes the `FileStream` if one has been opened, and line 194 exits the program.

Performance Tip 17.1

Close each file explicitly when the program no longer needs to reference the file. This can reduce resource usage in programs that continue executing long after they finish using a specific file. The practice of explicitly closing files also improves program clarity.

Performance Tip 17.2

Releasing resources explicitly when they are no longer needed makes them immediately available for reuse by the program, thus improving resource utilization.

In the sample execution for the program in Fig. 17.12–Fig. 17.13, we entered information for five accounts (Fig. 17.14). The program does not depict how the data records are rendered in the file. To verify that the file has been created successfully, in the next section, we create a program to read and display the file.

Account Number	First Name	Last Name	Balance
100	Nancy	Brown	-25.54
200	Stacey	Dunn	314.33
300	Doug	Barker	0.00
400	Dave	Smith	258.34
500	Sam	Stone	34.98

Fig. 17.14 Sample data for the program of Fig. 17.12–Fig. 17.13.

17.6 Reading Data from a Sequential-Access File

Data are stored in files so that they can be retrieved for processing when they are needed. The previous section demonstrated how to create a file for use in sequential-access applications. In this section, we discuss how to read (or retrieve) data sequentially from a file.

Class `Form1` (Fig. 17.15) reads records from the file created by the program in Fig. 17.12–Fig. 17.13, then displays the contents of each record. Much of the code in this example is similar to that of Fig. 17.12–Fig. 17.13, so we discuss only the unique aspects of the application.

```
// Fig. 17.15: Form1.h
// Reading a sequential-access file.

#pragma once


namespace ReadSequentialAccessFile
{
   using namespace System;
   using namespace System::ComponentModel;
   using namespace System::Collections;
   using namespace System::Windows::Forms;
   using namespace System::Data;
   using namespace System::Drawing;
   using namespace System::IO;
   using namespace System::Runtime::Serialization;
   using namespace System::Runtime::Serialization::Formatters::Binary;
   using namespace BankLibrary;   // Deitel namespace

   /// <summary>
   /// Summary for Form1
   ///
   /// WARNING: If you change the name of this class, you will need to
   ///          change the 'Resource File Name' property for the managed
   ///          resource compiler tool associated with all .resx files
   ///          this class depends on.  Otherwise, the designers will not
   ///          be able to interact properly with localized resources
   ///          associated with this form.
   /// </summary>
   public __gc class Form1 : public BankUIForm
   {
   public:
      Form1(void)
      {
         InitializeComponent();
      }

   protected:
      void Dispose(Boolean disposing)
      {
         if (disposing && components)
         {
            components->Dispose();
         }
         __super::Dispose(disposing);
      }
   private: System::Windows::Forms::Button *  openButton;
   private: System::Windows::Forms::Button *  nextButton;

   // stream through which serializable data are read from file
   private: FileStream *input;

```

Fig. 17.15 ReadSequentialAccessFile reads a sequential-access file. (Part 1 of 3.)

```
   // object for deserializing Record in binary format
   private: static BinaryFormatter *reader = new BinaryFormatter();

   private:
      /// <summary>
      /// Required designer variable.
      /// </summary>
      System::ComponentModel::Container * components;

   // Visual Studio .NET generated GUI code

   // invoked when user clicks Open File button
   private: System::Void openButton_Click(
               System::Object *  sender, System::EventArgs *  e)
            {
               // create dialog box enabling user to open file
               OpenFileDialog *fileChooser = new OpenFileDialog();
               Windows::Forms::DialogResult result =
                  fileChooser->ShowDialog();
               String *fileName; // name of file containing data

               // exit event handler if user clicked Cancel
               if ( result == DialogResult::Cancel )
                  return;

               // get specified file name
               fileName = fileChooser->FileName;
               ClearTextBoxes();

               // show error if user specified invalid file
               if ( ( fileName->Equals( S"" ) ) )
                  MessageBox::Show( S"Invalid File Name", S"Error",
                  MessageBoxButtons::OK, MessageBoxIcon::Error );
               else {

                  // create FileStream to obtain read access to file
                  input = new FileStream( fileName, FileMode::Open,
                     FileAccess::Read );

                  // enable next record button
                  nextButton->Enabled = true;
               } // end else
            } // end method openButton_Click

   // invoked when user clicks Next Record button
   private: System::Void nextButton_Click(
               System::Object *  sender, System::EventArgs *  e)
            {
               // deserialize Record and store data in TextBoxes
               try {

                  // get next Record available in file
```

Fig. 17.15 ReadSequentialAccessFile reads a sequential-access file. (Part 2 of 3.)

```
105                 Record *record = dynamic_cast< Record *>(
106                    reader->Deserialize( input ) );
107
108                 // store Record values in temporary string array
109                 String *values[] = { record->Account.ToString(),
110                    record->FirstName->ToString(),
111                    record->LastName->ToString(),
112                    record->Balance.ToString() };
113
114                 // copy string array values to TextBox values
115                 SetTextBoxValues( values );
116              } // end try
117
118              // handle exception when no Records in file
119              catch ( SerializationException * ) {
120
121                 // close FileStream if no Records in file
122                 input->Close();
123
124                 // enable Open File button
125                 openButton->Enabled = true;
126
127                 // disable Next Record button
128                 nextButton->Enabled = false;
129
130                 ClearTextBoxes();
131
132                 // notify user if no Records in file
133                 MessageBox::Show( S"No more records in file", S"",
134                    MessageBoxButtons::OK, MessageBoxIcon::Information );
135              } // end catch
136           } // end method nextButton_Click
137     };
138  }
```

Fig. 17.15 `ReadSequentialAccessFile` reads a sequential-access file. (Part 3 of 3.)

When the user clicks the **Open File** button, the program calls method `openButton_Click` (lines 65–95 of Fig. 17.15). Line 69 instantiates an object of class *`OpenFileDialog`*, and line 71 calls the object's *`ShowDialog`* method to display the **Open** dialog. (See the second screenshot in Fig. 17.16.) The behavior and GUI for this dialog and the `SaveFileDialog` are the same (except that **Save** is replaced by **Open**). If the user inputs a valid file name, lines 89–90 create a `FileStream` object and assign it to pointer `input`. We pass constant `FileMode::Open` as the second argument to the `FileStream` constructor. This constant indicates that the `FileStream` should open the file if the file exists or should throw a `FileNotFoundException` if the file does not exist. (In this example, the `FileStream` constructor will not throw a `FileNotFoundException`, because the `OpenFileDialog` requires the user to enter a name of a file that exists.) In the last example (Fig. 17.12–Fig. 17.13), we wrote text to the file, using a `FileStream` object with write-only access. In this example, (Fig. 17.15–Fig. 17.16), we specify read-only access to the file by passing constant `FileAccess::Read` as the third argument to the `FileStream` constructor.

```
// Fig. 17.16: Form1.cpp
// Entry point for application.

#include "stdafx.h"
#include "Form1.h"
#include <windows.h>

using namespace ReadSequentialAccessFile;

int APIENTRY _tWinMain(HINSTANCE hInstance,
                       HINSTANCE hPrevInstance,
                       LPTSTR    lpCmdLine,
                       int       nCmdShow)
{
   System::Threading::Thread::CurrentThread->ApartmentState =
      System::Threading::ApartmentState::STA;
   Application::Run(new Form1());
   return 0;
} // end _tWinMain
```

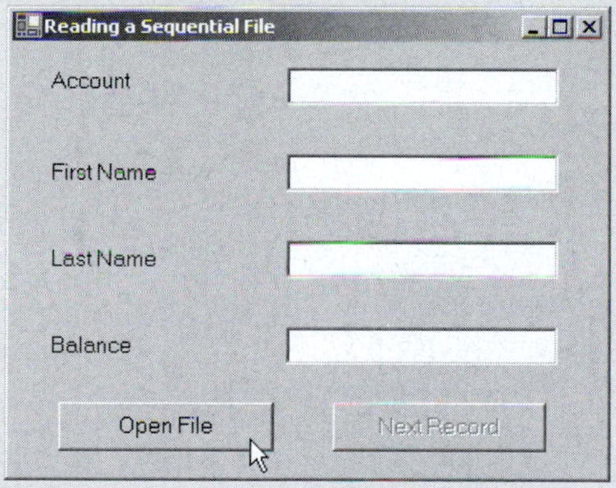

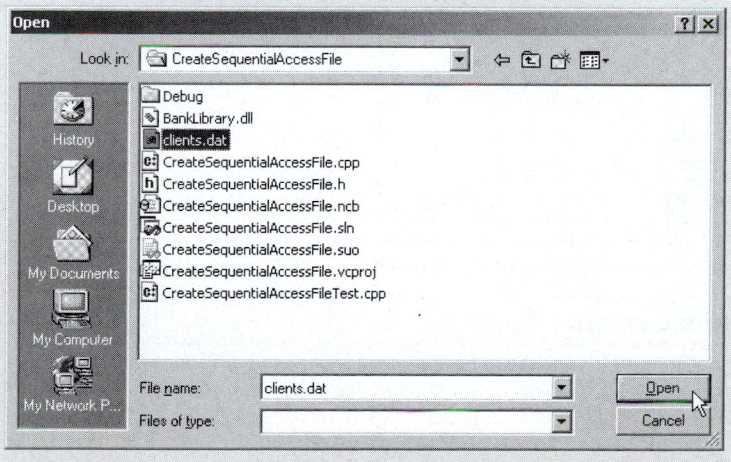

Fig. 17.16 `ReadSequentialAccessFile` entry point. (Part 1 of 2.)

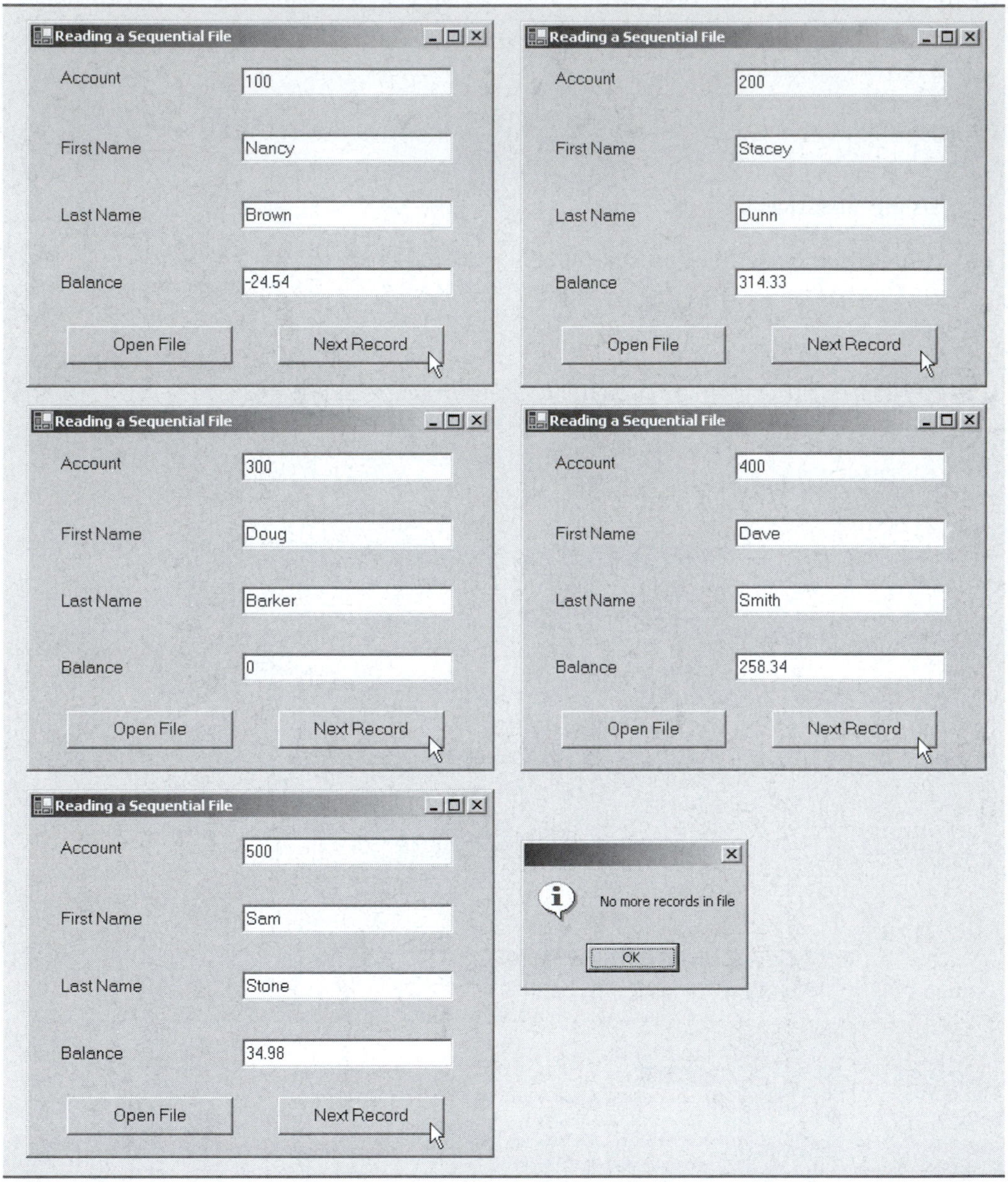

Fig. 17.16 `ReadSequentialAccessFile` entry point. (Part 2 of 2.)

Error-Prevention Tip 17.1

Open a file with the `FileAccess::Read` *file-open mode if the contents of the file should not be modified. This prevents unintentional modification of the file's contents.*

When the user clicks the **Next Record** button, the program calls method `nextButton_Click` (lines 98–136), which reads the next record from the user-specified file. (The user must click **Next Record** after opening the file to view the first record.) Line

106 calls method `Deserialize` of the `BinaryFormatter` object to read the next record and casts the result to a `Record`—this cast is necessary, because `Deserialize` returns a pointer of type `Object`. Lines 109–115 then display the `Record` values in the `TextBoxes`. When method `Deserialize` attempts to deserialize a record that does not exist in the file (i.e., the program has displayed all file records), the method throws a `SerializationException`. The `catch` block (lines 119–135) that handles this exception closes the `FileStream` object (line 122) and notifies the user that there are no more records (lines 133–134).

To retrieve data sequentially from a file, programs normally start from the beginning of the file, reading data consecutively until the desired data are found. It sometimes is necessary to process a file sequentially several times (from the beginning of the file) during the execution of a program. A `FileStream` object can reposition its *file-position pointer* (which contains the byte number of the next byte to be read from or written to the file) to any position in the file—we show this feature when we introduce random-access file-processing applications. When a `FileStream` object is opened, its file-position pointer is set to zero (i.e., the beginning of the file)

Performance Tip 17.3

It is time-consuming to close and reopen a file for the purpose of moving the file-position pointer to the file's beginning. Doing so frequently could slow program performance.

Credit Inquiry Program

We now present a more substantial program (Fig. 17.17–Fig. 17.18) that builds on the concepts employed in Fig. 17.15–Fig. 17.16. Class `Form1` (Fig. 17.17) is a credit-inquiry program that enables a credit manager to display account information for those customers with credit balances (i.e., customers to whom the company owes money), zero balances (i.e., customers who do not owe the company money) and debit balances (i.e., customers who owe the company money for previously received goods and services). Note that line 48 (Fig. 17.17) declares a *`RichTextBox`* that will display the account information. `RichTextBoxes` provide more functionality than do regular `TextBoxes`—for example, `RichTextBoxes` offer method *`Find`* for searching individual strings and method *`LoadFile`* for displaying file contents. Class `RichTextBox` does not inherit from class `TextBox`; rather, both classes inherit directly from `abstract` class *`System::Windows::Forms::TextBoxBase`*. We use a `RichTextBox` in this example, because a `RichTextBox` displays multiple lines of text by default, whereas a regular `TextBox` displays only one. Alternatively, we could have specified that a `TextBox` object display multiple lines of text by setting its `Multiline` property to `true`.

```
1  // Fig. 17.17: Form1.h
2  // Read a file sequentially and display contents based on
3  // account type specified by user (credit, debit or zero balances).
4
5  #pragma once
6
7
```

Fig. 17.17 `CreditInquiry` demonstrates reading and displaying contents from a sequential-access file. (Part 1 of 6.)

```
namespace CreditInquiry
{
   using namespace System;
   using namespace System::ComponentModel;
   using namespace System::Collections;
   using namespace System::Windows::Forms;
   using namespace System::Data;
   using namespace System::Drawing;
   using namespace System::IO;
   using namespace System::Runtime::Serialization;
   using namespace System::Runtime::Serialization::Formatters::Binary;
   using namespace BankLibrary;   // Deitel namespace

   /// <summary>
   /// Summary for Form1
   ///
   /// WARNING: If you change the name of this class, you will need to
   ///          change the 'Resource File Name' property for the managed
   ///          resource compiler tool associated with all .resx files
   ///          this class depends on.  Otherwise, the designers will not
   ///          be able to interact properly with localized resources
   ///          associated with this form.
   /// </summary>
   public __gc class Form1 : public System::Windows::Forms::Form
   {
   public:
      Form1(void)
      {
         InitializeComponent();
      }

   protected:
      void Dispose(Boolean disposing)
      {
         if (disposing && components)
         {
            components->Dispose();
         }
         __super::Dispose(disposing);
      }
   private: System::Windows::Forms::RichTextBox *  displayTextBox;

   private: System::Windows::Forms::Button *  doneButton;
   private: System::Windows::Forms::Button *  zeroButton;
   private: System::Windows::Forms::Button *  debitButton;
   private: System::Windows::Forms::Button *  creditButton;
   private: System::Windows::Forms::Button *  openButton;

   // stream through which serializable data are read from file
   private: FileStream *input;

```

Fig. 17.17 `CreditInquiry` demonstrates reading and displaying contents from a sequential-access file. (Part 2 of 6.)

```
   // object for deserializing Record in binary format
   private: static BinaryFormatter *reader = new BinaryFormatter();

   // name of file that stores credit, debit and zero balances
   private: String *fileName;

   private:
      /// <summary>
      /// Required designer variable.
      /// </summary>
      System::ComponentModel::Container * components;

   // Visual Studio .NET generated GUI code

   // invoked when user clicks Open File button
   private: System::Void openButton_Click(
               System::Object * sender, System::EventArgs * e)
            {
               // create dialog box enabling user to open file
               OpenFileDialog *fileChooser = new OpenFileDialog();
               Windows::Forms::DialogResult result =
                  fileChooser->ShowDialog();

               // exit event handler if user clicked Cancel
               if ( result == DialogResult::Cancel )
                  return;

               // get name from user
               fileName = fileChooser->FileName;

               // show error if user specified invalid file
               if ( fileName->Equals( S"" ) )
                  MessageBox::Show( S"Invalid File Name", S"Error",
                  MessageBoxButtons::OK, MessageBoxIcon::Error );
               else {

                  // enable all GUI buttons, disable Open File button
                  openButton->Enabled = false;
                  creditButton->Enabled = true;
                  debitButton->Enabled = true;
                  zeroButton->Enabled = true;
               } // end else
            } // end method openButton_Click

   // invoked when user clicks Credit Balances,
   // Debit Balances or Zero Balances button
   private: System::Void get_Click(
               System::Object * sender, System::EventArgs * e)
            {
               // convert sender explicitly to object of type button
               Button *senderButton = dynamic_cast< Button* >( sender );

```

Fig. 17.17 `CreditInquiry` demonstrates reading and displaying contents from a sequential-access file. (Part 3 of 6.)

```
            // get text from clicked Button, which stores account type
            String *accountType = senderButton->Text;

            // read and display file information
            try {

               // close file from previous operation
               if ( input != NULL )
                  input->Close();

               // create FileStream to obtain read access to file
               input = new FileStream( fileName, FileMode::Open,
                  FileAccess::Read );

               displayTextBox->Text = S"The accounts are:\r\n";

               // traverse file until end of file
               while ( true ) {

                  // get next Record available in file
                  Record *record = dynamic_cast< Record * >(
                     reader->Deserialize( input ) );

                  // store record's last field in balance
                  double balance = record->Balance;

                  // determine whether to display balance
                  if ( ShouldDisplay( balance, accountType ) ) {

                     // display record
                     String *output = String::Concat(
                        ( record->Account ).ToString(), S"\t",
                        record->FirstName, S"\t", record->LastName,
                        S"        ", S"\t" );

                     // display balance with correct monetary format
                     output = String::Concat( output, String::Format(
                        S"{0:F}", balance.ToString() ), S"\r\n" );

                     // copy output to screen
                     displayTextBox->Text = String::Concat(
                        displayTextBox->Text, output );
                  } // end if
               } // end while
            } // end try

            // handle exception when file cannot be closed
            catch ( IOException * ) {
               MessageBox::Show( S"Cannot Close File", S"Error",
                  MessageBoxButtons::OK, MessageBoxIcon::Error );
            } // end catch

```

Fig. 17.17 `CreditInquiry` demonstrates reading and displaying contents from a sequential-access file. (Part 4 of 6.)

```
            // handle exception when no more records
            catch ( SerializationException * ) {

               // close FileStream if no Records in file
               input->Close();
            } // end catch
         } // end method get_Click

   // invoked when user clicks Done button
   private: System::Void doneButton_Click(
            System::Object *  sender, System::EventArgs *  e)
         {
            // determine whether file exists
            if ( input != NULL ) {

               // close file
               try {
                  input->Close();
               } // end try

               // handle exception if FileStream does not exist
               catch ( IOException * ) {

                  // notify user of error closing file
                  MessageBox::Show( S"Cannot close file", S"Error",
                     MessageBoxButtons::OK, MessageBoxIcon::Error );
               } // end catch
            } // end if

            Application::Exit();
         } // end method doneButton_Click

   private:

      // determine whether to display given record
      bool ShouldDisplay( double balance, String *accountType )
      {
         if ( balance > 0 ) {

            // display credit balances
            if ( accountType->Equals( S"Credit Balances" ) )
               return true;
         } // end if
         else if ( balance < 0 ) {

            // display debit balances
            if ( accountType->Equals( S"Debit Balances" ) )
               return true;
         } // end if
         else { // balance == 0

```

Fig. 17.17 CreditInquiry demonstrates reading and displaying contents from a sequential-access file. (Part 5 of 6.)

```
            // display
            if ( accountType->Equals( S"Zero Balances" ) )
               return true;
         } // end else

         return false;
      } // end method ShouldDisplay
   };
}
```

Fig. 17.17 `CreditInquiry` demonstrates reading and displaying contents from a sequential-access file. (Part 6 of 6.)

The program in Fig. 17.17–Fig. 17.18 displays buttons that enable a credit manager to obtain credit information. The **Open File** button opens a file for gathering data. The **Credit Balances** button displays a list of accounts that have credit balances, the **Debit Balances** button displays a list of accounts that have debit balances, and the **Zero Balances** button displays a list of accounts that have zero balances. The **Done** button exits the application.

```
// Fig. 17.18: Form1.cpp
// Entry point for application.

#include "stdafx.h"
#include "Form1.h"
#include <windows.h>

using namespace CreditInquiry;

int APIENTRY _tWinMain(HINSTANCE hInstance,
                       HINSTANCE hPrevInstance,
                       LPTSTR    lpCmdLine,
                       int       nCmdShow)
{
   System::Threading::Thread::CurrentThread->ApartmentState =
      System::Threading::ApartmentState::STA;
   Application::Run(new Form1());
   return 0;
} // end _tWinMain
```

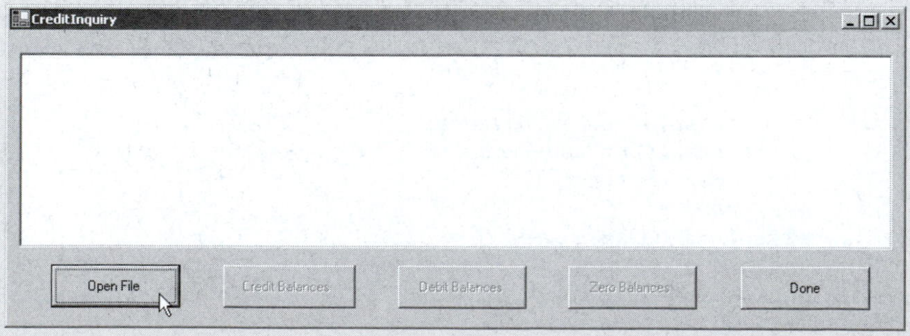

Fig. 17.18 `CreditInquiry` entry point. (Part 1 of 2.)

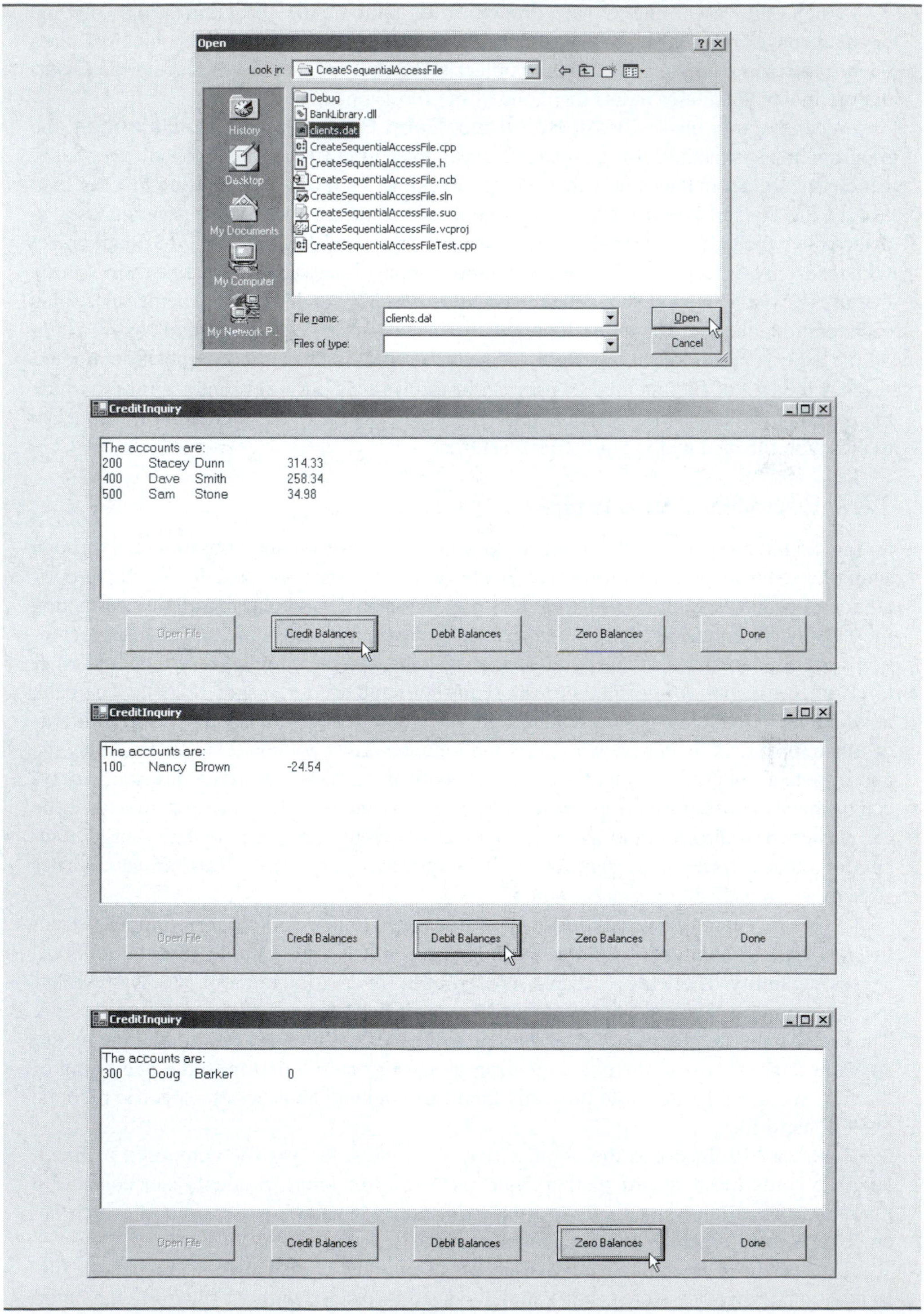

Fig. 17.18 `CreditInquiry` entry point. (Part 2 of 2.)

When the user clicks the **Open File** button, the program calls method `openButton_Click` (lines 74–101 of Fig. 17.17). Line 78 instantiates an object of class `OpenFileDialog`, and line 80 calls the object's `ShowDialog` method to display the **Open** dialog, in which the user inputs the name of the file to open.

When the user clicks **Credit Balances**, **Debit Balances** or **Zero Balances**, the program invokes method `get_Click` (lines 105–169). Line 109 casts the `sender` parameter, which is a pointer to the `Object` that sent the event, to a `Button` pointer. Line 112 can then extract the `Button` object's text into variable `accountType`, which the program uses to determine which GUI `Button` the user clicked. Lines 122–123 create a `FileStream` object with read-only file access and assign it to pointer `input`. Lines 128–154 define a `while` loop that uses `private` method `ShouldDisplay` (lines 198–220) to determine whether to display each record in the file. The `while` loop obtains each record by calling method `Deserialize` of the `FileStream` object repeatedly (lines 131–132). When the file-position pointer reaches the end of file, method `Deserialize` throws a `SerializationException`, which the `catch` block in lines 164–168 handles. Line 167 calls the `Close` method of `FileStream` to close the file, and method `get_Click` returns.

17.7 Random-Access Files

So far, we have explained how to create sequential-access files and how to search through such files to locate particular information. However, sequential-access files are inappropriate for so-called *"instant-access" applications*, in which a particular record of information must be located immediately. Popular instant-access applications include airline-reservation systems, banking systems, point-of-sale systems, automated-teller machines and other kinds of *transaction-processing systems* requiring rapid access to specific data. The bank at which an individual has an account might have hundreds of thousands or even millions of other customers; however, when that individual uses an automated teller machine, the appropriate account is checked for sufficient funds in seconds. This type of instant access can be made possible using *random-access files*. Individual records of a random-access file can be accessed directly (and quickly), without searching through potentially large numbers of other records, as is necessary with sequential-access files. Random-access files sometimes are called *direct-access files*.

As we discussed earlier in this chapter, the .NET Framework does not impose structure on files, so applications that use random-access files must implement the random-access capability. There are a variety of techniques for creating random-access files. Perhaps the simplest involves requiring that all records in a file be of a uniform, fixed length. The use of fixed-length records enables a program to calculate (as a function of the record size and the record key) the exact location of any record in relation to the beginning of the file. We soon demonstrate how this facilitates immediate access to specific records, even in large files.

Figure 17.19 illustrates the organization of a random-access file composed of fixed-length records (each record in this figure is 100 bytes long). Students can consider a random-access file as analogous to a railroad train with many cars, some of which are empty and some of which contain contents.

Data can be inserted into a random-access file without destroying other data in the file. In addition, previously stored data can be updated or deleted without rewriting the entire file. In the following sections, we explain how to create a random-access file, write data to

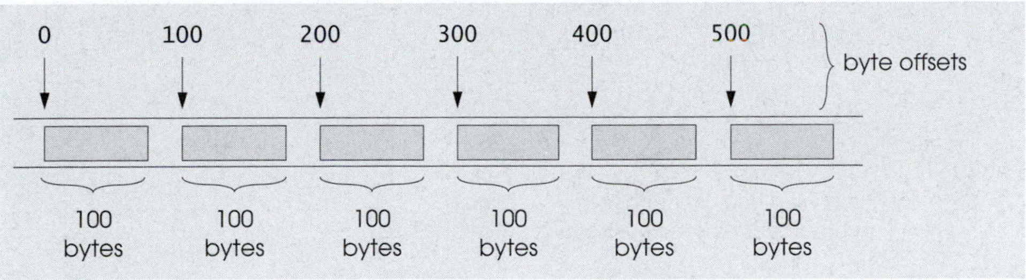

Fig. 17.19 Random-access file with fixed-length records.

that file, read data both sequentially and randomly, update data and delete data that are no longer needed.

Figure 17.20–Fig. 17.21 contain class `RandomAccessRecord`, which is used in the random-access file-processing applications in this chapter. This class also belongs to the `BankLibrary` DLL—i.e., it is part of the project that contains classes `BankUIForm` and `Record`. (When adding class `RandomAccessRecord` to the project containing `BankUIForm` and `Record`, remember to rebuild the project.)

```
// Fig. 17.20: RandomAccessRecord.h
// Data-record class for random-access applications.

#pragma once

#using <mscorlib.dll>

using namespace System;

// length of firstName and lastName
#define CHAR_ARRAY_LENGTH 15

#define SIZE_OF_CHAR sizeof( Char )
#define SIZE_OF_INT32 sizeof( Int32 )
#define SIZE_OF_DOUBLE sizeof( Double )

namespace BankLibrary
{
   public __gc class RandomAccessRecord
   {
   public:

      // length of record
      static const int SIZE = ( SIZE_OF_INT32 + 2 * (
         SIZE_OF_CHAR * CHAR_ARRAY_LENGTH ) + SIZE_OF_DOUBLE );

      // default constructor sets members to default values
      RandomAccessRecord();
      RandomAccessRecord( int, String *, String *, double );

```

Fig. 17.20 Data-record class for random-access applications. (Part 1 of 3.)

```
      // get method of property Account
      __property int get_Account()
      {
         return account;
      }

      // set method of property Account
      __property void set_Account( int value )
      {
         account = value;
      }

      // get method of property FirstName
      __property String *get_FirstName()
      {
         return new String( firstName );
      }

      // set method of property FirstName
      __property void set_FirstName( String *value )
      {
         // determine length of string parameter
         int stringSize = value->Length;

         // firstName string representation
         String *firstNameString = value;

         // append spaces to string parameter if too short
         if ( stringSize <= CHAR_ARRAY_LENGTH ) {
            firstNameString = String::Concat( value, new String( ' ',
               CHAR_ARRAY_LENGTH - stringSize ) );
         } // end if
         else {

            // remove characters from string parameter if too long
            firstNameString = value->Substring( 0, CHAR_ARRAY_LENGTH );
         } // end else

         // convert string parameter to char array
         firstName = firstNameString->ToCharArray();

      } // end set

      // get method of property LastName
      __property String *get_LastName()
      {
         return new String( lastName );
      }

      // set method of property LastName
      __property void set_LastName( String *value )
      {
```

Fig. 17.20 Data-record class for random-access applications. (Part 2 of 3.)

```
         // determine length of string parameter
         int stringSize = value->Length;

         // lastName string representation
         String *lastNameString = value;

         // append spaces to string parameter if too short
         if ( stringSize <= CHAR_ARRAY_LENGTH ) {
            lastNameString = String::Concat( value, new String( ' ',
               CHAR_ARRAY_LENGTH - stringSize ) );
         } // end if
         else {

            // remove characters from string parameter if too long
            lastNameString = value->Substring( 0, CHAR_ARRAY_LENGTH );
         } // end if

         // convert string parameter to char array
         lastName = lastNameString->ToCharArray();

      } // end set

      // get method of property Balance
      __property double get_Balance()
      {
         return balance;
      }

      // set method of property Balance
      __property void set_Balance( double value )
      {
         balance = value;
      }

   private:

      // record data
      int account;
      __wchar_t firstName __gc[];
      __wchar_t lastName __gc[];
      double balance;
   }; // end class RandomAccessRecord
} // end namespace BankLibrary
```

Fig. 17.20 Data-record class for random-access applications. (Part 3 of 3.)

```
// Fig. 17.21: RandomAccessRecord.cpp
// Method definitions for class RandomAccessRecord.

#include "stdafx.h"
#include "RandomAccessRecord.h"

```

Fig. 17.21 `RandomAccessRecord` class method definitions. (Part 1 of 2.)

```
using namespace BankLibrary;

// default constructor sets members to default values
RandomAccessRecord::RandomAccessRecord()
{
   firstName = new __wchar_t __gc[ CHAR_ARRAY_LENGTH ];
   lastName = new __wchar_t __gc[ CHAR_ARRAY_LENGTH ];
   FirstName = "";
   LastName = "";
   Account = 0;
   Balance = 0.0;
}

// overloaded counstructor sets members to parameter values
RandomAccessRecord::RandomAccessRecord( int accountValue,
   String *firstNameValue, String *lastNameValue,
   double balanceValue )
{
   Account = accountValue;
   FirstName = firstNameValue;
   LastName = lastNameValue;
   Balance = balanceValue;
} // end constructor
```

Fig. 17.21 RandomAccessRecord class method definitions. (Part 2 of 2.)

Like class Record (Fig. 17.10–Fig. 17.11), class RandomAccessRecord contains private data members (lines 120–123 of Fig. 17.20) for storing record information, two constructors for setting these members to default or to parameter-specified values, and properties for accessing these members. However, class RandomAccessRecord does not contain attribute [Serializable] before its class definition. We do not serialize this class, because the .NET Framework does not provide a means to obtain an object's size at runtime. This means that, if we serialize the class, we cannot guarantee a fixed-length record size.

Instead of serializing the class, we fix the length of the private data members, then write those data as a byte stream to the file. To fix this length, the set methods of properties FirstName (lines 50–72) and LastName (lines 75–103) ensure that members firstName and lastName are __wchar_t arrays of exactly 15 elements. Each set method receives as an argument a String * representing the first name and last name, respectively. If the String referenced by the String * parameter contains fewer than 15 characters, the property's set method copies the String's values to the __wchar_t array, then populates the remainder with spaces. If the String contains more than 15 characters, the set method stores only the first 15 characters of the String into the __wchar_t array. [*Note*: The String is truncated for convenience. In a commercial application, truncation of data may not be acceptable. One solution is to store any truncated data in another location. Another, more expensive, solution is to set the size of fields so large that data will never have to be truncated. If all else fails, alternative methods of data storage may have to be considered.]

Notice that rather than use the numeric constant 15 in the set methods, we use *symbolic constant* CHAR_ARRAY_LENGTH, which is defined in line 11. We do this so that we can easily change this number in the future, if necessary. Symbolic constants—constants represented as symbols—are defined using *preprocessor directive* `#define`. The format for the `#define` preprocessor directive is

> `#define` *identifier replacement-text*

When this line appears in a file, all subsequent occurrences (except those inside a string) of *identifier* in that file will be replaced by *replacement-text* before the program is compiled. Thus, all occurrences of `CHAR_ARRAY_LENGTH` are replaced by numeric constant `15` before the program is compiled.

Lines 13–15 declare symbolic constants `SIZE_OF_CHAR`, `SIZE_OF_INT32` and `SIZE_OF_DOUBLE` in a similar manner. The preprocessor will replace each constant with a call to *unary operator* `sizeof` that determines the size of its respective type (e.g., `sizeof( Int32 )` returns the size, in bytes, of an object of type `Int32`). We use the `sizeof` operator to ensure that we use the correct number of bytes to store each record.

Lines 24–25 declare `const SIZE`, which specifies the record's length. Each record contains `account` (4-byte `int`, or `Int32`), `firstName` and `lastName` (two 15-element `__wchar_t` arrays, where each `__wchar_t`, or `Char`, occupies two bytes, resulting in a total of 60 bytes) and `balance` (8-byte `double`, or `Double`). In this example, each record (i.e., the four `private` data members that our programs will read to and write from files) occupies 72 bytes (4 bytes + 60 bytes + 8 bytes). [*Note*: We create `SIZE` as a `const` data member rather than a symbolic constant because we use this value multiple times in the following examples.]

17.8 Creating a Random-Access File

Consider the following problem statement for a credit-processing application:

> *Create a transaction-processing program capable of storing a maximum of 100 fixed-length records for a company that can have a maximum of 100 customers. Each record consists of an account number (which acts as the record key), a last name, a first name and a balance. The program can update an account, create an account and delete an account.*

The next several sections introduce the techniques necessary to create this credit-processing program. We now discuss the program used to create the random-access file that the remainder of the programs in this chapter use to manipulate data. Class `CreateRandomAccessFile` (Fig. 17.22–Fig. 17.23) creates a random-access file.

```
// Fig. 17.22: CreateRandomAccessFile.h
// Creating a random access file.

#pragma once

#using <mscorlib.dll>
#using <system.windows.forms.dll>

using namespace System;
using namespace System::IO;
using namespace System::Windows::Forms;
using namespace BankLibrary;   // Deitel namespace

```

Fig. 17.22 Creating files for random-access file-processing applications. (Part 1 of 2.)

```
// number of records to write to disk
#define NUMBER_OF_RECORDS 100

public __gc class CreateRandomAccessFile : public Form
{
public:
   void SaveFile();
}; // end class CreateRandomAccessFile
```

Fig. 17.22 Creating files for random-access file-processing applications. (Part 2 of 2.)

```
// Fig. 17.23: CreateRandomAccessFile.cpp
// Method definitions for class CreateRandomAccessFile.

#include "stdafx.h"
#include "CreateRandomAccessFile.h"

// write records to disk
void CreateRandomAccessFile::SaveFile()
{
   // record for writing to disk
   RandomAccessRecord *blankRecord = new RandomAccessRecord();

   // stream through which serializable data are written to file
   FileStream *fileOutput = NULL;

   // stream for writing bytes to file
   BinaryWriter *binaryOutput = NULL;

   // create dialog box enabling user to save file
   SaveFileDialog *fileChooser = new SaveFileDialog();
   Windows::Forms::DialogResult result = fileChooser->ShowDialog();

   // get file name from user
   String *fileName = fileChooser->FileName;

   // exit event handler if user clicked Cancel
   if ( result == DialogResult::Cancel )
      return;

   // show error if user specified invalid file
   if ( fileName->Equals( S"" ) )
      MessageBox::Show( S"Invalid File Name", S"Error",
      MessageBoxButtons::OK, MessageBoxIcon::Error );
   else {

      // write records to file
      try {

         // create FileStream to hold records
         fileOutput = new FileStream( fileName,
            FileMode::Create, FileAccess::Write );
```

Fig. 17.23 `CreateRandomAccessFile` class method definitions. (Part 1 of 2.)

```
42
43          // set length of file
44          fileOutput->SetLength( RandomAccessRecord::SIZE *
45             NUMBER_OF_RECORDS );
46
47          // create object for writing bytes to file
48          binaryOutput = new BinaryWriter( fileOutput );
49
50          // write empty records to file
51          for ( int i = 0; i < NUMBER_OF_RECORDS; i++ ) {
52
53             // set file position pointer in file
54             fileOutput->Position = i * RandomAccessRecord::SIZE;
55
56             // write blank record to file
57             binaryOutput->Write( blankRecord->Account );
58             binaryOutput->Write( blankRecord->FirstName );
59             binaryOutput->Write( blankRecord->LastName );
60             binaryOutput->Write( blankRecord->Balance );
61          } // end for
62
63          // notify user of success
64          MessageBox::Show( S"File Created", S"Success",
65             MessageBoxButtons::OK, MessageBoxIcon::Information );
66       } // end try
67
68       // handle exception if error occurs during writing
69       catch ( IOException *fileException ) {
70
71          // notify user of error
72          MessageBox::Show( fileException->Message, S"Error",
73             MessageBoxButtons::OK, MessageBoxIcon::Error );
74       } // end catch
75    } // end else
76
77    // close FileStream
78    if ( fileOutput == NULL )
79       fileOutput->Close();
80
81    // close BinaryWriter
82    if ( binaryOutput == NULL )
83       binaryOutput->Close();
84 } // end method SaveFile
```

Fig. 17.23 `CreateRandomAccessFile` class method definitions. (Part 2 of 2.)

Function `_tmain` (line 11 of Fig. 17.24) starts the application, which creates a random-access file by calling the user-defined method `SaveFile` (lines 8–84 of Fig. 17.23). Method `SaveFile` populates a file with 100 copies of the default (i.e., empty) values for `private` data members `account`, `firstName`, `lastName` and `balance` of class `RandomAccessRecord`. Lines 20–21 of Fig. 17.23 create and display the `SaveFileDialog`, which enables a user to specify the file to which the program writes data. Lines 40–41 instantiate the `FileStream`. Note that line 41 passes constant `FileMode::Create`, which either creates the specified file (if the file does not exist), or overwrites the specified file (if it does exist). Lines 44–45 set the `FileStream`'s length, which is equal to the size of an individual `RandomAccessRecord` (obtained through constant `RandomAccess-Record::SIZE`) multiplied by the number of records we want to copy (obtained through constant `NUMBER_OF_RECORDS` (line 15 of Fig. 17.22), which we set to value `100`).

```
// Fig. 17.24: CreateRandom.cpp
// Entry point for application.

#include "stdafx.h"
#include "CreateRandomAccessFile.h"

#using <mscorlib.dll>

using namespace System;

int _tmain()
{
   // create random file, then save to disk
   CreateRandomAccessFile *file = new CreateRandomAccessFile();
   file->SaveFile();

   return 0;
} // end _tmain
```

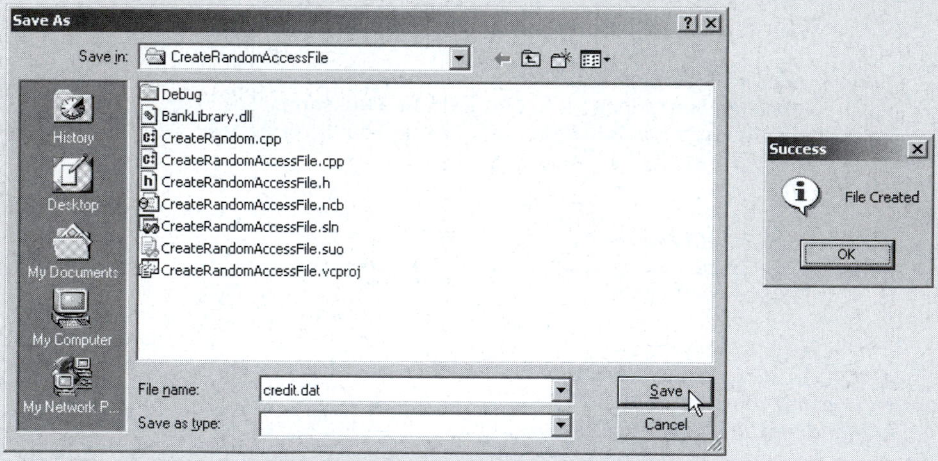

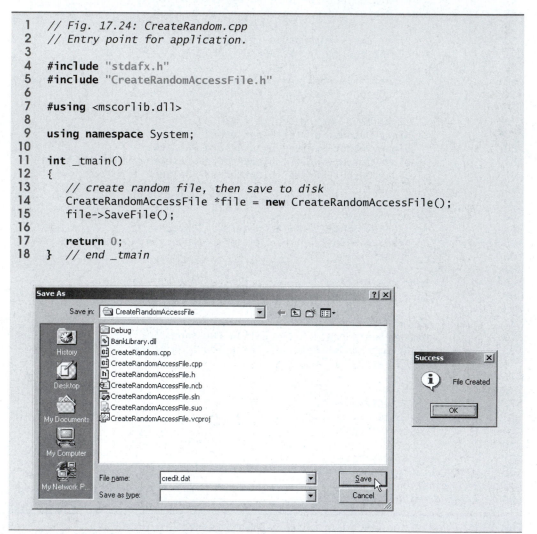

Fig. 17.24 Creating a new random-access file.

Class *BinaryWriter* of namespace `System::IO` provides methods for writing bytes to streams. The `BinaryWriter` constructor takes as an argument a pointer to an instance of class `Stream`, through which the `BinaryWriter` can write bytes. Class `FileStream` provides methods for writing streams to files and inherits from class `Stream`, so we can pass the `FileStream` pointer as an argument to the `BinaryWriter` constructor (line 48 of Fig. 17.23). Now, we can use the `BinaryWriter` to write bytes directly to the file.

Lines 51–61 populate the file with 100 copies of the empty record values (i.e., default values for `private` data members of class `RandomAccessRecord`). Line 54 changes the file-position pointer to specify the location in the file at which to write the next empty record. Now that we are working with a random-access file, we must set the file-pointer explicitly, using the `FileStream` object's `Position` property. This property receives as an argument a `long` value describing where to position the pointer relative to the beginning of the file—in this example, we set the pointer so that it advances a number of bytes that is equal to the record size (obtained by `RandomAccessRecord::SIZE`). Lines 57–60 call method *`Write`* of the `BinaryWriter` object to write the data. Method `Write` is an overloaded method that receives as an argument any primitive data type, then writes that type to a stream of bytes. After the `for` loop exits, lines 78–83 close the `FileStream` and `BinaryWriter` objects.

17.9 Writing Data "Randomly" to a Random-Access File

Now that we have created an empty random-access file, we use class `Form1` (Fig. 17.25) to write data to that file. When a user clicks the **Open File** button, the program invokes method `openButton_Click` (lines 65–107 of Fig. 17.25), which displays the `OpenFileDialog` for specifying the file in which to serialize data (lines 69–71); the program then uses the specified file to create a `FileStream` object with write-only access (lines 90–91). Line 94 uses the `FileStream` pointer to instantiate an object of class `BinaryWriter`, enabling the program to write bytes to files. We used the same approach when working with class `CreateRandomAccessFile` (Fig. 17.22–Fig. 17.23).

```
1   // Fig. 17.25: Form1.h
2   // Write data to a random-access file.
3
4   #pragma once
5
6   // number of RandomAccessRecords to write to disk
7   #define NUMBER_OF_RECORDS 100
8
9   namespace WriteRandomAccessFile
10  {
11     using namespace System;
12     using namespace System::ComponentModel;
13     using namespace System::Collections;
14     using namespace System::Windows::Forms;
15     using namespace System::Data;
16     using namespace System::Drawing;
17     using namespace System::IO;
18     using namespace BankLibrary;   // Deitel namespace
19
20     /// <summary>
21     /// Summary for Form1
22     ///
23     /// WARNING: If you change the name of this class, you will need to
24     ///          change the 'Resource File Name' property for the managed
25     ///          resource compiler tool associated with all .resx files
```

Fig. 17.25 Writing records to random-access files. (Part 1 of 4.)

```
   ///          this class depends on.  Otherwise, the designers will not
   ///          be able to interact properly with localized resources
   ///          associated with this form.
   /// </summary>
   public __gc class Form1 : public BankUIForm
   {
   public:
      Form1(void)
      {
         InitializeComponent();
      }

   protected:
      void Dispose(Boolean disposing)
      {
         if (disposing && components)
         {
            components->Dispose();
         }
         __super::Dispose(disposing);
      }
   private: System::Windows::Forms::Button *  openButton;
   private: System::Windows::Forms::Button *  enterButton;

   // stream through which data are written to file
   private: FileStream *fileOutput;

   // stream for writing bytes to file
   private: BinaryWriter *binaryOutput;

   private:
      /// <summary>
      /// Required designer variable.
      /// </summary>
      System::ComponentModel::Container * components;

   // Visual Studio .NET generated code

   // invoked when user clicks Open File button
   private: System::Void openButton_Click(
               System::Object *  sender, System::EventArgs *  e)
            {
               // create dialog box enabling user to open file
               OpenFileDialog *fileChooser = new OpenFileDialog();
               Windows::Forms::DialogResult result =
                  fileChooser->ShowDialog();

               // get file name from user
               String *fileName = fileChooser->FileName;

               // exit event handler if user clicked Cancel
               if ( result == DialogResult::Cancel )
                  return;
```

Fig. 17.25 Writing records to random-access files. (Part 2 of 4.)

```

            // show error if user specified invalid file
            if ( fileName->Equals( S"" ) )
               MessageBox::Show( S"Invalid File Name", S"Error",
                  MessageBoxButtons::OK, MessageBoxIcon::Error );
            else {

               // open file if file already exists
               try {

                  // create FileStream to hold records
                  fileOutput = new FileStream( fileName,
                     FileMode::Open, FileAccess::Write );

                  // create object for writing bytes to file
                  binaryOutput = new BinaryWriter( fileOutput );

                  // disable Open File button and enable Enter button
                  openButton->Enabled = false;
                  enterButton->Enabled = true;
               } // end try

               // notify user if file does not exist
               catch ( IOException * ) {
                  MessageBox::Show( S"File Does Not Exits", S"Error",
                     MessageBoxButtons::OK, MessageBoxIcon::Error );
               } // end catch
            } // end else
         } // end method openButton_Click

   // invoked when user clicks Enter button
   private: System::Void enterButton_Click(
            System::Object *  sender, System::EventArgs *  e)
         {
            // TextBox values string array
            String *values[] = GetTextBoxValues();

            // write record to file at appropriate position
            try {

               // get account number value from TextBox
               int accountNumber = Int32::Parse(
                  values[ TextBoxIndices::ACCOUNT ] );

               // determine whether accountNumber is valid
               if ( accountNumber > 0 &&
                  accountNumber <= NUMBER_OF_RECORDS ) {

                  // move file position pointer
                  fileOutput->Seek( ( accountNumber - 1 ) *
                     RandomAccessRecord::SIZE, SeekOrigin::Begin );

```

Fig. 17.25 Writing records to random-access files. (Part 3 of 4.)

```
                        // write data to file
                        binaryOutput->Write( accountNumber );
                        binaryOutput->Write(
                           values[ TextBoxIndices::FIRST ] );
                        binaryOutput->Write(
                           values[ TextBoxIndices::LAST ] );
                        binaryOutput->Write( Double::Parse(
                           values[ TextBoxIndices::BALANCE ] ) );
                  } // end if
                  else {

                     // notify user if invalid account number
                     MessageBox::Show( S"Invalid Account Number",
                        S"Error", MessageBoxButtons::OK,
                        MessageBoxIcon::Error);
                  } // end else
               } // end try

               // handle number-format exception
               catch ( FormatException * ) {

                  // notify if error occurs when formatting numbers
                  MessageBox::Show( S"Invalid Account/Balance", S"Error",
                     MessageBoxButtons::OK, MessageBoxIcon::Error );

                  return;
               } // end catch


               ClearTextBoxes(); // clear text box values
            } // end method enterButton_Click
   };
}
```

Fig. 17.25 Writing records to random-access files. (Part 4 of 4.)

```
// Fig. 17.26: Form1.cpp
// Entry point for application.

#include "stdafx.h"
#include "Form1.h"
#include <windows.h>

using namespace WriteRandomAccessFile;

int APIENTRY _tWinMain(HINSTANCE hInstance,
                       HINSTANCE hPrevInstance,
                       LPTSTR    lpCmdLine,
                       int       nCmdShow)
{
   System::Threading::Thread::CurrentThread->ApartmentState =
      System::Threading::ApartmentState::STA;
```

Fig. 17.26 `WriteRandomAccessFile` entry point. (Part 1 of 3.)

```
    Application::Run(new Form1());
    return 0;
} // end _tWinMain
```

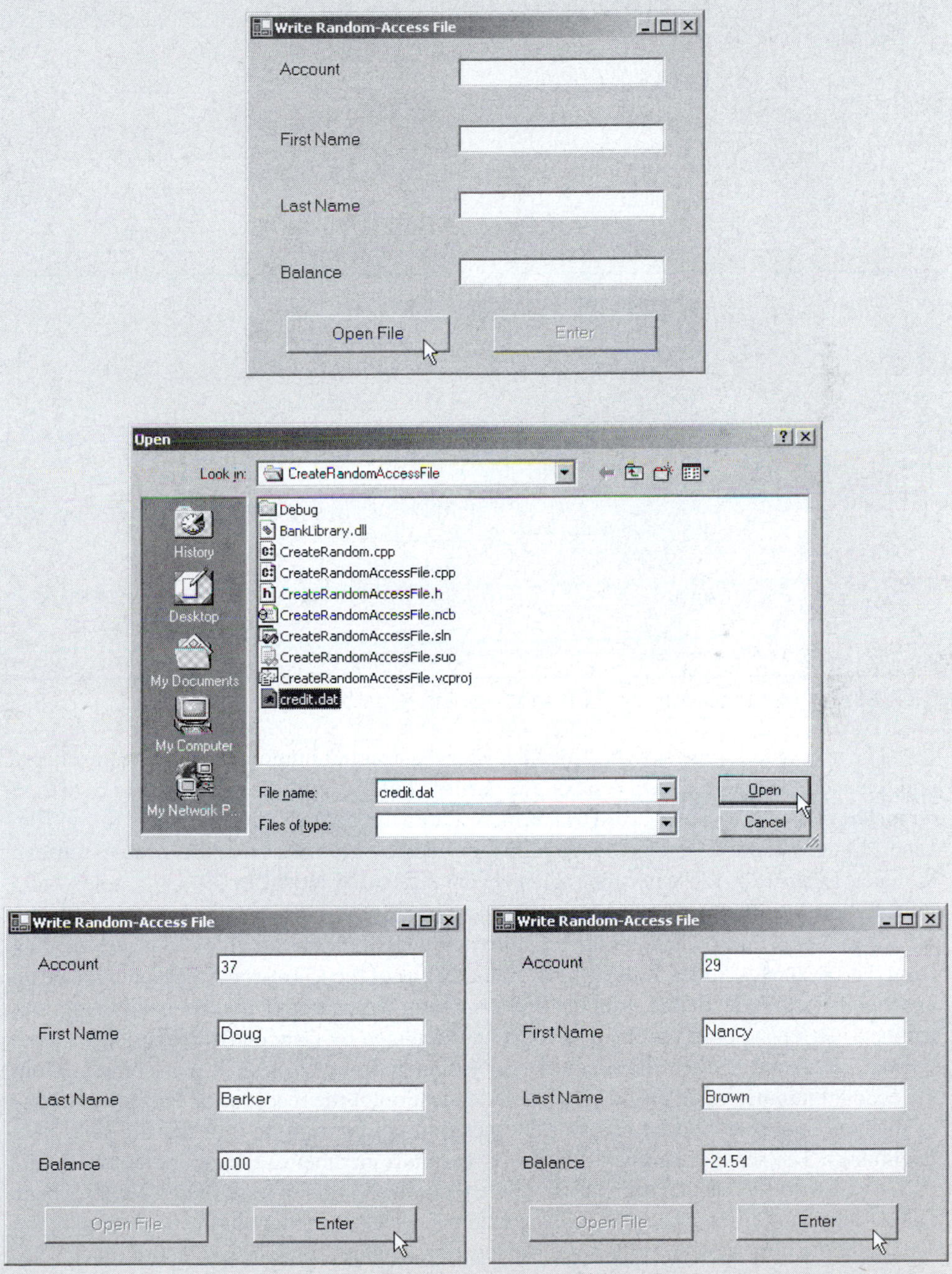

Fig. 17.26 `WriteRandomAccessFile` entry point. (Part 2 of 3.)

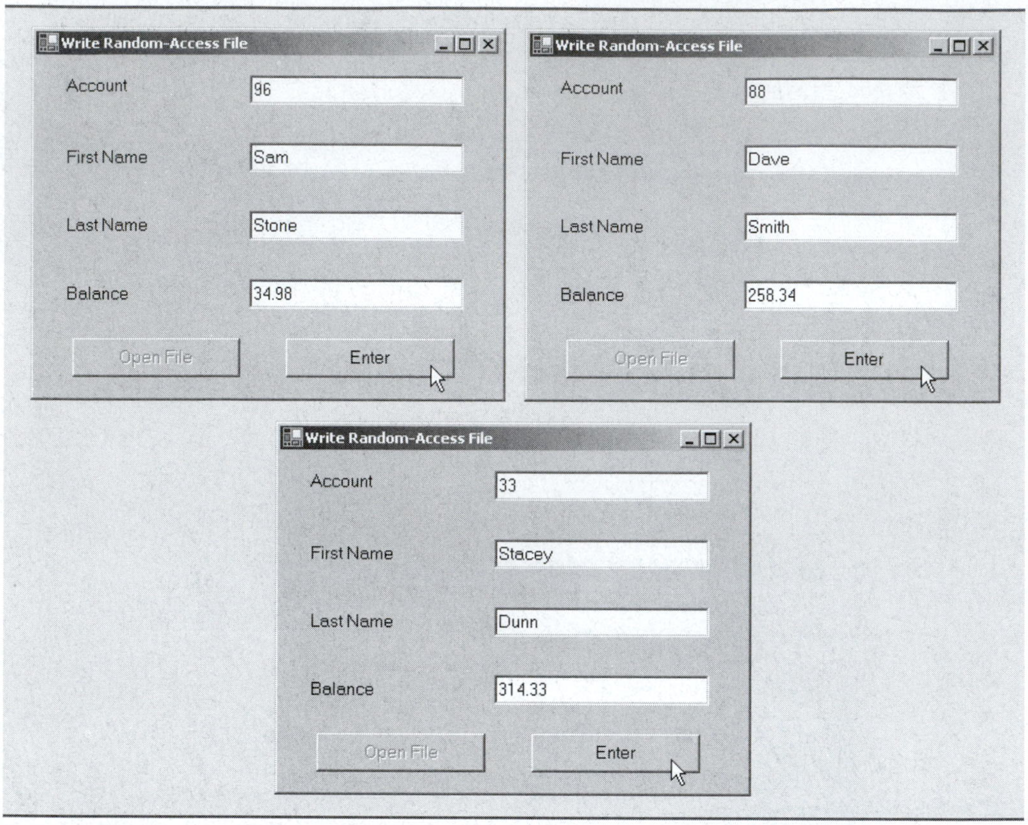

Fig. 17.26 `WriteRandomAccessFile` entry point. (Part 3 of 3.)

The user enters values in the `TextBox`es for the account number, first name, last name and balance. When the user clicks the **Enter** button, the program invokes method `enterButton_Click` (lines 110–161), which writes the data in the `TextBox`es to the file. Line 114 calls method `GetTextBoxValues` (provided by base class `BankUIForm`) to retrieve the data. Lines 124–125 determine whether the **Account Number** `TextBox` holds valid information (i.e., the account number is in the range `1`–`100`).

Class `Form1` must calculate the location in the `FileStream` at which to insert the data from the `TextBox`es. Lines 128–129 use method *`Seek`* of the `FileStream` object to locate an exact point in the file. In this case, method `Seek` sets the position of the file-position pointer for the `FileStream` object to the byte location calculated by `( accountNumber - 1 ) * RandomAccessRecord::SIZE`. The account numbers range from `1` to `100`, so we subtract `1` from the account number when calculating the byte location of the record. For example, our use of method `Seek` sets the first record's file-position pointer to byte 0 of the file (the file's beginning). The second argument to method `Seek` is a member of the enumeration *`SeekOrigin`* and specifies the location at which the method should begin seeking. We use `const` *`SeekOrigin::Begin`*, because we want the method to seek in relation to the beginning of the file. After the program determines the file location at which to place the record, lines 132–138 write the record to the file, using the `BinaryWriter` (discussed in the previous section).

17.10 Reading Data Sequentially from a Random-Access File

In the previous sections, we created a random-access file and wrote data to that file. Here, we develop a program (Fig. 17.27–Fig. 17.28) that opens the file, reads records from it and displays only the records that contain data (i.e., those records in which the account number is not zero). This program also provides an additional benefit. You should attempt to determine what it is—we will reveal it at the end of this section.

```
// Fig. 17.27: Form1.h
// Reads and displays random-access file contents.

#pragma once


namespace ReadRandomAccessFile
{
   using namespace System;
   using namespace System::ComponentModel;
   using namespace System::Collections;
   using namespace System::Windows::Forms;
   using namespace System::Data;
   using namespace System::Drawing;
   using namespace System::IO;
   using namespace BankLibrary;   // Deitel namespace

   /// <summary>
   /// Summary for Form1
   ///
   /// WARNING: If you change the name of this class, you will need to
   ///          change the 'Resource File Name' property for the managed
   ///          resource compiler tool associated with all .resx files
   ///          this class depends on.  Otherwise, the designers will not
   ///          be able to interact properly with localized resources
   ///          associated with this form.
   /// </summary>
   public __gc class Form1 : public BankUIForm
   {
   public:
      Form1(void)
      {
         InitializeComponent();
      }

   protected:
      void Dispose(Boolean disposing)
      {
         if (disposing && components)
         {
            components->Dispose();
         }
         __super::Dispose(disposing);
      }
```

Fig. 17.27 Reading records from random-access files sequentially. (Part 1 of 4.)

```
      private: System::Windows::Forms::Button *  openButton;
      private: System::Windows::Forms::Button *  nextButton;

      // stream through which data are read from file
      private: FileStream *fileInput;

      // stream for reading bytes from file
      private: BinaryReader *binaryInput;

      // index of current record to be displayed
      private: int currentRecordIndex;

      private:
         /// <summary>
         /// Required designer variable.
         /// </summary>
         System::ComponentModel::Container * components;

      // Visual Studio .NET generated GUI code

      // invoked when user clicks Open File button
      private: System::Void openButton_Click(
                  System::Object *  sender, System::EventArgs *  e)
               {
                  // create dialog box enabling user to open file
                  OpenFileDialog *fileChooser = new OpenFileDialog();
                  Windows::Forms::DialogResult result =
                     fileChooser->ShowDialog();

                  // get file name from user
                  String *fileName = fileChooser->FileName;

                  // exit eventhandler if user clicked Cancel
                  if ( result == DialogResult::Cancel )
                     return;

                  // show error if user specified invalid file
                  if ( fileName->Equals( S"" ) )
                     MessageBox::Show( S"Invalid File Name", S"Error",
                        MessageBoxButtons::OK, MessageBoxIcon::Error );
                  else {

                     // create FileStream to obtain read access to file
                     fileInput = new FileStream( fileName,
                        FileMode::Open, FileAccess::Read );

                     // use FileStream for BinaryWriter to read from file
                     binaryInput = new BinaryReader( fileInput );

                     openButton->Enabled = false; // disable Open File button
                     nextButton->Enabled = true; // enable Next button

                     currentRecordIndex = 0;
```

Fig. 17.27 Reading records from random-access files sequentially. (Part 2 of 4.)

```
                  ClearTextBoxes();
               } // end else
            } // end method openButton_Click

   // invoked when user clicks Next button
   private: System::Void nextButton_Click(
               System::Object *  sender, System::EventArgs *  e)
            {
               // record to store file data
               RandomAccessRecord *record = new RandomAccessRecord();

               // read record and store data in TextBoxes
               try {

                  // get next record available in file
                  while ( record->Account == 0 ) {

                     // set file position pointer to next record in file
                     fileInput->Seek(
                        currentRecordIndex * RandomAccessRecord::SIZE,
                        SeekOrigin::Begin );

                     currentRecordIndex += 1;

                     // read data from record
                     record->Account = binaryInput->ReadInt32();
                     record->FirstName = binaryInput->ReadString();
                     record->LastName = binaryInput->ReadString();
                     record->Balance = binaryInput->ReadDouble();
                  } // end while

                  // store record values in temporary string array
                  String *values[] = {
                     record->Account.ToString(),
                     record->FirstName->ToString(),
                     record->LastName->ToString(),
                     record->Balance.ToString() };

                  // copy string array values to TextBox values
                  SetTextBoxValues( values );
               } // end try

               // handle exception when no records in file
               catch ( IOException * ) {

                  // close streams if no records in file
                  fileInput->Close();
                  binaryInput->Close();

                  openButton->Enabled = true; // enable Open File button
                  nextButton->Enabled = false; // disable Next button
                  ClearTextBoxes();

```

Fig. 17.27 Reading records from random-access files sequentially. (Part 3 of 4.)

```
151                         // notify user if no records in file
152                         MessageBox::Show( S"No more records in file", S"",
153                            MessageBoxButtons::OK, MessageBoxIcon::Information );
154                      } // end catch
155                   } // end method nextButton_Click
156    };
157 }
```

Fig. 17.27 Reading records from random-access files sequentially. (Part 4 of 4.)

When the user clicks the **Open File** button, class `Form1` invokes method `openButton_Click` (lines 66–100 of Fig. 17.27), which displays the `OpenFileDialog` for specifying the file from which to read data. Lines 88–89 instantiate a `FileStream` object that opens a file with read-only access. Line 92 creates an instance of class *`BinaryReader`*, which reads bytes from a stream. We pass the `FileStream` pointer as an argument to the `BinaryReader` constructor, thus enabling the `BinaryReader` to read bytes from the file.

```
// Fig. 17.28: Form1.cpp
// Entry point for application.

#include "stdafx.h"
#include "Form1.h"
#include <windows.h>

using namespace ReadRandomAccessFile;

int APIENTRY _tWinMain(HINSTANCE hInstance,
                       HINSTANCE hPrevInstance,
                       LPTSTR    lpCmdLine,
                       int       nCmdShow)
{
   System::Threading::Thread::CurrentThread->ApartmentState =
      System::Threading::ApartmentState::STA;
   Application::Run(new Form1());
   return 0;
} // end _tWinMain
```

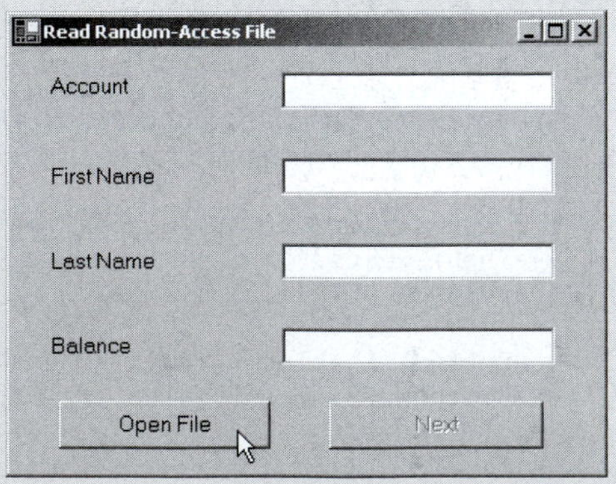

Fig. 17.28 `ReadRandomAccessFile` entry point. (Part 1 of 3.)

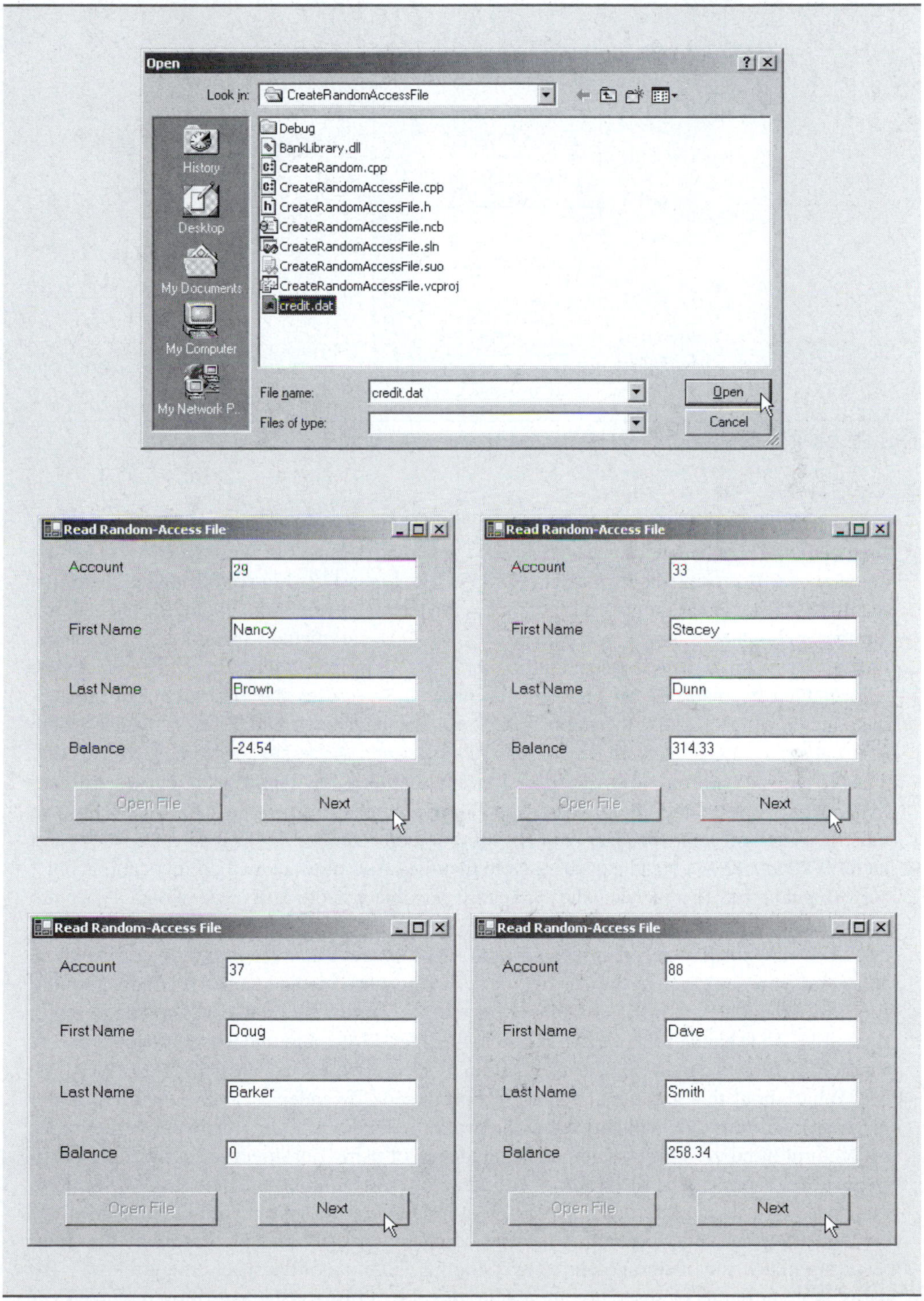

Fig. 17.28 `ReadRandomAccessFile` entry point. (Part 2 of 3.)

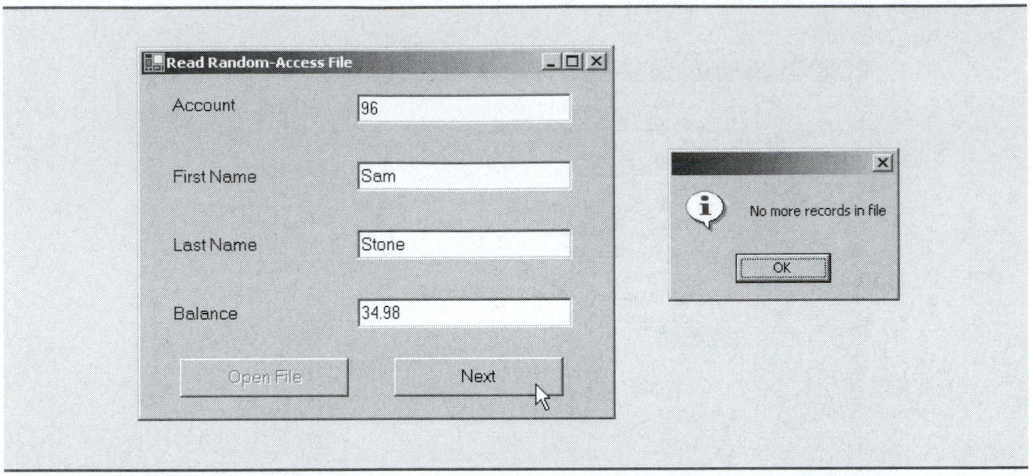

Fig. 17.28 `ReadRandomAccessFile` entry point. (Part 3 of 3.)

When the user clicks the **Next** button, the program calls method `nextButton_Click` (lines 103–155), which reads the next record from the file. Line 107 instantiates a `RandomAccessRecord` for storing the record data from the file. Lines 113–127 read from the file until a record that has a non-zero account number is reached. (`0` is the initial value for the account number and indicates an empty record.) Lines 116–118 call method `Seek` of the `FileStream` object, which moves the file-position pointer to the appropriate place in the file where the record must be read. To accomplish this, method `Seek` uses the `int` value `currentRecordIndex`, which contains the number of records that have been read. Lines 123–126 use the `BinaryReader` object to store the file data in the `RandomAccessRecord` object. Recall that class `BinaryWriter` provides overloaded `Write` methods for writing data. However, class `BinaryReader` does not provide overloaded `Read` methods to read data. This means that we must use method *`ReadInt32`* to read an `int`, method *`ReadString`* to read a `String *` and method *`ReadDouble`* to read a `double`. Note that the order of these method invocations must correspond to the order in which the `BinaryWriter` object wrote each piece of data. When the `BinaryReader` reads a valid account number (i.e., a non-zero value), the loop terminates, and lines 130–137 display the record values in the `TextBoxes`. When the program has displayed all records, method `Seek` throws an `IOException` (because method `Seek` tries to position the file-position pointer to a location that is beyond the end-of-file marker). The `catch` block (lines 141–154) handles this exception by closing the `FileStream` and `BinaryReader` objects (lines 144–145) and notifying the user that no more records exist (lines 152–153).

What about that additional benefit we promised? If readers examine the GUI as the program executes, they will notice that the program displays the records in ascending order by account number! This is a simple consequence of using our direct-access techniques to store these records in the file. Sorting with direct-access techniques is also fast. We achieve this speed by making the file large enough to hold every possible record that a user might create. Of course, this means that the file could be sparsely occupied most of the time, resulting in a waste of storage. Here is yet another example of the space/time trade-off: By using large amounts of space, we are able to develop a fast sorting algorithm.

17.11 Case Study: A Transaction-Processing Program

We now develop a substantial transaction-processing program (Fig. 17.29–Fig. 17.37), using a random-access file to achieve "instant-access" processing. The program maintains a bank's account information. Users of this program can add new accounts, update existing accounts and delete accounts that are no longer needed. First, we discuss the transaction-processing behavior (i.e., the class that enables the addition, updating and removal of accounts). We then discuss the GUI, which contains windows that display the account information and enable the user to invoke the application's transaction-processing behavior. Note that this example is only a simple transaction-processing program. More information about processing transactions in .NET can be found at

```
msdn.microsoft.com/library/default.asp?url=/library/en-us/cpguide/
html/cpconprocessingtransactions.asp
```

Transaction-Processing Behavior

In this case study, we create class `Transaction` (Fig. 17.29–Fig. 17.30), which acts as a proxy to handle all transaction processing. Rather than providing the transaction-processing behavior themselves, the objects in this application use an instance of `Transaction` which acts as a proxy to provide the necessary functionality. By using a proxy, we can encapsulate transaction-processing behavior in only one class, enabling various other classes in our application to reuse this behavior. Furthermore, if we decide to modify this behavior, we need modify only the proxy (i.e., class `Transaction`), instead of having to modify the behavior of each class that uses the proxy.

```
// Fig. 17.29: Transaction.h
// Handles record transactions.

#pragma once

#using <mscorlib.dll>

using namespace System;
using namespace System::IO;
using namespace System::Windows::Forms;
using namespace BankLibrary;   // Deitel namespace

// number of records to write to disk
#define NUMBER_OF_RECORDS 100

public __gc class Transaction
{
public:
   void OpenFile( String * );
   RandomAccessRecord *GetRecord( String * );
   bool AddRecord( RandomAccessRecord *, int );

private:

```

Fig. 17.29 Record-transaction class for the transaction-processor program. (Part 1 of 2.)

```
   // stream through which data moves to and from file
   FileStream *file;

   // stream for reading bytes from file
   BinaryReader *binaryInput;

   // stream for writing bytes to file
   BinaryWriter *binaryOutput;
}; // end class Transaction
```

Fig. 17.29 Record-transaction class for the transaction-processor program. (Part 2 of 2.)

```
// Fig. 17.30: Transaction.cpp
// Method definitions for class Transaction.

#include "stdafx.h"
#include "Transaction.h"

// create/open file containing empty records
void Transaction::OpenFile( String *fileName )
{
   // write empty records to file
   try {

      // create FileStream from new file or existing file
      file = new FileStream( fileName, FileMode::OpenOrCreate );

      // use FileStream for BinaryWriter to read bytes from file
      binaryInput = new BinaryReader( file );

      // use FileStream for BinaryWriter to write bytes to file
      binaryOutput = new BinaryWriter( file );

      // determine whether file has just been created
      if ( file->Length == 0 ) {

         // record to be written to file
         RandomAccessRecord *blankRecord =
            new RandomAccessRecord();

         // new record can hold NUMBER_OF_RECORDS records
         file->SetLength( RandomAccessRecord::SIZE *
            NUMBER_OF_RECORDS );

         // write blank records to file
         for ( int i = 1; i <= NUMBER_OF_RECORDS; i++ )
            AddRecord( blankRecord, i );

      } // end if
   } // end try

```

Fig. 17.30 `Transaction` class handles record transactions. (Part 1 of 3.)

```
      // notify user of error during writing of blank records
      catch ( IOException *fileException ) {
         MessageBox::Show( fileException->Message, S"Error",
            MessageBoxButtons::OK, MessageBoxIcon::Error );
      } // end catch
   } // end method OpenFile

   // retrieve record depending on whether account is valid
   RandomAccessRecord *Transaction::GetRecord(
      String *accountValue )
   {
      // store file data associated with account in record
      try {

         // record to store file data
         RandomAccessRecord *record = new RandomAccessRecord();

         // get value from TextBox's account field
         int accountNumber = Int32::Parse( accountValue );

         // if account is invalid, do not read data
         if ( accountNumber < 1 || accountNumber > NUMBER_OF_RECORDS ) {

            // set record's account field with account number
            record->Account = accountNumber;
         } // end if

         // get data from file if account is valid
         else {

            // locate position in file where record exists
            file->Seek( ( accountNumber - 1 ) *
               RandomAccessRecord::SIZE, SeekOrigin::Begin );

            // read data from record
            record->Account = binaryInput->ReadInt32();
            record->FirstName = binaryInput->ReadString();
            record->LastName = binaryInput->ReadString();
            record->Balance = binaryInput->ReadDouble();
         } // end else

         return record;
      } // end try

      // notify user of error during reading
      catch ( IOException *fileException ) {
         MessageBox::Show( fileException->Message, S"Error",
            MessageBoxButtons::OK, MessageBoxIcon::Error );
      } // end catch

      return 0;
   } // end method GetRecord

```

Fig. 17.30 `Transaction` class handles record transactions. (Part 2 of 3.)

```
93  // add record to file at position determined by accountNumber
94  bool Transaction::AddRecord( RandomAccessRecord *record,
95     int accountNumber )
96  {
97     // write record to file
98     try {
99
100       // move file position pointer to appropriate position
101       file->Seek( ( accountNumber - 1 ) *
102          RandomAccessRecord::SIZE, SeekOrigin::Begin );
103
104       // write data to file
105       binaryOutput->Write( record->Account );
106       binaryOutput->Write( record->FirstName );
107       binaryOutput->Write( record->LastName );
108       binaryOutput->Write( record->Balance );
109    } // end try
110
111    // notify user if error occurs during writing
112    catch ( IOException *fileException ) {
113       MessageBox::Show( fileException->Message, S"Error",
114          MessageBoxButtons::OK, MessageBoxIcon::Error );
115
116       return false; // failure
117    } // end catch
118
119    return true; // success
120 } // end method AddRecord
```

Fig. 17.30 `Transaction` class handles record transactions. (Part 3 of 3.)

Class `Transaction` contains methods `OpenFile`, `GetRecord` and `AddRecord`. Method `OpenFile` (lines 8–45 of Fig. 17.30) uses constant `FileMode::OpenOrCreate` (line 14) to create a `FileStream` object from either an existing file or one not yet created. Lines 17 and 20 use this `FileStream` to create `BinaryReader` and `BinaryWriter` objects for reading and writing bytes to the file, respectively. If the file is new, lines 26–35 populate the `FileStream` object with empty records. Lines 26–27 create a new `RandomAccessRecord` (with account number `0`). The `for` loop in lines 34–35 then adds this empty record to every position in the file (i.e., for account numbers in range `1–NUMBER_OF_RECORDS`).

Method `GetRecord` (lines 48–91) returns the record associated with the account-number parameter. Line 55 instantiates a `RandomAccessRecord` object that will store the file data. If the account parameter is valid, lines 71–72 call method `Seek` of the `FileStream` object, which uses the parameter to calculate the position of the specified record in the file. Lines 75–78 then call methods `ReadInt32`, `ReadString` and `ReadDouble` of the `BinaryReader` object to store the file data in the `RandomAccessRecord` object. Line 81 returns the `RandomAccessRecord` object. We used these techniques in Section 17.10.

Method `AddRecord` (lines 94–120) inserts a record into the file. Lines 101–102 call method `Seek` of the `FileStream` object, which uses the `accountNumber` parameter to locate the position at which to insert the record in the file. Lines 105–108 call the overloaded

`Write` methods of the `BinaryWriter` object to write the `RandomAccessRecord` object's data to the file. We used these techniques in Section 17.9. Note that, if an error occurs when adding the record (i.e., either the `FileStream` or the `BinaryWriter` throws an `IOException`), lines 112–114 notify the user of the error and return `false` (failure).

Transaction-Processor GUI

The GUI for this program uses a multiple-document interface. Class `Form1` (Fig. 17.31) is the parent window; it contains corresponding child windows `StartDialog` (Fig. 17.33), `NewDialog` (Fig. 17.35), `UpdateDialog` (Fig. 17.36) and `DeleteDialog` (Fig. 17.37). `StartDialog` allows the user to open a file containing account information and provides access to the `NewDialog`, `UpdateDialog` and `DeleteDialog` internal frames. These frames allow users to update, create and delete records, respectively.

Initially, `Form1` displays the `StartDialog` object; this window provides the user with various options. It contains four buttons, which enable the user to create or open a file, create a record, update an existing record or delete an existing record.

```
// Fig. 17.31: Form1.h
// MDI parent for transaction-processor application.

#pragma once

#include "StartDialog.h"

namespace TransactionProcessor
{
   using namespace System;
   using namespace System::ComponentModel;
   using namespace System::Collections;
   using namespace System::Windows::Forms;
   using namespace System::Data;
   using namespace System::Drawing;

   /// <summary>
   /// Summary for Form1
   ///
   /// WARNING: If you change the name of this class, you will need to
   ///          change the 'Resource File Name' property for the managed
   ///          resource compiler tool associated with all .resx files
   ///          this class depends on.  Otherwise, the designers will not
   ///          be able to interact properly with localized resources
   ///          associated with this form.
   /// </summary>
   public __gc class Form1 : public System::Windows::Forms::Form
   {
   public:
      Form1(void)
      {
         InitializeComponent();

```

Fig. 17.31 `TransactionProcessor` demonstrates the transaction-processor application. (Part 1 of 2.)

```
            startDialog = new StartDialog();
            startDialog->MdiParent = this;
            startDialog->Show();
         }

      protected:
         void Dispose(Boolean disposing)
         {
            if (disposing && components)
            {
               components->Dispose();
            }
            __super::Dispose(disposing);
         }

      // pointer to StartDialog
      private: StartDialog *startDialog;

      private:
         /// <summary>
         /// Required designer variable.
         /// </summary>
         System::ComponentModel::Container * components;

      // Visual Studio .NET generated GUI code
      };
}
```

Fig. 17.31 `TransactionProcessor` demonstrates the transaction-processor application. (Part 2 of 2.)

```
// Fig. 17.32: Form1.cpp
// Entry point for application.

#include "stdafx.h"
#include "Form1.h"
#include <windows.h>

using namespace TransactionProcessor;

int APIENTRY _tWinMain(HINSTANCE hInstance,
                       HINSTANCE hPrevInstance,
                       LPTSTR    lpCmdLine,
                       int       nCmdShow)
{
   System::Threading::Thread::CurrentThread->ApartmentState =
      System::Threading::ApartmentState::STA;
   Application::Run(new Form1());
   return 0;
} // end _tWinMain
```

Fig. 17.32 `TransactionProcessor` entry point.

Before the user can modify records, the user must either create or open a file. When the user clicks the **New/Open File** button, the program calls method `openButton_Click` (lines 77–134 of Fig. 17.33), which opens a file that the application uses for modifying records. Lines 81–97 display the `OpenFileDialog` for specifying the file from which to read data, then use this file to create the `FileStream` object. Note that line 87 sets property `CheckFileExists` of the `OpenFileDialog` object to `false`—this enables the user to create a file if the specified file does not exist. If this property were `true` (its default value), the dialog would notify the user that the specified file does not exist, thus preventing the user from creating a file.

```
1  // Fig. 17.33: StartDialog.h
2  // Initial dialog box displayed to user. Provides buttons for
3  // creating/opening file and for adding, updating and removing
4  // records from file.
5
6  #pragma once
7
8  using namespace System;
9  using namespace System::ComponentModel;
10 using namespace System::Collections;
11 using namespace System::Windows::Forms;
12 using namespace System::Data;
13 using namespace System::Drawing;
14 using namespace BankLibrary;    // Deitel namespace
15
16 #include “NewDialog.h”
17 #include “UpdateDialog.h”
18 #include “DeleteDialog.h”
19 #include “MyDelegate.h”
20
21 namespace TransactionProcessor
22 {
23    /// <summary>
24    /// Summary for StartDialog
25    ///
26    /// WARNING: If you change the name of this class, you will need to
27    ///          change the 'Resource File Name' property for the managed
28    ///          resource compiler tool associated with all .resx files
29    ///          this class depends on.  Otherwise, the designers will not
30    ///          be able to interact properly with localized resources
31    ///          associated with this form.
32    /// </summary>
33    public __gc class StartDialog : public System::Windows::Forms::Form
34    {
35    public:
36       StartDialog(void)
37       {
38          InitializeComponent();
39       }
40
```

Fig. 17.33 `StartDialog` class enables users to access dialog boxes associated with various transactions. (Part 1 of 5.)

```
   protected:
      void Dispose(Boolean disposing)
      {
         if (disposing && components)
         {
            components->Dispose();
         }
         __super::Dispose(disposing);
      }
   private: System::Windows::Forms::Button *  updateButton;
   private: System::Windows::Forms::Button *  newButton;
   private: System::Windows::Forms::Button *  deleteButton;
   private: System::Windows::Forms::Button *  openButton;

   private: System::ComponentModel::IContainer *  components;

   // pointer to dialog box for adding record
   private: NewDialog *newDialog;

   // pointer to dialog box for updating record
   private: UpdateDialog *updateDialog;

   // pointer to dialog box for removing record
   private: DeleteDialog *deleteDialog;

   // pointer to object that handles transactions
   private: Transaction *transactionProxy;

   private:
      /// <summary>
      /// Required designer variable.
      /// </summary>

   // Visual Studio .NET generated GUI code

   // invoked when user clicks New/Open File button
   private: System::Void openButton_Click(
               System::Object *  sender, System::EventArgs *  e)
            {
               // create dialog box enabling user to create or open file
               OpenFileDialog *fileChooser = new OpenFileDialog();
               Windows::Forms::DialogResult result;
               String *fileName;

               // enable user to create file if file does not exist
               fileChooser->Title = S"Create File / Open File";
               fileChooser->CheckFileExists = false;

               // show dialog box to user
               result = fileChooser->ShowDialog();

```

Fig. 17.33 `StartDialog` class enables users to access dialog boxes associated with various transactions. (Part 2 of 5.)

```
            // exit event handler if user clicked Cancel
            if ( result == DialogResult::Cancel )
               return;

            // get file name from user
            fileName = fileChooser->FileName;

            // show error if user specified invalid file
            if ( fileName->Equals( S"" ) )
               MessageBox::Show( S"Invalid File Name", S"Error",
                  MessageBoxButtons::OK, MessageBoxIcon::Error );

            // open or create file if user specified valid file
            else {

               // create Transaction with specified file
               transactionProxy = new Transaction();
               transactionProxy->OpenFile( fileName );

               // enable GUI buttons except for New/Open File button
               newButton->Enabled = true;
               updateButton->Enabled = true;
               deleteButton->Enabled = true;
               openButton->Enabled = false;

               // instantiate dialog box for creating records
               newDialog = new NewDialog( transactionProxy,
                  new MyDelegate( this, ShowStartDialog ) );

               // instantiate dialog box for updating records
               updateDialog = new UpdateDialog( transactionProxy,
                  new MyDelegate( this, ShowStartDialog ) );

               // instantiate dialog box for removing records
               deleteDialog = new DeleteDialog( transactionProxy,
                  new MyDelegate( this, ShowStartDialog ) );

               // set StartDialog as MdiParent for dialog boxes
               newDialog->MdiParent = this->MdiParent;
               updateDialog->MdiParent = this->MdiParent;
               deleteDialog->MdiParent = this->MdiParent;
            } // end else
         } // end method openButton_Click

   // invoked when user clicks New Record button
   private: System::Void newButton_Click(
            System::Object *  sender, System::EventArgs *  e)
         {
            Hide(); // hide StartDialog
            newDialog->Show(); // show NewDialog
         } // end method newButton_Click

```

Fig. 17.33 `StartDialog` class enables users to access dialog boxes associated with various transactions. (Part 3 of 5.)

```
    private: System::Void updateButton_Click(
                System::Object *  sender, System::EventArgs *  e)
             {
                Hide(); // hide StartDialog
                updateDialog->Show(); // show UpdateDialog
             } // end method updateButton_Click

    private: System::Void deleteButton_Click(
                System::Object *  sender, System::EventArgs *  e)
             {
                Hide(); // hide StartDialog
                deleteDialog->Show(); // show DeleteDialog
             }  // end method deleteButton_Click

    protected:

       void ShowStartDialog()
       {
          Show();
       }
    };
}
```

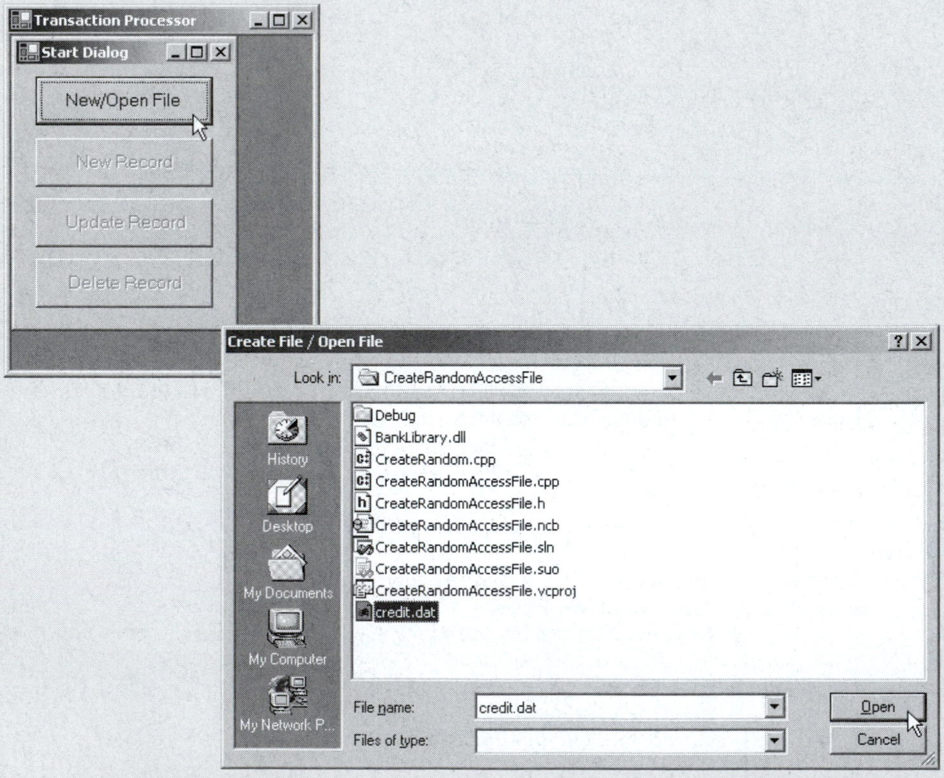

Fig. 17.33 `StartDialog` class enables users to access dialog boxes associated with various transactions. (Part 4 of 5.)

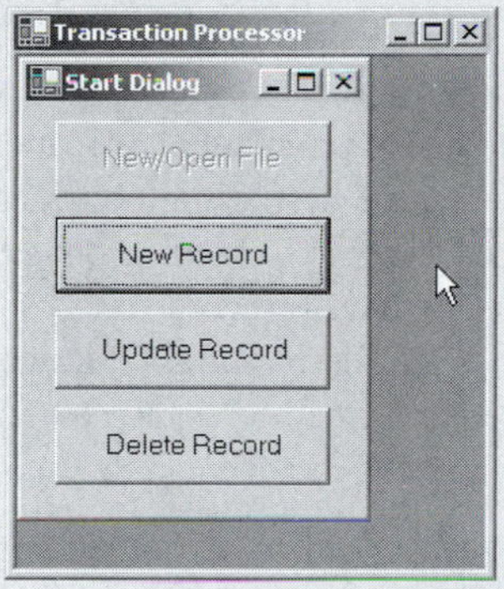

Fig. 17.33 `StartDialog` class enables users to access dialog boxes associated with various transactions. (Part 5 of 5.)

If the user specifies a file name, line 108 (of Fig. 17.33) instantiates an object of class `Transaction` (Fig. 17.29–Fig. 17.30), which acts as the proxy for creating, reading records from and writing records to random-access files. Line 109 calls `Transaction`'s method `OpenFile`, which either creates or opens the specified file, depending on whether the file does not exist or exists.

Class `StartDialog` also creates internal windows that enable the user to create, update and delete records. We do not use the default constructor; instead, we use an overloaded constructor that takes as arguments the `Transaction` object and a delegate object that points to method `ShowStartDialog` (lines 160–163). Each child window uses the second delegate parameter to display the `StartDialog` GUI when the user closes a child window. Lines 118–127 instantiate objects of classes `UpdateDialog`, `NewDialogForm` and `DeleteDialog`, which serve as the child windows.

When the user clicks the **New Record** button in the **Start Dialog**, the program invokes method `newButton_Click` of class `StartDialog` (lines 137–142 of Fig. 17.33), which displays the `NewDialogForm` internal frame (Fig. 17.35). Class `NewDialogForm` enables the user to create records in the file that `StartDialog` opened (or created). Line 6 of Fig. 17.34 defines `MyDelegate` as a delegate to a method that does not return a value and has no parameters; method `ShowStartDialog` of class `StartDialog` (Fig. 17.33, lines 160–163) conforms to these requirements. Class `NewDialogForm` receives a `MyDelegate` pointer, which points to this method as a parameter—therefore, `NewDialogForm` can invoke this method to display the `StartDialog` when the user exits the `NewDialogForm`. Classes `UpdateDialog` and `DeleteDialog` also receive `MyDelegate` pointers as arguments, enabling them to display `StartDialog` after completing their tasks.

```
1  // Fig. 17.34: MyDelegate.h
2  // Declares MyDelegate as a delegate with no input or return values.
3
4  #pragma once
5
6  __delegate void MyDelegate();
```

Fig. 17.34 Delegate declaration used in transaction-processor case study.

After the user enters data in the `TextBoxes` of the `NewDialogForm` and clicks the **Save Record** button, the program invokes method `saveButton_Click` (lines 83–97 of Fig. 17.35) to write the record to disk. Lines 86–88 call method `GetRecord` of the `Transaction` object, which should return an empty `RandomAccessRecord`. If method `GetRecord` returns a `RandomAccessRecord` that contains data, the user is attempting to overwrite that `RandomAccessRecord` with a new one. Line 92 calls `private` method `InsertRecord` (lines 102–144). If the user is attempting to overwrite an existing record, lines 113–115 notify the user that the record already exists and return from the method. Otherwise, the `RandomAccessRecord` is empty, and method `InsertRecord` calls method `AddRecord` of the `Transaction` object (lines 130–131), which adds the newly created `RandomAccessRecord` to the file.

```
1  // Fig. 17.35: NewDialog.h
2  // Enables user to insert new record into file.
3
4  #pragma once
5
6  using namespace System;
7  using namespace System::ComponentModel;
8  using namespace System::Collections;
9  using namespace System::Windows::Forms;
10 using namespace System::Data;
11 using namespace System::Drawing;
12 using namespace BankLibrary;   // Deitel namespace
13
14 #include "Transaction.h"
15 #include "MyDelegate.h"
16
17 namespace TransactionProcessor
18 {
19    /// <summary>
20    /// Summary for NewDialog
21    ///
22    /// WARNING: If you change the name of this class, you will need to
23    ///          change the 'Resource File Name' property for the managed
24    ///          resource compiler tool associated with all .resx files
25    ///          this class depends on.  Otherwise, the designers will not
26    ///          be able to interact properly with localized resources
27    ///          associated with this form.
28    /// </summary>
29    public __gc class NewDialog : public BankUIForm
30    {
31    public:
32       NewDialog(void)
33       {
34          InitializeComponent();
35       }
36
37       NewDialog( Transaction *transactionProxyValue,
38          MyDelegate *delegateValue )
39       {
```

Fig. 17.35 `NewDialog` class allows users to create new records. (Part 1 of 4.)

```
         InitializeComponent();
         showPreviousWindow = delegateValue;

         // instantiate object that handles transactions
         transactionProxy = transactionProxyValue;
      }

   protected:
      void Dispose(Boolean disposing)
      {
         if (disposing && components)
         {
            components->Dispose();
         }
         __super::Dispose(disposing);
      }
   private: System::Windows::Forms::Button *  saveButton;
   private: System::Windows::Forms::Button *  cancelButton;

   // delegate for method that displays previous window
   public: MyDelegate *showPreviousWindow;

   // pointer to object that handles transactions
   private: Transaction *transactionProxy;

   private:
      /// <summary>
      /// Required designer variable.
      /// </summary>
      System::ComponentModel::Container* components;

   // Visual Studio .NET generated GUI code

   // invoked when user clicks Cancel button
   private: System::Void cancelButton_Click(
               System::Object *  sender, System::EventArgs *  e)
            {
               Hide();
               ClearTextBoxes();
               showPreviousWindow->Invoke();
            } // end method cancelButton_Click

   // invoked when user clicks Save Record button
   private: System::Void saveButton_Click(
               System::Object *  sender, System::EventArgs *  e)
            {
               RandomAccessRecord *record =
                  transactionProxy->GetRecord( GetTextBoxValues()
                  [ TextBoxIndices::ACCOUNT ] );

               // if record exists, add it to file
               if ( record != NULL )
                  InsertRecord( record );
```

Fig. 17.35 NewDialog class allows users to create new records. (Part 2 of 4.)

```

            Hide();
            ClearTextBoxes();
            showPreviousWindow->Invoke();
         } // end method saveButton_Click

private:

   // insert record in file at position specified by accountNumber
   void InsertRecord( RandomAccessRecord *record )
   {
      //store TextBox values in string array
      String *textBoxValues[] = GetTextBoxValues();

      // store TextBox account field
      int accountNumber = Int32::Parse(
         textBoxValues[ TextBoxIndices::ACCOUNT ] );

      // notify user and return if record account is not empty
      if ( record->Account != 0 ) {
         MessageBox::Show(
            S"Record Already Exists or Invalid Number", S"Error",
            MessageBoxButtons::OK, MessageBoxIcon::Error );

         return;
      } // end if

      // store values in record
      record->Account = accountNumber;
      record->FirstName = textBoxValues[ TextBoxIndices::FIRST ];
      record->LastName = textBoxValues[ TextBoxIndices::LAST ];
      record->Balance = Double::Parse(
         textBoxValues[ TextBoxIndices::BALANCE ] );

      // add record to file
      try {

         if ( transactionProxy->AddRecord(
            record, accountNumber ) == false )

            return; // if error
      } // end try

      // notify user if error occurs in parameter mismatch
      catch ( FormatException * ) {
         MessageBox::Show( S"Invalid Balance", S"Error",
            MessageBoxButtons::OK, MessageBoxIcon::Error );
      } // end catch

      MessageBox::Show( S"Record Created", S"Success",
         MessageBoxButtons::OK, MessageBoxIcon::Information );
   } // end method InsertRecord
};
```

Fig. 17.35 NewDialog class allows users to create new records. (Part 3 of 4.)

```
}
```

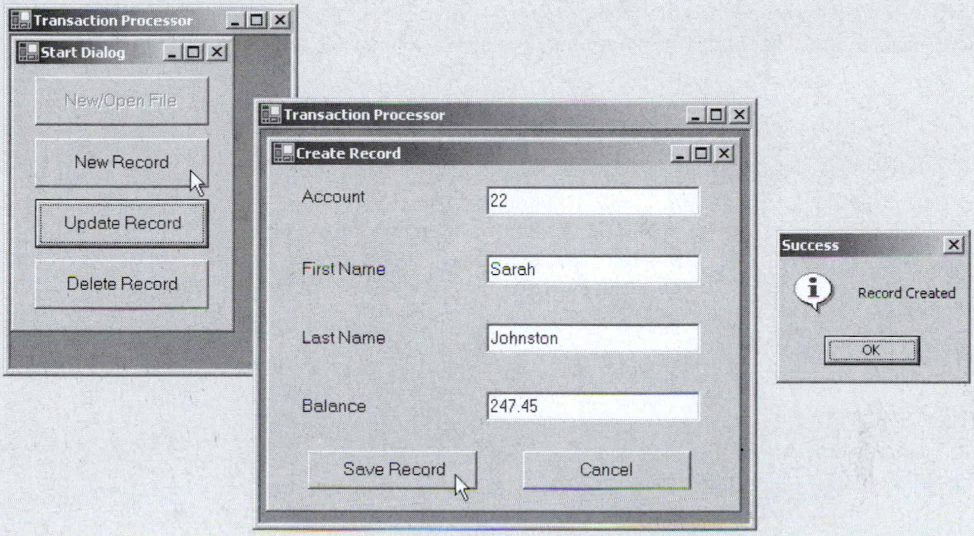

Fig. 17.35 `NewDialog` class allows users to create new records. (Part 4 of 4.)

When the user clicks the **Update Record** button in the **Start Dialog**, the program invokes method `updateButton_Click` of class `StartDialog` (Fig. 17.33, lines 144–149), which displays the `UpdateDialog` internal frame (Fig. 17.36). Class `UpdateDialog` enables the user to update existing records in the file.

To update a record, the user must enter the account number associated with that record. When the user presses *Enter*, `UpdateDialog` calls method `accountTextBox_KeyDown` (lines 77–113 of Fig. 17.36) to display the record contents. This method calls method `GetRecord` of the `Transaction` object (lines 84–86) to retrieve the specified `RandomAccessRecord`. If the record is not empty, lines 96–103 populate the `TextBoxes` with the `RandomAccessRecord` values.

```
1  // Fig. 17.36: UpdateDialog.h
2  // Enables user to update records in file.
3
4  #pragma once
5
6  using namespace System;
7  using namespace System::ComponentModel;
8  using namespace System::Collections;
9  using namespace System::Windows::Forms;
10 using namespace System::Data;
11 using namespace System::Drawing;
12 using namespace BankLibrary;    // Deitel namespace
13
```

Fig. 17.36 `UpdateDialog` class allows users to update records in transaction-processor case study. (Part 1 of 6.)

```
#include "Transaction.h"
#include "MyDelegate.h"

namespace TransactionProcessor
{
   /// <summary>
   /// Summary for UpdateDialog
   ///
   /// WARNING: If you change the name of this class, you will need to
   ///          change the 'Resource File Name' property for the managed
   ///          resource compiler tool associated with all .resx files
   ///          this class depends on.  Otherwise, the designers will not
   ///          be able to interact properly with localized resources
   ///          associated with this form.
   /// </summary>
   public __gc class UpdateDialog : public BankUIForm
   {
   public:
      UpdateDialog(void)
      {
         InitializeComponent();
      }

      // initialize components and set members to parameter values
      UpdateDialog( Transaction *transactionProxyValue,
         MyDelegate *delegateValue )
      {
         InitializeComponent();
         showPreviousWindow = delegateValue;

         // instantiate object that handles transactions
         transactionProxy = transactionProxyValue;
      }

   protected:
      void Dispose(Boolean disposing)
      {
         if (disposing && components)
         {
            components->Dispose();
         }
         __super::Dispose(disposing);
      }
   private: System::Windows::Forms::Button *  saveButton;
   private: System::Windows::Forms::TextBox *  transactionTextBox;
   private: System::Windows::Forms::Label *  transactionLabel;
   private: System::Windows::Forms::Button *  cancelButton;

   // pointer to object that handles transactions
   private: Transaction *transactionProxy;

```

Fig. 17.36 `UpdateDialog` class allows users to update records in transaction-processor case study. (Part 2 of 6.)

```
      // delegate for method that displays previous window
      private: MyDelegate *showPreviousWindow;

      private:
         /// <summary>
         /// Required designer variable.
         /// </summary>
         System::ComponentModel::Container* components;

      // Visual Studio .NET generated GUI code

      // invoked when user enters text in account TextBox
      private: System::Void accountTextBox_KeyDown(System::Object *  sender,
                  System::Windows::Forms::KeyEventArgs *  e)
               {
                  // determine whether user pressed Enter key
                  if ( e->KeyCode == Keys::Enter ) {

                     // retrieve record associated with account from file
                     RandomAccessRecord *record =
                        transactionProxy->GetRecord( GetTextBoxValues()
                        [ TextBoxIndices::ACCOUNT ] );

                     // return if record does not exist
                     if ( record == 0 )
                        return;

                     // determine whether record is empty
                     if ( record->Account != 0 ) {

                        // store record values in string array
                        String *values[] = { record->Account.ToString(),
                           record->FirstName->ToString(),
                           record->LastName->ToString(),
                           record->Balance.ToString() };

                        // copy string array value to TextBox values
                        SetTextBoxValues( values );
                        transactionTextBox->Text = S"[Charge or Payment]";

                     } // end if
                     else {

                        // notify user if record does not exist
                        MessageBox::Show( S"Record Does Not Exist", S"Error",
                           MessageBoxButtons::OK, MessageBoxIcon::Error );
                     } // end else
                  } // end if
               } // end method accountTextBox_KeyDown

```

Fig. 17.36 `UpdateDialog` class allows users to update records in transaction-processor case study. (Part 3 of 6.)

```
   // invoked when user enters text in transaction TextBox
   private: System::Void transactionTextBox_KeyDown(
               System::Object *  sender,
               System::Windows::Forms::KeyEventArgs *  e)
            {
               // determine whether user pressed Enter key
               if ( e->KeyCode == Keys::Enter ) {

                  // calculate balance using transaction TextBox value
                  try {

                     // retrieve record associated with account from file
                     RandomAccessRecord *record =
                        transactionProxy->GetRecord( GetTextBoxValues()
                        [ TextBoxIndices::ACCOUNT ] );

                     // get transaction TextBox value
                     double transactionValue =
                        Double::Parse( transactionTextBox->Text );

                     // calculate new balance (old balance + transaction)
                     double newBalance =
                        record->Balance + transactionValue;

                     // store record values in string array
                     String *values[] = { record->Account.ToString(),
                        record->FirstName->ToString(),
                        record->LastName->ToString(),
                        newBalance.ToString() };

                     // copy string array value to TextBox values
                     SetTextBoxValues( values );

                     // clear transaction TextBox
                     transactionTextBox->Text = S"";
                  } // end try

                  // notify user if error occurs in parameter mismatch
                  catch ( FormatException * ) {
                     MessageBox::Show( S"Invalid Transaction", S"Error",
                        MessageBoxButtons::OK, MessageBoxIcon::Error );
                  } // end catch
               } // end if
            } // end method transactionTextBox_KeyDown

   // invoked when user clicks Save Changes button
   private: System::Void saveButton_Click(
               System::Object *  sender, System::EventArgs *  e)
            {
               RandomAccessRecord *record =
                  transactionProxy->GetRecord( GetTextBoxValues()
                  [ TextBoxIndices::ACCOUNT ] );
```

Fig. 17.36 UpdateDialog class allows users to update records in transaction-processor case study. (Part 4 of 6.)

```

               // if record exists, update in file
               if ( record != 0 )
                  UpdateRecord( record );

               Hide();
               ClearTextBoxes();
               showPreviousWindow->Invoke();
            }  // end method saveButton_Click

   // invoked when user clicks Cancel button
   private: System::Void cancelButton_Click(
               System::Object *  sender, System::EventArgs *  e)
            {
               Hide();
               ClearTextBoxes();
               showPreviousWindow->Invoke();
            } // end method cancelButton_Click

   public:

      // update record in file at position specified by accountNumber
      void UpdateRecord( RandomAccessRecord *record )
      {
         // store TextBox values in record and write record to file
         try {
            int accountNumber = record->Account;
            String *values[] = GetTextBoxValues();

            // store values in record
            record->Account = accountNumber;
            record->FirstName = values[ TextBoxIndices::FIRST ];
            record->LastName = values[ TextBoxIndices::LAST ];
            record->Balance = Double::Parse(
               values[ TextBoxIndices::BALANCE ] );

            // add record to file
            if ( transactionProxy->AddRecord(
               record, accountNumber ) == false )

               return; // if error
         } // end try

         // notify user if error occurs in parameter mismatch
         catch ( FormatException * ) {
            MessageBox::Show( S"Invalid Balance", S"Error",
               MessageBoxButtons::OK, MessageBoxIcon::Error );
            return;
         } // end catch

         MessageBox::Show( S"Record Updated", S"Success",
            MessageBoxButtons::OK, MessageBoxIcon::Information );
```

Fig. 17.36 `UpdateDialog` class allows users to update records in transaction-processor case study. (Part 5 of 6.)

```
        } // end method UpdateRecord
    };
}
```

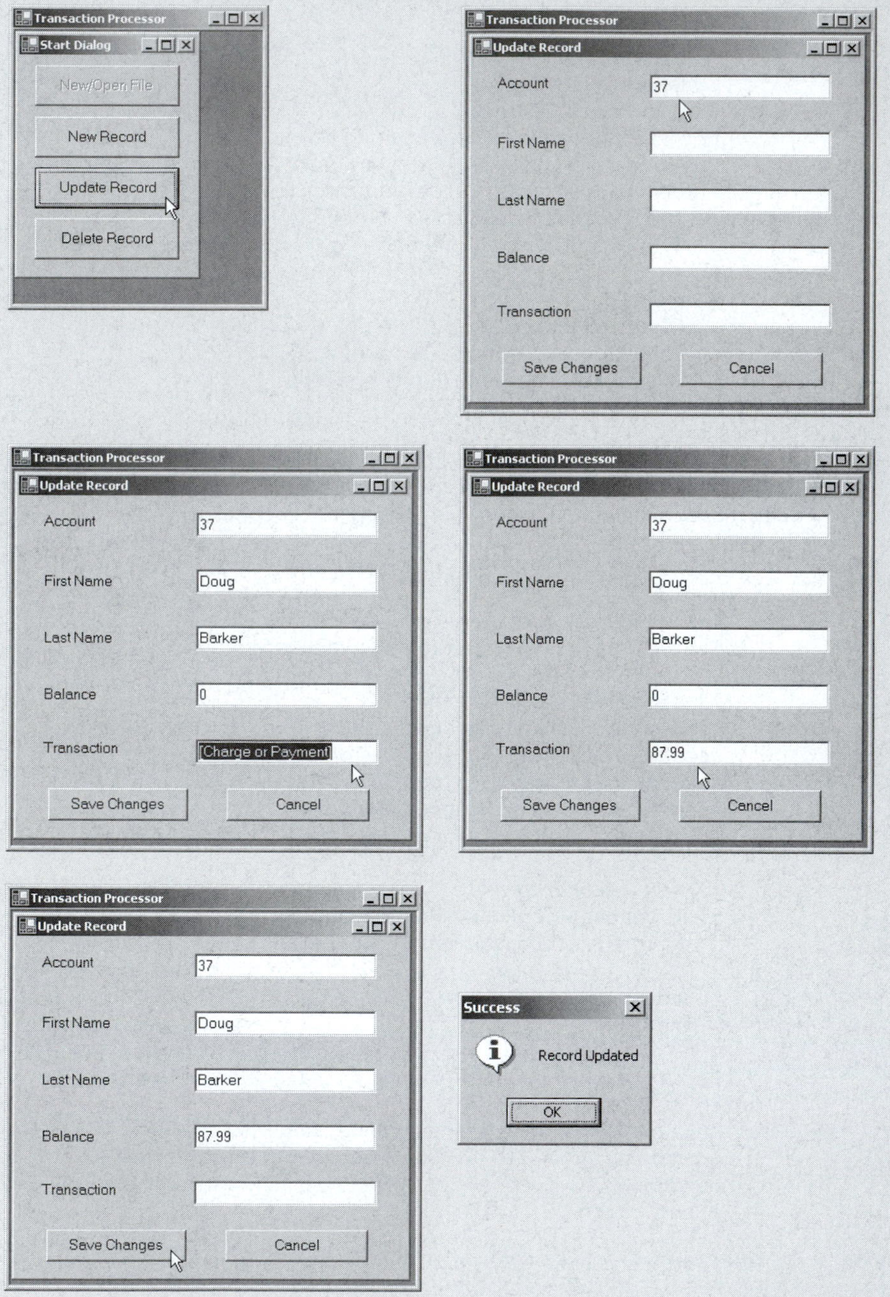

Fig. 17.36 `UpdateDialog` class allows users to update records in transaction-processor case study. (Part 6 of 6.)

The **Transaction** `TextBox` initially contains the string **[Charge or Payment]**. The user should select this text, type the transaction amount (a positive value for a charge or a negative value for a payment), then press *Enter*. The program calls method `transactionTextBox_KeyDown` (lines 116–158) to add the user-specified transaction amount to the current balance.

The user clicks the **Save Changes** button to write the altered contents of the `TextBoxes` to the file. (Note that pressing **Save Changes** does not update the **Balance** field—the user must press *Enter* to update this field before pressing **Save Changes**.) When the user clicks **Save Changes**, the program invokes method `saveButton_Click` (lines 161–175), which calls `private` method `UpdateRecord` (lines 189–219). This method calls method `AddRecord` of the `Transaction` object (lines 204–205) to store the `TextBox` values in a `RandomAccessRecord` and overwrite the existing file record with the `RandomAccessRecord` containing the new data.

When the user clicks the **Delete Record** button of the **Start Dialog**, the program invokes method `deleteButton_Click` of class `StartDialog` (Fig. 17.33, lines 151–156), which displays the `DeleteDialog` internal frame (Fig. 17.37). Class `DeleteDialog` enables the user to remove existing records from the file. To remove a record, the user must enter the account number associated with that record. When the user clicks the **Delete Record** button (now, from the `DeleteDialog` internal frame), `DeleteDialog` calls method `deleteButton_Click` (lines 77–89 of Fig. 17.37). This method calls method `DeleteRecord` (lines 102–133), which ensures that the record to be deleted exists, then calls method `AddRecord` of the `Transaction` object (lines 119–120) to overwrite the file record with an empty one.

```
1   // Fig. 17.37: DeleteDialog.h
2   // Enables user to delete records in file.
3
4   #pragma once
5
6   using namespace System;
7   using namespace System::ComponentModel;
8   using namespace System::Collections;
9   using namespace System::Windows::Forms;
10  using namespace System::Data;
11  using namespace System::Drawing;
12  using namespace BankLibrary;   // Deitel namespace
13
14  #include "Transaction.h"
15  #include "MyDelegate.h"
16
17  namespace TransactionProcessor
18  {
19     /// <summary>
20     /// Summary for DeleteDialog
21     ///
22     /// WARNING: If you change the name of this class, you will need to
23     ///          change the 'Resource File Name' property for the managed
```

Fig. 17.37 `DeleteDialog` class allows users to delete records from files in the transaction-processor case study. (Part 1 of 4.)

```
   ///         resource compiler tool associated with all .resx files
   ///         this class depends on.  Otherwise, the designers will not
   ///         be able to interact properly with localized resources
   ///         associated with this form.
   /// </summary>
   public __gc class DeleteDialog : public System::Windows::Forms::Form
   {
   public:
      DeleteDialog(void)
      {
         InitializeComponent();
      }

      // initialize components and set members to parameter values
      DeleteDialog( Transaction *transactionProxyValue,
         MyDelegate *delegateValue )
      {
         InitializeComponent();
         showPreviousWindow = delegateValue;

         // instantiate object that handles transactions
         transactionProxy = transactionProxyValue;
      }

   protected:
      void Dispose(Boolean disposing)
      {
         if (disposing && components)
         {
            components->Dispose();
         }
         __super::Dispose(disposing);
      }
   private: System::Windows::Forms::Label *  accountLabel;
   private: System::Windows::Forms::Button *  cancelButton;
   private: System::Windows::Forms::TextBox *  accountTextBox;
   private: System::Windows::Forms::Button *  deleteButton;

   // pointer to object that handles transactions
   private: Transaction *transactionProxy;

   // delegate for method that displays previous window
   private: MyDelegate *showPreviousWindow;

   private:
      /// <summary>
      /// Required designer variable.
      /// </summary>
      System::ComponentModel::Container* components;

   // Visual Studio .NET generated GUI code

```

Fig. 17.37 `DeleteDialog` class allows users to delete records from files in the transaction-processor case study. (Part 2 of 4.)

```
   // invoked when user clicks Delete Record button
   private: System::Void deleteButton_Click(
            System::Object *  sender, System::EventArgs *  e)
         {
            RandomAccessRecord *record =
               transactionProxy->GetRecord( accountTextBox->Text );

            // if record exists, delete it in file
            if ( record != NULL )
               DeleteRecord( record );

            this->Hide();
            showPreviousWindow->Invoke();
         } // end method deleteButton_Click

   // invoked when user clicks Cancel button
   private: System::Void cancelButton_Click(
            System::Object *  sender, System::EventArgs *  e)
         {
            this->Hide();
            showPreviousWindow->Invoke();
         } // end method cancelButton_Click

   public:

      // delete record in file at position specified by accountNumber
      void DeleteRecord( RandomAccessRecord *record )
      {
         int accountNumber = record->Account;

         // display error message if record does not exist
         if ( record->Account == 0 ) {
            MessageBox::Show( S"Record Does Not Exist", S"Error",
               MessageBoxButtons::OK, MessageBoxIcon::Error );
            accountTextBox->Clear();

            return;
         } // end if

         // create blank record
         record = new RandomAccessRecord();

         // write over file record with empty record
         if ( transactionProxy->AddRecord(
            record, accountNumber ) == true )

            // notify user of successful deletion
            MessageBox::Show( S"Record Deleted", S"Success",
               MessageBoxButtons::OK, MessageBoxIcon::Information );
         else

```

Fig. 17.37 `DeleteDialog` class allows users to delete records from files in the transaction-processor case study. (Part 3 of 4.)

```
            // notify user of failure
            MessageBox::Show( S"Record could not be deleted",
               S"Error", MessageBoxButtons::OK,
               MessageBoxIcon::Error );

         accountTextBox->Clear();
      } // end method DeleteRecord
   };
}
```

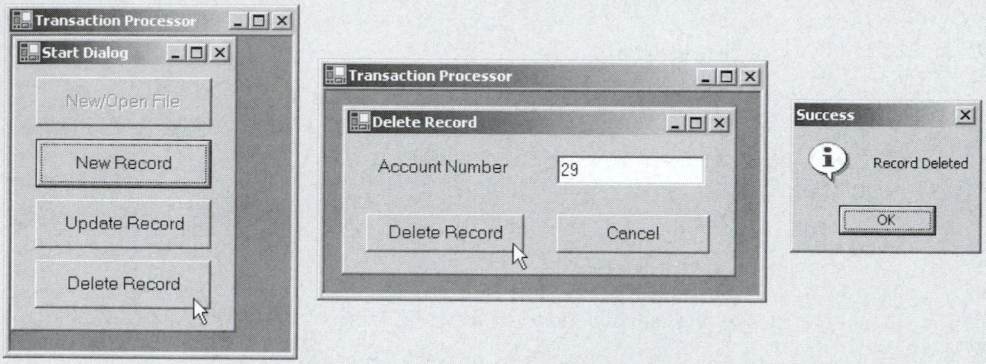

Fig. 17.37 `DeleteDialog` class allows users to delete records from files in the transaction-processor case study. (Part 4 of 4.)

In this chapter, we demonstrated how to read data from files and write data to files via both sequential-access and random-access file-processing techniques. Using class `BinaryFormatter`, we serialized and deserialized objects to and from streams; we then employed `FileStream`, `BinaryWriter` and `BinaryReader` to transfer the objects' byte representation to and from files. In Chapter 18, we discuss *Extensible Markup Language (XML)*, a widely supported technology for describing data. Using XML, we can describe any type of data, such as mathematical formulas, music and financial reports.

SUMMARY

- All data items processed by a computer ultimately are reduced to combinations of zeros and ones.
- The smallest data items that computers support are called bits and can assume either the value `0` or the value `1`.
- Digits, letters and special symbols are referred to as characters. The set of all characters used to write programs and represent data items on a particular computer is called that computer's character set. Every character in a computer's character set is represented as a pattern of `1`s and `0`s (characters in `System::String` objects are Unicode characters, which are composed of 2 bytes or 16 bits).
- A record is a group of related fields.
- At least one field in a record is chosen as a record key, which identifies that record as belonging to a particular person or entity and distinguishes that record from all other records in the file.
- A file is a group of related records.
- Files are used for long-term retention of large amounts of data and can store those data even after the program that created the data terminates.

- Data maintained in files often are called persistent data.
- Sometimes, a group of related files is called a database.
- A collection of programs designed to create and manage databases is called a database management system (DBMS).
- Class `File` enables programs to obtain information about a file.
- Class `Directory` enables programs to obtain information about a directory.
- Class `FileStream` provides method `Seek` for repositioning the file-position pointer (the byte number of the next byte in the file to be read or written) to any position in the file.
- The .NET Framework views each file as a sequential stream of bytes.
- Streams provide communication channels between files and programs.
- When a file is opened, an object is created, and a stream is associated with the object.
- To retrieve data sequentially from a file, programs normally start from the beginning of the file, reading all data consecutively until the desired data are found.
- Each file ends in some machine-dependent form of end-of-file marker.
- Objects of classes `OpenFileDialog` and `SaveFileDialog` are used for selecting files to open and save, respectively. Method `ShowDialog` of these classes displays that dialog.
- When displayed, both an `OpenFileDialog` and a `SaveFileDialog` prevent the user from interacting with any other program window until the dialog is closed. Dialogs that behave in this fashion are called modal dialogs.
- To perform file processing in MC++, the namespace `System::IO` must be referenced. This namespace includes definitions for stream classes such as `StreamReader`, `StreamWriter` and `FileStream`. Files are opened by creating objects of these stream classes.
- Programmers can use members of the `FileAccess` enumeration to control users' access to files.
- The .NET Framework imposes no structure on files (i.e., concepts like that of a "record" do not exist). The programmer must structure each file appropriately to meet the requirements of an application.
- The most common type of file organization is the sequential file, in which records typically are stored in order by the record-key field.
- With a sequential-access file, each successive input/output request reads or writes the next consecutive set of data in the file.
- Instant data access is possible with random-access files. A program can access individual records of a random-access file directly (and quickly) without searching through other records. Random-access files sometimes are called direct-access files.
- With a random-access file, each successive input/output request can be directed to any part of the file, which can be any distance from the part of the file referenced in the previous request.
- There are a variety of techniques for creating random-access files. Perhaps the simplest involves requiring that all records in a file be of the same fixed length.
- The use of fixed-length records makes it easy for a program to calculate (as a function of the record size and the record key) the exact location of any record in relation to the beginning of the file
- Data can be inserted into a random-access file without destroying other data in the file. Users can also update or delete previously stored data without rewriting the entire file.
- Random-access file-processing programs rarely write a single field to a file. Normally, they write one object at a time.
- `BinaryFormatter` uses methods `Serialize` and `Deserialize` to write and to read objects, respectively. Method `Serialize` writes the object's representation to a stream. Method `Deserialize` reads this representation from a stream and reconstructs the original object.

- Only classes with the `Serializable` attribute can be serialized to and deserialized from streams.
- Methods `Serialize` and `Deserialize` each require a `Stream` object as a parameter, enabling the `BinaryFormatter` to access the correct stream.
- Class `BinaryReader` and `BinaryWriter` provide methods for reading and writing bytes to streams, respectively. The `BinaryReader` and `BinaryWriter` constructors receive as arguments references to instances of class `System::IO::Stream`.
- Class `FileStream` inherits from class `Stream`, so we can pass the `FileStream` object as an argument to either the `BinaryReader` or `BinaryWriter` constructor to create an object that can transfer bytes directly to or from a file.
- Sorting with direct-access techniques is fast. This speed is achieved by making the file large enough to hold every possible record that might be created. Of course, this means that the file could be sparsely occupied most of the time, possibly wasting memory.

TERMINOLOGY

attribute
binary digit (bit)
`BinaryFormatter` class
`BinaryReader` class
`BinaryWriter` class
bit manipulation
`BufferedStream` class
character
character set
`Close` method of class `StreamReader`
closing a file
`Console` class
`Copy` method of class `File`
`Create` method of class `File`
`CreateDirectory` method of `Directory`
`CreateText` method of class `File`
data hierarchy
database
database management system (DBMS)
`Delete` method of class `Directory`
`Delete` method of class `File`
`Deserialize` method of `BinaryFormatter`
direct-access files
`Directory` class
`DirectoryInfo` class
end-of-file marker
`Error` property of class `Console`
escape sequence
`Exists` method of class `Directory`
field
file
`File` class
`FileAccess` enumeration
file-position pointer
file-processing programs
`FileStream` class
fixed-length records
`GetCreationTime` method of class `Directory`
`GetCreationTime` method of class `File`
`GetDirectories` method of class `Directory`
`GetFiles` method of class `Directory`
`GetLastAccessTime` method of `Directory`
`GetLastAccessTime` method of class `File`
`GetLastWriteTime` method of class `Directory`
`GetLastWriteTime` method of class `File`
`In` property of class `Console`
`IOException`
"instant-access" application
Managed C++ Class Library project
`MemoryStream` class
modal dialog
`Move` method of class `Directory`
`Move` method of class `File`
`Open` method of class `File`
`OpenFileDialog` class
`OpenRead` method of class `File`
`OpenText` method of class `File`
`OpenWrite` method of class `File`
`Out` property of class `Console`
pattern of `1`s and `0`s
persistent data
random-access file
`Read` method of class `Console`
`ReadDouble` method of `BinaryReader`
`ReadInt32` method of `BinaryReader`
`ReadLine` method of class `Console`
`ReadLine` method of class `StreamReader`
`ReadString` method of `BinaryReader`
record
record key

regular expression
`SaveFileDialog` class
secondary storage devices
`Seek` method of class `FileStream`
`SeekOrigin` enumeration
separator character
sequential-access file
`Serializable` attribute
`SerializationException`
`Serialize` method of class `BinaryFormatter`
`ShowDialog` method of class `OpenFileDialog`
`ShowDialog` method of class `SaveFileDialog`
standard error-stream object
standard input-stream object
standard output-stream object
`Stream` class
stream of bytes
stream processing
`StreamReader` class
`StreamWriter` class
`System::IO` namespace
`System::Runtime::Serialization::Formatters::Binary` namespace
`TextReader` class
`TextWriter` class
transaction-processing system
`Write` method of class `BinaryWriter`
`Write` method of class `Console`
`Write` method of class `StreamWriter`
`WriteLine` method of class `Console`
`WriteLine` method of class `StreamWriter`

SELF-REVIEW EXERCISES

17.1 State whether each of the following is *true* or *false*. If *false*, explain why.

a) Creating instances of classes `File` and `Directory` is impossible.
b) Typically, a sequential file stores records in order by the record-key field.
c) Class `StreamReader` inherits from class `Stream`.
d) Objects of any class can be serialized to a file.
e) Searching a random-access file sequentially to find a specific record is unnecessary.
f) Method `Seek` of class `FileStream` always seeks relative to the beginning of a file.
g) The .NET Framework provides class `Record` to store records for random-access file-processing applications.
h) Banking systems, point-of-sale systems and automated-teller machines are types of transaction-processing systems.
i) Classes `StreamReader` and `StreamWriter` can be used with sequential-access files.
j) Instantiating objects of type `Stream` is not allowed because `Stream` is an abstract class.

17.2 Fill in the blanks in each of the following statements:

a) Ultimately, all data items processed by a computer are reduced to combinations of ________ and ________.
b) The smallest data item a computer can process is called a(n) ________.
c) A(n) ________ is a group of related records.
d) Digits, letters and special symbols are collectively referred to as ________.
e) Sometimes, a group of related files is called a(n) ________.
f) `StreamReader` method ________ reads a line of text from a file.
g) `StreamWriter` method ________ writes a line of text to a file.
h) Method `Serialize` of class `BinaryFormatter` takes a(n) ________ and a(n) ________ as arguments.
i) The ________ namespace contains most of MC++'s file-processing classes.
j) The ________ namespace contains the `BinaryFormatter` class.

ANSWERS TO SELF-REVIEW EXERCISES

17.1 a) True. b) True. c) False. `StreamReader` inherits from `TextReader`. d) False. Only objects of classes with the `Serializable` attribute can be serialized. e) True. f) False. It seeks relative to the `SeekOrigin` enumeration member that is passed as one of the arguments. g) False. The .NET Framework imposes no structure on a file, so the concept of a "record" does not exist. h.) True. i) True. j) True.

17.2 a) 1s, 0s. b) bit. c) file. d) characters. e) database. f) `ReadLine`. g) `WriteLine`. h) `Stream`, `Object`. i) `System::IO`. j) `System::Runtime::Serialization::Formatters::Binary`.

EXERCISES

17.3 Create a program that stores student grades in a text file. The file should contain the name, ID number, class taken and grade of every student. Allow the user to load a grade file and display its contents in a read-only textbox. The entries should be displayed as follows:

```
LastName, FirstName:  ID#  Class  Grade
```

We list some sample data below:

```
Jones, Bob: 1 "Introduction to Computer Science" "A-"
Johnson, Sarah: 2 "Data Structures" "B+"
Smith, Sam: 3 "Data Structures" "C"
```

17.4 Modify the previous program to use objects of a class that can be serialized to and deserialized from a file. Ensure fixed-length records by fixing the lengths of the fields `LastName`, `FirstName`, `Class` and `Grade`.

17.5 Extend classes `StreamReader` and `StreamWriter`. Make the class that derives from `StreamReader` have methods `ReadInteger`, `ReadBoolean` and `ReadString`. Make the class that derives from `StreamWriter` have methods `WriteInteger`, `WriteBoolean` and `WriteString`. Think about how to design the writing methods so that the reading methods will be able to read what was written. Design `WriteInteger` and `WriteBoolean` to write strings of uniform size, so that `ReadInteger` and `ReadBoolean` can read those values accurately. Make sure `ReadString` and `WriteString` use the same character(s) to separate strings.

17.6 Create a program that combines the ideas of Fig. 17.12–Fig. 17.13 and Fig. 17.15–Fig. 17.16 to allow a user to write records to and read records from a file. Add an extra field of type `bool` to the record to indicate whether the account has overdraft protection.

17.7 In commercial data processing, it is common to have several files in each application system. In an accounts receivable system, for example, there is generally a master file containing detailed information about each customer, such as the customer's name, address, telephone number, outstanding balance, credit limit, discount terms, contract arrangements and possibly a condensed history of recent purchases and cash payments.

As transactions occur (i.e., sales are made and cash payments arrive in the mail), they are entered into a file. At the end of each business period (i.e., a month for some companies, a week for others and a day in some cases), the file of transactions (`trans.dat`) is applied to the master file (`oldmast.dat`), thus updating each account's record of purchases and payments. During an updating run, the master file is rewritten as a new file (`newmast.dat`), which then is used at the end of the next business period to begin the updating process again.

File-matching programs must deal with certain problems that do not exist in single-file programs. For example, a match does not always occur. A customer on the master file might not have made any purchases or cash payments in the current business period, and, therefore, no record for this customer will appear on the transaction file. Similarly, a customer who did make some purchases or cash payments might have just moved to the community, and the company might not have had a chance to create a master record for this customer.

When a match occurs (i.e., records with the same account number appear on both the master file and the transaction file), add the dollar amount on the transaction file to the current balance on the master file and write the `newmast.dat` record. (Assume that purchases are indicated by positive amounts on the transaction file and that payments are indicated by negative amounts.) When there is a master record for a particular account, but no corresponding transaction record, simply write the master record to `newmast.dat`. When there is a transaction record, but no corresponding master record, print the message "`Unmatched transaction record for account number...`" (fill in the account number from the transaction record).

17.8 You are the owner of a hardware store and need to keep an inventory of the different tools you sell, how many of each are currently in stock and the cost of each. Write a program that initializes the random-access file `hardware.dat` to 100 empty records, lets you input data relating to each tool, enables you to list all your tools, lets you delete a record for a tool that you no longer have and lets you update any information in the file. The tool identification number should be the record number. Use the information in Fig. 17.38 to start your file.

Record #	Tool name	Quantity	Price
3	Electric sander	18	35.99
19	Hammer	128	10.00
26	Jig saw	16	14.25
39	Lawn mower	10	79.50
56	Power saw	8	89.99
76	Screwdriver	236	4.99
81	Sledge hammer	32	19.75
88	Wrench	65	6.48

Fig. 17.38 Inventory of a hardware store.

18

Extensible Markup Language (XML)

Objectives

- To mark up data using XML.
- To understand the concept of an XML namespace.
- To understand the relationship between DTDs, Schemas and XML.
- To create Schemas.
- To create and use simple XSLT documents.
- To transform XML documents into XHTML, using class `XslTransform`.

Knowing trees, I understand the meaning of patience.
Knowing grass, I can appreciate persistence.
Hal Borland

Like everything metaphysical, the harmony between thought and reality is to be found in the grammar of the language.
Ludwig Wittgenstein

I played with an idea and grew willful, tossed it into the air; transformed it; let it escape and recaptured it; made it iridescent with fancy, and winged it with paradox.
Oscar Wilde

Outline

18.1 Introduction

The *Extensible Markup Language* (XML) was developed in 1996 by the World Wide Web Consortium's (W3C's) XML Working Group. XML is a portable, widely supported, *open* (i.e., non-proprietary) *technology* for describing data. XML is becoming the standard for storing data that is exchanged between applications. Using XML, document authors can describe any type of data, including mathematical formulas, software-configuration instructions, music, recipes and financial reports. XML documents are readable by both humans and machines.

The .NET Framework uses XML extensively. The Framework Class Library (FCL) provides a set of XML-related classes. Much of Visual Studio .NET's internal implementation employs XML. Visual Studio .NET also includes an XML editor and validator.[1] In this chapter, we introduce XML, XML-related technologies and key classes for creating and manipulating XML documents.

18.2 XML Documents

In this section, we present our first XML document, which describes an article (Fig. 18.1). [*Note:* The line numbers shown are not part of the XML document.]

```
<?xml version = "1.0"?>

<!-- Fig. 18.1: article.xml      -->
<!-- Article structured with XML. -->
```

Fig. 18.1 XML used to mark up an article. (Part 1 of 2.)

1. For more information about XML in Visual Studio .NET, visit `msdn.microsoft.com/library/default.asp?url=/library/en-us/vsintro7/html/vxorixmlinvisualstudio.asp`.

```
5
6   <article>
7
8      <title>Simple XML</title>
9
10     <date>August 6, 2003</date>
11
12     <author>
13        <firstName>Su</firstName>
14        <lastName>Fari</lastName>
15     </author>
16
17     <summary>XML is pretty easy.</summary>
18
19     <content>In this chapter, we present a wide variety of examples
20        that use XML.
21     </content>
22
23  </article>
```

Fig. 18.1 XML used to mark up an article. (Part 2 of 2.)

This document begins with an optional *XML declaration* (line 1), which identifies the document as an XML document. The `version` *information parameter* specifies the version of XML that is used in the document. XML comments (lines 3–4), which begin with `<!--` and end with `-->`, can be placed almost anywhere in an XML document. As in an MC++ program, comments are used in XML for documentation purposes.

Common Programming Error 18.1

Placing any characters, including white space, before the XML declaration is a syntax error.

Portability Tip 18.1

Although the XML declaration is optional, documents should include the declaration to identify the version of XML used. Otherwise, in the future, a document that lacks an XML declaration might be assumed to conform to the latest version of XML, and errors could result.

In XML, data are marked up with *tags*, which are names enclosed in *angle brackets* (<>). Tags are used in pairs to delimit character data (e.g., `Simple XML` in line 8). A tag that begins *markup* (i.e., XML data) is called a *start tag*; a tag that terminates markup is called an *end tag*. Examples of start tags are `<article>` and `<title>` (lines 6 and 8, respectively). End tags differ from start tags in that they contain a *forward slash* (/) character immediately after the < character. Examples of end tags are `</title>` and `</article>` (lines 8 and 23, respectively). XML documents can contain any number of tags.

Common Programming Error 18.2

Failure to provide a corresponding end tag for a start tag is a syntax error.

Individual units of markup (i.e., everything from a start tag through its corresponding end tag) are called *elements*. An XML document includes one element (called a root element or document element) that contains all other elements. The root element must be the first element after the XML declaration. In Fig. 18.1, `article` (line 6) is the root element. Elements are nested within each other to form hierarchies—with the root element at the top of the hierarchy. This allows document authors to create explicit relationships between data. For example, elements `title`, `date`, `author`, `summary` and `content` are nested within `article`. Elements `firstName` and `lastName` are nested within `author`.

Common Programming Error 18.3

Attempting to create more than one root element in an XML document is a syntax error.

Element `title` (line 8) contains the title of the article, `Simple XML`, as character data. Similarly, `date` (line 10), `summary` (line 17) and `content` (lines 19–21) contain as character data the date, summary and content, respectively. XML element names can be of any length and may contain letters, digits, underscores, hyphens and periods—they must begin with a letter or an underscore.

Common Programming Error 18.4

XML is case sensitive. The use of the wrong case for an XML element name (in a begin tag, end tag, etc.) is a syntax error.

By itself, this document is simply a text file named `article.xml`. Although it is not required, most XML documents end in the file extension *`.xml`*. Processing XML documents requires a program called an *XML parser* (also called an *XML processor*). Parsers are responsible for checking an XML document's syntax and making the XML document's data available to applications. XML parsers are built into such applications as Visual Studio .NET or are available for download over the Internet. Popular parsers include Microsoft's *MSXML* (`msdn.microsoft.com/library/default.asp?url=/library/en-us/xmlsdk/htm/sdk_intro_6g53.asp`), the Apache Software Foundation's *Xerces* (`xml.apache.org`) and IBM's *XML4J* (`www-106.ibm.com/developerworks/xml/library/x-xml4j/`). In this chapter, we use MSXML.

When the user loads `article.xml` into Internet Explorer (IE),[2] MSXML parses the document and passes the parsed data to IE. IE then uses a built-in *style sheet* to format the data. Notice that the resulting format of the data (Fig. 18.2) is similar to the format of the XML document shown in Fig. 18.1. As we soon demonstrate, style sheets play an important and powerful role in the transformation of XML data into formats suitable for display.

Notice the minus (**–**) and plus (**+**) signs in Fig. 18.2. Although these are not part of the XML document, IE places them next to all *container elements* (i.e., elements that contain other elements). Container elements also are called *parent elements*. A minus sign indicates that the parent element's *child elements* (i.e., nested elements) are being displayed. When clicked, IE collapses the container element and hides its children, and the minus sign becomes a plus sign. Conversely, clicking a plus sign expands the container element and changes the plus sign to a minus sign. This behavior is similar to the viewing of the directory structure on a Windows system using Windows Explorer. In fact, a directory structure often is modeled as a series of tree structures, in which each drive letter (e.g., `C:`, etc.) represents the *root* of a tree. Each folder is a *node* in the tree. Parsers often place XML data into trees to facilitate efficient manipulation, as discussed in Section 18.4.

---

2. IE 5 and higher.

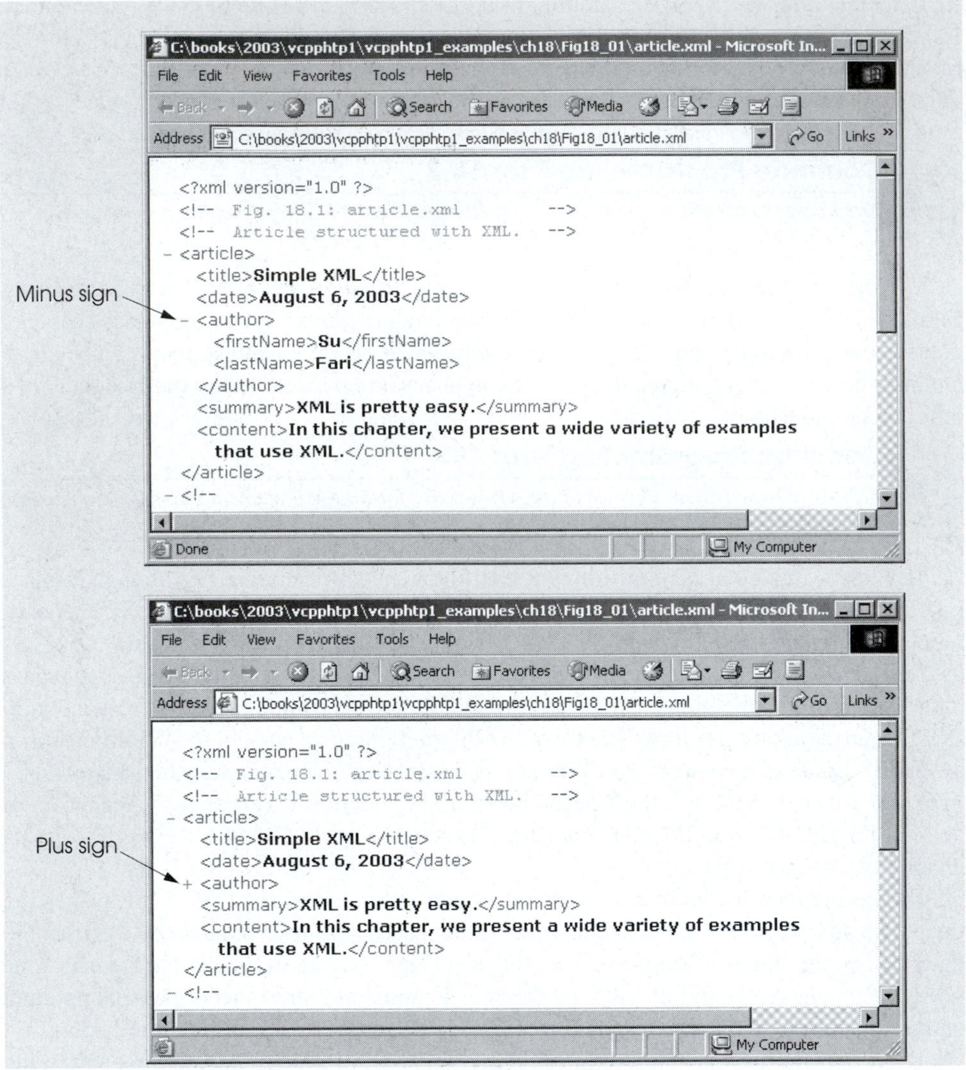
C:\books\2003\vcpphtp1\vcpphtp1_examples\ch18\Fig18_01\article.xml - Microsoft In...
Minus sign
<?xml version="1.0" ?>
<!-- Fig. 18.1: article.xml -->
<!-- Article structured with XML. -->
- <article>
<title>Simple XML</title>
<date>August 6, 2003</date>
- <author>
<firstName>Su</firstName>
<lastName>Fari</lastName>
</author>
<summary>XML is pretty easy.</summary>
<content>In this chapter, we present a wide variety of examples that use XML.</content>
</article>
Plus sign
+ <author>
My Computer

Fig. 18.2 `article.xml` displayed by Internet Explorer.

Common Programming Error 18.5

Nesting XML tags improperly is a syntax error. For example, `<x><y>hello</x></y>` *is an error, because the child element's ending tag (*`</y>`*) must precede the parent element's ending tag (*`</x>`*).*

We now present a second XML document (Fig. 18.3), which marks up a business letter. This document contains significantly more data than did the previous XML document.

Root element `letter` (lines 6–45) contains the child elements `contact` (lines 7–16 and 18–27), `salutation` (line 29), `paragraph` (lines 31–36 and 38–40), `closing` (line 42) and `signature` (line 44). In addition to being placed between tags, data also can be placed in *attributes*, which are name-value pairs separated by = in start tags. Elements can have

```
1  <?xml version = "1.0"?>
2
3  <!-- Fig. 18.3: letter.xml                    -->
4  <!-- Business letter formatted with XML. -->
5
6  <letter>
7     <contact type = "from">
8        <name>Jane Doe</name>
9        <address1>Box 12345</address1>
10       <address2>15 Any Ave.</address2>
11       <city>Othertown</city>
12       <state>Otherstate</state>
13       <zip>67890</zip>
14       <phone>555-4321</phone>
15       <flag gender = "F" />
16    </contact>
17
18    <contact type = "to">
19       <name>John Doe</name>
20       <address1>123 Main St.</address1>
21       <address2></address2>
22       <city>Anytown</city>
23       <state>Anystate</state>
24       <zip>12345</zip>
25       <phone>555-1234</phone>
26       <flag gender = "M" />
27    </contact>
28
29    <salutation>Dear Sir:</salutation>
30
31    <paragraph>It is our privilege to inform you about our new
32       database managed with <technology>XML</technology>. This
33       new system allows you to reduce the load on
34       your inventory list server by having the client machine
35       perform the work of sorting and filtering the data.
36    </paragraph>
37
38    <paragraph>Please visit our Web site for availability
39       and pricing.
40    </paragraph>
41
42    <closing>Sincerely</closing>
43
44    <signature>Ms. Doe</signature>
45 </letter>
```

Fig. 18.3 XML used to mark up a business letter.

any number of attributes in their start tags. The first `contact` element (lines 7–16) has attribute `type` with *attribute value* `"from"`, which indicates that this `contact` element marks up information about the letter's sender. The second `contact` element (lines 18–27) has attribute `type` with value `"to"`, which indicates that this `contact` element marks up information about the letter's recipient. Like element names, attribute names can be of any length; may contain letters, digits, underscores, hyphens and periods; and must begin with either a letter or underscore character. A `contact` element contains a contact's name, address, phone number and gender. Element `salutation` (line 29) marks up the letter's salutation. Lines 31–40 mark up the letter's body with `paragraph` elements. Elements `closing` (line 42) and `signature` (line 44) mark up the closing sentence and the signature of the letter's author, respectively.

Common Programming Error 18.6

Failure to enclose attribute values in either double ("") or single ('') quotes is a syntax error.

Common Programming Error 18.7

Attempting to provide two attributes with the same name for an element is a syntax error.

In line 15, we introduce empty element `flag`, which indicates the gender of the contact. Empty elements do not contain character data (i.e., they do not contain text between the start and end tags). Such elements are closed either by placing a slash at the end of the element (as shown in line 15) or by explicitly writing a closing tag, as in

```
<flag gender = "F"></flag>
```

Notice that element `address2` in line 21 also contains no data. Thus, we could safely change line 21 to `<address2 />`. However, it probably would not be wise to omit the element entirely, as it may be required by some *DTD* (Document Type Definition) or *Schema*. We discuss these in detail in Section 18.5.

18.3 XML Namespaces

The .NET Framework provides groups class libraries into namespaces. These namespaces prevent *naming collisions* between programmer-defined identifiers and identifiers in class libraries. For example, we might use class `Book` to represent information on one of our publications; however, a stamp collector might use class `Book` to represent a book of stamps. A naming collision would occur if we use these two classes in the same assembly, without using namespaces to differentiate them.

Like the .NET Framework, XML also provides *namespaces*, which provide a means of uniquely identifying XML elements. In addition, XML-based languages—called *vocabularies*, such as XML Schema (Section 18.5) and Extensible Stylesheet Language (Section 18.6)—often use namespaces to identify their elements.

Elements are differentiated via *namespace prefixes*, which identify the namespace to which an element belongs. For example,

```
<deitel:book>Visual C++ .NET</deitel:book>
```

qualifies element `book` with namespace prefix `deitel`. This indicates that element `book` is part of namespace `deitel`. Document authors can use any name for a namespace prefix except the reserved namespace prefix *`xml`*.

Common Programming Error 18.8

Attempting to create a namespace prefix named `xml` in any mixture of case is a syntax error.

The markup in Fig. 18.4 demonstrates namespaces. This XML document contains two `file` elements that are differentiated via namespaces.

```
1  <?xml version = "1.0"?>
2
3  <!-- Fig. 18.4: namespace.xml  -->
4  <!-- Demonstrating namespaces. -->
5
6  <text:directory xmlns:text = "urn:deitel:textInfo"
7     xmlns:image = "urn:deitel:imageInfo">
8
9     <text:file filename = "book.xml">
10       <text:description>A book list</text:description>
11    </text:file>
12
13    <image:file filename = "funny.jpg">
14       <image:description>A funny picture</image:description>
15       <image:size width = "200" height = "100" />
16    </image:file>
17
18 </text:directory>
```

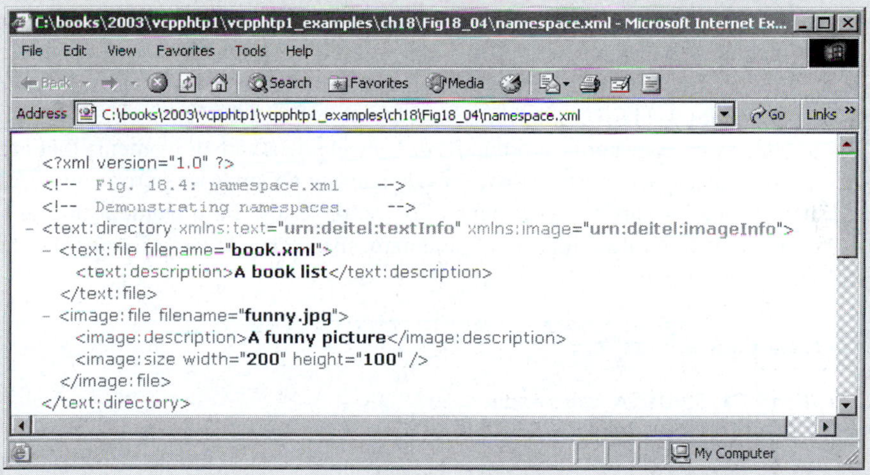

Fig. 18.4 XML namespaces demonstration.

Software Engineering Observation 18.1

A programmer has the option of qualifying an attribute with a namespace prefix. However, doing so is not required, because attributes always are associated with elements that would already be qualified with a namespace.

Lines 6–7 (Fig. 18.4) use attribute *`xmlns`* to create two namespace prefixes: `text` and `image`. Each namespace prefix is bound to a series of characters called a *uniform resource identifier (URI)* that uniquely identifies the namespace. Document authors create their own namespace prefixes and URIs. Notice that we use the `text` namespace prefix on the same line that the prefix is created (line 6).

To ensure that namespaces are unique, document authors must provide unique URIs. Here, we use the text `urn:deitel:textInfo` and `urn:deitel:imageInfo` as URIs. A common practice is to use *Uniform Resource Locators (URLs)* for URIs, because the domain names (such as `www.deitel.com`) used in URLs are guaranteed to be unique. For example, lines 6–7 could have been written as

```
<text:directory xmlns:text =
   "http://www.deitel.com/xmlns-text"
   xmlns:image = "http://www.deitel.com/xmlns-image">
```

In this example, we use URLs related to the Deitel & Associates, Inc, domain name to identify namespaces. The XML parser never visits these URLs—they simply represent a series of characters used to differentiate names. The URLs need not refer to actual Web pages or be properly formed.

Lines 9–11 use the namespace prefix `text` to qualify elements `file` and `description` as belonging to the namespace `"urn:deitel:textInfo"`. Notice that the namespace prefix `text` is applied to the end tags as well. Lines 13–16 apply namespace prefix `image` to elements `file`, `description` and `size`.

To eliminate the need to precede each element with a namespace prefix, document authors can specify a *default namespace*. Figure 18.5 demonstrates default namespaces.

Line 6 (Fig. 18.5) declares a default namespace using attribute `xmlns` with a URI as its value. Once we define this default namespace, child elements belonging to the namespace need not be qualified by a namespace prefix. Element `file` (line 9–11) is in the namespace `urn:deitel:textInfo`. Compare this to Fig. 18.4, where we prefixed `file` and `description` with `text` (lines 9–11).

The default namespace applies to the `directory` element and all elements that are not qualified with a namespace prefix. However, we can use a namespace prefix to specify a different namespace for particular elements. For example, the `file` element in line 13 is prefixed with `image` to indicate that it is in the namespace `urn:deitel:imageInfo`, rather than the default namespace.

```
1  <?xml version = "1.0"?>
2
3  <!-- Fig. 18.5: defaultnamespace.xml  -->
4  <!-- Using default namespaces.        -->
5
6  <directory xmlns = "urn:deitel:textInfo"
7     xmlns:image = "urn:deitel:imageInfo">
8
9     <file filename = "book.xml">
10       <description>A book list</description>
11    </file>
12
13    <image:file filename = "funny.jpg">
14       <image:description>A funny picture</image:description>
15       <image:size width = "200" height = "100" />
16    </image:file>
17
18 </directory>
```

Fig. 18.5 Default namespaces demonstration. (Part 1 of 2.)

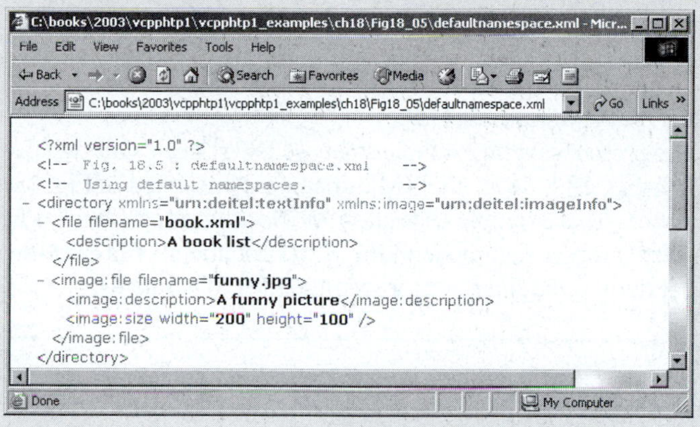

Fig. 18.5 Default namespaces demonstration. (Part 2 of 2.)

18.4 Document Object Model (DOM)

Although XML documents are text files, retrieving data from them via sequential-file access techniques is neither practical nor efficient, especially in situations where data must be added or deleted dynamically.

Upon successful parsing of documents, some XML parsers store document data as tree structures in memory. Figure 18.6 illustrates the tree structure for the document `article.xml` discussed in Fig. 18.1. This hierarchical tree structure is called a *Document Object Model (DOM)* tree, and an XML parser that creates this type of structure is known as a *DOM parser*. The DOM tree represents each component of the XML document (e.g., `article`, `date`, `firstName`, etc.) as a node in the tree. Nodes (such as `author`) that contain other nodes (called *child nodes*) are called *parent nodes*. Nodes that have the same parent (such as `firstName` and `lastName`) are called *sibling nodes*. A node's *descendant nodes* include that node's children, its children's children and so on. Similarly, a node's *ancestor nodes* include that node's parent, its parent's parent and so on. Every DOM tree has a single *root node* that contains all other nodes in the document, such as comments and elements.

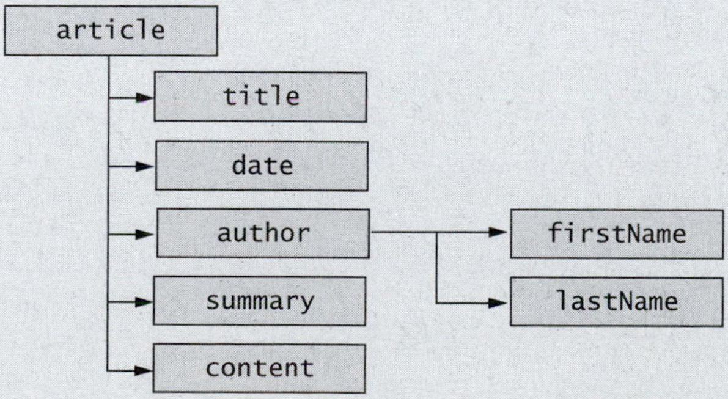

Fig. 18.6 Tree structure for Fig. 18.1.

Classes for creating, reading and manipulating XML documents are located in namespace *System::Xml*. This namespace also contains additional namespaces that contain other XML-related classes.

Creating DOM Trees Programmatically

In this section, we present several examples that use DOM trees. Our first example, the program in Fig. 18.7–Fig. 18.8, loads the XML document presented in Fig. 18.1 and displays its data in a text box. This example uses class *XmlNodeReader* (derived from *XmlReader*), which iterates through each node in the XML document. Class XmlReader is an abstract class that defines the interface for reading XML documents.

```
// Fig. 18.7: Form1.h
// Reading an XML document.

#pragma once


namespace XmlReaderTest
{
   using namespace System;
   using namespace System::ComponentModel;
   using namespace System::Collections;
   using namespace System::Windows::Forms;
   using namespace System::Data;
   using namespace System::Drawing;
   using namespace System::Xml;

   /// <summary>
   /// Summary for Form1
   ///
   /// WARNING: If you change the name of this class, you will need to
   ///          change the 'Resource File Name' property for the managed
   ///          resource compiler tool associated with all .resx files
   ///          this class depends on.  Otherwise, the designers will not
   ///          be able to interact properly with localized resources
   ///          associated with this form.
   /// </summary>
   public __gc class Form1 : public System::Windows::Forms::Form
   {
   public:
      Form1(void)
      {
         InitializeComponent();
         PrintXml();
      }

   protected:
      void Dispose(Boolean disposing)
      {
         if (disposing && components)
         {
```

Fig. 18.7 Iterating through an XML document. (Part 1 of 3.)

```
            components->Dispose();
         }
         __super::Dispose(disposing);
      }
   private: System::Windows::Forms::TextBox *  outputTextBox;

   private:
      /// <summary>
      /// Required designer variable.
      /// </summary>
      System::ComponentModel::Container * components;

   // Visual Studio .NET generated GUI code

   private:

      void PrintXml()
      {
         // create and load XMLDocument
         XmlDocument *document = new XmlDocument();
         document->Load( S"article.xml" );

         // create XmlNodeReader for document
         XmlNodeReader *reader = new XmlNodeReader( document );

         // show form before outputTextBox is populated
         this->Show();

         // tree depth is -1, no indentation
         int depth = -1;

         // display each node's content
         while ( reader->Read() ) {

            switch ( reader->NodeType ) {

               // if Element, display its name
               case XmlNodeType::Element:

                  // increase tab depth
                  depth++;
                  TabOutput( depth );
                  outputTextBox->AppendText( String::Concat(
                     S"<", reader->Name, S">\r\n" ) );

                  // if empty element, decrease depth
                  if ( reader->IsEmptyElement )
                     depth--;

                  break;

               // if Comment, display it
               case XmlNodeType::Comment:
```

Fig. 18.7 Iterating through an XML document. (Part 2 of 3.)

```
                  TabOutput( depth );
                  outputTextBox->AppendText( String::Concat(
                     S"<!--", reader->Value, S"-->\r\n" ) );
                  break;

               // if Text, display it
               case XmlNodeType::Text:
                  TabOutput( depth );
                  outputTextBox->AppendText( String::Concat(
                     S"\t", reader->Value, S"\r\n" ) );
                  break;

               // if XML declaration, display it
               case XmlNodeType::XmlDeclaration:
                  TabOutput( depth );
                  outputTextBox->AppendText( String::Concat( S"<?",
                     reader->Name, S" ", reader->Value, S" ?>\r\n" ) );
                  break;

               // if EndElement, display it and decrement depth
               case XmlNodeType::EndElement:
                  TabOutput( depth );
                  outputTextBox->AppendText( String::Concat(
                     S"</", reader->Name, S">\r\n" ) );
                  depth--;
                  break;

            } // end switch
         } // end while
      } // end method PrintXml

   private:

      // insert tabs
      void TabOutput( int number )
      {
         for ( int i = 0; i < number; i++ )
            outputTextBox->AppendText( S"\t" );
      } // end method TabOutput
   };
}
```

Fig. 18.7 Iterating through an XML document. (Part 3 of 3.)

```
// Fig. 18.8: Form1.cpp
// Entry point for application.

#include "stdafx.h"
#include "Form1.h"
#include <windows.h>

using namespace XmlReaderTest;
```

Fig. 18.8 `XmlReaderTest` entry point. (Part 1 of 2.)

```

int APIENTRY _tWinMain(HINSTANCE hInstance,
                       HINSTANCE hPrevInstance,
                       LPTSTR    lpCmdLine,
                       int       nCmdShow)
{
   System::Threading::Thread::CurrentThread->ApartmentState =
      System::Threading::ApartmentState::STA;
   Application::Run(new Form1());
   return 0;
} // end _tWinMain
```

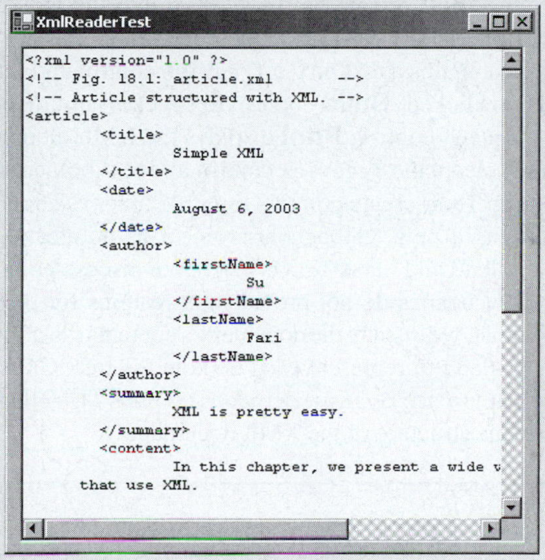
XmlReaderTest
<?xml version="1.0" ?>
<!-- Fig. 18.1: article.xml -->
<!-- Article structured with XML. -->
<article>
<title>
Simple XML
</title>
<date>
August 6, 2003
</date>
<author>
<firstName>
Su
</firstName>
<lastName>
Fari
</lastName>
</author>
<summary>
XML is pretty easy.
</summary>
<content>
In this chapter, we present a wide v
that use XML.

Fig. 18.8 `XmlReaderTest` entry point. (Part 2 of 2.)

Line 15 (Fig. 18.7) includes the `System::Xml` namespace, which contains the XML classes used in this example. Line 60 (Fig. 18.7) creates a pointer to an *`XmlDocument`* object that conceptually represents an empty XML document. The XML document `article.xml` is parsed and loaded into this `XmlDocument` object when method *`Load`* is invoked in line 61. Once an XML document is loaded into an `XmlDocument` object, its data can be read and manipulated programmatically. In this example, we read each node in the `XmlDocument`, which represents the DOM tree. In later examples, we demonstrate how to manipulate node values.

Line 64 creates an `XmlNodeReader` and assigns it to pointer `reader`, which enables us to read one node at a time from the `XmlDocument`. Method *`Read`* of `XmlNodeReader` reads one node from the DOM tree. Placing this statement in the `while` loop (lines 73–122) makes `reader` read all the document nodes. The `switch` statement (lines 75–121) processes each node. Either the *`Name`* property (line 84), which contains the node's name, or the *`Value`* property (line 96), which contains the node's data, is formatted and concatenated to the `String` displayed in `outputTextBox`. The *`NodeType`* property contains the node type (specifying whether the node is an element, comment, text, etc.). Notice that each `case` specifies a node type, using *`XmlNodeType`* enumeration constants.

Notice that the displayed output emphasizes the structure of the XML document. Variable `depth` (line 70) sets the number of tab characters used to indent each element. The depth is incremented each time an `Element` type is encountered and is decremented each time an `EndElement` or empty element is encountered. We use a similar technique in the next example to emphasize the tree structure of the XML document in the display. Notice that our line breaks use the character sequence `"\r\n"`, which denotes a carriage return followed by a line feed. This is the standard line break for Windows-based applications and controls.

Manipulating DOM Trees Programmatically

The program in Fig. 18.9–Fig. 18.10 demonstrates how to manipulate DOM trees programmatically. This program loads `letter.xml` (Fig. 18.3) into the DOM tree, then creates a second DOM tree that duplicates the DOM tree containing `letter.xml`'s contents. The GUI for this application contains a text box, a `TreeView` control and three buttons—**Build**, **Print** and **Reset**. When clicked, **Build** copies `letter.xml` and displays the document's tree structure in the `TreeView` control, **Print** displays the XML element values and names in a text box and **Reset** clears the `TreeView` control and text box content.

Lines 62 and 65 (Fig. 18.9) create pointers to `XmlDocuments` `source` and `copy`. Line 39 in the constructor assigns a new `XmlDocument` object to pointer `source`. Line 40 then invokes method `Load` to load and parse `letter.xml`. We discuss pointer `copy` shortly.

Unfortunately, `XmlDocuments` do not provide any features for displaying their content graphically. In this example, we display the document's contents via a `TreeView` control. We use objects of class `TreeNode` to represent each node in the tree. Class `TreeView` and class `TreeNode` are part of namespace `System::Windows::Forms`. `TreeNodes` are added to the `TreeView` to emphasize the structure of the XML document.

```
1   // Fig. 18.9: Form1.h
2   // Demonstrates DOM tree manipulation.
3
4   #pragma once
5
6
7   namespace XmlDom
8   {
9      using namespace System;
10     using namespace System::ComponentModel;
11     using namespace System::Collections;
12     using namespace System::Windows::Forms;
13     using namespace System::Data;
14     using namespace System::Drawing;
15     using namespace System::IO;
16     using namespace System::Xml;
17
18     // contains TempFileCollection
19     using namespace System::CodeDom::Compiler;
20
21     /// <summary>
22     /// Summary for Form1
23     ///
```

Fig. 18.9 DOM structure of an XML document illustrated by a class. (Part 1 of 6.)

```
   /// WARNING: If you change the name of this class, you will need to
   ///          change the 'Resource File Name' property for the managed
   ///          resource compiler tool associated with all .resx files
   ///          this class depends on.  Otherwise, the designers will not
   ///          be able to interact properly with localized resources
   ///          associated with this form.
   /// </summary>
   public __gc class Form1 : public System::Windows::Forms::Form
   {
   public:
      Form1(void)
      {
         InitializeComponent();

         // create XmlDocument and load letter.xml
         source = new XmlDocument();
         source->Load( S"letter.xml" );

         // initialize pointers to 0
         copy = 0;
         tree = 0;
      }

   protected:
      void Dispose(Boolean disposing)
      {
         if (disposing && components)
         {
            components->Dispose();
         }
         __super::Dispose(disposing);
      }
   private: System::Windows::Forms::Button *  resetButton;
   private: System::Windows::Forms::Button *  buildButton;
   private: System::Windows::Forms::TreeView *  xmlTreeView;
   private: System::Windows::Forms::TextBox *  consoleTextBox;
   private: System::Windows::Forms::Button *  printButton;

   private: XmlDocument *source; // pointer to "XML document"

   // pointer copy of source's "XML document"
   private: XmlDocument *copy;

   private: TreeNode *tree; // TreeNode pointer

   private:
      /// <summary>
      /// Required designer variable.
      /// </summary>
      System::ComponentModel::Container * components;

   // Visual Studio .NET generated GUI code

```

Fig. 18.9 DOM structure of an XML document illustrated by a class. (Part 2 of 6.)

```
   // event handler for buildButton click event
   private: System::Void buildButton_Click(
               System::Object *  sender, System::EventArgs *  e)
            {
               // determine if copy has been built already
               if ( copy != 0 )
                  return;  // document already exists

               // instantiate XmlDocument and TreeNode
               copy = new XmlDocument();
               tree = new TreeNode();

               // add root node name to TreeNode and add
               // TreeNode to TreeView control
               tree->Text = source->Name;      // assigns #root
               xmlTreeView->Nodes->Add( tree );

               // build node and tree hierarchy
               BuildTree( source, copy, tree );

               printButton->Enabled = true;
               resetButton->Enabled = true;
            } // end method buildButton_Click

   // event handler for printButton click event
   private: System::Void printButton_Click(
               System::Object *  sender, System::EventArgs *  e)
            {
               // exit if copy does not point to an XmlDocument
               if ( copy == 0 )
                  return;

               // create temporary XML file
               TempFileCollection *file = new TempFileCollection();

               // create file that is deleted at program termination
               String *filename = file->AddExtension( S"xml", false );

               // write XML data to disk
               XmlTextWriter *writer = new XmlTextWriter( filename,
                  System::Text::Encoding::UTF8 );
               copy->WriteTo( writer );
               writer->Close();

               // parse and load temporary XML document
               XmlTextReader *reader = new XmlTextReader( filename );

               // read, format and display data
               while ( reader->Read() ) {

                  if ( reader->NodeType == XmlNodeType::EndElement )
                     consoleTextBox->AppendText( S"/" );

```

Fig. 18.9 DOM structure of an XML document illustrated by a class. (Part 3 of 6.)

```
               if ( reader->Name != String::Empty )
                  consoleTextBox->AppendText(
                     String::Concat( reader->Name, S"\r\n" ) );

               if ( reader->Value != String::Empty )
                  consoleTextBox->AppendText(
                     String::Concat( S"\t", reader->Value, S"\r\n" ) );
            } // end while

            reader->Close();
         } // end method printButton_Click

   // handle resetButton click event
   private: System::Void resetButton_Click(
            System::Object *  sender, System::EventArgs *  e)
         {
            // remove TreeView nodes
            if ( tree != 0 )
               xmlTreeView->Nodes->Remove( tree );

            xmlTreeView->Refresh(); // force TreeView update

            // delete XmlDocument and tree
            copy = 0;
            tree = 0;

            consoleTextBox->Text = S"";  // clear text box

            printButton->Enabled = false;
            resetButton->Enabled = false;
         } // end method resetButton_Click

   private:

      // construct DOM tree
      void BuildTree( XmlNode *xmlSourceNode,
         XmlNode *document, TreeNode *treeNode )
      {
         // create XmlNodeReader to access XML document
         XmlNodeReader *nodeReader = new XmlNodeReader( xmlSourceNode );

         // represents current node in DOM tree
         XmlNode *currentNode = 0;

         // treeNode to add to existing tree
         TreeNode *newNode = new TreeNode();

         // points to modified node type for CreateNode
         XmlNodeType modifiedNodeType;

         while ( nodeReader->Read() ) {

```

Fig. 18.9 DOM structure of an XML document illustrated by a class. (Part 4 of 6.)

```
            // get current node type
            modifiedNodeType = nodeReader->NodeType;

            // check for EndElement, store as Element
            if ( modifiedNodeType == XmlNodeType::EndElement )
               modifiedNodeType = XmlNodeType::Element;

            // create node copy
            currentNode = copy->CreateNode( modifiedNodeType,
               nodeReader->Name, nodeReader->NamespaceURI );

            // build tree based on node type
            switch ( nodeReader->NodeType ) {

               // if Text node, add its value to tree
               case XmlNodeType::Text:
                  newNode->Text = nodeReader->Value;
                  treeNode->Nodes->Add( newNode );

                  // append Text node value to currentNode data
                  dynamic_cast< XmlText * >( currentNode )->
                     AppendData( nodeReader->Value );
                  document->AppendChild( currentNode );
                  break;

               // if EndElement, move up tree
               case XmlNodeType::EndElement:
                  document = document->ParentNode;
                  treeNode = treeNode->Parent;
                  break;

               // if new element, add name and traverse tree
               case XmlNodeType::Element:

                  // determine if element contains content
                  if ( !nodeReader->IsEmptyElement ) {

                     // assign node text, add newNode as child
                     newNode->Text = nodeReader->Name;
                     treeNode->Nodes->Add( newNode );

                     // set treeNode to last child
                     treeNode = newNode;

                     document->AppendChild( currentNode );
                     document = document->LastChild;
                  } // end if

                  // do not traverse empty elements
                  else {

                     // assign NodeType string to newNode
```

Fig. 18.9 DOM structure of an XML document illustrated by a class. (Part 5 of 6.)

```
                        newNode->Text =
                           __box( nodeReader->NodeType )->ToString();

                        treeNode->Nodes->Add( newNode );
                        document->AppendChild( currentNode );
                     } // end else

                     break;

                  // all other types, display node type
                  default:
                     newNode->Text =
                        __box( nodeReader->NodeType )->ToString();
                     treeNode->Nodes->Add( newNode );
                     document->AppendChild( currentNode );
                     break;
               } // end switch

               newNode = new TreeNode();
            } // end while

            // update the TreeView control
            xmlTreeView->ExpandAll();
            xmlTreeView->Refresh();
         } // end method BuildTree
   };
}
```

Fig. 18.9 DOM structure of an XML document illustrated by a class. (Part 6 of 6.)

```
// Fig. 18.10: Form1.cpp
// Entry point for application.

#include "stdafx.h"
#include "Form1.h"
#include <windows.h>

using namespace XmlDom;

int APIENTRY _tWinMain(HINSTANCE hInstance,
                       HINSTANCE hPrevInstance,
                       LPTSTR    lpCmdLine,
                       int       nCmdShow)
{
   System::Threading::Thread::CurrentThread->ApartmentState =
      System::Threading::ApartmentState::STA;
   Application::Run(new Form1());
   return 0;
} // end _tWinMain
```

Fig. 18.10 `XmlDom` entry point. (Part 1 of 2.)

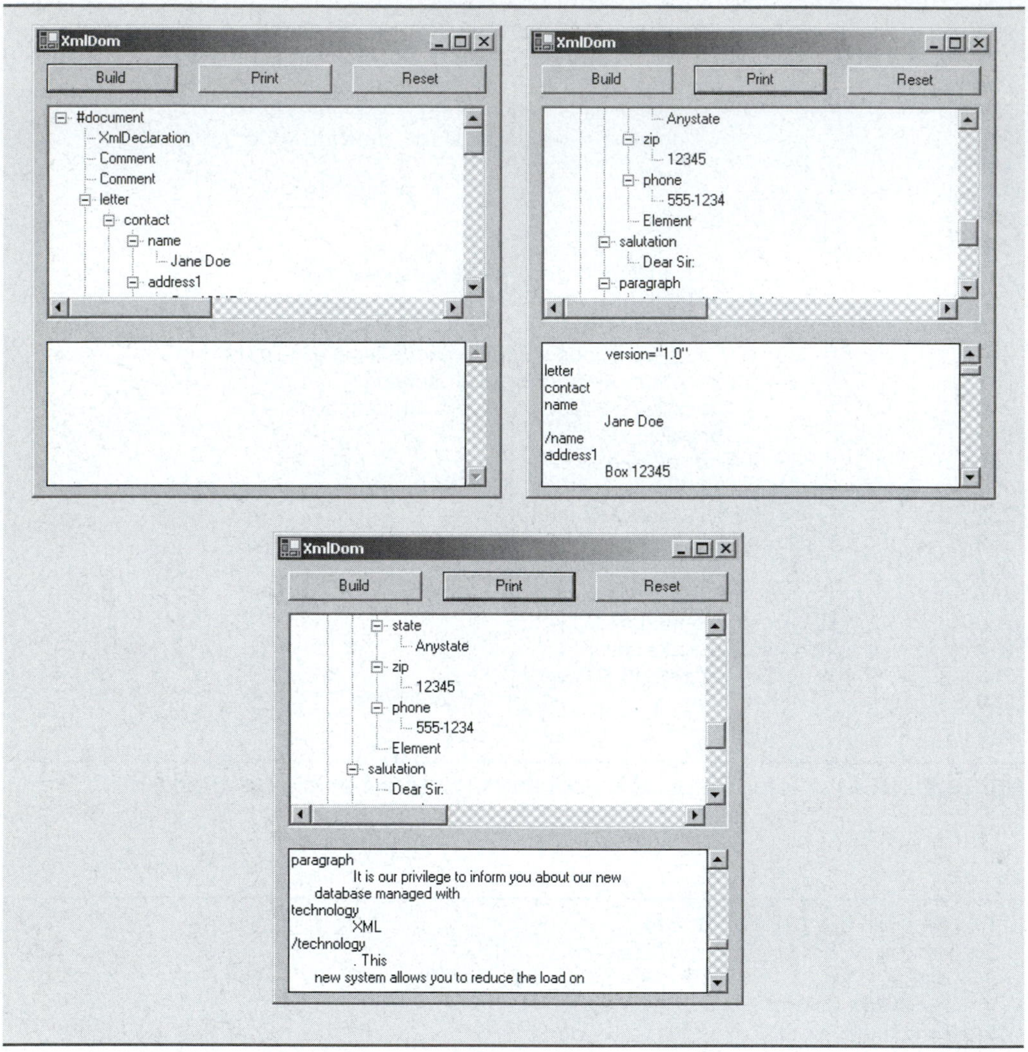

Fig. 18.10 `XmlDom` entry point. (Part 2 of 2.)

When clicked, button **Build** triggers event handler `buildButton_Click` (lines 78–99), which copies `letter.xml` dynamically. The new `XmlDocument` and `TreeNodes` (i.e., the nodes used for graphical representation in the `TreeView`) are created in lines 86–87. Line 91 retrieves the `Name` of the node pointed to by `source` (i.e., `#document`, which represents the document root) and assigns it to `tree`'s `Text` property. This `TreeNode` then is inserted into the `TreeView` control's node list. Method `Add` is called to add each new `TreeNode` to the `TreeView`'s `Nodes` collection (line 92). Line 95 calls method `BuildTree` to copy the `XMLDocument` pointed to by `source` and to update the `TreeView`.

Method `BuildTree` (line 165–258) receives an `XmlNode` representing the source node, an empty `XmlNode` and a `treeNode` to place in the DOM tree. Parameter `treeNode` points to the current location in the tree (i.e., the `TreeNode` most recently added to the `TreeView` control). Line 169 instantiates a new `XmlNodeReader` for iterating through the

DOM tree. Lines 172 and 175 declare XmlNode and TreeNode pointers that indicate the next nodes added to document (i.e., the DOM tree pointed to by copy) and treeNode. Lines 180–253 iterate through each node in the tree.

Lines 190–191 create a node containing a copy of the current nodeReader node. Method *CreateNode* of XmlDocument takes a NodeType, a Name and a *NamespaceURI* as arguments. The NodeType cannot be an EndElement or method CreateNode throws an ArgumentOutOfRangeException. If the NodeType is of type EndElement, lines 186–187 assign modifiedNodeType type Element.

The switch statement in lines 194–250 determines the node type, creates and adds nodes to the TreeView and updates the DOM tree.When a text node is encountered, the new TreeNode's newNode's Text property is assigned the current node's value. This TreeNode is added to the TreeView control. Lines 202–204 downcast currentNode to XmlText and append the node's value. The currentNode then is appended to the document. Lines 208–211 match an EndElement node type. This case moves up the tree, because the end of an element has been encountered. The *ParentNode* and *Parent* properties retrieve the document's and treeNode's parents, respectively.

Line 214 matches Element node types. Each nonempty Element (line 217) increases the depth of the tree; thus, we assign the current nodeReader's Name to the newNode's Text property and add the newNode to the treeNode node list. Lines 220–224 reorder the nodes in the node list to ensure that newNode is the last TreeNode in the node list. XmlNode currentNode is appended to document as the last child, and document is set to its *LastChild*, which is the child we just added. For an empty element (line 231), we assign to the newNode's Text property the String representation of the NodeType. Next, the newNode is added to the treeNode node list. Line 238 appends the currentNode to the document. The default case assigns the string representation of the node type to the NewNode Text property, adds the newNode to the TreeNode node list and appends the currentNode to the document.

After building the DOM trees, the TreeNode node list displays in the TreeView control. Clicking the nodes (i.e., the + or - boxes) in the TreeView either expands or collapses them. Clicking **Print** invokes event handler printButton_Click (lines 102–140). Lines 110 and 113 create a temporary file for storing the XML. Line 110 creates an instance of class *TempFileCollection* (namespace *System::CodeDom::Compiler*). This class can be used to create and delete temporary files (i.e., files that store short-lived information). Line 113 calls TempFileCollection method *AddExtension*. We use a version of this method that accepts two arguments. The first argument is a String * that specifies the file extension of the file to create—in this case, "xml". The second argument is a bool that specifies whether temporary files of this type (xml) should be kept after being used (i.e., when the TempFileCollection object is destroyed). We pass the value false, indicating that the temporary files (of type xml) should be deleted when the TempFileCollection is destroyed (i.e., goes out of scope). Method AddExtension returns the filename that it has just created, which we store in String * filename.

Lines 116–117 then create an XmlTextWriter for streaming the XML data to disk. The first argument to the XmlTextWriter constructor is the filename that it will use to output the data (filename). The second argument passed to the XmlTextWriter constructor specifies the encoding to use. We specify *UTF-8,* an 8-bit encoding for Unicode characters. For more information about Unicode, refer to Appendix D.

Line 118 calls method *`WriteTo`* to write the XML representation to the *`XmlTextWriter`* stream. Line 122 creates an *`XmlTextReader`* to read from the file. The `while` loop (line 125–137) reads each node in the DOM tree and writes tag names and character data to the text box. If it is an end element, a slash is concatenated. If the node has a `Name` or `Value`, that name or value is concatenated to the textbox text.

The **Reset** button's event handler, `resetButton_Click` (lines 143–160), deletes both dynamically generated trees and updates the `TreeView` control's display. Pointer `copy` is assigned `0` (to allow its tree to be garbage collected in line 153), and the `TreeNode` node list pointer `tree` is assigned `0`.

XPath Expressions

Although `XmlReader` includes methods for reading and modifying node values, it is not the most efficient means of locating data in a DOM tree. The .NET framework provides class *`XPathNavigator`* in namespace *`System::Xml::XPath`* for iterating through node lists that match search criteria, which are written as *XPath expressions*. XPath (XML Path Language) provides a syntax for locating specific nodes in XML documents effectively and efficiently. XPath is a string-based language of expressions used by XML and many of its related technologies (such as XSLT, discussed in Section 18.6).

Figure 18.11–Fig. 18.12 demonstrate how to navigate through an XML document with an `XPathNavigator`. Like Fig. 18.9–Fig. 18.10, this program uses a `TreeView` control and `TreeNode` objects to display the XML document's structure. However, instead of displaying the entire DOM tree, the `TreeNode` node list is updated each time the `XPathNavigator` is positioned to a new node. Nodes are added to and deleted from the `TreeView` to reflect the `XPathNavigator`'s location in the DOM tree. The XML document `sports.xml` that we use in this example is presented in Fig. 18.13.

This program (Fig. 18.11–Fig. 18.12) loads XML document `sports.xml` (Fig. 18.13) into an *`XPathDocument`* object by passing the document's file name to the `XPathDocument` constructor (line 36 of Fig. 18.11). Method *`CreateNavigator`* (line 39) creates and returns an `XPathNavigator` pointer to the `XPathDocument`'s tree structure.

The navigation methods of `XPathNavigator` used in Fig. 18.11 are *`MoveToFirstChild`* (line 96), *`MoveToParent`* (line 123), *`MoveToNext`* (line 150) and *`MoveToPrevious`* (line 178). Each method performs the action that its name implies. Method `MoveToFirstChild` moves to the first child of the node pointed to by the `XPathNavigator`, `MoveToParent` moves to the parent node of the node pointed to by the `XPathNavigator`, `MoveToNext` moves to the next sibling of the node pointed to by the `XPathNavigator` and `MoveToPrevious` moves to the previous sibling of the node pointed to by the `XPathNavigator`. Each method returns a `bool` indicating whether the move was successful. We display a warning in a `MessageBox` whenever a move operation fails. Each of the `XPathNavigator` methods is called in the event handler of the button that matches the method name (e.g., button **First Child** triggers `firstChildButton_Click` (line 90), which calls `MoveToFirstChild`).

Whenever we move forward via the `XPathNavigator`, as with `MoveToFirstChild` and `MoveToNext`, nodes are added to the `TreeNode` node list. Method `DetermineType` is a `private` method (defined in lines 243–256) that determines whether to assign the `Node`'s `Name` property or `Value` property to the `TreeNode` (lines 249 and 254). Whenever `MoveToParent` is called, all children of the parent node are removed from the display.

Similarly, a call to `MoveToPrevious` removes the current sibling node. Note that the nodes are removed only from the `TreeView`, not from the tree representation of the document.

```
// Fig. 18.11: Form1.h
// Demonstrates Class XPathNavigator.

#pragma once


namespace PathNavigator
{
   using namespace System;
   using namespace System::ComponentModel;
   using namespace System::Collections;
   using namespace System::Windows::Forms;
   using namespace System::Data;
   using namespace System::Drawing;
   using namespace System::Xml;
   using namespace System::Xml::XPath; // contains XPathNavigator

   /// <summary>
   /// Summary for Form1
   ///
   /// WARNING: If you change the name of this class, you will need to
   ///          change the 'Resource File Name' property for the managed
   ///          resource compiler tool associated with all .resx files
   ///          this class depends on.  Otherwise, the designers will not
   ///          be able to interact properly with localized resources
   ///          associated with this form.
   /// </summary>
   public __gc class Form1 : public System::Windows::Forms::Form
   {
   public:
      Form1(void)
      {
         InitializeComponent();

         // load in XML document
         document = new XPathDocument( S"sports.xml" );

         // create navigator
         xpath = document->CreateNavigator();

         // create root node for TreeNodes
         tree = new TreeNode();
         tree->Text = __box( xpath->NodeType )->ToString();  // #root
         pathTreeViewer->Nodes->Add( tree );       // add tree

         // update TreeView control
         pathTreeViewer->ExpandAll();
         pathTreeViewer->Refresh();
         pathTreeViewer->SelectedNode = tree;     // highlight root
      }
```

Fig. 18.11 `XPathNavigator` class used to navigate selected nodes. (Part 1 of 5.)

```
      protected:
         void Dispose(Boolean disposing)
         {
            if (disposing && components)
            {
               components->Dispose();
            }
            __super::Dispose(disposing);
         }
      private: System::Windows::Forms::Button *  firstChildButton;
      private: System::Windows::Forms::Button *  parentButton;
      private: System::Windows::Forms::Button *  nextButton;
      private: System::Windows::Forms::Button *  previousButton;
      private: System::Windows::Forms::Button *  selectButton;
      private: System::Windows::Forms::TreeView *  pathTreeViewer;
      private: System::Windows::Forms::ComboBox *  selectComboBox;
      private: System::Windows::Forms::TextBox *  selectTreeViewer;
      private: System::Windows::Forms::GroupBox *  navigateBox;
      private: System::Windows::Forms::GroupBox *  locateBox;

      // navigator to traverse document
      private: XPathNavigator *xpath;

      // points to document for use by XPathNavigator
      private: XPathDocument *document;

      // points to TreeNode list used by TreeView control
      private: TreeNode *tree;

      private:
         /// <summary>
         /// Required designer variable.
         /// </summary>
         System::ComponentModel::Container * components;

      // Visual Studio .NET generated GUI code

      // traverse to first child
      private: System::Void firstChildButton_Click(
                  System::Object *  sender, System::EventArgs *  e)
               {
                  TreeNode *newTreeNode;

                  // move to first child
                  if ( xpath->MoveToFirstChild() )   {
                     newTreeNode = new TreeNode(); // create new node

                     // set node's Text property to either
                     // navigator's name or value
                     DetermineType( newTreeNode, xpath );

```

Fig. 18.11 XPathNavigator class used to navigate selected nodes. (Part 2 of 5.)

```
            // add node to TreeNode node list
            tree->Nodes->Add( newTreeNode );
            tree = newTreeNode; // assign tree newTreeNode

            // update TreeView control
            pathTreeViewer->ExpandAll();
            pathTreeViewer->Refresh();
            pathTreeViewer->SelectedNode = tree;
         } // end if
         else // node has no children
            MessageBox::Show( S"Current Node has no children.",
               S"", MessageBoxButtons::OK,
               MessageBoxIcon::Information );
      } // end method firstChildButton_Click

   // traverse to node's parent on parentButton click event
   private: System::Void parentButton_Click(
         System::Object *  sender, System::EventArgs *  e)
      {
         // move to parent
         if ( xpath->MoveToParent() ) {
            tree = tree->Parent;

            // get number of child nodes, not including subtrees
            int count = tree->GetNodeCount( false );

            // remove all children
            tree->Nodes->Clear();

            // update TreeView control
            pathTreeViewer->ExpandAll();
            pathTreeViewer->Refresh();
            pathTreeViewer->SelectedNode = tree;
         } // end if
         else // if node has no parent (root node)
            MessageBox::Show( S"Current node has no parent.", S"",
               MessageBoxButtons::OK,
               MessageBoxIcon::Information );
      } // end method parentButton_Click

   // find next sibling on nextButton click event
   private: System::Void nextButton_Click(
         System::Object *  sender, System::EventArgs *  e)
      {
         TreeNode *newTreeNode = 0, *newNode = 0;

         // move to next sibling
         if ( xpath->MoveToNext() ) {
            newTreeNode = tree->Parent; // get parent node

            newNode = new TreeNode(); // create new node
            DetermineType( newNode, xpath );
            newTreeNode->Nodes->Add( newNode );
```

Fig. 18.11 `XPathNavigator` class used to navigate selected nodes. (Part 3 of 5.)

```

               // set current position for display
               tree = newNode;

               // update TreeView control
               pathTreeViewer->ExpandAll();
               pathTreeViewer->Refresh();
               pathTreeViewer->SelectedNode = tree;
            } // end if
            else // node has no additional siblings
               MessageBox::Show( S"Current node is last sibling.",
                  S"", MessageBoxButtons::OK,
                  MessageBoxIcon::Information );
         } // end method nextButton_Click

// get previous sibling on previousButton click
private: System::Void previousButton_Click(
            System::Object *  sender, System::EventArgs *  e)
         {
            TreeNode *parentTreeNode = 0;

            // move to previous sibling
            if ( xpath->MoveToPrevious() ) {
               parentTreeNode = tree->Parent; // get parent node

               // delete current node
               parentTreeNode->Nodes->Remove( tree );

               // move to previous node
               tree = parentTreeNode->LastNode;

               // update TreeView control
               pathTreeViewer->ExpandAll();
               pathTreeViewer->Refresh();
               pathTreeViewer->SelectedNode = tree;
            } // end if
            else // if current node has no previous siblings
               MessageBox::Show( S"Current node is first sibling.",
                  S"", MessageBoxButtons::OK,
                  MessageBoxIcon::Information );
         } // end method previousButton_Click

// process selectButton click event
private: System::Void selectButton_Click(
            System::Object *  sender, System::EventArgs *  e)
         {
            XPathNodeIterator *iterator; // enables node iteration

            // get specified node from ComboBox
            try {
               iterator = xpath->Select( selectComboBox->Text );
               DisplayIterator( iterator ); // print selection
            } // end try
```

Fig. 18.11 XPathNavigator class used to navigate selected nodes. (Part 4 of 5.)

```

            // catch invalid expressions
            catch ( ArgumentException *argumentException ) {
               MessageBox::Show( argumentException->Message,
                  S"Error", MessageBoxButtons::OK,
                  MessageBoxIcon::Error );
            } // end catch

            // catch empty expressions
            catch ( XPathException * ) {
               MessageBox::Show( S"Please select an expression",
                  S"Error", MessageBoxButtons::OK,
                  MessageBoxIcon::Error );
            } // end catch
         } // end method selectButton_Click

   private:

      // print values for XPathNodeIterator
      void DisplayIterator( XPathNodeIterator *iterator )
      {
         selectTreeViewer->Text = S"";

         // prints selected node's values
         while ( iterator->MoveNext() ) {
            selectTreeViewer->Text =
               String::Concat( selectTreeViewer->Text,
               iterator->Current->Value->Trim(), S"\r\n" );
         } // end while
      } // end method DisplayIterator

   private:

      // determine if TreeNode should display current node name or value
      void DetermineType( TreeNode *node, XPathNavigator *xPath )
      {
         // if Element, get its name
         if ( xPath->NodeType == XPathNodeType::Element ) {

            // get current node name, remove white space
            node->Text = xPath->Name->Trim();
         } // end if
         else {

            // get current node value, remove white space
            node->Text = xPath->Value->Trim();
         } // end else
      } // end method DetermineType
   };
}
```

Fig. 18.11 `XPathNavigator` class used to navigate selected nodes. (Part 5 of 5.)

The other event handler corresponds to button **Select** (line 199–223). Method `Select` (line 206) takes search criteria in the form of either an `XPathExpression` or a `String *` that represents an XPath expression and returns as an `XPathNodeIterator` object any nodes that match the search criteria. The XPath expressions provided by this program's combo box are summarized in Fig. 18.14. The `catch` blocks in lines 211–222 catch any exceptions (`ArgumentException` or `XPathException`) that can occur if the user enters an invalid or empty expression.

```
// Fig. 18.12: PathNavigatorTest.cpp
// Entry point for application.

#include "stdafx.h"
#include "Form1.h"
#include <windows.h>

using namespace PathNavigator;

int APIENTRY _tWinMain(HINSTANCE hInstance,
                       HINSTANCE hPrevInstance,
                       LPTSTR    lpCmdLine,
                       int       nCmdShow)
{
   System::Threading::Thread::CurrentThread->ApartmentState =
      System::Threading::ApartmentState::STA;
   Application::Run(new Form1());
   return 0;
} // end _tWinMain
```

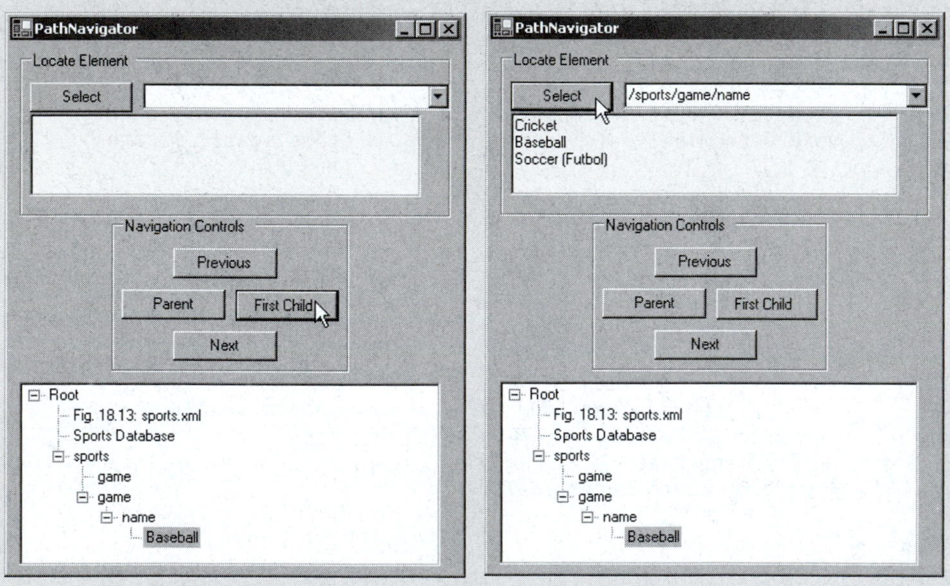

Fig. 18.12 `PathNavigator` entry point. (Part 1 of 2.)

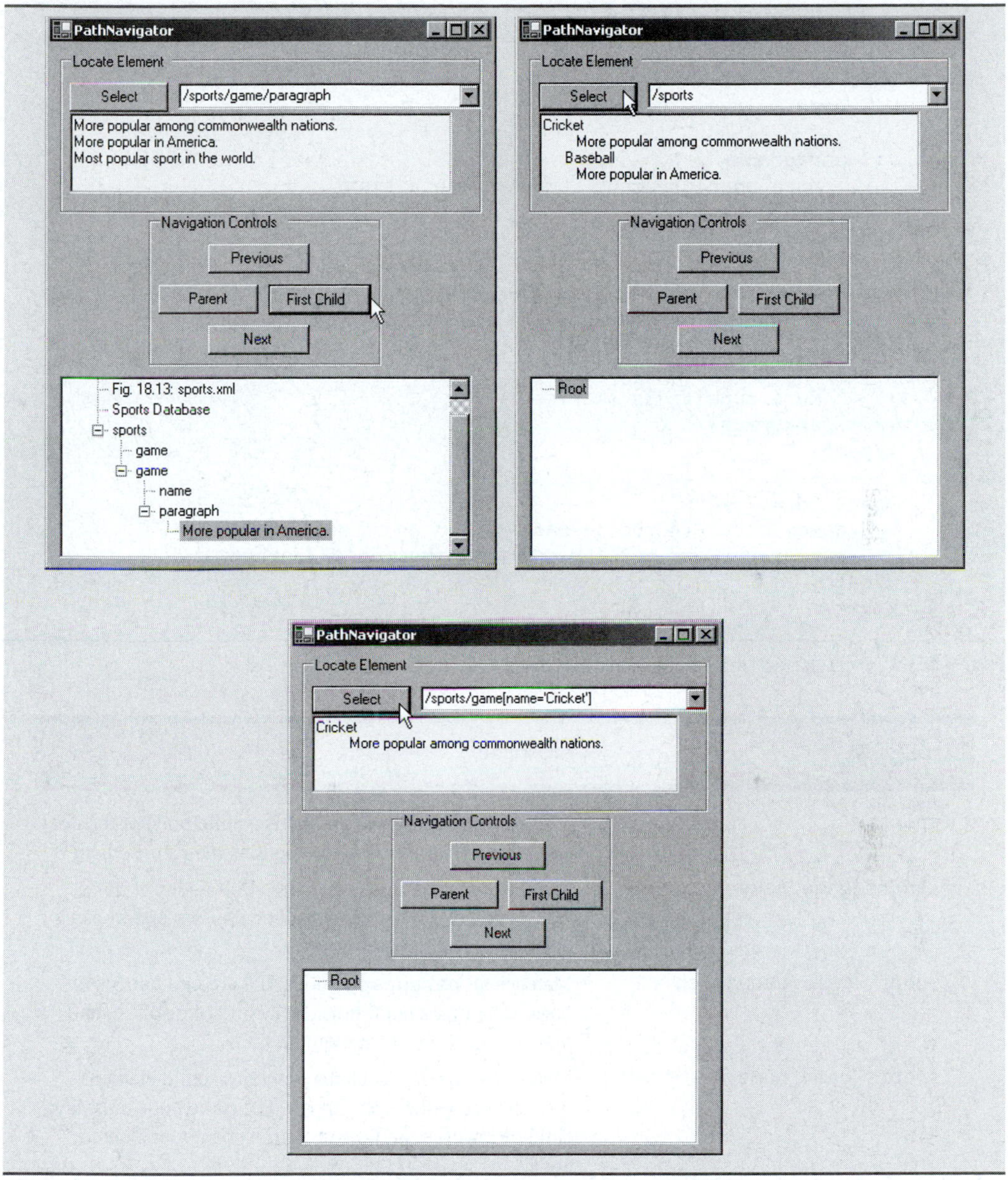

Fig. 18.12 `PathNavigator` entry point. (Part 2 of 2.)

```
<?xml version = "1.0"?>

<!-- Fig. 18.13: sports.xml  -->
<!-- Sports Database         -->

```

Fig. 18.13 XML document that describes various sports. (Part 1 of 2.)

```
<sports>

  <game id = "783">
     <name>Cricket</name>

     <paragraph>
        More popular among Commonwealth nations.
     </paragraph>
  </game>

  <game id = "239">
     <name>Baseball</name>

     <paragraph>
        More popular in America.
     </paragraph>
  </game>

  <game id = "418">
     <name>Soccer (Futbol)</name>
     <paragraph>Most popular sport in the world</paragraph>
  </game>
</sports>
```

Fig. 18.13 XML document that describes various sports. (Part 2 of 2.)

Expression	Description
`/sports`	Matches the `sports` node that is a child node of the document root node. This node contains the root element.
`/sports/game/name`	Matches all `name` nodes that are child nodes of `game`. The `game` node must be a child of `sports` and `sports` must be a root element node.
`/sports/game/paragraph`	Matches all `paragraph` nodes that are child nodes of `game`. The `game` node must be a child of `sports`, and `sports` must be a root element node.
`/sports/game[name='Cricket']`	Matches all `game` nodes that contain a child element `name` whose value is `Cricket`. The `game` node must be a child of `sports`, and `sports` must be a root element node.

Fig. 18.14 XPath expressions and descriptions used in Fig. 18.11–Fig. 18.12.

Method `DisplayIterator` (defined in lines 228–238 of Fig. 18.11) appends the node values from the given `XPathNodeIterator` to the `selectTreeViewer` text box. Note that we call the `String` method `Trim` to remove unnecessary white space. Method *`MoveNext`* (line 233) advances to the next node, which can be accessed via property *`Current`* (line 236).

18.5 Document Type Definitions (DTDs), Schemas and Validation

XML documents can reference optional documents that specify how the XML documents should be structured. These optional documents are called Document Type Definitions (DTDs) and *Schemas*. When a DTD or Schema document is provided, some parsers (called *validating parsers)* can read the DTD or Schema and check the XML document's structure against it. If the XML document conforms to the DTD or Schema, then the XML document is *valid*. Parsers that cannot check for document conformity against the DTD or Schema are called *non-validating parsers*. If an XML parser (validating or non-validating) is able to process an XML document (that does not reference a DTD or Schema), the XML document is considered to be *well formed* (i.e., it is syntactically correct). By definition, a valid XML document is also a well-formed XML document. If a document is not well formed, parsing halts, and the parser issues an error.

Software Engineering Observation 18.2

DTD and Schema documents are essential components for XML documents used in business-to-business (B2B) transactions and mission-critical systems. These documents help ensure that XML documents are valid.

Software Engineering Observation 18.3

XML document content can be structured in many different ways, so an application cannot determine whether the document it receives is complete, is missing data or is ordered properly. DTDs and Schemas solve this problem by providing an extensible means of describing a document's contents. An application can use a DTD or Schema document to perform a validity check on the document's contents.

18.5.1 Document Type Definitions

Document type definitions (DTDs) provide a means for type-checking XML documents and thus for verifying their *validity* (confirming that elements contain the proper attributes, elements are in the proper sequence, etc.). DTDs use *EBNF* (*Extended Backus-Naur Form*) *grammar* to describe an XML document's content. XML parsers need additional functionality to read EBNF grammar, because it is not XML syntax. Although DTDs are optional, they can be used to ensure document conformity. The DTD in Fig. 18.15 defines the set of rules (i.e., the grammar) for structuring the business letter document contained in Fig. 18.16.

Portability Tip 18.2

DTDs can ensure consistency among XML documents generated by different programs.

```
<!-- Fig. 18.15: letter.dtd       -->
<!-- DTD document for letter.xml. -->

<!ELEMENT letter ( contact+, salutation, paragraph+,
   closing, signature )>

<!ELEMENT contact ( name, address1, address2, city, state,
   zip, phone, flag )>
```

Fig. 18.15 Document Type Definition (DTD) for a business letter. (Part 1 of 2.)

```
9  <!ATTLIST contact type CDATA #IMPLIED>
10
11 <!ELEMENT name ( #PCDATA )>
12 <!ELEMENT address1 ( #PCDATA )>
13 <!ELEMENT address2 ( #PCDATA )>
14 <!ELEMENT city ( #PCDATA )>
15 <!ELEMENT state ( #PCDATA )>
16 <!ELEMENT zip ( #PCDATA )>
17 <!ELEMENT phone ( #PCDATA )>
18 <!ELEMENT flag EMPTY>
19 <!ATTLIST flag gender (M | F) "M">
20
21 <!ELEMENT salutation ( #PCDATA )>
22 <!ELEMENT closing ( #PCDATA )>
23 <!ELEMENT paragraph ( #PCDATA )>
24 <!ELEMENT signature ( #PCDATA )>
```

Fig. 18.15 Document Type Definition (DTD) for a business letter. (Part 2 of 2.)

Lines 4–5 use the *ELEMENT element type declaration* to define rules for element `letter`. In this case, `letter` contains one or more `contact` elements, one `salutation` element, one or more `paragraph` elements, one `closing` element and one `signature` element, in that sequence. The *plus sign* (+) *occurrence indicator* specifies that an element must occur one or more times. Other indicators include the *asterisk* (*), which indicates an optional element that can occur any number of times, and the *question mark* (?), which indicates an optional element that can occur at most once. If an occurrence indicator is omitted, exactly one occurrence is expected.

The `contact` element declaration (lines 7–8) specifies that it contains the `name`, `address1`, `address2`, `city`, `state`, `zip`, `phone` and `flag` elements—in that order. Exactly one occurrence of each is expected.

Line 9 uses the *ATTLIST attribute-list declaration* to define an attribute (i.e., `type`) for the `contact` element. Keyword *#IMPLIED* specifies that, if the parser finds a `contact` element without a `type` attribute, the application can provide a value or ignore the missing attribute. The absence of a `type` attribute cannot invalidate the document. Other types of default values include *#REQUIRED* and *#FIXED*. Keyword `#REQUIRED` specifies that the attribute must be present in the document; keyword `#FIXED` specifies that the attribute (if present) must always be assigned a specific value. For example,

```
<!ATTLIST address zip #FIXED "01757">
```

indicates that the value `01757` must be used for attribute `zip`; otherwise, the document is invalid. If the attribute is not present, then the parser, by default, uses the fixed value that is specified in the `ATTLIST` declaration. Flag *CDATA* specifies that attribute `type` contains a `String` that is not processed by the parser, but instead is passed to the application as is.

Software Engineering Observation 18.4

DTD syntax does not provide any mechanism for describing an element's (or attribute's) data type.

Flag *#PCDATA* (line 11) specifies that the element can store *parsed character data* (i.e., text). Parsed character data cannot contain markup. The characters *less than* (<) and *amper-*

sand (&) must be replaced by their *entities* (i.e., < and &). See Appendix G, XHTML Special Characters, for a list of predefined entities.

Line 18 declares an empty element named `flag`. Keyword *EMPTY* specifies that the element cannot contain character data. Empty elements commonly are used for their attributes.

Line 19 presents an *enumerated attribute type*, which declare a list of possible values an attribute can have. The attribute must be assigned a value from this list to conform to the DTD. Enumerated type values are separated by pipe characters (`|`). Line 19 contains an enumerated attribute type declaration that allows attribute `gender` to have either the value `M` or `F`. A default value of `"M"` is specified to the right of the element attribute type.

Common Programming Error 18.9

Any element, attribute or relationship not explicitly declared by a DTD results in an invalid document.

XML documents must explicitly reference a DTD against which they are going to be validated. Figure 18.16 is an XML document that conforms to `letter.dtd` (Fig. 18.15).

```
<?xml version = "1.0"?>

<!-- Fig. 18.16: letter2.xml            -->
<!-- Business letter formatted with XML -->

<!DOCTYPE letter SYSTEM "letter.dtd">

<letter>
   <contact type = "from">
      <name>Jane Doe</name>
      <address1>Box 12345</address1>
      <address2>15 Any Ave.</address2>
      <city>Othertown</city>
      <state>Otherstate</state>
      <zip>67890</zip>
      <phone>555-4321</phone>
      <flag gender = "F" />
   </contact>

   <contact type = "to">
      <name>John Doe</name>
      <address1>123 Main St.</address1>
      <address2></address2>
      <city>Anytown</city>
      <state>Anystate</state>
      <zip>12345</zip>
      <phone>555-1234</phone>
      <flag gender = "M" />
   </contact>

   <salutation>Dear Sir:</salutation>

   <paragraph>It is our privilege to inform you about our new
      database managed with XML. This new system
```

Fig. 18.16 XML document referencing its associated DTD. (Part 1 of 2.)

```
35          allows you to reduce the load on your inventory list
36          server by having the client machine perform the work of
37          sorting and filtering the data.
38       </paragraph>
39
40       <paragraph>Please visit our Web site for availability
41          and pricing.
42       </paragraph>
43       <closing>Sincerely</closing>
44       <signature>Ms. Doe</signature>
45    </letter>
```

Fig. 18.16 XML document referencing its associated DTD. (Part 2 of 2.)

This XML document is similar to that in Fig. 18.3. Line 6 references a DTD file. This markup contains three pieces: the name of the root element (`letter` in line 8) to which the DTD is applied, the keyword *`SYSTEM`* (which in this case denotes an *external DTD*—a DTD defined in a separate file) and the DTD's name and location (i.e., `letter.dtd` in the current directory). Though almost any file extension can be used, DTD documents typically end with the *`.dtd`* extension.

Various tools (many of which are free) check document conformity against DTDs and Schemas (discussed momentarily). Figure 18.17 shows the results of the validation of `letter2.xml` using Microsoft's *XML Validator*. Visit `www.w3.org/XML/Schema.html` for a list of validating tools. Microsoft's XML Validator is available free for download from `msdn.microsoft.com/downloads/samples/Internet/xml/xml_validator/sample.asp`.

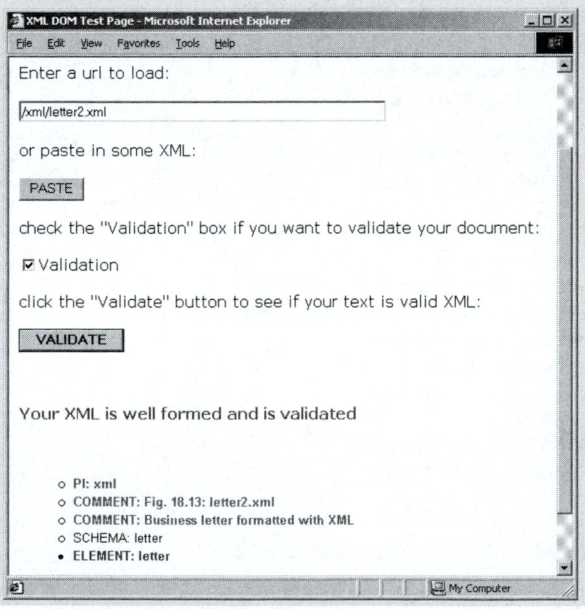

Fig. 18.17 XML Validator validates an XML document against a DTD.

Microsoft's XML Validator can validate XML documents against DTDs locally or by uploading the documents to the XML Validator Web site. Here, `letter2.xml` and `letter.dtd` are placed in folder `C:\XML\`. This XML document (`letter2.xml`) is well formed and conforms to `letter.dtd`.

XML documents that fail validation might still be well-formed documents. When a document fails to conform to a DTD or Schema, Microsoft XML Validator displays an error message. For example, the DTD in Fig. 18.15 indicates that the `contacts` element must contain child element `name`. If the document omits this child element, the document is well formed, but not valid. In such a scenario, Microsoft XML Validator displays the error message shown in Fig. 18.18.

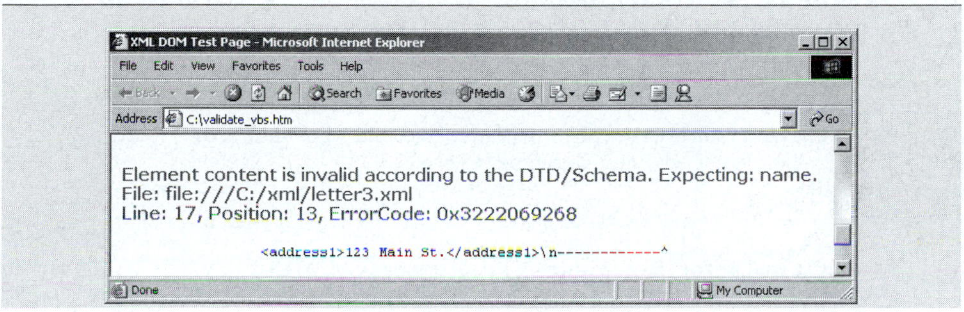

Fig. 18.18 XML Validator displaying an error message.

MC++ programs can use MSXML to validate XML documents against DTDs. For information on how to accomplish this, visit:

```
msdn.microsoft.com/library/en-us/cpguide/html/
cpconvalidationagainstdtdwithxmlvalidatingreader.asp
```

Schemas are the preferred means of defining structures for XML documents in .NET. Although several types of Schema exist, the two most popular are Microsoft Schema and W3C Schema. We begin our discussion of Schemas in the next section.

18.5.2 Microsoft XML Schema[3]

In this section, we introduce an alternative to DTDs—called Schemas—for defining an XML document's structure. Many developers in the XML community feel that DTDs are not flexible enough to meet today's programming needs. For example, DTDs cannot be manipulated (e.g., searched, programmatically modified, etc.) in the same manner that XML documents can, because DTDs are not XML documents. Furthermore, DTDs do not provide features for describing an element's (or attribute's) data type.

Unlike DTDs, Schemas do not use Extended Backus-Naur Form (EBNF) grammar. Instead, Schemas are XML documents which can be manipulated (e.g., elements can be added or removed, etc.) like any other XML document. As with DTDs, Schemas require validating parsers.

3. W3C Schema, which we discuss in Section 18.5.3, is emerging as the industry standard for describing an XML document's structure. Within the next two years, we expect most developers will be using W3C Schema.

In this section, we focus on Microsoft's *XML Schema* vocabulary. Figure 18.19 presents an XML document that conforms to the Microsoft Schema document shown in Fig. 18.20. By convention, Microsoft XML Schema documents use the file extension `.xdr`, which is short for *XML-Data Reduced*. Line 6 (Fig. 18.19) references the Schema document `book.xdr`. A document using a Microsoft XML Schema uses attribute `xmlns` to reference its schema through a URI which begins with `x-schema` followed by a colon (`:`) and the name of the schema document.

```
1  <?xml version = "1.0"?>
2
3  <!-- Fig. 18.19: bookxdr.xml             -->
4  <!-- XML file that marks up book data. -->
5
6  <books xmlns = "x-schema:book.xdr">
7     <book>
8        <title>Visual C++ .NET: A Managed Code Approach for
9           Experienced Programmers</title>
10    </book>
11
12    <book>
13       <title>C# for Experienced Programmers</title>
14    </book>
15
16    <book>
17       <title>Visual Basic .NET for Experienced Programmers
18       </title>
19    </book>
20
21    <book>
22       <title>Java Web Services for Experienced Programmers
23       </title>
24    </book>
25
26    <book>
27       <title>Web Services: A Technical Introduction</title>
28    </book>
29 </books>
```

Fig. 18.19 XML document that conforms to a Microsoft Schema document.

```
<?xml version = "1.0"?>

<!-- Fig. 18.20: book.xdr                         -->
<!-- Schema document to which book.xml conforms. -->

<Schema xmlns = "urn:schemas-microsoft-com:xml-data">
   <ElementType name = "title" content = "textOnly"
      model = "closed" />

```

Fig. 18.20 Microsoft Schema file that contains the structure to which `bookxdr.xml` conforms. (Part 1 of 2.)

```
10      <ElementType name = "book" content = "eltOnly" model = "closed">
11         <element type = "title" minOccurs = "1" maxOccurs = "1" />
12      </ElementType>
13
14      <ElementType name = "books" content = "eltOnly" model = "closed">
15         <element type = "book" minOccurs = "0" maxOccurs = "*" />
16      </ElementType>
17   </Schema>
```

Fig. 18.20 Microsoft Schema file that contains the structure to which `bookxdr.xml` conforms. (Part 2 of 2.)

Software Engineering Observation 18.5

Schemas are XML documents that conform to DTDs, which define the structure of a Schema. These DTDs, which are bundled with the parser, are used to validate the Schemas that authors create.

Software Engineering Observation 18.6

Many organizations and individuals are creating DTDs and Schemas for a broad range of categories (e.g., financial transactions, medical prescriptions, etc.). Often, these collections—called repositories*—are available free for download from the Web.*[4]

In line 6 of Fig. 18.20, root element *Schema* begins the Schema markup. Microsoft Schemas use the namespace URI *"urn:schemas-microsoft-com:xml-data"*. Lines 7–8 use element *ElementType* to define element `title`. Attribute *content* specifies that this element contains parsed character data (i.e., text only). Setting the *model attribute* to *"closed"* specifies that the element can only contain elements defined in the specified Schema. Line 10 defines element `book`; this element's `content` is "elements only" (i.e., *eltOnly*). This means that the element cannot contain mixed content (i.e., text and other elements). Within the `ElementType` element named `book`, the *element* element indicates that `title` is a `child` element of `book`. Attributes *minOccurs* and *maxOccurs* are set to `"1"`, indicating that a `book` element must contain exactly one `title` element. The asterisk (*) in line 15 indicates that the Schema permits any number of `book` elements in element `books`. We discuss how to validate `bookxdr.xml` against `book.xdr` in Section 18.5.4.

18.5.3 W3C XML Schema[5]

In this section, we focus on *W3C XML Schema*[6]—the schema that the W3C created. W3C XML Schema is a *Recommendation* (i.e., a stable release suitable for use in industry). Figure 18.21 shows a Schema-valid XML document named `bookxsd.xml` and Fig. 18.22 shows the W3C XML Schema document (`book.xsd`) that defines the structure for `bookxsd.xml`. Although Schema authors can use virtually any filename extension, W3C XML Schemas typically use the *.xsd* extension. We discuss how to validate `bookxsd.xml` against `book.xsd` in the next section.

---

4. See, for example, `opengis.net/schema.htm`.
5. We provide a detailed treatment of W3C Schema in *XML for Experienced Programmers* (late 2003).
6. For the latest on W3C XML Schema, visit `www.w3.org/XML/Schema`.

```
<?xml version = "1.0"?>

<!-- Fig. 18.21: bookxsd.xml                        -->
<!-- Document that conforms to W3C XML Schema. -->

<deitel:books xmlns:deitel = "http://www.deitel.com/booklist">
   <book>
      <title>Perl How to Program</title>
   </book>
   <book>
      <title>Python How to Program</title>
   </book>
</deitel:books>
```

Fig. 18.21 XML document that conforms to W3C XML Schema.

```
1  <?xml version = "1.0"?>
2
3  <!-- Fig. 18.22: book.xsd            -->
4  <!-- Simple W3C XML Schema document. -->
5
6  <xsd:schema xmlns:xsd = "http://www.w3.org/2001/XMLSchema"
7     xmlns:deitel = "http://www.deitel.com/booklist"
8     targetNamespace = "http://www.deitel.com/booklist">
9
10    <xsd:element name = "books" type = "deitel:BooksType"/>
11
12    <xsd:complexType name = "BooksType">
13       <xsd:sequence>
14          <xsd:element name = "book" type = "deitel:BookType"
15          minOccurs = "1" maxOccurs = "unbounded"/>
16       </xsd:sequence>
17    </xsd:complexType>
18
19    <xsd:complexType name = "BookType">
20       <xsd:sequence>
21          <xsd:element name = "title" type = "xsd:string"/>
22       </xsd:sequence>
23    </xsd:complexType>
24
25 </xsd:schema>
```

Fig. 18.22 XSD Schema document to which `bookxsd.xml` conforms.

W3C XML Schemas use the namespace URI *`www.w3.org/2001/XMLSchema`* and often use *namespace prefix `xsd`* (line 6 in Fig. 18.22). Root element *`schema`* (line 6) contains elements that define the XML document's structure. Line 7 binds the URI `http://www.deitel.com/booklist` to namespace prefix `deitel`. Line 8 specifies the *`targetNamespace`*, which is the namespace for elements and attributes that this schema defines.

In W3C XML Schema, element *`element`* (line 10) defines an element. Attributes *`name`* and *`type`* specify the `element`'s name and data type, respectively. In this case, the name of the element is `books` and the data type is `deitel:BooksType`. Any element (e.g., books) that contains attributes or child elements must define a *complex type*, which defines each attribute and child element. Type deitel:BooksType (lines 12–17) is an example of a complex type. We prefix BooksType with deitel, because this is a complex type that we have created, not an existing W3C XML Schema complex type.

Lines 12–17 use element *complexType* to define type BooksType (used in line 10). Here, we define BooksType as an element type that has a child element named book. Because book also contains a child element, its type must be a complex type (e.g., BookType, which we define later). Attribute *minOccurs* specifies that books must contain a minimum of one book element. Attribute *maxOccurs*, having value *unbounded* (line 15), specifies that books may have any number of book child elements. Element *sequence* specifies the order of elements in the complex type.

Lines 19–23 define the complexType BookType. Line 21 defines element title with type *xsd:string*. When an element has a *simple type* such as xsd:string, it is prohibited from containing attributes and child elements. W3C XML Schema provides a large number of data types, such as *xsd:date* for dates, *xsd:int* for integers, *xsd:double* for floating-point numbers and *xsd:time* for time.

Good Programming Practice 18.1

By convention, W3C XML Schema authors use namespace prefixes xsd *or* xs *when referring to the URI* http://www.w3.org/2001/XMLSchema.

18.5.4 Schema Validation in Visual C++ .NET

In this section, we present an MC++ application (Fig. 18.23–Fig. 18.24) that uses classes from the .NET Framework Class Library to validate the XML documents presented in the last two sections against their respective Schemas. We use an instance of *XmlValidatingReader* to perform the validation.

```
// Fig. 18.23: Form1.h
// Validating XML documents against Schemas.

#pragma once


namespace ValidationTest
{
   using namespace System;
   using namespace System::ComponentModel;
   using namespace System::Collections;
   using namespace System::Windows::Forms;
   using namespace System::Data;
   using namespace System::Drawing;
   using namespace System::Xml;
   using namespace System::Windows::Forms;
   using namespace System::Xml::Schema;  // contains Schema classes

   /// <summary>
   /// Summary for Form1
```

Fig. 18.23 Schema-validation example. (Part 1 of 4.)

```
   ///
   /// WARNING: If you change the name of this class, you will need to
   ///          change the 'Resource File Name' property for the managed
   ///          resource compiler tool associated with all .resx files
   ///          this class depends on.  Otherwise, the designers will not
   ///          be able to interact properly with localized resources
   ///          associated with this form.
   /// </summary>
   public __gc class Form1 : public System::Windows::Forms::Form
   {
   public:
      Form1(void)
      {
         InitializeComponent();

         valid = true;  // assume document is valid

         // get Schema(s) for validation
         schemas = new XmlSchemaCollection();
         schemas->Add( S"book", S"book.xdr" );
         schemas->Add( S"http://www.deitel.com/booklist", S"book.xsd" );
      }

   protected:
      void Dispose(Boolean disposing)
      {
         if (disposing && components)
         {
            components->Dispose();
         }
         __super::Dispose(disposing);
      }
   private: System::Windows::Forms::Button *  validateButton;
   private: System::Windows::Forms::Label *  consoleLabel;
   private: System::Windows::Forms::ComboBox *  filesComboBox;

   private: XmlSchemaCollection *schemas;  // Schemas collection
   private: bool valid;                    // validation result

   private:
      /// <summary>
      /// Required designer variable.
      /// </summary>
      System::ComponentModel::Container * components;

   // Visual Studio .NET generated GUI code

   // handle validateButton click event
   private: System::Void validateButton_Click(
               System::Object *  sender, System::EventArgs *  e)
            {
               try {

```

Fig. 18.23 Schema-validation example. (Part 2 of 4.)

```
            // get XML document
            XmlTextReader *reader =
               new XmlTextReader( filesComboBox->Text );

            // get validator
            XmlValidatingReader *validator =
               new XmlValidatingReader( reader );

            // assign Schema(s)
            validator->Schemas->Add( schemas );

            // set validation type
            validator->ValidationType = ValidationType::Auto;

            // register event handler for validation error(s)
            validator->ValidationEventHandler +=
               new ValidationEventHandler( this, ValidationError );

            // validate document node-by-node
            while ( validator->Read() ) ; // empty body

            // check validation result
            if ( valid )
               consoleLabel->Text = S"Document is valid";

            valid = true; // reset variable

            // close reader stream
            validator->Close();
         } // end try

         // no filename has been specified
         catch ( ArgumentException * ) {
            MessageBox::Show( S"Please specify a filename",
               S"Error", MessageBoxButtons::OK,
               MessageBoxIcon::Error );
         } // end catch

         // an invalid filename has been specified
         catch ( System::IO::IOException *fileException ) {
            MessageBox::Show( fileException->Message,
               S"Error", MessageBoxButtons::OK,
               MessageBoxIcon::Error );
         } // end catch
      } // end method validateButton_Click

   private:

      // event handler for validation error
      void ValidationError( Object *sender,
         ValidationEventArgs *arguments )
      {
         consoleLabel->Text = arguments->Message;
```

Fig. 18.23 Schema-validation example. (Part 3 of 4.)

```
127             valid = false; // validation failed
128          } // end method ValidationError
129       };
130    }
```

Fig. 18.23 Schema-validation example. (Part 4 of 4.)

```
// Fig. 18.24: Form1.cpp
// Entry point for application.

#include "stdafx.h"
#include "Form1.h"
#include <windows.h>

using namespace ValidationTest;

int APIENTRY _tWinMain(HINSTANCE hInstance,
                       HINSTANCE hPrevInstance,
                       LPTSTR    lpCmdLine,
                       int       nCmdShow)
{
   System::Threading::Thread::CurrentThread->ApartmentState =
      System::Threading::ApartmentState::STA;
   Application::Run(new Form1());
   return 0;
} // end _tWinMain
```

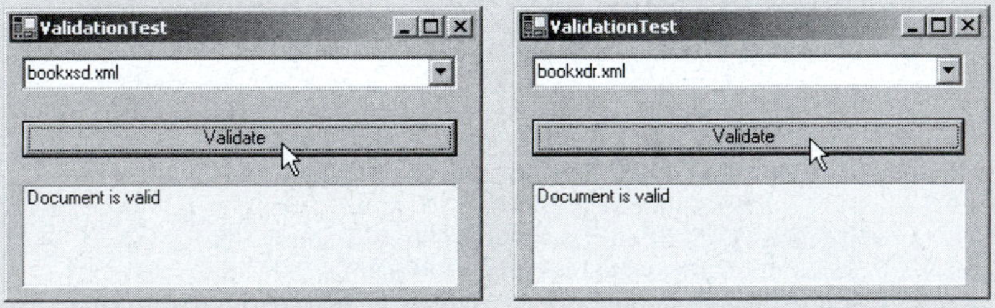

Fig. 18.24 `ValidationTest` entry point.

Line 39 (Fig. 18.23) creates an *`XmlSchemaCollection`* pointer named `schemas`. Line 40 calls method *`Add`* to add an *`XmlSchema`* object to the Schema collection. Method `Add` is passed a name that identifies the Schema (i.e., `"book"`) and the name of the Schema file (i.e., `"book.xdr"`). Line 41 calls method `Add` to add a W3C XML Schema. The first argument specifies the namespace URI (i.e., line 8 of Fig. 18.22) and the second argument identifies the schema file (i.e., `"book.xsd"`). This is the Schema that is used to validate `bookxsd.xml`.

Lines 75–76 create an `XmlTextReader` for the file that the user selected from `filesComboBox`. The XML document to be validated against a Schema contained in the `XmlSchemaCollection` must be passed to the `XmlValidatingReader` constructor (79–80). The `catch` blocks in lines 106–117 handle any exceptions (`ArgumentException` or `IOException`) that can occur if the user enters no filename or an invalid filename in `filesComboBox`.

Line 83 Adds the Schema collection pointed to by `schemas` to the *`Schemas`* *property*. This property sets the Schema used to validate the document. The *`ValidationType`* property (line 86) is set to the *`ValidationType`* enumeration constant for `Automatically` identifying the Schema's type (i.e., XDR or XSD). Lines 89–90 register method `ValidationError` with *`ValidationEventHandler`*. Method `ValidationError` (lines 123–128) is called if the document is invalid or if an error occurs, such as if the document cannot be found. Failure to register a method with `ValidationEventHandler` causes an exception to be thrown when the document is missing or invalid.

Validation is performed node-by-node, by calling the method *`Read`* (line 93). Each call to `Read` validates the next node in the document. The loop terminates either when all nodes have been validated successfully (and `valid` is still `true`) or a node fails validation (and `valid` has been set to `false` in line 127). When validated against their respective Schemas, the XML documents in Fig. 18.19 and Fig. 18.21 validate successfully.

Figure 18.25 and Fig. 18.26 list two XML documents that fail to conform to `book.xdr` and `book.xsd`, respectively. In both documents, an extra `title` element within a `book` element invalidates the documents. In Figure 18.25 and Figure 18.26, the extra elements are found in lines 9 and 21, respectively. Although both documents are invalid, they are well formed.

```
1   <?xml version = "1.0"?>
2
3  <!-- Fig. 18.25: bookxsdfail.xml                       -->
4  <!-- Document that does not conforms to W3C Schema. -->
5
6  <deitel:books xmlns:deitel = "http://www.deitel.com/booklist">
7     <book>
8        <title>Java Web Services for Experienced Programmers</title>
9        <title>C# for Experienced Programmers</title>
10    </book>
11    <book>
12       <title>Visual C++ .NET: A Managed Code Approach</title>
13    </book>
14 </deitel:books>
```

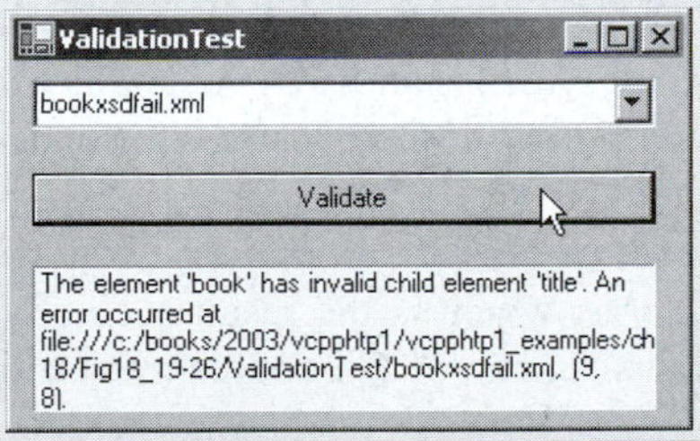
ValidationTest
bookxsdfail.xml
Validate
The element 'book' has invalid child element 'title'. An error occurred at file:///c:/books/2003/vcpphtp1/vcpphtp1_examples/ch18/Fig18_19-26/ValidationTest/bookxsdfail.xml, (9, 8).

Fig. 18.25 XML document that does not conform to the XSD schema of Fig. 18.22.

```
1  <?xml version = "1.0"?>
2
3  <!-- Fig. 18.26: bookxdrfail.xml                          -->
```

Fig. 18.26 XML file that does not conform to the Schema in Fig. 18.20. (Part 1 of 2.)

```
<!-- XML file that does not conform to Schema book.xdr. -->

<books xmlns = "x-schema:book.xdr">
   <book>
      <title>Web Services: A Technical Introduction</title>
   </book>

   <book>
      <title>Java Web Services for Experienced Programmers</title>
   </book>

   <book>
      <title>Visual Basic .NET for Experienced Programmers</title>
   </book>

   <book>
      <title>C++ How to Program, 4/e</title>
      <title>Python How to Program</title>
   </book>

   <book>
      <title>C# for Experienced Programmers</title>
   </book>
</books>
```

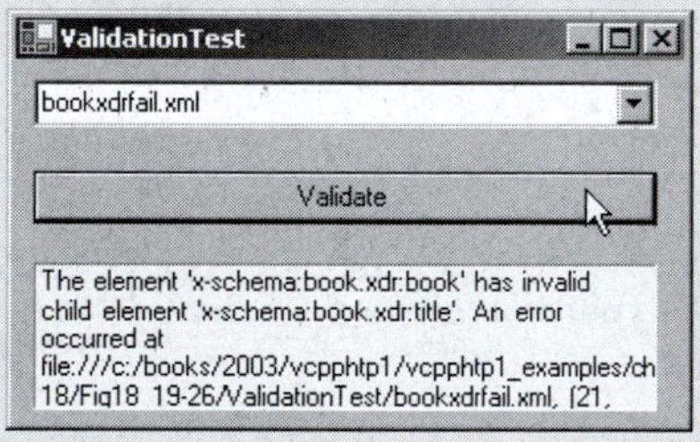
ValidationTest
bookxdrfail.xml
Validate
The element 'x-schema:book.xdr:book' has invalid child element 'x-schema:book.xdr:title'. An error occurred at file:///c:/books/2003/vcpphtp1/vcpphtp1_examples/ch18/Fig18 19-26/ValidationTest/bookxdrfail.xml, (21,

Fig. 18.26 XML file that does not conform to the Schema in Fig. 18.20. (Part 2 of 2.)

18.6 Extensible Stylesheet Language and `XslTransform`

Extensible Stylesheet Language (XSL) is an XML vocabulary for formatting XML data. In this section, we discuss the portion of XSL that creates formatted text-based documents (including other XML documents) from XML documents. This process is called a *transformation* and involves two tree structures: the *source tree*, which is the XML document being transformed, and the *result tree*, which is the result (i.e., any text-based format such as XHTML or XML) of the transformation.[7] The source tree is not modified when a transformation occurs.

To perform transformations, an XSLT processor is required. Popular XSLT processors include Microsoft's MSXML and the Apache Software Foundation's *Xalan*

7. Extensible HyperText Markup Language (XHTML) is the W3C technical recommendation that replaces HTML for marking up content for the Web. For more information on XHTML, see the XHTML Appendices E and F, and visit `www.w3.org`.

(`xml.apache.org`). The XML document, shown in Fig. 18.27, is transformed by MSXML into an XHTML document (Fig. 18.28).

```
1  <?xml version = "1.0"?>
2
3  <!-- Fig. 18.27: sorting.xml              -->
4  <!-- Usage of elements and attributes. -->
5
6  <?xml:stylesheet type = "text/xsl" href = "sorting.xsl"?>
7
8  <book isbn = "999-99999-9-X">
9     <title>Deitel&apos;s XML Primer</title>
10
11    <author>
12       <firstName>Paul</firstName>
13       <lastName>Deitel</lastName>
14    </author>
15
16    <chapters>
17       <frontMatter>
18          <preface pages = "2"/>
19          <contents pages = "5"/>
20          <illustrations pages = "4"/>
21       </frontMatter>
22
23       <chapter number = "3" pages = "44">
24          Advanced XML</chapter>
25       <chapter number = "2" pages = "35">
26          Intermediate XML</chapter>
27       <appendix number = "B" pages = "26">
28          Parsers and Tools</appendix>
29       <appendix number = "A" pages = "7">
30          Entities</appendix>
31       <chapter number = "1" pages = "28">
32          XML Fundamentals</chapter>
33    </chapters>
34
35    <media type = "CD"/>
36 </book>
```

Fig. 18.27 XML document containing book information.

Line 6 is a *processing instruction* (*PI*), which contains application-specific information that is embedded into the XML document. In this particular case, the processing instruction is specific to IE and specifies the location of an XSLT document with which to transform the XML document. The characters *<?* and *?>* delimit a processing instruction, which consists of a *PI target* (e.g., `xml:stylesheet`) and *PI value* (e.g., `type = "text/xsl" href = "sorting.xsl"`). The portion of this particular PI value that follows `href` specifies the name and location of the style sheet to apply—in this case, `sorting.xsl`, which is located in the same directory as this XML document.

Fig. 18.28 presents the XSLT document (`sorting.xsl`) that transforms `sorting.xml` (Fig. 18.27) to XHTML.

Performance Tip 18.1

Using Internet Explorer on the client to process XSLT documents conserves server resources by using the client's processing power (instead of having the server process XSLT documents for multiple clients).

Line 1 of Fig. 18.28 contains the XML declaration. Recall that an XSL document is an XML document. Lines 6–7 contain the `xsl:stylesheet` root element. Attribute *`version`* specifies the version of XSLT to which this document conforms. Namespace prefix `xsl` is defined and is bound to the XSLT URI defined by the W3C. When processed, lines 10–13 write the document type declaration to the result tree. Attribute *`method`* is assigned `"xml"`, which indicates that XML is being output to the result tree. Attribute *`omit-xml-declaration`* is assigned `"no"`, which outputs an XML declaration to the result tree. Attribute *`doctype-system`* and *`doctype-public`* write the `Doctype` DTD information to the result tree.

```
1  <?xml version = "1.0"?>
2
3  <!-- Fig. 18.28: sorting.xsl                       -->
4  <!-- Transformation of book information into XHTML. -->
5
6  <xsl:stylesheet version = "1.0"
7     xmlns:xsl = "http://www.w3.org/1999/XSL/Transform">
8
9     <!-- write XML declaration and DOCTYPE DTD information -->
10    <xsl:output method = "xml" omit-xml-declaration = "no"
11       doctype-system =
12          "http://www.w3.org/TR/xhtml1/DTD/xhtml1-strict.dtd"
13       doctype-public = "-//W3C//DTD XHTML 1.0 Strict//EN"/>
14
15    <!-- match document root -->
16    <xsl:template match = "/">
17       <html xmlns = "http://www.w3.org/1999/xhtml">
18          <xsl:apply-templates/>
19       </html>
20    </xsl:template>
21
22    <!-- match book -->
23    <xsl:template match = "book">
24       <head>
25          <title>ISBN <xsl:value-of select = "@isbn" /> -
26             <xsl:value-of select = "title" /></title>
27       </head>
28
29       <body>
30          <h1 style = "color: blue">
31             <xsl:value-of select = "title"/></h1>
32
```

Fig. 18.28 XSL document that transforms `sorting.xml` (Fig. 18.27) into XHTML. (Part 1 of 3.)

```
         <h2 style = "color: blue">by <xsl:value-of
            select = "author/lastName" />,
            <xsl:value-of select = "author/firstName" /></h2>

         <table style =
            "border-style: groove; background-color: wheat">

            <xsl:for-each select = "chapters/frontMatter/*">
               <tr>
                  <td style = "text-align: right">
                     <xsl:value-of select = "name()" />
                  </td>

                  <td>
                    ( <xsl:value-of select = "@pages" /> pages )
                  </td>
               </tr>
            </xsl:for-each>

            <xsl:for-each select = "chapters/chapter">
               <xsl:sort select = "@number" data-type = "number"
                    order = "ascending" />
               <tr>
                  <td style = "text-align: right">
                     Chapter <xsl:value-of select = "@number" />
                  </td>

                  <td>
                     ( <xsl:value-of select = "@pages" /> pages )
                  </td>
               </tr>
            </xsl:for-each>

            <xsl:for-each select = "chapters/appendix">
               <xsl:sort select = "@number" data-type = "text"
                    order = "ascending" />
               <tr>
                  <td style = "text-align: right">
                     Appendix <xsl:value-of select = "@number" />
                  </td>

                  <td>
                     ( <xsl:value-of select = "@pages" /> pages )
                  </td>
               </tr>
            </xsl:for-each>
         </table>

         <br /><p style = "color: blue">Pages:
            <xsl:variable name = "pagecount"
               select = "sum(chapters//*/@pages)" />
            <xsl:value-of select = "$pagecount" />
```

Fig. 18.28 XSL document that transforms `sorting.xml` (Fig. 18.27) into XHTML. (Part 2 of 3.)

```
85            <br />Media Type:
86               <xsl:value-of select = "media/@type" /></p>
87         </body>
88      </xsl:template>
89
90   </xsl:stylesheet>
```

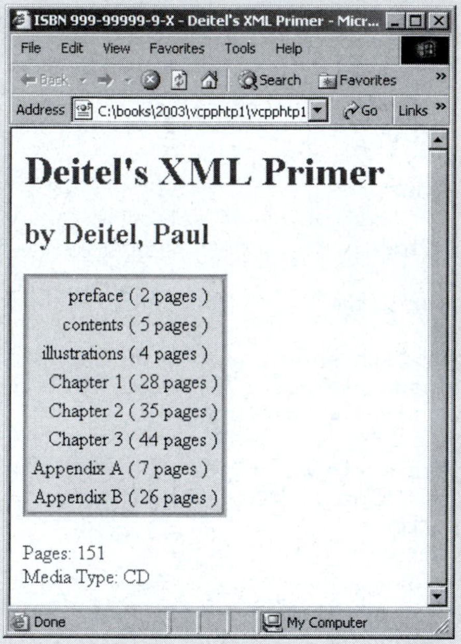

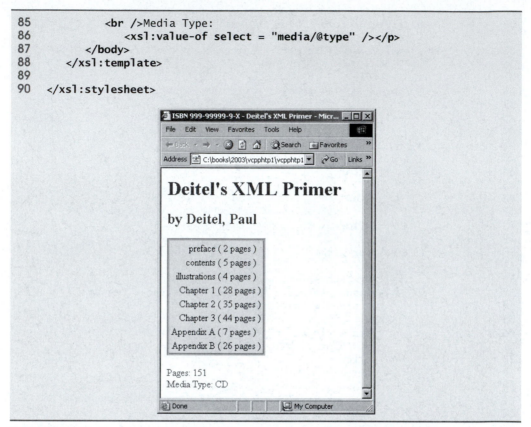

Fig. 18.28 XSL document that transforms `sorting.xml` (Fig. 18.27) into XHTML. (Part 3 of 3.)

XSLT documents contain one or more ***`xsl:template`*** elements that specify which information is output to the result tree. The template in line 16 ***`match`***es the source tree's document root. When the document root is encountered, this template is applied, and any text marked up by this element that is not in the namespace pointed to by `xsl` is output to the result tree. Line 18 calls for all the `templates` that match children of the document root to be applied. Line 23 specifies a `template` that `matches` element `book`.

Lines 25–26 create the title for the XHTML document. We use the ISBN of the book from attribute `isbn` and the contents of element `title` to create the title string **ISBN 999-99999-9-X - Deitel's XML Primer**. Element `xsl:value-of` selects the `book` element's `isbn` attribute.

Lines 33–35 create a header element that contains the book's author. The *context node* (i.e., the current node being processed) is `book`, so the XPath expression `author/lastName` selects the author's last name, and the expression `author/firstName` selects the author's first name.

Line 40 selects each element that is a child of element `frontMatter` (indicated by an asterisk). Line 43 calls *node-set function **`name`*** to retrieve the current node's element name (e.g., `preface`). The current node is the context node specified in the `xsl:for-each` (line 40).

Lines 53–54 sort `chapters` by number in ascending order. Attribute `select` selects the value of context node `chapter`'s attribute `number`. Attribute *`data-type`*, having value `"number"`, specifies a numeric sort, and attribute *`order`* specifies `"ascending"` order. Attribute `data-type` also can be assigned the value *`"text"`* (line 67), and attribute `order` also may be assigned the value *`"descending"`*.

Lines 82–83 use an *XSL variable* to store the value of the book's page count and output it to the result tree. Attribute `name` specifies the variable's name, and attribute `select` assigns it a value. Function *`sum`* totals the values for all `page` attribute values. The two slashes between `chapters` and `*` indicate that all descendant nodes of `chapters` are searched for elements that contain an attribute named `pages`.

The *`System::Xml::Xsl`* namespace provides classes for applying XSLT style sheets to XML documents. Specifically, an object of class *`XslTransform`* can be used to perform the transformation.

Figure 18.29–Fig. 18.30 apply a style sheet (`sports.xsl`) to `sports.xml` (Fig. 18.13). The transformation result is written to a text box and to a file. We also load the results in IE to show the transformation results rendered as HTML.

```
// Fig. 18.29: Form1.h
// Applying a style sheet to an XML document.

#pragma once


namespace TransformTest
{
   using namespace System;
   using namespace System::ComponentModel;
   using namespace System::Collections;
   using namespace System::Windows::Forms;
   using namespace System::Data;
   using namespace System::Drawing;
   using namespace System::Xml;
   using namespace System::Xml::XPath;
   using namespace System::Xml::Xsl;
   using namespace System::IO;

   /// <summary>
   /// Summary for Form1
   ///
   /// WARNING: If you change the name of this class, you will need to
   ///          change the 'Resource File Name' property for the managed
   ///          resource compiler tool associated with all .resx files
   ///          this class depends on.  Otherwise, the designers will not
   ///          be able to interact properly with localized resources
   ///          associated with this form.
   /// </summary>
   public __gc class Form1 : public System::Windows::Forms::Form
   {
   public:
```

Fig. 18.29 XSL style sheet applied to an XML document. (Part 1 of 3.)

```
      Form1(void)
      {
         InitializeComponent();

         // load XML data
         document = new XmlDocument();
         document->Load( S"sports.xml" );

         // create navigator
         navigator = document->CreateNavigator();

         // load style sheet
         transformer = new XslTransform();
         transformer->Load( S"sports.xsl" );
      }

   protected:
      void Dispose(Boolean disposing)
      {
         if (disposing && components)
         {
            components->Dispose();
         }
         __super::Dispose(disposing);
      }
   private: System::Windows::Forms::TextBox *  consoleTextBox;
   private: System::Windows::Forms::Button *  transformButton;

   private: XmlDocument *document;      // Xml document root
   private: XPathNavigator *navigator; // navigate document
   private: XslTransform *transformer; // transform document
   private: StringWriter *output;      // display document

   private:
      /// <summary>
      /// Required designer variable.
      /// </summary>
      System::ComponentModel::Container * components;

   // Visual Studio .NET generated GUI code

   // transformButton click event
   private: System::Void transformButton_Click(
               System::Object *  sender, System::EventArgs *  e)
            {
               // transform XML data
               output = new StringWriter();
               transformer->Transform( navigator, 0, output );

               // display transformation in text box
               consoleTextBox->Text = output->ToString();

```

Fig. 18.29 XSL style sheet applied to an XML document. (Part 2 of 3.)

```
            // write transformation result to disk
            FileStream *stream = new FileStream( S"sports.html",
               FileMode::Create );
            StreamWriter *writer = new StreamWriter( stream );
            writer->Write( output->ToString() );

            // close streams
            writer->Close();
            output->Close();
         } // end method transformButton_Click
   };
}
```

Fig. 18.29 XSL style sheet applied to an XML document. (Part 3 of 3.)

```
// Fig. 18.30: Form1.cpp
// Entry point for application.

#include "stdafx.h"
#include "Form1.h"
#include <windows.h>

using namespace TransformTest;

int APIENTRY _tWinMain(HINSTANCE hInstance,
                       HINSTANCE hPrevInstance,
                       LPTSTR    lpCmdLine,
                       int       nCmdShow)
{
   System::Threading::Thread::CurrentThread->ApartmentState =
      System::Threading::ApartmentState::STA;
   Application::Run(new Form1());
   return 0;
} // end _tWinMain
```

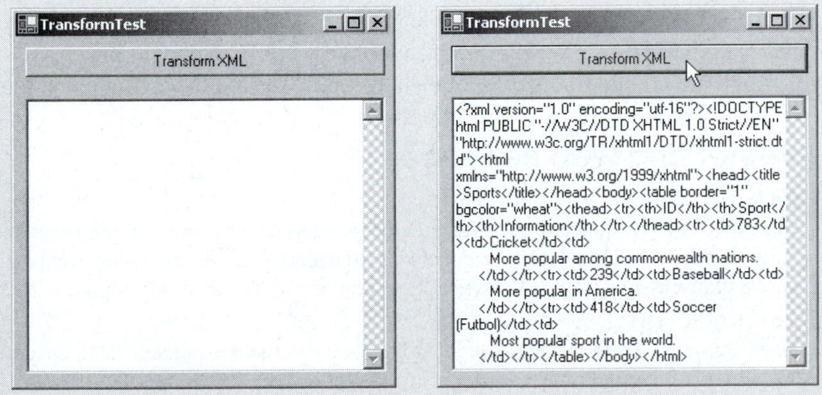

Fig. 18.30 `TransformTest` entry point. (Part 1 of 2.)

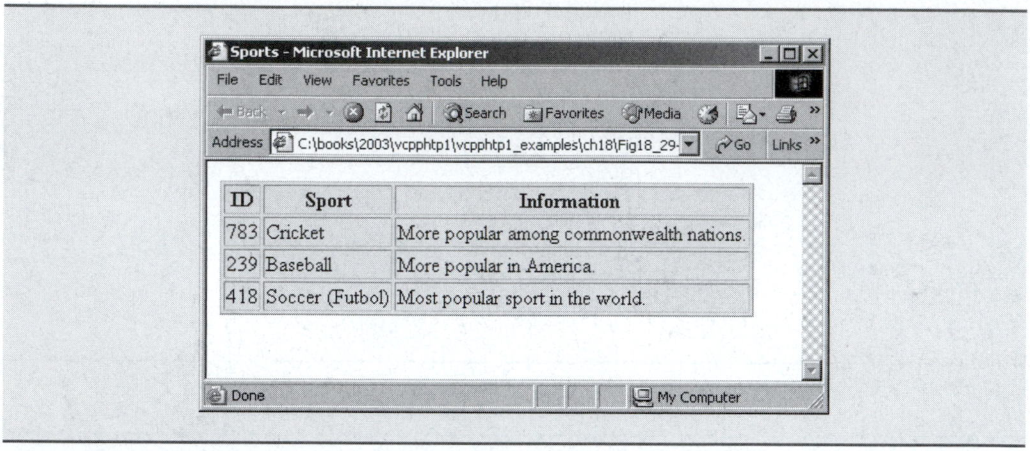

Fig. 18.30 `TransformTest` entry point. (Part 2 of 2.)

Line 63 (Fig. 18.29) declares `XslTransform` pointer `transformer`. An object of this type is necessary to transform the XML data to another format. In line 39, the XML document is parsed and loaded into memory with a call to method `Load`. Method `CreateNavigator` is called in line 42 to create an `XPathNavigator` object, which is used to navigate the XML document during the transformation. A call to method *`Load`* of class `XslTransform` (line 46) parses and loads the style sheet that this application uses. The argument that is passed contains the name and location of the style sheet.

Event handler `transformButton_Click` (lines 75–94) calls method *`Transform`* of class `XslTransform` to apply the style sheet (`sports.xsl`) to `sports.xml` (line 80). This method takes three arguments: An `XPathNavigator` (created from `sports.xml`'s `XmlDocument`), an instance of class *`XsltArgumentList`*, which is a list of `String *` parameters that can be applied to a style sheet—`0`, in this case—and an instance of a derived class of `TextWriter` (in this example, an instance of class `StringWriter`). The results of the transformation are stored in the `StringWriter` object pointed to by `output`. Lines 86–89 write the transformation results to disk. The third screen shot depicts the created XHTML document when it is rendered in IE.

In this chapter, we studied the Extensible Markup Language and several of its related technologies. In Chapter 19, Database, SQL and ADO .NET, we begin our discussion of databases, which are crucial to the development of multi-tier Web-based applications.

18.7 Internet and Web Resources

`www.w3.org/xml`

The W3C (World Wide Web Consortium) facilitates the development of common protocols to ensure interoperability on the Web. Their XML page includes information about upcoming events, publications, software and discussion groups. Visit this site to read about the latest developments in XML.

`www.w3.org/TR/REC-xml`

This W3C page contains a short introduction to XML as well as the most recent XML specification.

`www.w3.org/XML/1999/XML-in-10-points`

This W3C page describes the basics of XML in ten simple points. It is a useful page for those new to XML.

`www.xml.org`
`xml.org` is a reference for XML, DTDs, schemas and namespaces.

`www.w3.org/style/XSL`
This W3C page provides information on XSL, including such topics as XSL development, learning XSL, XSL-enabled tools, XSL specification, FAQs and XSL history.

`www.w3.org/TR`
This is the W3C technical reports and publications page. It contains links to working drafts, proposed recommendations and other resources.

`www.xmlbooks.com`
This site provides a list of XML books recommended by Charles Goldfarb, one of the original designers of GML (General Markup Language), from which SGML is derived.

`www.xml-zone.com`
The Development Exchange XML Zone is a complete resource for XML information. This site includes an FAQ, news, articles and links to other XML sites and newsgroups.

`wdvl.internet.com/Authoring/Languages/XML`
Web Developer's Virtual Library XML site includes tutorials, an FAQ, the latest news and extensive links to XML sites and software downloads.

`www.xml.com`
`XML.com` provides the latest news and information about XML, conference listings, links to XML Web resources organized by topic, tools and other resources.

`msdn.microsoft.com/xml/default.asp`
The MSDN Online XML Development Center features articles on XML, Ask the Experts chat sessions, samples and demos, newsgroups and other helpful information.

`msdn.microsoft.com/downloads/samples/Internet/xml/xml_validator/sample.asp`
Microsoft's XML validator, which can be downloaded from this site, can validate both online and offline documents.

`www.oasis-open.org/cover/xml.html`
The SGML/XML Web Page is an extensive resource that includes links to several FAQs, online resources, industry initiatives, demos, conferences and tutorials.

`www-106.ibm.com/developerworks/xml`
The IBM XML Zone site is a great resource for developers. It provides news, tools, a library, case studies and information about events and standards.

`developer.netscape.com/tech/xml`
The XML and Metadata Developer Central site has demos, technical notes and news articles related to XML.

`www.ucc.ie/xml`
This site is a detailed XML FAQ. Developers can check out responses to some popular questions or submit their own questions through the site.

SUMMARY

- XML is a widely supported, open (i.e., non-proprietary) technology for data exchange. XML is quickly becoming the standard by which applications maintain data.
- XML is highly portable. Any text editor that supports ASCII or Unicode characters can render or display XML documents. XML elements describe the data they contain, so they are both human and machine readable.
- XML permits document authors to create custom markup for virtually any type of information. This extensibility enables document authors to create entirely new markup languages, ones that

describe specific types of data, including mathematical formulas, chemical molecular structures, music, recipes, etc.

- The processing of XML documents—which programs typically store in files whose names end with the `.xml` extension—requires a program called an XML parser. A parser is responsible for identifying components of XML documents and for then storing those components in a data structure for manipulation.
- An XML document can reference another optional document that defines the XML document's structure. Two types of optional structure-defining documents are Document Type Definitions (DTDs) and XML Schemas.
- An XML document begins with an optional XML declaration, which identifies the document as an XML document. The `version` information parameter specifies the version of XML syntax that is used in the document.
- XML comments begin with `<!--` and end with `-->`. Data is marked up with tags whose names are enclosed in angle brackets (<>). Tags are used in pairs to delimit markup. A tag that begins markup is called a start tag; a tag that terminates markup is called an end tag. End tags differ from start tags in that they contain a forward slash (`/`) character.
- Individual units of markup are called elements, which are the most fundamental XML building blocks. XML documents contain one element, called a root element, that contains every other element in the document. Elements are embedded or nested within each other to form hierarchies, with the root element at the top of the hierarchy.
- In addition to being placed between tags, data also can be placed in attributes, which are name–value pairs in start tags. Elements can have any number of attributes.
- XML allows document authors to create their own tags, so naming collisions can occur. As in the .NET Framework, XML namespaces provide a means for document authors to prevent collisions. Namespace prefixes are prepended to elements to specify the namespace to which the element belongs.
- Each namespace prefix is bound to a uniform resource identifier (`URI`) that uniquely identifies the namespace. Document authors create their own namespace prefixes. Virtually any name can be used as a namespace prefix except the reserved namespace prefix `xml`.
- To eliminate the need to place a namespace prefix in each element, document authors can specify a default namespace for an element and its children.
- When an XML parser successfully parses a document, the parser stores a tree structure containing the document's data in memory. This hierarchical tree structure is called a Document Object Model (DOM) tree. The DOM tree represents each component of the XML document as a node in the tree. The DOM tree has a single root node that contains all other nodes in the document.
- Namespace `System::Xml` contains classes for creating, reading and manipulating XML documents.
- Class `XmlReader` is an `abstract` class that defines the interface for reading XML documents.
- `XmlReader`-derived class `XmlNodeReader` iterates through each node in the XML document.
- An `XmlDocument` object conceptually represents an empty XML document.
- Method `CreateNode` of `XmlDocument` takes a `NodeType`, a `Name` and a `NamespaceURI` as arguments.
- XML documents are parsed and loaded into an `XmlDocument` object when method `Load` is invoked. Once an XML document is loaded into an `XmlDocument`, its data can be read and manipulated programmatically.
- An `XmlNodeReader` allows us to read one node at a time from an `XmlDocument`.

- Method Read of XmlReader reads one node from the DOM tree.
- The Name property contains the node's name, the Value property contains the node's data and the NodeType property contains the node type (i.e., element, comment, text, etc.).
- An XmlTextWriter streams XML data to a stream. Method WriteTo writes an XML representation to an XmlTextWriter stream.
- An XmlTextReader reads XML data from a stream.
- Class XPathNavigator in the System::Xml::XPath namespace can iterate through node lists that match search criteria, written as an XPath expression.
- XPath (XML Path Language) provides a syntax for locating specific nodes in XML documents effectively and efficiently. XPath is a string-based language of expressions used by XML and many of its related technologies.
- Navigation methods of XPathNavigator are MoveToFirstChild, MoveToParent, MoveToNext and MoveToPrevious.
- Whereas XML contains only data, XSLT is capable of converting XML into any text-based document (including another XML document). XSLT documents typically have the extension .xsl.
- When transforming an XML document via XSLT, two tree structures are involved: the source tree, which is the XML document being transformed, and the result tree, which is the result (e.g., XHTML) of the transformation.
- The node-set function name retrieves the current node's element name.
- Attribute select selects the value of context node's attribute.
- XML documents can be transformed programmatically through MC++. The System::Xml::Xsl namespace facilitates the application of XSLT style sheets to XML documents.
- Class XsltArgumentList is a list of String parameters that can be applied to a style sheet.

TERMINOLOGY

@ character
Add method of class XmlSchemaCollection
ancestor node
asterisk (*) occurrence indicator
ATTLIST
attribute
attribute node
attribute value
CDATA character data
child element
child node
container element
context node
CreateNavigator method of class XPathDocument
CreateNode method of class XmlDocument
Current property of XPathNodeIterator
data-type attribute
default namespace
descendant node
doctype-public attribute
doctype-system attribute
document root
Document Type Definition (DTD)
DOM (Document Object Model)
EBNF (Extended Backus-Naur Form) grammar
ELEMENT element type declaration
empty element
EMPTY keyword
end tag
Extensible Stylesheet Language (XSL)
external DTD
forward slash
#IMPLIED flag
invalid document
IsEmptyElement property of class XmlNodeReader
LastChild property of class XmlNode
Load method of class XmlDocument
markup
match attribute
maxOccurs attribute
method attribute
minOccurs attribute

MoveToFirstChild property of class XPathNavigator
MoveToNext property of XPathNavigator
MoveToParent property of class XPathNavigator
MoveToPrevious property of class XPathNavigator
MoveToRoot property of XPathNavigator
MSXML parser
name attribute
name node-set function
Name property of class XmlNodeReader
namespace prefix
node
Nodes collection
node-set function
NodeType property
nonvalidating XML parser
occurrence indicator
omit-xml-declaration attribute
order attribute
parent node
Parent property of class TreeNode
#PCDATA flag
property
parsed character data
parser
PI (processing instruction)
PI target
PI value
plus-sign (+) occurrence indicator
processing instruction
question-mark (?) occurrence indicator
Read method of XmlNodeReader
recursive descent
reserved namespace prefix xml
result tree
root element
root node
Schema element
schema property
Schemas property of XmlSchemaCollection
select attribute
Select method of class XPathNavigator
sibling node
single-quote character (')
source tree
style sheet
sum function
SYSTEM flag
System::Xml namespace
System::Xml::Schema namespace
text node
Transform method of class XslTransform
tree-based model
type attribute
validating XML parser
ValidatingReader class
ValidationEventHandler class
ValidationType property of class XmlValidatingReader
ValidationType::Auto constant
value property
version attribute
version information parameter
W3C XML Schema
well-formed document
.xdr extension
XML (Extensible Markup Language)
XML declaration
.xml file extension
xml namespace
XML node
XML processor
XML Schema
XML Validator
XmlDocument class
XmlNodeReader class
XmlNodeType enumeration
XmlNodeType::Comment constant
XmlNodeType::Element constant
XmlNodeType::EndElement constant
XmlNodeType::Text constant
XmlNodeType::XmlDeclaration constant
xmlns attribute
XmlPathNodeIterator class
XmlReader class
XmlSchema class
XmlSchemaCollection collection
XmlTextWriter class
XPathExpression class
XPathNavigator class
.xsl extension
XSL Transformations (XSLT)
XSL variable
xsl:apply-templates element
xsl:for-each element
xsl:output element
xsl:sort element
xsl:stylesheet element

`xsl:template` element
`xsl:value-of` element
`XslTransform` class
`XsltTextWriter` class

SELF-REVIEW EXERCISES

18.1 Which of the following are valid XML element names?

a) `yearBorn`
b) `year.Born`
c) `year Born`
d) `year-Born1`
e) `2_year_born`
f) `--year/born`
g) `year*born`
h) `.year_born`
i) `_year_born_`
j) `y_e-a_r-b_o-r_n`

18.2 State whether the following are *true* or *false*. If *false*, explain why.

a) XML is a technology for creating markup languages.
b) XML markup is delimited by forward and backward slashes (/ and \).
c) All XML start tags must have corresponding end tags.
d) Parsers check an XML document's syntax.
e) XML does not support namespaces.
f) When creating new XML elements, document authors must use the set of XML tags provided by the W3C.
g) The pound character (#), the dollar sign ($), ampersand (&), greater-than (>) and less-than (<) are examples of XML reserved characters.

18.3 Fill in the blanks for each of the following statements:

a) ________ help prevent naming collisions.
b) ________ embed application-specific information into an XML document.
c) ________ is Microsoft's XML parser.
d) XSL element ________ writes a `DOCTYPE` to the result tree.
e) Microsoft XML Schema documents have root element ________.
f) To define an attribute in a DTD, ________ is used.
g) XSL element ________ is the root element in an XSL document.
h) XSL element ________ selects specific XML elements using repetition.

18.4 State which of the following statements are true and which are false. If false, explain why.

a) XML is not case sensitive.
b) Schemas are the preferred means of defining structures for XML documents in .NET.
c) DTDs are a vocabulary of XML.
d) Schema is a technology for locating information in an XML document.

18.5 In Fig. 18.1, we subdivided the `author` element into more detailed pieces. How might you subdivide the `date` element?

18.6 Write a processing instruction that includes the stylesheet `wap.xsl` for use in Internet Explorer.

18.7 Fill in the blanks in each of the following statements:

a) Nodes that contain other nodes are called ________ nodes.
b) Nodes that are peers are called ________ nodes.
c) Class `XmlDocument` is analogous to the ________ of a tree.
d) Method ________ adds an `XmlNode` to an `XmlTree` as a child of the current node.

18.8 Write an XPath expression that locates `contact` nodes in `letter.xml` (Fig. 18.3).

18.9 Describe the `Select` method of `XPathNavigator`.

ANSWERS TO SELF-REVIEW EXERCISES

18.1 a, b, d, i, j. [Choice c is incorrect because it contains a space. Choice e is incorrect because the first character is a number. Choice f is incorrect because it contains a forward slash (/) and does not begin with a letter or underscore. Choice g is incorrect because it contains an asterisk (*); Choice h is incorrect because the first character is a period (.) and does not begin with a letter or underscore.]

18.2 a) True. b) False. In an XML document, markup text is delimited by angle brackets (< and >), with a forward slash in the end tag. c) True. d) True. e) False. XML does support namespaces. f) False. When creating new tags, document authors can use any valid name except the reserved word `xml` (also `XML`, `Xml` etc.). g) False. XML reserved characters include the ampersand (&), the left-angle bracket (<) and the right-angle bracket (>), but not # and $.

18.3 a) namespaces. b) processing instructions. c) MSXML. d) `xsl:output`. e) `Schema`. f) `ATTLIST`. g) `xsl:stylesheet`. h) `xsl:for-each`.

18.4 a) False. XML is case sensitive. b) True. c) False. DTDs use EBNF grammar which is not XML syntax. d) False. XPath is a technology for locating information in an XML document.

18.5
```
<date>
   <month>August</month>
   <day>6</day>
   <year>2003</year>
</date>.
```

18.6 `<?xsl:stylesheet type = "text/xsl" href = "wap.xsl"?>`

18.7 a) parent. b) sibling. c) root. d) `AppendChild`.

18.8 `/letter/contact`.

18.9 `Select` takes either an `XPathExpression` or a `String` argument containing an `XPathExpression` to select nodes referenced by the navigator.

EXERCISES

18.10 Create an XML document that marks up the nutrition facts for a package of cookies. A package of cookies has a serving size of 1 package and the following nutritional value per serving: 260 calories, 100 fat calories, 11 grams of fat, 2 grams of saturated fat, 5 milligrams of cholesterol, 210 milligrams of sodium, 36 grams of total carbohydrates, 2 grams of fiber, 15 grams of sugars and 5 grams of protein. Name this document `nutrition.xml`. Load the XML document into Internet Explorer [*Hint*: Your markup should contain elements describing the product name, serving size/amount, calories, sodium, cholesterol, proteins, etc. Mark up each nutrition fact/ingredient listed above.

18.11 Write an XSLT style sheet for your solution to Exercise 18.10 that displays the nutritional facts in an XHTML table. Modify Fig. 18.29–Fig. 18.30 (application `TransformTest`) to output an XHTML file, `nutrition.html`. Render `nutrition.html` in a Web browser.

18.12 Write a Microsoft Schema for Fig. 18.27.

18.13 Alter Fig. 18.23–Fig. 18.24 (application `ValidationTest`) to include a list of Schemas in a drop-down box, along with the list of XML files. Allow the user to test for whether any XML file on the list satisfies a specific Schema. Use `books.xml`, `books.xsd`, `nutrition.xml`, `nutrition.xsd` and `fail.xml`.

18.14 Modify `XmlReaderTest` (Fig. 18.7–Fig. 18.8) to display `letter.xml` (Fig. 18.3) in a `TreeView`, instead of in a text box.

18.15 Modify Fig. 18.28 (`sorting.xsl`) to sort each section (i.e., frontmatter, chapters and appendices) by page number rather than by chapter number. Save the modified document as `sorting_byPage.xsl`.

18.16 Modify `TransformTest` (Fig. 18.29–Fig. 18.30) to take in `sorting.xml` (Fig. 18.27), `sorting.xsl` (Fig. 18.28) and `sorting_byPage.xsl`, and print the XHTML document resulting from the transform of `sorting.xml` into two XHTML files, `sorting_byPage.html` and `sorting_byPage.html`.

19

Database, SQL and ADO .NET

Objectives

- To understand the relational database model.
- To understand basic database queries that use SQL (Structured Query Language).
- To understand and use ADO .NET's disconnected model.
- To use the classes and interfaces of namespace `System::Data` to manipulate databases.
- To use the classes and interfaces of namespace `System::Data::OleDb`.

It is a capital mistake to theorize before one has data.
Arthur Conan Doyle

Now go, write it before them in a table, and note it in a book, that it may be for the time to come for ever and ever.
The Holy Bible: The Old Testament

Let's look at the record.
Alfred Emanuel Smith

Get your facts first, and then you can distort them as much as you please.
Mark Twain

I like two kinds of men: domestic and foreign.
Mae West

Outline

19.1 Introduction

A *database* is an integrated collection of data. Many different strategies exist for organizing data in databases to facilitate easy access to and manipulation of the data. A *database management system* (*DBMS*) provides mechanisms for storing and organizing data in a manner that is consistent with the database's format. Database management systems enable programmers to access and store data without worrying about the internal representation of databases.

Today's most popular database systems are *relational databases*. Almost universally, relational databases use a language called *SQL*—pronounced as its individual letters or as "sequel"—to perform *queries* (i.e., to request information that satisfies given criteria) and to manipulate data. [*Note*: The writing in this chapter assumes that SQL is pronounced as its individual letters. For this reason, we often precede SQL with the article "an," as in "an SQL database" or "an SQL statement."]

Some popular enterprise-level relational database systems include Microsoft SQL Server, Oracle,™ Sybase,™ DB2,™ Informix™ and MySQL™. This chapter presents examples using Microsoft Access—a relational database system that is packaged with

Microsoft Office. We provide the reader with links to more information about these products at the end of this chapter.

A programming language connects to, and interacts with, a relational database via an *interface*—software that facilitates communication between a database management system and a program. Many Visual C++ .NET programmers communicate with databases and manipulate their data through *Microsoft ActiveX Data Objects*™ (ADO) or *ADO .NET*.

19.2 Relational Database Model

The *relational database model* is a logical representation of data that allows relationships among data to be considered without concern for the physical structure of the data. A relational database is composed of *tables*. Figure 19.1 illustrates an example table that might be used in a personnel system. The table name is `Employee`, and its primary purpose is to illustrate the specific attributes of various employees. Tables are composed of *rows*, and rows are composed of *columns* in which values are stored. This table consists of six rows. The `number` column of each row in the table is the *primary key* for referencing data in the table. A primary key is a column (or group of columns) in a table that contain(s) unique data—i.e, data that is not duplicated in other rows of that table. This guarantees that each row can be identified by at least one distinct value. Examples of primary-keys are columns that contain Social Security numbers, employee IDs and part numbers in an inventory system. The rows of Fig. 19.1 are *ordered* by primary key. In this case, the rows are listed in increasing order (they also could be listed in decreasing order).

number	name	department	salary	location
23603	Jones	413	1100	New Jersey
24568	Kerwin	413	2000	New Jersey
34589	Larson	642	1800	Los Angeles
35761	Myers	611	1400	Orlando
47132	Neumann	413	9000	New Jersey
78321	Stephens	611	8500	Orlando

Row — Primary key — Column

Fig. 19.1 Relational-database structure of an `Employee` table.

Each column of the table represents a different data attribute. Rows normally are unique (by primary key) within a table, but other particular column values might appear in multiple rows. For example, three different rows in the `Employee` table's `Department` column contain the number 413.

Often, different users of a database are interested in different data and different relationships among those data. Some users require only subsets of the table columns. To obtain table subsets, we use SQL statements to specify certain data we wish to *select* from a table. SQL provides a complete set of statements (including `SELECT`) that enable programmers to define complex *queries* to select data from a table. The result of a query is another table, commonly called a *result set* (or *record set*). For example, we might select data from the table in Fig. 19.1 to generate a new result set (table) containing only the location of each department. This resulting table appears in Fig. 19.2. SQL queries are discussed in detail in Section 19.4.

department	location
413	New Jersey
611	Orlando
642	Los Angeles

Fig. 19.2 Result of selecting `Department` and `Location` data from the `Employee` table.

19.3 Relational Database Overview: Books Database

The next section provides an overview of SQL in the context of a sample `Books` database that we created for this chapter. However, before we discuss SQL, we must explain the various tables of the `Books` database. We use this database to introduce various database concepts, including the use of SQL to manipulate and obtain useful information from the database.

The database consists of four tables: `Authors`, `Publishers`, `AuthorISBN` and `Titles`. The `Authors` table (described in Fig. 19.3) consists of three columns that maintain each author's unique ID number, first name and last name. that maintain each author's unique ID number, first name and last name. Figure 19.4 contains sample data from the `Authors` table of the `Books` database.

Column	Description
`authorID`	Author's ID number in the database. In the `Books` database, this integral column is defined as *autoincremented*. For each new row inserted in this table, the database increments the `authorID` value, ensuring that each row has a unique `authorID`. This column represents the table's primary key.
`firstName`	Author's first name (a string).
`lastName`	Author's last name (a string).

Fig. 19.3 `Authors` table from `Books`.

`authorID`	`firstName`	`lastName`
1	Harvey	Deitel
2	Paul	Deitel
3	Tem	Nieto
4	Kate	Steinbuhler

Fig. 19.4 Data from the `Authors` table of `Books`. (Part 1 of 2.)

authorID	firstName	lastName
5	Sean	Santry
6	Ted	Lin
7	Praveen	Sadhu
8	David	McPhie
9	Cheryl	Yaeger
10	Marina	Zlatkina
11	Ben	Wiedermann
12	Jonathan	Liperi
13	Jeffrey	Listfield
14	Jeffrey	Hamm
15	Christina	Courtemarche

Fig. 19.4 Data from the `Authors` table of `Books`. (Part 2 of 2.)

The `Publishers` table (described in Fig. 19.5) consists of two columns, representing each publisher's unique ID and name. Figure 19.6 contains the data from the `Publishers` table of the `Books` database.

Column	Description
`publisherID`	The publisher's ID number in the database. This auto-incremented integral column is the table's primary-key.
`publisherName`	The name of the publisher (a string).

Fig. 19.5 `Publishers` table from `Books`.

publisherID	publisherName
1	Prentice Hall
2	Prentice Hall PTG

Fig. 19.6 Data from the `Publishers` table of `Books`.

The `AuthorISBN` table (described in Fig. 19.7) consists of two columns that maintain the authors' ID numbers and the corresponding ISBN numbers of their books. This table helps associate the names of the authors with the titles of their books. Figure 19.8 contains a portion of the data from the `AuthorISBN` table of the `Books` database. ISBN is an abbreviation for "International Standard Book Number"—a numbering scheme by which publishers worldwide assign every book a unique identification number. [*Note*: To save space, we have split the contents of this figure into two columns, each containing the `authorID` and `isbn` column.]

Column	Description
`authorID`	The author's ID number, which allows the database to associate each book with a specific author. This integer ID must also appear in the `Authors` table.
`isbn`	The ISBN number for a book (a string).

Fig. 19.7 `AuthorISBN` table from `Books`.

authorID	isbn	authorID	isbn
1	0130895725	2	0139163050
1	0132261197	2	013028419x
1	0130895717	2	0130161438
1	0135289106	2	0130856118
1	0139163050	2	0130125075
1	013028419x	2	0138993947
1	0130161438	2	0130852473
1	0130856118	2	0130829277
1	0130125075	2	0134569555
1	0138993947	2	0130829293
1	0130852473	2	0130284173
1	0130829277	2	0130284181
1	0134569555	2	0130895601
1	0130829293	2	0132261197
1	0130284173	2	0130895717
1	0130284181	2	0135289106
1	0130895601	3	013028419x
2	0130895725	3	0130161438
3	0130856118	3	0130284173
3	0134569555	3	0130284181
3	0130829293	4	0130895601

Fig. 19.8 Data from `AuthorISBN` table in `Books`.

The `Titles` table (described in Fig. 19.9) consists of seven columns that maintain general information about the books in the database. This information includes each book's ISBN number, title, edition number, copyright year and publisher's ID number, as well as the name of a file containing an image of the book cover and, finally, each book's price. Figure 19.10 contains a portion of the data from the `Titles` table.

Column	Description
`isbn`	ISBN number of the book (a string).
`title`	Title of the book (a string).
`editionNumber`	Edition number of the book (a string).
`copyright`	Copyright year of the book (an integer).
`publisherID`	Publisher's ID number (an integer). This value must correspond to an ID number in the `Publishers` table.
`imageFile`	Name of the file containing the book's cover image (a string).
`price`	Suggested retail price of the book (a real number). [*Note*: The prices shown in this database are for example purposes only.]

Fig. 19.9 `Titles` table from `Books`.

isbn	title	edition-Number	publisher-ID	copy-right	imageFile	price
013045821X	Visual C++ .NET: A Managed Code Approach for Experienced Programmers	1	1	2003	`vcppfxp.jpg`	$69.95
0130923613	Python How to Program	1	1	2002	`python.jpg`	$69.95
0130622214	C# How to Program	1	1	2002	`cshtp.jpg`	$69.95
0130341517	Java How to Program	4	1	2002	`jhtp4.jpg`	$69.95
0130649341	The Complete Java Training Course	4	2	2002	`javactc4.jpg`	$109.95
0130895601	Advanced Java 2 Platform How to Program	1	1	2002	`advjhtp1.jpg`	$69.95
0130308978	Internet and World Wide Web How to Program	2	1	2002	`iw3htp2.jpg`	$69.95
0130293636	Visual Basic .NET How to Program	2	1	2002	`vbnet.jpg`	$69.95
0130895725	C How to Program	3	1	2001	`chtp3.jpg`	$69.95

Fig. 19.10 Data from the `Titles` table of `Books`. (Part 1 of 2.)

isbn	title	edition-Number	publisher-ID	copy-right	imageFile	price
0130895717	C++ How to Program	3	1	2001	cpphtp3.jpg	$69.95
013028419X	e-Business and e-Commerce How to Program	1	1	2001	ebechtp1.jpg	$69.95
0130622265	Wireless Internet and Mobile Business How to Program	1	1	2001	wireless.jpg	$69.95
0130284181	Perl How to Program	1	1	2001	perlhtp1.jpg	$69.95
0130284173	XML How to Program	1	1	2001	xmlhtp1.jpg	$69.95

Fig. 19.10 Data from the `Titles` table of `Books`. (Part 2 of 2.)

Figure 19.11 illustrates the relationships among the tables in the `Books` database. The first line in each table is the table's name. The column whose name appears in italics is that table's primary key. A table's primary key uniquely identifies each row in the table. Every row must have a value in the primary-key column, and the value must be unique. This is known as the *Rule of Entity Integrity*. Note that the `AuthorISBN` table contains two columns whose names are italicized. This indicates that these two columns form a *compound primary key*—each row in the table must have a unique `authorID`–`isbn` combination. For example, several rows might have an `authorID` of `2`, and several rows might have an `isbn` of `0130895601`, but only one row can have both an `authorID` of `2` and an `isbn` of `0130895601`.

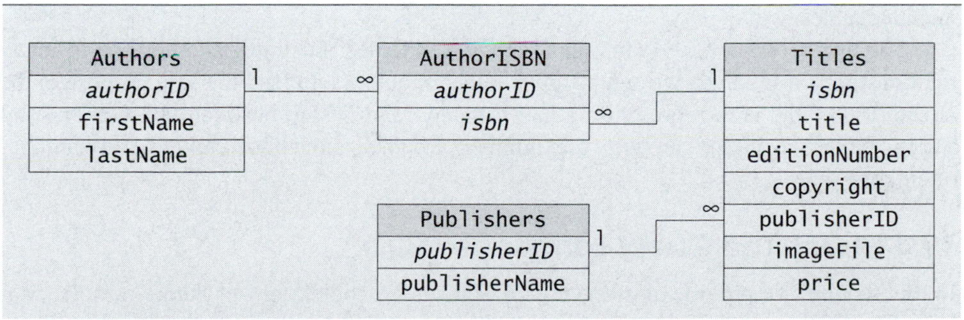

Fig. 19.11 Table relationships in `Books`.

Common Programming Error 19.1

Failure to provide a value for the primary key in every row breaks the Rule of Entity Integrity and causes the DBMS to report an error.

Common Programming Error 19.2

Providing duplicate values for the primary key of multiple rows causes the DBMS to report an error.

The lines connecting the tables in Fig. 19.11 represent the *relationships* among the tables. Consider the line between the `Publishers` and `Titles` tables. On the `Publishers` end of the line, there is a `1`, and on the `Titles` end, there is an infinity (∞) symbol. This line indicates a *one-to-many relationship*, in which every publisher in the `Publishers` table can have an arbitrarily large number of books in the `Titles` table. Note that the relationship line links the `publisherID` column in the `Publishers` table to the `publisherID` column in `Titles` table. In the `Titles` table, the `publisherID` column is a *foreign key*—a column that has the value of the primary key of another table (e.g., `publisherID` in the `Publishers` table). Programmers specify *foreign key constraints* when creating a table. The foreign key constraint helps maintain the *Rule of Referential Integrity*: Every foreign key must appear as another table's primary key. Foreign keys enable information from multiple tables to be *joined* together for analysis purposes. There is a one-to-many relationship between a primary key and its corresponding foreign key. This means that a foreign key value can appear many times in its own table, but must appear exactly once (as the primary key) in another table. The line between the tables represents the link between the foreign key in one table and the primary key in another table.

Common Programming Error 19.3

Providing a foreign-key value that does not appear as a primary-key value in another table breaks the Rule of Referential Integrity and causes the DBMS to report an error.

The line between the `AuthorISBN` and `Authors` tables indicates that, for each author in the `Authors` table, the `AuthorISBN` table can contain an arbitrary number of ISBNs for books written by that author. The `authorID` column in the `AuthorISBN` table is a foreign key of the `authorID` column (the primary key) of the `Authors` table. Note, again, that the line between the tables links the foreign key in table `AuthorISBN` to the corresponding primary key in table `Authors`. The `AuthorISBN` table links information in the `Titles` and `Authors` tables.

The line between the `Titles` and `AuthorISBN` tables illustrates another one-to-many relationship; a title can be written by any number of authors. In fact, the sole purpose of the `AuthorISBN` table is to represent a many-to-many relationship between the `Authors` and `Titles` tables; an author can write any number of books, and a book can have any number of authors.

19.4 Structured Query Language (SQL)

In this section, we provide an overview of SQL in the context of our `Books` sample database. The SQL queries discussed here form the foundation for the SQL used in the chapter examples.

Figure 19.12 lists SQL keywords and provides a description of each. In the next several subsections, we discuss these SQL keywords in the context of complete SQL queries. Other SQL keywords exist, but are beyond the scope of this text. [*Note*: To locate additional information on SQL, please refer to the book's bibliography.]

SQL keyword	Description
SELECT	Selects (retrieves) columns from one or more tables.
FROM	Specifies tables from which to get columns or delete rows. Required in every SELECT and DELETE.
WHERE	Specifies criteria that determine the rows to be retrieved.
INNER JOIN	Merge rows from multiple tables.
GROUP BY	Specifies criteria for grouping rows.
ORDER BY	Specifies criteria for ordering rows.
INSERT	Inserts data into a specified table.
UPDATE	Updates data in a specified table.
DELETE	Deletes data from a specified table.

Fig. 19.12 SQL query keywords.

19.4.1 Basic SELECT Query

Let us consider several SQL queries that extract information from database Books. A typical SQL query "selects" information from one or more tables in a database. Such selections are performed by *SELECT queries*. The basic format for a SELECT query is

```
SELECT * FROM tableName
```

In this query, the asterisk (*) indicates that all columns from the *tableName* table of the database should be selected. For example, to select the entire contents of the Authors table (i.e., all data depicted in Fig. 19.4), use the query

```
SELECT * FROM Authors
```

To select specific columns from a table, replace the asterisk (*) with a comma-separated list containing the names of the columns to select. For example, to select only the columns authorID and lastName for all rows in the Authors table, use the query

```
SELECT authorID, lastName FROM Authors
```

Figure 19.13 presents the data returned by the query. If a column name contains spaces, the entire column name must be enclosed in square brackets ([]) in the query. For example, if the column name is first name, it must appear in the query as [first name].

authorID	lastName	authorID	lastName
1	Deitel	4	Steinbuhler
2	Deitel	5	Santry
3	Nieto	6	Lin

Fig. 19.13 authorID and lastName from the Authors table. (Part 1 of 2.)

authorID	lastName	authorID	lastName
7	Sadhu	12	Liperi
8	McPhie	13	Listfield
9	Yaeger	14	Hamm
10	Zlatkina	15	Courtemarche
11	Wiedermann		

Fig. 19.13 `authorID` and `lastName` from the `Authors` table. (Part 2 of 2.)

Good Programming Practice 19.1

Some DBMSs do not allow spaces or dashes (–) to be used in column names. To maximize the compatibility of your database, use underscores (_) to separate words in column names (as well as in table names, database names, etc.)

Common Programming Error 19.4

If a program assumes that an SQL statement using the asterisk (*) to select columns always returns those columns in the same order, the program could process the result set incorrectly. If the column order in the database table(s) changes, the order of the columns in the result set would change accordingly.

Performance Tip 19.1

If a program does not know the order of columns in a result set, the program must process the columns by name. This could require a linear search of the column names in the result set. If users specify the column names that they wish to select from a table (or several tables), the application receiving the result set knows the order of the columns in advance. When this occurs, the program can process the data more efficiently, because columns can be accessed directly by column number.

19.4.2 WHERE Clause

In most cases, users search a database for rows that satisfy certain *selection criteria*. Only rows that match the selection criteria are selected. SQL uses the optional *`WHERE` clause* in a `SELECT` query to specify the selection criteria for the query. The simplest format for a `SELECT` query that includes selection criteria is

SELECT *columnName1*, *columnName2*, ... **FROM** *tableName* **WHERE** *criteria*

For example, to select the `title`, `editionNumber` and `copyright` columns from those rows of table `Titles` in which the `copyright` date is greater than `2001`, use the query

```
SELECT title, editionNumber, copyright
FROM Titles
WHERE copyright > 2001
```

Figure 19.14 shows the result set of the preceding query. [*Note*: When we construct a query for use in MC++, we simply create a `String *` containing the entire query. However, when we display queries in the text, we often use multiple lines and indentation to enhance readability.]

title	editionNumber	copyright
Visual C++ .NET: A Managed Code Approach for Experienced Programmers	1	2003
Internet and World Wide Web How to Program	2	2002
Java How to Program	4	2002
The Complete Java Training Course	4	2002
Advanced Java 2 Platform How to Program	1	2002
C# How To Program	1	2002
Python How to Program	1	2002
Visual Basic .NET How to Program	2	2002

Fig. 19.14 Titles with copyrights after 2001 from table `Titles`.

The `WHERE` clause condition can contain operators such as <, >, <=, >=, =, <> and *LIKE*.[1] Operator `LIKE` is used for *pattern matching* with wildcard characters *asterisk* (*) and *question mark* (?). Pattern matching allows SQL to search for strings that "match a pattern."

A pattern that contains an asterisk (*) searches for strings in which zero or more characters take the asterisk character's place in the pattern. For example, the following query locates all authors whose last names start with the letter `D`:

```
SELECT authorID, firstName, lastName
FROM Authors
WHERE lastName LIKE 'D*'
```

The preceding query selects the two rows shown in Fig. 19.15, because two of the authors in our database have last names that begin with the letter `D` (followed by zero or more characters). The * in the `WHERE` clause's `LIKE` pattern indicates that any number of characters can appear after the letter `D` in the `lastName` column. Notice that the pattern string is surrounded by single-quote characters.

authorID	firstName	lastName
1	Harvey	Deitel
2	Paul	Deitel

Fig. 19.15 Authors from the `Authors` table whose last names start with `D`.

Portability Tip 19.1

Not all database management systems support the `LIKE` *operator, so be sure to read the DBMS's documentation carefully before employing this operator.*

1. Information about other `WHERE` clause operators can be found at: `www.bayconggroup.com/sql_command_reference.htm` and `www.firstsql.com/tutor2.htm`

Portability Tip 19.2

*Most database management systems use the % character in place of the * character in* `LIKE` *expressions.*

Portability Tip 19.3

In most database management systems, string data are case sensitive.

Portability Tip 19.4

In some database management systems, table names and column names are case sensitive.

A pattern string including a question mark (?) character searches for strings in which exactly one character takes the question mark's place in the pattern. For example, the following query locates all authors whose last names start with any character (specified with ?), followed by the letter `i`, followed by any number of additional characters (specified with *):

```
SELECT authorID, firstName, lastName
FROM Authors
WHERE lastName LIKE '?i*'
```

The preceding query produces the rows listed in Fig. 19.16; five authors in our database have last names in which the letter `i` is the second letter.

authorID	firstName	lastName
3	Tem	Nieto
6	Ted	Lin
11	Ben	Wiedermann
12	Jonathan	Liperi
13	Jeffrey	Listfield

Fig. 19.16 Authors from table `Authors` whose last names contain `i` as the second letter.

Portability Tip 19.5

Many database management systems use the _ character in place of the ? character in `LIKE` *expressions.*

19.4.3 ORDER BY Clause

The results of a query can be arranged in ascending or descending order using the optional *`ORDER BY` clause*. The simplest forms for an `ORDER BY` clause are

SELECT *columnName1*, *columnName2*, ... **FROM** *columnName* **ORDER BY** *column* **ASC**
SELECT *columnName1*, *columnName2*, ... **FROM** *columnName* **ORDER BY** *column* **DESC**

where ASC specifies ascending order (lowest to highest), DESC specifies descending order (highest to lowest) and *column* specifies the column whose values determine the sorting order.

For example, to obtain a list of authors arranged in ascending order by last name (Fig. 19.17), use the query:

```
SELECT authorID, firstName, lastName
FROM Authors
ORDER BY lastName ASC
```

Note that the default sorting order is ascending; therefore, ASC is optional.

authorID	firstName	lastName
15	Christina	Courtemarche
2	Paul	Deitel
1	Harvey	Deitel
14	Jeffrey	Hamm
6	Ted	Lin
12	Jonathan	Liperi
13	Jeffrey	Listfield
8	David	McPhie
3	Tem	Nieto
7	Praveen	Sadhu
5	Sean	Santry
4	Kate	Steinbuhler
11	Ben	Wiedermann
9	Cheryl	Yaeger
10	Marina	Zlatkina

Fig. 19.17 Authors from table Authors in ascending order by lastName.

To obtain the same list of authors arranged in descending order by last name (Fig. 19.18), use the query:

```
SELECT authorID, firstName, lastName
FROM Authors
ORDER BY lastName DESC
```

The ORDER BY clause also can be used to order rows by multiple columns. Such queries are written in the form

ORDER BY *column1 sortingOrder*, *column2 sortingOrder*, ...

where *sortingOrder* is either ASC or DESC. Note that the *sortingOrder* does not have to be identical for each column.

authorID	firstName	lastName
10	Marina	Zlatkina
9	Cheryl	Yaeger
11	Ben	Wiedermann
4	Kate	Steinbuhler
5	Sean	Santry
7	Praveen	Sadhu
3	Tem	Nieto
8	David	McPhie
13	Jeffrey	Listfield
12	Jonathan	Liperi
6	Ted	Lin
14	Jeffrey	Hamm
2	Paul	Deitel
1	Harvey	Deitel
15	Christina	Courtemarche

Fig. 19.18 Authors from table `Authors` in descending order by `lastName`.

For example, the query

```
SELECT authorID, firstName, lastName
FROM Authors
ORDER BY lastName, firstName
```

sorts all authors in ascending order by last name, then by first name. This means that, if any authors have the same last name, their rows are returned sorted by first name (Fig. 19.19).

authorID	firstName	lastName
15	Christina	Courtemarche
1	Harvey	Deitel
2	Paul	Deitel
14	Jeffrey	Hamm
6	Ted	Lin
12	Jonathan	Liperi
13	Jeffrey	Listfield
8	David	McPhie
3	Tem	Nieto

Fig. 19.19 Authors from table `Authors` in ascending order by `lastName` and by `firstName`. (Part 1 of 2.)

authorID	firstName	lastName
7	Praveen	Sadhu
5	Sean	Santry
4	Kate	Steinbuhler
11	Ben	Wiedermann
9	Cheryl	Yaeger
10	Marina	Zlatkina

Fig. 19.19 Authors from table `Authors` in ascending order by `lastName` and by `firstName`. (Part 2 of 2.)

The `WHERE` and `ORDER BY` clauses can be combined in one query. For example, the query

```
SELECT isbn, title, editionNumber, copyright, price
FROM Titles
WHERE title
LIKE '*How to Program' ORDER BY title ASC
```

returns the ISBN, title, edition number, copyright and price of each book in the `Titles` table that has a `title` ending with "`How to Program`"; it lists these rows in ascending order by `title`. The results of the query are depicted in Fig. 19.20.

isbn	title	edition-Number	copy-right	price
0130895601	Advanced Java 2 Platform How to Program	1	2002	$69.95
0131180436	C How to Program	1	1992	$69.95
0130895725	C How to Program	3	2001	$69.95
0132261197	C How to Program	2	1994	$49.95
0130622214	C# How To Program	1	2002	$69.95
0135289106	C++ How to Program	2	1998	$49.95
0131173340	C++ How to Program	1	1994	$69.95
0130895717	C++ How to Program	3	2001	$69.95
013028419X	e-Business and e-Commerce How to Program	1	2001	$69.95
0130308978	Internet and World Wide Web How to Program	2	2002	$69.95
0130161438	Internet and World Wide Web How to Program	1	2000	$69.95

Fig. 19.20 Books from table `Titles` whose titles end with `How to Program`, in ascending order by `Title`. (Part 1 of 2.)

isbn	title	edition-Number	copy-right	price
0130341517	Java How to Program	4	2002	$69.95
0136325890	Java How to Program	1	1998	$49.95
0130284181	Perl How to Program	1	2001	$69.95
0130923613	Python How to Program	1	2002	$69.95
0130293636	Visual Basic .NET How to Program	2	2002	$69.95
0134569555	Visual Basic 6 How to Program	1	1999	$69.95
0130622265	Wireless Internet and Mobile Business How to Program	1	2001	$69.95
0130284173	XML How to Program	1	2001	$69.95

Fig. 19.20 Books from table `Titles` whose titles end with `How to Program`, in ascending order by `Title`. (Part 2 of 2.)

19.4.4 Merging Data from Multiple Tables: INNER JOIN

Database designers often split related data into separate tables to ensure that a database does not store data redundantly. For example, the `Books` database has tables `Authors` and `Titles`. We use an `AuthorISBN` table to provide "links" between authors and their corresponding titles. If we did not separate this information into individual tables, we would need to include author information with each entry in the `Titles` table. This would result in the database storing duplicate author information for authors who wrote multiple books.

Often, it is necessary for analysis purposes to merge data from multiple tables into a single set of data. Referred to as *joining* the tables, this can be accomplished via an *`INNER JOIN`* operation in the `SELECT` query. An `INNER JOIN` merges rows from two or more tables by testing for matching values in a column that is common to the tables. The simplest format for an `INNER JOIN` clause is:

```
SELECT columnName1, columnName2, ...
FROM table1
INNER JOIN table2
   ON table1.columnName = table2.columnName
```

The `ON` clause specifies the columns from each table that are compared to determine which rows are merged. For example, the following query produces a list of authors accompanied by the ISBN numbers for books written by each author:

```
SELECT firstName, lastName, isbn
FROM Authors
INNER JOIN AuthorISBN
   ON Authors.authorID = AuthorISBN.authorID
ORDER BY lastName, firstName
```

The query merges the `firstName` and `lastName` columns from table `Authors` with the `isbn` column from table `AuthorISBN`, sorting the results in ascending order by `lastName` and `firstName`. Notice the use of the syntax *tableName.columnName* in the `ON` clause. This syntax (called a *qualified name*) specifies the columns from each table that should be compared to join the tables. The "*tableName.*" syntax is required if the columns have the same name in both tables. The same syntax can be used in any query to distinguish among columns in different tables that have the same name. Qualified names that start with the database name can be used to perform cross-database queries.

Software Engineering Observation 19.1

If an SQL statement includes columns from multiple tables that have the same name, the statement must precede those column names with their table names and the dot operator (e.g., `Authors.authorID`*).*

Common Programming Error 19.5

In a query, failure to provide qualified names for columns that have the same name in two or more tables is an error.

Figure 19.21 depicts a portion of the results of the preceding query, ordered by `lastName` and `firstName`.

firstName	lastName	isbn	firstName	lastName	isbn
Harvey	Deitel	0130895601	Paul	Deitel	0134569555
Harvey	Deitel	0130284181	Paul	Deitel	0130829277
Harvey	Deitel	0130284173	Paul	Deitel	0130852473
Harvey	Deitel	0130852473	Tem	Nieto	0130284181
Harvey	Deitel	0138993947	Tem	Nieto	0130284173
Harvey	Deitel	0130856118	Tem	Nieto	0130829293
Paul	Deitel	0130284181	Tem	Nieto	0134569555
Paul	Deitel	0130284173	Tem	Nieto	0130856118
Paul	Deitel	0130829293	Tem	Nieto	0130161438

Fig. 19.21 Authors from table `Authors` and ISBN numbers of the authors' books, sorted in ascending order by `lastName` and `firstName`.

19.4.5 Joining Data from Tables `Authors`, `AuthorISBN`, `Titles` and `Publishers`

The `Books` database contains one predefined query (`TitleAuthor`), which selects as its results the title, ISBN number, author's first name, author's last name, copyright year and publisher's name for each book in the database. For books that have multiple authors, the query produces a separate composite row for each author. The `TitleAuthor` query is depicted in Fig. 19.22. Figure 19.23 contains a portion of the query result.

```
SELECT Titles.title, Titles.isbn, Authors.firstName,
    Authors.lastName, Titles.copyright,
     Publishers.publisherName
FROM
( Publishers INNER JOIN Titles
      ON Publishers.publisherID = Titles.publisherID )
   INNER JOIN
   ( Authors INNER JOIN AuthorISBN
   ON Authors.authorID = AuthorISBN.authorID )
ON Titles.isbn = AuthorISBN.isbn
ORDER BY Titles.title
```

Fig. 19.22 `TitleAuthor` query of `Books` database.

title	isbn	firstName	lastName	copyright	publisherName
Advanced Java 2 Platform How to Program	0130895601	Paul	Deitel	2002	Prentice Hall
Advanced Java 2 Platform How to Program	0130895601	Harvey	Deitel	2002	Prentice Hall
Advanced Java 2 Platform How to Program	0130895601	Sean	Santry	2002	Prentice Hall
C How to Program	0131180436	Harvey	Deitel	1992	Prentice Hall
C How to Program	0131180436	Paul	Deitel	1992	Prentice Hall
C How to Program	0132261197	Harvey	Deitel	1994	Prentice Hall
C How to Program	0132261197	Paul	Deitel	1994	Prentice Hall
C How to Program	0130895725	Harvey	Deitel	2001	Prentice Hall
C How to Program	0130895725	Paul	Deitel	2001	Prentice Hall
C# How To Program	0130622214	Tem	Nieto	2002	Prentice Hall
C# How To Program	0130622214	Paul	Deitel	2002	Prentice Hall
C# How To Program	0130622214	Jeffrey	Listfield	2002	Prentice Hall
C# How To Program	0130622214	Cheryl	Yaeger	2002	Prentice Hall
C# How To Program	0130622214	Marina	Zlatkina	2002	Prentice Hall
C# How To Program	0130622214	Harvey	Deitel	2002	Prentice Hall
C++ How to Program	0130895717	Paul	Deitel	2001	Prentice Hall
C++ How to Program	0130895717	Harvey	Deitel	2001	Prentice Hall
C++ How to Program	0131173340	Paul	Deitel	1994	Prentice Hall
C++ How to Program	0131173340	Harvey	Deitel	1994	Prentice Hall
C++ How to Program	0135289106	Harvey	Deitel	1998	Prentice Hall
C++ How to Program	0135289106	Paul	Deitel	1998	Prentice Hall

Fig. 19.23 Portion of the result set produced by the query in Fig. 19.22. (Part 1 of 2.)

title	isbn	firstName	lastName	copyright	publisherName
e-Business and e-Commerce for Managers	0130323640	Harvey	Deitel	2000	Prentice Hall
e-Business and e-Commerce for Managers	0130323640	Kate	Steinbuhler	2000	Prentice Hall
e-Business and e-Commerce for Managers	0130323640	Paul	Deitel	2000	Prentice Hall
e-Business and e-Commerce How to Program	013028419X	Harvey	Deitel	2001	Prentice Hall
e-Business and e-Commerce How to Program	013028419X	Paul	Deitel	2001	Prentice Hall
e-Business and e-Commerce How to Program	013028419X	Tem	Nieto	2001	Prentice Hall

Fig. 19.23 Portion of the result set produced by the query in Fig. 19.22. (Part 2 of 2.)

We added indentation to the query in Fig. 19.22 to make the query more readable. Let us now break down the query into its various parts. Lines 1–3 contain a comma-separated list of the columns that the query returns; the order of the columns from left to right specifies the columns' order in the returned table. This query selects columns `title` and `isbn` from table `Titles`, columns `firstName` and `lastName` from table `Authors`, column `copyright` from table `Titles` and column `publisherName` from table `Publishers`. For purposes of clarity, we qualified each column name with its table name (e.g., `Titles.isbn`).

Lines 5–10 specify the `INNER JOIN` operations used to combine information from the various tables. There are three `INNER JOIN` operations. It is important to note that, although an `INNER JOIN` is performed on two tables, either of those two tables can be the result of another query or another `INNER JOIN`. We use parentheses to nest the `INNER JOIN` operations; SQL evaluates the innermost set of parentheses first, then moves outward. We begin with the `INNER JOIN`:

```
( Publishers INNER JOIN Titles
   ON Publishers.publisherID = Titles.publisherID )
```

which joins the `Publishers` table and the `Titles` table `ON` the condition that the `publisherID` numbers in each table match. The resulting temporary table contains information about each book and its publisher.

The other nested set of parentheses contains the `INNER JOIN`:

```
( Authors INNER JOIN AuthorISBN ON
   Authors.AuthorID = AuthorISBN.AuthorID )
```

which joins the `Authors` table and the `AuthorISBN` table `ON` the condition that the `authorID` columns in each table match. Remember that the `AuthorISBN` table has multiple entries for `ISBN` numbers of books that have more than one author. The third `INNER JOIN`:

```
( Publishers INNER JOIN Titles
   ON Publishers.publisherID = Titles.publisherID )
INNER JOIN
( Authors INNER JOIN AuthorISBN
   ON Authors.authorID = AuthorISBN.authorID )
ON Titles.isbn = AuthorISBN.isbn
```

joins the two temporary tables produced by the two parenthesized inner joins `ON` the condition that the `Titles.isbn` column for each row in the first temporary table matches the corresponding `AuthorISBN.isbn` column for each row in the second temporary table. The result of all these `INNER JOIN` operations is a temporary table from which the appropriate columns are selected to produce the results of the query. Finally, line 11 of the query indicates that all the rows should be sorted in ascending order (the default) by title.

19.4.6 INSERT Statement

The *`INSERT`* statement inserts a new row in a table. The basic form for this statement is

```
INSERT INTO tableName ( columnName1, columnName2, ..., columnNameN )
   VALUES ( value1, value2, ..., valueN )
```

where *tableName* is the table in which to insert the row. The *tableName* is followed by a comma-separated list of column names in parentheses. The list of column names is followed by the SQL keyword `VALUES` and a comma-separated list of values in parentheses. The specified values in this list must match the column names listed after the table name in both order and type (for example, if *columnName1* is specified as the `firstName` column, then *value1* should be a string in single quotes representing the first name). The `INSERT` statement

```
INSERT INTO Authors ( firstName, lastName )
   VALUES ( 'Sue', 'Smith' )
```

inserts a row into the `Authors` table. The first comma-separated list indicates that the statement provides data for the `firstName` and `lastName` columns. The corresponding values to insert, which are contained in the second comma-separated list, are `'Sue'` and `'Smith'`. We do not specify an `authorID` in this example, because `authorID` is an auto-increment column in the database. Every new row that we add to this table is assigned a unique `authorID` value that is the next value in the auto-increment sequence (i.e., 1, 2, 3, etc.). In this case, `Sue Smith` would be assigned `authorID` number 16. Figure 19.24 shows the `Authors` table after we perform the `INSERT` operation.

authorID	firstName	lastName
1	Harvey	Deitel
2	Paul	Deitel
3	Tem	Nieto

Fig. 19.24 `Authors` after an `INSERT` operation to add a row. (Part 1 of 2.)

authorID	firstName	lastName
4	Kate	Steinbuhler
5	Sean	Santry
6	Ted	Lin
7	Praveen	Sadhu
8	David	McPhie
9	Cheryl	Yaeger
10	Marina	Zlatkina
11	Ben	Wiedermann
12	Jonathan	Liperi
13	Jeffrey	Listfield
14	Jeffrey	Hamm
15	Christina	Courtemarche
16	Sue	Smith

Fig. 19.24 `Authors` after an `INSERT` operation to add a row. (Part 2 of 2.)

Common Programming Error 19.6

SQL statements use the single-quote (`'`) character as a delimiter for strings. To specify a string containing a single quote (such as O'Malley) in an SQL statement, the string must include two single quotes in the position where the single-quote character should appear in the string (e.g., `'O''Malley'`). The first of the two single-quote characters acts as an escape character for the second. Failure to escape single-quote characters in a string that is part of an SQL statement is an SQL syntax error.

Note that if the values being specified in the `INSERT` statement match the name and type of all required columns in the table (i.e., one value of the correct type is specified for each required column), it is possible to omit the list of column names. For example, the `INSERT` statement above can be also written as

```
INSERT INTO Authors VALUES ( 'Sue', 'Smith' )
```

The `authorID` column is autoincremented, so it is not necessary to specify a value for it. The values in the list that follows keyword `VALUES` are then assigned to the remaining columns, `firstName` and `lastName`, in the order they occur (i.e., `'Sue'` is assigned to `firstName` and `'Smith'` is assigned to `lastName`).

Good Programming Practice 19.2

Although the shorthand version of `INSERT` statements can be convenient, avoid using it. Specifying a list of column names not only improves program clarity, but helps prevent program errors that could arise if the columns in a table are changed.

19.4.7 UPDATE Statement

An *UPDATE* statement modifies data in a table. The simplest form for an UPDATE statement is

```
UPDATE tableName
   SET columnName1 = value1, columnName2 = value2, ..., columnNameN = valueN
   WHERE criteria
```

where *tableName* is the table in which to update a row (or rows). The *tableName* is followed by keyword *SET* and a comma-separated list of column name/value pairs written in the format *columnName = value*. The WHERE clause specifies the criteria used to determine which row(s) to update. For example, the UPDATE statement:

```
UPDATE Authors
   SET lastName = 'Jones'
   WHERE lastName = 'Smith' AND firstName = 'Sue'
```

updates a row in the Authors table. The statement indicates that lastName will be assigned the new value Jones for the row in which lastName currently is equal to Smith and firstName is equal to Sue. If we know the authorID in advance of the UPDATE operation (possibly because we searched for the row previously), the WHERE clause could be simplified as follows:

```
WHERE AuthorID = 16
```

Figure 19.25 depicts the Authors table after we perform the UPDATE operation.

authorID	firstName	lastName
1	Harvey	Deitel
2	Paul	Deitel
3	Tem	Nieto
4	Kate	Steinbuhler
5	Sean	Santry
6	Ted	Lin
7	Praveen	Sadhu
8	David	McPhie
9	Cheryl	Yaeger
10	Marina	Zlatkina
11	Ben	Wiedermann
12	Jonathan	Liperi
13	Jeffrey	Listfield
14	Jeffrey	Hamm
15	Christina	Courtemarche
16	Sue	Jones

Fig. 19.25 Table Authors after an UPDATE operation to change a row.

Note that specifying a `WHERE` clause in an `UPDATE` statement is optional. If no `WHERE` clause is specified, the update will be performed on every row in the table. This is a powerful, but dangerous, feature. For example, imagine that there is a 15% off sale for all Deitel books. The following query would update all book prices accordingly

```
UPDATE Titles
   SET price = 0.85 * price
```

Common Programming Error 19.7

Failure to use a `WHERE` clause with an `UPDATE` statement could lead to logic errors. If an update does not apply to every row in the table, be sure to specify the correct `WHERE` clause.

19.4.8 DELETE Statement

An SQL *`DELETE`* statement removes data from a table. The simplest form for a `DELETE` statement is

```
DELETE FROM tableName WHERE criteria
```

where *tableName* is the table from which to delete a row (or rows). The `WHERE` clause specifies the criteria used to determine which row(s) to delete. For example, the `DELETE` statement

```
DELETE FROM Authors
   WHERE lastName = 'Jones' AND firstName = 'Sue'
```

deletes the row for `Sue Jones` from the `Authors` table.

Common Programming Error 19.8

`WHERE` clauses can match multiple rows. When deleting rows from a database, be sure to define a `WHERE` clause that matches only the rows to be deleted.

Figure 19.26 depicts the `Authors` table after we perform the `DELETE` operation.

authorID	firstName	lastName
1	Harvey	Deitel
2	Paul	Deitel
3	Tem	Nieto
4	Kate	Steinbuhler
5	Sean	Santry
6	Ted	Lin
7	Praveen	Sadhu
8	David	McPhie
9	Cheryl	Yaeger
10	Marina	Zlatkina

Fig. 19.26 Table `Authors` after a `DELETE` operation to remove a row. (Part 1 of 2.)

authorID	firstName	lastName
11	Ben	Wiedermann
12	Jonathan	Liperi
13	Jeffrey	Listfield
14	Jeffrey	Hamm
15	Christina	Courtemarche

Fig. 19.26 Table `Authors` after a `DELETE` operation to remove a row. (Part 2 of 2.)

As with `UPDATE` statements, the `WHERE` clause in a `DELETE` statement is optional. If no `WHERE` clause is specified, all rows in the table will be deleted! This is a dangerously powerful feature. Use caution when coding `DELETE` statements.

19.5 ADO .NET Object Model

The ADO .NET object model provides an API for accessing database systems programmatically. ADO .NET was created for the .NET Framework and is an improvement to *ActiveX Data Objects*™ (ADO).

Namespace ***`System::Data`*** is the root namespace for the ADO .NET API. The primary namespaces for ADO .NET, ***`System::Data::OleDb`*** and ***`System::Data::SqlClient`***, contain classes that enable programs to connect with and modify *data sources*. A data source is a location that contains data, such as a database. The namespace `System::Data::OleDb` contains classes that are designed to work with any data source, whereas the namespace `System::Data::SqlClient` contains classes that are optimized to work with Microsoft SQL Server databases.

Instances of class ***`System::Data::DataSet`***, which consist of a set of `DataTable`s and relationships among those `DataTable`s, represent *caches* of data—data that a program stores temporarily in local memory. The structure of a `DataSet` mimics the structure of a relational database. An advantage of using class `DataSet` is that it is *disconnected*—the program does not need a persistent connection to the data source to work with data in a `DataSet`. The program connects to the data source only during the initial population of the `DataSet` and then to store any changes made in the `DataSet`. Hence, the program does not require any active, permanent connection to the data source.

Instances of class ***`OleDbConnection`*** (namespace `System::Data::OleDb`) represent connections to a data source. An instance of class ***`OleDbDataAdapter`*** connects to a data source through an instance of class `OleDbConnection` and can populate a `DataSet` with data from that data source. We discuss the details of creating and populating `DataSet`s later in this chapter. An instance of class ***`OleDbCommand`*** (namespace `System::Data::OleDb`) represents arbitrary SQL to be executed on a data source. A program can use instances of class `OleDbCommand` to manipulate a data source through an `OleDbConnection`. The programmer must close the active connection to the data source explicitly once no further changes are to be made. Unlike `DataSet`s, `OleDbCommand` objects do not cache data in local memory.

19.6 Programming with ADO .NET: Extracting Information from a Database

In this section, we present two examples that introduce how to connect to a database, query the database and display the results of the query. The database used in these examples is the Microsoft Access `Books` database that we have discussed throughout this chapter. It can be found in the project directory for the application of Fig. 19.27–Fig. 19.28. Each program must specify the location of this database on the computer's hard drive.[2]

19.6.1 Connecting to and Querying an Access Data Source

The first example (Fig. 19.27–Fig. 19.28) performs a simple query on the `Books` database that retrieves the entire `Authors` table and displays the data in a *`DataGrid`* (a `System::Windows::Forms` control class that can display information from a data source, such as a table, in a GUI). The program illustrates the process of connecting to the database, querying the database and displaying the results in a `DataGrid`. The discussion following the example presents the key aspects of the program. [*Note*: We present all Visual Studio's auto-generated code in Fig. 19.27 so that readers are aware of the code that Visual Studio generates for the example.]

```
1  // Fig. 19.27: Form1.h
2  // Displays data from a database table.
3
4  #pragma once
5
6
7  namespace TableDisplay
8  {
9     using namespace System;
10    using namespace System::ComponentModel;
11    using namespace System::Collections;
12    using namespace System::Windows::Forms;
13    using namespace System::Data;
14    using namespace System::Drawing;
15    using namespace System::Data;
16
17    /// <summary>
18    /// Summary for Form1
19    ///
20    /// WARNING: If you change the name of this class, you will need to
21    ///          change the 'Resource File Name' property for the managed
22    ///          resource compiler tool associated with all .resx files
```

Fig. 19.27 Accessing and displaying a database's data. (Part 1 of 6.)

2. When a connection is added to a database using Visual Studio .NET, the exact path of the database is specified in the code. If the database or application is moved, the application will not be able to execute. The exact path created for the first application is shown on lines 103–114 of Fig. 19.27. For the code provided on the book's CD, we have modified these lines so that the programs will run from any location, provided that the database remains in the application's directory.

```
   ///         this class depends on.  Otherwise, the designers will not
   ///         be able to interact properly with localized resources
   ///         associated with this form.
   /// </summary>
   public __gc class Form1 : public System::Windows::Forms::Form
   {
   public:
      Form1(void)
      {
         InitializeComponent();

         // fill dataSet1 with data
         oleDbDataAdapter1->Fill( dataSet1, S"Authors" );

         // bind data in Users table in dataSet1 to dataGrid1
         dataGrid1->SetDataBinding( dataSet1, S"Authors" );
      }

   protected:
      void Dispose(Boolean disposing)
      {
         if (disposing && components)
         {
            components->Dispose();
         }
         __super::Dispose(disposing);
      }
   private: System::Windows::Forms::DataGrid *  dataGrid1;
   private: System::Data::OleDb::OleDbConnection *  oleDbConnection1;
   private: System::Data::OleDb::OleDbDataAdapter *  oleDbDataAdapter1;
   private: System::Data::OleDb::OleDbCommand *  oleDbSelectCommand1;
   private: System::Data::OleDb::OleDbCommand *  oleDbInsertCommand1;
   private: System::Data::OleDb::OleDbCommand *  oleDbUpdateCommand1;
   private: System::Data::OleDb::OleDbCommand *  oleDbDeleteCommand1;
   private: System::Data::DataSet *  dataSet1;

   private:
      /// <summary>
      /// Required designer variable.
      /// </summary>
      System::ComponentModel::Container * components;

      /// <summary>
      /// Required method for Designer support - do not modify
      /// the contents of this method with the code editor.
      /// </summary>
      void InitializeComponent(void)
      {
         this->dataGrid1 = new System::Windows::Forms::DataGrid();
         this->oleDbConnection1 =
            new System::Data::OleDb::OleDbConnection();
         this->oleDbDataAdapter1 =
            new System::Data::OleDb::OleDbDataAdapter();
```

Fig. 19.27 Accessing and displaying a database's data. (Part 2 of 6.)

```
         this->oleDbSelectCommand1 =
            new System::Data::OleDb::OleDbCommand();
         this->oleDbInsertCommand1 =
            new System::Data::OleDb::OleDbCommand();
         this->oleDbUpdateCommand1 =
            new System::Data::OleDb::OleDbCommand();
         this->oleDbDeleteCommand1 =
            new System::Data::OleDb::OleDbCommand();
         this->dataSet1 = new System::Data::DataSet();
         (__try_cast<System::ComponentModel::ISupportInitialize *  >
            (this->dataGrid1))->BeginInit();
         (__try_cast<System::ComponentModel::ISupportInitialize *  >
            (this->dataSet1))->BeginInit();
         this->SuspendLayout();
         //
         // dataGrid1
         //
         this->dataGrid1->DataMember = S"";
         this->dataGrid1->HeaderForeColor =
            System::Drawing::SystemColors::ControlText;
         this->dataGrid1->Location = System::Drawing::Point(16, 16);
         this->dataGrid1->Name = S"dataGrid1";
         this->dataGrid1->Size = System::Drawing::Size(264, 248);
         this->dataGrid1->TabIndex = 0;
         //
         // oleDbConnection1
         //
         this->oleDbConnection1->ConnectionString =
            S"Jet OLEDB:Global Partial Bulk Ops=2;Jet OLEDB:Registry "
            S"Path=;Jet OLEDB:Database Locking Mode=1;Data Source="
            S"\"C:\\Books\\2003\\vcpphtp1\\vcpphtp1_examples\\ch19\\"
            S"Fig19_27-28\\TableDisplay\\Books.mdb\";Jet OLEDB:Engine "
            S"Type=5;Provider=\"Microsoft.Jet.OLEDB.4.0\";Jet OLEDB:"
            S"System database=;Jet OLEDB:SFP=False;persist security "
            S"info=False;Extended Properties=;Mode=Share Deny None;"
            S"Jet OLEDB:Encrypt Database=False;Jet OLEDB:Create System "
            S"Database=False;Jet OLEDB:Don\'t Copy Locale on Compact="
            S"False;Jet OLEDB:Compact Without Replica Repair=False;"
            S"User ID=Admin;Jet OLEDB:Global Bulk Transactions=1";
         //
         // oleDbDataAdapter1
         //
         this->oleDbDataAdapter1->DeleteCommand =
            this->oleDbDeleteCommand1;
         this->oleDbDataAdapter1->InsertCommand =
            this->oleDbInsertCommand1;
         this->oleDbDataAdapter1->SelectCommand =
            this->oleDbSelectCommand1;
         System::Data::Common::DataTableMapping* __mcTemp__1[] =
            new System::Data::Common::DataTableMapping*[1];
         System::Data::Common::DataColumnMapping* __mcTemp__2[] =
            new System::Data::Common::DataColumnMapping*[3];
         __mcTemp__2[0] = new System::Data::Common::DataColumnMapping(
```

Fig. 19.27 Accessing and displaying a database's data. (Part 3 of 6.)

```
         S"authorID", S"authorID");
      __mcTemp__2[1] = new System::Data::Common::DataColumnMapping(
         S"firstName", S"firstName");
      __mcTemp__2[2] = new System::Data::Common::DataColumnMapping(
         S"lastName", S"lastName");
      __mcTemp__1[0] = new System::Data::Common::DataTableMapping(
         S"Table", S"Authors", __mcTemp__2);
      this->oleDbDataAdapter1->TableMappings->AddRange(__mcTemp__1);
      this->oleDbDataAdapter1->UpdateCommand =
         this->oleDbUpdateCommand1;
      //
      // oleDbSelectCommand1
      //
      this->oleDbSelectCommand1->CommandText =
         S"SELECT authorID, firstName, lastName FROM Authors";
      this->oleDbSelectCommand1->Connection = this->oleDbConnection1;
      //
      // oleDbInsertCommand1
      //
      this->oleDbInsertCommand1->CommandText =
         S"SELECT authorID, firstName, lastName FROM Authors";
      this->oleDbInsertCommand1->Connection = this->oleDbConnection1;
      this->oleDbInsertCommand1->Parameters->Add(
         new System::Data::OleDb::OleDbParameter(S"firstName",
         System::Data::OleDb::OleDbType::VarWChar, 50, S"firstName"));
      this->oleDbInsertCommand1->Parameters->Add(n
         ew System::Data::OleDb::OleDbParameter(S"lastName",
         System::Data::OleDb::OleDbType::VarWChar, 50, S"lastName"));
      //
      // oleDbUpdateCommand1
      //
      this->oleDbUpdateCommand1->CommandText = S"UPDATE Authors SET "
         S"firstName = \?, lastName = \? WHERE (authorID = \?) AND "
         S"(firstName = \? OR \? IS NULL AND firstName IS NULL) AND "
         S"(lastName = \? OR \? IS NULL AND lastName IS NULL)";
      this->oleDbUpdateCommand1->Connection = this->oleDbConnection1;
      this->oleDbUpdateCommand1->Parameters->Add(
         new System::Data::OleDb::OleDbParameter(S"firstName",
         System::Data::OleDb::OleDbType::VarWChar, 50, S"firstName"));
      this->oleDbUpdateCommand1->Parameters->Add(
         new System::Data::OleDb::OleDbParameter(S"lastName",
         System::Data::OleDb::OleDbType::VarWChar, 50, S"lastName"));
      this->oleDbUpdateCommand1->Parameters->Add(
         new System::Data::OleDb::OleDbParameter(S"Original_authorID",
         System::Data::OleDb::OleDbType::Integer, 0,
         System::Data::ParameterDirection::Input, false,
         (System::Byte)0, (System::Byte)0, S"authorID",
         System::Data::DataRowVersion::Original, 0));
      this->oleDbUpdateCommand1->Parameters->Add(
         new System::Data::OleDb::OleDbParameter(S"Original_firstName",
         System::Data::OleDb::OleDbType::VarWChar, 50,
         System::Data::ParameterDirection::Input, false,
         (System::Byte)0, (System::Byte)0, S"firstName",
```

Fig. 19.27 Accessing and displaying a database's data. (Part 4 of 6.)

```
   System::Data::DataRowVersion::Original, 0));
this->oleDbUpdateCommand1->Parameters->Add(
   new System::Data::OleDb::OleDbParameter(
   S"Original_firstName1",
   System::Data::OleDb::OleDbType::VarWChar, 50,
   System::Data::ParameterDirection::Input, false,
   (System::Byte)0, (System::Byte)0, S"firstName",
   System::Data::DataRowVersion::Original, 0));
this->oleDbUpdateCommand1->Parameters->Add(
   new System::Data::OleDb::OleDbParameter(S"Original_lastName",
   System::Data::OleDb::OleDbType::VarWChar, 50,
   System::Data::ParameterDirection::Input, false,
   (System::Byte)0, (System::Byte)0, S"lastName",
   System::Data::DataRowVersion::Original, 0));
this->oleDbUpdateCommand1->Parameters->Add(
   new System::Data::OleDb::OleDbParameter(S"Original_lastName1",
   System::Data::OleDb::OleDbType::VarWChar, 50,
   System::Data::ParameterDirection::Input, false,
   (System::Byte)0, (System::Byte)0, S"lastName",
   System::Data::DataRowVersion::Original, 0));
//
// oleDbDeleteCommand1
//
this->oleDbDeleteCommand1->CommandText = S"DELETE FROM Authors "
   S"WHERE (authorID = \?) AND (firstName = \? OR \? IS NULL "
   S"AND firstName IS NULL) AND (lastName = \? OR \? IS NULL "
   S"AND lastName IS NULL)";
this->oleDbDeleteCommand1->Connection = this->oleDbConnection1;
this->oleDbDeleteCommand1->Parameters->Add(
   new System::Data::OleDb::OleDbParameter(S"Original_authorID",
   System::Data::OleDb::OleDbType::Integer, 0,
   System::Data::ParameterDirection::Input, false,
   (System::Byte)0, (System::Byte)0, S"authorID",
   System::Data::DataRowVersion::Original, 0));
this->oleDbDeleteCommand1->Parameters->Add(
   new System::Data::OleDb::OleDbParameter(S"Original_firstName",
   System::Data::OleDb::OleDbType::VarWChar, 50,
   System::Data::ParameterDirection::Input, false,
   (System::Byte)0, (System::Byte)0, S"firstName",
   System::Data::DataRowVersion::Original, 0));
this->oleDbDeleteCommand1->Parameters->Add(
   new System::Data::OleDb::OleDbParameter(
   S"Original_firstName1",
   System::Data::OleDb::OleDbType::VarWChar, 50,
   System::Data::ParameterDirection::Input, false,
   (System::Byte)0, (System::Byte)0, S"firstName",
   System::Data::DataRowVersion::Original, 0));
this->oleDbDeleteCommand1->Parameters->Add(
   new System::Data::OleDb::OleDbParameter(S"Original_lastName",
   System::Data::OleDb::OleDbType::VarWChar, 50,
   System::Data::ParameterDirection::Input, false,
   (System::Byte)0, (System::Byte)0, S"lastName",
   System::Data::DataRowVersion::Original, 0));
```

Fig. 19.27 Accessing and displaying a database's data. (Part 5 of 6.)

```
         this->oleDbDeleteCommand1->Parameters->Add(
            new System::Data::OleDb::OleDbParameter(S"Original_lastName1",
            System::Data::OleDb::OleDbType::VarWChar, 50,
            System::Data::ParameterDirection::Input, false,
            (System::Byte)0, (System::Byte)0, S"lastName",
            System::Data::DataRowVersion::Original, 0));
         //
         // dataSet1
         //
         this->dataSet1->DataSetName = S"NewDataSet";
         this->dataSet1->Locale =
            new System::Globalization::CultureInfo(S"en-US");
         //
         // Form1
         //
         this->AutoScaleBaseSize = System::Drawing::Size(5, 13);
         this->ClientSize = System::Drawing::Size(292, 273);
         this->Controls->Add(this->dataGrid1);
         this->Name = S"Form1";
         this->Text = S"TableDisplay";
         (__try_cast<System::ComponentModel::ISupportInitialize *  >
            (this->dataGrid1))->EndInit();
         (__try_cast<System::ComponentModel::ISupportInitialize *  >
            (this->dataSet1))->EndInit();
         this->ResumeLayout(false);

      } // end method InitializeComponent
   };
}
```

Fig. 19.27 Accessing and displaying a database's data. (Part 6 of 6.)

```
// Fig. 19.28: Form1.cpp
// Entry point for application.

#include "stdafx.h"
#include "Form1.h"
#include <windows.h>

using namespace TableDisplay;

int APIENTRY _tWinMain(HINSTANCE hInstance,
                       HINSTANCE hPrevInstance,
                       LPTSTR    lpCmdLine,
                       int       nCmdShow)
{
   System::Threading::Thread::CurrentThread->ApartmentState =
      System::Threading::ApartmentState::STA;
   Application::Run(new Form1());
   return 0;
} // end _tWinMain
```

Fig. 19.28 `TableDisplay` entry point. (Part 1 of 2.)

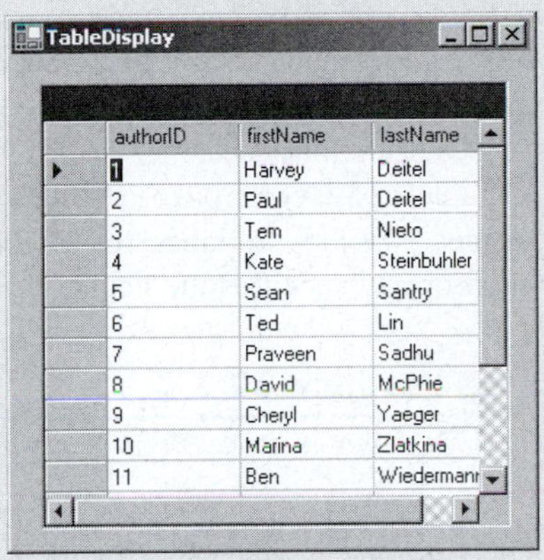

Fig. 19.28 `TableDisplay` entry point. (Part 2 of 2.)

This example uses an Access database. To register the `Books` database as a data source, select **View > Server Explorer**. Right click the **Data Connections** node in the **Server Explorer**, then click **Add Connection...**. In the **Provider** tab of the window that appears, choose **Microsoft Jet 4.0 OLE DB Provider**, which is the driver for Access databases. In the **Connection** tab, click the ellipses button (...) to the right of the text box for the database name, which opens the **Select Access Database** window. Go to the appropriate folder, select the `Books` database and click **OK**. Now, this database is listed as a connection in the **Server Explorer**. Drag this database node onto the Windows Form. This creates an `OleDbConnection` to the source, which the Windows Form designer displays as `oleDbConnection1`. A prompt is then displayed asking for the formatting of the password in the source code. Select **Don't Include Password** because there is no password for the `Books` database.

Next, drag an `OleDbDataAdapter` from the **Toolbox**'s **Data** group onto the Windows Form designer. This displays the **Data Adapter Configuration Wizard** for configuring the `OleDbDataAdapter` instance with a custom query for populating a `DataSet`. Click **Next** to select a connection to use. From the drop-down list, select the connection created in the previous step and click **Next**. The resulting screen allows us to choose how the `OleDbDataAdapter` should access the database. Keep the default **Use SQL Statement** option, then click **Next**. Click the **Query Builder** button, select the **Authors** table from the **Add** menu and **Close** that menu. Place a check mark in the **All Columns** box from the **Authors** window. Notice how that particular window lists all columns of the **Authors** table. Finally, click **OK**, then **Finish** to complete the step.

Next, we must create a `DataSet` to store the query result. To do so, drag `DataSet` from the **Data** group in the **Toolbox**. This displays the **Add DataSet** window. Choose the **Untyped DataSet (no schema)**, because the query with which we populate the `DataSet` dictates the `DataSet`'s *schema*, or structure.

Figure 19.27 shows all the code generated by Visual Studio. Normally, we omit this code, because it usually only contains GUI-related code. In this case, however, the code contains database functionality that we must discuss. Furthermore, we have left the default naming conventions of Visual Studio in this example to demonstrate the exact format of the auto-generated code that Visual Studio creates. Normally, we would change these names to conform to our programming conventions and style. The code generated by Visual Studio has also been formatted for presentation purposes.

Line 51 (Fig. 19.27) declares a System::Data::OleDb::OleDbConnection to the source, oleDbConnection1. Lines 103–114 initialize the oleDbConnection for this program. The ConnectionString property specifies the database file on the computer's hard drive.

Good Programming Practice 19.3

Use clear, descriptive variable names in code. This makes programs easier to understand.

Line 57 declares a DataSet to store the query result. An instance of class OleDbDataAdapter populates the DataSet in this example with data from the Books database. The OleDbDataAdapter properties *DeleteCommand* (lines 118–119), *InsertCommand* (lines 120–121), *SelectCommand* (lines 122–123) and *UpdateCommand* (lines 137–138) are OleDbCommand objects that specify how the OleDbDataAdapter deletes, inserts, selects and updates data in the database, respectively.

Each OleDbCommand object must have an OleDbConnection through which the OleDbCommand can communicate with the database. Property Connection of the OleDbConnection is set to the Books database. For oleDbSelectCommand1, line 164 sets the Connection property, and lines 160–163 set the CommandText. Property *CommandText* of class OleDbCommand is a String * representing the SQL that the OleDbCommand object executes.

Although Visual Studio generates most of this program's code, we enter code in the Form1 constructor (lines 30–39) for populating dataSet1 using an OleDbDataAdapter. Line 35 in the constructor populates dataSet1 using an OleDbDataAdapter. Line 35 calls OleDbDataAdapter method *Fill* to retrieve information from the database associated with the OleDbConnection, placing the information in the DataSet provided as an argument. This information will be stored in the DataSet in the form of a table. DataSets can contain many tables, so we provide a name for this table as the second argument to method Fill. We use the name Authors for simplicity, because this is the name of the table in the database that we are retrieving data from.

Line 38 invokes DataGrid method *SetDataBinding* to bind the DataGrid to a data source. The first argument is the DataSet—in this case, dataSet1—whose data the DataGrid should display. The second argument is a String * representing the name of the table within the DataSet we want to bind to the DataGrid. Once this line executes, the DataGrid is filled with the information in the DataSet—the number of rows and number of columns are set from the information in dataSet1.

Once the DataGrid is filled with the information, the data can be sorted in ascending or descending order by clicking a column name in the DataGrid (e.g., firstName). Note that this is simply a feature of DataGrids. Each time the user performs such a sorting operation, the program is not performing another query on the database. Rather, it is simply sorting the data that has already been returned.

19.6.2 Querying the Books Database

The example in Fig. 19.29–Fig. 19.30 demonstrates how to execute SELECT queries on database Books.mdb and display the results. Although Fig. 19.29 uses only SELECT to query the data, the same program could be used to execute many different SQL statements if we made a few modifications.

```
// Fig. 19.29: Form1.h
// Displays the contents of the authors database.

#pragma once


namespace DisplayQueryResults
{
   using namespace System;
   using namespace System::ComponentModel;
   using namespace System::Collections;
   using namespace System::Windows::Forms;
   using namespace System::Data;
   using namespace System::Drawing;
   using namespace System::Data;
   using namespace System::Data::OleDb;

   /// <summary>
   /// Summary for Form1
   ///
   /// WARNING: If you change the name of this class, you will need to
   ///          change the 'Resource File Name' property for the managed
   ///          resource compiler tool associated with all .resx files
   ///          this class depends on.  Otherwise, the designers will not
   ///          be able to interact properly with localized resources
   ///          associated with this form.
   /// </summary>
   public __gc class Form1 : public System::Windows::Forms::Form
   {
   public:
      Form1(void)
      {
         InitializeComponent();
      }

   protected:
      void Dispose(Boolean disposing)
      {
         if (disposing && components)
         {
            components->Dispose();
         }
         __super::Dispose(disposing);
      }
   private: System::Windows::Forms::TextBox *  queryTextBox;
```

Fig. 19.29 Execute SQL statements on a database. (Part 1 of 2.)

```
   private: System::Windows::Forms::Button *  submitButton;
   private: System::Windows::Forms::DataGrid *  dataGrid1;
   private: System::Data::OleDb::OleDbConnection *  oleDbConnection1;
   private: System::Data::OleDb::OleDbDataAdapter *  oleDbDataAdapter1;
   private: System::Data::OleDb::OleDbCommand *  oleDbSelectCommand1;
   private: System::Data::OleDb::OleDbCommand *  oleDbInsertCommand1;
   private: System::Data::OleDb::OleDbCommand *  oleDbUpdateCommand1;
   private: System::Data::OleDb::OleDbCommand *  oleDbDeleteCommand1;
   private: System::Data::DataSet *  dataSet1;

   private:
      /// <summary>
      /// Required designer variable.
      /// </summary>
      System::ComponentModel::Container * components;

   // Visual Studio .NET generated GUI code

   // perform SQL query on data
   private: System::Void submitButton_Click(
               System::Object *  sender, System::EventArgs *  e)
            {
               try {

                  // set the text of the SQL query to what the user typed
                  oleDbDataAdapter1->SelectCommand->CommandText =
                     queryTextBox->Text;

                  // clear the DataSet from the previous operation
                  dataSet1->Clear();

                  if ( dataSet1->Tables->get_Item( S"Results" ) )
                  {
                     dataSet1->Tables->get_Item(
                        S"Results" )->Columns->Clear();
                  }

                  // fill the data set with the information that results
                  // from the SQL query
                  oleDbDataAdapter1->Fill( dataSet1, S"Results" );

                  // bind the DataGrid to the contents of the DatSet
                  dataGrid1->SetDataBinding( dataSet1, S"Results" );
               } // end try
               catch ( OleDbException *oleException ) {
                  MessageBox::Show(
                     oleException->Message, S"Invalid query",
                     MessageBoxButtons::OK, MessageBoxIcon::Error );
               } // end catch
            } // end method submitButton_Click
   };
}
```

Fig. 19.29 Execute SQL statements on a database. (Part 2 of 2.)

```
// Fig. 19.30: Form1.cpp
// Entry point for application.

#include "stdafx.h"
#include "Form1.h"
#include <windows.h>

using namespace DisplayQueryResults;

int APIENTRY _tWinMain(HINSTANCE hInstance,
                       HINSTANCE hPrevInstance,
                       LPTSTR    lpCmdLine,
                       int       nCmdShow)
{
   System::Threading::Thread::CurrentThread->ApartmentState =
      System::Threading::ApartmentState::STA;
   Application::Run(new Form1());
   return 0;
} // end _tWinMain
```

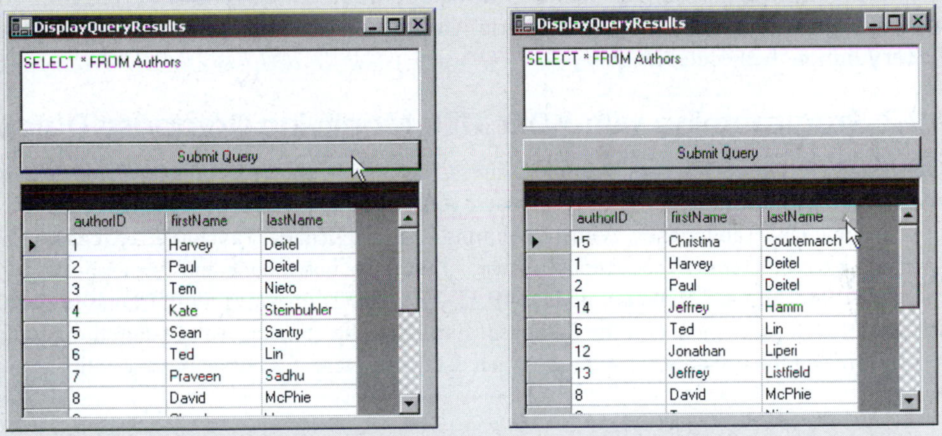

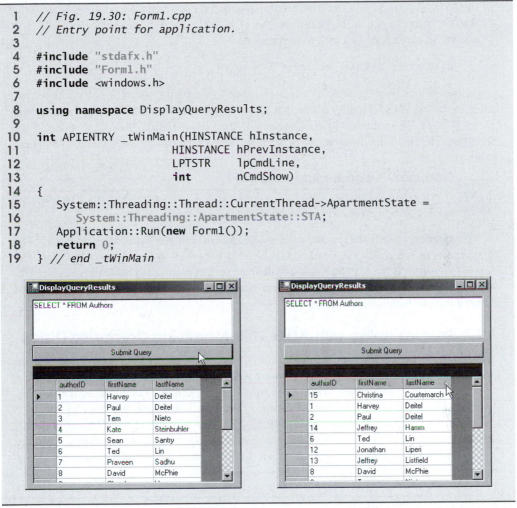

Fig. 19.30 `DisplayQueryResults` entry point.

Method `submitButton_Click` is the key part of this program. When the program invokes this event handler, lines 71–72 (Fig. 19.29) assign the `SELECT` query entered by the user into `queryTextBox` to `OleDbDataAdapter`'s `SelectCommand` property. This `String *` is parsed into an SQL query and executed on the database via the `OleDbDataAdapter`'s `Fill` method (line 85). As we discussed in the previous section, method `Fill` places data from the database into `dataSet1`.

Notice that before calling `Fill` we first call `DataSet` method *`Clear`* (line 75). This method removes all the data stored in the `DataSet`. This ensures that the data currently displayed in the `DataGrid` is only from the most recently executed query. If we did not call method `Clear`, new data would simply be appended to the `DataGrid`. Clearing the `DataSet` in this way, however, does not remove the columns displayed in the `DataGrid`. These columns need to be cleared if the user wants to enter a query whose result would have different columns than what is currently displayed. Lines 79–80 clear any previous columns of the `DataSet`. To do this, we first need to access the table from the previous query (the `"Results"` table), which is stored in the `DataSet`'s `Tables` property. The specific `"Results"` table is accessed with the expression

```
dataSet1->Tables->get_Item( S"Results" )
```

Line 80 then uses the table's `Columns` property to clear the columns of the `"Results"` table in the `DataGrid`. Finally, notice that lines 79–80 have been placed in an `if` statement (lines 77–81). These lines will only execute if there is already a `"Results"` table in the `DataSet`. The first time the application is run, the `DataSet` does not yet have an `"Results"` table.

Common Programming Error 19.9

If a `DataSet` has been `Fill`ed at least once, forgetting to call a `DataSet`'s `Clear` method before calling method `Fill` again could lead to logic errors.

To display, or redisplay, contents in the `DataGrid`, use method `SetDataBinding`. The first argument is the data source to be displayed in the table—a `DataSet`, in this case. The second argument is the `String *` name of the data source member to be displayed (line 88). Readers can try entering their own queries in the text box, then pressing the **Submit Query** button to execute the query.

19.7 Programming with ADO .NET: Modifying Database Data

Our next example implements a simple address-book application that enables the user to insert, locate and update rows in the Microsoft Access database `Addressbook`. The database contains one table (`addresses`) with 11 columns—`id`, `firstname`, `lastname`, `address`, `city`, `stateorprovince`, `postalcode`, `country`, `emailaddress`, `homephone` and `faxnumber`.

The `Addressbook` application (Fig. 19.31–Fig. 19.32) provides a GUI enabling users to execute SQL statements on the database. Earlier in the chapter, we presented examples demonstrating the use of `SELECT` queries on a database. Here, that same functionality is provided.

```
// Fig. 19.31: Form1.h
// Using SQL statements to manipulate a database.

#pragma once



namespace AddressBook
{
   using namespace System;
   using namespace System::ComponentModel;
   using namespace System::Collections;
   using namespace System::Windows::Forms;
   using namespace System::Data;
   using namespace System::Drawing;
   using namespace System::Data::OleDb;
```

Fig. 19.31 Modifying a database. (Part 1 of 8.)

```

   /// <summary>
   /// Summary for Form1
   ///
   /// WARNING: If you change the name of this class, you will need to
   ///          change the 'Resource File Name' property for the managed
   ///          resource compiler tool associated with all .resx files
   ///          this class depends on.  Otherwise, the designers will not
   ///          be able to interact properly with localized resources
   ///          associated with this form.
   /// </summary>
   public __gc class Form1 : public System::Windows::Forms::Form
   {
   public:
      Form1(void)
      {
         InitializeComponent();
         oleDbConnection1->Open();  // open connection
      }

   protected:
      void Dispose(Boolean disposing)
      {
         if (disposing && components)
         {
            components->Dispose();
         }
         __super::Dispose(disposing);
      }
   private: System::Windows::Forms::Button *  findButton;
   private: System::Windows::Forms::Button *  addButton;
   private: System::Windows::Forms::Button *  updateButton;
   private: System::Windows::Forms::Button *  clearButton;
   private: System::Windows::Forms::Button *  helpButton;
   private: System::Windows::Forms::Label *  idLabel;
   private: System::Windows::Forms::TextBox *  idTextBox;
   private: System::Windows::Forms::Label *  firstLabel;
   private: System::Windows::Forms::TextBox *  firstTextBox;
   private: System::Windows::Forms::Label *  lastLabel;
   private: System::Windows::Forms::TextBox *  lastTextBox;
   private: System::Windows::Forms::Label *  addressLabel;
   private: System::Windows::Forms::Label *  cityLabel;
   private: System::Windows::Forms::TextBox *  addressTextBox;
   private: System::Windows::Forms::TextBox *  cityTextBox;
   private: System::Windows::Forms::Label *  stateLabel;
   private: System::Windows::Forms::TextBox *  stateTextBox;
   private: System::Windows::Forms::Label *  postalLabel;
   private: System::Windows::Forms::Label *  countryLabel;
   private: System::Windows::Forms::Label *  emailLabel;
   private: System::Windows::Forms::Label *  homeLabel;
   private: System::Windows::Forms::Label *  faxLabel;
   private: System::Windows::Forms::TextBox *  postalTextBox;
   private: System::Windows::Forms::TextBox *  countryTextBox;
```

Fig. 19.31 Modifying a database. (Part 2 of 8.)

```
    private: System::Windows::Forms::TextBox *  emailTextBox;
    private: System::Windows::Forms::TextBox *  homeTextBox;
    private: System::Windows::Forms::TextBox *  faxTextBox;
    private: System::Windows::Forms::TextBox *  statusTextBox;
    private: System::Data::OleDb::OleDbConnection *  oleDbConnection1;
    private: System::Data::OleDb::OleDbDataAdapter *  oleDbDataAdapter1;
    private: System::Data::OleDb::OleDbCommand *  oleDbSelectCommand1;
    private: System::Data::OleDb::OleDbCommand *  oleDbInsertCommand1;
    private: System::Data::OleDb::OleDbCommand *  oleDbUpdateCommand1;
    private: System::Data::OleDb::OleDbCommand *  oleDbDeleteCommand1;
    private: System::Data::DataSet *  dataSet1;

    private:
      /// <summary>
      /// Required designer variable.
      /// </summary>
      System::ComponentModel::Container * components;

    // Visual Studio .NET generated GUI code

    private: System::Void findButton_Click(
                System::Object *  sender, System::EventArgs *  e)
             {
                try {

                   if ( !lastTextBox->Text->Equals( String::Empty ) ) {

                      // clear the DataSet from the last operation
                      dataSet1->Clear();

                      // create SQL query to find the contact with the
                      // specified last name
                      oleDbDataAdapter1->SelectCommand->CommandText =
                         String::Concat( S"SELECT * FROM addresses WHERE ",
                         S"lastname = '", lastTextBox->Text, S"'" );

                      // fill dataSet1 with the rows resulting from query
                      oleDbDataAdapter1->Fill( dataSet1 );

                      // display information
                      Display( dataSet1 );
                      statusTextBox->AppendText(
                         S"\r\nQuery successful\r\n" );
                   } // end if
                   else
                      lastTextBox->Text =
                         S"Enter last name here and press Find";
                } // end try

                catch ( OleDbException *oleException ) {
                   MessageBox::Show( oleException->Message, S"Error",
                      MessageBoxButtons::OK, MessageBoxIcon::Error );
                } // end catch
```

Fig. 19.31 Modifying a database. (Part 3 of 8.)

```

            catch ( InvalidOperationException *invalidException ) {
               MessageBox::Show( invalidException->Message, S"Error",
                  MessageBoxButtons::OK, MessageBoxIcon::Error );
            } // end catch
         } // end method findButton_Click

private: System::Void addButton_Click(
            System::Object *  sender, System::EventArgs *  e)
         {
            try {

               if ( !lastTextBox->Text->Equals( String::Empty ) &&
                  !firstTextBox->Text->Equals( String::Empty ) &&
                  !addressTextBox->Text->Equals( String::Empty ) &&
                  !cityTextBox->Text->Equals( String::Empty ) &&
                  !stateTextBox->Text->Equals( String::Empty ) &&
                  !postalTextBox->Text->Equals( String::Empty ) &&
                  !countryTextBox->Text->Equals( String::Empty ) &&
                  !emailTextBox->Text->Equals( String::Empty ) &&
                  !homeTextBox->Text->Equals( String::Empty ) &&
                  !faxTextBox->Text->Equals( String::Empty ) ) {

                  // create the SQL query to insert a row
                  oleDbDataAdapter1->InsertCommand->CommandText =
                     String::Concat( S"INSERT INTO addresses (",
                     S"firstname, lastname, address, city, ",
                     S"stateorprovince, postalcode, country, ",
                     S"emailaddress, homephone, faxnumber",
                     S") VALUES ('",
                     firstTextBox->Text, S"', '",
                     lastTextBox->Text, S"', '",
                     addressTextBox->Text, S"', '",
                     cityTextBox->Text, S"', '",
                     stateTextBox->Text, S"', '",
                     postalTextBox->Text, S"', '",
                     countryTextBox->Text, S"', '",
                     emailTextBox->Text, S"', '",
                     homeTextBox->Text, S"', '",
                     faxTextBox->Text, S"')" );

                  // notify the user the query is being sent
                  statusTextBox->AppendText( String::Concat(
                     S"\r\nSending query: ",
                     oleDbDataAdapter1->InsertCommand->CommandText,
                     S"\r\n" ) );

                  // send query
                  oleDbDataAdapter1->InsertCommand->ExecuteNonQuery();

                  statusTextBox->AppendText(
                     S"\r\nQuery successful\r\n" );
               } // end if
```

Fig. 19.31 Modifying a database. (Part 4 of 8.)

```
               else
                  statusTextBox->AppendText(
                     S"\r\nAll fields are required.\r\n" );
            } // end try

            catch ( OleDbException *oleException ) {
               MessageBox::Show( oleException->Message, S"Error",
                  MessageBoxButtons::OK, MessageBoxIcon::Error );
            } // end catch
         } // end method addButton_Click

private: System::Void updateButton_Click(
            System::Object *  sender, System::EventArgs *  e)
         {
            try {

               // make sure the user has already found the row
               // he or she wishes to update
               if ( !idTextBox->Text->Equals( String::Empty ) ) {

                  // make sure user has not left any other fields blank
                  if ( !lastTextBox->Text->Equals( String::Empty ) &&
                     !firstTextBox->Text->Equals( String::Empty ) &&
                     !addressTextBox->Text->Equals( String::Empty ) &&
                     !cityTextBox->Text->Equals( String::Empty ) &&
                     !stateTextBox->Text->Equals( String::Empty ) &&
                     !postalTextBox->Text->Equals( String::Empty ) &&
                     !countryTextBox->Text->Equals( String::Empty ) &&
                     !emailTextBox->Text->Equals( String::Empty ) &&
                     !homeTextBox->Text->Equals( String::Empty ) &&
                     !faxTextBox->Text->Equals( String::Empty ) ) {

                     // set the SQL query to update all the columns in
                     // the table where the id number matches the id
                     // in idTextBox
                     oleDbDataAdapter1->UpdateCommand->CommandText =
                        String::Concat( S"UPDATE addresses SET ",
                        S"firstname ='", firstTextBox->Text,
                        S"', lastname='", lastTextBox->Text,
                        S"', address='", addressTextBox->Text,
                        S"', city='", cityTextBox->Text,
                        S"', stateorprovince='", stateTextBox->Text,
                        S"', postalcode='", postalTextBox->Text,
                        S"', country='", countryTextBox->Text,
                        S"', emailaddress='", emailTextBox->Text,
                        S"', homephone='", homeTextBox->Text,
                        S"', faxnumber='", faxTextBox->Text,
                        S"' WHERE id=", idTextBox->Text );

                     // notify the user the query is being set
                     statusTextBox->AppendText( String::Concat(
                        S"\r\nSending query: ",
```

Fig. 19.31 Modifying a database. (Part 5 of 8.)

```
                 oleDbDataAdapter1->UpdateCommand->CommandText,
                 S"\r\n" ) );

               // execute query
               oleDbDataAdapter1->UpdateCommand->
                 ExecuteNonQuery();

               statusTextBox->AppendText(
                 S"\r\nQuery successful\r\n" );
             } // end if
             else
               statusTextBox->AppendText(
                 S"\r\nAll fields are required.\r\n" );

           } // end if
           else
             statusTextBox->AppendText( String::Concat(
               S"\r\nYou may only update an existing row. ",
               S"Use Find to locate the row, then modify ",
               S"the information and press Update.\r\n" ) );
         } // end try

         catch ( OleDbException *oleException ) {
           MessageBox::Show( oleException->Message, S"Error",
             MessageBoxButtons::OK, MessageBoxIcon::Error );
         } // end catch
       } // end method updateButton_Click

 private: System::Void clearButton_Click(
         System::Object *  sender, System::EventArgs *  e)
       {
         idTextBox->Clear();
         ClearTextBoxes();
       } // end method clearButton_Click

 // end method helpButton_Click
 private: System::Void helpButton_Click(
         System::Object *  sender, System::EventArgs *  e)
       {
         statusTextBox->AppendText( String::Concat(
           S"\r\nClick Find to locate a row\r\n",
           S"Click Add to insert a new row.\r\n",
           S"Click Update to update the information in a row",
           S"\r\nClick Clear to empty the textboxes" ) );
       }

private:

   void Display( DataSet *dataSet )
   {
     try {

```

Fig. 19.31 Modifying a database. (Part 6 of 8.)

```
         // get the first DataTable - there will always be one
         DataTable *dataTable = dataSet->Tables->Item[ 0 ];

         if ( dataTable->Rows->Count != 0 ) {

            int rowNumber = Convert::ToInt32(
               dataTable->Rows->Item[ 0 ]->Item[ 0 ] );

            idTextBox->Text = rowNumber.ToString();
            firstTextBox->Text = dataTable->Rows->Item[ 0 ]->
               Item[ 1 ]->ToString();
            lastTextBox->Text =  dataTable->Rows->Item[ 0 ]->
               Item[ 2 ]->ToString();
            addressTextBox->Text = dataTable->Rows->Item[ 0 ]->
               Item[ 3 ]->ToString();
            cityTextBox->Text = dataTable->Rows->Item[ 0 ]->
               Item[ 4 ]->ToString();
            stateTextBox->Text = dataTable->Rows->Item[ 0 ]->
               Item[ 5 ]->ToString();
            postalTextBox->Text = dataTable->Rows->Item[ 0 ]->
               Item[ 6 ]->ToString();
            countryTextBox->Text = dataTable->Rows->Item[ 0 ]->
               Item[ 7 ]->ToString();
            emailTextBox->Text = dataTable->Rows->Item[ 0 ]->
               Item[ 8 ]->ToString();
            homeTextBox->Text = dataTable->Rows->Item[ 0 ]->
               Item[ 9 ]->ToString();
            faxTextBox->Text = dataTable->Rows->Item[ 0 ]->
               Item[ 10 ]->ToString();
         } // end if
         else
            statusTextBox->AppendText( S"\r\nNo row found\r\n" );
      } // end try

      catch ( OleDbException *oleException ) {
         MessageBox::Show( oleException->Message, S"Error",
            MessageBoxButtons::OK, MessageBoxIcon::Error );
      } // end catch
   } // end method Display

private:

   void ClearTextBoxes()
   {
      firstTextBox->Clear();
      lastTextBox->Clear();
      addressTextBox->Clear();
      cityTextBox->Clear();
      stateTextBox->Clear();
      postalTextBox->Clear();
      countryTextBox->Clear();
      emailTextBox->Clear();
      homeTextBox->Clear();
```

Fig. 19.31 Modifying a database. (Part 7 of 8.)

```
        faxTextBox->Clear();
     } // end method ClearTextBoxes
  };
}
```

Fig. 19.31 Modifying a database. (Part 8 of 8.)

```
// Fig. 19.32: Form1.cpp
// Entry point for application.

#include "stdafx.h"
#include "Form1.h"
#include <windows.h>

using namespace AddressBook;

int APIENTRY _tWinMain(HINSTANCE hInstance,
                       HINSTANCE hPrevInstance,
                       LPTSTR    lpCmdLine,
                       int       nCmdShow)
{
   System::Threading::Thread::CurrentThread->ApartmentState =
      System::Threading::ApartmentState::STA;
   Application::Run(new Form1());
   return 0;
} // end _tWinMain
```

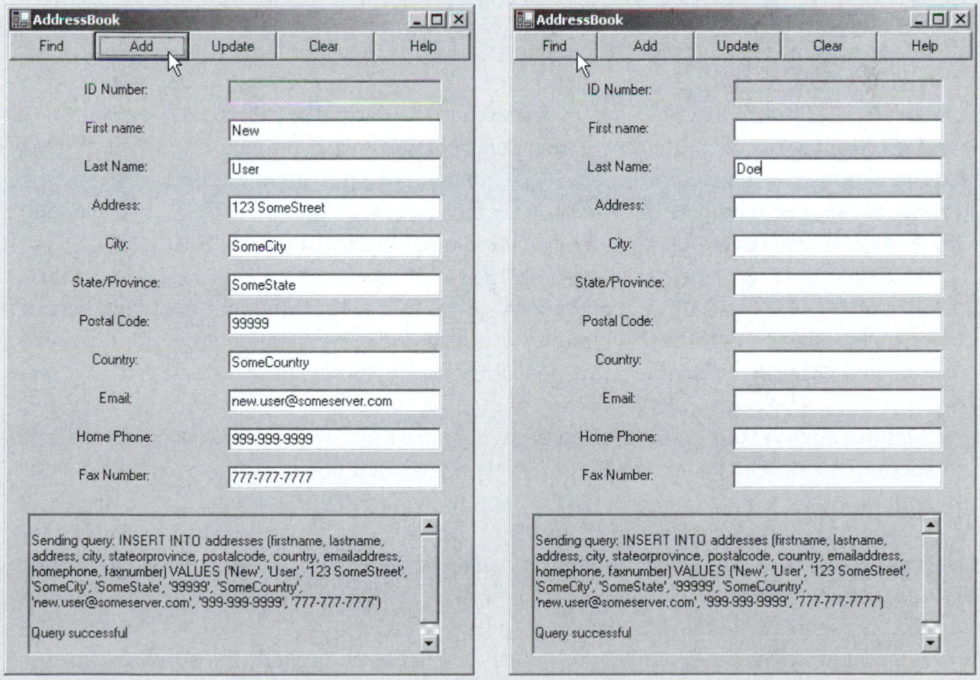

Fig. 19.32 `AddressBook` entry point. (Part 1 of 2.)

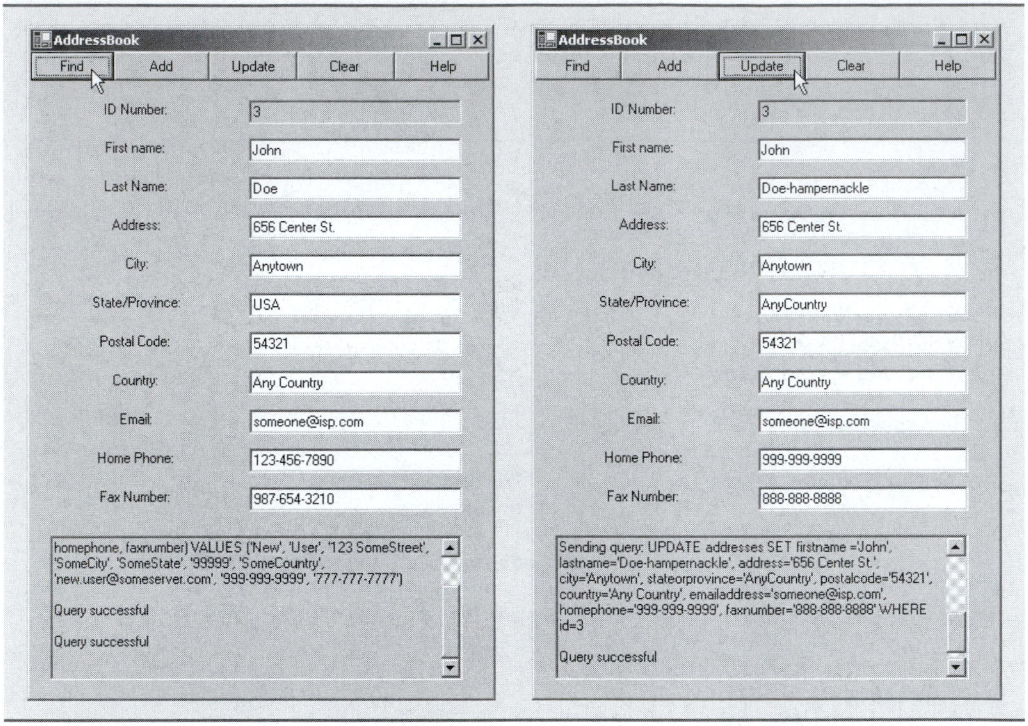

Fig. 19.32 `AddressBook` entry point. (Part 2 of 2.)

Event handler `findButton_Click` (lines 89–127 of Fig. 19.31) performs the query for the row associated with the string in `lastTextBox`. This represents the last name of the person whose data the user wishes to retrieve. Line 97 invokes method `Clear` of class `DataSet` to empty the `DataSet` of any prior data. Lines 101–103 then modify the text of the SQL query to perform the appropriate `SELECT` operation. This statement is executed by the `OleDbDataAdapter` method `Fill` (line 106), which is passed the `DataSet` as an argument. Finally, the `TextBoxes` are updated with a call to method `Display` (line 109).

Methods `addButton_Click` (lines 129–184) and `updateButton_Click` (lines 186–253) perform `INSERT` and `UPDATE` operations, respectively. Each method uses members of class `OleDbCommand` to perform operations on a database. The instance properties `InsertCommand` and `UpdateCommand` of class `OleDbDataAdapter` are instances of class `OleDbCommand`.

Method `addButton_Click` sets property `CommandText` of `InsertCommand` to execute the appropriate `INSERT` statement (lines 146–161). Method `updateButton_Click` sets this property of `UpdateCommand` to execute the appropriate `UPDATE` statement (lines 210–222).

Method *`ExecuteNonQuery`* of class `OleDbCommand` performs the action specified by `CommandText`. Hence, the `INSERT` statement defined in lines 146–161 is executed when line 170 invokes method `ExecuteNonQuery`. Similarly, the `UPDATE` statement defined in lines 210–222 is executed by `ExecuteNonQuery` (line 231–232).

If the user specifies invalid input for any available command, the `OleDbException` exception that is raised is handled in a `catch` block (lines 118–121, 180–183 and 249–252). For simplicity, we display the error in a `MessageBox`.

Method `Display` (lines 275–317) updates the user interface with data from the newly retrieved address-book row. Line 280 obtains a `DataTable` from the `DataSet`'s `Tables` collection. This `DataTable` contains the results of our SQL query. Line 282 determines whether the query returned any rows. Property ***`Rows`*** of class `DataTable` provides access to all rows retrieved by the query. Property `Rows` is similar to a two-dimensional rectangular array. Lines 284–285 retrieve the field with index *0, 0* (i.e., the first row's first column of data) and store the value in variable `rowNumber`. Lines 287–307 then retrieve the remaining data from the `DataTable` to populate the user interface.

When clicked, the application's **Help** button prints instructions at the bottom of the application window (lines 266–270). The event handler for this button is `helpButton_Click`. The `Clear` button clears the text from the `TextBoxes`. This event handler is defined in the method `clearButton_Click` (lines 255–260) and uses the utility method `ClearTextBoxes` (lines 321–333).

19.8 Reading and Writing XML Files

A powerful feature of ADO .NET is its ability to convert data stored in a data source to XML. Class `DataSet` of namespace `System::Data` provides methods ***`WriteXml`***, ***`ReadXml`*** and ***`GetXml`***, which enable developers to create XML documents from data sources and to convert data from XML into data sources. The application in Fig. 19.33–Fig. 19.34 populates a `DataSet` with statistics about baseball players, then writes the data to a file as XML. The application also displays the XML in a `TextBox`. For more information about XML, refer to Chapter 18.

```
// Fig. 19.33: Form1.h
// Demonstrates generating XML from an ADO.NET DataSet.

#pragma once


namespace DatabaseXMLWriter
{
   using namespace System;
   using namespace System::ComponentModel;
   using namespace System::Collections;
   using namespace System::Windows::Forms;
   using namespace System::Data;
   using namespace System::Drawing;
   using namespace System::Data::OleDb;

   /// <summary>
   /// Summary for Form1
   ///
   /// WARNING: If you change the name of this class, you will need to
   ///          change the 'Resource File Name' property for the managed
```

Fig. 19.33 Application that writes `DataSet` XML representation to a file. (Part 1 of 3.)

```
   ///         resource compiler tool associated with all .resx files
   ///         this class depends on.  Otherwise, the designers will not
   ///         be able to interact properly with localized resources
   ///         associated with this form.
   /// </summary>
   public __gc class Form1 : public System::Windows::Forms::Form
   {
   public:
      Form1(void)
      {
         InitializeComponent();

         this->baseballConnection->Open();  // open connection

         // fill DataSet with data from OleDbDataAdapter
         playersDataAdapter->Fill( playersDataSet, S"Players" );

         // bind DataGrid to DataSet
         playersDataGrid->SetDataBinding( playersDataSet, S"Players" );
      }

   protected:
      void Dispose(Boolean disposing)
      {
         if (disposing && components)
         {
            components->Dispose();
         }
         __super::Dispose(disposing);
      }
   private: System::Windows::Forms::Button *  writeButton;
   private: System::Windows::Forms::DataGrid *  playersDataGrid;
   private: System::Windows::Forms::TextBox *  outputTextBox;
   private: System::Data::OleDb::OleDbConnection *  baseballConnection;
   private: System::Data::DataSet *  playersDataSet;
   private: System::Data::OleDb::OleDbDataAdapter *  playersDataAdapter;
   private: System::Data::OleDb::OleDbCommand *  oleDbSelectCommand1;
   private: System::Data::OleDb::OleDbCommand *  oleDbInsertCommand1;
   private: System::Data::OleDb::OleDbCommand *  oleDbUpdateCommand1;
   private: System::Data::OleDb::OleDbCommand *  oleDbDeleteCommand1;

   private:
      /// <summary>
      /// Required designer variable.
      /// </summary>
      System::ComponentModel::Container * components;

   // Visual Studio .NET generated GUI code

   // write XML representation of DataSet when button clicked
   private: System::Void writeButton_Click(
               System::Object *  sender, System::EventArgs *  e)
            {
```

Fig. 19.33 Application that writes `DataSet` XML representation to a file. (Part 2 of 3.)

```
            // write XML representation of DataSet to file
            playersDataSet->WriteXml( S"Players.xml" );

            // display XML in TextBox
            outputTextBox->Text = String::Concat(
               S"Writing the following XML:\r\n",
               playersDataSet->GetXml(), S"\r\n" );
         } // end method writeButton_Click
   };
}
```

Fig. 19.33 Application that writes `DataSet` XML representation to a file. (Part 3 of 3.)

```
// Fig. 19.34: Form1.cpp
// Entry point for application.

#include "stdafx.h"
#include "Form1.h"
#include <windows.h>

using namespace DatabaseXMLWriter;

int APIENTRY _tWinMain(HINSTANCE hInstance,
                       HINSTANCE hPrevInstance,
                       LPTSTR    lpCmdLine,
                       int       nCmdShow)
{
   System::Threading::Thread::CurrentThread->ApartmentState =
      System::Threading::ApartmentState::STA;
   Application::Run(new Form1());
   return 0;
} // end _tWinMain
```

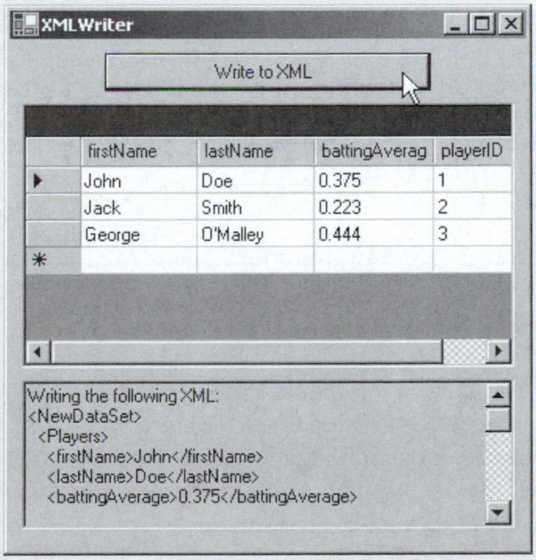

Fig. 19.34 `DatabaseXMLWriter` entry point.

The Form1 constructor (lines 30–41 of Fig. 19.33) establishes a connection to the Baseball database in line 34. The database has one table (Players) that consists of 4 columns—playerID, firstName, lastName and battingAverage. Line 37 calls method Fill of class OleDbDataAdapter to populate playersDataSet with data from the Players table in the Baseball database. Line 40 binds playersDataGrid to playersDataSet to display the information to the user.

Method writeButton_Click defines the event handler for the **Write to XML** button. When the user clicks this button, line 76 invokes DataSet method WriteXml, which generates an XML representation of the data contained in the DataSet and writes the XML to the specified file. Figure 19.35 depicts this XML representation. Each Players element represents a row in the Players table. The firstName, lastName, battingAverage and playerID elements correspond to the columns of the same names in the Players table. Method GetXml returns a String * representing the DataSet's data in XML form. Lines 79–81 append the XML String * to outputTextBox.

```
<?xml version="1.0" standalone="yes"?>
<NewDataSet>
   <Players>
      <firstName>John</firstName>
      <lastName>Doe</lastName>
      <battingAverage>0.375</battingAverage>
      <playerID>1</playerID>
   </Players>

   <Players>
      <firstName>Jack</firstName>
      <lastName>Smith</lastName>
      <battingAverage>0.223</battingAverage>
      <playerID>2</playerID>
   </Players>

   <Players>
      <firstName>George</firstName>
      <lastName>O'Malley</lastName>
      <battingAverage>0.444</battingAverage>
      <playerID>3</playerID>
   </Players>
</NewDataSet>
```

Fig. 19.35 XML document generated from DataSet in DatabaseXMLWriter.

In this chapter, we discussed the fundamentals of SQL and Visual C++ .NET's database capabilities. We learned that Visual C++ .NET programmers can communicate with databases and manipulate their data through *Microsoft ActiveX Data Objects*™ (ADO), via *ADO .NET*. In Chapter 20, we introduce Web services, which allow remote software to interact with methods and objects on a Web server.

19.9 Internet and Web Resources

`www.microsoft.com/office/access`

The Microsoft Access home page contains product information, purchase information and information about using the software.

`www.microsoft.com/sql`

The official Microsoft SQL Server home page contains information about this family of products.

`msdn.microsoft.com/sqlserver`

The MSDN Library contains additional developer information about Microsoft SQL Server.

`www.oracle.com`

The official Oracle Corporation home page contains information about the Oracle9*i* database.

`www.sybase.com`

The official Sybase Inc. home page contains information about their database servers.

`www-3.ibm.com/software/data/db2`

The official IBM DB2 home page contains product information, purchase information and support information for this family of products.

`www-3.ibm.com/software/data/informix`

The official IBM Informix home page contains product information, purchase information and support information for this family of products.

`www.mysql.com`

The official MySQL home page contains information about this open source database.

SUMMARY

- A database is an integrated collection of data. A database management system (DBMS) provides mechanisms for storing and organizing data.
- Today's most popular database systems are relational databases.
- A language called SQL is used almost universally with relational-database systems to perform queries and manipulate data.
- A programming language connects to, and interacts with, relational databases via an interface—software that facilitates communications between a database management system and a program.
- Visual C++ programmers communicate with databases and manipulate their data via ADO .NET.
- A relational database is composed of tables. Tables are composed of rows and columns.
- A primary key contains unique data, data that is not duplicated in other rows of a table.
- Each column in a table represents a different data attribute.
- A primary key can be composed of more than one column in a table.
- SQL provides a complete set of commands, enabling programmers to define complex queries to select data from a table. The results of a query commonly are called result sets (or record sets).
- A one-to-many relationship between tables indicates that a row in one table can have many corresponding rows in a separate table.
- A foreign key is a column(s) in one table that have the same values as the primary key for another table.
- The basic format for a `SELECT` query is:

  `SELECT * FROM` *tableName*

  where the asterisk (*) indicates that all columns from *tableName* should be selected, and *tableName* specifies the table in the database from which the data will be selected.

- To select specific columns from a table, replace the asterisk (*) with a comma-separated list of the column to select.
- Programmers process result sets by knowing in advance the order of the columns in the result set. Specifying the column names to select guarantees that the columns are returned in the specified order, even if the actual order of the columns in the database table(s) changes.
- The optional WHERE clause in a SELECT query specifies the selection criteria for the query. The simplest format for a SELECT query with selection criteria is:

  SELECT *columnName1*, *columnName2*, ... **FROM** *tableName* **WHERE** *criteria*

- The WHERE clause condition can contain operators <, >, <=, >=, =, <> and LIKE. Operator LIKE is used for pattern matching with wildcard characters asterisk (*) and question mark (?).
- A pattern string containing an asterisk character (*) searches for strings in which zero or more characters appear in the asterisk character's location in the pattern.
- A pattern string containing a question mark (?) searches for strings in which exactly one character appears in the question mark's position in the pattern.
- The results of a query can be arranged in ascending or descending order via the optional ORDER BY clause. The simplest form of an ORDER BY clause is:

  SELECT *columnName1*, *columnName2*, ... **FROM** *tableName* **ORDER BY** *column* **ASC**
  SELECT *columnName1*, *columnName2*, ... **FROM** *tableName* **ORDER BY** *column* **DESC**

  where ASC specifies ascending order, DESC specifies descending order and *column* specifies the column to be sorted. The default sorting order is ascending, so ASC is optional.
- An ORDER BY clause also can sort rows by multiple columns. Such queries are written in the form:

  ORDER BY *column1 sortingOrder*, *column2 sortingOrder*, ...

- The WHERE and ORDER BY clauses can be combined in one query.
- A join merges data from two tables by testing for matching values in columns that are common to both tables. The simplest format of a join is:

  SELECT *columnName1*, *columnName2*, ...
  FROM *table1* **INNER JOIN** *table2*
  ON *table1*.*columnName* = *table2*.*columnName*

  in which the WHERE clause specifies the columns from each table that should be compared to determine which rows are merged. These columns normally represent the primary key in one table and the corresponding foreign key in another table.
- If an SQL statement uses columns that have the same name in multiple tables, the statement must fully qualify the column name by preceding it with its table name and the dot operator (.).
- An INSERT statement inserts a new row in a table. The simplest form for this statement is:

  INSERT INTO *tableName* (*columnName1*, *columnName2*, ..., *columnNameN*)
  VALUES (*value1*, *value2*, ..., *valueN*)

  where *tableName* is the table in which to insert the row. The *tableName* is followed by a comma-separated list of column names in parentheses. The list of column names is followed by the SQL keyword VALUES and a comma-separated list of values in parentheses.
- SQL statements use a single quote (') as a delimiter for strings. To specify a string containing a single quote in an SQL statement, the single quote must be escaped with another single quote.
- An UPDATE statement modifies data in a table. The simplest form for an UPDATE statement is:

UPDATE *tableName*
  SET *columnName1* = *value1*, *columnName2* = *value2*, ..., *columnNameN* = *valueN*
  WHERE *criteria*

where *tableName* is the table in which to update a row (or rows). The *tableName* is followed by keyword SET and a comma-separated list of column-name/value pairs, written in the format *columnName* = *value*. The WHERE *criteria* determine the row(s) to update.

- A DELETE statement removes data from a table. The simplest form for a DELETE statement is:

  DELETE FROM *tableName* **WHERE** *criteria*

  where *tableName* is the table from which to delete a row (or rows). The WHERE *criteria* determine which row(s) to delete.
- System::Data, System::Data::OleDb and System::Data::SqlClient are the three main namespaces in ADO .NET.
- Class DataSet is from the System::Data namespace. Instances of this class represent in-memory caches of data.
- The advantage of using class DataSet is that it is a way to modify the contents of a data source without having to maintain an active connection.
- If a DataSet needs to be named, use the instance property DataSetName.
- Method Clear of class DataSet is called to empty the DataSet of any prior data. DataColumnMappings converts data from a database to a DataSet, and vice versa.
- One approach to ADO .NET programming uses OleDbCommand of the System::Data::OleDb namespace. In this approach, SQL statements are executed directly on the data source.
- OleDbCommand instance property Connection is set to the OleDbConnection that the command will be executed on, and the instance property CommandText is set to the SQL query that will be executed on the database.
- Property CommandText of class OleDbCommand is the String representing the SQL statement to be executed.
- Method ExecuteNonQuery of class OleDbCommand is called to perform the action specified by CommandText on the database.
- Instance property Parameters of class OleDbCommand is a collection of OleDbParameter objects. Adding them to an OleDbCommand is an optional way to add parameters in a command, instead of creating a lengthy, complex command string.
- OleDbCommands commands are what the OleDbDataAdapter executes on the database in the form of SQL queries.
- OleDbDataAdapter method Fill retrieves information from the database associated with the OleDbConnection and places this information in the DataSet provided as an argument.
- The instance properties InsertCommand and UpdateCommand of class OleDbDataAdapter are instances of class OleDbCommand.
- DataGrid is a System::Windows::Forms control that can display a data source in a GUI.
- DataGrid method SetDataBinding binds a DataGrid to a data source.
- A powerful feature of ADO .NET is its ability to convert data stored in a data source to XML, and vice versa.
- Method WriteXml of class DataSet writes the XML representation of the DataSet instance to the first argument passed to it. This method has several overloaded versions that allow programmers to specify an output source and a character encoding for the data.

- Method ReadXml of class DataSet reads the XML representation of the first argument passed to it into its own DataSet. This method has several overloaded versions that allow programmers to specify an input source and a character encoding for the data.

TERMINOLOGY

* SQL wildcard character
? SQL wildcard character
ADO.NET
AND
ascending order (ASC)
asterisk (*)
cache
Clear method of DataSet
column
column number
CommandText method of OleDbCommand
connect to a database
data provider
database
database management system (DBMS)
database table
DataGrid class
DataSet class
DELETE statement
DeleteCommand property of OleDbAdapter
descending order (DESC)
disconnected model
ExecuteNonQuery method of OleDbCommand
Fill method of OleDbAdapter
foreign key
FROM
GetXml method of DataSet
GROUP BY
infinity symbol
INNER JOIN
INSERT INTO statement
InsertCommand property of OleDbAdapter
interface to interact with a database
joining tables
LIKE
many-to-many relationship
match the selection criteria
merge data from tables
OleDbCommand class
OleDbConnection class
OleDbDataAdapter class
one-to-many relationship
ORDER BY
pattern matching
primary key
qualified name
query
query a database
ReadXml method of DataSet
record set
relational database
relational database model
relational database table
result set
row
rows to be retrieved
Rule of Entity Integrity
Rule of Referential Integrity
SELECT statement
select all columns from a table
SelectCommand property of OleDbAdapter
selection criteria
SET
SetDataBinding method of DataGrid
single-quote character
SQL (Structured Query Language)
SQL keyword
SQL query
SQL statement
square brackets in a query
System::Data namespace
System::Data::OleDb namespace
System::Data::SqlClient namespace
table
table column
table in which row will be updated
table row
UPDATE statement
UpdateCommand property of OleDbAdapter
VALUES
WHERE
WriteXml method of DataSet

SELF-REVIEW EXERCISES

19.1 Fill in the blanks in each of the following statements:

a) The most popular database query language is ________.
b) A table in a database consists of ________ and ________.
c) Databases can be manipulated in MC++ as ________ objects.
d) Class ________ enables programmers to display data in DataSets graphically.
e) SQL keyword ________ is followed by selection criteria that specify the rows to select in a query.
f) SQL keyword ________ specifies the order in which rows are sorted in a query.
g) Selecting data from multiple database tables is called ________ the data.
h) A(n) ________ is an integrated collection of data that is centrally controlled.
i) A(n) ________ is a column in a table for which every entry has a unique value in another table and where the column in the other table is the primary key for that table.
j) Namespace ________ contains special classes and interfaces for manipulating SQLServer databases.
k) Namespace ________ provides general interfacing to a database.

19.2 State which of the following are *true* or *false*. If *false*, explain why.

a) An advantage of using class `DataSet` is that it is disconnected—the program does not need a persistent connection to the data source to work with data in a `DataSet`.
b) SQL can implicitly determine the column being referred to in a query when there are two columns with the same name from two or mores tables.
c) Only the `UPDATE` SQL statement can make changes to a database.
d) Providing a foreign-key value that does not appear as a primary-key value in another table breaks the Rule of Referential Integrity.
e) `SELECT` queries can merge data from multiple tables.
f) The `DELETE` statement deletes only one row in a table.
g) An `OleDbDataAdapter` can `Fill` a `DataSet`.
h) Class `DataSet` of namespace `System::Data` provides methods that enable developers to create XML documents from data sources.

ANSWERS TO SELF-REVIEW EXERCISES

19.1 a) SQL. b) rows, columns. c) `DataSet`. d) `DataGrid`. e) `WHERE`. f) `ORDER BY`. g) joining. h) database. i) foreign key. j) `System::Data::SqlClient`. k) `System::Data::OleDb`.

19.2 a) True. b) False. In a query, failure to provide fully qualified names for columns with the same name in two or more tables is an error. c) False. `INSERT` and `DELETE` change the database, as well. d) True. e) True. f) False. The `DELETE` statement deletes all rows matching its `WHERE` clause or all rows in the table if no `WHERE` clause is coded. g) True. h) True.

EXERCISES

19.3 Using the techniques shown in this chapter, define a complete query application for the `Authors` table. Provide a series of predefined queries with an appropriate name for each query displayed in a `System::Windows::Forms::ComboBox`. Also, allow users to supply their own queries and add them to the `ComboBox`. Provide any queries you feel are appropriate.

19.4 Using the techniques shown in this chapter, define a complete query application for the `Books` database. Provide a series of predefined queries with an appropriate name for each query displayed in a `System::Windows::Forms::ComboBox`. Also, allow users to supply their own queries and add them to the `ComboBox`. Provide the following predefined queries:

a) Select all authors from the `Authors` table.
b) Select all publishers from the `Publishers` table.
c) Select a specific author and list all books for that author. Include the title, year and ISBN number. Order the information alphabetically by title.
d) Select a specific publisher and list all books published by that publisher. Include the title, year and ISBN number. Order the information alphabetically by title.
e) Provide any other queries you feel are appropriate.

19.5 Modify Exercise 19.4 to define a complete database-manipulation application for the `Books` database. In addition to the querying capabilities, application should allow users to edit existing data and add new data to the database. Allow the user to edit the database in the following ways:

a) Add a new author.
b) Edit the existing information for an author.
c) Add a new title for an author (remember that the book must have an entry in the `AuthorISBN` table). Be sure to specify the publisher of the title.
d) Add a new publisher.
e) Edit the existing information for a publisher.

For each of the preceding database manipulations, design an appropriate GUI to allow the user to perform the data manipulation.

19.6 Modify the address-book example of Fig. 19.33–Fig. 19.34 to enable each address-book entry to contain multiple addresses, phone numbers and e-mail addresses. The user should be able to view multiple addresses, phone numbers and e-mail addresses. [*Note:* This is a large exercise that requires substantial modifications to the original classes in the address-book example.]

19.7 Create an application that allows the user to modify all data of a database. The user should be able to find, modify and create entries. The GUI should include buttons **Accept Changes** and **Reject Changes**. Modifications to the data source should be made when the user clicks **Accept Changes**, by the invoking of method `Update` of the `OleDbDataAdapter` object.

19.8 Write a program that allows the user to modify a database graphically through an XML text editor. The GUI should be able to display the contents of the database and commit any changes in the XML text to the database.

20

Web Services

Objectives

- To understand what a Web service is.
- To understand the elements that compose a Web service, such as service descriptions and discovery files.
- To create Web services.
- To create a client that uses a Web service.
- To understand session tracking in Web services.
- To pass user-defined data types between Web services and Web clients.

A client is to me a mere unit, a factor in a problem.
Sir Arthur Conan Doyle

...if the simplest things of nature have a message that you understand, rejoice, for your soul is alive.
Eleonora Duse

Protocol is everything.
Françoise Giuliani

They also serve who only stand and wait.
John Milton

Outline

20.1 Introduction[1]

Throughout this book, we have created dynamic link libraries (DLLs) to facilitate software reusability and modularity—the cornerstones of good object-oriented programming. However, without remoting technologies such as Distributed Component Object Model (DCOM), Remote Procedure Call (RPC) or .NET remoting, the use of DLLs is limited by the fact that DLLs must reside on the same machine as the programs that use them. This chapter introduces *Web services* (sometimes called *XML Web services*) to promote software reusability in distributed systems. Distributed-systems technologies allow applications to execute across multiple computers on a network. A Web service is an application that enables distributed computing by allowing one machine to call methods on other machines via common data formats and protocols, such as XML (Chapter 18). In .NET, these method calls are implemented via the *Simple Object Access Protocol (SOAP)*, an XML-

1. Internet Information Services (IIS) must be running to create a Web service in Visual Studio .NET. Information on installing and running IIS can be found on our Web site (`www.deitel.com`).

based protocol describing how to mark up requests and responses so that they can be transferred via protocols such as Hypertext Transfer Protocol (HTTP). Using SOAP, applications represent and transmit data in a standardized format—XML. The underlying implementation of the Web service is irrelevant to clients using the Web service.

Microsoft is encouraging software vendors and e-businesses to deploy Web services. As more and more people worldwide connect to the Internet via networks, applications that call methods across a network become more practical. Earlier in this text, we discussed the merits of object-oriented programming. Web services represent the next step in object-oriented programming: Instead of developing software from a small number of class libraries provided at one location, programmers can access countless libraries in multiple locations.

This technology also makes it easier for businesses to collaborate and grow together. By purchasing Web services that are relevant to their businesses, companies that create applications can spend less time coding and more time developing new products from existing components. In addition, e-businesses can employ Web services to provide their customers with an enhanced shopping experience. As a simple example, consider an online music store that enables users to purchase music CDs or to obtain information about artists. Now, suppose that another company that sells concert tickets provides a Web service that reports the dates of upcoming concerts by various artists and allows users to buy concert tickets. By licensing the concert-ticket Web service for use on its site, the online music store can sell concert tickets to its customers, a service that likely will result in increased traffic at its site. The company that sells concert tickets also benefits from the business relationship. In addition to selling more tickets, the company receives revenue from the online music store in exchange for the use of its Web service. Visual Studio and the .NET Framework provide a simple way to create Web services like the one discussed in this example.

In this chapter, we begin with a brief introduction to Web content and Web protocols. We then explore the steps involved in both creating and accessing Web services. For each example, we provide the code for the Web service, then give an example of an application that might use the Web service. Our initial examples are designed to offer a brief introduction to Web services and how they work in Visual Studio .NET. In later sections, we move on to demonstrate more sophisticated Web services.

20.2 HTTP Request Types

HTTP defines several request types (also known as *request methods*), each of which specifies how a client requests information from a server. The two most common are *get* and *post*. These request types retrieve and send client form data from and to a Web server. A form is an HTML element that may contain text fields, radio buttons, check boxes and other GUI components that allow users to enter data into a Web page. Forms can also contain hidden fields, not exposed as GUI components. A *get* request is used to send data to the server. A *post* request also is used to send data to the server. A *get* request sends form data as part of the URL (e.g., `www.searchsomething.com/search?query=`*userquery*). In this fictitious request, the information following the `?` (`query=`*userquery*) indicates user-specified input. For example, if the user performs a search on "Massachusetts," the last part of the URL would be `?query=Massachusetts`. A *get* request limits the *query string* (e.g., `query=Massachusetts`) to a pre-defined number of characters. This limit varies from server to server. If the query string exceeds this limit, a *post* request must be used.

Software Engineering Observation 20.1

The data sent in a post *request is not part of the URL and cannot be seen by users. Forms that contain many fields often are submitted via a* post *request. Sensitive form fields, such as passwords, usually are sent using this request type.*

An HTTP request often sends data to a *server-side form handler* that processes the data. For example, when a user participates in a Web-based survey, the Web server receives the information specified in the form as part of the request and processes the survey in the form handler.

Browsers often *cache* (save on a local disk) Web pages for quick reloading, to reduce the amount of data that the browser needs to download. However, browsers typically do not cache the responses to *post* requests, because subsequent *post* requests might not contain the same information. For example, users participating in a Web-based survey may request the same Web page. Each user's response changes the overall results of the survey; thus, the information presented in the resulting Web page is different for each request.

Web browsers normally cache the server's responses to *get* requests. A static Web page, such as a course syllabus, is cached in the event that the user requests the same resource again.

20.3 Multi-Tier Architecture

A Web server is part of a *multi-tier application*, sometimes referred to as an *n*-tier application. Multi-tier applications divide functionality into separate tiers (i.e., logical groupings of functionality). Tiers can be located on the same computer or on separate computers. Figure 20.1 presents the basic structure of a three-tier application.

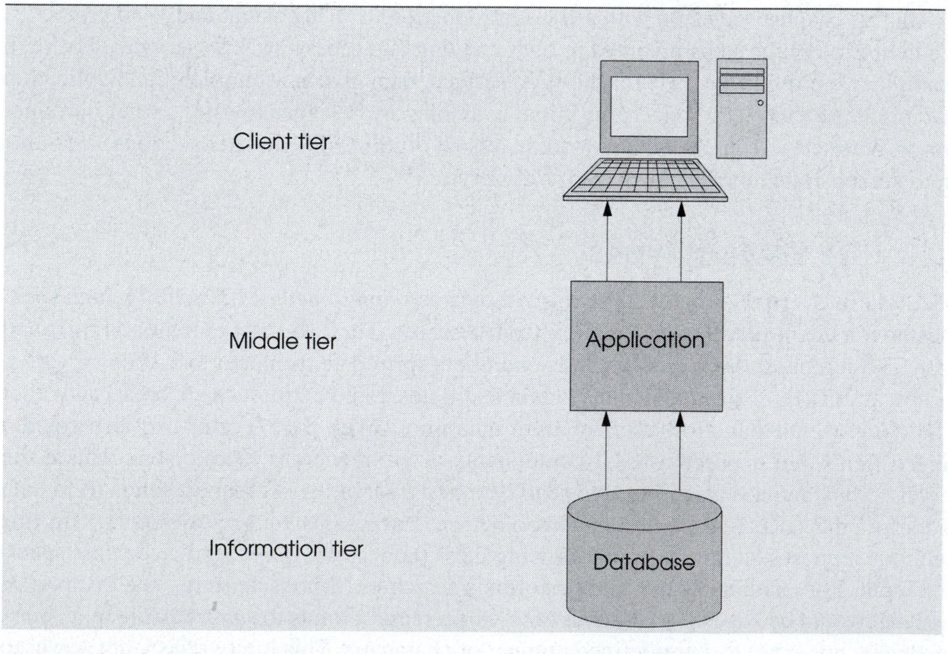

Fig. 20.1 Three-tier application model.

The *information tier* (also called the *data tier* or the *bottom tier*) maintains data for the application. This tier typically stores data in a *relational database management system (RDBMS)*. For example, a retail store might have a database of product information, such as descriptions, prices and quantities in stock. The same database also might contain customer information, such as user names for logging into the online store, billing addresses and credit-card numbers.

The *middle tier* implements *business logic* and *presentation logic* to control interactions between application clients and application data. The middle tier acts as an intermediary between data in the information tier and the application clients. The middle-tier *controller logic* (business logic) processes client requests from the top tier (e.g., a request to view a product catalog) and retrieves data from the database. The middle-tier presentation logic then processes data from the information tier and presents the content to the client. In Web-based applications, the middle tier presentation logic typically presents content as HTML documents.

Business logic in the middle tier enforces *business rules* and ensures that data is reliable before updating the database or presenting data to a user. Business rules dictate how clients can and cannot access application data and how applications process data.

The *client tier*, or *top tier*, is the application's user interface. Users interact directly with the application through the user interface. The client interacts with the middle tier to make requests and to retrieve data from the information tier. The client then displays to the user the data retrieved from the middle tier.

20.4 Accessing Web Servers

To request documents from Web servers, users must know the URLs at which those documents reside. A URL contains a machine name (called a *host name*) on which the Web server resides. Users can request documents from *local Web servers* (i.e., ones residing on user's machines) or *remote Web servers* (i.e., ones residing on machines across a network).

Local Web servers can be accessed in two ways: Through the machine name, or through `localhost`—a host name that references the local machine. We use `localhost` in this chapter. To determine the machine name in Windows 2000, right click **My Computer**, and select **Properties** from the context menu to display the **System Properties** dialog. In the dialog, click **Network Identification**. The **Full computer name:** field in the **System Properties** window displays the computer name. In Windows XP, select **Start > Control Panel > Switch to Classic View > System** to view the **System Properties** dialog. In the dialog, select the **Computer Name** tab.

A domain name represents a group of hosts on the Internet; it combines with a host name (e.g., www—World Wide Web) and a *top-level domain (TLD)* to form a *fully qualified host name*, which provides a user-friendly way to identify a site on the Internet. In a fully qualified host name, the TLD often describes the type of organization that owns the domain name. For example, the `com` TLD usually refers to a commercial business, whereas the `org` TLD usually refers to a nonprofit organization. In addition, each country has its own TLD, such as `cn` for China, `et` for Ethiopia, `om` for Oman and `us` for the United States.

Each fully qualified host name is assigned a unique address called an *IP address*, which is much like the street address of a house. Just as people use street addresses to locate houses or businesses in a city, computers use IP addresses to locate other computers on the Internet. A *domain name system (DNS) server*, a computer that maintains a database of host names and their corresponding IP addresses, translates fully qualified host names to IP addresses. This translation is referred to as a *DNS lookup*. For example, to access the Deitel Web site, type the host name (`www.deitel.com`) into a Web browser. The DNS server translates `www.deitel.com` into the IP address of the Deitel Web server (i.e., `63.110.43.82`). The IP address of `localhost` is always `127.0.0.1`.

20.5 Simple HTTP Transaction

Before exploring Web-based applications development further, a basic understanding of networking and the World Wide Web is necessary. In this section, we examine the inner workings of the *Hypertext Transfer Protocol (HTTP)* and discuss what occurs behind the scenes when a browser displays a Web page. HTTP is a protocol that specifies a set of *methods* and *headers* that allow clients and servers to interact and exchange information in a uniform and predictable way.

In their simplest form, Web pages are HTML documents—plain-text files that contain markings (*markup* or *tags*) describing the structures of the documents. For example, the HTML markup

```
<title>My Web Page</title>
```

indicates that the text contained between the `<title>` *start tag* and the `</title>` *end tag* is the Web page's title. HTML documents also can contain *hyperlinks*, which enable users to navigate their Web browsers to other Web pages. When the user activates a hyperlink (usually by clicking it with the mouse), the requested Web page (or different part of the same Web page) is loaded into the user's browser window.

Any HTML document available on the Web has a *Uniform Resource Locator (URL)*, which indicates the location of a resource. The URL contains information that directs Web browsers to the document. Computers that run *Web server* software provide such resources. Microsoft *Internet Information Services* (*IIS*) is the Web server that programmers use when developing Web services in Visual Studio .NET.

Let us examine the components of the following URL:

```
http://www.deitel.com/books/downloads.htm
```

The `http://` indicates that the resource is to be obtained via HTTP. The middle portion—`www.deitel.com`—is the fully qualified *host name* of the server. The host name is the name of the computer on which the resource resides. This computer usually is referred to as the *host*, because it houses and maintains resources. The host name `www.deitel.com` is translated into an *IP address* (`63.110.43.82`) that identifies the server in a manner similar to that by which a telephone number uniquely defines a particular phone line. The translation of the host name into an IP address normally is performed by a *domain name system (DNS) server*—a computer that maintains a database of host names and their corresponding IP addresses. This translation operation is called a *DNS lookup*.

The remainder of the URL provides the name and location of the requested resource, `/books/downloads.htm` (an HTML document). This portion of the URL specifies both the name of the resource (`downloads.htm`) and its path, or location (`/books`), on the Web server. The path could specify the location of an actual directory on the Web server's file system. However, for security reasons, paths often specify the locations of *virtual directo-*

ries. In such systems, the server translates each virtual directory into a real location on the server (or on another computer on the server's network), thus hiding the true location of a resource. Furthermore, some resources are created dynamically and do not reside anywhere on the server computer. The host name in the URL for such a resource specifies the correct server, and the path and resource information identify the location of the resource with which to respond to the client's request.

When given a URL, a browser performs a simple HTTP transaction to retrieve and display a Web page. Figure 20.2 illustrates this transaction in detail. The transaction consists of interaction between the Web browser (the client side) and the Web-server application (the server side).

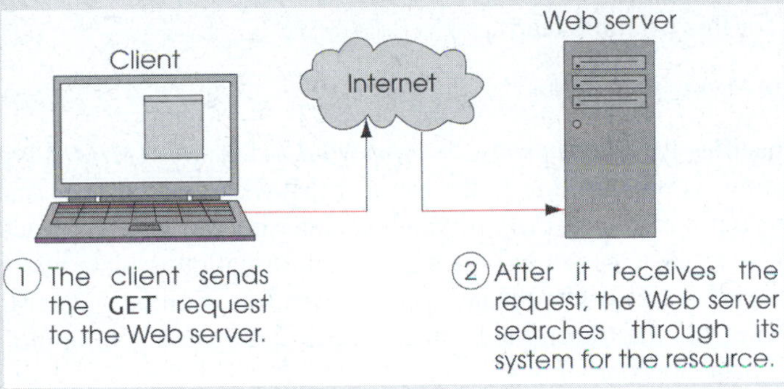

Fig. 20.2 Web server/client interaction. Step 1: The GET request, `GET /books/downloads.htm HTTP/1.1`.

In Fig. 20.2, the Web browser sends an HTTP request to the server. The request (in its simplest form) is

```
GET /books/downloads.htm HTTP/1.1
```

The word *GET* is an *HTTP method* indicating that the client wishes to obtain a resource from the server. The remainder of the request provides the path name of the resource and the protocol's name and version number (`HTTP/1.1`).

Any server that understands HTTP (version 1.1) can translate this request and respond appropriately. Figure 20.3 depicts a Web server's response when it a successful request. The server first responds by sending a line of text that indicates the HTTP version, followed by a numeric code and phrase, both of which describe the status of the transaction. For example,

```
HTTP/1.1 200 OK
```

indicates success, whereas

```
HTTP/1.1 404 Not found
```

informs the client that the Web server could not locate the requested resource.

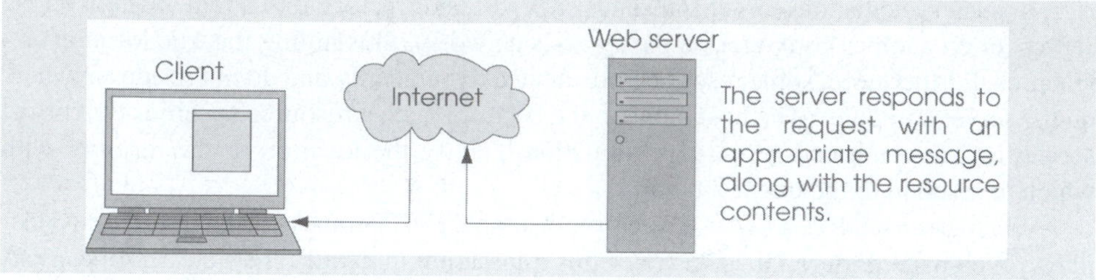

Fig. 20.3 Web server/client interaction. Step 2: The HTTP response, `HTTP/1.1 200 OK`.

The server then sends one or more *HTTP headers,* which provide information about the data that will be sent. In this case, the server is sending an HTML text document, so the HTTP header for this example reads

```
Content-type: text/html
```

This header specifies the *Multipurpose Internet Mail Extensions* (*MIME*) type of the content that the server is transmitting to the browser. MIME is an Internet standard used to identify various types of data so that programs can interpret those data correctly. For example, the MIME type `text/plain` indicates that the information is plain text, which a Web browser can display directly without any special formatting. Similarly, the MIME type `image/gif` indicates that the transmitted content is a GIF image, enabling the Web browser to display the image appropriately.

The set of headers is followed by a blank line, which indicates to the client that the server is finished sending HTTP headers. The server then sends the contents of the requested HTML document (`downloads.htm`). The server terminates the connection when the transfer of the resource is complete. At this point, the client-side browser parses the HTML it has received and *renders* (or displays) the results.

20.6 ASP (Active Server Pages) .NET

Microsoft's *Active Server Pages (ASP) .NET*, an integral part of the .NET initiative, is a technology for creating dynamic Web content marked up as HTML. Like Windows applications, Web pages built with ASP .NET are designed using Visual Studio .NET. ASP .NET developers can create multi-tier, database-intensive applications quickly by employing .NET's object-oriented languages and the FCL's *Web controls*. Web controls are similar to the controls in Windows applications, but are designed specifically for Web pages. ASP .NET is a sophisticated technology—it includes optimizations for performance, testing and security.

Unfortunately, Visual Studio .NET does not currently have the tools that allow developers to create ASP .NET Web applications easily in Visual C++ .NET. However, tools *are* available that enable Visual C++ .NET developers to create Web services that use ASP .NET technology. Such Web services are sometimes referred to as *ASP .NET Web services*. Using ASP .NET to build a Web service provides several benefits. First, ASP .NET itself is built upon the .NET Framework, which allows the Web service to employ features of the CLR, such as memory management, interoperability and software reuse. The Web service also benefits from the ASP .NET optimizations mentioned earlier.

When a developer creates Web services using ASP .NET and Visual Studio .NET, many programming details are hidden. In the next section, we will see examples of this.

20.7 .NET Web Services Basics

As we mentioned earlier, a Web service is an application stored on one machine that can be accessed on another machine over a network. Due to the nature of this relationship, the machine on which the Web service resides commonly is referred to as a *remote machine*. The application that accesses the Web service sends a method call to the remote machine, which processes the call and sends a response to the application. This kind of distributed computing benefits various systems, including those without access to certain data and those lacking the processing power necessary to perform specific computations.

A Web service is, in its simplest form, a class. In previous chapters, when we wanted to include a class in a project, we would either define the class in our project or add a reference to the compiled DLL. This compiled DLL was placed in the `Debug` directory of an application by default. As a result, all pieces of our application resided on one machine. When a client uses a Web service, the class (and its compiled DLL) is stored on a remote machine—a compiled version of this class is not placed in the current application's directory.

Most requests to and responses from Web services created with Visual Studio .NET are transmitted via SOAP. This means that any client capable of generating and processing SOAP messages can use a Web service, regardless of the language in which the Web service is written. SOAP will be discussed more in Section 20.8.

Web services have important implications for *business-to-business (B2B) transactions* (i.e., transactions that occur between two or more businesses). Now, instead of using proprietary applications, businesses can conduct transactions via Web services—a much simpler and more efficient means of conducting business. Web services and SOAP are platform independent, so companies can collaborate and use Web services without worrying about the compatibility of various technologies or programming languages. In this way, Web services are an inexpensive, readily available solution to facilitate B2B transactions.

To create a Web service in Visual Studio .NET, a developer first creates a project of type ***ASP .NET Web Service***. Visual Studio .NET then generates files to contain the Web service code (which implements the Web service), an *ASMX file* (which provides documentation for the Web service) and a DISCO file (which potential clients use to discover the Web service). Figure 20.4 displays the different files that comprise a Web service. We discuss these files in more detail shortly. [*Note*: When a developer creates an application in Visual Studio .NET, the IDE typically generates several files. We have chosen to show only those files that are specific to Web-services applications.]

When a developer creates an **ASP .NET Web Service** application, Visual Studio .NET provides code files to contain the Web service class and any other code that is part of the Web service implementation. The Web service class defines all methods that the Web service exposes to remote applications. Any methods that the developer wants to incorporate in the Web service are added to this class. Developers must tag as a *Web method* each method that they want to expose. We demonstrate how to tag Web methods later in this chapter.

Software Engineering Observation 20.2

By default, Visual Studio .NET creates only one `.h` *and one* `.cpp` *file for the Web service implementation. More complex Web services can contain many code files.*

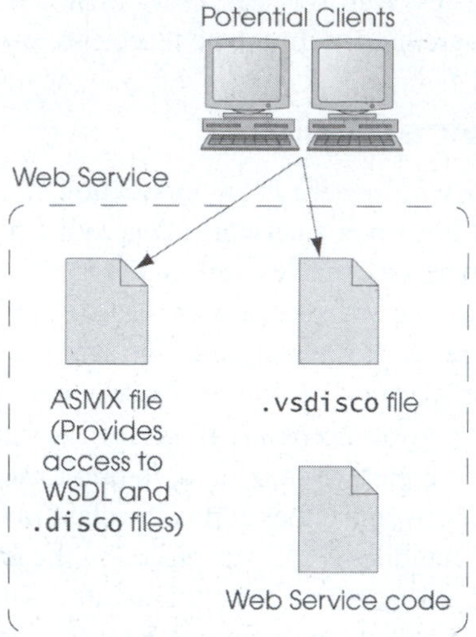

Fig. 20.4 Web service components.

Once the developer adds the necessary programming logic to the Web service code file and successfully compiles the Web service, a client application can consume the Web service. However, clients must be able to find the Web service and learn about its capabilities. *Discovery of Web services* (*DISCO*) is a Microsoft-specific technology used to locate Web services in a particular directory on a server. There are four types of discovery files: `.disco` files, `.vsdisco` files, `.discomap` and `.map` files. `.vsdisco` files are placed in the Web service application directory, whereas `.disco` files are accessed via the ASMX page. All four DISCO files contain XML that can help clients locate Web service files. A `.disco` file contains markup that specifies references to various Web services' documents. A `.vsdisco` file is slightly different. Rather than containing markup about Web services, this desired markup is generated when the file is requested. Markup containing references to Web services' documents will be generated and returned to the user. When a potential client requests a `.vsdisco` file, the .NET Framework analyzes the directory in which the `.vsdisco` file is located, as well as that directory's subdirectories. The .NET Framework then generates markup (using the same syntax as that of a `.disco` file) that contains references to all Web services in that directory and the directory's subdirectories. If this markup is generated, but not stored in the `.vsdisco` file, then what information is contained in the `.vsdisco` file? Developers can specify in the `.vsdisco` file certain directories that should not be searched when the file is requested.[a] Normally, the `.vsdisco` file contains only markup specifying which directories should not be searched. It is important to note that developers usually do not view `.vsdisco` markup. Although a developer can open a `.vsdisco` file in a text editor and examine its markup, `.vsdisco` files are intended to be requested (i.e., viewed in a browser), as these files will be primarily accessed by clients over the Web. Every time this occurs, new markup is generated and displayed.

The reader might be wondering why a developer would want to use one type of DISCO file over another. Developers benefit from `.vsdisco` files, because the files contain a small amount of data and provide up-to-date information on the Web service files provided by a server. However, `.vsdisco` files generate more overhead than `.disco` files do, because a search must be performed every time a `.vsdisco` file is accessed. Thus, some developers find it more convenient to keep `.disco` files up-to-date manually. Many systems use both files. As we discuss later in this section, Web services created using ASP .NET contain the functionality to generate a `.disco` file when it is requested. This `.disco` file contains references to files in the current Web service only.[2] Thus, a developer typically places a `.vsdisco` file at the root of a server; when accessed, this file locates the `.disco` files for Web services on the system and uses these `.disco` files' markup to return information about the entire system.

Once a client locates a Web service, the client must access details regarding the Web service's functionality and how to use that functionality. For this purpose, Web services normally contain a *service description*. A service description is an XML document that conforms to the *Web Service Description Language (WSDL)*—an XML vocabulary that defines the methods that the Web service makes available and the ways in which clients can interact with those methods. The WSDL document also specifies lower-level information that clients might need, such as the required formats for requests and responses.

Although WSDL documents supply this information, WSDL can be difficult to understand. Visual Studio .NET generates an ASMX file when a Web service is constructed to offer a more understandable description of the Web service. Files with an *`.asmx`* extension are ASP .NET Web service files. Such files can be viewed in a Web browser and contain descriptions of Web service methods and ways to test these methods. The ASMX file also indicates the compiled assembly, which contains the implementation of the Web service. When the Web server receives a request for the Web service, it calls the ASMX file, which, in turn, invokes the Web-service implementation. To view more technical information about the Web service, developers can access the WSDL file (which also is generated by ASP .NET). We will demonstrate how to do this shortly.

The ASMX file in Fig. 20.5 displays information about the `HugeInteger` Web service. This Web service, which we use as an example, is designed to perform calculations with integers that contain a maximum of 100 digits. (Most programming languages cannot easily perform calculations using integers this large.) The Web service provides client applications with methods that take two "huge integers" and determine which one is larger or smaller, whether the two numbers are equal, their sum and their difference. Notice that the top of the page provides a link to the Web service's ***Service Description***. Visual Studio .NET generates the WSDL service description. Client programs can use the service description to confirm the correctness of method calls when the client programs are compiled.

Rather than creating an actual WSDL file, ASP .NET generates WSDL information dynamically. If a client requests the Web service's WSDL file (either by appending *`?WSDL`* to the ASMX file's URL or by clicking the **Service Description** link), ASP .NET generates the WSDL description, which is then returned to the client and displayed in the Web browser. The WSDL file is generated when it is requested, so clients can be sure that the WSDL contains the most current information.[b]

The programmer should not alter the service description, because it defines how a Web service works. When a user clicks the **Service Description** link at the top of the ASMX page, WSDL is displayed that defines the service description for this Web service (Fig. 20.6).

2. Although in this instance `.disco` files contain references to files in only one Web service, both `.disco` files can contain references to files in several Web services.

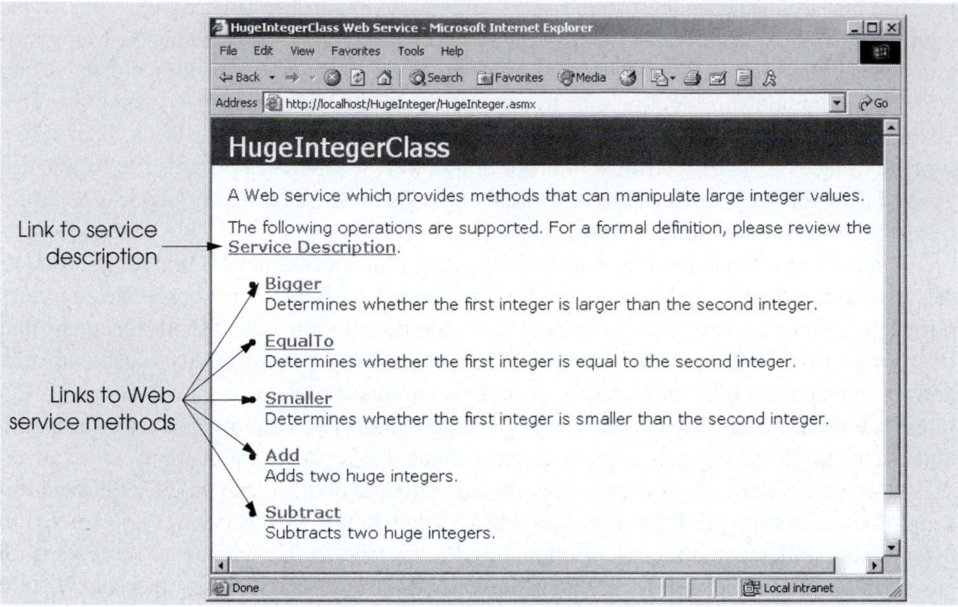

Fig. 20.5 ASMX file rendered in a Web browser.

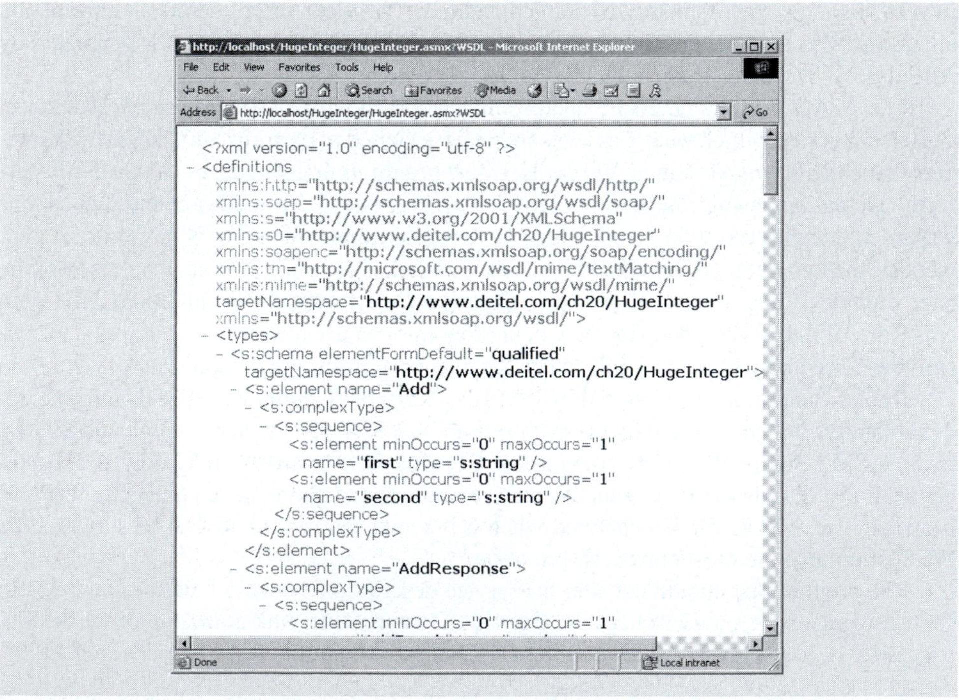

Fig. 20.6 Service description for a Web service.

As mentioned earlier, the `.disco` file for the Web service is accessed via the ASMX page. Like WSDL data, the `.disco` information for an ASP .NET Web service is not a physical file.[3] The .NET Framework generates this file when a client requests it, by appending *`?DISCO`* to the ASMX's URL. Readers might be wondering why someone would access a `.disco` file this way—if potential clients know the URL of the Web service's ASMX file, then they have discovered the Web service already. However, `.disco` files also may be accessed when a client requests a `.vsdisco` file. For instance, recall that accessing a `.vsdisco` file causes the .NET Framework to search for Web services. When this occurs, the .NET Framework actually searches for ASMX files, `.disco` files and `.vsdisco` files.[c] This way, the information in a `.disco` file may be returned to a potential client that does *not* know the URL of any ASMX files on this machine. The resulting data that is returned from accessing a `.disco` file is placed into the `.discomap` file, another type of DISCO file mentioned earlier.

Below the **Service Description** link, the ASMX page shown in Fig. 20.5 lists the methods that the Web service offers. Clicking any method name requests a test page that describes the method (Fig. 20.7). After explaining the method's arguments, the test page allows users to test the method by entering the proper parameters and clicking **Invoke**. (We discuss the process of testing a Web service method shortly.) Below the **Invoke** button, the page displays sample request-and-response messages using SOAP, HTTP GET and HTTP POST. These protocols are the three options for sending and receiving messages in Web services. The protocol that transmits request and response messages also is known as the Web service's *wire format*, because it defines how information is sent "along the wire." SOAP is the more commonly used wire format, because both HTTP GET and HTTP POST are tied to HTTP, whereas SOAP can be sent along other transport protocols.

Figure 20.7 depicts the test page for the `HugeInteger` method `Bigger`. From this page, users can test the method by entering values in the **first:** and **second:** fields, then clicking **Invoke**. The method executes, and a new Web browser window opens to display an XML document that contains the result (Fig. 20.8).

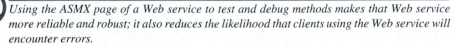

Error-Prevention Tip 20.1

Using the ASMX page of a Web service to test and debug methods makes that Web service more reliable and robust; it also reduces the likelihood that clients using the Web service will encounter errors.

Now that we have discussed the different files that comprise a .NET Web service, let us examine a .NET Web service client (Fig. 20.9). A .NET client can be any type of .NET application, such as a Windows program or a console application. Developers can consume Web services from their applications by the process of *adding a Web reference*. This process adds files to the client application that enable the client to access the Web service. To add a Web reference in Visual Studio .NET, the developer right-clicks the project name in the **Solution Explorer** and selects option **Add Web Reference...**. In the resulting dialog, the developer specifies the Web service to consume. Visual Studio .NET then adds an appropriate Web reference to the client application. We will demonstrate adding Web references in more detail in Section 20.9.

---

3. It is common for XML documents to be created dynamically and manipulated programmatically, but never saved to disk.

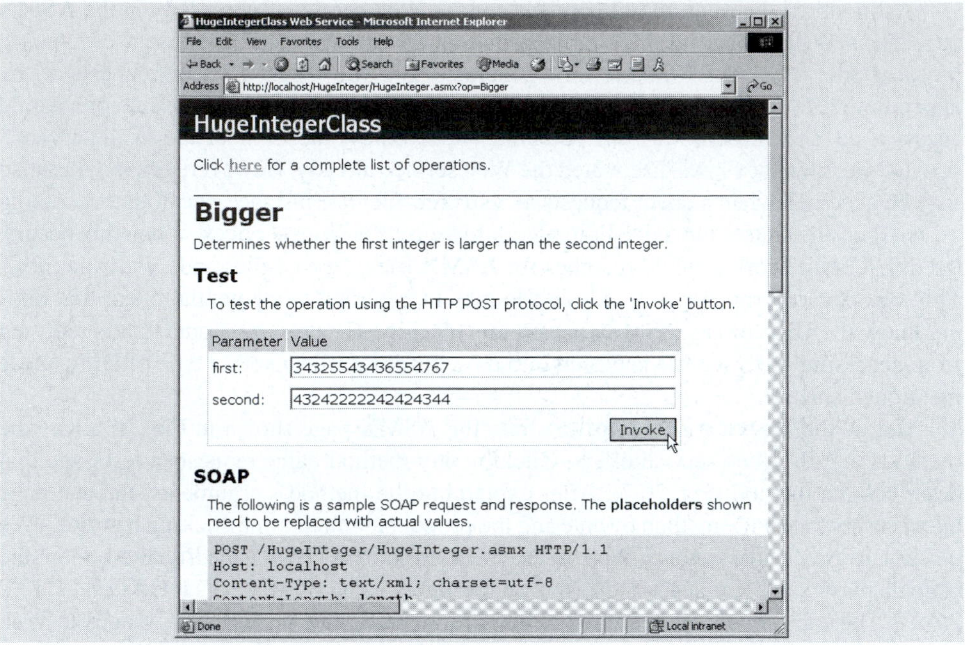

Fig. 20.7 Invoking a Web service method from a Web browser.

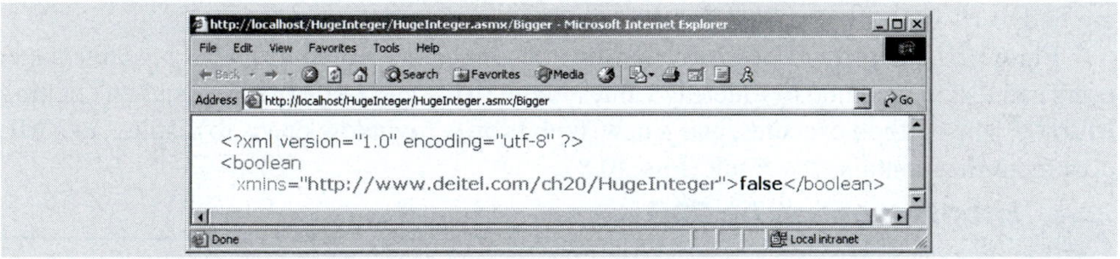

Fig. 20.8 Results of invoking a Web service method from a Web browser.

When developers specify the Web service they want to consume, Visual Studio .NET accesses the Web service's WSDL file and makes a copy of it, which will be stored as a file in the project folder.[4] The information in the WSDL file is used to create the *proxy class*, which handles all the "plumbing" required for Web service method calls. Whenever the client application calls a Web service method, the application actually calls a corresponding method in the proxy class. This method takes the name and arguments of the Web service method that is being called, then formats them so that they can be sent as a request in a SOAP message. The Web service receives this request and executes the method call, sending back the result as another SOAP message. When the client application receives the SOAP message containing the response, the proxy class decodes it and formats the results

4. A copy of the WSDL file provides the client application with local access to the Web service's description. To ensure that the WSDL file is current, Visual Studio .NET provides an **Update Web Reference** option, which updates the files in the `Web References` folder.

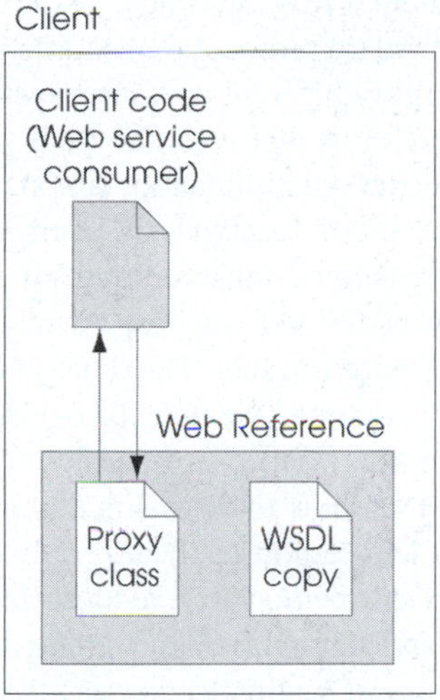

Fig. 20.9 .NET Web service client after Web reference has been added.

so that the client application can access them. The information is then returned to the client. Figure 20.10 depicts interactions among the client code, proxy and Web service.

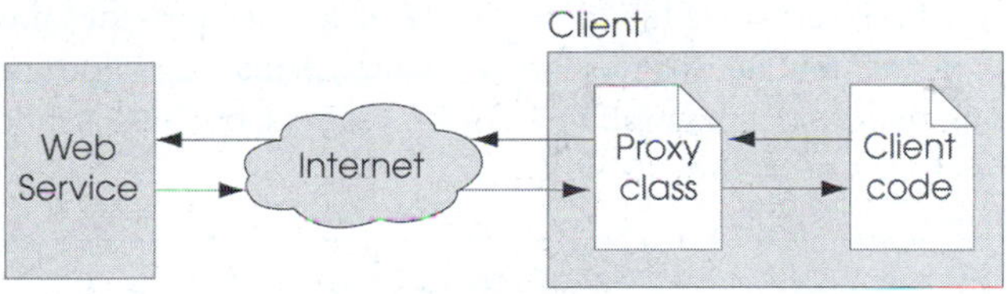

Fig. 20.10 Interaction between Web service and Web service client.

Just as .NET clients contain proxy classes to handle SOAP requests/responses, .NET Web services include their own proxy-like functionality. However, this functionality is provided by the .NET Framework, rather than being contained in a physical file (as is the proxy for the client).

It is important to note that the .NET environment hides from the programmer most of the details we have just discussed. Many aspects of Web service creation and consumption—such as generating WSDL, ASMX files, proxy classes and DISCO files—are handled by Visual Studio .NET and ASP .NET. Although developers are relieved of the tedious process of creating these files, they can still modify the files if necessary.

20.8 Simple Object Access Protocol (SOAP) and Web Services

The *Simple Object Access Protocol (SOAP)* is a platform-independent protocol that uses XML to make remote-procedure calls over HTTP. Each request and response is packaged in a *SOAP message*—an XML message that contains all the information necessary to process its contents. SOAP messages are quite popular, because they are written in the easy-to-understand and platform-independent XML. Similarly, HTTP was chosen to transmit SOAP messages, because HTTP is a standard protocol for sending information across the Internet. The use of XML and HTTP enables different operating systems to send and receive SOAP messages. Another benefit of HTTP is that it can be used with networks that contain *firewalls*—security barriers that restrict communication among networks.

SOAP supports an extensive set of data types. Readers should note that the wire format used to transmit requests and responses must support all data types passed between the applications. Web services that use SOAP support a wider variety of data types than do Web services that employ other wire formats. The data types supported by SOAP include most basic data types (such as `int`), plus `DataSet`, `DateTime`, `XmlNode` and several others. SOAP also permits the transmission of arrays of all these types. In addition, user-defined types can be used—we demonstrate how to do this in Section 20.13.

Applications send requests and responses to and from Web services via SOAP. When a program invokes a Web-service method, the request and all relevant information are packaged in a SOAP message and sent to the appropriate destination. When the Web service receives the SOAP message, it begins to process the contents (contained in *SOAP envelope*), which specify the method that the client wishes to execute and any arguments the client is passing to that method. After the Web service receives this request and parses it, the proper method is called with the specified arguments (if there are any), and the response is sent back to the client in another SOAP message. The client parses the response to retrieve the result of the method call.

The SOAP request portrayed in Fig. 20.11 was taken directly from the `Bigger` method of the `HugeInteger` Web service (Fig. 20.7). This Web service provides programmers with several methods that manipulate integers larger than those that can be stored in a `long` variable. Most programmers do not manipulate SOAP messages, but instead allow the Web service to handle the details of transmission.

```
POST /HugeIntegerWebService/HugeInteger.asmx HTTP/1.1
Host: localhost
Content-Type: text/xml; charset=utf-8
Content-Length: length
SOAPAction: "http://www.deitel.com/ch20/Bigger"

<?xml version="1.0" encoding="utf-8"?>

<soap:Envelope
   xmlns:xsi="http://www.w3.org/2001/XMLSchema-instance"
   xmlns:xsd="http://www.w3.org/2001/XMLSchema"
   xmlns:soap="http://schemas.xmlsoap.org/soap/envelope/">

   <soap:Body>
      <Bigger xmlns="http://www.deitel.com/ch20/">
         <first>string</first>
         <second>string</second>
      </Bigger>
   </soap:Body>

</soap:Envelope>
```

Fig. 20.11 SOAP request for the `HugeInteger` Web service.

Figure 20.11 displays a standard SOAP request that is created when a client wishes to execute the `HugeInteger` Web service's method `Bigger`. When a request to a Web service causes such a SOAP request to be created, the elements `first` and `second`'s character data (`strings`) would contain the actual values that the user entered (lines 16–17). If this envelope contained the request from Fig. 20.7, element `first` and element `second` would contain the values entered in Fig. 20.7. Placeholder `length` (line 4) would contain the length of this SOAP message.

20.9 Publishing and Consuming Web Services

This section presents an example of creating (also known as *publishing*) and using (also known as *consuming*) a Web service. We will walk the reader through the creation of both a Web service and a Web service client. Figure 20.12 and Fig. 20.13 present the implementation files for the `HugeInteger` Web service (Fig. 20.5). The name of the Web service is based on the name of the class that defines it (in this case, `HugeInteger`). This Web service is designed to perform calculations with integers that contain a maximum of 100 digits. As we mentioned earlier, `long` variables cannot handle integers of this size (i.e., an overflow would occur). The Web service provides a client with methods that take two "huge integers" and determine which one is larger or smaller, whether the two numbers are equal, their sum or their difference. The reader can think of these methods as services that one application provides for the programmers of other applications (hence, the term "Web services"). Any programmer can access this Web service, use its methods and thus avoid writing over 200 lines of code.

```
// Fig. 20.12: HugeIntegerClass.h
// HugeInteger Web service.

#pragma once

using namespace System;
using namespace System::Web;
using namespace System::Web::Services;
using namespace System::Text;

namespace HugeInteger
{
   /// WARNING: If you change the name of this class, you will need to
   ///          change the 'Resource File Name' property for the managed
   ///          resource compiler tool associated with all .resx files
   ///          this class depends on.  Otherwise, the designers will not
   ///          be able to interact properly with localized resources
   ///          associated with this form.

   // performs operations on large integers
   [ WebServiceAttribute(
      Namespace = "http://www.deitel.com/ch20/HugeInteger",
      Description = "A Web service which provides methods that"
      " can manipulate large integer values." ) ]
```

Fig. 20.12 `HugeIntegerClass` header file. (Part 1 of 3.)

```
   public __gc
      class HugeIntegerClass : public System::Web::Services::WebService
   {

   public:
      HugeIntegerClass()
      {
         InitializeComponent();
         number = new int __gc[ MAXIMUM ];
      }
   protected:
      void Dispose(Boolean disposing)
      {
         if (disposing && components)
         {
            components->Dispose();
         }
         __super::Dispose(disposing);
      }

   private:
      /// <summary>
      /// Required designer variable.
      /// </summary>
      System::ComponentModel::Container * components;

      /// <summary>
      /// Required method for Designer support - do not modify
      /// the contents of this method with the code editor.
      /// </summary>
      void InitializeComponent()
      {
      }

   public:

      int number __gc[];

      // indexed property that accepts an integer parameter
      __property int get_Index( int index )
      {
         return number[ index ];
      }

      __property void set_Index( int index, int value )
      {
         number[ index ] = value;
      }

      String *ToString();

      HugeIntegerClass *FromString( String *integer );

```

Fig. 20.12 HugeIntegerClass header file. (Part 2 of 3.)

```
      [ WebMethod( Description = "Adds two huge integers." ) ]
      String *Add( String *first, String *second );

      [ WebMethod ( Description = "Subtracts two huge integers." ) ]
      String *Subtract( String *first, String *second );

      [ WebMethod( Description = "Determines whether the first"
         "integer is larger than the second integer." ) ]
      bool Bigger( String *first, String *second );

      [ WebMethod( Description = "Determines whether the"
         "first integer is smaller than the second integer." ) ]
      bool Smaller( String *first, String *second );

      [ WebMethod( Description = "Determines whether the"
         "first integer is equal to the second integer." ) ]
      bool EqualTo( String *first, String *second );

   private:
      static const int MAXIMUM = 100;
      void Borrow( HugeIntegerClass *integer, int place );
   };
}
```

Fig. 20.12 `HugeIntegerClass` header file. (Part 3 of 3.)

```
// Fig. 20.13: HugeIntegerClass.cpp
// HugeInteger Web service.

#include "stdafx.h"
#include "HugeIntegerClass.h"
#include "Global.asax.h"

namespace HugeInteger
{
   // returns String * representation of HugeIntegerClass
   String *HugeIntegerClass::ToString()
   {
      StringBuilder *returnString = new StringBuilder();

      int digit;

      for ( int i = 0; i < number->Length; i++ ) {
         digit = number[ i ];

         returnString->Insert( 0, digit );
      } // end for

      return returnString->ToString();
   } // end method ToString

```

Fig. 20.13 `HugeInteger` Web service. (Part 1 of 4.)

```
   // creates HugeIntegerClass based on argument
   HugeIntegerClass *HugeIntegerClass::FromString( String *integer )
   {
      HugeIntegerClass *parsedInteger = new HugeIntegerClass();

      for ( int i = 0; i < integer->Length; i++ )
         parsedInteger->Index[ i ] = Int32::Parse( integer->
            Chars[ integer->Length - i - 1 ].ToString() );

      return parsedInteger;
   } // end method FromString

   // WebMethod that performs integer addition
   // represented by string * arguments
   String *HugeIntegerClass::Add( String *first, String *second )
   {
      int carry = 0;

      HugeIntegerClass *operand1 = FromString( first );
      HugeIntegerClass *operand2 = FromString( second );

      // store result of addition
      HugeIntegerClass *result = new HugeIntegerClass();

      // perform addition algorithm for each digit
      for ( int i = 0; i < MAXIMUM; i++ ) {

         // add two digits in same columnresult is their sum,
         // plus carry from previous operation modulus 10
         result->Index[ i ] = ( operand1->Index[ i ] +
            operand2->Index[ i ] + carry ) % 10;

         // store remainder of dividing sums of two digits by 10
         carry = ( operand1->Index[ i ] + operand2->Index[ i ]
            + carry ) / 10;
      } // end for

      return result->ToString();
   } // end method Add

   // WebMethod that performs the subtraction of integers
   // represented by String * arguments
   String *HugeIntegerClass::Subtract( String *first, String *second )
   {
      HugeIntegerClass *operand1 = FromString( first );
      HugeIntegerClass *operand2 = FromString( second );
      HugeIntegerClass *result = new HugeIntegerClass();

      // subtract top digit from bottom digit
      for ( int i = 0; i < MAXIMUM; i++ ) {

```

Fig. 20.13 HugeInteger Web service. (Part 2 of 4.)

```
         // if top digit is smaller than bottom
         // digit we need to borrow
         if ( operand1->Index[ i ] < operand2->Index[ i ] )
            Borrow( operand1, i );

         // subtract bottom from top
         result->Index[ i ] = operand1->Index[ i ] - operand2->Index[ i ];
      } // end for

      return result->ToString();
   } // end method Subtract

   // borrows 1 from next digit
   void HugeIntegerClass::Borrow( HugeIntegerClass *integer, int place )
   {
      // if no place to borrow from, signal problem
      if ( place >= MAXIMUM - 1 )
         throw new ArgumentException();

      // otherwise if next digit is zero, borrow left digit
      else if ( integer->Index[ place + 1 ] == 0 )
         Borrow( integer, place + 1 );

      // add ten to current place because we borrowed and
      // subtract one from previous digit
      // - this is digit borrowed from
      integer->Index[ place ] += 10;
      integer->Index[ place + 1 ] -= 1;
   } // end method Borrow

   // WebMethod that returns true if first integer is bigger than second
   bool HugeIntegerClass::Bigger( String *first, String *second )
   {
      __wchar_t zeroes __gc[] = { '0' };

      try {

         // if elimination of all zeroes from result
         // of subtraction is an empty string, numbers are equal,
         // so return false, otherwise return true
         if ( Subtract( first, second )->Trim( zeroes ) == "" )
            return false;
         else
            return true;
      } // end try

      // if ArgumentException occurs, first number
      // was smaller, so return false
      catch ( ArgumentException * ) {
         return false;
      } // end catch
   } // end method Bigger

```

Fig. 20.13 HugeInteger Web service. (Part 3 of 4.)

```
    // WebMethod returns true if first integer is
    // smaller than second
    bool HugeIntegerClass::Smaller( String *first, String *second )
    {
       // if second is bigger than first, then first is
       // smaller than second
       return Bigger( second, first );
    } // end method Smaller

    // WebMethod that returns true if two integers are equal
    bool HugeIntegerClass::EqualTo( String *first, String *second )
    {
       // if either first is bigger than second, or first is
       // smaller than second, they are not equal
       if ( Bigger( first, second ) || Smaller( first, second ) )
          return false;
       else
          return true;
    } // end method EqualTo
};
```

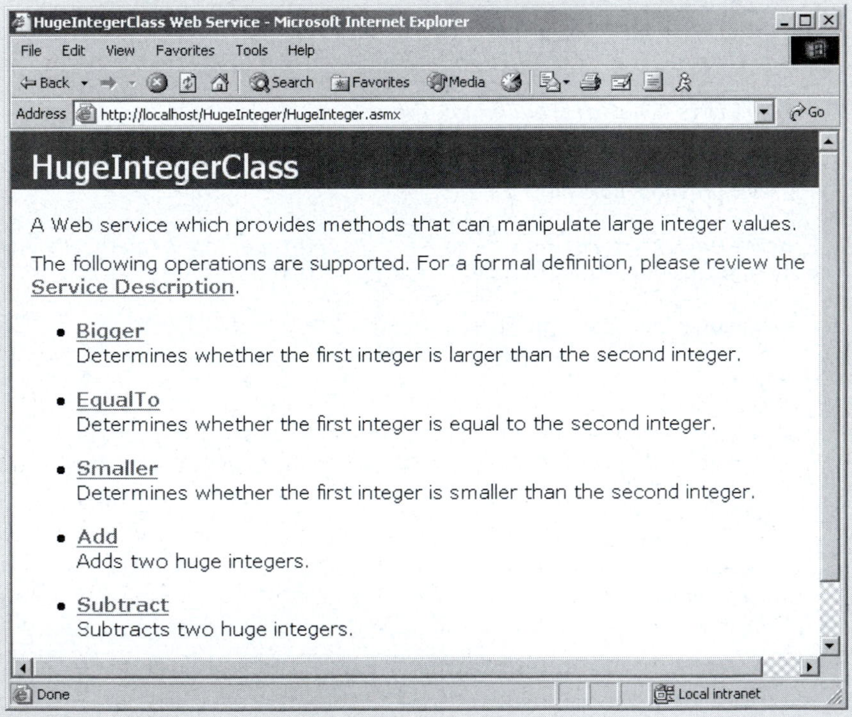

Fig. 20.13 `HugeInteger` Web service. (Part 4 of 4.)

In Fig. 20.12, line 22 assigns the Web service namespace to `www.deitel.com/ch20/HugeInteger`, to identify this Web service uniquely. The namespace is specified via the *`Namespace`* property of attribute *`WebServiceAttribute`*. Each Web service has a default namespace (`http://tempuri.org`), which is adequate for testing, but should be replaced before the Web service is deployed in real-world situations. In lines 23–24, we use property *`Description`* to provide information about our Web service that appears in the ASMX file. Line 26 specifies that our class derives from *`WebService`* (located in namespace *`System::Web::Services`*). By default, Visual Studio .NET defines our Web service so that it inherits from the `WebService` class. Although a Web-service class is not required to subclass `WebService`, class `WebService` provides members that are useful for obtaining information about the client and about the Web service itself. For instance, class `WebService` contains a `Session` object, which we will use later to store a user's information between Web service method calls. Several methods in class `HugeInteger` are tagged with *`WebMethod`* attributes, which *expose* the methods so that they can be called remotely. When this attribute is absent, the method is not accessible through the Web service. Notice that the `WebMethod` attribute, like attribute `WebServiceAttribute`, contains a `Description` property, which provides to the ASMX page information about the method. Readers can see these descriptions in the output of Fig. 20.13.

Good Programming Practice 20.1

Specify a namespace (e.g., a URL) for each Web service so that it can be uniquely identified.

Good Programming Practice 20.2

Specify descriptions for all Web services and Web-service methods so that clients can obtain additional information about the Web service and its contents.

Common Programming Error 20.1

Attempting to call a remote method from a Web service if the method is not declared with the `WebMethod` attribute is a compilation error.

Common Programming Error 20.2

Web-service methods cannot be declared `static`, or a compilation error occurs. For a client to access a Web-service method, an instance of that Web service must exist.

Lines 64–72 (Fig. 20.12) define an indexed property for our class. This enables us to access any digit in `HugeInteger` as if we were accessing it through array `number`. Lines 40–64 and 68–87 (Fig. 20.13) define `WebMethods` `Add` and `Subtract`, which perform addition and subtraction, respectively. Method `Borrow` (lines 90–105) handles the case in which the digit in the left operand is smaller than the corresponding digit in the right operand. For instance, when we subtract 19 from 32, we usually go digit by digit, starting from the right. The number 2 is smaller than 9, so we add 10 to 2 (resulting in 12), which subtracts 9, resulting in 3 for the rightmost digit in the solution. We then subtract 1 from the next digit over (3), making it 2. The corresponding digit in the right operand is now the "1" in 19. The subtraction of 1 from 2 is 1, making the corresponding digit in the result 1. The final result, when both resulting digits are combined, is 13. Method `Borrow` adds 10 to the appropriate digit and subtracts 1 from the digit to its left. This is a utility method that is not intended to be called remotely, so it is not qualified with attribute `WebMethod`.

The screen capture in Fig. 20.13 is identical to the one in Fig. 20.5. A client application can invoke only the five methods listed in the screen shot (i.e., the methods qualified with the `WebMethod` attribute).

Now, let us demonstrate how to create this Web service. To begin, we must create a project of type **ASP .NET Web Service**. By default, Web services are placed in the Web server's `wwwroot` directory on the server (`localhost`).

Visual Studio .NET generates a header file and a `.cpp` file named after the project. The Web service is defined in a namespace named after the project. The class in the header file is named `Class1` by default, but we changed this to the more descriptive `HugeInteger-Class`. The `.cpp` file contains a sample method `HelloWorld`. We replaced this method with our own code for the `HugeInteger` project. Note that the ASMX file contains only the line:

```
<%@ WebService Class=HugeInteger.HugeIntegerClass %>
```

indicating the class that defines our Web service.[5] This is the extent of the information that this file must contain.

Creating a Client to Consume the Web Service

Now that we have defined our Web service, we demonstrate how to use it. First, a client application must be created. In this first example, we create a Windows application as our client. Once this application has been created, the client must add a proxy class for accessing the Web service. Recall that a proxy class (or proxy) is a class created from the Web service's WSDL file that enables the client to call Web-service methods over the Internet. The proxy class handles all the "plumbing" required for Web-service method calls. Whenever a call is made in the client application to a Web-service method, the application actually calls a corresponding method in the proxy class. This method takes the name of the method and its arguments; it then formats them so that they can be sent as a request in a SOAP message. The Web service receives this request and executes the method call, sending back the result as another SOAP message. When the client application receives the SOAP message containing the response, the proxy class decodes it and formats the results so that they are understandable to the client. This information then is returned to the client. It is important to note that the proxy class essentially is hidden from the programmer. We cannot view it in the **Solution Explorer**. The purpose of the proxy class is to make it seem to clients that they are calling the Web-service methods directly. It is rarely necessary for the client to view or manipulate the proxy class.

The next example demonstrates how to create a Web-service client and its corresponding proxy class. We must begin by creating a project and adding a Web reference to that project. For simplicity, all our applications are MC++ applications. When we add a Web reference to a client application, the proxy class is created. The client then creates an instance of the proxy class, which is used to call methods included in the Web service.

To create a proxy class in Visual Studio .NET, right click the **References** folder in **Solution Explorer** and select **Add Web Reference...** (Fig. 20.14). In the **Add Web Reference** dialog that appears (Fig. 20.15), click **Web services on the local machine**. This will locate any web references stored on the local Web server (`http://localhost`, whose physical path is `C:\Inetpub\wwwroot`). Select the `HugeInteger` Web service from the list of available Web services (Fig. 20.16). We now can add the Web reference by

5. The <%@ and %> symbols delimit an *ASP directive*. An ASP directive sets the environment used by the ASP script by assigning values to keywords (e.g., assigning the class name to keyword `Class`).

entering `HugeInteger` in the textbox labeled **Web reference name:** and clicking the button **Add Reference** (Fig. 20.17). This adds `WebService.h`, a WSDL file and the proxy class `HugeInteger.h` to the **Solution Explorer** (Fig. 20.18). The header file `WebService.h` contains `#include` directives for the proxy class. The programmer should include `WebService.h` explicitly via `#include` to use the proxy class.

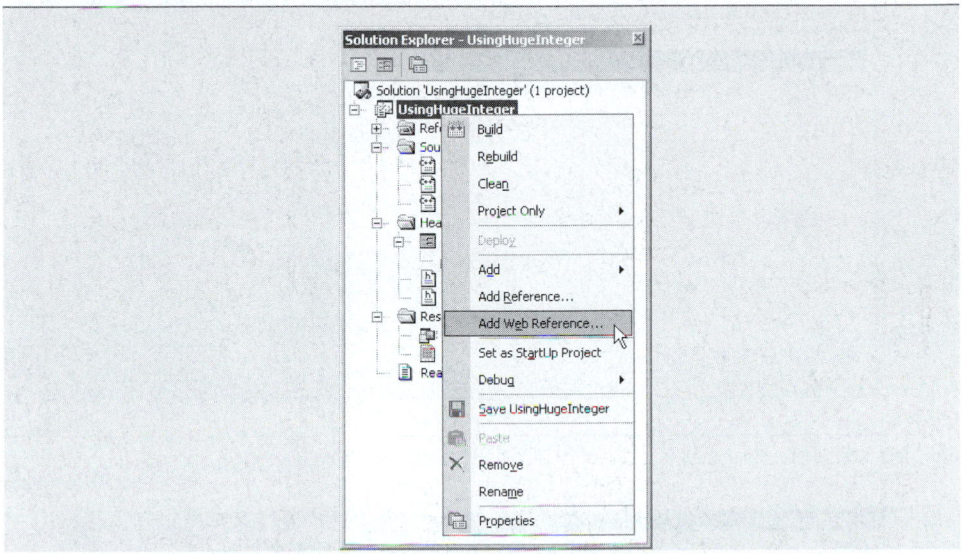

Fig. 20.14 Adding a Web-service reference to a project.

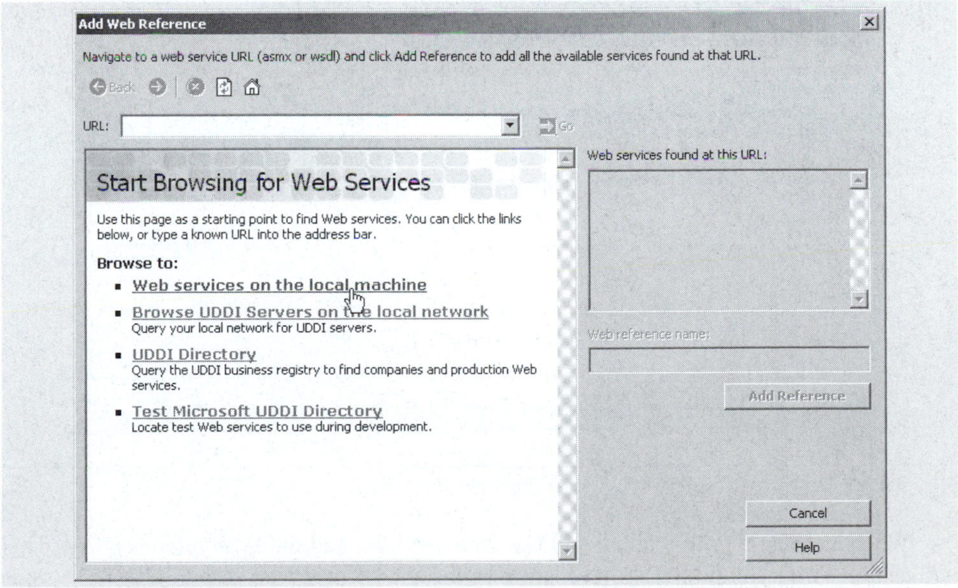

Fig. 20.15 **Add Web Reference** dialog.

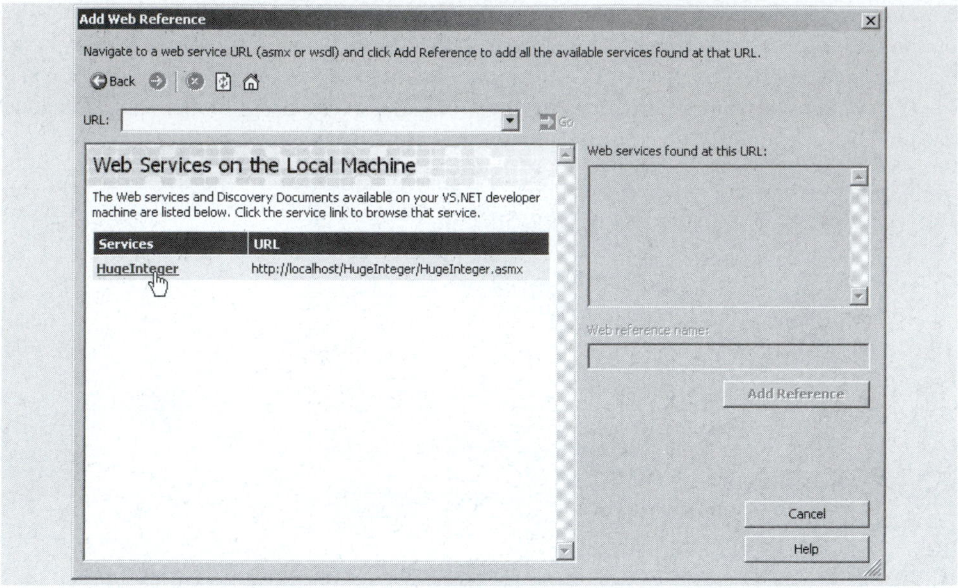

Fig. 20.16 Web services located on `localhost`.

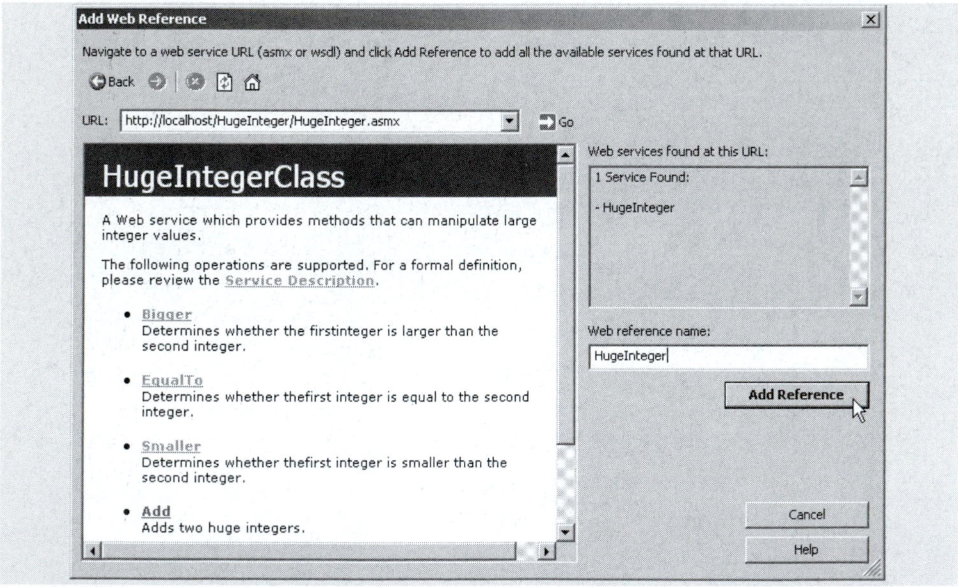

Fig. 20.17 Web reference selection and description.

When creating a program that will use Web services, add the Web reference first. This will enable Visual Studio .NET to recognize an instance of the Web-service class. The steps that we described previously work well if the programmer knows the appropriate Web-services reference. However, what if we are trying to locate a new Web service? There are a few

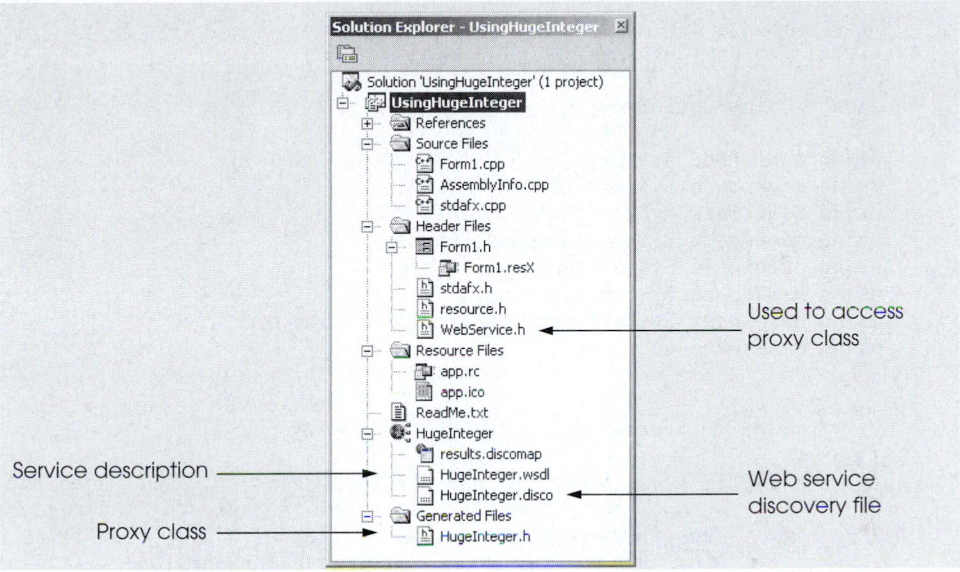

Fig. 20.18 **Solution Explorer** after adding a Web reference to a project.

technologies that facilitate this process. Two common technologies are: *Universal Description, Discovery and Integration* (*UDDI*) and Discovery files (DISCO). We discussed DISCO in Section 20.7.[6] UDDI is an ongoing project for developing a set of specifications that define how Web services should be published so that programmers searching for Web services can find them. Microsoft and its partners are working on this ongoing project to help programmers at various companies locate Web services that conform to certain specifications, allowing developers to find different Web services through search engines. UDDI describes Web services; it then organizes this information in a central location. Although UDDI is beyond the scope of what we are teaching, you can learn more about this project and view a demonstration by visiting `www.uddi.org` and `uddi.microsoft.com`. These sites contain search tools that make finding Web services fast and easy.

Once the Web reference is added, the client can access the Web service through our proxy. The application in Fig. 20.19–Fig. 20.20 uses the `HugeInteger` Web service to perform computations with positive integers up to `100` digits long. [*Note*: If using the example downloaded from `www.deitel.com`, the reader might need to regenerate the proxy. This action can be performed by right-clicking the WSDL file in the **Solution Explorer** and selecting option **Update Web Reference**.]

```
// Fig. 20.19: Form1.h
// Using the HugeInteger Web service.

#pragma once
```

Fig. 20.19 Using the `HugeInteger` Web service. (Part 1 of 5.)

6. One newer discovery technology, WS-Inspection, will be discussed in detail in Section 20.14.1.

```

#include "WebService.h"

namespace UsingHugeInteger
{
   using namespace System;
   using namespace System::ComponentModel;
   using namespace System::Collections;
   using namespace System::Windows::Forms;
   using namespace System::Data;
   using namespace System::Drawing;
   using namespace System::Web::Services::Protocols;
   using namespace HugeInteger;

   /// <summary>
   /// Summary for Form1
   ///
   /// WARNING: If you change the name of this class, you will need to
   ///          change the 'Resource File Name' property for the managed
   ///          resource compiler tool associated with all .resx files
   ///          this class depends on.  Otherwise, the designers will not
   ///          be able to interact properly with localized resources
   ///          associated with this form.
   /// </summary>
   public __gc class Form1 : public System::Windows::Forms::Form
   {
   public:
      Form1(void)
      {
         InitializeComponent();

         // instantiate remoteInteger
         remoteInteger = new HugeIntegerClass();
      }

   protected:
      void Dispose(Boolean disposing)
      {
         if (disposing && components)
         {
            components->Dispose();
         }
         __super::Dispose(disposing);
      }
   private: System::Windows::Forms::Label *  promptLabel;
   private: System::Windows::Forms::TextBox *  firstTextBox;
   private: System::Windows::Forms::TextBox *  secondTextBox;
   private: System::Windows::Forms::Button *  addButton;
   private: System::Windows::Forms::Button *  subtractButton;
   private: System::Windows::Forms::Button *  biggerButton;
   private: System::Windows::Forms::Button *  smallerButton;
   private: System::Windows::Forms::Button *  equalButton;
   private: System::Windows::Forms::Label *  resultLabel;
```

Fig. 20.19 Using the `HugeInteger` Web service. (Part 2 of 5.)

```

   // declare a pointer to a Web service
   private: HugeIntegerClass *remoteInteger;

   private: static __wchar_t zeroes __gc[] = { '0' };

   private:
      /// <summary>
      /// Required designer variable.
      /// </summary>
      System::ComponentModel::Container * components;

   // Visual Studio .NET generated GUI code

   // checks whether two numbers user input are equal
   private: System::Void equalButton_Click(
            System::Object *  sender, System::EventArgs *  e)
         {
            // make sure HugeIntegers do not exceed 100 digits
            if ( CheckSize( firstTextBox, secondTextBox ) )
               return;

            // call Web-service method to determine
            // whether integers are equal
            if ( remoteInteger->EqualTo(
               firstTextBox->Text, secondTextBox->Text ) )

               resultLabel->Text = String::Concat(
                  firstTextBox->Text->TrimStart( zeroes ),
                  S" is equal to ",
                  secondTextBox->Text->TrimStart( zeroes ) );

            else
               resultLabel->Text = String::Concat(
                  firstTextBox->Text->TrimStart( zeroes ),
                  S" is NOT equal to ",
                  secondTextBox->Text->TrimStart( zeroes ) );
         } // end method equalButton_Click

   // checks whether first integer input by user is smaller than second
   private: System::Void smallerButton_Click(
            System::Object *  sender, System::EventArgs *  e)
         {
            // make sure HugeIntegers do not exceed 100 digits
            if ( CheckSize( firstTextBox, secondTextBox ) )
               return;

            // call Web-service method to determine whether first
            // integer is smaller than second
            if ( remoteInteger->Smaller(
               firstTextBox->Text, secondTextBox->Text ) )

```

Fig. 20.19 Using the `HugeInteger` Web service. (Part 3 of 5.)

```
                resultLabel->Text = String::Concat(
                   firstTextBox->Text->TrimStart( zeroes ),
                   S" is smaller than ",
                   secondTextBox->Text->TrimStart( zeroes ) );
             else
                resultLabel->Text = String::Concat(
                   firstTextBox->Text->TrimStart( zeroes ),
                   S" is NOT smaller than ",
                   secondTextBox->Text->TrimStart( zeroes ) );
          } // end method smallerButton_Click

   // checks whether first integer input by user is bigger than second
   private: System::Void biggerButton_Click(
             System::Object *  sender, System::EventArgs *  e)
          {
             // make sure HugeIntegers do not exceed 100 digits
             if ( CheckSize( firstTextBox, secondTextBox ) )
                return;

             // call Web-service method to determine whether first
             // integer is larger than the second
             if ( remoteInteger->Bigger(
                firstTextBox->Text, secondTextBox->Text ) )

                resultLabel->Text = String::Concat(
                   firstTextBox->Text->TrimStart( zeroes ),
                   S" is larger than ",
                   secondTextBox->Text->TrimStart( zeroes ) );
             else
                resultLabel->Text = String::Concat(
                   firstTextBox->Text->TrimStart( zeroes ),
                   S" is NOT larger than ",
                   secondTextBox->Text->TrimStart( zeroes ) );
          } // end method biggerButton_Click

   // subtract second integer from first
   private: System::Void subtractButton_Click(
             System::Object *  sender, System::EventArgs *  e)
          {
             // make sure HugeIntegers do not exceed 100 digits
             if ( CheckSize( firstTextBox, secondTextBox ) )
                return;

             // perform subtraction
             try {
                String *result = remoteInteger->Subtract(
                   firstTextBox->Text,
                   secondTextBox->Text )->TrimStart( zeroes );

                resultLabel->Text =
                   ( ( result == S"" ) ? S"0" : result );
             } // end try

```

Fig. 20.19 Using the `HugeInteger` Web service. (Part 4 of 5.)

```
                  // if WebMethod throws an exception, then first
                  // argument was smaller than second
                  catch( SoapException * ) {
                     MessageBox::Show(
                        S"First argument was smaller than the second" );
                  } // end try
               } // end method subtractButton_Click

      // adds two integers input by user
      private: System::Void addButton_Click(
                  System::Object *  sender, System::EventArgs *  e)
               {
                  // make sure HugeInteger does not exceed 100 digits
                  // and is not situation where both integers are 100
                  // digits long--result in overflow
                  if ( firstTextBox->Text->Length > 100 ||
                     secondTextBox->Text->Length > 100 ||
                     ( firstTextBox->Text->Length == 100 &&
                     secondTextBox->Text->Length == 100 ) ) {
                     MessageBox::Show( String::Concat(
                        S"HugeIntegers must not be more ",
                        S"than 100 digits\nBoth integers cannot be of",
                        S" length 100: this causes an overflow",
                        S"Error", MessageBoxButtons::OK,
                        MessageBoxIcon::Information ) );

                     return;
                  } // end if

                  // perform addition
                  resultLabel->Text = remoteInteger->Add( firstTextBox->Text,
                     secondTextBox->Text )->TrimStart( zeroes )->ToString();
               } // end method addButton_Click

      private:

         // determines whether size of integers is too big
         bool CheckSize( TextBox *first, TextBox *second )
         {
            if ( first->Text->Length > 100 || second->Text->Length > 100 ) {
               MessageBox::Show( String::Concat( S"HugeIntegers must ",
                  S"be no more than 100 digits" ), S"Error",
                  MessageBoxButtons::OK, MessageBoxIcon::Information );
               return true;
            } // end if

            return false;
         } // end method CheckSize
      };
   }
```

Fig. 20.19 Using the `HugeInteger` Web service. (Part 5 of 5.)

```cpp
// Fig. 20.20: Form1.cpp
// Entry point for application.

#include "stdafx.h"
#include "Form1.h"
#include <windows.h>

using namespace UsingHugeInteger;

int APIENTRY _tWinMain(HINSTANCE hInstance,
                       HINSTANCE hPrevInstance,
                       LPTSTR    lpCmdLine,
                       int       nCmdShow)
{
   System::Threading::Thread::CurrentThread->ApartmentState =
      System::Threading::ApartmentState::STA;
   Application::Run(new Form1());
   return 0;
} // end _tWinMain
```

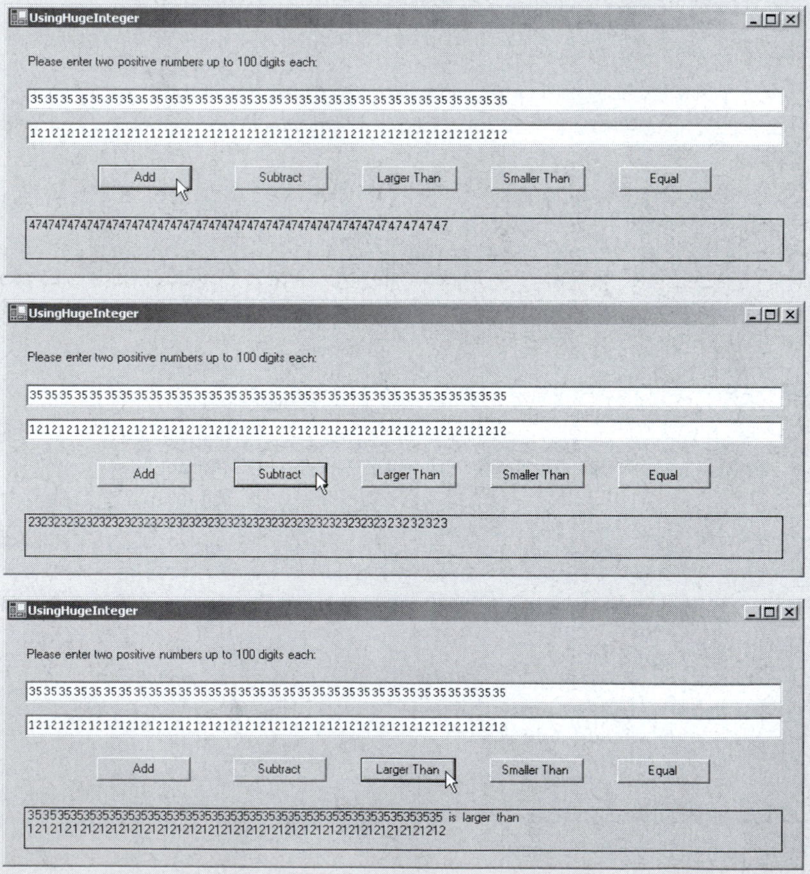

Fig. 20.20 `HugeInteger` Web-service demonstration.

The user inputs two integers, each up to 100 digits long. Clicking a button invokes a remote method to perform the appropriate calculation and return the result. The return value of each operation is displayed, and all leading zeroes are eliminated via `String` method `TrimStart`. Note that `UsingHugeInteger` does not have the capability to perform operations with 100-digit numbers. Instead, it creates `String *` representations of these numbers and passes them as arguments to Web-service methods that handle such tasks for us.

Line 6 of Fig. 20.19 includes our `WebService.h` header file. Line 37 of Fig. 20.19 instantiates `remoteInteger`, an instance of the proxy class (defined in `HugeInteger.h`, which is included in `WebService.h`). Method `equalButton_Click` (lines 73–95) uses `remoteInteger` to call Web-service method `EqualTo` to determine whether the integers are equal. Methods `smallerButton_Click` (lines 98–119), `biggerButton_Click` (lines 122–143), `subtractButton_Click` (lines 146–169) and `addButton_Click` (lines 172–195) invoke Web-service methods `Smaller` (lines 107–108), `Bigger` (lines 131–132), `Subtract` (lines 155–157) and `Add` (line 193–194) using `remoteInteger`.

20.10 Session Tracking

Originally, critics accused the Internet and e-businesses of failing to provide the customized services typically experienced in brick-and-mortar stores. To address this problem, e-businesses began to establish mechanisms by which they could personalize users' browsing experiences, tailoring content to individual users while enabling them to bypass irrelevant information. Businesses achieve this level of service by tracking each customer's movement through the Internet and combining the collected data with information that the consumer provides, including billing information, personal preferences, interests and hobbies.

Personalization makes it possible for e-businesses to communicate effectively with their customers and improves users' ability to locate desired products and services. Companies that provide content of particular interest to users can establish relationships with customers and build on those relationships over time. Futhermore, by targeting consumers with personal offers, advertisements, promotions and services, e-businesses create customer loyalty. At Web sites such as `MSN.com` and `CNN.com`, sophisticated technology allows visitors to customize home pages to suit their individual needs and preferences. Similarly, online shopping sites often store personal information for customers and target them with notifications and special offers tailored to their interests. Such services can create customer bases that visit sites more frequently and make purchases from those sites more regularly.

A trade-off exists, however, between personalized e-business service and *privacy protection*. Whereas some consumers embrace the idea of tailored content, others fear the release of information that they provide to e-businesses or that is collected about them by tracking technologies will have adverse consequences on their lives. Consumers and privacy advocates ask: What if the e-businesses to which we give personal data sell or give that information to other organizations without our knowledge? What if we do not want our actions on the Internet—a supposedly anonymous medium—to be tracked and recorded by unknown parties? What if unauthorized parties gain access to sensitive private data, such as credit-card numbers or medical history? All these are questions that must be debated and addressed by consumers, e-businesses and lawmakers, alike.

To provide personalized services to consumers, e-businesses must be able to recognize specific clients when they request information from a site. As we have discussed, HTTP enables the request/response system on which the Web operates. Unfortunately, HTTP is a stateless protocol—it does not support persistent connections that would enable Web servers to maintain state information for particular clients. This means that Web servers have no capacity to determine whether a request comes from a particular client or whether the same or different clients generate a series of requests. To circumvent this problem, sites such as `MSN.com` and `CNN.com` provide mechanisms by which they identify individual clients. A *session ID* represents a unique client on the Internet. If the client leaves a site and later returns, the client will be recognized as the same user. To help the server distinguish among clients, each client must identify itself to the server. The tracking of individual clients, known as *session tracking*, can be achieved in one of a number of ways. One popular technique uses cookies (Section 20.10.1); another employs .NET's `HttpSessionState` object (Section 20.10.2). Additional session-tracking techniques include the use of hidden form elements and URL rewriting. Using hidden form elements, the application writes its session-tracking data into a form in the Web page that it returns to the client in response to a prior request. When the user submits the form in the new Web page, all the form data, including the hidden fields, are sent to the form handler on the Web server. When a Web site employs URL rewriting, the site embeds session-tracking information directly in the URLs of the hyperlinks that the user clicks to send subsequent requests to the Web server.

20.10.1 Cookies

A popular way to customize Web pages for particular users is via *cookies*. A cookie is a text file that a Web site stores on an individual's computer to enable the site to track that individual's actions and preferences. The first time a user visits the Web site, the user's computer might receive a cookie that contains a unique identifier for that user. This cookie is reactivated each subsequent time the user visits that site. The Web site uses this cookie to identify the user and to store information, such as the user's zip code or other data that might facilitate the distribution of user-specific content. The collected information is intended to be an anonymous record for personalizing the user's future visits to the site. Cookies in a shopping application might store unique identifiers for users. When a user performs a task resulting in a request to the Web server, such as adding items to an online shopping cart, the server receives a cookie containing the user's unique identifier. The server then uses the unique identifier to locate the user's shopping cart and perform any necessary processing.

In addition to identifying users, cookies also can indicate a client's preferences. When a Web application receives a communication from a client, the application could examine the cookie(s) it sent to the client during previous communications, identify the client's preferences and immediately display products that are of interest to the client.

Every HTTP-based interaction between a client and a server includes a header that contains information either about the request (when the communication is from the client to the server) or about the response (when the communication is from the server to the client). When a Web application receives a request, the header includes such information as the request type (e.g., `GET`) and any cookies that the server has stored on the client machine. When the server formulates its response, the header information includes any cookies that the server wants to store on the client computer, as well as such information as the MIME type of the response.

Programmers can set an *expiration date* for a cookie—the Web browser maintains the cookie until the expiration date. The expiration date of a cookie can be set via the cookie's

`Expires` property of class `HttpCookie`, which is used to implement cookies in .NET. When the browser requests a resource from a Web server, cookies previously sent to the client by that Web server are returned to the Web server as part of the request. Cookies are deleted when they expire. We summarize some commonly used `HttpCookie` properties in Fig. 20.21.

Properties	Description
`Domain`	A string that contains the cookie's domain (i.e., the domain of the Web server from which the cookie was downloaded). This determines which Web servers can receive the cookie. By default, cookies are sent to the Web server that originally sent the cookie to the client.
`Expires`	A `DateTime` object indicating when the browser can delete the cookie.
`Name`	A string containing the cookie's name.
`Path`	A string containing the URL prefix for the cookie. Cookies can be "targeted" to specific URLs that include directories on the Web server, enabling the programmer to specify the location of the cookie. By default, a cookie is returned to services that operate in the same directory as the service that sent the cookie or a subdirectory of that directory.
`Secure`	A boolean value indicating whether the cookie should be transmitted using a secure protocol.
`Value`	A string containing the cookie's value.

Fig. 20.21 `HttpCookie` properties.

20.10.2 Session Tracking with `HttpSessionState`

The .NET Framework provides session-tracking capabilities with the `HttpSessionState` class. Every Web-service application includes an `HttpSessionState` object, which is accessible through property `Session` of class `WebService`. When a Web service method is called, an `HttpSessionState` object is created and assigned to the Web service's `Session` property. We often refer to the property `Session` as the `Session` object.

Software Engineering Observation 20.3

Visual C++ .NET Web-based applications must not use data members to maintain client-state information, because clients accessing that Web application in parallel might overwrite the shared data members. Web applications should maintain client-state information in `HttpSessionState` objects, because such objects are specific to each client.

An `HttpSessionState` object can store key-value pairs, where the key contains the name of a session attribute, and the value contains that attribute's value. In session terminology, these are called *session items*, and they are placed into an `HttpSessionState` object by calling method `Add`. One of the primary benefits of using `HttpSessionState` objects is that `HttpSessionState` objects can store any type of object as an attribute value. This provides programmers with increased flexibility in determining the type of state information they wish to maintain for their clients. If the application calls method `Add` to add an attribute that has the same name as an attribute previously stored in a session, the object associated with that attribute is replaced.

Figure 20.22 lists some common `HttpSessionState` properties. Property *`SessionID`* contains the *session's unique ID*. The first time a client connects to the Web server, the Web server generates the client's session ID. Property *`Timeout`* specifies the maximum amount of time that an `HttpSessionState` object can be inactive before it is discarded.

Properties	Description
`Count`	The number of key-value pairs in the `Session` object.
`IsNewSession`	Indicates whether this is a new session (i.e., whether the session was created when the page was loaded).
`IsReadOnly`	Indicates whether the `Session` object is read-only.
`Keys`	A collection containing the `Session` object's keys.
`SessionID`	The session's unique ID.
`Timeout`	The maximum number of minutes during which a session can be inactive (i.e., no requests are made) before the session expires. By default, this property is set to 20 minutes.

Fig. 20.22 `HttpSessionState` properties.

20.11 Session Tracking in Web Services

In this section, we incorporate session tracking into a Web service. Sometimes, it makes sense for client applications to call several methods from the same Web service or to call some methods several times. It would be beneficial for the Web service to maintain state information for the client. Using session tracking can be helpful, because information that is stored as part of the session will not need to be passed back and forth between the Web service and the client. This will not only cause the client application to run faster, but it will require less effort on the part of the programmer (who likely will have to pass less information to a Web-service method).

Storing session information also can provide for a more intuitive Web service. In the following example, we create a Web service designed to assist with the computations involved in playing a game of Blackjack (Fig. 20.23–Fig. 20.26). We then use this Web service to create a dealer for a game of Blackjack. This dealer handles the details for our deck of cards. The information is stored as part of the session, so that one set of cards does not get mixed up with another deck of cards being used by another client application. Our example uses the casino Blackjack rules that follow:

> *The dealer and the player each receive two cards. The player's cards are dealt face up. Only one of the dealer's cards is dealt face up. Then, the player can begin taking additional cards, one at a time. These cards are dealt face up, and the player decides when to stop taking cards. If the sum of the player's cards exceeds 21, the game is over, and the player loses. When the player is satisfied with the current set of cards, the player "stays" (i.e., stops taking cards), and the dealer's hidden card is revealed. If the dealer's total is less than 17, the dealer must take another card; otherwise, the dealer must stay. The dealer must continue to take cards until the sum of the dealer's cards is greater than or equal to 17. If the dealer exceeds 21, the player*

wins. Otherwise, the hand with the higher point total wins. If both sets of cards have the same point total, the game is a "push" (i.e., a tie), and no one wins. Finally, if a player's first two cards total 21, the player immediately wins. This type of win is known as a "Blackjack."

The Web service that we create provides methods to deal a card and to count cards in a hand, determining a value for a specific hand. Each card is represented by a string in the form "`face suit`," where `face` is a digit that represents the face of the card, and `suit` is a digit that represents the suit of the card. After the Web service is created, we create a Windows application that uses these methods to implement a game of Blackjack.

```
// Fig. 20.23: BlackjackClass.h
// Blackjack Web service which manipulates a deck of cards.

#pragma once

using namespace System;
using namespace System::Web;
using namespace System::Web::Services;

namespace Blackjack
{
   /// WARNING: If you change the name of this class, you will need to
   ///          change the 'Resource File Name' property for the managed
   ///          resource compiler tool associated with all .resx files
   ///          this class depends on.  Otherwise, the designers will not
   ///          be able to interact properly with localized resources
   ///          associated with this form.
   [ WebServiceAttribute(
      Namespace = "http://www.deitel.com/ch20/Blackjack",
      Description = "A Web service that provides methods "
      "to manipulate a deck of cards." ) ]
   public __gc
      class BlackjackClass : public System::Web::Services::WebService
   {

   public:
      BlackjackClass()
      {
         InitializeComponent();
      }
   protected:
      void Dispose(Boolean disposing)
      {
         if (disposing && components)
         {
            components->Dispose();
         }
         __super::Dispose(disposing);
      }

   private:
      /// <summary>
```

Fig. 20.23 `BlackjackClass` class header file. (Part 1 of 2.)

```
      /// Required designer variable.
      /// </summary>
      System::ComponentModel::Container * components;

      /// <summary>
      /// Required method for Designer support - do not modify
      /// the contents of this method with the code editor.
      /// </summary>
      void InitializeComponent()
      {
      }

   public:

      [ WebMethod( EnableSession = true,
         Description = "Deals the next card in the deck." ) ]
      String *DealCard();

      [ WebMethod( EnableSession = true,
         Description = "Create and shuffle a deck of cards." ) ]
      void Shuffle();

      [ WebMethod( Description = "Compute a "
         "numerical value for the current hand." ) ]
      int CountCards( String *dealt );
   };
}
```

Fig. 20.23 BlackjackClass class header file. (Part 2 of 2.)

```
// Fig. 20.24: BlackjackClass.cpp
// Blackjack Web service which manipulates a deck of cards.

#include "stdafx.h"
#include "BlackjackClass.h"
#include "Global.asax.h"

namespace Blackjack
{
   // deal new card
   String *BlackjackClass::DealCard()
   {
      String *card = S"2 2";

      // get client's deck
      ArrayList* deck = dynamic_cast< ArrayList* >(
         Session->Item[ S"deck" ] );
      card = Convert::ToString( deck->Item[ 0 ] );
      deck->RemoveAt( 0 );

      return card;
   } // end method DealCard
```

Fig. 20.24 Blackjack Web service. (Part 1 of 3.)

```
   void BlackjackClass::Shuffle()
   {
      Random *randomObject = new Random();

      ArrayList *deck = new ArrayList();

      // generate all possible cards
      for ( int i = 1; i < 14; i++ ) {

         for ( int j = 0; j < 4; j++ ) {
            deck->Add( String::Concat( Convert::ToString( i ),
               S" ", Convert::ToString( j ) ) );
         } // end for
      } // end for

      // swap each card with another card randomly
      for ( int i = 0; i < deck->Count; i++ ) {
         int newIndex = randomObject->Next( deck->Count );
         Object *temporary = deck->Item[ i ];
         deck->Item[ i ] = deck->Item[ newIndex ];
         deck->Item[ newIndex ] = temporary;
      } // end for

      // add this deck to user's session state
      Session->Item[ S"deck" ] = deck;
   } // end method Shuffle

   // computes value of hand
   int BlackjackClass::CountCards( String *dealt )
   {
      // split string containing cards
      __wchar_t tab __gc[] = { '\t' };
      String *cards[] = dealt->Split( tab );
      int total = 0, face, aceCount = 0;

      String *drawn;

      for ( int i = 0; i < cards->Length; i++ ) {
         drawn = cards[ i ];

         // get face of card
         face = Int32::Parse(
            drawn->Substring( 0, drawn->IndexOf( S" " ) ) );

         switch ( face ) {

            // if ace, increment number of aces in hand
            case 1:
               aceCount++;
               break;
```

Fig. 20.24 Blackjack Web service. (Part 2 of 3.)

```
            // if Jack, Queen or King, add 10 to total
            case 11: case 12: case 13:
               total += 10;
               break;

            // otherwise, add value of face
            default:
               total += face;
               break;
         } // end switch
      } // end for

      // if any aces, calculate optimum total
      if ( aceCount > 0 ) {

         // if it is possible to count one ace as 11, and rest
         // 1 each, do so; otherwise, count all aces as 1 each
         if ( total + 11 + aceCount - 1 <= 21 )
            total += 11 + aceCount - 1;
         else
            total += aceCount;
      } // end if

      return total;
   } // end method CountCards
};
```

Fig. 20.24 `Blackjack` Web service. (Part 3 of 3.)

Lines 57–59 of Fig. 20.23 declare method `DealCard` as a `WebMethod`, with property *`EnableSession`* set to `true` (line 57). This property needs to be set to `true` to maintain session information. This simple step provides an important advantage to our Web service. The Web service now can use the `HttpSessionState` object's property `Session` to maintain the deck of cards for each client application that wishes to use this Web service. We can use `Session` to store objects for a specific client between method calls.

As we will discuss shortly, method `DealCard` removes a card from the deck and returns it to the client. If we were not using a session variable, the deck of cards would need to be passed back and forth with each method call. Not only does the use of session state make the method easier to call (it now requires no arguments), but we avoid the overhead that would occur from sending this information back and forth, making our Web service faster.

In our current implementation, we simply have methods that use session variables. The Web service, however, still cannot ascertain which session variables belong to which user. This is an important point—if the Web service cannot uniquely identify a user, it has failed to perform session tracking properly. If the same client called method `DealCard` twice, two different decks would be manipulated (as if two different users had called `DealCard`). To identify various users, the Web service creates a cookie for each user. Unfortunately, the Web service has no way of determining whether cookies are enabled on the client's machine. If the client application wishes to use this Web service, the client must accept this cookie in a *`CookieContainer`* object. We discuss this more when we look into the client application that uses the `Blackjack` Web service.

Method DealCard (lines 11–22 of Fig. 20.24) obtains the current user's deck as an *ArrayList* from the Web service's Session object (lines 16–17). You can think of an ArrayList as a dynamic array (i.e., its size can change at runtime). Class ArrayList is discussed in greater detail in Chapter 22, Data Structures and Collections. The class's method Add places an Object * at the end of the ArrayList. Method DealCard then removes the top card from the deck (line 19) and returns the card's value as a String pointer (line 21).

Method Shuffle (lines 24–49) generates an ArrayList representing a card deck, shuffles it and stores the shuffled cards in the client's Session object. Lines 31–37 include for loops to generate Strings in the form "face suit" to represent each possible card in a deck. Lines 40–45 shuffle the re-created deck by swapping each card with another card in the deck. Line 48 adds the ArrayList to the Session object to maintain the deck between method calls.

Method CountCards (lines 52–99) counts the values of the cards in a hand by trying to attain the highest score possible without going over 21. Precautions need to be taken when calculating the value of the cards, because an ace can be counted as either 1 or 11, and all face cards count as 10.

The string dealt is tokenized (i.e., broken up) into its individual cards by calling String * method Split and passing it an array that contains the tab character. The for loop (line 61–85) counts the value of each card. Lines 65–66 retrieve the first integer—the face—and use that value as input to the switch statement in line 68. If the card is 1 (an ace), the program increments variable aceCount. An ace can have two values, so additional logic is required to process aces. If the card is a 13, 12 or 11 (King, Queen or Jack), the program adds 10 to the total. If the card is anything else, the program increases the total by that value.

In lines 88–96, the aces are counted after all the other cards. If several aces are included in a hand, only one can be counted as 11. (If two were counted as 11, we would already have a hand value of 22, which is a losing hand.) We then determine whether we can count an ace as 11 without exceeding 21. If this is possible, line 93 adjusts the total accordingly. Otherwise, line 95 adjusts the total by counting each ace as 1 point.

Method CountCards attempts to maximize the value of the current cards without exceeding 21. Imagine, for example, that the dealer has a 7, then receives an ace. The new total could be either 8 or 18. However, CountCards always tries the maximize the value of the cards without going over 21, so the new total is 18.

Creating a Client to Consume the Blackjack Web Service

Now we use the Blackjack Web service in a Windows application called BlackjackGame (Fig. 20.25–Fig. 20.26). This program uses an instance of BlackjackWebService to represent the dealer, calling its DealCard and CountCards methods. The Web service keeps track of both the player's and the dealer's cards (i.e., all the cards that have been dealt).

```
// Fig. 20.25: Form1.h
// Blackjack game that uses the Blackjack Web service.

#pragma once
```

Fig. 20.25 Blackjack game that uses the Blackjack Web service. (Part 1 of 8.)

```


namespace BlackjackGame
{
   using namespace System;
   using namespace System::ComponentModel;
   using namespace System::Collections;
   using namespace System::Windows::Forms;
   using namespace System::Data;
   using namespace System::Drawing;
   using namespace System::Collections;
   using namespace System::Net;
   using namespace Blackjack;

   /// <summary>
   /// Summary for Form1
   ///
   /// WARNING: If you change the name of this class, you will need to
   ///          change the 'Resource File Name' property for the managed
   ///          resource compiler tool associated with all .resx files
   ///          this class depends on.  Otherwise, the designers will not
   ///          be able to interact properly with localized resources
   ///          associated with this form.
   /// </summary>
   public __gc class Form1 : public System::Windows::Forms::Form
   {
   public:
      Form1(void)
      {
         InitializeComponent();

         dealer = new BlackjackClass();

         // allow session state
         dealer->CookieContainer = new CookieContainer();

         cardBoxes = new ArrayList();

         // put PictureBoxes into cardBoxes
         cardBoxes->Add( pictureBox1 );
         cardBoxes->Add( pictureBox2 );
         cardBoxes->Add( pictureBox3 );
         cardBoxes->Add( pictureBox4 );
         cardBoxes->Add( pictureBox5 );
         cardBoxes->Add( pictureBox6 );
         cardBoxes->Add( pictureBox7 );
         cardBoxes->Add( pictureBox8 );
         cardBoxes->Add( pictureBox9 );
         cardBoxes->Add( pictureBox10 );
         cardBoxes->Add( pictureBox11 );
         cardBoxes->Add( pictureBox12 );
         cardBoxes->Add( pictureBox13 );
         cardBoxes->Add( pictureBox14 );
```

Fig. 20.25 Blackjack game that uses the `Blackjack` Web service. (Part 2 of 8.)

```
         cardBoxes->Add( pictureBox15 );
         cardBoxes->Add( pictureBox16 );
         cardBoxes->Add( pictureBox17 );
         cardBoxes->Add( pictureBox18 );
         cardBoxes->Add( pictureBox19 );
         cardBoxes->Add( pictureBox20 );
         cardBoxes->Add( pictureBox21 );
         cardBoxes->Add( pictureBox22 );
      }

   protected:
      void Dispose(Boolean disposing)
      {
         if (disposing && components)
         {
            components->Dispose();
         }
         __super::Dispose(disposing);
      }
   private: System::Windows::Forms::PictureBox *  pictureBox1;
   private: System::Windows::Forms::PictureBox *  pictureBox2;
   private: System::Windows::Forms::PictureBox *  pictureBox3;
   private: System::Windows::Forms::PictureBox *  pictureBox4;
   private: System::Windows::Forms::PictureBox *  pictureBox5;
   private: System::Windows::Forms::PictureBox *  pictureBox6;
   private: System::Windows::Forms::PictureBox *  pictureBox7;
   private: System::Windows::Forms::PictureBox *  pictureBox8;
   private: System::Windows::Forms::PictureBox *  pictureBox9;
   private: System::Windows::Forms::PictureBox *  pictureBox10;
   private: System::Windows::Forms::PictureBox *  pictureBox11;
   private: System::Windows::Forms::PictureBox *  pictureBox12;
   private: System::Windows::Forms::PictureBox *  pictureBox13;
   private: System::Windows::Forms::PictureBox *  pictureBox14;
   private: System::Windows::Forms::PictureBox *  pictureBox15;
   private: System::Windows::Forms::PictureBox *  pictureBox16;
   private: System::Windows::Forms::PictureBox *  pictureBox17;
   private: System::Windows::Forms::PictureBox *  pictureBox18;
   private: System::Windows::Forms::PictureBox *  pictureBox19;
   private: System::Windows::Forms::PictureBox *  pictureBox20;
   private: System::Windows::Forms::PictureBox *  pictureBox21;
   private: System::Windows::Forms::PictureBox *  pictureBox22;

   private: System::Windows::Forms::Button *  dealButton;
   private: System::Windows::Forms::Button *  hitButton;
   private: System::Windows::Forms::Button *  stayButton;

   private: BlackjackClass *dealer;
   private: String *dealersCards, *playersCards;
   private: ArrayList *cardBoxes;
   private: int playerCard, dealerCard;

```

Fig. 20.25 Blackjack game that uses the `Blackjack` Web service. (Part 3 of 8.)

```
   // labels displaying game status, dealer and player
   private: System::Windows::Forms::Label *  statusLabel;
   private: System::Windows::Forms::Label *  dealerLabel;
   private: System::Windows::Forms::Label *  playerLabel;

   public: __value enum GameStatus : int { PUSH, LOSE, WIN, BLACKJACK };

   private:
      /// <summary>
      /// Required designer variable.
      /// </summary>
      System::ComponentModel::Container * components;

   // Visual Studio .NET generated GUI code

   // deals cards to dealer while dealer's total is less than 17,
   // then computes value of each hand and determines winner
   private: System::Void stayButton_Click(
               System::Object *  sender, System::EventArgs *  e)
         {
            stayButton->Enabled = false;
            hitButton->Enabled = false;
            dealButton->Enabled = true;
            DealerPlay();
         }  // end method stayButton_Click

   private:

      // process dealers turn
      void DealerPlay()
      {

         // while value of dealer's hand is below 17,
         // dealer must take cards
         while ( dealer->CountCards( dealersCards ) < 17 ) {
            dealersCards = String::Concat(
               dealersCards, S"\t", dealer->DealCard() );
            DisplayCard( dealerCard, S"" );
            dealerCard++;
            MessageBox::Show( S"Dealer takes a card" );
         } // end while

         int dealersTotal = dealer->CountCards( dealersCards );
         int playersTotal = dealer->CountCards( playersCards );

         // if dealer busted, player wins
         if ( dealersTotal > 21 ) {
            GameOver( GameStatus::WIN );

            return;
         } // end if

```

Fig. 20.25 Blackjack game that uses the `Blackjack` Web service. (Part 4 of 8.)

```
         // if dealer and player have not exceeded 21,
         // higher score wins; equal scores is a push.
         if ( dealersTotal > playersTotal )
            GameOver( GameStatus::LOSE );
         else if ( playersTotal > dealersTotal )
            GameOver( GameStatus::WIN );
         else
            GameOver( GameStatus::PUSH );
      } // end method DealerPlay

   // deal another card to player
   private: System::Void hitButton_Click(
               System::Object *  sender, System::EventArgs *  e)
            {
               // get player another card
               String *card = dealer->DealCard();
               playersCards = String::Concat( playersCards, S"\t", card );
               DisplayCard( playerCard, card );
               playerCard++;

               int total = dealer->CountCards( playersCards );

               // if player exceeds 21, house wins
               if ( total > 21 )
                  GameOver( GameStatus::LOSE );

               // if player has 21, they cannot take more cards
               // the dealer plays
               if ( total == 21 ) {
                  hitButton->Enabled = false;
                  DealerPlay();
               } // end if
            } // end method hitButton_Click

   // deal two cards each to dealer and player
   private: System::Void dealButton_Click(
               System::Object *  sender, System::EventArgs *  e)
            {
               String *card;

               // clear card images
               for ( int i = 0; i < cardBoxes->Count; i++ )
                  ( dynamic_cast< PictureBox* >(
                     cardBoxes->Item[ i ] ) )->Image = 0;

               // clear status from previous game
               statusLabel->Text = S"";

               // shuffle cards
               dealer->Shuffle();

               // deal two cards to player
               playersCards = dealer->DealCard();
```

Fig. 20.25 Blackjack game that uses the `Blackjack` Web service. (Part 5 of 8.)

```
            DisplayCard( 11, playersCards );
            card = dealer->DealCard();
            DisplayCard( 12, card );
            playersCards = String::Concat( playersCards, S"\t", card );

            // deal two cards to dealer, only display face
            // of first card
            dealersCards = dealer->DealCard();
            DisplayCard( 0, dealersCards );
            card = dealer->DealCard();
            DisplayCard( 1, S"" );
            dealersCards = String::Concat( dealersCards, S"\t", card );

            stayButton->Enabled = true;
            hitButton->Enabled = true;
            dealButton->Enabled = false;

            int dealersTotal = dealer->CountCards( dealersCards );
            int playersTotal = dealer->CountCards( playersCards );

            // if hands equal 21, it is a push
            if ( dealersTotal == playersTotal && dealersTotal == 21 )
               GameOver( GameStatus::PUSH );

            // if player has 21 player wins with blackjack
            else if ( playersTotal == 21 )
               GameOver( GameStatus::BLACKJACK );

            // if dealer has 21, dealer wins
            else if ( dealersTotal == 21 )
               GameOver( GameStatus::LOSE );

            dealerCard = 2;
            playerCard = 13;
         } // end method dealButton_Click

public:

   // displays card represented by cardValue in
   // PictureBox with number card
   void DisplayCard( int card, String *cardValue )
   {
      // retrieve appropriate PictureBox from ArrayList
      PictureBox *displayBox = dynamic_cast< PictureBox* >(
         cardBoxes->Item[ card ] );

      // if string representing card is empty,
      // set displayBox to display back of card
      if ( cardValue == S"" ) {
         displayBox->Image =
            Image::FromFile( S"blackjack_images\\cardback.png" );

```

Fig. 20.25 Blackjack game that uses the `Blackjack` Web service. (Part 6 of 8.)

```
            return;
         } // end if

         // retrieve face value of card from cardValue
         int faceNumber = Int32::Parse( cardValue->Substring( 0,
            cardValue->IndexOf( S" " ) ) );

         String *face = faceNumber.ToString();

         // retrieve the suit of the card from cardValue
         String *suit = cardValue->Substring(
            cardValue->IndexOf( S" " ) + 1 );

         __wchar_t suitLetter;

         // determine if suit is other than clubs
         switch ( Convert::ToInt32( suit ) ) {

            // suit is clubs
            case 0:
               suitLetter = 'c';
               break;

            // suit is diamonds
            case 1:
               suitLetter = 'd';
               break;

            // suit is hearts
            case 2:
               suitLetter = 'h';
               break;

            // else suit is spades
            default:
               suitLetter = 's';
               break;
         } // end switch

         // set displayBox to display appropriate image
         displayBox->Image = Image::FromFile(
            String::Concat( S"blackjack_images\\", face,
            Char::ToString( suitLetter ), S".png" ) );
      } // end method DisplayCard

   public:

      // displays all player cards and shows
      // appropriate game status message
      void GameOver( GameStatus winner )
      {
         __wchar_t tab __gc[] = { '\t' };
         String *cards[] = dealersCards->Split( tab );
```

Fig. 20.25 Blackjack game that uses the `Blackjack` Web service. (Part 7 of 8.)

```

         for ( int i = 0; i < cards->Length; i++ )
            DisplayCard( i, cards[ i ] );

         // push
         if ( winner == GameStatus::PUSH )
            statusLabel->Text = S"It's a tie!";

         // player loses
         else if ( winner == GameStatus::LOSE )
            statusLabel->Text = S"You Lose Try Again!";

         // player wins
         else if ( winner == GameStatus::WIN )
            statusLabel->Text = S"You Win!";

         // player has won with blackjack
         else
            statusLabel->Text = S"BlackJack!";

         stayButton->Enabled = false;
         hitButton->Enabled = false;
         dealButton->Enabled = true;
      } // end method GameOver
   };
}
```

Fig. 20.25 Blackjack game that uses the `Blackjack` Web service. (Part 8 of 8.)

```
// Fig. 20.26: Form1.cpp
// Entry point for application.

#include "stdafx.h"
#include "Form1.h"
#include <windows.h>

using namespace BlackjackGame;

int APIENTRY _tWinMain(HINSTANCE hInstance,
                       HINSTANCE hPrevInstance,
                       LPTSTR    lpCmdLine,
                       int       nCmdShow)
{
   System::Threading::Thread::CurrentThread->ApartmentState =
      System::Threading::ApartmentState::STA;
   Application::Run(new Form1());
   return 0;
} // end _tWinMain
```

Fig. 20.26 Blackjack game demonstration. (Part 1 of 3.)

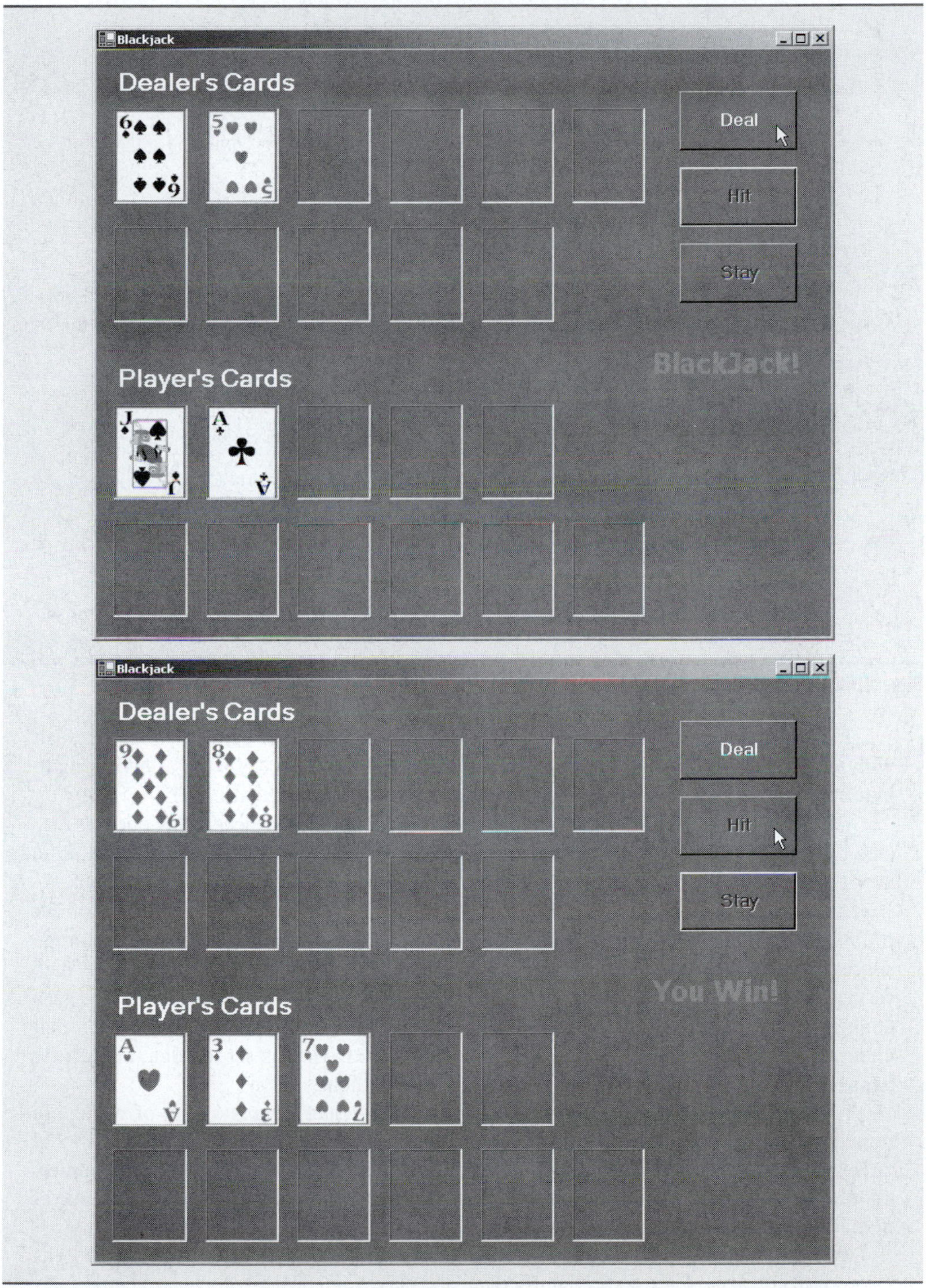

Fig. 20.26 Blackjack game demonstration. (Part 2 of 3.)

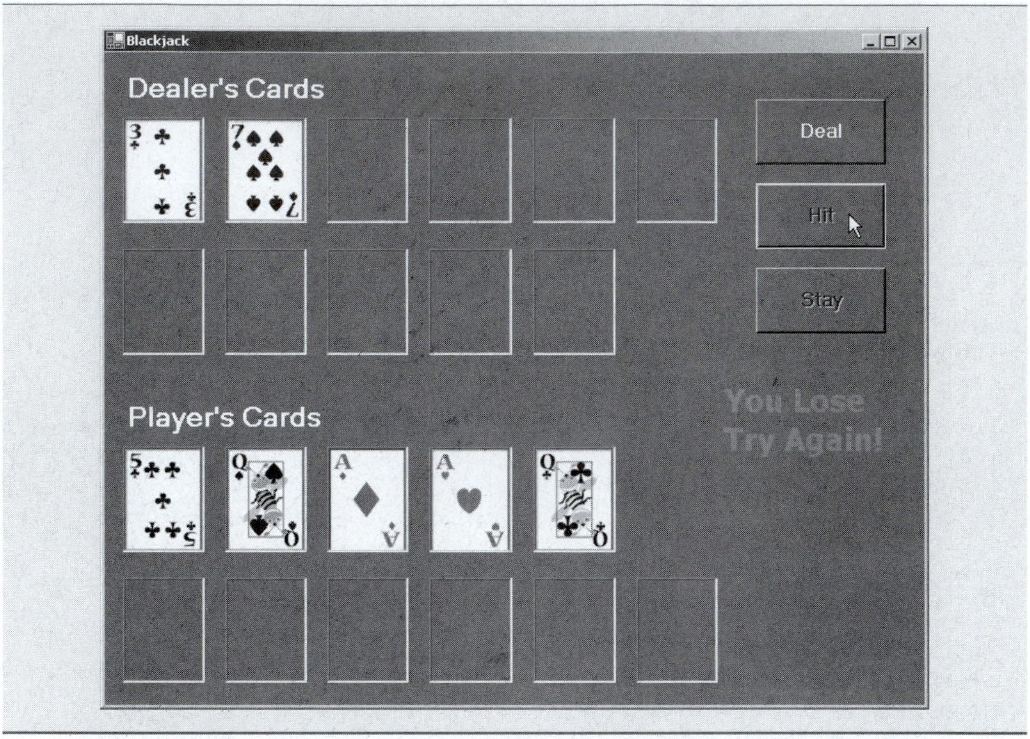

Fig. 20.26 Blackjack game demonstration. (Part 3 of 3.)

Each player has 11 `PictureBoxes`—the maximum number of cards that can be dealt without exceeding 21. These `PictureBoxes` are placed in an `ArrayList`, allowing us to index the `ArrayList` to determine which `PictureBox` displays the card image.

Previously, we mentioned that the client must provide a way to accept any cookies created by the Web service to identify users. Line 39 in the constructor (Fig. 20.25) creates a new `CookieContainer` object for the `CookieContainer` property of `dealer`. The `CookieContainer` property is a member of class *`SoapHttpClientProtocol`*, the base class of our proxy. Class *`CookieContainer`* (defined in namespace `System::Net`) acts as a storage space for an object of the `HttpCookie` class. Creating the `CookieContainer` allows the Web service to maintain session state for the current client. This `CookieContainer` stores a `Cookie` with a unique identifier that the server can use to recognize the client when that client makes future requests. By default, the `CookieContainer` is set to `NULL`, and a new `Session` object is created by the Web service for each client.

Method `GameOver` (lines 315–342) displays all the dealer's cards (many of which are turned face down during the game) and shows the appropriate message in the status `PictureBox`. Method `GameOver` receives as an argument a member of the `GameStatus` enumeration (defined in line 114 of Fig. 20.25). The enumeration represents whether the player tied, lost or won the game; its four members are `PUSH`, `LOSE`, `WIN` and `BLACKJACK`.

When the player clicks the **Deal** button (event handler in lines 196–248), all the `PictureBoxes` are cleared, the deck is shuffled and the player and dealer receive two cards each. If both obtain scores of 21, method `GameOver` is called and is passed `GameStatus::PUSH`. If only the player has 21, `GameOver` is called and is passed `GameStatus::BLACKJACK`. If only the dealer has 21, method `GameOver` is called and is passed `GameStatus::LOSE`.

Finally, if `GameOver` is not called, the player can take additional cards by clicking the **Hit** button (event handler in lines 172–193). Each time a player clicks **Hit**, the player is dealt one card, which is displayed in the GUI. If the player exceeds 21, the game is over, and the player loses. If the player has exactly 21, the player is not allowed to take any more cards.

Players can click the **Stay** button to indicate that they do not want to risk being dealt another card. In the event handler for this event (lines 126–133), all three buttons are disabled, and method `DealerPlay` is called. This method (lines 138–169) causes the dealer to keep taking cards until the dealer's hand is worth 17 or more. If the dealer's hand exceeds 21, the player wins; otherwise, the values of the hands are compared, and `GameOver` is called with the appropriate argument.

Method `DisplayCard` (lines 254–309) retrieves the appropriate card image. It takes as arguments an integer representing the index of the `PictureBox` in the `ArrayList` that must have its image set and a string representing the card. An empty string indicates that we wish to display the back of a card; otherwise, the program extracts the face and suit from the `String` object and uses this information to find the correct image. The `switch` statement (lines 282–303) converts the number representing the suit into an integer and assigns the appropriate character to `suitLetter` (`c` for Clubs, `d` for Diamonds, `h` for Hearts and `s` for Spades). The character `suitLetter` completes the image's file name.

20.12 Case Study: Temperature-Information Application

This case study discusses both a Web service that presents weather forecasts for various cities around the United States and a Windows application that employs the Web service. The Web service uses networking capabilities to display the forecasts; it parses a Web page containing the required information, then extracts weather-forecast data.

First, we present Web service `TemperatureServer` in Fig. 20.27 and Fig. 20.28. This Web service reads a Web page and collects information about the temperature and weather conditions in several American cities. [*Note*: At the time of publication, this program runs in the manner that we describe. However, if changes are made to the Web page from which the program retrieves data, the program might work differently or not at all. Please check our Web site at `www.deitel.com` for updates.]

```
// Fig. 20.27: TemperatureServerClass.h
// TemperatureServer Web service that extracts weather
// information from a Web page.

#pragma once

#include "CityWeather.h"

using namespace System;
using namespace System::Web;
using namespace System::Web::Services;
using namespace System::IO;
using namespace System::Net;
```

Fig. 20.27 `TemperatureServer` class header file. (Part 1 of 3.)

```
namespace TemperatureServer
{
   /// WARNING: If you change the name of this class, you will need to
   ///          change the 'Resource File Name' property for the managed
   ///          resource compiler tool associated with all .resx files
   ///          this class depends on.  Otherwise, the designers will not
   ///          be able to interact properly with localized resources
   ///          associated with this form.
   [ WebServiceAttribute( Namespace =
      "http://www.deitel.com/ch20/TemperatureServer",
      Description = "A Web service that provides information "
      "from the National Weather Service." ) ]
   public __gc class TemperatureServerClass :
      public System::Web::Services::WebService
   {

   public:
      TemperatureServerClass()
      {
         InitializeComponent();
      }
   protected:
      void Dispose(Boolean disposing)
      {
         if (disposing && components)
         {
            components->Dispose();
         }
         __super::Dispose(disposing);
      }

   private:
      /// <summary>
      /// Required designer variable.
      /// </summary>
      System::ComponentModel::Container * components;

      /// <summary>
      /// Required method for Designer support - do not modify
      /// the contents of this method with the code editor.
      /// </summary>
      void InitializeComponent()
      {
      }

   public:

      [ WebMethod( EnableSession = true, Description = "Method "
         "to read information from the weather service." ) ]
      void UpdateWeatherConditions();

```

Fig. 20.27 `TemperatureServer` class header file. (Part 2 of 3.)

```
      [ WebMethod( EnableSession = true, Description =
         "Method to retrieve a list of cities." ) ]
      String *Cities()[];

      [ WebMethod( EnableSession = true, Description = "Method"
         " to retrieve weather descriptions for a list "
         "of cities." ) ]
      String *Descriptions()[];

      [ WebMethod( EnableSession = true, Description = "Method "
         "to retrieve the temperature for a list of cities." ) ]
      String *Temperatures()[];

   };
}
```

Fig. 20.27 `TemperatureServer` class header file. (Part 3 of 3.)

```
// Fig. 20.28: TemperatureServerClass.cpp
// TemperatureServer Web service that extracts weather
// information from a Web page.

#include "stdafx.h"
#include "TemperatureServerClass.h"
#include "Global.asax.h"

namespace TemperatureServer
{
   void TemperatureServerClass::UpdateWeatherConditions()
   {
      // create WebClient to get access to Web page
      WebClient *myClient = new WebClient();
      ArrayList *cityList = new ArrayList();

      // get StreamReader for response so we can read page
      StreamReader *input = new StreamReader(
         myClient->OpenRead(
         S"http://iwin.nws.noaa.gov/iwin/us/traveler.html" ) );

      String *separator = S"TAV12";

      // locate line that starts with "TAV12"
      while ( !input->ReadLine()->StartsWith( separator ) )
         ; // do nothing

      // day format and night format
      String *dayFormat =
         S"CITY            WEA     HI/LO   WEA     HI/LO";
      String *nightFormat =
         S"CITY            WEA     LO/HI   WEA     LO/HI";
      String *inputLine = S"";

```

Fig. 20.28 `TemperatureServer` Web service. (Part 1 of 3.)

```
      // locate header that begins weather information
      do {
         inputLine = input->ReadLine();
      } while ( !inputLine->Equals( dayFormat ) &&
         !inputLine->Equals( nightFormat ) );

      // get first city's data
      inputLine = input->ReadLine();

      while ( inputLine->Length > 28 ) {

         // create CityWeather object for city
         CityWeather *weather = new CityWeather(
            inputLine->Substring( 0, 16 ),
            inputLine->Substring( 16, 7 ),
            inputLine->Substring( 23, 7 ) );

         // add to List
         cityList->Add( weather );

         // get next city's data
         inputLine = input->ReadLine();
      } // end while

      // close connection to NWS server
      input->Close();

      // add city list to user session
      Session->Add( S"cityList", cityList );
   } // end method UpdateWeatherConditions

   // gets all city names
   String *TemperatureServerClass::Cities()[]
   {
      ArrayList *cityList =
         dynamic_cast< ArrayList * >( Session->Item[ S"cityList" ] );
      String *cities[] = new String*[ cityList->Count ];

      // retrieve names for cities
      for ( int i = 0; i < cityList->Count; i++ ) {
         CityWeather* weather =
            dynamic_cast< CityWeather * >( cityList->Item[ i ] );

         cities[ i ] = weather->CityName;
      } // end for

      return cities;
   } // end method Cities

   // gets all city descriptions
   String *TemperatureServerClass::Descriptions()[]
   {
```

Fig. 20.28 TemperatureServer Web service. (Part 2 of 3.)

```
87        ArrayList *cityList =
88           dynamic_cast< ArrayList* >( Session->Item[ S"cityList" ] );
89        String *descriptions[] = new String*[ cityList->Count ];
90
91        // retrieve weather descriptions for all cities
92        for ( int i = 0; i < cityList->Count; i++ ) {
93           CityWeather *weather =
94              dynamic_cast< CityWeather* >( cityList->Item[ i ] );
95
96           descriptions[ i ] = weather->Description;
97        } // end for
98
99        return descriptions;
100    } // end method Descriptions
101
102    // obtains each city temperature
103    String *TemperatureServerClass::Temperatures()[]
104    {
105       ArrayList *cityList =
106          dynamic_cast< ArrayList* >( Session->Item[ S"cityList" ] );
107       String *temperatures[] = new String*[ cityList->Count ];
108
109       // retrieve temperatures for all cities
110       for ( int i = 0; i < cityList->Count; i++ ) {
111          CityWeather *weather =
112             dynamic_cast< CityWeather* >( cityList->Item[ i ] ) ;
113          temperatures[ i ] = weather->Temperature;
114       } // end for
115
116       return temperatures;
117    } // end method Temperatures
118 };
```

Fig. 20.28 `TemperatureServer` Web service. (Part 3 of 3.)

Method `UpdateWeatherConditions`, which gathers weather data from a Web page, is the first `WebMethod` that a client must call from the Web service. The service also provides `WebMethods Cities`, `Descriptions` and `Temperatures`, which return different kinds of forecast-related information. If one of these three methods is called before method `UpdateWeatherConditions` reads weather information from the Web page, no data will be returned to the client.

When `UpdateWeatherConditions` (lines 11–64 of Fig. 20.28) is invoked, the method connects to a Web site containing the traveler's forecasts from the National Weather Service (NWS). Line 14 creates a ***`WebClient`*** object, which we use because the `WebClient` class is designed for interaction with a source specified by a URL. In this case, the URL for the NWS page is `http://iwin.nws.noaa.gov/iwin/us/traveler.html`. Lines 19–20 call `WebClient` method ***`OpenRead`***; the method retrieves a `Stream` from the URL containing the weather information and then uses this `Stream` to create a `StreamReader` object. Using a `StreamReader` object, the program can read the Web page's HTML markup line by line.

The section of the Web page in which we are interested starts with the string "`TAV12`." Therefore, lines 25–26 read the HTML markup one line at a time until this string is encountered. Once the string "TAV12" is reached, the do...while statement (lines 36–39) continues to read the page one line at a time until it finds the header line (i.e., the line at the beginning of the forecast table). This line starts with either dayFormat, indicating day format, or nightFormat, indicating night format. The line could be in either format; therefore, the statement checks for both. Line 42 reads the next line from the page, which is the first line containing temperature information.

The while statement (lines 44–57) creates a new CityWeather object to represent the current city. It parses the string containing the current weather data, separating the city name, the weather condition and the temperature. The CityWeather object is added to cityList (an ArrayList that contains a list of the cities, their descriptions and their current temperatures); then the next line from the page is read and stored in inputLine for the next iteration. This process continues until the length of the string read from the Web page is less than or equal to 28. This signals the end of the temperature section. Line 63 adds cityList to the Session object so that the values are maintained between method calls.

Method Cities (lines 67–82) creates an array of strings that can contain as many string elements as there are elements in cityList. Line 69–70 obtains the list of cities from the Session object. Lines 74–79 iterate through each CityWeather object in cityList and insert the city name into the array, which is returned in line 81. Methods Descriptions (lines 85–100) and Temperatures (lines 103–117) behave similarly, except that they return weather descriptions and temperatures, respectively.

Figure 20.29 and Fig. 20.30 contain the code listing for the CityWeather class. The constructor takes three arguments: The city's name, the weather description and the current temperature. The class provides the read-only properties CityName, Temperature and Description so that these values can be retrieved by the Web service.

```
// Fig. 20.29: CityWeather.h
// CityWeather class header file.

#using <mscorlib.dll>

using namespace System;

public __gc class CityWeather
{
public:
   CityWeather( String *city, String *information,
      String *degrees );

   // city name
   __property String *get_CityName()
   {
      return cityName;
   }

   // city temperature
   __property String *get_Temperature()
   {
```

Fig. 20.29 CityWeather class header file. (Part 1 of 2.)

```
      return temperature;
   }

   // forecast description
   __property String *get_Description()
   {
      return description;
   }

private:
   String *cityName;
   String *temperature;
   String *description;
}; // end class CityWeather
```

Fig. 20.29 `CityWeather` class header file. (Part 2 of 2.)

```
// Fig. 20.30: CityWeather.cpp
// Class representing the weather information for one city.

#include "stdafx.h"
#include "CityWeather.h"

CityWeather::CityWeather(
   String *city, String *information, String *degrees )
{
   cityName = city;
   description = information;
   temperature = degrees;
}
```

Fig. 20.30 Class that stores weather information about a city.

Creating a Client to Consume the `TemperatureServer` *Web Service*

`TemperatureClient` (Fig. 20.31–Fig. 20.32) is a Windows application that uses the `TemperatureServer` Web service to display weather information in a graphical and easy-to-read manner. The application consists of 34 `Label`s, which are placed in two columns. Each `Label` displays the weather information for a different city.

```
// Fig. 20.31: Form1.h
// Class that displays weather information that it receives
// from a Web service.

#pragma once


namespace TemperatureClient
{
   using namespace System;
   using namespace System::ComponentModel;
```

Fig. 20.31 Receiving temperature and weather data from a Web service. (Part 1 of 5.)

```
using namespace System::Collections;
using namespace System::Windows::Forms;
using namespace System::Data;
using namespace System::Drawing;
using namespace System::Collections;
using namespace System::Net;
using namespace TemperatureServer;

/// <summary>
/// Summary for Form1
///
/// WARNING: If you change the name of this class, you will need to
///          change the 'Resource File Name' property for the managed
///          resource compiler tool associated with all .resx files
///          this class depends on.  Otherwise, the designers will not
///          be able to interact properly with localized resources
///          associated with this form.
/// </summary>
public __gc class Form1 : public System::Windows::Forms::Form
{
public:
   Form1(void)
   {
      InitializeComponent();

      TemperatureServerClass *server = new TemperatureServerClass();
      server->CookieContainer = new CookieContainer();
      server->UpdateWeatherConditions();

      String *cities[] = server->Cities();
      String *descriptions[] = server->Descriptions();
      String *temperatures[] = server->Temperatures();

      label35->BackgroundImage = new Bitmap( S"images\\header.png" );
      label36->BackgroundImage = new Bitmap( S"images\\header.png" );

      // create Hashtable and populate it with every label
      Hashtable *cityLabels = new Hashtable();
      cityLabels->Add( __box( 1 ), label1 );
      cityLabels->Add( __box( 2 ), label2 );
      cityLabels->Add( __box( 3 ), label3 );
      cityLabels->Add( __box( 4 ), label4 );
      cityLabels->Add( __box( 5 ), label5 );
      cityLabels->Add( __box( 6 ), label6 );
      cityLabels->Add( __box( 7 ), label7 );
      cityLabels->Add( __box( 8 ), label8 );
      cityLabels->Add( __box( 9 ), label9 );
      cityLabels->Add( __box( 10 ), label10 );
      cityLabels->Add( __box( 11 ), label11 );
      cityLabels->Add( __box( 12 ), label12 );
      cityLabels->Add( __box( 13 ), label13 );
      cityLabels->Add( __box( 14 ), label14 );
      cityLabels->Add( __box( 15 ), label15 );
```

Fig. 20.31 Receiving temperature and weather data from a Web service. (Part 2 of 5.)

```
      cityLabels->Add( __box( 16 ), label16 );
      cityLabels->Add( __box( 17 ), label17 );
      cityLabels->Add( __box( 18 ), label18 );
      cityLabels->Add( __box( 19 ), label19 );
      cityLabels->Add( __box( 20 ), label20 );
      cityLabels->Add( __box( 21 ), label21 );
      cityLabels->Add( __box( 22 ), label22 );
      cityLabels->Add( __box( 23 ), label23 );
      cityLabels->Add( __box( 24 ), label24 );
      cityLabels->Add( __box( 25 ), label25 );
      cityLabels->Add( __box( 26 ), label26 );
      cityLabels->Add( __box( 27 ), label27 );
      cityLabels->Add( __box( 28 ), label28 );
      cityLabels->Add( __box( 29 ), label29 );
      cityLabels->Add( __box( 30 ), label30 );
      cityLabels->Add( __box( 31 ), label31 );
      cityLabels->Add( __box( 32 ), label32 );
      cityLabels->Add( __box( 33 ), label33 );
      cityLabels->Add( __box( 34 ), label34 );

      // create Hashtable and populate with all weather conditions
      Hashtable *weather = new Hashtable();
      weather->Add( S"SUNNY", S"sunny" );
      weather->Add( S"PTCLDY", S"pcloudy" );
      weather->Add( S"CLOUDY", S"mcloudy" );
      weather->Add( S"MOCLDY", S"mcloudy" );
      weather->Add( S"TSTRMS", S"rain" );
      weather->Add( S"RAIN", S"rain" );
      weather->Add( S"SNOW", S"snow" );
      weather->Add( S"VRYHOT", S"vryhot" );
      weather->Add( S"FAIR", S"fair" );
      weather->Add( S"RNSNOW", S"rnsnow" );
      weather->Add( S"SHWRS", S"showers" );
      weather->Add( S"WINDY", S"windy" );
      weather->Add( S"NOINFO", S"noinfo" );
      weather->Add( S"MISG", S"noinfo" );
      weather->Add( S"DRZL", S"rain" );
      weather->Add( S"HAZE", S"noinfo" );
      weather->Add( S"SMOKE", S"mcloudy" );

      Bitmap *background = new Bitmap( S"images\\back.png" );
      Drawing::Font *font = new Drawing::Font(
         S"Courier New", 8, FontStyle::Bold );

      // for every city
      for ( int i = 0; i < cities->Length; i++ ) {

         // use Hashtable cityLabels to find the next Label
         Label *currentCity = dynamic_cast< Label* >(
            cityLabels->Item[ __box( i + 1 ) ] );

         try {

```

Fig. 20.31 Receiving temperature and weather data from a Web service. (Part 3 of 5.)

```
                // set current Label's image to image
                // corresponding to the city's weather condition -
                // find correct image name in Hashtable weather
                currentCity->Image = new Bitmap( String::Concat(
                   S"images\\", dynamic_cast< String* >(
                   weather->Item[ descriptions[ i ]->Trim() ] ),
                   S".png" ) );

             } // end try
             catch( Exception * ) {
                currentCity->Image = new Bitmap( S"images\\noinfo.png" );
             } // end catch

             // set background image, font and forecolor
             // of Label
             currentCity->BackgroundImage = background;
             currentCity->Font = font;
             currentCity->ForeColor = Color::White;

             // set label's text to city name
             currentCity->Text = String::Concat(
                S"\r\n", cities[ i ], S" ", temperatures[ i ] );
          } // end for
       }

    protected:
       void Dispose(Boolean disposing)
       {
          if (disposing && components)
          {
             components->Dispose();
          }
          __super::Dispose(disposing);
       }
    private: System::Windows::Forms::Label *  label1;
    private: System::Windows::Forms::Label *  label2;
    private: System::Windows::Forms::Label *  label3;
    private: System::Windows::Forms::Label *  label4;
    private: System::Windows::Forms::Label *  label5;
    private: System::Windows::Forms::Label *  label6;
    private: System::Windows::Forms::Label *  label7;
    private: System::Windows::Forms::Label *  label8;
    private: System::Windows::Forms::Label *  label9;
    private: System::Windows::Forms::Label *  label10;
    private: System::Windows::Forms::Label *  label11;
    private: System::Windows::Forms::Label *  label12;
    private: System::Windows::Forms::Label *  label13;
    private: System::Windows::Forms::Label *  label14;
    private: System::Windows::Forms::Label *  label15;
    private: System::Windows::Forms::Label *  label16;
    private: System::Windows::Forms::Label *  label17;
    private: System::Windows::Forms::Label *  label18;
    private: System::Windows::Forms::Label *  label19;
```

Fig. 20.31 Receiving temperature and weather data from a Web service. (Part 4 of 5.)

```
   private: System::Windows::Forms::Label *  label20;
   private: System::Windows::Forms::Label *  label21;
   private: System::Windows::Forms::Label *  label22;
   private: System::Windows::Forms::Label *  label23;
   private: System::Windows::Forms::Label *  label24;
   private: System::Windows::Forms::Label *  label25;
   private: System::Windows::Forms::Label *  label26;
   private: System::Windows::Forms::Label *  label27;
   private: System::Windows::Forms::Label *  label28;
   private: System::Windows::Forms::Label *  label29;
   private: System::Windows::Forms::Label *  label30;
   private: System::Windows::Forms::Label *  label31;
   private: System::Windows::Forms::Label *  label32;
   private: System::Windows::Forms::Label *  label33;
   private: System::Windows::Forms::Label *  label34;
   private: System::Windows::Forms::Label *  label35;
   private: System::Windows::Forms::Label *  label36;

   private:
      /// <summary>
      /// Required designer variable.
      /// </summary>
      System::ComponentModel::Container * components;

   // Visual Studio .NET generated GUI code
   };
}
```

Fig. 20.31 Receiving temperature and weather data from a Web service. (Part 5 of 5.)

```
// Fig. 20.32: Form1.cpp
// Entry point for application.

#include "stdafx.h"
#include "Form1.h"
#include <windows.h>

using namespace TemperatureClient;

int APIENTRY _tWinMain(HINSTANCE hInstance,
                       HINSTANCE hPrevInstance,
                       LPTSTR    lpCmdLine,
                       int       nCmdShow)
{
   System::Threading::Thread::CurrentThread->ApartmentState =
      System::Threading::ApartmentState::STA;
   Application::Run(new Form1());
   return 0;
} // end _tWinMain
```

Fig. 20.32 `TemperatureClient` entry point. (Part 1 of 2.)

Fig. 20.32 `TemperatureClient` entry point. (Part 2 of 2.)

Lines 37–39 of the constructor (Fig. 20.31) instantiate a `TemperatureServer` object, create a new `CookieContainer` object and update the weather data by calling method `UpdateWeatherConditions`. Lines 41–43 call `TemperatureServer` methods `Cities`, `Descriptions` and `Temperatures` to retrieve the city's weather and description information. The application presents weather data for many cities, so we must establish a way to organize the information in the `Label`s and to ensure that each weather description is accompanied by an appropriate image. To address these concerns, the program uses class `Hashtable` (discussed further in Chapter 22, Data Structures and Collections) to store all the `Label`s and weather descriptions and the names of their corresponding images. A `Hashtable` stores key-value pairs, in which both the key and the value can be any type of object. Method `Add` adds a key-value pair to a `Hashtable`. The class also provides an indexed array to return the key value on which the `Hashtable` is indexed. Line 49 creates a `Hashtable` object, and lines 50–83 add the `Label`s to the `Hashtable`, using the numbers `1` through `34` as keys. Then line 86 creates a second `Hashtable` object (`weather`) to contain pairs of weather conditions and the images associated with those conditions. Note that a given weather description does not necessarily correspond to the name of the PNG file containing the correct image. For example, both `"TSTRMS"` and `"RAIN"` weather conditions use the `rain.png` file.

Lines 110–140 set each `Label` so that it contains a city name, the current temperature in the city and an image corresponding to the weather condition for that city. Lines 113–114 use the indexed property of `Hashtable` to retrieve the next `Label` by passing as an argument the current value of `i` plus `1`. We add `1` because the `Hashtable` indexed property begins at 0, despite the fact that both the labels and the `Hashtable` keys are numbered from 1–34.

Lines 121–124 set the `Label`'s image to the PNG image that corresponds to the city's weather condition. The application does this by retrieving the name of the PNG image from `Hashtable weather`. The program eliminates any spaces in the description string by calling `String` method `Trim`. Lines 133–139 set several `Labels`' properties to achieve the visual effect seen in the output. For each label, we specify a blue-and-black background image (line 133). Lines 138–139 set each label's text so that it displays the correct information for each city (i.e., the city's name and temperature).

20.13 User-Defined Types in Web Services

The Web service discussed in the previous section returns arrays of strings. It would be much more convenient if `TemperatureServer` could return an array of `CityWeather` objects, instead of an array of strings. Fortunately, it is possible to define and employ user-defined types (also known as *custom types*) in a Web service. These types can be passed into or returned from Web-service methods. Web-service clients also can use these user-defined types, because the proxy class created for the client contains these type definitions. There are, however, some subtleties to keep in mind when using user-defined types in Web services; we point these out as we encounter them in the next example.

The case study in this section presents a math-tutoring program. The Web service generates random equations of type `Equation`. The client inputs information about the kind of mathematical example that the user wants (addition, subtraction or multiplication) and the skill level of the user (1 creates equations using one-digit numbers, 2 specifies more difficult equations involving two-digit numbers and 3 specifies the most difficult equations, containing three-digit numbers). It then generates an equation consisting of random numbers that have the proper number of digits. The client receives the `Equation` and displays the sample questions to the user.

We mentioned earlier that all data types passed to and from Web services must be supported by SOAP. How, then, can SOAP support a type that is not even created yet? In Chapter 17, Files and Streams, we discussed the serializing of data types, which enables them to be written to files. Similarly, custom types that are sent to or from a Web service are serialized, enabling them to be passed in XML format. This process is referred to as *XML serialization*.

When defining objects to be returned from Web-service methods, there are several subtleties to understand. For example, any object returned by a Web-service method must have a default constructor. Although all objects can be instantiated via a default constructor (even if this constructor is not defined explicitly), a class returned from a Web service must have an explicitly defined constructor, even if its body is empty.

Common Programming Error 20.3

Failure to define explicitly a default constructor for a type being used in a Web service results in a runtime error.

A few additional requirements apply to custom types in Web services. Any members of our user-defined type that we wish to access on the client side must be declared `public`. We also must define both the *get* and the *set* methods of any properties that we wish to access at runtime. The Web service needs to have ways both to retrieve and to manipulate such properties, because objects of the user-defined type will be converted into XML (when the objects are serialized), then converted back to objects (when they are deserialized). During serialization, the property value must be read (through the *get* method); during deserialization, the property value of the new object must be set (through the *set* method). If only one method is present, the client application will not have access to the property.

Common Programming Error 20.4

Defining only the get *or the* set *method of a property for a user-defined type being used in a Web service results in a property that is inaccessible to the client.*

Common Programming Error 20.5

Clients of a Web service can access only that service's `public` *members. To allow access to* `private` *data, the programmer should provide* `public` *properties.*

Figure 20.33 and Fig. 20.34 display class `Equation`. The constructor that is called (lines 16–36 of Fig. 20.34) takes three arguments—two integers representing the left and right operands and a string representing the algebraic operation to carry out. We define a default constructor (lines 8–13) that assigns default values to the class data members. The constructor sets the `left`, `right` and `operation` fields; then it calculates the appropriate result. We do not use this default constructor, but it must be defined in the program.

```
// Fig. 20.33: Equation.h
// Equation class header file.

#pragma once

#using <mscorlib.dll>

using namespace System;

public __gc class Equation
{
public:
   Equation();
   Equation( int leftValue, int rightValue, String *operationType );
   String *ToString();

   // property returning string representing left-hand side
   __property String *get_LeftHandSide()
   {
```

Fig. 20.33 `Equation` class header file. (Part 1 of 3.)

```
        return String::Concat( Left.ToString(), S" ",
           Operation, S" ", Right.ToString() );
     }

     __property void set_LeftHandSide( String *value ) {}

     // property returning string representing right-hand side
     __property String *get_RightHandSide()
     {
        return Result.ToString();
     }

     __property void set_RightHandSide( String *value ) {}

     // left operand get and set property
     __property int get_Left()
     {
        return left;
     }

     __property void set_Left( int value )
     {
        left = value;
     }

     // right operand get and set property
     __property int get_Right()
     {
        return right;
     }

     __property void set_Right( int value )
     {
        right = value;
     }

     // get and set property of result of applying
     // operation to left and right operands
     __property int get_Result()
     {
        return result;
     }

     __property void set_Result( int value )
     {
        result = value;
     }

     // get and set property for operation
     __property String *get_Operation()
     {
        return operation;
     }
```

Fig. 20.33 Equation class header file. (Part 2 of 3.)

```
    __property void set_Operation( String *value )
    {
       operation = value;
    }

private:
    int left, right, result;
    String *operation;
}; // end class Equation
```

Fig. 20.33 Equation class header file. (Part 3 of 3.)

```
// Fig. 20.34: Equation.cpp
// Class Equation contains information about an equation.

#include "stdafx.h"
#include "Equation.h"

// required default constructor
Equation::Equation()
{
   Left = 0;
   Right = 0;
   Operation = S"+";
}

// constructor for class Equation
Equation::Equation( int leftValue, int rightValue, String *operationType )
{
   Left = leftValue;
   Right = rightValue;
   Operation = operationType;

   switch ( operationType->Chars[ 0 ] ) {

      case '+':
         Result = Left + Right;
         break;
      case '-':
         Result = Left - Right;
         break;
      case '*':
         Result = Left * Right;
         break;
      default:
         break;
   } // end switch
}

String *Equation::ToString()
{
```

Fig. 20.34 Class that stores equation information. (Part 1 of 2.)

```
      return String::Concat( Left.ToString(), S" ", Operation,
         S" ", Right.ToString(), S" = ", Result.ToString() );
   }
```

Fig. 20.34 Class that stores equation information. (Part 2 of 2.)

Class `Equation` defines properties `LeftHandSide`, `RightHandSide`, `Left`, `Right`, `Operation` and `Result`. The program does not need to modify the values of some of these properties, but implementation for the *set* method must be provided. `LeftHandSide` returns a string representing everything to the left of the "=" sign, and `RightHandSide` returns a string representing everything to the right of the "=" sign. `Left` returns the `int` to the left of the operator (known as the left operand), and `Right` returns the `int` to the right of the operator (known as the right operand). `Result` returns the answer to the equation, and `Operation` returns the operator. The program does not actually need the `RightHandSide` property, but we have chosen to include it in case other clients choose to use it. Figure 20.35–Fig. 20.36 present the `EquationGenerator` Web service that creates random, customized `Equations`.

```
// Fig. 20.35: EquationGeneratorClass.h
// EquationGeneratorClass header file.

#pragma once

#include "Equation.h"

using namespace System;
using namespace System::Web;
using namespace System::Web::Services;

namespace EquationGenerator
{
   /// WARNING: If you change the name of this class, you will need to
   ///          change the 'Resource File Name' property for the managed
   ///          resource compiler tool associated with all .resx files
   ///          this class depends on.  Otherwise, the designers will not
   ///          be able to interact properly with localized resources
   ///          associated with this form.
   [ WebService(
      Namespace = "http://www.deitel.com/ch20/EquationGenerator",
      Description = "A Web service that generates questions "
      "based on the specified mathematical operation and "
      "level of difficulty chosen." ) ]
   public __gc class EquationGeneratorClass :
      public System::Web::Services::WebService
   {

   public:
      EquationGeneratorClass()
      {
```

Fig. 20.35 Web service that generates random equations. (Part 1 of 2.)

```
            InitializeComponent();
        }
    protected:
        void Dispose(Boolean disposing)
        {
            if (disposing && components)
            {
                components->Dispose();
            }
            __super::Dispose(disposing);
        }

    private:
        /// <summary>
        /// Required designer variable.
        /// </summary>
        System::ComponentModel::Container * components;

        /// <summary>
        /// Required method for Designer support - do not modify
        /// the contents of this method with the code editor.
        /// </summary>
        void InitializeComponent()
        {
        }

    public:

        [ WebMethod ( Description =
            "Method that generates a random equation." ) ]
        Equation *GenerateEquation( String *operation, int level );
    };
}
```

Fig. 20.35 Web service that generates random equations. (Part 2 of 2.)

```
// Fig. 20.36: EquationGeneratorClass.cpp
// Web service to generate random equations based on a
// specified operation and difficulty level.

#include "stdafx.h"
#include "EquationGeneratorClass.h"
#include "Global.asax.h"

namespace EquationGenerator
{
    Equation *EquationGeneratorClass::GenerateEquation(
        String *operation, int level )
    {
        // find maximum and minimum number to be used
        int maximum = static_cast< int >( Math::Pow( 10, level ) );
        int minimum = static_cast< int >( Math::Pow( 10, level - 1 ) );
```

Fig. 20.36 Web service that generates random equations. (Part 1 of 2.)

```

      Random *random = new Random();

      // create equation consisting of two random numbers
      // between minimum and maximum parameters
      Equation *equation = new Equation(
         random->Next( minimum, maximum ),
         random->Next( minimum, maximum ), operation );

      return equation;
   } // end method GenerateEquation
};
```

Fig. 20.36 Web service that generates random equations. (Part 2 of 2.)

Web service `EquationGenerator` contains only one Web-service method, `Generate-Equation`. This method takes as arguments a string representing the operation we wish to perform and an integer representing the desired difficulty level of the equation. Figure 20.37 demonstrates the result of executing a test call of this Web service. Notice that the return value from our Web-service method is marked up as XML. However, this example differs from previous ones in that the XML specifies the values for all `public` fields of the object that is being returned. The return object has been serialized into XML. Our proxy class takes this return value and deserializes it into an object (containing only the `public` data from the original object) that is then passed back to the client.

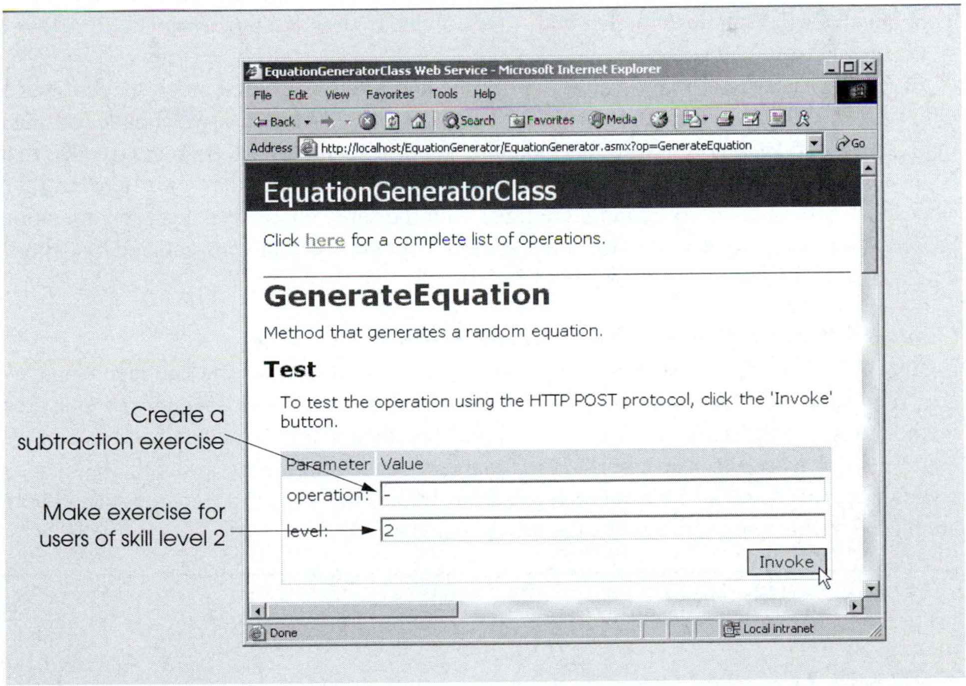

Fig. 20.37 Returning an object from a Web-service method. (Part 1 of 2.)

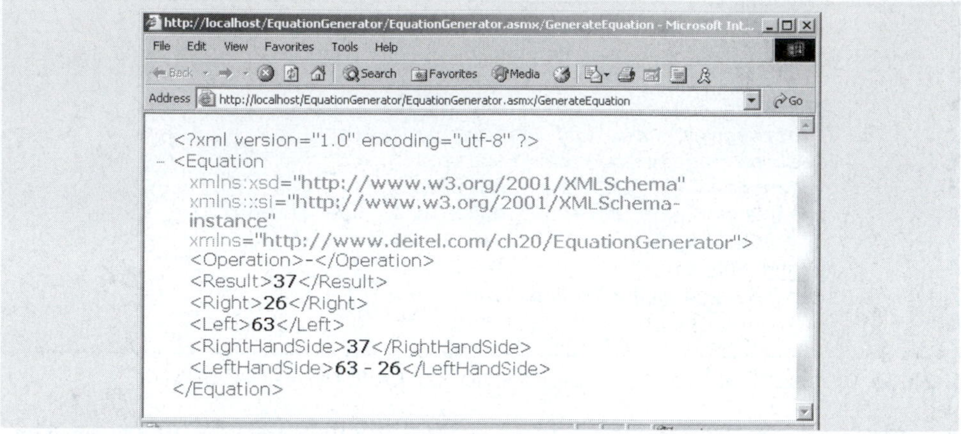

Fig. 20.37 Returning an object from a Web-service method. (Part 2 of 2.)

Lines 15–16 (of Fig. 20.36) define the lower and upper bounds for the random numbers that the method generates. To set these limits, the program first calls `static` method `Pow` of class `Math`—this method raises its first argument to the power of its second argument. Integer `maximum` represents the upper bound for a randomly generated number. The program raises `10` to the power of the specified `level` argument, then passes this value as the upper bound. For instance, if `level` is `1`, `maximum` is `10`; if `level` is `2`, `maximum` is `100`; and so on. Variable `minimum`'s value is determined by raising `10` to a power one less than `level`. This calculates the smallest number with `level` digits. If `level` is `2`, `minimum` is `10`; if `level` is `3`, `minimum` is `100` and so on.

Lines 22–24 create a new `Equation` object. The program calls `Random` method `Next`, which returns an integer that is greater than or equal to a specified lower bound, but less than a specified upper bound. In this example, `Random` generates a left operand value that is greater than or equal to `minimum`, but less than `maximum` (i.e., a number with `level` digits). The right operand is another random number with the same characteristics. The operation passed to the `Equation` constructor is the `String * operation` that was received by `GenerateEquation`. The new `Equation` object is returned.

Creating a Client to Consume the `EquationGenerator` *Web Service*

Figure 20.38–Fig. 20.39 list the math-tutoring application that uses the `EquationGenerator` Web service. The application calls `EquationGeneratorClass`'s `GenerateEquation` method to create an `Equation` object. The application then displays the left-hand side of the `Equation` and waits for user input. In this example, the program accesses both class `EquationGeneratorClass` and class `Equation` from within the `localhost` namespace—both are placed in this namespace when the proxy is generated.

```
// Fig. 20.38: Form1.h
// Math-tutor program.

#pragma once
```

Fig. 20.38 Math-tutor application. (Part 1 of 4.)

```

#include "WebService.h"

namespace MathTutor
{
   using namespace System;
   using namespace System::ComponentModel;
   using namespace System::Collections;
   using namespace System::Windows::Forms;
   using namespace System::Data;
   using namespace System::Drawing;
   using namespace EquationGenerator;

   /// <summary>
   /// Summary for Form1
   ///
   /// WARNING: If you change the name of this class, you will need to
   ///          change the 'Resource File Name' property for the managed
   ///          resource compiler tool associated with all .resx files
   ///          this class depends on.  Otherwise, the designers will not
   ///          be able to interact properly with localized resources
   ///          associated with this form.
   /// </summary>
   public __gc class Form1 : public System::Windows::Forms::Form
   {
   public:
      Form1(void)
      {
         generator = new EquationGeneratorClass();
         InitializeComponent();
      }

   protected:
      void Dispose(Boolean disposing)
      {
         if (disposing && components)
         {
            components->Dispose();
         }
         __super::Dispose(disposing);
      }
   private: System::Windows::Forms::Panel *  panel1;
   private: System::Windows::Forms::RadioButton *  oneRadioButton;
   private: System::Windows::Forms::RadioButton *  twoRadioButton;
   private: System::Windows::Forms::RadioButton *  threeRadioButton;

   private: System::Windows::Forms::Panel *  panel2;
   private: System::Windows::Forms::RadioButton *  addRadioButton;
   private: System::Windows::Forms::RadioButton *  subtractRadioButton;
   private: System::Windows::Forms::RadioButton *  multiplyRadioButton;

   private: System::Windows::Forms::Label *  questionLabel;
   private: System::Windows::Forms::TextBox *  answerTextBox;
```

Fig. 20.38 Math-tutor application. (Part 2 of 4.)

```
   private: System::Windows::Forms::Button *  generateButton;
   private: System::Windows::Forms::Button *  okButton;

   private: static int level = 1;

   private: Equation *equation;
   private: EquationGeneratorClass *generator;
   private: static String *operation = S"+";

   private:
      /// <summary>
      /// Required designer variable.
      /// </summary>
      System::ComponentModel::Container * components;

   // Visual Studio .NET generated GUI code

   // generates new equation on click event
   private: System::Void generateButton_Click(
            System::Object *  sender, System::EventArgs *  e)
         {
            // generate equation using current operation and level
            equation = generator->GenerateEquation( operation, level );

            // display left-hand side of equation
            questionLabel->Text = equation->LeftHandSide;

            okButton->Enabled = true;
            answerTextBox->Enabled = true;
         } // end method generateButton_Click

   // check users answer
   private: System::Void okButton_Click(
            System::Object *  sender, System::EventArgs *  e)
         {
            try {

               // determine correct result from Equation object
               int answer = equation->Result;

               // get user's answer
               int myAnswer = Int32::Parse( answerTextBox->Text );

               // test if user's answer is correct
               if ( answer == myAnswer ) {
                  questionLabel->Text = S"";
                  answerTextBox->Text = S"";
                  okButton->Enabled = false;
                  MessageBox::Show( S"Correct! Good job!" );
               } // end if
               else
                  MessageBox::Show( S"Incorrect. Try again." );
            } // end try
```

Fig. 20.38 Math-tutor application. (Part 3 of 4.)

```
                  catch ( FormatException * ){
                     MessageBox::Show( S"Please enter an integer answer." );
                  } // end catch
               } // end method okButton_Click

      // set the selected operation
      private: System::Void operationRadioButtons_Click(
                  System::Object *  sender, System::EventArgs *  e)
               {
                  RadioButton *item = dynamic_cast< RadioButton* >( sender );

                  // set the operation to be the appropriate symbol
                  if ( item == addRadioButton )
                     operation = S"+";
                  else if ( item == subtractRadioButton )
                     operation = S"-";
                  else
                     operation = S"*";

                  generateButton->Text = String::Concat( S"Generate ",
                     item->Text, S" Example" );
               } // end method operationRadioButtons_Click

      // set the current level
      private: System::Void levelRadioButtons_Click(
                  System::Object *  sender, System::EventArgs *  e)
               {
                  if ( sender == oneRadioButton )
                     level = 1;
                  else if ( sender == twoRadioButton )
                     level = 2;
                  else
                     level = 3;
               } // end method levelRadioButtons_Click
   };
}
```

Fig. 20.38 Math-tutor application. (Part 4 of 4.)

```
// Fig. 20.39: Form1.cpp
// Math-tutor entry point.

#include "stdafx.h"
#include "Form1.h"
#include <windows.h>

using namespace MathTutor;

int APIENTRY _tWinMain(HINSTANCE hInstance,
                     HINSTANCE hPrevInstance,
                     LPTSTR    lpCmdLine,
                     int       nCmdShow)
```

Fig. 20.39 Math-tutor entry point. (Part 1 of 2.)

```
{
   System::Threading::Thread::CurrentThread->ApartmentState =
      System::Threading::ApartmentState::STA;
   Application::Run(new Form1());
   return 0;
} // end _tWinMain
```

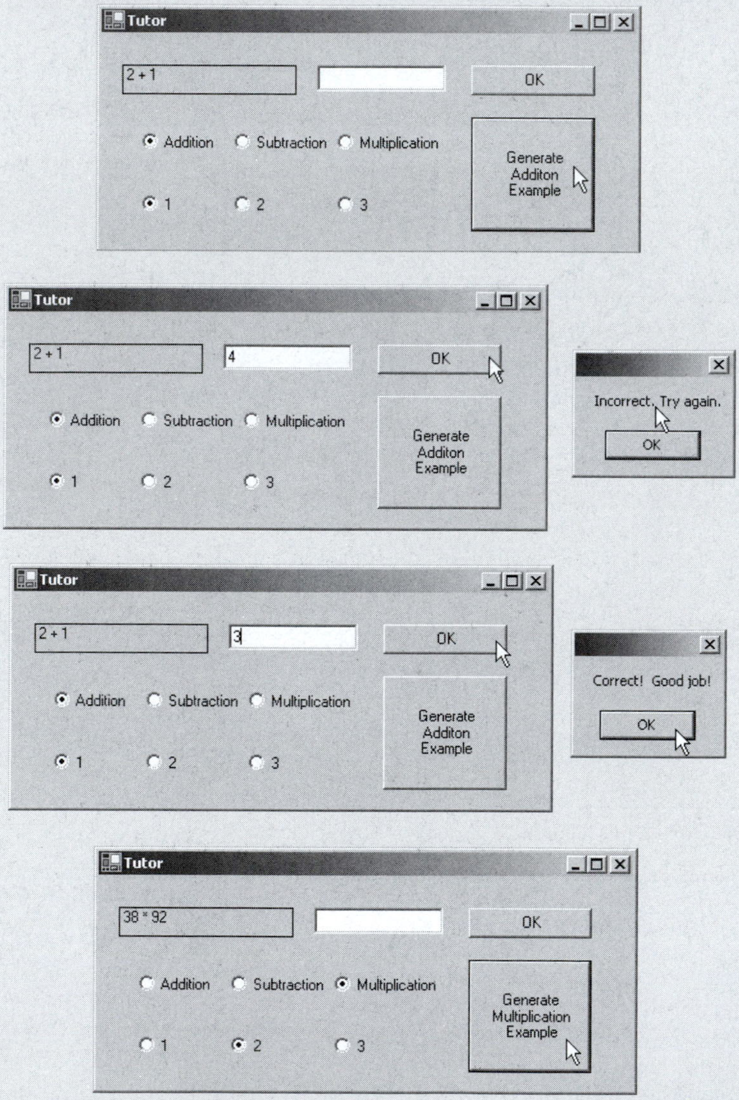

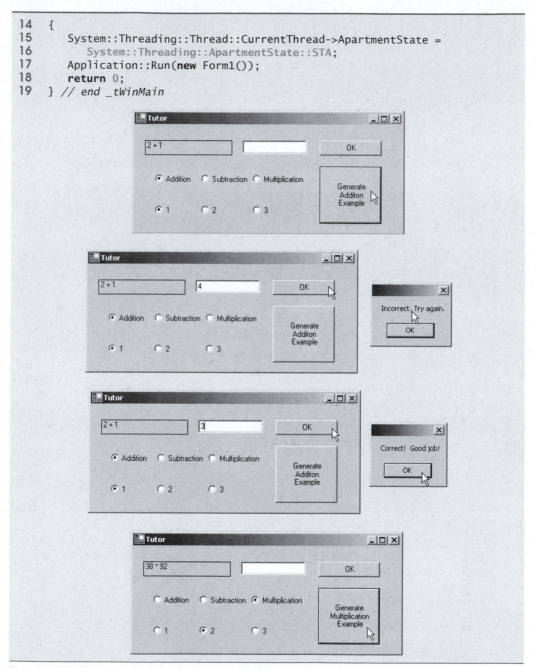

Fig. 20.39 Math-tutor entry point. (Part 2 of 2.)

The math-tutoring application displays a question and waits for input. The default setting for the difficulty level is **1**, but the user can change this at any time by choosing a level from the bottom row of `RadioButtons`. Clicking any of the level options invokes `levelRadioButtons_Click` (lines 135–144), which sets integer `level` to the level selected by the user. Although the default setting for the question type is **Addition**, the user also can change this at any time by selecting one of the top row of `RadioButtons`. Doing so invokes the `operationRadioButtons_Click` (lines 117–132) event handler, which sets string `operation` so that it contains the symbol corresponding to the user's selection.

Event handler `generateButton_Click` (lines 76–87) invokes `Generator` method `GenerateEquation`. The left-hand side of the equation is displayed in `questionLabel` (line 83), and `okButton` is enabled so that the user can enter an answer. When the user clicks **OK**, `okButton_Click` (lines 90–114) checks for whether the user provided the correct answer.

20.14 Global XML Web Services Architecture (GXA)

Web-services technologies are designed to be simple and open, containing only the necessary features to transmit data between applications across a network. However, as organizations begin to use Web services in enterprise systems, core standards such as SOAP, WSDL and UDDI do not provide sufficient support for Web services. For example, how can Web-services transmissions be secured? How are SOAP messages routed from one location to another? How does one company locate another company's Web services? How are partner relationships and Web-services interactions managed electronically?

To address such problems, Microsoft and its partners have created the *Global XML Web Services Architecture* (*GXA*), a series of specifications that extend SOAP and provide additional capabilities to Web services developers. Microsoft designed the specifications to supply the higher-level functionality that businesses require to implement complex Web services. GXA provides a general-purpose architecture, meaning that the specifications can be used in various Web service scenarios, regardless of complexity. The specifications are modular—therefore, they can be used separately or together to extend the functionality of GXA as needed. Microsoft plans to submit the GXA specifications for standardization, which will establish GXA as an open architecture.[d]

GXA specifications include *WS-Security*, *WS-Inspection*, *WS-Routing* and *WS-Referral*.[7] WS-Inspection helps programmers locate Web services' WSDL files and UDDI descriptions. WS-Routing allows developers to define routing information for a SOAP message. Developers can use WS-Routing to indicate in a SOAP envelope the path that a SOAP message should take.[e] WS-Referral enables developers to modify routing information dynamically (i.e., a SOAP message's path may be changed as the SOAP message moves from one location to another).[f] WS-Security provides security for Web-services transmissions.

Figure 20.40 illustrates the relationships among the specifications. Note that each specification enhances SOAP and that each specification is its own unit. The following sections discuss each specification in detail. New specifications are currently being developed and added to GXA. We will discuss some of these newer specifications in Section 20.14.4.

---

7. GXA includes several specifications. To provide an in-depth introduction to GXA, we discuss only the specifications in Fig. 20.40. Information about all the GXA specifications can be found at `msdn.microsoft.com/library/default.asp?url=/library/en-us/dnglobspec/html/wsspecsover.asp`.

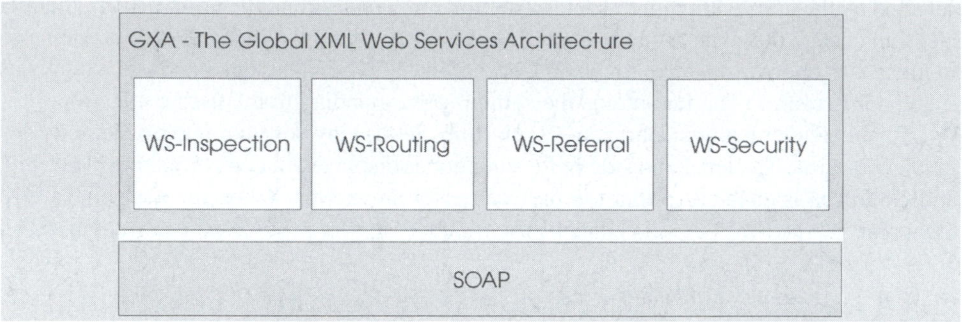

Fig. 20.40 SOAP provides the base for GXA specifications.

20.14.1 WS-Inspection[8]

WS-Inspection is a GXA specification created by Microsoft and IBM that addresses Web services discovery. WS-Inspection defines a syntax for creating *WS-Inspection documents*, which provide references to Web services available on a particular server. WS-Inspection's syntax is XML-based, so WS-Inspection documents contain references that are easy to understand, maintain and format into useful links.

UDDI allows developers to discover Web services by searching registries for services with specific capabilities. Why, then, would an organization want to use WS-Inspection? Whereas UDDI enables developers to discover Web services on the basis of functionality, WS-Inspection enables developers to discover Web services on the basis of location (i.e., Web services at a specific server). For example, some companies maintain relationships with partners that involve using each other's Web services. In these situations, a company might have access to a partner's server and might want to determine what Web services are available at that server. WS-Inspection is ideal for this purpose. WS-Inspection has a similar purpose to that of DISCO. WS-Inspection is, in fact, expected by some to replace DISCO in the future.

WS-Inspection information is stored in a document with a `.wsil` extension, known as a *WS-Inspection file* or a *WS-Inspection document*. WS-Inspection markup uses a *`service`* element to describe a Web service. The `service` element contains additional elements that provide further information about the Web service—including the *`name`* element, which identifies the service within the WSIL document; the *`abstract`* element, which provides a text description of the service; and a *`description`* element, which supplies references to service-description documents (usually WSDL files). In addition to the `service` element, a WSIL document can contain *`link`* elements, which supply links to other WSIL documents.

The WS-Inspection specification also includes *bindings*—i.e., extensions to WS-Inspection—that provide additional information to a `description` or a `link` element. Current bindings include the *WSDL binding* and the *UDDI binding*. The WSDL binding enables more specific referencing of a WSDL service description. For instance, a WSDL file can contain descriptions for several Web services; the WSDL binding enables the

8. Information in this section is based primarily on K. Ballinger, et al., "Web Services Inspection Language (WS-Inspection) 1.0." <`msdn.microsoft.com/library/en-us/dnglobspec/html/ws-inspection.asp`>.

developer to specify one specific service within such a file. The UDDI binding enables the referencing of UDDI entries. Due to WS-Inspection's extensible nature, more bindings can be created as they are needed.

For WS-Inspection files to be useful, they must be easily accessible to developers searching for Web services. One way to make a WS-Inspection file available is to name the file `inspection.wsil` and place it in a standard location—this is usually the root directory of a Web server, which is the topmost folder on the server that contains the organization's Web services. Placing a WSIL file in the root directory is sometimes referred to as *publishing the file*. Another way of providing access to an inspection document is to include a link to the document on a company's Web site. This is sometimes referred to as the *Linked* technique.[8]

20.14.2 WS-Routing[9]

WS-Routing is a specification for defining the path of a SOAP message. A SOAP message may stop at many locations when going from the sender to the receiver. These locations can be quite different in nature, so we will use the general term *intermediary* to designate a stop on the SOAP message path. Some intermediaries are known as *SOAP nodes*, which are applications or programming components that understand and process SOAP messages. Using WS-Routing, developers can specify exactly where a SOAP message should go, where it should stop along the way and the order in which the stops should be made. WS-Routing also enables developers to define the paths of SOAP-message responses.

SOAP allows developers to indicate a series of intermediaries through which a SOAP message should pass, but it is difficult to specify the order in which the message reaches these intermediaries. This is because a SOAP message can be transmitted over various transport protocols, and each transport protocol defines its own way of specifying a message path. For example, a SOAP message might travel across HTTP from its sender to an intermediary, then travel across SMTP from the intermediary to the final recipient—it would be complex and difficult to define the SOAP message's path in relation to all possible transport protocols. A developer can specify the message path by "binding" a SOAP message to a particular transport protocol, then using that protocol to define the message's path. However, this means that the SOAP message can travel only over that particular protocol.

WS-Routing provides a solution to this problem by enabling developers to specify a message path, regardless of the transport mechanism. The WS-Routing specification defines a syntax that developers can include in the header of a SOAP message. The syntax's elements can specify the message's ultimate destination (using the *`to`* element), its point of origin (using the *`from`* element) and any intermediaries (using the *`via`* element). WS-Routing also provides the *`fwd`* and *`rev`* elements, which specify the forward and reverse message path, respectively, and the *`id`* and *`relatesTo`* elements, which enable a message to reference another message. This could be useful when an error message (known as a *fault message*, or *fault*) is being sent in response to another message. The `id` and `relatesTo` elements can be used in the fault message to reference the original message that caused the error. The `fwd` element contains a list of `via` elements, which specify inter-

9. Information in this section is based primarily on H. Nielsen and S. Thatte, "Web Services Routing Protocol (WS-Routing)," October 2001 <`msdn.microsoft.com/library/en-us/dnglobspec/html/ws-routing.asp`>.

mediaries; the order of the via elements indicates the order in which the intermediaries should be reached.

When the message arrives at an intermediary (or its final destination), the receiver follows an algorithm to process the message. The receiver removes the first via element from the fwd element and determines whether the message has arrived at the proper intermediary. If so, the message is forwarded to the next receiver (specified by the next via element). If the removed via element does not reference the message's current location, an error message is returned to the original sender. If the removed via element was the last via element, the message is forwarded to the final destination, which is specified by the to element.

If an intermediary receives a message with no via elements (or no fwd element), the intermediary analyzes the to element to determine whether the current location is the final destination. If it is, the message has reached its final destination. If not, a fault is generated.

The reverse message path is generated as the message travels from the sender to the receiver (provided that the rev element exists in the SOAP header). For example, when an intermediary removes the first via element from the fwd element, a corresponding via element is added to the rev element. Thus, the WS-Routing information for the return path is created as the message moves from intermediary to intermediary.

Figure 20.41 illustrates the actions of a SOAP message that contains WS-Routing information. [*Note*: The WS-Routing information in this figure is not displayed in its actual XML-based format.] The SOAP message begins at location A. Notice that A is specified in the from element, and E, the destination of this message, is specified in the to element. The path is specified in element fwd, which, in this case, indicates that the message should stop at intermediaries B, C and D, in that order. Notice that, as the message travels from one intermediary to the next, the current location is removed from the fwd element and added to the rev element. Keep in the mind that the SOAP header is, in fact, being modified as it moves from one intermediary to another.

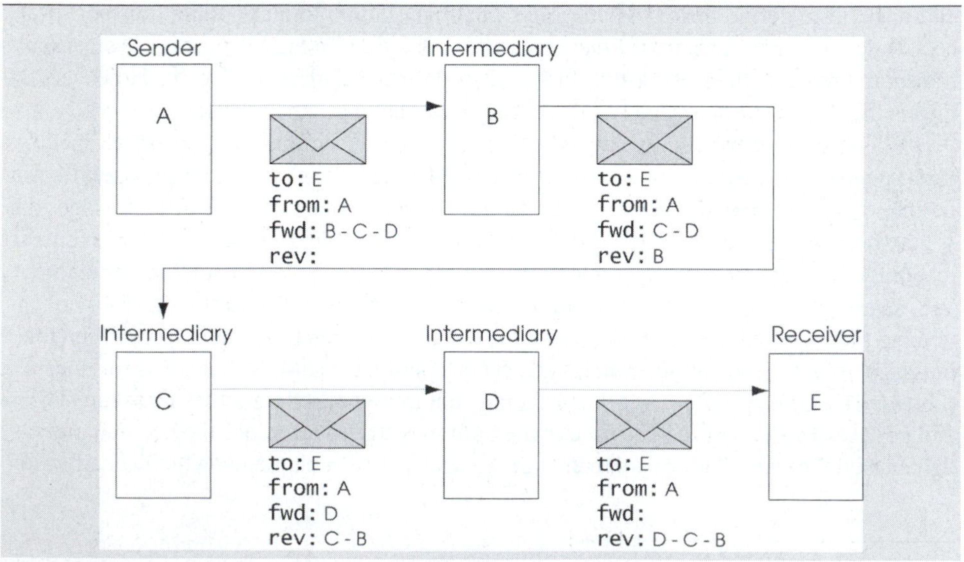

Fig. 20.41 SOAP message with WS-Routing information.

20.14.3 WS-Referral[10]

The previous section discussed WS-Routing, which enables developers to specify the path of a SOAP message. However, it is not necessary to define a SOAP message's entire path before the message leaves its sender. When an intermediary receives a message that does not have a specified next intermediary, that intermediary uses its own built-in routing information (referred to as *routing entries*), along with the ultimate destination indicated in the SOAP message, to determine the next intermediary. The message then is forwarded to the appropriate intermediary.

It is sometimes essential for a developer to modify an intermediary's routing entries. For instance, the developer might want to remove an unnecessary intermediary from the message path or inform other intermediaries of a new intermediary that can be used. WS-Referral is a specification for modifying routing entries and, thus, the paths of SOAP messages. WS-Referral can be used to modify only the routing entries of intermediaries known as SOAP routers. A *SOAP router* is a SOAP node that relays SOAP messages.[h] SOAP routers have the ability to process WS-Referral statements, which are discussed momentarily. WS-Referral can provide different SOAP routers with information about each other, which enables a SOAP message path to be changed dynamically.

The *WS-Referral Statement* is a statement used to modify routing entries. A WS-Referral statement contains a *for* element, which specifies the SOAP routers to which the statement should be applied. If a SOAP router receives a WS-Referral statement for which it is listed in the for element, the statement then is applied to that SOAP router. After the for element, an *if* element appears, which contains the conditions under which the statement should be applied. If the if element conditions are met, the message is sent to the next SOAP router, which is specified in a *go* element. WS-Referral statements are normally used to add or remove SOAP routers from a path.

WS-Referral statements can be delivered to a SOAP router in one of two ways. The first method, called a *WS-Referral Registration Message Exchange*, involves placing the WS-Referral statement in the body of a SOAP message, then sending the message to a SOAP router. In this scenario, the SOAP message is known as a *WS-Referral registration*. The SOAP router either can accept or reject the statement. The second method, known as *WS-Referral Header*, involves sending the WS-Referral statement in the header of a SOAP message.

In some situations, developers want to know what WS-Referral statements have been delivered to a SOAP router. For this purpose, WS-Referral provides the *WS-Referral Query Message Exchange*. Using WS-Referral Query Message Exchange, a query is sent (via a SOAP message) to a SOAP router. This query, which is stored in the body of the SOAP message, can be used to determine what WS-Referral statements are located at the SOAP router. The SOAP router returns a response message containing results of the query.

---

10. Information in this section is based primarily on H. Nielsen, et al., "Web Services Referral Protocol (WS-Referral)," October 2001 <msdn.microsoft.com/library/en-us/dnglobspec/html/ws-referral.asp>. Note that this document is in draft form and is therefore likely to change in the future.

20.14.4 WS-Security[11]

WS-Security provides SOAP extensions that enable a developer to build secure Web services. Web services developers have numerous security options, but most do not address Web services-specific security issues. Low-level security options, such as firewall-based rules, Secure Sockets Layer (SSL) and Virtual Private Networks (VPN), do not provide ways of authenticating messages and are ill equipped to secure large numbers of SOAP messages sent to multiple intermediaries over different transport protocols.[12] ASP .NET can provide authentication, but this authentication can be used only with HTTP; Web service messages transmitted over different protocols would require an alternate form of authentication.

Developers also can employ high-level options to ensure Web services security. One option is to leverage the capabilities of the .NET Framework. The FCL provides classes that enable developers to modify SOAP messages as they are sent back and forth between the Web service and the client. The developer can use this functionality to encrypt and decrypt information in the SOAP message at various stages of the message transmission.

Although these solutions provide security and are relatively simple, none are designed for the particular security needs of Web services. Microsoft, IBM and Verisign have developed various specifications to address Web services security. WS-Security (Web Services Security Language) is a SOAP-based specification that enables developers to enhance the security of SOAP messages. The specification enables developers to authenticate Web service users and ensure that messages remain private (*message confidentiality*) and unmodified (*message integrity*).

WS-Security defines ways of authenticating users by attaching security tokens to SOAP messages. WS-Security is extensible; therefore, it supports multiple security-token formats. The specification is designed to be compatible with commonly used security models. WS-Security also can be used in conjunction with *XML Signature* and *XML Encryption*, which are W3C security technologies used to specify digital signatures and encrypt data, respectively.[i]

This chapter familiarized readers with the creation of Web services, which enable users to request and receive data via the Internet. In the next chapter, we discuss the low-level details of how data are sent from one location to another. (This process is called networking.) Topics discussed in the next chapter include the implementation of servers and clients and the sending of data via sockets.

SUMMARY

- A Web service is an application that enables distributed computing by allowing one machine to call methods on other machines via common data formats and protocols, such as XML and HTTP.

---

11. Information in this section is based primarily on B. Atkinson, et al., "Web Services Security (WS-Security)," April 2002 <msdn.microsoft.com/library/en-us/dnglobspec/html/ws-security.asp>.

12. *SSL* is a non-proprietary protocol commonly used to secure communication between two computers on the Internet and the Web. A *VPN* connects multiple networks, wireless users and other remote users. VPNs use the Internet infrastructure that is already in place. More information on Internet security and Web services security can be found in our *Web Services: A Technical Introduction* publication.

- In .NET, these method calls are implemented through the Simple Object Access Protocol (SOAP), an XML-based protocol describing how to mark up requests and responses so that they can be transferred via protocols such as HTTP.
- Using SOAP, applications represent and transmit data in a standardized format—XML.
- The underlying implementation of the Web service is irrelevant to clients using the Web service.
- To create a Web service in Visual Studio .NET, a developer first creates a project of type **ASP .NET Web Service**. Visual Studio .NET then generates files to contain the Web service code (which implements the Web service), an ASMX file (which provides documentation for the Web service) and a DISCO file (which potential clients use to discover the Web service).
- The Web service class defines all methods that the Web service exposes to remote applications. Any methods (or additional classes) that the developer wants to incorporate in the Web service are added to this class.
- Developers must tag as a Web method each method that they want to expose.
- Once the developer adds the necessary programming logic to the Web service code file and successfully compiles the application, a client application can consume the Web service. However, clients must be able to find the Web service and learn about its capabilities.
- Discovery of Web services (DISCO) is a Microsoft-specific technology used to locate Web services in a particular directory on a server.
- There are four types of discovery files: `.disco` files, `.vsdisco` files, `.discomap` and `.map` files. All four DISCO files contain XML that can help clients locate Web service files.
- A `.disco` file contains markup that specifies references to various Web services' documents.
- A `.vsdisco` file, on the other hand, returns markup (which also contains references to Web services' documents) when requested.
- A service description is an XML document that conforms to the Web Service Description Language (WSDL), an XML vocabulary that defines the methods that the Web service makes available and the ways in which clients can interact with those methods.
- The WSDL document also specifies lower-level information that clients might need, such as the required formats for requests and responses.
- The ASMX page lists the methods that the Web service offers.
- Clicking any method name requests a test page that describes the method and provides the client with the ability to test the method.
- The test page displays sample request-and-response messages using SOAP, HTTP GET and HTTP POST.
- These protocols are the three options for sending and receiving messages in Web services.
- The protocol that transmits request and response messages also is known as the Web service's wire format, because it defines how information is sent "along the wire."
- Developers can consume Web services from their applications by the process of adding a Web reference. This process adds files to the client application that enable the client to access the Web service.
- When developers specify the Web service they want to consume, Visual Studio .NET accesses the Web service's WSDL file and makes a copy of it, which will be stored as a file in the project folder.
- The information in the WSDL file is used to create the proxy class, which handles all the "plumbing" required for Web service method calls.
- Whenever the client application calls a Web service method, the application actually calls a corresponding method in the proxy class.

- Web services used by e-businesses can personalize users' browsing experiences, tailoring content to individual users while enabling them to bypass irrelevant information.
- Personalization makes it possible for e-businesses to communicate effectively with their customers and improves users' ability to locate desired products and services.
- A trade-off exists, however, between personalized e-business service and privacy protection.
- To provide personalized services to consumers, e-businesses must be able to recognize specific clients when they request information from a site.
- A session ID represents a unique client on the Internet.
- The tracking of individual clients, known as session tracking, can be achieved in one of a number of ways.
- One popular technique uses cookies; another employs .NET's `HttpSessionState` object.
- A cookie is a text file that a Web site stores on an individual's computer to enable the site to track that individual's actions and preferences.
- Visual C++ provides session-tracking capabilities with the `HttpSessionState` class.
- Every Web-service application includes an `HttpSessionState` object, which is accessible through property `Session` of class `WebService`.
- When a Web service method is called, an `HttpSessionState` object is created and assigned to the Web service's `Session` property.
- Storing session information also can provide for a more intuitive Web service.
- A `WebMethod` must have property `EnableSession` set to `true` to maintain session information.
- The Web service then can use an `HttpSessionState` object (called `Session`) to store objects for a specific client between method calls.
- It is possible to define and employ user-defined types (also known as custom types) in a Web service.
- User-defined types can be passed into or returned from Web-service methods.
- Web-service clients also can use these user-defined types, because the proxy class created for the client contains these type definitions.
- When defining objects to be returned from Web-service methods, there are several subtleties to understand. For example, any object returned by a Web-service method must have a default constructor.
- Although all objects can be instantiated via a default constructor (even if this constructor is not defined explicitly), a class returned from a Web service must have an explicitly defined constructor, even if its body is empty.
- Any variables of our user-defined type that we wish to access on the client side must be declared `public`.
- We also must define both the *get* and the *set* methods of any properties that we wish to access at runtime. The Web service needs to have ways both to retrieve and to manipulate such properties, because objects of the user-defined type will be converted into XML (when the objects are serialized), then converted back to objects (when they are deserialized).
- During serialization, the property value must be read (through the *get* method); during deserialization, the property value of the new object must be set (through the *set* method). If only one method is present, the client application will not have access to the property.
- Microsoft's Global XML Web Services Architecture (GXA) is a set of specifications that provides higher-level functionality necessary to implement complex Web services.
- WS-Inspection defines a syntax for creating WS-Inspection documents, which provide references to Web services available on a particular server.

- WS-Routing is a specification for defining a SOAP message's path from sender to final recipient.
- WS-Referral can be used to modify routing entries and, thus, the paths of SOAP messages.
- WS-Security enables developers to enhance Web services security by authenticating users and ensuring that messages remain private (message confidentiality) and unmodified (message integrity).

TERMINOLOGY

`abstract` element in WS-Inspection
Active Server Pages (ASP) .NET
adding a Web reference
`ArrayList` class
ASMX file
ASP .NET Web service
binding
bottom tier
business logic
business-to-business (B2B) transactions
cache
client tier
consuming a Web service
controller logic
cookie
`CookieContainer` class
`CookieContainer` class
Count property of class `HttpSessionState`
data tier
`description` element in WS-Inspection
`Description` property of a `WebService` attribute
Discovery of Web services (DISCO)
DNS lookup
domain name
domain name system (DNS) server
`EnableSession` property of a `WebMethod` attribute
end tag
expiration date
`Expires` property of class `HttpCookie`
exposing a method
fault
fault message
firewall
`for` element in WS-Referral
`from` element in WS-Routing
fully qualified host name
`fwd` element in WS-Routing
get request
Global XML Web Services Architecture (GXA)
`go` element in WS-Referral
host
host name
host name
HTTP header
HTTP method
`HttpCookie` class
`HttpSessionState` class
hyperlink
Hypertext Transfer Protocol (HTTP)
`id` element in WS-Routing
`if` element in WS-Referral
information tier
intermediary
Internet Information Services (IIS)
IP (Internet Protocol) address
`IsNewSession` property of `HttpSessionState`
`IsReadOnly` property of `HttpSessionState`
`Keys` property of class `HttpSessionState`
`link` element in WS-Inspection
Linked technique
local Web server
`localhost`
markup
message confidentiality
message integrity
Multipurpose Internet Mail Extensions (MIME)
multi-tier application
`name` element in WS-Inspection
`Namespace` property of a `WebService` attribute
n-tier application
`OpenRead` method of class `WebClient`
personalization
post request
presentation logic
privacy protection
proxy class
publishing a Web service
publishing the file
query string
`relatesTo` element in WS-Routing
relational database management system (RDBMS)
remote machine
remote Web server
rendering a Web page
request method

rev element in WS-Routing
routing entry
server-side form handler
service description
service element in WS-Inspection
session ID
session item
Session property of class WebService
session tracking
SessionID property of HttpSessionState
Simple Object Access Protocol (SOAP)
SOAP envelope
SOAP message
SOAP node
SOAP router
start tag
System::Web::Services namespace
tag
Timeout property of class HttpSessionState
to element in WS-Routing
top tier
top-level domain (TLD)
TrustBridge
UDDI binding
Uniform Resource Locator (URL)
Universal Description, Discovery and Integration (UDDI)
via element in WS-Routing
virtual directory
Web control
Web method
Web server
Web service
Web Service Description Language (WSDL)
WebClient class
WebMethod attribute
WebService class
WebServiceAttribute attribute
wire format
WS-Authorization
WSDL binding
WS-Federation
WS-Inspection
WS-Inspection document
WS-Inspection file
WS-Policy
WS-Privacy
WS-Referral
WS-Referral Header
WS-Referral Query Message Exchange
WS-Referral registration
WS-Referral Registration Message Exchange
WS-Referral Statement
WS-Routing
WS-Secure Conversation
WS-Security
WS-Trust
XHTML document
XML Encryption
XML serialization
XML Signature
XML Web service

SELF-REVIEW EXERCISES

20.1 State whether each of the following is *true* or *false*. If *false*, explain why.

a) The purpose of a Web service is to create objects that are instantiated and used on the local machine.
b) A Web server is required to create Web services and make them available.
c) The purpose of the proxy class is to make it seem to clients that they are calling the Web-service methods directly.
d) Most requests to and responses from Web services created with Visual Studio .NET are transmitted via HTTP GET.
e) A client can use only Web-service methods that are tagged with the WebMethod attribute.
f) To enable session tracking in a Web-service method, the programmer sets the EnableSession property to true in the WebMethod attribute. No other action is required.
g) An application can use only one Web service.
h) All data types passed to and from Web services must be supported by SOAP.
i) WebMethods methods cannot be declared static.
j) A user-defined type used in a Web service must define both get and set methods for any property that will be accessed in an application.

20.2 Fill in the blanks for each of the following statements:

a) When messages are sent between an application and a Web service, each message is placed in a(n) ________.
b) A Web service can inherit from class ________.
c) Translation of a host name into an IP address is performed by a(n) ________.
d) The protocol used by a Web service to send and receive messages is usually known as the ________.
e) ________ is a technology used to locate Web services in a particular directory on a server.
f) Class ________ is designed for interaction with resources identified by a URL.
g) To add a description for a Web service method in an ASMX page, the ________ property of the `WebService` attribute is used.
h) Sending objects between a Web service and a client requires ________ of the object.
i) A(n) ________ represents a unique client on the Internet.
j) Cookies are deleted when they ________.

ANSWERS TO SELF-REVIEW EXERCISES

20.1 a) False. Web services are used to execute methods on remote machines. The Web service receives the parameters it needs to execute a particular method, executes the method and returns the result to the caller. b) True. c) True. d) False. Most requests to and responses from Web services created with Visual Studio .NET are transmitted via SOAP. e) True. f) False. A `CookieContainer` also must be created on the client side. g) False. An application can use as many Web services as it needs. h) True. i) True. j) True.

20.2 a) SOAP message. b) `WebService`. c) DNS server. d) wire format. e) DISCO. f) `WebClient`. g) `Description`. h) XML serialization. i) session ID. j) expire.

EXERCISES

20.3 Modify the `Blackjack` Web service example in Section 20.11 to include a class `Card`. Have `DealCard` return an object of type `Card`. Also, have the client application keep track of what cards have been dealt, using `Cards`. Your card class should include properties to determine the face and suit of the card.

20.4 Modify the `TemperatureServer` example in Section 20.12 so that it returns an array of `CityWeather` objects that the client application uses to display the weather information.

20.5 Modify the Web service in the math-tutor example in Section 20.13 so that it includes a method that calculates how "close" the player is to the correct answer. The client application should provide the correct answer only after a user has offered numerous answers that were far from the correct one. Use your best judgment regarding what constitutes being "close" to the right answer. Remember that there should be a different formula for one-digit, two-digit and three-digit numbers. Also, give the program the capability of suggesting that users try a lower difficulty level if the users are consistently wrong.

20.6 Create a Web service that stores phone-book entries in a database. Give the user the capability to enter new contacts and to find contacts by last name. Pass only primitive types as arguments to the Web service. [*Hint:* You can create a Web service that accesses a database using the same techniques learned in Chapter 19. For Web services, however, place the database in a Databases folder on the root directory of the Web server.]

20.7 Modify Exercise 20.6 so that it uses a class named `PhoneBookEntry`. The client application should provide objects of type `PhoneBookEntry` to the Web service when adding contacts and should receive objects of type `PhoneBookEntry` when searching for contacts.

WORKS CITED

a. A. Skonnard, "Publishing and Discovering Web Services with DISCO and UDDI," *MSDN Library* February 2002 <msdn.microsoft.com/msdnmag/issues/02/02/xml/xml0202.asp>.

b. R. Tabor, *Microsoft® .NET XML Web Services* (Indianapolis, IN: Sams Publishing 2002) 48.

c. "Deploying XML Web Services in Managed Code," *MSDN Library* <msdn.microsoft.com/library/default.asp?url=/library/en-us/vbcon/html/vbtskDeployingWebServices.asp>.

d. "An Introduction to GXA: Global XML Web Services Architecture," *MSDN Library* February 2002 <msdn.microsoft.com/library/en-us/dngxa/html/gloxmlws500.asp>.

e. "Web Services Specifications," *MSDN Library* <msdn.microsoft.com/library/default.asp?url=/library/en-us/dnglobspec/html/wsspecsover.asp>.

f. H. Nielsen, et al., "Web Services Referral Protocol (WS-Referral)," October 2001 <msdn.microsoft.com/library/en-us/dnglobspec/html/ws-referral.asp>.

g. S. Short, *Building XML Web Services for the Microsoft .NET Platform* (Redmond, WA: Microsoft Press 2002).

h. "Web Services Referral Specification Index Page," <msdn.microsoft.com/library/default.asp?url=/library/en-us/dnglobspec/html/wsreferspecindex.asp>.

i. "Web Services Specifications," *MSDN Library* <msdn.microsoft.com/library/default.asp?url=/library/en-us/dnglobspec/html/wsspecsover.asp>.

21

Networking: Streams-Based Sockets and Datagrams

Objectives

- To implement Visual C++ .NET networking applications that use sockets and datagrams.
- To understand how to implement Visual C++ .NET clients and servers that communicate with one another.
- To understand how to implement network-based collaborative applications.
- To construct a multithreaded server.

If the presence of electricity can be made visible in any part of a circuit, I see no reason why intelligence may not be transmitted instantaneously by electricity.
Samuel F. B. Morse

Mr. Watson, come here, I want you.
Alexander Graham Bell

What networks of railroads, highways and canals were in another age, the networks of telecommunications, information and computerization … are today.
Bruno Kreisky, Austrian Chancellor

Science may never come up with a better office-communication system than the coffee break.
Earl Wilson

Outline

21.1 Introduction

The Internet and the World Wide Web have generated a great deal of excitement in the business and computing communities. The Internet ties the "information world" together; the Web makes the Internet easy to use while providing the flair of multimedia. Organizations see both the Internet and the Web as crucial to their information-systems strategies. The .NET Framework offers a number of built-in networking capabilities that facilitate Internet-based and Web-based applications development. Visual C++ .NET not only can specify parallelism through multithreading, but also can enable programs to search the Web for information and collaborate with programs running on other computers internationally.

In Chapter 20, we began our presentation of Visual C++ .NET's networking and distributed-computing capabilities. We discussed Web Services, a high-level networking technology that enables programmers to develop distributed applications in Visual C++ .NET. In this chapter, we focus on the networking technologies that support Visual C++ .NET's Web services capabilities and can be used to build distributed applications.

Our discussion of networking focuses on both sides of a *client/server relationship*. The *client* requests that some action be performed; the *server* performs the action and responds to the client. A common implementation of this request-response model is between Web browsers and Web servers. When users select Web sites that they wish to view through a browser (the client application), the browser makes a request to the appropriate Web server (the server application). The server normally responds to the client by sending the appropriate HTML Web pages.

The networking capabilities of the .NET Framework are grouped into several namespaces. The fundamental networking capabilities are defined by classes and interfaces of namespace *`System::Net::Sockets`*. Through this namespace, Visual C++ .NET offers *socket-based communications*, which enable developers to view networking as if it were file I/O. This means that a program can read from a *socket* (network connection) or write to a socket as easily as it can read from or write to a file. Sockets are the fundamental way to perform network communications in the .NET Framework. The term "socket" refers to the Berkeley Sockets Interface, which was developed in 1978 for network programming with UNIX and was popularized by C and C++ programmers.

The classes and interfaces of namespace `System::Net::Sockets` also offer *packet-based communications*, through which individual *packets* of information are transmitted. When data are sent across a network, the data are first broken up into *packets*—small amounts of data. Each packet contains a few bytes of the original data, as well as other information (called *header information*), including its origin and its destination. This is a common method of transmitting audio and video over the Internet. In this chapter, we show how to create and manipulate sockets and how to communicate via packets of data.

Socket-based communications in Visual C++ .NET employ *stream sockets*. With stream sockets, a *process* (running program) establishes a *connection* to another process (that is running on the same machine or on a different machine). While the connection is in place, data flows between the processes in continuous *streams*. For this reason, stream sockets are said to provide a *connection-oriented service*. The popular *TCP (Transmission Control Protocol)* facilitates stream-socket transmission.

By contrast, packet-based communications in Visual C++ .NET employ *datagram sockets*, through which individual packets of information are transmitted. Unlike TCP, the protocol used to enable datagram sockets—*UDP*, the *User Datagram Protocol*—is a *connectionless service* and does not guarantee that packets will arrive in any particular order. In fact, packets can be lost or duplicated and can arrive out of sequence. Applications that use UDP often require significant extra programming to deal with these problems. UDP is most appropriate for network applications that do not require the error checking and reliability of TCP. For example, several online multi-player games use UDP, because speed is more important than perfect accuracy in these types of applications. Stream sockets and the TCP protocol will be the most desirable method of communication for the vast majority of Visual C++ .NET programmers.

Performance Tip 21.1

Connectionless services generally offer better performance but less reliability than do connection-oriented services.

Portability Tip 21.1

The TCP protocol and its related set of protocols enable intercommunication among a wide variety of heterogeneous computer systems (i.e., computer systems with different processors and different operating systems).

21.2 Establishing a Simple Server (Using Stream Sockets)

Typically, with TCP and stream sockets, a server "waits" for a connection request from a client. Often, the server program contains a control statement or block of code that executes continuously until the server receives a request. On receiving a request, the server establishes a connection with the client. The server then uses this connection to handle future requests from that client and to send data to the client.

Establishing a simple server with TCP and stream sockets in MC++ requires five steps. The first step is to create an object of class `TcpListener`, which belongs to namespace `System::Net::Sockets`. This class represents a TCP stream socket through which a server can listen for requests. A call to the `TcpListener` constructor, such as

```
TcpListener *server = new TcpListener(
   new IPAddress( static_cast< __int64 >( 0 ) ), port );
```

binds (assigns) the server to the specified *port number* on the local machine.

A port number identifies a process at a given *network address*, also known as an *Internet Protocol Address* (*IP Address*). IP addresses identify computers on the Internet. In fact, Web-site names, such as `www.deitel.com`, are aliases for IP addresses. Any process that performs networking identifies itself via an *IP address/port number pair*. Hence, no two processes can have the same port number at a given IP address. The explicit binding of a socket to a port (using method *`Bind`* of class `Socket`) is usually unnecessary, because class `TcpListener` and other classes discussed in this chapter perform this binding and other socket-initialization operations for you.

Software Engineering Observation 21.1

Port numbers can have values between 0 and 65535. Many operating systems reserve port numbers below 1024 for system services (such as e-mail and Web servers). Applications must be granted special privileges to use these reserved port numbers. Usually, a server-side application should not specify port numbers below 1024 as connection ports, because some operating systems might reserve these numbers.

Common Programming Error 21.1

Attempting to bind to a port that has already been assigned is a logic error.

To receive requests, the `TcpListener` first must listen for them. The second step in our connection process is to call `TcpListener`'s *`Start`* method, so the `TcpListener` begins listening for connection requests. The third step establishes the connection between the server and client. The server listens indefinitely for a request—i.e., the execution of the server-side application waits until some client attempts to connect to it. The server creates a connection to the client upon receipt of a connection request. An object of class *`System::Net::Sockets::Socket`* manages each connection to the client. Method *`AcceptSocket`* of class `TcpListener` waits for a connection request, then creates a connection when a request is received. This method returns a `Socket` object upon connection, as in the statement

```
Socket *connection = server->AcceptSocket();
```

When the server receives a request, method `AcceptSocket` calls method *`Accept`* of the `TcpListener`'s underlying `Socket` to make the connection. This is an example of how Visual C++ .NET hides networking complexity from you. You can write the preceding statement into a server-side program, then allow the classes of namespace `System:: Net::Sockets` to handle the details of accepting requests and establishing connections.

Step 4 is the processing phase, in which the server and the client communicate via methods *`Receive`* and *`Send`* of class `Socket`. Note that these methods can be used only when the server and client are connected. By contrast, through `Socket` methods *`SendTo`* and *`ReceiveFrom`*, UDP and datagram sockets can be used when no connection exists.

The fifth step is the connection-termination phase. When the client and server have finished communicating, the server uses method *`Close`* of the `Socket` object to close the connection. Most servers then return to Step 2 (i.e., wait for another client's connection request).

One problem associated with the server scheme described in this section is that step four *blocks* other requests while processing a client's request, so that no other client can connect with the server while the code that defines the processing phase is executing. The most common technique for addressing this problem is to use multithreaded servers, which place the processing-phase code in a separate thread. When the server receives a connection request, the server *spawns*, or creates, a `Thread` to process the connection, leaving its

`TcpListener` (or `Socket`) free to receive other connections. This newly created `Thread` is also assigned a new `Socket` (with a different port number) that it can use to communicate with its client.

Software Engineering Observation 21.2

Using the .NET Framework's multithreading capabilities, we can create servers that can manage simultaneous connections with multiple clients. This multithreaded-server architecture is precisely what popular UNIX and Windows network servers use.

Software Engineering Observation 21.3

A multithreaded server can be implemented to create a thread that manages network I/O across a pointer to a `Socket` *object returned by method* `AcceptSocket`*. A multithreaded server also can be implemented to maintain a pool of threads that manage network I/O across newly created* `Socket`*s.*

Performance Tip 21.2

In high-performance systems with abundant memory, a multithreaded server can be implemented to create a pool of threads. These threads can be assigned quickly to handle network I/O across each multiple `Socket`*. Thus, when a connection is received, the server does not incur the overhead of thread creation.*

21.3 Establishing a Simple Client (Using Stream Sockets)

Four steps are required to create simple TCP-stream-socket clients. The first step is to create an object of class *`TcpClient`* (which belongs to namespace `System::Net::Sockets`) to connect to the server. This connection is established through method *`Connect`* of class `TcpClient`. One overloaded version of this method receives two arguments—the server's IP address and the port number—as in the following code:

```
TcpClient *client = new TcpClient();
client->Connect( serverAddress, serverPort );
```

Here, `serverPort` is an `int` that represents the server's port number; `serverAddress` can be either an *`IPAddress`* instance (that encapsulates the server's IP address) or a `String *` that specifies the server's hostname. Alternatively, the programmer could pass a pointer to an object of class *`IPEndPoint`*, which represents an IP address/port number pair, to a different overload of method `Connect`. Method `Connect` of class `TcpClient` calls method *`Connect`* of class `Socket` to establish the connection. If the connection is successful, method `TcpClient::Connect` returns a positive integer; otherwise, it returns `0`.

In Step 2, the `TcpClient` uses its method *`GetStream`* to get a *`NetworkStream`* so that it can write to and read from the server. `NetworkStream` methods *`WriteByte`* and *`Write`* can be used to output individual bytes or sets of bytes to the server, respectively; similarly, `NetworkStream` methods *`ReadByte`* and *`Read`* can be used to input individual bytes or sets of bytes from the server, respectively.

The third step is the processing phase, in which the client and the server communicate. In this phase, the client uses methods `Read`, `ReadByte`, `Write` and `WriteByte` of class `NetworkStream` to perform the appropriate communications. Using a process similar to that used by servers, a client can employ threads to prevent blocking of communications with other servers while processing data from one connection.

After the transmission is complete, step four requires the client to close the connection by calling method *`Close`* of the `NetworkStream` object. This closes the underlying `Socket` (if the `NetworkStream` has a pointer to that `Socket`). Then, the client calls method *`Close`* of class `TcpClient` to terminate the TCP connection.

Good Programming Practice 21.1

Leaving socket objects open after you have finished using them wastes resources. Remember to close each socket explicitly using method `Close`.

21.4 Client/Server Interaction with Stream-Socket Connections

The applications in Fig. 21.1–Fig. 21.2 and Fig. 21.3–Fig. 21.4 use the classes and techniques discussed in the previous two sections to construct a simple *client/server chat application*. The server waits for a client's request to make a connection. When a client application connects to the server, the server application sends an array of bytes to the client, indicating that the connection was successful. The client then displays a message notifying the user that a connection has been established.

Both the client and the server applications contain `TextBoxes` that enable users to type messages and send them to the other application. When either the client or the server sends message `"TERMINATE"`, the connection between the client and the server terminates. The server then waits for another client to request a connection. Fig. 21.1–Fig. 21.2 and Fig. 21.3–Fig. 21.4 provide the code for classes `Server` and `Client`, respectively. Fig. 21.4 also contains screen captures displaying the execution between the client and the server.

We begin by discussing the `Server` (Fig. 21.1–Fig. 21.2). In the constructor, line 39 (Fig. 21.1) creates a `Thread` that will accept connections from clients. Line 40 starts the `Thread`, which invokes method `RunServer` (lines 108–187). Method `RunServer` initializes the server to receive connection requests and process connections. Lines 118–119 instantiate the `TcpListener` to listen for a connection request from a client at port `4500` (Step 1). Line 122 then calls method `Start` of the `TcpListener` object, which causes the `TcpListener` to begin waiting for requests (Step 2).

```
1  // Fig. 21.1: Form1.h
2  // Set up a Server that will receive a connection from a client,
3  // send a string to the client, and close the connection.
4
5  #pragma once
6
7
8  namespace Server
9  {
10    using namespace System;
11    using namespace System::ComponentModel;
12    using namespace System::Collections;
13    using namespace System::Windows::Forms;
14    using namespace System::Data;
15    using namespace System::Drawing;
16    using namespace System::Threading;
17    using namespace System::Net;
```

Fig. 21.1 Server portion of a client/server stream-socket connection. (Part 1 of 5.)

```
   using namespace System::Net::Sockets;
   using namespace System::IO;

   /// <summary>
   /// Summary for Form1
   ///
   /// WARNING: If you change the name of this class, you will need to
   ///          change the 'Resource File Name' property for the managed
   ///          resource compiler tool associated with all .resx files
   ///          this class depends on.  Otherwise, the designers will not
   ///          be able to interact properly with localized resources
   ///          associated with this form.
   /// </summary>
   public __gc class Form1 : public System::Windows::Forms::Form
   {
   public:
      Form1(void)
      {
         InitializeComponent();

         // create a new thread from the server
         readThread = new Thread( new ThreadStart( this, RunServer ) );
         readThread->Start();
      }

   protected:
      void Dispose(Boolean disposing)
      {
         if (disposing && components)
         {
            components->Dispose();
         }
         __super::Dispose(disposing);
      }
   private: System::Windows::Forms::TextBox *  displayTextBox;
   private: System::Windows::Forms::TextBox *  inputTextBox;

   private: Socket *connection;
   private: Thread *readThread;

   private: NetworkStream *socketStream;
   private: BinaryWriter *writer;
   private: BinaryReader *reader;

   private:
      /// <summary>
      /// Required designer variable.
      /// </summary>
      System::ComponentModel::Container * components;

   // Visual Studio .NET generated code

```

Fig. 21.1 Server portion of a client/server stream-socket connection. (Part 2 of 5.)

```
   private: System::Void Form1_Closing(System::Object *  sender,
               System::ComponentModel::CancelEventArgs *  e)
            {
               System::Environment::Exit( System::Environment::ExitCode );
            }

   // sends the text typed at the server to the client
   private: System::Void inputTextBox_KeyDown(System::Object *  sender,
               System::Windows::Forms::KeyEventArgs *  e)
            {
               // sends the text to the client
               try {

                  if ( e->KeyCode == Keys::Enter && connection != NULL ) {
                     writer->Write( String::Concat( S"SERVER>>> ",
                        inputTextBox->Text ) );

                     displayTextBox->Text = String::Concat(
                        displayTextBox->Text, S"\r\nSERVER>>> ",
                        inputTextBox->Text );

                     // if the user at the server signaled termination
                     // sever the connection to the client
                     if ( inputTextBox->Text->Equals( S"TERMINATE" ) )
                        connection->Close();

                     inputTextBox->Clear();
                  } // end if
               } // end try
               catch ( SocketException * ) {
                  displayTextBox->Text = String::Concat(
                     displayTextBox->Text, S"\nError writing object" );
               } // end catch
            } // end method inputTextBox_KeyDown

   public:

      // allows a client to connect and displays the text it sends
      void RunServer()
      {
         TcpListener *listener;
         int counter = 1;

         // wait for a client connection and display the text
         // that the client sends
         try {

            // Step 1: create TcpListener
            listener = new TcpListener(
               new IPAddress( static_cast< __int64 >( 0 ) ), 4500 );

            // Step 2: TcpListener waits for connection request
            listener->Start();
```

Fig. 21.1 Server portion of a client/server stream-socket connection. (Part 3 of 5.)

```

         // Step 3: establish connection upon client request
         while ( true ) {
            displayTextBox->Text = S"Waiting for connection\r\n";

            // accept an incoming connection
            connection = listener->AcceptSocket();

            // create NetworkStream object associated with socket
            socketStream = new NetworkStream( connection );

            // create objects for transferring data across stream
            writer = new BinaryWriter( socketStream );
            reader = new BinaryReader( socketStream );

            displayTextBox->Text = String::Concat(
               displayTextBox->Text, S"Connection ",
               counter.ToString(), S" received.\r\n" );

            // inform client that connection was successfull
            writer->Write( S"SERVER>>> Connection successful" );

            inputTextBox->ReadOnly = false;
            String *theReply = S"";

            // Step 4: read String data sent from client
            do {

               try {

                  // read the string sent to the server
                  theReply = reader->ReadString();

                  // display the message
                  displayTextBox->Text = String::Concat(
                     displayTextBox->Text, S"\r\n", theReply );
               } // end try

               // handle exception if error reading data
               catch ( Exception * ) {
                  break;
               } // end catch

            } while ( !theReply->Equals( S"CLIENT>>> TERMINATE" )
               && connection->Connected );

            displayTextBox->Text = String::Concat(
               displayTextBox->Text,
               S"\r\nUser terminated connection" );

            // Step 5: close connection
            inputTextBox->ReadOnly = true;
            writer->Close();
```

Fig. 21.1 Server portion of a client/server stream-socket connection. (Part 4 of 5.)

```
176                 reader->Close();
177                 socketStream->Close();
178                 connection->Close();
179
180                 ++counter;
181              } // end while
182           } // end try
183
184           catch ( Exception *error ) {
185              MessageBox::Show( error->ToString() );
186           } // end catch
187        } // end method RunServer
188     };
189  }
```

Fig. 21.1 Server portion of a client/server stream-socket connection. (Part 5 of 5.)

```
// Fig. 21.2: Form1.cpp
// Entry point for application.

#include "stdafx.h"
#include "Form1.h"
#include <windows.h>

using namespace Server;

int APIENTRY _tWinMain(HINSTANCE hInstance,
                       HINSTANCE hPrevInstance,
                       LPTSTR    lpCmdLine,
                       int       nCmdShow)
{
   System::Threading::Thread::CurrentThread->ApartmentState =
      System::Threading::ApartmentState::STA;
   Application::Run(new Form1());
   return 0;
} // end _tWinMain
```

Fig. 21.2 Server entry point.

Lines 125–181 declare an infinite loop that establishes connections requested by clients (Step 3). Line 129 calls method `AcceptSocket` of the `TcpListener` object, which returns a pointer to a `Socket` object upon successful connection. The thread in which method `AcceptSocket` is called stops executing until a connection is established. The `Socket` object will manage the connection. Line 132 passes this `Socket` pointer as an argument to the constructor of a `NetworkStream` object. Class `NetworkStream` provides access to streams across a network—in this example, the `NetworkStream` object provides access to the `Socket` connection. Lines 135–136 create instances of the *`BinaryWriter`* and *BinaryReader* classes for writing and reading data. We pass the NetworkStream object as an argument to each constructor; BinaryWriter can write bytes to a NetworkStream, and BinaryReader can read bytes from a NetworkStream. Lines 138–140 append text to the TextBox, indicating that a connection was received.

BinaryWriter method *Write* has many overloaded versions, which enable the method to write various types to a stream. (You might remember that we used these overloaded methods in Chapter 17 to write record data to files.) Line 143 uses method Write to send to the client a String * notifying the user of a successful connection. Lines 149–167 declare a do…while statement that executes until the server receives a message (i.e., CLIENT>>> TERMINATE) indicating connection termination. Line 154 uses BinaryReader method *ReadString* to read a String * from the stream (Step 4). (You might remember that we also used this method in Chapter 17 to read records' first-names and last-names from files.) Method ReadString blocks until a String * is read. To prevent the whole server from blocking, we use a separate Thread to execute method RunServer. This thread is created and started on lines 39–40. The while statement loops until there is more information to read—this results in I/O blocking, which causes the program always to appear frozen. However, if we run this portion of the program in a separate Thread, the user can interact with the Windows Form and send messages while the program waits in the background for incoming messages.

When the chat is complete, lines 175–178 close the BinaryWriter, BinaryReader, NetworkStream and Socket (Step 5) by invoking their respective Close methods. The server then waits for another client connection request by returning to the beginning of the while loop (line 125).

When the user of the server application enters a string in the TextBox and presses the *Enter* key, event handler inputTextBox_KeyDown (lines 77–103) reads the string and sends it via method Write of class BinaryWriter. If a user terminates the server application, line 94 calls method Close of the Socket object to close the connection.

Lines 70–74 define the Form1_Closing event handler for the Closing event. The event closes the application and uses System::Environment::Exit method with parameter System::Environment::ExitCode to terminate all threads. Method Exit of class Environment closes all threads associated with the application.

Figure 21.3–Fig. 21.4 list the code for the Client application. Like the Server application, the Client application creates a Thread (lines 37–38 of Fig. 21.3) in its constructor to handle all incoming messages. Client method RunClient (lines 100–164) connects to the Server, receives data from the Server and stores data that will be sent to the Server (this data will be sent when the user presses *Enter* in event handler inputTextBox_KeyDown). Lines 110–111 instantiate a TcpClient object, then call its method Connect to establish a connection (Step 1). The first argument to method Connect is the name of the server—in our case, the server's name is *"localhost"*, meaning that the server is located on the same machine as the client. The localhost is also known as the *loopback IP address* and is equivalent to the IP address *127.0.0.1*. This value sends the data transmission back to the sender's IP address. [*Note*: We chose to demonstrate the client/server relationship by connecting between programs that are executing on the same computer (localhost). Normally, this argument would contain the Internet address of another computer.] The second argument to method Connect is the server port number. This number must match the port number at which the server waits for connections.

```
// Fig. 21.3: Form1.h
// Set up a Client that will read information sent
// from a Server and display the information.

#pragma once


namespace Client
{
   using namespace System;
   using namespace System::ComponentModel;
   using namespace System::Collections;
   using namespace System::Windows::Forms;
   using namespace System::Data;
   using namespace System::Drawing;
   using namespace System::Threading;
   using namespace System::Net::Sockets;
   using namespace System::IO;

   /// <summary>
   /// Summary for Form1
   ///
   /// WARNING: If you change the name of this class, you will need to
   ///          change the 'Resource File Name' property for the managed
   ///          resource compiler tool associated with all .resx files
   ///          this class depends on.  Otherwise, the designers will not
   ///          be able to interact properly with localized resources
   ///          associated with this form.
   /// </summary>
   public __gc class Form1 : public System::Windows::Forms::Form
   {
   public:
      Form1(void)
      {
         InitializeComponent();

         readThread = new Thread( new ThreadStart( this, RunClient ) );
         readThread->Start();
      }

   protected:
      void Dispose(Boolean disposing)
      {
         if (disposing && components)
         {
            components->Dispose();
         }
         __super::Dispose(disposing);
      }
   private: System::Windows::Forms::TextBox *  inputTextBox;
   private: System::Windows::Forms::TextBox *  displayTextBox;

   private: NetworkStream *clientStream;
```

Fig. 21.3 Client portion of a client/server stream-socket connection. (Part 1 of 4.)

```
   private: BinaryWriter *writer;
   private: BinaryReader *reader;

   private: String *message;

   private: Thread *readThread;

   private:
      /// <summary>
      /// Required designer variable.
      /// </summary>
      System::ComponentModel::Container * components;

   // Visual Studio .NET generated GUI code

   private: System::Void Form1_Closing(System::Object *  sender,
            System::ComponentModel::CancelEventArgs *  e)
         {
            System::Environment::Exit( System::Environment::ExitCode );
         }

   // sends text the user typed to server
   private: System::Void inputTextBox_KeyDown(System::Object *  sender,
            System::Windows::Forms::KeyEventArgs *  e)
         {
            try {

               if ( e->KeyCode == Keys::Enter ) {
                  writer->Write( String::Concat(
                     S"CLIENT>>> ", inputTextBox->Text ) );

                  displayTextBox->Text = String::Concat(
                     displayTextBox->Text, S"\r\nCLIENT>>> ",
                     inputTextBox->Text );

                  inputTextBox->Clear();
               } // end if
            } // end try
            catch ( SocketException * ) {
               displayTextBox->Text = String::Concat(
                  displayTextBox->Text, S"\nError writing object" );
            } // end catch
         } // end method inputTextBox_KeyDown
   public:

      // connect to server and display server-generated text
      void RunClient()
      {
         TcpClient *client;

         // instantiate TcpClient for sending data to server
         try {
```

Fig. 21.3 Client portion of a client/server stream-socket connection. (Part 2 of 4.)

```
         displayTextBox->Text = String::Concat(
            displayTextBox->Text, S"Attempting connection\r\n" );

         // Step 1: create TcpClient and connect to server
         client = new TcpClient();
         client->Connect( S"localhost", 4500 );

         // Step 2: get NetworkStream associated with TcpClient
         clientStream = client->GetStream();

         // create objects for writing and reading across stream
         writer = new BinaryWriter( clientStream );
         reader = new BinaryReader( clientStream );

         displayTextBox->Text = String::Concat(
            displayTextBox->Text, S"\r\nGot I/O streams\r\n" );

         inputTextBox->ReadOnly = false;

         // loop until server signals termination
         do {

            // Step 3: processing phase
            try {

               // read message from server
               message = reader->ReadString();
               displayTextBox->Text = String::Concat(
                  displayTextBox->Text, S"\r\n", message );
            } // end try

            // handle exception if error in reading server data
            catch ( Exception * ) {
               System::Environment::Exit(
                  System::Environment::ExitCode );
            } // end catch

         } while ( !message->Equals( S"CLIENT>>> TERMINATE" ) );

         displayTextBox->Text = String::Concat(
            displayTextBox->Text,
            S"\r\nClosing connection->\r\n" );

         // Step 4: close connection
         writer->Close();
         reader->Close();
         clientStream->Close();
         client->Close();

         Application::Exit();
      } // end try
```

Fig. 21.3 Client portion of a client/server stream-socket connection. (Part 3 of 4.)

```
         // handle exception if error in establishing connection
         catch ( Exception *error ) {
            MessageBox::Show( error->ToString() );

            Application::Exit();
         } // end catch
      } // end method RunClient
   };
}
```

Fig. 21.3 Client portion of a client/server stream-socket connection. (Part 4 of 4.)

```
// Fig. 21.4: Form1.cpp
// Entry point for application.

#include "stdafx.h"
#include "Form1.h"
#include <windows.h>

using namespace Client;

int APIENTRY _tWinMain(HINSTANCE hInstance,
                       HINSTANCE hPrevInstance,
                       LPTSTR    lpCmdLine,
                       int       nCmdShow)
{
   System::Threading::Thread::CurrentThread->ApartmentState =
      System::Threading::ApartmentState::STA;
   Application::Run(new Form1());
   return 0;
} // end _tWinMain
```

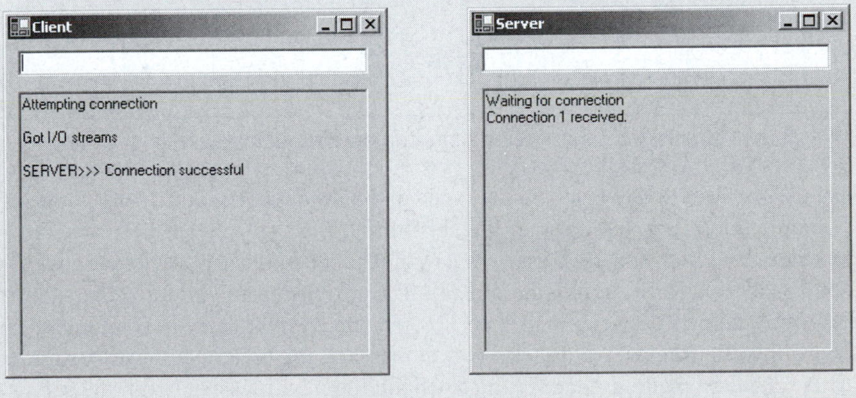

Fig. 21.4 Demonstrating a client/server stream-socket connection. (Part 1 of 2.)

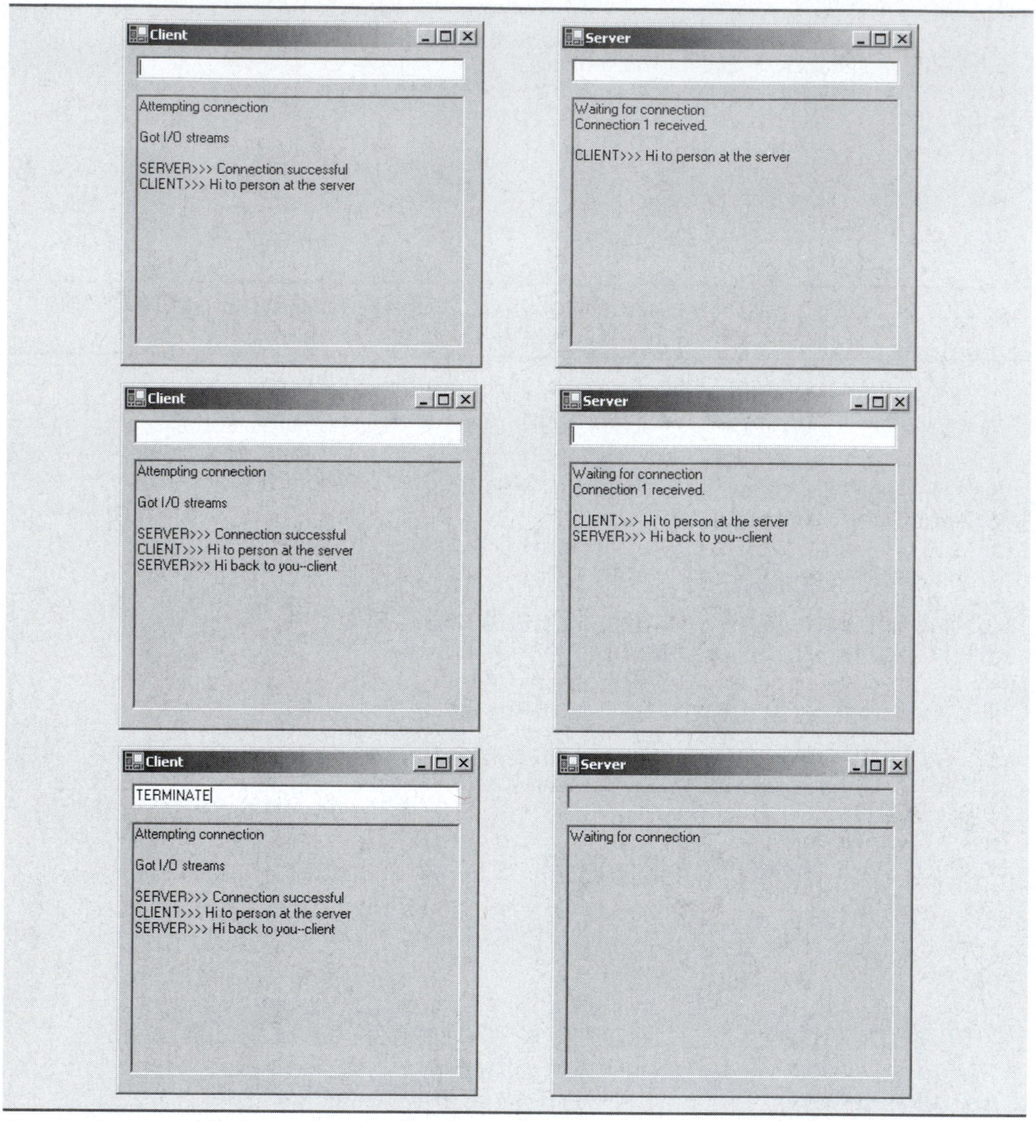

Fig. 21.4 Demonstrating a client/server stream-socket connection. (Part 2 of 2.)

The `Client` uses a `NetworkStream` to send data to and receive data from the server. The client obtains the `NetworkStream` in line 114 through a call to `TcpClient` method `GetStream` (Step 2). Lines 117–118 create a `BinaryWriter` and a `BinaryReader` with which data sent back and forth across the stream. These objects are initialized to the stream returned from method `GetStream` on line 114. The `do...while` statement in lines 126–143 loops until the client receives the termination message (`SERVER>>> TERMINATE`). Line 132 uses `BinaryReader` method `ReadString` to obtain the next message from the server (Step 3). Lines 133–134 display the message, and lines 150–153 close the `BinaryWriter`, `BinaryReader`, `NetworkStream` and `TcpClient` objects (Step 4) after the receiving loop terminates.

When the user of the client application enters a string in the `TextBox` and presses the *Enter* key, the event handler `inputTextBox_KeyDown` (lines 76–96) reads the string from the `TextBox` and sends it via `BinaryWriter` method `Write` (lines 82–83).

Notice that, in this client/server application, the `Server` receives a connection, processes it, closes it and waits for the next one. In a real-world application, a server would likely receive a connection, set up the connection to be processed as a separate thread of execution and wait for new connections. The separate threads that process existing connections can continue to execute while the `Server` concentrates on new connection requests.

21.5 Connectionless Client/Server Interaction with Datagrams

Up to this point, we have discussed connection-oriented, streams-based transmission. Now, we consider connectionless transmission using datagrams.

Connection-oriented transmission is similar to interaction over a telephone system, in which a user dials a number and is *connected* to the telephone of the party desired. The system maintains the connection for the duration of the phone call, regardless of whether the users are speaking. By contrast, connectionless transmission via *datagrams* more closely resembles the method by which the postal service carries and delivers mail. Connectionless transmission bundles and sends information in *packets* called datagrams, which can be thought of as similar to posted letters. If a large message will not fit in one envelope, that message is broken into separate message pieces and placed in separate, sequentially numbered envelopes. All the letters are mailed at once. The letters might arrive in order, out of order or not at all. The person at the receiving end reassembles the message pieces into sequential order before attempting to interpret the message. If the message is small enough to fit in one envelope, the sequencing problem is eliminated, but it is still possible that the message will never arrive. (Unlike with postal mail, duplicates of datagrams could reach receiving computers.) .NET provides the *`UdpClient`* class for connectionless transmission. Like `TcpListener` and `TcpClient`, `UdpClient` uses methods from class `Socket`. The `UdpClient` methods *`Send`* and *`Receive`* are used to transmit data with `Socket`'s `SendTo` method and to read data with `Socket`'s `ReceiveFrom` method, respectively.

The programs in Fig. 21.5–Fig. 21.6 (`Server`) and Fig. 21.7–Fig. 21.8 (`Client`) use datagrams to send *packets* of information between a client and server applications. In the `Client` application, the user types a message into a `TextBox` and presses *Enter*. The client converts the message to a `Byte` array and sends it to the server. The server receives the packet and displays the packet's information; it then *echoes*, or returns, the packet back to the client. When the client receives the packet, the client displays the packet's information. In this example (Fig. 21.5–Fig. 21.8), the implementations of the `Server` and `Client` are similar to the `Server` and `Client` created earlier (in Fig. 21.1–Fig. 21.4).

The code in Fig. 21.5–Fig. 21.6 defines the `Server` for this application. Line 38 (Fig. 21.5) in the constructor for the `Server` creates an instance of the `UdpClient` class that receives data at port `4600`. This initializes the underlying `Socket` for communications. Line 39 creates an instance of class `IPEndPoint` to hold the IP address and port number of the client that transmit to `Server`. The first argument to the constructor of `IPEndPoint` is an `IPAddress` object pointer; the second argument to the constructor for `IPEndPoint` is the port number of the endpoint. These values are both `0`, because we need only instantiate an empty `IPEndPoint` object. The IP addresses and port numbers of clients are copied into the `IPEndPoint` when datagrams are received from clients.

```
// Fig. 21.5: Form1.h
// Set up a Server that will receive packets from a
// client and send packets to a client.

#pragma once


namespace Server
{
   using namespace System;
   using namespace System::ComponentModel;
   using namespace System::Collections;
   using namespace System::Windows::Forms;
   using namespace System::Data;
   using namespace System::Drawing;
   using namespace System::Net;
   using namespace System::Net::Sockets;
   using namespace System::Threading;
   using namespace System::Text;

   /// <summary>
   /// Summary for Form1
   ///
   /// WARNING: If you change the name of this class, you will need to
   ///          change the 'Resource File Name' property for the managed
   ///          resource compiler tool associated with all .resx files
   ///          this class depends on.  Otherwise, the designers will not
   ///          be able to interact properly with localized resources
   ///          associated with this form.
   /// </summary>
   public __gc class Form1 : public System::Windows::Forms::Form
   {
   public:
      Form1(void)
      {
         InitializeComponent();

         client = new UdpClient( 4600 );
         receivePoint = new IPEndPoint(
            new IPAddress( static_cast< __int64 >( 0 ) ), 0 );
         Thread *readThread = new Thread(
            new ThreadStart( this, WaitForPackets ) );

         readThread->Start();
      }

   protected:
      void Dispose(Boolean disposing)
      {
         if (disposing && components)
         {
            components->Dispose();
         }
```

Fig. 21.5 Server-side portion of connectionless client/server computing. (Part 1 of 2.)

```
54           __super::Dispose(disposing);
55        }
56     private: System::Windows::Forms::TextBox *  displayTextBox;
57
58     private: UdpClient *client;
59     private: IPEndPoint *receivePoint;
60
61     private:
62        /// <summary>
63        /// Required designer variable.
64        /// </summary>
65        System::ComponentModel::Container * components;
66
67     // Visual Studio .NET generated GUI code
68
69     // shut down the server
70     private: System::Void Form1_Closing(System::Object *  sender,
71                 System::ComponentModel::CancelEventArgs *  e)
72              {
73                 System::Environment::Exit( System::Environment::ExitCode );
74              }
75
76     public:
77
78        // wait for a packet to arrive
79        void WaitForPackets()
80        {
81           while ( true ) {
82
83              // set up packet
84              Byte data __gc[] = client->Receive( &receivePoint );
85
86              displayTextBox->Text = String::Concat( displayTextBox->Text,
87                 S"\r\nPacket received:", S"\r\nLength: ",
88                 data->Length.ToString(), S"\r\nContaining: ",
89                 System::Text::Encoding::ASCII->GetString( data ) );
90
91              // echo information from packet back to client
92              displayTextBox->Text = String::Concat( displayTextBox->Text,
93                 S"\r\n\r\nEcho data back to client..." );
94
95              client->Send( data, data->Length, receivePoint );
96              displayTextBox->Text = String::Concat(
97                 displayTextBox->Text, S"\r\nPacket sent\r\n" );
98           } // end while
99        } // end method WaitForPackets
100    };
101 }
```

Fig. 21.5 Server-side portion of connectionless client/server computing. (Part 2 of 2.)

Lines 41–44 create and start a thread to execute method `WaitForPackets` (lines 79–99). This method executes an infinite loop while waiting for data to arrive at the `Server`. We use a separate thread so that the `Server` can perform other tasks. When information

```
// Fig. 21.6: Form1.cpp
// Entry point for application.

#include "stdafx.h"
#include "Form1.h"
#include <windows.h>

using namespace Server;

int APIENTRY _tWinMain(HINSTANCE hInstance,
                       HINSTANCE hPrevInstance,
                       LPTSTR    lpCmdLine,
                       int       nCmdShow)
{
   System::Threading::Thread::CurrentThread->ApartmentState =
      System::Threading::ApartmentState::STA;
   Application::Run(new Form1());
   return 0;
} // end _tWinMain
```

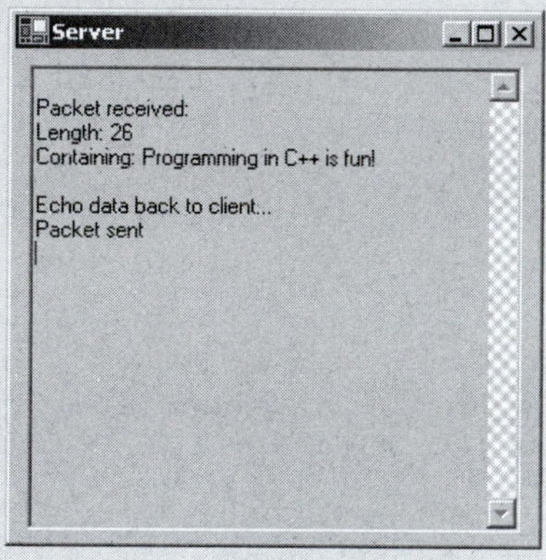

Fig. 21.6 Server entry point.

arrives, the `UdpClient` method `Receive` (line 84) receives a `Byte` array from the client. We pass `Receive` a pointer to the `IPEndPoint` object created in the constructor; this provides the method with an `IPEndPoint` into which the program copies the client's IP address and port number. This program will compile and run without an exception even if the pointer to the `IPEndPoint` object is `NULL`, because method `Receive` initializes the `IPEndPoint` to contain the IP address and port number of the packet sender (in this case, the `Server`).

Good Programming Practice 21.2

Initialize all pointers to objects (with a value other than `NULL`). This protects code from methods that do not check their parameters for `NULL` pointers.

Lines 86–93 update the `Server`'s display to include the packet's information and content. Line 95 echoes the data back to the client, using `UdpClient` method `Send`. This version of `Send` takes three arguments: the `Byte` array to send, an `int` representing the array's length and the `IPEndPoint` to which to send the data. We use array `data` returned by method

Receive as the data, the length of array data as the length and the IPEndPoint passed to method Receive as the data's destination. The IP address and port number of the client that sent the data to Server are stored in receivePoint, so simply passing receivePoint to Send allows Server to respond to the client.

The Client (Fig. 21.7–Fig. 21.8) works similarly to the Server, except that the Client object sends packets only when the user types a message in a TextBox and presses the *Enter* key. When this occurs, the program calls event handler inputTextBox_KeyDown (lines 76–98 of Fig. 21.7). Lines 89–90 convert the string that the user entered in the TextBox to a Byte array. Line 93 calls UdpClient method Send to send the Byte array to the Server that is located on localhost (i.e., the same machine). We specify the port as 4600, which we know to be Server's port.

```
1  // Fig. 21.7: Form1.h
2  // Set up a Client that sends packets to a server and receives
3  // packets from a server.
4
5  #pragma once
6
7
8  namespace Client
9  {
10    using namespace System;
11    using namespace System::ComponentModel;
12    using namespace System::Collections;
13    using namespace System::Windows::Forms;
14    using namespace System::Data;
15    using namespace System::Drawing;
16    using namespace System::Net;
17    using namespace System::Net::Sockets;
18    using namespace System::Threading;
19
20    /// <summary>
21    /// Summary for Form1
22    ///
23    /// WARNING: If you change the name of this class, you will need to
24    ///          change the 'Resource File Name' property for the managed
25    ///          resource compiler tool associated with all .resx files
26    ///          this class depends on.  Otherwise, the designers will not
27    ///          be able to interact properly with localized resources
28    ///          associated with this form.
29    /// </summary>
30    public __gc class Form1 : public System::Windows::Forms::Form
31    {
32    public:
33       Form1(void)
34       {
35          InitializeComponent();
36
37          receivePoint = new IPEndPoint(
38             new IPAddress( static_cast< __int64 >( 0 ) ), 0 );
```

Fig. 21.7 Client portion of connectionless client/server computing. (Part 1 of 3.)

```
         client = new UdpClient( 4601 );
         Thread *thread =
            new Thread( new ThreadStart( this, WaitForPackets ) );
         thread->Start();
      }

   protected:
      void Dispose(Boolean disposing)
      {
         if (disposing && components)
         {
            components->Dispose();
         }
         __super::Dispose(disposing);
      }
   private: System::Windows::Forms::TextBox *  displayTextBox;
   private: System::Windows::Forms::TextBox *  inputTextBox;

   private: UdpClient *client;
   private: IPEndPoint *receivePoint;

   private:
      /// <summary>
      /// Required designer variable.
      /// </summary>
      System::ComponentModel::Container * components;

   // Visual Studio .NET generated GUI code

   // shut down the client
   private: System::Void Form1_Closing(System::Object *  sender,
               System::ComponentModel::CancelEventArgs *  e)
            {
               System::Environment::Exit( System::Environment::ExitCode );
            }

   // send a packet
   private: System::Void inputTextBox_KeyDown(System::Object *  sender,
               System::Windows::Forms::KeyEventArgs *  e)
            {
               if ( e->KeyCode == Keys::Enter ) {

                  // create packet (datagram) as string
                  String *packet = inputTextBox->Text;

                  displayTextBox->Text = String::Concat(
                     displayTextBox->Text,
                     S"\r\nSending packet containing: ", packet );

                  // convert packet string to byte array
                  Byte data __gc[] =
                     System::Text::Encoding::ASCII->GetBytes( packet );

```

Fig. 21.7 Client portion of connectionless client/server computing. (Part 2 of 3.)

```
                  // send packet to server on port 4600
                  client->Send( data, data->Length, S"localhost", 4600 );
                  displayTextBox->Text = String::Concat(
                     displayTextBox->Text, S"\r\nPacket sent\r\n" );
                  inputTextBox->Clear();
               } // end if
            } // end method inputTextBox_KeyDown

   public:

      // wait for packets to arrive
      void WaitForPackets()
      {
         while ( true ) {

            // receive byte array from server
            Byte data __gc[]= client->Receive( &receivePoint );

            // output packet data to TextBox
            displayTextBox->Text = String::Concat(
               displayTextBox->Text, S"\r\nPacket received:",
               S"\r\nLength: ", data->Length.ToString(),
               S"\r\nContaining: ",
               System::Text::Encoding::ASCII->GetString( data ),
               S"\r\n" );
         } // end while
      } // end method WaitForPackets
   };
}
```

Fig. 21.7 Client portion of connectionless client/server computing. (Part 3 of 3.)

```
// Fig. 21.8: Form1.cpp
// Entry point for application.

#include "stdafx.h"
#include "Form1.h"
#include <windows.h>

using namespace Client;

int APIENTRY _tWinMain(HINSTANCE hInstance,
                       HINSTANCE hPrevInstance,
                       LPTSTR    lpCmdLine,
                       int       nCmdShow)
{
   System::Threading::Thread::CurrentThread->ApartmentState =
      System::Threading::ApartmentState::STA;
   Application::Run(new Form1());
   return 0;
} // end _tWinMain
```

Fig. 21.8 `Client` entry point. (Part 1 of 2.)

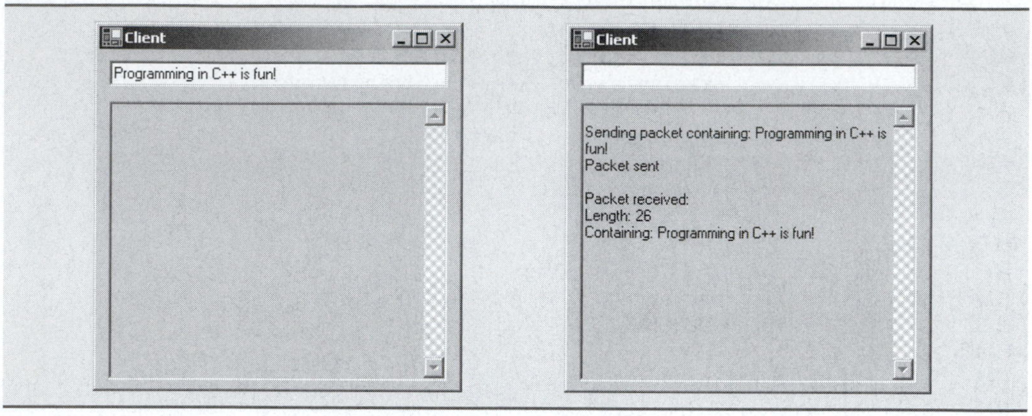

Fig. 21.8 `Client` entry point. (Part 2 of 2.)

Line 39 instantiates a `UdpClient` object to receive packets at port `4601`—we choose port `4601` because the `Server` already occupies port `4600`. Lines 40–42 create and start a thread to execute the `Client`'s `WiatForPackets` method (lines 103–118). This method uses an infinite loop to wait for these packets. The `UdpClient` method `Receive` blocks until a packet of data is received (line 108). The blocking performed by method `Receive` does not prevent the `Client` from performing other services (e.g., handling user input), because a separate thread runs method `WaitForPackets`.

When a packet arrives, lines 111–116 display its contents in the `TextBox`. The user can type information into the `Client` window's `TextBox` and press the *Enter* key at any time, even while a packet is being received. The event handler for the `TextBox` processes the event and sends the data to the server.

21.6 Client/Server Tic-Tac-Toe Using a Multithreaded Server

In this section, we present our capstone networking example—the popular game Tic-Tac-Toe, implemented with stream sockets and client/server techniques. The program consists of a `Server` application (Fig. 21.9–Fig. 21.11) and two `Client` applications (Fig. 21.14–Fig. 21.15); `Server`, which inherits from interface `TicTacToeServer` (Fig. 21.9), allows the `Clients` to connect to the server and play Tic-Tac-Toe. We depict the output in Fig. 21.15. When the server receives a client connection, lines 99–108 of Fig. 21.10 create an instance of class `Player` (Fig. 21.12–Fig. 21.13) to process the client in a separate thread of execution. This enables the server to handle requests from both clients. The server assigns value `"X"` to the first client that connects (player `X` makes the first move), then assigns value `"O"` to the second client. Throughout the game, the server maintains information regarding the status of the board so that the server can validate players' requested moves. However, neither the server nor the client can establish whether a player has won the game—in this application, method `GameOver` (lines 171–175 of Fig. 21.10) always returns `false`. We leave it to the reader to implement functionality that enables the application to determine a winner. Each `Client` maintains its own GUI version of the Tic-Tac-Toe board to display the game. The clients can place marks only in empty squares on the board. Class `Square` (Fig. 21.16–Fig. 21.17) is used to define squares on the Tic-Tac-Toe board.

```
// Fig. 21.9: TicTacToeServer.h
// Interface that Server class implements.

#pragma once

#using <mscorlib.dll>

using namespace System;

public __gc __interface TicTacToeServer
{
public:

   // determine if the game is over
   bool GameOver();

   // appends the argument to text in displayTextBox
   void Display( String * );

   // determine if a move is valid
   bool ValidMove( int, int );

   __property bool get_IsDisconnected();
}; // end interface TicTacToeServer
```

Fig. 21.9 TicTacToeServer interface.

Server (Fig. 21.10–Fig. 21.11) uses its constructor (lines 32–45 of Fig. 21.10) to create a Byte array to store the moves the players have made (line 36). The program creates an array of two Player pointers (line 38) and an array of two Thread pointers (line 39). Each element in both arrays corresponds to a Tic-Tac-Toe player. Variable currentPlayer is set to 0, which corresponds to player "X" (line 40). In our program, player "X" makes the first move. Lines 43–44 create and start Thread getPlayers, which the Server uses to accept connections so that the current Thread does not block while awaiting players.

```
1  // Fig. 21.10: Form1.h
2  // This class maintains a game of Tic-Tac-Toe for two clients.
3
4  #pragma once
5
6  #include "TicTacToeServer.h"
7  #include "Player.h"
8
9  namespace Server
10 {
11    using namespace System;
12    using namespace System::ComponentModel;
13    using namespace System::Collections;
14    using namespace System::Windows::Forms;
15    using namespace System::Data;
```

Fig. 21.10 Server side of a client/server Tic-Tac-Toe program. (Part 1 of 5.)

```
using namespace System::Drawing;

/// <summary>
/// Summary for Form1
///
/// WARNING: If you change the name of this class, you will need to
///          change the 'Resource File Name' property for the managed
///          resource compiler tool associated with all .resx files
///          this class depends on.  Otherwise, the designers will not
///          be able to interact properly with localized resources
///          associated with this form.
/// </summary>
public __gc class Form1 :
   public System::Windows::Forms::Form, public TicTacToeServer
{
public:
   Form1(void)
   {
      InitializeComponent();

      board = new Byte[ 9 ];

      players = new Player*[ 2 ];
      playerThreads = new Thread*[ 2 ];
      currentPlayer = 0;

      // accept connections on a different thread
      getPlayers = new Thread( new ThreadStart( this, SetUp ) );
      getPlayers->Start();
   }

protected:
   void Dispose(Boolean disposing)
   {
      if (disposing && components)
      {
         components->Dispose();
      }
      __super::Dispose(disposing);
   }
private: System::Windows::Forms::TextBox *  displayTextBox;

private: Byte board __gc[];

private: Player *players __gc[];
private: Thread *playerThreads __gc[];

private: TcpListener *listener;
private: int currentPlayer;
private: Thread *getPlayers;

private: static bool disconnected = false;

```

Fig. 21.10 Server side of a client/server Tic-Tac-Toe program. (Part 2 of 5.)

```
   private:
      /// <summary>
      /// Required designer variable.
      /// </summary>
      System::ComponentModel::Container * components;

   // Visual Studio .NET generated GUI code

   private: System::Void Form1_Closing(System::Object *  sender,
            System::ComponentModel::CancelEventArgs *  e)
         {
            disconnected = true;
         }

   public:

      __property bool get_IsDisconnected()
      {
         return disconnected;
      }

      // accepts connections from 2 players
      void SetUp()
      {
         // set up Socket
         listener = new TcpListener(
            new IPAddress( static_cast< __int64 >( 0 ) ), 4500 );
         listener->Start();

         // accept first player and start a thread for him or her
         players[ 0 ] = new Player( listener->AcceptSocket(), this, 0 );
         playerThreads[ 0 ] = new Thread(
            new ThreadStart( players[ 0 ], &Player::Run ) );
         playerThreads[ 0 ]->Start();

         // accept second player and start a thread for him or her
         players[ 1 ] = new Player( listener->AcceptSocket(), this, 1 );
         playerThreads[ 1 ] =
            new Thread( new ThreadStart( players[ 1 ], &Player::Run ) );
         playerThreads[ 1 ]->Start();

         // let the first player know that the other player has connected
         Monitor::Enter( players[ 0 ] );
         players[ 0 ]->ThreadSuspended = false;
         Monitor::Pulse( players[ 0 ] );
         Monitor::Exit( players[ 0 ] );
      } // end method SetUp

      // appends the argument to text in displayTextBox
      void Display( String *message )
      {
         displayTextBox->AppendText( String::Concat( message, S"\r\n" ) );
      }
```

Fig. 21.10 Server side of a client/server Tic-Tac-Toe program. (Part 3 of 5.)

```

   // determine if a move is valid
   bool ValidMove( int location, int player )
   {
      // prevent another thread from making a move
      Monitor::Enter( this );

      // while it is not the current player's turn, wait
      while ( player != currentPlayer )
         Monitor::Wait( this );

      // if the desired square is not occupied
      if ( !IsOccupied( location ) ) {

         // set the board to contain the current player's mark
         board[ location ] = ( currentPlayer == 0 ? 'X' : 'O' );

         // set the currentPlayer to be the other player
         currentPlayer = ( currentPlayer + 1 ) % 2;

         // notify the other player of the move
         players[ currentPlayer ]->OtherPlayerMoved( location );

         // alert the other player it's time to move
         Monitor::Pulse( this );
         Monitor::Exit( this );

         return true;
      } // end if
      else {

         // allow another move attempt
         Monitor::Pulse( this );
         Monitor::Exit( this );

         return false;
      } // end else
   } // end method ValidMove

   // determines whether the specified square is occupied
   bool IsOccupied( int location )
   {
      if ( board[ location ] == 'X' || board[ location ] == 'O' )
         return true;
      else
         return false;
   }

   // determines if the game is over
   bool GameOver()
   {
      // place code here to test for a winner of the game
      return false;
```

Fig. 21.10 Server side of a client/server Tic-Tac-Toe program. (Part 4 of 5.)

```
175       }
176    };
177 }
```

Fig. 21.10 Server side of a client/server Tic-Tac-Toe program. (Part 5 of 5.)

```
// Fig. 21.11: Form1.cpp
// Entry point for application.

#include "stdafx.h"
#include "Form1.h"
#include <windows.h>

using namespace Server;

int APIENTRY _tWinMain(HINSTANCE hInstance,
                       HINSTANCE hPrevInstance,
                       LPTSTR    lpCmdLine,
                       int       nCmdShow)
{
   System::Threading::Thread::CurrentThread->ApartmentState =
      System::Threading::ApartmentState::STA;
   Application::Run(new Form1());
   return 0;
} // end _tWinMain
```

Fig. 21.11 Server entry point.

Thread `getPlayers` executes method `SetUp` (lines 91–115), which creates a `TcpListener` object to listen for requests on port `4500` (lines 94–95). This object then listens for connection requests from the first and second players. Lines 99 and 105 instantiate `Player` objects representing the players, and lines 100–101 and 106–107 create two `Threads` that execute the `Run` methods of each `Player` object.

The `Player` constructor (Fig. 21.13, lines 7–23) receives as arguments a pointer to the `Socket` object (i.e., the connection to the client), a pointer to the `Server` object (as a `TicTacToeServer` pointer) and an `int` indicating the mark (`"X"` or `"O"`) used by that player. In this case study, `Server` calls `Player` method `Run` (lines 35–102) after instantiating a `Player` object. Lines 40–48 notify the server of a successful connection and send to the client the `__wchar_t` that the client will place on the board when making a move. If `Run` is executing for `Player "X"`, lines 52–63 execute, causing `Player "X"` to wait for a second player to connect. Lines 58–59 define a `while` loop that suspends the `Player "X" Thread` until the server signals that `Player "O"` has connected. The server notifies the `Player` of the connection by setting the `Player`'s `threadSuspended` variable to `false` (line 112 of Fig. 21.10). When `threadSuspended` becomes `false`, `Player` exits the `while` loop in lines 58–59 (Fig. 21.13).

Method `Run` executes the `while` statement (lines 67–95), enabling the user to play the game. Each iteration of this statement waits for the client to send an `int` specifying where on the board to place the `"X"` or `"O"`—the `Player` then places the mark on the board, if the specified mark location is valid (e.g., that location does not already contain a mark). Note that the `while` statement continues execution only if `bool` variable `done` is `false`. This variable only becomes `true` when `Server` method `GameOver` returns `true` (lines 93–94). Thus, the loop will not terminate because we do not implement the logic to determine when the game is over. However, method `Run` may return prematurely if `Server` property `IsDisconnected` is `true` (line 73). This variable is set to `true` by event handler `Form1_Closing` of the `Server`, which is invoked when the `Server`'s form is closed.

```
// Fig. 21.12: Player.h
// This class processes a single Tic-Tac-Toe client
// in a separate thread of execution.

#pragma once

#include "TicTacToeServer.h"

#using <mscorlib.dll>

using namespace System;
using namespace System::Net;
using namespace System::Net::Sockets;
using namespace System::Threading;
using namespace System::IO;

public __gc class Player
{
public:
   Player( Socket *, TicTacToeServer *, int );
   void OtherPlayerMoved( int );
   void Run();

   __property bool get_ThreadSuspended()
   {
      return threadSuspended;
   }

   __property void set_ThreadSuspended( bool value )
   {
      threadSuspended = value;
   }

private:
   Socket *connection;
   NetworkStream *socketStream;
   TicTacToeServer *server;
   BinaryWriter *writer;
   BinaryReader *reader;

   int number;
   __wchar_t mark;
   static bool threadSuspended = true;
}; // end class Player
```

Fig. 21.12 `Player` class represents a single player connected to the server.

```
// Fig. 21.13: Player.cpp
// Method definitions for class Player.

#include "stdafx.h"
#include "Player.h"

Player::Player( Socket *socket, TicTacToeServer *serverValue,
   int newNumber )
{
   mark = ( newNumber == 0 ? 'X' : 'O' );

   connection = socket;

   server = serverValue;
   number = newNumber;

   // create NetworkStream object for Socket
   socketStream = new NetworkStream( connection );

   // create Streams for reading/writing bytes
   writer = new BinaryWriter( socketStream );
   reader = new BinaryReader( socketStream );
} // end constructor

// signal other player of move
void Player::OtherPlayerMoved( int location )
{
   // signal that opponent moved
   writer->Write( S"Opponent moved" );
   writer->Write( location ); // send location of move
}

// allows the players to make moves and receives moves
// from other player
void Player::Run()
{
   bool done = false;

   // display on the server that a connection was made
   server->Display( String::Concat( S"Player ",
      ( number == 0 ? S"X" : S"O" ), S" connected" ) );

   // send the current player's mark to the server
   writer->Write( mark );

   // if number equals 0 then this player is X, so send
   writer->Write( String::Concat( S"Player ", ( number == 0 ?
      S"X connected\r\n" : S"O connected, please wait\r\n" ) ) );

   // wait for another player to arrive
   if ( mark == 'X' ) {
      writer->Write( S"Waiting for another player" );

```

Fig. 21.13 Player class method definitions. (Part 1 of 2.)

```
54        // wait for notification from server that another
55        // player has connected
56        Monitor::Enter( this );
57
58        while ( threadSuspended )
59           Monitor::Wait( this );
60
61        writer->Write( S"Other player connected. Your move" );
62        Monitor::Pulse( this );
63        Monitor::Exit( this );
64     } // end if
65
66     // play game
67     while ( !done ) {
68
69        // wait for data to become available
70        while ( connection->Available == 0 ) {
71           Thread::Sleep( 1000 );
72
73           if ( server->IsDisconnected )
74              return;
75        } // end while
76
77        // receive data
78        int location = reader->ReadInt32();
79
80        // if the move is valid, display the move on the
81        // server and signal the move is valid
82        if ( server->ValidMove( location, number ) ) {
83           server->Display( String::Concat(
84              S"loc: ", location.ToString() ) );
85           writer->Write( S"Valid move." );
86        } // end if
87
88        // signal the move is invalid
89        else
90           writer->Write( S"Invalid move, try again" );
91
92        // if game is over, set done to true to exit while loop
93        if ( server->GameOver() )
94           done = true;
95     } // end while
96
97     // close the socket connection
98     writer->Close();
99     reader->Close();
100    socketStream->Close();
101    connection->Close();
102 } // end method Run
```

Fig. 21.13 `Player` class method definitions. (Part 2 of 2.)

Line 70 (Fig. 21.13) begins a `while` statement that loops until `Socket` property *`Available`* indicates that there is information to receive from the `Socket` (or until the server disconnects from the client). Socket property Available contains the amount of data, in bytes, that has been received. If there is no information, the thread goes to sleep for one second. Upon awakening, the thread uses property IsDisconnected to determine whether server variable disconnect is true. If the value is true, the Thread exits the method (thus terminating the Thread); otherwise, the Thread loops again. However, if property Available indicates that there is data to receive, the while loop of lines 70–75 terminates, enabling the information to be processed.

This information contains an int representing the location in which the client wants to place a mark. Line 78 calls method ReadInt32 of the BinaryReader object (which reads from the NetworkStream created with the Socket) to read this int (or Int32). Line 82 then passes the int to Server method ValidMove. If this method validates the move, the Player places the mark in the desired location.

Method ValidMove (lines 124–159 of Fig. 21.10) sends to the client a message indicating whether the move was valid. Locations on the board correspond to numbers from 0–8 (0–2 for the first row, 3–5 for the second and 6–8 for the third). All statements in method ValidMove are enclosed in Monitor::Enter and Monitor::Exit statements that allow only one move to be attempted at a time. This prevents two players from modifying the game's state information simultaneously. If the Player attempting to validate a move is not the current player (i.e., the one allowed to make a move), that Player is placed in a *wait* state until it is that Player's turn to move (line 131). If the user attempts to place a mark in a location that already contains a mark, method ValidMove returns false. However, if the user has selected an unoccupied location (line 134), line 137 places the mark on the local representation of the board. Line 143 notifies the other Player that a move has been made, and line 146 invokes the Pulse method so that the waiting Player can validate a move. The method then returns true to indicate that the move is valid.

When a Client application (Fig. 21.14–Fig. 21.15) executes, it creates a TextBox to display messages from the server and the Tic-Tac-Toe board representation. The board is created out of nine Square objects (Fig. 21.16–Fig. 21.17) that contain Panels on which the user can click, indicating the position on the board in which to place a mark. The Client's constructor (lines 33–65 of Fig. 21.14) opens a connection to the server (line 56) and obtains a pointer to the connection's associated NetworkStream object from TcpClient (line 57). Lines 63–64 start a thread to read messages sent from the server to the client. The server passes messages (e.g., whether each move is valid) to method ProcessMessage (lines 196–238). If the message indicates that a move is valid (line 201), the client sets its mark to the current square (the square that the user clicked) and repaints the board. If the message indicates that a move is invalid (line 209), the client notifies the user to click a different square. If the message indicates that the opponent made a move (line 216), line 219 reads from the server an int specifying where on the board the client should place the opponent's mark.

```
1  // Fig. 21.14: Form1.h
2  // Client for the TicTacToe program.
3
4  #pragma once
5
```

Fig. 21.14 Client side of client/server Tic-Tac-Toe program. (Part 1 of 6.)

```
#include "Square.h"

namespace Client
{
   using namespace System;
   using namespace System::ComponentModel;
   using namespace System::Collections;
   using namespace System::Windows::Forms;
   using namespace System::Data;
   using namespace System::Drawing;
   using namespace System::Net::Sockets;
   using namespace System::Threading;
   using namespace System::IO;

   /// <summary>
   /// Summary for Form1
   ///
   /// WARNING: If you change the name of this class, you will need to
   ///          change the 'Resource File Name' property for the managed
   ///          resource compiler tool associated with all .resx files
   ///          this class depends on.  Otherwise, the designers will not
   ///          be able to interact properly with localized resources
   ///          associated with this form.
   /// </summary>
   public __gc class Form1 : public System::Windows::Forms::Form
   {
   public:
      Form1(void)
      {
         InitializeComponent();

         board = new Square* __gc[ 3, 3 ];

         // create 9 Square objects and place them on the board
         board[ 0, 0 ] = new Square( panel1, ' ', 0 );
         board[ 0, 1 ] = new Square( panel2, ' ', 1 );
         board[ 0, 2 ] = new Square( panel3, ' ', 2 );
         board[ 1, 0 ] = new Square( panel4, ' ', 3 );
         board[ 1, 1 ] = new Square( panel5, ' ', 4 );
         board[ 1, 2 ] = new Square( panel6, ' ', 5 );
         board[ 2, 0 ] = new Square( panel7, ' ', 6 );
         board[ 2, 1 ] = new Square( panel8, ' ', 7 );
         board[ 2, 2 ] = new Square( panel9, ' ', 8 );

         // create a SolidBrush for writing on the Squares
         brush = new SolidBrush( Color::Black );

         // Make connection to sever and get the associated
         // network stream. Start separate thread to allow this
         // program to continually update its output in textbox.
         connection = new TcpClient( S"localhost", 4500 );
         stream = connection->GetStream();

```

Fig. 21.14 Client side of client/server Tic-Tac-Toe program. (Part 2 of 6.)

```
         writer = new BinaryWriter( stream );
         reader = new BinaryReader( stream );

         // start a new thread for sending and receiving messages
         outputThread = new Thread( new ThreadStart( this, Run ) );
         outputThread->Start();
      } // end constructor

   protected:
      void Dispose(Boolean disposing)
      {
         if (disposing && components)
         {
            components->Dispose();
         }
         __super::Dispose(disposing);
      }
   private: System::Windows::Forms::Label *  idLabel;

   private: System::Windows::Forms::TextBox *  displayTextBox;

   private: System::Windows::Forms::Panel *  panel1;
   private: System::Windows::Forms::Panel *  panel2;
   private: System::Windows::Forms::Panel *  panel3;
   private: System::Windows::Forms::Panel *  panel4;
   private: System::Windows::Forms::Panel *  panel5;
   private: System::Windows::Forms::Panel *  panel6;
   private: System::Windows::Forms::Panel *  panel7;
   private: System::Windows::Forms::Panel *  panel8;
   private: System::Windows::Forms::Panel *  panel9;

   private: Square *board __gc[ , ];
   private: Square *currentSquare;

   private: Thread *outputThread;

   private: TcpClient *connection;
   private: NetworkStream *stream;
   private: BinaryWriter *writer;
   private: BinaryReader *reader;

   private: __wchar_t myMark;
   private: bool myTurn;

   private: SolidBrush *brush;

   private: static bool done = false;

   private:
      /// <summary>
      /// Required designer variable.
      /// </summary>
      System::ComponentModel::Container * components;
```

Fig. 21.14 Client side of client/server Tic-Tac-Toe program. (Part 3 of 6.)

```

   // Visual Studio .NET generated GUI code

   private: System::Void Form1_Paint(System::Object *  sender,
               System::Windows::Forms::PaintEventArgs *  e)
            {
               PaintSquares();
            }

   private: System::Void Form1_Closing(System::Object *  sender,
               System::ComponentModel::CancelEventArgs *  e)
            {
               done = true;
            }

   // send location of the clicked square to server
   private: System::Void square_MouseUp(System::Object *  sender,
               System::Windows::Forms::MouseEventArgs *  e)
            {
               // for each square check if that square was clicked
               for ( int row = 0; row < 3; row++ )

                  for ( int column = 0; column < 3; column++ )

                     if ( board[ row, column ]->SquarePanel == sender ) {
                        CurrentSquare = board[ row, column ];

                        // send the move to the server
                        SendClickedSquare(
                           board[ row, column ]->Location );
                     }
            } // end method square_MouseUp

   public:

      // write-only property for the current square
      __property void set_CurrentSquare( Square *value )
      {
         currentSquare = value;
      }


      // draws the mark of each square
      void PaintSquares()
      {
         Graphics *g;

         // draw the appropriate mark on each panel
         for ( int row = 0; row < 3; row++ )

            for ( int column = 0; column < 3; column++ ) {

```

Fig. 21.14 Client side of client/server Tic-Tac-Toe program. (Part 4 of 6.)

```
            // get the Graphics for each Panel
            g = board[ row, column ]->SquarePanel->CreateGraphics();

            // draw the appropriate letter on the panel
            g->DrawString( __box( board[ row, column ]->Mark ),
               this->Font, brush, 8, 8 );
         } // end for
   } // end method PaintSquares

   // control thread that allows continuous update of the textbox
   void Run()
   {
      // first get players's mark (X or O)
      myMark = reader->ReadChar();
      idLabel->Text = String::Concat( S"You are player \"",
         __box( myMark ), S"\"" );
      myTurn = ( myMark == 'X' ? true : false );

      // process incoming messages
      try {

         // receive messages sent to client
         while ( true )
            ProcessMessage( reader->ReadString() );
      } // end try
      catch ( EndOfStreamException * ) {
         MessageBox::Show( S"Server is down, game over", S"Error",
            MessageBoxButtons::OK, MessageBoxIcon::Error );
      } // end catch
   } // end method Run

   // process messages sent to client
   void ProcessMessage( String *message )
   {
      // if the move player sent to the server is valid
      // update the display, set that square's mark to be
      // the mark of the current player and repaint the board
      if ( message->Equals( S"Valid move." ) ) {
         displayTextBox->AppendText( S"Valid move, please wait.\r\n" );
         currentSquare->Mark = myMark;
         PaintSquares();
      } // end if

      // if the move is invalid, display that and it is now
      // this player's turn again
      else if ( message->Equals( S"Invalid move, try again" ) )  {
         displayTextBox->AppendText(
            String::Concat( message, S"\r\n" ) );
         myTurn = true;
      } // end else

      // if opponent moved
      else if ( message->Equals( S"Opponent moved" ) ) {
```

Fig. 21.14 Client side of client/server Tic-Tac-Toe program. (Part 5 of 6.)

```
                    // find location of their move
                    int location = reader->ReadInt32();

                    // set that square to have the opponents mark and
                    // repaint the board
                    board[ location / 3, location % 3 ]->Mark =
                       ( myMark == 'X' ? 'O' : 'X' );
                    PaintSquares();

                    displayTextBox->AppendText(
                       S"Opponent moved.  Your turn.\r\n" );

                    // it is now this player's turn
                    myTurn = true;
                 } // end else

                 // display the message
                 else
                    displayTextBox->AppendText(
                       String::Concat( message, S"\r\n" ) );
              } // end method ProcessMessage

              // sends the server the number of the clicked square
              void SendClickedSquare( int location )
              {
                 // if it is the current player's move right now
                 if ( myTurn ) {

                    // send the location of the move to the server
                    writer->Write( location );

                    // it is now the other player's turn
                    myTurn = false;
                 } // end if
              }
           };
        }
```

Fig. 21.14 Client side of client/server Tic-Tac-Toe program. (Part 6 of 6.)

```
// Fig. 21.15: Form1.cpp
// Entry point for application.

#include "stdafx.h"
#include "Form1.h"
#include <windows.h>

using namespace Client;

int APIENTRY _tWinMain(HINSTANCE hInstance,
                       HINSTANCE hPrevInstance,
```

Fig. 21.15 `Client` entry point. (Part 1 of 3.)

```
                      LPTSTR    lpCmdLine,
                      int       nCmdShow)
{
   System::Threading::Thread::CurrentThread->ApartmentState =
      System::Threading::ApartmentState::STA;
   Application::Run(new Form1());
   return 0;
} // end _tWinMain
```

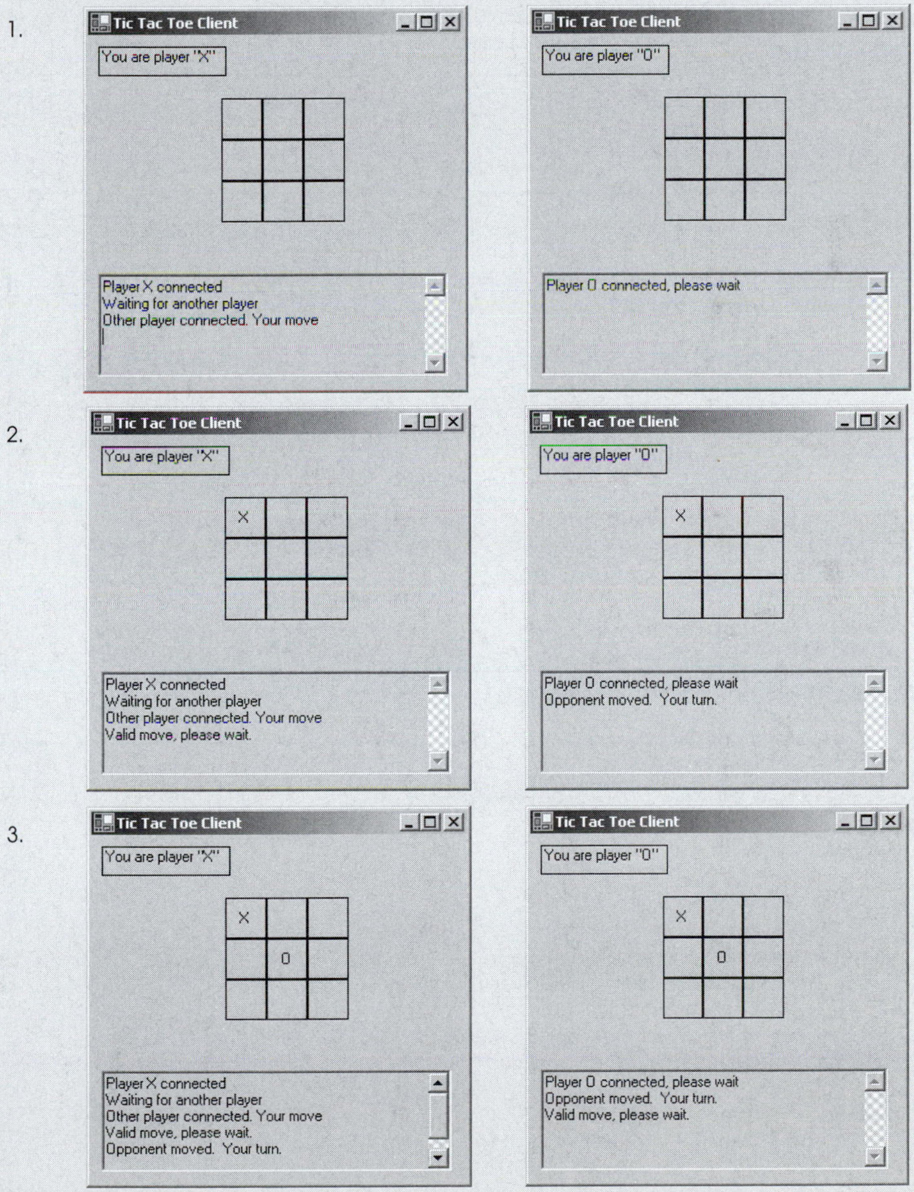

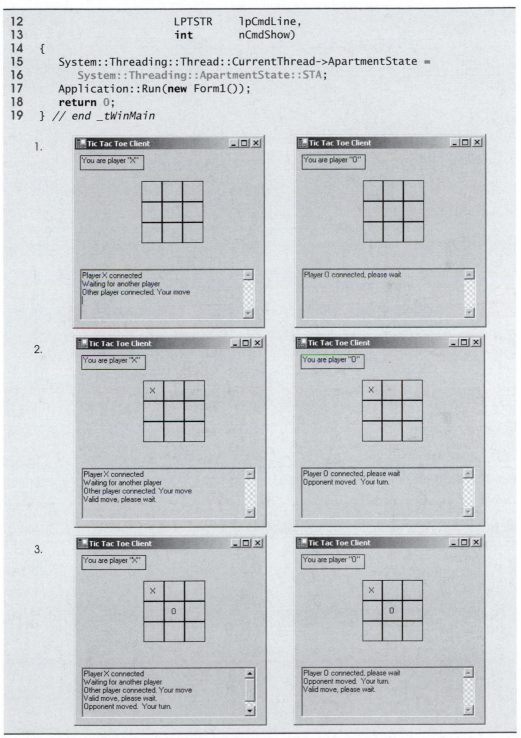

Fig. 21.15 `Client` entry point. (Part 2 of 3.)

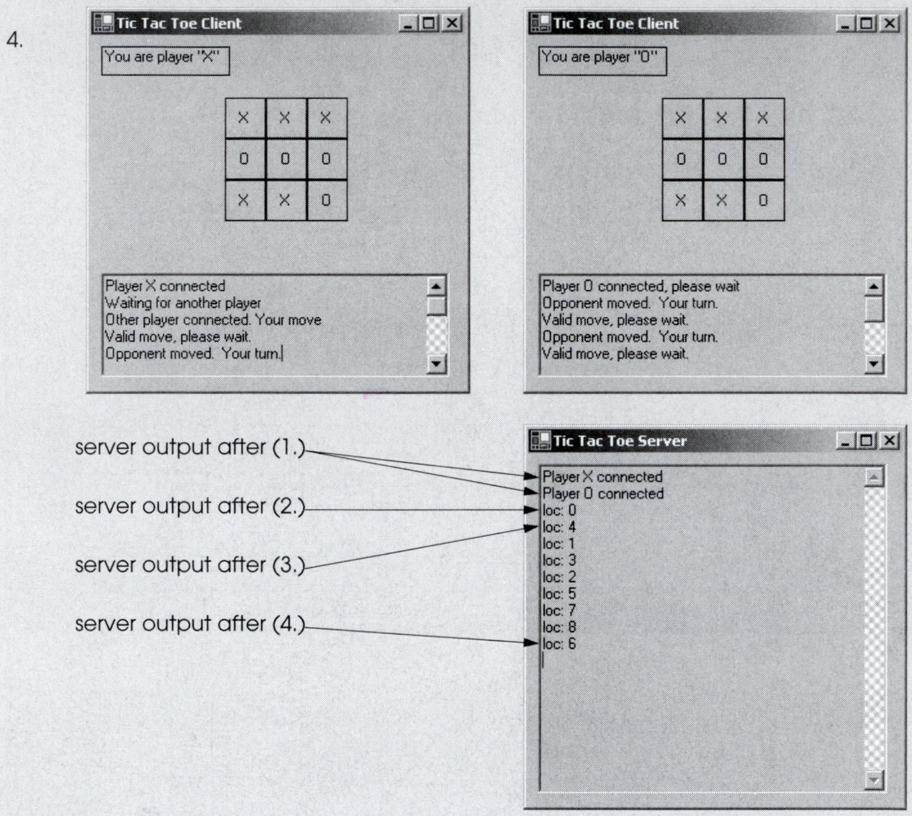

Fig. 21.15 `Client` entry point. (Part 3 of 3.)

```
// Fig. 21.16: Square.h
// A Square on the TicTacToe board.

#pragma once

#using <mscorlib.dll>

using namespace System;
using namespace System::Windows::Forms;

// the representation of a square in a tic-tac-toe grid
public __gc class Square
{
public:
   Square( Panel *, __wchar_t, int );

```

Fig. 21.16 `Square` class represents a square on the Tic-Tac-Toe board. (Part 1 of 2.)

```
   // property SquarePanel;
   // the panel which the square represents
   __property Panel *get_SquarePanel()
   {
      return panel;
   } // end property SquarePanel

   // property Mark; the mark of the square
   __property __wchar_t get_Mark()
   {
      return mark;
   }

   __property void set_Mark( __wchar_t value )
   {
      mark = value;
   } // end property Mark

   // property Location; the square's location on the board
   __property int get_Location()
   {
      return location;
   } // property Location

private:
   Panel *panel;
   __wchar_t mark;
   int location;
}; // end class Square
```

Fig. 21.16 Square class represents a square on the Tic-Tac-Toe board. (Part 2 of 2.)

```
// Fig. 21.17: Square.cpp
// Method definitions for class Square.

#include "stdafx.h"
#include "Square.h"

// constructor
Square::Square( Panel *newPanel, __wchar_t newMark, int newLocation )
{
   panel = newPanel;
   mark = newMark;
   location = newLocation;
}
```

Fig. 21.17 Square class method definitions.

In this chapter, we discussed how to use .NET Framework's networking technologies by providing both connection-oriented (i.e., streams-based) transmission and connectionless (i.e., packet-based) transmission. We showed how to create a simple server and client via stream sockets, then showed how to create a multithreaded server. In Chapter 22, Data

Structures and Collections, we discuss how to store data dynamically, and we discuss several of the key classes that belong to the `System::Collections` namespace.

SUMMARY

- Sockets are the fundamental way to perform network communications in the .NET Framework. The term "socket" refers to the Berkeley Sockets Interface, which was developed in 1978 to facilitate network programming with UNIX and was popularized by C and C++ programmers.
- The two most popular types of sockets are stream sockets and datagram sockets.
- Stream sockets provide a connection-oriented service, meaning that one process establishes a connection to another process and that data can flow between the processes in continuous streams.
- Datagram sockets provide a connectionless service that uses messages to transmit data. Connectionless services generally offer greater performance but less reliability than connection-oriented services.
- Transmission Control Protocol (TCP) is the preferred protocol for stream sockets. It is a reliable and relatively fast way to send data through a network.
- The User Datagram Protocol (UDP) is the preferred protocol for datagram sockets. UDP is unreliable. There is no guarantee that packets sent with UDP will arrive in the order in which they were sent or that they will arrive at all.
- Establishing a simple server with TCP and stream sockets in Visual C++ .NET requires five steps. Step 1 is to create a `TcpListener` object. This class represents a TCP stream socket that a server can use to receive connections.
- To receive connections, the `TcpListener` must be listening for them. For the `TcpListener` to listen for client connections, its `Start` method must be called (Step 2).
- `TcpListener` method `AcceptSocket` blocks indefinitely until a connection is established, at which point it returns a `Socket` (Step 3).
- Step 4 is the processing phase, in which the server and the client communicate via methods `Read` and `Write` via a `NetworkStream` object.
- When the client and server have finished communicating, the server closes the connection with the `Close` method on the `Socket` (Step 5). Most servers will then, by means of a control loop, return to the `AcceptSocket` call step to wait for another client's connection.
- A port number is a numeric ID number that a process uses to identify itself at a given network address, also known as an Internet Protocol Address (IP Address).
- An individual process running on a computer is identified by an IP address/port number pair. Hence, no two processes can have the same port number at a given IP address.
- Establishing a simple client requires four steps. In Step 1, we create a `TcpClient` to connect to the server. This connection is established through a call to the `TcpClient` method `Connect` containing two arguments—the server's IP address and the port number.
- In Step 2, the `TcpClient` uses method `GetStream` to get a `Stream` to write to and read from the server.
- Step 3 is the processing phase, in which the client and the server communicate.
- Step 4 has the client close the connection by calling the `Close` method on the `NetworkStream`.
- `NetworkStream` methods `WriteByte` and `Write` can be used to output individual bytes or sets of bytes to the server, respectively.
- `NetworkStream` methods `ReadByte` and `Read` can be used to read individual bytes or sets of bytes from the server, respectively.

- Class UdpClient is provided for connectionless transmission of data.
- Class UdpClient methods Send and Receive are used to transmit data.
- Class IPAddress represents an Internet Protocol address.
- Class IPEndPoint represents an endpoint on a network.
- Multithreaded servers can manage many simultaneous connections with multiple clients.

TERMINOLOGY

127.0.0.1
AcceptSocket method of class TcpListener
BinaryReader class
BinaryWriter class
Bind method of class Socket
binding a server to a port
block until connection received
client
client/server chat
client/server model
Close method of class Socket
Close method of class TcpClient
collaborative applications
Connect method of class TcpListener
connection
connection port
connectionless service
connectionless transmission with datagrams
connection-oriented service
connection-oriented, streams-based transmission
datagram
datagram socket
e-mail
Exit method of class Environment
ExitCode property of class Environment
GetStream method of class Socket
Internet Protocol Addresses (IP Address)
IP Address
IPAddress class
IPEndPoint class
localhost
loopback IP address
network address
NetworkStream class
packet
port number
protocol
Read method of class NetworkStream
ReadByte method of NetworkStream
ReadString method of BinaryReader
receive a connection
Receive method of class Socket
Receive method of class UdpClient
ReceiveFrom method of class Socket
Send method of class Socket
Send method of class UdpClient
SendTo method of class Socket
server
server Internet address
server port number
socket
Socket class
socket-based communications
Start method of class TcpListener
stream
stream socket
streams-based transmission
System::Net namespace
System::Net::Sockets namespace
TcpClient class
TcpListener class
Transmission Control Protocol (TCP)
UdpClient class
User Datagram Protocol (UDP)
Web server
Write method of class BinaryWriter
Write method of class NetworkStream
WriteByte method of class NetworkStream

SELF-REVIEW EXERCISES

21.1 State whether each of the following is *true* or *false*. If *false*, explain why.

a) UDP is a connection-oriented protocol.
b) With stream sockets, a process establishes a connection to another process.
c) Datagram-packet transmission over a network is reliable—packets are guaranteed to arrive in sequence.

d) The `localhost` is also known as the loopback IP address.
e) Each `TcpListener` can accept only one connection.
f) A `TcpListener` can listen for connections at more than one port at a time.
g) A `UdpClient` can send information only to one particular port.
h) Method `ReturnStream` of class `TcpClient` creates a `NetworkStream` that can be used to read and write data over a connection.
i) Clients need to know the port number at which the server is waiting for connections.

21.2 Fill in the blanks in each of the following statements:
a) Many of .NET's networking classes are contained in namespaces ________ and ________.
b) Class ________ is used for unreliable but fast datagram transmission.
c) An object of class ________ represents an Internet Protocol (IP) address.
d) The two types of sockets we discussed in this chapter are ________ sockets and ________ sockets.
e) The acronym TCP stands for ________.
f) Class ________ listens for connections from clients.
g) Class ________ connects to servers.
h) Class ________ provides access to stream data on a network.

ANSWERS TO SELF-REVIEW EXERCISES

21.1 a) False. UDP is a connectionless protocol, and TCP is a connection-oriented protocol. b) True. c) False. Packets can be lost, arrive out of order or even be duplicated. d) True. e) False. `TcpListener` `AcceptSocket` may be called as often as necessary—each call will accept a new connection. f) False. A `TcpListener` can listen for connections at only one port at a time. g) False. A `UdpClient` can send information to any port represented by an `IPEndPoint`. h) False. Method `GetStream` of class `TcpClient` creates a `NetworkStream` that can be used to read and write data over a connection. i) True.

21.2 a) `System::Net`, `System::Net::Sockets`. b) `UdpClient`. c) `IPAddress`. d) stream, datagram. e) Transmission Control Protocol. f) `TcpListener`. g) `TcpClient`. h) `NetworkStream`.

EXERCISES

21.3 Use a socket connection to allow a client to specify a file name and have the server send the contents of the file or indicate that the file does not exist. Allow the client to modify the file contents and to send the file back to the server for storage.

21.4 Multithreaded servers are quite popular today, especially because of the increasing use of multiprocessing servers (i.e., servers with more than one processor unit). Modify the simple server application presented in Section 21.4 to be a multithreaded server. Then, use several client applications and have each of them connect to the server simultaneously.

21.5 Create a client/server application for the game of Hangman, using socket connections. The server should randomly pick a word or phrase from a file or a database. After connecting, the client should be allowed to begin guessing. If a client guesses incorrectly five times, the game is over. Display the original phrase or word on the server. Display underscores (for letters that have not been guessed yet) and the letters that have been guessed in the word or phrase on the client. [*Note:* You do not need to draw the hangman for this exercise, simply display the number of incorrect guesses to the user.]

21.6 Modify the previous exercise to be a connectionless game using datagrams.

21.7 *(Modifications to the Multithreaded Tic-Tac-Toe Program)* The programs of Fig. 21.9–Fig. 21.17 implement a multithreaded, client/server version of the game Tic-Tac-Toe. Our goal in developing this game was to demonstrate a multithreaded server that could process multiple connections from clients at the same time. The server in the example is really a mediator between the two clients—it makes sure that each move is valid and that each client moves in the proper order. The server does not determine who won or lost or whether there was a draw. Also, there is no capability to allow a new game to be played or to terminate an existing game.

The following is a list of suggested modifications to the multithreaded Tic-Tac-Toe application:

a) Modify the `Server` to test for a win, loss or draw on each move in the game. When the game is over, send a message to each client that indicates the result of the game.
b) Modify the `Client` to display a button that, when clicked, allows the client to play another game. The button should be enabled only when a game completes. Note that both the `Client` and the `Server` must be modified to reset the board and all state information. Also, the other `Client` should be notified of a new game, so that client can reset its board and state information.
c) Modify the `Client` to provide a button that allows a client to terminate the program at any time. When the button is clicked, the server and the other client should be notified. The server should then wait for a connection from another client so that a new game can begin.

21.8 *(Networked Morse Code)* Perhaps the most famous of all coding schemes is the Morse code, developed by Samuel Morse in 1832 for use with the telegraph system. The Morse code assigns a series of dots and dashes to each letter of the alphabet, each digit, and a few special characters (such as period, comma, colon and semicolon). In sound-oriented systems, the dot represents a short sound and the dash represents a long sound. Other representations of dots and dashes are used with light-oriented systems and signal-flag systems.

Separation between words is indicated by a space, or, quite simply, the absence of a dot or dash. In a sound-oriented system, a space is indicated by a short period of time during which no sound is transmitted. The international version of the Morse code appears in Fig. 21.18.

Character	Code	Character	Code
A	•-	N	-•
B	-•••	O	---
C	-•-•	P	•--•
D	-••	Q	--•-
E	•	R	•-•
F	••-•	S	•••
G	--•	T	-
H	••••	U	••-
I	••	V	•••-
J	•---	W	•--
K	-•-	X	-••-
L	•-••	Y	-•--
M	--	Z	--••

Fig. 21.18 English letters of the alphabet and decimal digits as expressed in international Morse code. (Part 1 of 2.)

Character	Code	Character	Code
Digits			
1	•----	6	-••••
2	••---	7	--•••
3	•••--	8	---••
4	••••-	9	----•
5	•••••	0	-----

Fig. 21.18 English letters of the alphabet and decimal digits as expressed in international Morse code. (Part 2 of 2.)

Write an application that reads an English-language phrase and encodes the phrase into Morse code. Also, write a program that reads a phrase in Morse code and converts the phrase into the English-language equivalent. Use one blank between each Morse-coded letter and three blanks between each Morse-coded word. Then, enable these two applications to send Morse Code messages to each other through a multithreaded-server application. Each application should allow the user to type normal characters into a `TextBox`. The application should then translate the characters into Morse Code and send the coded message through the server to the other client. When messages are received, they should be decoded and displayed as normal characters and as Morse Code. The application should have two `TextBox`es: one for displaying the other client's messages, and one for typing.

22

Data Structures and Collections

Objectives

- To form linked data structures that use pointers, self-referential classes and recursion.
- To create and manipulate dynamic data structures, such as linked lists, queues, stacks and binary trees.
- To understand various important applications of linked data structures.
- To understand how to create reusable data structures with classes, inheritance and composition.

Much that I bound, I could not free;
Much that I freed returned to me.
Lee Wilson Dodd

'Will you walk a little faster?' said a whiting to a snail,
'There's a porpoise close behind us, and he's treading on my tail.'
Lewis Carroll

There is always room at the top.
Daniel Webster

Push on—keep moving.
Thomas Morton

I think that I shall never see
A poem lovely as a tree.
Joyce Kilmer

Outline

22.1 Introduction

The *data structures* that we have studied thus far have had fixed size, such as single- and double-subscripted arrays. This chapter introduces *dynamic data structures* that grow and shrink during execution time. *Linked lists* are collections of data items that are logically "lined up in a row"—users can make insertions and deletions anywhere in a linked list. *Stacks* are important in compilers and operating systems because insertions and deletions are made at only one end—the *top*. *Queues* represent waiting lines; insertions are made at the back (also referred to as the *tail*) of a queue, and deletions are made from the front (also referred to as the *head*) of a queue. *Binary trees* facilitate high-speed searching and sorting of data, efficient elimination of duplicate data items, representation of file system directories and compilation of expressions into machine language. These data structures have many other interesting applications as well.

We will discuss each of the major types of data structures and implement programs that create and manipulate them. We use classes, inheritance and composition to create and package these data structures for reusability and maintainability.

The chapter examples are practical programs that will be useful in more advanced courses and in industrial applications. The programs devote special attention to pointer manipulation and focus on it.

22.2 Self-Referential Classes

A *self-referential class* contains a pointer member that points to an object of the same class type. For example, the class definition in Fig. 22.1 defines a type, `Node`. This type has two `private` data members—integer member `data` and pointer member `next`. Member `next` points to an object of type `Node`, an object of the same type as the one being declared here—hence, the term "self-referential class." Member `next` is referred to as a *link* (i.e., `next` can be used to "tie" an object of type `Node` to another object of the same type). Class `Node` also has two properties: one for variable `data` (named `Data`), and another for variable `next` (named `Next`). Self-referential objects can be linked together to form useful data structures, such as lists, queues, stacks and trees. Figure 22.2 illustrates two self-referential objects linked together to form a list. A backslash (representing a null pointer) is placed in the link member of the second self-referential object to indicate that the link does not point to another object. The slash is for illustration purposes; it does not correspond to the backslash character. A null pointer normally indicates the end of a data structure. [*Note*: Readers should recall that in MC++, `0` represents a null pointer. However, throughout this chapter, we use `NULL` in place of `0`. `NULL` is defined in a number of headers, including `tchar.h`, and is interchangeable with `0`.]

Common Programming Error 22.1

Not setting the link in the last node of a list (or other linear data structure) to `NULL` *is a common logic error.*

```
// Fig. 22.1: NodeClass.cpp
// Example demonstrating a node class.

public __gc class Node
{
public:
   Node( int d )
   {
      // constructor body
   }

   __property int get_Data()
   {
      // get body
   }

   __property void set_Data( int newData )
   {
      // set body
   }

   __property Node *get_Next()
   {
      // get body
   }

   __property void set_Next( Node *newNext )
   {
      // set body
   }

private:
   int data;
   Node *next;
}; // end class Node
```

Fig. 22.1 Sample self-referential `Node` class definition.

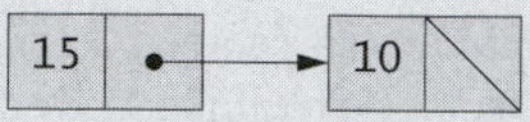

Fig. 22.2 Two self-referential class objects linked together.

Creating and maintaining dynamic data structures requires *dynamic memory allocation*—a program's ability to obtain more memory space at execution time to hold new nodes and to release space no longer needed. As we have already learned, MC++ programs do not explicitly release dynamically allocated memory. Rather, the CLR performs automatic garbage collection of managed objects.

The limit for dynamic memory allocation can be as large as the amount of available disk space in a virtual-memory system. Often, the limits are much smaller, because the computer's available memory must be shared among many users.

Operator `new` is essential to dynamic memory allocation. Operator `new` takes as an operand the type of the object being dynamically allocated and returns a pointer to a newly created object of that type. For example, the statement

```
Node *nodeToAdd = new Node( 10 );
```

allocates the appropriate amount of memory to store a `Node` and stores a pointer to this object in `nodeToAdd`. If no memory is available, `new` throws an `OutOfMemoryException`. The `10` is the `Node` object's data.

The following sections discuss lists, stacks, queues and trees. These data structures are created and maintained with dynamic memory allocation and self-referential classes.

Good Programming Practice 22.1

When creating a large number of objects, test for an `OutOfMemoryException`*. Perform appropriate error processing if the requested memory is not allocated.*

22.3 Linked Lists

A *linked list* is a linear collection (i.e., a sequence) of self-referential class objects, called *nodes,* connected by pointer links—hence, the term "linked" list. A program accesses a linked list via a pointer to the first node of the list. Each subsequent node is accessed via the link-pointer member stored in the previous node. By convention, the link pointer in the last node of a list is set to `NULL` to mark the end of the list. Data are stored in a linked list dynamically—that is, each node is created as necessary. A node can contain data of any type, including objects of other classes. Stacks and queues are also linear data structures, and they are constrained versions of linked lists. Trees are nonlinear data structures.

Lists of data can be stored in arrays, but linked lists provide several advantages. A linked list is appropriate when the number of data elements to be represented in the data structure is unpredictable. Unlike a linked list, the size of a conventional array cannot be altered, because the array size is fixed at creation time. Conventional arrays can become full, but linked lists become full only when the system has insufficient memory to satisfy dynamic storage allocation requests.

Performance Tip 22.1

An array can be declared to contain more elements than the number of items expected, at the expense of wasting memory. Linked lists may provide better memory utilization in these situations and they allow the program to adapt at run time.

Performance Tip 22.2

After locating the insertion point for a new item in a sorted linked list, inserting an element in the list is fast—only two pointers have to be modified. All existing nodes remain at their current locations in memory.

Performance Tip 22.3

The elements of an array are stored contiguously in memory to allow immediate access to any array element—the address of any element can be calculated directly from its offset from the beginning of the array. Linked lists do not afford such immediate access to their elements—an element can be accessed only by traversing the list from the front.

Memory does not normally store linked list nodes contiguously. Rather, the nodes are logically contiguous. Figure 22.3 illustrates a linked list with several nodes. Variable `firstNode` is a pointer to the first node in the list (containing value `H`), and variable `lastNode` is a pointer to the last node in the list (containing value `Q`). A programmer would use pointers `firstNode` and `lastNode` to access the front and back of the list, respectively.

Performance Tip 22.4

Using dynamic memory allocation (instead of arrays) for data structures that grow and shrink at execution time can save memory. Keep in mind, however, that pointers occupy space, and that dynamic memory allocation incurs the overhead of method calls.

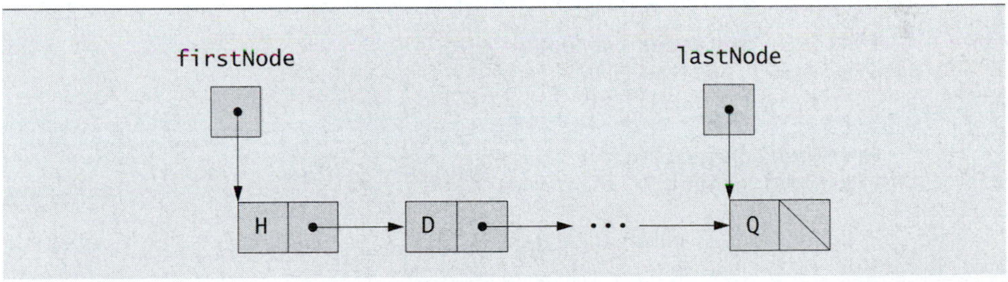

Fig. 22.3 Graphical representation of a linked list.

The program of Fig. 22.4–Fig. 22.10 uses an object of class `List` to manipulate a list of miscellaneous object types. Function `_tmain` in `ListTest.cpp` (Fig. 22.10) creates a list of objects, inserts objects at the beginning of the list using `List` method `InsertAtFront`, inserts objects at the end of the list using `List` method `InsertAtBack`, deletes objects from the front of the list using `List` method `RemoveFromFront` and deletes objects from the end of the list using `List` method `RemoveFromBack`. Each insertion and deletion operation invokes `List` method `Print` to display the current list contents. A detailed discussion of the program follows. If an attempt is made to remove an item from an empty list, an `EmptyListException` occurs.

Performance Tip 22.5

Insertion and deletion in a sorted array can be time consuming—all the elements following the inserted or deleted element must be shifted appropriately.

The program contains three classes—`ListNode` (Fig. 22.4–Fig. 22.5), `List` (Fig. 22.6–Fig. 22.7) and `EmptyListException` (Fig. 22.8–Fig. 22.9). These classes create a linked-list library (defined in namespace `LinkedListLibrary`) that can be reused throughout this chapter.

Encapsulated in each `List` object is a linked list of `ListNode` objects. Class `ListNode` (Fig. 22.4–Fig. 22.5) consists of two member variables—`data` and `next`. Member `data` can point to any object. Member `next` stores a pointer to the next `ListNode` object in the linked list. A `List` accesses the `ListNode` member variables via the properties `Data` (lines 31–34 of Fig. 22.4) and `Next` (lines 21–24), respectively.

```
1   // Fig. 22.4: ListNode.h
2   // Class ListNode represents one node in a list.
3
4   #pragma once
5
6   #include <tchar.h>
7
8   #using <mscorlib.dll>
9
10  using namespace System;
11
12  namespace LinkedListLibrary
13  {
14     // class to represent one node in a list
15     public __gc class ListNode
16     {
17     public:
18        ListNode( Object * );
19        ListNode( Object *, ListNode * );
20
21        __property ListNode *get_Next()
22        {
23           return next;
24        }
25
26        __property void set_Next( ListNode *value )
27        {
28           next = value;
29        }
30
31        __property Object *get_Data()
32        {
33           return data;
34        }
35
```

Fig. 22.4 `ListNode` class represents one node in a list. (Part 1 of 2.)

```
    private:
        Object *data;
        ListNode *next;
    }; // end class ListNode
} // end namespace LinkedListLibrary
```

Fig. 22.4 `ListNode` class represents one node in a list. (Part 2 of 2.)

```
// Fig. 22.5: ListNode.cpp
// Method definitions for class ListNode.

#include "stdafx.h"
#include "ListNode.h"

using namespace LinkedListLibrary;

// constructor to create ListNode that points to dataValue
// and is last node in list
ListNode::ListNode( Object *dataValue )
{
   data = dataValue;
   next = NULL;
}

// constructor to create ListNode that points to dataValue
// and points to next ListNode in List
ListNode::ListNode( Object *dataValue, ListNode *nextNode )
{
   data = dataValue;
   next = nextNode;
}
```

Fig. 22.5 `ListNode` class method definitions.

Common Programming Error 22.2

Attempting to use the object pointed to by a link pointer without checking if the pointer is `NULL` *first is a common mistake.*

Class `List` contains `private` members `firstNode` (a pointer to the first `ListNode` in a `List`) and `lastNode` (a pointer to the last `ListNode` in a `List`). The constructors (lines 10–14 and 17–21 of Fig. 22.7) initialize both pointers to `NULL`. `InsertAtFront` (lines 26–36), `InsertAtBack` (lines 41–53), `RemoveFromFront` (lines 56–74) and `RemoveFromBack` (lines 77–104) are the primary methods of class `List`. Each method uses `Monitor` methods `Enter` and `Exit` to ensure that `List` objects are *multithread safe* when used in a multithreaded program. If one thread is modifying the contents of a `List` object, no other thread can modify the same `List` object at the same time. Method `IsEmpty` (lines 107–114) is a predicate method that determines whether the list is empty (i.e., the pointer to the first node of the list is `NULL`). Predicate methods typically test a condition and do not modify the object on which they are called. If the list is empty, method `IsEmpty` returns `true`; otherwise, it returns `false`. Method `Print` (lines 117–140) displays the list's contents. Both `IsEmpty` and `Print` also use methods `Monitor::Enter` and `Monitor::Exit` so that the state of the list does not change while those methods are performing their tasks.

```
// Fig. 22.6: List.h
// Class List represents a linked list of ListNodes.

#pragma once

#include "ListNode.h"
#include "EmptyListException.h"

namespace LinkedListLibrary
{
   // class List definition
   public __gc class List
   {
   public:
      List( String * );
      List();

      void InsertAtFront( Object * );
      void InsertAtBack( Object * );

      Object *RemoveFromFront();
      Object *RemoveFromBack();

      bool IsEmpty();
      virtual void Print();

   private:
      ListNode *firstNode;
      ListNode *lastNode;
      String *name;    // string like "list" to display
   }; // end class List
} // end namespace LinkedListLibrary
```

Fig. 22.6 `List` class represents a linked list of `ListNode`s.

```
// Fig. 22.7: List.cpp
// Method definitions for class List.

#include "stdafx.h"
#include "List.h"

using namespace LinkedListLibrary;

// construct empty List with specified name
List::List( String *listName )
{
   name = listName;
   firstNode = lastNode = NULL;
}
```

Fig. 22.7 `List` class method definitions. (Part 1 of 4.)

```

// construct empty List with "list" as its name
List::List()
{
   name = S"list";
   firstNode = lastNode = NULL;
}

// Insert object at front of List. If List is empty,
// firstNode and lastNode will point to same object.
// Otherwise, firstNode points to the new node.
void List::InsertAtFront( Object *insertItem )
{
   Monitor::Enter( this );

   if( IsEmpty() )
      firstNode = lastNode = new ListNode( insertItem );
   else
      firstNode = new ListNode( insertItem, firstNode );

   Monitor::Exit( this );
} // end method InsertAtFront

// Insert object at end of List.  If List is empty,
// firstNode and lastNode will point to same object.
// Otherwise, lastNode's Next property points to new node.
void List::InsertAtBack( Object *insertItem )
{
   Monitor::Enter ( this );

   if ( IsEmpty() )
      firstNode = lastNode = new ListNode( insertItem );
   else {
      lastNode->Next = new ListNode( insertItem );
      lastNode = lastNode->Next;
   } // end else

   Monitor::Exit( this );
} // end method InsertAtBack

// remove first node from List
Object *List::RemoveFromFront()
{
   Monitor::Enter ( this );

   if ( IsEmpty() )
      throw new EmptyListException( name );

   Object *removeItem = firstNode->Data; // retrieve data

   // reset firstNode and lastNode pointers
   if ( firstNode == lastNode )
      firstNode = lastNode = NULL;
```

Fig. 22.7 List class method definitions. (Part 2 of 4.)

```
   else
      firstNode = firstNode->Next;

   Monitor::Exit( this );

   return removeItem; // return removed data
} // end method RemoveFromFront

// remove last node from List
Object *List::RemoveFromBack()
{
   Monitor::Enter ( this );

   if ( IsEmpty() )
      throw new EmptyListException( name );

   Object *removeItem = lastNode->Data; // retrieve data

   // reset firstNode and lastNode pointers
   if ( firstNode == lastNode )
      firstNode = lastNode = NULL;
   else {
      ListNode *current = firstNode;

      // loop while current node is not the new lastNode
      while ( current->Next != lastNode )
         current = current->Next; // move to next node

      // current is now the new lastNode
      lastNode = current;
      current->Next = NULL;
   } // end else

   Monitor::Exit( this );

   return removeItem; // return removed data
} // end method RemoveFromBack

// return true if List is emtpy
bool List::IsEmpty()
{
   Monitor::Enter( this );
   bool isEmpty = ( firstNode == NULL );
   Monitor::Exit( this );

   return isEmpty;
} // end method IsEmpty

// output List contents
void List::Print()
{
   Monitor::Enter( this );

```

Fig. 22.7 List class method definitions. (Part 3 of 4.)

```
   if ( IsEmpty() ) {
      Console::WriteLine( String::Concat( S"Empty ", name ) );
      Monitor::Exit( this );
      return;
   } // end if

   Console::Write( String::Concat( S"The ", name, S" is: " ) );

   ListNode *current = firstNode;

   // output current node data while not at end of list
   while ( current != NULL ) {
      Console::Write( String::Concat( current->Data, S" " ) );
      current = current->Next;
   } // end while

   Console::WriteLine( S"\n" );

   Monitor::Exit( this );
} // end method Print
```

Fig. 22.7 `List` class method definitions. (Part 4 of 4.)

Class `EmptyListException` (Fig. 22.8-Fig. 22.9) defines an exception class to handle illegal operations on an empty `List`.

```
// Fig. 22.8: EmpytListException.h
// Class EmptyListException declaration.

#pragma once

#using <mscorlib.dll>

using namespace System;
using namespace System::Threading;

namespace LinkedListLibrary
{
   // class EmptyListException definition
   public __gc class EmptyListException :  public ApplicationException
   {
   public:
      EmptyListException( String * );
   }; // end class EmptyListExeption
} // end namespace LinkedListLibrary
```

Fig. 22.8 `EmptyListException` is raised when the list is empty.

```
// Fig. 22.9: EmptyListException.cpp
// Class EmptyListException method definitions.

```

Fig. 22.9 `EmptyListException` class method definitions. (Part 1 of 2.)

```
#include "stdafx.h"
#include "EmptyListException.h"

using namespace LinkedListLibrary;

EmptyListException::EmptyListException( String *name ) :
   ApplicationException( String::Concat(
      S"The ", name, S" is empty" ) )
{
}
```

Fig. 22.9 `EmptyListException` class method definitions. (Part 2 of 2.)

`ListTest.cpp` (Fig. 22.10) uses the `LinkedListLibrary.dll` assembly created in Fig. 22.4–Fig. 22.9 to create and manipulate a linked list. (Review Section 8.16 to learn how to add a reference to an assembly.) Line 13 creates a new instance of type `List` named `list`. Lines 16–19 create data to add to the list. Lines 22–29 use `List` insertion methods to insert these objects and use `List` method `Print` to output the contents of `list` after each insertion. Note that the primitive data types (i.e., `aBoolean`, `aCharacter` and `anInteger`) must be boxed as `Objects` before being passed to the `List` insertion methods.

```
1  // Fig. 22.10: ListTest.cpp
2  // Testing class List.
3
4  #include "stdafx.h"
5
6  #using <mscorlib.dll>
7
8  using namespace System;
9  using namespace LinkedListLibrary;
10
11 int _tmain()
12 {
13    List *list = new List();    // create List container
14
15    // create data to store in List
16    bool aBoolean = true;
17    __wchar_t aCharacter = '$';
18    int anInteger = 34567;
19    String *aString = S"hello";
20
21    // use List insert methods
22    list->InsertAtFront( __box( aBoolean ) );
23    list->Print();
24    list->InsertAtFront( __box( aCharacter ) );
25    list->Print();
26    list->InsertAtBack( __box( anInteger ) );
27    list->Print();
28    list->InsertAtBack( aString );
29    list->Print();
30
```

Fig. 22.10 `ListTest.cpp` demonstrates the linked list. (Part 1 of 2.)

```
      // use List remove methods
      Object *removedObject;

      // remove data from list and print after each removal
      try {
         removedObject = list->RemoveFromFront();
         Console::WriteLine( String::Concat( removedObject, S" removed" ) );
         list->Print();

         removedObject = list->RemoveFromFront();
         Console::WriteLine( String::Concat( removedObject, S" removed" ) );
         list->Print();

         removedObject = list->RemoveFromBack();
         Console::WriteLine( String::Concat( removedObject, S" removed" ) );
         list->Print();

         removedObject = list->RemoveFromBack();
         Console::WriteLine( String::Concat( removedObject, S" removed" ) );
         list->Print();
      } // end try

      // process exception if list empty when attempt is made to remove item
      catch ( EmptyListException *emptyListException ) {
         Console::Error->WriteLine( String::Concat( S"\n",
            emptyListException ) );
      } // end catch

      return 0;
   } // end _tmain
```

```
The list is: True

The list is: $ True

The list is: $ True 34567

The list is: $ True 34567 hello

$ removed
The list is: True 34567 hello

True removed
The list is: 34567 hello

hello removed
The list is: 34567

34567 removed
Emtpy list
```

Fig. 22.10 `ListTest.cpp` demonstrates the linked list. (Part 2 of 2.)

The code inside the try block (lines 35–51) removes objects via List deletion methods, outputs the object removed and outputs list after every deletion. If there is an attempt to remove an object from an empty list, this try block catches the EmptyListException. Note that ListTest.cpp uses namespace LinkedListLibrary (line 9); thus, ListTest.cpp must reference the DLL created by the LinkedListLibrary class library (line 9).

Over the next several pages, we discuss each of the methods of class List in detail. Method InsertAtFront (Fig. 22.7, lines 26–36) places a new node at the front of the list. The method consists of three steps (illustrated in Fig. 22.11):

1. Call IsEmpty to determine whether the list is empty (line 30 of Fig. 22.7).
2. If the list is empty, set both firstNode and lastNode to point to a new ListNode initialized with insertItem (line 31). The ListNode constructor in lines 11–15 (of Fig. 22.5) sets variable data to the Object pointer passed as the first argument and sets the next pointer to NULL.
3. If the list is not empty, the new node is "threaded" (not to be confused with *multithreading*) into the list by setting firstNode to point to a new ListNode object initialized with insertItem and firstNode (line 33 of Fig. 22.7). When this ListNode constructor (lines 19–23 of Fig. 22.5) executes, it sets variable data to point to the same object pointed to by the first argument and performs the insertion by setting the next pointer to the ListNode passed as the second argument.

Figure 22.11 illustrates method InsertAtFront. Part (a) of the figure shows the list and the new node during the InsertAtFront operation and before the threading of the new node into the list. The dotted arrows in part (b) illustrate *Step 3* of the InsertAtFront operation, which enables the node containing 12 to become the new list front.

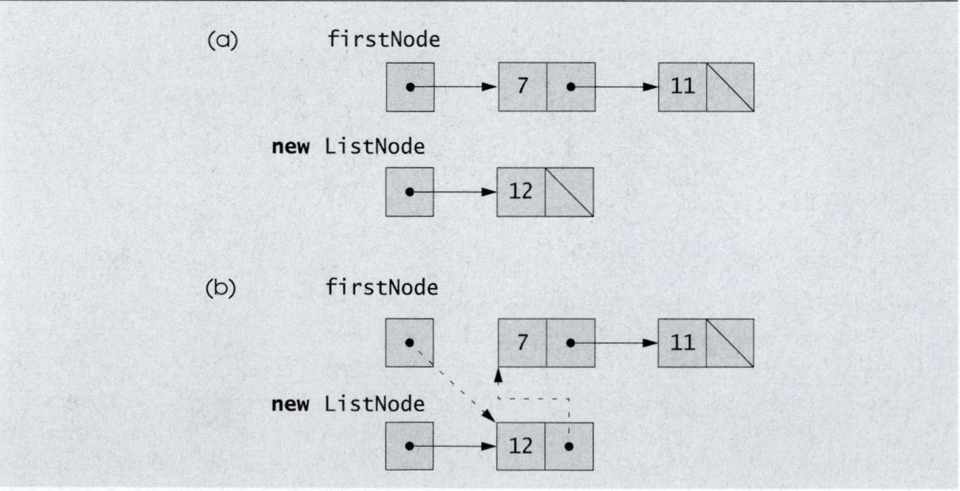

Fig. 22.11 Graphical representation of the InsertAtFront operation.

Method InsertAtBack (Fig. 22.7, lines 41–53) places a new node at the back of the list. The method consists of three steps (illustrated in Fig. 22.12):

1. Call `IsEmpty` to determine whether the list is empty (line 45).
2. If the list is empty, set both `firstNode` and `lastNode` to point to a new `ListNode` initialized with `insertItem` (line 46). The `ListNode` constructor in lines 11–15 (of Fig. 22.5) sets variable `data` to the `Object` pointer passed as the first argument and sets the `next` pointer to `NULL`.
3. If the list is not empty, thread the new node into the list by setting `lastNode` and `lastNode->next` to point to a new `ListNode` object initialized with `insertItem` (lines 48–49 of Fig. 22.7). When the `ListNode` constructor (lines 11–15 of Fig. 22.5) executes, it sets variable `data` to the `Object` pointer passed as an argument and sets the `next` pointer to `NULL`.

Figure 22.12 illustrates an `InsertAtBack` operation. Part a) of the figure shows the list and the new node during the `InsertAtBack` operation and before the new node has been threaded into the list. The dotted arrows in part b) illustrate the steps of method `InsertAtBack` that enable a new node to be added to the end of a list that is not empty.

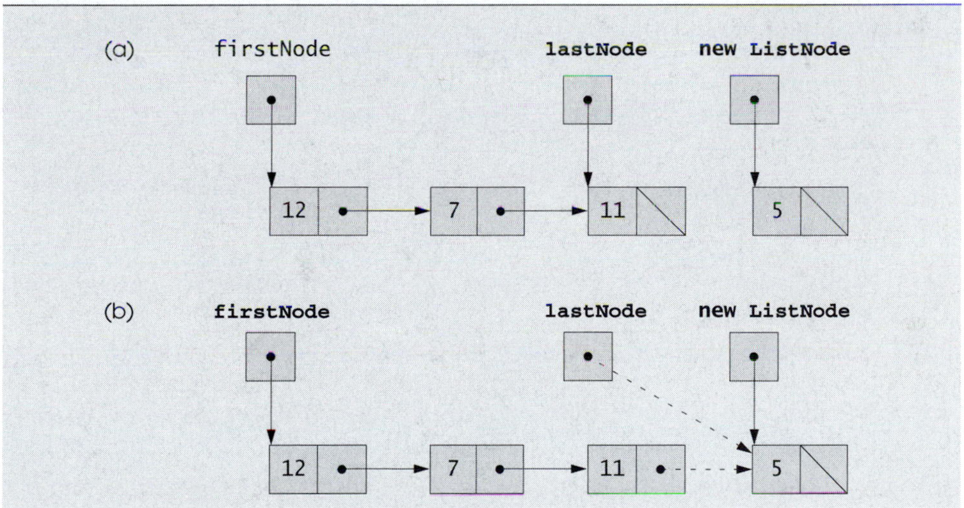

Fig. 22.12 Graphical representation of the `InsertAtBack` operation.

Method `RemoveFromFront` (Fig. 22.7, lines 56–74) removes the front node of the list and returns a pointer to the removed data. The method throws an `EmptyListException` (line 61) if the programmer tries to remove a node from an empty list. Otherwise, the method returns a pointer to the removed data. The method consists of four steps (illustrated in Fig. 22.13):

1. Assign `firstNode->Data` (the data being removed from the list) to pointer `removeItem` (line 63 of Fig. 22.7).
2. If the objects to which `firstNode` and `lastNode` point are the same object (line 66), the list has only one element prior to the removal attempt. In this case, the method sets `firstNode` and `lastNode` to `NULL` (line 67) to “dethread” (remove) the node from the list (leaving the list empty).

3. If the list has more than one node prior to removal, then the method leaves pointer `lastNode` as is and simply assigns `firstNode->Next` to pointer `firstNode` (line 69). Thus, `firstNode` points to the node that was the second node prior to the `RemoveFromFront` call.
4. Return the `removeItem` pointer.

Notice that method `RemoveFromFront` returns a pointer to the object that has been removed from the list (`removeItem`). To delete the object, the programmer must do it explicitly (i.e., set `removeItem` to `NULL`). Figure 22.13 illustrates method `RemoveFromFront`. Part a) illustrates the list before the removal operation. Part b) shows actual pointer manipulations.

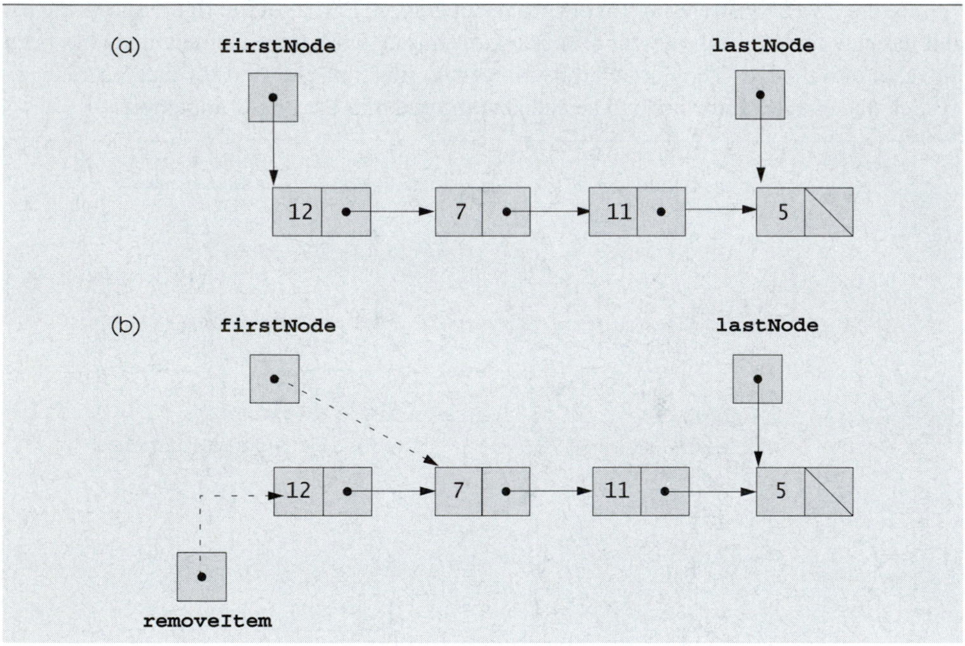

Fig. 22.13 Graphical representation of the `RemoveFromFront` operation.

Common Programming Error 22.3

Forgetting to delete an object that has been removed from a linked list is a common error.

Method `RemoveFromBack` (Fig. 22.7, lines 77–104) removes the last node of a list and returns a pointer to the removed data. The method throws an `EmptyListException` (line 82) if the program attempts to remove a node from an empty list. The method consists of several steps (illustrated in Fig. 22.14):

1. Assign `lastNode->Data` (the data being removed from the list) to pointer `removeItem` (line 84).
2. If the objects to which `firstNode` and `lastNode` point are the same object (line 87), the list has only one element prior to the removal attempt. In this case, the

method sets `firstNode` and `lastNode` to `NULL` (line 88) to dethread (remove) that node from the list (leaving the list empty).

3. If the list has more than one node prior to removal, create the `ListNode` pointer `current` and assign it `firstNode` (line 90).
4. Now "walk the list" with `current` until it points to the node before the last node. The `while` loop (lines 93–94) assigns `current->Next` to pointer `current` as long as `current->Next` is not equal to `lastNode`.
5. After locating the second-to-last node, assign `current` to `lastNode` (line 97) to dethread the last node from the list.
6. Set `current->Next` to `NULL` (line 98) in the new last node of the list to ensure proper list termination.
7. Return the `removeItem` pointer (line 103).

Notice that (as with method `RemoveFromFront`) method `RemoveFromBack` returns a pointer to the object that has been removed from the list (`removeItem`). To delete the object, the programmer must explicitly set `removeItem` to `NULL`. Figure 22.14 illustrates method `RemoveFromBack`. Part a) illustrates the list before the removal operation. Part b) shows the actual pointer manipulations.

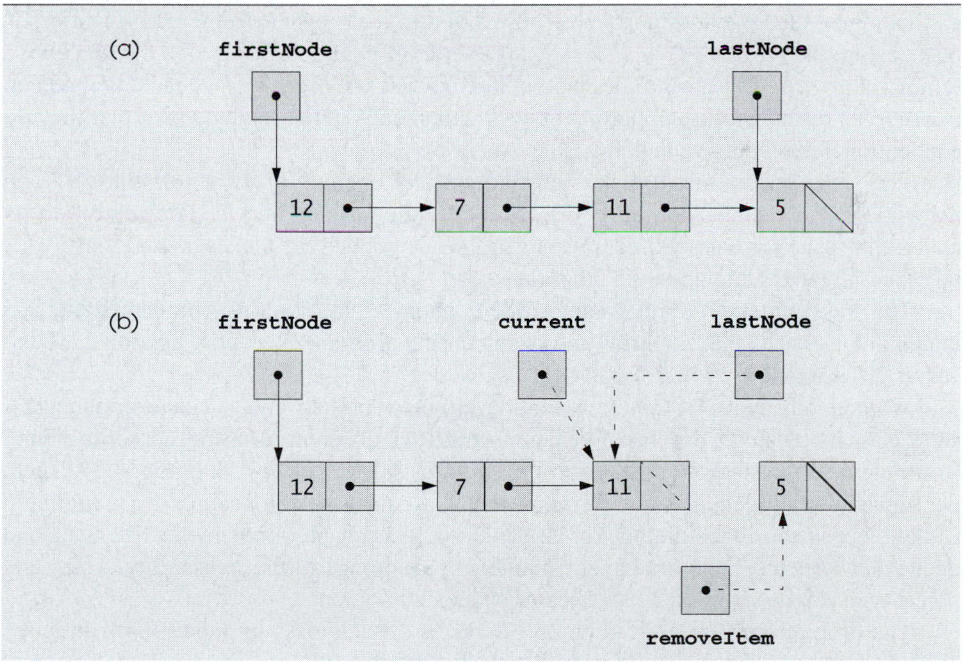

Fig. 22.14 Graphical representation of the `RemoveFromBack` operation.

Method `Print` (Fig. 22.7, lines 117–140) first checks for whether the list is empty (line 121). If so, `Print` displays output consisting of the string `"Empty "` and the list's `name`, then returns control to the calling method. Otherwise, `Print` outputs the data in the list. The method prints a string consisting of the string "The ", the name and the string " is: ". Then, line 129 creates ListNode pointer current and initializes it with firstNode. While current is not NULL, there are more items in the list. Therefore, the method prints current->Data (line 133), then assigns current->Next to current (line 134) to move to the next node in the list. Note that, if the link in the last node of the list is not NULL, the printing algorithm will erroneously attempt to print past the end of the list. The printing algorithm is identical for linked lists, stacks and queues.

22.4 Stacks

A *stack* is a constrained version of a linked list—a stack takes new nodes and releases nodes only at the top. For this reason, a stack is referred to as a *last-in, first-out* (*LIFO*) data structure. The link member in the bottom (i.e., last) node of the stack is set to NULL to indicate the bottom of the stack.

The primary operations to manipulate a stack are *push* and *pop*. Operation push adds a new node to the top of the stack. Operation pop removes a node from the top of the stack and returns the item from the popped node.

Stacks have many interesting applications. For example, when a program calls a method, the called method must know how to return to its caller, so the return address is pushed onto the *program execution stack*. If a series of method calls occurs, the successive return values are pushed onto the stack in last-in, first-out order so that each method can return to its caller. Stacks support recursive method calls in the same manner that they do conventional nonrecursive method calls.

The program-execution stack contains the space created for local variables on each invocation of a method during a program's execution. When the method returns to its caller, the space for that method's local variables is popped off the stack, and those variables are no longer known to the program.

The *System::Collections* namespace contains class *Stack* for implementing and manipulating stacks that can grow and shrink during program execution. Section 22.7 discusses class Stack.

We take advantage of the close relationship between lists and stacks to implement a stack class by reusing a list class. We demonstrate two different forms of reusability. First, we implement the stack class by inheriting from class List of Fig. 22.6–Fig. 22.7. Then, we implement an identically performing stack class through composition by including a List object as a private member of a stack class. This chapter implements list, stack and queue data structures to store Object pointers to encourage further reusability. Thus, any object type can be stored in a list, stack or queue.

The program of Fig. 22.15–Fig. 22.17 creates a stack class by inheriting from class List of Fig. 22.6–Fig. 22.7. We want the stack to have methods Push, Pop, IsEmpty and Print. Essentially, these are the methods InsertAtFront, RemoveFromFront, IsEmpty and Print of class List. Of course, class List contains other methods (such as InsertAtBack and RemoveFromBack) that we would rather not make accessible through the public interface of the stack. It is important to remember that all methods in the public interface of class List are also public methods of the derived class StackInheritance (Fig. 22.15–Fig. 22.16).

```
// Fig. 22.15: StackInheritance.h
// Implementing a stack by inheriting from class List.

#pragma once

#using <mscorlib.dll>

using namespace System;
using namespace LinkedListLibrary;

// class StackInheritance inherits class List's capabilities
public __gc class StackInheritance : public List
{
public:
   StackInheritance();
   void Push( Object * );
   Object *Pop();
}; // end class StackInheritance
```

Fig. 22.15 `StackInheritance` extends class `List`.

```
// Fig. 22.16: StackInheritance.cpp
// Method definitions for class StackInheritance.

#include "stdafx.h"
#include "StackInheritance.h"

// pass name "stack" to List constructor
StackInheritance::StackInheritance() : List( S"stack" )
{
}

// place dataValue at top of stack by inserting
// dataValue at front of linked list
void StackInheritance::Push( Object *dataValue )
{
   InsertAtFront( dataValue );
}

// remove item from top of stack by removing
// item at front of linked list
Object *StackInheritance::Pop()
{
   return RemoveFromFront();
}
```

Fig. 22.16 `StackInheritance` class method definitions.

When we implement the stack's methods, we have each `StackInheritance` method call the appropriate `List` method—method `Push` calls `InsertAtFront`, method `Pop` calls `RemoveFromFront`. Class `StackInheritance` does not define methods `IsEmpty` and `Print`, because `StackInheritance` inherits these methods from class `List` into `StackInheritance`'s `public` interface. The methods in class `StackInheritance` do not use methods `Monitor::Enter` and `Monitor::Exit`. Each of the methods in this class calls a method from class `List` that uses `Monitor` methods `Enter` and `Exit`. If two threads call `Push` on the same stack object, only one of the threads at a time will be able to call `List` method `InsertAtFront`. Note that class `StackInheritance` uses namespace `LinkedListLibrary` (line 9 of Fig. 22.15).; thus, the solution that defines `StackInheritance` must reference the DLL created by the `LinkedListLibrary` class library (line 9).

`StackInheritanceTest.cpp`'s `_tmain` function (Fig. 22.17) uses class `StackInheritance` to instantiate a stack of `Objects` called `stack`. Lines 16–19 define the data that will be pushed onto the stack and popped off the stack. The program pushes onto the stack (at lines 22, 24, 26 and 28) a `bool` containing `true`, a `__wchar_t` containing `$`, an `int` containing `34567` and a `String *` containing `hello`. An infinite `while` loop (lines 34–39) pops the elements from the stack. The program uses method `Print` (inherited from class `List`) to output the contents of the stack after each operation (line 38). When there are no objects left to pop, the infinite loop forces method `Pop` to throw an `EmptyListException`. The program then displays the exception's stack trace (line 44), which shows the program execution stack at the time the exception occurred.

```
1  // Fig. 22.17: StackInheritanceTest.cpp
2  // Testing class StackInheritance.
3
4  #include "stdafx.h"
5  #include "StackInheritance.h"
6
7  #using <mscorlib.dll>
8
9  using namespace System;
10
11 int _tmain()
12 {
13    StackInheritance *stack = new StackInheritance();
14
15    // create objects to store in the stack
16    bool aBoolean = true;
17    __wchar_t aCharacter = '$';
18    int anInteger = 34567;
19    String *aString = S"hello";
20
21    // use method Push to add items to stack
22    stack->Push( __box( aBoolean ) );
23    stack->Print();
24    stack->Push( __box( aCharacter ) );
25    stack->Print();
26    stack->Push( __box( anInteger ) );
27    stack->Print();
28    stack->Push( aString );
29    stack->Print();
30
31    // use method Pop to remove items from stack
32    try {
33
```

Fig. 22.17 `StackInheritanceTest` program. (Part 1 of 2.)

```
      while ( true ) {
         Object *removedObject = stack->Pop();
         Console::WriteLine(
            String::Concat ( removedObject,S" popped" ) );
         stack->Print();
      } // end while
   } // end try

   // if exception occurs, print stack trace
   catch ( EmptyListException *emptyListException ) {
      Console::Error->WriteLine( emptyListException->StackTrace );
   } // end catch

   return 0;
} // end _tmain
```

```
The stack is: True

The stack is: $ True

The stack is: 34567 $ True

The stack is: hello 34567 $ True

hello popped
The stack is: 34567 $ True

34567 popped
The stack is: $ True

$ popped
The stack is: True

True popped
Empty stack
   at LinkedListLibrary.List.RemoveFromFront()
   at StackInheritance.Pop()
      in c:\ch22\fig22_15-17\stackinheritancetest\stackinheritance.cpp:line 23
   at main()
      in c:\ch22\fig22_15-17\stackinheritancetest\
         stackinheritancetest.cpp:line 35
```

Fig. 22.17 `StackInheritanceTest` program. (Part 2 of 2.)

Another way to implement a stack class is by reusing a list class through composition. The class in Fig. 22.18–Fig. 22.19 uses a `private` object of class `List` (line 21 of Fig. 22.18) in the definition of class `StackComposition`. Composition enables us to hide the methods of class `List` that should not be in our stack's `public` interface by providing `public` interface methods only to the required `List` methods. This class implements each stack method by delegating its work to an appropriate `List` method. In particular, `StackComposition` calls `List` methods `InsertAtFront`, `RemoveFromFront`, `IsEmpty` and `Print`. In this example, we do not show sample output for class `StackComposition`, because the only difference in the test program is that we change the type of the stack from `StackInheritance` to `StackComposition`. If you execute the application, you will see that the output (before the stack trace occurs) is identical.

```
// Fig. 22.18: StackComposition.h
// StackComposition definition with composed List object.

#pragma once

#using <mscorlib.dll>

using namespace System;
using namespace LinkedListLibrary;

public __gc class StackComposition
{
public:
   StackComposition();
   void Push( Object * );
   Object *Pop();
   bool IsEmpty();
   void Print();

private:
   List *stack;
}; // end class StackComposition
```

Fig. 22.18 `StackComposition` class encapsulates functionality of class `List`.

```
// Fig. 22.19: StackComposition.cpp
// Method definitions for class StackComposition.

#include "stdafx.h"
#include "StackComposition.h"

// construct empty stack
StackComposition::StackComposition()
{
   stack = new List( S"stack" );
}

// add object to stack
void StackComposition::Push( Object *dataValue )
{
   stack->InsertAtFront( dataValue );
}

// remove object from stack
Object *StackComposition::Pop()
{
   return stack->RemoveFromFront();
}
```

Fig. 22.19 `StackComposition` class method definitions. (Part 1 of 2.)

```
// determine wheater stack is empty
bool StackComposition::IsEmpty()
{
   return stack->IsEmpty();
}

// output stack contents
void StackComposition::Print()
{
   stack->Print();
}
```

Fig. 22.19 `StackComposition` class method definitions. (Part 2 of 2.)

22.5 Queues

Another common data structure is the *queue*. A queue is similar to a checkout line in a supermarket—the first person in line is served first, customers enter the line only at the end, and they wait to be served. Queue nodes are removed only from the *head* of the queue and are inserted only at the *tail* of the queue. For this reason, a queue is a *first-in, first-out* (*FIFO*) data structure. The insert and remove operations are known as *enqueue* and *dequeue*.

Queues have many applications in computer systems. Most computers have only a single processor, so they cannot serve more than one user at a time. Entries for the other users are placed in a queue. The entry at the front of the queue receives the first available service. Each entry gradually advances to the front of the queue as users receive service.

Queues also support print spooling. A multiuser environment might have only one printer. Several users may send output to the printer. If the printer is busy, users may still generate other outputs, which are "spooled" to disk (much as thread is wound onto a spool), where they wait in a queue until the printer becomes available.

Information packets also wait in queues in computer networks. Each time a packet arrives at a network node, the routing node must route it to the next node on the network along the path to the packet's final destination. The routing node routes one packet at a time, so additional packets are enqueued until the router can route them.

A file server in a computer network handles file access requests from many clients throughout the network. Servers have a limited capacity to service requests from clients. When client requests exceed that capacity, the requests wait in queues.

The program of Fig. 22.20–Fig. 22.22 creates a queue class through inheritance from a list class. We want the `QueueInheritance` class (Fig. 22.20–Fig. 22.21) to have methods `Enqueue`, `Dequeue`, `IsEmpty` and `Print`. Note that these methods are essentially the `InsertAtBack`, `RemoveFromFront`, `IsEmpty` and `Print` methods of class `List`. Of course, the list class contains other methods (such as `InsertAtFront` and `RemoveFromBack`) that we would rather not make accessible through the `public` interface to the queue class. Remember that all methods in the `public` interface of the `List` class are also `public` methods of the derived class `QueueInheritance`.

When we implement the queue's methods, we have each `QueueInheritance` method call the appropriate `List` method—method `Enqueue` calls `InsertAtBack`, method `Dequeue` calls `RemoveFromFront`, and `IsEmpty` and `Print` calls invoke their base-class versions. Class `QueueInheritance` does not define methods `IsEmpty` and

```
1 // Fig. 22.20: QueueInheritance.h
2 // Implementing a queue by inheriting from class List.
3
4 #pragma once
5
6 #using <mscorlib.dll>
7
8 using namespace System;
9 using namespace LinkedListLibrary;
10
11 // class QueueInheritance inherits List's capabilities
12 public __gc class QueueInheritance : public List
13 {
14 public:
15    QueueInheritance();
16    void Enqueue( Object * );
17    Object * Dequeue();
18 }; // end of QueueInheritance
```

Fig. 22.20 QueueInheritance extends class List.

```
// Fig. 22.21: QueueInheritance.cpp
// Method definitions for class QueueInheritance.

#include "stdafx.h"
#include "QueueInheritance.h"

// pass name "queue" to List constructor
QueueInheritance::QueueInheritance() : List( S"queue" )
{
}

// place dataValue at end of queue by inserting
// dataValue at end of linked list
void QueueInheritance::Enqueue( Object *dataValue )
{
   InsertAtBack( dataValue );
}

// remove item from front of queue by removng
// item at front of linked list
Object* QueueInheritance::Dequeue()
{
   return RemoveFromFront();
}
```

Fig. 22.21 QueueInheritance class method definitions.

Print, because QueueInheritance inherits these methods from class List into QueueInheritance's public interface. Also, the methods in class QueueInheritance do not use methods Monitor::Enter and Monitor::Exit. Each of the methods in this class calls a method from class List that already uses Monitor methods Enter and Exit. Note that class QueueInheritance uses namespace LinkedListLibrary (line 9 of Fig. 22.20); thus, the solution that defines `QueueInheritance` must reference the DLL created by the `LinkedListLibrary` class library (line 9).

`QueueTest.cpp`'s `_tmain` method (Fig. 22.22) uses class `QueueInheritance` to instantiate a queue of `Objects` called `queue`. Lines 16–19 define the data that will be enqueued and dequeued. The program enqueues (in lines 22, 24, 26 and 28) a `bool` containing `true`, a `__wchar_t` containing `$`, an `int` containing `34567` and a `String *` containing `hello`.

```
1  // Fig. 22.22: QueueTest.cpp
2  // Testing class QueueInheritance.
3
4  #include "stdafx.h"
5  #include "QueueInheritance.h"
6
7  #using <mscorlib.dll>
8
9  using namespace System;
10
11 int _tmain()
12 {
13    QueueInheritance *queue = new QueueInheritance();
14
15    // create objects to store in the stack
16    bool aBoolean = true;
17    __wchar_t aCharacter = '$';
18    int anInteger = 34567;
19    String *aString = S"hello";
20
21    // use method Enqueue to add items to queue
22    queue->Enqueue( __box( aBoolean ) );
23    queue->Print();
24    queue->Enqueue( __box( aCharacter ) );
25    queue->Print();
26    queue->Enqueue( __box( anInteger ) );
27    queue->Print();
28    queue->Enqueue( aString );
29    queue->Print();
30
31    // use method Dequeue to remove items from queue
32    Object *removedObject = NULL;
33
34    // remove items from queue
35    try {
36
37       while ( true ) {
38          removedObject = queue->Dequeue();
39          Console::WriteLine(
40             String::Concat( removedObject, S" dequeue" ) );
41          queue->Print();
42       } // end while
43    } // end try
44
```

Fig. 22.22 Inheritance used to create a queue. (Part 1 of 2.)

```
45      // if exception occurs, print stack trace
46      catch( EmptyListException *emptyListException ) {
47         Console::Error->WriteLine( emptyListException->StackTrace );
48      } // end catch
49
50      return 0;
51   } // end _tmain
```

```
The queue is: True

The queue is: True $

The queue is: True $ 34567

The queue is: True $ 34567 hello

True dequeue
The queue is: $ 34567 hello

$ dequeue
The queue is: 34567 hello

34567 dequeue
The queue is: hello

hello dequeue
Empty queue
   at LinkedListLibrary.List.RemoveFromFront()
   at QueueInheritance.Dequeue()
      in c:\ch22\fig22_20-22\queuetest\queueinheritance.cpp:line 23
   at main()
      in c:\ch22\fig22_20-22\queuetest\queuetest.cpp:line 38
```

Fig. 22.22 Inheritance used to create a queue. (Part 2 of 2.)

An infinite `while` loop (lines 37–42) dequeues the elements from the queue in FIFO order. The program uses method `Print` (inherited from class `List`) to output the contents of the queue after each operation. When there are no objects left to dequeue, the infinite loop forces method `Dequeue` to throw an `EmptyListException`. The program then displays the exception's stack trace (line 47), which shows the program execution stack at the time the exception occurred.

22.6 Trees

Linked lists, stacks and queues are *linear data structures* (i.e., *sequences*). A *tree* is a nonlinear, two-dimensional data structure with special properties. Tree nodes contain two or more links. This section discusses *binary trees* (Fig. 22.23)—trees whose nodes all contain two links (of which none, one or both might be `NULL`). The *root node* is the first node in a tree. Each link in the root node points to a *child.* The *left child* is the first node in the *left subtree,* and the *right child* is the first node in the *right subtree.* The children of a specific node are called *siblings.* A node with no children is a *leaf node.* Computer scientists normally draw trees from the root node down—exactly the opposite of the way most trees grow in nature.

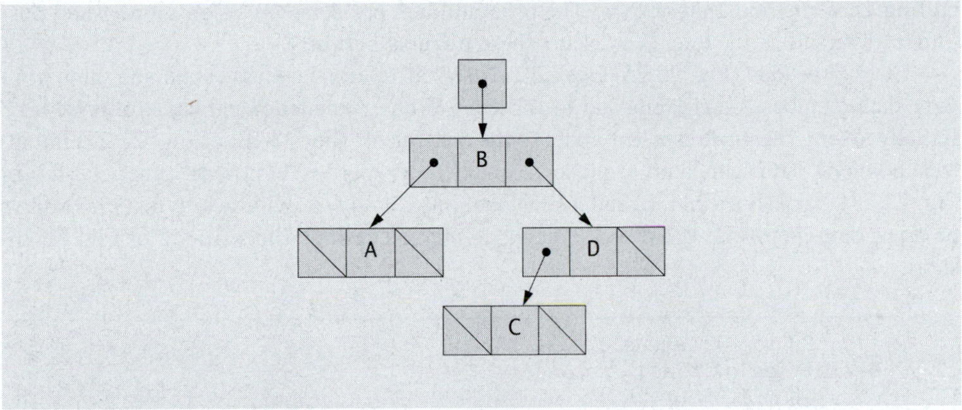

Fig. 22.23 Graphical representation of a binary tree.

Common Programming Error 22.4

Not setting to `NULL` *the links in leaf nodes of a tree is a common logic error.*

In our binary tree example, we create a special binary tree called a *binary search tree*. A binary search tree (with no duplicate node values) has the characteristic that the values in any left subtree are less than the value in the subtree's parent node, and the values in any right subtree are greater than the value in the subtree's parent node. Figure 22.24 illustrates a binary search tree with 12 integer values. Note that the shape of the binary search tree that corresponds to a set of data can depend on the order in which the values are inserted into the tree.

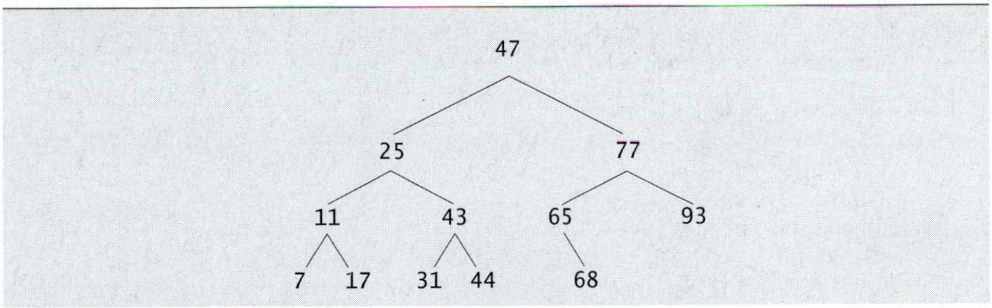

Fig. 22.24 Binary search tree containing 12 values.

22.6.1 Binary Search Tree of Integer Values

The application of Fig. 22.25–Fig. 22.29 creates a binary search tree of integers and traverses it (i.e., walks through all its nodes) in three ways—using recursive *inorder, preorder* and *postorder traversals*. The program generates 10 random numbers and inserts each into the tree. Fig. 22.27–Fig. 22.28 defines class `Tree`. Fig. 22.29 defines `TreeTest.cpp` to demonstrate class `Tree`. Function `_tmain` instantiates an empty `Tree` object, then randomly generates 10 integers and inserts each value into the binary tree by calling `Tree` method `InsertNode`. The program then performs preorder, inorder and postorder traversals of the tree. We discuss these traversals shortly.

Class `TreeNode` (Fig. 22.25–Fig. 22.26) is a self-referential class containing three `private` data members—`leftNode` and `rightNode` (of type `TreeNode`) and `data` (of type `int`). Initially, every `TreeNode` is a leaf node, so the constructor (lines 8–12 of Fig. 22.26) initializes pointers `leftNode` and `rightNode` to `NULL`. Properties `LeftNode` (lines 17–25 of Fig. 22.25), `Data` (lines 28–36) and `RightNode` (lines 39–47) provide access to a `ListNode`'s `private` data members. We discuss `TreeNode` method `Insert` (lines 16–42 of Fig. 22.26) shortly.

```
1  // Fig. 22.25: TreeNode.h
2  // Definition of class TreeNode.
3
4  #pragma once
5
6  #using <mscorlib.dll>
7
8  using namespace System;
9  using namespace System::Threading;
10
11 public __gc class TreeNode
12 {
13 public:
14    TreeNode( int );
15
16    // LeftNode property
17    __property TreeNode *get_LeftNode()
18    {
19       return leftNode;
20    }
21
22    __property void set_LeftNode( TreeNode *value )
23    {
24       leftNode = value;
25    }
26
27    // Data property
28    __property int get_Data()
29    {
30       return data;
31    }
32
33    __property void set_Data( int value )
34    {
35       data = value;
36    }
37
38    // RightNode property
39    __property TreeNode *get_RightNode()
40    {
```

Fig. 22.25 `TreeNode` class represents one node in a binary tree. (Part 1 of 2.)

```
      return rightNode;
   }

   __property void set_RightNode( TreeNode *value )
   {
      rightNode = value;
   }

   void Insert( int );

private:
   TreeNode *leftNode;
   int data;
   TreeNode *rightNode;
}; // end class TreeNode
```

Fig. 22.25 TreeNode class represents one node in a binary tree. (Part 2 of 2.)

```
// Fig. 22.26: TreeNode.cpp
// Method definitions for class TreeNode.

#include "stdafx.h"
#include "TreeNode.h"

// initialize data and make this a leaf node
TreeNode::TreeNode( int nodeData )
{
   data = nodeData;
   leftNode = rightNode = NULL; // node has no children
}

// insert TreeNode into Tree that contains nodes;
// ignore duplicate values
void TreeNode::Insert( int insertValue )
{
   // insert in left subtree
   if ( insertValue < data ) {

      // insert new TreeNode
      if ( leftNode == NULL )
         leftNode = new TreeNode( insertValue );

      // continue traversing left subtree
      else
         leftNode->Insert( insertValue );
   } // end if

   // insert in right subtree
   else if ( insertValue > data ) {

```

Fig. 22.26 TreeNode class method definitions. (Part 1 of 2.)

```
      // insert new TreeNode
      if ( rightNode == NULL )
         rightNode = new TreeNode( insertValue );

      // continue traversing right subtree
      else
         rightNode->Insert( insertValue );
   } // end else

} // end method Insert
```

Fig. 22.26 `TreeNode` class method definitions. (Part 2 of 2.)

Class `Tree` (Fig. 22.27–Fig. 22.28) manipulates objects of class `TreeNode`. Class `Tree` has as `private` member `root` (line 18 of Fig. 22.27)—a pointer to the root node of the tree. The class contains `public` method `InsertNode` (lines 16–25 of Fig. 22.28) to insert a new node in the tree and `public` methods `PreorderTraversal` (lines 28–33), `InorderTraversal` (lines 52–57) and `PostorderTraversal` (lines 76–81) to begin traversals of the tree. Each of these methods calls a separate recursive utility method to perform the traversal operations on the internal representation of the tree. The `Tree` constructor (lines 8–11) initializes `root` to `NULL` to indicate that the tree initially is empty.

```
1  // Fig. 22.27: Tree.h
2  // Definition of class Tree.
3
4  #pragma once
5
6  #include "TreeNode.h"
7
8  public __gc class Tree
9  {
10 public:
11    Tree();
12    void InsertNode( int );
13    void PreorderTraversal();
14    void InorderTraversal();
15    void PostorderTraversal();
16
17 private:
18    TreeNode *root;
19    void PreorderHelper( TreeNode * );
20    void InorderHelper( TreeNode * );
21    void PostorderHelper( TreeNode * );
22 }; // end class Tree
```

Fig. 22.27 `Tree` class represents a binary tree of `TreeNode`s.

```
1  // Fig. 22.28: Tree.cpp
2  // Method definitions for class Tree.
3
```

Fig. 22.28 `Tree` class method definitions. (Part 1 of 3.)

```
#include "stdafx.h"
#include "Tree.h"

// construct an empty Tree of integers
Tree::Tree()
{
   root = NULL;
}

// Insert a new node in the binary search tree.
// If the root node is NULL, create the root node here.
// Otherwise, call the insert method of clas TreeNode.
void Tree::InsertNode( int insertValue )
{
   Monitor::Enter( this );

   if ( root == NULL )
      root = new TreeNode( insertValue );
   else root->Insert( insertValue );

   Monitor::Exit( this );
} // end method InsertNode

// begin preorder traversal
void Tree::PreorderTraversal()
{
   Monitor::Enter( this );
   PreorderHelper( root );
   Monitor::Exit( this );
} // end method PreorderTraversal

// recursive method to perform preorder traversal
void Tree::PreorderHelper( TreeNode *node )
{
   if ( node == NULL )
      return;

   // output node data
   Console::Write( String::Concat( node->Data.ToString(), S" " ) );

   // traverse left subtree
   PreorderHelper( node->LeftNode );

   // traverse right subtree
   PreorderHelper( node->RightNode );
} // end method PreorderHelper

// begin inorder traversal
void Tree::InorderTraversal()
{
   Monitor::Enter( this );
   InorderHelper( root );
```

Fig. 22.28 Tree class method definitions. (Part 2 of 3.)

```
   Monitor::Exit( this );
} // end method InorderTraversal

// recursive method to perform inorder traversal
void Tree::InorderHelper( TreeNode *node )
{
   if ( node == NULL )
      return;

   // traverse left subtree
   InorderHelper( node->LeftNode );

   // output node data
   Console::Write( String::Concat( node->Data.ToString(), S" " ) );

   // traverse right subtree
   InorderHelper( node->RightNode );
} // end method InorderHelper

// begin postorder taversal
void Tree::PostorderTraversal()
{
   Monitor::Enter( this );
   PostorderHelper( root );
   Monitor::Exit( this );
} // end method PostorderTraversal

// recursive method to perform postorder traversal
void Tree::PostorderHelper( TreeNode *node )
{
   if ( node == NULL )
      return;

   // traverse left subtree
   PostorderHelper( node->LeftNode );

   // traverse right subtree
   PostorderHelper( node->RightNode );

   // output node data
   Console::Write( String::Concat ( node->Data.ToString(), S" " ) );
} // end method PostorderHelper
```

Fig. 22.28 Tree class method definitions. (Part 3 of 3.)

```
// Fig. 22.29: TreeTest.cpp
// This program tests class Tree.

#include "stdafx.h"
#include "Tree.h"

#using <mscorlib.dll>
```

Fig. 22.29 TreeTest.cpp creates and traverses a binary tree. (Part 1 of 2.)

```

using namespace System;

int _tmain()
{
   Tree *tree = new Tree();
   int insertValue;

   Console::WriteLine( S"Inserting values: " );
   Random *random = new Random();

   // insert 10 random integers from 0-99 in tree
   for ( int i = 1; i <= 10; i++ ) {
      insertValue = random->Next( 100 );
      Console::Write(
         String::Concat( insertValue.ToString(), S" " ) );

      tree->InsertNode( insertValue );
   } // end for

   // perform preorder traversal of tree
   Console::WriteLine( S"\n\nPreorder traversal" );
   tree->PreorderTraversal();

   // perform inorder traversal of tree
   Console::WriteLine( S"\n\nInorder traversal" );
   tree->InorderTraversal();

   // perform postorder traversal of tree
   Console::WriteLine( S"\n\nPostorder traversal" );
   tree->PostorderTraversal();
   Console::WriteLine();

   return 0;
} // end _tmain
```

```
Inserting values:
70 90 75 23 98 76 19 98 96 56

Preorder traversal
70 23 19 56 90 75 76 98 96

Inorder traversal
19 23 56 70 75 76 90 96 98

Postorder traversal
19 56 23 76 75 96 98 90 70
```

Fig. 22.29 `TreeTest.cpp` creates and traverses a binary tree. (Part 2 of 2.)

The `Tree` class's method `InsertNode` (lines 16–25) first locks the `Tree` object for thread safety, then checks for whether the tree is empty. If so, line 21 allocates a new `TreeNode`, initializes the node with the integer being inserted in the tree and assigns the new node to `root`. If the tree is not empty, `InsertNode` calls `TreeNode` method `Insert` (lines 16–42 of Fig. 22.26), which recursively determines the location for the new node in the tree and inserts the node at that location. *In a binary search tree, a node can be inserted only as a leaf node.*

The `TreeNode` method `Insert` compares the value to insert with the `data` value in the root node. If the insert value is less than the root-node data, the program checks for whether the left subtree is empty (line 22 of Fig. 22.26). If so, line 23 allocates a new `TreeNode`, initializes it with the integer being inserted and assigns the new node to pointer `leftNode`; otherwise, line 27 recursively calls `Insert` for the left subtree to insert the value into the left subtree. If the insert value is greater than the root-node data, the program checks for whether the right subtree is empty (line 34). If so, line 35 allocates a new `TreeNode`, initializes it with the integer being inserted and assigns the new node to pointer `rightNode`; otherwise, line 39 recursively calls `Insert` for the right subtree to insert the value in the right subtree.

Methods `InorderTraversal`, `PreorderTraversal` and `PostorderTraversal` call helper methods `InorderHelper` (lines 60–73 of Fig. 22.28), `PreorderHelper` (lines 36–49) and `PostorderHelper` (lines 84–97), respectively, to traverse the tree and print the node values. The purpose of the helper methods in class `Tree` is to allow the programmer to start a traversal without the need to obtain a pointer to the `root` node first, then call the recursive method with that pointer. Methods `InorderTraversal`, `PreorderTraversal` and `PostorderTraversal` simply take the `private` pointer `root` and pass it to the appropriate helper method to initiate a traversal of the tree. For the following discussion, we use the binary search tree shown in Fig. 22.30.Method `InorderHelper` (lines 60–73) defines the steps for an inorder traversal. Those steps are as follows:

1. If the argument is `NULL`, return immediately.
2. Traverse the left subtree with a call to `InorderHelper` (line 66 of Fig. 22.28).
3. Process the value in the node (line 69).
4. Traverse the right subtree with a call to `InorderHelper` (line 72).

The inorder traversal does not process the value in a node until the values in that node's left subtree are processed. The inorder traversal of the tree in Fig. 22.30 is

```
6 13 17 27 33 42 48
```

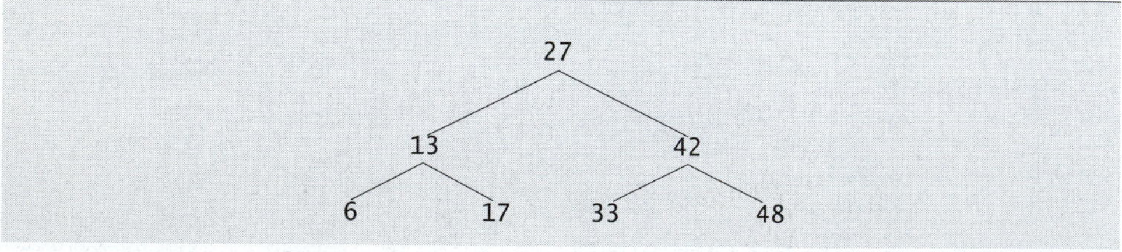

Fig. 22.30 Binary search tree.

Note that the inorder traversal of a binary search tree prints the node values in ascending order. The process of creating a binary search tree actually sorts the data—thus, this process is called the *binary tree sort*.

Method `PreorderHelper` (lines 36–49) defines the steps for a preorder traversal. Those steps are as follows:

1. If the argument is `NULL`, return immediately.
2. Process the value in the node (line 42).
3. Traverse the left subtree with a call to `PreorderHelper` (line 45).
4. Traverse the right subtree with a call to `PreorderHelper` (line 48).

The preorder traversal processes the value in each node as the node is visited. After processing the value in a given node, the preorder traversal processes the values in the left subtree, then the values in the right subtree. The preorder traversal of the tree in Fig. 22.30 is

```
27 13 6 17 42 33 48
```

Method `PostorderHelper` (lines 84–97) defines the steps for a postorder traversal. Those steps are as follows:

1. If the argument is `NULL`, return immediately.
2. Traverse the left subtree with a call to `PostorderHelper` (line 90).
3. Traverse the right subtree with a call to `PostorderHelper` (line 93).
4. Process the value in the node (line 96).

The postorder traversal processes the value in each node after the values of all that node's children are processed. The postorder traversal of the tree in Fig. 22.30 is

```
6 17 13 33 48 42 27
```

The binary search tree facilitates *duplicate elimination*. While building a tree, the insertion operation recognizes attempts to insert a duplicate value, because a duplicate follows the same "go left" or "go right" decisions on each comparison as the original value did. Thus, the insertion operation eventually compares the duplicate with a node containing the same value. At this point, the insertion operation might simply discard the duplicate value.

Searching a binary tree for a value that matches a key value is fast, especially for *tightly packed* trees. In a tightly packed tree, each level contains about twice as many elements as the previous level. Figure 22.30 shows a tightly packed binary tree. A binary search tree with n elements has a minimum of $\log_2 n$ levels. Thus, at most $\log_2 n$ comparisons are required either to find a match or to determine that no match exists. Searching a (tightly packed) 1000-element binary search tree requires at most 10 comparisons, because $2^{10} > 1000$. Searching a (tightly packed) 1,000,000-element binary search tree requires at most 20 comparisons, because $2^{20} > 1{,}000{,}000$.

22.6.2 Binary Search Tree of `IComparable` Objects

The binary tree example in Section 22.6.1 works nicely when all the data is of type `int`. Suppose that you want to manipulate a binary tree of double values. You could rewrite the `TreeNode` and `Tree` classes with different names and customize the classes to manipulate double values. Similarly, for each data type you could create customized versions of classes `TreeNode` and `Tree`. This results in a proliferation of code, which can become difficult to manage and maintain. The C++ programming language provides a technology, called *tem-*

plates, that enables us to write a class definition once, then have the compiler generate new versions of the class for any data type we choose.

Ideally, we would like to define the functionality of a binary tree once and reuse that functionality for many data types. Languages like Java and C++ provide polymorphic capabilities that enable all objects to be manipulated in a uniform manner. Using such capabilities enables us to design a more flexible data structure.

In our next example, we take advantage of C++'s polymorphic capabilities by implementing `TreeNode` and `Tree` classes that manipulate objects of any type that implements interface ***`IComparable`*** (namespace `System`). It is imperative that we be able to compare objects stored in a binary search, so that we can determine the path to the insertion point of a new node. Classes that implement `IComparable` define method ***`CompareTo`***, which compares the object that invokes the method with the object that the method receives as an argument. The method returns an `int` value less than zero if the calling object is less than the argument object, zero if the objects are equal and a positive value if the calling object is greater than the argument object. Also, both the calling and argument objects must be of the same data type; otherwise, the method throws an `ArgumentException`. Many of the data types we have used throughout this book implement interface `IComparable`.

The program of Fig. 22.31–Fig. 22.35 enhances the program from Section 22.6.1 to manipulate `IComparable` objects. One restriction on the new versions of classes `TreeNode` and `Tree` in Fig. 22.31–Fig. 22.34 is that each `Tree` object can contain objects of only one data type (e.g., all `String` pointers or all `double`s). If a program attempts to insert multiple data types in the same `Tree` object, `ArgumentException`s will occur. We modified only nine lines of code in class `TreeNode` (lines 16, 30, 35, 51 and 55 of Fig. 22.31 and lines 8, 16, 19 and 31 of Fig. 22.32) and two lines of code in class `Tree` (line 12 of Fig. 22.33 and line 16 of Fig. 22.34) to enable processing of `IComparable` objects. With the exception of lines 19 and 31 (of Fig. 22.32), all other changes simply replaced the type `int` with the type `IComparable *`. Lines 19 and 31 previously used the < and > operators to compare the value being inserted with the value in a given node. These lines now compare `IComparable` objects via the interface's method `CompareTo`, then test the method's return value to determine whether it is less than zero (the calling object is less than the argument object) or greater than zero (the calling object is greater than the argument object), respectively.

```
1  // Fig. 22.31: TreeNode2.h
2  // Definition of class TreeNode for IComparable objects.
3
4  #pragma once
5
6  #using <mscorlib.dll>
7
8  using namespace System;
9  using namespace System::Threading;
10
11 public __gc class TreeNode
12 {
13 public:
```

Fig. 22.31 `TreeNode` class for manipulating `IComparable` objects. (Part 1 of 2.)

```

   // initialize data and make this a leaf node
   TreeNode( IComparable * );

   // property LeftNode
   __property TreeNode *get_LeftNode()
   {
      return leftNode;
   }

   __property void set_LeftNode( TreeNode *value )
   {
      leftNode = value;
   }

   // property Data
   __property IComparable *get_Data()
   {
      return data;
   }

   __property void set_Data( IComparable *value )
   {
      data = value;
   }

   // property RightNode
   __property TreeNode *get_RightNode()
   {
      return rightNode;
   }

   __property void set_RightNode( TreeNode *value )
   {
      rightNode = value;
   }

   void Insert( IComparable * );

private:
   TreeNode *leftNode;
   IComparable *data;
   TreeNode *rightNode;
}; // end class TreeNode
```

Fig. 22.31 `TreeNode` class for manipulating `IComparable` objects. (Part 2 of 2.)

```
// Fig. 22.32: TreeNode2.cpp
// Method definitions for class TreeNode.

#include "stdafx.h"
#include "TreeNode2.h"
```

Fig. 22.32 `TreeNode` class method definitions. (Part 1 of 2.)

```

// initialize data and make this a leaf node
TreeNode::TreeNode( IComparable *nodeData )
{
   data = nodeData;
   leftNode = rightNode = NULL; // node has no children
}

// insert TreeNode into Tree that contains nodes;
// ignore duplicate values
void TreeNode::Insert( IComparable *insertValue )
{
   // insert in left subtree
   if ( insertValue->CompareTo( data ) < 0 ) {

      // insert new TreeNode
      if ( leftNode == NULL )
         leftNode = new TreeNode( insertValue );

      // continue traversing left subtree
      else
         leftNode->Insert( insertValue );
   } // end if

   // insert in right subtree
   else if ( insertValue->CompareTo( data ) > 0 ) {

      // insert new TreeNOde
      if ( rightNode == NULL )
         rightNode = new TreeNode( insertValue );

      // continue traversing right subtree
      else
         rightNode->Insert( insertValue );
   } // end else
} // end method Insert
```

Fig. 22.32 TreeNode class method definitions. (Part 2 of 2.)

```
// Fig. 22.33: Tree2.h
// Definition of class Tree for IComparable objects.

#pragma once

#include "TreeNode2.h"

public __gc class Tree
{
public:
   Tree();
   void InsertNode( IComparable * );
```

Fig. 22.33 Tree class for manipulating IComparable objects. (Part 1 of 2.)

```
    void PreorderTraversal();
    void PreorderHelper( TreeNode * );
    void InorderTraversal();
    void InorderHelper( TreeNode * );
    void PostorderTraversal();
    void PostorderHelper( TreeNode * );

private:
    TreeNode *root;
}; // end class Tree
```

Fig. 22.33 Tree class for manipulating IComparable objects. (Part 2 of 2.)

```
// Fig. 22.34: Tree2.cpp
// Method definitions for class Tree.

#include "stdafx.h"
#include "Tree2.h"

// construct an empty Tree of integers
Tree::Tree()
{
    root = NULL;
}

// Insert a new node in the binary search tree.
// If the root node is NULL, create the root node here.
// Otherwise, call the insert method of class TreeNode.
void Tree::InsertNode( IComparable *insertValue )
{
    Monitor::Enter( this );

    if ( root == NULL )
        root = new TreeNode( insertValue );
    else root->Insert( insertValue );

    Monitor::Exit( this );
}

// begin preorder traversal
void Tree::PreorderTraversal()
{
    Monitor::Enter( this );
    PreorderHelper( root );
    Monitor::Exit( this );
} // end method PreorderTraversal

// recursive method to perform preorder traversal
void Tree::PreorderHelper( TreeNode *node )
{
```

Fig. 22.34 Tree class method definitions. (Part 1 of 3.)

```
   if ( node == NULL )
      return;

   // output node data
   Console::Write( String::Concat( node->Data->ToString(), S" " ) );

   // traverse left subtree
   PreorderHelper( node->LeftNode );

   // traverse right subtree
   PreorderHelper( node->RightNode );
} // end method PreorderHelper

// begin inorder traversal
void Tree::InorderTraversal()
{
   Monitor::Enter( this );
   InorderHelper( root );
   Monitor::Exit( this );
} // end method InorderTraversal

// recursive method to perform inorder traversal
void Tree::InorderHelper( TreeNode *node )
{
   if ( node == NULL )
      return;

   // traverse left subtree
   InorderHelper( node->LeftNode );

   // output node data
   Console::Write( String::Concat( node->Data->ToString(), S" " ) );

   // traverse right subtree
   InorderHelper( node->RightNode );
} // end method InorderHelper

// begin post order traversal
void Tree::PostorderTraversal()
{
   Monitor::Enter( this );
   PostorderHelper( root );
   Monitor::Exit( this );
} // end method PostorderTraversal

// recursive method to perform postorder traversal
void Tree::PostorderHelper( TreeNode *node )
{
   if ( node == NULL )
      return;

   // traverse left subtre
   PostorderHelper( node->LeftNode );
```

Fig. 22.34 Tree class method definitions. (Part 2 of 3.)

```

   // traverse right subtree
   PostorderHelper( node->RightNode );

   // output node data
   Console::Write( String::Concat( node->Data->ToString(), S" " ) );
} // end method PostorderHelper
```

Fig. 22.34 Tree class method definitions. (Part 3 of 3.)

TreeTest2.cpp (Fig. 22.35) creates three Tree objects to store int, double and String * values, all of which the .NET Framework defines as IComparable types. The program populates the trees with the values in arrays intArray (line 16), doubleArray (line 17) and stringArray (lines 18–19), respectively.

Method PopulateTree (lines 40–52) receives an Array containing the initializer values for the Tree, a Tree into which the array elements will be placed and a String * representing the Tree name as arguments, then inserts each Array element into the Tree. Method TraverseTree (lines 55–72) receives a Tree and a String * representing the Tree name as arguments, then outputs the preorder, inorder and postorder traversals of the Tree. Note that the inorder traversal of each Tree outputs the data in sorted order regardless of the data type stored in the Tree. Our polymorphic implementation of class Tree invokes the appropriate data type's CompareTo method to trace the path to each value's insertion point by using the standard binary search tree insertion rules. Also, notice that the Tree of String pointers appears in alphabetical order.

```
1  // Fig. 22.35: TreeTest2.cpp
2  // Entry point for application.
3
4  #include "stdafx.h"
5  #include "Tree2.h"
6
7  #using <mscorlib.dll>
8
9  using namespace System;
10
11 void PopulateTree( Array *array, Tree *tree, String *name );
12 void TraverseTree( Tree *, String * );
13
14 int _tmain()
15 {
16    int intArray __gc[] = { 8, 2, 4, 3, 1, 7, 5, 6 };
17    double doubleArray __gc[] = { 8.8, 2.2, 4.4, 3.3, 1.1, 7.7, 5.5, 6.6 };
18    String *stringArray[] = { S"eight", S"two", S"four",
19       S"three", S"one", S"seven", S"five", S"six" };
20
```

Fig. 22.35 TreeTest2.cpp demonstrates class Tree with IComparable objects. (Part 1 of 3.)

```
   // create int Tree
   Tree *intTree = new Tree();
   PopulateTree( intArray, intTree, S"intTree" );
   TraverseTree( intTree, S"intTree" );

   // create double Tree
   Tree *doubleTree = new Tree();
   PopulateTree( doubleArray, doubleTree, S"doubleTree" );
   TraverseTree( doubleTree, S"doubleTree" );

   // create String Tree
   Tree *stringTree = new Tree();
   PopulateTree( stringArray, stringTree, S"stringTree" );
   TraverseTree( stringTree, S"stringTree" );

   return 0;
} // end _tmain

// populate Tree with array elements
void PopulateTree( Array *array, Tree *tree, String *name )
{
   Console::WriteLine( String::Concat( S"\nInserting into ",
      name, S":" ) );

   IComparable *data;

   for ( int i = 0; i < array->Length; i++ ) {
      data = dynamic_cast< IComparable * >( array->Item[ i ] );
      Console::Write( String::Concat( data->ToString(), S" " ) );
      tree->InsertNode( data );
   } // end for
} // end function PopulateTree

// perform traversals
void TraverseTree( Tree *tree, String *treeType )
{
   // perform preorder traversal of tree
   Console::WriteLine( String::Concat(
      S"\n\nPreorder traversal of ", treeType ) );
   tree->PreorderTraversal();

   // perform inorder traversal of tree
   Console::WriteLine( String::Concat(
      S"\n\nInorder traversal of ", treeType ) );
   tree->InorderTraversal();

   // perform postorder traversal of tree
   Console::WriteLine( String::Concat(
      S"\n\nPostorder traversal of ", treeType ) );
   tree->PostorderTraversal();
   Console::WriteLine( S"\n" );
} // end function TraverseTree
```

Fig. 22.35 `TreeTest2.cpp` demonstrates class `Tree` with `IComparable` objects. (Part 2 of 3.)

```
Inserting into intTree:
8 2 4 3 1 7 5 6

Preorder traversal of intTree
8 2 1 4 3 7 5 6

Inorder traversal of intTree
1 2 3 4 5 6 7 8

Postorder traversal of intTree
1 3 6 5 7 4 2 8


Inserting into doubleTree:
8.8 2.2 4.4 3.3 1.1 7.7 5.5 6.6

Preorder traversal of doubleTree
8.8 2.2 1.1 4.4 3.3 7.7 5.5 6.6

Inorder traversal of doubleTree
1.1 2.2 3.3 4.4 5.5 6.6 7.7 8.8

Postorder traversal of doubleTree
1.1 3.3 6.6 5.5 7.7 4.4 2.2 8.8


Inserting into stringTree:
eight two four three one seven five six

Preorder traversal of stringTree
eight two four five three one seven six

Inorder traversal of stringTree
eight five four one seven six three two

Postorder traversal of stringTree
five six seven one three four two eight
```

Fig. 22.35 `TreeTest2.cpp` demonstrates class `Tree` with `IComparable` objects. (Part 3 of 3.)

22.7 Collection Classes

The previous sections of this chapter discussed how to create and manipulate data structures. The discussion was "low level," in the sense that we painstakingly created each element of each data structure dynamically with `new` and modified the data structures by directly manipulating their elements and pointers to their elements. In this section, we consider the prepackaged data-structure classes provided by the .NET Framework. These classes are known as *collection classes*—they store collections of data. Each instance of one of these classes is known as a *collection*, which is a set of items.

With collection classes, instead of creating data structures, the programmer simply uses existing data structures, without concern for how the data structures are implemented.

This methodology is a marvelous example of code reuse. Programmers can code faster and can expect excellent performance, maximizing execution speed and minimizing memory consumption.

Some examples of collections are the cards you hold in a card game, your favorite songs stored in your computer and the real-estate records in your local registry of deeds (which map book numbers and page numbers to property owners). The .NET Framework provides several collections. We demonstrate four collection classes—*Array*, *ArrayList*, *Stack* and *Hashtable*—all from namespace System::Collections, plus built-in array capabilities. In addition, namespace System::Collections provides several other data structures, including *BitArray* (a collection of true/false values), *Queue* and *SortedList* (a collection of key/value pairs that are sorted by key and can be accessed either by key or by index).

The .NET Framework provides ready-to-go, reusable components; you do not need to write your own collection classes. The collections are standardized, so applications can share them easily, without having to be concerned with the details of their implementation. These collections are written for broad reuse. They are tuned for rapid execution and for efficient use of memory. As new data structures and algorithms are developed that fit this framework, a large base of programmers already will be familiar with the interfaces and algorithms implemented by those data structures.

22.7.1 Class Array

Chapter 7, Arrays, presented basic array-processing capabilities, and many subsequent chapters used the techniques shown there. We discussed briefly that all arrays inherit from class Array (namespace System). We also discussed Array property Length that specifies the number of elements in an array. In addition, class Array provides static methods that implement algorithms for processing arrays. Typically, class Array overloads these methods to provide multiple options for performing algorithms. For example, Array method *Reverse* can reverse the order of the elements in an entire array or can reverse the elements in a specified range of elements in an array. For a complete list of class Array's static methods and their overloaded versions, see the online documentation for the class.[1] Figure 22.36–Figure 22.38 demonstrates several static methods of class Array.

```
// Fig. 22.36: UsingArray.h
// Using Array class to perform common array manipulations.

#pragma once

#using <mscorlib.dll>
#using <system.drawing.dll>
#using <system.windows.forms.dll>

using namespace System;
```

Fig. 22.36 UsingArray class demonstrates class Array. (Part 1 of 2.)

1. The online documentation for class Array can be found at msdn.microsoft.com/library/default.asp?url=/library/en-us/cpref/html/frlrfsystemarrayclasstopic.asp.

```
using namespace System::Windows::Forms;
using namespace System::Collections;

public __gc class UsingArray
{
public:
   void Start();

private:
   static int intValues __gc[] = { 1, 2, 3, 4, 5, 6 };
   static double doubleValues __gc[] = { 8.4, 9.3, 0.2, 7.9, 3.4 };
   int intValuesCopy __gc[];
   String *output;
   void PrintArray();
}; // end class UsingArray
```

Fig. 22.36 UsingArray class demonstrates class Array. (Part 2 of 2.)

```
// Fig. 22.37: UsingArray.cpp
// Method definitions for class UsingArray.

#include "stdafx.h"
#include "UsingArray.h"

// method to build and display program output
void UsingArray::Start()
{
   intValuesCopy = new int __gc[ intValues->Length ];

   output = S"Initial Array values:\n";
   PrintArray(); // output initial array contents

   // sort doubleValues
   Array::Sort( doubleValues );

   // copy intValues into intValuesCopy
   Array::Copy( intValues, intValuesCopy, intValues->Length );

   output = String::Concat( output,
      S"\nArray values after Sort and Copy:\n" );
   PrintArray(); // output array contents
   output = String::Concat( output, S"\n" );

   // search for 5 in intValues
   int result = Array::BinarySearch( intValues, __box( 5 ) );
   output = String::Concat( output,
      ( result >= 0 ? String::Concat( S"5 found at element ",
      result.ToString() ) : S"5 not found" ), S" in intValues\n" );

   // search for 8763 in intValues
   result = Array::BinarySearch( intValues, __box( 8763 ) );
```

Fig. 22.37 UsingArray class method definitions. (Part 1 of 2.)

```
      output = String::Concat( output,
         ( result >= 0 ? S"8763 found at element ",
         result.ToString() : S"8763 not found" ), S" in intValues\n" );

      MessageBox::Show( output, S"Using Class Array",
         MessageBoxButtons::OK, MessageBoxIcon::Information );
   } // end method Start

   // append array content to output string
   void UsingArray::PrintArray()
   {
      output = String::Concat( output, S"doubleValues: " );

      double element;

      for ( int i = 0; i < doubleValues->Length; i++ ) {
         element = doubleValues[ i ];
         output = String::Concat( output, element.ToString(), S" " );
      } // end for

      output = String::Concat( output, S"\nintValues: " );

      int intElement;

      for( int j = 0; j < intValues->Length; j++ ) {
         intElement = intValues[ j ];
         output = String::Concat( output, intElement.ToString(), S" " );
      } // end for

      output = String::Concat( output, S"\nintValuesCopy: " );

      int intCopy;

      for( int n = 0; n < intValuesCopy->Length; n++ ) {
         intCopy = intValuesCopy[ n ];
         output = String::Concat( output, intCopy.ToString(), S" " );
      } // end for

      output = String::Concat( output, S"\n" );
   } // end method PrintArray
```

Fig. 22.37 UsingArray class method definitions. (Part 2 of 2.)

```
   // Fig. 22.38: UsingArrayTest.cpp
   // Entry point for application.

   #include "stdafx.h"
   #include "UsingArray.h"

   #using <mscorlib.dll>

   using namespace System;
```

Fig. 22.38 UsingArrayTest.cpp demonstrates class Array. (Part 1 of 2.)

```
int _tmain()
{
   UsingArray *application = new UsingArray();
   application->Start();

   return 0;
} // end _tmain
```

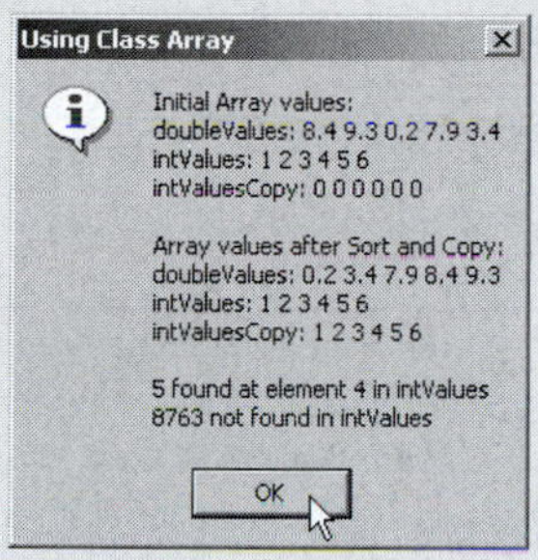
Using Class Array
Initial Array values:
doubleValues: 8.4 9.3 0.2 7.9 3.4
intValues: 1 2 3 4 5 6
intValuesCopy: 0 0 0 0 0 0
Array values after Sort and Copy:
doubleValues: 0.2 3.4 7.9 8.4 9.3
intValues: 1 2 3 4 5 6
intValuesCopy: 1 2 3 4 5 6
5 found at element 4 in intValues
8763 not found in intValues
OK

Fig. 22.38 `UsingArrayTest.cpp` demonstrates class Array. (Part 2 of 2.)

Line 16 (of Fig. 22.37) uses `static Array` method *`Sort`* to sort an array of `double` values. When this method returns, the array contains its original elements, but sorted in ascending order.

Lines 19 uses `static Array` method *`Copy`* to copy elements from array `intValues` into array `intValuesCopy`. The first argument is the array to copy (`intValues`), the second argument is the destination array (`intValuesCopy`) and the third argument is an integer representing the number of elements to copy (in this case, `intValues.Length` specifies all elements).

Lines 27 and 33 invoke `static Array` method *`BinarySearch`* to perform binary searches on array `intValues`. Method `BinarySearch` receives the *sorted* array in which to search and the key for which to search. The method returns the index in the array at which it finds the key (or a negative number if the key was not found).

Other `static Array` methods include *`Clear`* (to set a range of elements to `0` or `NULL`), *`CreateInstance`* (to create a new array of a specified data type), *`IndexOf`* (to locate the first occurrence of an object in an array or portion of an array) and *`LastIndexOf`* (to locate the last occurrence of an object in an array or portion of an array).

22.7.2 Class `ArrayList`

In most programming languages, conventional arrays have a fixed size—they cannot be changed dynamically to conform to an application's execution-time memory requirements. In some applications, this fixed-size feature presents a problem for programmers. They must choose between using fixed-size arrays that are large enough to store the maximum number of elements the program could require and using dynamic data structures that can grow and shrink the amount of memory required to store data in response to the changing requirements of a program at execution time.

The .NET Framework's *`ArrayList`* collection mimics the functionality of conventional arrays, yet provides dynamic resizing of the collection through the class's methods.

At any time an ArrayList contains a certain number of elements less than or equal to its *capacity*—the number of elements currently reserved for an ArrayList. A program can manipulate the capacity with ArrayList property *Capacity*. If an ArrayList needs to grow, it by default doubles its current Capacity.

Performance Tip 22.6

As with linked lists, inserting additional elements into an ArrayList *whose current size is less than its capacity is a fast operation.*

Performance Tip 22.7

It is a slow operation to insert an element into an ArrayList *that needs to grow larger to accommodate a new element.*

Performance Tip 22.8

If storage is at a premium, use method TrimToSize *of class* ArrayList *to trim an* ArrayList *to its exact size. This will optimize an* ArrayList*'s memory use. Be careful—if the program needs to insert additional elements, the process will be slower because the* ArrayList *must grow dynamically (trimming leaves no room for growth).*

Performance Tip 22.9

The default capacity increment, doubling the size of the ArrayList*, might seem to waste storage, but doubling is an efficient way for an* ArrayList *to grow quickly to "about the right size." This is a much more efficient use of time than growing the* ArrayList *by one element at a time in response to insert operations.*

ArrayLists store pointers to Objects. All classes derive from class Object, so an ArrayList can contain objects of any type. Figure 22.39 lists some useful methods of class ArrayList.

Method	Description
Add	Adds an Object to the ArrayList. Returns an int specifying the index at which the Object was added.
Clear	Removes all the elements from the ArrayList.
Contains	Returns true if the specified Object is in the ArrayList; false otherwise.
IndexOf	Returns the index of the first occurrence of the specified Object in the ArrayList.
Insert	Inserts an Object at the specified index.
Remove	Removes the first occurrence of the specified Object.
RemoveAt	Removes an object at the specified index.
RemoveRange	Removes a specified number of elements starting at a specified index in the ArrayList.
Sort	Sorts the ArrayList.
TrimToSize	Sets the Capacity of the ArrayList to be the number of elements the ArrayList currently contains.

Fig. 22.39 Some methods of class ArrayList.

Figure 22.40–Fig. 22.41 demonstrate class `ArrayList` and several of its methods. Users can type a string into the user interface's `TextBox`, then press a button representing an `ArrayList` method to see that method's functionality. A `TextBox` displays messages indicating each operation's results.

```
// Fig. 22.40: Form1.h
// Demonstrating ArrayList functionality.

#pragma once


namespace ArrayListTest
{
   using namespace System;
   using namespace System::ComponentModel;
   using namespace System::Collections;
   using namespace System::Windows::Forms;
   using namespace System::Data;
   using namespace System::Drawing;
   using namespace System::Text;

   /// <summary>
   /// Summary for Form1
   ///
   /// WARNING: If you change the name of this class, you will need to
   ///          change the 'Resource File Name' property for the managed
   ///          resource compiler tool associated with all .resx files
   ///          this class depends on.  Otherwise, the designers will not
   ///          be able to interact properly with localized resources
   ///          associated with this form.
   /// </summary>
   public __gc class Form1 : public System::Windows::Forms::Form
   {
   public:
      Form1(void)
      {
         InitializeComponent();
      }

   protected:
      void Dispose(Boolean disposing)
      {
         if (disposing && components)
         {
            components->Dispose();
         }
         __super::Dispose(disposing);
      }
   private: System::Windows::Forms::Button *  addButton;
   private: System::Windows::Forms::Button *  removeButton;
   private: System::Windows::Forms::Button *  firstButton;
   private: System::Windows::Forms::Button *  lastButton;
```

Fig. 22.40 `ArrayListTest` demonstrates class `ArrayList`. (Part 1 of 4.)

```
   private: System::Windows::Forms::Button *  isEmptyButton;
   private: System::Windows::Forms::Button *  containsButton;
   private: System::Windows::Forms::Button *  locationButton;
   private: System::Windows::Forms::Button *  trimButton;
   private: System::Windows::Forms::Button *  statisticsButton;
   private: System::Windows::Forms::Button *  displayButton;
   private: System::Windows::Forms::TextBox *  inputTextBox;
   private: System::Windows::Forms::TextBox *  consoleTextBox;
   private: System::Windows::Forms::Label *  inputLabel;

   // ArrayList for manipulating strings
   private: static ArrayList *arrayList = new ArrayList( 1 );

   private:
      /// <summary>
      /// Required designer variable.
      /// </summary>
      System::ComponentModel::Container * components;

   // Visual Studio .NET generated GUI code

   // add item to end of arrayList
   private: System::Void addButton_Click(
            System::Object *  sender, System::EventArgs *  e)
         {
            arrayList->Add( inputTextBox->Text );
            consoleTextBox->Text = String::Concat(
               S"Added to end: ", inputTextBox->Text );
            inputTextBox->Clear();
         } // end method addButton_Click

   // remove specified item from arrayList
   private: System::Void removeButton_Click(
            System::Object *  sender, System::EventArgs *  e)
         {
            arrayList->Remove( inputTextBox->Text );
            consoleTextBox->Text = String::Concat( S"Removed: ",
               inputTextBox->Text );
            inputTextBox->Clear();
         } // end method removeButton_Click

   // display first element
   private: System::Void firstButton_Click(
            System::Object *  sender, System::EventArgs *  e)
         {
            // get first element
            try {
               consoleTextBox->Text = String::Concat(
                  S"First element: ", arrayList->Item[ 0 ] );
            } // end try

```

Fig. 22.40 `ArrayListTest` demonstrates class `ArrayList`. (Part 2 of 4.)

```
               // show exception if no elements in arrrayList
               catch ( ArgumentOutOfRangeException *outOfRange ) {
                  consoleTextBox->Text = outOfRange->ToString();
               } // end catch
            } // end method firstButton_Click

   // display last element
   private: System::Void lastButton_Click(
               System::Object *  sender, System::EventArgs *  e)
            {
               // get last element
               try {
                  consoleTextBox->Text =
                     String::Concat( S"Last element: ",
                     arrayList->Item[ arrayList->Count - 1 ] );
               } // end try

               // show exception if no elements in arrrayList
               catch ( ArgumentOutOfRangeException *outOfRange ) {
                  consoleTextBox->Text = outOfRange->ToString();
               } // end catch
            } // end method lastButton_Click

   // determine whether arrayList is empty
   private: System::Void isEmptyButton_Click(
               System::Object *  sender, System::EventArgs *  e)
            {
               consoleTextBox->Text = ( arrayList->Count == 0 ?
                  S"arrayList is empty" : S"arrayList is not empty" );
            } // end method isEmptyButton_Click

   // determine whether arrayList contains specified object
   private: System::Void containsButton_Click(
               System::Object *  sender, System::EventArgs *  e)
            {
               if ( arrayList->Contains( inputTextBox->Text ) )
                  consoleTextBox->Text = String::Concat(
                     S"arrayList contains ", inputTextBox->Text );
               else
                  consoleTextBox->Text = String::Concat(
                     inputTextBox->Text, S" not found" );
            } // end method containsButton_Click

   // determine location of specified object
   private: System::Void locationButton_Click(
               System::Object *  sender, System::EventArgs *  e)
            {
               consoleTextBox->Text = String::Concat(
                  S"Element is at location ",
                  arrayList->IndexOf( inputTextBox->Text ).ToString() );
            } // end method locationButton_Click

```

Fig. 22.40 `ArrayListTest` demonstrates class `ArrayList`. (Part 3 of 4.)

```
    // trim arrayList to current size
    private: System::Void trimButton_Click(
                System::Object *  sender, System::EventArgs *  e)
             {
                arrayList->TrimToSize();
                consoleTextBox->Text = S"Vector trimmed to size";
             } // end method trimButton_Click

    // show arrayList current size and capacity
    private: System::Void statisticsButton_Click(
                System::Object *  sender, System::EventArgs *  e)
             {
                consoleTextBox->Text = String::Concat( S"Size = ",
                   arrayList->Count.ToString(),
                   S"; capacity = ", arrayList->Capacity.ToString() );
             } // end method statisticsButton_Click

    // display contents of arrayList
    private: System::Void displayButton_Click(
                System::Object *  sender, System::EventArgs *  e)
             {
                IEnumerator *enumerator = arrayList->GetEnumerator();
                StringBuilder *buffer = new StringBuilder();

                while ( enumerator->MoveNext() )
                   buffer->Append( String::Concat(
                      enumerator->Current, S"  " ) );

                consoleTextBox->Text = buffer->ToString();
             } // end method displayButton_Click
   };
}
```

Fig. 22.40 ArrayListTest demonstrates class ArrayList. (Part 4 of 4.)

```
// Fig. 22.41: Form1.cpp
// Entry point for application.

#include "stdafx.h"
#include "Form1.h"
#include <windows.h>

using namespace ArrayListTest;

int APIENTRY _tWinMain(HINSTANCE hInstance,
                       HINSTANCE hPrevInstance,
                       LPTSTR    lpCmdLine,
                       int       nCmdShow)
{
   System::Threading::Thread::CurrentThread->ApartmentState =
      System::Threading::ApartmentState::STA;
   Application::Run(new Form1());
```

Fig. 22.41 ArrayListTest entry point. (Part 1 of 2.)

```
        return 0;
    } // end _tWinMain
```

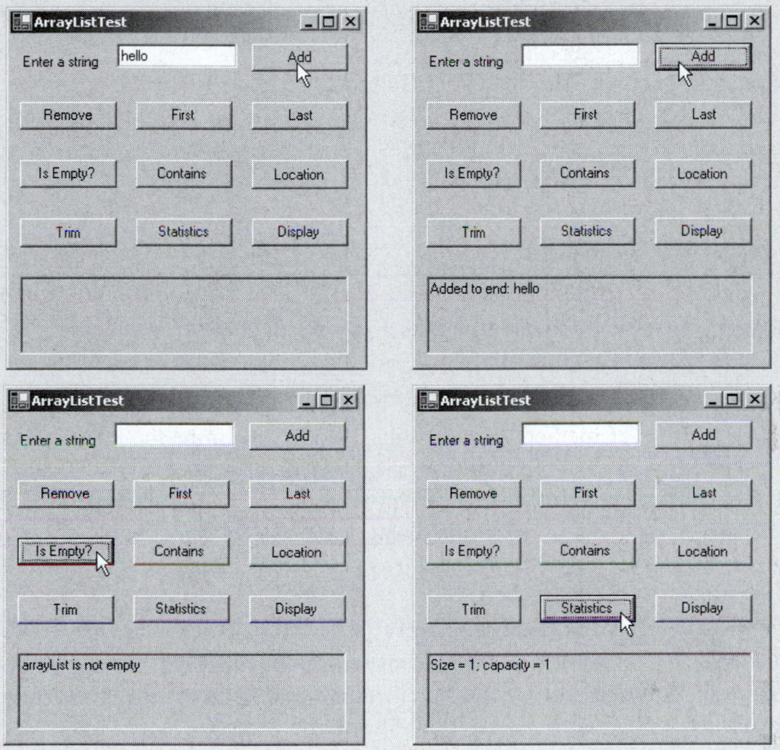

Fig. 22.41 `ArrayListTest` entry point. (Part 2 of 2.)

The `ArrayList` in this example stores `String` pointers that users input in the `TextBox`. Line 59 (of Fig. 22.40) creates an `ArrayList` with an initial capacity of one element. This `ArrayList` will double in size each time the user fills the array and attempts to add another element.

`ArrayList` method *Add* appends a new element at the end of an `ArrayList`. When the user clicks **Add**, event handler `addButton_Click` (lines 70–77 of Fig. 22.40) invokes method `Add` (line 73) to append the `String *` in the `inputTextBox` to the `ArrayList`.

`ArrayList` method *`Remove`* deletes a specified item from an `ArrayList`. When the user clicks **Remove**, event handler `removeButton_Click` (line 80–87) invokes `Remove` (line 83) to remove the `String *` specified in the `inputTextBox` from the `ArrayList`. If the object passed to `Remove` is in the `ArrayList`, the first occurrence of that object is removed, and all subsequent elements shift toward the beginning of the `ArrayList` to fill the empty position.

You cannot access `ArrayList` elements as you do conventional array elements, by following the `ArrayList` pointer name with the array subscript operator (`[]`) and the desired index of the element (e.g., `arrayList[ 0 ]`). Rather, programmers can access `ArrayList` elements by following the `ArrayList` indexed property `Item` with the array subscript operator (`[]`) and the desired index of the element (e.g., `arrayList->Item[0]`).

Event handlers `firstButton_Click` (lines 90–103) and `lastButton_Click` (lines 106–120) use `ArrayList` property `Item` to retrieve the first element (line 96) and last element (line 112), respectively. An `ArgumentOutOfRangeException` occurs if the specified index is not both greater than `0` and less than the number of elements currently stored in the `ArrayList`.

Event handler `isEmptyButton_Click` (lines 123–128) uses `ArrayList` property *`Count`* (line 126) to determine whether the `ArrayList` is empty. Event handler `containsButton_Click` (lines 131–140) uses `ArrayList` method *`Contains`* (line 134) to determine whether the given object is currently in the `ArrayList`. If so, the method returns `true`; otherwise, it returns `false`.

Performance Tip 22.10

`ArrayList` method `Contains` performs a linear search, which is a costly operation for large `ArrayList`s. If the `ArrayList` is sorted, use `ArrayList` method `BinarySearch` to perform a more efficient search.

When the user clicks **Location**, event handler `locationButton_Click` (lines 143–149) invokes `ArrayList` method *`IndexOf`* (line 148) to determine the index of a particular object in the `ArrayList`. `IndexOf` returns `-1` if the element is not found.

When the user clicks **Trim**, event handler `trimButton_Click` (lines 152–157) invokes method *`TrimToSize`* (line 155) to set the `Capacity` property to equal the `Count` property. This reduces the storage capacity of the `ArrayList` to the exact number of elements currently in the `ArrayList`.

When the user clicks **Statistics**, `statisticsButton_Click` (lines 160–166) uses the `Count` and `Capacity` properties to display the current number of elements in the `ArrayList` and the maximum number of elements that can be stored without allocating more memory to the `ArrayList`.

When the user clicks **Display**, `displayButton_Click` (lines 169–180) outputs the contents of the `ArrayList`. This event handler uses an *`IEnumerator`* (sometimes called an *enumerator* or an *iterator*) to traverse the elements of an `ArrayList` one element at a time. Interface `IEnumerator` defines methods *`MoveNext`* and *`Reset`* and property *`Current`*. `MoveNext` moves the enumerator to the next element in the `ArrayList`. The first call to `MoveNext` positions the enumerator at the first element of the `ArrayList`. `MoveNext` returns `true` if there is at least one more element in the `ArrayList`; otherwise, the method returns `false`. Method `Reset` positions the enumerator before the first element of the `ArrayList`. Methods `MoveNext` and `Reset` throw an `InvalidOperationException` if the contents of the collection are modified in any way after the enumerator's creation. Property `Current` returns the object at the current location in the `ArrayList`.

Line 172 creates an `IEnumerator` called `enumerator` and assigns it the result of calling `ArrayList` method *`GetEnumerator`*. Lines 175–177 iterate while `MoveNext` returns `true`, retrieve the current item via property `Current` and append it to `buffer`. When the loop terminates, line 179 displays the contents of `buffer`.

22.7.3 Class Stack

The `Stack` class, as its name implies, implements a stack data structure. This class provides much of the functionality that we defined in our implementation in Section 22.4. Refer to that section for a discussion of stack-data structure concepts. The application in Fig. 22.42–

Fig. 22.43 provides a GUI that enables the user to test many `Stack` methods. Line 35 of the `StackTest` constructor (Fig. 22.42) creates a `Stack` with the default initial capacity (10 elements).

```
1  // Fig. 22.42: Form1.h
2  // Demonstrates class Stack of namespace System::Collections.
3
4  #pragma once
5
6
7  namespace StackTest
8  {
9     using namespace System;
10    using namespace System::ComponentModel;
11    using namespace System::Collections;
12    using namespace System::Windows::Forms;
13    using namespace System::Data;
14    using namespace System::Drawing;
15    using namespace System::Text;
16
17    /// <summary>
18    /// Summary for Form1
19    ///
20    /// WARNING: If you change the name of this class, you will need to
21    ///          change the 'Resource File Name' property for the managed
22    ///          resource compiler tool associated with all .resx files
23    ///          this class depends on.  Otherwise, the designers will not
24    ///          be able to interact properly with localized resources
25    ///          associated with this form.
26    /// </summary>
27    public __gc class Form1 : public System::Windows::Forms::Form
28    {
29    public:
30       Form1(void)
31       {
32          InitializeComponent();
33
34          // create Stack
35          stack = new Stack();
36       }
37
38    protected:
39       void Dispose(Boolean disposing)
40       {
41          if (disposing && components)
42          {
43             components->Dispose();
44          }
45          __super::Dispose(disposing);
46       }
47    private: System::Windows::Forms::Label *  inputLabel;
48    private: System::Windows::Forms::TextBox *  inputTextBox;
```

Fig. 22.42 `StackTest` demonstrates class `Stack`. (Part 1 of 3.)

```
   private: System::Windows::Forms::Button *  pushButton;
   private: System::Windows::Forms::Button *  popButton;
   private: System::Windows::Forms::Button *  peekButton;
   private: System::Windows::Forms::Button *  isEmptyButton;
   private: System::Windows::Forms::Button *  searchButton;
   private: System::Windows::Forms::Button *  displayButton;
   private: System::Windows::Forms::Label *  statusLabel;

   private: Stack *stack;

   private:
      /// <summary>
      /// Required designer variable.
      /// </summary>
      System::ComponentModel::Container * components;

   // Visual Studio .NET generated GUI code

   // push element onto stack
   private: System::Void pushButton_Click(
               System::Object *  sender, System::EventArgs *  e)
            {
               stack->Push( inputTextBox->Text );
               statusLabel->Text = String::Concat( S"Pushed: ",
                  inputTextBox->Text );
            } // end method pushButton_Click

   // pop element from stack
   private: System::Void popButton_Click(
               System::Object *  sender, System::EventArgs *  e)
            {
               // pop element
               try {
                  statusLabel->Text = String::Concat( S"Popped: ",
                     stack->Pop() );
               } // end try

               // print message if stack is empty
               catch ( InvalidOperationException *invalidOperation ) {
                  statusLabel->Text = invalidOperation->ToString();
               } // end catch
            } // end method popButton_Click

   // peek at top element of stack
   private: System::Void peekButton_Click(
               System::Object *  sender, System::EventArgs *  e)
            {
               // view top element
               try {
                  statusLabel->Text = String::Concat( S"Top: ",
                     stack->Peek() );
               } // end try

```

Fig. 22.42 StackTest demonstrates class Stack. (Part 2 of 3.)

```
               // print message if stack is empty
               catch ( InvalidOperationException *invalidOperation ) {
                  statusLabel->Text = invalidOperation->ToString();
               } // end catch
            } // end method peekButton_Click

   // determine whether stack is empty
   private: System::Void isEmptyButton_Click(
               System::Object *  sender, System::EventArgs *  e)
            {
               statusLabel->Text = ( stack->Count == 0 ?
                  S"Stack is empty" : S"Stack is not empty" );
            } // end method isEmptyButton_Click

   // determine whether specified element is on stack
   private: System::Void searchButton_Click(
               System::Object *  sender, System::EventArgs *  e)
            {
               String *result = stack->Contains( inputTextBox->Text ) ?
                  S" found" : S" not found";

               statusLabel->Text = String::Concat( inputTextBox->Text,
                  result );
            } // end method searchButton_Click

   // display stack contents
   private: System::Void displayButton_Click(
               System::Object *  sender, System::EventArgs *  e)
            {
               IEnumerator *enumerator = stack->GetEnumerator();
               StringBuilder *buffer = new StringBuilder();

               // while the enumerator can move on to the next element
               // print that element out
               while ( enumerator->MoveNext() )
                  buffer->Append( String::Concat( enumerator->Current,
                     S" " ) );

               statusLabel->Text = buffer->ToString();
            } // end method displayButton_Click
   };
}
```

Fig. 22.42 StackTest demonstrates class Stack. (Part 3 of 3.)

```
// Fig. 22.43: Form1.cpp
// Entry point for application.

#include "stdafx.h"
#include "Form1.h"
#include <windows.h>

```

Fig. 22.43 StackTest entry point. (Part 1 of 2.)

```
using namespace StackTest;

int APIENTRY _tWinMain(HINSTANCE hInstance,
                       HINSTANCE hPrevInstance,
                       LPTSTR    lpCmdLine,
                       int       nCmdShow)
{
   System::Threading::Thread::CurrentThread->ApartmentState =
      System::Threading::ApartmentState::STA;
   Application::Run(new Form1());
   return 0;
} // end _tWinMain
```

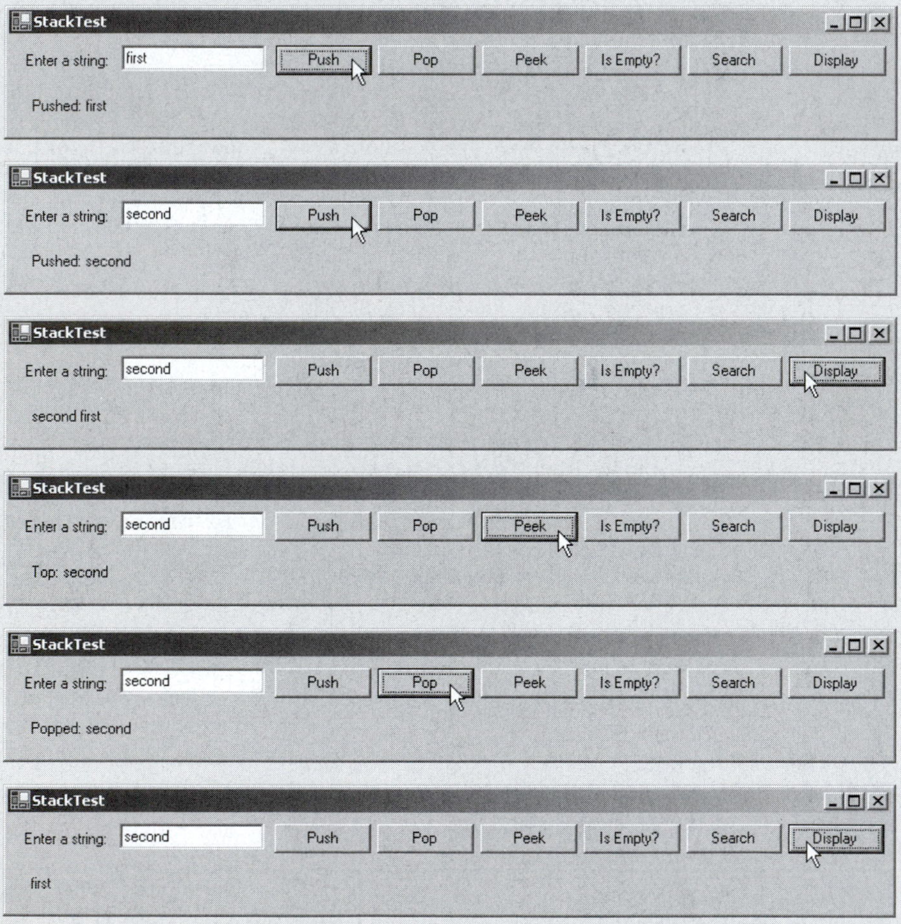

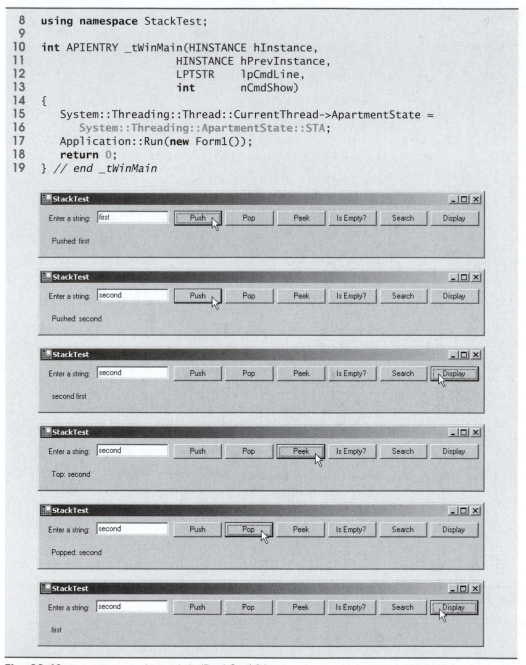

Fig. 22.43 `StackTest` entry point. (Part 2 of 2.)

As one might expect, class `Stack` has methods `Push` and `Pop` to perform the basic stack operations. Method ***`Push`*** takes an `Object` as an argument and adds it to the top of the `Stack`. If the number of items on the `Stack` (the `Count` property) is equal to the capacity at the time of the `Push` operation, the `Stack` grows to accommodate more

`Objects`. Event handler `pushButton_Click` (lines 68–74 of Fig. 22.42) uses method `Push` to add a user-specified string to the stack (line 71).

Method *Pop* takes no arguments. This method removes and returns the object currently on top of the `Stack`. Event handler `popButton_Click` (lines 77–90) calls method `Pop` (line 83) to remove an object from the `Stack`. An `InvalidOperationException` occurs if the `Stack` is empty when the program calls `Pop`.

Method *Peek* returns the value of the top stack element, but does not remove the element from the `Stack`. We use `Peek` in line 99 in event handler `peekButton_Click` (lines 93–106) to view the object on top of the `Stack`. As with `Pop`, an `InvalidOperationException` occurs if the `Stack` is empty when the program calls `Peek`.

Common Programming Error 22.5

Attempting to `Peek` or `Pop` an empty `Stack` (a `Stack` whose `Count` property equals 0) causes an `InvalidOperationException`.

Event handler `isEmptyButton_Click` (lines 109–114) determines whether the `Stack` is empty by comparing the `Stack`'s `Count` property to 0. If it is 0, the `Stack` is empty; otherwise, it is not. Event handler `searchButton_Click` (lines 117–125) uses `Stack` method `Contains` (lines 120–121) to determine whether the `Stack` contains the object specified as its argument. `Contains` returns `true` if the `Stack` contains the specified object, `false` otherwise.

Event handler `displayButton_Click` (lines 128–141) uses an `IEnumerator` to traverse the `Stack` and display its contents.

22.7.4 Class `Hashtable`

Object-oriented programming languages facilitate the creating of new types. When a program creates objects of new or existing types, it then needs to manage those objects efficiently. This includes sorting and retrieving objects. Sorting and retrieving information with arrays is efficient if some aspect of your data directly matches the key value and if those keys are unique and tightly packed. If you have 100 employees with nine-digit Social Security numbers and you want to store and retrieve employee data by using the Social Security number as a key, it would nominally require an array with 999,999,999 elements, because there are 999,999,999 unique nine-digit numbers. This is impractical for virtually all applications that key on Social Security numbers. If you could have an array that large, you could get extremely high performance storing and retrieving employee records by simply using the Social Security number as the array index.

A large variety of applications have this problem—namely, that either the keys are of the wrong type (i.e., not nonnegative integers), or they are of the right type, but they are sparsely spread over a large range.

What is needed is a high-speed scheme for converting keys such as Social Security numbers and inventory part numbers into unique array subscripts. Then, when an application needs to store something, the scheme could convert the application key rapidly into a subscript and the record of information could be stored at that location in the array. Retrieval occurs the same way—once the application has a key for which it wants to retrieve the data record, the application simply applies the conversion to the key, which produces the array subscript where the data resides in the array and retrieves the data.

The scheme we describe here is the basis of a technique called *hashing*. Why the name? Because, when we convert a key into an array subscript, we literally scramble the bits, forming a kind of "mishmash" number. The number actually has no real significance beyond its usefulness in storing and retrieving this particular data record.

A glitch in the scheme occurs when *collisions* occur [i.e., two different keys "hash into" the same cell (or element) in the array]. We cannot sort two different data records into the same space, so we need to find an alternative home for all records beyond the first that hash to a particular array subscript. Many schemes exist for doing this. One is to "hash again" (i.e., to reapply the hashing transformation to the key to provide a next candidate cell in the array). The hashing process is designed to be quite random, so the assumption is that, with just a few hashes, an available cell will be found.

Another scheme uses one hash to locate the first candidate cell. If the cell is occupied, successive cells are searched linearly until an available cell is found. Retrieval works the same way—the key is hashed once, the resulting cell is checked for whether it contains the desired data. If it does, the search is complete. If it does not, successive cells are searched linearly until the desired item(s) are found.

The most popular solution to hash-table collisions is to have each cell of the table be a hash "bucket," typically a linked list of all the key/value pairs that hash to that cell. This is the solution that the .NET Framework's *`Hashtable`* class implements.

The *load factor* is one factor that affects the performance of hashing schemes. The load factor is the ratio of the number of occupied cells in the hash table to the size of the hash table. The closer the ratio gets to 1.0, the greater the chance of collisions.

Performance Tip 22.11

The load factor in a hash table is a classic example of a space/time trade-off: By increasing the load factor, we get better memory utilization, but the program runs slower due to increased hashing collisions. By decreasing the load factor, we get better program speed because of reduced hashing collisions, but we get poorer memory utilization because a larger portion of the hash table remains empty.

Programming hash tables properly is too complex for most casual programmers. Computer science students study hashing schemes thoroughly in courses called "Data Structures" and "Algorithms." Recognizing the value of hashing, .NET provides class `Hashtable` and some related features to enable programmers to take advantage of hashing without the complex details.

The preceding sentence is profoundly important in our study of object-oriented programming. Classes encapsulate and hide complexity (i.e., implementation details) and offer user-friendly interfaces. Crafting classes to do this properly is one of the most valued skills in the field of object-oriented programming.

A *hash function* performs a calculation that determines where to place data in the hashtable. The hash function is applied to the key in a key/value pair of objects. Class `Hashtable` can accept any object as a key. For this reason, class `Object` defines method *`GetHashCode`*, which all objects in MC++ inherit. Most classes that are candidates to be used as keys in a hash table override this method to provide one that performs efficient hashcode calculations for a specific data type. For example, a `String` has a hashcode calculation that is based on the contents of the `String`. Figure 22.44–Fig. 22.47 demonstrate several methods of class `Hashtable`.

```
// Fig. 22.44: Employee.h
// Employee class for hashtable demonstration.

#pragma once

#using <mscorlib.dll>

using namespace System;

public __gc class Employee
{
public:
   Employee( String *, String * );
   String *ToString();

private:
   String *first, *last;
}; // end class Employee
```

Fig. 22.44 `Employee` class represents a single employee.

```
// Fig. 22.45: Employee.cpp
// Method definitions for class Employee.

#include "stdafx.h"
#include "Employee.h"

// constructor
Employee::Employee( String *fName, String *lName )
{
   first = fName;
   last = lName;
}

// return Employee first and last names as string
String *Employee::ToString()
{
   return String::Concat( first, S" ", last );
}
```

Fig. 22.45 `Employee` class method definitions.

```
// Fig. 22.46: Form1.h
// Demonstrate class Hashtable of namespace System::Collections.

#pragma once

#include "Employee.h"

namespace HashTableTest
{
```

Fig. 22.46 `HashTableTest` demonstrates class `Hashtable`. (Part 1 of 5.)

```
using namespace System;
using namespace System::ComponentModel;
using namespace System::Collections;
using namespace System::Windows::Forms;
using namespace System::Data;
using namespace System::Drawing;
using namespace System::Text;

/// <summary>
/// Summary for Form1
///
/// WARNING: If you change the name of this class, you will need to
///          change the 'Resource File Name' property for the managed
///          resource compiler tool associated with all .resx files
///          this class depends on.  Otherwise, the designers will not
///          be able to interact properly with localized resources
///          associated with this form.
/// </summary>
public __gc class Form1 : public System::Windows::Forms::Form
{
public:
   Form1(void)
   {
      InitializeComponent();

      // create Hashtable object
      table = new Hashtable();
   }

protected:
   void Dispose(Boolean disposing)
   {
      if (disposing && components)
      {
         components->Dispose();
      }
      __super::Dispose(disposing);
   }
private: System::Windows::Forms::Label *  lastNameLabel;
private: System::Windows::Forms::Button *  addButton;
private: System::Windows::Forms::TextBox *  lastNameTextBox;
private: System::Windows::Forms::Button *  listKeysButton;
private: System::Windows::Forms::Button *  removeButton;
private: System::Windows::Forms::TextBox *  consoleTextBox;
private: System::Windows::Forms::Button *  containsKeyButton;
private: System::Windows::Forms::Button *  getButton;
private: System::Windows::Forms::Label *  firstNameLabel;
private: System::Windows::Forms::Button *  listObjectsButton;
private: System::Windows::Forms::Label *  statusLabel;
private: System::Windows::Forms::TextBox *  firstNameTextBox;
private: System::Windows::Forms::Button *  clearTableButton;
private: System::Windows::Forms::Button *  emptyButton;

```

Fig. 22.46 `HashTableTest` demonstrates class `Hashtable`. (Part 2 of 5.)

```
   // Hashtable to demonstrate functionality
   private: Hashtable *table;

   private:
      /// <summary>
      /// Required designer variable.
      /// </summary>
      System::ComponentModel::Container * components;

   // Visual Studio .NET generated GUI code

   // add last name and Employee Object *to table
   private: System::Void addButton_Click(
               System::Object *  sender, System::EventArgs *  e)
            {
               Employee *employee = new Employee( firstNameTextBox->Text,
                  lastNameTextBox->Text );

               // add new key/value pair
               try {
                  table->Add( lastNameTextBox->Text, employee );
                  statusLabel->Text = String::Concat( S"Put: ",
                     employee->ToString() );
               } // end try

               // if key is NULL or already in table, output message
               catch ( ArgumentException *argumentException ) {
                  statusLabel->Text = argumentException->ToString();
               } // end catch
            } // end method addButton_Click

   // get object for given key
   private: System::Void getButton_Click(
               System::Object *  sender, System::EventArgs *  e)
            {
               Object *result = table->Item[ lastNameTextBox->Text ];

               if ( result != NULL )
                  statusLabel->Text = String::Concat( S"Get: ",
                  result->ToString() );
               else
                  statusLabel->Text = String::Concat( S"Get: ",
                  lastNameTextBox->Text, S" not in table" );
            } // end method getButton_Click

   // remove key/value pair from table
   private: System::Void removeButton_Click(
               System::Object *  sender, System::EventArgs *  e)
            {
               table->Remove( lastNameTextBox->Text );
               statusLabel->Text = S"Object *Removed";
            } // end method removeButton_Click

```

Fig. 22.46 `HashTableTest` demonstrates class `Hashtable`. (Part 3 of 5.)

```
   // determine whether table is empty
   private: System::Void emptyButton_Click(
               System::Object *  sender, System::EventArgs *  e)
            {
               statusLabel->Text = String::Concat( S"Table is ",
                  ( table->Count == 0 ? S"empty" : S"not empty" ) );
            } // end method emptyButton_Click

   // determine whether table contains specified key
   private: System::Void containsKeyButton_Click(
               System::Object *  sender, System::EventArgs *  e)
            {
               statusLabel->Text = String::Concat( S"Contains key: ",
                  table->ContainsKey(
                  lastNameTextBox->Text ).ToString() );
            } // end method containsKeyButton_Click

   // discard all table contents
   private: System::Void clearTableButton_Click(
               System::Object *  sender, System::EventArgs *  e)
            {
               table->Clear();
               statusLabel->Text = S"Clear: Table is now empty";
            } // end method clearTableButton_Click

   // display list of objects in table
   private: System::Void listObjectsButton_Click(
               System::Object *  sender, System::EventArgs *  e)
            {
               IDictionaryEnumerator *enumerator = table->GetEnumerator();
               StringBuilder *buffer = new StringBuilder();

               while ( enumerator->MoveNext() )
                  buffer->Append( String::Concat( enumerator->Value,
                  S"\r\n" ) );

               consoleTextBox->Text = buffer->ToString();
               statusLabel->Text = S"";
            } // end method listObjectsButton_Click

   // display list of keys in table
   private: System::Void listKeysButton_Click(
               System::Object *  sender, System::EventArgs *  e)
            {
               IDictionaryEnumerator *enumerator = table->GetEnumerator();
               StringBuilder *buffer = new StringBuilder();

               while ( enumerator->MoveNext() )
                  buffer->Append( String::Concat( enumerator->Key,
                  S"\r\n" ) );

               consoleTextBox->Text = buffer->ToString();
               statusLabel->Text = S"";
```

Fig. 22.46 `HashTableTest` demonstrates class `Hashtable`. (Part 4 of 5.)

```
               } // end method listKeysButton_Click
   };
}
```

Fig. 22.46 `HashTableTest` demonstrates class `Hashtable`. (Part 5 of 5.)

```
// Fig. 22.47: Form1.cpp
// Entry point for application.

#include "stdafx.h"
#include "Form1.h"
#include <windows.h>

using namespace HashTableTest;

int APIENTRY _tWinMain(HINSTANCE hInstance,
                       HINSTANCE hPrevInstance,
                       LPTSTR    lpCmdLine,
                       int       nCmdShow)
{
   System::Threading::Thread::CurrentThread->ApartmentState =
      System::Threading::ApartmentState::STA;
   Application::Run(new Form1());
   return 0;
} // end _tWinMain
```

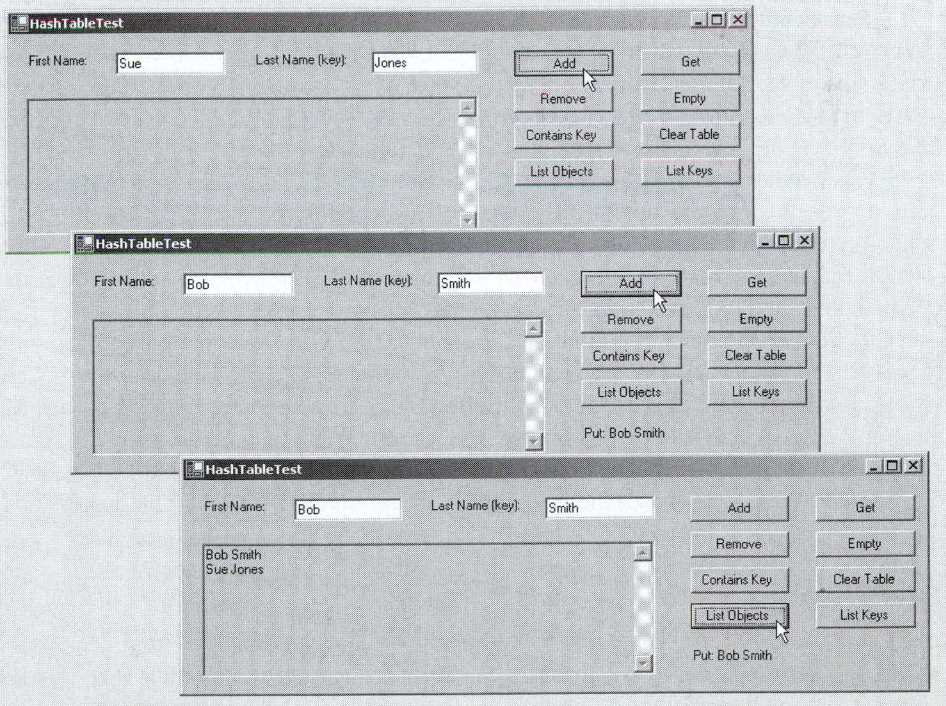

Fig. 22.47 `HashTableTest` entry point. (Part 1 of 2.)

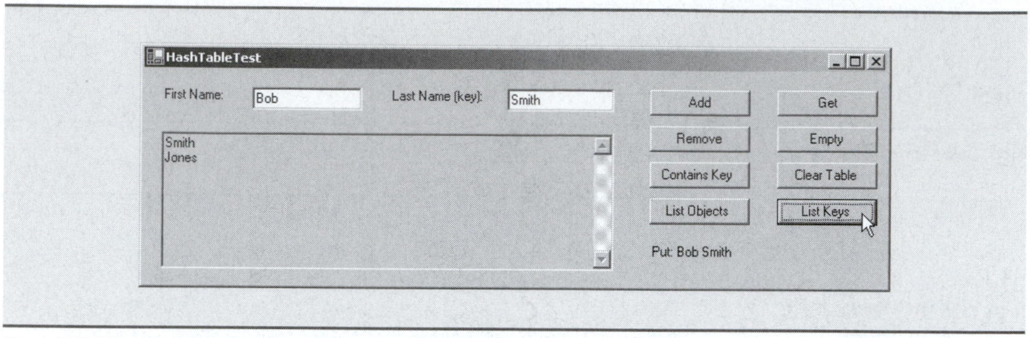

Fig. 22.47 `HashTableTest` entry point. (Part 2 of 2.)

Event handler `addButton_Click` (lines 75–92 of Fig. 22.46) reads the first name and last name of an employee from the user interface, creates an object of class `Employee` (Fig. 22.44–Fig. 22.45) and adds that `Employee` to the `Hashtable` with method *`Add`* (line 83). This method receives two arguments—a key object, and a value object. In this example, the key is the last name of the `Employee` (a `String *`), and the value is the corresponding `Employee` pointer. An `ArgumentException` occurs if the `Hashtable` already contains the key or if the key is `NULL`.

Event handler `getButton_Click` (lines 95–106) retrieves the object associated with a specific key, using the `Hashtable`'s *`Item`* property as shown in line 98. The expression in parentheses is the key for which the `Hashtable` should return the corresponding object. If the key is not found, the result is `NULL`.

Event handler `removeButton_Click` (lines 109–114) invokes `Hashtable` method *`Remove`* to delete a key and its associated object from the `Hashtable`. If the key does not exist in the table, nothing happens.

Event handler `emptyButton_Click` (lines 117–122) uses `Hashtable` property *`Count`* to determine whether the `Hashtable` is empty (i.e., `Count` is `0`).

Event handler `containsKeyButton_Click` (lines 125–131) invokes `Hashtable` method *`ContainsKey`* to find out whether the `Hashtable` contains the specified key. If so, the method returns `true`; otherwise, it returns `false`.

Event handler `clearTableButton_Click` (lines 134–139) invokes `Hashtable` method *`Clear`* to delete all `Hashtable` entries.

Class `Hashtable` provides method `GetEnumerator`, which returns an enumerator of type *`IDictionaryEnumerator`*, which derives from `IEnumerator`. Such enumerators provide properties *`Key`* and *`Value`* to access the information for a key/value pair. The event handler in lines 142–154 (`listObjectsButton_Click`) uses the `Value` property of the enumerator to output the objects in the `Hashtable`. The event handler in lines 157–169 (`listKeysButton_Click`) uses the `Key` property of the enumerator to output the keys in the `Hashtable`.

SUMMARY

- Dynamic data structures can grow and shrink at execution time.
- Creating and maintaining dynamic data structures requires dynamic memory allocation—the ability for a program to obtain more memory at execution time (to hold new nodes) and to release memory no longer needed.

- The limit for dynamic memory allocation can be as large as the available physical memory in the computer or the amount of available disk space in a virtual-memory system.
- Memory can be allocated dynamically with operator `new`. Operator `new` takes as an operand the type of the object being dynamically allocated and returns a pointer to a newly created object of that type. If no memory is available, `new` throws an `OutOfMemoryException`.
- A self-referential class contains a data member that points to an object of the same class type. Self-referential objects can be linked to form useful data structures, such as lists, queues, stacks and trees.
- A linked list is a linear collection (i.e., a sequence) of self-referential class objects called nodes, connected by pointer links.
- A node can contain data of any type, including objects of other classes.
- A linked list is accessed via a pointer to the first node of the list. Each subsequent node is accessed via the link-pointer member stored in the previous node.
- By convention, the link pointer in the last node of a list is set to `NULL` to mark the end of the list.
- Stacks are important in compilers and operating systems.
- A stack is a constrained version of a linked list—new nodes can be added to a stack and removed from a stack only at the top. A stack is referred to as a last-in, first-out (LIFO) data structure.
- The primary stack operations are push and pop. Operation push adds a new node to the top of the stack. Operation pop removes a node from the top of the stack and returns the data object from the popped node.
- Queues represent waiting lines. Insertions occur at the back (also referred to as the tail) of a queue, and deletions occur from the front (also referred to as the head) of a queue.
- A queue is similar to a checkout line in a supermarket: The first person in line is served first; other customers enter the line only at the end and wait to be served.
- Queue nodes are removed only from the head of the queue and are inserted only at the tail of the queue. For this reason, a queue is referred to as a first-in, first-out (FIFO) data structure.
- The insert and remove operations for a queue are known as enqueue and dequeue.
- Binary trees facilitate high-speed searching and sorting of data.
- Tree nodes contain two or more links.
- A binary tree is a tree whose nodes all contain two links. The root node is the first node in a tree.
- Each link in the root node points to a child. The left child is the first node in the left subtree and the right child is the first node in the right subtree.
- The children of a node are called siblings. A node with no children is called a leaf node.
- A binary search tree (with no duplicate node values) has the characteristic that the values in any left subtree are less than the values in that subtree's parent node and the values in any right subtree are greater than the values in that subtree's parent node.
- In a binary search tree, a node can be inserted only as a leaf node.
- An inorder traversal of a binary search tree processes the node values in ascending order.
- The process of creating a binary search tree actually sorts the data—hence, the term "binary tree sort."
- In a preorder traversal, the value in each node is processed as the node is visited. After the value in a given node is processed, the values in the left subtree are processed, then the values in the right subtree are processed.
- In a postorder traversal, the value in each node is processed after the node's left and right subtrees are processed.

- The binary search tree facilitates duplicate elimination. As the tree is created, attempts to insert a duplicate value are recognized because a duplicate follows the same "go left" or "go right" decisions on each comparison that the original value did. Thus, the duplicate eventually is compared with a node containing the same value. The duplicate value may simply be discarded at this point.
- Class `ArrayList` can be used as a dynamically growing array.
- `ArrayList` method `Add` adds an `Object` to the `ArrayList`.
- `ArrayList` method `Remove` removes the first occurrence of the specified `Object` from the `ArrayList`.
- `ArrayList` elements can be accessed by following the `ArrayList` indexed property `Item` with the array subscript operator (`[]`) and the desired index of the element.
- Class `Stack` is provided in the `System::Collections` namespace.
- `Stack` method `Push` performs the push operation on the `Stack`.
- `Stack` method `Pop` performs the pop operation on the `Stack`.
- Class `Hashtable` is provided in the `System::Collections` namespace.
- `Hashtable` method `Add` adds a key/value pair to the `Hashtable`.
- Any class that implements the `IEnumerator` interface must define methods `MoveNext` and `Reset` and the `Current` property.
- Method `MoveNext` must be called before the `Current` property is accessed for the first time.
- Methods `MoveNext` and `Reset` throw an `InvalidOperationException` if the contents of the collection were modified in any way after the enumerator's creation.

TERMINOLOGY

`Add` method of class `ArrayList`
`Add` method of class `Hashtable`
`ArgumentException`
`ArrayList` class
binary search tree
binary tree
binary tree sort
`BinarySearch` method of class `Array`
`BinarySearch` method of class `ArrayList`
`BitArray` class
`Capacity` property of class `ArrayList`
child
`Clear` method of class `Array`
`Clear` method of class `ArrayList`
`Clear` method of class `Hashtable`
collection
collection class
`CompareTo` method of class `IComparable`
`Contains` method of class `ArrayList`
`Contains` method of class `Stack`
`ContainsKey` method of class `Hashtable`
`Copy` method of class `Array`
`Count` property of class `ArrayList`
`Count` property of class `Stack`
`CreateInstance` method of class `Array`
`Current` property of interface `IEnumerator`
data structures
dequeue
duplicate elimination
dynamic data structures
enqueue
enumerator
`GetEnumerator` method of class `ArrayList`
`GetEnumerator` method of class `Hashtable`
`GetHashCode` method of class `Object`
hashing
`Hashtable` class
head of a queue
`IComparable` interface
`IDictionaryEnumerator` interface
`IEnumerator` interface
`IndexOf` method of class `Array`
`IndexOf` method of class `ArrayList`
inorder traversal
`InvalidOperationException`
`Item` property of class `ArrayList`
`Item` property of class `Hashtable`
iterator
`LastIndexOf` method of class `Array`
leaf node

left child
left subtree
linear data structure
linked list
load factor
`MoveNext` method of interface `IEnumerator`
multithread safe
`Peek` method of class `Stack`
`Pop` method of class `Stack`
postorder traversal
preorder traversal
`Push` method of class `Stack`
queue
`Queue` class
`Remove` method of class `ArrayList`
`Remove` method of class `Hashtable`
`RemoveAt` method of class `ArrayList`
`RemoveRange` method of class `ArrayList`
`Reset` method of interface `IEnumerator`
`Reverse` method of class Array
right child
right subtree
root node
searching
self-referential class
sequence
sibling
`Sort` method of class `Array`
`Sort` method of class `ArrayList`
`SortedList` class
sorting
stack
`Stack` class
`System::Collections` namespace
tail of a queue
`TrimToSize` method of class `ArrayList`
waiting line

SELF-REVIEW EXERCISES

22.1 State whether each of the following is *true* or *false*. If *false*, explain why.

a) In a queue, the first item to be added is the last item to be removed.
b) Trees can have no more than two child nodes per node.
c) A tree node with no children is called a leaf node.
d) Class `Stack` is in the `System::Collections` namespace.
e) A class implementing interface `IEnumerator` must define only methods `MoveNext` and `Reset`.
f) A hashtable stores key/value pairs.
g) Linked list nodes are stored contiguously in memory.
h) The primary operations of the stack data structure are enqueue and dequeue.
i) Lists, stacks and queues are linear data structures.

22.2 Fill in the blanks in each of the following statements:

a) A(n) ________ class is used to define nodes that form dynamic data structures, which can grow and shrink at execution time.
b) Operator ________ allocates memory dynamically; this operator returns a pointer to the allocated memory.
c) A(n) ________ is a constrained version of a linked list in which nodes can be inserted and deleted only from the start of the list; this data structure returns node values in last-in, first-out order.
d) A queue is a(n) ________ data structure, because the first nodes inserted are the first nodes removed.
e) A(n) ________ is a constrained version of a linked list in which nodes can be inserted only at the end of the list and deleted only from the start of the list.
f) A(n) ________ is a nonlinear, two-dimensional data structure that contains nodes with two or more links.
g) The nodes of a(n) ________ tree contain two link members.
h) `IEnumerator` method ________ advances the enumerator to the next item.

i) The tree-traversal algorithm that processes the node, then processes all the nodes to its left followed by all the nodes to its right is called ________.
j) If the collection it references was altered after the enumerator's creation, calling method `Reset` will cause a(n) ________.

ANSWERS TO SELF-REVIEW EXERCISES

22.1 a) False. A queue is a first-in, first-out data structure—the first item added is the first item removed. b) False. In general, trees may have as many child nodes per node as is necessary. Only binary trees are restricted to no more than two child nodes per node. c) True. d) True. e) False. The class must also implement property `Current`. f) True. g) False. Linked-list nodes are logically contiguous, but they need not be stored in a physically contiguous memory space. h) False. Those are the primary operations of a queue. The primary operations of a stack are push and pop. i) True.

22.2 a) self-referential. b) `new`. c) stack. d) first-in, first-out (FIFO). e) queue. f) tree. g) binary. h) `MoveNext`. i) preorder. j) `InvalidOperationException`.

EXERCISES

22.3 Write a program that merges two ordered list objects of integers into a single ordered list object of integers. Method `Merge` of class `ListMerge` should receive references to each of the list objects to be merged and should return a reference to the merged list object.

22.4 Write a program that inputs a line of text and uses a stack object to print the line reversed.

22.5 Write a program that uses a stack to determine whether a string is a palindrome (i.e., the string is spelled identically backward and forward). The program should ignore spaces and punctuation.

22.6 Stacks are used by compilers to help in the process of evaluating expressions and in generating machine language code. In this and the next exercise, we investigate how compilers evaluate arithmetic expressions consisting only of constants, operators and parentheses.

Humans generally write expressions like `3 + 4` and `7 / 9`, in which the operator (`+` or `/` here) is written between its operands—this is called *infix notation.* Computers "prefer" *postfix notation*, in which the operator is written to the right of its two operands. The preceding infix expressions would appear in postfix notation as `3 4 +` and `7 9 /`, respectively.

To evaluate a complex infix expression, a compiler would first convert the expression to postfix notation, then evaluate the postfix version of the expression. Each of these algorithms requires only a single left-to-right pass of the expression. Each algorithm uses a stack object in support of its operation, and in each algorithm the stack is used for a different purpose.

In this exercise, you will write a MC++ version of the infix-to-postfix conversion algorithm. In the next exercise, you will write a MC++ version of the postfix expression evaluation algorithm. In a later exercise, you will discover that code you write in this exercise can help you implement a complete working compiler.

Write class `InfixToPostfixConverter` to convert an ordinary infix arithmetic expression (assume a valid expression is entered), with single-digit integers, such as

```
(6 + 2) * 5 - 8 / 4
```

to a postfix expression. The postfix version of the preceding infix expression (note that no parentheses are needed) is

```
6 2 + 5 * 8 4 / -
```

The program should read the expression into `StringBuilder infix`, then use class `StackComposition` (implemented in Fig. 22.18–Fig. 22.19) to help create the postfix expression in `StringBuilder postfix`. The algorithm for creating a postfix expression is as follows:

a) Push a left parenthesis `'('` on the stack.
b) Append a right parenthesis `')'` to the end of `infix`.
c) While the stack is not empty, read `infix` from left to right and do the following:
    If the current character in `infix` is a digit, append it to `postfix`.
    If the current character in `infix` is a left parenthesis, push it onto the stack.
    If the current character in `infix` is an operator:
        Pop operators (if there are any) at the top of the stack while they have equal or higher precedence than the current operator, and append the popped operators to `postfix`.
        Push the current character in `infix` onto the stack.
    If the current character in `infix` is a right parenthesis:
        Pop operators from the top of the stack and append them to `postfix` until a left parenthesis is at the top of the stack.
        Pop (and discard) the left parenthesis from the stack.

The following arithmetic operations are allowed in an expression:

+ addition
- subtraction
* multiplication
/ division
^ exponentiation
% modulus

Some of the methods you may want to provide in your program follow:

a) Method `ConvertToPostfix`, which converts the infix expression to postfix notation.
b) Method `IsOperator`, which determines whether `c` is an operator.
c) Method `Precedence`, which determines whether the precedence of `operator1` (from the infix expression) is less than, equal to or greater than the precedence of `operator2` (from the stack). The method returns `true` if `operator1` has lower precedence than `operator2`. Otherwise, `false` is returned.
d) Add this method to the class definition for class `StackComposition`.

22.7 Write class `PostfixEvaluator`, which evaluates a postfix expression (assume it is valid) such as

```
6 2 + 5 * 8 4 / -
```

The program should read a postfix expression consisting of digits and operators into a `StringBuilder`. Using class `StackComposition` from Exercise 22.6, the program should scan the expression and evaluate it. The algorithm is as follows:

a) Append a right parenthesis (`')'`) to the end of the postfix expression. When the right-parenthesis character is encountered, no further processing is necessary.
b) When the right-parenthesis character has not been encountered, read the expression from left to right.
    If the current character is a digit do the following:
        Push its integer value on the stack (the integer value of a digit character is its value in the computer's character set minus the value of `'0'` in Unicode).
    Otherwise, if the current character is an *operator*:
        Pop the two top elements of the stack into variables `x` and `y`.
        Calculate `y` *operator* `x`.
        Push the result of the calculation onto the stack.
c) When the right parenthesis is encountered in the expression, pop the top value of the stack. This is the result of the postfix expression.

[*Note*: In b) above (based on the sample expression at the beginning of this exercises), if the operator is `'/'`, the top of the stack is 2 and the next element in the stack is 8, then pop 2 into `x`, pop 8 into `y`, evaluate `8 / 2` and push the result, 4, back on the stack. This note also applies to operator `'-'`.] The arithmetic operations allowed in an expression are:

+ addition
- subtraction
* multiplication
/ division
^ exponentiation
% modulus

You may want to provide the following methods:

a) Method `EvaluatePostfixExpression`, which evaluates the postfix expression.
b) Method `Calculate`, which evaluates the expression `op1` *operator* `op2`.

22.8 (*Binary Tree Delete*) In this exercise, we discuss deleting items from binary search trees. The deletion algorithm is not as straightforward as the insertion algorithm. There are three cases that are encountered when deleting an item—the item is contained in a leaf node (i.e., it has no children), the item is contained in a node that has one child or the item is contained in a node that has two children.

If the item to be deleted is contained in a leaf node, the node is deleted and the reference in the parent node is set to null.

If the item to be deleted is contained in a node with one child, the reference in the parent node is set to reference the child node and the node containing the data item is deleted. This causes the child node to take the place of the deleted node in the tree.

The last case is the most difficult. When a node with two children is deleted, another node in the tree must take its place. However, the reference in the parent node simply cannot be assigned to reference one of the children of the node to be deleted. In most cases, the resulting binary search tree would not adhere to the following characteristic of binary search trees (with no duplicate values): *The values in any left subtree are less than the value in the parent node, and the values in any right subtree are greater than the value in the parent node.*

Which node is used as a *replacement node* to maintain this characteristic—either the node containing the largest value in the tree less than the value in the node being deleted, or the node containing the smallest value in the tree greater than the value in the node being deleted. Let us consider the node with the smaller value. In a binary search tree, the largest value less than a parent's value is located in the left subtree of the parent node and is guaranteed to be contained in the rightmost node of the subtree. This node is located by walking down the left subtree to the right until the reference to the right child of the current node is null. We are now referencing the replacement node which is either a leaf node or a node with one child to its left. If the replacement node is a leaf node, the steps to perform the deletion are as follows:

a) Store the reference to the node to be deleted in a temporary reference variable.
b) Set the reference in the parent of the node being deleted to reference the replacement node.
c) Set the reference in the parent of the replacement node to null.
d) Set the reference to the right subtree in the replacement node to reference the right subtree of the node to be deleted.
e) Set the reference to the left subtree in the replacement node to reference the left subtree of the node to be deleted.

The deletion steps for a replacement node with a left child are similar to those for a replacement node with no children, but the algorithm also must move the child into the replacement node's position in the tree. If the replacement node is a node with a left child, the steps to perform the deletion are as follows:

a) Store the reference to the node to be deleted in a temporary reference variable.

b) Set the reference in the parent of the node being deleted to reference the replacement node.
c) Set the reference in the parent of the replacement node reference to the left child of the replacement node.
d) Set the reference to the right subtree in the replacement node reference to the right subtree of the node to be deleted.
e) Set the reference to the left subtree in the replacement node to reference the left subtree of the node to be deleted.

Write method `DeleteNode`, which takes as its argument the value to be deleted. Method `DeleteNode` should locate in the tree the node containing the value to be deleted and use the algorithms discussed here to delete the node. If the value is not found in the tree, the method should print a message that indicates whether the value is deleted. Modify the program of Fig. 22.29 to use this method. After deleting an item, call the methods `InorderTraversal`, `PreorderTraversal` and `PostorderTraversal` to confirm that the delete operation was performed correctly.

22.9 (*Level-Order Binary Tree Traversal*) The application in Fig. 22.25–Fig. 22.29 illustrated three recursive methods of traversing a binary tree—inorder, preorder, and postorder traversals. This exercise presents the *level-order traversal* of a binary tree, in which the node values are printed level by level, starting at the root-node level. The nodes on each level are printed from left to right. The level-order traversal is not a recursive algorithm. It uses a queue object to control the output of the nodes. The algorithm is as follows:

a) Insert the root node in the queue.
b) While there are nodes left in the queue, do the following:
   Get the next node in the queue.
   Print the node's value.
   If the reference to the left child of the node is not null:
      Insert the left child node in the queue.
   If the reference to the right child of the node is not null:
      Insert the right child node in the queue.

Write method `LevelorderTraversal` to perform a level-order traversal of a binary tree object. Modify the program of Fig. 22.29 to use this method. [*Note*: You also will need to use the queue-processing methods of Fig. 22.20–Fig. 22.21 in this program.]

A

Operator Precedence Chart

MC++ operators are shown in decreasing order of precedence from top to bottom, with each level of precedence separated by a horizontal line.

Operator	Type	Associativity
`::`	binary scope resolution	left-to-right
`::`	unary scope resolution	
`[]`	element access	left-to-right
`.`	member selection via object	
`->`	member selection via pointer	
`++`	unary post-increment	
`--`	unary post-decrement	
`typeid`	run-time type information	
`dynamic_cast< type >`	run-time type-checked cast	
`static_cast< type >`	compile-time type-checked cast	
`reinterpret_cast< type >`	cast for non-standard conversions	
`const_cast< type >`	cast away `const`-ness	
`++`	unary pre-increment	right-to-left
`--`	unary pre-decrement	
`+`	unary plus	
`-`	unary minus	
`!`	unary logical negation	

Fig. A.1 Operator precedence chart. (Part 1 of 3.)

Operator	Type	Associativity
`~`	unary bitwise complement	right-to-left
(*type*)	C-style unary cast	
`sizeof`	determine size in bytes	
`&`	address	
`*`	dereference	
`new`	dynamic memory allocation	
`new[]`	dynamic array allocation	
`delete`	dynamic memory deallocation	
`delete[]`	dynamic array deallocation	
`.*`	pointer to member via object	left-to-right
`->*`	pointer to member via pointer	
`*`	multiplication	left-to-right
`/`	division	
`%`	modulus	
`+`	addition	left-to-right
`-`	subtraction	
`<<`	bitwise left shift	left-to-right
`>>`	bitwise right shift	
`<`	relational less than	left-to-right
`<=`	relational less than or equal to	
`>`	relational greater than	
`>=`	relational greater than or equal to	
`==`	relational is equal to	left-to-right
`!=`	relational is not equal to	
`&`	bitwise AND	left-to-right
`^`	bitwise exclusive OR	left-to-right
		bitwise inclusive OR	left-to-right
`&&`	logical AND	left-to-right
||	logical OR	left-to-right
`?:`	ternary conditional	right-to-left

Fig. A.1 Operator precedence chart. (Part 2 of 3.)

Operator	Type	Associativity
=	assignment	right-to-left
+=	addition assignment	
-=	subtraction assignment	
*=	multiplication assignment	
/=	division assignment	
%=	modulus assignment	
&=	bitwise AND assignment	
^=	bitwse exclusive OR assignment	
|=	bitwise inclusive OR assignment	
<<=	bitwise left shift assignment	
>>=	bitwise right shift assignment	
,	comma	left-to-right

Fig. A.1 Operator precedence chart. (Part 3 of 3.)

B

Number Systems

Objectives

- To understand basic number system concepts, such as base, positional value and symbol value.
- To understand how to work with numbers represented in the binary, octal and hexadecimal number systems.
- To abbreviate binary numbers as octal numbers or hexadecimal numbers.
- To convert octal numbers and hexadecimal numbers to binary numbers.
- To convert back and forth between decimal numbers and their binary, octal and hexadecimal equivalents.
- To understand binary arithmetic and how negative binary numbers are represented in twos-complement notation.

Here are only numbers ratified.
William Shakespeare

Nature has some sort of arithmetic-geometrical coordinate system, because nature has all kinds of models. What we experience of nature is in models, and all of nature's models are so beautiful.
It struck me that nature's system must be a real beauty, because in chemistry we find that the associations are always in beautiful whole numbers—there are no fractions.
Richard Buckminster Fuller

Outline

B.1 Introduction

In this appendix, we introduce the key number systems that programmers use, especially when they are working on software projects that require close interaction with "machine-level" hardware. Projects like this include operating systems, computer networking software, compilers, database systems and applications requiring high performance.

When we write an integer such as 227 or –63 in a program, the number is assumed to be in the *decimal (base 10) number system*. The *digits* in the decimal number system are 0, 1, 2, 3, 4, 5, 6, 7, 8, and 9. The lowest digit is 0 and the highest digit is 9—one less than the *base* of 10. Internally, computers use the *binary (base 2) number system*. The binary number system has only two digits, namely 0 and 1. Its lowest digit is 0 and its highest digit is 1—one less than the base of 2. Fig. B.1 summarizes the digits used in the binary, octal, decimal and hexadecimal number systems.

As we will see, binary numbers tend to be much longer than their decimal equivalents. Programmers who work in assembly languages and in high-level languages that enable programmers to reach down to the "machine level" find it cumbersome to work with binary numbers. So two other number systems—the *octal number system (base 8)* and the *hexadecimal number system (base 16)*—are popular, primarily because they make it convenient to abbreviate binary numbers.

In the octal number system, the digits range from 0 to 7. Both the binary number system and the octal number system have fewer digits than the decimal number system, so their digits are the same as the corresponding digits in decimal.

The hexadecimal number system poses a problem because it requires sixteen digits—a lowest digit of 0 and a highest digit with a value equivalent to decimal 15 (one less than the base of 16). By convention, we use the letters A through F to represent the hexadecimal digits corresponding to decimal values 10 through 15. Thus, in hexadecimal, we can have numbers like 876 consisting solely of decimal-like digits, numbers like 8A55F consisting of digits and letters, and numbers like FFE consisting solely of letters. Occasionally, a hexadecimal number spells a common word, such as FACE or FEED—this can appear strange to programmers accustomed to working with numbers. Fig. B.2 summarizes each of the number systems.

Binary digit	Octal digit	Decimal digit	Hexadecimal digit
0	0	0	0
1	1	1	1
	2	2	2
	3	3	3
	4	4	4
	5	5	5
	6	6	6
	7	7	7
		8	8
		9	9
			A (decimal value of 10)
			B (decimal value of 11)
			C (decimal value of 12)
			D (decimal value of 13)
			E (decimal value of 14)
			F (decimal value of 15)

Fig. B.1 Digits of the binary, octal, decimal and hexadecimal number systems.

Attribute	Binary	Octal	Decimal	Hexadecimal
Base	2	8	10	16
Lowest digit	0	0	0	0
Highest digit	1	7	9	F

Fig. B.2 Comparison of the binary, octal, decimal and hexadecimal number systems.

Each of these number systems uses *positional notation*—each position in which a digit is written has a different positional value. For example, in the decimal number 937 (the 9, the 3, and the 7 are referred to as symbol values), we say that the 7 is written in the ones position, the 3 is written in the tens position, and the 9 is written in the hundreds position. Notice that each of these positions is a power of the base (base 10) and that these powers begin at 0 and increase by 1 as we move left in the number (Fig. B.3).

For longer decimal numbers, the next positions to the left would be the thousands position (10 to the 3rd power), the ten-thousands position (10 to the 4th power), the hundred-thousands position (10 to the 5th power), the millions position (10 to the 6th power), the ten-millions position (10 to the 7th power) and so on.

In the binary number 101, we say that the rightmost 1 is written in the ones position, the 0 is written in the twos position, and the leftmost 1 is written in the fours position.

Notice that each of these positions is a power of the base (base 2), and that these powers begin at 0 and increase by 1 as we move left in the number (Fig. B.4).

Positional values in the decimal number system			
Decimal digit	9	3	7
Position name	Hundreds	Tens	Ones
Positional value	100	10	1
Positional value as a power of the base (10)	10^2	10^1	10^0

Fig. B.3 Positional values in the decimal number system.

Positional values in the binary number system			
Binary digit	1	0	1
Position name	Fours	Twos	Ones
Positional value	4	2	1
Positional value as a power of the base (2)	2^2	2^1	2^0

Fig. B.4 Positional values in the binary number system.

For longer binary numbers, the next positions to the left would be the eights position (2 to the 3rd power), the sixteens position (2 to the 4th power), the thirty-twos position (2 to the 5th power), the sixty-fours position (2 to the 6th power) and so on.

In the octal number 425, we say that the 5 is written in the ones position, the 2 is written in the eights position, and the 4 is written in the sixty-fours position. Notice that each of these positions is a power of the base (base 8) and that these powers begin at 0 and increase by 1 as we move left in the number (Fig. B.5).

Positional values in the octal number system			
Decimal digit	4	2	5
Position name	Sixty-fours	Eights	Ones
Positional value	64	8	1
Positional value as a power of the base (8)	8^2	8^1	8^0

Fig. B.5 Positional values in the octal number system.

For longer octal numbers, the next positions to the left would be the five-hundred-and-twelves position (8 to the 3rd power), the four-thousand-and-ninety-sixes position (8 to the 4th power), the thirty-two-thousand-seven-hundred-and-sixty-eights position (8 to the 5th power) and so on.

In the hexadecimal number 3DA, we say that the A is written in the ones position, the D is written in the sixteens position, and the 3 is written in the two-hundred-and-fifty-sixes position. Notice that each of these positions is a power of the base (base 16) and that these powers begin at 0 and increase by 1 as we move left in the number (Fig. B.6).

Positional values in the hexadecimal number system			
Decimal digit	3	D	A
Position name	Two-hundred-and-fifty-sixes	Sixteens	Ones
Positional value	256	16	1
Positional value as a power of the base (16)	16^2	16^1	16^0

Fig. B.6 Positional values in the hexadecimal number system.

For longer hexadecimal numbers, the next positions to the left would be the four-thousand-and-ninety-sixes position (16 to the 3rd power), the sixty-five-thousand-five-hundred-and-thirty-sixes position (16 to the 4th power) and so on.

B.2 Abbreviating Binary Numbers as Octal Numbers and Hexadecimal Numbers

The main use for octal and hexadecimal numbers in computing is for abbreviating lengthy binary representations. Figure B.7 highlights the fact that lengthy binary numbers can be expressed concisely in number systems with bases higher than that of the binary number system.

Decimal number	Binary representation	Octal representation	Hexadecimal representation
0	0	0	0
1	1	1	1
2	10	2	2
3	11	3	3
4	100	4	4
5	101	5	5
6	110	6	6

Fig. B.7 Decimal, binary, octal and hexadecimal equivalents. (Part 1 of 2.)

Decimal number	Binary representation	Octal representation	Hexadecimal representation
7	111	7	7
8	1000	10	8
9	1001	11	9
10	1010	12	A
11	1011	13	B
12	1100	14	C
13	1101	15	D
14	1110	16	E
15	1111	17	F
16	10000	20	10

Fig. B.7 Decimal, binary, octal and hexadecimal equivalents. (Part 2 of 2.)

A particularly important relationship that both the octal number system and the hexadecimal number system have to the binary system is that the bases of octal and hexadecimal (8 and 16 respectively) are powers of the base of the binary number system (base 2). Consider the following 12-digit binary number and its octal and hexadecimal equivalents. See if you can determine how this relationship makes it convenient to abbreviate binary numbers in octal or hexadecimal. The answer follows the numbers.

Binary Number	Octal equivalent	Hexadecimal equivalent
100011010001	4321	8D1

To see how the binary number converts easily to octal, simply break the 12-digit binary number into groups of three consecutive bits each, and write those groups over the corresponding digits of the octal number as follows

```
100   011   010   001
4     3     2     1
```

Notice that the octal digit you have written under each group of thee bits corresponds precisely to the octal equivalent of that 3-digit binary number as shown in Fig. B.7.

The same kind of relationship may be observed in converting numbers from binary to hexadecimal. In particular, break the 12-digit binary number into groups of four consecutive bits each, and write those groups over the corresponding digits of the hexadecimal number as follows

```
1000   1101   0001
8      D      1
```

Notice that the hexadecimal digit you wrote under each group of four bits corresponds precisely to the hexadecimal equivalent of that 4-digit binary number as shown in Fig. B.7.

B.3 Converting Octal Numbers and Hexadecimal Numbers to Binary Numbers

In the previous section, we saw how to convert binary numbers to their octal and hexadecimal equivalents by forming groups of binary digits and simply rewriting these groups as their equivalent octal digit values or hexadecimal digit values. This process may be used in reverse to produce the binary equivalent of a given octal or hexadecimal number.

For example, the octal number 653 is converted to binary simply by writing the 6 as its 3-digit binary equivalent 110, the 5 as its 3-digit binary equivalent 101, and the 3 as its 3-digit binary equivalent 011 to form the 9-digit binary number 110101011.

The hexadecimal number FAD5 is converted to binary simply by writing the F as its 4-digit binary equivalent 1111, the A as its 4-digit binary equivalent 1010, the D as its 4-digit binary equivalent 1101, and the 5 as its 4-digit binary equivalent 0101 to form the 16-digit 1111101011010101.

B.4 Converting from Binary, Octal or Hexadecimal to Decimal

We are accustomed to working in decimal, so it is often convenient to convert a binary, octal or hexadecimal number to decimal to get a sense of what the number is "really" worth. Our diagrams in Section B.1 express the positional values in decimal. To convert a number to decimal from another base, multiply the decimal equivalent of each digit by its positional value, and sum these products. For example, the binary number 110101 is converted to decimal 53, as shown in Fig. B.8.

Converting a binary number to decimal

Positional values:	32	16	8	4	2	1
Symbol values:	1	1	0	1	0	1
Products:	1*32=32	1*16=16	0*8=0	1*4=4	0*2=0	1*1=1
Sum:	= 32 + 16 + 0 + 4 + 0 + 1 = 53					

Fig. B.8 Converting a binary number to decimal.

To convert octal 7614 to decimal 3980, we use the same technique, this time using appropriate octal positional values, as shown in Fig. B.9.

Converting an octal number to decimal

Positional values:	512	64	8	1
Symbol values:	7	6	1	4
Products	7*512=3584	6*64=384	1*8=8	4*1=4
Sum:	= 3584 + 384 + 8 + 4 = 3980			

Fig. B.9 Converting an octal number to decimal.

To convert hexadecimal AD3B to decimal 44347, we use the same technique, this time using appropriate hexadecimal positional values, as shown in Fig. B.10.

Converting a hexadecimal number to decimal

Positional values:	4096	256	16	1
Symbol values:	A	D	3	B
Products	A*4096=40960	D*256=3328	3*16=48	B*1=11
Sum:	= 40960 + 3328 + 48 + 11 = 44347			

Fig. B.10 Converting a hexadecimal number to decimal.

B.5 Converting from Decimal to Binary, Octal or Hexadecimal

The conversions of the previous section follow naturally from the positional notation conventions. Converting from decimal to binary, octal or hexadecimal also follows these conventions.

Suppose we wish to convert decimal 57 to binary. We begin by writing the positional values of the columns right to left until we reach a column whose positional value is greater than the decimal number. We do not need that column, so we discard it. Thus, we first write

Positional values: 64 32 16 8 4 2 1

Then, we discard the column with positional value 64, leaving

Positional values: 32 16 8 4 2 1

Next we work from the leftmost column to the right. We divide 32 into 57 and observe that there is one 32 in 57 with a remainder of 25, so we write 1 in the 32 column. We divide 16 into 25 and observe that there is one 16 in 25 with a remainder of 9 and write 1 in the 16 column. We divide 8 into 9 and observe that there is one 8 in 9 with a remainder of 1. The next two columns each produce quotients of zero when their positional values are divided into 1 so we write 0s in the 4 and 2 columns. Finally, 1 into 1 is 1, so we write 1 in the 1 column. This yields

Positional values:	32	16	8	4	2	1
Symbol values:	1	1	1	0	0	1

and thus decimal 57 is equivalent to binary 111001.

To convert decimal 103 to octal, we begin by writing the positional values of the columns until we reach a column whose positional value is greater than the decimal number. We do not need that column, so we discard it. Thus, we first write

Positional values: 512 64 8 1

Then, we discard the column with positional value 512, yielding

Positional values: 64 8 1

Next, we work from the leftmost column to the right. We divide 64 into 103 and observe that there is one 64 in 103 with a remainder of 39, so we write 1 in the 64 column. We divide 8 into 39 and observe that there are four 8s in 39 with a remainder of 7 and write 4 in the 8 column. Finally, we divide 1 into 7 and observe that there are seven 1s in 7 with no remainder, so we write 7 in the 1 column. This yields

```
Positional values: 64  8  1
Symbol values:      1  4  7
```

and thus decimal 103 is equivalent to octal 147.

To convert decimal 375 to hexadecimal, we begin by writing the positional values of the columns until we reach a column whose positional value is greater than the decimal number. We do not need that column, so we discard it. Thus, we first write

```
Positional values: 4096   256    16     1
```

Then, we discard the column with positional value 4096, yielding

```
Positional values: 256     16     1
```

Next, we work from the leftmost column to the right. We divide 256 into 375 and observe that there is one 256 in 375 with a remainder of 119, so we write 1 in the 256 column. We divide 16 into 119 and observe that there are seven 16s in 119 with a remainder of 7 and write 7 in the 16 column. Finally, we divide 1 into 7 and observe that there are seven 1s in 7 with no remainder, so we write 7 in the 1 column. This yields

```
Positional values: 256  16  1
Symbol values:       1   7  1
```

and thus decimal 375 is equivalent to hexadecimal 177.

B.6 Negative Binary Numbers: Twos-Complement Notation

The discussion in this appendix has been focussed on positive numbers. In this section, we explain how computers represent negative numbers in *twos-complement notation*. First we explain how the twos complement of a binary number is formed,then we show why it represents the negative value of the given binary number.

Consider a 32-bit integer. Suppose

```
int number = 13;
```

The 32-bit representation of `number` is

```
00000000 00000000 00000000 00001101
```

To form the negative of `number`, we first form its *ones complement* by applying MC++'s bitwise complement operator (~), which is also called the *bitwise NOT operator*:

```
onesComplement = ~number;
```

Internally, `onesComplement` is now `number` with each of its bits reversed—ones become zeros and zeros become ones, as follows:

```
number:
00000000 00000000 00000000 00001101

onesComplement:
11111111 11111111 11111111 11110010
```

To form the twos complement of `number`, we simply add one to `number`'s ones complement. Thus

```
Twos complement of number:
11111111 11111111 11111111 11110011
```

Now if this is in fact equal to –13, we should be able to add it to binary 13 and obtain the result 0. Let us try this:

```
 00000000 00000000 00000000 00001101
+11111111 11111111 11111111 11110011
------------------------------------
 00000000 00000000 00000000 00000000
```

The carry bit coming out of the leftmost column is discarded, and we indeed get zero as a result. If we add the ones complement of a number to the number, the result would be all 1s. The key to getting a result of all zeros is that the twos complement is 1 more than the ones complement. The addition of 1 causes each column to add to 0 with a carry of 1. The carry keeps moving leftward until it is discarded from the leftmost bit, and hence the resulting number is all zeros.

Computers actually perform a subtraction such as

```
x = a - number;
```

by adding the twos complement of `number` to `a` as follows:

```
x = a + ( onesComplement + 1 );
```

Suppose `a` is 27 and `number` is 13 as before. If the twos complement of `number` is actually the negative of `number`, then adding the twos complement of value to `a` should produce the result 14. Let us try this:

```
a (i.e., 27)                 00000000 00000000 00000000 00011011
+( onesComplement + 1 )     +11111111 11111111 11111111 11110011
                            ------------------------------------
                             00000000 00000000 00000000 00001110
```

which is indeed equal to 14.

SUMMARY

- When we write an integer such as 19 or 227 or –63 in a program, the number is automatically assumed to be in the decimal (base-10) number system.
- The digits in the decimal number system are 0, 1, 2, 3, 4, 5, 6, 7, 8, and 9. The lowest digit is 0 and the highest digit is 9—one less than the base of 10.

- Internally, computers use the binary (base 2) number system. The binary number system has only two digits, namely 0 and 1. Its lowest digit is 0 and its highest digit is 1—one less than the base of 2.
- The octal number system (base 8) and the hexadecimal number system (base 16) are popular primarily because they make it convenient to abbreviate binary numbers. The digits of the octal number system range from 0 to 7.
- The hexadecimal number system poses a problem because it requires sixteen digits—a lowest digit of 0 and a highest digit with a value equivalent to decimal 15 (one less than the base of 16).
- By convention, we use the letters A through F to represent the hexadecimal digits corresponding to decimal values 10 through 15.
- Each number system uses positional notation—each position in which a digit is written has a different positional value.
- A particularly important relationship that both the octal number system and the hexadecimal number system have to the binary system is that the bases of octal and hexadecimal (8 and 16 respectively) are powers of the base of the binary number system (base 2).
- To convert an octal number to a binary number, simply replace each octal digit with its three-digit binary equivalent.
- To convert a hexadecimal number to a binary number, simply replace each hexadecimal digit with its four-digit binary equivalent.
- We are accustomed to working in decimal, so it is convenient to convert a binary, octal or hexadecimal number to decimal to get a sense of the number's "real" worth.
- To convert a number to decimal from another base, multiply the decimal equivalent of each digit by its positional value, and sum these products.
- Computers represent negative numbers using twos-complement notation.
- To form the negative of a value in binary, first form its ones complement by applying MC++'s bitwise complement operator (~). This reverses the bits of the value.
- To form the twos complement of a value, simply add one to the value's ones complement.

C

ASCII Character Set

	0	1	2	3	4	5	6	7	8	9
0	nul	soh	stx	etx	eot	enq	ack	bel	bs	ht
1	nl	vt	ff	cr	so	si	dle	dc1	dc2	dc3
2	dc4	nak	syn	etb	can	em	sub	esc	fs	gs
3	rs	us	sp	!	"	#	$	%	&	‘
4	(	)	*	+	,	-	.	/	0	1
5	2	3	4	5	6	7	8	9	:	;
6	<	=	>	?	@	A	B	C	D	E
7	F	G	H	I	J	K	L	M	N	O
8	P	Q	R	S	T	U	V	W	X	Y
9	Z	[	\	]	^	_	’	a	b	c
10	d	e	f	g	h	i	j	k	l	m
11	n	o	p	q	r	s	t	u	v	w
12	x	y	z	{	|	}	~	del		

Fig. C.1 ASCII character set.

The digits at the left of the table are the left digits of the decimal equivalent (0–127) of the character code, and the digits at the top of the table are the right digits of the character code. For example, the character code for “F” is 70, and the character code for “&” is 38.

Most users of this book are interested in the ASCII character set used to represent English characters on many computers. The ASCII character set is a subset of the Unicode character set used to represent characters from most of the world’s languages. For more information on the Unicode character set, see Appendix D.

D

Unicode

Objectives

- To become familiar with Unicode.
- To discuss the mission of the Unicode Consortium.
- To discuss the design basis of Unicode.
- To understand the three Unicode encoding forms: UTF-8, UTF-16 and UTF-32.
- To introduce characters and glyphs.
- To discuss the advantages and disadvantages of using Unicode.
- To provide a brief tour of the Unicode Consortium's Web site.

Outline

D.1 Introduction

The use of inconsistent character *encodings* (i.e., numeric values associated with characters) when developing global software products causes serious problems because computers process information using numbers. For example, the character "a" is converted to a numeric value so that a computer can manipulate that piece of data. Many countries and corporations have developed their own encoding systems that are incompatible with the encoding systems of other countries and corporations. For example, the Microsoft Windows operating system assigns the value 0xC0 to the character "A with a grave accent," while the Apple Macintosh operating system assigns that same value to an upside-down question mark. This results in the misrepresentation and possible corruption of data, because the data is not processed as intended.

In the absence of a widely implemented universal character encoding standard, global software developers had to *localize* their products extensively before distribution. Localization includes the language translation and cultural adaptation of content. The process of localization usually includes significant modifications to the source code (such as the conversion of numeric values and the underlying assumptions made by programmers), which results in increased costs and delays releasing the software. For example, some English-speaking programmers might design global software products assuming that a single character can be represented by one byte. However, when those products are localized for Asian markets, the programmer's assumptions are no longer valid; thus, the majority, if not the entirety, of the code needs to be rewritten. Localization is necessary with each release of a version. By the time a software product is localized for a particular market, a newer version, which needs to be localized as well, may be ready for distribution. As a result, it is cumbersome and costly to produce and distribute global software products in a market where there is no universal character-encoding standard.

In response to this situation, the *Unicode Standard*, an encoding standard that facilitates the production and distribution of software, was created. The Unicode Standard outlines a specification to produce consistent encoding of the world's characters and *symbols*. Software products that handle text encoded in the Unicode Standard need to be localized, but the localization process is simpler and more efficient because the numeric values need not be converted and the assumptions made by programmers about the character encoding are universal. The Unicode Standard is maintained by a nonprofit organization called the

Unicode Consortium, whose members include Apple, IBM, Microsoft, Oracle, Sun Microsystems, Sybase and many others.

When the Consortium envisioned and developed the Unicode Standard, they wanted an encoding system that was *universal*, *efficient*, *uniform* and *unambiguous*. A universal encoding system encompasses all commonly used characters. An efficient encoding system allows text files to be parsed easily. A uniform encoding system assigns fixed values to all characters. An unambiguous encoding system represents a given character in a consistent manner. These four terms are referred to as the Unicode Standard *design basis*.

D.2 Unicode Transformation Formats

Although Unicode incorporates the limited ASCII *character set* (i.e., a collection of characters), it encompasses a more comprehensive character set. In ASCII, each character is represented by a byte containing 0s and 1s. One byte is capable of storing the binary numbers from 0 to 255. Each character is assigned a number between 0 and 255; thus, ASCII-based systems can support only 256 characters, a tiny fraction of the world's characters. Unicode extends the ASCII character set by encoding the vast majority of the world's characters. The Unicode Standard encodes all those characters in a uniform numerical space from 0 to 10FFFF hexadecimal. An implementation will express these numbers in one of several transformation formats, choosing the one that best fits the particular application at hand.

Three such formats are in use, called *UTF-8*, *UTF-16* and *UTF-32*, depending on the size of the units—in *bits*—being used. UTF-8, a variable-width encoding form, requires one to four bytes to express each Unicode character. UTF-8 data consists of 8-bit bytes (sequences of one, two, three or four bytes, depending on the character being encoded) and is well suited for ASCII-based systems, where there is a predominance of one-byte characters (ASCII represents characters as one byte). Currently, UTF-8 is widely implemented in UNIX systems and in databases. [*Note*: Currently, Internet Explorer 5.5 and Netscape Communicator 6 support only UTF-8, so document authors should use UTF-8 for encoding XML and XHTML documents.]

The variable-width UTF-16 encoding form expresses Unicode characters in units of 16 bits (i.e., as two adjacent bytes, or a short integer in many machines). Most characters of Unicode are expressed in a single 16-bit unit. However, characters with values above FFFF hexadecimal are expressed with an ordered pair of 16-bit units called *surrogates*. Surrogates are 16-bit integers in the range D800 through DFFF, which are used solely for the purpose of "escaping" into higher-numbered characters. Approximately one million characters can be expressed in this manner. Although a surrogate pair requires 32 bits to represent characters, it is space-efficient to use these 16-bit units. Surrogates are rare characters in current implementations. Many string-handling implementations are written in terms of UTF-16. [*Note*: Details and sample code for UTF-16 handling are available on the Unicode Consortium Web site at `www.unicode.org`.]

Implementations that require significant use of rare characters or entire scripts encoded above FFFF hexadecimal should use UTF-32, a 32-bit, fixed-width encoding form that usually requires twice as much memory as UTF-16 encoded characters. The major advantage of the fixed-width UTF-32 encoding form is that it expresses all characters uniformly, so it is easy to handle in arrays.

There are few guidelines that state when to use a particular encoding form. The best encoding form to use depends on computer systems and business protocols, not on the data.

Typically, the UTF-8 encoding form should be used where computer systems and business protocols require data to be handled in 8-bit units, particularly in legacy systems being upgraded, because it often simplifies changes to existing programs. For this reason, UTF-8 has become the encoding form of choice on the Internet. Likewise, UTF-16 is the encoding form of choice on Microsoft Windows applications. UTF-32 is likely to become more widely used in the future as more characters are encoded with values above FFFF hexadecimal. Also, UTF-32 requires less sophisticated handling than UTF-16 in the presence of surrogate pairs. Figure D.1 shows the different ways in which the three encoding forms handle character encoding.

Character	UTF-8	UTF-16	UTF-32
LATIN CAPITAL LETTER A	0x41	0x0041	0x00000041
GREEK CAPITAL LETTER ALPHA	0xCD 0x91	0x0391	0x00000391
CJK UNIFIED IDEOGRAPH-4E95	0xE4 0xBA 0x95	0x4E95	0x00004E95
OLD ITALIC LETTER A	0xF0 0x80 0x83 0x80	0xDC00 0xDF00	0x00010300

Fig. D.1 Correlation between the three encoding forms.

D.3 Characters and Glyphs

The Unicode Standard consists of *characters*—written components (i.e., alphabetic letters, numerals, punctuation marks, accent marks, etc.) that can be represented by numeric values. Examples of characters include U+0041 LATIN CAPITAL LETTER A. In the first character representation, U+*yyyy* is a *code value*, in which U+ refers to Unicode code values, as opposed to other hexadecimal values. The *yyyy* represents a four-digit hexadecimal number of an encoded character. Code values are bit combinations that represent encoded characters. Characters are represented using *glyphs*, various shapes, fonts and sizes for displaying characters. There are no code values for glyphs in the Unicode Standard. Examples of glyphs are shown in Fig. D.2.

Fig. D.2 Various glyphs of the character A.

The Unicode Standard encompasses the alphabets, ideographs, syllabaries, punctuation marks, *diacritics*, mathematical operators, etc. that comprise the written languages and scripts of the world. A diacritic is a special mark added to a character to distinguish it from another letter or to indicate an accent (e.g., in Spanish, the tilde "~" above the character "n"). Currently, Unicode provides code values for 94,140 character representations, with more than 880,000 code values reserved for future expansion.

D.4 Advantages and Disadvantages of Unicode

The Unicode Standard has several significant advantages that promote its use. One is the impact it has on the performance of the international economy. Unicode standardizes the characters for the world's writing systems to a uniform model that promotes transferring and sharing data. Programs developed using such a schema maintain their accuracy because each character has a single definition (i.e., *a* is always U+0061, *%* is always U+0025). This enables corporations to manage the high demands of international markets by processing different writing systems at the same time. Also, all characters can be managed in an identical manner, thus avoiding any confusion caused by different character code architectures. Moreover, managing data in a consistent manner eliminates data corruption, because data can be sorted, searched and manipulated using a consistent process.

Another advantage of the Unicode Standard is *portability* (i.e., the ability to execute software on disparate computers or with disparate operating systems). Most operating systems, databases, programming languages and Web browsers currently support, or are planning to support, Unicode. Additionally, Unicode includes more characters than any other character set in common use (although it does not yet include all the world's characters).

A disadvantage of the Unicode Standard is the amount of memory required by UTF-16 and UTF-32. ASCII character sets are 8 bits in length, so they require less storage than the default 16-bit Unicode character set. However, the *double-byte character set (DBCS)* and the *multi-byte character set (MBCS)* that encode Asian characters (ideographs) require two to four bytes, respectively. In such instances, the UTF-16 or the UTF-32 encoding forms may be used with little hindrance on memory and performance.

D.5 Unicode Consortium's Web Site

If you would like to learn more about the Unicode Standard, visit `www.unicode.org`. This site provides a wealth of information about the Unicode Standard. Currently, the home page is organized into various sections: *New to Unicode*, *General Information*, *The Consortium*, *The Unicode Standard*, *Work in Progress* and *For Members*.

The *New to Unicode* section consists of two subsections: ***What is Unicode?*** and ***How to Use this Site***. The first subsection provides a technical introduction to Unicode by describing design principles, character interpretations and assignments, text processing and Unicode conformance. This subsection is recommended reading for anyone new to Unicode. Also, this subsection provides a list of related links that provide the reader with additional information about Unicode. The **How to Use this Site** subsection contains information about using and navigating the site as well hyperlinks to additional resources.

The *General Information* section contains seven subsections: ***Where is My Character?***, ***Display Problems?***, ***Useful Resources***, ***Enabled Products***, ***Technical Notes***, ***Mail Lists*** and ***Conferences***. The main areas covered in this section include a link to the Unicode code charts (a complete listing of code values) assembled by the Unicode Consortium, as well as a detailed outline on how to locate an encoded character in the code chart. Also, the section contains advice on how to configure different operating systems and Web browsers so that the Unicode characters can be viewed properly. Moreover, from this section, the user can navigate to other sites that provide information on various topics such as, fonts, linguistics and other standards such as the *Armenian Standards Page* and the *Chinese GB 18030 Encoding Standard*.

The Consortium section consists of five subsections: ***Who We Are***, ***Our Members***, ***How to Join***, ***Press Info*** and ***Contact Us***. This section provides a list of the current Unicode Consortium members as well as information on how to become a member. Privileges for each member type—*full*, *associate*, *specialist* and *individual*—and the fees assessed to each member are listed here.

The Unicode Standard section consists of nine subsections: ***Start Here***, ***Latest Version***, ***Technical Reports***, ***Code Charts***, ***Unicode Data***, ***Updates & Errata***, ***Unicode Policies***, ***Glossary*** and ***FAQ***. This section describes the updates applied to the latest version of the Unicode Standard, as well as categorizing all defined encoding. The user can learn how the latest version has been modified to encompass more features and capabilities. For instance, one enhancement of Version 3.1 is that it contains additional encoded characters. Also, if users are unfamiliar with vocabulary terms used by the Unicode Consortium, then they can navigate to the **Glossary** subsection.

The *Work in Progress* section consists of three subsections: ***Calendar of Meetings***, ***Proposed Characters*** and ***Submitting Proposals***. This section presents the user with a catalog of the recent characters included into the Unicode Standard scheme as well as those characters being considered for inclusion. If users determine that a character has been overlooked, then they can submit a written proposal for the inclusion of that character. The **Submitting Proposals** subsection contains strict guidelines that must be adhered to when submitting written proposals.

The *For Members* section consists of two subsections: ***Member Resources*** and ***Working Documents***. These subsections are password protected; only consortium members can access these links.

D.6 Using Unicode

The MC++ application in Fig. D.3–Fig. D.4 displays the text "Welcome to Unicode!" in eight different languages: English, French, German, Japanese, Portuguese, Russian, Spanish and Simplified Chinese. The necessary characters are specified using their UTF-16 encoding values. [*Note*: The Unicode Consortium's Web site contains a link to code charts that lists the 16-bit Unicode code values.]

```
// Fig. D.3: Form1.h
// Using unicode encoding.

#pragma once


namespace Unicode
{
   using namespace System;
   using namespace System::ComponentModel;
   using namespace System::Collections;
   using namespace System::Windows::Forms;
   using namespace System::Data;
   using namespace System::Drawing;
```

Fig. D.3 `Unicode::Form1` class demonstrates Unicode values for multiple languages. (Part 1 of 4.)

```

   /// <summary>
   /// Summary for Form1
   ///
   /// WARNING: If you change the name of this class, you will need to
   ///          change the 'Resource File Name' property for the managed
   ///          resource compiler tool associated with all .resx files
   ///          this class depends on.  Otherwise, the designers will not
   ///          be able to interact properly with localized resources
   ///          associated with this form.
   /// </summary>
   public __gc class Form1 : public System::Windows::Forms::Form
   {
   public:
      Form1(void)
      {
         InitializeComponent();
      }

   protected:
      void Dispose(Boolean disposing)
      {
         if (disposing && components)
         {
            components->Dispose();
         }
         __super::Dispose(disposing);
      }
   private: System::Windows::Forms::Label *  lblChinese;
   private: System::Windows::Forms::Label *  lblSpanish;
   private: System::Windows::Forms::Label *  lblRussian;
   private: System::Windows::Forms::Label *  lblPortuguese;
   private: System::Windows::Forms::Label *  lblJapanese;
   private: System::Windows::Forms::Label *  lblGerman;
   private: System::Windows::Forms::Label *  lblFrench;
   private: System::Windows::Forms::Label *  lblEnglish;

   private:
      /// <summary>
      /// Required designer variable.
      /// </summary>
      System::ComponentModel::Container * components;

   // Visual Studio .NET generated GUI code

   private: System::Void Form1_Load(
               System::Object *  sender, System::EventArgs *  e)
            {
               // exclamation point
               __wchar_t exclamation = 0x0021;
```

Fig. D.3 `Unicode::Form1` class demonstrates Unicode values for multiple languages. (Part 2 of 4.)

```
      // English
      __wchar_t english __gc[] = { 0x0057, 0x0065, 0x006C,
         0x0063, 0x006F, 0x006D, 0x0065, 0x0020, 0x0074, 0x006F,
         0x0020 };

      lblEnglish->Text = String::Concat( new String( english ),
         S"Unicode", exclamation.ToString() );

      // French
      __wchar_t french __gc[] = { 0x0042, 0x0069, 0x0065, 0x006E,
         0x0076, 0x0065, 0x006E, 0x0075, 0x0065, 0x0020, 0x0061,
         0x0075, 0x0020 };

      lblFrench->Text = String::Concat( new String( french ),
         S"Unicode", exclamation.ToString() );

      // German
     __wchar_t german __gc[] = { 0x0057, 0x0069, 0x006C, 0x006B,
         0x006F, 0x006D, 0x006D, 0x0065, 0x006E, 0x0020, 0x007A,
         0x0075, 0x0020 };

      lblGerman->Text =  String::Concat( new String( german ),
         S"Unicode", exclamation.ToString() );

      // Japanese
      __wchar_t japanese __gc[] = { 0x3078,  0x3087, 0x3045,
         0x3053, 0x305D, 0x0021 };

      lblJapanese->Text = String::Concat( S"Unicode",
         new String( japanese ) );

      // Portuguese
      __wchar_t portuguese __gc[] = { 0x0053, 0x0065, 0x006A,
         0x0061, 0x0020, 0x0062, 0x0065, 0x006D, 0x0020, 0x0076,
         0x0069, 0x006E, 0x0064, 0x006F, 0x0020, 0x0061,
         0x0020 };

      lblPortuguese->Text = String::Concat( new String(
         portuguese ), S"Unicode", exclamation.ToString() );

      // Russian
      __wchar_t russian __gc[] = { 0x0414, 0x043E, 0x0431,
         0x0440, 0x043E, 0x0020, 0x043F, 0x043E, 0x0436, 0x0430,
         0x043B, 0x043E, 0x0432, 0x0430, 0x0442, 0x044A, 0x0020,
         0x0432, 0x0020 };

      lblRussian->Text = String::Concat( new String( russian ),
         S"Unicode", exclamation.ToString() );

```

Fig. D.3 `Unicode::Form1` class demonstrates Unicode values for multiple languages. (Part 3 of 4.)

```
            // Spanish
            __wchar_t spanish __gc[] = { 0x0042, 0x0069, 0x0065,
               0x006E, 0x0076, 0x0065, 0x006E, 0x0069, 0x0064, 0x006F,
               0x0020, 0x0061, 0x0020 };

            lblSpanish->Text = String::Concat( new String( spanish ),
               S"Unicode", exclamation.ToString() );

            // Simplified Chinese
            __wchar_t chinese __gc[] = { 0x6B22, 0x8FCE, 0x4F7F,
               0x7528, 0x0020 };

            lblChinese->Text = String::Concat( new String( chinese ),
               S"Unicode", exclamation.ToString() );
         } // end method Form1_Load
   };
}
```

Fig. D.3 `Unicode::Form1` class demonstrates Unicode values for multiple languages. (Part 4 of 4.)

```
// Fig. D.4: Form1.cpp
// Entry point for application.

#include "stdafx.h"
#include "Form1.h"
#include <windows.h>

using namespace Unicode;

int APIENTRY _tWinMain(HINSTANCE hInstance,
                       HINSTANCE hPrevInstance,
                       LPTSTR    lpCmdLine,
                       int       nCmdShow)
{
   System::Threading::Thread::CurrentThread->ApartmentState =
      System::Threading::ApartmentState::STA;
   Application::Run(new Form1());
   return 0;
}
```

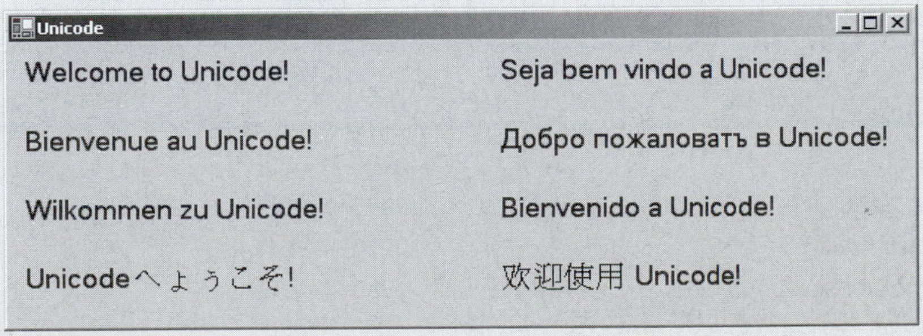

Fig. D.4 `Unicode::Form1` class driver.

Lines 67–69 contain the hexadecimal codes for the English text. The **Code Charts** page on the Unicode Consortium Web site contains a document that lists the code values for the **Basic Latin** *block* (or category), which includes the English alphabet. The first seven hexadecimal codes in lines 67–69 equate to "**Welcome** ". For specifying hexadecimal values in MC++, the format `0x`*yyyy* is used, where *yyyy* represents the hexadecimal number. For example, the letter "W" (with hexadecimal code `0057`) is denoted by `0x0057`. Line 69 contains the hexadecimal for the *space* character (`0x0020`). Lines 71–72 create a new string from the character array and append the word "Unicode." "Unicode" is not encoded because it is a registered trademark and has no equivalent translation in most languages. Line 72also uses variable `exclamation` (line 64), a `__wchar_t` containing the `0x0021` notation for the exclamation mark (`!`).

The remaining welcome messages (lines 74–128) contain the Unicode values for the other seven languages. The code values used for the French, German, Portuguese and Spanish text are located in the **Basic Latin** block, the code values used for the Simplified Chinese text are located in the **CJK Unified Ideographs** block, the code values used for the Russian text are located in the **Cyrillic** block and the code values used for the Japanese text are located in the **Hiragana** block.

[*Note*: To render the Asian characters in a Windows application, you may need to install the proper language files on your computer. To do this in Windows 2000, open the **Regional Options** dialog from the **Control Panel** (**Start > Settings > Control Panel**). At the bottom of the **General** tab is a list of languages. Check the **Japanese** and the **Traditional Chinese** checkboxes, and press **Apply**. Follow the directions of the install wizard to install the languages. For additional assistance, visit `www.unicode.org/help/display_problems.html`.]

D.7 Character Ranges

The Unicode Standard assigns code values, which range from `0000` (**Basic Latin**) to `E007F` (***Tags***), to the written characters of the world. Currently, there are code values for 94,140 characters. To simplify the search for a character and its associated code value, the Unicode Standard generally groups code values by *script* and function (i.e., Latin characters are grouped in a block, mathematical operators are grouped in another block, etc.). As a rule, a script is a single writing system that is used for multiple languages (e.g., the Latin script is used for English, French, Spanish, etc.). The **Code Charts** page on the Unicode Consortium Web site lists all the defined blocks and their respective code values. Figure D.5 lists some blocks (scripts) from the Web site and their ranges of code values.

Script	Range of Code Values
Arabic	`U+0600-U+06FF`
Basic Latin	`U+0000-U+007F`
Bengali (India)	`U+0980-U+09FF`
Cherokee (Native America)	`U+13A0-U+13FF`

Fig. D.5 Some character ranges. (Part 1 of 2.)

Script	Range of Code Values
CJK Unified Ideographs (East Asia)	U+4E00–U+9FAF
Cyrillic (Russia and Eastern Europe)	U+0400–U+04FF
Ethiopic	U+1200–U+137F
Greek	U+0370–U+03FF
Hangul Jamo (Korea)	U+1100–U+11FF
Hebrew	U+0590–U+05FF
Hiragana (Japan)	U+3040–U+309F
Khmer (Cambodia)	U+1780–U+17FF
Lao (Laos)	U+0E80–U+0EFF
Mongolian	U+1800–U+18AF
Myanmar	U+1000–U+109F
Ogham (Ireland)	U+1680–U+169F
Runic (Germany and Scandinavia)	U+16A0–U+16FF
Sinhala (Sri Lanka)	U+0D80–U+0DFF
Telugu (India)	U+0C00–U+0C7F
Thai	U+0E00–U+0E7F

Fig. D.5 Some character ranges. (Part 2 of 2.)

SUMMARY

- Before Unicode, software developers were plagued by the use of inconsistent character encoding (i.e., numeric values for characters).
- Most countries and organizations had their own encoding systems, which were incompatible. A good example is the different encoding systems on the Windows and Macintosh platforms.
- Computers process data by converting characters to numeric values. For instance, the character "a" is converted to a numeric value so that a computer can manipulate that piece of data.
- Without Unicode, localization of global software requires significant modifications to the source code, which results in increased cost and in delays releasing the product. Localization is necessary with each release of a version.
- By the time a software product is localized for a particular market, a newer version, which needs to be localized as well, is ready for distribution. As a result, it is cumbersome and costly to produce and distribute global software products in a market where there is no universal character encoding standard.
- The Unicode Consortium developed the Unicode Standard in response to the serious problems created by multiple character encodings and the use of those encodings.
- The Unicode Standard facilitates the production and distribution of localized software. It outlines a specification for the consistent encoding of the world's characters and symbols.
- Software products that handle text encoded in the Unicode Standard need to be localized, but the localization process is simpler and more efficient because the numeric values need not be converted.
- The Unicode Standard is designed to be universal, efficient, uniform and unambiguous.

- A universal encoding system encompasses all commonly used characters; an efficient encoding system parses text files easily; a uniform encoding system assigns fixed values to all characters; and an unambiguous encoding system represents the same character for any given value.
- Unicode extends the limited ASCII character set to include all the major characters of the world.
- Unicode makes use of three Unicode Transformation Formats (UTF): UTF-8, UTF-16 and UTF-32, each of which may be appropriate for use in different contexts.
- UTF-8 data consists of 8-bit bytes (sequences of one, two, three or four bytes depending on the character being encoded) and is well suited for ASCII-based systems when there is a predominance of one-byte characters (ASCII represents characters as one-byte).
- UTF-8 is a variable-width encoding form that is more compact for text involving mostly Latin characters and ASCII punctuation.
- UTF-16 is the default encoding form of the Unicode Standard. It is a variable-width encoding form that uses 16-bit code units instead of bytes. Most characters are represented by a single unit, but some characters require surrogate pairs.
- Surrogates are 16-bit integers in the range D800 through DFFF, which are used solely for the purpose of "escaping" into higher-numbered characters.
- Without surrogate pairs, the UTF-16 encoding form can only encompass 65,000 characters, but with the surrogate pairs, this is expanded to include over a million characters.
- UTF-32 is a 32-bit encoding form. The major advantage of the fixed-width encoding form is that it uniformly expresses all characters, so that they are easy to handle in arrays and so forth.
- The Unicode Standard consists of characters. A character is any written component that can be represented by a numeric value.
- Characters are represented using glyphs, various shapes, fonts and sizes for displaying characters.
- Code values are bit combinations that represent encoded characters.
- The Unicode notation for a code value is U+*yyyy* in which U+ refers to the Unicode code values, as opposed to other hexadecimal values. The *yyyy* represents a four-digit hexadecimal number.
- When specifying hexadecimal values in MC++, the format `0x`*yyyy* is used, where *yyyy* represents the hexadecimal number.
- Currently, the Unicode Standard provides code values for 94,140 character representations.
- An advantage of the Unicode Standard is its impact on the overall performance of the international economy. Applications that conform to an encoding standard can be processed easily by computers anywhere.
- Another advantage of the Unicode Standard is its portability. Applications written in Unicode can easily be transferred to different operating systems, databases, Web browsers, etc.
- Most companies currently support, or are planning to support, Unicode.
- To obtain more information about the Unicode Standard and the Unicode Consortium, visit `www.unicode.org`. It contains a link to the code charts, which contain the 16-bit code values for the currently encoded characters.

E

Introduction to XHTML: Part 1

Objectives

- To understand important components of XHTML documents.
- To use XHTML to create World Wide Web pages.
- To add images to Web pages.
- To understand how to create and use hyperlinks to navigate Web pages.
- To mark up lists of information.

To read between the lines was easier than to follow the text.
Aristophanes

Outline

E.1 Introduction

In this appendix, we introduce *XHTML*[1]—the *Extensible HyperText Markup Language*. In the next appendix, Introduction to XHTML: Part 2, we introduce more sophisticated XHTML techniques, such as *tables*, which are particularly useful for structuring information from *databases* (i.e., software that stores structured sets of data). In this appendix, we do not present any MC++ programming.

Unlike procedural programming languages such as C, Fortran, Cobol and Visual Basic, XHTML is a *markup language* that specifies the format of text that is displayed in a Web browser, such as Microsoft's Internet Explorer or Netscape's Communicator.

One key issue when using XHTML[2] is the separation of the *presentation of a document* (i.e., the document's appearance when rendered by a browser) from the *structure of the document's information*. Throughout this appendix and the next, we will discuss this issue in depth.

E.2 Editing XHTML

In this appendix, we write XHTML in its *source-code form*. We create *XHTML documents* by typing them in with a text editor (e.g., *Notepad*, *Wordpad*, *vi* or *emacs*), saving the documents with either an `.html` or `.htm` file-name extension.

---

1. XHTML has replaced the HyperText Markup Language (HTML) as the primary means of describing Web content. XHTML provides more robust, richer and more extensible features than HTML. For more on XHTML/HTML, visit `www.w3.org/markup`.
2. The XHTML examples presented in this appendix are based on the XHTML 1.0 Recommendation.

Good Programming Practice E.1

Assign documents file names that describe their functionality. This practice can help you identify documents faster. It also helps people who want to link to a page, by giving them an easy-to-remember name. For example, if you are writing an XHTML document that contains product information, you might want to call it `products.html`.

Machines running specialized software called a *Web server* store XHTML documents. Clients (e.g., Web browsers) request specific *resources*, such as the XHTML documents, from the Web server. For example, typing `www.deitel.com/books/downloads.htm` into a Web browser's address field requests `downloads.htm` from the Web server running at `www.deitel.com`. This document is located in a directory named `books`.

E.3 First XHTML Example

In this appendix and the next, we present XHTML markup and provide screen captures that show how Internet Explorer renders (i.e., displays) the XHTML. Every XHTML document we show has line numbers for the reader's convenience. These line numbers are not part of the XHTML documents.

Our first example (Fig. E.1) is an XHTML document named `main.html` that displays the message `Welcome to XHTML!` in the browser.

The key line in the program is line 14, which tells the browser to display `Welcome to XHTML!` Now let us consider each line of the program.

Lines 1–3 are required in XHTML documents to conform with proper XHTML syntax. For now, copy and paste these lines into each XHTML document you create. The meaning of these lines is discussed in detail in Chapter 18, Extensible Markup Language (XML).

Lines 5–6 are *XHTML comments*. XHTML document creators insert comments to improve markup readability and describe the content of a document. Comments also help other people read and understand an XHTML document's markup and content. Comments do not cause the browser to perform any action when the user loads the XHTML document into the Web browser to view the document. XHTML comments always start with `<!--` and end with `-->`. Each of our XHTML examples includes comments that specify the figure number and file name and provide a brief description of the example's purpose. Subsequent examples include comments in the markup, especially to highlight new features.

Good Programming Practice E.2

Place comments throughout your markup. Comments help other programmers understand the markup, assist in debugging and list useful information that you do not want the browser to render. Comments also help you understand your own markup when you revisit a document for modifications or updates in the future.

```
1  <?xml version = "1.0"?>
2  <!DOCTYPE html PUBLIC "-//W3C//DTD XHTML 1.0 Strict//EN"
3     "http://www.w3.org/TR/xhtml1/DTD/xhtml1-strict.dtd">
4
5  <!-- Fig. E.1: main.html -->
6  <!-- Our first Web page. -->
7
```

Fig. E.1 First XHTML example. (Part 1 of 2.)

```
8  <html xmlns = "http://www.w3.org/1999/xhtml">
9     <head>
10       <title>Welcome</title>
11    </head>
12
13    <body>
14       <p>Welcome to XHTML!</p>
15    </body>
16 </html>
```

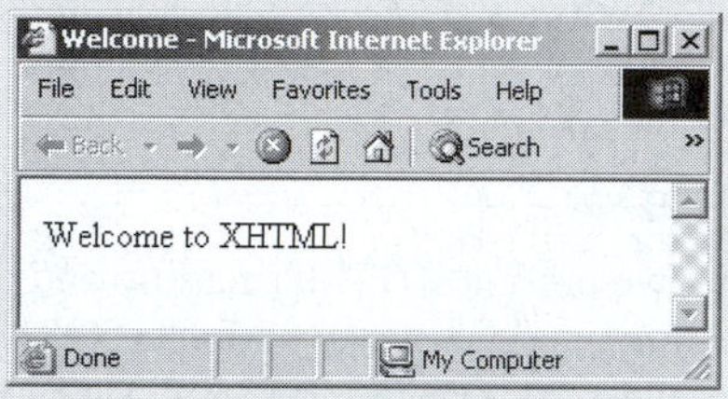

Fig. E.1 First XHTML example. (Part 2 of 2.)

XHTML markup contains text that represents the content of a document and *elements* that specify a document's structure. Some important elements of an XHTML document include the `html` element, the *head* element and the *body* element. The `html` element encloses the *head section* (represented by the *head element*) and the *body section* (represented by the *body element*). The head section contains information about the XHTML document, such as the *title* of the document. The head section also can contain special document-formatting instructions called *style sheets* and client-side programs called *scripts* for creating dynamic Web pages. The body section contains the page's content that the browser displays when the user visits the Web page.

XHTML documents delimit an element with *start* and *end* tags. A start tag consists of the element name in angle brackets (e.g., `<html>`). An end tag consists of the element name preceded by a / in angle brackets (e.g., `</html>`). In this example, lines 8 and 16 define the start and end of the `html` element. Note that the end tag in line 16 has the same name as the start tag, but is preceded by a / inside the angle brackets. Many start tags define *attributes* that provide additional information about an element. Browsers can use this additional information to determine how to process the element. Each attribute has a *name* and a *value* separated by an equal sign (=). Line 8 specifies a required attribute (`xmlns`) and value (`http://www.w3.org/1999/xhtml`) for the `html` element in an XHTML document. For now, simply copy and paste the `html` element start tag in line 8 into your XHTML documents. We discuss the details of the `html` element's `xmlns` attribute in Chapter 18, Extensible Markup Language (XML).

Common Programming Error E.1

Not enclosing attribute values in either single or double quotes is a syntax error.

Common Programming Error E.2

Using uppercase letters in an XHTML element or attribute name is a syntax error.

An XHTML document divides the `html` element into two sections—head and body. Lines 9–11 define the Web page's head section with a `head` element. Line 10 specifies a `title` element. This is called a *nested element*, because it is enclosed in the `head` element's start and end tags. The `head` element also is a nested element, because it is enclosed in the `html` element's start and end tags. The `title` element describes the Web page. Titles usually appear in the *title bar* at the top of the browser window and also as the text identifying a page when users add the page to their list of **Favorites** or **Bookmarks**, which enable users to return to their favorite sites. Search engines (i.e., sites that allow users to search the Web) also use the `title` for cataloging purposes.

Good Programming Practice E.3

Indenting nested elements emphasizes a document's structure and promotes readability.

Common Programming Error E.3

XHTML does not permit tags to overlap—a nested element's end tag must appear in the document before the enclosing element's end tag. For example, the nested XHTML tags `<head><title>hello</head></title>` *cause a syntax error, because the enclosing* `head` *element's ending* `</head>` *tag appears before the nested* `title` *element's ending* `</title>` *tag.*

Good Programming Practice E.4

Use a consistent `title` *naming convention for all pages on a site. For example, if a site is named "Bailey's Web Site," then the* `title` *of the main page might be "Bailey's Web Site—Links." This practice can help users better understand the Web site's structure.*

Line 13 opens the document's *body* element. The body section of an XHTML document specifies the document's content, which may include text and tags.

Some tags, such as the *paragraph tags* (<p> and </p>) in line 14, mark up text for display in a browser. All text placed between the <p> and </p> tags form one paragraph. When the browser renders a paragraph, a blank line usually precedes and follows paragraph text.

This document ends with two closing tags (lines 15–16). These tags close the body and `html` elements, respectively. The ending </html> tag in an XHTML document informs the browser that the XHTML markup is complete.

To view this example in Internet Explorer, perform the following steps:

1. Copy the Appendix E examples onto your machine by downloading the examples from `www.deitel.com`.
2. Launch Internet Explorer, and select **Open...** from the **File** Menu. This displays the **Open** dialog.
3. Click the **Open** dialog's **Browse...** button to display the **Microsoft Internet Explorer** file dialog.
4. Navigate to the directory containing the Appendix E examples and select the file `main.html`; then, click **Open**.
5. Click **OK** to have Internet Explorer render the document. Other examples are opened in a similar manner.

At this point your browser window should appear similar to the sample screen capture shown in Fig. E.1. (Note that we resized the browser window to save space on the page of this book.)

E.4 W3C XHTML Validation Service

Programming Web-based applications can be complex, and XHTML documents must be written correctly to ensure that browsers process them properly. To promote correctly written documents, the World Wide Web Consortium (W3C) provides a *validation service* (`validator.w3.org`) for checking a document's syntax. Documents can be validated either from a URL that specifies the location of the file or by uploading a file to the site `validator.w3.org/file-upload.html`. Uploading a file copies the file from the user's computer to another computer on the Internet. Figure E.2 shows `main.html` (Fig. E.1) being uploaded for validation. Although the W3C's Web page indicates that the service name is **HTML Validation Service**,[3] the validation service is able to validate the syntax of XHTML documents. All the XHTML examples in this book have been validated successfully through `validator.w3.org`.

By clicking **Browse...**, users can select files on their own computers for upload. After selecting a file, clicking the **Validate this document** button uploads and validates the file. Figure E.3 shows the results of validating `main.html`. This document does not contain any syntax errors. If a document does contain syntax errors, the Validation Service displays error messages describing the errors.

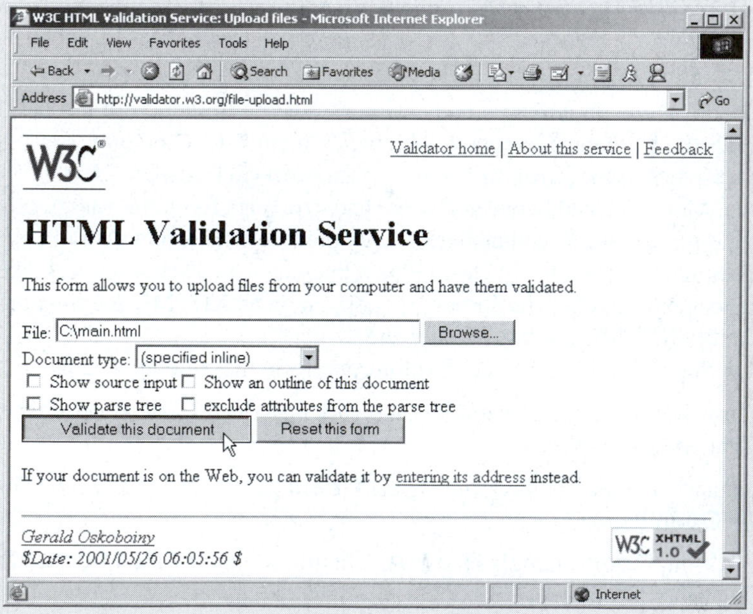

Fig. E.2 Validating an XHTML document. (Courtesy of World Wide Web Consortium (W3C).)

3. HTML (HyperText Markup Language) is the predecessor of XHTML designed for marking up Web content. HTML is a deprecated technology.

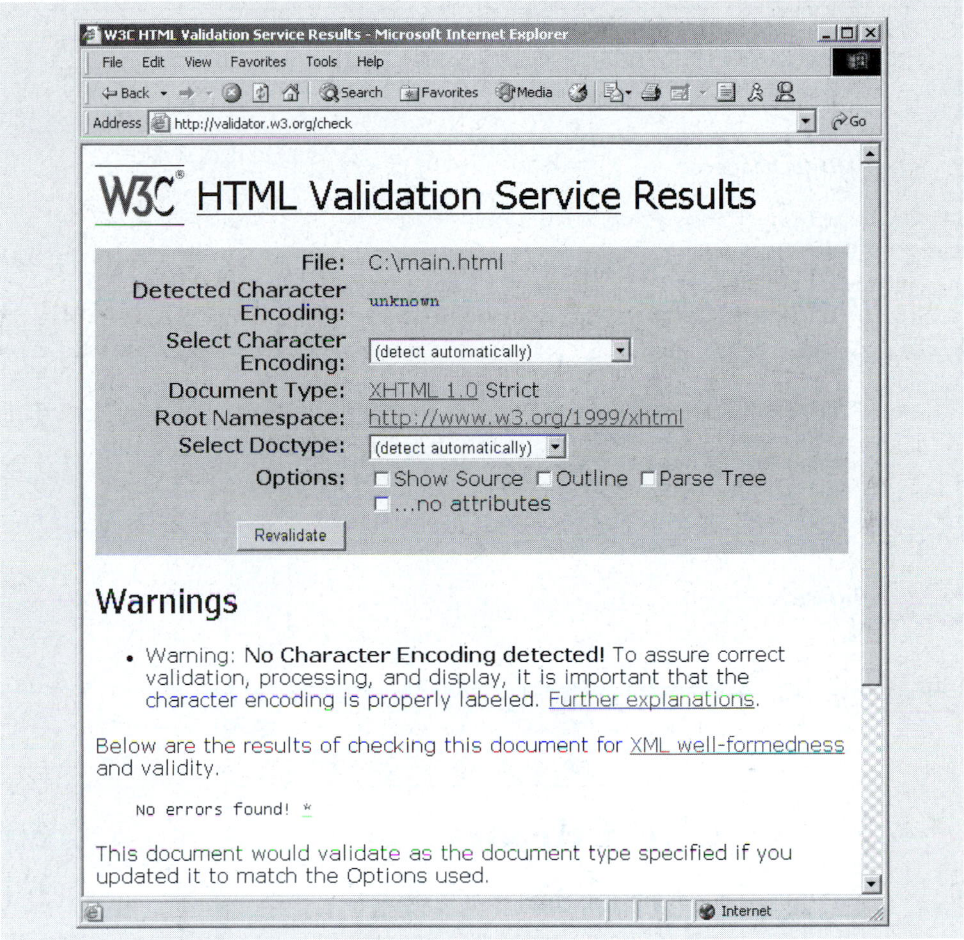

Fig. E.3 XHTML validation results. (Courtesy of World Wide Web Consortium (W3C).)

Error-Prevention Tip E.1

Use a validation service, such as the W3C HTML Validation Service, to confirm that an XHTML document is syntactically correct.

E.5 Headers

Some text in an XHTML document may be more important than some other. For example, the text in this section is considered more important than a footnote. XHTML provides six *headers*, called *header elements*, for specifying the relative importance of information. Figure E.4 demonstrates these elements (`h1` through `h6`).

Portability Tip E.1

The text size used to display each header element can vary significantly between browsers.

```
1  <?xml version = "1.0"?>
2  <!DOCTYPE html PUBLIC "-//W3C//DTD XHTML 1.0 Strict//EN"
3     "http://www.w3.org/TR/xhtml1/DTD/xhtml1-strict.dtd">
4
5  <!-- Fig. E.4: header.html -->
6  <!-- XHTML headers.        -->
7
8  <html xmlns = "http://www.w3.org/1999/xhtml">
9     <head>
10       <title>Headers</title>
11    </head>
12
13    <body>
14
15       <h1>Level 1 Header</h1>
16       <h2>Level 2 header</h2>
17       <h3>Level 3 header</h3>
18       <h4>Level 4 header</h4>
19       <h5>Level 5 header</h5>
20       <h6>Level 6 header</h6>
21
22    </body>
23 </html>
```

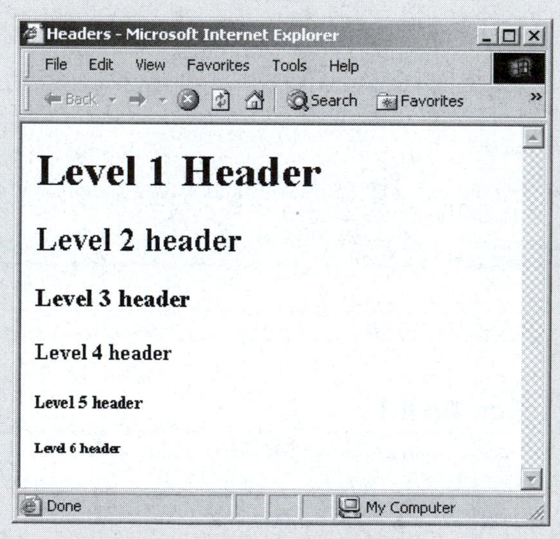

Fig. E.4 Header elements h1 through h6.

Header element h1 (line 15) is considered the most significant header and is rendered in a larger font than the other five headers (lines 16–20). Each successive header element (i.e., h2, h3, etc.) is rendered in a smaller font.

Look-and-Feel Observation E.1

Placing a header at the top of every XHTML page helps viewers understand the purpose of each page.

Look-and-Feel Observation E.2

Use larger headers to emphasize more important sections of a Web page.

E.6 Linking

One of the most important XHTML features is the *hyperlink,* which references (or *links* to) other resources, such as XHTML documents and images. In XHTML, both text and images can act as hyperlinks. Web browsers typically underline text hyperlinks and color their text blue by default, so that users can distinguish hyperlinks from plain text. In Fig. E.5, we create text hyperlinks to four different Web sites.

Line 17 introduces the `<strong>` tag. Browsers typically display text marked up with `<strong>` in a bold font.

```
1  <?xml version = "1.0"?>
2  <!DOCTYPE html PUBLIC "-//W3C//DTD XHTML 1.0 Strict//EN"
3     "http://www.w3.org/TR/xhtml1/DTD/xhtml1-strict.dtd">
4
5  <!-- Fig. E.5: links.html         -->
6  <!-- Introduction to hyperlinks. -->
7
8  <html xmlns = "http://www.w3.org/1999/xhtml">
9     <head>
10       <title>Links</title>
11    </head>
12
13    <body>
14
15       <h1>Here are my favorite sites</h1>
16
17       <p><strong>Click a name to go to that page.</strong></p>
18
19       <!-- create four text hyperlinks -->
20       <p>
21          <a href = "http://www.deitel.com">Deitel</a>
22       </p>
23
24       <p>
25          <a href = "http://www.prenhall.com">Prentice Hall</a>
26       </p>
27
28       <p>
29          <a href = "http://www.yahoo.com">Yahoo!</a>
30       </p>
31
32       <p>
33          <a href = "http://www.usatoday.com">USA Today</a>
34       </p>
35
36    </body>
37 </html>
```

Fig. E.5 Linking to other Web pages. (Part 1 of 2.)

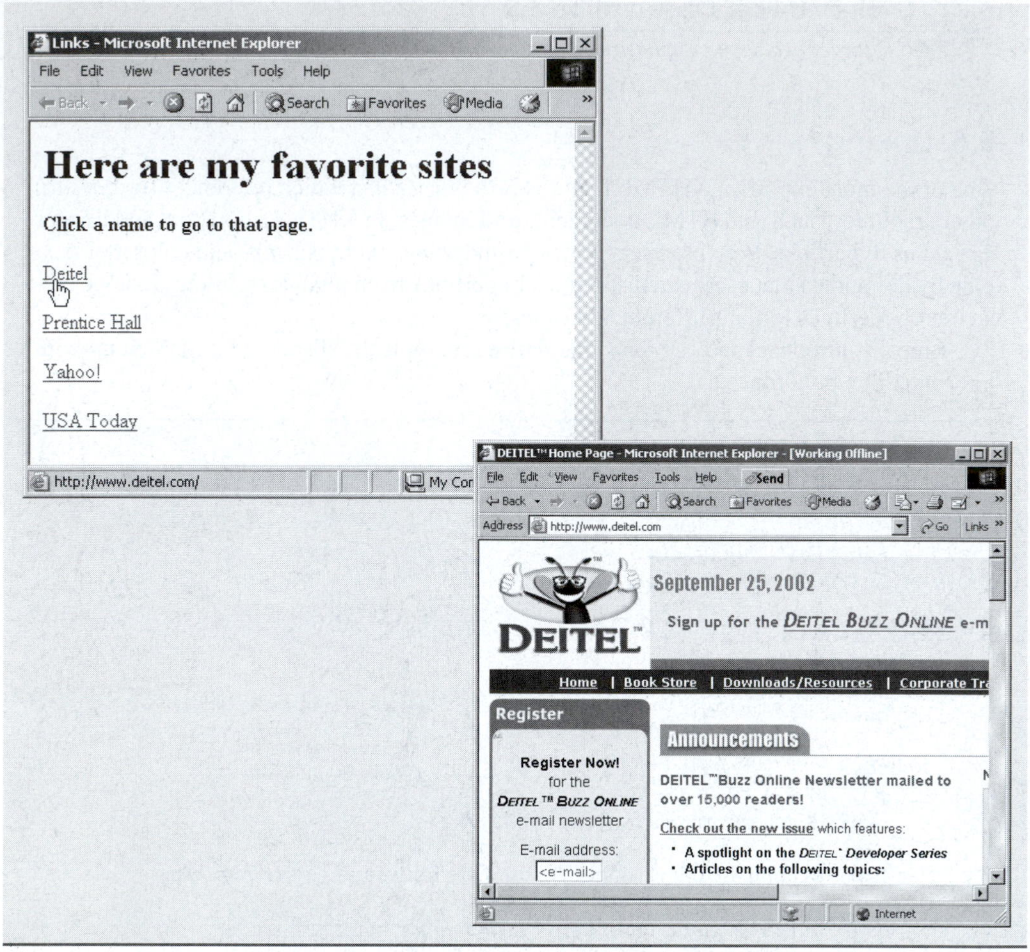

Fig. E.5 Linking to other Web pages. (Part 2 of 2.)

Links are created with the `a` (*anchor*) *element*. Line 21 defines a hyperlink that links the text `Deitel` to the URL assigned to attribute *`href`*, which specifies the location of a linked resource, such as a Web page, a file or an e-mail address. This particular anchor element links to a Web page located at `http://www.deitel.com`. When a URL does not indicate a specific document on the Web site, the Web server returns a default Web page. This page often is called `index.html`; however, most Web servers can be configured to to use any file as the default Web page for the site. (Open `http://www.deitel.com` in one browser window and `http://www.deitel.com/index.html` in a second browser window to confirm that they are identical.) If the Web server cannot locate a requested document, the server returns an error indication to the Web browser, and the browser displays an error message to the user.

Anchors can link to e-mail addresses through a *`mailto:`* URL. When someone clicks this type of anchored link, most browsers launch the default e-mail program (e.g., Outlook Express) to enable the user to write an e-mail message to the linked address. Figure E.6 demonstrates this type of anchor.

```
1  <?xml version = "1.0"?>
2  <!DOCTYPE html PUBLIC "-//W3C//DTD XHTML 1.0 Strict//EN"
3     "http://www.w3.org/TR/xhtml1/DTD/xhtml1-strict.dtd">
4
5  <!-- Fig. E.6: contact.html   -->
6  <!-- Adding email hyperlinks. -->
7
8  <html xmlns = "http://www.w3.org/1999/xhtml">
9     <head>
10       <title>Contact Page</title>
11       </title>
12    </head>
13
14    <body>
15
16       <p>My email address is
17          <a href = "mailto:deitel@deitel.com">
18             deitel@deitel.com
19          </a>
20          . Click the address and your browser will
21          open an e-mail message and address it to me.
22       </p>
23    </body>
24 </html>
```

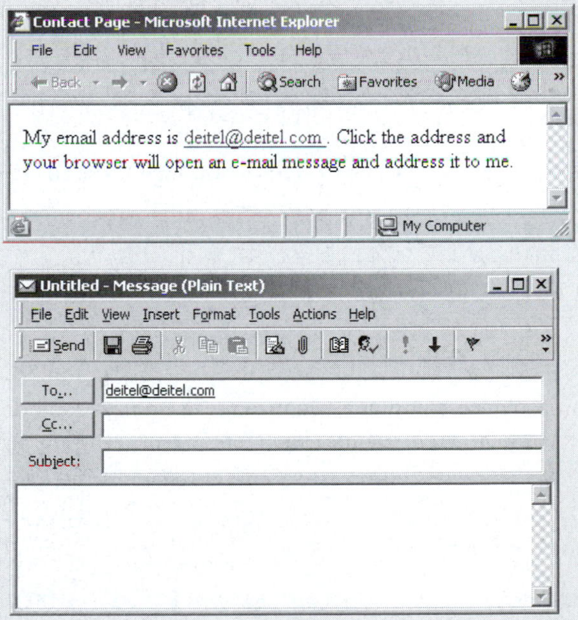

Fig. E.6 Linking to an e-mail address.

Lines 17–19 contain an e-mail link. The form of an e-mail anchor is `<a href = "mailto:`*emailaddress*`">...</a>`. In this case, we link to the e-mail address `deitel@deitel.com`.

E.7 Images

The examples discussed so far demonstrated how to mark up documents that contain only text. However, most Web pages contain both text and images. In fact, images are an equal and essential part of Web-page design. The two most popular image formats used by Web developers are Graphics Interchange Format (GIF) and Joint Photographic Experts Group (JPEG) images. Users can create images through specialized pieces of software, such as Adobe PhotoShop Elements and Jasc Paint Shop Pro (`www.jasc.com`). Images may also be acquired from various Web sites, such as `gallery.yahoo.com`. Figure E.7 demonstrates how to incorporate images into Web pages.

Lines 16–17 use an *`img`* element to insert an image in the document. The image file's location is specified with the `img` element's *`src`* attribute. In this case, the image is located in the same directory as this XHTML document, so only the image's file name is required. Optional attributes *`width`* and *`height`* specify the image's width and height, respectively. The document author can scale an image by increasing or decreasing the values of the image `width` and `height` attributes. If these attributes are omitted, the browser uses the image's actual width and height. Images are measured in *pixels* ("picture elements"), which represent dots of color on the screen. The image in Fig. E.7 is `300` pixels wide and `300` pixels high.

Good Programming Practice E.5

Always include the `width` and the `height` of an image inside the `<img>` tag. When the browser loads the XHTML file, it will know immediately from these attributes how much screen space to provide for the image and will lay out the page properly, even before it downloads the image.

```
1  <?xml version = "1.0"?>
2  <!DOCTYPE html PUBLIC "-//W3C//DTD XHTML 1.0 Strict//EN"
3     "http://www.w3.org/TR/xhtml1/DTD/xhtml1-strict.dtd">
4
5  <!-- Fig. E.7: picture.html     -->
6  <!-- Adding images with XHTML. -->
7
8  <html xmlns = "http://www.w3.org/1999/xhtml">
9     <head>
10       <title>Images</title>
11    </head>
12
13    <body>
14
15       <p>
16          <img src = "pyramid.jpg" height = "300" width = "300"
17             alt = "digital art of a pyramid" />
18
19          <img src = "spaceship.jpg" height = "300" width = "300"
20             alt = "digital art of a spaceship" />
21       </p>
22
23    </body>
24 </html>
```

Fig. E.7 Placing images in XHTML files. (Part 1 of 2.)

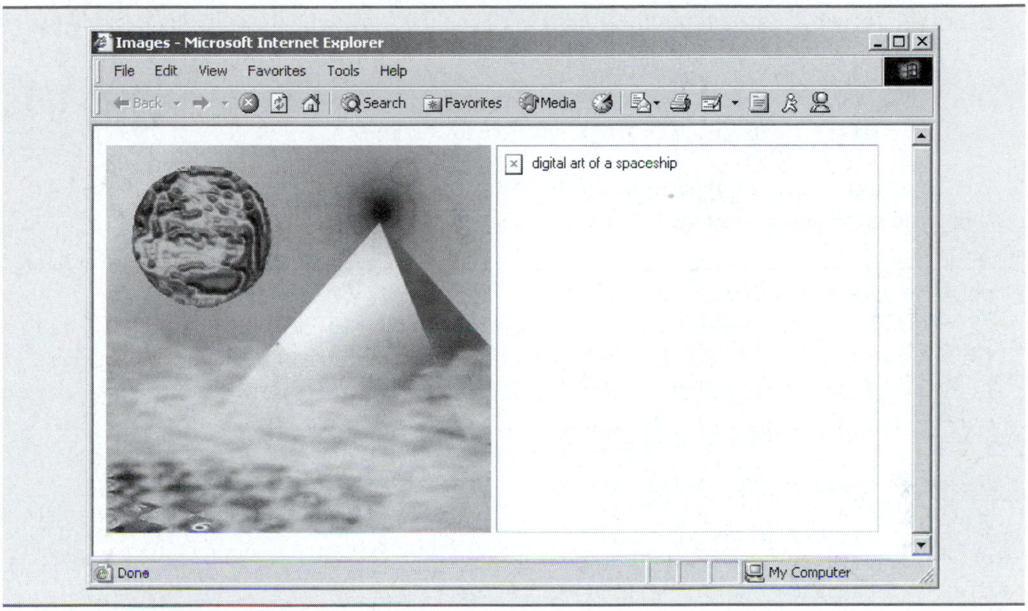

Fig. E.7 Placing images in XHTML files. (Part 2 of 2.)

Performance Tip E.1

Including the width *and* height *attributes in an* <img> *tag will help the browser load and render pages faster.*

Common Programming Error E.4

Entering new dimensions for an image that change its inherent width-to-height ratio distorts the appearance of the image. For example, if your image is 200 pixels wide and 100 pixels high, you should ensure that any new dimensions have a 2:1 width-to-height ratio.

Every img element in an XHTML document has an alt attribute. If a browser cannot render an image, the browser displays the alt attribute's value. A browser might not be able to render an image for several reasons. It might not support images—as is the case with a *text-based browser* (i.e., a browser that can display only text)—or the client might have disabled image viewing to reduce download time. Figure E.7 shows Internet Explorer rendering the alt attribute's value when a document references a nonexistent image file (spaceship.jpg).

The alt attribute is important for creating *accessible* Web pages for users with disabilities, especially those with vision impairments and text-based browsers. Specialized software called *speech synthesizers* often are used by people with disabilities. These software applications "speak" the alt attribute's value so that the user knows what the browser is displaying.

Some XHTML elements (called *empty elements*) contain only attributes and do not mark up text (i.e., text is not placed between the start and end tags). Empty elements (e.g., img) must be terminated, either by using the *forward slash character* (/) inside the closing right angle bracket (>) of the start tag or by explicitly including the end tag. When using the forward slash character, we add a space before the forward slash to improve readability (as shown at the ends of lines 17 and 20). Rather than using the forward slash character, lines 19–20 could be written with a closing </img> tag as follows:

```
<img src = "spaceship.jpg" height = "300" width = "300"
   alt = "digital art of a spaceship"></img>
```

By using images as hyperlinks, Web developers can create graphical Web pages that link to other resources. In Fig. E.8, we create six different image hyperlinks.

```
<?xml version = "1.0"?>
<!DOCTYPE html PUBLIC "-//W3C//DTD XHTML 1.0 Strict//EN"
   "http://www.w3.org/TR/xhtml1/DTD/xhtml1-strict.dtd">

<!-- Fig. E.8: nav.html                -->
<!-- Using images as link anchors. -->

<html xmlns = "http://www.w3.org/1999/xhtml">
   <head>
      <title>Navigation Bar
      </title>
   </head>

   <body>

      <p>
         <a href = "links.html">
            <img src = "buttons/links.jpg" width = "65"
               height = "50" alt = "Links Page" />
         </a><br />

         <a href = "list.html">
            <img src = "buttons/list.jpg" width = "65"
               height = "50" alt = "List Example Page" />
         </a><br />

         <a href = "contact.html">
            <img src = "buttons/contact.jpg" width = "65"
               height = "50" alt = "Contact Page" />
         </a><br />

         <a href = "header.html">
            <img src = "buttons/header.jpg" width = "65"
               height = "50" alt = "Header Page" />
         </a><br />

         <a href = "table.html">
            <img src = "buttons/table.jpg" width = "65"
               height = "50" alt = "Table Page" />
         </a><br />

         <a href = "form.html">
            <img src = "buttons/form.jpg" width = "65"
```

Fig. E.8 Using images as link anchors. (Part 1 of 2.)

```
44                    height = "50" alt = "Feedback Form" />
45                </a><br />
46            </p>
47
48        </body>
49    </html>
```

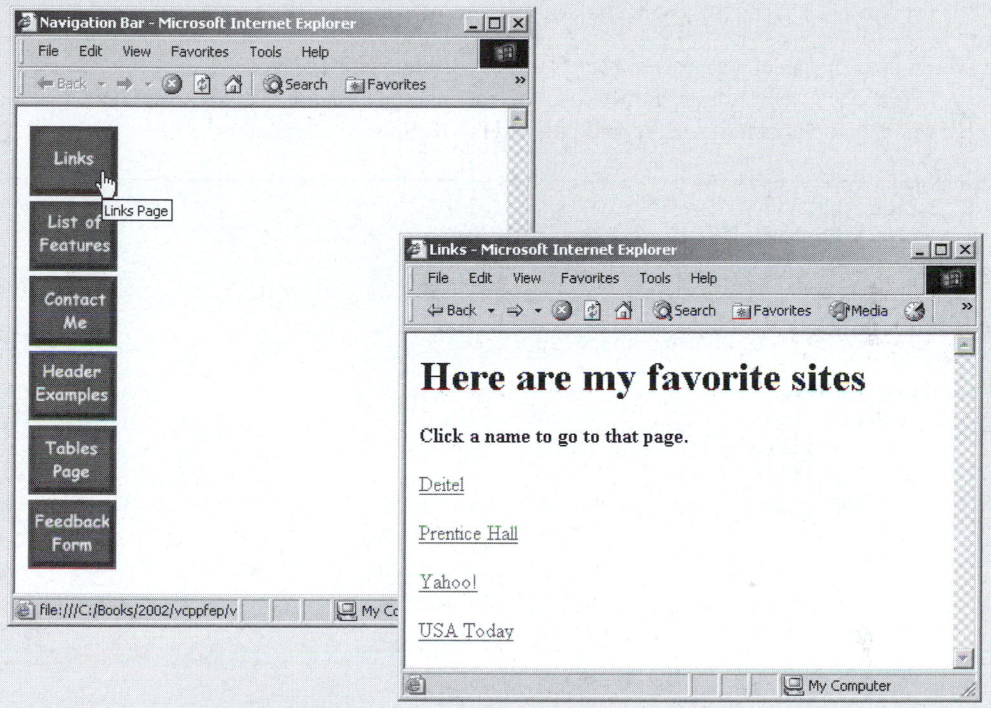

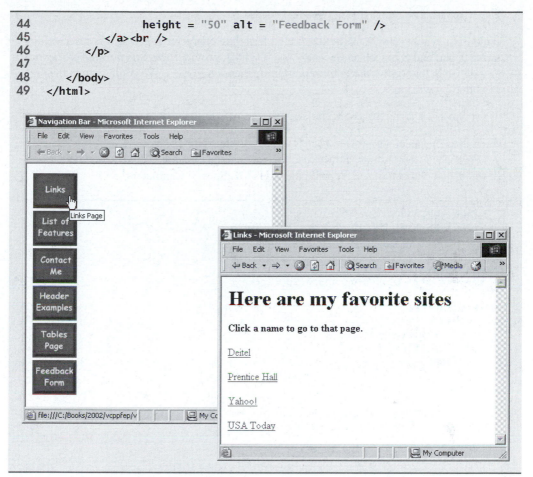

Fig. E.8 Using images as link anchors. (Part 2 of 2.)

Lines 17–20 create an *image hyperlink* by nesting an `img` element within an anchor (`a`) element. The value of the `img` element's `src` attribute value specifies that this image (`links.jpg`) resides in a directory named `buttons`. The `buttons` directory and the XHTML document are in the same directory. Images from other Web documents also can be referenced (after obtaining permission from the document's owner) by setting the `src` attribute to the name and location of the image.

In line 20, we introduce the ***br** element*, which most browsers render as a *line break*. Any markup or text following a `br` element is rendered on the next line. Like the `img` element, `br` is an example of an empty element terminated with a forward slash. We add a space before the forward slash to enhance readability.

E.8 Special Characters and More Line Breaks

When marking up text, certain characters or symbols (e.g., <) may be difficult to embed directly into an XHTML document. Some keyboards may not provide these symbols, or the presence of these symbols may cause syntax errors. For example, the markup

```
<p>if x < 10 then increment x by 1</p>
```

results in a syntax error, because it uses the less-than character (<), which is reserved for start tags and end tags such as <p> and </p>. XHTML provides *special characters* or *entity references* (in the form &*code*;) for representing these characters. We could correct the previous line by writing

```
<p>if x &lt; 10 then increment x by 1</p>
```

which uses the special character *<* for the less-than symbol.

Figure E.9 demonstrates how to use special characters in an XHTML document. For a list of special characters, see Appendix G, XHTML Special Characters.

```
<?xml version = "1.0"?>
<!DOCTYPE html PUBLIC "-//W3C//DTD XHTML 1.0 Strict//EN"
   "http://www.w3.org/TR/xhtml1/DTD/xhtml1-strict.dtd">

<!-- Fig. E.9: contact2.html        -->
<!-- Inserting special characters. -->

<html xmlns = "http://www.w3.org/1999/xhtml">
   <head>
      <title>Contact Page
      </title>
   </head>

   <body>

      <!-- special characters are    -->
      <!-- entered using form &code; -->
      <p>
         Click
         <a href = "mailto:deitel@deitel.com">here
         </a> to open an e-mail message addressed to
         deitel@deitel.com.
      </p>

      <hr /> <!-- inserts a horizontal rule -->

      <p>All information on this site is <strong>&copy;</strong>
         Deitel <strong>&amp;</strong> Associates, Inc. 2003.</p>

      <!-- to strike through text use <del> tags   -->
      <!-- to subscript text use <sub> tags        -->
      <!-- to superscript text use <sup> tags      -->
      <!-- these tags are nested inside other tags -->
      <p><del>You may download 3.14 x 10<sup>2</sup>
         characters worth of information from this site.</del>
         Only <sub>one</sub> download per hour is permitted.</p>

      <p>Note: <strong>&lt; &frac14;</strong> of the information
         presented here is updated daily.</p>
```

Fig. E.9 Inserting special characters into XHTML. (Part 1 of 2.)

```
40
41      </body>
42   </html>
```

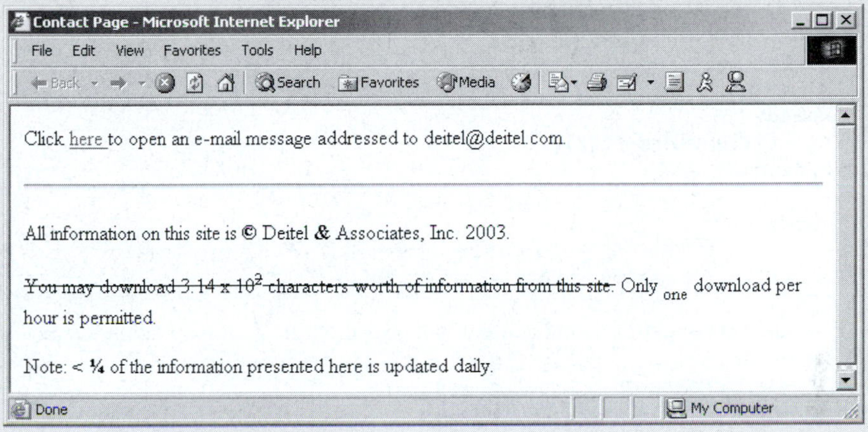

Fig. E.9 Inserting special characters into XHTML. (Part 2 of 2.)

Lines 27–28 contain other special characters, which are expressed as either word abbreviations (e.g., `amp` for ampersand and `copy` for copyright) or *hexadecimal (hex)* values (e.g., `&` is the hexadecimal representation of `&`). Hexadecimal numbers are base-16 numbers—digits in a hexadecimal number have values from 0 to 15 (a total of 16 different values). The letters A–F represent the hexadecimal digits corresponding to decimal values 10–15. Thus, in hexadecimal notation we can have numbers like 876 consisting solely of decimal-like digits, numbers like DA19F consisting of digits and letters, and numbers like DCB consisting solely of letters. We discuss hexadecimal numbers in detail in Appendix B, Number Systems.

In lines 34–36, we introduce three new elements. Most browsers render the *`del`* element as strike-through text. With this format, users can easily indicate document revisions. To *superscript* text (i.e., raise text on a line with a decreased font size) or *subscript* text (i.e., lower text on a line with a decreased font size), use the *`sup`* and *`sub`* elements, respectively. We also use special characters `<` for a less-than sign and *`¼`* for the fraction 1/4 (line 38).

In addition to special characters, this document introduces a *horizontal rule*, indicated by the *`<hr />`* tag in line 25. Most browsers render a horizontal rule as a horizontal line. The `<hr />` tag also inserts a line break above and below the horizontal line.

E.9 Unordered Lists

Up to this point, we have presented basic XHTML elements and attributes for linking to resources, creating headers, using special characters and incorporating images. In this section, we discuss how to organize information on a Web page using lists. In Appendix F, Introduction to XHTML: Part 2, we introduce another feature for organizing information, called a table. Figure E.10 displays text in an *unordered list* (i.e., a list that does not order

```
<?xml version = "1.0"?>
<!DOCTYPE html PUBLIC "-//W3C//DTD XHTML 1.0 Strict//EN"
   "http://www.w3.org/TR/xhtml1/DTD/xhtml1-strict.dtd">

<!-- Fig. E.10: links2.html                  -->
<!-- Unordered list containing hyperlinks. -->

<html xmlns = "http://www.w3.org/1999/xhtml">
   <head>
      <title>Links</title>
   </head>

   <body>

      <h1>Here are my favorite sites</h1>

      <p><strong>Click on a name to go to that page.</strong></p>

      <!-- create an unordered list -->
      <ul>

         <!-- add four list items -->
         <li><a href = "http://www.deitel.com">Deitel</a></li>

         <li><a href = "http://www.w3.org">W3C</a></li>

         <li><a href = "http://www.yahoo.com">Yahoo!</a></li>

         <li><a href = "http://www.cnn.com">CNN</a></li>

       </ul>

   </body>
</html>
```

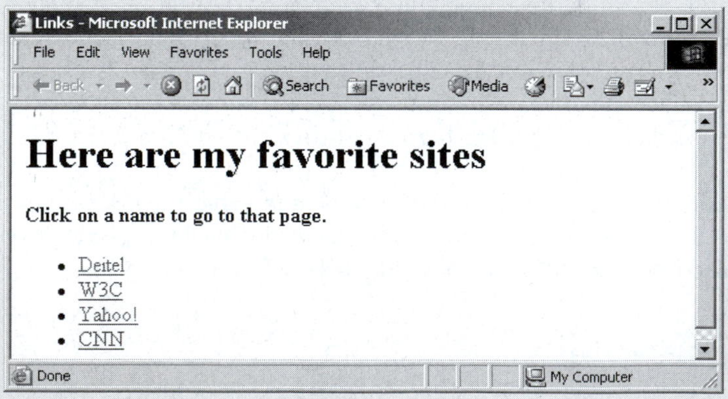

Fig. E.10 Unordered lists in XHTML.

its items by letter or number). The *unordered list element* `ul` creates a list in which each item begins with a bullet symbol (called a *disc*).

Each entry in an unordered list (element *ul* in line 20) is an *li* (*list item*) element (lines 23, 25, 27 and 29). Most Web browsers render these elements with a line break and a bullet symbol indented from the beginning of the new line.

E.10 Nested and Ordered Lists

Lists may be nested to represent hierarchical relationships, as in an outline format. Figure E.11 demonstrates nested lists and *ordered lists* (i.e., list that order their items by letter or number).

The first ordered list begins in line 33. Attribute *type* specifies the *sequence type* (i.e., the set of numbers or letters used in the ordered list). In this case, setting type to "I" specifies upper-case roman numerals. Line 47 begins the second ordered list and sets attribute type to "a", specifying lowercase letters for the list items. The last ordered list (lines 71–75) does not use attribute type. By default, the list's items are enumerated from one to three.

A Web browser indents each nested list to indicate a hierarchal relationship. By default, the items in the outermost unordered list (line 18) are preceded by discs. List items nested inside the unordered list of line 18 are preceded by *circles*. Although not demonstrated in this example, subsequent nested list items are preceded by *squares*. Unordered list items may be explicitly set to discs, circles or squares by setting the ul element's type attribute to *"disc"*, *"circle"* or *"square"*, respectively.

```
1   <?xml version = "1.0"?>
2   <!DOCTYPE html PUBLIC "-//W3C//DTD XHTML 1.0 Transitional//EN"
3      "http://www.w3.org/TR/xhtml1/DTD/xhtml1-transitional.dtd">
4
5   <!-- Fig. E.11: list.html                   -->
6   <!-- Advanced Lists: nested and ordered. -->
7
8   <html xmlns = "http://www.w3.org/1999/xhtml">
9      <head>
10        <title>Lists</title>
11     </head>
12
13     <body>
14
15        <h1>The Best Features of the Internet</h1>
16
17        <!-- create an unordered list -->
18        <ul>
19           <li>You can meet new people from countries around
20              the world.</li>
21
22           <li>
23              You have access to new media as it becomes public:
24
25              <!-- start nested list, use modified bullets -->
26              <!-- list ends with closing </ul> tag        -->
27              <ul>
28                 <li>New games</li>
```

Fig. E.11 Nested and ordered lists in XHTML. (Part 1 of 3.)

```
               <li>
                  New applications

                  <!-- ordered nested list -->
                  <ol type = "I">
                     <li>For business</li>
                     <li>For pleasure</li>
                  </ol>

               </li>

               <li>Around the clock news</li>
               <li>Search engines</li>
               <li>Shopping</li>
               <li>
                  Programming

                  <!-- another nested ordered list -->
                  <ol type = "a">
                     <li>XML</li>
                     <li>Visual C++</li>
                     <li>XHTML</li>
                     <li>Scripts</li>
                     <li>New languages</li>
                  </ol>

               </li>

            </ul> <!-- ends nested list started in line 27 -->

         </li>

         <li>Links</li>
         <li>Keeping in touch with old friends</li>
         <li>It is the technology of the future!</li>

      </ul>   <!-- ends unordered list started in line 18 -->

      <h1>My 3 Favorite <em>CEOs</em></h1>

      <!-- ol elements without type attribute have -->
      <!-- numeric sequence type (i.e., 1, 2, ...) -->
      <ol>
         <li>Ant Chovy</li>
         <li>CeCe Sharp</li>
         <li>Albert Antstein</li>
      </ol>

   </body>
</html>
```

Fig. E.11 Nested and ordered lists in XHTML. (Part 2 of 3.)

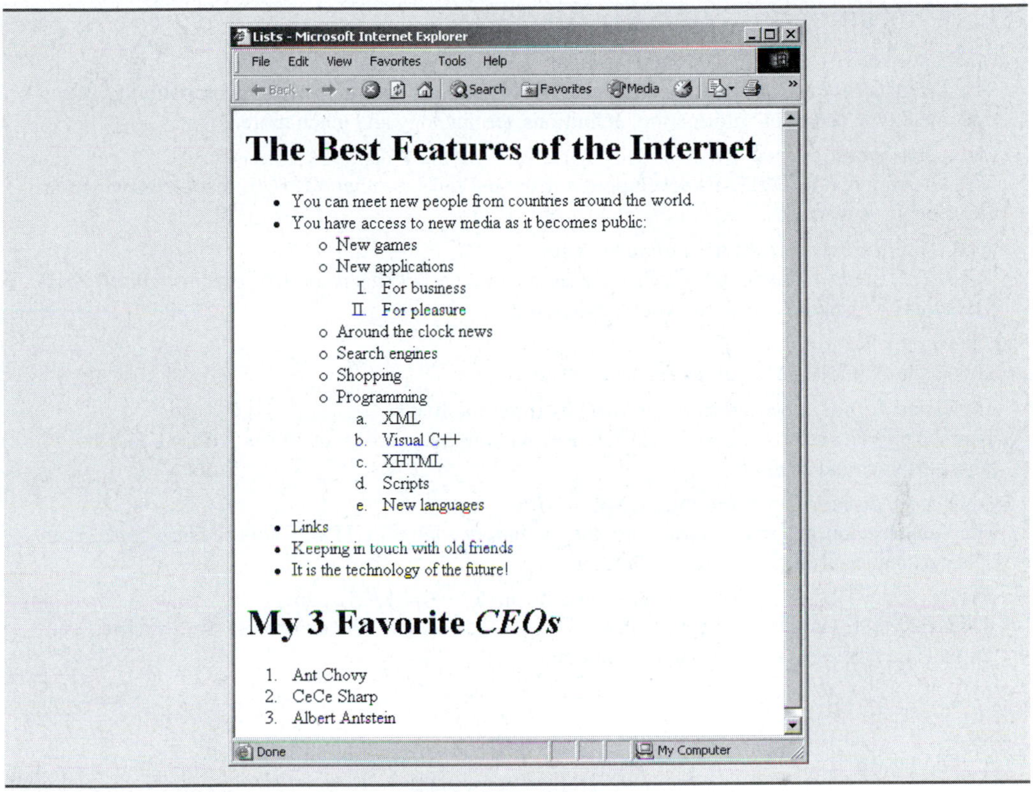

Fig. E.11 Nested and ordered lists in XHTML. (Part 3 of 3.)

[*Note:* XHTML is based on HTML (HyperText Markup Language)—a legacy technology of the World Wide Web Consortium (W3C).] In HTML, it was common to specify the document's content, structure and formatting. Formatting might specify where the browser places an element in a Web page or the fonts and colors used to display an element. The so-called *strict* form of XHTML allows only a document's content and structure to appear in a valid XHTML document, and not that document's formatting. Our first several examples used only the strict form of XHTML. In fact, the purpose of lines 2–3 in each of the examples before Fig. E.11 was to indicate to the browser that each document conformed to the strict XHTML definition. This enables the browser to confirm that the document is valid. There are other XHTML document types as well. This particular example uses the XHTML *transitional* document type. This document type exists to enable XHTML document creators to use legacy HTML technologies in an XHTML document. In this example, the `type` attribute of the `ol` element (lines 33 and 47) is a legacy HTML technology. Changing lines 2–3, as shown in this example, enables us to demonstrate ordered lists with different numbering formats. Normally, such formatting is specified with style sheets. Most examples in this book adhere to strict HTML form.

Error-Prevention Tip E.2

Most current browsers attempt to render XHTML documents, even if they are invalid.

E.11 Internet and Web Resources

`www.w3.org/TR/xhtml1`

The *XHTML 1.0 Recommendation* contains XHTML 1.0 general information, compatibility issues, document type definition information, definitions, terminology and much more.

`www.xhtml.org`

XHTML.org provides XHTML development news and links to other XHTML resources, which include books and articles.

`www.w3schools.com/xhtml/default.asp`

The *XHTML School* provides XHTML quizzes and references. This page also contains links to XHTML syntax, validation and document type definitions.

`validator.w3.org`

This is the W3C XHTML validation-service site.

`hotwired.lycos.com/webmonkey/00/50/index2a.html`

This site provides an article about XHTML. Key sections of the article overview XHTML and discuss tags, attributes and anchors.

`wdvl.com/Authoring/Languages/XML/XHTML`

The Web Developers Virtual Library provides an introduction to XHTML. This site also contains articles, examples and links to other technologies.

`www.w3.org/TR/1999/xhtml-modularization-19990406/DTD/doc`

The XHTML 1.0 DTD documentation site provides links to DTD documentation for the strict, transitional and frameset document-type definitions.

SUMMARY

- XHTML (Extensible Hypertext Markup Language) is a markup language for creating Web pages.
- In XHTML, text is marked up with elements, delimited by tags that are names contained in pairs of angle brackets.
- Some elements may contain additional markup called attributes, which provide additional information about the element.
- A key issue when using XHTML is the separation of the presentation of a document (i.e., the document's appearance when rendered by a browser) from the structure of the information in the document.
- A machine that runs specialized piece of software called a Web server stores XHTML documents.
- Validation services (e.g., `validator.w3.org`) ensure that an XHTML document is syntactically correct.
- XHTML documents that are syntactically correct are guaranteed to render properly. XHTML documents that contain syntax errors may not display properly.
- Every XHTML document contains a start `<html>` tag and an end `</html>` tag.
- Comments in XHTML always begin with `<!--` and end with `-->`. The browser ignores all text inside a comment.
- Every XHTML document has a `head` element, which generally contains information, such as a title, and a `body` element, which contains the page content.
- Information in the `head` element generally is not rendered in the display window, but it could be made available to the user through other means.

- The `title` element names a Web page. The title usually appears in the colored bar (called the title bar) at the top of the browser window and also appears as the text identifying a page when users add your page to their list of **Favorites** or **Bookmarks**.
- The body of an XHTML document is the area in which the document's content is placed. The content may include text and tags.
- All text placed between the <p> and </p> tags forms one paragraph.
- The `<strong>` tag renders text in a bold font.
- XHTML provides six headers (`h1` through `h6`) for specifying the relative importance of information.
- Header element `h1` is considered the most significant header and is rendered in a larger font than the other five headers. Each successive header element (i.e., `h2`, `h3`, etc.) is rendered in a smaller font.
- Users can insert links with the `a` (anchor) element. The most important attribute for the `a` element is `href`, which specifies the resource (e.g., page, file or e-mail address) being linked.
- Web browsers typically underline text hyperlinks and color them blue by default.
- Anchors can link to an e-mail address, using a `mailto` URL. When someone clicks this type of anchored link, most browsers launch the default e-mail program (e.g., Outlook Express) to initiate an e-mail message to the linked address.
- The `img` element's `src` attribute specifies an image's location.
- Optional attributes `width` and `height` specify the image width and height, respectively.
- Images are measured in pixels ("picture elements"), which represent dots of color on the screen.
- Every `img` element in a valid XHTML document must have an `alt` attribute, which contains text that is displayed if the client cannot render the image.
- The `alt` attribute makes Web pages more accessible to users with disabilities, especially those with vision impairments.
- Some XHTML elements are empty elements that contain only attributes and do not mark up text.
- Empty elements (e.g., `img`) must be terminated, either by using the forward slash character (`/`) or by explicitly writing an end tag.
- The `br` element causes most browsers to render a line break. Any markup or text following a `br` element is rendered on the next line.
- XHTML provides special characters or entity references (in the form &*code*;) for representing characters that cannot be marked up. For example, the special character `<` represents the less-than symbol.
- Most browsers render a horizontal rule, indicated by the `<hr />` tag, as a horizontal line. The `hr` element also inserts a line break above and below the horizontal line.
- The unordered list element `ul` creates a list in which each item in the list begins with a bullet symbol (called a disc).
- Each entry in an unordered list is an `li` (list item) element. Most Web browsers render these elements with a line break and a bullet symbol at the beginning of the line.
- Lists may be nested to represent hierarchical data relationships. Attribute `type` specifies the sequence type (i.e., the set of numbers or letters used in the ordered list).

7

Introduction to XHTML: Part 2

Objectives

- To create tables with rows and columns of data.
- To control table formatting.
- To create and use forms.
- To create and use image maps to aid in Web-page navigation.
- To make Web pages accessible to search engines through `<meta>` tags.
- To use the `frameset` element to display multiple Web pages in a single browser window.

Yea, from the table of my memory
I'll wipe away all trivial fond records.
William Shakespeare

Outline

F.1 Introduction

In the previous appendix, we introduced XHTML. We built several complete Web pages featuring text, hyperlinks, images, horizontal rules and line breaks. In this appendix, we discuss more substantial XHTML features, including presentation of information in *tables* and *incorporating forms* for collecting information from a Web-page visitor. We also introduce *internal linking* and *image maps* for enhancing Web-page navigation and *frames* for displaying multiple documents in the browser. By the end of this appendix, you will be familiar with the most commonly used XHTML features and will be able to create more complex Web documents. In this appendix, we do not present any MC++ programming.

F.2 Basic XHTML Tables

This section presents the XHTML *table*—a frequently used feature that organizes data into rows and columns. Our first example (Fig. F.1) uses a table with six rows and two columns to display price information for fruit.

```
<?xml version = "1.0"?>
<!DOCTYPE html PUBLIC "-//W3C//DTD XHTML 1.0 Strict//EN"
   "http://www.w3.org/TR/xhtml1/DTD/xhtml1-strict.dtd">

<!-- Fig. F.1: table1.html    -->
<!-- Creating a basic table. -->

<html xmlns = "http://www.w3.org/1999/xhtml">
   <head>
      <title>A simple XHTML table</title>
   </head>
```

Fig. F.1 XHTML table. (Part 1 of 3.)

```

   <body>

      <!-- the <table> tag begins table -->
      <table border = "1" width = "40%"
         summary = "This table provides information about
            the price of fruit">

         <!-- <caption> tag summarizes table's   -->
         <!-- contents to help visually impaired -->
         <caption><strong>Price of Fruit</strong></caption>

         <!-- <thead> is first section of table -->
         <!-- it formats table header area      -->
         <thead>
            <tr> <!-- <tr> inserts one table row -->
               <th>Fruit</th> <!-- insert heading cell -->
               <th>Price</th>
            </tr>
         </thead>

         <!-- all table content is enclosed within <tbody> -->
         <tbody>
            <tr>
               <td>Apple</td> <!-- insert data cell -->
               <td>$0.25</td>
            </tr>

            <tr>
               <td>Orange</td>
               <td>$0.50</td>
            </tr>

            <tr>
               <td>Banana</td>
               <td>$1.00</td>
            </tr>

            <tr>
               <td>Pineapple</td>
               <td>$2.00</td>
            </tr>
         </tbody>

         <!-- <tfoot> is last section of table -->
         <!-- it formats table footer          -->
         <tfoot>
            <tr>
               <th>Total</th>
               <th>$3.75</th>
            </tr>
         </tfoot>

```

Fig. F.1 XHTML table. (Part 2 of 3.)

```
65          </table>
66
67       </body>
68    </html>
```

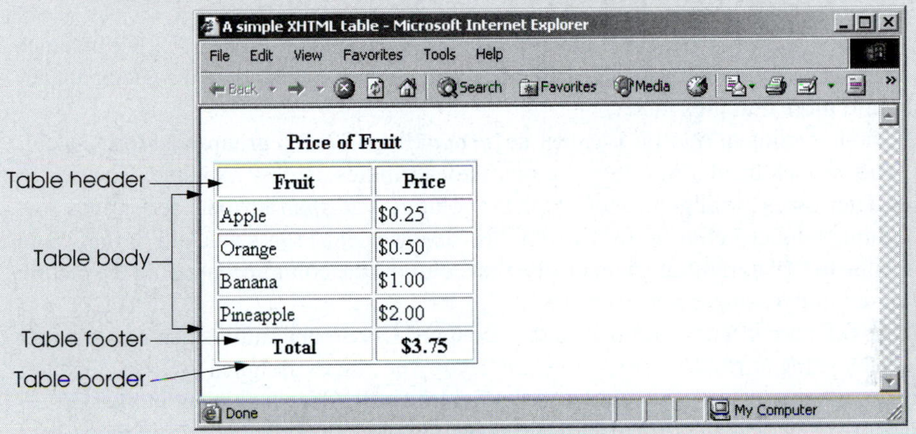

Fig. F.1 XHTML table. (Part 3 of 3.)

Tables are defined with the `table` element. Lines 16–18 specify the start tag for a table element that has several attributes. The ***border*** attribute specifies the table's border width in pixels. To create a table without a border, set `border` to `"0"`. This example assigns attribute `width` `"40%"`, to set the table's width to 40 percent of the browser's width. A developer can also set attribute `width` to a specified number of pixels.

Error-Prevention Tip F.1

Try resizing the browser window to see how the width of the window affects the width of the table.

As its name implies, attribute ***summary*** (line 17) describes the table's contents. Speech devices use this attribute to make the table more accessible to users with visual impairments. The ***caption*** element (line 22) describes the table's content and helps text-based browsers interpret the table data. Text inside the `<caption>` tag is rendered above the table by most browsers. Attribute `summary` and element `caption` are two of many XHTML features that make Web pages more accessible to users with disabilities.

A table has three distinct sections—*head*, *body* and *foot*. The head section (or *header cell*) is defined with a ***thead*** element (lines 26–31), which contains header information, such as column names. Each ***tr*** element (lines 27–30) defines an individual *table row*. The columns in the head section are defined with `th` elements. Most browsers center text formatted by `th` (table header column) elements and display it in bold. Table header elements are nested inside table row elements.

The body section, or *table body*, contains the table's primary data. The table body (lines 34–54) is defined in a `tbody` element. *Data cells* contain individual pieces of data and are defined with `td` (*table data*) elements.

The foot section (lines 58–63) is defined with a *tfoot* (table foot) element and represents a footer. Text commonly placed in the footer includes calculation results and footnotes. Like other sections, the foot section can contain table rows and each row can contain columns.

F.3 Intermediate XHTML Tables and Formatting

In the previous section, we explored the structure of a basic table. In Fig. F.2, we enhance our discussion of tables by introducing elements and attributes that allow the document author to build more complex tables.

The table begins in line 17. Element *colgroup* (lines 22–27) groups and formats columns. The *col* element (line 26) specifies two attributes in this example. The *align* attribute determines the alignment of text in the column. The *span* attribute determines how many columns the *col* element formats. In this case, we set `align`'s value to `"right"` and `span`'s value to `"1"` to right-align text in the first column (the column containing the picture of the camel in the sample screen capture).

Table cells are sized to fit the data they contain. Document authors can create larger data cells by using attributes *rowspan* and *colspan*. The values assigned to these attributes specify the number of rows or columns occupied by a cell. The `th` element in lines 36–39 uses the attribute `rowspan = "2"` to allow the cell containing the picture of the python to use two vertically adjacent cells (thus, the cell *spans* two rows). The `th` element in lines 42–45 uses the attribute `colspan = "4"` to widen the header cell (containing `Python comparison` and `Approximate as of 12/2001`) to span four cells.

```
1  <?xml version = "1.0"?>
2  <!DOCTYPE html PUBLIC "-//W3C//DTD XHTML 1.0 Strict//EN"
3     "http://www.w3.org/TR/xhtml1/DTD/xhtml1-strict.dtd">
4
5  <!-- Fig. F.2: table2.html      -->
6  <!-- Intermediate table design. -->
7
8  <html xmlns = "http://www.w3.org/1999/xhtml">
9     <head>
10       <title>Tables</title>
11    </head>
12
13    <body>
14
15       <h1>Table Example Page</h1>
16
17       <table border = "1">
18          <caption>Here is a more complex sample table.</caption>
19
20          <!-- <colgroup> and <col> tags are used to -->
21          <!-- format entire columns                 -->
22          <colgroup>
23
```

Fig. F.2 Complex XHTML table. (Part 1 of 3.)

```
            <!-- span attribute determines how many columns -->
            <!-- the <col> tag affects                      -->
            <col align = "right" span = "1" />
         </colgroup>

         <thead>

            <!-- rowspans and colspans merge the specified    -->
            <!-- number of cells vertically or horizontally   -->
            <tr>

               <!-- merge two rows -->
               <th rowspan = "2">
                  <img src = "snake.gif" width = "220"
                     height = "100" alt = "python picture" />
               </th>

               <!-- merge four columns -->
               <th colspan = "4" valign = "top">
                  <h1>Python comparison</h1><br />
                  <p>Approximate as of 12/2001</p>
               </th>
            </tr>

            <tr valign = "bottom">
               <th>Average Length (Feet)</th>
               <th>Indigenous region</th>
               <th>Arboreal?</th>
            </tr>

         </thead>

         <tbody>

            <tr>
               <th>Indian Python</th>
               <td>20</td>
               <td>southeast Asia</td>
               <td rowspan = "2">Indian Python</td>
            </tr>

            <tr>
               <th>Royal Python</th>
               <td>4</td>
               <td>equatorial West Africa</td>
            </tr>

         </tbody>

      </table>

   </body>
</html>
```

Fig. F.2 Complex XHTML table. (Part 2 of 3.)

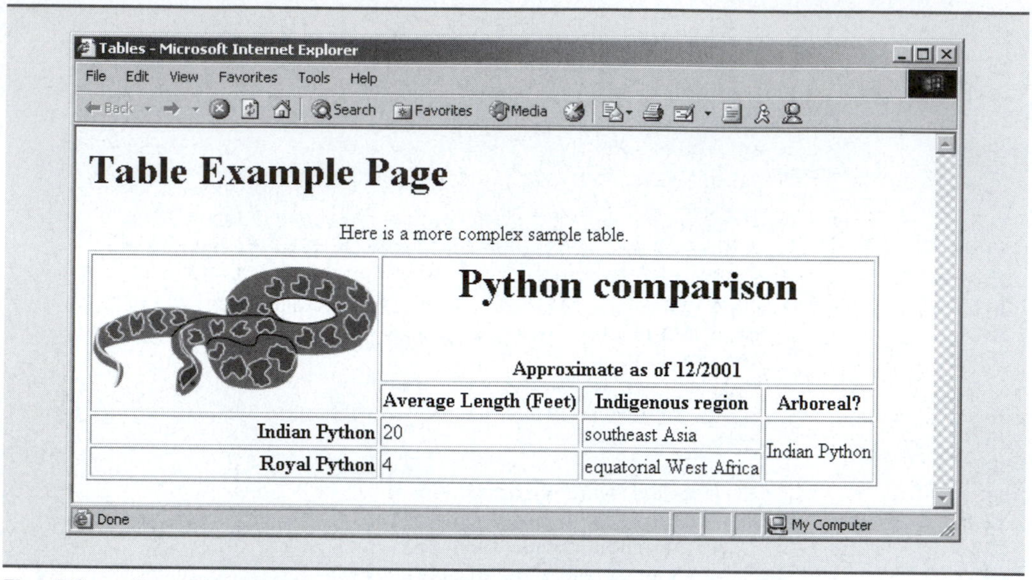

Fig. F.2 Complex XHTML table. (Part 3 of 3.)

Common Programming Error F.1

When using `colspan` *and* `rowspan` *to adjust the size of table data cells, keep in mind that the modified cells will occupy more than one column or row; other rows or columns of the table must compensate for the extra rows or columns spanned by individual cells. If you do not, the formatting of your table will be distorted, and you could inadvertently create more columns and rows than you originally intended.*

Line 42 introduces attribute `valign`, which aligns data vertically and may be assigned one of four values—`"top"` aligns data with the top of the cell, `"middle"` vertically centers data (the default for all data and header cells), `"bottom"` aligns data with the bottom of the cell and `"baseline"` ignores the fonts used for the row data and sets the bottom of all text in the row on a common *baseline* (i.e., the horizontal line to which each character in a word is aligned).

F.4 Basic XHTML Forms

When browsing Web sites, users often need to provide information such as e-mail addresses, search keywords and zip codes. XHTML provides a mechanism, called a *form*, for collecting such user information.

Data that users enter on a Web page normally is sent to a Web server that provides access to a site's resources (e.g., XHTML documents or images). These resources are located either on the same machine as the Web server or on a machine that the Web server can access through the network. When a browser requests a Web page or file that is located on a server, the server processes the request and returns the requested resource. A request contains the name and path of the desired resource and the method of communication (called a *protocol*). XHTML documents use the HyperText Transfer Protocol (HTTP).

Figure F.3 sends the form data to the Web server, which passes the form data to a *CGI* (*Common Gateway Interface*) script (i.e., a program) written in Perl, C or some other language. The script processes the data received from the Web server and typically returns information to the Web server. The Web server then sends the information in the form of an XHTML document to the Web browser. [*Note*: This example demonstrates client-side functionality. If the form is submitted (by clicking **Submit Your Entries**), an error occurs.]

Forms can contain visual and non-visual components. Visual components include clickable buttons and other graphical user interface components with which users interact. Non-visual components, called *hidden inputs*, store any data that the document author specifies, such as e-mail addresses and XHTML document file names that act as links. The form begins in line 23 with the `form` element. Attribute `method` specifies how the form's data is sent to the Web server.

```
1  <?xml version = "1.0"?>
2  <!DOCTYPE html PUBLIC "-//W3C//DTD XHTML 1.0 Strict//EN"
3     "http://www.w3.org/TR/xhtml1/DTD/xhtml1-strict.dtd">
4
5  <!-- Fig. F.3: form.html     -->
6  <!-- Form design example 1. -->
7
8  <html xmlns = "http://www.w3.org/1999/xhtml">
9     <head>
10       <title>Forms</title>
11    </head>
12
13    <body>
14
15       <h1>Feedback Form</h1>
16
17       <p>Please fill out this form to help
18          us improve our site.</p>
19
20       <!-- <form> tag begins form, gives -->
21       <!-- method of sending information -->
22       <!-- and location of form scripts  -->
23       <form method = "post" action = "/cgi-bin/formmail">
24
25          <p>
26
27             <!-- hidden inputs contain non-visual -->
28             <!-- information                      -->
29             <input type = "hidden" name = "recipient"
30                value = "deitel@deitel.com" />
31
32             <input type = "hidden" name = "subject"
33                value = "Feedback Form" />
34
35             <input type = "hidden" name = "redirect"
36                value = "main.html" />
37          </p>
38
```

Fig. F.3 Simple form with hidden fields and a textbox. (Part 1 of 2.)

```
         <!-- <input type = "text"> inserts text box -->
         <p>
            <label>Name:
               <input name = "name" type = "text" size = "25"
                  maxlength = "30" />
            </label>
         </p>

         <p>

            <!-- input types "submit" and "reset" -->
            <!-- insert buttons for submitting    -->
            <!-- and clearing form's contents     -->
            <input type = "submit" value =
               "Submit Your Entries" />

            <input type = "reset" value =
               "Clear Your Entries" />
         </p>

      </form>

   </body>
</html>
```

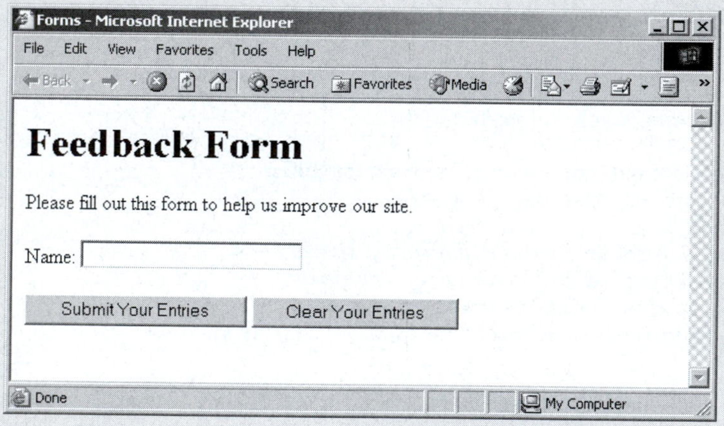

Fig. F.3 Simple form with hidden fields and a textbox. (Part 2 of 2.)

Using `method = "post"` appends form data to the browser request, which contains the protocol (i.e., HTTP) and the requested resource's URL. Scripts located on the Web server's computer (or on a computer accessible through the network) can access the form data sent as part of the request. For example, a script may take the form information and update an electronic mailing list. The other possible value, `method = "get"`, appends the form data directly to the end of the URL. For example, the URL `/cgi-bin/formmail` might have the form information `name = bob` appended to it.

The *action* attribute in the <form> tag specifies the URL of a script on the Web server; in this case, it specifies a script that e-mails form data to an address. Most Internet Service Providers (ISPs) have a script like this on their site; ask the Web-site system administrator how to set up an XHTML document to use its script correctly.

Lines 29–36 define three *input* elements that specify data to provide to the script that processes the form (also called the *form handler*). These three input elements have *type* attribute "hidden", which allows the document author to send form data that is not entered by a user to a script.

The three hidden inputs are an e-mail address to which the data will be sent, the e-mail's subject line and a URL where the browser will be redirected after submitting the form. Two other input attributes are *name*, which identifies the input element, and *value*, which provides the value that will be sent (or posted) to the Web server.

Good Programming Practice F.1

Place hidden input elements at the beginning of a form, immediately after the opening <form> tag. This placement allows document authors to locate hidden input elements quickly.

We introduce another type of input in lines 38–39. The *"text"* input inserts a *text box* into the form. Users can type data in text boxes. The *label* element (lines 37–40) provides users with information about the input element's purpose.

Common Programming Error F.2

Forgetting to include a label element for each form element is a design error. Without these labels, users cannot determine the purpose of individual form elements.

The input element's *size* attribute specifies the number of characters visible in the text box. Optional attribute *maxlength* limits the number of characters input into the text box. In this case, the user is not permitted to type more than 30 characters into the text box.

There are two types of input elements in lines 52–56. The *"submit"* input element is a button. When the user presses a "submit" button, the browser sends the data in the form to the Web server for processing. The *value attribute* sets the text displayed on the button (the default value is **Submit**). The *"reset"* input element allows a user to reset all form elements to their default values. The value attribute of the "reset" input element sets the text displayed on the button. (The default value is **Reset**.)

F.5 More Complex XHTML Forms

In the previous section, we introduced basic forms. In this section, we introduce elements and attributes for creating more complex forms. Figure F.4 contains a form that solicits user feedback about a Web site.

The *textarea* element (lines 42–44) inserts a multiline text box, called a *textarea*, into the form. The number of rows is specified with the *rows attribute* and the number of columns (i.e., characters) is specified with the *cols attribute*. In this example, the textarea is four rows high and 36 characters wide. To display default text in the text area, place the text between the <textarea> and </textarea> tags. Default text can be specified in other input types, such as textboxes, by using the value attribute.

The *"password"* input in lines 52–53 inserts a password box with the specified `size`. A password box allows users to enter sensitive information, such as credit-card numbers and passwords, by "masking" the information input with asterisks. The actual value input is sent to the Web server, not the asterisks that mask the input.

Lines 60–78 introduce the *checkbox* `form` element. Checkboxes enable users to select from a set of options. When a user selects a checkbox, a check mark appears in the check box. Otherwise, the checkbox remains empty. Each *"checkbox"* `input` creates a new checkbox. Checkboxes can be used individually or in groups. Checkboxes that belong to a group are assigned the same `name` (in this case, `"thingsliked"`).

```
1  <?xml version = "1.0"?>
2  <!DOCTYPE html PUBLIC "-//W3C//DTD XHTML 1.0 Strict//EN"
3     "http://www.w3.org/TR/xhtml1/DTD/xhtml1-strict.dtd">
4
5  <!-- Fig. F.4: form2.html   -->
6  <!-- Form design example 2. -->
7
8  <html xmlns = "http://www.w3.org/1999/xhtml">
9     <head>
10       <title>Forms</title>
11    </head>
12
13    <body>
14
15       <h1>Feedback Form</h1>
16
17       <p>Please fill out this form to help
18          us improve our site.</p>
19
20       <form method = "post" action = "/cgi-bin/formmail">
21
22          <p>
23             <input type = "hidden" name = "recipient"
24                value = "deitel@deitel.com" />
25
26             <input type = "hidden" name = "subject"
27                value = "Feedback Form" />
28
29             <input type = "hidden" name = "redirect"
30                value = "main.html" />
31          </p>
32
33          <p>
34             <label>Name:
35                <input name = "name" type = "text" size = "25" />
36             </label>
37          </p>
38
39          <!-- <textarea> creates multiline textbox -->
40          <p>
41             <label>Comments:<br />
```

Fig. F.4 Form with textareas, password boxes and checkboxes. (Part 1 of 3.)

```
               <textarea name = "comments" rows = "4"
                  cols = "36">Enter your comments here.
               </textarea>
            </label></p>

         <!-- <input type = "password"> inserts -->
         <!-- textboxwhose display is masked    -->
         <!-- with asterisk characters -->
         <p>
            <label>E-mail Address:
               <input name = "email" type = "password"
                  size = "25" />
            </label>
         </p>

         <p>
            <strong>Things you liked:</strong><br />

            <label>Site design
            <input name = "thingsliked" type = "checkbox"
               value = "Design" /></label>

            <label>Links
            <input name = "thingsliked" type = "checkbox"
               value = "Links" /></label>

            <label>Ease of use
            <input name = "thingsliked" type = "checkbox"
               value = "Ease" /></label>

            <label>Images
            <input name = "thingsliked" type = "checkbox"
               value = "Images" /></label>

            <label>Source code
            <input name = "thingsliked" type = "checkbox"
               value = "Code" /></label>
         </p>

         <p>
            <input type = "submit" value =
               "Submit Your Entries" />

            <input type = "reset" value =
               "Clear Your Entries" />
         </p>

      </form>

   </body>
</html>
```

Fig. F.4 Form with textareas, password boxes and checkboxes. (Part 2 of 3.)

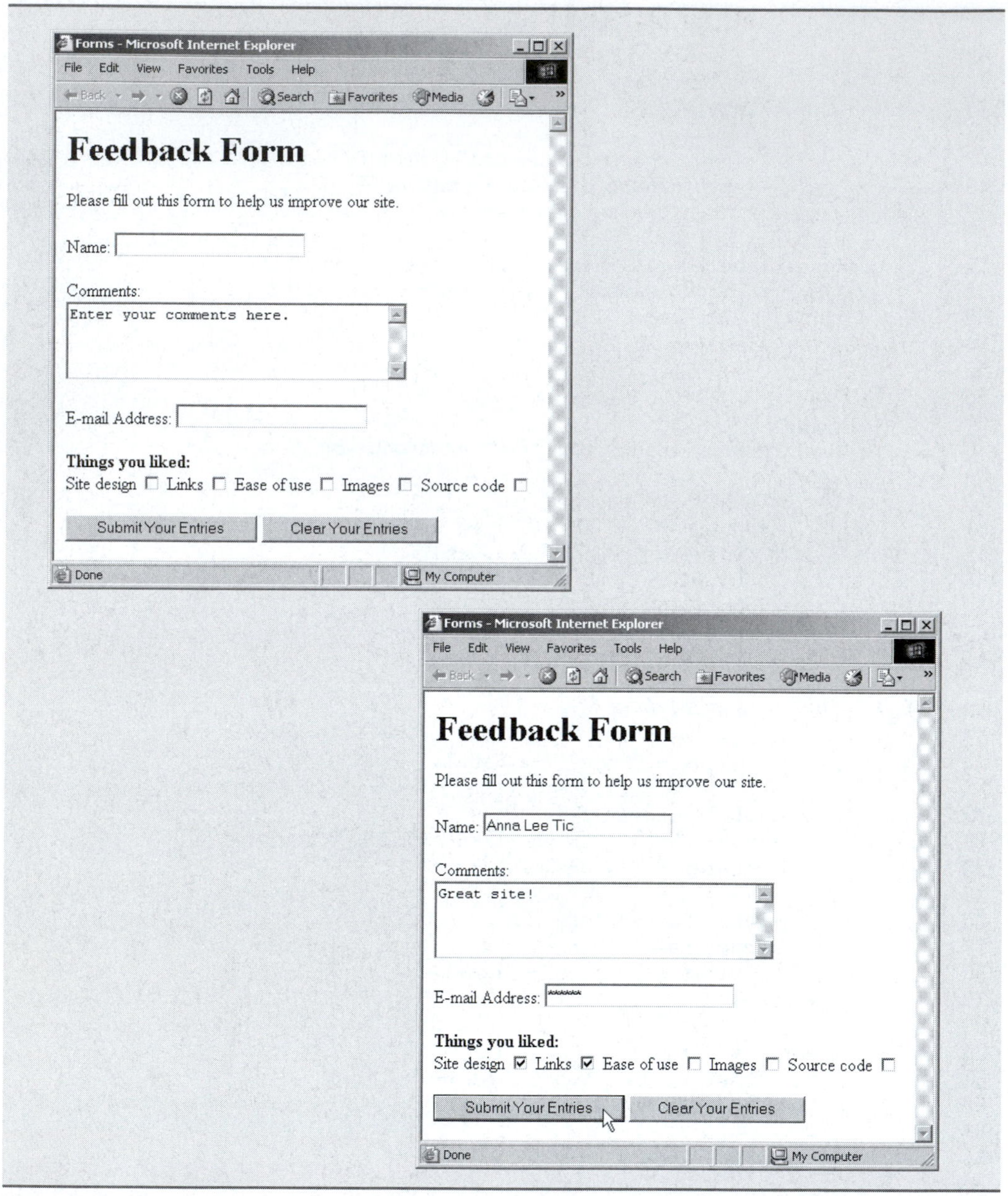

Fig. F.4 Form with textareas, password boxes and checkboxes. (Part 3 of 3.)

Common Programming Error F.3

When your `form` has several checkboxes with the same `name`, you must make sure that they have different `values`, or the scripts running on the Web server will not be able to distinguish between them.

We continue our discussion of forms by presenting a third example that introduces several more form elements from which users can make selections (Fig. F.5). In this example, we introduce two new `input` types. The first type is the *radio button* (lines 90–113), specified with type `"radio"`. Radio buttons are similar to checkboxes, except that only one radio button in a group of radio buttons may be selected at any time. All radio buttons in a group have the same `name` attribute; they are distinguished by their different `value` attributes. The attribute–value pair *checked = "checked"* (line 92) indicates which radio button, if any, is selected initially. The `checked` attribute also applies to checkboxes.

```
1  <?xml version = "1.0"?>
2  <!DOCTYPE html PUBLIC "-//W3C//DTD XHTML 1.0 Strict//EN"
3     "http://www.w3.org/TR/xhtml1/DTD/xhtml1-strict.dtd">
4
5  <!-- Fig. F.5: form3.html   -->
6  <!-- Form design example 3. -->
7
8  <html xmlns = "http://www.w3.org/1999/xhtml">
9     <head>
10       <title>Forms</title>
11    </head>
12
13    <body>
14
15       <h1>Feedback Form</h1>
16
17       <p>Please fill out this form to help
18          us improve our site.</p>
19
20       <form method = "post" action = "/cgi-bin/formmail">
21
22          <p>
23             <input type = "hidden" name = "recipient"
24                value = "deitel@deitel.com" />
25
26             <input type = "hidden" name = "subject"
27                value = "Feedback Form" />
28
29             <input type = "hidden" name = "redirect"
30                value = "main.html" />
31          </p>
32
33          <p>
34             <label>Name:
35                <input name = "name" type = "text" size = "25" />
36             </label>
37          </p>
38
39          <p>
40             <label>Comments:<br />
41                <textarea name = "comments" rows = "4"
42                   cols = "36"></textarea>
43             </label>
44          </p>
45
```

Fig. F.5 Form including radio buttons and drop-down lists. (Part 1 of 4.)

```
         <p>
            <label>E-mail Address:
               <input name = "email" type = "password"
                  size = "25" />
            </label>
         </p>

         <p>
            <strong>Things you liked:</strong><br />

            <label>Site design
               <input name = "thingsliked" type = "checkbox"
                  value = "Design" />
            </label>

            <label>Links
               <input name = "thingsliked" type = "checkbox"
                  value = "Links" />
            </label>

            <label>Ease of use
               <input name = "thingsliked" type = "checkbox"
                  value = "Ease" />
            </label>

            <label>Images
               <input name = "thingsliked" type = "checkbox"
                  value = "Images" />
            </label>

            <label>Source code
               <input name = "thingsliked" type = "checkbox"
                  value = "Code" />
            </label>

         </p>

         <!-- <input type = "radio" /> creates one radio   -->
         <!-- button. The difference between radio buttons -->
         <!-- and checkboxes is that only one radio button -->
         <!-- in a group can be selected.                  -->
         <p>
            <strong>How did you get to our site?:</strong><br />

            <label>Search engine
               <input name = "howtosite" type = "radio"
                  value = "search engine" checked = "checked" />
            </label>

            <label>Links from another site
               <input name = "howtosite" type = "radio"
                  value = "link" />
            </label>
```

Fig. F.5 Form including radio buttons and drop-down lists. (Part 2 of 4.)

```

            <label>Deitel.com Web site
               <input name = "howtosite" type = "radio"
                  value = "deitel.com" />
            </label>

            <label>Reference in a book
               <input name = "howtosite" type = "radio"
                  value = "book" />
            </label>

            <label>Other
               <input name = "howtosite" type = "radio"
                  value = "other" />
            </label>

         </p>

         <p>
            <label>Rate our site:

                <!-- <select> tag presents a drop-down -->
                <!-- list with choices indicated by    -->
                <!-- <option> tags                     -->
               <select name = "rating">
                  <option selected = "selected">Amazing</option>
                  <option>10</option>
                  <option>9</option>
                  <option>8</option>
                  <option>7</option>
                  <option>6</option>
                  <option>5</option>
                  <option>4</option>
                  <option>3</option>
                  <option>2</option>
                  <option>1</option>
                  <option>Awful</option>
               </select>

            </label>
         </p>

         <p>
            <input type = "submit" value =
               "Submit Your Entries" />

            <input type = "reset" value = "Clear Your Entries" />
         </p>

      </form>

   </body>
</html>
```

Fig. F.5 Form including radio buttons and drop-down lists. (Part 3 of 4.)

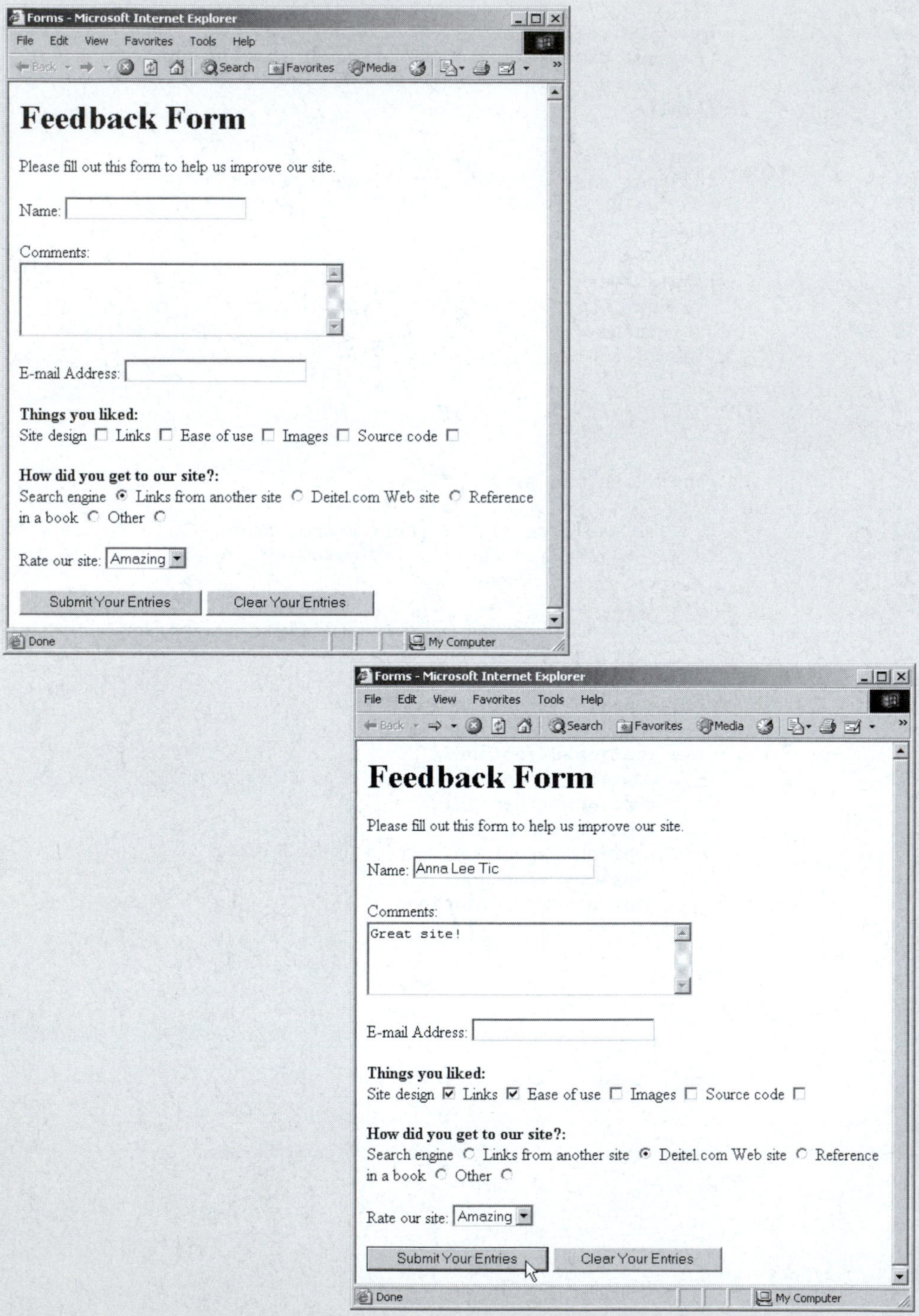

Fig. F.5 Form including radio buttons and drop-down lists. (Part 4 of 4.)

Common Programming Error F.4

When using a group of radio buttons in a form, forgetting to set the `name` attributes to the same name lets the user select all the radio buttons at the same time, which is a logic error.

The `select` element (lines 123–136) provides a drop-down list from which the user can select an item. The `name` attribute identifies the drop-down list. The `option` element (lines 124–135) adds items to the drop-down list. The `option` element's *`selected` attribute* specifies which item initially is displayed as the selected item in the `select` element.

F.6 Internal Linking

In Appendix E, we discussed how to hyperlink one Web page to another. Figure F.6 introduces *internal linking*—a mechanism that enables the user to jump between locations in the same document. Internal linking is useful for long documents that contain many sections. Clicking an internal link enables users to find a section without scrolling through the entire document.

```
<?xml version = "1.0"?>
<!DOCTYPE html PUBLIC "-//W3C//DTD XHTML 1.0 Strict//EN"
   "http://www.w3.org/TR/xhtml1/DTD/xhtml1-strict.dtd">

<!-- Fig. F.6: links.html -->
<!-- Internal linking.    -->

<html xmlns = "http://www.w3.org/1999/xhtml">
   <head>
      <title>List</title>
   </head>

   <body>

      <!-- <a name = ".."></a> creates internal hyperlink -->
      <p><a name = "features"></a></p>

      <h1>The Best Features of the Internet</h1>

      <!-- address of internal link is "#linkname" -->
      <p>
         <a href = "#ceos">Go to <em>Favorite CEOs</em></a>
      </p>

      <ul>
         <li>You can meet people from countries
            around the world.</li>

         <li>You have access to new media as it becomes public:

            <ul>
               <li>New games</li>
               <li>New applications
```

Fig. F.6 Internal hyperlinks used to make pages more easily navigable. (Part 1 of 3.)

```

                        <ul>
                           <li>For Business</li>
                           <li>For Pleasure</li>
                        </ul>

                     </li>

                     <li>Around the clock news</li>
                     <li>Search Engines</li>
                     <li>Shopping</li>
                     <li>Programming

                        <ul>
                           <li>XHTML</li>
                           <li>Visual C++</li>
                           <li>Java</li>
                           <li>Scripts</li>
                           <li>New languages</li>
                        </ul>

                     </li>
                  </ul>

               </li>

               <li>Links</li>
               <li>Keeping in touch with old friends</li>
               <li>It is the technology of the future!</li>
            </ul>

            <!-- named anchor -->
            <p><a name = "ceos"></a></p>

            <h1>My 3 Favorite <em>CEOs</em></h1>

            <p>

               <!-- internal hyperlink to features -->
               <a href = "#features">
                  Go to <em>Favorite Features</em>
               </a>
            </p>

            <ol>
               <li>Ant Chovy</li>
               <li>CeCe Sharp</li>
               <li>Albert Antstein</li>
            </ol>

         </body>
      </html>
```

Fig. F.6 Internal hyperlinks used to make pages more easily navigable. (Part 2 of 3.)

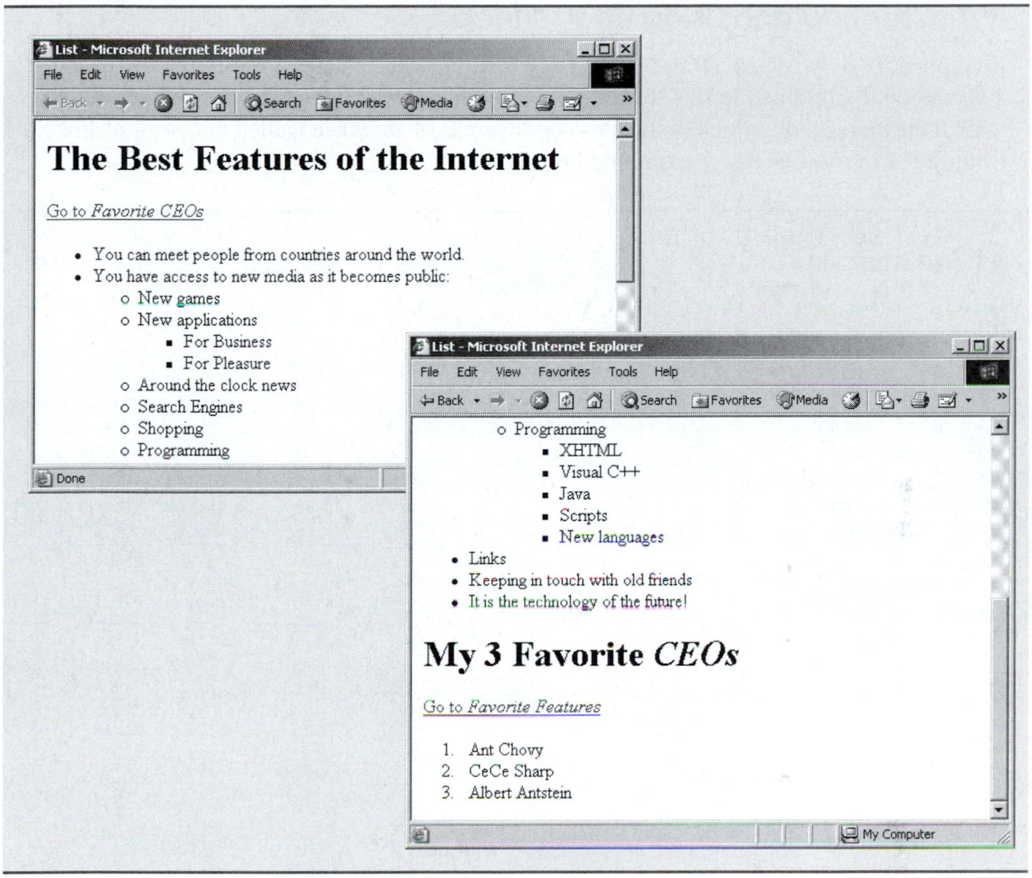

Fig. F.6 Internal hyperlinks used to make pages more easily navigable. (Part 3 of 3.)

Line 16 contains a *named anchor* (called `features`) for an internal hyperlink. To link to this type of anchor inside the same Web page, the `href` attribute of another anchor element includes the named anchor preceded with a pound sign (as in `#features`). Lines 73–74 contain a hyperlink with the anchor `features` as its target. Selecting this hyperlink in a Web browser scrolls the browser window to the `features` anchor in line 16.

Look-and-Feel Observation F.1

Internal hyperlinks are useful in XHTML documents that contain large amounts of information. Internal links to various sections on the page make it easier for users to navigate the page: They do not have to scroll to find a specific section.

Although not demonstrated in this example, a hyperlink can specify an internal link in another document by specifying the document name followed by a pound sign and the named anchor, as in

```
href = "page.html#name"
```

For example, to link to a named anchor called `booklist` in `books.html`, `href` is assigned `"books.html#booklist"`.

F.7 Creating and Using Image Maps

In Appendix E, we demonstrated how images can be used as hyperlinks to link to other resources on the Internet. In this section, we introduce another technique for image linking, called the *image map*, which designates certain areas of an image (called *hotspots*) as links. Figure F.7 introduces image maps and hotspots.

```
<?xml version = "1.0" ?>
<!DOCTYPE html PUBLIC "-//W3C//DTD XHTML 1.0 Strict//EN"
   "http://www.w3.org/TR/xhtml1/DTD/xhtml1-strict.dtd">

<!-- Fig. F.7: picture.html          -->
<!-- Creating and using image maps. -->

<html xmlns = "http://www.w3.org/1999/xhtml">
   <head>
      <title>Image Map
      </title>
   </head>

   <body>

      <p>

         <!-- <map> tag defines image map -->
         <map id = "picture">

            <!-- shape = "rect" indicates rectangular  -->
            <!-- area, with coordinates for upper-left -->
            <!-- and lower-right corners               -->
            <area href = "form.html" shape = "rect"
               coords = "2,123,54,143"
               alt = "Go to the feedback form" />

            <area href = "contact.html" shape = "rect"
               coords = "126,122,198,143"
               alt = "Go to the contact page" />

            <area href = "main.html" shape = "rect"
               coords = "3,7,61,25" alt = "Go to the homepage" />

            <area href = "links.html" shape = "rect"
               coords = "168,5,197,25"
               alt = "Go to the links page" />

            <!-- value "poly" creates hotspot in shape -->
            <!-- of polygon, defined by coords         -->
            <area shape = "poly" alt = "E-mail the Deitels"
               coords = "162,25,154,39,158,54,169,51,183,39,161,26"
               href = "mailto:deitel@deitel.com" />

```

Fig. F.7 Image with links anchored to an image map. (Part 1 of 2.)

```
45             <!-- shape = "circle" indicates a circular -->
46             <!-- area with the given center and radius -->
47             <area href = "mailto:deitel@deitel.com"
48                shape = "circle" coords = "100,36,33"
49                alt = "E-mail the Deitels" />
50          </map>
51
52          <!-- <img src =... usemap = "#id"> indicates that -->
53          <!-- specified image map is used with this image  -->
54          <img src = "deitel.gif" width = "200" height = "144"
55             alt = "Deitel logo" usemap = "#picture" />
56       </p>
57
58    </body>
59 </html>
```

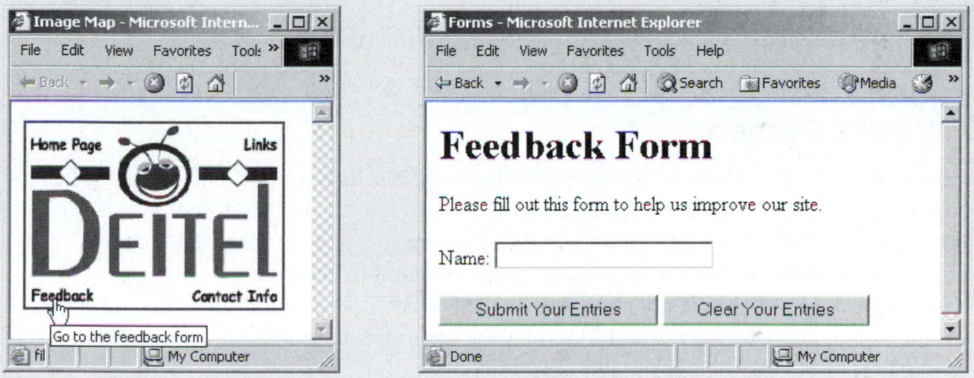

Fig. F.7 Image with links anchored to an image map. (Part 2 of 2.)

Lines 19–50 define an image map via a *`map`* element. Attribute *`id`* (line 19) identifies the image map. If `id` is omitted, the map cannot be referenced by an image. Shortly, we discuss how to reference an image map. Hotspots are defined with *`area`* elements (as shown in lines 24–26). Attribute `href` (line 24) specifies the link's target (i.e., the resource to which to link). Attributes *`shape`* (line 24) and *`coords`* (line 25) specify the hotspot's shape and coordinates, respectively. Attribute `alt` (line 26) provides alternative text for the link.

Common Programming Error F.5

Not specifying an `id` attribute for a `map` element prevents an `img` element from using the `map`'s `area` elements to define hotspots.

The markup in lines 24–26 creates a *rectangular hotspot* (`shape = "rect"`) for the *coordinates* specified in the `coords` attribute. A coordinate pair consists of two numbers representing the location of a point on the *x*-axis and the *y*-axis, respectively. The *x*-axis extends horizontally and the *y*-axis extends vertically from the upper-left corner of the image. Every point on an image has a unique *x–y* coordinate. For rectangular hotspots, the required coordinates are those of the upper-left and lower-right corners of the rectangle. In this case, the upper-left corner of the rectangle is located at 2 on the *x*-axis and 123 on the *y*-axis, annotated as *(2, 123)*. The lower-right corner of the rectangle is at *(54, 143)*. Coordinates are measured in pixels.

Common Programming Error F.6

Overlapping the coordinates of an image map causes the browser to render the first hotspot it encounters for the area.

The map `area` (lines 41–43) assigns the `shape` attribute *"poly"* to create a hotspot in the shape of a polygon, using the coordinates in attribute `coords`. These coordinates represent each *vertex*, or corner, of the polygon. The browser connects these points with lines to form the hotspot's area.

The map `area` (lines 47–49) assigns the `shape` attribute *"circle"* to create a *circular hotspot*. In this case, the `coords` attribute specifies the circle's center coordinates and the circle's radius, in pixels.

To use an image map with an `img` element, the `img` element's *usemap* attribute is assigned the `id` of a `map`. Lines 54–55 reference the image map named `"picture"`. The image map is located within the same document, so internal linking is used.

F.8 meta Elements

People use search engines to find useful Web sites. Search engines usually catalog sites by following links from page to page and saving identification and classification information for each page. One way that search engines catalog pages is by reading the content in each page's *meta* elements, which specify information about a document.

Two important attributes of the `meta` element are *name*, which identifies the type of `meta` element and *content*, which provides the information search engines use to catalog pages. Figure F.8 introduces the `meta` element.

Lines 14–16 demonstrate a *"keywords"* `meta` element. The *content* attribute of such a `meta` element provides search engines with a list of words that describe a page. These words are compared with words in search requests. Thus, including `meta` elements and their `content` information can draw more viewers to your site.

```
1  <?xml version = "1.0"?>
2  <!DOCTYPE html PUBLIC "-//W3C//DTD XHTML 1.0 Strict//EN"
3     "http://www.w3.org/TR/xhtml1/DTD/xhtml1-strict.dtd">
4
5  <!-- Fig. F.8: main.html -->
6  <!-- Using meta tags.    -->
7
8  <html xmlns = "http://www.w3.org/1999/xhtml">
9     <head>
10       <title>Welcome</title>
11
12       <!-- <meta> tags provide search engines with -->
13       <!-- information used to catalog site        -->
14       <meta name = "keywords" content = "Web page, design,
15          XHTML, tutorial, personal, help, index, form,
16          contact, feedback, list, links, frame, deitel" />
```

Fig. F.8 meta used to provide keywords and a description. (Part 1 of 2.)

```
17
18          <meta name = "description" content = "This Web site will
19             help you learn the basics of XHTML and Web page design
20             through the use of interactive examples and
21             instruction." />
22
23       </head>
24
25       <body>
26
27          <h1>Welcome to Our Web Site!</h1>
28
29          <p>
30             We have designed this site to teach about the wonders
31             of <strong><em>XHTML</em></strong>. <em>XHTML</em> is
32             better equipped than <em>HTML</em> to represent complex
33             data on the Internet. <em>XHTML</em> takes advantage of
34             XML's strict syntax to ensure well-formedness. Soon you
35             will know about many of the great new features of
36             <em>XHTML.</em>
37          </p>
38
39         <p>Have Fun With the Site!</p>
40
41       </body>
42    </html>
```

Fig. F.8 `meta` used to provide keywords and a description. (Part 2 of 2.)

Lines 18–21 demonstrate a *"description"* `meta` element. The `content` attribute of such a `meta` element provides a three- to four-line description of a site, written in sentence form. Search engines also use this description to catalog your site and sometimes display this information as part of the search results.

Software Engineering Observation F.1

`meta` elements are not visible to users and must be placed inside the `head` section of your XHTML document. If `meta` elements are not placed in this section, they will not be read by search engines.

F.9 `frameset` Element

All of the Web pages we have presented in this book have the ability to link to other pages, but can display only one page at a time. Figure F.9 uses *frames*, which allow the browser to display more than one XHTML document simultaneously, to display the documents in Fig. F.8 and Fig. F.10.

Most of our prior examples adhered to the strict XHTML document type. This particular example uses the *frameset* document type—a special XHTML document type specifically for framesets. This new document type is specified in lines 2–3 and is required for documents that define framesets.

A document that defines a frameset normally consists of an `html` element that contains a `head` element and a *`frameset`* element. The *`<frameset>`* tag (line 24) informs the browser that the page contains frames. Attribute *`cols`* specifies the frameset's column layout. The value of `cols` gives the width of each frame, either in pixels or as a percentage of the browser width. In this case, the attribute `cols = "110,*"` informs the browser that there are two vertical frames. The first frame extends `110` pixels from the left edge of the browser window, and the second frame fills the remainder of the browser width (as indicated by the asterisk). Similarly, `frameset` attribute *`rows`* can be used to specify the number of rows and the size of each row in a frameset.

```
1  <?xml version = "1.0"?>
2  <!DOCTYPE html PUBLIC "-//W3C//DTD XHTML 1.0 Frameset//EN"
3     "http://www.w3.org/TR/xhtml1/DTD/xhtml1-frameset.dtd">
4
5  <!-- Fig. F.9: index.html -->
6  <!-- XHTML frames I.      -->
7
8  <html xmlns = "http://www.w3.org/1999/xhtml">
9     <head>
10       <title>Main</title>
11
12       <meta name = "keywords" content = "Webpage, design,
13          XHTML, tutorial, personal, help, index, form,
14          contact, feedback, list, links, frame, deitel" />
15
16       <meta name = "description" content = "This Web site will
17          help you learn the basics of XHTML and Web page design
18          through the use of interactive examples
19          and instruction." />
20
21    </head>
22
23    <!-- <frameset> tag sets frame dimensions -->
24    <frameset cols = "110,*">
25
26       <!-- frame elements specify which pages -->
27       <!-- are loaded into given frame        -->
28       <frame name = "leftframe" src = "nav.html" />
29       <frame name = "main" src = "main.html" />
30
31       <noframes>
32          <p>This page uses frames, but your browser does not
33          support them.</p>
34
35          <p>Please, <a href = "nav.html">follow this link to
36          browse our site without frames</a>.</p>
37       </noframes>
38
39    </frameset>
40 </html>
```

Fig. F.9 Web document containing two frames—navigation and content. (Part 1 of 2.)

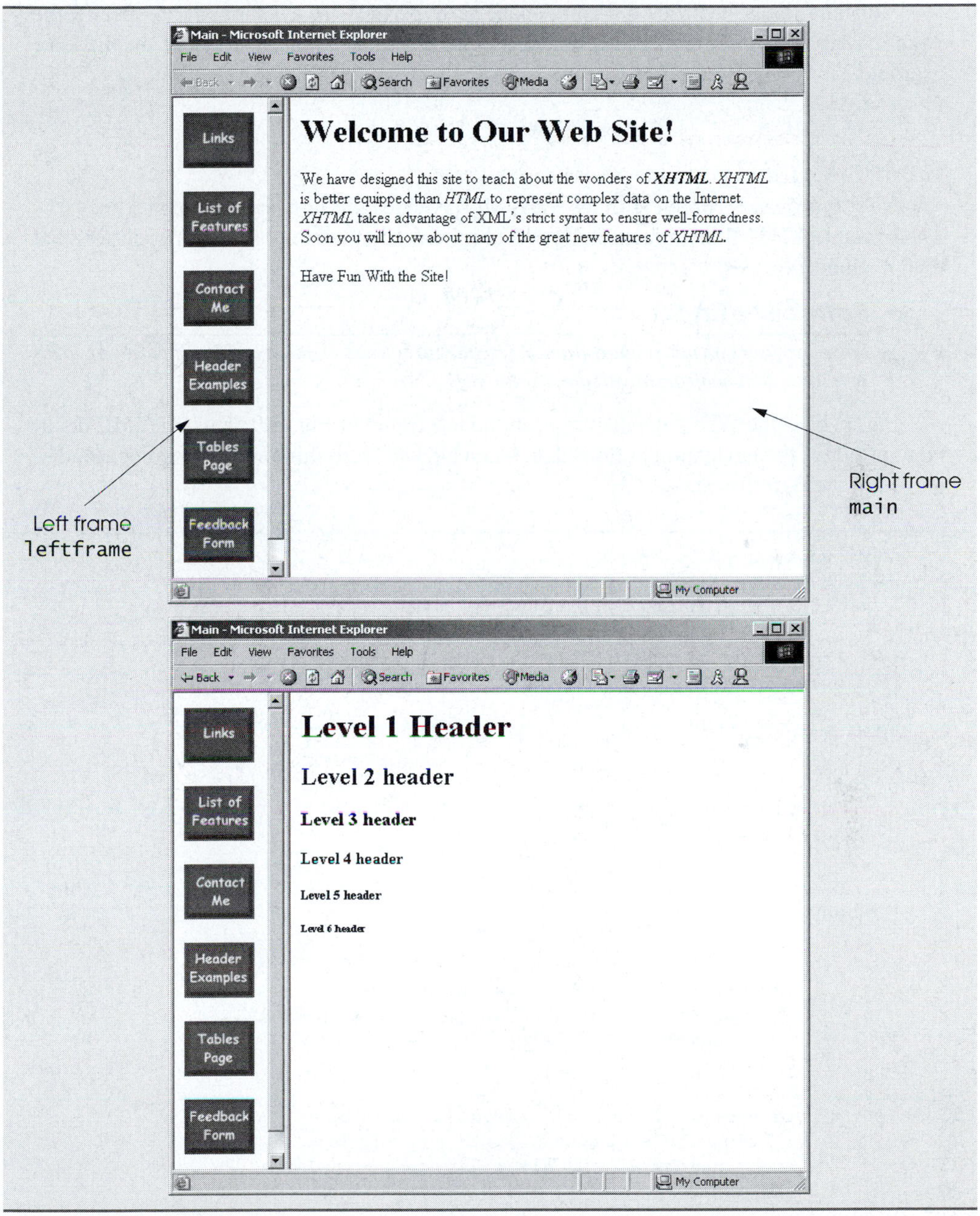

Fig. F.9 Web document containing two frames—navigation and content. (Part 2 of 2.)

The documents that will be loaded into the `frameset` are specified with *`frame`* elements (lines 28–29 in this example). Attribute `src` specifies the URL of the page to display in the frame. Each frame has `name` and `src` attributes. The first frame (which covers `110` pixels on the left side of the `frameset`) is named `leftframe` and displays the page `nav.html` (Fig. F.10). The second frame is named `main` and displays the page `main.html`.

Attribute name identifies a frame, enabling hyperlinks in a frameset to specify the *target* frame in which a linked document should display when the user clicks the link. For example,

```
<a href = "links.html" target = "main">
```

loads links.html in the frame whose name is "main".

Not all browsers support frames. XHTML provides the *noframes* element (lines 31–37) to enable XHTML document designers to specify alternative content for browsers that do not support frames.

Portability Tip F.1

Some browsers do not support frames. Use the noframes *element inside a* frameset *to direct users to a nonframed version of your site.*

Fig. F.10 is the Web page displayed in the left frame of Fig. F.9. This XHTML document provides the navigation buttons that, when clicked, determine which document is displayed in the right frame.

```
<?xml version = "1.0"?>
<!DOCTYPE html PUBLIC "-//W3C//DTD XHTML 1.0 Transitional//EN"
   "http://www.w3.org/TR/xhtml1/DTD/xhtml1-transitional.dtd">

<!-- Fig. F.10: nav.html              -->
<!-- Using images as link anchors. -->

<html xmlns = "http://www.w3.org/1999/xhtml">

   <head>
      <title>Navigation Bar
      </title>
   </head>

   <body>

      <p>
         <a href = "links.html" target = "main">
            <img src = "buttons/links.jpg" width = "65"
               height = "50" alt = "Links Page" />
         </a><br />

         <a href = "list.html" target = "main">
            <img src = "buttons/list.jpg" width = "65"
               height = "50" alt = "List Example Page" />
         </a><br />

         <a href = "contact.html" target = "main">
            <img src = "buttons/contact.jpg" width = "65"
               height = "50" alt = "Contact Page" />
         </a><br />

```

Fig. F.10 XHTML document displayed in the left frame of Fig. F.9. (Part 1 of 2.)

```
33            <a href = "header.html" target = "main">
34               <img src = "buttons/header.jpg" width = "65"
35                  height = "50" alt = "Header Page" />
36            </a><br />
37
38            <a href = "table1.html" target = "main">
39               <img src = "buttons/table.jpg" width = "65"
40                  height = "50" alt = "Table Page" />
41            </a><br />
42
43            <a href = "form.html" target = "main">
44               <img src = "buttons/form.jpg" width = "65"
45                  height = "50" alt = "Feedback Form" />
46            </a><br />
47         </p>
48
49      </body>
50   </html>
```

Fig. F.10 XHTML document displayed in the left frame of Fig. F.9. (Part 2 of 2.)

Line 29 (Fig. F.9) displays the XHTML page in Fig. F.10. Anchor attribute `target` (line 18 in Fig. F.10) specifies that the linked documents are loaded in frame `main` (line 30 in Fig. F.9). A `target` can be set to a number of preset values: `"_blank"` loads the page into a new browser window, `"_self"` loads the page into the frame in which the anchor element appears and `"_top"` loads the page into the full browser window (i.e., removes the `frameset`).

F.10 Nested framesets

You can use the `frameset` element to create more complex layouts in a Web page by nesting `framesets`, as in Fig. F.11. The nested `frameset` in this example displays the XHTML documents in Fig. F.7, Fig. F.8 and Fig. F.10.

```
<?xml version = "1.0"?>
<!DOCTYPE html PUBLIC "-//W3C//DTD XHTML 1.0 Frameset//EN"
   "http://www.w3.org/TR/xhtml1/DTD/xhtml1-frameset.dtd">

<!-- Fig. F.11: index2.html -->
<!-- XHTML frames II.       -->

<html xmlns = "http://www.w3.org/1999/xhtml">
   <head>
      <title>Main</title>

      <meta name = "keywords" content = "Webpage, design,
         XHTML, tutorial, personal, help, index, form,
         contact, feedback, list, links, frame, deitel" />

      <meta name = "description" content = "This Web site will
```

Fig. F.11 Framed Web site with a nested frameset. (Part 1 of 2.)

```
17             help you learn the basics of XHTML and Web page design
18             through the use of interactive examples
19             and instruction." />
20
21       </head>
22
23       <frameset cols = "110,*">
24          <frame name = "leftframe" src = "nav.html" />
25
26          <!-- nested framesets are used to change -->
27          <!-- formatting and layout of frameset  -->
28          <frameset rows = "175,*">
29             <frame name = "picture" src = "picture.html" />
30             <frame name = "main" src = "main.html" />
31          </frameset>
32
33          <noframes>
34             <p>This page uses frames, but your browser does not
35             support them.</p>
36
37             <p>Please, <a href = "nav.html">follow this link to
38             browse our site without frames</a>.</p>
39          </noframes>
40
41       </frameset>
42    </html>
```

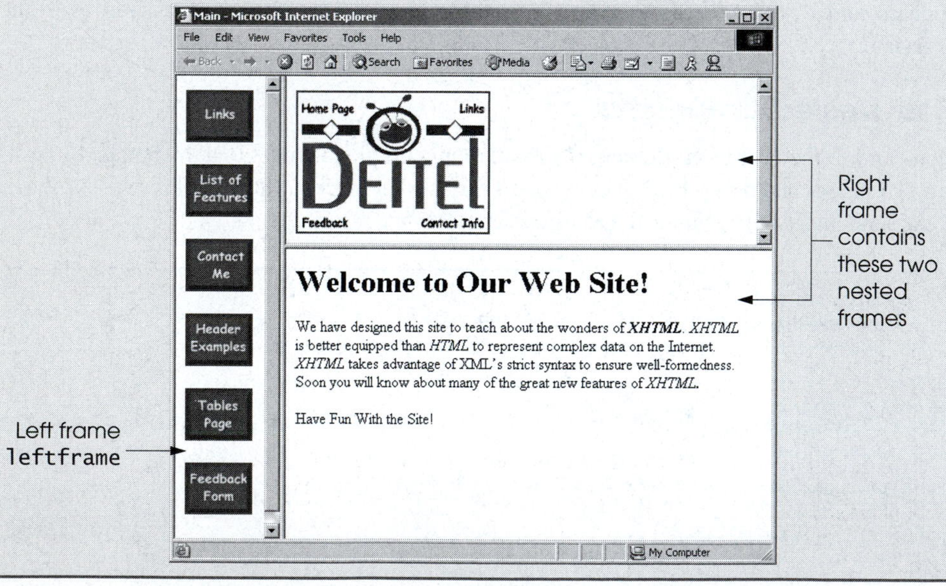

Fig. F.11 Framed Web site with a nested frameset. (Part 2 of 2.)

The outer frameset element (lines 23–41) defines two columns. The left frame extends over the first 110 pixels from the left edge of the browser, and the right frame occupies the rest of the window's width. The `frame` element in line 24 specifies that the document `nav.html` (Fig. F.10) will be displayed in the left column.

Lines 28–31 define a nested `frameset` element for the second column of the outer frameset. This `frameset` defines two rows. The first row extends 175 pixels from the top of the browser window, and the second occupies the remainder of the browser window's height, as is indicated by `rows = "175,*"`. The `frame` element in line 29 specifies that the first row of the nested `frameset` will display `picture.html` (Fig. F.7). The `frame` element in line 30 specifies that the second row of the nested `frameset` will display `main.html` (Fig. F.8).

Error-Prevention Tip F.2

When using nested `frameset` elements, indent every level of `<frame>` tag. This practice makes the page clearer and easier to debug.

In this appendix, we presented XHTML for marking up information in tables, creating forms for gathering user input, linking to sections within the same document, using `<meta>` tags and creating frames.

F.11 Internet and Web Resources

`www.gself.com/xadv/`
This site contains lessons teaching various XHTML features, such as links, tables, frames and forms. Users can e-mail questions or comments to the creator of the lessons.

`www.vbxml.com/xhtml/articles/xhtml_tables`
The *VBXML.com* Web site contains a tutorial on creating XHTML tables.

`www.webreference.com/xml/reference/xhtml.html`
This Web page contains a list of the frequently used XHTML tags, such as header tags, table tags, frame tags and form tags. It also provides a description of each tag.

SUMMARY

- XHTML tables mark up tabular data and are one of the most frequently used features in XHTML. The `table` element defines an XHTML table.
- Attribute `border` specifies the table's border width, in pixels. Tables without borders set this attribute to `"0"`.
- Element `summary` summarizes the table's contents and is used by speech devices to make the table more accessible to users with visual impairments.
- Element `caption` describes the table's content. The text inside the `<caption>` tag is rendered above the table in most browsers.
- A table can be split into three distinct sections: head (`thead`), body (`tbody`) and foot (`tfoot`).
- The head section contains such information as table titles and column headers.
- The table body contains the primary table data. The table foot contains secondary information, such as footnotes.
- Element `tr`, or table row, defines individual table rows.
- Element `th` defines a header cell. Text in `th` elements usually is centered and displayed in bold by most browsers. This element can be present in any section of the table.
- Data within a row are defined with `td`, or table data, elements.
- Element `colgroup` groups and formats columns. Each `col` element can format any number of columns (specified with the `span` attribute).

- The document author has the ability to merge data cells with the `rowspan` and `colspan` attributes. The values assigned to these attributes specify the number of rows or columns occupied by the cell. These attributes can be placed inside any data-cell tag.
- XHTML provides forms for collecting information from users.
- Forms contain visual components, such as buttons that users click. Forms may also contain non-visual components, called hidden inputs, which are used to store any data, such as e-mail addresses and XHTML document file names used for linking. A form begins with the `form` element.
- Attribute `method` specifies how the form's data is sent to the Web server.
- The `"text"` input inserts a textbox into the form. Textboxes allow the user to input data.
- The `input` element's `size` attribute specifies the number of characters visible in the `input` element. Optional attribute `maxlength` limits the number of characters input into a textbox.
- The `"submit"` input submits the data entered in the form to the Web server for processing. Most Web browsers create a button that submits the form data when clicked.
- The `"reset"` input allows a user to reset all `form` elements to their default values.
- The `textarea` element inserts a multiline textbox, called a textarea, into a form. The number of rows in the textarea is specified with the `rows` attribute, the number of columns (i.e., characters) with the `cols` attribute.
- The `"password"` input inserts a password box into a form. A password box allows users to enter sensitive information, such as credit-card numbers and passwords, by "masking" the information input with another character.
- Asterisks are the masking character used for most password boxes. The actual value input is sent to the Web server, not the asterisks that mask the input.
- The "`checkbox`" input allows the user to make a selection. When the checkbox is selected, a check mark appears in the checkbox. Otherwise, the checkbox is empty.
- Checkboxes can be used individually and in groups. Checkboxes that are part of the same group have the same `name`.
- A radio button is similar in function and use to a checkbox, except that only one radio button in a group can be selected at any time. All radio buttons in a group have the same `name` attribute value, but different attribute `values`.
- The "`select`" input provides a drop-down list of items. The `name` attribute identifies the drop-down list. The `option` element adds items to the drop-down list. The `selected` attribute, like the `checked` attribute for radio buttons and checkboxes, specifies which list item is displayed initially.
- Image maps designate certain sections of an image as links. These links are more properly called hotspots.
- Image maps are defined with `map` elements. Attribute `id` identifies the image map. Hotspots are defined with the `area` element.
- Attribute `href` specifies the link's target. Attributes `shape` and `coords` specify the hotspot's shape and coordinates, respectively, and `alt` provides alternative text.
- One way that search engines catalog pages is by reading the `meta` elements's contents.
- Two important attributes of the `meta` element are `name`, which identifies the type of `meta` element, and `content`, which provides information a search engine uses to catalog a page.
- Frames allow the browser to display more than one XHTML document simultaneously.
- The `frameset` element informs the browser that the page contains frames.
- Not all browsers support frames. XHTML provides the `noframes` element to specify alternative content for browsers that do not support frames.

G

XHTML Special Characters

The table in Fig. G.1 shows many commonly used XHTML special characters—called *character entity references* by the World Wide Web Consortium. For a complete list of character entity references, see the site:

```
www.w3.org/TR/REC-html40/sgml/entities.html
```

Character	XHTML encoding	Character	XHTML encoding
non-breaking space	` `	ê	`ê`
§	`§`	ì	`ì`
©	`©`	í	`í`
®	`®`	î	`î`
π	`¼`	ñ	`ñ`
∫	`½`	ò	`ò`
Ω	`¾`	ó	`ó`
à	`à`	ô	`ô`
á	`á`	õ	`õ`
â	`â`	÷	`÷`
ã	`ã`	ù	`ù`
å	`å`	ú	`ú`
ç	`ç`	û	`û`
è	`è`	•	`•`
é	`é`	™	`™`

Fig. G.1 XHTML special characters.

H

XHTML Colors

Colors may be specified by using a standard name (such as aqua) or a hexadecimal RGB value (such as #00FFFF for aqua). Of the six hexadecimal digits in an RGB value, the first two represent the amount of red in the color, the middle two represent the amount of green in the color and the last two represent the amount of blue in the color. For example, black is the absence of color and is defined by #000000, whereas white is the maximum amount of red, green and blue and is defined by #FFFFFF. Pure red is #FF0000, pure green (which is called lime) is #00FF00 and pure blue is #0000FF. Note that green in the standard is defined as #008000. Figure H.1 contains the XHTML standard color set. Figure H.2 contains the XHTML extended color set.

Color name	Value	Color name	Value
aqua	#00FFFF	navy	#000080
black	#000000	olive	#808000
blue	#0000FF	purple	#800080
fuchsia	#FF00FF	red	#FF0000
gray	#808080	silver	#C0C0C0
green	#008000	teal	#008080
lime	#00FF00	yellow	#FFFF00
maroon	#800000	white	#FFFFFF

Fig. H.1 XHTML standard colors and hexadecimal RGB values.

Color name	Value	Color name	Value
aliceblue	#F0F8FF	dimgray	#696969
antiquewhite	#FAEBD7	dodgerblue	#1E90FF
aquamarine	#7FFFD4	firebrick	#B22222
azure	#F0FFFF	floralwhite	#FFFAF0
beige	#F5F5DC	forestgreen	#228B22
bisque	#FFE4C4	gainsboro	#DCDCDC
blanchedalmond	#FFEBCD	ghostwhite	#F8F8FF
blueviolet	#8A2BE2	gold	#FFD700
brown	#A52A2A	goldenrod	#DAA520
burlywood	#DEB887	greenyellow	#ADFF2F
cadetblue	#5F9EA0	honeydew	#F0FFF0
chartreuse	#7FFF00	hotpink	#FF69B4
chocolate	#D2691E	indianred	#CD5C5C
coral	#FF7F50	indigo	#4B0082
cornflowerblue	#6495ED	ivory	#FFFFF0
cornsilk	#FFF8DC	khaki	#F0E68C
crimson	#DC1436	lavender	#E6E6FA
cyan	#00FFFF	lavenderblush	#FFF0F5
darkblue	#00008B	lawngreen	#7CFC00
darkcyan	#008B8B	lemonchiffon	#FFFACD
darkgoldenrod	#B8860B	lightblue	#ADD8E6
darkgray	#A9A9A9	lightcoral	#F08080
darkgreen	#006400	lightcyan	#E0FFFF
darkkhaki	#BDB76B	lightgoldenrodyellow	#FAFAD2
darkmagenta	#8B008B	lightgreen	#90EE90
darkolivegreen	#556B2F	lightgrey	#D3D3D3
darkorange	#FF8C00	lightpink	#FFB6C1
darkorchid	#9932CC	lightsalmon	#FFA07A
darkred	#8B0000	lightseagreen	#20B2AA
darksalmon	#E9967A	lightskyblue	#87CEFA
darkseagreen	#8FBC8F	lightslategray	#778899
darkslateblue	#483D8B	lightsteelblue	#B0C4DE
darkslategray	#2F4F4F	lightyellow	#FFFFE0
darkturquoise	#00CED1	limegreen	#32CD32
darkviolet	#9400D3	mediumaquamarine	#66CDAA
deeppink	#FF1493	mediumblue	#0000CD
deepskyblue	#00BFFF	mediumorchid	#BA55D3

Fig. H.2 XHTML extended colors and hexadecimal RGB values. (Part 1 of 2.)

Color name	Value	Color name	Value
mediumpurple	#9370DB	plum	#DDA0DD
mediumseagreen	#3CB371	powderblue	#B0E0E6
mediumslateblue	#7B68EE	rosybrown	#BC8F8F
mediumspringgreen	#00FA9A	royalblue	#4169E1
mediumturquoise	#48D1CC	saddlebrown	#8B4513
mediumvioletred	#C71585	salmon	#FA8072
midnightblue	#191970	sandybrown	#F4A460
mintcream	#F5FFFA	seagreen	#2E8B57
mistyrose	#FFE4E1	seashell	#FFF5EE
moccasin	#FFE4B5	sienna	#A0522D
navajowhite	#FFDEAD	skyblue	#87CEEB
oldlace	#FDF5E6	slateblue	#6A5ACD
olivedrab	#6B8E23	slategray	#708090
orange	#FFA500	snow	#FFFAFA
orangered	#FF4500	springgreen	#00FF7F
orchid	#DA70D6	steelblue	#4682B4
palegoldenrod	#EEE8AA	tan	#D2B48C
palegreen	#98FB98	thistle	#D8BFD8
paleturquoise	#AFEEEE	tomato	#FF6347
palevioletred	#DB7093	turquoise	#40E0D0
papayawhip	#FFEFD5	violet	#EE82EE
peachpuff	#FFDAB9	wheat	#F5DEB3
peru	#CD853F	whitesmoke	#F5F5F5
pink	#FFC0CB	yellowgreen	#9ACD32

Fig. H.2 XHTML extended colors and hexadecimal RGB values. (Part 2 of 2.)

7

Bit Manipulation

Objectives

- To understand the concept of bit manipulation.
- To be able to use bitwise operators.
- To be able to use class `BitArray` to perform bit manipulation.

Outline

I.1 Introduction

In this appendix, we present an extensive discussion of bit manipulation and the *bitwise operators* that enable it. We also discuss class `BitArray`, from which we create objects useful for manipulating sets of bits.

I.2 Bit Manipulation and the Bitwise Operators

MC++ provides extensive bit-manipulation capabilities for programmers who must work at the "bits-and-bytes" level. Operating systems, test-equipment software, networking software and many other kinds of software require that programmers communicate "directly with the hardware." In this section and the next, we discuss MC++'s bit-manipulation capabilities. After introducing MC++'s bitwise operators, we demonstrate the use of the operators in live-code examples.

Computers represent data internally as sequences of bits. Arithmetic Logic Units (ALUs), Central Processing Units (CPUs) and other pieces of hardware in a computer process data as bits or groups of bits. Each bit can assume either the value `0` or the value `1`. On all systems, a sequence of 8 bits forms a *byte*—the standard storage unit for a variable of type `char`. Other data types require larger numbers of bytes for storage. The bitwise operators manipulate the bits of integral operands (`char`, `short`, `int` and `long`; both `signed` and `unsigned`). Unsigned integers are normally used with the bitwise operators. Note that the discussion of bitwise operators in this section illustrates the binary representations of the integer operands. For a detailed explanation of the binary (also called base-2) number system, see Appendix B, Number Systems.

The operators *bitwise AND* (&), *bitwise inclusive OR* (|) and *bitwise exclusive OR* (^) operate similarly to their logical counterparts, except that the bitwise versions operate on the level of bits. The bitwise AND operator sets each bit in the result to 1 if the corresponding bits in both operands are 1 (Fig. I.2). The bitwise inclusive OR operator sets each bit in the result to 1 if the corresponding bits in either (or both) operand(s) are 1 (Fig. I.3). The bitwise exclusive OR operator sets each bit in the result to 1 if the corresponding bit in exactly one operand is 1 (Fig. I.4). Exclusive OR is also known as *XOR*.

The *left-shift* (<<) operator shifts the bits of its left operand to the left by the number of bits specified in its right operand. The *right-shift* (>>) operator shifts the bits in its left operand to the right by the number of bits specified in its right operand. If the left operand is negative, `1`s are shifted in from the left, whereas, if the left operand is positive `0`s are shifted in from the left. The bitwise *complement* (~) operator sets all `0` bits in its operand to `1` and all `1` bits to `0` in the result; this process sometimes is referred to as "taking the *ones complement* of the value." A detailed discussion of each bitwise operator appears in the examples that follow. The bitwise operators and their functions are summarized in Fig. I.1.

Operator	Name	Description
&	bitwise AND	Each bit in the result is set to 1 if the corresponding bits in the two operands are both 1. Otherwise, the bit is set to 0.
|	bitwise inclusive OR	Each bit in the result is set to 1 if at least one of the corresponding bits in the two operands is 1. Otherwise, the bit is set to 0.
^	bitwise exclusive OR	Each bit in the result is set to 1 if exactly one of the corresponding bits in the two operands is 1. Otherwise, the bit is set to 0.
<<	left shift	Shifts the bits of the first operand to the left by the number of bits specified by the second operand; fill from the right with 0 bits.
>>	right shift	Shifts the bits of the first operand to the right by the number of bits specified by the second operand. If the first operand is negative, 1s are shifted in from the left; otherwise, 0s are shifted in from the left.
~	complement	All 0 bits are set to 1, and all 1 bits are set to 0.

Fig. I.1 Bitwise operators.

Bit 1	Bit 2	Bit 1 & Bit 2
0	0	0
1	0	0
0	1	0
1	1	1

Fig. I.2 Results of combining two bits with the bitwise AND operator (&).

Bit 1	Bit 2	Bit 1 | Bit 2
0	0	0
1	0	1
0	1	1
1	1	1

Fig. I.3 Results of combining two bits with the bitwise inclusive OR operator (|).

Bit 1	Bit 2	Bit 1 ^ Bit 2
0	0	0
1	0	1
0	1	1
1	1	0

Fig. I.4 Results of combining two bits with the bitwise exclusive OR operator (^).

When using the bitwise operators, it is useful to display values in their binary representations to illustrate the effects of these operators. The application in Fig. I.5—Fig. I.6 displays integers in their binary representations as groups of eight bits each. Method `GetBits` (lines 86–107 of Fig. I.5) of class `PrintBits::Form1` uses the bitwise AND operator (line 96) to combine variable `number` with variable `displayMask`. Often, the bitwise AND operator is used with a *mask* operand—an integer value with specific bits set to `1`. Masks hide some bits in a value and select other bits. In line 88, `GetBits` assigns mask variable `displayMask` the value `1 << 31` (`10000000 00000000 00000000 00000000`). The left-shift operator shifts the value `1` from the low-order (rightmost) bit to the high-order (leftmost) bit in `displayMask` and fills in `0` bits from the right. The second operand is 31, so 31 bits (each is `0`) are filled in from the right. The word "fill," in this context, means that we add a bit to the right end and delete one from the left end. Every time we add a `0` to the right end, we remove the bit at the left end.

The statement in line 96 determines whether a `1` or a `0` should be appended to `StringBuilder *output` for the leftmost bit of variable `number`. When `number` and `displayMask` are combined using `&`, all the bits except the high-order bit in variable `number` are "masked off" (hidden), because any bit ANDed with `0` yields `0`. If the leftmost bit is `0`, `number & displayMask` evaluates to `0`, and `0` is appended; otherwise, `1` is appended. Line 100 then left shifts variable `number` one bit with the expression `number <<= 1`. (This is equivalent to `number = number << 1`.) These steps are repeated for each bit in variable `number`. At the end of method `GetBits`, line 106 returns the `String *` representation of the `StringBuilder`.

```
1  // Fig. I.5: Form1.h
2  // Printing the bits that constitute an integer.
3
4  #pragma once
5
6
7  namespace PrintBits
8  {
9     using namespace System;
10    using namespace System::ComponentModel;
11    using namespace System::Collections;
12    using namespace System::Windows::Forms;
```

Fig. I.5 `PrintBits::Form1` class displays the bit representation of an integer. (Part 1 of 3.)

```
using namespace System::Data;
using namespace System::Drawing;
using namespace System::Text;

/// <summary>
/// Summary for Form1
///
/// WARNING: If you change the name of this class, you will need to
///          change the 'Resource File Name' property for the managed
///          resource compiler tool associated with all .resx files
///          this class depends on.  Otherwise, the designers will not
///          be able to interact properly with localized resources
///          associated with this form.
/// </summary>
public __gc class Form1 : public System::Windows::Forms::Form
{
public:
   Form1(void)
   {
      InitializeComponent();
   }

protected:
   void Dispose(Boolean disposing)
   {
      if (disposing && components)
      {
         components->Dispose();
      }
      __super::Dispose(disposing);
   }
private: System::Windows::Forms::Label *  promptLabel;
private: System::Windows::Forms::Label *  viewLabel;

// for user input
private: System::Windows::Forms::TextBox *  inputTextBox;

// bit representation displayed here
private: System::Windows::Forms::Label *  displayLabel;

private:
   /// <summary>
   /// Required designer variable.
   /// </summary>
   System::ComponentModel::Container * components;

// Visual Studio .NET generated GUI code

// process integer when user presses Enter
private: System::Void inputTextBox_KeyDown(System::Object *  sender,
         System::Windows::Forms::KeyEventArgs *  e)
      {
```

Fig. I.5 `PrintBits::Form1` class displays the bit representation of an integer. (Part 2 of 3.)

```
               // if user pressed Enter
               if ( e->KeyCode == Keys::Enter ) {

                  // test whether user enetered an integer
                  try {
                     displayLabel->Text = GetBits(
                        Convert::ToInt32( inputTextBox->Text ) );
                  }

                  // if value is not integer, exception is thrown
                  catch ( FormatException * ) {
                     MessageBox::Show(
                        S"Please Enter an Integer", S"Error",
                        MessageBoxButtons::OK, MessageBoxIcon::Error );
                  } // end catch
               } // end if
            } // end method inputTextBox_KeyDown

   public:

      // convert integer to its bit representation
      String* GetBits( int number )
      {
         int displayMask = 1 << 31;

         StringBuilder *output = new StringBuilder();

         // get each bit, add space every 8 bits for display formatting
         for ( int c = 1; c <= 32; c++ ) {

            // append 0 or 1 depending on result of masking
            output->Append( ( number & displayMask ) == 0 ? S"0" : S"1" );

            // shift left so that mask will find bit of
            // next digit during next iteration of loop
            number <<= 1;

            if ( c % 8 == 0 )
               output->Append( S" " );
         } // end for

         return output->ToString();
      } // end method GetBits
   };
}
```

Fig. I.5 `PrintBits::Form1` class displays the bit representation of an integer. (Part 3 of 3.)

```
// Fig. I.6: Form1.cpp
// Entry point for application.

```

Fig. I.6 `PrintBits::Form1` class driver. (Part 1 of 2.)

```
#include "stdafx.h"
#include "Form1.h"
#include <windows.h>

using namespace PrintBits;

int APIENTRY _tWinMain(HINSTANCE hInstance,
                       HINSTANCE hPrevInstance,
                       LPTSTR    lpCmdLine,
                       int       nCmdShow)
{
   System::Threading::Thread::CurrentThread->ApartmentState =
      System::Threading::ApartmentState::STA;
   Application::Run(new Form1());
   return 0;
}
```

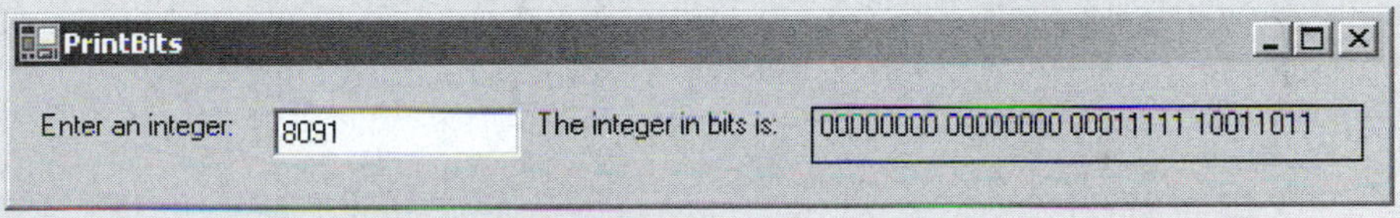

Fig. I.6 `PrintBits::Form1` class driver. (Part 2 of 2.)

Common Programming Error I.1

Using the logical AND operator (&&) in place of the bitwise AND operator (&) is a common programming error.

Common Programming Error I.2

Using the logical OR operator (||) in place of the bitwise inclusive OR operator (|) is a common programming error.

The application in Fig. I.7–Fig. I.8 demonstrates the bitwise AND operator, the bitwise inclusive OR operator, the bitwise exclusive OR operator and the bitwise complement operator. The program uses method `GetBits` (lines 161–182 of Fig. I.7), which returns a `String *` that contains the bit representation of its integer argument. Users enter values into `TextBox`es and press the button corresponding to the operation they would like to test. The program displays the result in both integer and bit representations.

```
// Fig. I.7: Form1.h
// A class that demonstrates miscellaneous bit operations.

#pragma once


namespace BitOperations
{
```

Fig. I.7 Demonstrating the bitwise AND, bitwise inclusive OR, bitwise exclusive OR and bitwise complement operators. (Part 1 of 5.)

```
using namespace System;
using namespace System::ComponentModel;
using namespace System::Collections;
using namespace System::Windows::Forms;
using namespace System::Data;
using namespace System::Drawing;
using namespace System::Text;

/// <summary>
/// Summary for Form1
///
/// WARNING: If you change the name of this class, you will need to
///          change the 'Resource File Name' property for the managed
///          resource compiler tool associated with all .resx files
///          this class depends on.  Otherwise, the designers will not
///          be able to interact properly with localized resources
///          associated with this form.
/// </summary>
public __gc class Form1 : public System::Windows::Forms::Form
{
public:
   Form1(void)
   {
      InitializeComponent();
   }

protected:
   void Dispose(Boolean disposing)
   {
      if (disposing && components)
      {
         components->Dispose();
      }
      __super::Dispose(disposing);
   }
private: System::Windows::Forms::Label *  promptLabel;
private: System::Windows::Forms::Label *  representationLabel;
private: System::Windows::Forms::Label *  value1Label;
private: System::Windows::Forms::Label *  value2Label;
private: System::Windows::Forms::Label *  resultLabel;

// display bit reprentations
private: System::Windows::Forms::Label *  bit1Label;
private: System::Windows::Forms::Label *  bit2Label;
private: System::Windows::Forms::Label *  resultBitLabel;

// user inputs two integers
private: System::Windows::Forms::TextBox *  bit1TextBox;
private: System::Windows::Forms::TextBox *  bit2TextBox;

private: System::Windows::Forms::TextBox *  resultTextBox;

```

Fig. I.7 Demonstrating the bitwise AND, bitwise inclusive OR, bitwise exclusive OR and bitwise complement operators. (Part 2 of 5.)

```
   // allow user to perform bit operations
   private: System::Windows::Forms::Button *  andButton;
   private: System::Windows::Forms::Button *  inclusiveOrButton;
   private: System::Windows::Forms::Button *  exclusiveOrButton;
   private: System::Windows::Forms::Button *  complementButton;

   private: int value1, value2;

   private:
      /// <summary>
      /// Required designer variable.
      /// </summary>
      System::ComponentModel::Container * components;

   // Visual Studio .NET generated GUI code

   // AND
   private: System::Void andButton_Click(
            System::Object *  sender, System::EventArgs *  e)
         {
            try {
               SetFields();

               // update resultTextBox
               resultTextBox->Text = ( value1 & value2 ).ToString();
               resultBitLabel->Text = GetBits( value1 & value2 );
            }

            // if value is not integer, exception is thrown
            catch ( FormatException * ) {
               MessageBox::Show(
                  S"Please Enter Two Integers", S"Error",
                  MessageBoxButtons::OK, MessageBoxIcon::Error );
            } // end catch
         } // end method andButton_Click

   // inclusive OR
   private: System::Void inclusiveOrButton_Click(
            System::Object *  sender, System::EventArgs *  e)
         {
            try {
               SetFields();

               // update resultTextBox
               resultTextBox->Text = ( value1 | value2 ).ToString();
               resultBitLabel->Text = GetBits( value1 | value2 );
            }

            // if value is not integer, exception is thrown
            catch ( FormatException * ) {
               MessageBox::Show(
                  S"Please Enter Two Integers", S"Error",
```

Fig. I.7 Demonstrating the bitwise AND, bitwise inclusive OR, bitwise exclusive OR and bitwise complement operators. (Part 3 of 5.)

```
                     MessageBoxButtons::OK, MessageBoxIcon::Error );
               } // end catch
            } // end method inclusiveOrButton_Click

   // exclusive OR
   private: System::Void exclusiveOrButton_Click(
               System::Object *  sender, System::EventArgs *  e)
            {
               try {
                  SetFields();

                  // update resultTextBox
                  resultTextBox->Text = ( value1 ^ value2 ).ToString();
                  resultBitLabel->Text = GetBits( value1 ^ value2 );
               }

               // if value is not integer, exception is thrown
               catch ( FormatException * ) {
                  MessageBox::Show(
                     S"Please Enter Two Integers", S"Error",
                     MessageBoxButtons::OK, MessageBoxIcon::Error );
               } // end catch
            } // end method exclusiveOrButton_Click

   // complement of first integer
   private: System::Void complementButton_Click(
               System::Object *  sender, System::EventArgs *  e)
            {
               try {
                  value1 = Convert::ToInt32( bit1TextBox->Text );
                  bit1Label->Text = GetBits( value1 );

                  // update resultTextBox
                  resultTextBox->Text = ( ~value1 ).ToString();
                  resultBitLabel->Text = GetBits( ~value1 );
               }

               // if value is not integer, exception is thrown
               catch ( FormatException * ) {
                  MessageBox::Show(
                     S"Please Enter Two Integers", S"Error",
                     MessageBoxButtons::OK, MessageBoxIcon::Error );
               } // end catch
            } // end method complementButton_Click

   public:

      // convert integer to its bit representation
      String *GetBits( int number )
      {
         int displayMask = 1 << 31;

```

Fig. I.7 Demonstrating the bitwise AND, bitwise inclusive OR, bitwise exclusive OR and bitwise complement operators. (Part 4 of 5.)

```
            StringBuilder *output = new StringBuilder();

            // get each bit, add space every 8 bits for display formatting
            for ( int c = 1; c <= 32; c++ ) {

               // append 0 or 1 depending on the result of masking
               output->Append( ( number & displayMask ) == 0 ? S"0" : S"1" );

               // shift left so that mask will find bit of
               // next digit in the next iteration of loop
               number <<= 1;

               if ( c % 8 == 0 )
                  output->Append( S" " );
            } // end for

            return output->ToString();
         } // end method GetBits

         // set fields of Form
         void SetFields()
         {
            // retrieve input values
            value1 = Convert::ToInt32( bit1TextBox->Text );
            value2 = Convert::ToInt32( bit2TextBox->Text );

            // set labels to display bit representations of integers
            bit1Label->Text = GetBits( value1 );
            bit2Label->Text = GetBits( value2 );
         } // end method SetFields
      };
}
```

Fig. I.7 Demonstrating the bitwise AND, bitwise inclusive OR, bitwise exclusive OR and bitwise complement operators. (Part 5 of 5.)

```
// Fig. I.8: Form1.cpp
// Entry point for application.

#include "stdafx.h"
#include "Form1.h"
#include <windows.h>

using namespace BitOperations;

int APIENTRY _tWinMain(HINSTANCE hInstance,
                       HINSTANCE hPrevInstance,
                       LPTSTR    lpCmdLine,
                       int       nCmdShow)
{
   System::Threading::Thread::CurrentThread->ApartmentState =
      System::Threading::ApartmentState::STA;
```

Fig. I.8 `BitOperations` class driver. (Part 1 of 2.)

```
    Application::Run(new Form1());
    return 0;
}
```

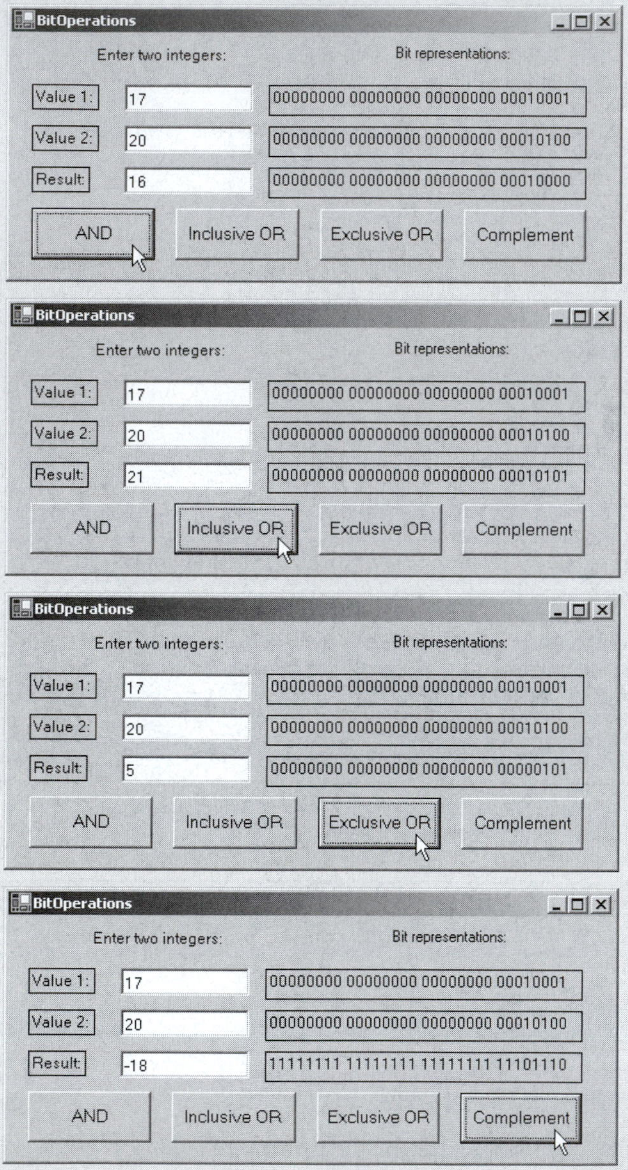

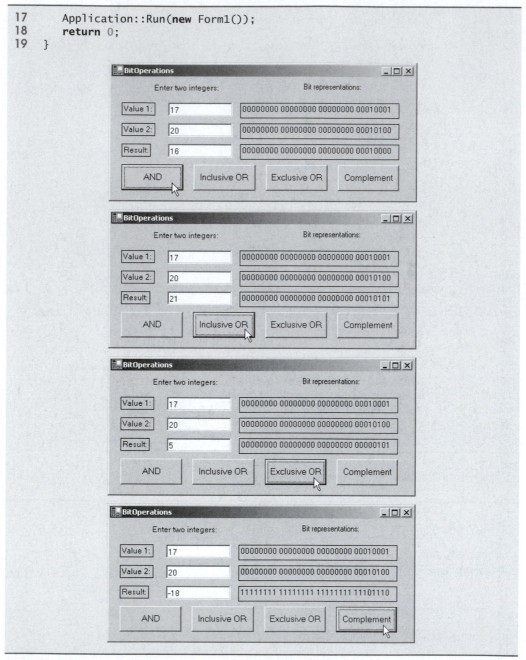

Fig. I.8 `BitOperations` class driver. (Part 2 of 2.)

The first output window of Fig. I.8 shows the results of combining the value `17` and the value `20` through the bitwise AND operator (&); the result is `16`. The second output window shows the results of combining the value `17` and the value `20` through the bitwise OR operator; the result is `21`. The third output shows the results of combining the value `17` and the value 20 through the exclusive OR operator; the result is 5. The fourth output window shows the results of taking the ones complement of the value 17. The result is -18.

The program in Fig. I.9–Fig. I.10 demonstrates the use of the left-shift operator (<<) and the right-shift operator (>>). Method GetBits (Fig. I.9, lines 135–157) returns a String* containing the bit representation of an integer value passed to it as an argument. When users enter an integer in a TextBox and press *Enter*, the program displays the bit representation of the specified integer in a Label.

```
1  // Fig. I.9: Form1.h
2  // Demonstrates bitshift operators.
3
4  #pragma once
5
6
7  namespace BitShift
8  {
9     using namespace System;
10    using namespace System::ComponentModel;
11    using namespace System::Collections;
12    using namespace System::Windows::Forms;
13    using namespace System::Data;
14    using namespace System::Drawing;
15    using namespace System::Text;
16
17    /// <summary>
18    /// Summary for Form1
19    ///
20    /// WARNING: If you change the name of this class, you will need to
21    ///          change the 'Resource File Name' property for the managed
22    ///          resource compiler tool associated with all .resx files
23    ///          this class depends on.  Otherwise, the designers will not
24    ///          be able to interact properly with localized resources
25    ///          associated with this form.
26    /// </summary>
27    public __gc class Form1 : public System::Windows::Forms::Form
28    {
29    public:
30       Form1(void)
31       {
32          InitializeComponent();
33       }
34
35    protected:
36       void Dispose(Boolean disposing)
37       {
38          if (disposing && components)
39          {
40             components->Dispose();
41          }
42          __super::Dispose(disposing);
43       }
```

Fig. I.9 BitShift::Form1 class demonstrates the bitshift operators. (Part 1 of 4.)

```
   private: System::Windows::Forms::Label *  inputLabel;

   // accepts user input
   private: System::Windows::Forms::TextBox *  inputTextBox;

   // displays integer in bits
   private: System::Windows::Forms::Label *  displayLabel;
   private: System::Windows::Forms::Button *  leftButton;
   private: System::Windows::Forms::Button *  rightButton;

   private:
      /// <summary>
      /// Required designer variable.
      /// </summary>
      System::ComponentModel::Container * components;

   // Visual Studio .NET generated GUI code

   // process user input
   private: System::Void inputTextBox_KeyDown(System::Object *  sender,
            System::Windows::Forms::KeyEventArgs *  e)
         {
            try {

               if ( e->KeyCode == Keys::Enter )
                  displayLabel->Text = GetBits( Convert::ToInt32(
                     inputTextBox->Text ) );
            }

            // if value is not integer, exception is thrown
            catch ( FormatException * ) {
               MessageBox::Show( S"Please Enter an Integer", S"Error",
                  MessageBoxButtons::OK, MessageBoxIcon::Error );
            } // end catch
         } // end method inputTextBox_KeyDown

   // do left shift
   private: System::Void leftButton_Click(
            System::Object *  sender, System::EventArgs *  e)
         {
            try {

               // retrieve user input
               int number = Convert::ToInt32( inputTextBox->Text );

               // do left shift operation
               number <<= 1;

               // convert to integer and display in textbox
               inputTextBox->Text = number.ToString();

               // display bits in label
               displayLabel->Text = GetBits( number );
```

Fig. I.9 `BitShift::Form1` class demonstrates the bitshift operators. (Part 2 of 4.)

```
            }

            // if value is not integer, exception is thrown
            catch ( FormatException * ) {
               MessageBox::Show( S"Please Enter an Integer", S"Error",
                  MessageBoxButtons::OK, MessageBoxIcon::Error );
            } // end catch
         } // end method leftButton_Click

   // do right shift
   private: System::Void rightButton_Click(
            System::Object *  sender, System::EventArgs *  e)
         {
            try {

               // retrieve user input
               int number = Convert::ToInt32( inputTextBox->Text );

               // do right shift operation
               number >>= 1;

               // convert to integer and display in textbox
               inputTextBox->Text = number.ToString();

               // display bits in label
               displayLabel->Text = GetBits( number );
            }

            // if value is not integer, exception is thrown
            catch ( FormatException * ) {
               MessageBox::Show( S"Please Enter an Integer", S"Error",
                  MessageBoxButtons::OK, MessageBoxIcon::Error );
            } // end catch
         } // end method rightButton_Click

   private:

      // convert integer to its bit representation
      String* GetBits( int number )
      {
         int displayMask = 1 << 31;

         StringBuilder *output = new StringBuilder();

         // get each bit, add space every 8 bits for display formatting
         for ( int c = 1; c <= 32; c++ ) {

            // append a 0 or 1 depending on the result of masking
            output->Append(
               ( number & displayMask ) == 0 ? S"0" : S"1" );

            // shift left so that mask will find bit of
            // next digit during next iteration of loop
```

Fig. I.9 BitShift::Form1 class demonstrates the bitshift operators. (Part 3 of 4.)

```
            number <<= 1;

            if ( c % 8 == 0 )
               output->Append( S" " );
         } // end for

         return output->ToString();
      } // end method GetBits
   };
}
```

Fig. I.9 `BitShift::Form1` class demonstrates the bitshift operators. (Part 4 of 4.)

```
// Fig. I.10: Form1.cpp
// Entry point for application.

#include "stdafx.h"
#include "Form1.h"
#include <windows.h>

using namespace BitShift;

int APIENTRY _tWinMain(HINSTANCE hInstance,
                       HINSTANCE hPrevInstance,
                       LPTSTR    lpCmdLine,
                       int       nCmdShow)
{
   System::Threading::Thread::CurrentThread->ApartmentState =
      System::Threading::ApartmentState::STA;
   Application::Run(new Form1());
   return 0;
}
```

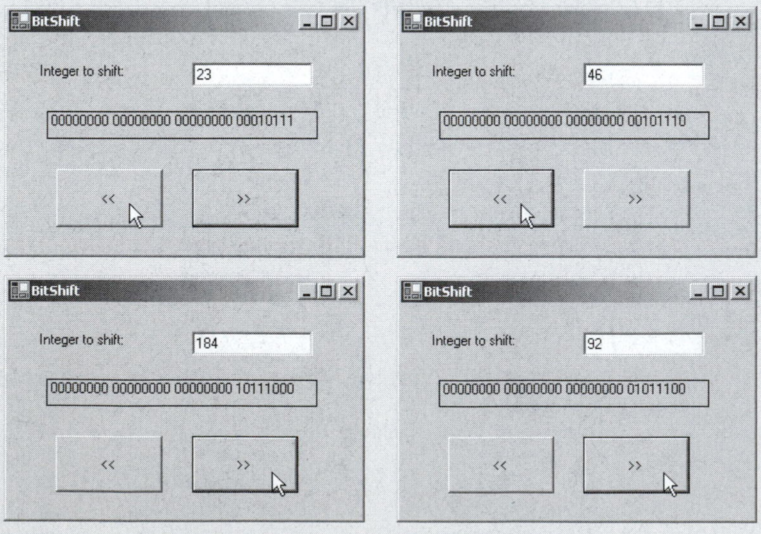

Fig. I.10 `BitShift::Form1` class driver.

Each shift operator has its own button on the application's GUI. As a user clicks each button, the bits in the integer shift left or right by one bit. The `TextBox` and `Label` display the new integer value and new bit representation, respectively.

The left-shift operator (<<) shifts the bits of its left operand to the left by the number of bits specified in its right operand. The rightmost bits are replaced with `0`s; `1`s shifted off the left are lost. The first two output windows in Fig. I.10 demonstrate the left-shift operator. To produce the output, the user entered the value `23` and clicked the left-shift button, resulting in the value `46`.

The right-shift operator (>>) shifts the bits of its left operand to the right by the number of bits specified in its right operand. `0`s replace vacated bits on the left side if the number is positive, and `1`s replace the vacated bits if the number is negative. Any `1`s shifted off the right are lost. The third and fourth output windows depict the result of shifting `184` to the right once.

Each bitwise operator (except the bitwise complement operator) has a corresponding assignment operator. Figure I.11 describes these *bitwise assignment operators*, which are used in a manner similar to the arithmetic assignment operators introduced in Chapter 4, Control Statements: Part 1.

Bitwise assignment operators	
&=	Bitwise AND assignment operator.
|=	Bitwise inclusive OR assignment operator.
^=	Bitwise exclusive OR assignment operator.
<<=	Left-shift assignment operator.
>>=	Right-shift assignment operator.

Fig. I.11 Bitwise assignment operators.

I.3 Class `BitArray`

Class *`BitArray`* (located in namespace `System::Collections`) facilitates the creation and manipulation of *bit sets*, which programmers often use to represent a set of *boolean flags*. A boolean flag is a variable that keeps track of a certain boolean decision. `BitArray`s are resizable dynamically—more bits can be added once a `BitArray` object is created, causing the object to grow to accommodate the additional bits.

Class `BitArray` provides several constructors, one of which accepts an `int` as an argument. The `int` specifies the number of bits that the `BitArray` represents, all of which are initially set to `false`.

Method *`Set`* of `BitArray` can change the value of an individual bit; it accepts the index of the bit to change and its new `bool` value. Class `BitArray` also includes an indexer that allows us to get and set individual bit values. The indexer returns `true` if the specified bit is on (i.e., the bit has value 1) and returns `false` otherwise (i.e., the bit has value 0 or "off").

Class `BitArray` method *`And`* performs a bitwise AND between two `BitArray`s and returns the `BitArray` result of the operation. Methods *`Or`* and *`Xor`* perform bitwise inclusive OR and bitwise exclusive OR operations, respectively. Class `BitArray` also provides a *`Length`* property, which returns the number of elements in the `BitArray`.

Figure I.12–Fig. I.13 demonstrates the *Sieve of Eratosthenes*, which is a technique for finding prime numbers. A prime number is an integer larger than 1 that is divisible evenly only by itself and one. The Sieve of Eratosthenes operates as follows:

1. *Create an array with all elements initialized to 1 (true). Array elements with prime subscripts remain 1. All other array elements eventually are set to 0.*
2. *Starting with array subscript 2 (subscript 1 must not be prime), every time an array element is found with a value of 1, loop through the remainder of the array and set to 0 every element whose subscript is a multiple of the subscript for the element with value 1. For example, for array subscript 2, all elements after 2 in the array that are multiples of 2 are set to 0 (subscripts 4, 6, 8, 10, etc.); for array subscript 3, all elements after 3 in the array that are multiples of 3 are set to 0 (subscripts 6, 9, 12, 15, etc.); and so on.*

At the end of this process, the subscripts of the array elements that are 1 are prime numbers. The list of prime numbers can then be displayed by locating and printing these subscripts.

```
// Fig. I.12: Form1.h
// Implements Sieve of Eratosthenes using class BitArray.

#pragma once


namespace BitArrayTest
{
   using namespace System;
   using namespace System::ComponentModel;
   using namespace System::Collections;
   using namespace System::Windows::Forms;
   using namespace System::Data;
   using namespace System::Drawing;

   /// <summary>
   /// Summary for Form1
   ///
   /// WARNING: If you change the name of this class, you will need to
   ///          change the 'Resource File Name' property for the managed
   ///          resource compiler tool associated with all .resx files
   ///          this class depends on.  Otherwise, the designers will not
   ///          be able to interact properly with localized resources
   ///          associated with this form.
   /// </summary>
   public __gc class Form1 : public System::Windows::Forms::Form
   {
   public:
      Form1(void)
      {
         InitializeComponent();

```

Fig. I.12 `BitArrayTest::Form1` class implements the Sieve of Eratosthenes, using class `BitArray`. (Part 1 of 3.)

```
         // create BitArray and set all bits to true
         sieve = new BitArray( 1024 );
         sieve->SetAll( true );

         int finalBit = static_cast< int >( Math::Sqrt( sieve->Length ) );

         // perform sieve operation
         for ( int i = 2; i < finalBit; i++ )

            if ( sieve->Get( i ) )

               for ( int j = 2 * i; j < sieve->Length; j += i )
                  sieve->Set( j, false );

         int counter = 0;

         // display prime numbers
         for ( int i = 2; i < sieve->Length; i++ )

            if ( sieve->Get( i ) )
               outputTextBox->AppendText( String::Concat( i.ToString(),
                  ( ++counter % 7 == 0 ? S"\r\n" : S"   " ) ) );
      }

   protected:
      void Dispose(Boolean disposing)
      {
         if (disposing && components)
         {
            components->Dispose();
         }
         __super::Dispose(disposing);
      }
   private: System::Windows::Forms::Label *  promptLabel;

   // user inputs integer
   private: System::Windows::Forms::TextBox *  inputTextBox;

   // display prime numbers
   private: System::Windows::Forms::TextBox *  outputTextBox;

   // displays whether input integer is prime
   private: System::Windows::Forms::Label *  displayLabel;

   private:  BitArray *sieve;

   private:
      /// <summary>
      /// Required designer variable.
      /// </summary>
      System::ComponentModel::Container * components;

```

Fig. I.12 `BitArrayTest::Form1` class implements the Sieve of Eratosthenes, using class `BitArray`. (Part 2 of 3.)

```
  // Visual Studio .NET generated code

  // end method inputTextBox_KeyDown
  private: System::Void inputTextBox_KeyDown(System::Object *  sender,
          System::Windows::Forms::KeyEventArgs *  e)
        {
          // if user pressed Enter
          if ( e->KeyCode == Keys::Enter ) {

            try {
              int number = Convert::ToInt32( inputTextBox->Text );

              // if sieve is true at index of integer
              // input by user, then number is prime
              if ( sieve->Get( number ) )
                displayLabel->Text = String::Concat(
                  number.ToString(), S" is a prime number" );
              else
                displayLabel->Text = String::Concat(
                  number.ToString(), S" is not a prime number" );
            }

            // if value is not integer, exception is thrown
            catch ( FormatException * ) {
              MessageBox::Show(
                S"Please Enter an Integer", S"Error",
                MessageBoxButtons::OK, MessageBoxIcon::Error );
            } // end catch

            // if value is not in range, exception is thrown
            catch ( ArgumentOutOfRangeException * ) {
              MessageBox::Show( S"Not in valid range", S"Error",
                MessageBoxButtons::OK, MessageBoxIcon::Error );
            } // end catch
          } // end if
        }
  };
}
```

Fig. I.12 `BitArrayTest::Form1` class implements the Sieve of Eratosthenes, using class `BitArray`. (Part 3 of 3.)

```
// Fig. I.13: Form1.cpp
// Entry point for application.

#include "stdafx.h"
#include "Form1.h"
#include <windows.h>

using namespace BitArrayTest;

```

Fig. I.13 `BitArrayTest::Form1` class driver. (Part 1 of 2.)

```
int APIENTRY _tWinMain(HINSTANCE hInstance,
                       HINSTANCE hPrevInstance,
                       LPTSTR    lpCmdLine,
                       int       nCmdShow)
{
   System::Threading::Thread::CurrentThread->ApartmentState =
      System::Threading::ApartmentState::STA;
   Application::Run(new Form1());
   return 0;
}
```

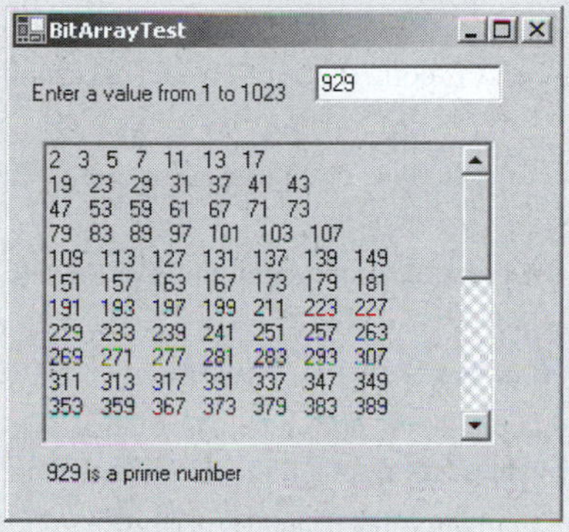

Fig. I.13 `BitArrayTest::Form1` class driver. (Part 2 of 2.)

We use a `BitArray` to implement the algorithm. The program displays the prime numbers in the range 1–1023 in a `TextBox`. The program also provides a `TextBox` in which users can type any number from 1–1023 to determine whether that number is prime. (In which case, it displays a message indicating that the number is prime.)

The statement in line 34 (of Fig. I.12) creates a `BitArray` of `1024` bits. `BitArray` method *`SetAll`* sets all the bits to `true` in line 35; then, lines 37–45 determine all prime numbers occurring between 1 and 1023. The integer `finalBit` determines when the algorithm is complete.

When the user inputs a number and presses *Enter*, line 99 tests whether the input number is prime. This line uses the *`Get`* method of class `BitArray`, which takes a number and returns the value of that bit in the array. Lines 100–101 and 103–104 display an appropriate response.

SUMMARY

- Computers represent data internally as sequences of bits. Each bit can assume the value 0 or the value 1.
- On all systems, a sequence of 8 bits forms a byte—the standard storage unit for a variable of type `char`. Other data types require larger numbers of bytes for storage.
- The bitwise AND operator sets each bit in the result to 1 if the corresponding bits in both operands are 1.
- Often, the bitwise AND operator is used with a mask operand—an integer value with specific bits set to 1. Masks hide some bits in a value and select other bits.

- The bitwise inclusive OR operator sets each bit in the result to 1 if the corresponding bit in either (or both) operand(s) are 1.
- The bitwise exclusive OR operator sets each bit in the result to 1 if the corresponding bit in exactly one operand is 1. Exclusive OR is also known as XOR.
- The left-shift (<<) operator shifts the bits of its left operand to the left by the number of bits specified in its right operand.
- The right-shift (>>) operator shifts the bits in its left operand to the right by the number of bits specified in its right operand. If the left operand is negative, `1`s are shifted in from the left, whereas, if the left operand is positive, `0`s are shifted in from the left.
- The bitwise complement (~) operator sets all `0` bits in its operand to `1` in the result and sets all `1` bits to `0` in the result; this process is sometimes referred to as "taking the ones complement of the value."
- Each bitwise operator (except the bitwise complement operator) has a corresponding assignment operator.
- Class `BitArray` facilitates the creation and manipulation of bit sets, which programmers often use to represent a set of boolean flags.
- A boolean flag is a variable that keeps track of a certain boolean decision.
- `BitArray`s are resizable dynamically—more bits can be added once a `BitArray` object is created, causing the object to grow to accommodate the additional bits.
- Method `Set` of `BitArray` can change the value of an individual bit—it accepts the index of the bit to change and the `bool` value to which the bit should change.
- `BitArray` method `And` performs a bitwise AND between two `BitArray`s. It returns the `BitArray` that is the result of performing this operation.
- Methods `Or` and `Xor`, perform bitwise inclusive OR and bitwise exclusive OR, respectively.
- `BitArray` method `SetAll` sets all the bits in the `BitArray` to `true`.

Bibliography

Albahari, B., P. Drayton and B. Merrill. *C# Essentials*. Cambridge, MA: O'Reilly & Associates, 2001.

Anderson, R., A. Homer, R. Howard and D. Sussman. *A Preview of Active Server Pages+*. Birmingham, UK: Wrox Press, 2001.

Anderson, R., B. Francis, A. Homer, R. Howard, D. Sussman and K. Watson. *ASP .NET*. Chicago, IL: Wrox Press, Inc., 2001.

Archer, T. *Inside C#*. Redmond, WA: Microsoft Press, 2001.

Blaha, M. R., W. J. Premerlani and J. E. Rumbaugh. "Relational Database Design Using an Object-Oriented Methodology." *Communications of the ACM*. Vol. 31, No. 4, April 1988, 414–427.

Carr, D. F. "Dave Winer: The President of Userland and SOAP Co-Creator Surveys the Changing Scene." *Internet World*. March 2001, 53–58.

Carr, D. "Hitting a High Note." *Internet World*. March 2001, 71.

Carr, D. "Slippery SOAP." *Internet World*. March 2001, 72–74.

Challa, S. and Laksberg, A. *Essential Guide to Managed Extensions for C++*. Berkeley, CA: Apress, 2002.

Chappel, D. "A Standard for Web Services: SOAP vs. ebXML." *Application Development Trends*, February 2001, 17.

Chappel, D. "Coming Soon: The Biggest Platform Ever." *Application Development Trends Magazine*, May 2001, 15.

Codd, E. F. "A Relational Model of Data for Large Shared Data Banks." *Communications of the ACM*, June 1970.

Codd, E. F. "Fatal Flaws in SQL." *Datamation*, Vol. 34, No. 16, August 15, 1988, 45–48.

Codd, E. F. "Further Normalization of the Data Base Relational Model." *Courant Computer Science Symposia*, Vol. 6, *Data Base Systems*. Upper Saddle River, N.J.: Prentice Hall, 1972.

Conard, J., P. Dengler, B. Francis, J. Glynn, B. Harvey, B. Hollis, R. Ramachandran, J. Schenken, S. Short and C. Ullman. *Introducing .NET*. Birmingham, UK: Wrox Press, 2000.

Corera, A., Fraser, S., McLean, S., Kumar, N., Robinson, S., Sarang, P.G. and Gentile, S. *Visual C++ .NET: A Primer for C++ Developers*. Birmingham, United Kingdon: Wrox Press, 2002.

Correia, E. J. "Visual Studio .NET to Speak in Tongues." *Software Development Times*, April 2001, 12.

Cornell, G. and J. Morrison. *Moving to VB .NET: Strategies, Concepts, and Code.* Berkeley, CA: Apress Publishing, 2001.

Date, C. J. *An Introduction to Database Systems, Seventh Edition.* Reading, MA: Addison-Wesley Publishing, 2000.

Davydov, M. "The Road to the Future of Web Services." *Intelligent Enterprise.* May 2001, 50–52.

Deitel, H. M., P. J. Deitel, T. R. Nieto, J. Lisfield, C. Yaeger, M. and Zlatkina. *C# How To Program.* Upper Saddle River, NJ: Prentice Hall, 2002.

Deitel, H. M. *Operating Systems, Second Edition.* Reading, MA: Addison Wesley Publishing, 1990.

Deitel, H. M. and P. J. Deitel. *Java How To Program, Fifth Edition.* Upper Saddle River, NJ: Prentice Hall, 2003.

Deitel, H. M., P. J. Deitel and T. R. Nieto. *Visual Basic .NET How To Program, Second Edition.* Upper Saddle River, NJ: Prentice Hall, 2001.

Deitel, H. M., P. J. Deitel, C. Couremarche, J. Liperi, T. R. Nieto, C. and Yaeger. *Visual C++ .NET: A Managed Code Approach for Experienced Programmers.* Upper Saddle River, NJ: Prentice Hall, 2002.

Deitel, H. M., P. J. Deitel, T. R. Nieto, T. M. Lin and P. Sadhu. *XML How To Program.* Upper Saddle River, NJ: Prentice Hall, 2001.

Dejong, J. "Microsoft's Clout Drives Web Services." *Software Development Times*, March 2001, 29, 31.

Dejong, J. "One-Stop Shopping: A Favored Method." *Software Development Times*, February 2001, 20.

Dejong, J. "Raising the Bar." *Software Development Times*, March 2001, 29–30.

Erlanger. L. "Dissecting .NET." *Internet World*, March 2001, 30–36.

Erlanger. L. ".NET Services." *Internet World*, March 2001, 47.

Esposito, D. "Data Grid In-Place Editing." *MSDN Magazine*, June 2001, 37–45.

Esposito, D. "Server-Side ASP .NET Data Binding: Part 2: Customizing the Data Grid Control." *MSDN Magazine*, April 2001, 33–45.

Finlay, D. "GoXML Native Database Clusters Data, Reduces Seek Time." *Software Development Times*, March 2001, 5.

Finlay, D. "New York Prepares for .NET Conference." *Software Development Times*, June 2001, 23.

Finlay, D. "UDDI Works on Classification, Taxonomy Issues." *Software Development Times*, March 2001, 3.

Fontana, J. "What You Get in .NET." *Network World*, April 2001, 75.

Galli, P. and R. Holland. ".NET Taking Shape, But Developers Still Wary." *eWeek*, June 2001, pages 9, 13.

Gillen, A. "Sun's Answer to .NET." *EntMag*, March 2001, 38.

Gillen, A. "What a Year It's Been." *EntMag*, December 2000, 54.

Gladwin, L. C. "Microsoft, eBay Strike Web Services Deal." *Computer World*, March 2001, 22.

Grimes, R. "Make COM Programming a Breeze with New Feature in Visual Studio .NET." *MSDN Magazine*, April 2001, 48–62.

Grimes, R. *Programming with Managed Extensions for Visual C++ .NET.* Redmond, Washington: Microsoft Press, 2003.

Gunnerson, E. *A Programmer's Introduction to C#: Second Edition.* New York, NY: Apress, 2001.

Harvey, B., S. Robinson, J. Templeman and K. Watson. *C# Programming With the Public Beta.* Birmingham, UK: Wrox Press, 2000.

Holland, R. "Microsoft Scales Back VB Changes." *eWeek*, April 2001, 16.

Holland, R. "Tools Case Transition to .NET Platform." *eWeek*, March 2001, 21.

Hulme, G, V. "XML Specification May Ease PKI Integration." *Information Week*, December 2000, 38.

Hutchinson, J. "Can't Fit Another Byte." *Network Computing*, March 2001, 14.

Jepson, B. "Applying .NET to Web Services." *Web Techniques*, May 2001, 49–54.

Jones, B. *Sams Teach Yourself C# in 21 Days*. Indianapolis, IN: Sams Publishing, 2002.

Karney. J. ".NET Devices." *Internet World*, March 2001, 49–50.

Kiely, D. "Doing .NET In Internet Time." *Information Week*, December 2000, 137–138, 142–144, 148.

Kirtland, M. "The Programmable Web: Web Services Provides Building Blocks for the Microsoft .NET Framework." *MSDN Magazine*, September 2000 <msdn.microsoft.com/msdnmag/issues/0900/WebPlatform/WebPlatform.asp>.

Levitt, J. "Plug-And-Play Redefined." *Information Week*, April 2001, 63–68.

McCright, J. S. and D. Callaghan. "Lotus Pushes Domino Services." *eWeek*, June 2001, 14.

Michaelis, M. and P. Spokas. *C# Developer's Headstart*. New York, NY: Osbourne/McGraw-Hill, 2001.

"Microsoft Chimes in with New C Sharp Programming Language." Xephon Web site. June 30, 2000 <www.xephon.com/news/00063019.html>.

Microsoft Corporation, *Microsoft C# Language Specifications*. Redmond, VA: Microsoft Press, 2001.

Microsoft Developer Network Documentation. Visual Studio .NET CD-ROM, 2001.

Microsoft Developer Network Library. .NET Framework SDK. Microsoft Web site <msdn.microsoft.com/library/default.asp>.

Moran, B. "Questions, Answers, and Tips." *SQL Server Magazine*, April 2001, 19–20.

Mueller, J. *Visual C++ .NET Developer's Guide*. New York, NY: McGraw-Hill Publishing, 2002.

MySQL Manual. MySQL Web site <www.mysql.com/doc/>.

Olsen, A. and Templeman, J. *Microsoft Visual C++ .NET Step By Step*. Redmond. Washington: Microsoft Press, 2003.

Oracle Technology Network Documentation. Oracle Web site. <otn.oracle.com/docs/content.html>.

Otey, M. "Me Too .NET." *SQL Server Magazine*. April 2001, 7.

Papa, J. "Revisiting the Ad-Hoc Data Display Web Application." *MSDN Magazine*, June 2001, 27–33.

Pappas, C. and Murray, W. *The Complete Reference Visual C++ .NET*. New York, NY: McGraw-Hill Publishing, 2002.

Powell, R. and R. Weeks. *C# and the .NET Framework: The C# Perspective*. Indianapolis, IN: Sams Publishing, 2002.

Pratschner, S. "Simplifying Deployment and Solving DLL Hell with the .NET Framework." *MSDN Library*, September 2000 <msdn.microsoft.com/library/techart/dplywithnet.htm>.

Prosise, J. "Wicked Code." *MSDN Magazine*, April 2001, 121–127.

Reeves, R. *C++/C# Programmer's Guide for Windows 2000*. Upper Saddle River, NJ: Prentice Hall, 2002.

Relational Technology, *INGRES Overview*. Alameda, CA: Relational Technology, 1988.

Ricadela, A. "IBM Readies XML Middleware." *Information Week*, December 2000, 155.

Ricadela, A. and P. McDougall. "eBay Deal Helps Microsoft Sell .NET Strategy." *Information Week*, March 2001, 33.

Richter, J. "An Introduction to Delegates." *MSDN Magazine*, April 2001, 107–111.

Richter, J. "Delegates, Part 2." *MSDN Magazine*, June 2001, 133–139.

Rizzo, T. "Let's Talk Web Services." *Internet World*, April 2001, 4–5.

Rizzo, T. "Moving to Square One." *Internet World*, March 2001, 4–5.

Robinson, S., O. Cornes, J. Glynn, B. Harvey, C. McQueen, J. Moemeka, C. Nagel, M. Skinner and K. Watson. *Professional C#*. Birmingham, UK: Wrox Press, 2001.

Rollman, R. "XML Q & A." *SQL Server Magazine*, April 2001, 57–58.

Rubinstein, D. "Suit Settled, Acrimony Remains." *Software Development Times*, February 2001, 1, 8.

Rubinstein, D. "Play It Again, XML." *Software Development Times*, March 2001, 12.

Scott, G. "Adjusting to Adversity." *EntMag*, March 2001, 38.

Scott, G. "Putting on the Breaks." *EntMag*, December 2000, 54.

Sells, C. "Managed Extensions Bring .NET CLR Support to C++." *MSDN Magazine*. July 2001, 115–122.

Seltzer, L. "Standards and .NET." *Internet World*, March 2001, 75–76.

Shohoud, Y. "Tracing, Logging, and Threading Made Easy with .NET." *MSDN Magazine*, July 2001, 60–72.

Sliwa, C. "Microsoft Backs Off Changes to VB .NET." *Computer World*, April 2001, 14.

Songini, Marc. "Despite Tough Times, Novell Users Remain Upbeat." *Computer World*, March 2001, 22.

Spencer, K. "Cleaning House." *SQL Server Magazine*, April 2001, 61–62.

Spencer, K. "Windows Forms in Visual Basic .NET." *MSDN Magazine*, April 2001, 25–45.

Stonebraker, M. "Operating System Support for Database Management." *Communications of the ACM*, Vol. 24, No. 7, July 1981, 412–418.

Surveyor. J. ".NET Framework." *Internet World*, March 2001, 43–44.

Tapang, C. C. "New Definition Languages Expose Your COM Objects to SOAP Clients." *MSDN Magazine*, April 2001, 85–89.

Thai, T. and H. Q. Lam. *.NET Framework*. Cambridge, MA: O'Reilly & Associates, Inc., 2001.

Troelsen, A. *C# and the .NET Platform*. New York, NY: Apress, 2001.

Utley, C. *A Programmer's Introduction to Visual Basic .NET*. Indianapolis, IN: Sams Publishing, 2001.

Visual Studio .NET ADO .NET Overview. Microsoft Developers Network Web site <`msdn.microsoft.com/vstudio/nextgen/technology/adoplusdefault.asp`>.

Ward, K. "Microsoft Attempts to Demystify .NET." *EntMag*, December 2000, 1.

Waymire, R. "Answers from Microsoft." *SQL Server Magazine*, April 2001, 71–72.

Whitney, R. "XML for Analysis." *SQL Server Magazine*, April 2001, 63–66.

Wille, C. *Presenting C#*. Indianapolis, IN: Sams Publishing, 2000.

Winston, A. "A Distributed Database Primer." *UNIX World*, April 1988, 54–63.

Zeichick, A. "Microsoft Serious About Web Services." *Software Development Times*, March 2001, 3.

Index

Symbols

A

B

C

E

F

G

H

Q

R

T

U

X

Y

Z

End User License Agreements

Prentice Hall License Agreement and Limited Warranty

READ THE FOLLOWING TERMS AND CONDITIONS CAREFULLY BEFORE OPENING THIS SOFTWARE PACKAGE. THIS LEGAL DOCUMENT IS AN AGREEMENT BETWEEN YOU AND PRENTICE-HALL, INC. (THE "COMPANY"). BY OPENING THIS SEALED SOFTWARE PACKAGE, YOU ARE AGREEING TO BE BOUND BY THESE TERMS AND CONDITIONS. IF YOU DO NOT AGREE WITH THESE TERMS AND CONDITIONS, DO NOT OPEN THE SOFTWARE PACKAGE. PROMPTLY RETURN THE UNOPENED SOFTWARE PACKAGE AND ALL ACCOMPANYING ITEMS TO THE PLACE YOU OBTAINED THEM FOR A FULL REFUND OF ANY SUMS YOU HAVE PAID.

1. GRANT OF LICENSE: In consideration of your purchase of this book, and your agreement to abide by the terms and conditions of this Agreement, the Company grants to you a nonexclusive right to use and display the copy of the enclosed software program (hereinafter the "SOFTWARE") on a single computer (i.e., with a single CPU) at a single location so long as you comply with the terms of this Agreement. The Company reserves all rights not expressly granted to you under this Agreement.

2. OWNERSHIP OF SOFTWARE: You own only the magnetic or physical media (the enclosed media) on which the SOFTWARE is recorded or fixed, but the Company and the software developers retain all the rights, title, and ownership to the SOFTWARE recorded on the original media copy(ies) and all subsequent copies of the SOFTWARE, regardless of the form or media on which the original or other copies may exist. This license is not a sale of the original SOFTWARE or any copy to you.

3. COPY RESTRICTIONS: This SOFTWARE and the accompanying printed materials and user manual (the "Documentation") are the subject of copyright. The individual programs on the media are copyrighted by the authors of each program. Some of the programs on the media include separate licensing agreements. If you intend to use one of these programs, you must read and follow its accompanying license agreement. You may not copy the Documentation or the SOFTWARE, except that you may make a single copy of the SOFTWARE for backup or archival purposes only. You may be held legally responsible for any copying or copyright infringement which is caused or encouraged by your failure to abide by the terms of this restriction.

4. USE RESTRICTIONS: You may not network the SOFTWARE or otherwise use it on more than one computer or computer terminal at the same time. You may physically transfer the SOFTWARE from one computer to another provided that the SOFTWARE is used on only one computer at a time. You may not distribute copies of the SOFTWARE or Documentation to others. You may not reverse engineer, disassemble, decompile, modify, adapt, translate, or create derivative works based on the SOFTWARE or the Documentation without the prior written consent of the Company.

5. TRANSFER RESTRICTIONS: The enclosed SOFTWARE is licensed only to you and may not be transferred to any one else without the prior written consent of the Company. Any unauthorized transfer of the SOFTWARE shall result in the immediate termination of this Agreement.

6. TERMINATION: This license is effective until terminated. This license will terminate automatically without notice from the Company and become null and void if you fail to comply with any provisions or limitations of this license. Upon termination, you shall destroy the Documentation and all copies of the SOFTWARE. All provisions of this Agreement as to warranties, limitation of liability, remedies or damages, and our ownership rights shall survive termination.

7. MISCELLANEOUS: This Agreement shall be construed in accordance with the laws of the United States of America and the State of New York and shall benefit the Company, its affiliates, and assignees.

8. LIMITED WARRANTY AND DISCLAIMER OF WARRANTY: The Company warrants that the SOFTWARE, when properly used in accordance with the Documentation, will operate in substantial conformity with the description of the SOFTWARE set forth in the Documentation. The Company does not warrant that the SOFTWARE will meet your requirements or that the operation of the SOFTWARE will be uninterrupted or error-free. The Company warrants that the media on which the SOFTWARE is delivered shall be free from defects in materials and workmanship under normal use for a period of thirty (30) days from the date of your purchase. Your only remedy and the Company's only obligation under these limited warranties is, at the Company's option, return of the warranted item for a refund of any amounts paid by you or replacement of the item. Any replacement of SOFTWARE or media under the warranties shall not extend the original warranty period. The limited warranty set forth above shall not apply to any SOFTWARE which the Company determines in good faith has been subject to misuse, neglect, improper installation, repair, alteration, or damage by you. EXCEPT FOR THE EXPRESSED WARRANTIES SET FORTH ABOVE, THE COMPANY DISCLAIMS ALL WARRANTIES, EXPRESS OR IMPLIED, INCLUDING WITHOUT LIMITATION, THE IMPLIED WARRANTIES OF MERCHANTABILITY AND FITNESS FOR A PARTICULAR PURPOSE. EXCEPT FOR THE EXPRESS WARRANTY SET FORTH ABOVE, THE COMPANY DOES NOT WARRANT, GUARANTEE, OR MAKE ANY REPRESENTATION REGARDING THE USE OR THE RESULTS OF THE USE OF THE SOFTWARE IN TERMS OF ITS CORRECTNESS, ACCURACY, RELIABILITY, CURRENTNESS, OR OTHERWISE.

IN NO EVENT, SHALL THE COMPANY OR ITS EMPLOYEES, AGENTS, SUPPLIERS, OR CONTRACTORS BE LIABLE FOR ANY INCIDENTAL, INDIRECT, SPECIAL, OR CONSEQUENTIAL DAMAGES ARISING OUT OF OR IN CONNECTION

WITH THE LICENSE GRANTED UNDER THIS AGREEMENT, OR FOR LOSS OF USE, LOSS OF DATA, LOSS OF INCOME OR PROFIT, OR OTHER LOSSES, SUSTAINED AS A RESULT OF INJURY TO ANY PERSON, OR LOSS OF OR DAMAGE TO PROPERTY, OR CLAIMS OF THIRD PARTIES, EVEN IF THE COMPANY OR AN AUTHORIZED REPRESENTATIVE OF THE COMPANY HAS BEEN ADVISED OF THE POSSIBILITY OF SUCH DAMAGES. IN NO EVENT SHALL LIABILITY OF THE COMPANY FOR DAMAGES WITH RESPECT TO THE SOFTWARE EXCEED THE AMOUNTS ACTUALLY PAID BY YOU, IF ANY, FOR THE SOFTWARE.

SOME JURISDICTIONS DO NOT ALLOW THE LIMITATION OF IMPLIED WARRANTIES OR LIABILITY FOR INCIDENTAL, INDIRECT, SPECIAL, OR CONSEQUENTIAL DAMAGES, SO THE ABOVE LIMITATIONS MAY NOT ALWAYS APPLY. THE WARRANTIES IN THIS AGREEMENT GIVE YOU SPECIFIC LEGAL RIGHTS AND YOU MAY ALSO HAVE OTHER RIGHTS WHICH VARY IN ACCORDANCE WITH LOCAL LAW.

ACKNOWLEDGMENT

YOU ACKNOWLEDGE THAT YOU HAVE READ THIS AGREEMENT, UNDERSTAND IT, AND AGREE TO BE BOUND BY ITS TERMS AND CONDITIONS. YOU ALSO AGREE THAT THIS AGREEMENT IS THE COMPLETE AND EXCLUSIVE STATEMENT OF THE AGREEMENT BETWEEN YOU AND THE COMPANY AND SUPERSEDES ALL PROPOSALS OR PRIOR AGREEMENTS, ORAL, OR WRITTEN, AND ANY OTHER COMMUNICATIONS BETWEEN YOU AND THE COMPANY OR ANY REPRESENTATIVE OF THE COMPANY RELATING TO THE SUBJECT MATTER OF THIS AGREEMENT.

Should you have any questions concerning this Agreement or if you wish to contact the Company for any reason, please contact in writing at the address below.

Robin Short
Prentice Hall PTR
One Lake Street
Upper Saddle River, New Jersey 07458

Getting Started with Microsoft® Visual C++™ 6 with an Introduction to MFC

BOOK / CD-ROM

©2000, 163 pp., paper (0-13-016147-0)

Visual C++ .NET® How To Program

BOOK / CD-ROM

©2004, 1400 pp., paper (0-13-437377-4)

Written by the authors of the world's best-selling introductory/intermediate C and C++ textbooks, this comprehensive book thoroughly examines Visual C++® .NET. *Visual C++® .NET How to Program* begins with a strong foundation in the introductory and intermediate programming principles students will need in industry, including fundamental topics such as arrays, functions and control structures. Readers learn the concepts of object-oriented programming, including how to create reusable software components with classes and assemblies. The text then explores such essential topics as networking, databases, XML and multimedia. Graphical user interfaces are also extensively covered, giving students the tools to build compelling and fully interactive programs using the "drag-and-drop" techniques provided by the latest version of Visual Studio .NET, Visual Studio .NET 2003.

Advanced Java™ 2 Platform How to Program

BOOK / CD-ROM

©2002, 1811 pp., paper (0-13-089560-1)

Expanding on the world's best-selling Java textbook—*Java™ How to Program*—*Advanced Java™ 2 Platform How To Program* presents advanced Java topics for developing sophisticated, user-friendly GUIs; significant, scalable enterprise applications; wireless applications and distributed systems. Primarily based on Java 2 Enterprise Edition (J2EE), this textbook integrates technologies such as XML, JavaBeans, security, JDBC™, JavaServer Pages (JSP™), servlets, Remote Method Invocation (RMI), Enterprise JavaBeans™ (EJB) and design patterns into a production-quality system that allows developers to benefit from the leverage and platform independence Java 2 Enterprise Edition provides. The book also features the development of a complete, end-to-end e-business solution using advanced Java technologies. Additional topics include Swing, Java 2D and 3D, XML, design patterns, CORBA, Jini™, JavaSpaces™, Jiro™, Java Management Extensions (JMX) and Peer-to-Peer networking with an introduction to JXTA. This textbook also introduces the Java 2 Micro Edition (J2ME™) for building applications for handheld and wireless devices using MIDP and MIDlets. Wireless technologies covered include WAP, WML and i-mode.

C# How to Program

BOOK / CD-ROM

©2002, 1568 pp., paper (0-13-062221-4)

An exciting addition to the *How to Program Series, C# How to Program* provides a comprehensive introduction to Microsoft's new object-oriented language. C# builds on the skills already mastered by countless C++ and Java programmers, enabling them to create powerful Web applications and components—ranging from XML-based Web services on Microsoft's .NET platform to middle-tier business objects and system-level applications. *C# How to Program* begins with a strong foundation in the introductory- and intermediate-programming principles students will need in industry. It then explores such essential topics as object-oriented programming and exception handling. Graphical user interfaces are extensively covered, giving readers the tools to build compelling and fully interactive programs. Internet technologies such as XML, ADO .NET and Web services are covered as well as topics including regular expressions, multithreading, networking, databases, files and data structures.

Visual Basic® .NET How to Program Second Edition

BOOK / CD-ROM

©2002, 1400 pp., paper (0-13-029363-6)

Learn Visual Basic .NET programming from the ground up! The introduction of Microsoft's .NET Framework marks the beginning of major revisions to all of Microsoft's programming languages. This book provides a comprehensive introduction to the next version of Visual Basic—Visual Basic .NET—featuring extensive updates and increased functionality. *Visual Basic .NET How to Program, Second Edition* covers introductory programming techniques as well as more advanced topics, featuring enhanced treatment of developing Web-based applications. Other topics discussed include an extensive treatment of XML and wireless applications, databases, SQL and ADO .NET, Web forms, Web services and ASP .NET.

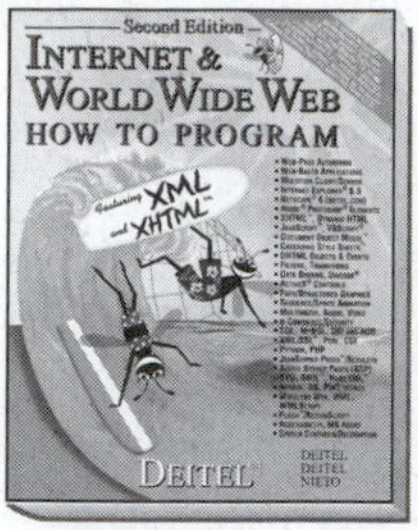

Second Edition
INTERNET & WORLD WIDE WEB HOW TO PROGRAM
DEITEL

Internet & World Wide Web How to Program, Second Edition

BOOK / CD-ROM

©2002, 1428 pp., paper (0-13-030897-8)

The revision of this groundbreaking book offers a thorough treatment of programming concepts that yield visible or audible results in Web pages and Web-based applications. This book discusses effective Web-based design, server- and client-side scripting, multitier Web-based applications development, ActiveX® controls and electronic commerce essentials. This book offers an alternative to traditional programming courses using markup languages (such as XHTML, Dynamic HTML and XML) and scripting languages (such as JavaScript, VBScript, Perl/CGI, Python and PHP) to teach the fundamentals of programming "wrapped in the metaphor of the Web." Updated material on `www.deitel.com` and `www.prenhall.com/deitel` provides additional resources for instructors who want to cover Microsoft® or non-Microsoft technologies. The Web site includes an extensive treatment of Netscape® 6 and alternate versions of the code from the Dynamic HTML chapters that will work with non-Microsoft environments as well.

Wireless Internet & Mobile Business How to Program

©2002, 1292 pp., paper (0-13-062226-5)

While the rapid expansion of wireless technologies, such as cell phones, pagers and personal digital assistants (PDAs), offers many new opportunities for businesses and programmers, it also presents numerous challenges related to issues such as security and standardization. This book offers a thorough treatment of both the management and technical aspects of this growing area, including coverage of current practices and future trends. The first half explores the business issues surrounding wireless technology and mobile business, including an overview of existing and developing communication technologies and the application of business principles to wireless devices. It also discusses location-based services and location-identifying technologies, a topic that is revisited throughout the book. Wireless payment, security, legal and social issues, international communications and more are also discussed. The book then turns to programming for the wireless Internet, exploring topics such as WAP (including 2.0), WML, WMLScript, XML, XHTML™, wireless Java programming (J2ME™), Web Clipping and more. Other topics covered include career resources, wireless marketing, accessibility, Palm™, PocketPC, Windows CE, i-mode, Bluetooth, MIDP, MIDlets, ASP, Microsoft .NET Mobile Framework, BREW™, multimedia, Flash™ and VBScript.

Python How to Program

BOOK / CD-ROM

©2002, 1376 pp., paper (0-13-092361-3)

This exciting new textbook provides a comprehensive introduction to Python—a powerful object-oriented programming language with clear syntax and the ability to bring together various technologies quickly and easily. This book covers introductory-programming techniques and more advanced topics such as graphical user interfaces, databases, wireless Internet programming, networking, security, process management, multithreading, XHTML, CSS, PSP and multimedia. Readers will learn principles that are applicable to both systems development and Web programming. The book features the consistent and applied pedagogy that the *How to Program Series* is known for, including the Deitels' signature *Live-Code* Approach, with thousands of lines of code in hundreds of working programs; hundreds of valuable programming tips identified with icons throughout the text; an extensive set of exercises, projects and case studies; two-color four-way syntax coloring and much more.

e-Business & e-Commerce for Managers

©2001, 794 pp., cloth (0-13-032364-0)

This comprehensive overview of building and managing e-businesses explores topics such as the decision to bring a business online, choosing a business model, accepting payments, marketing strategies and security, as well as many other important issues (such as career resources). The book features Web resources and online demonstrations that supplement the text and direct readers to additional materials. The book also includes an appendix that develops a complete Web-based shopping-cart application using HTML, JavaScript, VBScript, Active Server Pages, ADO, SQL, HTTP, XML and XSL. Plus, company-specific sections provide "real-world" examples of the concepts presented in the book.

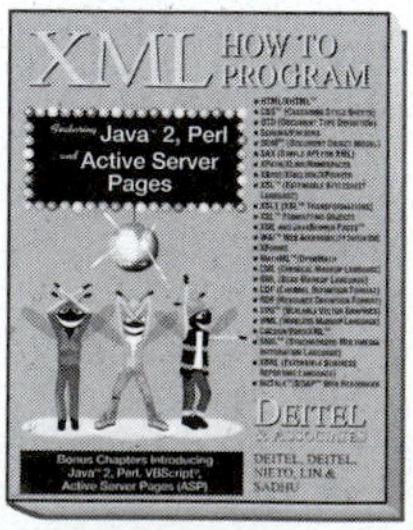

XML How to Program

BOOK / CD-ROM

©2001, 934 pp., paper (0-13-028417-3)

This book is a comprehensive guide to programming in XML. It teaches how to use XML to create customized tags and includes chapters that address markup languages for science and technology, multimedia, commerce and many other fields. Concise introductions to Java, JavaServer Pages, VBScript, Active Server Pages and Perl/CGI provide readers with the essentials of these programming languages and server-side development technologies to enable them to work effectively with XML. The book also covers cutting-edge topics such as XSL, DOM™ and SAX, plus a real-world e-commerce case study and a complete chapter on Web accessibility that addresses Voice XML. It includes tips such as Common Programming Errors, Software Engineering Observations, Portability Tips and Debugging Hints. Other topics covered include XHTML, CSS, DTD, schema, parsers, XPath, XLink, namespaces, XBase, XInclude, XPointer, XSLT, XSL Formatting Objects, JavaServer Pages, XForms, topic maps, X3D, MathML, OpenMath, CML, BML, CDF, RDF, SVG, Cocoon, WML, XBRL and BizTalk™ and SOAP™ Web resources.

Perl How to Program

BOOK / CD-ROM

©2001, 1057 pp., paper (0-13-028418-1)

This comprehensive guide to Perl programming emphasizes the use of the Common Gateway Interface (CGI) with Perl to create powerful, dynamic multi-tier Web-based client/server applications. The book begins with a clear and careful introduction to programming concepts at a level suitable for beginners, and proceeds through advanced topics such as references and complex data structures. Key Perl topics such as regular expressions and string manipulation are covered in detail. The authors address important and topical issues such as object-oriented programming, the Perl database interface (DBI), graphics and security. Also included is a treatment of XML, a bonus chapter introducing the Python programming language, supplemental material on career resources and a complete chapter on Web accessibility. The text includes tips such as Common Programming Errors, Software Engineering Observations, Portability Tips and Debugging Hints.

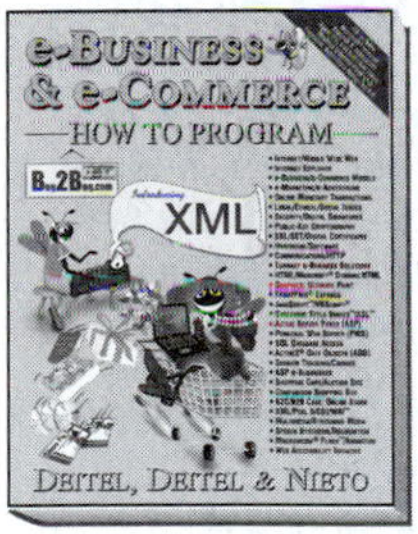

e-Business & e-Commerce How to Program

BOOK / CD-ROM

©2001, 1254 pp., paper (0-13-028419-X)

This innovative book explores programming technologies for developing Web-based e-business and e-commerce solutions, and covers e-business and e-commerce models and business issues. Readers learn a full range of options, from "build-your-own" to turnkey solutions. The book examines scores of the top e-businesses (examples include Amazon, eBay, Priceline, Travelocity, etc.), explaining the technical details of building successful e-business and e-commerce sites and their underlying business premises. Learn how to implement the dominant e-commerce models—shopping carts, auctions, name-your-own-price, comparison shopping and bots/ intelligent agents—by using markup languages (HTML, Dynamic HTML and XML), scripting languages (JavaScript, VBScript and Perl), server-side technologies (Active Server Pages and Perl/CGI) and database (SQL and ADO), security and online payment technologies. Updates are regularly posted to `www.deitel.com` and the book includes a CD-ROM with software tools, source code and live links.

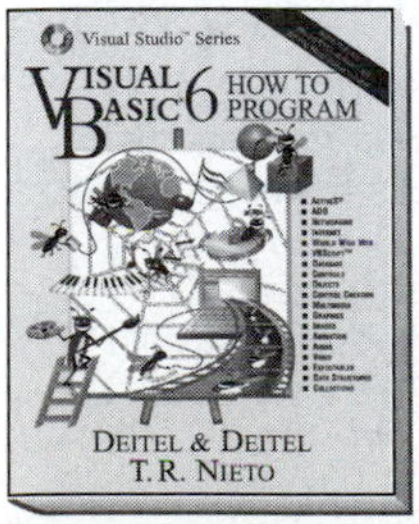

Visual Basic® 6 How to Program

BOOK / CD-ROM

©1999, 1015 pp., paper (0-13-456955-5)

Visual Basic® 6 How to Program was developed in cooperation with Microsoft to cover important topics such as graphical user interfaces (GUIs), multimedia, object-oriented programming, networking, database programming, VBScript®, COM/DCOM and ActiveX®.

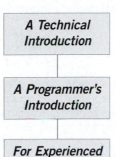

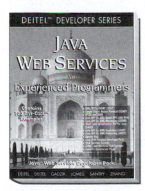

BOOK/MULTIMEDIA PACKAGES

The Complete C++ Training Course, Fourth Edition
(0-13-100252-X)

The Complete e-Business & e-Commerce Programming Training Course
(0-13-089549-0)

The Complete Java™ Training Course, Fifth Edition
(0-13-101766-7)

The Complete Perl Training Course
(0-13-089552-0)

The Complete Visual Basic® .NET Training Course, Second Edition
(0-13-042530-3)

The Complete Visual Basic® 6 Training Course
(0-13-082929-3)

The Complete C# Training Course
(0-13-064584-2)

The Complete Python Training Course
(0-13-067374-9)

The Complete Internet & World Wide Web Programming Training Course, Second Edition
(0-13-089550-4)

The Complete Wireless Internet & Mobile Business Programming Training Course
(0-13-062335-0)

The Complete XML Programming Training Course
(0-13-089557-1)

All of these ISBNs are retail ISBNs. College and university instructors should contact your local Prentice Hall representative or write to `cs@prenhall.com` *for the corresponding student edition ISBNs.*

If you would like to purchase the Cyber Classrooms separately...

Prentice Hall offers Multimedia Cyber Classroom CD-ROMs to accompany the *How to Program Series* texts for the topics listed at right. If you have already purchased one of these books and would like to purchase a stand-alone copy of the corresponding *Multimedia Cyber Classroom,* you can make your purchase at the following Web site:

www.informit.com/cyberclassrooms

C++ Multimedia Cyber Classroom, 4/E, ISBN # 0-13-100253-8

C# Multimedia Cyber Classroom, ask for product number 0-13-064587-7

e-Business & e-Commerce Cyber Classroom, ISBN # 0-13-089540-7

Internet & World Wide Web Cyber Classroom, 2/E, ISBN # 0-13-089559-8

Java Multimedia Cyber Classroom, 5/E, ISBN # 0-13-101769-1

Perl Multimedia Cyber Classroom, ISBN # 0-13-089553-9

Python Multimedia Cyber Classroom, ISBN # 0-13-067375-7

Visual Basic 6 Multimedia Cyber Classroom, ISBN # 0-13-083116-6

Visual Basic .NET Multimedia Cyber Classroom, 2/E, ISBN # 0-13-065193-1

XML Multimedia Cyber Classroom, ISBN # 0-13-089555-5

Wireless Internet & Mobile Business Programming Multimedia Cyber Classroom,ISBN # 0-13-062337-7

e-LEARNING • from Deitel & Associates, Inc.

Cyber Classrooms, Web-Based Training and Course Management Systems

DEITEL is committed to continuous research and development in e-Learning.

We are enhancing the *Multimedia Cyber Classroom* products to include more audio, pre- and post-assessment questions and Web-based labs with solutions for the benefit of professors and students alike. In addition, our *Multimedia Cyber Classroom* products, currently available in CD-ROM format, are being ported to Pearson's Premium CourseCompass course-management system—*a powerful e-platform for teaching and learning.* Many DEITEL® materials are available in WebCT, Blackboard and CourseCompass formats for colleges, and will soon be available for various corporate learning management systems. For more information on course management systems, please visit us on the Web at `www.prenhall.com/cms`.

WHAT'S COMING FROM THE DEITELS

Future Publications

Here are some new books we are considering for 2004/2005 release:

Simply Series: *Simply C++*

Computer Science Series: *Java Software Design, C++ Software Design.*

Internet and Web Programming Series: *Internet and World Wide Web How to Program 3/e; Open Source Software Development: Linux, Apache, MySQL, Perl and PHP.*

DEITEL® Developer Series: *ASP .NET with Visual Basic .NET, ASP .NET with C#.*

Object Technology Series: *OOAD with the UML, Design Patterns, Java and XML.*

Java Series: *Advanced Java™ 2 Platform How to Program 2/e.*

Operating Systems, Third Edition

This fall we will wrap up the first book in our new *Computer Science Series, Operating Systems, Third Edition.* This book will be entirely updated to reflect current core operating system concepts and design considerations. Using Java™ code to illustrate key points, *Operating Systems, 3/E* will introduce processes, concurrent programming, deadlock and indefinite postponement, mutual exclusion, physical and virtual memory, file systems, disk performance, distributed systems, security and more. To complement the discussion of operating system concepts, the book will feature extensive case studies on the latest operating systems, including the soon-to-be-released Linux kernel version 2.6 and the Windows XP operating system. This book covers all of the core topics and most elective topics recommended by the Joint Task Force on Computing Curricula 2001 developed by the IEEE Computer Society and ACM, making it an ideal textbook for undergraduate and early graduate operating systems courses.

Sign up now for the new *DEITEL® Buzz Online* newsletter at:
`www.deitel.com/newsletter/subscribe.html`

DEITEL® BUZZ ONLINE NEWSLETTER

Our official e-mail newsletter, the DEITEL® BUZZ ONLINE, is a free publication designed to keep you updated on our publishing program, instructor-led corporate training courses, hottest industry trends and topics and more.

Issues of our newsletter include:

- **Technology Spotlights** that feature articles and information on the hottest industry topics drawn directly from our publications or written during the research and development process.
- **Anecdotes** and/or **challenges** that allow our readers to interact with our newsletter and with us. We always welcome and appreciate your comments, answers and feedback. We will summarize all responses we receive in future issues.
- **Highlights** and **Announcements** on current and upcoming products that are of interest to professionals, students and instructors.
- Information on our **instructor-led corporate training courses delivered at organizations worldwide**. Complete course listings and special course highlights provide readers with additional details on DEITEL® training offerings.
- Our newsletter is available in both **full-color HTML** or **plain-text** formats depending on your viewing preferences and e-mail client capabilities.

www.deitel.com | Deitel/Prentice Hall | Deitel Kiosk on InformIT | Contact Us

Features

Simply Visual Basic .NET
Java How to Program, 5/E
DEITEL™ Buzz Online
Milestone: 20,000 Readers
Announcements:
Deitel Developer Series: Visual C++ .NET For Experienced Programmers
In the Next Issue
Feedback

A Note from the Authors

Welcome!

We are pleased to announce two new publications that will be available for January 2003 classes. *Simply Visual Basic .NET: An Application-Driven™ Tutorial Approach* is the first publication in the new Deitel *Simply...Series*. *Java How to Program 5/e* is a new edition of the world's best-selling Java textbook! This issue of the *DEITEL™ Buzz Online* overviews these new publications and includes links to excerpts from both books.

We welcome your feedback on this newsletter and hope you enjoy our fifth issue. Please e-mail your questions or comments about this newsletter to buzzfeedback@deitel.com.

We look forward to hearing from you!

Simply Visual Basic .NET Back to Top

Simply Visual Basic® .NET An APPLICATION-DRIVEN™ Tutorial Approach takes a different approach to teaching Visual Basic .NET from the ground up. This book combines the DEITEL™ signature LIVE CODE™ approach with a new APPLICATION-DRIVEN™ methodology, in which readers build real-world applications that incorporate Visual Basic .NET programming fundamentals. Using a step-by-step tutorial approach, readers begin learning the basics of programming. Each successive tutorial builds on previously learned concepts and introduces new programming features. Learn GUI design, controls, methods, functions, data types, control structures, procedures, arrays, object-oriented programming, strings and characters, sequential files and more in this comprehensive introduction to Visual Basic .NET. We also include higher-end topics such as database programming, graphics and multimedia and Web applications development.

Available for January 2003 Classes!
The first textbook in the new Deitel *Simply...Series* contains many new features including:

- **Step-by-step tutorials** show how to build and execute complete applications, from start to finish
- **APPLICATION-DRIVEN™** design includes 31 tutorials and 100+ exercises on real-word applications

Simply Visual Basic .NET: An Application-Driven Tutorial Approach
ISBN: 0131405535
Table of Contents
Preface
Pre-Order the book from the following Web sites:

- Learn about the history of Deitel & Associates, our brands, the bugs and more in the **Lore and Legends** section of the newsletter.
- **Hyperlinked Table of Contents** allows readers to navigate quickly through the newsletter by jumping directly to specific topics of interest.

To sign up for the *DEITEL® BUZZ ONLINE* newsletter, visit `www.deitel.com/newsletter/subscribe.html`.

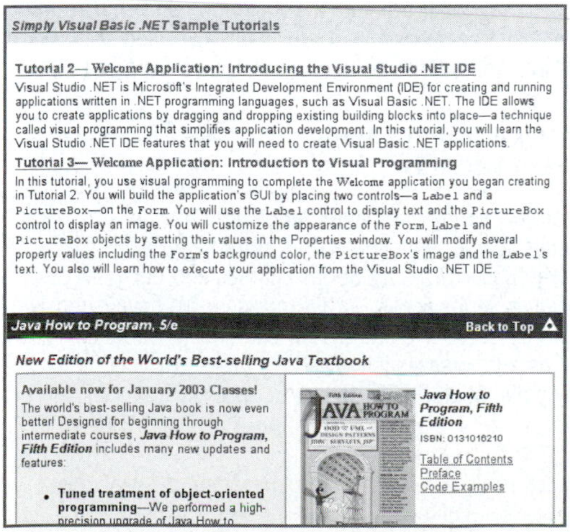

***Simply Visual Basic .NET* Sample Tutorials**

Tutorial 2— Welcome Application: Introducing the Visual Studio .NET IDE
Visual Studio .NET is Microsoft's Integrated Development Environment (IDE) for creating and running applications written in .NET programming languages, such as Visual Basic .NET. The IDE allows you to create applications by dragging and dropping existing building blocks into place—a technique called visual programming that simplifies application development. In this tutorial, you will learn the Visual Studio .NET IDE features that you will need to create Visual Basic .NET applications.

Tutorial 3— Welcome Application: Introduction to Visual Programming
In this tutorial, you use visual programming to complete the Welcome application you began creating in Tutorial 2. You will build the application's GUI by placing two controls—a `Label` and a `PictureBox`—on the `Form`. You will use the `Label` control to display text and the `PictureBox` control to display an image. You will customize the appearance of the `Form`, `Label` and `PictureBox` objects by setting their values in the Properties window. You will modify several property values including the `Form`'s background color, the `PictureBox`'s image and the `Label`'s text. You also will learn how to execute your application from the Visual Studio .NET IDE.

Java How to Program, 5/e Back to Top

New Edition of the World's Best-selling Java Textbook

Available now for January 2003 Classes!
The world's best-selling Java book is now even better! Designed for beginning through intermediate courses, ***Java How to Program, Fifth Edition*** includes many new updates and features:

- **Tuned treatment of object-oriented programming**—We performed a high-precision upgrade of Java How to

Java How to Program, Fifth Edition
ISBN: 0131016210
Table of Contents
Preface
Code Examples

Turn the page to find out more about Deitel & Associates!

The Deitels are the authors of best-selling Java™, C++, C#, C, Visual Basic® and Internet and World Wide Web books and multimedia packages.

Corporate Training Delivered Worldwide

Deitel & Associates, Inc. provides intensive, lecture-and-laboratory courses to organizations worldwide. The programming courses use our signature *Live-Code Approach*, presenting complete working programs.

Deitel & Associates, Inc. has trained over one million students and professionals worldwide through corporate training courses, public seminars, university teaching, *How to Program Series* textbooks, *Deitel® Developer Series* books, *Simply Series* textbooks, *Cyber Classroom Series* multimedia packages, *Complete Training Course Series* textbook and multimedia packages, broadcast-satellite courses and Web-based training.

Educational Consulting

Deitel & Associates, Inc. offers complete educational consulting services for corporate training programs and professional schools including:

- Curriculum design and development
- Preparation of Instructor Guides
- Customized courses and course materials
- Design and implementation of professional training certificate programs
- Instructor certification
- Train-the-trainers programs
- Delivery of software-related corporate training programs

Visit our Web site for more information on our corporate training curriculum and to purchase our training products.

www.deitel.com/training

Would you like to review upcoming publications?

If you are a professor or senior industry professional interested in being a reviewer of our forthcoming publications, please contact us by email at **deitel@deitel.com**. Insert "Content Reviewer" in the subject heading.

Are you interested in a career in computer education, publishing and training?

We offer a limited number of full-time positions available for college graduates in computer science, information systems, information technology, management information systems, English and communications, marketing, multimedia technology and other areas. Please check our Web site for the latest job postings or contact us by email at **deitel@deitel.com**. Insert "Full-time Job" in the subject heading.

Are you a Boston-area college student looking for an internship?

We have a limited number of competitive summer positions and 20-hr./week school-year opportunities for computer science, English and business majors. Students work at our worldwide headquarters west of Boston. We also offer full-time internships for students taking a semester off from school. This is an excellent opportunity for students looking to gain industry experience and earn money to pay for school. Please contact us by email at **deitel@deitel.com**. Insert "Internship" in the subject heading.

Would you like to explore contract training opportunities with us?

Deitel & Associates, Inc. is looking for contract instructors to teach software-related topics at our clients' sites in the United States and worldwide. Applicants should be experienced professional trainers or college professors. For more information, please visit **www.deitel.com** and send your resume to Abbey Deitel at **abbey.deitel@deitel.com**.

Are you a training company in need of quality course materials?

Corporate training companies worldwide use our *Complete Training Course Series* book and multimedia packages, our *Web-Based Training Series* courses and our *Deitel® Developer Series* books in their classes. We have extensive ancillary instructor materials for each of our products. For more details, please visit **www.deitel.com** or contact us by email at **deitel@deitel.com**.

Sign up now for the new *Deitel® Buzz Online* newsletter at:
www.deitel.com/newsletter/subscribe.html

LOOK HERE
for the latest buzz on
DEITEL PRODUCTS
from Prentice Hall.